AMERICA VOTES 18

A HANDBOOK OF CONTEMPORARY
AMERICAN ELECTION STATISTICS

COMPILED AND EDITED BY
RICHARD M. SCAMMON
and
ALICE V. McGILLIVRAY

1988

ELECTIONS RESEARCH CENTER

CONGRESSIONAL QUARTERLY WASHINGTON 1989

5508 Greystone Street
Chevy Chase, Maryland 20815

Copies available from: Congressional Quarterly Inc., 1414 22nd St. N.W., Washington, D.C. 20037

Printed in the United States of America

Library of Congress Catalog Card Number; 56-10132
International Standard Book Number: 0-87187-522-5

CONTENTS

Chicago, Detroit, Harris County (Texas), Los Angeles County, New York City and Philadelphia data will be found in the appropriate state sections.

INTRODUCTION

The eighteenth volume of AMERICA VOTES follows the general pattern used in the previous handbooks. The state chapter system is continued, with a profile sheet, map of the state by congressional districts, tables of the voting data by counties, time sequence vote for Congress where district boundaries have remained the same, note section with general election information and primary elections data. Also included within the appropriate state chapters are voting data for Chicago, Detroit, Harris county (Texas), New York City, Philadelphia and Los Angeles county, with voting division maps. In the chapters for the New England states, tables are included which list the voting by larger cities and towns except for Rhode Island which lists *all* cities and towns.

In past issues, the introductory pages of each state section have included postwar vote tables for the state-wide vote for Governor and Senator. In volume 18, a table with the state-wide postwar vote for President has been added. In the Presidential table, it should be noted that the plurality figures are calculated on a first-second party basis rather than being limited to a Republican-Democratic plurality as in the Senator and Governor tables. This conforms with the data shown on the national state-by-state Presidential vote tables.

The implementation of the 1980 Census for redistricting purposes led to changes in the congressional district lines in most states for 1982. Ten states redistricted between 1982 and 1984 and Ohio between 1984 and 1986. The congressional district maps for each state reflect these changes. Since voting data in each CD are carried back in time only to the point at which the district was set up with its present boundaries, data in the CD tables reflect these changes also. For earlier election results (and earlier boundaries) previous volumes of AMERICA VOTES should be consulted.

Attention of AMERICA VOTES 18 users is directed particularly to the note sections at the close of each chapter. Many special situations develop in the politics and elections of the various states and these are set out in detail in the individual state note sections. Distribution of the non-major party vote, recount tallies, withdrawal and substitution data, party nomenclature, boundary changes, discrepancies or corrections in the canvassed returns—these and similar special state situations are listed in the note sections.

AMERICA VOTES 18 carries United States tables of the state-by-state Presidential vote from 1920 through 1988 and data for the Presidential preference primaries from 1968 through 1988 by state and/or summary tables.

The AMERICA VOTES series draws from official state sources the raw material of American elections behavior. From that raw material is built a set of national reference volumes on American politics. To make these reference volumes of maximum efficiency in meeting the needs of its users, suggestions as to new materials, together with any corrections of data are solicited.

For AMERICA VOTES 18, as for its predecessors, it would be impossible to list all those to whom acknowledgement is due for aid in bringing this volume to the public. To all those who have helped in the preparation of this volume for publication must go the gratitude of the editors and of all those who will use this newest volume in the series.

Richard M. Scammon
Alice V. McGillivray

Washington, D.C.
September, 1989

UNITED STATES

POST ELECTION CHANGES

Following the 1988 General Election, and prior to September 1, 1989 there were nine changes in the membership of the 101st Congress.

SENATOR

J. Danforth Quayle (R) resigned in January 1989 following his election as Vice-President of the United States; Daniel R. Coats (R) was appointed in January 1989 to fill out two years of this term. A special election will be held in 1990 for the last two years of this term.

REPRESENTATIVES

3rd CD Alabama—Bill Nichols (D) died in December 1988; Glen Browder (D) was elected April 1989 to succeed him.

15th CD California—Tony Coelho (D) resigned in May 1989; this vacancy will be filled by a special election in November 1989 if no candidate receives a majority in the September 1989 all-party primary.

18th CD Flordia—Claude Pepper (D) died in May 1989; Ileana Ros-Lehtinen (R) was elected August 1989 to succeed him.

4th CD Indiana—Daniel R. Coats (R) resigned January 1989 upon being appointed Senator (see above); Jill L. Long (D) was elected March 1989 to succeed him.

5th CD Mississippi—Larkin Smith (R) died in August 1989; this vacancy will be filled by a special election in October 1989.

12th CD Texas—James C. Wright (D) resigned June 1989; this vacancy will be filled by a special election in September 1989.

18th CD Texas—Mickey Leland (D) died in August 1989; this vacancy will be filled by a special election in November 1989 with a later run-off election if no candidate receives a majority.

At-Large Wyoming—Richard Cheney (R) resigned in March 1989 to become Secretary of Defense; Craig Thomas (R) was elected April 1989 to succeed him.

UNITED STATES

SPECIAL ELECTIONS TO THE 100TH CONGRESS

Between the General Elections of 1986 and 1988 eight special elections were held to fill vacancies in the 100th Congress. Details of these special elections are listed below.

REPRESENTATIVES

CALIFORNIA 5TH CD

Sala Burton (D) died in February 1987; Nancy Pelosi (D) was elected June 1987 to fill out the remaining term for the 100th Congress.

April 7, 1987 Special All-Party Primary

38,927 Nancy Pelosi (D); 35,008 Harry G. Britt (D); 15,355 Bill Maher (D); 6,498 Doris M. Ward (D); 3,016 Harriet Ross (R); 2,896 Carol R. Silver (D); 1,755 Kevin W. Wadsworth (R); 1,712 Tom Spinosa (R); 1,262 Mike Garza (R); 447 Karen Edwards (Independent); 408 Sam Grove (Libertarian); 187 Theodore A. Zuur (Peace and Freedom); 164 Cathy Sedwick (Independent); 141 Brian Lantz (D).

June 2, 1987 Special Election

46,428 Nancy Pelosi (D); 22,478 Harriet Ross (R); 1,602 Karen Edwards (Independent); 1,105 Theodore A. Zuur (Peace and Freedom); 1,007 Sam Grove (Libertarian); 659 Cathy Sedwick (Independent).

CONNECTICUT 4TH CD

Stewart B. McKinney (R) died in May 1987; Christopher Shays (R) was elected August 1987 to fill out the remaining term for the 100th Congress.

July 21, 1987 Republican Primary

11,142 Christopher Shays; 7,740 John T. Becker; 7,185 Frank D. Rich; 2,876 John G. Metsopoulos.

July 21, 1987 Democratic Primary

13,422 Christine M. Niedermeier; 7,143 Margaret Morton; 4,954 Michael G. Morgan.

August 18, 1987 Special Election

50,518 Christopher Shays (R); 37,293 Christine M. Niedermeier (D); 524 Nicholas J. Tarzia (War Against AIDS); 28 scattered write-in.

ILLINOIS 21ST CD

Melvin Price (D) died in April 1988; Jerry F. Costello (D) was elected August 1988 to fill out the remaining term for the 100th Congress.

July 12, 1988 Republican Primary

Robert H. Gaffner, unopposed.

July 12, 1988 Democratic Primary

18,259 Jerry F. Costello; 2,062 Clarence Ellis.

August 9, 1988 Special Election

33,144 Jerry F. Costello (D); 31,257 Robert H. Gaffner (R); 1 scattered write-in.

UNITED STATES

LOUISIANA 4TH CD

Charles Roemer (D) resigned in March 1988 following his election to be Governor of Louisiana; Jim McCrery (R) was elected April 1988 to fill out the remaining term for the 100th Congress.

March 8, 1988 Special All-Party Primary

39,624 Jim McCrery (R); 24,220 Foster Campbell (D); 19,567 Stan Tiner (D); 16,829 June Phillips (D); 13,646 Claude Leach (D); 5,236 Marshall Jones (D); 3,827 Troy Bain (D); 2,018 Noel E. Byars (D); 567 Charles S. Martin (D); 288 Mitchell E. Marsh (D).

April 16, 1988 Special Election

63,590 Jim McCrery (R); 62,214 Foster Campbell (D).

NEW JERSEY 3RD CD

James J. Howard (D) died in March 1988; Frank Pallone (D) was elected November 1988 to fill out the remaining months of the term for the 100th Congress.

June 7, 1988 Republican Primary

16,816 Joseph Azzolina; 3,163 Scott M. Colabella.

June 7, 1988 Democratic Primary

Frank Pallone, unopposed.

November 8, 1988 Special Election

116,988 Frank Pallone (D); 106,489 Joseph Azzolina (R); 1,713 Laura Stewart (Libertarian).

TENNESSEE 2ND CD

John J. Duncan (R) died in June 1988; John J. Duncan, Jr. (R) was elected in November 1988 to fill out the remaining months of the term for the 100th Congress.

August 25, 1988 Republican Primary

John J. Duncan, Jr., unopposed.

August 25, 1988 Democratic Primary

3,357 Dudley W. Taylor; 418 John F. Bowen; 313 Robert R. Scott.

November 8, 1988 Special Election

92,929 John J. Duncan, Jr. (R); 70,576 Dudley W. Taylor (D); 2,114 Charles West (Independent); 1 scattered write-in.

UNITED STATES

TENNESSEE 5TH CD

Bill Boner (D) resigned in October 1987 following his election to be Mayor of Nashville, Tennessee; Bob Clement (D) was elected in January 1988 to fill out the remaining term for the 100th Congress.

December 3, 1987 Republican Primary

Terry Holcomb, unopposed.

December 3, 1987 Democratic Primary

43,868 Bob Clement; 39,745 Phil Bredesen; 16,128 Jane Eskind; 9,746 Walter T. Searcy; 187 Jo Ann North; 153 Dorothy N. Barker; 105 Doug Johnston; 53 Bobby Watts; 22 Howard A. Kent; 5 scattered write-in. North, Barker, Johnston, Watts and Kent had withdrawn from the race but their names were retained on the ballot.

January 19, 1988 Special Election

56,323 Bob Clement (D); 32,847 Terry Holcomb (R); 685 Suzanne Stewart (Independent); 601 Joe Driscoll (Independent); 34 scattered write-in.

VIRGINIA 5TH CD

W. C. Daniel (D) died in January 1988; L. F. Payne (D) was elected June 1988 to fill out the remaining term for the 100th Congress.

Candidates for both parties were nominated by local party conventions.

June 14, 1988 Special Election

55,469 L. F. Payne (D); 38,063 Linda Arey (R); 80 scattered write-in.

UNITED STATES

POPULAR VOTE FOR PRESIDENT 1920 TO 1988

Year	Total Vote	Republican Vote	Republican Candidate	Democratic Vote	Democratic Candidate	Other Vote	Plurality	Percentage Total Vote Rep.	Percentage Total Vote Dem.	Percentage Major Vote Rep.	Percentage Major Vote Dem.
1988	91,594,809	48,886,097	Bush, George	41,809,074	Dukakis, Michael S.	899,638	7,077,023 R	53.4%	45.6%	53.9%	46.1%
1984	92,652,842	54,455,075	Reagan, Ronald	37,577,185	Mondale, Walter F.	620,582	16,877,890 R	58.8%	40.6%	59.2%	40.8%
1980	86,515,221	43,904,153	Reagan, Ronald	35,483,883	Carter, Jimmy	7,127,185	8,420,270 R	50.7%	41.0%	55.3%	44.7%
1976	81,555,889	39,147,793	Ford, Gerald R.	40,830,763	Carter, Jimmy	1,577,333	1,682,970 D	48.0%	50.1%	48.9%	51.1%
1972	77,718,554	47,169,911	Nixon, Richard M.	29,170,383	McGovern, George S.	1,378,260	17,999,528 R	60.7%	37.5%	61.8%	38.2%
1968	73,211,875	31,785,480	Nixon, Richard M.	31,275,166	Humphrey, Hubert H.	10,151,229	510,314 R	43.4%	42.7%	50.4%	49.6%
1964	70,644,592	27,178,188	Goldwater, Barry M.	43,129,566	Johnson, Lyndon B.	336,838	15,951,378 D	38.5%	61.1%	38.7%	61.3%
1960	68,838,219	34,108,157	Nixon, Richard M.	34,226,731	Kennedy, John F.	503,331	118,574 D	49.5%	49.7%	49.9%	50.1%
1956	62,026,908	35,590,472	Eisenhower, Dwight D.	26,022,752	Stevenson, Adlai E.	413,684	9,567,720 R	57.4%	42.0%	57.8%	42.2%
1952	61,550,918	33,936,234	Eisenhower, Dwight D.	27,314,992	Stevenson, Adlai E.	299,692	6,621,242 R	55.1%	44.4%	55.4%	44.6%
1948	48,793,826	21,991,291	Dewey, Thomas E.	24,179,345	Truman, Harry S.	2,623,190	2,188,054 D	45.1%	49.6%	47.6%	52.4%
1944	47,976,670	22,017,617	Dewey, Thomas E.	25,612,610	Roosevelt, Franklin D.	346,443	3,594,993 D	45.9%	53.4%	46.2%	53.8%
1940	49,900,418	22,348,480	Willkie, Wendell	27,313,041	Roosevelt, Franklin D.	238,897	4,964,561 D	44.8%	54.7%	45.0%	55.0%
1936	45,654,763	16,684,231	Landon, Alfred M.	27,757,333	Roosevelt, Franklin D.	1,213,199	11,073,102 D	36.5%	60.8%	37.5%	62.5%
1932	39,758,759	15,760,684	Hoover, Herbert C.	22,829,501	Roosevelt, Franklin D.	1,168,574	7,068,817 D	39.6%	57.4%	40.8%	59.2%
1928	36,805,951	21,437,277	Hoover, Herbert C.	15,007,698	Smith, Alfred E.	360,976	6,429,579 R	58.2%	40.8%	58.8%	41.2%
1924	29,095,023	15,719,921	Coolidge, Calvin	8,386,704	Davis, John W.	4,988,398	7,333,217 R	54.0%	28.8%	65.2%	34.8%
1920	26,768,613	16,153,115	Harding, Warren G.	9,133,092	Cox, James M.	1,482,406	7,020,023 R	60.3%	34.1%	63.9%	36.1%

For detail of other vote see note section included with each U.S. summary table that follows.

ELECTORAL COLLEGE VOTE 1920 TO 1988

Year	Total	Republican	Democratic	Other
1988	538	426	111	1 BENTSEN
1984	538	525	13	—
1980	538	489	49	—
1976	538	240	297	1 REAGAN
1972	538	520	17	1 LIBERTARIAN
1968	538	301	191	46 AIP
1964	538	52	486	—
1960	537	219	303	15 BYRD
1956	531	457	73	1 JONES
1952	531	442	89	—
1948	531	189	303	39 SR
1944	531	99	432	—
1940	531	82	449	—
1936	531	8	523	—
1932	531	59	472	—
1928	531	444	87	—
1924	531	382	136	13 PROGRESSIVE
1920	531	404	127	—

PRESIDENT 1988

In West Virginia, one Democratic elector voted in the Electoral College for Lloyd Bentsen for President and Michael S. Dukakis for Vice-President.

In New York the Republican figures include Conservative votes and the Democratic figures include Liberal votes.

In Minnesota, the Republican candidates appear on the ballot as Independent-Republican, the Democratic as Democratic-Farmer-Labor. In many states various non-major party candidates appeared on the ballot with variations of the party designations given here, were listed as "Independent" or were carried with entirely different party labels.

In several states minor party Vice-Presidential candidates were different from those listed below.

The full list of candidates for President and Vice-President was:

48,886,097	George Bush and J. Danforth Quayle, *Republican.*
41,809,074	Michael S. Dukakis and Lloyd Bentsen, *Democratic.*
432,179	Ron Paul and Andre V. Marrou, *Libertarian.*
217,219	Lenora B. Fulani and Joyce Dattner, *New Alliance.*
47,047	David E. Duke and Floyd C. Parker, *Populist.*
30,905	Eugene J. McCarthy and Florence Rice, *Consumer.*
27,818	James C. Griffin and Charles J. Morsa, *American Independent.*
25,562	Lyndon H. LaRouche and Debra H. Freeman, *National Economic Recovery.*
20,504	William A. Marra and Joan Andrews, *Right to Life.*
18,693	Ed Winn and Barry Porster, *Workers League.*
15,604	James Warren and Kathleen Mickells, *Socialist Workers.*
10,370	Herbert Lewin and Vikki Murdock, *Peace and Freedom.*
8,002	Earl F. Dodge and George Ormsby, *Prohibition.*
7,846	Larry Holmes and Gloria LaRiva, *Workers World.*
3,882	Willa Kenoyer and Ron Ehrenreich, *Socialist.*
3,475	Delmar Dennis and Earl Jeppson, *American.*
1,949	Jack Herer and Dana Beal, *Grassroots.*
372	Louie G. Youngkeit with no Vice-Presidential candidate, *Independent.*
236	John G. Martin and Cleveland Sparrow, *Third World Assembly.*

The candidates listed above include all those who appeared on the ballot in at least one state. Republican, Democratic and New Alliance candidates appeared on the ballot in all fifty-one jurisdictions. The Libertarian nominees were on the ballot in all save four. Where identified by state authorities, write-in votes for minor party candidates are credited to their total above and listed in the individual state note sections. In addition to the votes listed, 21,041 scattered write-in votes were reported from various states and 6,934 votes were cast for "None of these Candidates" in Nevada.

UNITED STATES

PRESIDENT 1988

State	Electoral Vote Rep.	Electoral Vote Dem.	Electoral Vote Other	Total Vote	Republican	Democratic	Other	Plurality	Percentage Total Vote Rep.	Percentage Total Vote Dem.	Percentage Major Vote Rep.	Percentage Major Vote Dem
Alabama	9			1,378,476	815,576	549,506	13,394	266,070 R	59.2%	39.9%	59.7%	40.3%
Alaska	3			200,116	119,251	72,584	8,281	46,667 R	59.6%	36.3%	62.2%	37.8%
Arizona	7			1,171,873	702,541	454,029	15,303	248,512 R	60.0%	38.7%	60.7%	39.3%
Arkansas	6			827,738	466,578	349,237	11,923	117,341 R	56.4%	42.2%	57.2%	42.8%
California	47			9,887,065	5,054,917	4,702,233	129,915	352,684 R	51.1%	47.6%	51.8%	48.2%
Colorado	8			1,372,394	728,177	621,453	22,764	106,724 R	53.1%	45.3%	54.0%	46.0%
Connecticut	8			1,443,394	750,241	676,584	16,569	73,657 R	52.0%	46.9%	52.6%	47.4%
Delaware	3			249,891	139,639	108,647	1,605	30,992 R	55.9%	43.5%	56.2%	43.8%
Florida	21			4,302,313	2,618,885	1,656,701	26,727	962,184 R	60.9%	38.5%	61.3%	38.7%
Georgia	12			1,809,672	1,081,331	714,792	13,549	366,539 R	59.8%	39.5%	60.2%	39.8%
Hawaii		4		354,461	158,625	192,364	3,472	33,739 D	44.8%	54.3%	45.2%	54.8%
Idaho	4			408,968	253,881	147,272	7,815	106,609 R	62.1%	36.0%	63.3%	36.7%
Illinois	24			4,559,120	2,310,939	2,215,940	32,241	94,999 R	50.7%	48.6%	51.0%	49.0%
Indiana	12			2,168,621	1,297,763	860,643	10,215	437,120 R	59.8%	39.7%	60.1%	39.9%
Iowa		8		1,225,614	545,355	670,557	9,702	125,202 D	44.5%	54.7%	44.9%	55.1%
Kansas	7			993,044	554,049	422,636	16,359	131,413 R	55.8%	42.6%	56.7%	43.3%
Kentucky	9			1,322,517	734,281	580,368	7,868	153,913 R	55.5%	43.9%	55.9%	44.1%
Louisiana	10			1,628,202	883,702	717,460	27,040	166,242 R	54.3%	44.1%	55.2%	44.8%
Maine	4			555,035	307,131	243,569	4,335	63,562 R	55.3%	43.9%	55.8%	44.2%
Maryland	10			1,714,358	876,167	826,304	11,887	49,863 R	51.1%	48.2%	51.5%	48.5%
Massachusetts		13		2,632,805	1,194,635	1,401,415	36,755	206,780 D	45.4%	53.2%	46.0%	54.0%
Michigan	20			3,669,163	1,965,486	1,675,783	27,894	289,703 R	53.6%	45.7%	54.0%	46.0%
Minnesota		10		2,096,790	962,337	1,109,471	24,982	147,134 D	45.9%	52.9%	46.4%	53.6%
Mississippi	7			931,527	557,890	363,921	9,716	193,969 R	59.9%	39.1%	60.5%	39.5%
Missouri	11			2,093,713	1,084,953	1,001,619	7,141	83,334 R	51.8%	47.8%	52.0%	48.0%
Montana	4			365,674	190,412	168,936	6,326	21,476 R	52.1%	46.2%	53.0%	47.0%
Nebraska	5			661,465	397,956	259,235	4,274	138,721 R	60.2%	39.2%	60.6%	39.4%
Nevada	4			350,067	206,040	132,738	11,289	73,302 R	58.9%	37.9%	60.8%	39.2%
New Hampshire	4			451,074	281,537	163,696	5,841	117,841 R	62.4%	36.3%	63.2%	36.8%
New Jersey	16			3,099,553	1,743,192	1,320,352	36,009	422,840 R	56.2%	42.6%	56.9%	43.1%
New Mexico	5			521,287	270,341	244,497	6,449	25,844 R	51.9%	46.9%	52.5%	47.5%
New York		36		6,485,683	3,081,871	3,347,882	55,930	266,011 D	47.5%	51.6%	47.9%	52.1%
North Carolina	13			2,134,370	1,237,258	890,167	6,945	347,091 R	58.0%	41.7%	58.2%	41.8%
North Dakota	3			297,261	166,559	127,739	2,963	38,820 R	56.0%	43.0%	56.6%	43.4%
Ohio	23			4,393,699	2,416,549	1,939,629	37,521	476,920 R	55.0%	44.1%	55.5%	44.5%
Oklahoma	8			1,171,036	678,367	483,423	9,246	194,944 R	57.9%	41.3%	58.4%	41.6%
Oregon		7		1,201,694	560,126	616,206	25,362	56,080 D	46.6%	51.3%	47.6%	52.4%
Pennsylvania	25			4,536,251	2,300,087	2,194,944	41,220	105,143 R	50.7%	48.4%	51.2%	48.8%
Rhode Island		4		404,620	177,761	225,123	1,736	47,362 D	43.9%	55.6%	44.1%	55.9%
South Carolina	8			986,009	606,443	370,554	9,012	235,889 R	61.5%	37.6%	62.1%	37.9%
South Dakota	3			312,991	165,415	145,560	2,016	19,855 R	52.8%	46.5%	53.2%	46.8%
Tennessee	11			1,636,250	947,233	679,794	9,223	267,439 R	57.9%	41.5%	58.2%	41.8%
Texas	29			5,427,410	3,036,829	2,352,748	37,833	684,081 R	56.0%	43.3%	56.3%	43.7%
Utah	5			647,008	428,442	207,343	11,223	221,099 R	66.2%	32.0%	67.4%	32.6%
Vermont	3			243,328	124,331	115,775	3,222	8,556 R	51.1%	47.6%	51.8%	48.2%
Virginia	12			2,191,609	1,309,162	859,799	22,648	449,363 R	59.7%	39.2%	60.4%	39.6%
Washington		10		1,865,253	903,835	933,516	27,902	29,681 D	48.5%	50.0%	49.2%	50.8%
West Virginia		5	1	653,311	310,065	341,016	2,230	30,951 D	47.5%	52.2%	47.6%	52.4%
Wisconsin		11		2,191,608	1,047,499	1,126,794	17,315	79,295 D	47.8%	51.4%	48.2%	51.8%
Wyoming	3			176,551	106,867	67,113	2,571	39,754 R	60.5%	38.0%	61.4%	38.6%
Dist. of Col.		3		192,877	27,590	159,407	5,880	131,817 D	14.3%	82.6%	14.8%	85.2%
United States	426	111	1	91,594,809	48,886,097	41,809,074	899,638	7,077,023 R	53.4%	45.6%	53.9%	46.1%

PRESIDENT 1984

In New York the Republican figures include Conservative votes and the Democratic figures include Liberal votes.

In Minnesota, the Republican candidates appear on the ballot as Independent-Republican, the Democratic as Democratic-Farmer-Labor. In many states various non-major party candidates appeared on the ballot with variations of the party designations given here, were listed as "Independent" or "Non-Party", or were carried with entirely different party labels.

The Workers World candidate for President was Gavrielle Holmes in Ohio and Rhode Island; in several states minor party Vice-Presidential candidates were different from those listed below.

The full list of candidates for President and Vice-President was:

54,455,075	Ronald Reagan and George Bush, *Republican.*
37,577,185	Walter F. Mondale and Geraldine A. Ferraro, *Democratic.*
228,314	David Bergland and James A. Lewis, *Libertarian.*
78,807	Lyndon H. LaRouche and Billy M. Davis, *Independent.*
72,200	Sonia Johnson and Richard Walton, *Citizens.*
66,336	Bob Richards and Maureen Salaman, *Populist.*
46,868	Dennis L. Serrette and Nancy Ross, *Alliance.*
36,386	Gus Hall and Angela Davis, *Communist.*
24,706	Mel Mason and Matilde Zimmermann, *Socialist Workers.*
17,985	Larry Holmes and Gloria LaRiva, *Workers World.*
13,161	Delmar Dennis and Traves Brownlee, *American.*
10,801	Ed Winn and Helen Halyard, *Workers League.*
4,242	Earl F. Dodge and Warren C. Martin, *Prohibition.*
1,486	John B. Anderson and Grace Pierce, *National Unity.*
892	Gerald Baker and Ferris Alger, *Big Deal.*
825	Arthur J. Lowery and Raymond L. Garland, *United Sovreign Citizens.*

The candidates listed above are those who appeared on the ballot in at least one state. Where identified by state authorities, write-in votes for minor party candidates are credited to their total above and listed in the individual state note sections. In addition to the votes listed, 13,623 scattered write-in votes were reported from various states and 3,950 votes were cast for "None of these Candidates" in Nevada.

UNITED STATES

PRESIDENT 1984

	Electoral Vote			Total					Percentage			
									Total Vote		Major Vote	
State	Rep.	Dem.	Other	Vote	Republican	Democratic	Other	Plurality	Rep.	Dem.	Rep.	Dem.
Alabama	9			1,441,713	872,849	551,899	16,965	320,950 R	60.5%	38.3%	61.3%	38.7%
Alaska	3			207,605	138,377	62,007	7,221	76,370 R	66.7%	29.9%	69.1%	30.9%
Arizona	7			1,025,897	681,416	333,854	10,627	347,562 R	66.4%	32.5%	67.1%	32.9%
Arkansas	6			884,406	534,774	338,646	10,986	196,128 R	60.5%	38.3%	61.2%	38.8%
California	47			9,505,423	5,467,009	3,922,519	115,895	1,544,490 R	57.5%	41.3%	58.2%	41.8%
Colorado	8			1,295,380	821,817	454,975	18,588	366,842 R	63.4%	35.1%	64.4%	35.6%
Connecticut	8			1,466,900	890,877	569,597	6,426	321,280 R	60.7%	38.8%	61.0%	39.0%
Delaware	3			254,572	152,190	101,656	726	50,534 R	59.8%	39.9%	60.0%	40.0%
Florida	21			4,180,051	2,730,350	1,448,816	885	1,281,534 R	65.3%	34.7%	65.3%	34.7%
Georgia	12			1,776,120	1,068,722	706,628	770	362,094 R	60.2%	39.8%	60.2%	39.8%
Hawaii	4			335,846	185,050	147,154	3,642	37,896 R	55.1%	43.8%	55.7%	44.3%
Idaho	4			411,144	297,523	108,510	5,111	189,013 R	72.4%	26.4%	73.3%	26.7%
Illinois	24			4,819,088	2,707,103	2,086,499	25,486	620,604 R	56.2%	43.3%	56.5%	43.5%
Indiana	12			2,233,069	1,377,230	841,481	14,358	535,749 R	61.7%	37.7%	62.1%	37.9%
Iowa	8			1,319,805	703,088	605,620	11,097	97,468 R	53.3%	45.9%	53.7%	46.3%
Kansas	7			1,021,991	677,296	333,149	11,546	344,147 R	66.3%	32.6%	67.0%	33.0%
Kentucky	9			1,369,345	821,702	539,539	8,104	282,163 R	60.0%	39.4%	60.4%	39.6%
Louisiana	10			1,706,822	1,037,299	651,586	17,937	385,713 R	60.8%	38.2%	61.4%	38.6%
Maine	4			553,144	336,500	214,515	2,129	121,985 R	60.8%	38.8%	61.1%	38.9%
Maryland	10			1,675,873	879,918	787,935	8,020	91,983 R	52.5%	47.0%	52.8%	47.2%
Massachusetts	13			2,559,453	1,310,936	1,239,606	8,911	71,330 R	51.2%	48.4%	51.4%	48.6%
Michigan	20			3,801,658	2,251,571	1,529,638	20,449	721,933 R	59.2%	40.2%	59.5%	40.5%
Minnesota		10		2,084,449	1,032,603	1,036,364	15,482	3,761 D	49.5%	49.7%	49.9%	50.1%
Mississippi	7			941,104	582,377	352,192	6,535	230,185 R	61.9%	37.4%	62.3%	37.7%
Missouri	11			2,122,783	1,274,188	848,583	12	425,605 R	60.0%	40.0%	60.0%	40.0%
Montana	4			384,377	232,450	146,742	5,185	85,708 R	60.5%	38.2%	61.3%	38.7%
Nebraska	5			652,090	460,054	187,866	4,170	272,188 R	70.6%	28.8%	71.0%	29.0%
Nevada	4			286,667	188,770	91,655	6,242	97,115 R	65.8%	32.0%	67.3%	32.7%
New Hampshire	4			389,066	267,051	120,395	1,620	146,656 R	68.6%	30.9%	68.9%	31.1%
New Jersey	16			3,217,862	1,933,630	1,261,323	22,909	672,307 R	60.1%	39.2%	60.5%	39.5%
New Mexico	5			514,370	307,101	201,769	5,500	105,332 R	59.7%	39.2%	60.3%	39.7%
New York	36			6,806,810	3,664,763	3,119,609	22,438	545,154 R	53.8%	45.8%	54.0%	46.0%
North Carolina	13			2,175,361	1,346,481	824,287	4,593	522,194 R	61.9%	37.9%	62.0%	38.0%
North Dakota	3			308,971	200,336	104,429	4,206	95,907 R	64.8%	33.8%	65.7%	34.3%
Ohio	23			4,547,619	2,678,560	1,825,440	43,619	853,120 R	58.9%	40.1%	59.5%	40.5%
Oklahoma	8			1,255,676	861,530	385,080	9,066	476,450 R	68.6%	30.7%	69.1%	30.9%
Oregon	7			1,226,527	685,700	536,479	4,348	149,221 R	55.9%	43.7%	56.1%	43.9%
Pennsylvania	25			4,844,903	2,584,323	2,228,131	32,449	356,192 R	53.3%	46.0%	53.7%	46.3%
Rhode Island	4			410,492	212,080	197,106	1,306	14,974 R	51.7%	48.0%	51.8%	48.2%
South Carolina	8			968,529	615,539	344,459	8,531	271,080 R	63.6%	35.6%	64.1%	35.9%
South Dakota	3			317,867	200,267	116,113	1,487	84,154 R	63.0%	36.5%	63.3%	36.7%
Tennessee	11			1,711,994	990,212	711,714	10,068	278,498 R	57.8%	41.6%	58.2%	41.8%
Texas	29			5,397,571	3,433,428	1,949,276	14,867	1,484,152 R	63.6%	36.1%	63.8%	36.2%
Utah	5			629,656	469,105	155,369	5,182	313,736 R	74.5%	24.7%	75.1%	24.9%
Vermont	3			234,561	135,865	95,730	2,966	40,135 R	57.9%	40.8%	58.7%	41.3%
Virginia	12			2,146,635	1,337,078	796,250	13,307	540,828 R	62.3%	37.1%	62.7%	37.3%
Washington	10			1,883,910	1,051,670	807,352	24,888	244,318 R	55.8%	42.9%	56.6%	43.4%
West Virginia	6			735,742	405,483	328,125	2,134	77,358 R	55.1%	44.6%	55.3%	44.7%
Wisconsin	11			2,211,689	1,198,584	995,740	17,365	202,844 R	54.2%	45.0%	54.6%	45.4%
Wyoming	3			188,968	133,241	53,370	2,357	79,871 R	70.5%	28.2%	71.4%	28.6%
Dist. of Col.		3		211,288	29,009	180,408	1,871	151,399 D	13.7%	85.4%	13.9%	86.1%
United States	525	13	—	92,652,842	54,455,075	37,577,185	620,582	16,877,890 R	58.8%	40.6%	59.2%	40.8%

PRESIDENT 1980

In New York the Republican figures include Conservative votes and in a number of states candidates appeared on the ballot with variants of the party designations listed below, without any party designation, or with entirely different party names.

In several cases, Vice-Presidential nominees were different from those listed for most states and the Socialist Workers party nominee for President varied from state to state.

43,904,153	Ronald Reagan and George Bush, Republican.
35,483,883	Jimmy Carter and Walter F. Mondale, Democratic.
5,720,060	John B. Anderson and Patrick J. Lucey, Independent.
921,299	Edward E. Clark and David Koch, Libertarian.
234,294	Barry Commoner and LaDonna Harris, Citizens.
45,023	Gus Hall and Angela Davis, Communist.
41,268	John R. Rarick and Eileen M. Shearer, American Independent.
38,737	Clifton DeBerry and Matilde Zimmermann, Socialist Workers.
32,327	Ellen McCormack and Carroll Driscoll, Right to Life.
18,116	Maureen Smith and Elizabeth Barron, Peace and Freedom.
13,300	Deirdre Griswold and Larry Holmes, Workers World.
7,212	Benjamin C. Bubar and Earl F. Dodge, Statesman.
6,898	David McReynolds and Diane Drufenbrock, Socialist.
6,647	Percy L. Greaves and Frank L. Varnum, American.
6,272	Andrew Pulley and Matilde Zimmermann, Socialist Workers.
4,029	Richard Congress and Matilde Zimmermann, Socialist Workers.
3,694	Kurt Lynen and Harry Kieve, Middle Class.
1,718	Bill Gahres and J. F. Loughlin, Down With Lawyers.
1,555	Frank W. Shelton and George E. Jackson, American.
923	Martin E. Wendelken with no Vice-Presidential candidate, Independent.
296	Harley McLain and Jewelie Goeller, Natural Peoples.

In addition to these votes, 13,185 scattered write-in votes were reported from various states, 6,139 votes were cast in Minnesota for American party electors without designated national nominees, and 4,193 votes were cast for "None of these Candidates" in Nevada.

State-by-state vote details will be found in the individual state note sections and a supplementary state-by-state national table follows for all "other" candidates polling over 100,000 votes. An asterisk by the vote denotes write-in.

UNITED STATES

PRESIDENT 1980

State	Electoral Vote			Total					Percentage			
									Total Vote		Major Vote	
	Rep.	Dem.	Other	Vote	Republican	Democratic	Other	Plurality	Rep.	Dem.	Rep.	Dem.
Alabama	9			1,341,929	654,192	636,730	51,007	17,462 R	48.8%	47.4%	50.7%	49.3%
Alaska	3			158,445	86,112	41,842	30,491	44,270 R	54.3%	26.4%	67.3%	32.7%
Arizona	6			873,945	529,688	246,843	97,414	282,845 R	60.6%	28.2%	68.2%	31.8%
Arkansas	6			837,582	403,164	398,041	36,377	5,123 R	48.1%	47.5%	50.3%	49.7%
California	45			8,587,063	4,524,858	3,083,661	978,544	1,441,197 R	52.7%	35.9%	59.5%	40.5%
Colorado	7			1,184,415	652,264	367,973	164,178	284,291 R	55.1%	31.1%	63.9%	36.1%
Connecticut	8			1,406,285	677,210	541,732	187,343	135,478 R	48.2%	38.5%	55.6%	44.4%
Delaware	3			235,900	111,252	105,754	18,894	5,498 R	47.2%	44.8%	51.3%	48.7%
Florida	17			3,686,930	2,046,951	1,419,475	220,504	627,476 R	55.5%	38.5%	59.1%	40.9%
Georgia		12		1,596,695	654,168	890,733	51,794	236,565 D	41.0%	55.8%	42.3%	57.7%
Hawaii		4		303,287	130,112	135,879	37,296	5,767 D	42.9%	44.8%	48.9%	51.1%
Idaho	4			437,431	290,699	110,192	36,540	180,507 R	66.5%	25.2%	72.5%	27.5%
Illinois	26			4,749,721	2,358,049	1,981,413	410,259	376,636 R	49.6%	41.7%	54.3%	45.7%
Indiana	13			2,242,033	1,255,656	844,197	142,180	411,459 R	56.0%	37.7%	59.8%	40.2%
Iowa	8			1,317,661	676,026	508,672	132,963	167,354 R	51.3%	38.6%	57.1%	42.9%
Kansas	7			979,795	566,812	326,150	86,833	240,662 R	57.9%	33.3%	63.5%	36.5%
Kentucky	9			1,294,627	635,274	616,417	42,936	18,857 R	49.1%	47.6%	50.8%	49.2%
Louisiana	10			1,548,591	792,853	708,453	47,285	84,400 R	51.2%	45.7%	52.8%	47.2%
Maine	4			523,011	238,522	220,974	63,515	17,548 R	45.6%	42.3%	51.9%	48.1%
Maryland		10		1,540,496	680,606	726,161	133,729	45,555 D	44.2%	47.1%	48.4%	51.6%
Massachusetts	14			2,524,298	1,057,631	1,053,802	412,865	3,829 R	41.9%	41.7%	50.1%	49.9%
Michigan	21			3,909,725	1,915,225	1,661,532	332,968	253,693 R	49.0%	42.5%	53.5%	46.5%
Minnesota		10		2,051,980	873,268	954,174	224,538	80,906 D	42.6%	46.5%	47.8%	52.2%
Mississippi	7			892,620	441,089	429,281	22,250	11,808 R	49.4%	48.1%	50.7%	49.3%
Missouri	12			2,099,824	1,074,181	931,182	94,461	142,999 R	51.2%	44.3%	53.6%	46.4%
Montana	4			363,952	206,814	118,032	39,106	88,782 R	56.8%	32.4%	63.7%	36.3%
Nebraska	5			640,854	419,937	166,851	54,066	253,086 R	65.5%	26.0%	71.6%	28.4%
Nevada	3			247,885	155,017	66,666	26,202	88,351 R	62.5%	26.9%	69.9%	30.1%
New Hampshire	4			383,990	221,705	108,864	53,421	112,841 R	57.7%	28.4%	67.1%	32.9%
New Jersey	17			2,975,684	1,546,557	1,147,364	281,763	399,193 R	52.0%	38.6%	57.4%	42.6%
New Mexico	4			456,971	250,779	167,826	38,366	82,953 R	54.9%	36.7%	59.9%	40.1%
New York	41			6,201,959	2,893,831	2,728,372	579,756	165,459 R	46.7%	44.0%	51.5%	48.5%
North Carolina	13			1,855,833	915,018	875,635	65,180	39,383 R	49.3%	47.2%	51.1%	48.9%
North Dakota	3			301,545	193,695	79,189	28,661	114,506 R	64.2%	26.3%	71.0%	29.0%
Ohio	25			4,283,603	2,206,545	1,752,414	324,644	454,131 R	51.5%	40.9%	55.7%	44.3%
Oklahoma	8			1,149,708	695,570	402,026	52,112	293,544 R	60.5%	35.0%	63.4%	36.6%
Oregon	6			1,181,516	571,044	456,890	153,582	114,154 R	48.3%	38.7%	55.6%	44.4%
Pennsylvania	27			4,561,501	2,261,872	1,937,540	362,089	324,332 R	49.6%	42.5%	53.9%	46.1%
Rhode Island		4		416,072	154,793	198,342	62,937	43,549 D	37.2%	47.7%	43.8%	56.2%
South Carolina	8			894,071	441,841	430,385	21,845	11,456 R	49.4%	48.1%	50.7%	49.3%
South Dakota	4			327,703	198,343	103,855	25,505	94,488 R	60.5%	31.7%	65.6%	34.4%
Tennessee	10			1,617,616	787,761	783,051	46,804	4,710 R	48.7%	48.4%	50.1%	49.9%
Texas	26			4,541,636	2,510,705	1,881,147	149,784	629,558 R	55.3%	41.4%	57.2%	42.8%
Utah	4			604,222	439,687	124,266	40,269	315,421 R	72.8%	20.6%	78.0%	22.0%
Vermont	3			213,299	94,628	81,952	36,719	12,676 R	44.4%	38.4%	53.6%	46.4%
Virginia	12			1,866,032	989,609	752,174	124,249	237,435 R	53.0%	40.3%	56.8%	43.2%
Washington	9			1,742,394	865,244	650,193	226,957	215,051 R	49.7%	37.3%	57.1%	42.9%
West Virginia		6		737,715	334,206	367,462	36,047	33,256 D	45.3%	49.8%	47.6%	52.4%
Wisconsin	11			2,273,221	1,088,845	981,584	202,792	107,261 R	47.9%	43.2%	52.6%	47.4%
Wyoming	3			176,713	110,700	49,427	16,586	61,273 R	62.6%	28.0%	69.1%	30.9%
Dist. of Col.		3		175,237	23,545	131,113	20,579	107,568 D	13.4%	74.8%	15.2%	84.8%
United States	489	49	—	86,515,221	43,904,153	35,483,883	7,127,185	8,420,270 R	50.7%	41.0%	55.3%	44.7%

PRESIDENT 1976

In Washington, one Republican elector voted in the Electoral College for Ronald Reagan for President and Robert Dole for Vice-President.

In New York the Republican figures include Conservative votes and the Democratic figures include Liberal votes; in Vermont the Democratic figures include votes cast on the Independent Vermonters party ticket.

In a number of states candidates appeared on the ballot with variants of the party designations listed below and in several cases with entirely different party names.

The ballot designations for electors for Eugene J. McCarthy for President varied from state to state, as did the names of Vice-Presidential candidates running with him. In New Jersey, the Maddox Vice-Presidential candidate was Edmund O. Matzal.

The full list of candidates for President and Vice-President was:

40,830,763	Jimmy Carter and Walter F. Mondale, Democratic.
39,147,793	Gerald R. Ford and Robert Dole, Republican.
756,691	Eugene J. McCarthy with various Vice-Presidential candidates, Independent.
173,011	Roger L. MacBride and David D. Bergland, Libertarian.
170,531	Lester G. Maddox and William D. Dyke, American Independent.
160,773	Thomas J. Anderson and Rufus Shackelford, American.
91,314	Peter Camejo and Willie Mae Reid, Socialist Workers.
58,992	Gus Hall and Jarvis Tyner, Communist.
49,024	Margaret Wright and Benjamin Spock, People's.
40,043	Lyndon H. LaRouche and R. W. Evans, United States Labor.
15,934	Benjamin C. Bubar and Earl F. Dodge, Prohibition.
9,616	Julius Levin and Constance Blomen, Socialist Labor.
6,038	Frank P. Zeidler and J. Q. Brisben, Socialist.
361	Ernest L. Miller and Roy N. Eddy, Restoration.
36	Frank Taylor and Henry Swan, United American.

In addition to these votes, 39,861 scattered write-in votes were reported from various states and 5,108 votes were cast for "None of these Candidates" in Nevada.

UNITED STATES

PRESIDENT 1976

	Electoral Vote			Total					Percentage: Total Vote		Percentage: Major Vote	
State	Rep.	Dem.	Other	Vote	Republican	Democratic	Other	Plurality	Rep.	Dem.	Rep.	Dem.
Alabama		9		1,182,850	504,070	659,170	19,610	155,100 D	42.6%	55.7%	43.3%	56.7%
Alaska	3			123,574	71,555	44,058	7,961	27,497 R	57.9%	35.7%	61.9%	38.1%
Arizona	6			742,719	418,642	295,602	28,475	123,040 R	56.4%	39.8%	58.6%	41.4%
Arkansas		6		767,535	267,903	498,604	1,028	230,701 D	34.9%	65.0%	35.0%	65.0%
California	45			7,867,117	3,882,244	3,742,284	242,589	139,960 R	49.3%	47.6%	50.9%	49.1%
Colorado	7			1,081,554	584,367	460,353	36,834	124,014 R	54.0%	42.6%	55.9%	44.1%
Connecticut	8			1,381,526	719,261	647,895	14,370	71,366 R	52.1%	46.9%	52.6%	47.4%
Delaware		3		235,834	109,831	122,596	3,407	12,765 D	46.6%	52.0%	47.3%	52.7%
Florida		17		3,150,631	1,469,531	1,636,000	45,100	166,469 D	46.6%	51.9%	47.3%	52.7%
Georgia		12		1,467,458	483,743	979,409	4,306	495,666 D	33.0%	66.7%	33.1%	66.9%
Hawaii		4		291,301	140,003	147,375	3,923	7,372 D	48.1%	50.6%	48.7%	51.3%
Idaho	4			344,071	204,151	126,549	13,371	77,602 R	59.3%	36.8%	61.7%	38.3%
Illinois	26			4,718,914	2,364,269	2,271,295	83,350	92,974 R	50.1%	48.1%	51.0%	49.0%
Indiana	13			2,220,362	1,183,958	1,014,714	21,690	169,244 R	53.3%	45.7%	53.8%	46.2%
Iowa	8			1,279,306	632,863	619,931	26,512	12,932 R	49.5%	48.5%	50.5%	49.5%
Kansas	7			957,845	502,752	430,421	24,672	72,331 R	52.5%	44.9%	53.9%	46.1%
Kentucky		9		1,167,142	531,852	615,717	19,573	83,865 D	45.6%	52.8%	46.3%	53.7%
Louisiana		10		1,278,439	587,446	661,365	29,628	73,919 D	46.0%	51.7%	47.0%	53.0%
Maine	4			483,216	236,320	232,279	14,617	4,041 R	48.9%	48.1%	50.4%	49.6%
Maryland		10		1,439,897	672,661	759,612	7,624	86,951 D	46.7%	52.8%	47.0%	53.0%
Massachusetts		14		2,547,558	1,030,276	1,429,475	87,807	399,199 D	40.4%	56.1%	41.9%	58.1%
Michigan	21			3,653,749	1,893,742	1,696,714	63,293	197,028 R	51.8%	46.4%	52.7%	47.3%
Minnesota		10		1,949,931	819,395	1,070,440	60,096	251,045 D	42.0%	54.9%	43.4%	56.6%
Mississippi		7		769,361	366,846	381,309	21,206	14,463 D	47.7%	49.6%	49.0%	51.0%
Missouri		12		1,953,600	927,443	998,387	27,770	70,944 D	47.5%	51.1%	48.2%	51.8%
Montana	4			328,734	173,703	149,259	5,772	24,444 R	52.8%	45.4%	53.8%	46.2%
Nebraska	5			607,668	359,705	233,692	14,271	126,013 R	59.2%	38.5%	60.6%	39.4%
Nevada	3			201,876	101,273	92,479	8,124	8,794 R	50.2%	45.8%	52.3%	47.7%
New Hampshire	4			339,618	185,935	147,635	6,048	38,300 R	54.7%	43.5%	55.7%	44.3%
New Jersey	17			3,014,472	1,509,688	1,444,653	60,131	65,035 R	50.1%	47.9%	51.1%	48.9%
New Mexico	4			418,409	211,419	201,148	5,842	10,271 R	50.5%	48.1%	51.2%	48.8%
New York		41		6,534,170	3,100,791	3,389,558	43,821	288,767 D	47.5%	51.9%	47.8%	52.2%
North Carolina		13		1,678,914	741,960	927,365	9,589	185,405 D	44.2%	55.2%	44.4%	55.6%
North Dakota	3			297,188	153,470	136,078	7,640	17,392 R	51.6%	45.8%	53.0%	47.0%
Ohio		25		4,111,873	2,000,505	2,011,621	99,747	11,116 D	48.7%	48.9%	49.9%	50.1%
Oklahoma	8			1,092,251	545,708	532,442	14,101	13,266 R	50.0%	48.7%	50.6%	49.4%
Oregon	6			1,029,876	492,120	490,407	47,349	1,713 R	47.8%	47.6%	50.1%	49.9%
Pennsylvania		27		4,620,787	2,205,604	2,328,677	86,506	123,073 D	47.7%	50.4%	48.6%	51.4%
Rhode Island		4		411,170	181,249	227,636	2,285	46,387 D	44.1%	55.4%	44.3%	55.7%
South Carolina		8		802,583	346,149	450,807	5,627	104,658 D	43.1%	56.2%	43.4%	56.6%
South Dakota	4			300,678	151,505	147,068	2,105	4,437 R	50.4%	48.9%	50.7%	49.3%
Tennessee		10		1,476,345	633,969	825,879	16,497	191,910 D	42.9%	55.9%	43.4%	56.6%
Texas		26		4,071,884	1,953,300	2,082,319	36,265	129,019 D	48.0%	51.1%	48.4%	51.6%
Utah	4			541,198	337,908	182,110	21,180	155,798 R	62.4%	33.6%	65.0%	35.0%
Vermont	3			187,765	102,085	80,954	4,726	21,131 R	54.4%	43.1%	55.8%	44.2%
Virginia	12			1,697,094	836,554	813,896	46,644	22,658 R	49.3%	48.0%	50.7%	49.3%
Washington	8		1	1,555,534	777,732	717,323	60,479	60,409 R	50.0%	46.1%	52.0%	48.0%
West Virginia		6		750,964	314,760	435,914	290	121,154 D	41.9%	58.0%	41.9%	58.1%
Wisconsin		11		2,104,175	1,004,987	1,040,232	58,956	35,245 D	47.8%	49.4%	49.1%	50.9%
Wyoming	3			156,343	92,717	62,239	1,387	30,478 R	59.3%	39.8%	59.8%	40.2%
Dist. of Col.		3		168,830	27,873	137,818	3,139	109,945 D	16.5%	81.6%	16.8%	83.2%
United States	240	297	1	81,555,889	39,147,793	40,830,763	1,577,333	1,682,970 D	48.0%	50.1%	48.9%	51.1%

PRESIDENT 1972

In Virginia one Republican elector voted in the Electoral College for the Libertarian candidates for President and Vice-President.

In New York the Republican figures include Conservative votes and the Democratic figures include Liberal votes. In Alabama the Democratic figures include votes cast on the National Democratic Party of Alabama ticket, and in South Carolina include United Citizens Party votes.

In certain states candidates appeared on the ballot under party names other than those used below; for the Socialist Workers party the votes listed for Jenness and Pulley were actually cast for substitute candidates (Reed and DeBerry) or without named candidates in several states.

The Democratic Vice-Presidential candidate originally was Senator Thomas F. Eagleton; on his withdrawal shortly after the party convention, R. Sargent Shriver was named by the Democratic National Committee as candidate.

The full list of candidates for President and Vice-President was:

47,169,911	Richard M. Nixon and Spiro T. Agnew, Republican.
29,170,383	George S. McGovern and R. Sargent Shriver, Democratic.
1,099,482	John G. Schmitz and Thomas J. Anderson, American.
78,756	Benjamin Spock and Julius Hobson, People's.
66,677	Linda Jenness and Andrew Pulley, Socialist Workers.
53,814	Louis Fisher and Genevieve Gunderson, Socialist Labor.
25,595	Gus Hall and Jarvis Tyner, Communist.
13,505	E. Harold Munn and Marshall E. Uncapher, Prohibition.
3,673	John Hospers and Theodora Nathan, Libertarian.
1,743	John V. Mahalchik and Irving Homer, America First.
220	Gabriel Green and Daniel Fry, Universal.

In addition to the above, 34,795 scattered votes were reported from various states.

Vice-President Agnew resigned in October 1973 and Representative Gerald R. Ford of Michigan was nominated by President Nixon to fill the vacancy. In November (Senate) and December (House of Representatives) this action was approved by Congress.

In August 1974 President Nixon resigned and was succeeded by Vice-President Ford. In the same month Nelson A. Rockefeller, former Governor of New York, was nominated to be Vice-President and was confirmed by Congress in December 1974.

UNITED STATES

PRESIDENT 1972

	Electoral Vote			Total					Percentage			
									Total Vote		Major Vote	
State	Rep.	Dem.	Other	Vote	Republican	Democratic	Other	Plurality	Rep.	Dem.	Rep.	Dem.
Alabama	9			1,006,111	728,701	256,923	20,487	471,778 R	72.4%	25.5%	73.9%	26.1%
Alaska	3			95,219	55,349	32,967	6,903	22,382 R	58.1%	34.6%	62.7%	37.3%
Arizona	6			622,926	402,812	198,540	21,574	204,272 R	64.7%	31.9%	67.0%	33.0%
Arkansas	6			651,320	448,541	199,892	2,887	248,649 R	68.9%	30.7%	69.2%	30.8%
California	45			8,367,862	4,602,096	3,475,847	289,919	1,126,249 R	55.0%	41.5%	57.0%	43.0%
Colorado	7			953,884	597,189	329,980	26,715	267,209 R	62.6%	34.6%	64.4%	35.6%
Connecticut	8			1,384,277	810,763	555,498	18,016	255,265 R	58.6%	40.1%	59.3%	40.7%
Delaware	3			235,516	140,357	92,283	2,876	48,074 R	59.6%	39.2%	60.3%	39.7%
Florida	17			2,583,283	1,857,759	718,117	7,407	1,139,642 R	71.9%	27.8%	72.1%	27.9%
Georgia	12			1,174,772	881,496	289,529	3,747	591,967 R	75.0%	24.6%	75.3%	24.7%
Hawaii	4			270,274	168,865	101,409		67,456 R	62.5%	37.5%	62.5%	37.5%
Idaho	4			310,379	199,384	80,826	30,169	118,558 R	64.2%	26.0%	71.2%	28.8%
Illinois	26			4,723,236	2,788,179	1,913,472	21,585	874,707 R	59.0%	40.5%	59.3%	40.7%
Indiana	13			2,125,529	1,405,154	708,568	11,807	696,586 R	66.1%	33.3%	66.5%	33.5%
Iowa	8			1,225,944	706,207	496,206	23,531	210,001 R	57.6%	40.5%	58.7%	41.3%
Kansas	7			916,095	619,812	270,287	25,996	349,525 R	67.7%	29.5%	69.6%	30.4%
Kentucky	9			1,067,499	676,446	371,159	19,894	305,287 R	63.4%	34.8%	64.6%	35.4%
Louisiana	10			1,051,491	686,852	298,142	66,497	388,710 R	65.3%	28.4%	69.7%	30.3%
Maine	4			417,042	256,458	160,584		95,874 R	61.5%	38.5%	61.5%	38.5%
Maryland	10			1,353,812	829,305	505,781	18,726	323,524 R	61.3%	37.4%	62.1%	37.9%
Massachusetts		14		2,458,756	1,112,078	1,332,540	14,138	220,462 D	45.2%	54.2%	45.5%	54.5%
Michigan	21			3,489,727	1,961,721	1,459,435	68,571	502,286 R	56.2%	41.8%	57.3%	42.7%
Minnesota	10			1,741,652	898,269	802,346	41,037	95,923 R	51.6%	46.1%	52.8%	47.2%
Mississippi	7			645,963	505,125	126,782	14,056	378,343 R	78.2%	19.6%	79.9%	20.1%
Missouri	12			1,855,803	1,153,852	697,147	4,804	456,705 R	62.2%	37.6%	62.3%	37.7%
Montana	4			317,603	183,976	120,197	13,430	63,779 R	57.9%	37.8%	60.5%	39.5%
Nebraska	5			576,289	406,298	169,991		236,307 R	70.5%	29.5%	70.5%	29.5%
Nevada	3			181,766	115,750	66,016		49,734 R	63.7%	36.3%	63.7%	36.3%
New Hampshire	4			334,055	213,724	116,435	3,896	97,289 R	64.0%	34.9%	64.7%	35.3%
New Jersey	17			2,997,229	1,845,502	1,102,211	49,516	743,291 R	61.6%	36.8%	62.6%	37.4%
New Mexico	4			386,241	235,606	141,084	9,551	94,522 R	61.0%	36.5%	62.5%	37.5%
New York	41			7,165,919	4,192,778	2,951,084	22,057	1,241,694 R	58.5%	41.2%	58.7%	41.3%
North Carolina	13			1,518,612	1,054,889	438,705	25,018	616,184 R	69.5%	28.9%	70.6%	29.4%
North Dakota	3			280,514	174,109	100,384	6,021	73,725 R	62.1%	35.8%	63.4%	36.6%
Ohio	25			4,094,787	2,441,827	1,558,889	94,071	882,938 R	59.6%	38.1%	61.0%	39.0%
Oklahoma	8			1,029,900	759,025	247,147	23,728	511,878 R	73.7%	24.0%	75.4%	24.6%
Oregon	6			927,946	486,686	392,760	48,500	93,926 R	52.4%	42.3%	55.3%	44.7%
Pennsylvania	27			4,592,106	2,714,521	1,796,951	80,634	917,570 R	59.1%	39.1%	60.2%	39.8%
Rhode Island	4			415,808	220,383	194,645	780	25,738 R	53.0%	46.8%	53.1%	46.9%
South Carolina	8			673,960	477,044	186,824	10,092	290,220 R	70.8%	27.7%	71.9%	28.1%
South Dakota	4			307,415	166,476	139,945	994	26,531 R	54.2%	45.5%	54.3%	45.7%
Tennessee	10			1,201,182	813,147	357,293	30,742	455,854 R	67.7%	29.7%	69.5%	30.5%
Texas	26			3,471,281	2,298,896	1,154,289	18,096	1,144,607 R	66.2%	33.3%	66.6%	33.4%
Utah	4			478,476	323,643	126,284	28,549	197,359 R	67.6%	26.4%	71.9%	28.1%
Vermont	3			186,947	117,149	68,174	1,624	48,975 R	62.7%	36.5%	63.2%	36.8%
Virginia	11		1	1,457,019	988,493	438,887	29,639	549,606 R	67.8%	30.1%	69.3%	30.7%
Washington	9			1,470,847	837,135	568,334	65,378	268,801 R	56.9%	38.6%	59.6%	40.4%
West Virginia	6			762,399	484,964	277,435		207,529 R	63.6%	36.4%	63.6%	36.4%
Wisconsin	11			1,852,890	989,430	810,174	53,286	179,256 R	53.4%	43.7%	55.0%	45.0%
Wyoming	3			145,570	100,464	44,358	748	56,106 R	69.0%	30.5%	69.4%	30.6%
Dist. of Col.		3		163,421	35,226	127,627	568	92,401 D	21.6%	78.1%	21.6%	78.4%
United States	520	17	1	77,718,554	47,169,911	29,170,383	1,378,260	17,999,528 R	60.7%	37.5%	61.8%	38.2%

PRESIDENT 1968

In North Carolina one Republican elector voted in the Electoral College for the American Independent candidates for President and Vice-President.

In New York the Democratic figure includes Liberal votes and in Alabama the Democratic vote is the total of the Alabama Independent Democratic and National Democratic Party of Alabama vote. In certain states candidates appeared under variants of the party name used below and in most states the Vice-Presidential candidate of the American Independent party was listed as Marvin Griffin rather than Curtis E. LeMay.

The full list of candidates for President and Vice-President was:

31,785,480	Richard M. Nixon and Spiro T. Agnew, Republican.
31,275,166	Hubert H. Humphrey and Edmund S. Muskie, Democratic.
9,906,473	George C. Wallace and Curtis E. LeMay, American Independent.
52,588	Henning A. Blomen and George S. Taylor, Socialist Labor.
47,133	Dick Gregory, Peace and Freedom, with various Vice-Presidential candidates.
41,388	Fred Halstead and Paul Boutelle, Socialist Workers.
36,563	Eldridge Cleaver, Peace and Freedom, with various Vice-Presidential candidates.
25,552	Eugene J. McCarthy, under various titles and written-in, but without indication of Vice-Presidential candidates.
15,123	E. Harold Munn and Rolland E. Fisher, Prohibition.
1,519	Ventura Chavez and Adelicio Moya, People's Constitutional.
1,075	Charlene Mitchell and Michael Zagarell, Communist.
142	James Hensley and Roscoe B. MacKenna, Universal.
34	Richard K. Troxell and Merle Thayer, Constitution.
17	Kent M. Soeters and James P. Powers, Berkeley Defense Group.

In the vote listed above for Eldridge Cleaver, two states are included (California and Utah) in which only the party Vice-Presidential candidate appeared on the ballot.

In addition to these votes, 12,430 were cast for elector tickets for which there were no formal Presidential or Vice-Presidential candidates, and 11,192 scattered votes were reported from various states.

UNITED STATES

PRESIDENT 1968

State	Electoral Vote Rep.	Electoral Vote Dem.	Electoral Vote AIP	Total Vote	Republican	Democratic	AIP	Other	Plurality	Percentage Total Vote Rep.	Percentage Total Vote Dem.	Percentage Total Vote AIP
Alabama			10	1,049,922	146,923	196,579	691,425	14,995	494,846 A	14.0%	18.7%	65.9%
Alaska	3			83,035	37,600	35,411	10,024		2,189 R	45.3%	42.6%	12.1%
Arizona	5			486,936	266,721	170,514	46,573	3,128	96,207 R	54.8%	35.0%	9.6%
Arkansas			6	619,969	190,759	188,228	240,982		50,223 A	30.8%	30.4%	38.9%
California	40			7,251,587	3,467,664	3,244,318	487,270	52,335	223,346 R	47.8%	44.7%	6.7%
Colorado	6			811,199	409,345	335,174	60,813	5,867	74,171 R	50.5%	41.3%	7.5%
Connecticut		8		1,256,232	556,721	621,561	76,650	1,300	64,840 D	44.3%	49.5%	6.1%
Delaware	3			214,367	96,714	89,194	28,459		7,520 R	45.1%	41.6%	13.3%
Florida	14			2,187,805	886,804	676,794	624,207		210,010 R	40.5%	30.9%	28.5%
Georgia			12	1,250,266	380,111	334,440	535,550	165	155,439 A	30.4%	26.7%	42.8%
Hawaii		4		236,218	91,425	141,324	3,469		49,899 D	38.7%	59.8%	1.5%
Idaho	4			291,183	165,369	89,273	36,541		76,096 R	56.8%	30.7%	12.5%
Illinois	26			4,619,749	2,174,774	2,039,814	390,958	14,203	134,960 R	47.1%	44.2%	8.5%
Indiana	13			2,123,597	1,067,885	806,659	243,108	5,945	261,226 R	50.3%	38.0%	11.4%
Iowa	9			1,167,931	619,106	476,699	66,422	5,704	142,407 R	53.0%	40.8%	5.7%
Kansas	7			872,783	478,674	302,996	88,921	2,192	175,678 R	54.8%	34.7%	10.2%
Kentucky	9			1,055,893	462,411	397,541	193,098	2,843	64,870 R	43.8%	37.6%	18.3%
Louisiana			10	1,097,450	257,535	309,615	530,300		220,685 A	23.5%	28.2%	48.3%
Maine		4		392,936	169,254	217,312	6,370		48,058 D	43.1%	55.3%	1.6%
Maryland		10		1,235,039	517,995	538,310	178,734		20,315 D	41.9%	43.6%	14.5%
Massachusetts		14		2,331,752	766,844	1,469,218	87,088	8,602	702,374 D	32.9%	63.0%	3.7%
Michigan		21		3,306,250	1,370,665	1,593,082	331,968	10,535	222,417 D	41.5%	48.2%	10.0%
Minnesota		10		1,588,506	658,643	857,738	68,931	3,194	199,095 D	41.5%	54.0%	4.3%
Mississippi			7	654,509	88,516	150,644	415,349		264,705 A	13.5%	23.0%	63.5%
Missouri	12			1,809,502	811,932	791,444	206,126		20,488 R	44.9%	43.7%	11.4%
Montana	4			274,404	138,835	114,117	20,015	1,437	24,718 R	50.6%	41.6%	7.3%
Nebraska	5			536,851	321,163	170,784	44,904		150,379 R	59.8%	31.8%	8.4%
Nevada	3			154,218	73,188	60,598	20,432		12,590 R	47.5%	39.3%	13.2%
New Hampshire	4			297,298	154,903	130,589	11,173	633	24,314 R	52.1%	43.9%	3.8%
New Jersey	17			2,875,395	1,325,467	1,264,206	262,187	23,535	61,261 R	46.1%	44.0%	9.1%
New Mexico	4			327,350	169,692	130,081	25,737	1,840	39,611 R	51.8%	39.7%	7.9%
New York		43		6,791,688	3,007,932	3,378,470	358,864	46,422	370,538 D	44.3%	49.7%	5.3%
North Carolina	12		1	1,587,493	627,192	464,113	496,188		131,004 R	39.5%	29.2%	31.3%
North Dakota	4			247,882	138,669	94,769	14,244	200	43,900 R	55.9%	38.2%	5.7%
Ohio	26			3,959,698	1,791,014	1,700,586	467,495	603	90,428 R	45.2%	42.9%	11.8%
Oklahoma	8			943,086	449,697	301,658	191,731		148,039 R	47.7%	32.0%	20.3%
Oregon	6			819,622	408,433	358,866	49,683	2,640	49,567 R	49.8%	43.8%	6.1%
Pennsylvania		29		4,747,928	2,090,017	2,259,405	378,582	19,924	169,388 D	44.0%	47.6%	8.0%
Rhode Island		4		385,000	122,359	246,518	15,678	445	124,159 D	31.8%	64.0%	4.1%
South Carolina	8			666,978	254,062	197,486	215,430		38,632 R	38.1%	29.6%	32.3%
South Dakota	4			281,264	149,841	118,023	13,400		31,818 R	53.3%	42.0%	4.8%
Tennessee	11			1,248,617	472,592	351,233	424,792		47,800 R	37.8%	28.1%	34.0%
Texas		25		3,079,216	1,227,844	1,266,804	584,269	299	38,960 D	39.9%	41.1%	19.0%
Utah	4			422,568	238,728	156,665	26,906	269	82,063 R	56.5%	37.1%	6.4%
Vermont	3			161,404	85,142	70,255	5,104	903	14,887 R	52.8%	43.5%	3.2%
Virginia	12			1,361,491	590,319	442,387	321,833	6,952	147,932 R	43.4%	32.5%	23.6%
Washington		9		1,304,281	588,510	616,037	96,990	2,744	27,527 D	45.1%	47.2%	7.4%
West Virginia		7		754,206	307,555	374,091	72,560		66,536 D	40.8%	49.6%	9.6%
Wisconsin	12			1,691,538	809,997	748,804	127,835	4,902	61,193 R	47.9%	44.3%	7.6%
Wyoming	3			127,205	70,927	45,173	11,105		25,754 R	55.8%	35.5%	8.7%
Dist. of Col.		3		170,578	31,012	139,566			108,554 D	18.2%	81.8%	
United States	301	191	46	73,211,875	31,785,480	31,275,166	9,906,473	244,756	510,314 R	43.4%	42.7%	13.5%

PRESIDENT 1964

In New York the Democratic figure includes Liberal votes.

The full list of candidates for President and Vice-President was:

43,129,566	Lyndon B. Johnson and Hubert H. Humphrey, Democratic.
27,178,188	Barry M. Goldwater and William E. Miller, Republican.
45,219	Eric Hass and Henning A. Blomen, Socialist Labor.
32,720	Clifton DeBerry and Edward Shaw, Socialist Workers.
23,267	E. Harold Munn and Mark R. Shaw, Prohibition.
6,953	John Kasper and J. B. Stoner, National States Rights.
5,060	Joseph B. Lightburn and T. C. Billings, Constitution.
19	James Hensley and John O. Hopkins, Universal.

In addition, 210,732 votes were cast in Alabama for an unpledged Democratic elector ticket and 12,868 scattered votes were reported from various states.

UNITED STATES

PRESIDENT 1964

State	Electoral Vote Rep.	Electoral Vote Dem.	Electoral Vote Other	Total Vote	Republican	Democratic	Other	Plurality	Percentage Total Vote Rep.	Percentage Total Vote Dem.	Percentage Major Vote Rep.	Percentage Major Vote Dem.
Alabama	10			689,818	479,085		210,733	268,353 R	69.5%		100.0%	
Alaska		3		67,259	22,930	44,329		21,399 D	34.1%	65.9%	34.1%	65.9%
Arizona	5			480,770	242,535	237,753	482	4,782 R	50.4%	49.5%	50.5%	49.5%
Arkansas		6		560,426	243,264	314,197	2,965	70,933 D	43.4%	56.1%	43.6%	56.4%
California		40		7,057,586	2,879,108	4,171,877	6,601	1,292,769 D	40.8%	59.1%	40.8%	59.2%
Colorado		6		776,986	296,767	476,024	4,195	179,257 D	38.2%	61.3%	38.4%	61.6%
Connecticut		8		1,218,578	390,996	826,269	1,313	435,273 D	32.1%	67.8%	32.1%	67.9%
Delaware		3		201,320	78,078	122,704	538	44,626 D	38.8%	60.9%	38.9%	61.1%
Florida		14		1,854,481	905,941	948,540		42,599 D	48.9%	51.1%	48.9%	51.1%
Georgia	12			1,139,335	616,584	522,556	195	94,028 R	54.1%	45.9%	54.1%	45.9%
Hawaii		4		207,271	44,022	163,249		119,227 D	21.2%	78.8%	21.2%	78.8%
Idaho		4		292,477	143,557	148,920		5,363 D	49.1%	50.9%	49.1%	50.9%
Illinois		26		4,702,841	1,905,946	2,796,833	62	890,887 D	40.5%	59.5%	40.5%	59.5%
Indiana		13		2,091,606	911,118	1,170,848	9,640	259,730 D	43.6%	56.0%	43.8%	56.2%
Iowa		9		1,184,539	449,148	733,030	2,361	283,882 D	37.9%	61.9%	38.0%	62.0%
Kansas		7		857,901	386,579	464,028	7,294	77,449 D	45.1%	54.1%	45.4%	54.6%
Kentucky		9		1,046,105	372,977	669,659	3,469	296,682 D	35.7%	64.0%	35.8%	64.2%
Louisiana	10			896,293	509,225	387,068		122,157 R	56.8%	43.2%	56.8%	43.2%
Maine		4		380,965	118,701	262,264		143,563 D	31.2%	68.8%	31.2%	68.8%
Maryland		10		1,116,457	385,495	730,912	50	345,417 D	34.5%	65.5%	34.5%	65.5%
Massachusetts		14		2,344,798	549,727	1,786,422	8,649	1,236,695 D	23.4%	76.2%	23.5%	76.5%
Michigan		21		3,203,102	1,060,152	2,136,615	6,335	1,076,463 D	33.1%	66.7%	33.2%	66.8%
Minnesota		10		1,554,462	559,624	991,117	3,721	431,493 D	36.0%	63.8%	36.1%	63.9%
Mississippi	7			409,146	356,528	52,618		303,910 R	87.1%	12.9%	87.1%	12.9%
Missouri		12		1,817,879	653,535	1,164,344		510,809 D	36.0%	64.0%	36.0%	64.0%
Montana		4		278,628	113,032	164,246	1,350	51,214 D	40.6%	58.9%	40.8%	59.2%
Nebraska		5		584,154	276,847	307,307		30,460 D	47.4%	52.6%	47.4%	52.6%
Nevada		3		135,433	56,094	79,339		23,245 D	41.4%	58.6%	41.4%	58.6%
New Hampshire		4		288,093	104,029	184,064		80,035 D	36.1%	63.9%	36.1%	63.9%
New Jersey		17		2,847,663	964,174	1,868,231	15,258	904,057 D	33.9%	65.6%	34.0%	66.0%
New Mexico		4		328,645	132,838	194,015	1,792	61,177 D	40.4%	59.0%	40.6%	59.4%
New York		43		7,166,275	2,243,559	4,913,102	9,614	2,669,543 D	31.3%	68.6%	31.3%	68.7%
North Carolina		13		1,424,983	624,844	800,139		175,295 D	43.8%	56.2%	43.8%	56.2%
North Dakota		4		258,389	108,207	149,784	398	41,577 D	41.9%	58.0%	41.9%	58.1%
Ohio		26		3,969,196	1,470,865	2,498,331		1,027,466 D	37.1%	62.9%	37.1%	62.9%
Oklahoma		8		932,499	412,665	519,834		107,169 D	44.3%	55.7%	44.3%	55.7%
Oregon		6		786,305	282,779	501,017	2,509	218,238 D	36.0%	63.7%	36.1%	63.9%
Pennsylvania		29		4,822,690	1,673,657	3,130,954	18,079	1,457,297 D	34.7%	64.9%	34.8%	65.2%
Rhode Island		4		390,091	74,615	315,463	13	240,848 D	19.1%	80.9%	19.1%	80.9%
South Carolina	8			524,779	309,048	215,723	8	93,325 R	58.9%	41.1%	58.9%	41.1%
South Dakota		4		293,118	130,108	163,010		32,902 D	44.4%	55.6%	44.4%	55.6%
Tennessee		11		1,143,946	508,965	634,947	34	125,982 D	44.5%	55.5%	44.5%	55.5%
Texas		25		2,626,811	958,566	1,663,185	5,060	704,619 D	36.5%	63.3%	36.6%	63.4%
Utah		4		401,413	181,785	219,628		37,843 D	45.3%	54.7%	45.3%	54.7%
Vermont		3		163,089	54,942	108,127	20	53,185 D	33.7%	66.3%	33.7%	66.3%
Virginia		12		1,042,267	481,334	558,038	2,895	76,704 D	46.2%	53.5%	46.3%	53.7%
Washington		9		1,258,556	470,366	779,881	8,309	309,515 D	37.4%	62.0%	37.6%	62.4%
West Virginia		7		792,040	253,953	538,087		284,134 D	32.1%	67.9%	32.1%	67.9%
Wisconsin		12		1,691,815	638,495	1,050,424	2,896	411,929 D	37.7%	62.1%	37.8%	62.2%
Wyoming		3		142,716	61,998	80,718		18,720 D	43.4%	56.6%	43.4%	56.6%
Dist. of Col.		3		198,597	28,801	169,796		140,995 D	14.5%	85.5%	14.5%	85.5%
United States	52	486	—	70,644,592	27,178,188	43,129,566	336,838	15,951,378 D	38.5%	61.1%	38.7%	61.3%

PRESIDENT 1960

Senator Harry Flood Byrd received 15 votes for President in the Electoral College; these were the votes of 6 of the 11 Democratic electors in Alabama, all 8 unpledged Democratic electors in Mississippi, and one of the 8 Republican electors in Oklahoma. The Alabama and Mississippi electors also cast 14 votes for Senator Strom Thurmond for Vice-President; the single Oklahoma elector voted for Senator Barry M. Goldwater for Vice-President.

In New York the Democratic figure includes Liberal votes.

The full list of candidates for President and Vice-President was:

34,226,731	John F. Kennedy and Lyndon B. Johnson, Democratic.
34,108,157	Richard M. Nixon and Henry Cabot Lodge, Republican.
47,522	Eric Hass and Georgia Cozzini, Socialist Labor.
46,203	Rutherford L. Decker and E. Harold Munn, Prohibition.
44,977	Orval E. Faubus and John G. Crommelin, National States Rights.
40,165	Farrell Dobbs and Myra Tanner Weiss, Socialist Workers.
18,162	Charles L. Sullivan and Merritt B. Curtis, Constitution.
8,708	J. Bracken Lee and Kent H. Courtney, Conservative.
4,204	C. Benton Coiner and Edward J. Silverman, Conservative.
1,767	Lar Daly and B. M. Miller, Tax Cut.
1,485	Clennon King and Reginald Carter, Independent Afro-American.
1,401	Merritt B. Curtis and B. M. Miller, Constitution.

In addition, 169,572 votes were cast in Louisiana for Independent electors and 116,248 in Mississippi for an unpledged Democratic elector ticket. 539 votes were cast in Michigan for an Independent American ticket and 2,378 scattered votes were reported from various states.

UNITED STATES

PRESIDENT 1960

State	Electoral Vote			Total Vote	Republican	Democratic	Other	Plurality	Percentage			
									Total Vote		Major Vote	
	Rep.	Dem.	Other						Rep.	Dem.	Rep.	Dem.
Alabama		5	6	570,225	237,981	324,050	8,194	86,069 D	41.7%	56.8%	42.3%	57.7%
Alaska	3			60,762	30,953	29,809		1,144 R	50.9%	49.1%	50.9%	49.1%
Arizona	4			398,491	221,241	176,781	469	44,460 R	55.5%	44.4%	55.6%	44.4%
Arkansas		8		428,509	184,508	215,049	28,952	30,541 D	43.1%	50.2%	46.2%	53.8%
California	32			6,506,578	3,259,722	3,224,099	22,757	35,623 R	50.1%	49.6%	50.3%	49.7%
Colorado	6			736,236	402,242	330,629	3,365	71,613 R	54.6%	44.9%	54.9%	45.1%
Connecticut		8		1,222,883	565,813	657,055	15	91,242 D	46.3%	53.7%	46.3%	53.7%
Delaware		3		196,683	96,373	99,590	720	3,217 D	49.0%	50.6%	49.2%	50.8%
Florida	10			1,544,176	795,476	748,700		46,776 R	51.5%	48.5%	51.5%	48.5%
Georgia		12		733,349	274,472	458,638	239	184,166 D	37.4%	62.5%	37.4%	62.6%
Hawaii		3		184,705	92,295	92,410		115 D	50.0%	50.0%	50.0%	50.0%
Idaho	4			300,450	161,597	138,853		22,744 R	53.8%	46.2%	53.8%	46.2%
Illinois		27		4,757,409	2,368,988	2,377,846	10,575	8,858 D	49.8%	50.0%	49.9%	50.1%
Indiana	13			2,135,360	1,175,120	952,358	7,882	222,762 R	55.0%	44.6%	55.2%	44.8%
Iowa	10			1,273,810	722,381	550,565	864	171,816 R	56.7%	43.2%	56.7%	43.3%
Kansas	8			928,825	561,474	363,213	4,138	198,261 R	60.4%	39.1%	60.7%	39.3%
Kentucky	10			1,124,462	602,607	521,855		80,752 R	53.6%	46.4%	53.6%	46.4%
Louisiana		10		807,891	230,980	407,339	169,572	176,359 D	28.6%	50.4%	36.2%	63.8%
Maine	5			421,767	240,608	181,159		59,449 R	57.0%	43.0%	57.0%	43.0%
Maryland		9		1,055,349	489,538	565,808	3	76,270 D	46.4%	53.6%	46.4%	53.6%
Massachusetts		16		2,469,480	976,750	1,487,174	5,556	510,424 D	39.6%	60.2%	39.6%	60.4%
Michigan		20		3,318,097	1,620,428	1,687,269	10,400	66,841 D	48.8%	50.9%	49.0%	51.0%
Minnesota		11		1,541,887	757,915	779,933	4,039	22,018 D	49.2%	50.6%	49.3%	50.7%
Mississippi			8	298,171	73,561	108,362	116,248	7,886 U	24.7%	36.3%	40.4%	59.6%
Missouri		13		1,934,422	962,221	972,201		9,980 D	49.7%	50.3%	49.7%	50.3%
Montana	4			277,579	141,841	134,891	847	6,950 R	51.1%	48.6%	51.3%	48.7%
Nebraska	6			613,095	380,553	232,542		148,011 R	62.1%	37.9%	62.1%	37.9%
Nevada		3		107,267	52,387	54,880		2,493 D	48.8%	51.2%	48.8%	51.2%
New Hampshire	4			295,761	157,989	137,772		20,217 R	53.4%	46.6%	53.4%	46.6%
New Jersey		16		2,773,111	1,363,324	1,385,415	24,372	22,091 D	49.2%	50.0%	49.6%	50.4%
New Mexico		4		311,107	153,733	156,027	1,347	2,294 D	49.4%	50.2%	49.6%	50.4%
New York		45		7,291,079	3,446,419	3,830,085	14,575	383,666 D	47.3%	52.5%	47.4%	52.6%
North Carolina		14		1,368,556	655,420	713,136		57,716 D	47.9%	52.1%	47.9%	52.1%
North Dakota	4			278,431	154,310	123,963	158	30,347 R	55.4%	44.5%	55.5%	44.5%
Ohio	25			4,161,859	2,217,611	1,944,248		273,363 R	53.3%	46.7%	53.3%	46.7%
Oklahoma	7		1	903,150	533,039	370,111		162,928 R	59.0%	41.0%	59.0%	41.0%
Oregon	6			776,421	408,060	367,402	959	40,658 R	52.6%	47.3%	52.6%	47.4%
Pennsylvania		32		5,006,541	2,439,956	2,556,282	10,303	116,326 D	48.7%	51.1%	48.8%	51.2%
Rhode Island		4		405,535	147,502	258,032	1	110,530 D	36.4%	63.6%	36.4%	63.6%
South Carolina		8		386,688	188,558	198,129	1	9,571 D	48.8%	51.2%	48.8%	51.2%
South Dakota	4			306,487	178,417	128,070		50,347 R	58.2%	41.8%	58.2%	41.8%
Tennessee	11			1,051,792	556,577	481,453	13,762	75,124 R	52.9%	45.8%	53.6%	46.4%
Texas		24		2,311,084	1,121,310	1,167,567	22,207	46,257 D	48.5%	50.5%	49.0%	51.0%
Utah	4			374,709	205,361	169,248	100	36,113 R	54.8%	45.2%	54.8%	45.2%
Vermont	3			167,324	98,131	69,186	7	28,945 R	58.6%	41.3%	58.6%	41.4%
Virginia	12			771,449	404,521	362,327	4,601	42,194 R	52.4%	47.0%	52.8%	47.2%
Washington	9			1,241,572	629,273	599,298	13,001	29,975 R	50.7%	48.3%	51.2%	48.8%
West Virginia		8		837,781	395,995	441,786		45,791 D	47.3%	52.7%	47.3%	52.7%
Wisconsin	12			1,729,082	895,175	830,805	3,102	64,370 R	51.8%	48.0%	51.9%	48.1%
Wyoming	3			140,782	77,451	63,331		14,120 R	55.0%	45.0%	55.0%	45.0%
United States	219	303	15	68,838,219	34,108,157	34,226,731	503,331	118,574 D	49.5%	49.7%	49.9%	50.1%

PRESIDENT 1956

One of the 11 Democratic electors chosen in Alabama cast his Electoral College vote for Walter B. Jones and Herman Talmadge rather than for the national Democratic candidates.

The Republican figure in Mississippi includes votes cast for two elector tickets. In New York the Democratic figure includes Liberal votes.

The full list of candidates for President and Vice-President was:

35,590,472	Dwight D. Eisenhower and Richard M. Nixon, Republican.
26,022,752	Adlai E. Stevenson and Estes Kefauver, Democratic.
111,178	T. Coleman Andrews and Thomas H. Werdel, States Rights.
44,450	Eric Hass and Georgia Cozzini, Socialist Labor.
41,937	Enoch A. Holtwick and Edwin M. Cooper, Prohibition.
7,797	Farrell Dobbs and Myra Tanner Weiss, Socialist Workers.
2,657	Harry Flood Byrd and William E. Jenner, States Rights.
2,126	Darlington Hoopes and Samuel H. Friedman, Socialist.
1,829	Henry B. Krajewski and Anne Marie Yezo, American Third Party.
8	Gerald L. K. Smith and Charles F. Robertson, Christian Nationalist.

In addition, 196,318 votes were cast in Alabama, Louisiana, Mississippi, and South Carolina for Independent electors or for States Rights elector tickets not officially pledged to any candidate, and 5,384 scattered votes were reported from various states.

UNITED STATES

PRESIDENT 1956

	Electoral Vote			Total					Percentage			
									Total Vote		Major Vote	
State	Rep.	Dem.	Other	Vote	Republican	Democratic	Other	Plurality	Rep.	Dem.	Rep.	Dem.
Alabama		10	1	496,861	195,694	280,844	20,323	85,150 D	39.4%	56.5%	41.1%	58.9%
Alaska												
Arizona	4			290,173	176,990	112,880	303	64,110 R	61.0%	38.9%	61.1%	38.9%
Arkansas		8		406,572	186,287	213,277	7,008	26,990 D	45.8%	52.5%	46.6%	53.4%
California	32			5,466,355	3,027,668	2,420,135	18,552	607,533 R	55.4%	44.3%	55.6%	44.4%
Colorado	6			657,074	394,479	257,997	4,598	136,482 R	60.0%	39.3%	60.5%	39.5%
Connecticut	8			1,117,121	711,837	405,079	205	306,758 R	63.7%	36.3%	63.7%	36.3%
Delaware	3			177,988	98,057	79,421	510	18,636 R	55.1%	44.6%	55.3%	44.7%
Florida	10			1,125,762	643,849	480,371	1,542	163,478 R	57.2%	42.7%	57.3%	42.7%
Georgia		12		669,655	222,778	444,688	2,189	221,910 D	33.3%	66.4%	33.4%	66.6%
Hawaii												
Idaho	4			272,989	166,979	105,868	142	61,111 R	61.2%	38.8%	61.2%	38.8%
Illinois	27			4,407,407	2,623,327	1,775,682	8,398	847,645 R	59.5%	40.3%	59.6%	40.4%
Indiana	13			1,974,607	1,182,811	783,908	7,888	398,903 R	59.9%	39.7%	60.1%	39.9%
Iowa	10			1,234,564	729,187	501,858	3,519	227,329 R	59.1%	40.7%	59.2%	40.8%
Kansas	8			866,243	566,878	296,317	3,048	270,561 R	65.4%	34.2%	65.7%	34.3%
Kentucky	10			1,053,805	572,192	476,453	5,160	95,739 R	54.3%	45.2%	54.6%	45.4%
Louisiana	10			617,544	329,047	243,977	44,520	85,070 R	53.3%	39.5%	57.4%	42.6%
Maine	5			351,706	249,238	102,468		146,770 R	70.9%	29.1%	70.9%	29.1%
Maryland	9			932,827	559,738	372,613	476	187,125 R	60.0%	39.9%	60.0%	40.0%
Massachusetts	16			2,348,506	1,393,197	948,190	7,119	445,007 R	59.3%	40.4%	59.5%	40.5%
Michigan	20			3,080,468	1,713,647	1,359,898	6,923	353,749 R	55.6%	44.1%	55.8%	44.2%
Minnesota	11			1,340,005	719,302	617,525	3,178	101,777 R	53.7%	46.1%	53.8%	46.2%
Mississippi		8		248,104	60,685	144,453	42,966	83,768 D	24.5%	58.2%	29.6%	70.4%
Missouri		13		1,832,562	914,289	918,273		3,984 D	49.9%	50.1%	49.9%	50.1%
Montana	4			271,171	154,933	116,238		38,695 R	57.1%	42.9%	57.1%	42.9%
Nebraska	6			577,137	378,108	199,029		179,079 R	65.5%	34.5%	65.5%	34.5%
Nevada	3			96,689	56,049	40,640		15,409 R	58.0%	42.0%	58.0%	42.0%
New Hampshire	4			266,994	176,519	90,364	111	86,155 R	66.1%	33.8%	66.1%	33.9%
New Jersey	16			2,484,312	1,606,942	850,337	27,033	756,605 R	64.7%	34.2%	65.4%	34.6%
New Mexico	4			253,926	146,788	106,098	1,040	40,690 R	57.8%	41.8%	58.0%	42.0%
New York	45			7,095,971	4,345,506	2,747,944	2,521	1,597,562 R	61.2%	38.4%	61.3%	38.7%
North Carolina		14		1,165,592	575,062	590,530		15,468 D	49.3%	50.7%	49.3%	50.7%
North Dakota	4			253,991	156,766	96,742	483	60,024 R	61.7%	38.1%	61.8%	38.2%
Ohio	25			3,702,265	2,262,610	1,439,655		822,955 R	61.1%	38.9%	61.1%	38.9%
Oklahoma	8			859,350	473,769	385,581		88,188 R	55.1%	44.9%	55.1%	44.9%
Oregon	6			736,132	406,393	329,204	535	77,189 R	55.2%	44.7%	55.2%	44.8%
Pennsylvania	32			4,576,503	2,585,252	1,981,769	9,482	603,483 R	56.5%	43.3%	56.6%	43.4%
Rhode Island	4			387,609	225,819	161,790		64,029 R	58.3%	41.7%	58.3%	41.7%
South Carolina		8		300,583	75,700	136,372	88,511	47,863 D	25.2%	45.4%	35.7%	64.3%
South Dakota	4			293,857	171,569	122,288		49,281 R	58.4%	41.6%	58.4%	41.6%
Tennessee	11			939,404	462,288	456,507	20,609	5,781 R	49.2%	48.6%	50.3%	49.7%
Texas	24			1,955,168	1,080,619	859,958	14,591	220,661 R	55.3%	44.0%	55.7%	44.3%
Utah	4			333,995	215,631	118,364		97,267 R	64.6%	35.4%	64.6%	35.4%
Vermont	3			152,978	110,390	42,549	39	67,841 R	72.2%	27.8%	72.2%	27.8%
Virginia	12			697,978	386,459	267,760	43,759	118,699 R	55.4%	38.4%	59.1%	40.9%
Washington	9			1,150,889	620,430	523,002	7,457	97,428 R	53.9%	45.4%	54.3%	45.7%
West Virginia	8			830,831	449,297	381,534		67,763 R	54.1%	45.9%	54.1%	45.9%
Wisconsin	12			1,550,558	954,844	586,768	8,946	368,076 R	61.6%	37.8%	61.9%	38.1%
Wyoming	3			124,127	74,573	49,554		25,019 R	60.1%	39.9%	60.1%	39.9%
United States	457	73	1	62,026,908	35,590,472	26,022,752	413,684	9,567,720 R	57.4%	42.0%	57.8%	42.2%

PRESIDENT 1952

The Republican figure in South Carolina includes votes cast for two elector tickets; in Mississippi the Republican total is the vote cast for an Independent elector ticket "pledged to vote for the nominees of the National Republican Party". In New York the Democratic figure includes Liberal votes.

The full list of candidates for President and Vice-President was:

33,936,234	Dwight D. Eisenhower and Richard M. Nixon, Republican.
27,314,992	Adlai E. Stevenson and John J. Sparkman, Democratic.
140,023	Vincent Hallinan and Charlotta Bass, Progressive.
72,949	Stuart Hamblen and Enoch A. Holtwick, Prohibition.
30,267	Eric Hass and Stephen Emery, Socialist Labor.
20,203	Darlington Hoopes and Samuel H. Friedman, Socialist.
10,312	Farrell Dobbs and Myra Tanner Weiss, Socialist Workers.
4,203	Henry B. Krajewski and Frank Jenkins, Poor Man's Party.

In addition, 17,205 votes were cast for various elector tickets filed on behalf of General Douglas MacArthur, including Christian Nationalist (with Jack B. Tenney as candidate for Vice-President), Constitution (with Vivien Kellems), and America First (with Senator Harry Flood Byrd). In California, Missouri, and Texas the MacArthur vote was cast for two elector tickets. 4,530 scattered votes were reported from various states.

UNITED STATES

PRESIDENT 1952

State	Electoral Vote Rep.	Electoral Vote Dem.	Electoral Vote Other	Total Vote	Republican	Democratic	Other	Plurality	Percentage Total Vote Rep.	Percentage Total Vote Dem.	Percentage Major Vote Rep.	Percentage Major Vote Dem.
Alabama		11		426,120	149,231	275,075	1,814	125,844 D	35.0%	64.6%	35.2%	64.8%
Alaska												
Arizona	4			260,570	152,042	108,528		43,514 R	58.3%	41.7%	58.3%	41.7%
Arkansas		8		404,800	177,155	226,300	1,345	49,145 D	43.8%	55.9%	43.9%	56.1%
California	32			5,141,849	2,897,310	2,197,548	46,991	699,762 R	56.3%	42.7%	56.9%	43.1%
Colorado	6			630,103	379,782	245,504	4,817	134,278 R	60.3%	39.0%	60.7%	39.3%
Connecticut	8			1,096,911	611,012	481,649	4,250	129,363 R	55.7%	43.9%	55.9%	44.1%
Delaware	3			174,025	90,059	83,315	651	6,744 R	51.8%	47.9%	51.9%	48.1%
Florida	10			989,337	544,036	444,950	351	99,086 R	55.0%	45.0%	55.0%	45.0%
Georgia		12		655,785	198,961	456,823	1	257,862 D	30.3%	69.7%	30.3%	69.7%
Hawaii												
Idaho	4			276,254	180,707	95,081	466	85,626 R	65.4%	34.4%	65.5%	34.5%
Illinois	27			4,481,058	2,457,327	2,013,920	9,811	443,407 R	54.8%	44.9%	55.0%	45.0%
Indiana	13			1,955,049	1,136,259	801,530	17,260	334,729 R	58.1%	41.0%	58.6%	41.4%
Iowa	10			1,268,773	808,906	451,513	8,354	357,393 R	63.8%	35.6%	64.2%	35.8%
Kansas	8			896,166	616,302	273,296	6,568	343,006 R	68.8%	30.5%	69.3%	30.7%
Kentucky		10		993,148	495,029	495,729	2,390	700 D	49.8%	49.9%	50.0%	50.0%
Louisiana		10		651,952	306,925	345,027		38,102 D	47.1%	52.9%	47.1%	52.9%
Maine	5			351,786	232,353	118,806	627	113,547 R	66.0%	33.8%	66.2%	33.8%
Maryland	9			902,074	499,424	395,337	7,313	104,087 R	55.4%	43.8%	55.8%	44.2%
Massachusetts	16			2,383,398	1,292,325	1,083,525	7,548	208,800 R	54.2%	45.5%	54.4%	45.6%
Michigan	20			2,798,592	1,551,529	1,230,657	16,406	320,872 R	55.4%	44.0%	55.8%	44.2%
Minnesota	11			1,379,483	763,211	608,458	7,814	154,753 R	55.3%	44.1%	55.6%	44.4%
Mississippi		8		285,532	112,966	172,566		59,600 D	39.6%	60.4%	39.6%	60.4%
Missouri	13			1,892,062	959,429	929,830	2,803	29,599 R	50.7%	49.1%	50.8%	49.2%
Montana	4			265,037	157,394	106,213	1,430	51,181 R	59.4%	40.1%	59.7%	40.3%
Nebraska	6			609,660	421,603	188,057		233,546 R	69.2%	30.8%	69.2%	30.8%
Nevada	3			82,190	50,502	31,688		18,814 R	61.4%	38.6%	61.4%	38.6%
New Hampshire	4			272,950	166,287	106,663		59,624 R	60.9%	39.1%	60.9%	39.1%
New Jersey	16			2,418,554	1,373,613	1,015,902	29,039	357,711 R	56.8%	42.0%	57.5%	42.5%
New Mexico	4			238,608	132,170	105,661	777	26,509 R	55.4%	44.3%	55.6%	44.4%
New York	45			7,128,239	3,952,813	3,104,601	70,825	848,212 R	55.5%	43.6%	56.0%	44.0%
North Carolina		14		1,210,910	558,107	652,803		94,696 D	46.1%	53.9%	46.1%	53.9%
North Dakota	4			270,127	191,712	76,694	1,721	115,018 R	71.0%	28.4%	71.4%	28.6%
Ohio	25			3,700,758	2,100,391	1,600,367		500,024 R	56.8%	43.2%	56.8%	43.2%
Oklahoma	8			948,984	518,045	430,939		87,106 R	54.6%	45.4%	54.6%	45.4%
Oregon	6			695,059	420,815	270,579	3,665	150,236 R	60.5%	38.9%	60.9%	39.1%
Pennsylvania	32			4,580,969	2,415,789	2,146,269	18,911	269,520 R	52.7%	46.9%	53.0%	47.0%
Rhode Island	4			414,498	210,935	203,293	270	7,642 R	50.9%	49.0%	50.9%	49.1%
South Carolina		8		341,087	168,082	173,004	1	4,922 D	49.3%	50.7%	49.3%	50.7%
South Dakota	4			294,283	203,857	90,426		113,431 R	69.3%	30.7%	69.3%	30.7%
Tennessee	11			892,553	446,147	443,710	2,696	2,437 R	50.0%	49.7%	50.1%	49.9%
Texas	24			2,075,946	1,102,878	969,228	3,840	133,650 R	53.1%	46.7%	53.2%	46.8%
Utah	4			329,554	194,190	135,364		58,826 R	58.9%	41.1%	58.9%	41.1%
Vermont	3			153,557	109,717	43,355	485	66,362 R	71.5%	28.2%	71.7%	28.3%
Virginia	12			619,689	349,037	268,677	1,975	80,360 R	56.3%	43.4%	56.5%	43.5%
Washington	9			1,102,708	599,107	492,845	10,756	106,262 R	54.3%	44.7%	54.9%	45.1%
West Virginia		8		873,548	419,970	453,578		33,608 D	48.1%	51.9%	48.1%	51.9%
Wisconsin	12			1,607,370	979,744	622,175	5,451	357,569 R	61.0%	38.7%	61.2%	38.8%
Wyoming	3			129,253	81,049	47,934	270	33,115 R	62.7%	37.1%	62.8%	37.2%
United States	442	89	—	61,550,918	33,936,234	27,314,992	299,692	6,621,242 R	55.1%	44.4%	55.4%	44.6%

PRESIDENT 1948

The electoral votes of Alabama, Louisiana, Mississippi, and South Carolina were cast for the States Rights nominees. In addition, one of the 12 Democratic electors chosen in Tennessee cast his Electoral College vote for the States Rights nominees rather than for the national Democratic candidates.

In Alabama the Democratic electors were pledged to the States Rights candidates. There were no national Democratic electors on the ballot in that state.

The Republican figure in Mississippi includes votes cast for two elector tickets. In New York the Democratic figure includes Liberal votes.

The full list of candidates for President and Vice-President was:

24,179,345	Harry S. Truman and Alben W. Barkley, Democratic.
21,991,291	Thomas E. Dewey and Earl Warren, Republican.
1,176,125	Strom Thurmond and Fielding L. Wright, States Rights.
1,157,326	Henry A. Wallace and Glen H. Taylor, Progressive.
139,572	Norman Thomas and Tucker P. Smith, Socialist.
103,900	Claude A. Watson and Dale H. Learn, Prohibition.
29,241	Edward A. Teichert and Stephen Emery, Socialist Labor.
13,614	Farrell Dobbs and Grace Carlson, Socialist Workers.

In addition, 3,412 scattered votes were reported from various states.

UNITED STATES

PRESIDENT 1948

State	Electoral Vote Rep.	Electoral Vote Dem.	Electoral Vote Other	Total Vote	Republican	Democratic	Other	Plurality	Percentage Total Vote Rep.	Percentage Total Vote Dem.	Percentage Major Vote Rep.	Percentage Major Vote Dem.
Alabama			11	214,980	40,930		174,050	130,513 SR	19.0%		100.0%	
Alaska												
Arizona		4		177,065	77,597	95,251	4,217	17,654 D	43.8%	53.8%	44.9%	55.1%
Arkansas		9		242,475	50,959	149,659	41,857	98,700 D	21.0%	61.7%	25.4%	74.6%
California		25		4,021,538	1,895,269	1,913,134	213,135	17,865 D	47.1%	47.6%	49.8%	50.2%
Colorado		6		515,237	239,714	267,288	8,235	27,574 D	46.5%	51.9%	47.3%	52.7%
Connecticut	8			883,518	437,754	423,297	22,467	14,457 R	49.5%	47.9%	50.8%	49.2%
Delaware	3			139,073	69,588	67,813	1,672	1,775 R	50.0%	48.8%	50.6%	49.4%
Florida		8		577,643	194,280	281,988	101,375	87,708 D	33.6%	48.8%	40.8%	59.2%
Georgia		12		418,844	76,691	254,646	87,507	169,511 D	18.3%	60.8%	23.1%	76.9%
Hawaii												
Idaho		4		214,816	101,514	107,370	5,932	5,856 D	47.3%	50.0%	48.6%	51.4%
Illinois		28		3,984,046	1,961,103	1,994,715	28,228	33,612 D	49.2%	50.1%	49.6%	50.4%
Indiana	13			1,656,212	821,079	807,831	27,302	13,248 R	49.6%	48.8%	50.4%	49.6%
Iowa		10		1,038,264	494,018	522,380	21,866	28,362 D	47.6%	50.3%	48.6%	51.4%
Kansas	8			788,819	423,039	351,902	13,878	71,137 R	53.6%	44.6%	54.6%	45.4%
Kentucky		11		822,658	341,210	466,756	14,692	125,546 D	41.5%	56.7%	42.2%	57.8%
Louisiana			10	416,336	72,657	136,344	207,335	67,946 SR	17.5%	32.7%	34.8%	65.2%
Maine	5			264,787	150,234	111,916	2,637	38,318 R	56.7%	42.3%	57.3%	42.7%
Maryland	8			596,748	294,814	286,521	15,413	8,293 R	49.4%	48.0%	50.7%	49.3%
Massachusetts		16		2,107,146	909,370	1,151,788	45,988	242,418 D	43.2%	54.7%	44.1%	55.9%
Michigan	19			2,109,609	1,038,595	1,003,448	67,566	35,147 R	49.2%	47.6%	50.9%	49.1%
Minnesota		11		1,212,226	483,617	692,966	35,643	209,349 D	39.9%	57.2%	41.1%	58.9%
Mississippi			9	192,190	5,043	19,384	167,763	148,154 SR	2.6%	10.1%	20.6%	79.4%
Missouri		15		1,578,628	655,039	917,315	6,274	262,276 D	41.5%	58.1%	41.7%	58.3%
Montana		4		224,278	96,770	119,071	8,437	22,301 D	43.1%	53.1%	44.8%	55.2%
Nebraska	6			488,940	264,774	224,165	1	40,609 R	54.2%	45.8%	54.2%	45.8%
Nevada		3		62,117	29,357	31,291	1,469	1,934 D	47.3%	50.4%	48.4%	51.6%
New Hampshire	4			231,440	121,299	107,995	2,146	13,304 R	52.4%	46.7%	52.9%	47.1%
New Jersey	16			1,949,555	981,124	895,455	72,976	85,669 R	50.3%	45.9%	52.3%	47.7%
New Mexico		4		187,063	80,303	105,464	1,296	25,161 D	42.9%	56.4%	43.2%	56.8%
New York	47			6,177,337	2,841,163	2,780,204	555,970	60,959 R	46.0%	45.0%	50.5%	49.5%
North Carolina		14		791,209	258,572	459,070	73,567	200,498 D	32.7%	58.0%	36.0%	64.0%
North Dakota	4			220,716	115,139	95,812	9,765	19,327 R	52.2%	43.4%	54.6%	45.4%
Ohio		25		2,936,071	1,445,684	1,452,791	37,596	7,107 D	49.2%	49.5%	49.9%	50.1%
Oklahoma		10		721,599	268,817	452,782		183,965 D	37.3%	62.7%	37.3%	62.7%
Oregon	6			524,080	260,904	243,147	20,029	17,757 R	49.8%	46.4%	51.8%	48.2%
Pennsylvania	35			3,735,348	1,902,197	1,752,426	80,725	149,771 R	50.9%	46.9%	52.0%	48.0%
Rhode Island		4		327,702	135,787	188,736	3,179	52,949 D	41.4%	57.6%	41.8%	58.2%
South Carolina			8	142,571	5,386	34,423	102,762	68,184 SR	3.8%	24.1%	13.5%	86.5%
South Dakota	4			250,105	129,651	117,653	2,801	11,998 R	51.8%	47.0%	52.4%	47.6%
Tennessee		11	1	550,283	202,914	270,402	76,967	67,488 D	36.9%	49.1%	42.9%	57.1%
Texas		23		1,249,577	303,467	824,235	121,875	520,768 D	24.3%	66.0%	26.9%	73.1%
Utah		4		276,306	124,402	149,151	2,753	24,749 D	45.0%	54.0%	45.5%	54.5%
Vermont	3			123,382	75,926	45,557	1,899	30,369 R	61.5%	36.9%	62.5%	37.5%
Virginia		11		419,256	172,070	200,786	46,400	28,716 D	41.0%	47.9%	46.1%	53.9%
Washington		8		905,058	386,314	476,165	42,579	89,851 D	42.7%	52.6%	44.8%	55.2%
West Virginia		8		748,750	316,251	429,188	3,311	112,937 D	42.2%	57.3%	42.4%	57.6%
Wisconsin		12		1,276,800	590,959	647,310	38,531	56,351 D	46.3%	50.7%	47.7%	52.3%
Wyoming		3		101,425	47,947	52,354	1,124	4,407 D	47.3%	51.6%	47.8%	52.2%
United States	189	303	39	48,793,826	21,991,291	24,179,345	2,623,190	2,188,054 D	45.1%	49.6%	47.6%	52.4%

PRESIDENT 1944

The Republican figures in Georgia, Mississippi and South Carolina include votes cast for two elector tickets. The Democratic figure in Mississippi includes votes cast for two elector tickets and in New York includes American Labor and Liberal votes.

In South Carolina an uncommitted Southern Democratic elector ticket ran in second place ahead of the Republican candidates.

The full list of candidates for President and Vice-President was:

25,612,610	Franklin D. Roosevelt and Harry S. Truman, Democratic.
22,017,617	Thomas E. Dewey and John W. Bricker, Republican.
79,003	Norman Thomas and Darlington Hoopes, Socialist.
74,799	Claude A. Watson and Andrew Johnson, Prohibition.
45,191	Edward A. Teichert and Arla A. Albaugh, Socialist Labor.
1,780	Gerald L. K. Smith and Harry Romer, American First.

In addition, 135,444 votes were cast in Texas for a Texas Regulars elector ticket and 7,799 in South Carolina for an uncommitted Southern Democratic elector ticket. There were 2,447 scattered votes reported from various states.

UNITED STATES

PRESIDENT 1944

State	Electoral Vote Rep.	Electoral Vote Dem.	Electoral Vote Other	Total Vote	Republican	Democratic	Other	Plurality	Percentage Total Vote Rep.	Percentage Total Vote Dem.	Percentage Major Vote Rep.	Percentage Major Vote Dem.
Alabama		11		244,743	44,540	198,918	1,285	154,378 D	18.2%	81.3%	18.3%	81.7%
Alaska												
Arizona		4		137,634	56,287	80,926	421	24,639 D	40.9%	58.8%	41.0%	59.0%
Arkansas		9		212,954	63,551	148,965	438	85,414 D	29.8%	70.0%	29.9%	70.1%
California		25		3,520,875	1,512,965	1,988,564	19,346	475,599 D	43.0%	56.5%	43.2%	56.8%
Colorado	6			505,039	268,731	234,331	1,977	34,400 R	53.2%	46.4%	53.4%	46.6%
Connecticut		8		831,990	390,527	435,146	6,317	44,619 D	46.9%	52.3%	47.3%	52.7%
Delaware		3		125,361	56,747	68,166	448	11,419 D	45.3%	54.4%	45.4%	54.6%
Florida		8		482,803	143,215	339,377	211	196,162 D	29.7%	70.3%	29.7%	70.3%
Georgia		12		328,129	59,900	268,187	42	208,287 D	18.3%	81.7%	18.3%	81.7%
Hawaii												
Idaho		4		208,321	100,137	107,399	785	7,262 D	48.1%	51.6%	48.3%	51.7%
Illinois		28		4,036,061	1,939,314	2,079,479	17,268	140,165 D	48.0%	51.5%	48.3%	51.7%
Indiana	13			1,672,091	875,891	781,403	14,797	94,488 R	52.4%	46.7%	52.9%	47.1%
Iowa	10			1,052,599	547,267	499,876	5,456	47,391 R	52.0%	47.5%	52.3%	47.7%
Kansas	8			733,776	442,096	287,458	4,222	154,638 R	60.2%	39.2%	60.6%	39.4%
Kentucky		11		867,924	392,448	472,589	2,887	80,141 D	45.2%	54.5%	45.4%	54.6%
Louisiana		10		349,383	67,750	281,564	69	213,814 D	19.4%	80.6%	19.4%	80.6%
Maine	5			296,400	155,434	140,631	335	14,803 R	52.4%	47.4%	52.5%	47.5%
Maryland		8		608,439	292,949	315,490		22,541 D	48.1%	51.9%	48.1%	51.9%
Massachusetts		16		1,960,665	921,350	1,035,296	4,019	113,946 D	47.0%	52.8%	47.1%	52.9%
Michigan		19		2,205,223	1,084,423	1,106,899	13,901	22,476 D	49.2%	50.2%	49.5%	50.5%
Minnesota		11		1,125,504	527,416	589,864	8,224	62,448 D	46.9%	52.4%	47.2%	52.8%
Mississippi		9		180,234	11,613	168,621		157,008 D	6.4%	93.6%	6.4%	93.6%
Missouri		15		1,571,697	761,175	807,356	3,166	46,181 D	48.4%	51.4%	48.5%	51.5%
Montana		4		207,355	93,163	112,556	1,636	19,393 D	44.9%	54.3%	45.3%	54.7%
Nebraska	6			563,126	329,880	233,246		96,634 R	58.6%	41.4%	58.6%	41.4%
Nevada		3		54,234	24,611	29,623		5,012 D	45.4%	54.6%	45.4%	54.6%
New Hampshire		4		229,625	109,916	119,663	46	9,747 D	47.9%	52.1%	47.9%	52.1%
New Jersey		16		1,963,761	961,335	987,874	14,552	26,539 D	49.0%	50.3%	49.3%	50.7%
New Mexico		4		152,225	70,688	81,389	148	10,701 D	46.4%	53.5%	46.5%	53.5%
New York		47		6,316,790	2,987,647	3,304,238	24,905	316,591 D	47.3%	52.3%	47.5%	52.5%
North Carolina		14		790,554	263,155	527,399		264,244 D	33.3%	66.7%	33.3%	66.7%
North Dakota	4			220,182	118,535	100,144	1,503	18,391 R	53.8%	45.5%	54.2%	45.8%
Ohio	25			3,153,056	1,582,293	1,570,763		11,530 R	50.2%	49.8%	50.2%	49.8%
Oklahoma		10		722,636	319,424	401,549	1,663	82,125 D	44.2%	55.6%	44.3%	55.7%
Oregon		6		480,147	225,365	248,635	6,147	23,270 D	46.9%	51.8%	47.5%	52.5%
Pennsylvania		35		3,794,793	1,835,054	1,940,479	19,260	105,425 D	48.4%	51.1%	48.6%	51.4%
Rhode Island		4		299,276	123,487	175,356	433	51,869 D	41.3%	58.6%	41.3%	58.7%
South Carolina		8		103,382	4,617	90,601	8,164	82,802 D	4.5%	87.6%	4.8%	95.2%
South Dakota	4			232,076	135,365	96,711		38,654 R	58.3%	41.7%	58.3%	41.7%
Tennessee		12		510,692	200,311	308,707	1,674	108,396 D	39.2%	60.4%	39.4%	60.6%
Texas		23		1,150,334	191,423	821,605	137,306	630,182 D	16.6%	71.4%	18.9%	81.1%
Utah		4		248,319	97,891	150,088	340	52,197 D	39.4%	60.4%	39.5%	60.5%
Vermont	3			125,361	71,527	53,820	14	17,707 R	57.1%	42.9%	57.1%	42.9%
Virginia		11		388,485	145,243	242,276	966	97,033 D	37.4%	62.4%	37.5%	62.5%
Washington		8		856,328	361,689	486,774	7,865	125,085 D	42.2%	56.8%	42.6%	57.4%
West Virginia		8		715,596	322,819	392,777		69,958 D	45.1%	54.9%	45.1%	54.9%
Wisconsin	12			1,339,152	674,532	650,413	14,207	24,119 R	50.4%	48.6%	50.9%	49.1%
Wyoming	3			101,340	51,921	49,419		2,502 R	51.2%	48.8%	51.2%	48.8%
United States	99	432	—	47,976,670	22,017,617	25,612,610	346,443	3,594,993 D	45.9%	53.4%	46.2%	53.8%

PRESIDENT 1940

The Republican figures in Connecticut, Georgia, Mississippi and South Carolina include votes cast for two or three elector tickets. In New York the Democratic figure includes American Labor votes.

The full list of candidates for President and Vice-President was:

27,313,041	Franklin D. Roosevelt and Henry A. Wallace, Democratic.
22,348,480	Wendell Willkie and Charles L. McNary, Republican.
116,410	Norman Thomas and Maynard C. Krueger, Socialist.
58,708	Roger Babson and Edgar V. Moorman, Prohibition.
46,259	Earl Browder and James W. Ford, Communist.
14,892	John W. Aiken and Aaron M. Orange, Socialist Labor.

In addition, 545 votes were cast in North Dakota for the individual candidacy of Alfred Knutson and 2,083 scattered votes were reported from various states.

UNITED STATES

PRESIDENT 1940

State	Electoral Vote			Total Vote	Republican	Democratic	Other	Plurality	Percentage			
									Total Vote		Major Vote	
	Rep.	Dem.	Other						Rep.	Dem.	Rep.	Dem.
Alabama		11		294,219	42,184	250,726	1,309	208,542 D	14.3%	85.2%	14.4%	85.6%
Alaska												
Arizona		3		150,039	54,030	95,267	742	41,237 D	36.0%	63.5%	36.2%	63.8%
Arkansas		9		200,429	42,122	157,213	1,094	115,091 D	21.0%	78.4%	21.1%	78.9%
California		22		3,268,791	1,351,419	1,877,618	39,754	526,199 D	41.3%	57.4%	41.9%	58.1%
Colorado	6			549,004	279,576	265,554	3,874	14,022 R	50.9%	48.4%	51.3%	48.7%
Connecticut		8		781,502	361,819	417,621	2,062	55,802 D	46.3%	53.4%	46.4%	53.6%
Delaware		3		136,374	61,440	74,599	335	13,159 D	45.1%	54.7%	45.2%	54.8%
Florida		7		485,640	126,158	359,334	148	233,176 D	26.0%	74.0%	26.0%	74.0%
Georgia		12		312,686	46,495	265,194	997	218,699 D	14.9%	84.8%	14.9%	85.1%
Hawaii												
Idaho		4		235,168	106,553	127,842	773	21,289 D	45.3%	54.4%	45.5%	54.5%
Illinois		29		4,217,935	2,047,240	2,149,934	20,761	102,694 D	48.5%	51.0%	48.8%	51.2%
Indiana	14			1,782,747	899,466	874,063	9,218	25,403 R	50.5%	49.0%	50.7%	49.3%
Iowa	11			1,215,432	632,370	578,802	4,260	53,568 R	52.0%	47.6%	52.2%	47.8%
Kansas	9			860,297	489,169	364,725	6,403	124,444 R	56.9%	42.4%	57.3%	42.7%
Kentucky		11		970,163	410,384	557,322	2,457	146,938 D	42.3%	57.4%	42.4%	57.6%
Louisiana		10		372,305	52,446	319,751	108	267,305 D	14.1%	85.9%	14.1%	85.9%
Maine	5			320,840	163,951	156,478	411	7,473 R	51.1%	48.8%	51.2%	48.8%
Maryland		8		660,104	269,534	384,546	6,024	115,012 D	40.8%	58.3%	41.2%	58.8%
Massachusetts		17		2,026,993	939,700	1,076,522	10,771	136,822 D	46.4%	53.1%	46.6%	53.4%
Michigan	19			2,085,929	1,039,917	1,032,991	13,021	6,926 R	49.9%	49.5%	50.2%	49.8%
Minnesota		11		1,251,188	596,274	644,196	10,718	47,922 D	47.7%	51.5%	48.1%	51.9%
Mississippi		9		175,824	7,364	168,267	193	160,903 D	4.2%	95.7%	4.2%	95.8%
Missouri		15		1,833,729	871,009	958,476	4,244	87,467 D	47.5%	52.3%	47.6%	52.4%
Montana		4		247,873	99,579	145,698	2,596	46,119 D	40.2%	58.8%	40.6%	59.4%
Nebraska	7			615,878	352,201	263,677		88,524 R	57.2%	42.8%	57.2%	42.8%
Nevada		3		53,174	21,229	31,945		10,716 D	39.9%	60.1%	39.9%	60.1%
New Hampshire		4		235,419	110,127	125,292		15,165 D	46.8%	53.2%	46.8%	53.2%
New Jersey		16		1,972,552	945,475	1,016,808	10,269	71,333 D	47.9%	51.5%	48.2%	51.8%
New Mexico		3		183,258	79,315	103,699	244	24,384 D	43.3%	56.6%	43.3%	56.7%
New York		47		6,301,596	3,027,478	3,251,918	22,200	224,440 D	48.0%	51.6%	48.2%	51.8%
North Carolina		13		822,648	213,633	609,015		395,382 D	26.0%	74.0%	26.0%	74.0%
North Dakota	4			280,775	154,590	124,036	2,149	30,554 R	55.1%	44.2%	55.5%	44.5%
Ohio		26		3,319,912	1,586,773	1,733,139		146,366 D	47.8%	52.2%	47.8%	52.2%
Oklahoma		11		826,212	348,872	474,313	3,027	125,441 D	42.2%	57.4%	42.4%	57.6%
Oregon		5		481,240	219,555	258,415	3,270	38,860 D	45.6%	53.7%	45.9%	54.1%
Pennsylvania		36		4,078,714	1,889,848	2,171,035	17,831	281,187 D	46.3%	53.2%	46.5%	53.5%
Rhode Island		4		321,152	138,654	182,181	317	43,527 D	43.2%	56.7%	43.2%	56.8%
South Carolina		8		99,830	4,360	95,470		91,110 D	4.4%	95.6%	4.4%	95.6%
South Dakota	4			308,427	177,065	131,362		45,703 R	57.4%	42.6%	57.4%	42.6%
Tennessee		11		522,823	169,153	351,601	2,069	182,448 D	32.4%	67.3%	32.5%	67.5%
Texas		23		1,124,437	212,692	909,974	1,771	697,282 D	18.9%	80.9%	18.9%	81.1%
Utah		4		247,819	93,151	154,277	391	61,126 D	37.6%	62.3%	37.6%	62.4%
Vermont	3			143,062	78,371	64,269	422	14,102 R	54.8%	44.9%	54.9%	45.1%
Virginia		11		346,608	109,363	235,961	1,284	126,598 D	31.6%	68.1%	31.7%	68.3%
Washington		8		793,833	322,123	462,145	9,565	140,022 D	40.6%	58.2%	41.1%	58.9%
West Virginia		8		868,076	372,414	495,662		123,248 D	42.9%	57.1%	42.9%	57.1%
Wisconsin		12		1,405,522	679,206	704,821	21,495	25,615 D	48.3%	50.1%	49.1%	50.9%
Wyoming		3		112,240	52,633	59,287	320	6,654 D	46.9%	52.8%	47.0%	53.0%
United States	82	449	—	49,900,418	22,348,480	27,313,041	238,897	4,964,561 D	44.8%	54.7%	45.0%	55.0%

PRESIDENT 1936

The Republican figures in Delaware, Mississippi, and South Carolina include votes cast for two elector tickets. In New York the Democratic figure includes American Labor votes.

The full list of candidates for President and Vice-President was:

27,757,333	Franklin D. Roosevelt and John N. Garner, Democratic.
16,684,231	Alfred M. Landon and Frank Knox, Republican.
892,267	William Lemke and Thomas C. O'Brien, Union.
187,833	Norman Thomas and George A. Nelson, Socialist.
80,171	Earl Browder and James W. Ford, Communist.
37,677	D. Leigh Colvin and Claude A. Watson, Prohibition.
12,829	John W. Aiken and Emil F. Teichert, Socialist Labor.
1,598	William Dudley Pelley and Willard W. Kemp, Christian.

In addition, 824 scattered votes were reported from various states.

UNITED STATES

PRESIDENT 1936

State	Electoral Vote Rep.	Electoral Vote Dem.	Electoral Vote Other	Total Vote	Republican	Democratic	Other	Plurality	Percentage Total Vote Rep.	Percentage Total Vote Dem.	Percentage Major Vote Rep.	Percentage Major Vote Dem.
Alabama		11		275,744	35,358	238,196	2,190	202,838 D	12.8%	86.4%	12.9%	87.1%
Alaska												
Arizona		3		124,163	33,433	86,722	4,008	53,289 D	26.9%	69.8%	27.8%	72.2%
Arkansas		9		179,431	32,049	146,765	617	114,716 D	17.9%	81.8%	17.9%	82.1%
California		22		2,638,882	836,431	1,766,836	35,615	930,405 D	31.7%	67.0%	32.1%	67.9%
Colorado		6		488,685	181,267	295,021	12,397	113,754 D	37.1%	60.4%	38.1%	61.9%
Connecticut		8		690,723	278,685	382,129	29,909	103,444 D	40.3%	55.3%	42.2%	57.8%
Delaware		3		127,603	57,236	69,702	665	12,466 D	44.9%	54.6%	45.1%	54.9%
Florida		7		327,436	78,248	249,117	71	170,869 D	23.9%	76.1%	23.9%	76.1%
Georgia		12		293,170	36,943	255,363	864	218,420 D	12.6%	87.1%	12.6%	87.4%
Hawaii												
Idaho		4		199,617	66,256	125,683	7,678	59,427 D	33.2%	63.0%	34.5%	65.5%
Illinois		29		3,956,522	1,570,393	2,282,999	103,130	712,606 D	39.7%	57.7%	40.8%	59.2%
Indiana		14		1,650,897	691,570	934,974	24,353	243,404 D	41.9%	56.6%	42.5%	57.5%
Iowa		11		1,142,737	487,977	621,756	33,004	133,779 D	42.7%	54.4%	44.0%	56.0%
Kansas		9		865,507	397,727	464,520	3,260	66,793 D	46.0%	53.7%	46.1%	53.9%
Kentucky		11		926,214	369,702	541,944	14,568	172,242 D	39.9%	58.5%	40.6%	59.4%
Louisiana		10		329,778	36,791	292,894	93	256,103 D	11.2%	88.8%	11.2%	88.8%
Maine	5			304,240	168,823	126,333	9,084	42,490 R	55.5%	41.5%	57.2%	42.8%
Maryland		8		624,896	231,435	389,612	3,849	158,177 D	37.0%	62.3%	37.3%	62.7%
Massachusetts		17		1,840,357	768,613	942,716	129,028	174,103 D	41.8%	51.2%	44.9%	55.1%
Michigan		19		1,805,098	699,733	1,016,794	88,571	317,061 D	38.8%	56.3%	40.8%	59.2%
Minnesota		11		1,129,975	350,461	698,811	80,703	348,350 D	31.0%	61.8%	33.4%	66.6%
Mississippi		9		162,142	4,467	157,333	342	152,866 D	2.8%	97.0%	2.8%	97.2%
Missouri		15		1,828,635	697,891	1,111,043	19,701	413,152 D	38.2%	60.8%	38.6%	61.4%
Montana		4		230,502	63,598	159,690	7,214	96,092 D	27.6%	69.3%	28.5%	71.5%
Nebraska		7		608,023	247,731	347,445	12,847	99,714 D	40.7%	57.1%	41.6%	58.4%
Nevada		3		43,848	11,923	31,925		20,002 D	27.2%	72.8%	27.2%	72.8%
New Hampshire		4		218,114	104,642	108,460	5,012	3,818 D	48.0%	49.7%	49.1%	50.9%
New Jersey		16		1,820,437	720,322	1,083,850	16,265	363,528 D	39.6%	59.5%	39.9%	60.1%
New Mexico		3		169,135	61,727	106,037	1,371	44,310 D	36.5%	62.7%	36.8%	63.2%
New York		47		5,596,398	2,180,670	3,293,222	122,506	1,112,552 D	39.0%	58.8%	39.8%	60.2%
North Carolina		13		839,475	223,294	616,141	40	392,847 D	26.6%	73.4%	26.6%	73.4%
North Dakota		4		273,716	72,751	163,148	37,817	90,397 D	26.6%	59.6%	30.8%	69.2%
Ohio		26		3,012,660	1,127,855	1,747,140	137,665	619,285 D	37.4%	58.0%	39.2%	60.8%
Oklahoma		11		749,740	245,122	501,069	3,549	255,947 D	32.7%	66.8%	32.8%	67.2%
Oregon		5		414,021	122,706	266,733	24,582	144,027 D	29.6%	64.4%	31.5%	68.5%
Pennsylvania		36		4,138,105	1,690,300	2,353,788	94,017	663,488 D	40.8%	56.9%	41.8%	58.2%
Rhode Island		4		310,278	125,031	164,338	20,909	39,307 D	40.3%	53.0%	43.2%	56.8%
South Carolina		8		115,437	1,646	113,791		112,145 D	1.4%	98.6%	1.4%	98.6%
South Dakota		4		296,452	125,977	160,137	10,338	34,160 D	42.5%	54.0%	44.0%	56.0%
Tennessee		11		477,086	147,055	328,083	1,948	181,028 D	30.8%	68.8%	30.9%	69.1%
Texas		23		849,701	104,661	739,952	5,088	635,291 D	12.3%	87.1%	12.4%	87.6%
Utah		4		216,679	64,555	150,248	1,876	85,693 D	29.8%	69.3%	30.1%	69.9%
Vermont	3			143,689	81,023	62,124	542	18,899 R	56.4%	43.2%	56.6%	43.4%
Virginia		11		334,590	98,336	234,980	1,274	136,644 D	29.4%	70.2%	29.5%	70.5%
Washington		8		692,338	206,892	459,579	25,867	252,687 D	29.9%	66.4%	31.0%	69.0%
West Virginia		8		829,945	325,358	502,582	2,005	177,224 D	39.2%	60.6%	39.3%	60.7%
Wisconsin		12		1,258,560	380,828	802,984	74,748	422,156 D	30.3%	63.8%	32.2%	67.8%
Wyoming		3		103,382	38,739	62,624	2,019	23,885 D	37.5%	60.6%	38.2%	61.8%
United States	8	523	—	45,654,763	16,684,231	27,757,333	1,213,199	11,073,102 D	36.5%	60.8%	37.5%	62.5%

PRESIDENT 1932

The Republican figure in Mississippi includes votes cast for two elector tickets.

The full list of candidates for President and Vice-President was:

22,829,501	Franklin D. Roosevelt and John N. Garner, Democratic.
15,760,684	Herbert C. Hoover and Charles Curtis, Republican.
884,649	Norman Thomas and James H. Maurer, Socialist.
103,253	William Z. Foster and James W. Ford, Communist.
81,872	William D. Upshaw and Frank S. Regan, Prohibition.
53,247	William H. Harvey and Frank Hemenway, Liberty.
34,043	Verne L. Reynolds and John W. Aiken, Socialist Labor.
7,431	Jacob S. Coxey and Julius J. Reiter, Farmer-Labor.
1,645	John Zahnd and Florence Garvin, National.
740	James R. Cox and Victor C. Tisdal, Jobless.

In addition, 157 votes were cast for a Jacksonian elector ticket in Texas and 9 in Arizona for an Arizona Progressive Democratic Ticket. There were 1,528 scattered votes reported from various states.

UNITED STATES

PRESIDENT 1932

State	Electoral Vote Rep.	Electoral Vote Dem.	Electoral Vote Other	Total Vote	Republican	Democratic	Other	Plurality	Percentage Total Vote Rep.	Percentage Total Vote Dem.	Percentage Major Vote Rep.	Percentage Major Vote Dem.
Alabama		11		245,303	34,675	207,910	2,718	173,235 D	14.1%	84.8%	14.3%	85.7%
Alaska												
Arizona		3		118,251	36,104	79,264	2,883	43,160 D	30.5%	67.0%	31.3%	68.7%
Arkansas		9		216,569	27,465	186,829	2,275	159,364 D	12.7%	86.3%	12.8%	87.2%
California		22		2,266,972	847,902	1,324,157	94,913	476,255 D	37.4%	58.4%	39.0%	61.0%
Colorado		6		457,696	189,617	250,877	17,202	61,260 D	41.4%	54.8%	43.0%	57.0%
Connecticut	8			594,183	288,420	281,632	24,131	6,788 R	48.5%	47.4%	50.6%	49.4%
Delaware	3			112,901	57,073	54,319	1,509	2,754 R	50.6%	48.1%	51.2%	48.8%
Florida		7		276,943	69,170	206,307	1,466	137,137 D	25.0%	74.5%	25.1%	74.9%
Georgia		12		255,590	19,863	234,118	1,609	214,255 D	7.8%	91.6%	7.8%	92.2%
Hawaii												
Idaho		4		186,520	71,312	109,479	5,729	38,167 D	38.2%	58.7%	39.4%	60.6%
Illinois		29		3,407,926	1,432,756	1,882,304	92,866	449,548 D	42.0%	55.2%	43.2%	56.8%
Indiana		14		1,576,927	677,184	862,054	37,689	184,870 D	42.9%	54.7%	44.0%	56.0%
Iowa		11		1,036,687	414,433	598,019	24,235	183,586 D	40.0%	57.7%	40.9%	59.1%
Kansas		9		791,978	349,498	424,204	18,276	74,706 D	44.1%	53.6%	45.2%	54.8%
Kentucky		11		983,059	394,716	580,574	7,769	185,858 D	40.2%	59.1%	40.5%	59.5%
Louisiana		10		268,804	18,853	249,418	533	230,565 D	7.0%	92.8%	7.0%	93.0%
Maine	5			298,444	166,631	128,907	2,906	37,724 R	55.8%	43.2%	56.4%	43.6%
Maryland		8		511,054	184,184	314,314	12,556	130,130 D	36.0%	61.5%	36.9%	63.1%
Massachusetts		17		1,580,114	736,959	800,148	43,007	63,189 D	46.6%	50.6%	47.9%	52.1%
Michigan		19		1,664,765	739,894	871,700	53,171	131,806 D	44.4%	52.4%	45.9%	54.1%
Minnesota		11		1,002,843	363,959	600,806	38,078	236,847 D	36.3%	59.9%	37.7%	62.3%
Mississippi		9		146,034	5,180	140,168	686	134,988 D	3.5%	96.0%	3.6%	96.4%
Missouri		15		1,609,894	564,713	1,025,406	19,775	460,693 D	35.1%	63.7%	35.5%	64.5%
Montana		4		216,479	78,078	127,286	11,115	49,208 D	36.1%	58.8%	38.0%	62.0%
Nebraska		7		570,135	201,177	359,082	9,876	157,905 D	35.3%	63.0%	35.9%	64.1%
Nevada		3		41,430	12,674	28,756		16,082 D	30.6%	69.4%	30.6%	69.4%
New Hampshire	4			205,520	103,629	100,680	1,211	2,949 R	50.4%	49.0%	50.7%	49.3%
New Jersey		16		1,630,063	775,684	806,630	47,749	30,946 D	47.6%	49.5%	49.0%	51.0%
New Mexico		3		151,606	54,217	95,089	2,300	40,872 D	35.8%	62.7%	36.3%	63.7%
New York		47		4,688,614	1,937,963	2,534,959	215,692	596,996 D	41.3%	54.1%	43.3%	56.7%
North Carolina		13		711,498	208,344	497,566	5,588	289,222 D	29.3%	69.9%	29.5%	70.5%
North Dakota		4		256,290	71,772	178,350	6,168	106,578 D	28.0%	69.6%	28.7%	71.3%
Ohio		26		2,609,728	1,227,319	1,301,695	80,714	74,376 D	47.0%	49.9%	48.5%	51.5%
Oklahoma		11		704,633	188,165	516,468		328,303 D	26.7%	73.3%	26.7%	73.3%
Oregon		5		368,751	136,019	213,871	18,861	77,852 D	36.9%	58.0%	38.9%	61.1%
Pennsylvania	36			2,859,021	1,453,540	1,295,948	109,533	157,592 R	50.8%	45.3%	52.9%	47.1%
Rhode Island		4		266,170	115,266	146,604	4,300	31,338 D	43.3%	55.1%	44.0%	56.0%
South Carolina		8		104,407	1,978	102,347	82	100,369 D	1.9%	98.0%	1.9%	98.1%
South Dakota		4		288,438	99,212	183,515	5,711	84,303 D	34.4%	63.6%	35.1%	64.9%
Tennessee		11		390,273	126,752	259,473	4,048	132,721 D	32.5%	66.5%	32.8%	67.2%
Texas		23		874,382	98,218	771,109	5,055	672,891 D	11.2%	88.2%	11.3%	88.7%
Utah		4		206,578	84,795	116,750	5,033	31,955 D	41.0%	56.5%	42.1%	57.9%
Vermont	3			136,980	78,984	56,266	1,730	22,718 R	57.7%	41.1%	58.4%	41.6%
Virginia		11		297,942	89,637	203,979	4,326	114,342 D	30.1%	68.5%	30.5%	69.5%
Washington		8		614,814	208,645	353,260	52,909	144,615 D	33.9%	57.5%	37.1%	62.9%
West Virginia		8		743,774	330,731	405,124	7,919	74,393 D	44.5%	54.5%	44.9%	55.1%
Wisconsin		12		1,114,814	347,741	707,410	59,663	359,669 D	31.2%	63.5%	33.0%	67.0%
Wyoming		3		96,962	39,583	54,370	3,009	14,787 D	40.8%	56.1%	42.1%	57.9%
United States	59	472	—	39,758,759	15,760,684	22,829,501	1,168,574	7,068,817 D	39.6%	57.4%	40.8%	59.2%

PRESIDENT 1928

The Republican figures in Georgia, Mississippi, and South Carolina include votes cast for two or three elector tickets; in Pennsylvania the Communist total includes votes cast for two elector tickets.

The full list of candidates for President and Vice-President was:

21,437,277	Herbert C. Hoover and Charles Curtis, Republican.
15,007,698	Alfred E. Smith and Joseph T. Robinson, Democratic.
265,583	Norman Thomas and James H. Maurer, Socialist.
46,896	William Z. Foster and Benjamin Gitlow, Communist.
21,586	Verne L. Reynolds and Jeremiah D. Crowley, Socialist Labor.
20,101	William F. Varney and James A. Edgerton, Prohibition.
6,390	Frank E. Webb and L. R. Tillman, Farmer-Labor.

In addition, 420 scattered votes were reported from various states.

UNITED STATES

PRESIDENT 1928

State	Electoral Vote Rep.	Electoral Vote Dem.	Electoral Vote Other	Total Vote	Republican	Democratic	Other	Plurality	Percentage Total Vote Rep.	Percentage Total Vote Dem.	Percentage Major Vote Rep.	Percentage Major Vote Dem.
Alabama		12		248,981	120,725	127,796	460	7,071 D	48.5%	51.3%	48.6%	51.4%
Alaska												
Arizona	3			91,254	52,533	38,537	184	13,996 R	57.6%	42.2%	57.7%	42.3%
Arkansas		9		197,726	77,784	119,196	746	41,412 D	39.3%	60.3%	39.5%	60.5%
California	13			1,796,656	1,162,323	614,365	19,968	547,958 R	64.7%	34.2%	65.4%	34.6%
Colorado	6			392,242	253,872	133,131	5,239	120,741 R	64.7%	33.9%	65.6%	34.4%
Connecticut	7			553,118	296,641	252,085	4,392	44,556 R	53.6%	45.6%	54.1%	45.9%
Delaware	3			104,602	68,860	35,354	388	33,506 R	65.8%	33.8%	66.1%	33.9%
Florida	6			252,068	145,860	101,764	4,444	44,096 R	57.9%	40.4%	58.9%	41.1%
Georgia		14		231,592	101,800	129,604	188	27,804 D	44.0%	56.0%	44.0%	56.0%
Hawaii												
Idaho	4			151,541	97,322	52,926	1,293	44,396 R	64.2%	34.9%	64.8%	35.2%
Illinois	29			3,107,489	1,769,141	1,313,817	24,531	455,324 R	56.9%	42.3%	57.4%	42.6%
Indiana	15			1,421,314	848,290	562,691	10,333	285,599 R	59.7%	39.6%	60.1%	39.9%
Iowa	13			1,009,189	623,570	379,011	6,608	244,559 R	61.8%	37.6%	62.2%	37.8%
Kansas	10			713,200	513,672	193,003	6,525	320,669 R	72.0%	27.1%	72.7%	27.3%
Kentucky	13			940,521	558,064	381,070	1,387	176,994 R	59.3%	40.5%	59.4%	40.6%
Louisiana		10		215,833	51,160	164,655	18	113,495 D	23.7%	76.3%	23.7%	76.3%
Maine	6			262,170	179,923	81,179	1,068	98,744 R	68.6%	31.0%	68.9%	31.1%
Maryland	8			528,348	301,479	223,626	3,243	77,853 R	57.1%	42.3%	57.4%	42.6%
Massachusetts		18		1,577,823	775,566	792,758	9,499	17,192 D	49.2%	50.2%	49.5%	50.5%
Michigan	15			1,372,082	965,396	396,762	9,924	568,634 R	70.4%	28.9%	70.9%	29.1%
Minnesota	12			970,976	560,977	396,451	13,548	164,526 R	57.8%	40.8%	58.6%	41.4%
Mississippi		10		151,568	27,030	124,538		97,508 D	17.8%	82.2%	17.8%	82.2%
Missouri	18			1,500,845	834,080	662,684	4,081	171,396 R	55.6%	44.2%	55.7%	44.3%
Montana	4			194,108	113,300	78,578	2,230	34,722 R	58.4%	40.5%	59.0%	41.0%
Nebraska	8			547,128	345,745	197,950	3,433	147,795 R	63.2%	36.2%	63.6%	36.4%
Nevada	3			32,417	18,327	14,090		4,237 R	56.5%	43.5%	56.5%	43.5%
New Hampshire	4			196,757	115,404	80,715	638	34,689 R	58.7%	41.0%	58.8%	41.2%
New Jersey	14			1,549,381	926,050	616,517	6,814	309,533 R	59.8%	39.8%	60.0%	40.0%
New Mexico	3			118,077	69,708	48,211	158	21,497 R	59.0%	40.8%	59.1%	40.9%
New York	45			4,405,626	2,193,344	2,089,863	122,419	103,481 R	49.8%	47.4%	51.2%	48.8%
North Carolina	12			635,150	348,923	286,227		62,696 R	54.9%	45.1%	54.9%	45.1%
North Dakota	5			239,845	131,419	106,648	1,778	24,771 R	54.8%	44.5%	55.2%	44.8%
Ohio	24			2,508,346	1,627,546	864,210	16,590	763,336 R	64.9%	34.5%	65.3%	34.7%
Oklahoma	10			618,427	394,046	219,174	5,207	174,872 R	63.7%	35.4%	64.3%	35.7%
Oregon	5			319,942	205,341	109,223	5,378	96,118 R	64.2%	34.1%	65.3%	34.7%
Pennsylvania	38			3,150,612	2,055,382	1,067,586	27,644	987,796 R	65.2%	33.9%	65.8%	34.2%
Rhode Island		5		237,194	117,522	118,973	699	1,451 D	49.5%	50.2%	49.7%	50.3%
South Carolina		9		68,605	5,858	62,700	47	56,842 D	8.5%	91.4%	8.5%	91.5%
South Dakota	5			261,857	157,603	102,660	1,594	54,943 R	60.2%	39.2%	60.6%	39.4%
Tennessee	12			353,192	195,388	157,143	661	38,245 R	55.3%	44.5%	55.4%	44.6%
Texas	20			717,733	372,324	344,542	867	27,782 R	51.9%	48.0%	51.9%	48.1%
Utah	4			176,603	94,618	80,985	1,000	13,633 R	53.6%	45.9%	53.9%	46.1%
Vermont	4			135,191	90,404	44,440	347	45,964 R	66.9%	32.9%	67.0%	33.0%
Virginia	12			305,364	164,609	140,146	609	24,463 R	53.9%	45.9%	54.0%	46.0%
Washington	7			500,840	335,844	156,772	8,224	179,072 R	67.1%	31.3%	68.2%	31.8%
West Virginia	8			642,752	375,551	263,784	3,417	111,767 R	58.4%	41.0%	58.7%	41.3%
Wisconsin	13			1,016,831	544,205	450,259	22,367	93,946 R	53.5%	44.3%	54.7%	45.3%
Wyoming	3			82,835	52,748	29,299	788	23,449 R	63.7%	35.4%	64.3%	35.7%
United States	444	87	—	36,805,951	21,437,277	15,007,698	360,976	6,429,579 R	58.2%	40.8%	58.8%	41.2%

PRESIDENT 1924

Wisconsin's 13 electoral votes were cast for the Progressive nominees, and in eleven other states in the Midwest and West the Progressive candidates ran second. In several states the Progressive total includes votes cast for two or three elector tickets.

The full list of candidates for President and Vice-President was:

15,719,921	Calvin Coolidge and Charles G. Dawes, Republican.
8,386,704	John W. Davis and Charles W. Bryan, Democratic.
4,832,532	Robert M. LaFollette and Burton K. Wheeler, Progressive.
56,292	Herman P. Faris and Marie Caroline Brehm, Prohibition.
34,174	Frank T. Johns and Verne L. Reynolds, Socialist Labor.
33,360	William Z. Foster and Benjamin Gitlow, Communist.
24,340	Gilbert O. Nations and Leander L. Pickett, American.
2,948	William J. Wallace and John C. Lincoln, Commonwealth Land.

In addition, 4,752 scattered votes were reported from various states.

UNITED STATES

PRESIDENT 1924

State	Electoral Vote Rep.	Electoral Vote Dem.	Electoral Vote Other	Total Vote	Republican	Democratic	Progressive	Other	Plurality	Percentage Total Vote Rep.	Percentage Total Vote Dem.	Percentage Total Vote Prog.
Alabama		12		164,563	42,823	113,138	8,040	562	70,315 D	26.0%	68.8%	4.9%
Alaska												
Arizona	3			73,961	30,516	26,235	17,210		4,281 R	41.3%	35.5%	23.3%
Arkansas		9		138,540	40,583	84,790	13,167		44,207 D	29.3%	61.2%	9.5%
California	13			1,281,778	733,250	105,514	424,649	18,365	308,601 R	57.2%	8.2%	33.1%
Colorado	6			342,261	195,171	75,238	69,946	1,906	119,933 R	57.0%	22.0%	20.4%
Connecticut	7			400,396	246,322	110,184	42,416	1,474	136,138 R	61.5%	27.5%	10.6%
Delaware	3			90,885	52,441	33,445	4,979	20	18,996 R	57.7%	36.8%	5.5%
Florida		6		109,158	30,633	62,083	8,625	7,817	31,450 D	28.1%	56.9%	7.9%
Georgia		14		166,635	30,300	123,262	12,687	386	92,962 D	18.2%	74.0%	7.6%
Hawaii												
Idaho	4			147,690	69,791	23,951	53,948		15,843 R	47.3%	16.2%	36.5%
Illinois	29			2,470,067	1,453,321	576,975	432,027	7,744	876,346 R	58.8%	23.4%	17.5%
Indiana	15			1,272,390	703,042	492,245	71,700	5,403	210,797 R	55.3%	38.7%	5.6%
Iowa	13			976,770	537,458	160,382	274,448	4,482	263,010 R	55.0%	16.4%	28.1%
Kansas	10			662,456	407,671	156,320	98,461	4	251,351 R	61.5%	23.6%	14.9%
Kentucky	13			813,843	396,758	375,593	38,465	3,027	21,165 R	48.8%	46.2%	4.7%
Louisiana		10		121,951	24,670	93,218		4,063	68,548 D	20.2%	76.4%	
Maine	6			192,192	138,440	41,964	11,382	406	96,476 R	72.0%	21.8%	5.9%
Maryland	8			358,630	162,414	148,072	47,157	987	14,342 R	45.3%	41.3%	13.1%
Massachusetts	18			1,129,837	703,476	280,831	141,225	4,305	422,645 R	62.3%	24.9%	12.5%
Michigan	15			1,160,419	874,631	152,359	122,014	11,415	722,272 R	75.4%	13.1%	10.5%
Minnesota	12			822,146	420,759	55,913	339,192	6,282	81,567 R	51.2%	6.8%	41.3%
Mississippi		10		112,442	8,494	100,474	3,474		91,980 D	7.6%	89.4%	3.1%
Missouri	18			1,310,095	648,488	574,962	83,996	2,649	73,526 R	49.5%	43.9%	6.4%
Montana	4			174,425	74,138	33,805	66,124	358	8,014 R	42.5%	19.4%	37.9%
Nebraska	8			463,559	218,985	137,299	105,681	1,594	81,686 R	47.2%	29.6%	22.8%
Nevada	3			26,921	11,243	5,909	9,769		1,474 R	41.8%	21.9%	36.3%
New Hampshire	4			164,769	98,575	57,201	8,993		41,374 R	59.8%	34.7%	5.5%
New Jersey	14			1,088,054	676,277	298,043	109,028	4,706	378,234 R	62.2%	27.4%	10.0%
New Mexico	3			112,830	54,745	48,542	9,543		6,203 R	48.5%	43.0%	8.5%
New York	45			3,263,939	1,820,058	950,796	474,913	18,172	869,262 R	55.8%	29.1%	14.6%
North Carolina		12		481,608	190,754	284,190	6,651	13	93,436 D	39.6%	59.0%	1.4%
North Dakota	5			199,081	94,931	13,858	89,922	370	5,009 R	47.7%	7.0%	45.2%
Ohio	24			2,016,296	1,176,130	477,887	358,008	4,271	698,243 R	58.3%	23.7%	17.8%
Oklahoma		10		527,828	225,756	255,798	46,274		30,042 D	42.8%	48.5%	8.8%
Oregon	5			279,488	142,579	67,589	68,403	917	74,176 R	51.0%	24.2%	24.5%
Pennsylvania	38			2,144,850	1,401,481	409,192	307,567	26,610	992,289 R	65.3%	19.1%	14.3%
Rhode Island	5			210,115	125,286	76,606	7,628	595	48,680 R	59.6%	36.5%	3.6%
South Carolina		9		50,755	1,123	49,008	623	1	47,885 D	2.2%	96.6%	1.2%
South Dakota	5			203,868	101,299	27,214	75,355		25,944 R	49.7%	13.3%	37.0%
Tennessee		12		301,030	130,831	159,339	10,666	194	28,508 D	43.5%	52.9%	3.5%
Texas		20		657,054	130,794	483,381	42,879		352,587 D	19.9%	73.6%	6.5%
Utah	4			156,990	77,327	47,001	32,662		30,326 R	49.3%	29.9%	20.8%
Vermont	4			102,917	80,498	16,124	5,964	331	64,374 R	78.2%	15.7%	5.8%
Virginia		12		223,603	73,328	139,717	10,369	189	66,389 D	32.8%	62.5%	4.6%
Washington	7			421,549	220,224	42,842	150,727	7,756	69,497 R	52.2%	10.2%	35.8%
West Virginia	8			583,662	288,635	257,232	36,723	1,072	31,403 R	49.5%	44.1%	6.3%
Wisconsin			13	840,827	311,614	68,115	453,678	7,420	142,064 P	37.1%	8.1%	54.0%
Wyoming	3			79,900	41,858	12,868	25,174		16,684 R	52.4%	16.1%	31.5%
United States	382	136	13	29,095,023	15,719,921	8,386,704	4,832,532	155,866	7,333,217 R	54.0%	28.8%	16.6%

PRESIDENT 1920

The Republican figure in South Carolina includes votes cast for two elector tickets; the figure in Florida is the vote cast for the one elector candidate who ran on both Republican tickets in that state. In Washington, the total vote for minor party candidates exceeded that for the Democratic candidates, but the Democratic total was greater than that for any one of the minor party nominees.

The full list of candidates for President and Vice-President was:

16,153,115	Warren G. Harding and Calvin Coolidge, Republican.
9,133,092	James M. Cox and Franklin D. Roosevelt, Democratic.
915,490	Eugene V. Debs and Seymour Stedman, Socialist.
265,229	Parley P. Christensen and Max S. Hayes, Farmer-Labor.
189,339	Aaron S. Watkins and D. Leigh Colvin, Prohibition.
48,098	James Ferguson and William J. Hough, American.
30,594	William W. Cox and August Gillhaus, Socialist Labor.
5,833	Robert C. Macauley and Richard C. Barnum, Single Tax.

In addition, 27,309 votes were cast in Texas for a Black-and-Tan Republican elector ticket and 514 scattered votes were reported from various states.

UNITED STATES

PRESIDENT 1920

State	Electoral Vote Rep.	Electoral Vote Dem.	Electoral Vote Other	Total Vote	Republican	Democratic	Other	Plurality	Percentage Total Vote Rep.	Percentage Total Vote Dem.	Percentage Major Vote Rep.	Percentage Major Vote Dem.
Alabama		12		233,951	74,719	156,064	3,168	81,345 D	31.9%	66.7%	32.4%	67.6%
Alaska												
Arizona	3			66,803	37,016	29,546	241	7,470 R	55.4%	44.2%	55.6%	44.4%
Arkansas		9		183,871	72,316	106,427	5,128	34,111 D	39.3%	57.9%	40.5%	59.5%
California	13			943,463	624,992	229,191	89,280	395,801 R	66.2%	24.3%	73.2%	26.8%
Colorado	6			292,053	173,248	104,936	13,869	68,312 R	59.3%	35.9%	62.3%	37.7%
Connecticut	7			365,518	229,238	120,721	15,559	108,517 R	62.7%	33.0%	65.5%	34.5%
Delaware	3			94,875	52,858	39,911	2,106	12,947 R	55.7%	42.1%	57.0%	43.0%
Florida		6		145,684	44,853	90,515	10,316	45,662 D	30.8%	62.1%	33.1%	66.9%
Georgia		14		149,558	42,981	106,112	465	63,131 D	28.7%	71.0%	28.8%	71.2%
Hawaii												
Idaho	4			138,281	91,351	46,930		44,421 R	66.1%	33.9%	66.1%	33.9%
Illinois	29			2,094,714	1,420,480	534,395	139,839	886,085 R	67.8%	25.5%	72.7%	27.3%
Indiana	15			1,262,974	696,370	511,364	55,240	185,006 R	55.1%	40.5%	57.7%	42.3%
Iowa	13			894,959	634,674	227,804	32,481	406,870 R	70.9%	25.5%	73.6%	26.4%
Kansas	10			570,243	369,268	185,464	15,511	183,804 R	64.8%	32.5%	66.6%	33.4%
Kentucky		13		918,636	452,480	456,497	9,659	4,017 D	49.3%	49.7%	49.8%	50.2%
Louisiana		10		126,397	38,539	87,519	339	48,980 D	30.5%	69.2%	30.6%	69.4%
Maine	6			197,840	136,355	58,961	2,524	77,394 R	68.9%	29.8%	69.8%	30.2%
Maryland	8			428,443	236,117	180,626	11,700	55,491 R	55.1%	42.2%	56.7%	43.3%
Massachusetts	18			993,718	681,153	276,691	35,874	404,462 R	68.5%	27.8%	71.1%	28.9%
Michigan	15			1,048,411	762,865	233,450	52,096	529,415 R	72.8%	22.3%	76.6%	23.4%
Minnesota	12			735,838	519,421	142,994	73,423	376,427 R	70.6%	19.4%	78.4%	21.6%
Mississippi		10		82,351	11,576	69,136	1,639	57,560 D	14.1%	84.0%	14.3%	85.7%
Missouri	18			1,332,140	727,252	574,699	30,189	152,553 R	54.6%	43.1%	55.9%	44.1%
Montana	4			179,006	109,430	57,372	12,204	52,058 R	61.1%	32.1%	65.6%	34.4%
Nebraska	8			382,743	247,498	119,608	15,637	127,890 R	64.7%	31.3%	67.4%	32.6%
Nevada	3			27,194	15,479	9,851	1,864	5,628 R	56.9%	36.2%	61.1%	38.9%
New Hampshire	4			159,092	95,196	62,662	1,234	32,534 R	59.8%	39.4%	60.3%	39.7%
New Jersey	14			910,251	615,333	258,761	36,157	356,572 R	67.6%	28.4%	70.4%	29.6%
New Mexico	3			105,412	57,634	46,668	1,110	10,966 R	54.7%	44.3%	55.3%	44.7%
New York	45			2,898,513	1,871,167	781,238	246,108	1,089,929 R	64.6%	27.0%	70.5%	29.5%
North Carolina		12		538,649	232,819	305,367	463	72,548 D	43.2%	56.7%	43.3%	56.7%
North Dakota	5			205,786	160,082	37,422	8,282	122,660 R	77.8%	18.2%	81.1%	18.9%
Ohio	24			2,021,653	1,182,022	780,037	59,594	401,985 R	58.5%	38.6%	60.2%	39.8%
Oklahoma	10			485,678	243,840	216,122	25,716	27,718 R	50.2%	44.5%	53.0%	47.0%
Oregon	5			238,522	143,592	80,019	14,911	63,573 R	60.2%	33.5%	64.2%	35.8%
Pennsylvania	38			1,851,248	1,218,215	503,202	129,831	715,013 R	65.8%	27.2%	70.8%	29.2%
Rhode Island	5			167,981	107,463	55,062	5,456	52,401 R	64.0%	32.8%	66.1%	33.9%
South Carolina		9		66,808	2,610	64,170	28	61,560 D	3.9%	96.1%	3.9%	96.1%
South Dakota	5			182,237	110,692	35,938	35,607	74,754 R	60.7%	19.7%	75.5%	24.5%
Tennessee	12			428,036	219,229	206,558	2,249	12,671 R	51.2%	48.3%	51.5%	48.5%
Texas		20		486,109	114,658	287,920	83,531	173,262 D	23.6%	59.2%	28.5%	71.5%
Utah	4			145,828	81,555	56,639	7,634	24,916 R	55.9%	38.8%	59.0%	41.0%
Vermont	4			89,961	68,212	20,919	830	47,293 R	75.8%	23.3%	76.5%	23.5%
Virginia		12		231,000	87,456	141,670	1,874	54,214 D	37.9%	61.3%	38.2%	61.8%
Washington	7			398,715	223,137	84,298	91,280	138,839 R	56.0%	21.1%	72.6%	27.4%
West Virginia	8			509,936	282,007	220,785	7,144	61,222 R	55.3%	43.3%	56.1%	43.9%
Wisconsin	13			701,281	498,576	113,422	89,283	385,154 R	71.1%	16.2%	81.5%	18.5%
Wyoming	3			56,253	35,091	17,429	3,733	17,662 R	62.4%	31.0%	66.8%	33.2%
United States	404	127	—	26,768,613	16,153,115	9,133,092	1,482,406	7,020,023 R	60.3%	34.1%	63.9%	36.1%

1988 PRESIDENTIAL PRIMARIES

In 1988 thirty-six states and the District of Columbia held Presidential primaries though there was no Republican voting in New York and no Democratic voting in South Carolina.

In some jurisdictions balloting was for delegate slates linked to specific Presidential candidates; in others, electors indicated only a personal preference as to their party's nominee.

The tables included here give the major party primary vote in each state for those candidates on the ballot in at least twenty states. An asterisk in the table indicates votes written-in for a candidate not on the ballot.

Republican candidates on the ballot in at least one state were George Bush, Paul B. Conley, Robert Dole, Robert F. Drucker, Pierre duPont, Alexander M. Haig, William Horrigan, Jack F. Kemp, Michael S. Levinson, Isabell Masters, Mary Jane Rachner, Pat Robertson and Harold E. Stassen.

Democratic candidates on the ballot in at least one state were Frank Ahern, Douglas Applegate, Bruce Babbitt, Norbert G. Dennerll, Florenzo DiDonato, Charles R. Doty, Michael S. Dukakis, David E. Duke, William J. duPont, Richard A. Gephardt, Albert Gore, Jr., Gary W. Hart, Jesse L. Jackson, Richard B. Kay, William King, Claude R. Kirk, Stephen A. Koczak, Lyndon H. LaRouche, Stanley Lock, Angus W. McDonald, William A. Marra, Anthony R. Martin-Trigona, Edward T. O'Donnell, Conrad W. Roy, Cyril E. Sagan, Paul Simon, Frank L. Thomas, Osie Thorpe, James A. Traficant, A. A. VanPetten, Jennifer Alden Wesner, W. A. Williams and Irwin Zucker.

ALABAMA MARCH 8

Republican 137,807 Bush; 34,733 Dole; 29,772 Robertson; 10,557 Kemp; 392 duPont; 300 Haig.

Democratic 176,764 Jackson; 151,739 Gore; 31,306 Dukakis; 30,214 Gephardt; 7,530 Hart; 3,063 Simon; 2,410 Babbitt; 1,771 Uncommitted; 845 LaRouche.

ARKANSAS MARCH 8

Republican 32,114 Bush, 17,667 Dole; 12,918 Robertson; 3,499 Kemp; 1,402 Uncommitted; 359 duPont; 346 Haig.

Democratic 185,758 Gore; 94,103 Dukakis; 85,003 Jackson; 59,711 Gephardt; 35,553 Uncommitted; 18,630 Hart; 9,020 Simon; 4,805 Duke; 2,614 Babbitt; 2,347 LaRouche.

CALIFORNIA JUNE 7

Republican 1,856,273 Bush; 289,220 Dole; 94,779 Robertson; 115 scattered write-in.

Democratic 1,910,808 Dukakis; 1,102,093 Jackson; 56,645 Gore; 43,771 Simon; 25,417 LaRouche.

American Independent 9,792 James C. Griffin; 5,401 James Gritz; 3 scattered write-in.

Peace & Freedom 2,117 Lenora B. Fulani; 1,222 Shirley Isaacson; 1,042 Larry Holmes; 778 Herb Lewin; 411 Willa Kenoyer; 353 Al Hamburg; 6 scattered write-in.

CONNECTICUT MARCH 29

Republican 73,501 Bush; 21,005 Dole; 3,281 Kemp; 3,193 Uncommitted; 3,191 Robertson.

Democratic 140,291 Dukakis; 68,372 Jackson; 18,501 Gore; 5,761 Hart; 3,140 Simon; 2,370 Babbitt; 1,951 Uncommitted; 1,009 Gephardt.

1988 PRESIDENTIAL PRIMARIES

FLORIDA MARCH 8

Republican 559,820 Bush; 191,197 Dole; 95,826 Robertson; 41,795 Kemp; 6,726 duPont; 5,858 Haig.

Democratic 521,041 Dukakis; 254,912 Jackson; 182,861 Gephardt; 161,165 Gore; 79,088 Undecided; 36,315 Hart; 27,620 Simon; 10,296 Babbitt.

GEORGIA MARCH 8

Republican 215,516 Bush; 94,749 Dole; 65,163 Robertson; 23,409 Kemp; 1,309 duPont; 782 Haig.

Democratic 247,831 Jackson; 201,490 Gore; 97,179 Dukakis; 41,489 Gephardt; 15,852 Hart; 8,388 Simon; 7,276 Uncommitted; 3,247 Babbitt.

IDAHO MAY 24

Republican 55,464 Bush; 6,935 None of the Names Shown; 5,876 Robertson.

Democratic 37,696 Dukakis; 8,066 Jackson; 2,308 "None of the Names Shown"; 1,891 Gore; 1,409 Simon.

ILLINOIS MARCH 15

Republican 469,151 Bush; 309,253 Dole; 59,087 Robertson; 12,687 Kemp; 4,653 duPont; 3,806 Haig.

Democratic 635,219 Simon; 484,233 Jackson; 245,289 Dukakis; 77,265 Gore; 35,108 Gephardt; 12,769 Hart; 6,094 LaRouche; 4,953 Babbitt.

Solidarity 170 Lenora B. Fulani.

INDIANA MAY 3

Republican 351,829 Bush; 42,878 Dole; 28,712 Robertson; 14,236 Kemp.

Democratic 449,495 Dukakis; 145,021 Jackson; 21,865 Gore; 16,777 Gephardt; 12,550 Simon.

KENTUCKY MARCH 8

Republican 72,020 Bush; 27,868 Dole; 13,526 Robertson; 4,020 Kemp; 2,245 Uncommitted; 844 Stassen; 457 duPont; 422 Haig.

Democratic 145,988 Gore; 59,433 Dukakis; 49,667 Jackson; 28,982 Gephardt; 11,798 Hart; 10,465 Uncommitted; 9,393 Simon; 1,290 Babbitt; 681 LaRouche; 537 Martin-Trigona; 487 Kay.

LOUISIANA MARCH 8

Republican 83,687 Bush; 26,295 Robertson; 25,626 Dole; 7,722 Kemp; 853 duPont; 598 Haig.

Democratic 221,532 Jackson; 174,974 Gore; 95,667 Dukakis; 66,434 Gephardt; 26,442 Hart; 23,390 Duke; 5,155 Simon; 3,701 Ahern; 3,076 Babbitt; 1,681 LaRouche; 1,575 Dennerll; 823 Kay.

MARYLAND MARCH 8

Republican 107,026 Bush; 64,987 Dole; 12,860 Robertson; 11,909 Kemp; 2,551 duPont; 1,421 Haig.

Democratic 242,479 Dukakis; 152,642 Jackson; 46,063 Gore; 42,059 Gephardt; 16,513 Simon; 14,948 Uncommitted; 9,732 Hart; 4,750 Babbitt; 2,149 LaRouche.

1988 PRESIDENTIAL PRIMARIES

MASSACHUSETTS MARCH 8

Republican 141,113 Bush; 63,392 Dole; 16,791 Kemp; 10,891 Robertson; 3,522 duPont; 3,416 No Preference; 1,705 Haig; 351 scattered write-in.

Democratic 418,256 Dukakis; 133,141 Jackson; 72,944 Gephardt; 31,631 Gore; 26,176 Simon; 11,866 No Preference; 10,837 Hart; 4,222 Babbitt; 1,971 DiDonato; 998 LaRouche; 1,405 scattered write-in.

MISSISSIPPI MARCH 8

Republican 104,814 Bush; 26,855 Dole; 21,378 Robertson; 5,479 Kemp.

Democratic 160,651 Jackson; 120,364 Gore; 29,941 Dukakis; 19,693 Gephardt; 13,934 Hart; 9,384 Uncommitted; 2,118 Simon; 2,037 Babbitt; 1,295 LaRouche. Data given are for the amended returns.

MISSOURI MARCH 8

Republican 168,812 Bush; 164,394 Dole; 44,705 Robertson; 14,180 Kemp; 5,563 Uncommitted; 1,788 duPont; 858 Haig.

Democratic 305,287 Gephardt; 106,386 Jackson; 61,303 Dukakis; 21,433 Simon; 14,549 Gore; 7,607 Hart; 6,635 Uncommitted; 1,760 Duke; 1,377 Babbitt; 664 LaRouche; 372 Kay; 241 Koczak; 191 Dennerll.

MONTANA JUNE 7

Republican 63,098 Bush; 16,762 Dole; 6,520 No Preference.

Democratic 83,684 Dukakis; 26,908 Jackson; 4,083 No Preference; 3,369 Gephardt; 2,261 Gore; 1,566 Simon.

NEBRASKA MAY 10

Republican 138,784 Bush; 45,572 Dole; 10,334 Robertson; 8,423 Kemp; 936 scattered write-in.

Democratic 106,334 Dukakis; 43,380 Jackson; 4,948 Gephardt; 4,763 Uncommitted; 4,220 Hart; 2,519 Gore; 2,104 Simon; 416 LaRouche; 324 scattered write-in.

New Alliance 10 Lenora B. Fulani.

NEW HAMPSHIRE FEBRUARY 16

Republican 59,290 Bush; 44,797 Dole; 20,114 Kemp; 15,885 duPont; 14,775 Robertson; 481 Haig; 130 Stassen; 107 Conley; 107 Rachner; 83 Drucker; 76 Horrigan; 43 Levinson; 1,756 scattered write-in.

Democratic 44,112 Dukakis; 24,513 Gephardt; 21,094 Simon; 9,615 Jackson; 8,400 Gore; 5,644 Babbitt; 4,888 Hart; 1,349 William J. duPont; 264 Duke; 188 LaRouche; 142 Marra; 122 Roy; 84 DiDonato; 61 Martin-Trigona; 47 Koczak; 36 King; 33 O'Donnell; 33 Sagan; 28 Thomas; 25 Kirk; 22 Zucker; 18 Dennerll; 16 Thorpe; 10 VanPetten; 9 Lock; 2,759 scattered write-in.

NEW JERSEY JUNE 7

Republican 241,033 Bush.

Democratic 414,829 Dukakis; 213,705 Jackson; 18,062 Gore; 2,621 LaRouche; 2,594 Marra; 2,491 Duke.

1988 PRESIDENTIAL PRIMARIES

NEW MEXICO JUNE 7

Republican 69,359 Bush; 9,305 Dole; 5,350 Robertson; 2,569 Uncommitted; 2,161 Haig.

Democratic 114,968 Dukakis; 52,988 Jackson; 6,898 Hart; 4,747 Gore; 3,275 Uncommitted; 2,913 Babbitt; 2,821 Simon.

NEW YORK APRIL 19

Republican No Presidential primary held.

Democratic 801,457 Dukakis; 585,076 Jackson; 157,559 Gore; 17,011 Simon; 10,258 Uncommitted; 2,672 Gephardt; 1,153 LaRouche.

NORTH CAROLINA MARCH 8

Republican 124,260 Bush; 107,032 Dole; 26,861 Robertson; 11,361 Kemp; 2,797 No Preference; 944 duPont; 546 Haig.

Democratic 235,669 Gore; 224,177 Jackson; 137,993 Dukakis; 37,553 Gephardt; 16,381 Hart; 16,337 No Preference; 8,032 Simon; 3,816 Babbitt.

NORTH DAKOTA JUNE 14

Republican 37,062 Bush; 2,372 Rachner.

Democratic No candidate names appeared on the ballot. Tallied write-in votes were 2,890 Dukakis; 515 Jackson.

Libertarian 985 Ron Paul.

OHIO MAY 3

Republican 643,907 Bush slate; 94,650 Dole slate; 56,347 Robertson slate. The data given here are for the statewide at-large slates pledged to the candidates indicated.

Democratic 869,792 Dukakis slates; 378,866 Jackson slates; 29,931 Gore slates; 29,912 Traficant slates; 28,414 Hart slates; 25,068 Applegate slate; 15,524 Simon slates; 6,065 LaRouche slates. The data given here are the sum of the votes cast for delegate slates by Congressional District pledged to the candidates indicated. Only Dukakis and Gore had delegate slates in all twenty-one Congressional Districts.

OKLAHOMA MARCH 8

Republican 78,224 Bush; 73,016 Dole; 44,067 Robertson; 11,439 Kemp; 938 duPont; 715 Haig; 539 Masters.

Democratic 162,584 Gore; 82,596 Gephardt; 66,278 Dukakis; 52,417 Jackson; 14,336 Hart; 6,901 Simon; 2,388 Duke; 1,601 Babbitt; 1,078 LaRouche; 1,068 Koczak; 1,005 Doty; 475 Dennerll.

OREGON MAY 17

Republican 199,938 Bush; 49,128 Dole; 21,212 Robertson; 4,208 scattered write-in.

Democratic 221,048 Dukakis; 148,207 Jackson; 6,772 Gephardt; 5,445 Gore; 4,757 Simon; 1,562 LaRouche; 1,141 scattered write-in.

1988 PRESIDENTIAL PRIMARIES

PENNSYLVANIA APRIL 26

Republican 687,323 Bush; 103,763 Dole; 79,463 Robertson.

Democratic 1,002,480 Dukakis; 411,260 Jackson; 44,542 Gore; 20,473 Hart; 9,692 Simon; 7,546 Wesner; 7,254 Gephardt; 4,443 LaRouche.

RHODE ISLAND MARCH 8

Republican 10,401 Bush; 3,628 Dole; 911 Robertson; 792 Kemp; 174 Uncommitted; 80 duPont; 49 Haig.

Democratic 34,211 Dukakis; 7,445 Jackson; 2,028 Gephardt; 1,939 Gore; 1,395 Simon; 809 Uncommitted; 733 Hart; 469 Babbitt.

SOUTH CAROLINA MARCH 5

Republican 94,738 Bush; 40,265 Dole; 37,261 Robertson; 22,431 Kemp; 316 duPont; 177 Haig; 104 Stassen.

Democratic No Presidential primary held.

SOUTH DAKOTA FEBRUARY 23

Republican 51,599 Dole slate; 18,310 Robertson slate; 17,404 Bush slate; 4,290 Kemp slate; 1,226 Uncommitted slate; 576 duPont slate.

Democratic 31,184 Gephardt; 22,349 Dukakis; 5,993 Gore; 3,992 Simon; 3,875 Hart; 3,867 Jackson; 346 Babbitt.

TENNESSEE MARCH 8

Republican 152,515 Bush; 55,027 Dole; 32,015 Robertson; 10,911 Kemp; 2,340 Uncommitted; 777 Haig; 646 duPont; 21 scattered write-in.

Democratic 416,861 Gore; 119,248 Jackson; 19,348 Dukakis; 8,470 Gephardt; 4,706 Hart; 3,032 Uncommitted; 2,647 Simon; 1,946 Babbitt; 56 scattered write-in.

TEXAS MARCH 8

Republican 648,178 Bush; 155,449 Robertson; 140,795 Dole; 50,586 Kemp; 12,563 Uncommitted; 4,245 duPont; 3,140 Haig.

Democratic 579,713 Dukakis; 433,335 Jackson; 357,764 Gore; 240,158 Gephardt; 82,199 Hart; 34,499 Simon; 11,618 Babbitt; 9,013 LaRouche; 8,808 Duke; 6,238 Williams; 3,700 Dennerll.

VERMONT MARCH 1

Republican 23,565 Bush; 18,655 Dole; 2,452 Robertson; 1,877 Kemp; 808 duPont; 324 Haig; 151 scattered write-in.

Democratic 28,353 Dukakis; 13,044 Jackson; 3,910 Gephardt; 2,620 Simon; 2,055 Hart; 809 scattered write-in.

Liberty Union 199 Willa Kenoyer; 65 Herb Lewin; 25 scattered write-in.

1988 PRESIDENTIAL PRIMARIES

VIRGINIA MARCH 8

Republican 124,738 Bush; 60,921 Dole; 32,173 Robertson; 10,809 Kemp; 3,675 Uncommitted; 1,229 duPont; 597 Haig.

Democratic 164,709 Jackson; 81,419 Gore; 80,183 Dukakis; 15,935 Gephardt; 7,045 Simon; 6,266 Hart; 6,142 Uncommitted; 2,454 Babbitt; 746 LaRouche.

WEST VIRGINIA MAY 10

Republican 110,705 Bush; 15,600 Dole; 10,417 Robertson; 3,820 Kemp; 1,604 Stassen; 994 Conley.

Democratic 254,289 Dukakis; 45,788 Jackson; 11,573 Gore; 9,284 Hart; 6,130 Gephardt; 3,604 McDonald; 2,280 Simon; 1,978 Babbitt; 1,482 LaRouche; 1,383 Duke; 1,339 Dennerll; 967 Traficant.

WISCONSIN APRIL 5

Republican 295,295 Bush; 28,460 Dole; 24,798 Robertson; 4,915 Kemp; 2,372 Uninstructed Delegation; 1,554 Haig; 1,504 duPont; 396 scattered write-in.

Democratic 483,172 Dukakis; 285,995 Jackson; 176,712 Gore; 48,419 Simon; 7,996 Gephardt; 7,068 Hart; 2,554 Uninstructed Delegation; 2,353 Babbitt; 513 scattered write-in.

DISTRICT OF COLUMBIA MAY 3

Republican 5,890 Bush; 469 Dole; 268 Robertson; 93 scattered write-in.

Democratic 68,840 Jackson; 15,415 Dukakis; 769 Simon; 648 Gore; 300 Gephardt; 80 Thorpe.

1988 REPUBLICAN PREFERENCE PRIMARIES

Date		State	Total Vote	Bush	Dole	duPont	Haig	Kemp	Robertson	Other
Feb.	16	New Hampshire	157,644	59,290	44,797	15,885	481	20,114	14,775	2,302
	23	South Dakota	93,405	17,404	51,599	576		4,290	18,310	1,226
Mar.	1	Vermont	47,832	23,565	18,655	808	324	1,877	2,452	151
	5	South Carolina	195,292	94,738	40,265	316	177	22,431	37,261	104
	8	Alabama	213,561	137,807	34,733	392	300	10,557	29,772	
	8	Arkansas	68,305	32,114	17,667	359	346	3,499	12,918	1,402
	8	Florida	901,222	559,820	191,197	6,726	5,858	41,795	95,826	
	8	Georgia	400,928	215,516	94,749	1,309	782	23,409	65,163	
	8	Kentucky	121,402	72,020	27,868	457	422	4,020	13,526	3,089
	8	Louisiana	144,781	83,687	25,626	853	598	7,722	26,295	
	8	Maryland	200,754	107,026	64,987	2,551	1,421	11,909	12,860	
	8	Massachusetts	241,181	141,113	63,392	3,522	1,705	16,791	10,891	3,767
	8	Mississippi	158,526	104,814	26,855			5,479	21,378	
	8	Missouri	400,300	168,812	164,394	1,788	858	14,180	44,705	5,563
	8	North Carolina	273,801	124,260	107,032	944	546	11,361	26,861	2,797
	8	Oklahoma	208,938	78,224	73,016	938	715	11,439	44,067	539
	8	Rhode Island	16,035	10,401	3,628	80	49	792	911	174
	8	Tennessee	254,252	152,515	55,027	646	777	10,911	32,015	2,361
	8	Texas	1,014,956	648,178	140,795	4,245	3,140	50,586	155,449	12,563
	8	Virginia	234,142	124,738	60,921	1,229	597	10,809	32,173	3,675
	15	Illinois	858,637	469,151	309,253	4,653	3,806	12,687	59,087	
	29	Connecticut	104,171	73,501	21,005			3,281	3,191	3,193
April	5	Wisconsin	359,294	295,295	28,460	1,504	1,554	4,915	24,798	2,768
	19	New York	No Primary held							
	26	Pennsylvania	870,549	687,323	103,763				79,463	
May	3	Indiana	437,655	351,829	42,878			14,236	28,712	
	3	Ohio	794,904	643,907	94,650				56,347	
	3	District of Columbia	6,720	5,890	469				268	93
	10	Nebraska	204,049	138,784	45,572			8,423	10,334	936
	10	West Virginia	143,140	110,705	15,600			3,820	10,417	2,598
	17	Oregon	274,486	199,938	49,128				21,212	4,208
	24	Idaho	68,275	55,464					5,876	6,935
June	7	California	2,240,387	1,856,273	289,220				94,779	115
	7	Montana	86,380	63,098	16,762					6,520
	7	New Jersey	241,033	241,033						
	7	New Mexico	88,744	69,359	9,305		2,161		5,350	2,569
	14	North Dakota	39,434	37,062						2,372
			12,165,115	8,254,654	2,333,268	49,781	26,617	331,333	1,097,442	72,020

Other vote includes 34,950 Uncommitted; 12,733 No Preference; 6,935 "None of the Names Shown"; 2,682 Stassen; 2,479 Rachner; 2,372 Uninstructed Delegation; 1,101 Conley; 539 Masters; 83 Drucker; 76 Horrigan; 43 Levinson; 8,027 scattered.

1988 DEMOCRATIC PREFERENCE PRIMARIES

Date		State	Total Vote	Babbitt	Dukakis	Gephardt	Gore	Hart	Jackson	LaRouche	Simon	Other
Feb.	16	New Hampshire	123,512	5,644	44,112	24,513	8,400	4,888	9,615	188	21,094	5,058
	23	South Dakota	71,606	346	22,349	31,184	5,993	3,875	3,867		3,992	
Mar.	1	Vermont	50,791		28,353	3,910		2,055	13,044		2,620	809
	5	South Carolina	No Primary held									
	8	Alabama	405,642	2,410	31,306	30,214	151,739	7,530	176,764	845	3,063	1,771
	8	Arkansas	97,544	2,614	94,103	59,711	185,758	18,630	85,003	2,347	9,020	40,358
	8	Florida	1,273,298	10,296	521,041	182,861	161,165	36,315	254,912		27,620	79,088
	8	Georgia	622,752	3,247	97,179	41,489	201,490	15,852	247,831		8,388	7,276
	8	Kentucky	318,721	1,290	59,433	28,982	145,988	11,798	49,667	681	9,393	11,489
	8	Louisiana	624,450	3,076	95,667	66,434	174,974	26,442	221,532	1,681	5,155	29,489
	8	Maryland	531,335	4,750	242,479	42,059	46,063	9,732	152,642	2,149	16,513	14,948
	8	Massachusetts	713,447	4,222	418,256	72,944	31,631	10,837	133,141	998	26,176	15,242
	8	Mississippi	359,417	2,037	29,941	19,693	120,364	13,934	160,651	1,295	2,118	9,384
	8	Missouri	527,805	1,377	61,303	305,287	14,549	7,607	106,386	664	21,433	9,199
	8	North Carolina	679,958	3,816	137,993	37,553	235,669	16,381	224,177		8,032	16,337
	8	Oklahoma	392,727	1,601	66,278	82,596	162,584	14,336	52,417	1,078	6,901	4,936
	8	Rhode Island	49,029	469	34,211	2,028	1,939	733	7,445		1,395	809
	8	Tennessee	576,314	1,946	19,348	8,470	416,861	4,706	119,248		2,647	3,088
	8	Texas	1,767,045	11,618	579,713	240,158	357,764	82,199	433,335	9,013	34,499	18,746
	8	Virginia	364,899	2,454	80,183	15,935	81,419	6,266	164,709	746	7,045	6,142
	15	Illinois	1,500,930	4,953	245,289	35,108	77,265	12,769	484,233	6,094	635,219	
	29	Connecticut	241,395	2,370	140,291	1,009	18,501	5,761	68,372		3,140	1,951
April	5	Wisconsin	1,014,782	2,353	483,172	7,996	176,712	7,068	285,995		48,419	3,067
	19	New York	1,575,186		801,457	2,672	157,559		585,076	1,153	17,011	10,258
	26	Pennsylvania	1,507,690		1,002,480	7,254	44,542	20,473	411,260	4,443	9,692	7,546
May	3	Indiana	645,708		449,495	16,777	21,865		145,021		12,550	
	3	Ohio	1,383,572		869,792		29,931	28,414	378,866	6,065	15,524	54,980
	3	District of Columbia	86,052		15,415	300	648		68,840		769	80
	10	Nebraska	169,008		106,334	4,948	2,519	4,220	43,380	416	2,104	5,087
	10	West Virginia	340,097	1,978	254,289	6,130	11,573	9,284	45,788	1,482	2,280	7,293
	17	Oregon	388,932		221,048	6,772	5,445		148,207	1,562	4,757	1,141
	24	Idaho	51,370		37,696		1,891		8,066		1,409	2,308
June	7	California	3,138,734		1,910,808		56,645		1,102,093	25,417	43,771	
	7	Montana	121,871		83,684	3,369	2,261		26,908		1,566	4,083
	7	New Jersey	654,302		414,829		18,062		213,705	2,621		5,085
	7	New Mexico	188,610	2,913	114,968		4,747	6,898	52,988		2,821	3,275
	14	North Dakota	3,405		2,890				515			
			22,961,936	77,780	9,817,185	1,388,356	3,134,516	389,003	6,685,699	70,938	1,018,136	380,323

Other vote includes 116,262 Uncommitted; 79,088 Undecided; 45,289 Duke; 32,286 No Preference; 30,879 Traficant; 25,068 Applegate; 7,298 Dennerll; 7,546 Wesner; 6,238 Williams; 3,701 Ahern; 3,604 McDonald; 2,736 Marra; 2,554 Uninstructed Delegation; 2,308 "None of the Names Shown"; 2,055 DiDonato; 1,682 Kay; 1,356 Koczak; 1,349 duPont; 1,005 Doty; 598 Martin-Trigona; 122 Roy; 96 Thorpe; 36 King; 33 O'Donnell; 33 Sagan; 28 Thomas; 25 Kirk; 22 Zucker; 10 VanPetter; 9 Lock; 7,007 scattered.

1984 REPUBLICAN PREFERENCE PRIMARIES

Date		State	Total Vote	Reagan	Other
Feb.	28	New Hampshire	75,570	65,033	10,537
Mar.	6	Vermont	33,643	33,218	425
	13	Alabama	No Primary Held		
	13	Florida	344,150	344,150	—
	13	Georgia	50,793	50,793	—
	13	Massachusetts	65,937	58,996	6,941
	13	Rhode Island	2,235	2,028	207
	20	Illinois	595,078	594,742	336
	27	Connecticut	No Primary Held		
April	3	New York	No Primary Held		
	3	Wisconsin	294,813	280,608	14,205
	10	Pennsylvania	621,206	616,916	4,290
May	1	District of Columbia	5,692	5,692	—
	1	Tennessee	82,921	75,367	7,554
	5	Louisiana	16,687	14,964	1,723
	5	Texas	319,839	308,713	11,126
	8	Indiana	428,559	428,559	—
	8	Maryland	73,663	73,663	—
	8	North Carolina	No Primary Held		
	8	Ohio	658,169	658,169	—
	15	Nebraksa	146,648	145,245	1,403
	15	Oregon	243,346	238,594	4,752
	22	Idaho	105,687	97,450	8,237
June	5	California	1,874,975	1,874,897	78
	5	Montana	71,887	66,432	5,455
	5	New Jersey	240,054	240,054	—
	5	New Mexico	42,994	40,805	2,189
	5	South Dakota	No Primary Held		
	5	West Virginia	136,996	125,790	11,206
	12	North Dakota	44,109	44,109	
			6,575,651	6,484,987	90,664

Other vote includes 22,791 Uncommitted; 14,047 "Ronald Reagan No"; 12,749 Stassen; 10,383 No Preference; 8,237 "None of the Names Shown"; 360 Kelley; 252 Arnold; 202 Fernandez; 21,643 scattered.

1984 DEMOCRATIC PREFERENCE PRIMARIES

Date		State	Total Vote	Glenn	Hart	Jackson	LaRouche	McGovern	Mondale	Other
Feb.	28	New Hampshire	101,131	12,088	37,702	5,311	—	5,217	28,173	12,640
Mar.	6	Vermont	74,059	—	51,873	5,761	—	—	14,834	1,591
	13	Alabama	428,283	89,286	88,465	83,787	—	—	148,165	18,580
	13	Florida	1,182,190	128,209	463,799	144,263	—	17,614	394,350	33,955
	13	Georgia	684,541	122,744	186,903	143,730	—	11,321	208,588	11,255
	13	Massachusetts	630,962	45,456	245,943	31,824	—	134,341	160,893	12,505
	13	Rhode Island	44,511	2,249	20,011	3,875	—	2,146	15,338	892
	20	Illinois	1,659,425	19,800	584,579	348,843	—	25,336	670,951	9,916
	27	Connecticut	220,842	955	116,286	26,395	—	2,426	64,230	10,550
April	3	New York	1,387,950	15,941	380,564	355,541	—	4,547	621,581	9,776
	3	Wisconsin	635,768	6,398	282,435	62,524	—	10,166	261,374	12,871
	10	Pennsylvania	1,656,294	22,605	551,335	264,463	19,180	13,139	747,267	38,305
May	1	District of Columbia	102,731	—	7,305	69,106	—	—	26,320	—
	1	Tennessee	322,063	4,198	93,710	81,418	—	3,824	132,201	6,712
	5	Louisiana	318,810	—	79,593	136,707	4,970	3,158	71,162	23,220
	5	Texas	No Primary held							
	8	Indiana	716,955	16,046	299,491	98,190	—	—	293,413	9,815
	8	Maryland	506,886	6,238	123,365	129,387	7,836	5,796	215,222	19,042
	8	North Carolina	960,857	17,659	289,877	243,945	—	10,149	342,324	56,903
	8	Ohio	1,447,236	—	608,528	237,133	4,336	8,991	583,595	4,653
	15	Nebraska	148,855	—	86,582	13,495	1,227	1,561	39,635	6,355
	15	Oregon	399,679	10,831	233,638	37,106	5,943	—	110,374	1,787
	22	Idaho	54,722	—	31,737	3,104	1,196	—	16,460	2,225
June	5	California	2,970,903	96,770	1,155,499	546,693	52,647	69,926	1,049,342	26
	5	Montana	34,214	—	3,080*	388*	—	—	2,026*	28,720
	5	New Jersey	676,561	—	200,948	159,788	10,309	—	305,516	—
	5	New Mexico	187,403	—	87,610	22,168	3,330	5,143	67,675	1,477
	5	South Dakota	52,561	—	26,641	2,738	1,383	—	20,495	1,304
	5	West Virginia	369,245	—	137,866	24,697	7,274	—	198,776	632
	12	North Dakota	33,555	—	28,603	—	4,018	—	934	—
			18,009,192	617,473	6,503,968	3,282,380	123,649	334,801	6,811,214	335,707

Other vote includes 77,697 No Preference; 59,254 Uncommitted; 52,759 Askew; 51,437 Cranston; 33,684 Hollings; 9,815 Brewster; 9,261 "None of the Names Shown"; 8,014 Griser; 7,957 Willis; 4,847 Williams; 2,699 Kay; 1,855 Koczak; 632 Timinski; 132 Buchanan; 127 Beckman; 74 O'Donnell; 34 King; 25 Kreml; 24 Bagley; 24 Kirk; 21 Rudnicki; 20 Clendenan; 20 Sagan; 19 Caplette; 15,276 scattered.

1980 REPUBLICAN PREFERENCE PRIMARIES

Date		State	Total Vote	Anderson	Baker	Bush	Connally	Crane	Reagan	Other
Feb.	26	New Hampshire	147,157	14,458	18,943	33,443	2,239	2,618	72,983	2,473
Mar.	4	Massachusetts	400,826	122,987	19,366	124,365	4,714	4,669	115,334	9,391
	4	Vermont	65,611	19,030	8,055	14,226	884	1,238	19,720	2,458
	8	South Carolina	145,501	—	773	21,569	43,113	—	79,549	497
	11	Alabama	211,353	—	1,963	54,730	1,077	5,099	147,352	1,132
	11	Florida	614,995	56,636	6,345	185,996	4,958	12,000	345,699	3,361
	11	Georgia	200,171	16,853	1,571	25,293	2,388	6,308	146,500	1,258
	18	Illinois	1,130,081	415,193	7,051	124,057	4,548	24,865	547,355	7,012
	25	Connecticut	182,284	40,354	2,446	70,367	598	1,887	61,735	4,897
	25	New York	No Primary Held							
April	1	Kansas	285,398	51,924	3,603	35,838	2,067	1,367	179,739	10,860
	1	Wisconsin	907,853	248,623	3,298	276,164	2,312	2,951	364,898	9,607
	5	Louisiana	41,683	—	—	7,818	—	—	31,212	2,653
	22	Pennsylvania	1,241,411	26,890	30,846	626,759	10,656	—	527,916	18,344
May	3	Texas	526,769	—	—	249,819	—	—	268,798	8,152
	6	Indiana	568,313	56,342	—	92,955	—	—	419,016	—
	6	North Carolina	168,391	8,542	2,543	36,631	1,107	547	113,854	5,167
	6	Tennessee	195,210	8,722	—	35,274	—	1,574	144,625	5,015
	6	District of Columbia	7,529	2,025	—	4,973	—	270	—	261
	13	Maryland	167,303	16,244	—	68,389	—	2,113	80,557	—
	13	Nebraska	205,203	11,879	—	31,380	—	1,062	155,995	4,887
	20	Michigan	595,176	48,947	—	341,998	—	—	189,184	15,047
	20	Oregon	315,366	32,118	—	109,210	—	2,324	170,449	1,265
	27	Arkansas	No Primary Held							
	27	Idaho	134,879	13,130	5,416	—	—	1,024	111,868	3,441
	27	Kentucky	94,795	4,791	—	6,861	—	—	78,072	5,071
	27	Nevada	47,395	—	—	3,078	—	—	39,352	4,965
June	3	California	2,564,072	349,315	—	125,113	—	21,465	2,057,923	10,256
	3	Mississippi	25,751	—	—	2,105	—	—	23,028	618
	3	Montana	79,423	—	—	7,665	—	—	68,744	3,014
	3	New Jersey	277,977	—	—	47,447	—	—	225,959	4,571
	3	New Mexico	59,546	7,171	—	5,892	—	4,412	37,982	4,089
	3	Ohio	856,773	—	—	164,485	—	—	692,288	—
	3	Rhode Island	5,335	—	—	993	—	—	3,839	503
	3	South Dakota	82,905	—	—	3,691	—	—	72,861	6,353
	3	West Virginia	138,016	—	—	19,509	—	—	115,407	3,100
			12,690,451	1,572,174	112,219	2,958,093	80,661	97,793	7,709,793	159,718

Other vote includes 38,708 Uncommitted; 24,753 Stassen; 23,423 Fernandez; 15,161 No Preference; 9,321 "None of the Names Shown"; 7,298 Dole; 4,965 "None of These Candidates"; 4,357 Jacobson; 3,757 Kelley; 1,063 Yeager; 483 Carris; 355 Belluso; 311 Carlson; 244 Badgley; 67 Pickett; 25,452 scattered.

1980 DEMOCRATIC PREFERENCE PRIMARIES

Date		State	Total Vote	Brown	Carter	Kennedy	LaRouche	Other
Feb.	26	New Hampshire	111,930	10,743	52,692	41,745	2,326	4,424
Mar.	4	Massachusetts	907,323	31,498	260,401	590,393	—	25,031
	4	Vermont	39,703	—	29,015	10,135	—	553
	8	South Carolina	No Primary Held					
	11	Alabama	237,464	9,529	193,734	31,382	—	2,819
	11	Florida	1,098,003	53,474	666,321	254,727	—	123,481
	11	Georgia	384,780	7,255	338,772	32,315	513	5,925
	18	Illinois	1,201,067	39,168	780,787	359,875	19,192	2,045
	25	Connecticut	210,275	5,386	87,207	98,662	5,617	13,403
	25	New York	989,062	—	406,305	582,757	—	—
April	1	Kansas	193,918	9,434	109,807	61,318	—	13,359
	1	Wisconsin	629,619	74,496	353,662	189,520	6,896	5,045
	5	Louisiana	358,741	16,774	199,956	80,797	—	61,214
	22	Pennsylvania	1,613,551	37,669	732,332	736,854	—	106,696
May	3	Texas	1,377,354	35,585	770,390	314,129	—	257,250
	6	Indiana	589,441	—	398,949	190,492	—	—
	6	North Carolina	737,262	21,420	516,778	130,684	—	68,380
	6	Tennessee	294,680	5,612	221,658	53,258	925	13,227
	6	District of Columbia	64,150	—	23,697	39,561	892	—
	13	Maryland	477,090	14,313	226,528	181,091	4,388	50,770
	13	Nebraska	153,881	5,478	72,120	57,826	1,169	17,288
	20	Michigan	78,424	23,043	—	—	8,948	46,433
	20	Oregon	368,322	34,409	208,693	114,651	—	10,569
	27	Arkansas	448,290	—	269,375	78,542	—	100,373
	27	Idaho	50,482	2,078	31,383	11,087	—	5,934
	27	Kentucky	240,331	—	160,819	55,167	—	24,345
	27	Nevada	66,948	—	25,159	19,296	—	22,493
June	3	California	3,363,969	135,962	1,266,276	1,507,142	71,779	382,810
	3	Mississippi	No Primary Held					
	3	Montana	130,059	—	66,922	47,671	—	15,466
	3	New Jersey	560,908	—	212,387	315,109	13,913	19,499
	3	New Mexico	159,364	—	66,621	73,721	4,798	14,224
	3	Ohio	1,186,410	—	605,744	523,874	35,268	21,524
	3	Rhode Island	38,327	310	9,907	26,179	1,160	771
	3	South Dakota	68,763	—	31,251	33,418	—	4,094
	3	West Virginia	317,934	—	197,687	120,247	—	—
			18,747,825	573,636	9,593,335	6,963,625	177,784	1,439,445

Other vote includes 950,378 Uncommitted; 301,695 No Preference; 48,061 Kay; 48,032 Finch; 22,493 "None of These Candidates"; 13,857 "None of the Names Shown"; 4,002 Maddox; 2,255 Reaux; 609 Nuckols; 571 Ahern; 364 Rollinson; 47,128 Scattered.

1976 REPUBLICAN PREFERENCE PRIMARIES

Date		State	Total Vote	Ford	Reagan	Other
February	24	New Hampshire	111,674	55,156	53,569	2,949
March	2	Massachusetts	188,449	115,375	63,555	9,519
	2	Vermont	32,157	27,014	4,892	251
	9	Florida	609,819	321,982	287,837	–
	16	Illinois	775,893	456,750	311,295	7,848
	23	North Carolina	193,727	88,897	101,468	3,362
April	6	Wisconsin	591,812	326,869	262,126	2,817
	27	Pennsylvania	796,660	733,472	40,510	22,678
May	4	District of Columbia	No Primary			
	4	Georgia	188,472	59,801	128,671	–
	4	Indiana	631,292	307,513	323,779	–
	11	Nebraska	208,414	94,542	113,493	379
	11	West Virginia	155,692	88,386	67,306	–
	18	Maryland	165,971	96,291	69,680	–
	18	Michigan	1,062,814	690,180	364,052	8,582
	25	Arkansas	32,541	11,430	20,628	483
	25	Idaho	89,793	22,323	66,743	727
	25	Kentucky	133,528	67,976	62,683	2,869
	25	Nevada	47,749	13,747	31,637	2,365
	25	Oregon	298,535	150,181	136,691	11,663
	25	Tennessee	242,535	120,685	118,997	2,853
June	1	Montana	89,779	31,100	56,683	1,996
	1	Rhode Island	14,352	9,365	4,480	507
	1	South Dakota	84,077	36,976	43,068	4,033
	8	California	2,450,511	845,655	1,604,836	20
	8	New Jersey	242,122	242,122	–	–
	8	Ohio	935,757	516,111	419,646	–
			10,374,125	5,529,899	4,758,325	85,901

Other vote includes 7,582 Daly; 1,088 Klein; 42,514 scattered write-ins; 15,391 No Preference; 14,727 Uncommitted; 2,365 "None of These Candidates"; 2,234 "None of the Names Shown".

1976 DEMOCRATIC PREFERENCE PRIMARIES

Date		State	Total Vote	Bayh	Brown	Byrd	Carter	Church	Harris	Jackson	McCormack	Shriver	Udall	Wallace	Other
February	24	New Hampshire	82,381	12,510	–	–	23,373	–	8,863	1,857	1,007	6,743	18,710	1,061	8,257
March	2	Massachusetts	735,821	34,963	–	–	101,948	–	55,701	164,393	25,772	53,252	130,440	123,112	46,240
	2	Vermont	38,714	–	–	–	16,335	–	4,893	–	3,324	10,699	–	–	3,463
	9	Florida	1,300,330	8,750	–	5,042	448,844	4,906	5,397	310,944	7,595	7,084	27,235	396,820	77,713
	16	Illinois	1,311,914	–	–	–	630,915	–	98,862	–	–	214,024	–	361,798	6,315
	23	North Carolina	604,832	–	–	–	324,437	–	5,923	25,749	–	–	14,032	210,166	24,525
April	6	Wisconsin	740,528	1,255	–	–	271,220	–	8,185	47,605	26,982	5,097	263,771	92,460	23,953
	27	Pennsylvania	1,385,042	15,320	–	–	511,905	–	13,067	340,340	38,800	–	259,166	155,902	50,542
May	4	District of Columbia	33,291	–	–	–	10,521	–	461	–	–	–	6,999	–	15,310
	4	Georgia	502,471	824	–	3,628	419,272	2,477	699	3,358	635	1,378	9,755	57,594	2,851
	4	Indiana	614,389	–	–	–	417,480	–	–	72,080	31,708	–	–	93,121	–
	11	Nebraska	175,013	407	–	–	65,833	67,297	811	2,642	6,033	384	4,688	5,567	21,351
	11	West Virginia	372,577	–	–	331,639	–	–	–	–	–	–	–	40,938	–
	18	Maryland	591,746	–	286,672	–	219,404	–	6,841	13,956	7,907	–	32,790	24,176	–
	18	Michigan	708,666	–	–	–	307,559	–	4,081	10,332	7,623	5,738	305,134	49,204	18,995
	25	Arkansas	501,800	–	–	–	314,306	–	–	9,554	–	–	37,783	83,005	57,152
	25	Idaho	74,405	–	1,453	–	8,818	58,570	319	485	–	–	981	1,115	2,664
	25	Kentucky	306,006	–	–	–	181,690	–	–	8,186	17,061	–	33,262	51,540	14,267
	25	Nevada	75,242	–	39,671	–	17,567	6,778	–	1,896	–	–	2,237	2,490	4,603
	25	Oregon	432,632	743	106,812	–	115,310	145,394	1,344	5,298	3,753	–	11,747	5,797	36,434
	25	Tennessee	334,078	–	1,556	–	259,243	8,026	1,628	5,672	1,782	–	12,420	36,495	7,256
June	1	Montana	106,841	–	–	–	26,329	63,448	–	2,856	–	–	6,708	3,680	3,820
	1	Rhode Island	60,348	247	–	–	18,237	16,423	–	756	2,468	–	2,543	507	19,167
	1	South Dakota	58,671	–	–	–	24,186	–	573	558	4,561	–	19,510	1,412	7,871
	8	California	3,409,701	11,419	2,013,210	–	697,092	250,581	16,920	38,634	29,242	–	171,501	102,292	78,810
	8	New Jersey	360,839	–	–	–	210,655	49,034	–	31,820	21,774	–	–	31,183	16,373
	8	Ohio	1,134,374	–	–	–	593,130	157,884	–	35,404	–	–	240,342	63,953	43,661
			16,052,652	86,438	2,449,374	340,309	6,235,609	830,818	234,568	1,134,375	238,027	304,399	1,611,754	1,995,388	591,593

Other vote includes 88,254 Shapp; 61,992 Humphrey; 43,661 Donahey; 19,805 Kennedy; 8,717 Blessitt; 4,046 Bentsen; 3,935 Lunger; 3,574 Gray; 3,555 Lomento; 3,021 Rollinson; 2,305 Fifi Rockefeller; 2,288 Gonas; 1,829 Kelleher; 1,487 Ahern; 404 Sanford; 398 Bona; 371 Arnold; 351 Eisenman; 174 Clegg; 173 Schechter; 153 Roden; 49 Loewenherz; 205,019 Uncommitted; 81,971 No Preference; 42,304 scattered write-ins; 7,154 "None of the Names Shown"; 4,603 "None of These Candidates".

1972 REPUBLICAN PREFERENCE PRIMARIES

Date	State	Total Vote	Ashbrook	McCloskey	Nixon	Other
March 7	New Hampshire	117,208	11,362	23,190	79,239	3,417
14	Florida	414,207	36,617	17,312	360,278	–
21	Illinois	33,569	170	47	32,550	802
April 4	Wisconsin	286,444	2,604	3,651	277,601	2,588
25	Massachusetts	122,139	4,864	16,435	99,150	1,690
25	Pennsylvania	184,801	–	–	153,886	30,915
May 2	District of Columbia	No Slates Entered				
2	Indiana	417,069	–	–	417,069	–
2	Ohio	692,828	–	–	692,828	–
4	Tennessee	114,489	2,419	2,370	109,696	4
6	North Carolina	167,899	–	8,732	159,167	–
9	Nebraska	194,272	4,996	9,011	179,464	801
9	West Virginia	No Candidates Entered				
16	Maryland	115,249	6,718	9,223	99,308	–
16	Michigan	336,743	–	9,691	321,652	5,400
23	Rhode Island	5,611	175	337	4,953	146
23	Oregon	282,010	16,696	29,365	231,151	4,798
June 6	California	2,283,922	224,922	–	2,058,825	175
6	New Jersey	No Candidates Entered				
6	New Mexico	55,469	–	3,367	49,067	3,035
6	South Dakota	52,820	–	–	52,820	–
		5,876,749	311,543	132,731	5,378,704	53,771

Other vote includes 1,211 Paulsen; 52,559 Uncommitted, None, and scattered.

1972 DEMOCRATIC PREFERENCE PRIMARIES

Date	State	Total Vote	Chisholm	Humphrey	Jackson	McCarthy	McGovern	Muskie	Wallace	Other
March 7	New Hampshire	88,854	–	348	197	–	33,007	41,235	175	13,892
14	Florida	1,264,554	43,989	234,658	170,156	5,847	78,232	112,523	526,651	92,498
21	Illinois	1,225,144	777	1,476	442	444,260	3,687	766,914	7,017	571
April 4	Wisconsin	1,128,584	9,198	233,748	88,068	15,543	333,528	115,811	248,676	84,012
25	Massachusetts	618,516	22,398	48,929	8,499	8,736	325,673	131,709	45,807	26,765
25	Pennsylvania	1,374,839	306	481,900	38,767	–	280,861	279,983	292,437	585
May 2	District of Columbia	29,560	–	–	–	–	–	–	–	29,560
2	Indiana	751,458	–	354,244	–	–	–	87,719	309,495	–
2	Ohio	1,212,330	–	499,680	98,498	26,026	480,320	107,806	–	–
4	Tennessee	492,721	18,809	78,350	5,896	2,267	35,551	9,634	335,858	6,356
6	North Carolina	821,410	61,723	–	9,416	–	–	30,739	413,518	306,014
9	Nebraska	192,137	1,763	65,968	5,276	3,194	79,309	6,886	23,912	5,829
9	West Virginia	368,484	–	246,596	–	–	–	–	121,888	–
16	Maryland	568,131	12,602	151,981	17,728	4,691	126,978	13,363	219,687	21,101
16	Michigan	1,588,073	44,090	249,798	6,938	–	425,694	38,701	809,239	13,613
23	Rhode Island	37,864	–	7,701	138	245	15,603	7,838	5,802	537
23	Oregon	408,644	2,975	51,163	22,042	8,943	205,328	10,244	81,868	26,081
June 6	California	3,564,518	157,435	1,375,064	28,901	34,203	1,550,652	72,701	268,551	77,011
6	New Jersey	76,834	51,433	–	–	–	–	–	–	25,401
6	New Mexico	153,293	3,205	39,768	4,236	–	51,011	6,411	44,843	3,819
6	South Dakota	28,017	–	–	–	–	28,017	–	–	–
		15,993,965	430,703	4,121,372	505,198	553,955	4,053,451	1,840,217	3,755,424	733,645

Other vote includes 331,415 Sanford; 196,406 Lindsay; 79,446 Yorty; 37,401 Mills; 21,217 Fauntroy; 16,693 Kennedy; 11,798 Hartke; 8,286 Mink; 869 Coll; 30,114 Uncommitted, None, and scattered.

1968 REPUBLICAN PREFERENCE PRIMARIES

Date		State	Total Vote	Nixon	Reagan	Other
March	12	New Hampshire	103,938	80,666	—	23,272
April	2	Wisconsin	489,853	390,368	50,727	48,758
	23	Pennsylvania	287,573	171,815	7,934	107,824
	30	Massachusetts	106,521	27,447	1,770	77,304
May	7	Indiana	508,362	508,362	—	—
	7	Ohio	614,492	—	—	614,492
	14	Nebraska	200,476	140,336	42,703	17,437
	28	Florida	51,509	—	—	51,509
	28	Oregon	312,159	203,037	63,707	45,415
June	4	California	1,525,091	—	1,525,091	—
	4	New Jersey	88,592	71,809	2,737	14,046
	4	South Dakota	68,113	68,113	—	—
	11	Illinois	22,403	17,490	1,601	3,312
			4,379,082	1,679,443	1,696,270	1,003,369

Other vote includes 614,492 Rhodes; 164,340 Rockefeller; 31,598 Stassen; 31,465 Volpe; 3,830 Romney; 1,302 Americus; 1,223 Shafer; 527 Stone; 247 Hoover; 161 Watumull; 151 Evans; 73 Coy; 39 DuMont; 58,272 No Preference and 95,649 scattered.

1968 DEMOCRATIC PREFERENCE PRIMARIES

Date		State	Total Vote	McCarthy	Kennedy	Johnson	Humphrey	Other
March	12	New Hampshire	55,464	23,263	—	27,520	—	4,681
April	2	Wisconsin	733,002	412,160	46,507	253,696	3,605	17,034
	23	Pennsylvania	597,089	428,259	65,430	21,265	51,998	30,137
	30	Massachusetts	248,903	122,697	68,604	6,890	44,156	6,556
May	7	Indiana	776,513	209,695	328,118	—	—	238,700
	7	Ohio	549,140	—	—	549,140		
	14	Nebraska	162,611	50,655	84,102	9,187	12,087	6,580
	28	Florida	512,357	147,216	—	—	—	365,141
	28	Oregon	373,070	163,990	141,631	45,174	12,421	9,854
June	4	California	3,181,753	1,329,301	1,472,166	—	—	380,286
	4	New Jersey	27,446	9,906	8,603	—	5,578	3,359
	4	South Dakota	64,287	13,145	31,826	19,316	—	—
	11	Illinois	12,038	4,646	—	—	2,059	5,333
			7,293,673	2,914,933	2,246,987	383,048	131,904	1,616,801

Other vote includes 549,140 Young; 238,700 Branigin; 236,242 Smathers; 33,520 Wallace; 4,052 Edward M. Kennedy; 186 Crommelin; 170 Lee; 77 Gordon; 521,046 No Preference and 33,668 scattered.

ALABAMA

GOVERNOR

Guy Hunt (R). Elected 1986 to a four-year term.

SENATORS

Howell Heflin (D). Re-elected 1984 to a six-year term. Previously elected 1978.

Richard C. Shelby (D). Elected 1986 to a six-year term.

REPRESENTATIVES

1. H. L. Callahan (R)
2. William Dickinson (R)
3. Bill Nichols (D) (see page 1)
4. Tom Bevill (D)
5. Ronnie G. Flippo (D)
6. Ben Erdreich (D)
7. Claude Harris (D)

POSTWAR VOTE FOR PRESIDENT

								Percentage			
	Total	Republican		Democratic		Other		Total Vote		Major Vote	
Year	Vote	Vote	Candidate	Vote	Candidate	Vote	Plurality	Rep.	Dem.	Rep.	Dem.
1988	1,378,476	815,576	Bush, George	549,506	Dukakis, Michael S.	13,394	266,070 R	59.2%	39.9%	59.7%	40.3%
1984	1,441,713	872,849	Reagan, Ronald	551,899	Mondale, Walter F.	16,965	320,950 R	60.5%	38.3%	61.3%	38.7%
1980	1,341,929	654,192	Reagan, Ronald	636,730	Carter, Jimmy	51,007	17,462 R	48.8%	47.4%	50.7%	49.3%
1976	1,182,850	504,070	Ford, Gerald R.	659,170	Carter, Jimmy	19,610	155,100 D	42.6%	55.7%	43.3%	56.7%
1972	1,006,111	728,701	Nixon, Richard M.	256,923	McGovern, George S.	20,487	471,778 R	72.4%	25.5%	73.9%	26.1%
1968 **	1,049,922	146,923	Nixon, Richard M.	196,579	Humphrey, Hubert H.	706,420	494,846 A	14.0%	18.7%	42.8%	57.2%
1964 **	689,818	479,085	Goldwater, Barry M.		Johnson, Lyndon B.	210,733	268,353 R	69.5%		100.0%	
1960	570,225	237,981	Nixon, Richard M.	324,050	Kennedy, John F.	8,194	86,069 D	41.7%	56.8%	42.3%	57.7%
1956	496,861	195,694	Eisenhower, Dwight D.	280,844	Stevenson, Adlai E.	20,323	85,150 D	39.4%	56.5%	41.1%	58.9%
1952	426,120	149,231	Eisenhower, Dwight D.	275,075	Stevenson, Adlai E.	1,814	125,844 D	35.0%	64.6%	35.2%	64.8%
1948 **	214,980	40,930	Dewey, Thomas E.		Truman, Harry S.	174,050	130,513 SR	19.0%		100.0%	

In 1968 other vote was 691,425 American Independent (Wallace); 10,960 American Independent of Alabama; 4,022 Prohibition and 13 scattered. In 1964 and 1948 the national Democratic candidates were not represented on the ballot. In 1964 other vote was 210,732 Unpledged Democratic and 1 scattered. In 1948 other vote was 171,443 States Rights; 1,522 Progressive and 1,085 Prohibition.

POSTWAR VOTE FOR GOVERNOR

								Percentage			
	Total	Republican		Democratic		Other	Rep.-Dem.	Total Vote		Major Vote	
Year	Vote	Vote	Candidate	Vote	Candidate	Vote	Plurality	Rep.	Dem.	Rep.	Dem.
1986	1,236,230	696,203	Hunt, Guy	537,163	Baxley, Bill	2,864	159,040 R	56.3%	43.5%	56.4%	43.6%
1982	1,128,725	440,815	Folmar, Emory	650,538	Wallace, George C.	37,372	209,723 D	39.1%	57.6%	40.4%	59.6%
1978	760,474	196,963	Hunt, Guy	551,886	James, Forrest H.	11,625	354,923 D	25.9%	72.6%	26.3%	73.7%
1974	598,305	88,381	McCary, Elvin	497,574	Wallace, George C.	12,350	409,193 D	14.8%	83.2%	15.1%	84.9%
1970 **	854,952		—	637,046	Wallace, George C.	217,906	637,046 D		74.5%		100.0%
1966	848,101	262,943	Martin, James D.	537,505	Wallace, Mrs. George C.	47,653	274,562 D	31.0%	63.4%	32.8%	67.2%
1962	315,776		—	303,987	Wallace, George C.	11,789	303,987 D		96.3%		100.0%
1958	270,952	30,415	Longshore, W. L.	239,633	Patterson, John	904	209,218 D	11.2%	88.4%	11.3%	88.7%
1954	333,090	88,688	Amernethy, Tom	244,401	Folsom, James E.	1	155,713 D	26.6%	73.4%	26.6%	73.4%
1950	170,541	15,127	Crowder, John S.	155,414	Persons, Gordon		140,287 D	8.9%	91.1%	8.9%	91.1%
1946	197,324	22,362	Ward, Lyman	174,962	Folsom, James E.		152,600 D	11.3%	88.7%	11.3%	88.7%

In 1970 other vote was 125,491 National Democratic Party of Alabama (Cashin); 75,679 Independent (Shelton); 9,705 Prohibition (Couch); 3,534 Independent (Walter) and 3,497 Whig (Watts).

ALABAMA

POSTWAR VOTE FOR SENATOR

								Percentage			
	Total	Republican		Democratic		Other	Rep.-Dem.	Total Vote		Major Vote	
Year	Vote	Vote	Candidate	Vote	Candidate	Vote	Plurality	Rep.	Dem.	Rep.	Dem.
1986	1,211,953	602,537	Denton, Jeremiah	609,360	Shelby, Richard C.	56	6,823 D	49.7%	50.3%	49.7%	50.3%
1984	1,371,238	498,508	Smith, Albert L.	860,535	Heflin, Howell	12,195	362,027 D	36.4%	62.8%	36.7%	63.3%
1980	1,296,757	650,362	Denton, Jeremiah	610,175	Folsom, James E., Jr.	36,220	40,187 R	50.2%	47.1%	51.6%	48.4%
1978	582,025		—	547,054	Heflin, Howell	34,971	547,054 D		94.0%		100.0%
1978 S	731,614	316,170	Martin, James D.	401,852	Stewart, Donald W.	13,592	85,682 D	43.2%	54.9%	44.0%	56.0%
1974	523,290		—	501,541	Allen, James B.	21,749	501,541 D		95.8%		100.0%
1972	1,051,099	347,523	Blount, Winston M.	654,491	Sparkman, John J.	49,085	306,968 D	33.1%	62.3%	34.7%	65.3%
1968	912,708	201,227	Hooper, Perry	638,774	Allen, James B.	72,707	437,547 D	22.0%	70.0%	24.0%	76.0%
1966	802,608	313,018	Grenier, John	482,138	Sparkman, John J.	7,452	169,120 D	39.0%	60.1%	39.4%	60.6%
1962	397,079	195,134	Martin, James D.	201,937	Hill, Lister	8	6,803 D	49.1%	50.9%	49.1%	50.9%
1960	554,081	164,868	Elgin, Julian	389,196	Sparkman, John J.	17	224,328 D	29.8%	70.2%	29.8%	70.2%
1956	330,191		—	330,182	Hill, Lister	9	330,182 D		100.0%		100.0%
1954	314,459	55,110	Guin, J. Foy	259,348	Sparkman, John J.	1	204,238 D	17.5%	82.5%	17.5%	82.5%
1950 **	164,011		—	125,534	Hill, Lister	38,477	125,534 D		76.5%		100.0%
1948	220,875	35,341	Parsons, Paul G.	185,534	Sparkman, John J.		150,193 D	16.0%	84.0%	16.0%	84.0%
1946 S	163,217		—	163,217	Sparkman, John J.		163,217 D		100.0%		100.0%

The 1946 election and one of the 1978 elections were for short terms to fill vacancies. In 1950 other vote was Independent (Crommelin).

ALABAMA

Districts Established August 18, 1981

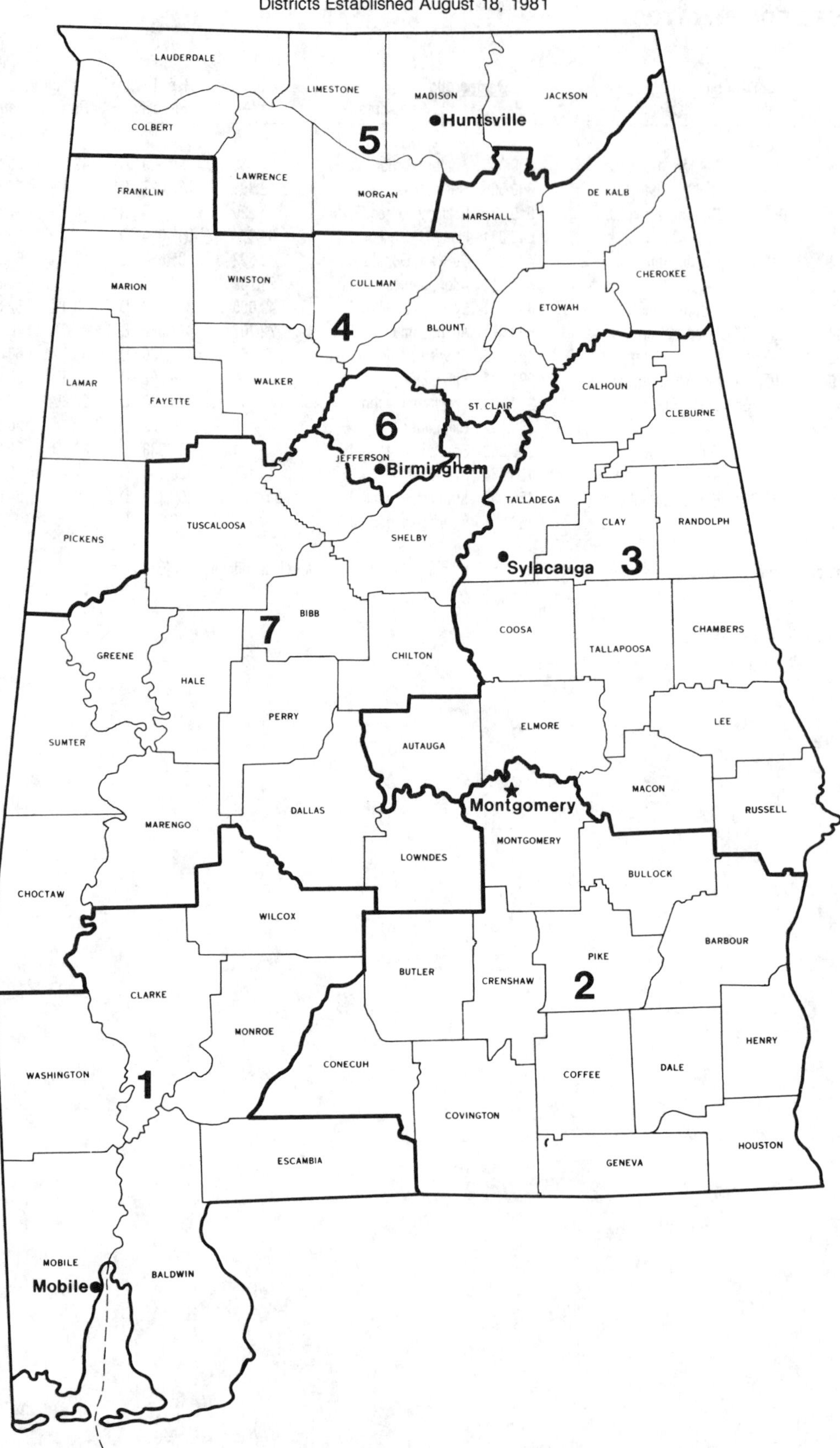

ALABAMA

PRESIDENT 1988

1980 Census Population	County	Total Vote	Republican	Democratic	Other	Rep.-Dem. Plurality	Percentage Total Vote Rep.	Percentage Total Vote Dem.	Percentage Major Vote Rep.	Percentage Major Vote Dem.
32,259	AUTAUGA	11,661	7,828	3,667	166	4,161 R	67.1%	31.4%	68.1%	31.9%
78,556	BALDWIN	35,598	25,933	9,271	394	16,662 R	72.8%	26.0%	73.7%	26.3%
24,756	BARBOUR	8,900	4,958	3,836	106	1,122 R	55.7%	43.1%	56.4%	43.6%
15,723	BIBB	5,146	2,885	2,244	17	641 R	56.1%	43.6%	56.2%	43.8%
36,459	BLOUNT	13,548	8,754	4,485	309	4,269 R	64.6%	33.1%	66.1%	33.9%
10,596	BULLOCK	4,584	1,421	3,122	41	1,701 D	31.0%	68.1%	31.3%	68.7%
21,680	BUTLER	7,460	3,923	3,465	72	458 R	52.6%	46.4%	53.1%	46.9%
119,761	CALHOUN	33,970	19,806	12,451	1,713	7,355 R	58.3%	36.7%	61.4%	38.6%
39,191	CHAMBERS	12,956	7,694	5,103	159	2,591 R	59.4%	39.4%	60.1%	39.9%
18,760	CHEROKEE	6,101	2,868	3,176	57	308 D	47.0%	52.1%	47.5%	52.5%
30,612	CHILTON	12,623	8,761	3,820	42	4,941 R	69.4%	30.3%	69.6%	30.4%
16,839	CHOCTAW	7,131	3,629	3,491	11	138 R	50.9%	49.0%	51.0%	49.0%
27,702	CLARKE	10,021	5,708	4,217	96	1,491 R	57.0%	42.1%	57.5%	42.5%
13,703	CLAY	5,239	3,496	1,602	141	1,894 R	66.7%	30.6%	68.6%	31.4%
12,595	CLEBURNE	4,491	3,071	1,383	37	1,688 R	68.4%	30.8%	68.9%	31.1%
38,533	COFFEE	13,357	8,890	4,319	148	4,571 R	66.6%	32.3%	67.3%	32.7%
54,519	COLBERT	18,409	7,775	10,397	237	2,622 D	42.2%	56.5%	42.8%	57.2%
15,884	CONECUH	6,357	3,256	3,022	79	234 R	51.2%	47.5%	51.9%	48.1%
11,377	COOSA	4,283	2,405	1,860	18	545 R	56.2%	43.4%	56.4%	43.6%
36,850	COVINGTON	12,075	8,130	3,845	100	4,285 R	67.3%	31.8%	67.9%	32.1%
14,110	CRENSHAW	4,478	2,617	1,836	25	781 R	58.4%	41.0%	58.8%	41.2%
61,642	CULLMAN	23,197	14,351	8,517	329	5,834 R	61.9%	36.7%	62.8%	37.2%
47,821	DALE	12,909	9,266	3,476	167	5,790 R	71.8%	26.9%	72.7%	27.3%
53,981	DALLAS	17,423	7,630	9,660	133	2,030 D	43.8%	55.4%	44.1%	55.9%
53,658	DE KALB	18,971	11,478	7,333	160	4,145 R	60.5%	38.7%	61.0%	39.0%
43,390	ELMORE	15,540	10,852	4,501	187	6,351 R	69.8%	29.0%	70.7%	29.3%
38,440	ESCAMBIA	10,954	6,807	4,020	127	2,787 R	62.1%	36.7%	62.9%	37.1%
103,057	ETOWAH	35,891	17,828	17,762	301	66 R	49.7%	49.5%	50.1%	49.9%
18,809	FAYETTE	7,557	4,338	3,186	33	1,152 R	57.4%	42.2%	57.7%	42.3%
28,350	FRANKLIN	10,241	5,146	4,961	134	185 R	50.2%	48.4%	50.9%	49.1%
24,253	GENEVA	8,472	5,703	2,685	84	3,018 R	67.3%	31.7%	68.0%	32.0%
11,021	GREENE	4,377	1,048	3,295	34	2,247 D	23.9%	75.3%	24.1%	75.9%
15,604	HALE	5,652	2,414	3,187	51	773 D	42.7%	56.4%	43.1%	56.9%
15,302	HENRY	5,844	3,613	2,206	25	1,407 R	61.8%	37.7%	62.1%	37.9%
74,632	HOUSTON	27,061	19,989	7,001	71	12,988 R	73.9%	25.9%	74.1%	25.9%
51,407	JACKSON	13,671	6,090	7,418	163	1,328 D	44.5%	54.3%	45.1%	54.9%
671,324	JEFFERSON	258,062	148,879	107,766	1,417	41,113 R	57.7%	41.8%	58.0%	42.0%
16,453	LAMAR	5,499	3,214	2,274	11	940 R	58.4%	41.4%	58.6%	41.4%
80,546	LAUDERDALE	26,190	12,942	12,862	386	80 R	49.4%	49.1%	50.2%	49.8%
30,170	LAWRENCE	8,417	3,616	4,646	155	1,030 D	43.0%	55.2%	43.8%	56.2%
76,283	LEE	26,685	17,180	9,078	427	8,102 R	64.4%	34.0%	65.4%	34.6%
46,005	LIMESTONE	14,760	9,086	5,455	219	3,631 R	61.6%	37.0%	62.5%	37.5%
13,253	LOWNDES	4,776	1,405	3,328	43	1,923 D	29.4%	69.7%	29.7%	70.3%
26,829	MACON	7,756	1,304	6,351	101	5,047 D	16.8%	81.9%	17.0%	83.0%
196,966	MADISON	79,894	53,575	25,800	519	27,775 R	67.1%	32.3%	67.5%	32.5%
25,047	MARENGO	8,725	4,241	4,402	82	161 D	48.6%	50.5%	49.1%	50.9%
30,041	MARION	10,497	5,955	4,505	37	1,450 R	56.7%	42.9%	56.9%	43.1%
65,622	MARSHALL	19,947	12,148	7,357	442	4,791 R	60.9%	36.9%	62.3%	37.7%
364,980	MOBILE	118,688	72,203	45,524	961	26,679 R	60.8%	38.4%	61.3%	38.7%
22,651	MONROE	8,954	5,379	3,509	66	1,870 R	60.1%	39.2%	60.5%	39.5%
197,038	MONTGOMERY	70,482	41,131	28,709	642	12,422 R	58.4%	40.7%	58.9%	41.1%
90,231	MORGAN	29,407	18,679	10,594	134	8,085 R	63.5%	36.0%	63.8%	36.2%
15,012	PERRY	5,758	2,107	3,574	77	1,467 D	36.6%	62.1%	37.1%	62.9%
21,481	PICKENS	6,982	3,851	3,107	24	744 R	55.2%	44.5%	55.3%	44.7%
28,050	PIKE	9,822	5,897	3,813	112	2,084 R	60.0%	38.8%	60.7%	39.3%
20,075	RANDOLPH	7,224	4,625	2,462	137	2,163 R	64.0%	34.1%	65.3%	34.7%
47,356	RUSSELL	13,087	6,333	6,589	165	256 D	48.4%	50.3%	49.0%	51.0%
41,205	ST. CLAIR	14,997	10,604	4,335	58	6,269 R	70.7%	28.9%	71.0%	29.0%
66,298	SHELBY	34,314	27,052	7,138	124	19,914 R	78.8%	20.8%	79.1%	20.9%
16,908	SUMTER	6,635	2,212	4,390	33	2,178 D	33.3%	66.2%	33.5%	66.5%

ALABAMA

PRESIDENT 1988

1980 Census Population	County	Total Vote	Republican	Democratic	Other	Rep.-Dem. Plurality	Percentage Total Vote Rep.	Percentage Total Vote Dem.	Percentage Major Vote Rep.	Percentage Major Vote Dem.
73,826	TALLADEGA	21,507	12,973	8,291	243	4,682 R	60.3%	38.6%	61.0%	39.0%
38,676	TALLAPOOSA	13,298	8,502	4,598	198	3,904 R	63.9%	34.6%	64.9%	35.1%
137,541	TUSCALOOSA	45,758	27,396	18,166	196	9,230 R	59.9%	39.7%	60.1%	39.9%
68,660	WALKER	22,700	11,011	11,338	351	327 D	48.5%	49.9%	49.3%	50.7%
16,821	WASHINGTON	7,164	3,741	3,402	21	339 R	52.2%	47.5%	52.4%	47.6%
14,755	WILCOX	5,118	1,739	3,369	10	1,630 D	34.0%	65.8%	34.0%	66.0%
21,953	WINSTON	9,225	6,235	2,954	36	3,281 R	67.6%	32.0%	67.9%	32.1%
3,893,888	TOTAL	1,378,476	815,576	549,506	13,394	266,070 R	59.2%	39.9%	59.7%	40.3%

ALABAMA

CONGRESS

CD	Year	Total Vote	Republican Vote	Republican Candidate	Democratic Vote	Democratic Candidate	Other Vote	Rep.-Dem. Plurality	Percentage Total Vote Rep.	Percentage Total Vote Dem.	Percentage Major Vote Rep.	Percentage Major Vote Dem.
1	1988	194,363	115,173	CALLAHAN, H. L.	77,670	TYSON, JOHN M.	1,520	37,503 R	59.3%	40.0%	59.7%	40.3%
1	1986	96,555	96,469	CALLAHAN, H. L.			86	96,469 R	99.9%		100.0%	
1	1984	200,934	102,479	CALLAHAN, H. L.	98,455	MCRIGHT, FRANK		4,024 R	51.0%	49.0%	51.0%	49.0%
1	1982	144,028	87,901	EDWARDS, JACK	54,315	GUDAC, STEVE	1,812	33,586 R	61.0%	37.7%	61.8%	38.2%
1	1980	117,221	111,089	EDWARDS, JACK			6,132	111,089 R	94.8%		100.0%	
1	1978	112,161	71,711	EDWARDS, JACK	40,450	NOONAN, L. W.		31,261 R	63.9%	36.1%	63.9%	36.1%
1	1976	157,170	98,257	EDWARDS, JACK	58,906	DAVENPORT, BILL	7	39,351 R	62.5%	37.5%	62.5%	37.5%
1	1974	102,066	60,710	EDWARDS, JACK	37,718	WILSON, AUGUSTA E.	3,638	22,992 R	59.5%	37.0%	61.7%	38.3%
1	1972	136,710	104,606	EDWARDS, JACK	24,357	MCCRORY, O. W.	7,747	80,249 R	76.5%	17.8%	81.1%	18.9%
2	1988	127,861	120,408	DICKINSON, WILLIAM			7,453	120,408 R	94.2%		100.0%	
2	1986	172,887	115,302	DICKINSON, WILLIAM	57,568	STONE, MERCER	17	57,734 R	66.7%	33.3%	66.7%	33.3%
2	1984	195,815	118,153	DICKINSON, WILLIAM	75,506	LEE, LARRY	2,156	42,647 R	60.3%	38.6%	61.0%	39.0%
2	1982	165,194	83,290	DICKINSON, WILLIAM	81,904	CAMP, BILLY JOE		1,386 R	50.4%	49.6%	50.4%	49.6%
2	1980	172,962	104,796	DICKINSON, WILLIAM	63,447	WYATT, CECIL	4,719	41,349 R	60.6%	36.7%	62.3%	37.7%
2	1978	107,265	57,924	DICKINSON, WILLIAM	49,341	MITCHELL, WENDELL		8,583 R	54.0%	46.0%	54.0%	46.0%
2	1976	156,362	90,069	DICKINSON, WILLIAM	66,288	KEAHEY, J. CAROLE	5	23,781 R	57.6%	42.4%	57.6%	42.4%
2	1974	81,818	54,089	DICKINSON, WILLIAM	27,729	CHISLER, CLAIR		26,360 R	66.1%	33.9%	66.1%	33.9%
2	1972	146,508	80,362	DICKINSON, WILLIAM	60,769	REEVES, BEN C.	5,377	19,593 R	54.9%	41.5%	56.9%	43.1%
3	1988	122,310			117,514	NICHOLS, BILL	4,796	117,514 D		96.1%		100.0%
3	1986	142,898	27,769	GUERIN, WHIT	115,127	NICHOLS, BILL	2	87,358 D	19.4%	80.6%	19.4%	80.6%
3	1984	125,102			120,357	NICHOLS, BILL	4,745	120,357 D		96.2%		100.0%
3	1982	104,784			100,864	NICHOLS, BILL	3,920	100,864 D		96.3%		100.0%
4	1988	137,149			131,880	BEVILL, TOM	5,269	131,880 D		96.2%		100.0%
4	1986	171,472	38,588	DESHAZO, A. L.	132,881	BEVILL, TOM	3	94,293 D	22.5%	77.5%	22.5%	77.5%
4	1984	120,106			120,106	BEVILL, TOM		120,106 D		100.0%		100.0%
4	1982	118,607			118,595	BEVILL, TOM	12	118,595 D		100.0%		100.0%
5	1988	186,623	64,491	MCDONALD, STAN	120,142	FLIPPO, RONNIE G.	1,990	55,651 D	34.6%	64.4%	34.9%	65.1%
5	1986	158,935	33,528	MCCARLEY, H. R.	125,406	FLIPPO, RONNIE G.	1	91,878 D	21.1%	78.9%	21.1%	78.9%
5	1984	146,575			140,542	FLIPPO, RONNIE G.	6,033	140,542 D		95.9%		100.0%
5	1982	134,880	24,593	YAMBREK, LEOPOLD	108,807	FLIPPO, RONNIE G.	1,480	84,214 D	18.2%	80.7%	18.4%	81.6%
5	1980	124,967			117,626	FLIPPO, RONNIE G.	7,341	117,626 D		94.1%		100.0%
5	1978	71,236			68,985	FLIPPO, RONNIE G.	2,251	68,985 D		96.8%		100.0%
5	1976	113,560			113,553	FLIPPO, RONNIE G.	7	113,553 D		100.0%		100.0%
5	1974	56,381			56,375	JONES, ROBERT E.	6	56,375 D		100.0%		100.0%
5	1972	136,553	33,352	SCHRADER, DIETER J.	101,303	JONES, ROBERT E.	1,898	67,951 D	24.4%	74.2%	24.8%	75.2%
8	1970	90,058			76,413	JONES, ROBERT E.	13,645	76,413 D		84.8%		100.0%
8	1968	112,449			85,528	JONES, ROBERT E.	26,921	85,528 D		76.1%		100.0%
8	1966	91,386	25,404	MAYHALL, DONALD G.	65,982	JONES, ROBERT E.		40,578 D	27.8%	72.2%	27.8%	72.2%
8	1964	43,842			43,842	JONES, ROBERT E.		43,842 D		100.0%		100.0%
6	1988	209,026	68,788	CADDIS, CHARLES	138,920	ERDREICH, BEN	1,318	70,132 D	32.9%	66.5%	33.1%	66.9%
6	1986	191,997	51,924	WILLIAMS, L. MORGAN	139,608	ERDREICH, BEN	465	87,684 D	27.0%	72.7%	27.1%	72.9%
6	1984	219,710	87,550	WAGGONER, J. T.	130,973	ERDREICH, BEN	1,187	43,423 D	39.8%	59.6%	40.1%	59.9%
6	1982	165,387	76,726	SMITH, ALBERT L.	88,029	ERDREICH, BEN	632	11,303 D	46.4%	53.2%	46.6%	53.4%
7	1988	200,966	63,372	BACON, JAMES E.	136,074	HARRIS, CLAUDE	1,520	72,702 D	31.5%	67.7%	31.8%	68.2%
7	1986	180,910	72,777	MCFARLAND, BILL	108,126	HARRIS, CLAUDE	7	35,349 D	40.2%	59.8%	40.2%	59.8%
7	1984	140,332			135,834	SHELBY, RICHARD C.	4,498	135,834 D		96.8%		100.0%
7	1982	128,139			124,070	SHELBY, RICHARD C.	4,069	124,070 D		96.8%		100.0%

ALABAMA

1988 GENERAL ELECTION

President Other vote was 8,460 Libertarian (Paul); 3,311 Independent (Fulani); 656 Independent (Warren); 461 Independent (Winn); 506 scattered write-in.

Congress Other vote was 1,483 Libertarian (Ament) and 37 scattered in CD 1; 7,352 Libertarian (King) and 101 scattered in CD 2; 4,793 Libertarian (Shockley) and 3 scattered in CD 3; 5,264 Libertarian (Sebastian) and 5 scattered in CD 4; 1,989 Libertarian (Palmer) and 1 scattered in CD 5; 1,092 Libertarian (Wingo) and 226 scattered in CD 6; 1,421 Libertarian (Barksdale) and 99 scattered in CD 7.

1988 PRIMARIES

JUNE 7 REPUBLICAN

Congress Unopposed in four CD's. No candidate in CD's 3 and 4. Contested as follows:

CD 7 3,783 James E. Bacon; 3,374 Sam Kelley.

JUNE 7 DEMOCRATIC

Congress Unopposed in five CD's. Janie B. Clarke, the unopposed candidate in CD 2, withdrew after the primary and no substitution was made. Contested as follows:

CD 3 70,087 Bill Nichols; 7,817 Ted McLaughlin.
CD 7 70,789 Claude Harris; 4,811 Wayne Sowell.

ALASKA

GOVERNOR

Steve Cowper (D). Elected 1986 to a four-year term.

SENATORS

Frank H. Murkowski (R). Re-elected 1986 to a six-year term. Previously elected 1980.

Ted Stevens (R). Re-elected 1984 to a six-year term. Previously elected 1978, 1972, and in 1970 to fill out term vacated by the death of Senator E. L.Bartlett; had been appointed December 1968 to fill this vacancy.

REPRESENTATIVE

At-Large. Don Young (R)

POSTWAR VOTE FOR PRESIDENT

		Republican		Democratic				Percentage			
	Total					Other		Total Vote		Major Vote	
Year	Vote	Vote	Candidate	Vote	Candidate	Vote	Plurality	Rep.	Dem.	Rep.	Dem.
1988	200,116	119,251	Bush, George	72,584	Dukakis, Michael S.	8,281	46,667 R	59.6%	36.3%	62.2%	37.8%
1984	207,605	138,377	Reagan, Ronald	62,007	Mondale, Walter F.	7,221	76,370 R	66.7%	29.9%	69.1%	30.9%
1980	158,445	86,112	Reagan, Ronald	41,842	Carter, Jimmy	30,491	44,270 R	54.3%	26.4%	67.3%	32.7%
1976	123,574	71,555	Ford, Gerald R.	44,058	Carter, Jimmy	7,961	27,497 R	57.9%	35.7%	61.9%	38.1%
1972	95,219	55,349	Nixon, Richard M.	32,967	McGovern, George S.	6,903	22,382 R	58.1%	34.6%	62.7%	37.3%
1968	83,035	37,600	Nixon, Richard M.	35,411	Humphrey, Hubert H.	10,024	2,189 R	45.3%	42.6%	51.5%	48.5%
1964	67,259	22,930	Goldwater, Barry M.	44,329	Johnson, Lyndon B.		21,399 D	34.1%	65.9%	34.1%	65.9%
1960	60,762	30,953	Nixon, Richard M.	29,809	Kennedy, John F.		1,144 R	50.9%	49.1%	50.9%	49.1%

Alaska was formally admitted to statehood in January 1959.

POSTWAR VOTE FOR GOVERNOR

		Republican		Democratic				Percentage			
	Total					Other	Rep.-Dem.	Total Vote		Major Vote	
Year	Vote	Vote	Candidate	Vote	Candidate	Vote	Plurality	Rep.	Dem.	Rep.	Dem.
1986	179,555	76,515	Sturgulewski, Arliss	84,943	Cowper, Steve	18,097	8,428 D	42.6%	47.3%	47.4%	52.6%
1982	194,885	72,291	Fink, Tom	89,918	Sheffield, Bill	32,676	17,627 D	37.1%	46.1%	44.6%	55.4%
1978 **	126,910	49,580	Hammond, Jay S.	25,656	Croft, Chancy	51,674	23,924 R	39.1%	20.2%	65.9%	34.1%
1974	96,163	45,840	Hammond, Jay S.	45,553	Egan, William A.	4,770	287 R	47.7%	47.4%	50.2%	49.8%
1970	80,779	37,264	Miller, Keith	42,309	Egan, William A.	1,206	5,045 D	46.1%	52.4%	46.8%	53.2%
1966	66,294	33,145	Hickel, Walter J.	32,065	Egan, William A.	1,084	1,080 R	50.0%	48.4%	50.8%	49.2%
1962	56,681	27,054	Stepovich, Mike	29,627	Egan, William A.		2,573 D	47.7%	52.3%	47.7%	52.3%
1958	48,968	19,299	Butrovich, John	29,189	Egan, William A.	480	9,890 D	39.4%	59.6%	39.8%	60.2%

In 1978 other vote was 33,555 Walter J. Hickel (write-in); 15,656 Tom Kelly (Alaskans for Kelly) and 2,463 Donald R. Wright (Alaskan Independence).

ALASKA

POSTWAR VOTE FOR SENATOR

Year	Total Vote	Republican Vote	Republican Candidate	Democratic Vote	Democratic Candidate	Other Vote	Rep.-Dem. Plurality	Percentage Total Vote Rep.	Percentage Total Vote Dem.	Percentage Major Vote Rep.	Percentage Major Vote Dem.
1986	180,801	97,674	Murkowski, Frank H.	79,727	Olds, Glenn	3,400	17,947 R	54.0%	44.1%	55.1%	44.9%
1984	206,438	146,919	Stevens, Ted	58,804	Havelock, John E.	715	88,115 R	71.2%	28.5%	71.4%	28.6%
1980	156,762	84,159	Murkowski, Frank H.	72,007	Gruening, Clark S.	596	12,152 R	53.7%	45.9%	53.9%	46.1%
1978	122,741	92,783	Stevens, Ted	29,574	Hobbs, Donald W.	384	63,209 R	75.6%	24.1%	75.8%	24.2%
1974	93,275	38,914	Lewis, C. R.	54,361	Gravel, Mike		15,447 D	41.7%	58.3%	41.7%	58.3%
1972	96,007	74,216	Stevens, Ted	21,791	Guess, Gene		52,425 R	77.3%	22.7%	77.3%	22.7%
1970 S	80,364	47,908	Stevens, Ted	32,456	Kay, Wendell P.		15,452 R	59.6%	40.4%	59.6%	40.4%
1968	80,931	30,286	Rasmuson, Elmer	36,527	Gravel, Mike	14,118	6,241 D	37.4%	45.1%	45.3%	54.7%
1966	65,250	15,961	McKinley, Lee L.	49,289	Bartlett, E. L.		33,328 D	24.5%	75.5%	24.5%	75.5%
1962	58,181	24,354	Stevens, Ted	33,827	Gruening, Ernest		9,473 D	41.9%	58.1%	41.9%	58.1%
1960	59,978	21,937	McKinley, Lee L.	38,041	Bartlett, E. L.		16,104 D	36.6%	63.4%	36.6%	63.4%
1958 S	49,525	23,462	Stepovich, Mike	26,063	Gruening, Ernest		2,601 D	47.4%	52.6%	47.4%	52.6%
1958 S	48,837	7,299	Robertson, R. E.	40,939	Bartlett, E. L.	599	33,640 D	14.9%	83.8%	15.1%	84.9%

The two 1958 elections were held to indeterminate terms and the Senate later determined by lot that Senator Gruening would serve four years, Senator Bartlett two. The 1970 election was for a short term to fill a vacancy.

ALASKA

(One At Large)
Election Districts Established February 16, 1984

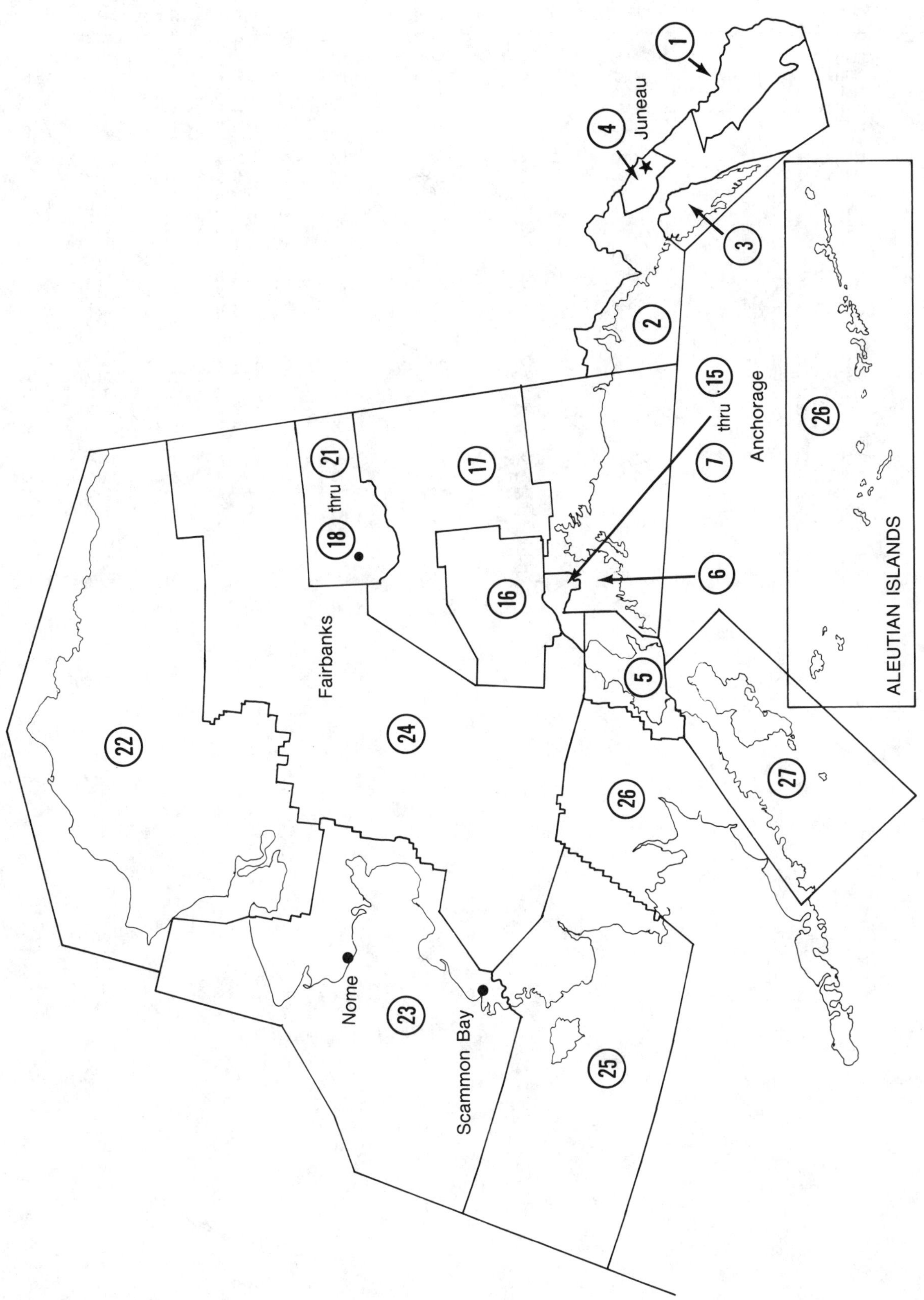

ALASKA

PRESIDENT 1988

1980 Census Population	District	Total Vote	Republican	Democratic	Other	Rep.-Dem. Plurality	Percentage Total Vote Rep.	Total Vote Dem.	Major Vote Rep.	Major Vote Dem.
	DISTRICT 1	8,010	4,564	3,167	279	1,397 R	57.0%	39.5%	59.0%	41.0%
	DISTRICT 2	4,342	2,274	1,879	189	395 R	52.4%	43.3%	54.8%	45.2%
	DISTRICT 3	4,355	2,313	1,884	158	429 R	53.1%	43.3%	55.1%	44.9%
	DISTRICT 4	12,385	5,963	6,057	365	94 D	48.1%	48.9%	49.6%	50.4%
	DISTRICT 5	11,372	6,874	3,696	802	3,178 R	60.4%	32.5%	65.0%	35.0%
	DISTRICT 6	4,060	2,347	1,543	170	804 R	57.8%	38.0%	60.3%	39.7%
	DISTRICT 7	6,186	3,806	2,088	292	1,718 R	61.5%	33.8%	64.6%	35.4%
	DISTRICT 8	11,778	7,629	3,815	334	3,814 R	64.8%	32.4%	66.7%	33.3%
	DISTRICT 9	11,195	6,876	3,980	339	2,896 R	61.4%	35.6%	63.3%	36.7%
	DISTRICT 10	10,361	6,241	3,786	334	2,455 R	60.2%	36.5%	62.2%	37.8%
	DISTRICT 11	6,022	3,189	2,590	243	599 R	53.0%	43.0%	55.2%	44.8%
	DISTRICT 12	7,506	3,511	3,733	262	222 D	46.8%	49.7%	48.5%	51.5%
	DISTRICT 13	7,877	4,968	2,643	266	2,325 R	63.1%	33.6%	65.3%	34.7%
	DISTRICT 14	9,829	6,164	3,387	278	2,777 R	62.7%	34.5%	64.5%	35.5%
	DISTRICT 15	13,085	8,949	3,726	410	5,223 R	68.4%	28.5%	70.6%	29.4%
	DISTRICT 16	13,816	8,851	4,174	791	4,677 R	64.1%	30.2%	68.0%	32.0%
	DISTRICT 17	4,681	3,093	1,302	286	1,791 R	66.1%	27.8%	70.4%	29.6%
	DISTRICT 18	8,001	5,998	1,674	329	4,324 R	75.0%	20.9%	78.2%	21.8%
	DISTRICT 19	7,689	4,485	2,737	467	1,748 R	58.3%	35.6%	62.1%	37.9%
	DISTRICT 20	9,114	5,225	3,389	500	1,836 R	57.3%	37.2%	60.7%	39.3%
	DISTRICT 21	6,282	3,127	2,816	339	311 R	49.8%	44.8%	52.6%	47.4%
	DISTRICT 22	3,391	1,861	1,377	153	484 R	54.9%	40.6%	57.5%	42.5%
	DISTRICT 23	3,413	1,898	1,390	125	508 R	55.6%	40.7%	57.7%	42.3%
	DISTRICT 24	3,363	1,818	1,381	164	437 R	54.1%	41.1%	56.8%	43.2%
	DISTRICT 25	3,145	1,611	1,430	104	181 R	51.2%	45.5%	53.0%	47.0%
	DISTRICT 26	4,674	2,959	1,568	147	1,391 R	63.3%	33.5%	65.4%	34.6%
	DISTRICT 27	4,184	2,657	1,372	155	1,285 R	63.5%	32.8%	65.9%	34.1%
369,117	TOTAL	200,116	119,251	72,584	8,281	46,667 R	59.6%	36.3%	62.2%	37.8%

ALASKA

CONGRESS

CD	Year	Total Vote	Republican Vote	Republican Candidate	Democratic Vote	Democratic Candidate	Other Vote	Rep.-Dem. Plurality	Percentage Total Vote Rep.	Percentage Total Vote Dem.	Percentage Major Vote Rep.	Percentage Major Vote Dem.
AL	1988	192,955	120,595	YOUNG, DON	71,881	GRUENSTEIN, PETER	479	48,714 R	62.5%	37.3%	62.7%	37.3%
AL	1986	180,277	101,799	YOUNG, DON	74,053	BEGICH, PEGGE	4,425	27,746 R	56.5%	41.1%	57.9%	42.1%
AL	1984	206,437	113,582	YOUNG, DON	86,052	BEGICH, PEGGE	6,803	27,530 R	55.0%	41.7%	56.9%	43.1%
AL	1982	181,084	128,274	YOUNG, DON	52,011	CARLSON, DAVE	799	76,263 R	70.8%	28.7%	71.2%	28.8%
AL	1980	154,618	114,089	YOUNG, DON	39,922	PARNELL, KEVIN	607	74,167 R	73.8%	25.8%	74.1%	25.9%
AL	1978	124,187	68,811	YOUNG, DON	55,176	RODEY, PATRICK	200	13,635 R	55.4%	44.4%	55.5%	44.5%
AL	1976	118,208	83,722	YOUNG, DON	34,194	HOPSON, EBEN	292	49,528 R	70.8%	28.9%	71.0%	29.0%
AL	1974	95,921	51,641	YOUNG, DON	44,280	HENSLEY, WILLIAM L.		7,361 R	53.8%	46.2%	53.8%	46.2%
AL	1972	95,401	41,750	YOUNG, DON	53,651	BEGICH, N. J.		11,901 D	43.8%	56.2%	43.8%	56.2%
AL	1970	80,084	35,947	MURKOWSKI, FRANK H.	44,137	BEGICH, N. J.		8,190 D	44.9%	55.1%	44.9%	55.1%
AL	1968	80,362	43,577	POLLOCK, HOWARD W.	36,785	BEGICH, N. J.		6,792 R	54.2%	45.8%	54.2%	45.8%
AL	1966	65,907	34,040	POLLOCK, HOWARD W.	31,867	RIVERS, RALPH J.		2,173 R	51.6%	48.4%	51.6%	48.4%
AL	1964	67,146	32,556	THOMAS, LOWELL	34,590	RIVERS, RALPH J.		2,034 D	48.5%	51.5%	48.5%	51.5%
AL	1962	58,591	26,638	THOMAS, LOWELL	31,953	RIVERS, RALPH J.		5,315 D	45.5%	54.5%	45.5%	54.5%
AL	1960	59,063	25,517	RETTIG, R. L.	33,546	RIVERS, RALPH J.		8,029 D	43.2%	56.8%	43.2%	56.8%
AL	1958	48,647	20,699	BENSON, HENRY A.	27,948	RIVERS, RALPH J.		7,249 D	42.5%	57.5%	42.5%	57.5%
AL	1956	28,266	9,332	GILLAM, BYRON A.	18,934	BARTLETT, E. L.		9,602 D	33.0%	67.0%	33.0%	67.0%
AL	1954	26,999	7,083	DIMOCK, BARBARA D.	19,916	BARTLETT, E. L.		12,833 D	26.2%	73.8%	26.2%	73.8%
AL	1952	25,112	10,893	REEVE, ROBERT C.	14,219	BARTLETT, E. L.		3,326 D	43.4%	56.6%	43.4%	56.6%
AL	1950	18,726	5,138	PETERSON, ALMER J.	13,588	BARTLETT, E. L.		8,450 D	27.4%	72.6%	27.4%	72.6%
AL	1948	22,309	4,789	STOCK, R. H.	17,520	BARTLETT, E. L.		12,731 D	21.5%	78.5%	21.5%	78.5%
AL	1946	16,384	4,868	PETERSON, ALMER J.	11,516	BARTLETT, E. L.		6,648 D	29.7%	70.3%	29.7%	70.3%

ALASKA

1980 Population not available for present districts created in February 1984.

1988 GENERAL ELECTION

President Other vote was 5,484 Libertarian (Paul); 1,024 New Alliance (Fulani); 816 Democrats for Economic Recovery (LaRouche); 957 scattered write-in.

Congress Other vote at-large was scattered. The data for Congress on the previous page include the postwar voting for Delegate from 1946 to 1956 and for Representative at-large since statehood.

1988 PRIMARIES

Alaska's primaries are completely open, with all candidates for an office carried on the ballot together; thus a voter may vote for a Republican for Governor, a Democrat for Senator, and so on. Actual nominations go to the highest Republican and the highest Democrat, as determined in this so-called "jungle primary".

AUGUST 23 REPUBLICAN

Congress Contested as follows:

AL 62,803 Don Young; 6,214 George W. Johnston.

AUGUST 23 DEMOCRATIC

Congress Contested as follows:

AL 40,040 Peter Gruenstein; 3,028 Eugene E. Vick; 1,840 Ryal White.

ARIZONA

GOVERNOR

Rose Mofford (D). Elected Secretary of State in 1986 and became Acting Governor in February 1988 on the impeachment of Governor Evan Mecham (R) by the Arizona House of Representatives. In April 1988 the Arizona Senate voted to convict Governor Mecham on the impeachment charges and Ms. Mofford became Governor.

SENATORS

Dennis DeConcini (D). Re-elected 1988 to a six-year term. Previously elected 1982, 1976.

John McCain (R). Elected 1986 to a six-year term.

REPRESENTATIVES

1. John J. Rhodes, III (R)
2. Morris K. Udall (D)
3. Bob Stump (R)
4. Jon Kyl (R)
5. Jim Kolbe (R)

POSTWAR VOTE FOR PRESIDENT

		Republican		Democratic				Percentage			
								Total Vote		Major Vote	
Year	Total Vote	Vote	Candidate	Vote	Candidate	Other Vote	Plurality	Rep.	Dem.	Rep.	Dem.
1988	1,171,873	702,541	Bush, George	454,029	Dukakis, Michael S.	15,303	248,512 R	60.0%	38.7%	60.7%	39.3%
1984	1,025,897	681,416	Reagan, Ronald	333,854	Mondale, Walter F.	10,627	347,562 R	66.4%	32.5%	67.1%	32.9%
1980	873,945	529,688	Reagan, Ronald	246,843	Carter, Jimmy	97,414	282,845 R	60.6%	28.2%	68.2%	31.8%
1976	742,719	418,642	Ford, Gerald R.	295,602	Carter, Jimmy	28,475	123,040 R	56.4%	39.8%	58.6%	41.4%
1972	622,926	402,812	Nixon, Richard M.	198,540	McGovern, George S.	21,574	204,272 R	64.7%	31.9%	67.0%	33.0%
1968	486,936	266,721	Nixon, Richard M.	170,514	Humphrey, Hubert H.	49,701	96,207 R	54.8%	35.0%	61.0%	39.0%
1964	480,770	242,535	Goldwater, Barry M.	237,753	Johnson, Lyndon B.	482	4,782 R	50.4%	49.5%	50.5%	49.5%
1960	398,491	221,241	Nixon, Richard M.	176,781	Kennedy, John F.	469	44,460 R	55.5%	44.4%	55.6%	44.4%
1956	290,173	176,990	Eisenhower, Dwight D.	112,880	Stevenson, Adlai E.	303	64,110 R	61.0%	38.9%	61.1%	38.9%
1952	260,570	152,042	Eisenhower, Dwight D.	108,528	Stevenson, Adlai E.		43,514 R	58.3%	41.7%	58.3%	41.7%
1948	177,065	77,597	Dewey, Thomas E.	95,251	Truman, Harry S.	4,217	17,654 D	43.8%	53.8%	44.9%	55.1%

POSTWAR VOTE FOR GOVERNOR

		Republican		Democratic				Percentage			
								Total Vote		Major Vote	
Year	Total Vote	Vote	Candidate	Vote	Candidate	Other Vote	Rep.-Dem. Plurality	Rep.	Dem.	Rep.	Dem.
1986 **	866,984	343,913	Mecham, Evan	298,986	Warner, Carolyn	224,085	44,927 R	39.7%	34.5%	53.5%	46.5%
1982	726,364	235,877	Corbet, Leo	453,795	Babbitt, Bruce	36,692	217,918 D	32.5%	62.5%	34.2%	65.8%
1978	538,556	241,093	Mecham, Evan	282,605	Babbitt, Bruce	14,858	41,512 D	44.8%	52.5%	46.0%	54.0%
1974	552,202	273,674	Williams, Russell	278,375	Castro, Raul H.	153	4,701 D	49.6%	50.4%	49.6%	50.4%
1970 **	411,409	209,522	Williams, John R.	201,887	Castro, Raul H.		7,635 R	50.9%	49.1%	50.9%	49.1%
1968	483,998	279,923	Williams, John R.	204,075	Goddard, Sam		75,848 R	57.8%	42.2%	57.8%	42.2%
1966	378,342	203,438	Williams, John R.	174,904	Goddard, Sam		28,534 R	53.8%	46.2%	53.8%	46.2%
1964	473,502	221,404	Kleindienst, Richard	252,098	Goddard, Sam		30,694 D	46.8%	53.2%	46.8%	53.2%
1962	365,841	200,578	Fannin, Paul	165,263	Goddard, Sam		35,315 R	54.8%	45.2%	54.8%	45.2%
1960	397,107	235,502	Fannin, Paul	161,605	Ackerman, Lee		73,897 R	59.3%	40.7%	59.3%	40.7%
1958	290,465	160,136	Fannin, Paul	130,329	Morrison, Robert		29,807 R	55.1%	44.9%	55.1%	44.9%
1956	288,592	116,744	Griffen, Horace B.	171,848	McFarland, Ernest W.		55,104 D	40.5%	59.5%	40.5%	59.5%
1954	243,970	115,866	Pyle, Howard	128,104	McFarland, Ernest W.		12,238 D	47.5%	52.5%	47.5%	52.5%
1952	260,285	156,592	Pyle, Howard	103,693	Haldiman, Joe C.		52,899 R	60.2%	39.8%	60.2%	39.8%
1950	195,227	99,109	Pyle, Howard	96,118	Frohmiller, Ana		2,991 R	50.8%	49.2%	50.8%	49.2%
1948	175,767	70,419	Brockett, Bruce	104,008	Garvey, Dan E.	1,340	33,589 D	40.1%	59.2%	40.4%	59.6%
1946	122,462	48,867	Brockett, Bruce	73,595	Osborn, Sidney P.		24,728 D	39.9%	60.1%	39.9%	60.1%

The term of office for Arizona's Governor was increased from two to four years effective with the 1970 election. In 1986 other vote was Bill Schulz (Independent).

ARIZONA

POSTWAR VOTE FOR SENATOR

		Republican		Democratic				Percentage			
	Total					Other	Rep.-Dem.	Total Vote		Major Vote	
Year	Vote	Vote	Candidate	Vote	Candidate	Vote	Plurality	Rep.	Dem.	Rep.	Dem.
1988	1,164,539	478,060	DeGreen, Keith	660,403	DeConcini, Dennis	26,076	182,343 D	41.1%	56.7%	42.0%	58.0%
1986	862,921	521,850	McCain, John	340,965	Kimball, Richard	106	180,885 R	60.5%	39.5%	60.5%	39.5%
1982	723,885	291,749	Dunn, Pete	411,970	DeConcini, Dennis	20,166	120,221 D	40.3%	56.9%	41.5%	58.5%
1980	874,238	432,371	Goldwater, Barry M.	422,972	Schulz, Bill	18,895	9,399 R	49.5%	48.4%	50.5%	49.5%
1976	741,210	321,236	Steiger, Sam	400,334	DeConcini, Dennis	19,640	79,098 D	43.3%	54.0%	44.5%	55.5%
1974	549,919	320,396	Goldwater, Barry M.	229,523	Marshall, Jonathan		90,873 R	58.3%	41.7%	58.3%	41.7%
1970	407,796	228,284	Fannin, Paul	179,512	Grossman, Sam		48,772 R	56.0%	44.0%	56.0%	44.0%
1968	479,945	274,607	Goldwater, Barry M.	205,338	Elson, Roy L.		69,269 R	57.2%	42.8%	57.2%	42.8%
1964	468,801	241,089	Fannin, Paul	227,712	Elson, Roy L.		13,377 R	51.4%	48.6%	51.4%	48.6%
1962	362,605	163,388	Mecham, Evan	199,217	Hayden, Carl		35,829 D	45.1%	54.9%	45.1%	54.9%
1958	293,623	164,593	Goldwater, Barry M.	129,030	McFarland, Ernest W.		35,563 R	56.1%	43.9%	56.1%	43.9%
1956	278,263	107,447	Jones, Ross F.	170,816	Hayden, Carl		63,369 D	38.6%	61.4%	38.6%	61.4%
1952	257,401	132,063	Goldwater, Barry M.	125,338	McFarland, Ernest W.		6,725 R	51.3%	48.7%	51.3%	48.7%
1950	185,092	68,846	Brockett, Bruce	116,246	Hayden, Carl		47,400 D	37.2%	62.8%	37.2%	62.8%
1946	116,239	35,022	Powers, Ward S.	80,415	McFarland, Ernest W.	802	45,393 D	30.1%	69.2%	30.3%	69.7%

ARIZONA

Districts Established April 2, 1982

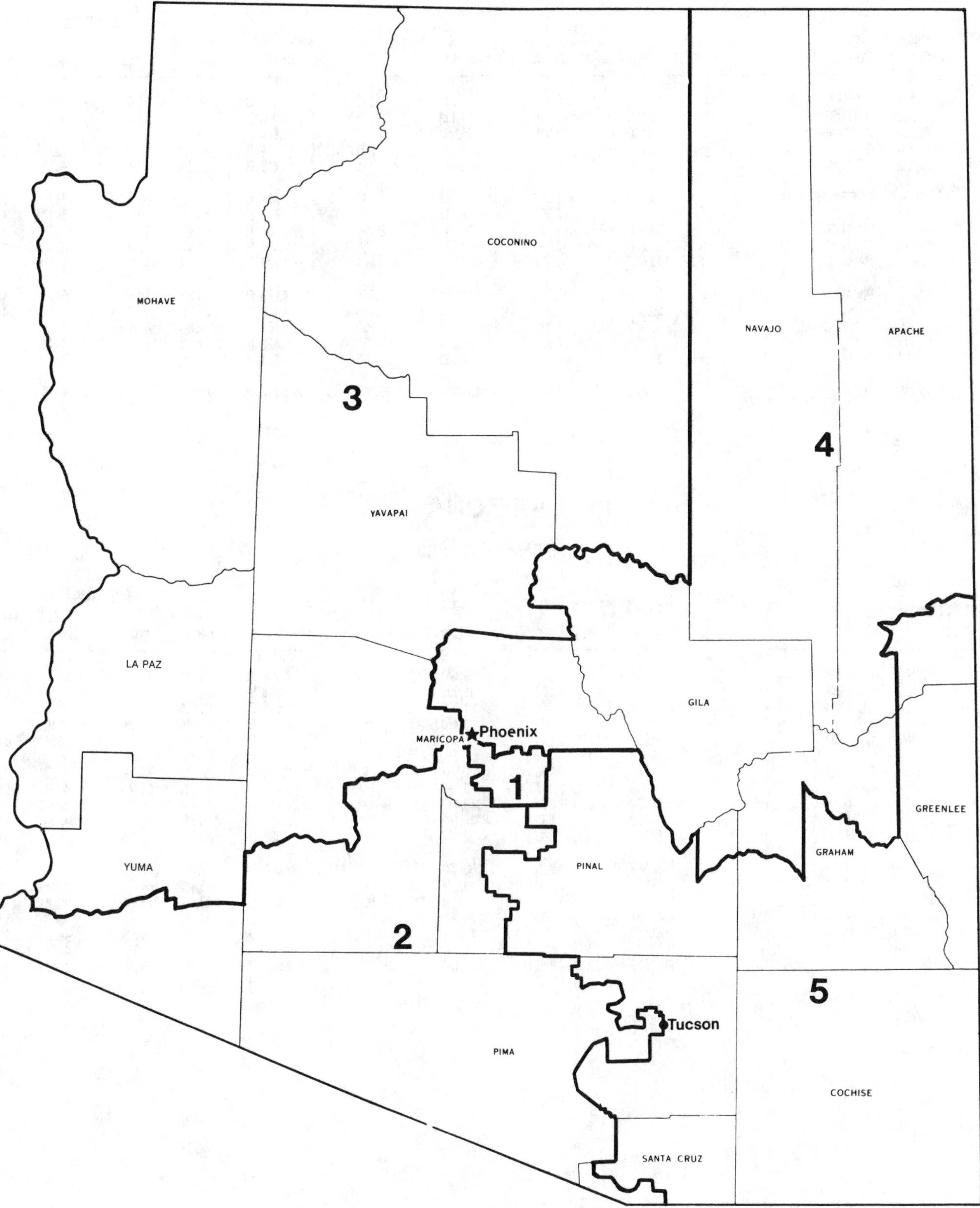

ARIZONA

PRESIDENT 1988

1980 Census Population	County	Total Vote	Republican	Democratic	Other	Rep.-Dem. Plurality	Percentage Total Vote Rep.	Total Vote Dem.	Major Vote Rep.	Major Vote Dem.
52,108	APACHE	14,544	5,347	8,944	253	3,597 D	36.8%	61.5%	37.4%	62.6%
85,686	COCHISE	28,050	15,815	11,812	423	4,003 R	56.4%	42.1%	57.2%	42.8%
75,008	COCONINO	32,140	16,649	14,660	831	1,989 R	51.8%	45.6%	53.2%	46.8%
37,080	GILA	15,299	7,861	7,147	291	714 R	51.4%	46.7%	52.4%	47.6%
22,862	GRAHAM	8,652	5,120	3,407	125	1,713 R	59.2%	39.4%	60.0%	40.0%
11,406	GREENLEE	3,302	1,526	1,733	43	207 D	46.2%	52.5%	46.8%	53.2%
12,557	LA PAZ	4,376	2,562	1,746	68	816 R	58.5%	39.9%	59.5%	40.5%
1,509,052	MARICOPA	681,518	442,337	230,952	8,229	211,385 R	64.9%	33.9%	65.7%	34.3%
55,865	MOHAVE	28,286	17,651	10,197	438	7,454 R	62.4%	36.0%	63.4%	36.6%
67,629	NAVAJO	19,677	10,393	9,023	261	1,370 R	52.8%	45.9%	53.5%	46.5%
531,443	PIMA	234,473	117,899	113,824	2,750	4,075 R	50.3%	48.5%	50.9%	49.1%
90,918	PINAL	29,180	14,966	13,850	364	1,116 R	51.3%	47.5%	51.9%	48.1%
20,459	SANTA CRUZ	6,690	3,320	3,268	102	52 R	49.6%	48.8%	50.4%	49.6%
68,145	YAVAPAI	43,206	27,842	14,514	850	13,328 R	64.4%	33.6%	65.7%	34.3%
77,997	YUMA	22,480	13,253	8,952	275	4,301 R	59.0%	39.8%	59.7%	40.3%
2,718,215	TOTAL	1,171,873	702,541	454,029	15,303	248,512 R	60.0%	38.7%	60.7%	39.3%

ARIZONA

SENATOR 1988

1980 Census Population	County	Total Vote	Republican	Democratic	Other	Rep.-Dem. Plurality	Percentage Total Vote Rep.	Total Vote Dem.	Major Vote Rep.	Major Vote Dem.
52,108	APACHE	14,602	3,318	10,871	413	7,553 D	22.7%	74.4%	23.4%	76.6%
85,686	COCHISE	28,338	8,604	19,002	732	10,398 D	30.4%	67.1%	31.2%	68.8%
75,008	COCONINO	32,098	9,644	21,203	1,251	11,559 D	30.0%	66.1%	31.3%	68.7%
37,080	GILA	15,486	5,327	9,770	389	4,443 D	34.4%	63.1%	35.3%	64.7%
22,862	GRAHAM	8,831	3,084	5,603	144	2,519 D	34.9%	63.4%	35.5%	64.5%
11,406	GREENLEE	3,387	796	2,551	40	1,755 D	23.5%	75.3%	23.8%	76.2%
12,557	LA PAZ	4,413	2,017	2,292	104	275 D	45.7%	51.9%	46.8%	53.2%
1,509,052	MARICOPA	674,874	319,561	340,814	14,499	21,253 D	47.4%	50.5%	48.4%	51.6%
55,865	MOHAVE	28,469	12,657	15,142	670	2,485 D	44.5%	53.2%	45.5%	54.5%
67,629	NAVAJO	19,877	7,043	12,439	395	5,396 D	35.4%	62.6%	36.2%	63.8%
531,443	PIMA	232,393	64,220	163,100	5,073	98,880 D	27.6%	70.2%	28.3%	71.7%
90,918	PINAL	29,628	9,906	19,082	640	9,176 D	33.4%	64.4%	34.2%	65.8%
20,459	SANTA CRUZ	6,666	1,702	4,817	147	3,115 D	25.5%	72.3%	26.1%	73.9%
68,145	YAVAPAI	43,037	20,382	21,460	1,195	1,078 D	47.4%	49.9%	48.7%	51.3%
77,997	YUMA	22,440	9,799	12,257	384	2,458 D	43.7%	54.6%	44.4%	55.6%
2,718,215	TOTAL	1,164,539	478,060	660,403	26,076	182,343 D	41.1%	56.7%	42.0%	58.0%

ARIZONA

CONGRESS

CD	Year	Total Vote	Republican Vote	Republican Candidate	Democratic Vote	Democratic Candidate	Other Vote	Rep.-Dem. Plurality	Percentage Total Vote Rep.	Percentage Total Vote Dem.	Percentage Major Vote Rep.	Percentage Major Vote Dem.
1	1988	256,027	184,639	RHODES, JOHN J., III	71,388	FILLMORE, JOHN M.		113,251 R	72.1%	27.9%	72.1%	27.9%
1	1986	178,533	127,370	RHODES, JOHN J., III	51,163	BRAUN, HARRY W.		76,207 R	71.3%	28.7%	71.3%	28.7%
1	1984	208,027	162,418	MCCAIN, JOHN	45,609	BRAUN, HARRY W.		116,809 R	78.1%	21.9%	78.1%	21.9%
1	1982	135,227	89,116	MCCAIN, JOHN	41,261	HEGARTY, WILLIAM E.	4,850	47,855 R	65.9%	30.5%	68.4%	31.6%
2	1988	136,204	36,309	SWEENEY, JOSEPH D.	99,895	UDALL, MORRIS K.		63,586 D	26.7%	73.3%	26.7%	73.3%
2	1986	105,407	24,522	CLARK, SHELDON	77,239	UDALL, MORRIS K.	3,646	52,717 D	23.3%	73.3%	24.1%	75.9%
2	1984	121,215			106,332	UDALL, MORRIS K.	14,883	106,332 D		87.7%		100.0%
2	1982	103,674	28,407	LAOS, ROY B.	73,468	UDALL, MORRIS K.	1,799	45,061 D	27.4%	70.9%	27.9%	72.1%
3	1988	253,330	174,453	STUMP, BOB	72,417	MOSS, DAVE	6,460	102,036 R	68.9%	28.6%	70.7%	29.3%
3	1986	146,462	146,462	STUMP, BOB				146,462 R	100.0%		100.0%	
3	1984	218,328	156,686	STUMP, BOB	57,748	SCHUSTER, BOB	3,894	98,938 R	71.8%	26.5%	73.1%	26.9%
3	1982	159,842	101,198	STUMP, BOB	58,644	BOSCH, PAT		42,554 R	63.3%	36.7%	63.3%	36.7%
4	1988	236,678	206,248	KYL, JON			30,430	206,248 R	87.1%		100.0%	
4	1986	188,833	121,939	KYL, JON	66,894	DAVIS, PHILIP R.		55,045 R	64.6%	35.4%	64.6%	35.4%
4	1984	167,615	167,558	RUDD, ELDON			57	167,558 R	100.0%		100.0%	
4	1982	145,466	95,620	RUDD, ELDON	44,182	EARLEY, WAYNE O.	5,664	51,438 R	65.7%	30.4%	68.4%	31.6%
5	1988	242,577	164,462	KOLBE, JIM	78,115	BELCHER, JUDITH E.		86,347 R	67.8%	32.2%	67.8%	32.2%
5	1986	184,495	119,647	KOLBE, JIM	64,848	IRELAND, JOEL		54,799 R	64.9%	35.1%	64.9%	35.1%
5	1984	227,938	116,075	KOLBE, JIM	109,871	MCNULTY, JIM	1,992	6,204 R	50.9%	48.2%	51.4%	48.6%
5	1982	166,802	80,531	KOLBE, JIM	82,938	MCNULTY, JIM	3,333	2,407 D	48.3%	49.7%	49.3%	50.7%

ARIZONA

1988 GENERAL ELECTION

President Other vote was 13,351 Libertarian (Paul); 1,662 New Alliance (Fulani); 159 Independent (McCarthy write-in); 113 Populist (Duke write-in); 18 American (Dennis write-in). Early canvass gave the American vote as 20.

Senator Other vote was 20,849 Libertarian (Tompkins); 5,195 New Alliance (Finkelstein); 32 Socialist Workers (Nebbia write-in). Early uncorrected canvass gave the Democratic (DeConcini) vote as 641,402.

Congress Other vote was Land-Water-Legacy (Parsons) in CD 3; Libertarian (Sprunk) in CD 4.

1988 PRIMARIES

SEPTEMBER 13 REPUBLICAN

Senator Keith DeGreen, unopposed.

Congress Unopposed in four CD's. Contested as follows:

CD 5 38,306 Jim Kolbe; 5,875 Walter Weber; 5,094 Al Rodriguez.

SEPTEMBER 13 DEMOCRATIC

Senator Dennis DeConcini, unopposed.

Congress Unopposed in three CD's. No candidate in CD 4. Contested as follows:

CD 1 21,111 John M. Fillmore; 6,584 Thane Read.

SEPTEMBER 13 LIBERTARIAN

Senator No candidates appeared on the ballot; there were 180 write-in votes for Rick Tompkins.

Congress No candidates appeared on the ballot in any CD's. In CD 4 there were 30 write-in votes for Gary Sprunk.

SEPTEMBER 13 NEW ALLIANCE

Senator No candidates appeared on the ballot; there were 6 write-in votes for Ed Finkelstein.

Congress No candidates appeared on the ballot in any CD's.

ARKANSAS

GOVERNOR

Bill Clinton (D). Re-elected 1986 to a four-year term. Previously elected 1984, 1982, 1978 to two-year terms.

SENATORS

Dale Bumpers (D). Re-elected 1986 to a six-year term. Previously elected 1980, 1974.

David H. Pryor (D). Re-elected 1984 to a six-year term. Previously elected 1978.

REPRESENTATIVES

1. William Alexander (D)
2. Tommy F. Robinson (D)**
3. John Hammerschmidt (R)
4. Beryl F. Anthony (D)

See note section.

POSTWAR VOTE FOR PRESIDENT

									Percentage			
									Total Vote		Major Vote	
	Total	Republican		Democratic		Other						
Year	Vote	Vote	Candidate	Vote	Candidate	Vote	Plurality		Rep.	Dem.	Rep.	Dem.
1988	827,738	466,578	Bush, George	349,237	Dukakis, Michael S.	11,923	117,341	R	56.4%	42.2%	57.2%	42.8%
1984	884,406	534,774	Reagan, Ronald	338,646	Mondale, Walter F.	10,986	196,128	R	60.5%	38.3%	61.2%	38.8%
1980	837,582	403,164	Reagan, Ronald	398,041	Carter, Jimmy	36,377	5,123	R	48.1%	47.5%	50.3%	49.7%
1976	767,535	267,903	Ford, Gerald R.	498,604	Carter, Jimmy	1,028	230,701	D	34.9%	65.0%	35.0%	65.0%
1972	651,320	448,541	Nixon, Richard M.	199,892	McGovern, George S.	2,887	248,649	R	68.9%	30.7%	69.2%	30.8%
1968 **	619,969	190,759	Nixon, Richard M.	188,228	Humphrey, Hubert H.	240,982	50,223	A	30.8%	30.4%	50.3%	49.7%
1964	560,426	243,264	Goldwater, Barry M.	314,197	Johnson, Lyndon B.	2,965	70,933	D	43.4%	56.1%	43.6%	56.4%
1960	428,509	184,508	Nixon, Richard M.	215,049	Kennedy, John F.	28,952	30,541	D	43.1%	50.2%	46.2%	53.8%
1956	406,572	186,287	Eisenhower, Dwight D.	213,277	Stevenson, Adlai E.	7,008	26,990	D	45.8%	52.5%	46.6%	53.4%
1952	404,800	177,155	Eisenhower, Dwight D.	226,300	Stevenson, Adlai E.	1,345	49,145	D	43.8%	55.9%	43.9%	56.1%
1948 **	242,475	50,959	Dewey, Thomas E.	149,659	Truman, Harry S.	41,857	98,700	D	21.0%	61.7%	25.4%	74.6%

In 1968 other vote was American (Wallace). In 1948 other vote was 40,068 States Rights; 1,037 Socialist; 751 Progressive and 1 Prohibition.

ARKANSAS

POSTWAR VOTE FOR GOVERNOR

Year	Total Vote	Republican Vote	Republican Candidate	Democratic Vote	Democratic Candidate	Other Vote	Rep.-Dem. Plurality	Percentage Total Vote Rep.	Total Vote Dem.	Major Vote Rep.	Major Vote Dem.
1986 * *	688,551	248,427	White, Frank D.	439,882	Clinton, Bill	242	191,455 D	36.1%	63.9%	36.1%	63.9%
1984	886,548	331,987	Freeman, Woody	554,561	Clinton, Bill		222,574 D	37.4%	62.6%	37.4%	62.6%
1982	789,351	357,496	White, Frank D.	431,855	Clinton, Bill		74,359 D	45.3%	54.7%	45.3%	54.7%
1980	838,925	435,684	White, Frank D.	403,241	Clinton, Bill		32,443 R	51.9%	48.1%	51.9%	48.1%
1978	528,912	193,746	Lowe, A. Lynn	335,101	Clinton, Bill	65	141,355 D	36.6%	63.4%	36.6%	63.4%
1976	726,949	121,716	Griffith, Leon	605,083	Pryor, David H.	150	483,367 D	16.7%	83.2%	16.7%	83.3%
1974	545,974	187,872	Coon, Ken	358,018	Pryor, David H.	84	170,146 D	34.4%	65.6%	34.4%	65.6%
1972	648,069	159,177	Blaylock, Len E.	488,892	Bumpers, Dale		329,715 D	24.6%	75.4%	24.6%	75.4%
1970	609,198	197,418	Rockefeller, Winthrop	375,648	Bumpers, Dale	36,132	178,230 D	32.4%	61.7%	34.4%	65.6%
1968	615,595	322,782	Rockefeller, Winthrop	292,813	Crank, Marion		29,969 R	52.4%	47.6%	52.4%	47.6%
1966	563,527	306,324	Rockefeller, Winthrop	257,203	Johnson, James D.		49,121 R	54.4%	45.6%	54.4%	45.6%
1964	592,113	254,561	Rockefeller, Winthrop	337,489	Faubus, Orval E.	63	82,928 D	43.0%	57.0%	43.0%	57.0%
1962	308,092	82,349	Ricketts, Willis	225,743	Faubus, Orval E.		143,394 D	26.7%	73.3%	26.7%	73.3%
1960	421,985	129,921	Britt, Henry M.	292,064	Faubus, Orval E.		162,143 D	30.8%	69.2%	30.8%	69.2%
1958	286,886	50,288	Johnson, George W.	236,598	Faubus, Orval E.		186,310 D	17.5%	82.5%	17.5%	82.5%
1956	399,012	77,215	Mitchell, Roy	321,797	Faubus, Orval E.		244,582 D	19.4%	80.6%	19.4%	80.6%
1954	335,176	127,004	Remmel, Pratt C.	208,121	Faubus, Orval E.	51	81,117 D	37.9%	62.1%	37.9%	62.1%
1952	391,592	49,292	Speck, Jefferson W.	342,292	Cherry, Francis	8	293,000 D	12.6%	87.4%	12.6%	87.4%
1950	317,087	50,309	Speck, Jefferson W.	266,778	McMath, Sidney S.		216,469 D	15.9%	84.1%	15.9%	84.1%
1948	249,301	26,500	Black, Charles R.	222,801	McMath, Sidney S.		196,301 D	10.6%	89.4%	10.6%	89.4%
1946	152,162	24,133	Mills, W. T.	128,029	Laney, Ben T.		103,896 D	15.9%	84.1%	15.9%	84.1%

The term of office for Arkansas' Governor was increased from two to four years effective with the 1986 election.

POSTWAR VOTE FOR SENATOR

Year	Total Vote	Republican Vote	Republican Candidate	Democratic Vote	Democratic Candidate	Other Vote	Rep.-Dem. Plurality	Percentage Total Vote Rep.	Total Vote Dem.	Major Vote Rep.	Major Vote Dem.
1986	695,487	262,313	Hutchinson, Asa	433,122	Bumpers, Dale	52	170,809 D	37.7%	62.3%	37.7%	62.3%
1984	875,956	373,615	Bethune, Ed	502,341	Pryor, David H.		128,726 D	42.7%	57.3%	42.7%	57.3%
1980	808,812	330,576	Clark, Bill	477,905	Bumpers, Dale	331	147,329 D	40.9%	59.1%	40.9%	59.1%
1978	522,239	84,722	Kelly, Tom	399,916	Pryor, David H.	37,601	315,194 D	16.2%	76.6%	17.5%	82.5%
1974	543,082	82,026	Jones, John H.	461,056	Bumpers, Dale		379,030 D	15.1%	84.9%	15.1%	84.9%
1972	634,636	248,238	Babbitt, Wayne H.	386,398	McClellan, John L.		138,160 D	39.1%	60.9%	39.1%	60.9%
1968	591,704	241,739	Bernard, Charles T.	349,965	Fulbright, J. W.		108,226 D	40.9%	59.1%	40.9%	59.1%
1966 * *			—		McClellan, John L.						
1962	312,880	98,013	Jones, Kenneth	214,867	Fulbright, J. W.		116,854 D	31.3%	68.7%	31.3%	68.7%
1960 * *			—		McClellan, John L.						
1956	399,695	68,016	Henley, Ben C.	331,679	Fulbright, J. W.		263,663 D	17.0%	83.0%	17.0%	83.0%
1954	291,058		—	291,058	McClellan, John L.		291,058 D		100.0%		100.0%
1950	302,582		—	302,582	Fulbright, J. W.		302,582 D		100.0%		100.0%
1948	216,401		—	216,401	McClellan, John L.		216,401 D		100.0%		100.0%

Senator McClellan was re-elected in 1966 and in 1960, but his vote was not canvassed in many counties.

ARKANSAS

Districts Established February 25, 1981

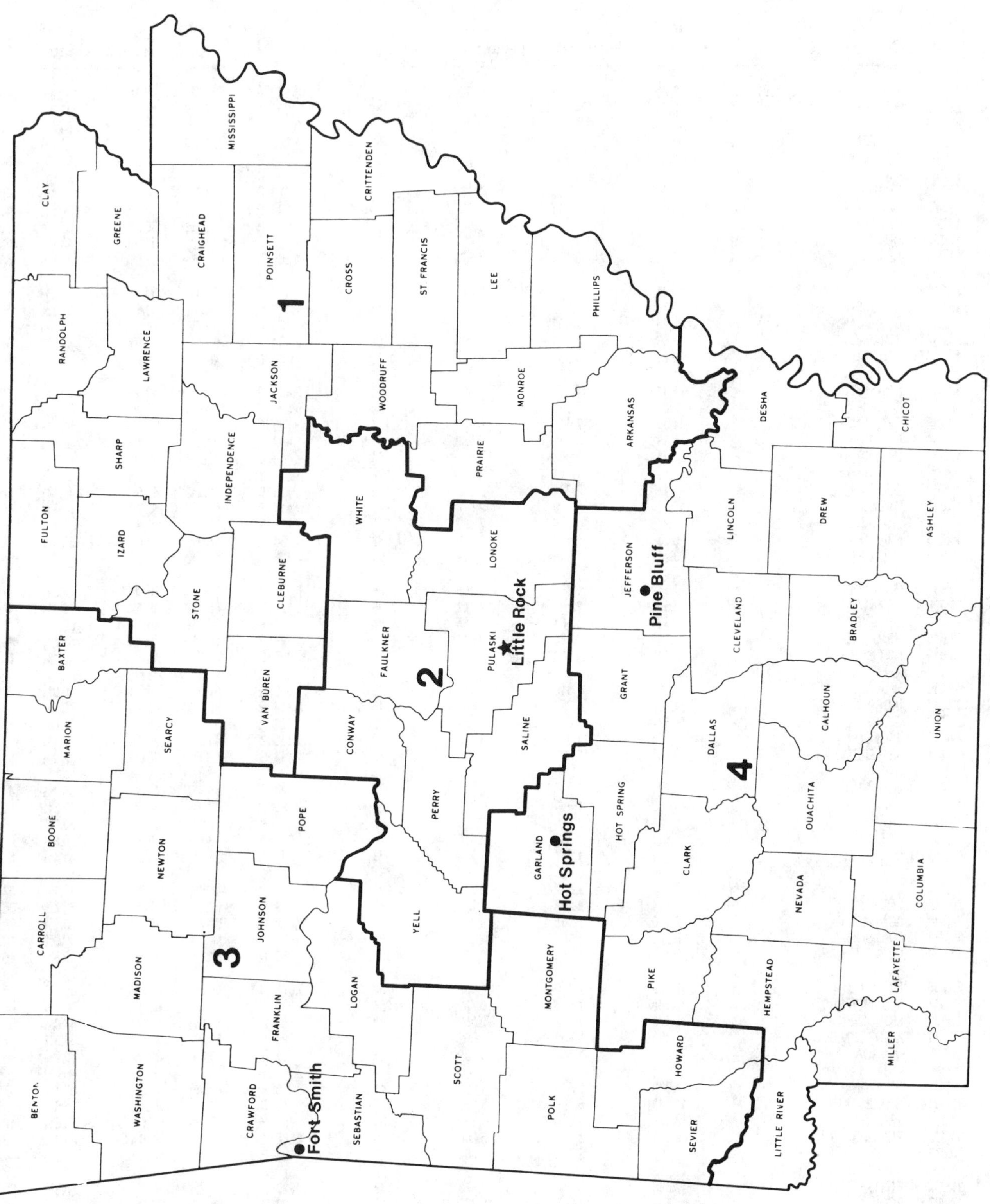

ARKANSAS

PRESIDENT 1988

1980 Census Population	County	Total Vote	Republican	Democratic	Other	Rep.-Dem. Plurality	Percentage Total Vote Rep.	Percentage Total Vote Dem.	Percentage Major Vote Rep.	Percentage Major Vote Dem.
24,175	ARKANSAS	7,205	4,007	3,075	123	932 R	55.6%	42.7%	56.6%	43.4%
26,538	ASHLEY	8,659	4,111	4,466	82	355 D	47.5%	51.6%	47.9%	52.1%
27,409	BAXTER	13,597	8,614	4,808	175	3,806 R	63.4%	35.4%	64.2%	35.8%
78,115	BENTON	34,110	24,295	9,399	416	14,896 R	71.2%	27.6%	72.1%	27.9%
26,067	BOONE	11,816	7,567	3,998	251	3,569 R	64.0%	33.8%	65.4%	34.6%
13,803	BRADLEY	4,269	2,089	2,167	13	78 D	48.9%	50.8%	49.1%	50.9%
6,079	CALHOUN	2,344	1,316	1,024	4	292 R	56.1%	43.7%	56.2%	43.8%
16,203	CARROLL	7,253	4,553	2,632	68	1,921 R	62.8%	36.3%	63.4%	36.6%
17,793	CHICOT	4,346	1,901	2,426	19	525 D	43.7%	55.8%	43.9%	56.1%
23,326	CLARK	8,130	3,389	4,675	66	1,286 D	41.7%	57.5%	42.0%	58.0%
20,616	CLAY	6,240	2,766	3,442	32	676 D	44.3%	55.2%	44.6%	55.4%
16,909	CLEBURNE	8,381	4,932	3,404	45	1,528 R	58.8%	40.6%	59.2%	40.8%
7,868	CLEVELAND	2,881	1,462	1,404	15	58 R	50.7%	48.7%	51.0%	49.0%
26,644	COLUMBIA	9,802	5,810	3,706	286	2,104 R	59.3%	37.8%	61.1%	38.9%
19,505	CONWAY	8,239	4,066	4,134	39	68 D	49.4%	50.2%	49.6%	50.4%
63,239	CRAIGHEAD	21,615	11,887	9,083	645	2,804 R	55.0%	42.0%	56.7%	43.3%
36,892	CRAWFORD	12,832	9,092	3,582	158	5,510 R	70.9%	27.9%	71.7%	28.3%
49,499	CRITTENDEN	14,384	7,441	6,702	241	739 R	51.7%	46.6%	52.6%	47.4%
20,434	CROSS	6,212	3,186	2,989	37	197 R	51.3%	48.1%	51.6%	48.4%
10,515	DALLAS	3,958	1,947	1,990	21	43 D	49.2%	50.3%	49.5%	50.5%
19,760	DESHA	5,435	2,334	2,859	242	525 D	42.9%	52.6%	44.9%	55.1%
17,910	DREW	5,620	2,995	2,578	47	417 R	53.3%	45.9%	53.7%	46.3%
46,192	FAULKNER	18,279	10,678	7,302	299	3,376 R	58.4%	39.9%	59.4%	40.6%
14,705	FRANKLIN	6,089	3,588	2,458	43	1,130 R	58.9%	40.4%	59.3%	40.7%
9,975	FULTON	3,957	1,918	2,018	21	100 D	48.5%	51.0%	48.7%	51.3%
70,531	GARLAND	31,642	19,281	11,406	955	7,875 R	60.9%	36.0%	62.8%	37.2%
13,008	GRANT	4,904	2,717	2,142	45	575 R	55.4%	43.7%	55.9%	44.1%
30,744	GREENE	10,310	5,161	5,065	84	96 R	50.1%	49.1%	50.5%	49.5%
23,635	HEMPSTEAD	7,799	3,938	3,841	20	97 R	50.5%	49.2%	50.6%	49.4%
26,819	HOT SPRING	9,405	4,181	5,090	134	909 D	44.5%	54.1%	45.1%	54.9%
13,459	HOWARD	4,337	2,510	1,818	9	692 R	57.9%	41.9%	58.0%	42.0%
30,147	INDEPENDENCE	11,208	6,637	4,523	48	2,114 R	59.2%	40.4%	59.5%	40.5%
10,768	IZARD	5,517	2,824	2,652	41	172 R	51.2%	48.1%	51.6%	48.4%
21,646	JACKSON	7,276	3,049	4,199	28	1,150 D	41.9%	57.7%	42.1%	57.9%
90,718	JEFFERSON	29,752	12,520	16,664	568	4,144 D	42.1%	56.0%	42.9%	57.1%
17,423	JOHNSON	6,941	4,046	2,818	77	1,228 R	58.3%	40.6%	58.9%	41.1%
10,213	LAFAYETTE	3,800	1,860	1,915	25	55 D	48.9%	50.4%	49.3%	50.7%
18,447	LAWRENCE	6,421	3,205	3,179	37	26 R	49.9%	49.5%	50.2%	49.8%
15,539	LEE	4,812	1,863	2,878	71	1,015 D	38.7%	59.8%	39.3%	60.7%
13,369	LINCOLN	3,794	1,557	2,204	33	647 D	41.0%	58.1%	41.4%	58.6%
13,952	LITTLE RIVER	5,119	2,347	2,740	32	393 D	45.8%	53.5%	46.1%	53.9%
20,144	LOGAN	3,504	2,203	1,254	47	949 R	62.9%	35.8%	63.7%	36.3%
34,518	LONOKE	12,090	7,215	4,786	89	2,429 R	59.7%	39.6%	60.1%	39.9%
11,373	MADISON	5,223	3,067	2,106	50	961 R	58.7%	40.3%	59.3%	40.7%
11,334	MARION	5,178	2,993	2,033	152	960 R	57.8%	39.3%	59.6%	40.4%
37,766	MILLER	12,629	7,110	5,437	82	1,673 R	56.3%	43.1%	56.7%	43.3%
59,517	MISSISSIPPI	14,888	7,841	6,759	288	1,082 R	52.7%	45.4%	53.7%	46.3%
14,052	MONROE	3,972	1,862	2,052	58	190 D	46.9%	51.7%	47.6%	52.4%
7,771	MONTGOMERY	3,129	1,752	1,362	15	390 R	56.0%	43.5%	56.3%	43.7%
11,097	NEVADA	3,459	1,714	1,732	13	18 D	49.6%	50.1%	49.7%	50.3%
7,756	NEWTON	4,039	2,504	1,489	46	1,015 R	62.0%	36.9%	62.7%	37.3%
30,541	OUACHITA	12,043	6,297	5,229	517	1,068 R	52.3%	43.4%	54.6%	45.4%
7,266	PERRY	3,128	1,627	1,470	31	157 R	52.0%	47.0%	52.5%	47.5%
34,772	PHILLIPS	9,861	3,892	5,580	389	1,688 D	39.5%	56.6%	41.1%	58.9%
10,373	PIKE	3,797	2,105	1,681	11	424 R	55.4%	44.3%	55.6%	44.4%
27,032	POINSETT	7,566	3,644	3,873	49	229 D	48.2%	51.2%	48.5%	51.5%
17,007	POLK	6,595	4,099	2,390	106	1,709 R	62.2%	36.2%	63.2%	36.8%
39,021	POPE	15,123	10,084	4,941	98	5,143 R	66.7%	32.7%	67.1%	32.9%
10,140	PRAIRIE	3,656	1,947	1,688	21	259 R	53.3%	46.2%	53.6%	46.4%
340,613	PULASKI	128,333	70,562	55,857	1,914	14,705 R	55.0%	43.5%	55.8%	44.2%

ARKANSAS

PRESIDENT 1988

1980 Census Population	County	Total Vote	Republican	Democratic	Other	Rep.-Dem. Plurality	Percentage Total Vote Rep.	Total Vote Dem.	Major Vote Rep.	Major Vote Dem.
16,834	RANDOLPH	5,418	2,560	2,781	77	221 D	47.2%	51.3%	47.9%	52.1%
30,858	ST. FRANCIS	8,980	4,298	4,656	26	358 D	47.9%	51.8%	48.0%	52.0%
53,161	SALINE	20,977	12,353	8,436	188	3,917 R	58.9%	40.2%	59.4%	40.6%
9,685	SCOTT	4,262	2,507	1,707	48	800 R	58.8%	40.1%	59.5%	40.5%
8,847	SEARCY	4,143	2,743	1,340	60	1,403 R	66.2%	32.3%	67.2%	32.8%
95,172	SEBASTIAN	34,432	24,426	9,684	322	14,742 R	70.9%	28.1%	71.6%	28.4%
14,060	SEVIER	4,327	2,254	2,037	36	217 R	52.1%	47.1%	52.5%	47.5%
14,607	SHARP	6,612	3,623	2,955	34	668 R	54.8%	44.7%	55.1%	44.9%
9,022	STONE	3,962	2,186	1,728	48	458 R	55.2%	43.6%	55.9%	44.1%
48,573	UNION	17,256	10,581	5,931	744	4,650 R	61.3%	34.4%	64.1%	35.9%
13,357	VAN BUREN	6,209	3,562	2,607	40	955 R	57.4%	42.0%	57.7%	42.3%
100,494	WASHINGTON	36,658	23,601	12,557	500	11,044 R	64.4%	34.3%	65.3%	34.7%
50,835	WHITE	18,234	11,094	6,957	183	4,137 R	60.8%	38.2%	61.5%	38.5%
11,222	WOODRUFF	3,034	1,097	1,924	13	827 D	36.2%	63.4%	36.3%	63.7%
17,026	YELL	6,331	3,535	2,763	33	772 R	55.8%	43.6%	56.1%	43.9%
2,286,435	TOTAL	827,738	466,578	349,237	11,923	117,341 R	56.4%	42.2%	57.2%	42.8%

ARKANSAS

CONGRESS

CD	Year	Total Vote	Republican Vote	Republican Candidate	Democratic Vote	Democratic Candidate	Other Vote	Rep.-Dem. Plurality	Percentage Total Vote Rep.	Percentage Total Vote Dem.	Percentage Major Vote Rep.	Percentage Major Vote Dem.
1	1988					ALEXANDER, WILLIAM						
1	1986	164,719	58,937	ALBIN, RICK	105,782	ALEXANDER, WILLIAM		46,845 D	35.8%	64.2%	35.8%	64.2%
1	1984	124,528			121,047	ALEXANDER, WILLIAM	3,481	121,047 D		97.2%		100.0%
1	1982	191,635	67,427	BANKS, CHUCK	124,208	ALEXANDER, WILLIAM		56,781 D	35.2%	64.8%	35.2%	64.8%
2	1988	202,364	33,475	CARPENTER, WARREN D.	168,889	ROBINSON, TOMMY F.		135,414 D	16.5%	83.5%	16.5%	83.5%
2	1986	170,146	41,247	HAMAKER, KEITH	128,822	ROBINSON, TOMMY F.	77	87,575 D	24.2%	75.7%	24.3%	75.7%
2	1984	219,079	90,841	PETTY, JUDY	103,165	ROBINSON, TOMMY F.	25,073	12,324 D	41.5%	47.1%	46.8%	53.2%
2	1982	179,688	96,775	BETHUNE, ED	82,913	GEORGE, CHARLES L.		13,862 R	53.9%	46.1%	53.9%	46.1%
3	1988	216,390	161,623	HAMMERSCHMIDT, JOHN	54,767	STEWART, DAVID		106,856 R	74.7%	25.3%	74.7%	25.3%
3	1986	181,856	145,127	HAMMERSCHMIDT, JOHN	36,729	SARGENT, SU		108,398 R	79.8%	20.2%	79.8%	20.2%
3	1984			HAMMERSCHMIDT, JOHN								
3	1982	202,998	133,909	HAMMERSCHMIDT, JOHN	69,089	MCDOUGAL, JIM		64,820 R	66.0%	34.0%	66.0%	34.0%
4	1988	187,166	57,658	BELL, ROGER N.	129,508	ANTHONY, BERYL F.		71,850 D	30.8%	69.2%	30.8%	69.2%
4	1986	148,924	22,980	KEELS, LAMAR	115,339	ANTHONY, BERYL F.	10,605	92,359 D	15.4%	77.4%	16.6%	83.4%
4	1984	119,639			117,123	ANTHONY, BERYL F.	2,516	117,123 D		97.9%		100.0%
4	1982	184,917	63,661	LESLIE, BOB	121,256	ANTHONY, BERYL F.		57,595 D	34.4%	65.6%	34.4%	65.6%

ARKANSAS

1988 GENERAL ELECTION

President Other vote was 5,146 Independent (Duke); 3,297 Independent (Paul); 2,161 Independent (Fulani); 1,319 Independent (Dodge). The vote in Logan county appears to be low, but the official certified returns are presented in the table.

Congress According to state law, votes are not required to be tabulated for unopposed candidates. In CD 2, Tommy F. Robinson was re-elected as a Democrat in November 1988 but in July 1989 announced his change of party affiliation to Republican.

1988 PRIMARIES

MARCH 8 REPUBLICAN

Congress Unopposed in two CD's. No candidate in CD 1. Contested as follows:

CD 2 6,648 Warren D. Carpenter; 6,347 M. Alan Waters.

MARCH 8 DEMOCRATIC

Congress Unopposed in two CD's. Contested as follows:

CD 1 94,978 William Alexander; 46,974 Darrell Glascock.
CD 3 46,620 David Stewart; 31,395 Jim Lingle.

CALIFORNIA

GOVERNOR

George Deukmejian (R). Re-elected 1986 to a four-year term. Previously elected 1982.

SENATORS

Alan Cranston (D). Re-elected 1986 to a six-year term. Previously elected 1980, 1974, 1968.

Pete Wilson (R). Re-elected 1988 to a six-year term. Previously elected 1982.

REPRESENTATIVES

1. Douglas H. Bosco (D)
2. Wally Herger (R)
3. Robert T. Matsui (D)
4. Vic Fazio (D)
5. Nancy Pelosi (D)
6. Barbara Boxer (D)
7. George Miller (D)
8. Ronald V. Dellums (D)
9. Fortmey Stark (D)
10. Don Edwards (D)
11. Tom Lantos (D)
12. Tom Campbell (R)
13. Norman Y. Mienta (D)
14. Norman D. Shumway (R)
15. Tony Coelho (D) (see page 1)
16. Leon E. Panetta (D)
17. Charles Pashayan (R)
18. Richard Lehman (D)
19. Robert J. Lagomarsino (R)
20. William M. Thomas (R)
21. Elton Gallegly (R)
22. Carlos J. Moorhead (R)
23. Anthony C. Beilenson (D)
24. Henry A. Waxman (D)
25. Edward R. Roybal (D)
26. Howard L. Berman (D)
27. Mel Levine (D)
28. Julian C. Dixon (D)
29. Augustus Hawkins (D)
30. Matthew G. Martinez (D)
31. Mervyn M. Dymally (D)
32. Glenn M. Anderson (D)
33. David Dreier (R)
34. Esteban Torres (D)
35. Jerry Lewis (R)
36. George E. Brown (D)
37. Al McCandless (R)
38. Robert K. Dornan (R)
39. William E. Dannemeyer (R)
40. Christopher Cox (R)
41. Bill Lowery (R)
42. Dana Rohrabacher (R)
43. Ron Packard (R)
44. Jim Bates (D)
45. Duncan L. Hunter (R)

POSTWAR VOTE FOR PRESIDENT

		Republican		Democratic					Percentage			
									Total Vote		Major Vote	
Year	Total Vote	Vote	Candidate	Vote	Candidate	Other Vote	Plurality		Rep.	Dem.	Rep.	Dem.
1988	9,887,065	5,054,917	Bush, George	4,702,233	Dukakis, Michael S.	129,915	352,684	R	51.1%	47.6%	51.8%	48.2%
1984	9,505,423	5,467,009	Reagan, Ronald	3,922,519	Mondale, Walter F.	115,895	1,544,490	R	57.5%	41.3%	58.2%	41.8%
1980	8,587,063	4,524,858	Reagan, Ronald	3,083,661	Carter, Jimmy	978,544	1,441,197	R	52.7%	35.9%	59.5%	40.5%
1976	7,867,117	3,882,244	Ford, Gerald R.	3,742,284	Carter, Jimmy	242,589	139,960	R	49.3%	47.6%	50.9%	49.1%
1972	8,367,862	4,602,096	Nixon, Richard M.	3,475,847	McGovern, George S.	289,919	1,126,249	R	55.0%	41.5%	57.0%	43.0%
1968	7,251,587	3,467,664	Nixon, Richard M.	3,244,318	Humphrey, Hubert H.	539,605	223,346	R	47.8%	44.7%	51.7%	48.3%
1964	7,057,586	2,879,108	Goldwater, Barry M.	4,171,877	Johnson, Lyndon B.	6,601	1,292,769	D	40.8%	59.1%	40.8%	59.2%
1960	6,506,578	3,259,722	Nixon, Richard M.	3,224,099	Kennedy, John F.	22,757	35,623	R	50.1%	49.6%	50.3%	49.7%
1956	5,466,355	3,027,668	Eisenhower, Dwight D.	2,420,135	Stevenson, Adlai E.	18,552	607,533	R	55.4%	44.3%	55.6%	44.4%
1952	5,141,849	2,897,310	Eisenhower, Dwight D.	2,197,548	Stevenson, Adlai E.	46,991	699,762	R	56.3%	42.7%	56.9%	43.1%
1948	4,021,538	1,895,269	Dewey, Thomas E.	1,913,134	Truman, Harry S.	213,135	17,865	D	47.1%	47.6%	49.8%	50.2%

CALIFORNIA

POSTWAR VOTE FOR GOVERNOR

Year	Total Vote	Republican Vote	Republican Candidate	Democratic Vote	Democratic Candidate	Other Vote	Rep.-Dem. Plurality	Percentage Total Vote Rep.	Percentage Total Vote Dem.	Percentage Major Vote Rep.	Percentage Major Vote Dem.
1986	7,443,551	4,506,601	Deukmejian, George	2,781,714	Bradley, Tom	155,236	1,724,887 R	60.5%	37.4%	61.8%	38.2%
1982	7,876,698	3,881,014	Deukmejian, George	3,787,669	Bradley, Tom	208,015	93,345 R	49.3%	48.1%	50.6%	49.4%
1978	6,922,378	2,526,534	Younger, Evelle J.	3,878,812	Brown, Edmund G., Jr.	517,032	1,352,278 D	36.5%	56.0%	39.4%	60.6%
1974	6,248,070	2,952,954	Flournoy, Houston I.	3,131,648	Brown, Edmund G., Jr.	163,468	178,694 D	47.3%	50.1%	48.5%	51.5%
1970	6,510,072	3,439,664	Reagan, Ronald	2,938,607	Unruh, Jess	131,801	501,057 R	52.8%	45.1%	53.9%	46.1%
1966	6,503,445	3,742,913	Reagan, Ronald	2,749,174	Brown, Edmund G.	11,358	993,739 R	57.6%	42.3%	57.7%	42.3%
1962	5,853,270	2,740,351	Nixon, Richard M.	3,037,109	Brown, Edmund G.	75,810	296,758 D	46.8%	51.9%	47.4%	52.6%
1958	5,255,777	2,110,911	Knowland, William F.	3,140,076	Brown, Edmund G.	4,790	1,029,165 D	40.2%	59.7%	40.2%	59.8%
1954	4,030,368	2,290,519	Knight, Goodwin J.	1,739,368	Graves, Richard P.	481	551,151 R	56.8%	43.2%	56.8%	43.2%
1950	3,796,090	2,461,754	Warren, Earl	1,333,856	Roosevelt, James	480	1,127,898 R	64.8%	35.1%	64.9%	35.1%
1946 * *	2,558,399	2,344,542	Warren, Earl		—	213,857	2,344,542 R	91.6%		100.0%	

In 1946 the Republican candidate won both major party nominations.

POSTWAR VOTE FOR SENATOR

Year	Total Vote	Republican Vote	Republican Candidate	Democratic Vote	Democratic Candidate	Other Vote	Rep.-Dem. Plurality	Percentage Total Vote Rep.	Percentage Total Vote Dem.	Percentage Major Vote Rep.	Percentage Major Vote Dem.
1988	9,743,598	5,143,409	Wilson, Pete	4,287,253	McCarthy, Leo	312,936	856,156 R	52.8%	44.0%	54.5%	45.5%
1986	7,398,549	3,541,804	Zschau, Ed	3,646,672	Cranston, Alan	210,073	104,868 D	47.9%	49.3%	49.3%	50.7%
1982	7,805,538	4,022,565	Wilson, Pete	3,494,968	Brown, Edmund G., Jr.	288,005	527,597 R	51.5%	44.8%	53.5%	46.5%
1980	8,327,481	3,093,426	Gann, Paul	4,705,399	Cranston, Alan	528,656	1,611,973 D	37.1%	56.5%	39.7%	60.3%
1976	7,472,268	3,748,973	Hayakawa, S. I.	3,502,862	Tunney, John V.	220,433	246,111 R	50.2%	46.9%	51.7%	48.3%
1974	6,102,432	2,210,267	Richardson, H. L.	3,693,160	Cranston, Alan	199,005	1,482,893 D	36.2%	60.5%	37.4%	62.6%
1970	6,492,157	2,877,617	Murphy, George	3,496,558	Tunney, John V.	117,982	618,941 D	44.3%	53.9%	45.1%	54.9%
1968	7,102,465	3,329,148	Rafferty, Max	3,680,352	Cranston, Alan	92,965	351,204 D	46.9%	51.8%	47.5%	52.5%
1964	7,041,821	3,628,555	Murphy, George	3,411,912	Salinger, Pierre	1,354	216,643 R	51.5%	48.5%	51.5%	48.5%
1962	5,647,952	3,180,483	Kuchel, Thomas H.	2,452,839	Richards, Richard	14,630	727,644 R	56.3%	43.4%	56.5%	43.5%
1958	5,135,221	2,204,337	Knight, Goodwin J.	2,927,693	Engle, Clair	3,191	723,356 D	42.9%	57.0%	43.0%	57.0%
1956	5,361,467	2,892,918	Kuchel, Thomas H.	2,445,816	Richards, Richard	22,733	447,102 R	54.0%	45.6%	54.2%	45.8%
1954 S	3,929,668	2,090,836	Kuchel, Thomas H.	1,788,071	Yorty, Samuel W.	50,761	302,765 R	53.2%	45.5%	53.9%	46.1%
1952 * *	4,542,548	3,982,448	Knowland, William F.		—	560,100	3,982,448 R	87.7%		100.0%	
1950	3,686,315	2,183,454	Nixon, Richard M.	1,502,507	Douglas, Helen	354	680,947 R	59.2%	40.8%	59.2%	40.8%
1946	2,639,465	1,428,067	Knowland, William F.	1,167,161	Rogers, Will	44,237	260,906 R	54.1%	44.2%	55.0%	45.0%

The 1954 election was for a short term to fill a vacancy. In 1952 the Republican candidate won both major party nominations.

CALIFORNIA

Districts Established January 2, 1983

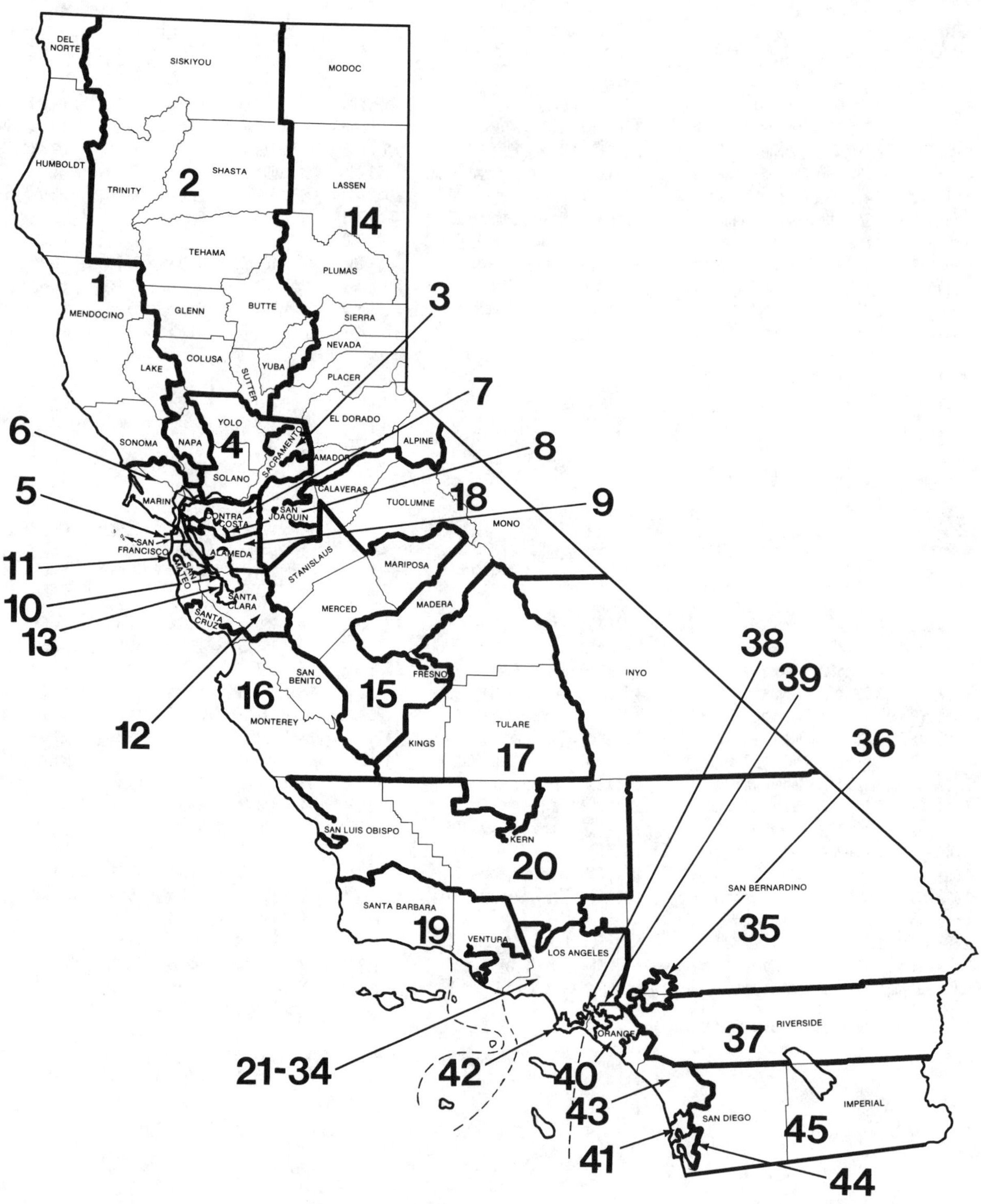

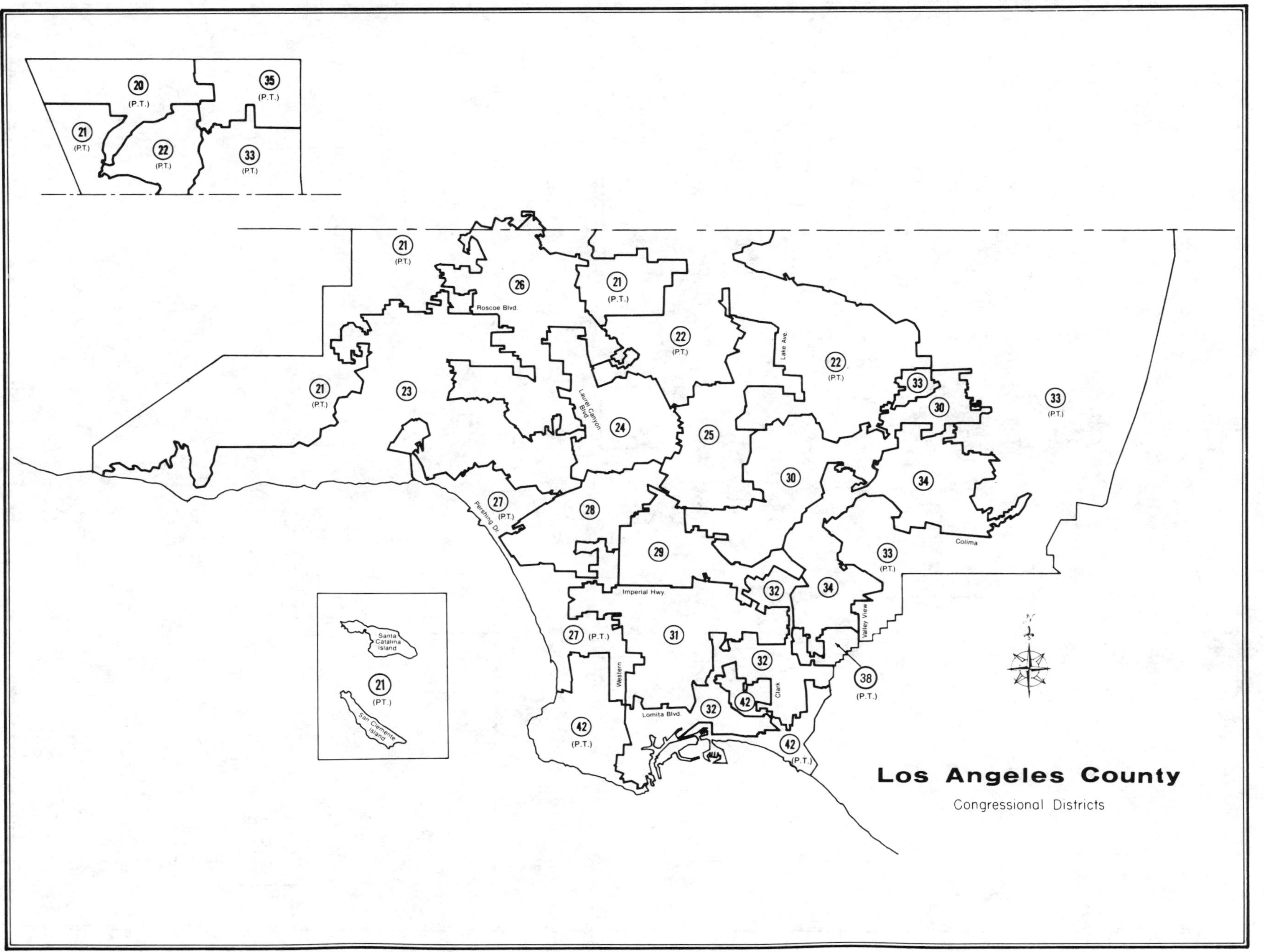
Los Angeles County
Congressional Districts
Roscoe Blvd.
Laurel Canyon Blvd
Lake Ave
Pershing Dr.
Imperial Hwy.
Western
Lomita Blvd.
Clark
Valley View
Colima
Santa Catalina Island
San Clemente Island

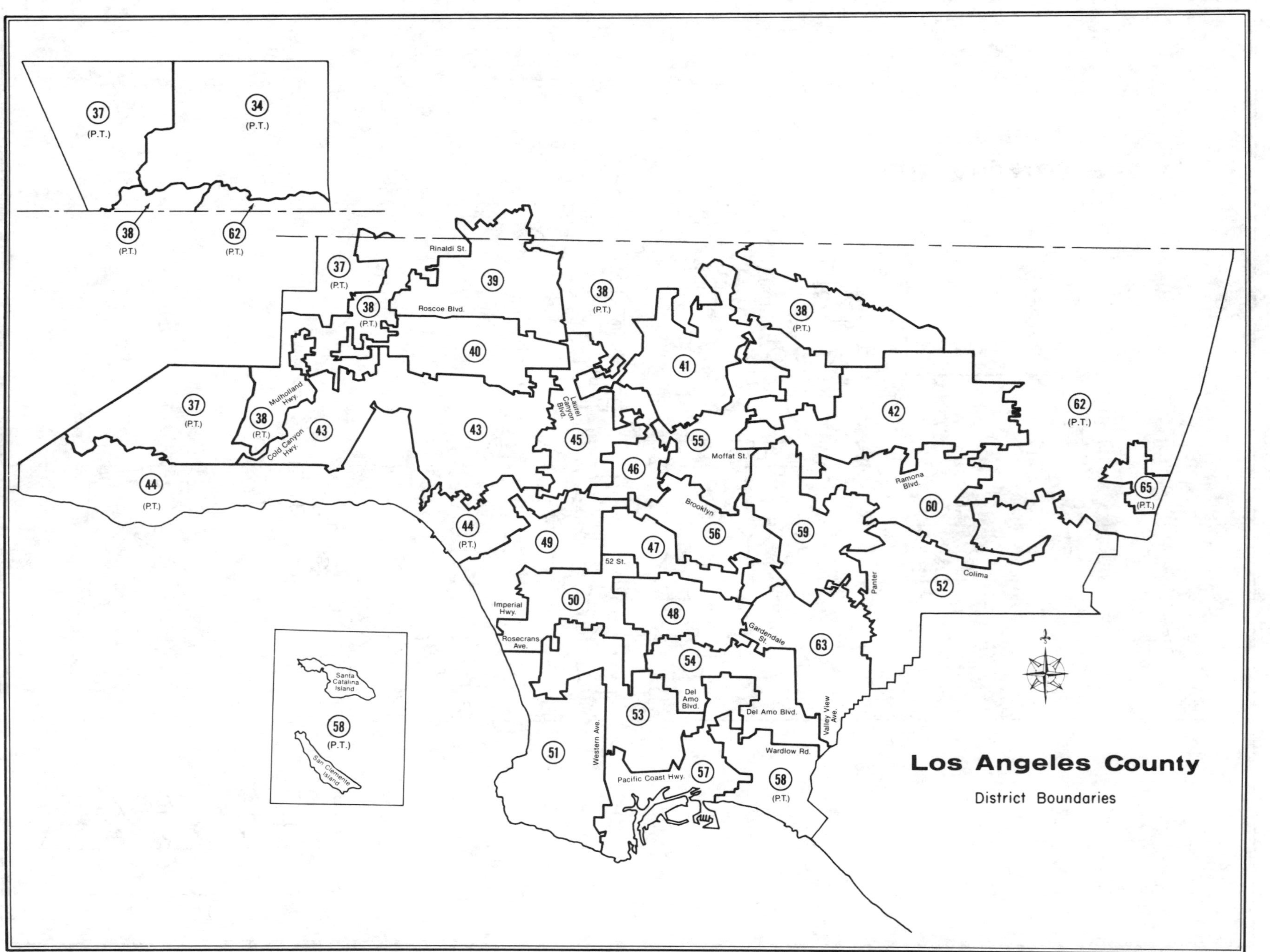
Los Angeles County
District Boundaries
Rinaldi St.
Roscoe Blvd.
Mulholland Hwy.
Cold Canyon Hwy.
Laurel Canyon Blvd.
Moffat St.
Brooklyn
Ramona Blvd.
Colima
Panter
52 St.
Imperial Hwy.
Rosecrans Ave.
Gardendale St.
Del Amo Blvd.
Del Amo Blvd.
Valley View Ave.
Wardlow Rd.
Western Ave.
Pacific Coast Hwy.
Santa Catalina Island
San Clemente Island
34 (P.T.)
37 (P.T.)
38 (P.T.)
39
40
41
42
43
44 (P.T.)
45
46
47
48
49
50
51
52
53
54
55
56
57
58 (P.T.)
59
60
62 (P.T.)
63
65 (P.T.)

CALIFORNIA

PRESIDENT 1988

1980 Census Population	County	Total Vote	Republican	Democratic	Other	Rep.-Dem. Plurality	Percentage Total Vote Rep.	Total Vote Dem.	Major Vote Rep.	Major Vote Dem.
1,105,379	ALAMEDA	478,998	162,815	310,283	5,900	147,468 D	34.0%	64.8%	34.4%	65.6%
1,097	ALPINE	552	306	230	16	76 R	55.4%	41.7%	57.1%	42.9%
19,314	AMADOR	12,338	6,893	5,197	248	1,696 R	55.9%	42.1%	57.0%	43.0%
143,851	BUTTE	71,631	40,143	30,406	1,082	9,737 R	56.0%	42.4%	56.9%	43.1%
20,710	CALAVERAS	13,574	7,640	5,674	260	1,966 R	56.3%	41.8%	57.4%	42.6%
12,791	COLUSA	5,172	3,077	2,022	73	1,055 R	59.5%	39.1%	60.3%	39.7%
656,380	CONTRA COSTA	331,511	158,652	169,411	3,448	10,759 D	47.9%	51.1%	48.4%	51.6%
18,217	DEL NORTE	7,468	3,714	3,587	167	127 R	49.7%	48.0%	50.9%	49.1%
85,812	EL DORADO	50,603	30,021	19,801	781	10,220 R	59.3%	39.1%	60.3%	39.7%
514,621	FRESNO	189,870	94,835	92,635	2,400	2,200 R	49.9%	48.8%	50.6%	49.4%
21,350	GLENN	7,966	4,944	2,894	128	2,050 R	62.1%	36.3%	63.1%	36.9%
108,514	HUMBOLDT	52,146	21,460	29,781	905	8,321 D	41.2%	57.1%	41.9%	58.1%
92,110	IMPERIAL	23,365	12,889	10,243	233	2,646 R	55.2%	43.8%	55.7%	44.3%
17,895	INYO	7,837	5,042	2,653	142	2,389 R	64.3%	33.9%	65.5%	34.5%
403,089	KERN	147,293	90,550	55,083	1,660	35,467 R	61.5%	37.4%	62.2%	37.8%
73,738	KINGS	21,482	12,118	9,142	222	2,976 R	56.4%	42.6%	57.0%	43.0%
36,366	LAKE	19,502	9,366	9,828	308	462 D	48.0%	50.4%	48.8%	51.2%
21,661	LASSEN	8,802	5,157	3,446	199	1,711 R	58.6%	39.2%	59.9%	40.1%
7,477,503	LOS ANGELES	2,644,671	1,239,716	1,372,352	32,603	132,636 D	46.9%	51.9%	47.5%	52.5%
63,116	MADERA	24,281	13,255	10,642	384	2,613 R	54.6%	43.8%	55.5%	44.5%
222,568	MARIN	117,920	46,855	69,394	1,671	22,539 D	39.7%	58.8%	40.3%	59.7%
11,108	MARIPOSA	6,910	3,768	2,998	144	770 R	54.5%	43.4%	55.7%	44.3%
66,738	MENDOCINO	30,947	12,979	17,152	816	4,173 D	41.9%	55.4%	43.1%	56.9%
134,560	MERCED	42,414	21,717	20,105	592	1,612 R	51.2%	47.4%	51.9%	48.1%
8,610	MODOC	4,017	2,518	1,416	83	1,102 R	62.7%	35.3%	64.0%	36.0%
8,577	MONO	3,547	2,177	1,284	86	893 R	61.4%	36.2%	62.9%	37.1%
290,444	MONTEREY	100,381	50,022	48,998	1,361	1,024 R	49.8%	48.8%	50.5%	49.5%
99,199	NAPA	46,290	23,235	22,283	772	952 R	50.2%	48.1%	51.0%	49.0%
51,645	NEVADA	37,023	21,383	14,980	660	6,403 R	57.8%	40.5%	58.8%	41.2%
1,932,709	ORANGE	865,307	586,230	269,013	10,064	317,217 R	67.7%	31.1%	68.5%	31.5%
117,247	PLACER	70,642	42,096	27,516	1,030	14,580 R	59.6%	39.0%	60.5%	39.5%
17,340	PLUMAS	9,015	4,603	4,251	161	352 R	51.1%	47.2%	52.0%	48.0%
663,166	RIVERSIDE	336,348	199,979	133,122	3,247	66,857 R	59.5%	39.6%	60.0%	40.0%
783,381	SACRAMENTO	395,690	201,832	188,557	5,301	13,275 R	51.0%	47.7%	51.7%	48.3%
25,005	SAN BENITO	10,308	5,578	4,559	171	1,019 R	54.1%	44.2%	55.0%	45.0%
895,016	SAN BERNARDINO	392,008	235,167	151,118	5,723	84,049 R	60.0%	38.5%	60.9%	39.1%
1,861,846	SAN DIEGO	869,195	523,143	333,264	12,788	189,879 R	60.2%	38.3%	61.1%	38.9%
678,974	SAN FRANCISCO	277,394	72,503	201,887	3,004	129,384 D	26.1%	72.8%	26.4%	73.6%
347,342	SAN JOAQUIN	138,453	75,309	61,699	1,445	13,610 R	54.4%	44.6%	55.0%	45.0%
155,435	SAN LUIS OBISPO	83,467	46,613	35,667	1,187	10,946 R	55.8%	42.7%	56.7%	43.3%
587,329	SAN MATEO	254,480	109,261	141,859	3,360	32,598 D	42.9%	55.7%	43.5%	56.5%
298,694	SANTA BARBARA	142,940	77,524	63,586	1,830	13,938 R	54.2%	44.5%	54.9%	45.1%
1,295,071	SANTA CLARA	541,528	254,442	277,810	9,276	23,368 D	47.0%	51.3%	47.8%	52.2%
188,141	SANTA CRUZ	102,611	37,728	63,133	1,750	25,405 D	36.8%	61.5%	37.4%	62.6%
115,715	SHASTA	54,585	32,402	21,171	1,012	11,231 R	59.4%	38.8%	60.5%	39.5%
3,073	SIERRA	1,696	860	791	45	69 R	50.7%	46.6%	52.1%	47.9%
39,732	SISKIYOU	17,797	9,056	8,365	376	691 R	50.9%	47.0%	52.0%	48.0%
235,203	SOLANO	106,088	50,314	54,344	1,430	4,030 D	47.4%	51.2%	48.1%	51.9%
299,681	SONOMA	161,583	67,725	91,262	2,596	23,537 D	41.9%	56.5%	42.6%	57.4%
265,900	STANISLAUS	97,315	51,648	44,685	982	6,963 R	53.1%	45.9%	53.6%	46.4%
52,246	SUTTER	20,898	14,100	6,557	241	7,543 R	67.5%	31.4%	68.3%	31.7%
38,888	TEHAMA	17,434	9,854	7,213	367	2,641 R	56.5%	41.4%	57.7%	42.3%
11,858	TRINITY	5,980	3,267	2,518	195	749 R	54.6%	42.1%	56.5%	43.5%
245,738	TULARE	78,669	46,891	30,711	1,067	16,180 R	59.6%	39.0%	60.4%	39.6%
33,928	TUOLUMNE	19,715	10,646	8,717	352	1,929 R	54.0%	44.2%	55.0%	45.0%
529,174	VENTURA	239,473	147,604	89,065	2,804	58,539 R	61.6%	37.2%	62.4%	37.6%
113,374	YOLO	53,372	22,358	30,429	585	8,071 D	41.9%	57.0%	42.4%	57.6%
49,733	YUBA	14,563	8,937	5,444	182	3,493 R	61.4%	37.4%	62.1%	37.9%
23,667,902	TOTAL	9,887,065	5,054,917	4,702,233	129,915	352,684 R	51.1%	47.6%	51.8%	48.2%

CALIFORNIA

SENATOR 1988

1980 Census Population	County	Total Vote	Republican	Democratic	Other	Rep.-Dem. Plurality	Percentage Total Vote Rep.	Total Vote Dem.	Major Vote Rep.	Major Vote Dem.
1,105,379	ALAMEDA	470,873	173,313	283,560	14,000	110,247 D	36.8%	60.2%	37.9%	62.1%
1,097	ALPINE	554	311	194	49	117 R	56.1%	35.0%	61.6%	38.4%
19,314	AMADOR	12,265	6,896	4,912	457	1,984 R	56.2%	40.0%	58.4%	41.6%
143,851	BUTTE	72,056	40,056	28,886	3,114	11,170 R	55.6%	40.1%	58.1%	41.9%
20,710	CALAVERAS	13,388	7,584	5,310	494	2,274 R	56.6%	39.7%	58.8%	41.2%
12,791	COLUSA	5,052	2,960	1,942	150	1,018 R	58.6%	38.4%	60.4%	39.6%
656,380	CONTRA COSTA	330,259	168,760	152,714	8,785	16,046 R	51.1%	46.2%	52.5%	47.5%
18,217	DEL NORTE	7,582	3,418	3,863	301	445 D	45.1%	50.9%	46.9%	53.1%
85,812	EL DORADO	50,709	30,738	17,986	1,985	12,752 R	60.6%	35.5%	63.1%	36.9%
514,621	FRESNO	187,371	99,315	81,733	6,323	17,582 R	53.0%	43.6%	54.9%	45.1%
21,350	GLENN	8,043	5,006	2,767	270	2,239 R	62.2%	34.4%	64.4%	35.6%
108,514	HUMBOLDT	51,411	19,384	30,472	1,555	11,088 D	37.7%	59.3%	38.9%	61.1%
92,110	IMPERIAL	23,667	12,391	10,099	1,177	2,292 R	52.4%	42.7%	55.1%	44.9%
17,895	INYO	7,627	4,986	2,425	216	2,561 R	65.4%	31.8%	67.3%	32.7%
403,089	KERN	150,254	91,303	53,415	5,536	37,888 R	60.8%	35.5%	63.1%	36.9%
73,738	KINGS	21,727	12,238	8,732	757	3,506 R	56.3%	40.2%	58.4%	41.6%
36,366	LAKE	19,478	9,516	9,210	752	306 R	48.9%	47.3%	50.8%	49.2%
21,661	LASSEN	8,698	4,780	3,541	377	1,239 R	55.0%	40.7%	57.4%	42.6%
7,477,503	LOS ANGELES	2,603,311	1,265,582	1,261,449	76,280	4,133 R	48.6%	48.5%	50.1%	49.9%
63,116	MADERA	23,437	13,324	9,117	996	4,207 R	56.9%	38.9%	59.4%	40.6%
222,568	MARIN	116,099	49,942	63,101	3,056	13,159 D	43.0%	54.4%	44.2%	55.8%
11,108	MARIPOSA	6,915	3,895	2,742	278	1,153 R	56.3%	39.7%	58.7%	41.3%
66,738	MENDOCINO	30,470	13,318	15,835	1,317	2,517 D	43.7%	52.0%	45.7%	54.3%
134,560	MERCED	39,416	20,513	17,247	1,656	3,266 R	52.0%	43.8%	54.3%	45.7%
8,610	MODOC	4,020	2,441	1,414	165	1,027 R	60.7%	35.2%	63.3%	36.7%
8,577	MONO	3,747	2,397	1,180	170	1,217 R	64.0%	31.5%	67.0%	33.0%
290,444	MONTEREY	100,621	50,136	46,401	4,084	3,735 R	49.8%	46.1%	51.9%	48.1%
99,199	NAPA	46,444	24,071	20,619	1,754	3,452 R	51.8%	44.4%	53.9%	46.1%
51,645	NEVADA	36,911	21,815	13,598	1,498	8,217 R	59.1%	36.8%	61.6%	38.4%
1,932,709	ORANGE	869,999	593,614	251,264	25,121	342,350 R	68.2%	28.9%	70.3%	29.7%
117,247	PLACER	70,587	42,643	25,243	2,701	17,400 R	60.4%	35.8%	62.8%	37.2%
17,340	PLUMAS	8,892	4,635	3,877	380	758 R	52.1%	43.6%	54.5%	45.5%
663,166	RIVERSIDE	334,404	195,956	128,422	10,026	67,534 R	58.6%	38.4%	60.4%	39.6%
783,381	SACRAMENTO	389,278	201,827	173,110	14,341	28,717 R	51.8%	44.5%	53.8%	46.2%
25,005	SAN BENITO	10,288	5,331	4,499	458	832 R	51.8%	43.7%	54.2%	45.8%
895,016	SAN BERNARDINO	388,256	230,772	143,465	14,019	87,307 R	59.4%	37.0%	61.7%	38.3%
1,861,846	SAN DIEGO	857,565	549,367	283,554	24,644	265,813 R	64.1%	33.1%	66.0%	34.0%
678,974	SAN FRANCISCO	243,527	70,102	167,613	5,812	97,511 D	28.8%	68.8%	29.5%	70.5%
347,342	SAN JOAQUIN	136,989	75,753	56,330	4,906	19,423 R	55.3%	41.1%	57.4%	42.6%
155,435	SAN LUIS OBISPO	85,101	49,564	32,452	3,085	17,112 R	58.2%	38.1%	60.4%	39.6%
587,329	SAN MATEO	245,918	111,187	125,724	9,007	14,537 D	45.2%	51.1%	46.9%	53.1%
298,694	SANTA BARBARA	142,985	81,282	56,916	4,787	24,366 R	56.8%	39.8%	58.8%	41.2%
1,295,071	SANTA CLARA	532,365	253,865	257,463	21,037	3,598 D	47.7%	48.4%	49.6%	50.4%
188,141	SANTA CRUZ	102,461	39,104	58,715	4,642	19,611 D	38.2%	57.3%	40.0%	60.0%
115,715	SHASTA	51,042	30,821	18,384	1,837	12,437 R	60.4%	36.0%	62.6%	37.4%
3,073	SIERRA	1,723	880	759	84	121 R	51.1%	44.1%	53.7%	46.3%
39,732	SISKIYOU	17,880	9,448	7,577	855	1,871 R	52.8%	42.4%	55.5%	44.5%
235,203	SOLANO	98,059	47,288	47,420	3,351	132 D	48.2%	48.4%	49.9%	50.1%
299,681	SONOMA	159,688	71,775	81,747	6,166	9,972 D	44.9%	51.2%	46.8%	53.2%
265,900	STANISLAUS	96,516	51,423	42,440	2,653	8,983 R	53.3%	44.0%	54.8%	45.2%
52,246	SUTTER	20,002	12,724	6,466	812	6,258 R	63.6%	32.3%	66.3%	33.7%
38,888	TEHAMA	17,934	10,338	6,916	680	3,422 R	57.6%	38.6%	59.9%	40.1%
11,858	TRINITY	6,178	3,337	2,459	382	878 R	54.0%	39.8%	57.6%	42.4%
245,738	TULARE	76,454	46,958	26,980	2,516	19,978 R	61.4%	35.3%	63.5%	36.5%
33,928	TUOLUMNE	19,321	10,781	7,892	648	2,889 R	55.8%	40.8%	57.7%	42.3%
529,174	VENTURA	239,727	149,958	81,831	7,938	68,127 R	62.6%	34.1%	64.7%	35.3%
113,374	YOLO	52,709	23,459	27,291	1,959	3,832 D	44.5%	51.8%	46.2%	53.8%
49,733	YUBA	15,345	8,828	5,980	537	2,848 R	57.5%	39.0%	59.6%	40.4%
23,667,902	TOTAL	9,743,598	5,143,409	4,287,253	312,936	856,156 R	52.8%	44.0%	54.5%	45.5%

LOS ANGELES COUNTY

PRESIDENT 1988

1980 Census Population	Assembly District	Total Vote	Republican	Democratic	Other	Rep.-Dem. Plurality	Percentage Total Vote Rep.	Total Vote Dem.	Major Vote Rep.	Major Vote Dem.
105,028	DISTRICT 34 (PART)	66,582	48,196	17,563	823	30,633 R	72.4%	26.4%	73.3%	26.7%
147,812	DISTRICT 37 (PART)	88,791	58,547	29,138	1,106	29,409 R	65.9%	32.8%	66.8%	33.2%
301,250	DISTRICT 38	141,624	83,744	56,204	1,676	27,540 R	59.1%	39.7%	59.8%	40.2%
295,331	DISTRICT 39	90,960	43,017	46,886	1,057	3,869 D	47.3%	51.5%	47.8%	52.2%
291,137	DISTRICT 40	108,582	45,273	61,970	1,339	16,697 D	41.7%	57.1%	42.2%	57.8%
294,121	DISTRICT 41	126,421	71,643	53,029	1,749	18,614 R	56.7%	41.9%	57.5%	42.5%
293,648	DISTRICT 42	119,539	73,919	44,004	1,616	29,915 R	61.8%	36.8%	62.7%	37.3%
291,647	DISTRICT 43	152,306	62,201	88,697	1,408	26,496 D	40.8%	58.2%	41.2%	58.8%
292,765	DISTRICT 44	145,794	51,733	92,507	1,554	40,774 D	35.5%	63.5%	35.9%	64.1%
293,863	DISTRICT 45	123,865	41,969	80,391	1,505	38,422 D	33.9%	64.9%	34.3%	65.7%
299,036	DISTRICT 46	49,049	17,573	30,662	814	13,089 D	35.8%	62.5%	36.4%	63.6%
291,099	DISTRICT 47	48,635	7,966	39,847	822	31,881 D	16.4%	81.9%	16.7%	83.3%
300,319	DISTRICT 48	61,941	10,487	50,720	734	40,233 D	16.9%	81.9%	17.1%	82.9%
290,012	DISTRICT 49	117,117	29,728	85,891	1,498	56,163 D	25.4%	73.3%	25.7%	74.3%
290,112	DISTRICT 50	93,197	22,598	69,075	1,524	46,477 D	24.2%	74.1%	24.7%	75.3%
301,650	DISTRICT 51	149,229	96,294	51,085	1,850	45,209 R	64.5%	34.2%	65.3%	34.7%
289,931	DISTRICT 52	123,166	78,138	43,619	1,409	34,519 R	63.4%	35.4%	64.2%	35.8%
296,057	DISTRICT 53	98,390	46,106	51,016	1,268	4,910 D	46.9%	51.9%	47.5%	52.5%
291,565	DISTRICT 54	97,330	42,433	53,817	1,080	11,384 D	43.6%	55.3%	44.1%	55.9%
292,183	DISTRICT 55	68,953	22,812	45,176	965	22,364 D	33.1%	65.5%	33.6%	66.4%
293,880	DISTRICT 56	35,141	8,979	25,702	460	16,723 D	25.6%	73.1%	25.9%	74.1%
300,113	DISTRICT 57	81,100	34,139	45,731	1,230	11,592 D	42.1%	56.4%	42.7%	57.3%
151,539	DISTRICT 58 (PART)	78,918	43,116	34,929	873	8,187 R	54.6%	44.3%	55.2%	44.8%
296,546	DISTRICT 59	89,840	38,939	50,135	766	11,196 D	43.3%	55.8%	43.7%	56.3%
296,707	DISTRICT 60	69,243	32,832	35,568	843	2,736 D	47.4%	51.4%	48.0%	52.0%
249,390	DISTRICT 62 (PART)	105,770	64,887	39,535	1,348	25,352 R	61.3%	37.4%	62.1%	37.9%
297,416	DISTRICT 63	99,678	55,921	42,824	933	13,097 R	56.1%	43.0%	56.6%	43.4%
43,512	DISTRICT 65 (PART)	13,344	6,526	6,631	187	105 D	48.9%	49.7%	49.6%	50.4%
7,477,669	TOTAL	2,644,671	1,239,716	1,372,352	32,603	132,636 D	46.9%	51.9%	47.5%	52.5%

LOS ANGELES COUNTY

SENATOR 1988

1980 Census Population	Assembly District	Total Vote	Republican	Democratic	Other	Rep.-Dem. Plurality	Percentage Total Vote Rep.	Total Vote Dem.	Major Vote Rep.	Major Vote Dem.
105,028	DISTRICT 34 (PART)	65,526	46,027	17,706	1,793	28,321 R	70.2%	27.0%	72.2%	27.8%
147,812	DISTRICT 37 (PART)	87,233	59,463	25,712	2,058	33,751 R	68.2%	29.5%	69.8%	30.2%
301,250	DISTRICT 38	139,476	85,327	50,478	3,671	34,849 R	61.2%	36.2%	62.8%	37.2%
295,331	DISTRICT 39	89,476	43,202	43,332	2,942	130 D	48.3%	48.4%	49.9%	50.1%
291,137	DISTRICT 40	106,053	48,860	54,147	3,046	5,287 D	46.1%	51.1%	47.4%	52.6%
294,121	DISTRICT 41	124,760	74,785	46,758	3,217	28,027 R	59.9%	37.5%	61.5%	38.5%
293,648	DISTRICT 42	118,651	75,952	39,580	3,119	36,372 R	64.0%	33.4%	65.7%	34.3%
291,647	DISTRICT 43	150,492	68,222	79,079	3,191	10,857 D	45.3%	52.5%	46.3%	53.7%
292,765	DISTRICT 44	143,809	55,872	84,737	3,200	28,865 D	38.9%	58.9%	39.7%	60.3%
293,863	DISTRICT 45	121,119	45,225	72,478	3,416	27,253 D	37.3%	59.8%	38.4%	61.6%
299,036	DISTRICT 46	48,150	18,336	27,980	1,834	9,644 D	38.1%	58.1%	39.6%	60.4%
291,099	DISTRICT 47	47,667	8,859	37,412	1,396	28,553 D	18.6%	78.5%	19.1%	80.9%
300,319	DISTRICT 48	61,397	10,377	49,052	1,968	38,675 D	16.9%	79.9%	17.5%	82.5%
290,012	DISTRICT 49	115,334	31,612	81,464	2,258	49,852 D	27.4%	70.6%	28.0%	72.0%
290,112	DISTRICT 50	91,342	23,595	65,579	2,168	41,984 D	25.8%	71.8%	26.5%	73.5%
301,650	DISTRICT 51	146,493	97,892	45,008	3,593	52,884 R	66.8%	30.7%	68.5%	31.5%
289,931	DISTRICT 52	121,523	78,066	40,002	3,455	38,064 R	64.2%	32.9%	66.1%	33.9%
296,057	DISTRICT 53	96,694	44,412	48,588	3,694	4,176 D	45.9%	50.2%	47.8%	52.2%
291,565	DISTRICT 54	95,906	42,124	51,613	2,169	9,489 D	43.9%	53.8%	44.9%	55.1%
292,183	DISTRICT 55	67,543	23,360	40,807	3,376	17,447 D	34.6%	60.4%	36.4%	63.6%
293,880	DISTRICT 56	34,440	8,894	23,407	2,139	14,513 D	25.8%	68.0%	27.5%	72.5%
300,113	DISTRICT 57	79,640	35,703	41,315	2,622	5,612 D	44.8%	51.9%	46.4%	53.6%
151,539	DISTRICT 58 (PART)	77,805	44,410	31,222	2,173	13,188 R	57.1%	40.1%	58.7%	41.3%
296,546	DISTRICT 59	88,449	37,277	47,427	3,745	10,150 D	42.1%	53.6%	44.0%	56.0%
296,707	DISTRICT 60	68,298	31,558	33,527	3,213	1,969 D	46.2%	49.1%	48.5%	51.5%
249,390	DISTRICT 62 (PART)	104,566	65,758	36,074	2,734	29,684 R	62.9%	34.5%	64.6%	35.4%
297,416	DISTRICT 63	98,272	53,740	40,900	3,632	12,840 R	54.7%	41.6%	56.8%	43.2%
43,512	DISTRICT 65 (PART)	13,173	6,674	6,065	434	609 R	50.7%	46.0%	52.4%	47.6%
7,477,669	TOTAL	2,603,311	1,265,582	1,261,449	76,280	4,133 R	48.6%	48.5%	50.1%	49.9%

CALIFORNIA

CONGRESS

CD	Year	Total Vote	Republican Vote	Republican Candidate	Democratic Vote	Democratic Candidate	Other Vote	Rep.-Dem. Plurality	Percentage Total Vote Rep.	Percentage Total Vote Dem.	Percentage Major Vote Rep.	Percentage Major Vote Dem.
1	1988	254,154	72,189	VANDERBILT, SAMUEL	159,815	BOSCO, DOUGLAS H.	22,150	87,626 D	28.4%	62.9%	31.1%	68.9%
1	1986	204,759	54,436	SAMPSON, FLOYD G.	138,174	BOSCO, DOUGLAS H.	12,149	83,738 D	26.6%	67.5%	28.3%	71.7%
1	1984	252,223	95,186	REDICK, DAVID	157,037	BOSCO, DOUGLAS H.		61,851 D	37.7%	62.3%	37.7%	62.3%
2	1988	236,351	139,010	HERGER, WALLY	91,088	MEYER, WAYNE	6,253	47,922 R	58.8%	38.5%	60.4%	39.6%
2	1986	188,414	109,758	HERGER, WALLY	74,602	SWENDIMAN, STEPHEN C.	4,054	35,156 R	58.3%	39.6%	59.5%	40.5%
2	1984	228,472	158,679	CHAPPIE, EUGENE A.	69,793	COZAD, HARRY		88,886 R	69.5%	30.5%	69.5%	30.5%
3	1988	257,766	74,296	LANDOWSKI, LOWELL	183,470	MATSUI, ROBERT T.		109,174 D	28.8%	71.2%	28.8%	71.2%
3	1986	208,974	50,265	LANDOWSKI, LOWELL	158,709	MATSUI, ROBERT T.		108,444 D	24.1%	75.9%	24.1%	75.9%
3	1984	131,565			131,369	MATSUI, ROBERT T.	196	131,369 D		99.9%		100.0%
4	1988	182,490			181,184	FAZIO, VIC	1,306	181,184 D		99.3%		100.0%
4	1986	182,960	54,596	HITE, JACK D.	128,364	FAZIO, VIC		73,768 D	29.8%	70.2%	29.8%	70.2%
4	1984	211,921	77,773	CANFIELD, ROGER B.	130,109	FAZIO, VIC	4,039	52,336 D	36.7%	61.4%	37.4%	62.6%
5	1988	174,758	33,692	O'NEILL, BRUCE M.	133,530	PELOSI, NANCY	7,536	99,838 D	19.3%	76.4%	20.1%	79.9%
5	1986	163,214	36,039	GARZA, MIKE	122,688	BURTON, SALA	4,487	86,649 D	22.1%	75.2%	22.7%	77.3%
5	1984	193,204	45,930	SPINOSA, TOM	139,692	BURTON, SALA	7,582	93,762 D	23.8%	72.3%	24.7%	75.3%
6	1988	240,819	64,174	STEINMETZ, WILLIAM	176,645	BOXER, BARBARA		112,471 D	26.6%	73.4%	26.6%	73.4%
6	1986	193,552	50,606	ERNST, FRANKLIN	142,946	BOXER, BARBARA		92,340 D	26.1%	73.9%	26.1%	73.9%
6	1984	239,096	71,011	BINDERUP, DOUGLAS	162,511	BOXER, BARBARA	5,574	91,500 D	29.7%	68.0%	30.4%	69.6%
7	1988	248,484	78,478	LAST, JEAN	170,006	MILLER, GEORGE		91,528 D	31.6%	68.4%	31.6%	68.4%
7	1986	186,553	62,379	THAKAR, ROSEMARY	124,174	MILLER, GEORGE		61,795 D	33.4%	66.6%	33.4%	66.6%
7	1984	241,244	78,985	THAKAR, ROSEMARY	158,306	MILLER, GEORGE	3,953	79,321 D	32.7%	65.6%	33.3%	66.7%
8	1988	245,196	76,531	CUDDIHY, JOHN J.	163,221	DELLUMS, RONALD V.	5,444	86,690 D	31.2%	66.6%	31.9%	68.1%
8	1986	202,935	76,850	EIGENBERG, STEVEN	121,790	DELLUMS, RONALD V.	4,295	44,940 D	37.9%	60.0%	38.7%	61.3%
8	1984	239,223	94,907	CONNOR, CHARLES	144,316	DELLUMS, RONALD V.		49,409 D	39.7%	60.3%	39.7%	60.3%
9	1988	209,522	56,656	HERTZ, HOWARD	152,866	STARK, FORTNEY		96,210 D	27.0%	73.0%	27.0%	73.0%
9	1986	162,790	49,300	WILLIAMS, DAVID M.	113,490	STARK, FORTNEY		64,190 D	30.3%	69.7%	30.3%	69.7%
9	1984	195,308	51,399	BEAVER, J. T.	136,511	STARK, FORTNEY	7,398	85,112 D	26.3%	69.9%	27.4%	72.6%
10	1988	165,301			142,500	EDWARDS, DON	22,801	142,500 D		86.2%		100.0%
10	1986	119,564	31,826	LA CRONE, MICHAEL R.	84,240	EDWARDS, DON	3,498	52,414 D	26.6%	70.5%	27.4%	72.6%
10	1984	164,177	56,256	HERRIOTT, BOB	102,469	EDWARDS, DON	5,452	46,213 D	34.3%	62.4%	35.4%	64.6%
11	1988	205,016	50,050	QURAISHI, G. M.	145,484	LANTOS, TOM	9,482	95,434 D	24.4%	71.0%	25.6%	74.4%
11	1986	151,695	39,315	QURAISHI, G. M.	112,380	LANTOS, TOM		73,065 D	25.9%	74.1%	25.9%	74.1%
11	1984	211,115	59,625	HICKEY, JOHN J.	147,607	LANTOS, TOM	3,883	87,982 D	28.2%	69.9%	28.8%	71.2%
12	1988	263,930	136,384	CAMPBELL, TOM	121,523	ESHOO, ANNA G.	6,023	14,861 R	51.7%	46.0%	52.9%	47.1%
12	1986	187,043	111,252	KONNYU, ERNEST L.	69,564	WEIL, LANCE T.	6,227	41,688 R	59.5%	37.2%	61.5%	38.5%
12	1984	252,693	155,795	ZSCHAU, ED	91,026	CARNOY, MARTIN	5,872	64,769 R	61.7%	36.0%	63.1%	36.9%
13	1988	214,522	63,959	SOMMER, LUKE	143,980	MINETA, NORMAN Y.	6,583	80,021 D	29.8%	67.1%	30.8%	69.2%
13	1986	154,450	46,754	NASH, BOB	107,696	MINETA, NORMAN Y.		60,942 D	30.3%	69.7%	30.3%	69.7%
13	1984	214,353	70,666	WILLIAMS, JOHN D.	139,851	MINETA, NORMAN Y.	3,836	69,185 D	33.0%	65.2%	33.6%	66.4%
14	1988	277,775	173,876	SHUMWAY, NORMAN D.	103,899	MALBERG, PATRICIA		69,977 R	62.6%	37.4%	62.6%	37.4%
14	1986	205,161	146,906	SHUMWAY, NORMAN D.	53,597	STEELE, BILL	4,658	93,309 R	71.6%	26.1%	73.3%	26.7%
14	1984	244,476	179,238	SHUMWAY, NORMAN D.	58,384	CARLSON, RUTH	6,854	120,854 R	73.3%	23.9%	75.4%	24.6%

CALIFORNIA

CONGRESS

CD	Year	Total Vote	Republican Vote	Republican Candidate	Democratic Vote	Democratic Candidate	Other Vote	Rep.-Dem. Plurality	Percentage Total Vote Rep.	Percentage Total Vote Dem.	Percentage Major Vote Rep.	Percentage Major Vote Dem.
15	1988	170,193	47,957	HARNER, CAROL	118,710	COELHO, TONY	3,526	70,753 D	28.2%	69.8%	28.8%	71.2%
15	1986	131,775	35,793	HARNER, CAROL	93,600	COELHO, TONY	2,382	57,807 D	27.2%	71.0%	27.7%	72.3%
15	1984	167,406	54,730	HARNER, CAROL	109,590	COELHO, TONY	3,086	54,860 D	32.7%	65.5%	33.3%	66.7%
16	1988	225,827	48,375	MONTEITH, STANLEY	177,452	PANETTA, LEON E.		129,077 D	21.4%	78.6%	21.4%	78.6%
16	1986	163,498	31,386	DARRIGO, LOUIS	128,151	PANETTA, LEON E.	3,961	96,765 D	19.2%	78.4%	19.7%	80.3%
16	1984	216,687	60,065	RAMSEY, PATRICIA S.	153,377	PANETTA, LEON E.	3,245	93,312 D	27.7%	70.8%	28.1%	71.9%
17	1988	181,298	129,568	PASHAYAN, CHARLES	51,730	LAVERY, VINCENT		77,838 R	71.5%	28.5%	71.5%	28.5%
17	1986	147,469	88,787	PASHAYAN, CHARLES	58,682	HARTNETT, JOHN		30,105 R	60.2%	39.8%	60.2%	39.8%
17	1984	177,690	128,802	PASHAYAN, CHARLES	48,888	LAKRITZ, SIMON		79,914 R	72.5%	27.5%	72.5%	27.5%
18	1988	179,749	54,034	LINN, DAVID A.	125,715	LEHMAN, RICHARD		71,681 D	30.1%	69.9%	30.1%	69.9%
18	1986	142,387	40,907	CREVELT, DAVID C.	101,480	LEHMAN, RICHARD		60,573 D	28.7%	71.3%	28.7%	71.3%
18	1984	190,525	62,339	EWEN, DALE L.	128,186	LEHMAN, RICHARD		65,847 D	32.7%	67.3%	32.7%	67.3%
19	1988	230,924	116,026	LAGOMARSINO, ROBERT J.	112,033	HART, GARY K.	2,865	3,993 R	50.2%	48.5%	50.9%	49.1%
19	1986	170,538	122,578	LAGOMARSINO, ROBERT J.	45,619	NORRIS, WAYNE B.	2,341	76,959 R	71.9%	26.8%	72.9%	27.1%
19	1984	227,626	153,187	LAGOMARSINO, ROBERT J.	70,278	CAREY, JAMES C.	4,161	82,909 R	67.3%	30.9%	68.6%	31.4%
20	1988	229,006	162,779	THOMAS, WILLIAM M.	62,037	REID, LITA	4,190	100,742 R	71.1%	27.1%	72.4%	27.6%
20	1986	179,016	129,989	THOMAS, WILLIAM M.	49,027	MOQUIN, JULES H.		80,962 R	72.6%	27.4%	72.6%	27.4%
20	1984	214,039	151,732	THOMAS, WILLIAM M.	62,307	LESAGE, MIKE		89,425 R	70.9%	29.1%	70.9%	29.1%
21	1988	262,671	181,413	GALLEGLY, ELTON	75,739	STEVENS, DONALD E.	5,519	105,674 R	69.1%	28.8%	70.5%	29.5%
21	1986	193,101	132,100	GALLEGLY, ELTON	54,497	SALDANA, GILBERT R.	6,504	77,603 R	68.4%	28.2%	70.8%	29.2%
21	1984	239,968	173,504	FIEDLER, BOBBI	62,085	DAVIS, CHARLES	4,379	111,419 R	72.3%	25.9%	73.6%	26.4%
22	1988	236,811	164,699	MOORHEAD, CARLOS J.	61,555	SIMMONS, JOHN G.	10,557	103,144 R	69.5%	26.0%	72.8%	27.2%
22	1986	191,176	141,096	MOORHEAD, CARLOS J.	44,036	SIMMONS, JOHN G.	6,044	97,060 R	73.8%	23.0%	76.2%	23.8%
22	1984	217,176	184,981	MOORHEAD, CARLOS J.			32,195	184,981 R	85.2%		100.0%	
23	1988	232,879	77,184	SALOMON, JIM	147,858	BEILENSON, ANTHONY C.	7,837	70,674 D	33.1%	63.5%	34.3%	65.7%
23	1986	184,754	58,746	WOOLVERTON, GEORGE	121,468	BEILENSON, ANTHONY C.	4,540	62,722 D	31.8%	65.7%	32.6%	67.4%
23	1984	228,134	84,093	PARRISH, CLAUDE	140,461	BEILENSON, ANTHONY C.	3,580	56,368 D	36.9%	61.6%	37.4%	62.6%
24	1988	155,071	36,835	COWLES, JOHN N.	112,038	WAXMAN, HENRY A.	6,198	75,203 D	23.8%	72.2%	24.7%	75.3%
24	1986	118,173			103,914	WAXMAN, HENRY A.	14,259	103,914 D		87.9%		100.0%
24	1984	153,607	51,010	ZERG, JERRY	97,340	WAXMAN, HENRY A.	5,257	46,330 D	33.2%	63.4%	34.4%	65.6%
25	1988	99,876			85,378	ROYBAL, EDWARD R.	14,498	85,378 D		85.5%		100.0%
25	1986	82,413	17,558	HARDY, GREGORY L.	62,692	ROYBAL, EDWARD R.	2,163	45,134 D	21.3%	76.1%	21.9%	78.1%
25	1984	103,602	24,968	BLOXOM, ROY D.	74,261	ROYBAL, EDWARD R.	4,373	49,293 D	24.1%	71.7%	25.2%	74.8%
26	1988	180,448	53,518	BRODERSON, G. C.	126,930	BERMAN, HOWARD L.		73,412 D	29.7%	70.3%	29.7%	70.3%
26	1986	150,753	52,662	KERNS, ROBERT M.	98,091	BERMAN, HOWARD L.		45,429 D	34.9%	65.1%	34.9%	65.1%
26	1984	186,452	69,372	OJEDA, MIRIAM	117,080	BERMAN, HOWARD L.		47,708 D	37.2%	62.8%	37.2%	62.8%
27	1988	220,335	65,307	GALBRAITH, DENNIS	148,814	LEVINE, MEL	6,214	83,507 D	29.6%	67.5%	30.5%	69.5%
27	1986	173,320	59,410	SCRIBNER, ROBERT B.	110,403	LEVINE, MEL	3,507	50,993 D	34.3%	63.7%	35.0%	65.0%
27	1984	212,781	88,896	SCRIBNER, ROBERT B.	116,933	LEVINE, MEL	6,952	28,037 D	41.8%	55.0%	43.2%	56.8%
28	1988	144,337	28,645	ADAMS, GEORGE	109,801	DIXON, JULIAN C.	5,891	81,156 D	19.8%	76.1%	20.7%	79.3%
28	1986	121,330	25,858	ADAMS, GEORGE	92,635	DIXON, JULIAN C.	2,837	66,777 D	21.3%	76.3%	21.8%	78.2%
28	1984	149,517	33,511	JETT, BEATRICE M.	113,076	DIXON, JULIAN C.	2,930	79,565 D	22.4%	75.6%	22.9%	77.1%
29	1988	106,436	14,543	FRANCO, REUBEN D.	88,169	HAWKINS, AUGUSTUS	3,724	73,626 D	13.7%	82.8%	14.2%	85.8%
29	1986	92,415	13,432	VAN DE BROOKE, JOHN	78,132	HAWKINS, AUGUSTUS	851	64,700 D	14.5%	84.5%	14.7%	85.3%
29	1984	125,559	16,781	GOTO, ECHO Y.	108,777	HAWKINS, AUGUSTUS	1	91,996 D	13.4%	86.6%	13.4%	86.6%

CALIFORNIA

CONGRESS

		Total	Republican		Democratic		Other	Rep.-Dem.	Percentage Total Vote		Percentage Major Vote	
CD	Year	Vote	Vote	Candidate	Vote	Candidate	Vote	Plurality	Rep.	Dem.	Rep.	Dem.
30	1988	120,644	43,833	RAMIREZ, RALPH R.	72,253	MARTINEZ, MATTHEW G.	4,558	28,420 D	36.3%	59.9%	37.8%	62.2%
30	1986	94,985	33,705	ALMQUIST, JOHN W.	59,369	MARTINEZ, MATTHEW G.	1,911	25,664 D	35.5%	62.5%	36.2%	63.8%
30	1984	124,333	53,900	GOMEZ, RICHARD	64,378	MARTINEZ, MATTHEW G.	6,055	10,478 D	43.4%	51.8%	45.6%	54.4%
31	1988	141,027	36,017	MAY, ARNOLD C.	100,919	DYMALLY, MERVYN M.	4,091	64,902 D	25.5%	71.6%	26.3%	73.7%
31	1986	109,800	30,322	MCMURRAY, JACK	77,126	DYMALLY, MERVYN M.	2,352	46,804 D	27.6%	70.2%	28.2%	71.8%
31	1984	142,349	41,691	MINTURN, HENRY C.	100,658	DYMALLY, MERVYN M.		58,967 D	29.3%	70.7%	29.3%	70.7%
32	1988	171,349	50,710	KAHN, SANFORD W.	114,666	ANDERSON, GLENN M.	5,973	63,956 D	29.6%	66.9%	30.7%	69.3%
32	1986	132,541	39,003	ROBERTSON, JOYCE M.	90,739	ANDERSON, GLENN M.	2,799	51,736 D	29.4%	68.5%	30.1%	69.9%
32	1984	169,716	62,176	FIOLA, ROGER E.	102,961	ANDERSON, GLENN M.	4,579	40,785 D	36.6%	60.7%	37.7%	62.3%
33	1988	219,383	151,704	DREIER, DAVID	57,586	GENTRY, NELSON	10,093	94,118 R	69.2%	26.2%	72.5%	27.5%
33	1986	165,353	118,541	DREIER, DAVID	44,312	HEMPEL, MONTY	2,500	74,229 R	71.7%	26.8%	72.8%	27.2%
33	1984	208,619	147,363	DREIER, DAVID	54,147	MCDONALD, CLAIRE K.	7,109	93,216 R	70.6%	26.0%	73.1%	26.9%
34	1988	145,727	50,954	HOUSE, CHARLES M.	92,087	TORRES, ESTEBAN	2,686	41,133 D	35.0%	63.2%	35.6%	64.4%
34	1986	110,063	43,659	HOUSE, CHARLES M.	66,404	TORRES, ESTEBAN		22,745 D	39.7%	60.3%	39.7%	60.3%
34	1984	145,527	58,467	JACKSON, PAUL R.	87,060	TORRES, ESTEBAN		28,593 D	40.2%	59.8%	40.2%	59.8%
35	1988	257,268	181,203	LEWIS, JERRY	71,186	SWEENEY, PAUL	4,879	110,017 R	70.4%	27.7%	71.8%	28.2%
35	1986	165,557	127,235	LEWIS, JERRY	38,322	HALL, R. SARGE		88,913 R	76.9%	23.1%	76.9%	23.1%
35	1984	206,467	176,477	LEWIS, JERRY			29,990	176,477 R	85.5%		100.0%	
36	1988	191,648	81,413	STARK, JOHN P.	103,493	BROWN, GEORGE E.	6,742	22,080 D	42.5%	54.0%	44.0%	56.0%
36	1986	136,778	58,660	HENLEY, BOB	78,118	BROWN, GEORGE E.		19,458 D	42.9%	57.1%	42.9%	57.1%
36	1984	184,661	80,212	STARK, JOHN P.	104,438	BROWN, GEORGE E.	11	24,226 D	43.4%	56.6%	43.4%	56.6%
37	1988	271,242	174,284	MCCANDLESS, AL	89,666	PEARSON, JOHNNY	7,292	84,618 R	64.3%	33.1%	66.0%	34.0%
37	1986	192,224	122,416	MCCANDLESS, AL	69,808	SKINNER, DAVID E.		52,608 R	63.7%	36.3%	63.7%	36.3%
37	1984	235,863	149,955	MCCANDLESS, AL	85,908	SKINNER, DAVID E.		64,047 R	63.6%	36.4%	63.6%	36.4%
38	1988	147,369	87,690	DORNAN, ROBERT K.	52,399	YUDELSON, JERRY	7,280	35,291 R	59.5%	35.6%	62.6%	37.4%
38	1986	119,464	66,032	DORNAN, ROBERT K.	50,625	ROBINSON, RICHARD	2,807	15,407 R	55.3%	42.4%	56.6%	43.4%
38	1984	162,797	86,545	DORNAN, ROBERT K.	73,231	PATTERSON, JERRY M.	3,021	13,314 R	53.2%	45.0%	54.2%	45.8%
39	1988	229,359	169,360	DANNEMEYER, WILLIAM E.	52,162	MARQUIS, DON E.	7,837	117,198 R	73.8%	22.7%	76.5%	23.5%
39	1986	176,732	131,603	DANNEMEYER, WILLIAM E.	42,377	VEST, DAVID D.	2,752	89,226 R	74.5%	24.0%	75.6%	24.4%
39	1984	230,677	175,788	DANNEMEYER, WILLIAM E.	54,889	WARD, ROBERT E.		120,899 R	76.2%	23.8%	76.2%	23.8%
40	1988	270,376	181,269	COX, CHRISTOPHER	80,782	LENNEY, LIDA	8,325	100,487 R	67.0%	29.9%	69.2%	30.8%
40	1986	200,518	119,829	BADHAM, ROBERT E.	75,664	SUMNER, BRUCE W.	5,025	44,165 R	59.8%	37.7%	61.3%	38.7%
40	1984	254,974	164,257	BADHAM, ROBERT E.	86,748	BRADFORD, CAROL A.	3,969	77,509 R	64.4%	34.0%	65.4%	34.6%
41	1988	285,761	187,380	LOWERY, BILL	88,192	KRIPKE, DAN	10,189	99,188 R	65.6%	30.9%	68.0%	32.0%
41	1986	196,933	133,566	LOWERY, BILL	59,816	KRIPKE, DAN	3,551	73,750 R	67.8%	30.4%	69.1%	30.9%
41	1984	253,855	161,068	LOWERY, BILL	85,475	SIMMONS, BOB	7,312	75,593 R	63.4%	33.7%	65.3%	34.7%
42	1988	238,621	153,280	ROHRABACHER, DANA	78,778	KIMBROUGH, GUY C.	6,563	74,502 R	64.2%	33.0%	66.1%	33.9%
42	1986	192,711	140,364	LUNGREN, DANIEL E.	47,586	BLACKBURN, MICHAEL P.	4,761	92,778 R	72.8%	24.7%	74.7%	25.3%
42	1984	243,619	177,783	LUNGREN, DANIEL E.	60,025	BROPHY, MARY L.	5,811	117,758 R	73.0%	24.6%	74.8%	25.2%
43	1988	282,529	202,478	PACKARD, RON	72,499	GREENEBAUM, HOWARD	7,552	129,979 R	71.7%	25.7%	73.6%	26.4%
43	1986	187,789	137,341	PACKARD, RON	45,078	CHIRRA, JOSEPH	5,370	92,263 R	73.1%	24.0%	75.3%	24.7%
43	1984	223,517	165,643	PACKARD, RON	50,996	HUMPHREYS, LOIS E.	6,878	114,647 R	74.1%	22.8%	76.5%	23.5%
44	1988	152,089	55,511	BUTTERFIELD, ROB	90,796	BATES, JIM	5,782	35,285 D	36.5%	59.7%	37.9%	62.1%
44	1986	109,844	36,359	MITCHELL, BILL	70,557	BATES, JIM	2,928	34,198 D	33.1%	64.2%	34.0%	66.0%
44	1984	142,563	39,977	CAMPBELL, NEILL	99,378	BATES, JIM	3,208	59,401 D	28.0%	69.7%	28.7%	71.3%

CALIFORNIA

CONGRESS

CD	Year	Total Vote	Republican Vote	Republican Candidate	Democratic Vote	Democratic Candidate	Other Vote	Rep.-Dem. Plurality	Percentage Total Vote Rep.	Percentage Total Vote Dem.	Percentage Major Vote Rep.	Percentage Major Vote Dem.
45	1988	224,903	166,451	HUNTER, DUNCAN L.	54,012	LEPISCOPO, PETE	4,440	112,439 R	74.0%	24.0%	75.5%	24.5%
45	1986	154,675	118,900	HUNTER, DUNCAN L.	32,800	RYAN, HEWITT F.	2,975	86,100 R	76.9%	21.2%	78.4%	21.6%
45	1984	198,307	149,011	HUNTER, DUNCAN L.	45,325	GUTHRIE, DAVID W.	3,971	103,686 R	75.1%	22.9%	76.7%	23.3%

CALIFORNIA

1988 GENERAL ELECTION

President Other vote was 70,105 Libertarian (Paul); 31,181 Independent (Fulani); 27,818 American Independent (Griffin); 483 Duke (write-in); 234 McCarthy (write-in); 58 Lewin (write-in); 11 Holmes (write-in); 25 scattered write-in.

Senator Other vote was 166,600 Peace and Freedom (Munzo); 79,997 Libertarian (Dean); 66,288 American Independent (Short); 51 Britton (write-in).

Congress Other vote was Peace and Freedom (Fried) in CD 1; Libertarian (Pendery) in CD 2; 1,245 Smith (write-in) and 61 MacKenzie (write-in) in CD 4; 3,975 Peace and Freedom (Zuur) and 3,561 Libertarian (Grove) in CD 5; Peace and Freedom (Condit) in CD 8; Libertarian (Watson) in CD 10; 4,683 Libertarian (Wade), 2,906 Peace and Freedom (Martinez) and 1,893 American Independent (Kudrovzeff) in CD 11; Libertarian (Grey) in CD 12; Libertarian (Webster) in CD 13; Libertarian (Harris) in CD 15; Libertarian (Donaldson) in CD 19; Libertarian (Bersohn) in CD 20; Libertarian (Jay) in CD 21; 6,298 Peace and Freedom (Isaacson) and 4,259 Libertarian (Brown) in CD 22; 4,503 Libertarian (Vernon), 3,316 Peace and Freedom (Honigsfeld) and 18 Meagher (write-in) in CD 23; 3,571 Peace and Freedom (Green) and 2,627 Libertarian (Abrahams) in CD 24; 8,746 Peace and Freedom (Reyes) and 5,752 Libertarian (Thie) in CD 25; Libertarian (Fulco) in CD 27; 3,080 Libertarian (Johnson) and 2,811 Peace and Freedom (Honigsfeld) in CD 28; Libertarian (Gilmore) in CD 29; 2,694 American Independent (Myers) and 1,864 Libertarian (Goldsworthy) in CD 30; Peace and Freedom (Duren) in CD 31; 4,032 Peace and Freedom (Murdock) and 1,941 Libertarian (Denny) in CD 32; 6,601 Libertarian (Lightfood) and 3,492 Peace and Freedom (Noonan) in CD 33; Libertarian (Swinney) in CD 34; Libertarian (Shuman) in CD 35; 3,382 Libertarian (Valentine) and 3,360 American Independent (Anderson) in CD 36; 7,169 Libertarian (Flickinger), 65 Rainsbury (write-in) and 58 Smith (write-in) in CD 37; 3,733 Libertarian (McKay) and 3,547 Peace and Freedom (German) in CD 38; 7,470 Libertarian (Connelly) and 367 Foster (write-in) in CD 39; 4,539 Libertarian (Bloxham), 3,699 Peace and Freedom (Farsai) and 87 Kelly (write-in) in CD 40; 5,336 Libertarian (Rider) and 4,853 Peace and Freedom (Weber) in CD 41; Peace and Freedom (Rose) in CD 42; Libertarian (Muhe) in CD 43; Libertarian (Thompson) in CD 44; Libertarian (Willis) in CD 45.

LOS ANGELES COUNTY

President Other vote was 15,182 Libertarian (Paul); 10,194 Independent (Fulani); 7,061 American Independent (Griffin); 107 Duke (write-in); 37 McCarthy (write-in); 21 Lewin (write-in); 1 Holmes (write-in). The total for the other vote column includes these 166 write-in votes not available by Assembly District.

Senator Other vote was 45,427 Peace and Freedom (Munoz); 17,458 Libertarian (Dean); 13,371 American Independent (Short); 24 Britton (write-in). The total for the other vote column includes these 24 write-in votes not available by Assembly District.

1988 PRIMARIES

JUNE 7 REPUBLICAN

Senator Pete Wilson, unopposed.

Congress Unopposed in twenty-two CD's. No candidate in CD's 4, 10 and 25. In CD 4 Larry T. Smith received 1,348 write-in votes but did not qualify; in CD 10 Arthur B. Chesnut received 317 write-in votes but did not qualify. Contested as follows:

CD 1 34,178 Samuel Vanderbilt; 12,976 Ruben Covarrubias.
CD 3 30,795 Lowell Landowski; 25,559 Donald S. Perdue.
CD 5 14,804 Bruce M. O'Neill; 7,775 Tom Spinosa.
CD 6 26,766 William Steinmetz; 9,154 Franklin Ernst.
CD 8 15,440 John J. Cuddihy; 14,603 Eric Garris.
CD 12 41,867 Tom Campbell; 30,162 Ernest L. Konnyu.
CD 13 21,188 Luke Sommer; 19,909 Jim Eskes.

CALIFORNIA

CD 16 23,073 Stanley Monteith; 22,819 Louis Darrigo.
CD 21 57,568 Elton Gallegly; 9,762 Sang Korman; 2,863 David Desko.
CD 22 67,378 Carlos J. Moorhead; 10,314 David R. Headrick.
CD 24 9,573 John N. Cowles; 4,883 Dean DeGruccio; 4,827 Sol Annenberg.
CD 30 9,056 Ralph R. Ramirez; 7,505 Michael M. Radlovic; 3,809 Robert S. Kowell.
CD 32 14,863 Sanford W. Kahn; 14,616 Lionel Allen.
CD 36 16,442 John P. Stark; 8,176 Dorothy R. Davis; 5,755 R. M. Barela; 2,822 Robert M. Kerns; 2,353 Doug Graham.
CD 37 58,589 Al McCandless; 11,897 Bud Mathewson.
CD 39 64,862 William E. Dannemeyer; 11,207 John M. Gullixson.
CD 40 30,713 Christopher Cox; 29,326 Dave Baker; 17,647 Nathan Rosenberg; 6,290 William Yacobozzi; 4,184 John Kelly; 4,089 John Hylton; 2,103 Kathleen B. Latham; 1,523 Patricia G. Kishel; 1,046 Charles S. DeVore; 814 Larry F. Sternberg; 725 Dave Williams; 670 Peer A. Swan; 460 Peter Buffa; 288 Adam W. Kiernik.
CD 41 63,485 Bill Lowery; 8,085 Rick Singer.
CD 42 27,507 Dana Rohrabacher; 17,128 Harriett M. Wieder; 15,911 Steve Horn; 6,581 Andrew J. Littlefair; 4,368 Robert Welbourn; 2,501 Tom Bauer; 2,236 Don Davis; 2,188 Jeffrey R. Burns.
CD 44 13,862 Rob Butterfield; 10,282 Luis Acle.

JUNE 7 DEMOCRATIC

Senator 2,367,067 Leo McCarthy; 220,331 John H. Abbott; 163,882 Robert J. Banuelos; 146,307 Charles Greene.

Congress Unopposed in twenty-nine CD's. Contested as follows:

CD 1 64,653 Douglas H. Bosco; 13,598 Lionel Gambill; 11,703 Neil B. Sinclair; 5,325 Darryl Cherney.
CD 10 48,276 Don Edwards; 9,863 Anselmo A. Chavez.
CD 12 30,963 Anna G. Eshoo; 26,099 Jim Garrison; 6,354 Sylvia Simmons; 3,970 Gary Bond; 3,901 Ernest R. Macias.
CD 15 50,248 Tony Coelho; 5,442 Gerry Mansell.
CD 16 76,452 Leon E. Panetta; 4,027 Arthur V. Dunn.
CD 23 67,802 Anthony C. Beilenson; 12,755 Val Marmillion.
CD 27 66,452 Mel Levine; 8,679 Ralph Cole.
CD 29 60,656 Augustus Hawkins; 6,504 Mervin Evans.
CD 30 33,615 Matthew G. Martinez; 12,088 Lily Chen.
CD 31 58,806 Mervyn M. Dymally; 10,037 Collin K. O'Brien.
CD 33 24,682 Nelson Gentry; 19,481 John Kraft.
CD 35 37,407 Paul Sweeney; 14,672 Barry Norton; 1 R. Sarge Hall (write-in).
CD 36 48,148 George E. Brown; 10,450 James D. Sparks.
CD 37 33,797 Johnny Pearson; 22,351 Paul Boyajian.
CD 40 26,769 Lida Lenney; 19,060 George H. Margolis.
CD 42 23,472 Guy C. Kimbrough; 17,735 Ada Unruh; 7,823 Dan Farrell.

JUNE 7 AMERICAN INDEPENDENT

Senator Merton D. Short, unopposed.

Congress Unopposed in all CD's in which candidates were entered.

JUNE 7 LIBERTARIAN

Senator Jack Dean, unopposed.

Congress Unopposed in all CD's in which candidates were entered.

CALIFORNIA

JUNE 7 PEACE AND FREEDOM

Senator 3,701 M. Elizabeth Munoz; 2,623 Gloria Garcia.

Congress Unopposed in all CD's in which candidates were entered.

COLORADO

GOVERNOR

Roy Romer (D). Elected 1986 to a four-year term.

SENATORS

William L. Armstrong (R). Re-elected 1984 to a six-year term. Previously elected 1978.

Timothy E. Wirth (D). Elected 1986 to a six-year term.

REPRESENTATIVES

1. Patricia Schroeder (D)
2. David Skaggs (D)
3. Ben N. Campbell (D)
4. Hank Brown (R)
5. Joel Hefley (R)
6. Daniel L. Schaefer (R)

POSTWAR VOTE FOR PRESIDENT

Year	Total Vote	Republican Vote	Republican Candidate	Democratic Vote	Democratic Candidate	Other Vote	Plurality	Percentage Total Vote Rep.	Total Vote Dem.	Major Vote Rep.	Major Vote Dem.
1988	1,372,394	728,177	Bush, George	621,453	Dukakis, Michael S.	22,764	106,724 R	53.1%	45.3%	54.0%	46.0%
1984	1,295,380	821,817	Reagan, Ronald	454,975	Mondale, Walter F.	18,588	366,842 R	63.4%	35.1%	64.4%	35.6%
1980	1,184,415	652,264	Reagan, Ronald	367,973	Carter, Jimmy	164,178	284,291 R	55.1%	31.1%	63.9%	36.1%
1976	1,081,554	584,367	Ford, Gerald R.	460,353	Carter, Jimmy	36,834	124,014 R	54.0%	42.6%	55.9%	44.1%
1972	953,884	597,189	Nixon, Richard M.	329,980	McGovern, George S.	26,715	267,209 R	62.6%	34.6%	64.4%	35.6%
1968	811,199	409,345	Nixon, Richard M.	335,174	Humphrey, Hubert H.	66,680	74,171 R	50.5%	41.3%	55.0%	45.0%
1964	776,986	296,767	Goldwater, Barry M.	476,024	Johnson, Lyndon B.	4,195	179,257 D	38.2%	61.3%	38.4%	61.6%
1960	736,236	402,242	Nixon, Richard M.	330,629	Kennedy, John F.	3,365	71,613 R	54.6%	44.9%	54.9%	45.1%
1956	657,074	394,479	Eisenhower, Dwight D.	257,997	Stevenson, Adlai E.	4,598	136,482 R	60.0%	39.3%	60.5%	39.5%
1952	630,103	379,782	Eisenhower, Dwight D.	245,504	Stevenson, Adlai E.	4,817	134,278 R	60.3%	39.0%	60.7%	39.3%
1948	515,237	239,714	Dewey, Thomas E.	267,288	Truman, Harry S.	8,235	27,574 D	46.5%	51.9%	47.3%	52.7%

POSTWAR VOTE FOR GOVERNOR

Year	Total Vote	Republican Vote	Republican Candidate	Democratic Vote	Democratic Candidate	Other Vote	Rep.-Dem. Plurality	Percentage Total Vote Rep.	Total Vote Dem.	Major Vote Rep.	Major Vote Dem.
1986	1,058,928	434,420	Strickland, Ted	616,325	Romer, Roy	8,183	181,905 D	41.0%	58.2%	41.3%	58.7%
1982	956,021	302,740	Fuhr, John D.	627,960	Lamm, Richard D.	25,321	325,220 D	31.7%	65.7%	32.5%	67.5%
1978	823,807	317,292	Strickland, Ted	483,985	Lamm, Richard D.	22,530	166,693 D	38.5%	58.7%	39.6%	60.4%
1974	828,968	378,698	Vanderhoof, John D.	441,408	Lamm, Richard D.	8,862	62,710 D	45.7%	53.2%	46.2%	53.8%
1970	668,496	350,690	Love, John A.	302,432	Hogan, Mark	15,374	48,258 R	52.5%	45.2%	53.7%	46.3%
1966	660,063	356,730	Love, John A.	287,132	Knous, Robert L.	16,201	69,598 R	54.0%	43.5%	55.4%	44.6%
1962	616,481	349,342	Love, John A.	262,890	McNichols, Stephen	4,249	86,452 R	56.7%	42.6%	57.1%	42.9%
1958 **	549,808	228,643	Burch, Palmer L.	321,165	McNichols, Stephen		92,522 D	41.6%	58.4%	41.6%	58.4%
1956	645,233	313,950	Brotzman, Donald G.	331,283	McNichols, Stephen		17,333 D	48.7%	51.3%	48.7%	51.3%
1954	489,540	227,335	Brotzman, Donald G.	262,205	Johnson, Ed C.		34,870 D	46.4%	53.6%	46.4%	53.6%
1952	613,034	349,924	Thornton, Dan	260,044	Metzger, John W.	3,066	89,880 R	57.1%	42.4%	57.4%	42.6%
1950	450,994	236,472	Thornton, Dan	212,976	Johnson, Walter	1,546	23,496 R	52.4%	47.2%	52.6%	47.4%
1948	501,680	168,928	Hamil, David A.	332,752	Knous, William Lee		163,824 D	33.7%	66.3%	33.7%	66.3%
1946	335,087	160,483	Lavington, Leon E.	174,604	Knous, William Lee		14,121 D	47.9%	52.1%	47.9%	52.1%

The term of office of Colorado's Governor was increased from two to four years effective with the 1958 election.

COLORADO

POSTWAR VOTE FOR SENATOR

		Republican		Democratic				Percentage			
	Total					Other	Rep.-Dem.	Total Vote		Major Vote	
Year	Vote	Vote	Candidate	Vote	Candidate	Vote	Plurality	Rep.	Dem.	Rep.	Dem.
1986	1,060,765	512,994	Kramer, Ken	529,449	Wirth, Timothy E.	18,322	16,455 D	48.4%	49.9%	49.2%	50.8%
1984	1,297,809	833,821	Armstrong, William L.	449,327	Dick, Nancy	14,661	384,494 R	64.2%	34.6%	65.0%	35.0%
1980	1,173,646	571,295	Buchanan, Mary E.	590,501	Hart, Gary W.	11,850	19,206 D	48.7%	50.3%	49.2%	50.8%
1978	819,150	480,596	Armstrong, William L.	330,247	Haskell, Floyd K.	8,307	150,349 R	58.7%	40.3%	59.3%	40.7%
1974	824,166	325,508	Dominick, Peter H.	471,691	Hart, Gary W.	26,967	146,183 D	39.5%	57.2%	40.8%	59.2%
1972	926,093	447,957	Allott, Gordon	457,545	Haskell, Floyd K.	20,591	9,588 D	48.4%	49.4%	49.5%	50.5%
1968	785,536	459,952	Dominick, Peter H.	325,584	McNichols, Stephen		134,368 R	58.6%	41.4%	58.6%	41.4%
1966	634,898	368,307	Allott, Gordon	266,259	Romer, Roy	332	102,048 R	58.0%	41.9%	58.0%	42.0%
1962	613,444	328,655	Dominick, Peter H.	279,586	Carroll, John A.	5,203	49,069 R	53.6%	45.6%	54.0%	46.0%
1960	727,633	389,428	Allott, Gordon	334,854	Knous, Robert L.	3,351	54,574 R	53.5%	46.0%	53.8%	46.2%
1956	636,974	317,102	Thornton, Dan	319,872	Carroll, John A.		2,770 D	49.8%	50.2%	49.8%	50.2%
1954	484,188	248,502	Allott, Gordon	235,686	Carroll, John A.		12,816 R	51.3%	48.7%	51.3%	48.7%
1950	450,176	239,734	Millikin, Eugene D.	210,442	Carroll, John A.		29,292 R	53.3%	46.7%	53.3%	46.7%
1948	510,121	165,069	Nicholson, W. F.	340,719	Johnson, Ed C.	4,333	175,650 D	32.4%	66.8%	32.6%	67.4%

COLORADO

Districts Established June 3, 1982

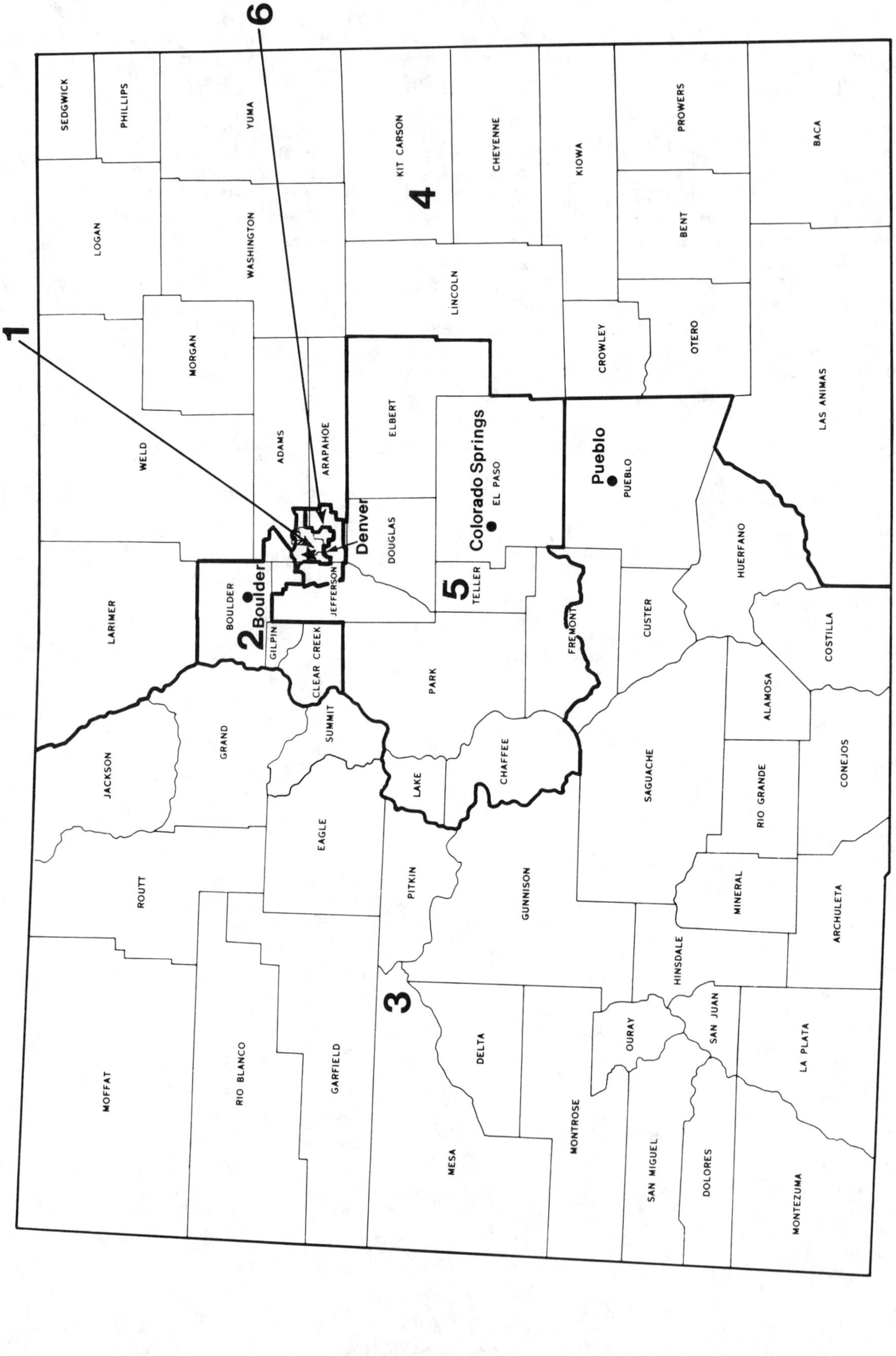

COLORADO

PRESIDENT 1988

1980 Census Population	County	Total Vote	Republican	Democratic	Other	Rep.-Dem. Plurality	Percentage Total Vote Rep.	Percentage Total Vote Dem.	Percentage Major Vote Rep.	Percentage Major Vote Dem.
245,944	ADAMS	94,094	43,163	49,464	1,467	6,301 D	45.9%	52.6%	46.6%	53.4%
11,799	ALAMOSA	4,780	2,567	2,146	67	421 R	53.7%	44.9%	54.5%	45.5%
293,621	ARAPAHOE	159,245	95,926	61,113	2,206	34,813 R	60.2%	38.4%	61.1%	38.9%
3,664	ARCHULETA	2,262	1,440	795	27	645 R	63.7%	35.1%	64.4%	35.6%
5,419	BACA	2,556	1,670	851	35	819 R	65.3%	33.3%	66.2%	33.8%
5,945	BENT	2,167	1,032	1,088	47	56 D	47.6%	50.2%	48.7%	51.3%
189,625	BOULDER	107,223	48,174	57,265	1,784	9,091 D	44.9%	53.4%	45.7%	54.3%
13,227	CHAFFEE	5,714	3,080	2,548	86	532 R	53.9%	44.6%	54.7%	45.3%
2,153	CHEYENNE	1,186	760	399	27	361 R	64.1%	33.6%	65.6%	34.4%
7,308	CLEAR CREEK	3,632	1,820	1,698	114	122 R	50.1%	46.8%	51.7%	48.3%
7,794	CONEJOS	3,447	1,445	1,976	26	531 D	41.9%	57.3%	42.2%	57.8%
3,071	COSTILLA	1,581	454	1,120	7	666 D	28.7%	70.8%	28.8%	71.2%
2,988	CROWLEY	1,500	862	630	8	232 R	57.5%	42.0%	57.8%	42.2%
1,528	CUSTER	1,084	753	310	21	443 R	69.5%	28.6%	70.8%	29.2%
21,225	DELTA	9,144	5,449	3,521	174	1,928 R	59.6%	38.5%	60.7%	39.3%
492,365	DENVER	209,430	77,753	127,173	4,504	49,420 D	37.1%	60.7%	37.9%	62.1%
1,658	DOLORES	732	488	230	14	258 R	66.7%	31.4%	68.0%	32.0%
25,153	DOUGLAS	24,350	17,035	6,931	384	10,104 R	70.0%	28.5%	71.1%	28.9%
13,320	EAGLE	7,809	4,366	3,314	129	1,052 R	55.9%	42.4%	56.8%	43.2%
6,850	ELBERT	4,448	2,805	1,566	77	1,239 R	63.1%	35.2%	64.2%	35.8%
309,424	EL PASO	138,466	96,965	39,995	1,506	56,970 R	70.0%	28.9%	70.8%	29.2%
28,676	FREMONT	13,088	7,623	5,278	187	2,345 R	58.2%	40.3%	59.1%	40.9%
22,514	GARFIELD	11,114	6,358	4,620	136	1,738 R	57.2%	41.6%	57.9%	42.1%
2,441	GILPIN	1,590	728	804	58	76 D	45.8%	50.6%	47.5%	52.5%
7,475	GRAND	3,838	2,306	1,451	81	855 R	60.1%	37.8%	61.4%	38.6%
10,689	GUNNISON	4,523	2,520	1,897	106	623 R	55.7%	41.9%	57.1%	42.9%
408	HINSDALE	407	295	111	1	184 R	72.5%	27.3%	72.7%	27.3%
6,440	HUERFANO	2,971	1,079	1,876	16	797 D	36.3%	63.1%	36.5%	63.5%
1,863	JACKSON	891	584	294	13	290 R	65.5%	33.0%	66.5%	33.5%
371,753	JEFFERSON	196,511	110,820	81,824	3,867	28,996 R	56.4%	41.6%	57.5%	42.5%
1,936	KIOWA	1,053	645	398	10	247 R	61.3%	37.8%	61.8%	38.2%
7,599	KIT CARSON	3,512	2,262	1,196	54	1,066 R	64.4%	34.1%	65.4%	34.6%
8,830	LAKE	2,543	969	1,516	58	547 D	38.1%	59.6%	39.0%	61.0%
27,424	LA PLATA	13,362	7,714	5,443	205	2,271 R	57.7%	40.7%	58.6%	41.4%
149,184	LARIMER	83,066	45,967	35,703	1,396	10,264 R	55.3%	43.0%	56.3%	43.7%
14,897	LAS ANIMAS	6,331	2,162	4,075	94	1,913 D	34.1%	64.4%	34.7%	65.3%
4,663	LINCOLN	2,249	1,356	874	19	482 R	60.3%	38.9%	60.8%	39.2%
19,800	LOGAN	7,975	4,485	3,382	108	1,103 R	56.2%	42.4%	57.0%	43.0%
81,530	MESA	37,155	22,150	14,372	633	7,778 R	59.6%	38.7%	60.6%	39.4%
804	MINERAL	394	217	174	3	43 R	55.1%	44.2%	55.5%	44.5%
13,133	MOFFAT	4,519	2,757	1,634	128	1,123 R	61.0%	36.2%	62.8%	37.2%
16,510	MONTEZUMA	6,551	4,208	2,233	110	1,975 R	64.2%	34.1%	65.3%	34.7%
24,352	MONTROSE	9,993	6,012	3,748	233	2,264 R	60.2%	37.5%	61.6%	38.4%
22,513	MORGAN	8,680	4,795	3,728	157	1,067 R	55.2%	42.9%	56.3%	43.7%
22,567	OTERO	8,299	4,265	3,910	124	355 R	51.4%	47.1%	52.2%	47.8%
1,925	OURAY	1,274	814	439	21	375 R	63.9%	34.5%	65.0%	35.0%
5,333	PARK	3,357	1,909	1,343	105	566 R	56.9%	40.0%	58.7%	41.3%
4,542	PHILLIPS	2,278	1,317	923	38	394 R	57.8%	40.5%	58.8%	41.2%
10,338	PITKIN	6,326	2,801	3,420	105	619 D	44.3%	54.1%	45.0%	55.0%
13,070	PROWERS	5,286	2,978	2,207	101	771 R	56.3%	41.8%	57.4%	42.6%
125,972	PUEBLO	53,318	20,119	32,788	411	12,669 D	37.7%	61.5%	38.0%	62.0%
6,255	RIO BLANCO	2,662	1,821	803	38	1,018 R	68.4%	30.2%	69.4%	30.6%
10,511	RIO GRANDE	4,235	2,626	1,545	64	1,081 R	62.0%	36.5%	63.0%	37.0%
13,404	ROUTT	6,319	3,264	2,922	133	342 R	51.7%	46.2%	52.8%	47.2%
3,935	SAGUACHE	2,013	945	1,033	35	88 D	46.9%	51.3%	47.8%	52.2%
833	SAN JUAN	417	210	192	15	18 R	50.4%	46.0%	52.2%	47.8%
3,192	SAN MIGUEL	1,839	798	961	80	163 D	43.4%	52.3%	45.4%	54.6%
3,266	SEDGWICK	1,545	921	611	13	310 R	59.6%	39.5%	60.1%	39.9%
8,848	SUMMIT	5,624	2,893	2,595	136	298 R	51.4%	46.1%	52.7%	47.3%
8,034	TELLER	5,500	3,760	1,656	84	2,104 R	68.4%	30.1%	69.4%	30.6%

COLORADO

PRESIDENT 1988

1980 Census Population	County	Total Vote	Republican	Democratic	Other	Rep.-Dem. Plurality	Percentage Total Vote Rep.	Percentage Total Vote Dem.	Percentage Major Vote Rep.	Percentage Major Vote Dem.
5,304	WASHINGTON	2,715	1,707	958	50	749 R	62.9%	35.3%	64.1%	35.9%
123,438	WELD	47,807	26,497	20,548	762	5,949 R	55.4%	43.0%	56.3%	43.7%
9,682	YUMA	4,414	2,513	1,835	66	678 R	56.9%	41.6%	57.8%	42.2%
2,889,964	TOTAL	1,372,394	728,177	621,453	22,764	106,724 R	53.1%	45.3%	54.0%	46.0%

COLORADO

CONGRESS

CD	Year	Total Vote	Republican Vote	Republican Candidate	Democratic Vote	Democratic Candidate	Other Vote	Rep.-Dem. Plurality	Percentage Total Vote Rep.	Percentage Total Vote Dem.	Percentage Major Vote Rep.	Percentage Major Vote Dem.
1	1988	191,509	57,587	WOOD, JOY	133,922	SCHROEDER, PATRICIA		76,335 D	30.1%	69.9%	30.1%	69.9%
1	1986	155,208	49,095	WOOD, JOY	106,113	SCHROEDER, PATRICIA		57,018 D	31.6%	68.4%	31.6%	68.4%
1	1984	203,873	73,993	DOWNS, MARY	126,348	SCHROEDER, PATRICIA	3,532	52,355 D	36.3%	62.0%	36.9%	63.1%
1	1982	157,597	59,009	DECKER, ARCH	94,969	SCHROEDER, PATRICIA	3,619	35,960 D	37.4%	60.3%	38.3%	61.7%
2	1988	235,015	87,578	BATH, DAVID	147,437	SKAGGS, DAVID		59,859 D	37.3%	62.7%	37.3%	62.7%
2	1986	177,255	86,032	NORTON, MICHAEL J.	91,223	SKAGGS, DAVID		5,191 D	48.5%	51.5%	48.5%	51.5%
2	1984	222,859	101,488	NORTON, MICHAEL J.	118,580	WIRTH, TIMOTHY E.	2,791	17,092 D	45.5%	53.2%	46.1%	53.9%
2	1982	163,654	59,590	BUECHNER, JOHN C.	101,202	WIRTH, TIMOTHY E.	2,862	41,612 D	36.4%	61.8%	37.1%	62.9%
3	1988	216,909	47,625	ZARTMAN, JIM	169,284	CAMPBELL, BEN N.		121,659 D	22.0%	78.0%	22.0%	78.0%
3	1986	183,861	88,508	STRANG, MICHAEL L.	95,353	CAMPBELL, BEN N.		6,845 D	48.1%	51.9%	48.1%	51.9%
3	1984	214,970	122,669	STRANG, MICHAEL L.	90,063	MITCHELL, W.	2,238	32,606 R	57.1%	41.9%	57.7%	42.3%
3	1982	172,889	77,410	WIENS, TOM	92,384	KOGOVSEK, RAY	3,095	14,974 D	44.8%	53.4%	45.6%	54.4%
4	1988	213,754	156,202	BROWN, HANK	57,552	VIGIL, CHARLES S.		98,650 R	73.1%	26.9%	73.1%	26.9%
4	1986	167,761	117,089	BROWN, HANK	50,672	SPRAGUE, DAVID		66,417 R	69.8%	30.2%	69.8%	30.2%
4	1984	205,930	146,469	BROWN, HANK	56,462	BATES, MARY F.	2,999	90,007 R	71.1%	27.4%	72.2%	27.8%
4	1982	151,300	105,550	BROWN, HANK	45,750	BISHOPP, CHARLES L.		59,800 R	69.8%	30.2%	69.8%	30.2%
5	1988	241,728	181,612	HEFLEY, JOEL	60,116	MITCHELL, JOHN J.		121,496 R	75.1%	24.9%	75.1%	24.9%
5	1986	173,641	121,153	HEFLEY, JOEL	52,488	STORY, BILL		68,665 R	69.8%	30.2%	69.8%	30.2%
5	1984	208,242	163,654	KRAMER, KEN	44,588	GEFFEN, WILLIAM		119,066 R	78.6%	21.4%	78.6%	21.4%
5	1982	141,871	84,479	KRAMER, KEN	57,392	CRONIN, TOM		27,087 R	59.5%	40.5%	59.5%	40.5%
6	1988	216,556	136,487	SCHAEFER, DANIEL L.	77,158	EZZARD, MARTHA M.	2,911	59,329 R	63.0%	35.6%	63.9%	36.1%
6	1986	160,531	104,359	SCHAEFER, DANIEL L.	53,834	NORRIS, CHUCK	2,338	50,525 R	65.0%	33.5%	66.0%	34.0%
6	1984	191,760	171,427	SCHAEFER, DANIEL L.			20,333	171,427 R	89.4%		100.0%	
6	1982	159,112	98,909	SWIGERT, JACK	56,598	HOGAN, STEVE	3,605	42,311 R	62.2%	35.6%	63.6%	36.4%

COLORADO

1988 GENERAL ELECTION

President Other vote was 15,482 Libertarian (Paul); 4,604 Prohibition (Dodge); 2,539 New Alliance (Fulani); 139 Duke (write-in).

Congress Other vote was Concerns of People (Heckman) in CD 6.

1988 PRIMARIES

AUGUST 9 REPUBLICAN

Congress Unopposed in four CD's. Contested as follows:

CD 2 8,001 David Bath; 6,956 Mary E. Buchanan.
CD 3 10,979 Jim Zartman; 9,470 Ken Neesham.

AUGUST 9 DEMOCRATIC

Congress Unopposed in all six CD's.

CONNECTICUT

GOVERNOR

William A. O'Neill (D). Re-elected 1986 to a four-year term. Previously elected 1982. Elected Lieutenant-Governor in 1978 and became Governor in December 1980 on the resignation of Governor Ella T. Grasso.

SENATORS

Christopher J. Dodd (D). Re-elected 1986 to a six-year term. Previously elected 1980.

Joseph I. Lieberman (D). Elected 1988 to a six-year term.

REPRESENTATIVES

1. Barbara B. Kennelly (D)
2. Samuel Gejdenson (D)
3. Bruce A. Morrison (D)
4. Christopher Shays (R)
5. John G. Rowland (R)
6. Nancy L. Johnson (R)

POSTWAR VOTE FOR PRESIDENT

		Republican		Democratic				Percentage			
	Total					Other		Total Vote		Major Vote	
Year	Vote	Vote	Candidate	Vote	Candidate	Vote	Plurality	Rep.	Dem.	Rep.	Dem.
1988	1,443,394	750,241	Bush, George	676,584	Dukakis, Michael S.	16,569	73,657 R	52.0%	46.9%	52.6%	47.4%
1984	1,466,900	890,877	Reagan, Ronald	569,597	Mondale, Walter F.	6,426	321,280 R	60.7%	38.8%	61.0%	39.0%
1980	1,406,285	677,210	Reagan, Ronald	541,732	Carter, Jimmy	187,343	135,478 R	48.2%	38.5%	55.6%	44.4%
1976	1,381,526	719,261	Ford, Gerald R.	647,895	Carter, Jimmy	14,370	71,366 R	52.1%	46.9%	52.6%	47.4%
1972	1,384,277	810,763	Nixon, Richard M.	555,498	McGovern, George S.	18,016	255,265 R	58.6%	40.1%	59.3%	40.7%
1968	1,256,232	556,721	Nixon, Richard M.	621,561	Humphrey, Hubert H.	77,950	64,840 D	44.3%	49.5%	47.2%	52.8%
1964	1,218,578	390,996	Goldwater, Barry M.	826,269	Johnson, Lyndon B.	1,313	435,273 D	32.1%	67.8%	32.1%	67.9%
1960	1,222,883	565,813	Nixon, Richard M.	657,055	Kennedy, John F.	15	91,242 D	46.3%	53.7%	46.3%	53.7%
1956	1,117,121	711,837	Eisenhower, Dwight D.	405,079	Stevenson, Adlai E.	205	306,758 R	63.7%	36.3%	63.7%	36.3%
1952	1,096,911	611,012	Eisenhower, Dwight D.	481,649	Stevenson, Adlai E.	4,250	129,363 R	55.7%	43.9%	55.9%	44.1%
1948	883,518	437,754	Dewey, Thomas E.	423,297	Truman, Harry S.	22,467	14,457 R	49.5%	47.9%	50.8%	49.2%

POSTWAR VOTE FOR GOVERNOR

		Republican		Democratic				Percentage			
	Total					Other	Rep.-Dem.	Total Vote		Major Vote	
Year	Vote	Vote	Candidate	Vote	Candidate	Vote	Plurality	Rep.	Dem.	Rep.	Dem.
1986	993,692	408,489	Belaga, Julie D.	575,638	O'Neill, William A.	9,565	167,149 D	41.1%	57.9%	41.5%	58.5%
1982	1,084,156	497,773	Rome, Lewis B.	578,264	O'Neill, William A.	8,119	80,491 D	45.9%	53.3%	46.3%	53.7%
1978	1,036,608	422,316	Sarasin, Ronald A.	613,109	Grasso, Ella T.	1,183	190,793 D	40.7%	59.1%	40.8%	59.2%
1974	1,102,773	440,169	Steele, Robert H.	643,490	Grasso, Ella T.	19,114	203,321 D	39.9%	58.4%	40.6%	59.4%
1970	1,082,797	582,160	Meskill, Thomas J.	500,561	Daddario, Emilio	76	81,599 R	53.8%	46.2%	53.8%	46.2%
1966	1,008,557	446,536	Gengras, E. Clayton	561,599	Dempsey, John N.	422	115,063 D	44.3%	55.7%	44.3%	55.7%
1962	1,031,902	482,852	Alsop, John	549,027	Dempsey, John N.	23	66,175 D	46.8%	53.2%	46.8%	53.2%
1958	974,509	360,644	Zeller, Fred R.	607,012	Ribicoff, Abraham A.	6,853	246,368 D	37.0%	62.3%	37.3%	62.7%
1954	936,753	460,528	Lodge, John D.	463,643	Ribicoff, Abraham A.	12,582	3,115 D	49.2%	49.5%	49.8%	50.2%
1950 **	878,735	436,418	Lodge, John D.	419,404	Bowles, Chester	22,913	17,014 R	49.7%	47.7%	51.0%	49.0%
1948	875,170	429,071	Shannon, James C.	431,296	Bowles, Chester	14,803	2,225 D	49.0%	49.3%	49.9%	50.1%
1946	683,831	371,852	McConaughy, J. L.	276,335	Snow, Wilbert	35,644	95,517 R	54.4%	40.4%	57.4%	42.6%

The term of office for Connecticut's Governor was increased from two to four years effective with the 1950 election.

CONNECTICUT

POSTWAR VOTE FOR SENATOR

Year	Total Vote	Republican Vote	Republican Candidate	Democratic Vote	Democratic Candidate	Other Vote	Rep.-Dem. Plurality	Percentage Total Vote Rep.	Percentage Total Vote Dem.	Percentage Major Vote Rep.	Percentage Major Vote Dem.
1988	1,383,526	678,454	Weicker, Lowell P.	688,499	Lieberman, Joseph I.	16,573	10,045 D	49.0%	49.8%	49.6%	50.4%
1986	976,933	340,438	Eddy, Roger W.	632,695	Dodd, Christopher J.	3,800	292,257 D	34.8%	64.8%	35.0%	65.0%
1982	1,083,613	545,987	Weicker, Lowell P.	499,146	Moffett, Anthony T.	38,480	46,841 R	50.4%	46.1%	52.2%	47.8%
1980	1,356,075	581,884	Buckley, James L.	763,969	Dodd, Christopher J.	10,222	182,085 D	42.9%	56.3%	43.2%	56.8%
1976	1,361,666	785,683	Weicker, Lowell P.	561,018	Schaffer, Gloria	14,965	224,665 R	57.7%	41.2%	58.3%	41.7%
1974	1,084,918	372,055	Brannen, James H.	690,820	Ribicoff, Abraham A.	22,043	318,765 D	34.3%	63.7%	35.0%	65.0%
1970	1,089,353	454,721	Weicker, Lowell P.	368,111	Duffey, Joseph D.	266,521	86,610 R	41.7%	33.8%	55.3%	44.7%
1968	1,206,537	551,455	May, Edwin H.	655,043	Ribicoff, Abraham A.	39	103,588 D	45.7%	54.3%	45.7%	54.3%
1964	1,208,163	426,939	Lodge, John D.	781,008	Dodd, Thomas J.	216	354,069 D	35.3%	64.6%	35.3%	64.7%
1962	1,029,301	501,694	Seely-Brown, Horace	527,522	Ribicoff, Abraham A.	85	25,828 D	48.7%	51.3%	48.7%	51.3%
1958	965,463	410,622	Purtell, William A.	554,841	Dodd, Thomas J.		144,219 D	42.5%	57.5%	42.5%	57.5%
1956	1,113,819	610,829	Bush, Prescott	479,460	Dodd, Thomas J.	23,530	131,369 R	54.8%	43.0%	56.0%	44.0%
1952	1,093,467	573,854	Purtell, William A.	485,066	Benton, William	34,547	88,788 R	52.5%	44.4%	54.2%	45.8%
1952 S	1,093,268	559,465	Bush, Prescott	530,505	Ribicoff, Abraham A.	3,298	28,960 R	51.2%	48.5%	51.3%	48.7%
1950	877,827	409,053	Talbot, Joseph E.	453,646	McMahon, Brien	15,128	44,593 D	46.6%	51.7%	47.4%	52.6%
1950 S	877,135	430,311	Bush, Prescott	431,413	Benton, William	15,411	1,102 D	49.1%	49.2%	49.9%	50.1%
1946	682,921	381,328	Baldwin, Raymond	276,424	Tone, Joseph M.	25,169	104,904 R	55.8%	40.5%	58.0%	42.0%

One each of the 1952 and 1950 elections was for a short term to fill a vacancy.

CONNECTICUT

Districts Established October 29, 1981

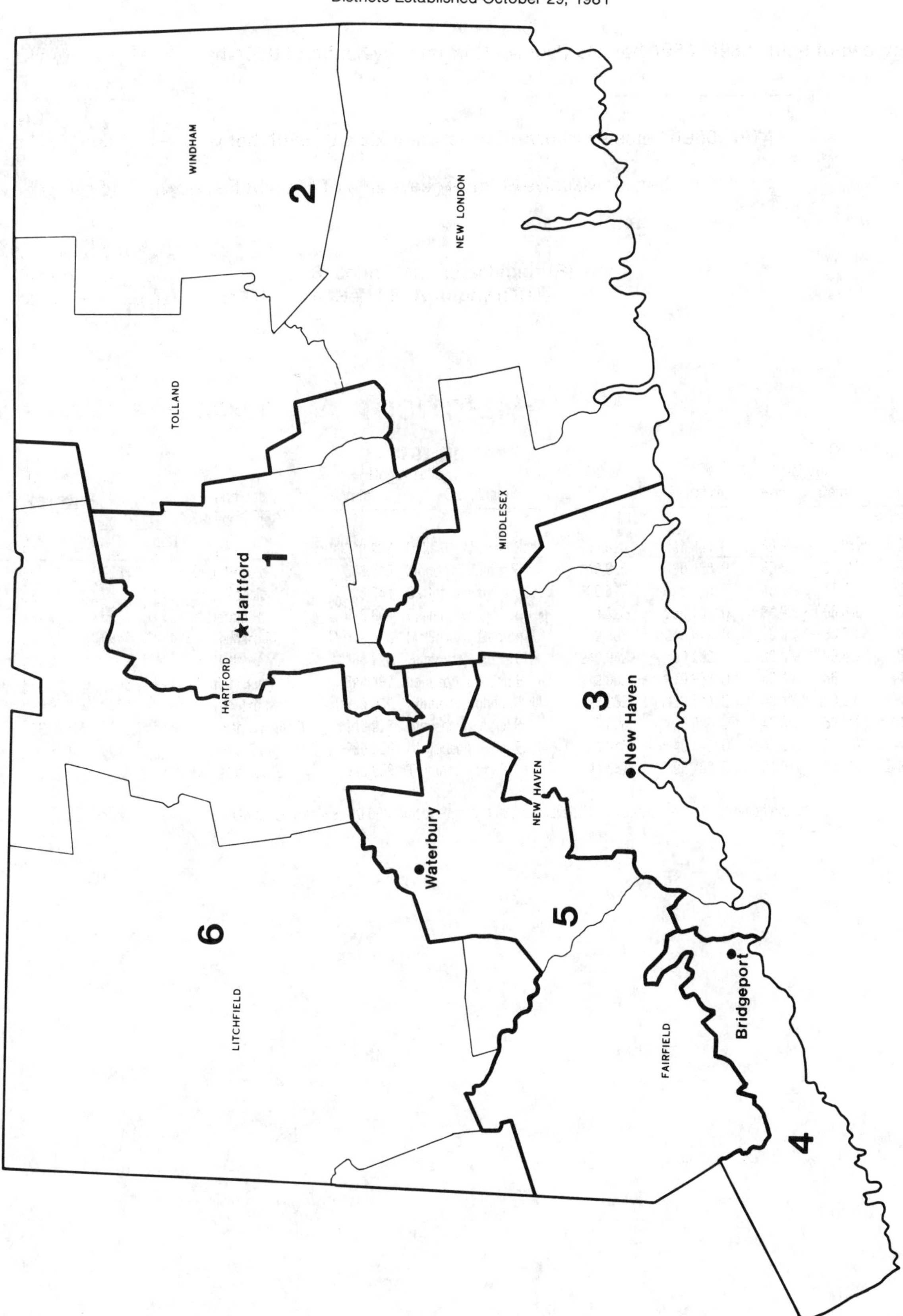

CONNECTICUT

PRESIDENT 1988

1980 Census Population	County	Total Vote	Republican	Democratic	Other	Rep.-Dem. Plurality	Percentage Total Vote Rep.	Percentage Total Vote Dem.	Percentage Major Vote Rep.	Percentage Major Vote Dem.
807,143	FAIRFIELD	374,627	221,316	149,630	3,681	71,686 R	59.1%	39.9%	59.7%	40.3%
807,766	HARTFORD	376,402	173,031	199,857	3,514	26,826 D	46.0%	53.1%	46.4%	53.6%
156,769	LITCHFIELD	80,113	44,637	34,227	1,249	10,410 R	55.7%	42.7%	56.6%	43.4%
129,017	MIDDLESEX	69,593	34,682	33,946	965	736 R	49.8%	48.8%	50.5%	49.5%
761,337	NEW HAVEN	341,811	174,251	163,153	4,407	11,098 R	51.0%	47.7%	51.6%	48.4%
238,409	NEW LONDON	103,011	52,681	48,882	1,448	3,799 R	51.1%	47.5%	51.9%	48.1%
114,823	TOLLAND	55,926	28,375	26,884	667	1,491 R	50.7%	48.1%	51.3%	48.7%
92,312	WINDHAM	41,904	21,268	20,005	631	1,263 R	50.8%	47.7%	51.5%	48.5%
3,107,576	TOTAL	1,443,394	750,241	676,584	16,569	73,657 R	52.0%	46.9%	52.6%	47.4%

CONNECTICUT

SENATOR 1988

1980 Census Population	County	Total Vote	Republican	Democratic	Other	Rep.-Dem. Plurality	Percentage Total Vote Rep.	Percentage Total Vote Dem.	Percentage Major Vote Rep.	Percentage Major Vote Dem.
807,143	FAIRFIELD	353,957	191,452	157,917	4,588	33,535 R	54.1%	44.6%	54.8%	45.2%
807,766	HARTFORD	364,722	171,324	189,692	3,706	18,368 D	47.0%	52.0%	47.5%	52.5%
156,769	LITCHFIELD	77,439	38,184	38,400	855	216 D	49.3%	49.6%	49.9%	50.1%
129,017	MIDDLESEX	66,944	33,309	32,912	723	397 R	49.8%	49.2%	50.3%	49.7%
761,337	NEW HAVEN	327,416	146,145	177,201	4,070	31,056 D	44.6%	54.1%	45.2%	54.8%
238,409	NEW LONDON	98,841	50,792	46,703	1,346	4,089 R	51.4%	47.3%	52.1%	47.9%
114,823	TOLLAND	54,566	27,525	26,448	593	1,077 R	50.4%	48.5%	51.0%	49.0%
92,312	WINDHAM	39,631	19,723	19,226	682	497 R	49.8%	48.5%	50.6%	49.4%
3,107,576	TOTAL	1,383,526	678,454	688,499	16,573	10,045 D	49.0%	49.8%	49.6%	50.4%

CONNECTICUT

PRESIDENT 1988

1980 Census Population	City/Town	Total Vote	Republican	Democratic	Other	Rep.-Dem. Plurality	Percentage Total Vote Rep.	Total Vote Dem.	Major Vote Rep.	Major Vote Dem.
19,039	ANSONIA	8,008	3,942	3,973	93	31 D	49.2%	49.6%	49.8%	50.2%
23,363	BRANFORD	13,253	7,068	6,007	178	1,061 R	53.3%	45.3%	54.1%	45.9%
142,546	BRIDGEPORT	41,442	17,084	23,831	527	6,747 D	41.2%	57.5%	41.8%	58.2%
57,370	BRISTOL	24,752	11,034	13,462	256	2,428 D	44.6%	54.4%	45.0%	55.0%
21,788	CHESHIRE	12,476	7,682	4,700	94	2,982 R	61.6%	37.7%	62.0%	38.0%
60,470	DANBURY	23,919	13,690	10,071	158	3,619 R	57.2%	42.1%	57.6%	42.4%
18,892	DARIEN	10,466	7,676	2,696	94	4,980 R	73.3%	25.8%	74.0%	26.0%
52,563	EAST HARTFORD	21,213	8,501	12,511	201	4,010 D	40.1%	59.0%	40.5%	59.5%
25,028	EAST HAVEN	10,518	5,804	4,432	282	1,372 R	55.2%	42.1%	56.7%	43.3%
42,695	ENFIELD	18,585	9,041	9,356	188	315 D	48.6%	50.3%	49.1%	50.9%
54,849	FAIRFIELD TOWN	29,459	17,786	11,336	337	6,450 R	60.4%	38.5%	61.1%	38.9%
24,327	GLASTONBURY	15,877	9,088	6,638	151	2,450 R	57.2%	41.8%	57.8%	42.2%
59,578	GREENWICH	30,690	20,158	10,205	327	9,953 R	65.7%	33.3%	66.4%	33.6%
41,062	GROTON	13,293	7,095	6,067	131	1,028 R	53.4%	45.6%	53.9%	46.1%
51,071	HAMDEN	26,318	12,869	13,054	395	185 D	48.9%	49.6%	49.6%	50.4%
136,392	HARTFORD CITY	35,878	8,100	27,295	483	19,195 D	22.6%	76.1%	22.9%	77.1%
49,761	MANCHESTER	25,114	12,009	12,891	214	882 D	47.8%	51.3%	48.2%	51.8%
20,634	MANSFIELD	6,980	2,522	4,380	78	1,858 D	36.1%	62.8%	36.5%	63.5%
57,118	MERIDEN	23,461	10,809	12,224	428	1,415 D	46.1%	52.1%	46.9%	53.1%
39,040	MIDDLETOWN	18,285	7,034	11,113	138	4,079 D	38.5%	60.8%	38.8%	61.2%
50,898	MILFORD	22,626	13,286	9,150	190	4,136 R	58.7%	40.4%	59.2%	40.8%
26,456	NAUGATUCK	11,136	6,147	4,857	132	1,290 R	55.2%	43.6%	55.9%	44.1%
73,840	NEW BRITAIN	25,707	9,569	15,843	295	6,274 D	37.2%	61.6%	37.7%	62.3%
126,109	NEW HAVEN CITY	44,069	11,616	31,951	502	20,335 D	26.4%	72.5%	26.7%	73.3%
28,841	NEWINGTON	15,487	7,238	8,109	140	871 D	46.7%	52.4%	47.2%	52.8%
28,842	NEW LONDON CITY	9,236	3,577	5,539	120	1,962 D	38.7%	60.0%	39.2%	60.8%
22,080	NORTH HAVEN	11,594	6,730	4,689	175	2,041 R	58.0%	40.4%	58.9%	41.1%
77,767	NORWALK	33,581	18,618	14,518	445	4,100 R	55.4%	43.2%	56.2%	43.8%
38,074	NORWICH	14,034	6,328	7,510	196	1,182 D	45.1%	53.5%	45.7%	54.3%
20,120	RIDGEFIELD	12,021	7,860	4,055	106	3,805 R	65.4%	33.7%	66.0%	34.0%
31,314	SHELTON	16,072	10,729	5,217	126	5,512 R	66.8%	32.5%	67.3%	32.7%
21,161	SIMSBURY	12,779	7,734	4,948	97	2,786 R	60.5%	38.7%	61.0%	39.0%
36,879	SOUTHINGTON	16,766	8,695	7,939	132	756 R	51.9%	47.4%	52.3%	47.7%
102,453	STAMFORD	46,198	24,877	20,773	548	4,104 R	53.8%	45.0%	54.5%	45.5%
50,541	STRATFORD	24,666	14,048	10,346	272	3,702 R	57.0%	41.9%	57.6%	42.4%
30,987	TORRINGTON	14,286	6,974	7,162	150	188 D	48.8%	50.1%	49.3%	50.7%
32,989	TRUMBULL	18,140	11,769	6,179	192	5,590 R	64.9%	34.1%	65.6%	34.4%
27,974	VERNON	12,925	6,604	6,206	115	398 R	51.1%	48.0%	51.6%	48.4%
37,274	WALLINGFORD	18,071	9,403	8,462	206	941 R	52.0%	46.8%	52.6%	47.4%
103,266	WATERBURY	39,166	20,018	18,202	946	1,816 R	51.1%	46.5%	52.4%	47.6%
61,301	WEST HARTFORD	35,985	16,482	19,311	192	2,829 D	45.8%	53.7%	46.0%	54.0%
53,184	WEST HAVEN	23,202	11,060	11,710	432	650 D	47.7%	50.5%	48.6%	51.4%
25,290	WESTPORT	14,710	8,051	6,519	140	1,532 R	54.7%	44.3%	55.3%	44.7%
26,013	WETHERSFIELD	15,518	8,070	7,275	173	795 R	52.0%	46.9%	52.6%	47.4%
21,062	WINDHAM TOWN	8,948	3,719	5,106	123	1,387 D	41.6%	57.1%	42.1%	57.9%
25,204	WINDSOR	13,354	6,161	7,067	126	906 D	46.1%	52.9%	46.6%	53.4%

CONNECTICUT

SENATOR 1988

1980 Census Population	City/Town	Total Vote	Republican	Democratic	Other	Rep.-Dem. Plurality	Percentage Total Vote Rep.	Percentage Total Vote Dem.	Percentage Major Vote Rep.	Percentage Major Vote Dem.
19,039	ANSONIA	7,637	3,256	4,293	88	1,037 D	42.6%	56.2%	43.1%	56.9%
23,363	BRANFORD	12,708	6,254	6,307	147	53 D	49.2%	49.6%	49.8%	50.2%
142,546	BRIDGEPORT	38,285	15,235	22,525	525	7,290 D	39.8%	58.8%	40.3%	59.7%
57,370	BRISTOL	23,915	9,857	13,822	236	3,965 D	41.2%	57.8%	41.6%	58.4%
21,788	CHESHIRE	12,207	6,505	5,607	95	898 R	53.3%	45.9%	53.7%	46.3%
60,470	DANBURY	22,228	11,043	10,945	240	98 R	49.7%	49.2%	50.2%	49.8%
18,892	DARIEN	9,825	6,172	3,526	127	2,646 R	62.8%	35.9%	63.6%	36.4%
52,563	EAST HARTFORD	20,607	8,342	12,072	193	3,730 D	40.5%	58.6%	40.9%	59.1%
25,028	EAST HAVEN	10,719	4,373	6,167	179	1,794 D	40.8%	57.5%	41.5%	58.5%
42,695	ENFIELD	17,890	7,751	9,932	207	2,181 D	43.3%	55.5%	43.8%	56.2%
54,849	FAIRFIELD TOWN	28,163	15,665	12,142	356	3,523 R	55.6%	43.1%	56.3%	43.7%
24,327	GLASTONBURY	15,616	8,839	6,631	146	2,208 R	56.6%	42.5%	57.1%	42.9%
59,578	GREENWICH	28,895	18,733	9,727	435	9,006 R	64.8%	33.7%	65.8%	34.2%
41,062	GROTON	12,750	6,840	5,740	170	1,100 R	53.6%	45.0%	54.4%	45.6%
51,071	HAMDEN	25,129	11,268	13,570	291	2,302 D	44.8%	54.0%	45.4%	54.6%
136,392	HARTFORD CITY	33,079	11,181	21,477	421	10,296 D	33.8%	64.9%	34.2%	65.8%
49,761	MANCHESTER	24,657	12,202	12,215	240	13 D	49.5%	49.5%	50.0%	50.0%
20,634	MANSFIELD	6,781	3,819	2,891	71	928 R	56.3%	42.6%	56.9%	43.1%
57,118	MERIDEN	22,196	9,564	12,258	374	2,694 D	43.1%	55.2%	43.8%	56.2%
39,040	MIDDLETOWN	17,073	7,956	8,910	207	954 D	46.6%	52.2%	47.2%	52.8%
50,898	MILFORD	21,714	10,178	11,309	227	1,131 D	46.9%	52.1%	47.4%	52.6%
26,456	NAUGATUCK	10,738	4,525	6,097	116	1,572 D	42.1%	56.8%	42.6%	57.4%
73,840	NEW BRITAIN	24,343	9,360	14,711	272	5,351 D	38.5%	60.4%	38.9%	61.1%
126,109	NEW HAVEN CITY	40,361	14,713	25,205	443	10,492 D	36.5%	62.4%	36.9%	63.1%
28,841	NEWINGTON	15,087	6,769	8,176	142	1,407 D	44.9%	54.2%	45.3%	54.7%
28,842	NEW LONDON CITY	8,649	3,969	4,534	146	565 D	45.9%	52.4%	46.7%	53.3%
22,080	NORTH HAVEN	11,118	5,263	5,733	122	470 D	47.3%	51.6%	47.9%	52.1%
77,767	NORWALK	31,322	16,898	13,954	470	2,944 R	53.9%	44.6%	54.8%	45.2%
38,074	NORWICH	13,471	6,358	6,888	225	530 D	47.2%	51.1%	48.0%	52.0%
20,120	RIDGEFIELD	11,532	7,165	4,229	138	2,936 R	62.1%	36.7%	62.9%	37.1%
31,314	SHELTON	15,491	7,900	7,441	150	459 R	51.0%	48.0%	51.5%	48.5%
21,161	SIMSBURY	12,568	7,618	4,827	123	2,791 R	60.6%	38.4%	61.2%	38.8%
36,879	SOUTHINGTON	16,327	7,472	8,667	188	1,195 D	45.8%	53.1%	46.3%	53.7%
102,453	STAMFORD	42,619	21,498	20,522	599	976 R	50.4%	48.2%	51.2%	48.8%
50,541	STRATFORD	23,722	11,521	11,916	285	395 D	48.6%	50.2%	49.2%	50.8%
30,987	TORRINGTON	13,871	5,829	7,901	141	2,072 D	42.0%	57.0%	42.5%	57.5%
32,989	TRUMBULL	17,323	9,286	7,820	217	1,466 R	53.6%	45.1%	54.3%	45.7%
27,974	VERNON	12,649	6,079	6,479	91	400 D	48.1%	51.2%	48.4%	51.6%
37,274	WALLINGFORD	17,477	7,739	9,546	192	1,807 D	44.3%	54.6%	44.8%	55.2%
103,266	WATERBURY	37,529	15,389	21,386	754	5,997 D	41.0%	57.0%	41.8%	58.2%
61,301	WEST HARTFORD	35,222	18,540	16,420	262	2,120 R	52.6%	46.6%	53.0%	47.0%
53,184	WEST HAVEN	21,958	8,307	13,344	307	5,037 D	37.8%	60.8%	38.4%	61.6%
25,290	WESTPORT	14,076	9,088	4,823	165	4,265 R	64.6%	34.3%	65.3%	34.7%
26,013	WETHERSFIELD	15,120	7,610	7,348	162	262 R	50.3%	48.6%	50.9%	49.1%
21,062	WINDHAM TOWN	8,446	3,782	4,550	114	768 D	44.8%	53.9%	45.4%	54.6%
25,204	WINDSOR	13,022	6,240	6,668	114	428 D	47.9%	51.2%	48.3%	51.7%

CONNECTICUT

CONGRESS

CD	Year	Total Vote	Republican Vote	Republican Candidate	Democratic Vote	Democratic Candidate	Other Vote	Rep.-Dem. Plurality	Percentage Total Vote Rep.	Total Vote Dem.	Major Vote Rep.	Major Vote Dem.
1	1988	228,448	51,985	ROBLES, MARIO	176,463	KENNELLY, BARBARA B.		124,478 D	22.8%	77.2%	22.8%	77.2%
1	1986	173,787	44,122	KLEIN, HERSCHEL A.	128,930	KENNELLY, BARBARA B.	735	84,808 D	25.4%	74.2%	25.5%	74.5%
1	1984	239,362	90,823	KLEIN, HERSCHEL A.	147,748	KENNELLY, BARBARA B.	791	56,925 D	37.9%	61.7%	38.1%	61.9%
1	1982	186,123	58,075	KLEIN, HERSCHEL A.	126,798	KENNELLY, BARBARA B.	1,250	68,723 D	31.2%	68.1%	31.4%	68.6%
2	1988	225,291	81,965	CARBERRY, GLENN	143,326	GEJDENSON, SAMUEL		61,361 D	36.4%	63.6%	36.4%	63.6%
2	1986	162,098	52,869	MULLEN, FRANCIS M.	109,229	GEJDENSON, SAMUEL		56,360 D	32.6%	67.4%	32.6%	67.4%
2	1984	228,253	103,119	KOONTZ, ROBERTA F.	124,110	GEJDENSON, SAMUEL	1,024	20,991 D	45.2%	54.4%	45.4%	54.6%
2	1982	170,814	74,294	GUGLIELMO, TONY	95,254	GEJDENSON, SAMUEL	1,266	20,960 D	43.5%	55.8%	43.8%	56.2%
3	1988	221,669	74,275	PATTON, GERARD B.	147,394	MORRISON, BRUCE A.		73,119 D	33.5%	66.5%	33.5%	66.5%
3	1986	164,087	49,806	DIETTE, ERNEST J.	114,276	MORRISON, BRUCE A.	5	64,470 D	30.4%	69.6%	30.4%	69.6%
3	1984	245,795	115,939	DENARDIS, LAWRENCE J.	129,230	MORRISON, BRUCE A.	626	13,291 D	47.2%	52.6%	47.3%	52.7%
3	1982	181,458	88,951	DENARDIS, LAWRENCE J.	90,638	MORRISON, BRUCE A.	1,869	1,687 D	49.0%	49.9%	49.5%	50.5%
4	1988	205,973	147,843	SHAYS, CHRISTOPHER	55,751	PEARSON, ROGER	2,379	92,092 R	71.8%	27.1%	72.6%	27.4%
4	1986	144,211	77,212	MCKINNEY, STEWART B.	66,999	NIEDERMEIER, CHRISTINE M.		10,213 R	53.5%	46.5%	53.5%	46.5%
4	1984	235,310	165,644	MCKINNEY, STEWART B.	69,666	ORMAN, JOHN M.		95,978 R	70.4%	29.6%	70.4%	29.6%
4	1982	165,907	93,660	MCKINNEY, STEWART B.	71,110	PHILLIPS, JOHN A.	1,137	22,550 R	56.5%	42.9%	56.8%	43.2%
5	1988	222,341	163,729	ROWLAND, JOHN G.	58,612	MARINAN, JOSEPH		105,117 R	73.6%	26.4%	73.6%	26.4%
5	1986	162,035	98,664	ROWLAND, JOHN G.	63,371	COHEN, JIM		35,293 R	60.9%	39.1%	60.9%	39.1%
5	1984	240,657	130,700	ROWLAND, JOHN G.	109,425	RATCHFORD, WILLIAM	532	21,275 R	54.3%	45.5%	54.4%	45.6%
5	1982	173,376	70,808	HANLON, NEAL B.	101,362	RATCHFORD, WILLIAM	1,206	30,554 D	40.8%	58.5%	41.1%	58.9%
6	1988	236,888	157,020	JOHNSON, NANCY L.	78,814	GRIFFIN, JAMES L.	1,054	78,206 R	66.3%	33.3%	66.6%	33.4%
6	1986	173,437	111,304	JOHNSON, NANCY L.	62,133	AMENTA, PAUL S.		49,171 R	64.2%	35.8%	64.2%	35.8%
6	1984	242,911	155,422	JOHNSON, NANCY L.	87,489	HOUSE, ARTHUR H.		67,933 R	64.0%	36.0%	64.0%	36.0%
6	1982	192,997	99,703	JOHNSON, NANCY L.	92,178	CURRY, WILLIAM E.	1,116	7,525 R	51.7%	47.8%	52.0%	48.0%

CONNECTICUT

In addition to the county-by-county figures, data are presented for selected Connecticut communities. Since not all jurisdictions of the state are listed in this special tabulation, state-wide totals are shown only with the county-by-county statistics.

1988 GENERAL ELECTION

President Other vote was 14,071 Libertarian (Paul); 2,491 New Alliance (Fulani); 7 Marra (write-in). Total for the other vote column includes these 7 write-in votes not available by county or city/town.

Senator Other vote was 12,409 Libertarian(Grayson); 4,154 New Alliance (Fisher); 10 Longo (write-in). Total for the other vote column includes these 10 write-in votes not available by county or city/town.

Congress Other vote was War Against Aids (Tarzia) in CD 4; Independent (Marietta) in CD 6.

1988 PRIMARIES

Party conventions nominate Connecticut candidates, subject to a system of "challenge" primaries. Any candidate who receives more than 20 percent of the convention vote is entitled to challenge the endorsed candidate in a primary. There were no challenge primary elections on September 14 for the U.S. Senate or the U. S. House of Representatives as all candidates for those offices were nominated by convention in July.

DELAWARE

GOVERNOR

Michael N. Castle (R). Re-elected 1988 to a four-year term. Previously elected 1984.

SENATORS

Joseph R. Biden (D). Re-elected 1984 to a six-year term. Previously elected 1978, 1972.

William V. Roth (R). Re-elected 1988 to a six-year term. Previously elected 1982, 1976, 1970.

REPRESENTATIVE

At-Large. Thomas R. Carper (D)

POSTWAR VOTE FOR PRESIDENT

								Percentage			
	Total	Republican		Democratic		Other		Total Vote		Major Vote	
Year	Vote	Vote	Candidate	Vote	Candidate	Vote	Plurality	Rep.	Dem.	Rep.	Dem.
1988	249,891	139,639	Bush, George	108,647	Dukakis, Michael S.	1,605	30,992 R	55.9%	43.5%	56.2%	43.8%
1984	254,572	152,190	Reagan, Ronald	101,656	Mondale, Walter F.	726	50,534 R	59.8%	39.9%	60.0%	40.0%
1980	235,900	111,252	Reagan, Ronald	105,754	Carter, Jimmy	18,894	5,498 R	47.2%	44.8%	51.3%	48.7%
1976	235,834	109,831	Ford, Gerald R.	122,596	Carter, Jimmy	3,407	12,765 D	46.6%	52.0%	47.3%	52.7%
1972	235,516	140,357	Nixon, Richard M.	92,283	McGovern, George S.	2,876	48,074 R	59.6%	39.2%	60.3%	39.7%
1968	214,367	96,714	Nixon, Richard M.	89,194	Humphrey, Hubert H.	28,459	7,520 R	45.1%	41.6%	52.0%	48.0%
1964	201,320	78,078	Goldwater, Barry M.	122,704	Johnson, Lyndon B.	538	44,626 D	38.8%	60.9%	38.9%	61.1%
1960	196,683	96,373	Nixon, Richard M.	99,590	Kennedy, John F.	720	3,217 D	49.0%	50.6%	49.2%	50.8%
1956	177,988	98,057	Eisenhower, Dwight D.	79,421	Stevenson, Adlai E.	510	18,636 R	55.1%	44.6%	55.3%	44.7%
1952	174,025	90,059	Eisenhower, Dwight D.	83,315	Stevenson, Adlai E.	651	6,744 R	51.8%	47.9%	51.9%	48.1%
1948	139,073	69,588	Dewey, Thomas E.	67,813	Truman, Harry S.	1,672	1,775 R	50.0%	48.8%	50.6%	49.4%

POSTWAR VOTE FOR GOVERNOR

								Percentage			
	Total	Republican		Democratic		Other	Rep.-Dem.	Total Vote		Major Vote	
Year	Vote	Vote	Candidate	Vote	Candidate	Vote	Plurality	Rep.	Dem.	Rep.	Dem.
1988	239,969	169,733	Castle, Michael N.	70,236	Kreshtoll, Jacob		99,497 R	70.7%	29.3%	70.7%	29.3%
1984	243,565	135,250	Castle, Michael N.	108,315	Quillen, William T.		26,935 R	55.5%	44.5%	55.5%	44.5%
1980	225,081	159,004	duPont, Pierre	64,217	Gordy, William J.	1,860	94,787 R	70.6%	28.5%	71.2%	28.8%
1976	229,563	130,531	duPont, Pierre	97,480	Tribbitt, Sherman W.	1,552	33,051 R	56.9%	42.5%	57.2%	42.8%
1972	228,722	109,583	Peterson, Russell W.	117,274	Tribbitt, Sherman W.	1,865	7,691 D	47.9%	51.3%	48.3%	51.7%
1968	206,834	104,474	Peterson, Russell W.	102,360	Terry, Charles L.		2,114 R	50.5%	49.5%	50.5%	49.5%
1964	200,171	97,374	Buckson, David P.	102,797	Terry, Charles L.		5,423 D	48.6%	51.4%	48.6%	51.4%
1960	194,835	94,043	Rollins, John W.	100,792	Carvel, Elbert N.		6,749 D	48.3%	51.7%	48.3%	51.7%
1956	177,012	91,965	Boggs, J. Caleb	85,047	McConnell, J. H.T.		6,918 R	52.0%	48.0%	52.0%	48.0%
1952	170,749	88,977	Boggs, J. Caleb	81,772	Carvel, Elbert N.		7,205 R	52.1%	47.9%	52.1%	47.9%
1948	140,335	64,996	George, Hyland P.	75,339	Carvel, Elbert N.		10,343 D	46.3%	53.7%	46.3%	53.7%

DELAWARE

POSTWAR VOTE FOR SENATOR

Year	Total Vote	Republican Vote	Republican Candidate	Democratic Vote	Democratic Candidate	Other Vote	Rep.-Dem. Plurality	Percentage Total Vote Rep.	Percentage Total Vote Dem.	Percentage Major Vote Rep.	Percentage Major Vote Dem.
1988	243,493	151,115	Roth, William V.	92,378	Woo, S. B.		58,737 R	62.1%	37.9%	62.1%	37.9%
1984	245,932	98,101	Burris, John M.	147,831	Biden, Joseph R.		49,730 D	39.9%	60.1%	39.9%	60.1%
1982	190,960	105,357	Roth, William V.	84,413	Levinson, David N.	1,190	20,944 R	55.2%	44.2%	55.5%	44.5%
1978	162,072	66,479	Baxter, James H.	93,930	Biden, Joseph R.	1,663	27,451 D	41.0%	58.0%	41.4%	58.6%
1976	224,859	125,502	Roth, William V.	98,055	Maloney, Thomas C.	1,302	27,447 R	55.8%	43.6%	56.1%	43.9%
1972	229,828	112,844	Boggs, J. Caleb	116,006	Biden, Joseph R.	978	3,162 D	49.1%	50.5%	49.3%	50.7%
1970	161,439	94,979	Roth, William V.	64,740	Zimmerman, Jacob	1,720	30,239 R	58.8%	40.1%	59.5%	40.5%
1966	164,549	97,268	Boggs, J. Caleb	67,281	Tunnell, James M., Jr.		29,987 R	59.1%	40.9%	59.1%	40.9%
1964	200,703	103,782	Williams, John J.	96,850	Carvel, Elbert N.	71	6,932 R	51.7%	48.3%	51.7%	48.3%
1960	194,964	98,874	Boggs, J. Caleb	96,090	Frear, J. Allen		2,784 R	50.7%	49.3%	50.7%	49.3%
1958	154,432	82,280	Williams, John J.	72,152	Carvel, Elbert N.		10,128 R	53.3%	46.7%	53.3%	46.7%
1954	144,900	62,389	Warburton, H. B.	82,511	Frear, J. Allen		20,122 D	43.1%	56.9%	43.1%	56.9%
1952	170,705	93,020	Williams, John J.	77,685	Bayard, A. I.duP.		15,335 R	54.5%	45.5%	54.5%	45.5%
1948	141,362	68,246	Buck, C. Douglas	71,888	Frear, J. Allen	1,228	3,642 D	48.3%	50.9%	48.7%	51.3%
1946	113,513	62,603	Williams, John J.	50,910	Tunnell, James M.		11,693 R	55.2%	44.8%	55.2%	44.8%

DELAWARE

One At Large

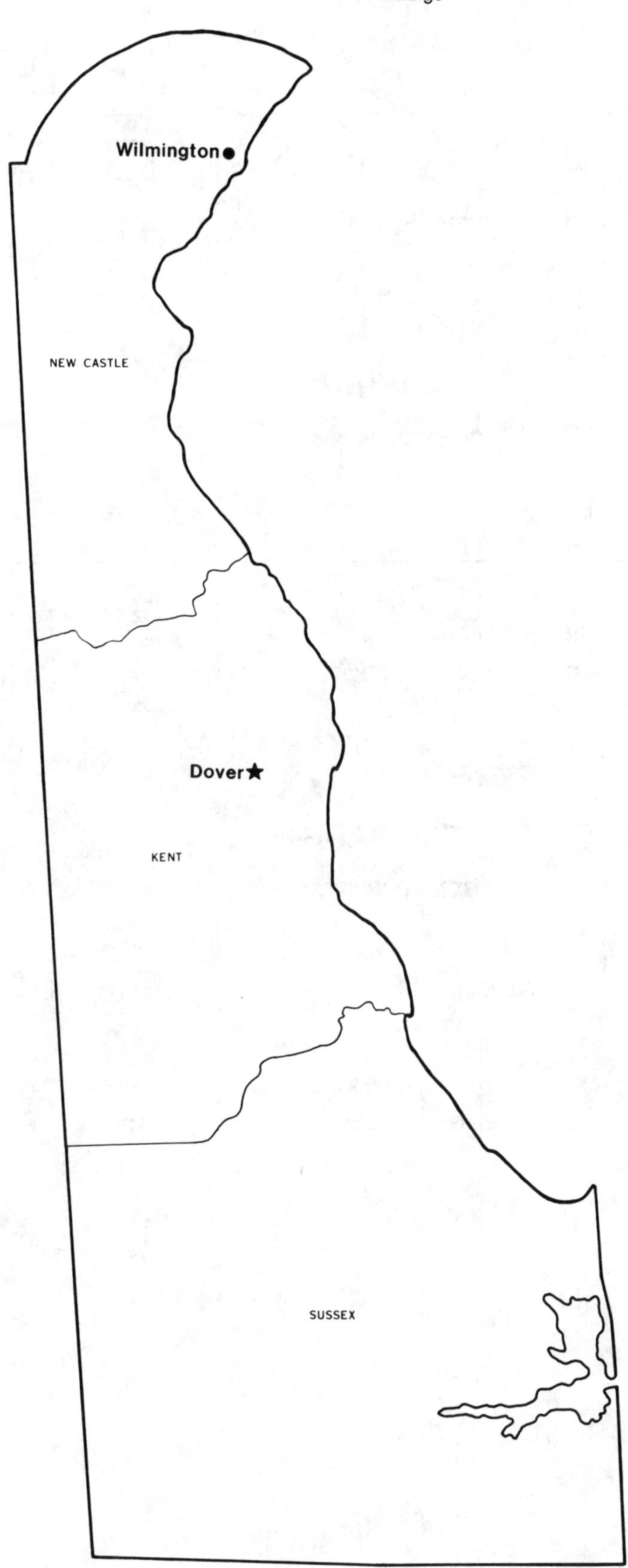

DELAWARE

PRESIDENT 1988

1980 Census Population	County	Total Vote	Republican	Democratic	Other	Rep.-Dem. Plurality	Percentage Total Vote Rep.	Percentage Total Vote Dem.	Percentage Major Vote Rep.	Percentage Major Vote Dem.
98,219	KENT	33,113	19,923	12,996	194	6,927 R	60.2%	39.2%	60.5%	39.5%
398,115	NEW CASTLE	173,003	92,587	79,147	1,269	13,440 R	53.5%	45.7%	53.9%	46.1%
98,004	SUSSEX	43,775	27,129	16,504	142	10,625 R	62.0%	37.7%	62.2%	37.8%
594,338	TOTAL	249,891	139,639	108,647	1,605	30,992 R	55.9%	43.5%	56.2%	43.8%

DELAWARE

GOVERNOR 1988

1980 Census Population	County	Total Vote	Republican	Democratic	Other	Rep.-Dem. Plurality	Percentage Total Vote Rep.	Percentage Total Vote Dem.	Percentage Major Vote Rep.	Percentage Major Vote Dem.
98,219	KENT	32,437	22,563	9,874		12,689 R	69.6%	30.4%	69.6%	30.4%
398,115	NEW CASTLE	165,496	115,866	49,630		66,236 R	70.0%	30.0%	70.0%	30.0%
98,004	SUSSEX	42,036	31,304	10,732		20,572 R	74.5%	25.5%	74.5%	25.5%
594,338	TOTAL	239,969	169,733	70,236		99,497 R	70.7%	29.3%	70.7%	29.3%

DELAWARE

SENATOR 1988

1980 Census Population	County	Total Vote	Republican	Democratic	Other	Rep.-Dem. Plurality	Percentage Total Vote Rep.	Percentage Total Vote Dem.	Percentage Major Vote Rep.	Percentage Major Vote Dem.
98,219	KENT	32,618	21,808	10,810		10,998 R	66.9%	33.1%	66.9%	33.1%
398,115	NEW CASTLE	168,206	99,798	68,408		31,390 R	59.3%	40.7%	59.3%	40.7%
98,004	SUSSEX	42,669	29,509	13,160		16,349 R	69.2%	30.8%	69.2%	30.8%
594,338	TOTAL	243,493	151,115	92,378		58,737 R	62.1%	37.9%	62.1%	37.9%

DELAWARE

CONGRESS

CD	Year	Total Vote	Republican Vote	Republican Candidate	Democratic Vote	Democratic Candidate	Other Vote	Rep.-Dem. Plurality	Percentage Total Vote Rep.	Percentage Total Vote Dem.	Percentage Major Vote Rep.	Percentage Major Vote Dem.
AL	1988	234,517	76,179	KRAPF, JAMES P.	158,338	CARPER, THOMAS R.		82,159 D	32.5%	67.5%	32.5%	67.5%
AL	1986	160,757	53,767	NEUBERGER, THOMAS S.	106,351	CARPER, THOMAS R.	639	52,584 D	33.4%	66.2%	33.6%	66.4%
AL	1984	243,014	100,650	DUPONT, ELISE	142,070	CARPER, THOMAS R.	294	41,420 D	41.4%	58.5%	41.5%	58.5%
AL	1982	188,064	87,153	EVANS, THOMAS B.	98,533	CARPER, THOMAS R.	2,378	11,380 D	46.3%	52.4%	46.9%	53.1%
AL	1980	216,629	133,842	EVANS, THOMAS B.	81,227	MAXWELL, ROBERT L.	1,560	52,615 R	61.8%	37.5%	62.2%	37.8%
AL	1978	157,566	91,689	EVANS, THOMAS B.	64,863	HINDES, GARY E.	1,014	26,826 R	58.2%	41.2%	58.6%	41.4%
AL	1976	214,799	110,677	EVANS, THOMAS B.	102,431	SHIPLEY, SAMUEL L.	1,691	8,246 R	51.5%	47.7%	51.9%	48.1%
AL	1974	160,328	93,826	DUPONT, PIERRE	63,490	SOLES, JAMES	3,012	30,336 R	58.5%	39.6%	59.6%	40.4%
AL	1972	225,851	141,237	DUPONT, PIERRE	83,230	HANDLOFF, NORMA	1,384	58,007 R	62.5%	36.9%	62.9%	37.1%
AL	1970	160,313	86,125	DUPONT, PIERRE	71,429	DANIELLO, JOHN D.	2,759	14,696 R	53.7%	44.6%	54.7%	45.3%
AL	1968	200,820	117,827	ROTH, WILLIAM V.	82,993	MCDOWELL, HARRIS B.		34,834 R	58.7%	41.3%	58.7%	41.3%
AL	1966	163,103	90,961	ROTH, WILLIAM V.	72,142	MCDOWELL, HARRIS B.		18,819 R	55.8%	44.2%	55.8%	44.2%
AL	1964	198,691	86,254	SNOWDEN, JAMES H.	112,361	MCDOWELL, HARRIS B.	76	26,107 D	43.4%	56.6%	43.4%	56.6%
AL	1962	153,356	71,934	WILLIAMS, WILMER F.	81,166	MCDOWELL, HARRIS B.	256	9,232 D	46.9%	52.9%	47.0%	53.0%
AL	1960	194,564	96,337	MCKINSTRY, JAMES T.	98,227	MCDOWELL, HARRIS B.		1,890 D	49.5%	50.5%	49.5%	50.5%
AL	1958	152,896	76,099	HASKELL, HARRY G.	76,797	MCDOWELL, HARRIS B.		698 D	49.8%	50.2%	49.8%	50.2%
AL	1956	176,182	91,538	HASKELL, HARRY G.	84,644	MCDOWELL, HARRIS B.		6,894 R	52.0%	48.0%	52.0%	48.0%
AL	1954	144,236	65,035	MARTIN, LILLIAN	79,201	MCDOWELL, HARRIS B.		14,166 D	45.1%	54.9%	45.1%	54.9%
AL	1952	170,015	88,285	WARBURTON, H. B.	81,730	SCANNELL, JOSEPH S.		6,555 R	51.9%	48.1%	51.9%	48.1%
AL	1950	129,404	73,313	BOGGS, J. CALEB	56,091	WINCHESTER, H. M.		17,222 R	56.7%	43.3%	56.7%	43.3%
AL	1948	140,535	71,127	BOGGS, J. CALEB	68,909	MCGUIGAN, J. CARL	499	2,218 R	50.6%	49.0%	50.8%	49.2%
AL	1946	112,621	63,516	BOGGS, J. CALEB	49,105	TRAYNOR, PHILIP A.		14,411 R	56.4%	43.6%	56.4%	43.6%

DELAWARE

1988 GENERAL ELECTION

President Other vote was 1,162 Libertarian (Paul); 443 New Alliance (Fulani).

Governor

Senator

Congress

1988 PRIMARIES

SEPTEMBER 10 REPUBLICAN

Governor Michael N. Castle, unopposed.

Senator William V. Roth, unopposed.

Congress Unopposed at-large.

SEPTEMBER 10 DEMOCRATIC

Governor Jacob Kreshtool, unopposed.

Senator 20,225 S. B. Woo; 20,154 Samuel S. Beard. Data given are for the re-count.

Congress Unopposed at-large.

FLORIDA

GOVERNOR

Bob Martinez (R). Elected 1986 to a four-year term.

SENATORS

Robert Graham (D). Elected 1986 to a six-year term.

Connie Mack (R). Elected 1988 to a six-year term.

REPRESENTATIVES

1. Earl D. Hutto (D)
2. Bill Grant (D)**
3. Charles E. Bennett (D)
4. Craig T. James (R)
5. Bill McCollum (R)
6. Clifford B. Stearns (R)
7. Sam M. Gibbons (D)
8. C. W.Young (R)
9. Michael Bilirakis (R)
10. Andrew P. Ireland (R)
11. Bill Nelson (D)
12. Tom Lewis (R)
13. Porter J. Goss (R)
14. Harry Johnston (D)
15. Clay Shaw (R)
16. Larry Smith (D)
17. William Lehman (D)
18. Claude Pepper (D) (see page 1)
19. Dante B. Fascell (D)

** See note section

POSTWAR VOTE FOR PRESIDENT

		Republican		Democratic				Percentage			
								Total Vote		Major Vote	
Year	Total Vote	Vote	Candidate	Vote	Candidate	Other Vote	Plurality	Rep.	Dem.	Rep.	Dem.
1988	4,302,313	2,618,885	Bush, George	1,656,701	Dukakis, Michael S.	26,727	962,184 R	60.9%	38.5%	61.3%	38.7%
1984	4,180,051	2,730,350	Reagan, Ronald	1,448,816	Mondale, Walter F.	885	1,281,534 R	65.3%	34.7%	65.3%	34.7%
1980	3,686,930	2,046,951	Reagan, Ronald	1,419,475	Carter, Jimmy	220,504	627,476 R	55.5%	38.5%	59.1%	40.9%
1976	3,150,631	1,469,531	Ford, Gerald R.	1,636,000	Carter, Jimmy	45,100	166,469 D	46.6%	51.9%	47.3%	52.7%
1972	2,583,283	1,857,759	Nixon, Richard M.	718,117	McGovern, George S.	7,407	1,139,642 R	71.9%	27.8%	72.1%	27.9%
1968 **	2,187,805	886,804	Nixon, Richard M.	676,794	Humphrey, Hubert H.	624,207	210,010 R	40.5%	30.9%	56.7%	43.3%
1964	1,854,481	905,941	Goldwater, Barry M.	948,540	Johnson, Lyndon B.		42,599 D	48.9%	51.1%	48.9%	51.1%
1960	1,544,176	795,476	Nixon, Richard M.	748,700	Kennedy, John F.		46,776 R	51.5%	48.5%	51.5%	48.5%
1956	1,125,762	643,849	Eisenhower, Dwight D.	480,371	Stevenson, Adlai E.	1,542	163,478 R	57.2%	42.7%	57.3%	42.7%
1952	989,337	544,036	Eisenhower, Dwight D.	444,950	Stevenson, Adlai E.	351	99,086 R	55.0%	45.0%	55.0%	45.0%
1948	577,643	194,280	Dewey, Thomas E.	281,988	Truman, Harry S.	101,375	87,708 D	33.6%	48.8%	40.8%	59.2%

In 1968 other vote was George Wallace party.

FLORIDA

POSTWAR VOTE FOR GOVERNOR

Year	Total Vote	Republican Vote	Republican Candidate	Democratic Vote	Democratic Candidate	Other Vote	Rep.-Dem. Plurality	Percentage Total Vote Rep.	Percentage Total Vote Dem.	Percentage Major Vote Rep.	Percentage Major Vote Dem.
1986	3,386,171	1,847,525	Martinez, Bob	1,538,620	Pajcic, Steve	26	308,905 R	54.6%	45.4%	54.6%	45.4%
1982	2,688,566	949,013	Bafalis, L. A.	1,739,553	Graham, Robert		790,540 D	35.3%	64.7%	35.3%	64.7%
1978	2,530,468	1,123,888	Eckerd, Jack M.	1,406,580	Graham, Robert		282,692 D	44.4%	55.6%	44.4%	55.6%
1974	1,828,392	709,438	Thomas, Jerry	1,118,954	Askew, Reubin		409,516 D	38.8%	61.2%	38.8%	61.2%
1970	1,730,813	746,243	Kirk, Claude R.	984,305	Askew, Reubin	265	238,062 D	43.1%	56.9%	43.1%	56.9%
1966	1,489,661	821,190	Kirk, Claude R.	668,233	High, Robert King	238	152,957 R	55.1%	44.9%	55.1%	44.9%
1964 S	1,663,481	686,297	Holley, Charles R.	933,554	Burns, Haydon	43,630	247,257 D	41.3%	56.1%	42.4%	57.6%
1960	1,419,343	569,936	Petersen, George C.	849,407	Bryant, Farris		279,471 D	40.2%	59.8%	40.2%	59.8%
1956	1,014,733	266,980	Washburne, W. A.	747,753	Collins, LeRoy		480,773 D	26.3%	73.7%	26.3%	73.7%
1954 S	357,783	69,852	Watson, J. Tom	287,769	Collins, LeRoy	162	217,917 D	19.5%	80.4%	19.5%	80.5%
1952	834,518	210,009	Swan, Harry S.	624,463	McCarty, Dan	46	414,454 D	25.2%	74.8%	25.2%	74.8%
1948	457,638	76,153	Acker, Bert Lee	381,459	Warren, Fuller	26	305,306 D	16.6%	83.4%	16.6%	83.4%

The 1954 election was for a short term to fill a vacancy. The 1964 election was for a two-year term to permit shifting the vote for Governor to non-Presidential years.

POSTWAR VOTE FOR SENATOR

Year	Total Vote	Republican Vote	Republican Candidate	Democratic Vote	Democratic Candidate	Other Vote	Rep.-Dem. Plurality	Percentage Total Vote Rep.	Percentage Total Vote Dem.	Percentage Major Vote Rep.	Percentage Major Vote Dem.
1988	4,068,209	2,051,071	Mack, Connie	2,016,553	MacKay, Buddy	585	34,518 R	50.4%	49.6%	50.4%	49.6%
1986	3,429,996	1,552,376	Hawkins, Paula	1,877,543	Graham, Robert	77	325,167 D	45.3%	54.7%	45.3%	54.7%
1982	2,653,419	1,015,330	Poole, Van B.	1,637,667	Chiles, Lawton	422	622,337 D	38.3%	61.7%	38.3%	61.7%
1980	3,528,028	1,822,460	Hawkins, Paula	1,705,409	Gunter, Bill	159	117,051 R	51.7%	48.3%	51.7%	48.3%
1976	2,857,534	1,057,886	Grady, John	1,799,518	Chiles, Lawton	130	741,632 D	37.0%	63.0%	37.0%	63.0%
1974	1,800,539	736,674	Eckerd, Jack M.	781,031	Stone, Richard	282,834	44,357 D	40.9%	43.4%	48.5%	51.5%
1970	1,675,378	772,817	Cramer, William C.	902,438	Chiles, Lawton	123	129,621 D	46.1%	53.9%	46.1%	53.9%
1968	2,024,136	1,131,499	Gurney, Edward J.	892,637	Collins, LeRoy		238,862 R	55.9%	44.1%	55.9%	44.1%
1964	1,560,337	562,212	Kirk, Claude R.	997,585	Holland, Spessard L.	540	435,373 D	36.0%	63.9%	36.0%	64.0%
1962	939,207	281,381	Rupert, Emerson H.	657,633	Smathers, George A.	193	376,252 D	30.0%	70.0%	30.0%	70.0%
1958	542,069	155,956	Hyzer, Leland	386,113	Holland, Spessard L.		230,157 D	28.8%	71.2%	28.8%	71.2%
1956	655,418		—	655,418	Smathers, George A.		655,418 D		100.0%		100.0%
1952	617,800		—	616,665	Holland, Pessard L.	1,135	616,665 D		99.8%		100.0%
1950	313,487	74,228	Booth, John P.	238,987	Smathers, George A.	272	164,759 D	23.7%	76.2%	23.7%	76.3%
1946	198,640	42,408	Schad, J. Harry	156,232	Holland, Spessard L.		113,824 D	21.3%	78.7%	21.3%	78.7%

FLORIDA

Districts Established May 21, 1982

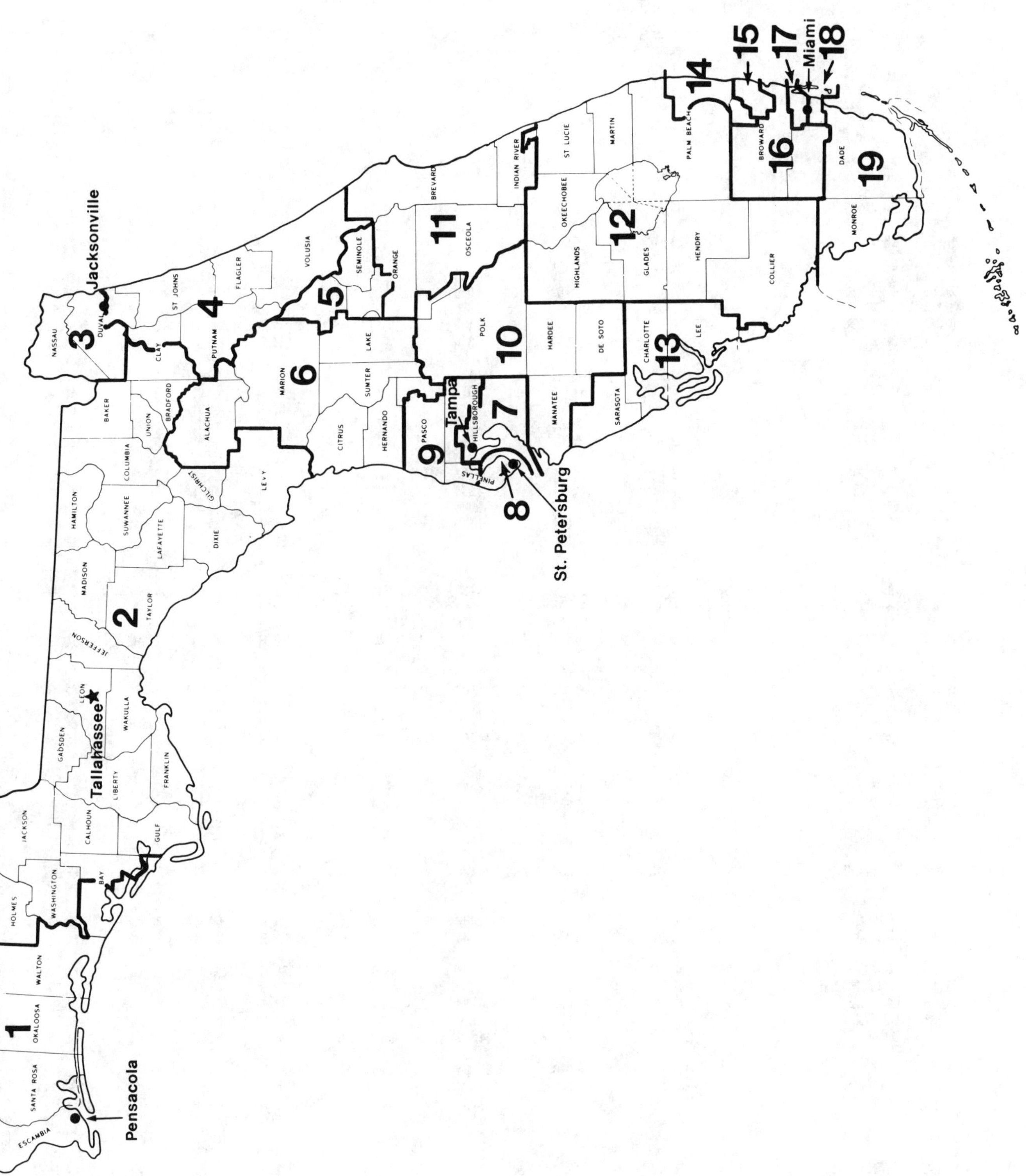

FLORIDA

PRESIDENT 1988

1980 Census Population	County	Total Vote	Republican	Democratic	Other	Rep.-Dem. Plurality	Percentage: Total Vote Rep.	Total Vote Dem.	Major Vote Rep.	Major Vote Dem.
151,348	ALACHUA	60,213	30,153	29,396	664	757 R	50.1%	48.8%	50.6%	49.4%
15,289	BAKER	4,781	3,418	1,355	8	2,063 R	71.5%	28.3%	71.6%	28.4%
97,740	BAY	43,851	31,796	11,603	452	20,193 R	72.5%	26.5%	73.3%	26.7%
20,023	BRADFORD	6,636	4,221	2,386	29	1,835 R	63.6%	36.0%	63.9%	36.1%
272,959	BREVARD	149,159	104,854	43,004	1,301	61,850 R	70.3%	28.8%	70.9%	29.1%
1,018,200	BROWARD	440,605	220,316	218,274	2,015	2,042 R	50.0%	49.5%	50.2%	49.8%
9,294	CALHOUN	3,784	2,422	1,329	33	1,093 R	64.0%	35.1%	64.6%	35.4%
58,460	CHARLOTTE	45,159	28,893	15,974	292	12,919 R	64.0%	35.4%	64.4%	35.6%
54,703	CITRUS	33,474	21,072	12,184	218	8,888 R	63.0%	36.4%	63.4%	36.6%
67,052	CLAY	33,837	25,942	7,773	122	18,169 R	76.7%	23.0%	76.9%	23.1%
85,971	COLLIER	51,980	38,920	12,769	291	26,151 R	74.9%	24.6%	75.3%	24.7%
35,399	COLUMBIA	11,916	7,761	4,073	82	3,688 R	65.1%	34.2%	65.6%	34.4%
1,625,781	DADE	490,265	270,937	216,970	2,358	53,967 R	55.3%	44.3%	55.5%	44.5%
19,039	DESOTO	6,464	4,243	2,181	40	2,062 R	65.6%	33.7%	66.0%	34.0%
7,751	DIXIE	3,397	2,031	1,366		665 R	59.8%	40.2%	59.8%	40.2%
571,003	DUVAL	203,979	128,081	74,894	1,004	53,187 R	62.8%	36.7%	63.1%	36.9%
233,794	ESCAMBIA	95,460	64,959	29,977	524	34,982 R	68.0%	31.4%	68.4%	31.6%
10,913	FLAGLER	10,782	6,504	4,244	34	2,260 R	60.3%	39.4%	60.5%	39.5%
7,661	FRANKLIN	3,269	1,913	1,283	73	630 R	58.5%	39.2%	59.9%	40.1%
41,565	GADSDEN	12,577	5,992	6,372	213	380 D	47.6%	50.7%	48.5%	51.5%
5,767	GILCHRIST	3,012	1,855	1,137	20	718 R	61.6%	37.7%	62.0%	38.0%
5,992	GLADES	2,593	1,547	1,034	12	513 R	59.7%	39.9%	59.9%	40.1%
10,658	GULF	4,872	3,042	1,688	142	1,354 R	62.4%	34.6%	64.3%	35.7%
8,761	HAMILTON	3,396	2,062	1,318	16	744 R	60.7%	38.8%	61.0%	39.0%
19,379	HARDEE	5,436	3,640	1,688	108	1,952 R	67.0%	31.1%	68.3%	31.7%
18,599	HENDRY	6,035	3,965	2,036	34	1,929 R	65.7%	33.7%	66.1%	33.9%
44,469	HERNANDO	36,863	21,195	15,437	231	5,758 R	57.5%	41.9%	57.9%	42.1%
47,526	HIGHLANDS	24,941	16,723	8,091	127	8,632 R	67.1%	32.4%	67.4%	32.6%
646,960	HILLSBOROUGH	250,716	150,151	99,014	1,551	51,137 R	59.9%	39.5%	60.3%	39.7%
14,723	HOLMES	5,900	4,225	1,639	36	2,586 R	71.6%	27.8%	72.0%	28.0%
59,896	INDIAN RIVER	35,333	24,630	10,451	252	14,179 R	69.7%	29.6%	70.2%	29.8%
39,154	JACKSON	13,513	8,405	5,008	100	3,397 R	62.2%	37.1%	62.7%	37.3%
10,703	JEFFERSON	4,398	2,326	2,055	17	271 R	52.9%	46.7%	53.1%	46.9%
4,035	LAFAYETTE	2,185	1,451	722	12	729 R	66.4%	33.0%	66.8%	33.2%
104,870	LAKE	54,572	37,327	16,766	479	20,561 R	68.4%	30.7%	69.0%	31.0%
205,266	LEE	128,936	87,303	40,725	908	46,578 R	67.7%	31.6%	68.2%	31.8%
148,655	LEON	70,158	36,055	33,472	631	2,583 R	51.4%	47.7%	51.9%	48.1%
19,870	LEVY	8,791	5,253	3,434	104	1,819 R	59.8%	39.1%	60.5%	39.5%
4,260	LIBERTY	2,177	1,421	709	47	712 R	65.3%	32.6%	66.7%	33.3%
14,894	MADISON	4,529	2,563	1,951	15	612 R	56.6%	43.1%	56.8%	43.2%
148,442	MANATEE	78,113	51,187	26,624	302	24,563 R	65.5%	34.1%	65.8%	34.2%
122,488	MARION	62,520	41,501	20,685	334	20,816 R	66.4%	33.1%	66.7%	33.3%
64,014	MARTIN	43,083	31,279	11,488	316	19,791 R	72.6%	26.7%	73.1%	26.9%
63,188	MONROE	26,405	15,928	10,157	320	5,771 R	60.3%	38.5%	61.1%	38.9%
32,894	NASSAU	12,575	8,374	4,143	58	4,231 R	66.6%	32.9%	66.9%	33.1%
109,920	OKALOOSA	50,462	40,389	9,753	320	30,636 R	80.0%	19.3%	80.5%	19.5%
20,264	OKEECHOBEE	7,791	4,736	3,007	48	1,729 R	60.8%	38.6%	61.2%	38.8%
471,016	ORANGE	172,770	117,237	54,023	1,510	63,214 R	67.9%	31.3%	68.5%	31.5%
49,287	OSCEOLA	31,381	21,355	9,812	214	11,543 R	68.1%	31.3%	68.5%	31.5%
576,863	PALM BEACH	327,217	181,495	144,199	1,523	37,296 R	55.5%	44.1%	55.7%	44.3%
193,643	PASCO	114,803	63,820	50,385	598	13,435 R	55.6%	43.9%	55.9%	44.1%
728,531	PINELLAS	365,370	211,049	152,420	1,901	58,629 R	57.8%	41.7%	58.1%	41.9%
321,652	POLK	116,040	77,104	38,249	687	38,855 R	66.4%	33.0%	66.8%	33.2%
50,549	PUTNAM	20,307	11,624	8,575	108	3,049 R	57.2%	42.2%	57.5%	42.5%
51,303	ST. JOHNS	27,347	19,189	8,002	156	11,187 R	70.2%	29.3%	70.6%	29.4%
87,182	ST. LUCIE	50,004	32,258	17,431	315	14,827 R	64.5%	34.9%	64.9%	35.1%
55,988	SANTA ROSA	24,424	19,021	5,259	144	13,762 R	77.9%	21.5%	78.3%	21.7%
202,251	SARASOTA	127,483	84,649	42,125	709	42,524 R	66.4%	33.0%	66.8%	33.2%
179,752	SEMINOLE	83,673	60,406	22,646	621	37,760 R	72.2%	27.1%	72.7%	27.3%
24,272	SUMTER	9,896	5,936	3,900	60	2,036 R	60.0%	39.4%	60.3%	39.7%

FLORIDA

PRESIDENT 1988

1980 Census Population	County	Total Vote	Republican	Democratic	Other	Rep.-Dem. Plurality	Percentage Total Vote Rep.	Total Vote Dem.	Major Vote Rep.	Major Vote Dem.
22,287	SUWANNEE	9,122	5,863	3,129	130	2,734 R	64.3%	34.3%	65.2%	34.8%
16,532	TAYLOR	5,875	4,057	1,763	55	2,294 R	69.1%	30.0%	69.7%	30.3%
10,166	UNION	2,349	1,644	691	14	953 R	70.0%	29.4%	70.4%	29.6%
258,762	VOLUSIA	131,182	74,195	55,469	1,518	18,726 R	56.6%	42.3%	57.2%	42.8%
10,887	WAKULLA	4,805	3,158	1,605	42	1,553 R	65.7%	33.4%	66.3%	33.7%
21,300	WALTON	10,808	7,490	3,235	83	4,255 R	69.3%	29.9%	69.8%	30.2%
14,509	WASHINGTON	6,564	4,374	2,144	46	2,230 R	66.6%	32.7%	67.1%	32.9%
9,746,324	TOTAL	4,302,313	2,618,885	1,656,701	26,727	962,184 R	60.9%	38.5%	61.3%	38.7%

FLORIDA

SENATOR 1988

1980 Census Population	County	Total Vote	Republican	Democratic	Other	Rep.-Dem. Plurality	Percentage			
							Total Vote		Major Vote	
							Rep.	Dem.	Rep.	Dem.
151,348	ALACHUA	61,032	18,826	42,206		23,380 D	30.8%	69.2%	30.8%	69.2%
15,289	BAKER	5,209	2,711	2,498		213 R	52.0%	48.0%	52.0%	48.0%
97,740	BAY	39,623	23,799	15,824		7,975 R	60.1%	39.9%	60.1%	39.9%
20,023	BRADFORD	6,709	2,943	3,766		823 D	43.9%	56.1%	43.9%	56.1%
272,959	BREVARD	154,810	90,378	64,431	1	25,947 R	58.4%	41.6%	58.4%	41.6%
1,018,200	BROWARD	410,780	171,290	239,490		68,200 D	41.7%	58.3%	41.7%	58.3%
9,294	CALHOUN	3,544	1,730	1,814		84 D	48.8%	51.2%	48.8%	51.2%
58,460	CHARLOTTE	44,133	23,831	20,302		3,529 R	54.0%	46.0%	54.0%	46.0%
54,703	CITRUS	36,511	16,455	20,056		3,601 D	45.1%	54.9%	45.1%	54.9%
67,052	CLAY	34,552	22,812	11,740		11,072 R	66.0%	34.0%	66.0%	34.0%
85,971	COLLIER	52,332	36,426	15,906		20,520 R	69.6%	30.4%	69.6%	30.4%
35,399	COLUMBIA	12,604	5,717	6,887		1,170 D	45.4%	54.6%	45.4%	54.6%
1,625,781	DADE	426,787	201,331	225,456		24,125 D	47.2%	52.8%	47.2%	52.8%
19,039	DESOTO	7,099	3,584	3,515		69 R	50.5%	49.5%	50.5%	49.5%
7,751	DIXIE	3,809	1,267	2,542		1,275 D	33.3%	66.7%	33.3%	66.7%
571,003	DUVAL	190,063	107,644	82,418	1	25,226 R	56.6%	43.4%	56.6%	43.4%
233,794	ESCAMBIA	90,038	56,107	33,930	1	22,177 R	62.3%	37.7%	62.3%	37.7%
10,913	FLAGLER	11,165	5,952	5,213		739 R	53.3%	46.7%	53.3%	46.7%
7,661	FRANKLIN	2,868	1,366	1,502		136 D	47.6%	52.4%	47.6%	52.4%
41,565	GADSDEN	11,617	4,106	7,511		3,405 D	35.3%	64.7%	35.3%	64.7%
5,767	GILCHRIST	3,266	1,133	2,133		1,000 D	34.7%	65.3%	34.7%	65.3%
5,992	GLADES	2,730	1,259	1,471		212 D	46.1%	53.9%	46.1%	53.9%
10,658	GULF	4,233	2,068	2,165		97 D	48.9%	51.1%	48.9%	51.1%
8,761	HAMILTON	3,177	1,276	1,890	11	614 D	40.2%	59.5%	40.3%	59.7%
19,379	HARDEE	5,089	2,508	2,581		73 D	49.3%	50.7%	49.3%	50.7%
18,599	HENDRY	6,439	3,396	3,043		353 R	52.7%	47.3%	52.7%	47.3%
44,469	HERNANDO	43,168	19,047	24,099	22	5,052 D	44.1%	55.8%	44.1%	55.9%
47,526	HIGHLANDS	26,688	14,158	12,530		1,628 R	53.1%	46.9%	53.1%	46.9%
646,960	HILLSBOROUGH	189,188	85,815	103,373		17,558 D	45.4%	54.6%	45.4%	54.6%
14,723	HOLMES	5,616	3,272	2,344		928 R	58.3%	41.7%	58.3%	41.7%
59,896	INDIAN RIVER	35,655	21,797	13,858		7,939 R	61.1%	38.9%	61.1%	38.9%
39,154	JACKSON	12,719	6,631	6,088		543 R	52.1%	47.9%	52.1%	47.9%
10,703	JEFFERSON	4,806	1,634	3,172		1,538 D	34.0%	66.0%	34.0%	66.0%
4,035	LAFAYETTE	2,129	827	1,297	5	470 D	38.8%	60.9%	38.9%	61.1%
104,870	LAKE	52,480	28,666	23,814		4,852 R	54.6%	45.4%	54.6%	45.4%
205,266	LEE	131,532	76,605	54,924	3	21,681 R	58.2%	41.8%	58.2%	41.8%
148,655	LEON	68,257	24,873	43,378	6	18,505 D	36.4%	63.6%	36.4%	63.6%
19,870	LEVY	8,534	3,356	5,178		1,822 D	39.3%	60.7%	39.3%	60.7%
4,260	LIBERTY	2,047	916	1,131		215 D	44.7%	55.3%	44.7%	55.3%
14,894	MADISON	5,020	1,998	3,022		1,024 D	39.8%	60.2%	39.8%	60.2%
148,442	MANATEE	83,348	43,165	39,887	296	3,278 R	51.8%	47.9%	52.0%	48.0%
122,488	MARION	64,779	30,500	34,279		3,779 D	47.1%	52.9%	47.1%	52.9%
64,014	MARTIN	39,729	24,639	15,090		9,549 R	62.0%	38.0%	62.0%	38.0%
63,188	MONROE	26,360	12,644	13,713	3	1,069 D	48.0%	52.0%	48.0%	52.0%
32,894	NASSAU	13,020	7,305	5,715		1,590 R	56.1%	43.9%	56.1%	43.9%
109,920	OKALOOSA	48,287	34,349	13,938		20,411 R	71.1%	28.9%	71.1%	28.9%
20,264	OKEECHOBEE	7,402	3,451	3,951		500 D	46.6%	53.4%	46.6%	53.4%
471,016	ORANGE	178,460	100,337	78,053	70	22,284 R	56.2%	43.7%	56.2%	43.8%
49,287	OSCEOLA	31,695	18,299	13,395	1	4,904 R	57.7%	42.3%	57.7%	42.3%
576,863	PALM BEACH	273,171	131,299	141,872		10,573 D	48.1%	51.9%	48.1%	51.9%
193,643	PASCO	117,066	52,377	64,688	1	12,311 D	44.7%	55.3%	44.7%	55.3%
728,531	PINELLAS	362,051	171,630	190,386	35	18,756 D	47.4%	52.6%	47.4%	52.6%
321,652	POLK	119,066	59,324	59,741	1	417 D	49.8%	50.2%	49.8%	50.2%
50,549	PUTNAM	21,843	9,288	12,555		3,267 D	42.5%	57.5%	42.5%	57.5%
51,303	ST. JOHNS	27,956	16,952	10,948	56	6,004 R	60.6%	39.2%	60.8%	39.2%
87,182	ST. LUCIE	42,292	23,463	18,829		4,634 R	55.5%	44.5%	55.5%	44.5%
55,988	SANTA ROSA	28,039	18,961	9,030	48	9,931 R	67.6%	32.2%	67.7%	32.3%
202,251	SARASOTA	111,366	58,030	53,333	3	4,697 R	52.1%	47.9%	52.1%	47.9%
179,752	SEMINOLE	84,954	50,736	34,216	2	16,520 R	59.7%	40.3%	59.7%	40.3%
24,272	SUMTER	8,855	3,545	5,310		1,765 D	40.0%	60.0%	40.0%	60.0%

FLORIDA

SENATOR 1988

1980 Census Population	County	Total Vote	Republican	Democratic	Other	Rep.-Dem. Plurality	Percentage Total Vote Rep.	Total Vote Dem.	Major Vote Rep.	Major Vote Dem.
22,287	SUWANNEE	8,801	4,008	4,793		785 D	45.5%	54.5%	45.5%	54.5%
16,532	TAYLOR	5,628	2,859	2,769		90 R	50.8%	49.2%	50.8%	49.2%
10,166	UNION	2,410	1,157	1,253		96 D	48.0%	52.0%	48.0%	52.0%
258,762	VOLUSIA	122,115	61,853	60,262		1,591 R	50.7%	49.3%	50.7%	49.3%
10,887	WAKULLA	5,064	2,213	2,834	17	621 D	43.7%	56.0%	43.8%	56.2%
21,300	WALTON	10,190	5,847	4,341	2	1,506 R	57.4%	42.6%	57.4%	42.6%
14,509	WASHINGTON	6,204	3,330	2,874		456 R	53.7%	46.3%	53.7%	46.3%
9,746,324	TOTAL	4,068,209	2,051,071	2,016,553	585	34,518 R	50.4%	49.6%	50.4%	49.6%

FLORIDA

CONGRESS

CD	Year	Total Vote	Republican Vote	Republican Candidate	Democratic Vote	Democratic Candidate	Other Vote	Rep.-Dem. Plurality	Percentage Total Vote Rep.	Percentage Total Vote Dem.	Percentage Major Vote Rep.	Percentage Major Vote Dem.
1	1988	212,983	70,534	ARMBRUSTER, E. D.	142,449	HUTTO, EARL D.		71,915 D	33.1%	66.9%	33.1%	66.9%
1	1986	152,991	55,459	NEUBECK, GREG	97,532	HUTTO, EARL D.		42,073 D	36.2%	63.8%	36.2%	63.8%
1	1984					HUTTO, EARL D.						
1	1982	110,942	28,373	BECHTOL, J. TERRYL	82,569	HUTTO, EARL D.		54,196 D	25.6%	74.4%	25.6%	74.4%
2	1988	134,621			134,269	GRANT, BILL	352	134,269 D		99.7%		100.0%
2	1986	110,766			110,141	GRANT, BILL	625	110,141 D		99.4%		100.0%
2	1984					FUQUA, DON						
2	1982	128,244	49,101	MCNEIL, RON	79,143	FUQUA, DON		30,042 D	38.3%	61.7%	38.3%	61.7%
3	1988					BENNETT, CHARLES E.						
3	1986					BENNETT, CHARLES E.						
3	1984					BENNETT, CHARLES E.						
3	1982	87,774	13,972	GRIMSLEY, GEORGE	73,802	BENNETT, CHARLES E.		59,830 D	15.9%	84.1%	15.9%	84.1%
4	1988	250,425	125,608	JAMES, CRAIG T.	124,817	CHAPPELL, WILLIAM V.		791 R	50.2%	49.8%	50.2%	49.8%
4	1986					CHAPPELL, WILLIAM V.						
4	1984	207,912	73,218	STARLING, ALTON H.	134,694	CHAPPELL, WILLIAM V.		61,476 D	35.2%	64.8%	35.2%	64.8%
4	1982	125,352	41,457	GAUDET, LARRY	83,895	CHAPPELL, WILLIAM V.		42,438 D	33.1%	66.9%	33.1%	66.9%
5	1988			MCCOLLUM, BILL								
5	1986			MCCOLLUM, BILL								
5	1984			MCCOLLUM, BILL								
5	1982	119,063	69,993	MCCOLLUM, BILL	49,070	BATCHELOR, DICK		20,923 R	58.8%	41.2%	58.8%	41.2%
6	1988	255,171	136,415	STEARNS, CLIFFORD B.	118,756	MILLS, JON		17,659 R	53.5%	46.5%	53.5%	46.5%
6	1986	204,667	61,069	GALLAGHER, LARRY	143,598	MACKAY, BUDDY		82,529 D	29.8%	70.2%	29.8%	70.2%
6	1984	168,583			167,409	MACKAY, BUDDY	1,174	167,409 D		99.3%		100.0%
6	1982	139,897	54,059	HAVILL, ED	85,825	MACKAY, BUDDY	13	31,766 D	38.6%	61.3%	38.6%	61.4%
7	1988					GIBBONS, SAM M.						
7	1986					GIBBONS, SAM M.						
7	1984	170,710	70,280	KAVOUKLIS, MICHAEL N.	100,430	GIBBONS, SAM M.		30,150 D	41.2%	58.8%	41.2%	58.8%
7	1982	114,963	29,632	AYERS, KEN	85,331	GIBBONS, SAM M.		55,699 D	25.8%	74.2%	25.8%	74.2%
8	1988	231,704	169,165	YOUNG, C. W.	62,539	WIMBISH, C. BETTE		106,626 R	73.0%	27.0%	73.0%	27.0%
8	1986			YOUNG, C. W.								
8	1984	229,946	184,553	YOUNG, C. W.	45,393	KENT, ROBERT		139,160 R	80.3%	19.7%	80.3%	19.7%
8	1982			YOUNG, C. W.								
9	1988	224,167	223,925	BILIRAKIS, MICHAEL			242	223,925 R	99.9%		100.0%	
9	1986	235,118	166,540	BILIRAKIS, MICHAEL	68,578	CAZARES, GABE		97,962 R	70.8%	29.2%	70.8%	29.2%
9	1984	243,493	191,343	BILIRAKIS, MICHAEL	52,150	WILSON, JACK		139,193 R	78.6%	21.4%	78.6%	21.4%
9	1982	185,742	95,009	BILIRAKIS, MICHAEL	90,697	SHELDON, GEORGE H.	36	4,312 R	51.2%	48.8%	51.2%	48.8%
10	1988	213,099	156,563	IRELAND, ANDREW P.	56,536	HIGGINBOTTOM, DAVID		100,027 R	73.5%	26.5%	73.5%	26.5%
10	1986	171,966	122,395	IRELAND, ANDREW P.	49,571	HIGGINBOTTOM, DAVID		72,824 R	71.2%	28.8%	71.2%	28.8%
10	1984	203,841	126,206	IRELAND, ANDREW P.	77,635	GLASS, PATRICIA M.		48,571 R	61.9%	38.1%	61.9%	38.1%
10	1982					IRELAND, ANDREW P.						
11	1988	276,763	108,373	TOLLEY, BILL	168,390	NELSON, BILL		60,017 D	39.2%	60.8%	39.2%	60.8%
11	1986	205,061	55,952	ELLIS, SCOTT	149,109	NELSON, BILL		93,157 D	27.3%	72.7%	27.3%	72.7%
11	1984	240,890	95,115	QUARTEL, ROB	145,764	NELSON, BILL	11	50,649 D	39.5%	60.5%	39.5%	60.5%
11	1982	144,168	42,422	ROBINSON, JOEL	101,746	NELSON, BILL		59,324 D	29.4%	70.6%	29.4%	70.6%
12	1988			LEWIS, TOM								
12	1986	151,180	150,244	LEWIS, TOM			936	150,244 R	99.4%		100.0%	
12	1984			LEWIS, TOM								
12	1982	155,806	81,893	LEWIS, TOM	73,913	CULVERHOUSE, BRAD		7,980 R	52.6%	47.4%	52.6%	47.4%

FLORIDA

CONGRESS

CD	Year	Total Vote	Republican Vote	Republican Candidate	Democratic Vote	Democratic Candidate	Other Vote	Rep.-Dem. Plurality	Percentage Total Vote Rep.	Percentage Total Vote Dem.	Percentage Major Vote Rep.	Percentage Major Vote Dem.
13	1988	324,870	231,170	GOSS, PORTER J.	93,700	CONWAY, JACK		137,470 R	71.2%	28.8%	71.2%	28.8%
13	1986	250,555	187,846	MACK, CONNIE	62,709	GILBERT, ADDISON S.		125,137 R	75.0%	25.0%	75.0%	25.0%
13	1984			MACK, CONNIE								
13	1982	204,190	132,951	MACK, CONNIE	71,239	STEVENS, DANA N.		61,712 R	65.1%	34.9%	65.1%	34.9%
14	1988	315,927	142,635	ADAMS, KEN	173,292	JOHNSTON, HARRY		30,657 D	45.1%	54.9%	45.1%	54.9%
14	1986	233,165	61,189	MARTIN, RICK	171,976	MICA, DAN		110,787 D	26.2%	73.8%	26.2%	73.8%
14	1984	277,861	123,926	ROSS, DON	153,935	MICA, DAN		30,009 D	44.6%	55.4%	44.6%	55.4%
14	1982	176,206	47,560	MITCHELL, STEVE	128,646	MICA, DAN		81,086 D	27.0%	73.0%	27.0%	73.0%
15	1988	199,836	132,090	SHAW, CLAY	67,746	KUHLE, MICHAEL A.		64,344 R	66.1%	33.9%	66.1%	33.9%
15	1986			SHAW, CLAY								
15	1984	194,930	128,097	SHAW, CLAY	66,833	HUMPHREY, BILL		61,264 R	65.7%	34.3%	65.7%	34.3%
15	1982	156,241	89,158	SHAW, CLAY	67,083	STACK, EDWARD J.		22,075 R	57.1%	42.9%	57.1%	42.9%
16	1988	220,493	67,461	SMITH, JOSEPH	153,032	SMITH, LARRY		85,571 D	30.6%	69.4%	30.6%	69.4%
16	1986	174,028	52,809	COLLINS, MARY	121,219	SMITH, LARRY		68,410 D	30.3%	69.7%	30.3%	69.7%
16	1984	192,313	83,903	BUSH, TOM	108,410	SMITH, LARRY		24,507 D	43.6%	56.4%	43.6%	56.4%
16	1982	135,346	43,458	BERKOWITZ, MAURICE	91,888	SMITH, LARRY		48,430 D	32.1%	67.9%	32.1%	67.9%
17	1988					LEHMAN, WILLIAM						
17	1986					LEHMAN, WILLIAM						
17	1984					LEHMAN, WILLIAM						
17	1982					LEHMAN, WILLIAM						
18	1988					PEPPER, CLAUDE						
18	1986	108,876	28,814	BRODIE, TOM	80,062	PEPPER, CLAUDE		51,248 D	26.5%	73.5%	26.5%	73.5%
18	1984	126,222	49,818	NUNEZ, RICARDO	76,404	PEPPER, CLAUDE		26,586 D	39.5%	60.5%	39.5%	60.5%
18	1982	101,379	29,196	NUNEZ, RICARDO	72,183	PEPPER, CLAUDE		42,987 D	28.8%	71.2%	28.8%	71.2%
19	1988	186,983	51,628	ROCHETEAU, RALPH C.	135,355	FASCELL, DANTE B.		83,727 D	27.6%	72.4%	27.6%	72.4%
19	1986	143,678	44,463	FLANAGAN, BILL	99,215	FASCELL, DANTE B.		54,752 D	30.9%	69.1%	30.9%	69.1%
19	1984	179,951	64,317	FLANAGAN, BILL	115,631	FASCELL, DANTE B.	3	51,314 D	35.7%	64.3%	35.7%	64.3%
19	1982	126,281	51,969	RINKER, GLENN	74,312	FASCELL, DANTE B.		22,343 D	41.2%	58.8%	41.2%	58.8%

FLORIDA

1988 GENERAL ELECTION

President Other vote was 19,796 Libertarian (Paul); 6,655 New Alliance (Fulani); 249 Duke (write-in); 14 Kenoyer (write-in); 13 scattered write-in. County and state-wide totals include special absentee ballots counted separately by court order.

Senator Other vote was Straus (write-in). Original unamended returns gave the Straus total as 385.

Congress Other vote was Prescott (write-in) in CD 2; Bigenho (write-in) in CD 9. In CD 2 Bill Grant was re-elected as a Democrat in November, 1988 but shortly after the election announced his change of party affiliation to Republican. In CD 10 Andrew P. Ireland was elected as a Democrat in 1982 and as a Republican in 1984, 1986 and 1988. According to state law, votes are not required to be tabulated for unopposed candidates.

1988 PRIMARIES

SEPTEMBER 6 REPUBLICAN

Senator 405,296 Connie Mack; 250,730 Robert W. Merkle.

Congress Unopposed in nine CD's. No candidate in CD's 2, 3, 7, 17 and 18. Contested as follows:

CD 4 19,275 Craig T. James; 10,380 Tom Visconti; 8,694 Ken C. McCarthy.
CD 6 13,355 Jim Cherry; 10,875 Clifford B. Stearns; 6,459 Roy Abshier; 5,984 Larry Gallagher; 2,317 Ken Stepp; 2,215 Norman F. Cates.
CD 11 17,137 Bill Tolley; 16,191 Rod Borum; 15,968 Ron Martin.
CD 13 36,875 Porter J. Goss; 27,958 L. A. Bafalis; 18,048 Jim Dozier; 6,835 Lee A. Coppock; 6,387 Brian Pappas.
CD 14 22,108 Ken Adams; 10,259 Reid Moore; 2,971 John L. Shudlick.

SEPTEMBER 6 DEMOCRATIC

Senator 383,721 Bill Gunter; 263,946 Buddy MacKay; 179,524 Dan Mica; 119,277 Patricia Frank; 51,387 Claude R. Kirk; 11,820 Fred Rader.

Congress Unopposed in eleven CD's. No candidate in CD's 5, 9, and 12. Contested as follows:

CD 1 72,508 Earl D. Hutto; 28,883 Durell Peaden.
CD 4 50,408 William V. Chappell; 21,541 Charley Roberts.
CD 13 26,066 Jack Conway; 7,968 Patricia Bidelman; 5,340 Martin A. Rosen.
CD 14 36,874 Harry Johnston; 26,116 Dorothy H. Wilken.
CD 19 35,630 Dante B. Fascell; 6,416 Wesley F. White.

OCTOBER 4 REPUBLICAN RUN-OFF

Congress

CD 6 15,205 Clifford B. Stearns; 12,882 Jim Cherry.
CD 11 9,590 Bill Tolley; 9,021 Rod Borum.
CD 13 49,292 Porter J. Goss; 19,413 L. A. Bafalis.

OCTOBER 4 DEMOCRATIC RUN-OFF

Senator 369,266 Buddy MacKay; 340,918 Bill Gunter.

GEORGIA

GOVERNOR

Joe Frank Harris (D). Re-elected 1986 to a four-year term. Previously elected 1982.

SENATORS

Wyche Fowler (D). Elected 1986 to a six-year term.

Sam Nunn (D). Re-elected 1984 to a six-year term. Previously elected 1978, 1972.

REPRESENTATIVES

1. Lindsay Thomas (D)
2. Charles Hatcher (D)
3. Richard Ray (D)
4. Ben Jones (D)
5. John Lewis (D)
6. Newt Gingrich (R)
7. George Darden (D)
8. J. Roy Rowland (D)
9. Ed Jenkins (D)
10. Doug Barnard (D)

POSTWAR VOTE FOR PRESIDENT

								Percentage			
	Total	Republican		Democratic		Other		Total Vote		Major Vote	
Year	Vote	Vote	Candidate	Vote	Candidate	Vote	Plurality	Rep.	Dem.	Rep.	Dem.
1988	1,809,672	1,081,331	Bush, George	714,792	Dukakis, Michael S.	13,549	366,539 R	59.8%	39.5%	60.2%	39.8%
1984	1,776,120	1,068,722	Reagan, Ronald	706,628	Mondale, Walter F.	770	362,094 R	60.2%	39.8%	60.2%	39.8%
1980	1,596,695	654,168	Reagan, Ronald	890,733	Carter, Jimmy	51,794	236,565 D	41.0%	55.8%	42.3%	57.7%
1976	1,467,458	483,743	Ford, Gerald R.	979,409	Carter, Jimmy	4,306	495,666 D	33.0%	66.7%	33.1%	66.9%
1972	1,174,772	881,496	Nixon, Richard M.	289,529	McGovern, George S.	3,747	591,967 R	75.0%	24.6%	75.3%	24.7%
1968 **	1,250,266	380,111	Nixon, Richard M.	334,440	Humphrey, Hubert H.	535,715	155,439 A	30.4%	26.7%	53.2%	46.8%
1964	1,139,335	616,584	Goldwater, Barry M.	522,556	Johnson, Lyndon B.	195	94,028 R	54.1%	45.9%	54.1%	45.9%
1960	733,349	274,472	Nixon, Richard M.	458,638	Kennedy, John F.	239	184,166 D	37.4%	62.5%	37.4%	62.6%
1956	669,655	222,778	Eisenhower, Dwight D.	444,688	Stevenson, Adlai E.	2,189	221,910 D	33.3%	66.4%	33.4%	66.6%
1952	655,785	198,961	Eisenhower, Dwight D.	456,823	Stevenson, Adlai E.	1	257,862 D	30.3%	69.7%	30.3%	69.7%
1948 **	418,844	76,691	Dewey, Thomas E.	254,646	Truman, Harry S.	87,507	169,511 D	18.3%	60.8%	23.1%	76.9%

In 1968 other vote was 535,550 American (Wallace) and 165 scattered. In 1948 other vote was 85,135 States Rights; 1,636 Progressive; 732 Prohibition; 3 Socialist and 1 scattered.

POSTWAR VOTE FOR GOVERNOR

								Percentage			
	Total	Republican		Democratic		Other	Rep.-Dem.	Total Vote		Major Vote	
Year	Vote	Vote	Candidate	Vote	Candidate	Vote	Plurality	Rep.	Dem.	Rep.	Dem.
1986	1,175,114	346,512	Davis, Guy	828,465	Harris, Joe Frank	137	481,953 D	29.5%	70.5%	29.5%	70.5%
1982	1,169,041	434,496	Bell, Robert H.	734,090	Harris, Joe Frank	455	299,594 D	37.2%	62.8%	37.2%	62.8%
1978	662,862	128,139	Cook, Rodney M.	534,572	Busbee, George	151	406,433 D	19.3%	80.6%	19.3%	80.7%
1974	936,438	289,113	Thompson, Ronnie	646,777	Busbee, George	548	357,664 D	30.9%	69.1%	30.9%	69.1%
1970	1,046,663	424,983	Suit, Hal	620,419	Carter, Jimmy	1,261	195,436 D	40.6%	59.3%	40.7%	59.3%
1966 **	975,019	453,665	Callaway, Howard H.	450,626	Maddox, Lester	70,728	3,039 R	46.5%	46.2%	50.2%	49.8%
1962	311,691		—	311,524	Sanders, Carl E.	167	311,524 D		99.9%		100.0%
1958	168,497		—	168,414	Vandiver, Ernest	83	168,414 D		100.0%		100.0%
1954	331,966		—	331,899	Griffin, Marvin	67	331,899 D		100.0%		100.0%
1950	234,430		—	230,771	Talmadge, Herman	3,659	230,771 D		98.4%		100.0%
1948 S	363,763		—	354,711	Talmadge, Herman	9,052	354,711 D		97.5%		100.0%
1946	145,403		—	143,279	Talmadge, Herman	2,124	143,279 D		98.5%		100.0%

The 1948 election was for a short term to fill a vacancy. In 1966, in the absence of a majority for any candidate, the State Legislature elected Lester Maddox to a four-year term.

GEORGIA

POSTWAR VOTE FOR SENATOR

Year	Total Vote	Republican Vote	Republican Candidate	Democratic Vote	Democratic Candidate	Other Vote	Rep.-Dem. Plurality	Percentage Total Vote Rep.	Percentage Total Vote Dem.	Percentage Major Vote Rep.	Percentage Major Vote Dem.
1986	1,225,008	601,241	Mattingly, Mack	623,707	Fowler, Wyche	60	22,466 D	49.1%	50.9%	49.1%	50.9%
1984	1,681,344	337,196	Hicks, Jon Michael	1,344,104	Nunn, Sam	44	1,006,908 D	20.1%	79.9%	20.1%	79.9%
1980	1,580,340	803,686	Mattingly, Mack	776,143	Talmadge, Herman	511	27,543 R	50.9%	49.1%	50.9%	49.1%
1978	645,164	108,808	Stokes, John W.	536,320	Nunn, Sam	36	427,512 D	16.9%	83.1%	16.9%	83.1%
1974	874,555	246,866	Johnson, Jerry R.	627,376	Talmadge, Herman	313	380,510 D	28.2%	71.7%	28.2%	71.8%
1972	1,178,708	542,331	Thompson, Fletcher	635,970	Nunn, Sam	407	93,639 D	46.0%	54.0%	46.0%	54.0%
1968	1,141,889	256,796	Patton, E. Earl	885,093	Talmadge, Herman		628,297 D	22.5%	77.5%	22.5%	77.5%
1966	622,371		—	622,043	Russell, Richard B.	328	622,043 D		99.9%		100.0%
1962	306,250		—	306,250	Talmadge, Herman		306,250 D		100.0%		100.0%
1960	576,495		—	576,140	Russell, Richard B.	355	576,140 D		99.9%		100.0%
1956	541,267		—	541,094	Talmadge, Herman	173	541,094 D		100.0%		100.0%
1954	333,936		—	333,917	Russell, Richard B.	19	333,917 D		100.0%		100.0%
1950	261,293		—	261,290	George, Walter F.	3	261,290 D		100.0%		100.0%
1948	362,504		—	362,104	Russell, Richard B.	400	362,104 D		99.9%		100.0%

GEORGIA

Districts Established August 24, 1982

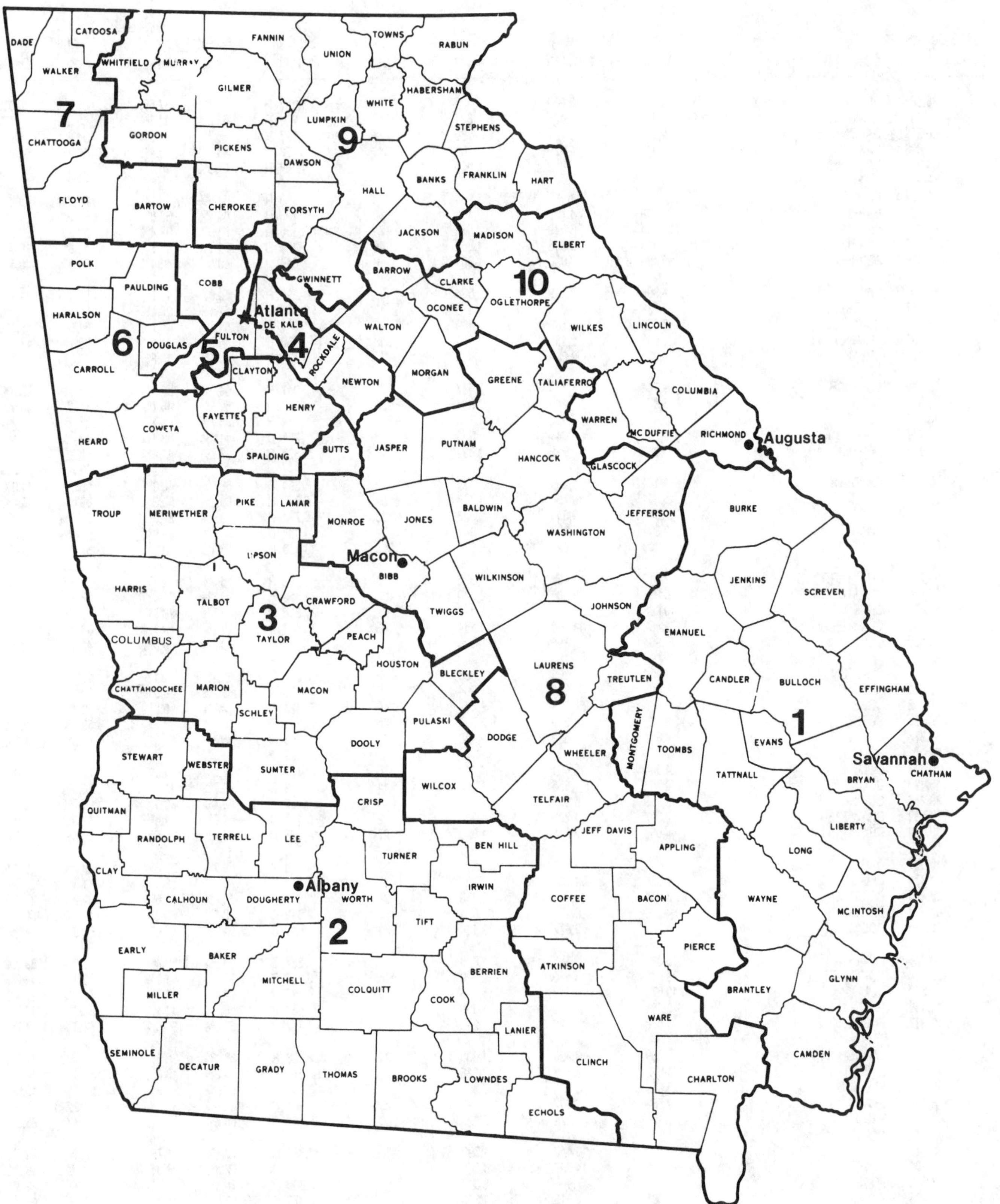

GEORGIA

PRESIDENT 1988

1980 Census Population	County	Total Vote	Republican	Democratic	Other	Rep.-Dem. Plurality	Percentage Total Vote Rep.	Percentage Total Vote Dem.	Percentage Major Vote Rep.	Percentage Major Vote Dem.
15,565	APPLING	4,859	3,000	1,837	22	1,163 R	61.7%	37.8%	62.0%	38.0%
6,141	ATKINSON	2,025	1,126	887	12	239 R	55.6%	43.8%	55.9%	44.1%
9,379	BACON	2,194	1,407	780	7	627 R	64.1%	35.6%	64.3%	35.7%
3,808	BAKER	1,348	629	707	12	78 D	46.7%	52.4%	47.1%	52.9%
34,686	BALDWIN	9,911	5,852	4,008	51	1,844 R	59.0%	40.4%	59.4%	40.6%
8,702	BANKS	2,582	1,590	984	8	606 R	61.6%	38.1%	61.8%	38.2%
21,354	BARROW	7,218	4,738	2,442	38	2,296 R	65.6%	33.8%	66.0%	34.0%
40,760	BARTOW	13,044	8,039	4,884	121	3,155 R	61.6%	37.4%	62.2%	37.8%
16,000	BEN HILL	3,918	2,005	1,867	46	138 R	51.2%	47.7%	51.8%	48.2%
13,525	BERRIEN	3,420	2,030	1,381	9	649 R	59.4%	40.4%	59.5%	40.5%
150,256	BIBB	44,396	22,179	22,084	133	95 R	50.0%	49.7%	50.1%	49.9%
10,767	BLECKLEY	3,138	1,950	1,175	13	775 R	62.1%	37.4%	62.4%	37.6%
8,701	BRANTLEY	3,007	1,539	1,450	18	89 R	51.2%	48.2%	51.5%	48.5%
15,255	BROOKS	3,649	2,136	1,500	13	636 R	58.5%	41.1%	58.7%	41.3%
10,175	BRYAN	4,235	2,802	1,423	10	1,379 R	66.2%	33.6%	66.3%	33.7%
35,785	BULLOCH	9,794	6,354	3,417	23	2,937 R	64.9%	34.9%	65.0%	35.0%
19,349	BURKE	5,872	2,988	2,861	23	127 R	50.9%	48.7%	51.1%	48.9%
13,665	BUTTS	3,924	2,184	1,730	10	454 R	55.7%	44.1%	55.8%	44.2%
5,717	CALHOUN	1,551	644	901	6	257 D	41.5%	58.1%	41.7%	58.3%
13,371	CAMDEN	5,050	2,913	2,090	47	823 R	57.7%	41.4%	58.2%	41.8%
7,518	CANDLER	2,144	1,261	877	6	384 R	58.8%	40.9%	59.0%	41.0%
56,346	CARROLL	15,541	10,754	4,706	81	6,048 R	69.2%	30.3%	69.6%	30.4%
36,991	CATOOSA	12,940	9,319	3,588	33	5,731 R	72.0%	27.7%	72.2%	27.8%
7,343	CHARLTON	2,304	1,327	943	34	384 R	57.6%	40.9%	58.5%	41.5%
202,226	CHATHAM	61,289	35,623	25,063	603	10,560 R	58.1%	40.9%	58.7%	41.3%
21,732	CHATTAHOOCHEE	817	454	362	1	92 R	55.6%	44.3%	55.6%	44.4%
21,856	CHATTOOGA	5,895	3,665	2,206	24	1,459 R	62.2%	37.4%	62.4%	37.6%
51,699	CHEROKEE	19,088	14,593	4,378	117	10,215 R	76.5%	22.9%	76.9%	23.1%
74,498	CLARKE	22,452	11,150	11,154	148	4 D	49.7%	49.7%	50.0%	50.0%
3,553	CLAY	994	398	595	1	197 D	40.0%	59.9%	40.1%	59.9%
150,357	CLAYTON	43,137	28,225	14,689	223	13,536 R	65.4%	34.1%	65.8%	34.2%
6,660	CLINCH	1,465	863	594	8	269 R	58.9%	40.5%	59.2%	40.8%
297,718	COBB	146,658	106,621	39,297	740	67,324 R	72.7%	26.8%	73.1%	26.9%
26,894	COFFEE	6,822	4,019	2,777	26	1,242 R	58.9%	40.7%	59.1%	40.9%
35,376	COLQUITT	8,691	5,653	2,998	40	2,655 R	65.0%	34.5%	65.3%	34.7%
40,118	COLUMBIA	21,094	16,401	4,617	76	11,784 R	77.8%	21.9%	78.0%	22.0%
13,490	COOK	2,792	1,555	1,226	11	329 R	55.7%	43.9%	55.9%	44.1%
39,268	COWETA	13,929	9,668	4,212	49	5,456 R	69.4%	30.2%	69.7%	30.3%
7,684	CRAWFORD	2,597	1,235	1,340	22	105 D	47.6%	51.6%	48.0%	52.0%
19,489	CRISP	4,633	2,916	1,690	27	1,226 R	62.9%	36.5%	63.3%	36.7%
12,318	DADE	3,671	2,539	1,120	12	1,419 R	69.2%	30.5%	69.4%	30.6%
4,774	DAWSON	2,686	1,908	761	17	1,147 R	71.0%	28.3%	71.5%	28.5%
25,495	DECATUR	6,241	3,866	2,348	27	1,518 R	61.9%	37.6%	62.2%	37.8%
483,024	DE KALB	184,250	90,179	92,521	1,550	2,342 D	48.9%	50.2%	49.4%	50.6%
16,955	DODGE	4,872	2,677	2,164	31	513 R	54.9%	44.4%	55.3%	44.7%
10,826	DOOLY	3,021	1,386	1,613	22	227 D	45.9%	53.4%	46.2%	53.8%
100,718	DOUGHERTY	30,517	15,520	12,579	2,418	2,941 R	50.9%	41.2%	55.2%	44.8%
54,573	DOUGLAS	18,678	13,493	5,086	99	8,407 R	72.2%	27.2%	72.6%	27.4%
13,158	EARLY	3,281	1,918	1,359	4	559 R	58.5%	41.4%	58.5%	41.5%
2,297	ECHOLS	670	422	245	3	177 R	63.0%	36.6%	63.3%	36.7%
18,327	EFFINGHAM	5,859	3,933	1,905	21	2,028 R	67.1%	32.5%	67.4%	32.6%
18,758	ELBERT	4,925	2,796	2,118	11	678 R	56.8%	43.0%	56.9%	43.1%
20,795	EMANUEL	5,988	3,530	2,387	71	1,143 R	59.0%	39.9%	59.7%	40.3%
8,428	EVANS	2,753	1,707	1,023	23	684 R	62.0%	37.2%	62.5%	37.5%
14,748	FANNIN	6,427	4,271	2,123	33	2,148 R	66.5%	33.0%	66.8%	33.2%
29,043	FAYETTE	21,123	16,443	4,593	87	11,850 R	77.8%	21.7%	78.2%	21.8%
79,800	FLOYD	23,386	14,697	8,548	141	6,149 R	62.8%	36.6%	63.2%	36.8%
27,958	FORSYTH	10,344	7,947	2,347	50	5,600 R	76.8%	22.7%	77.2%	22.8%
15,185	FRANKLIN	4,465	2,615	1,842	8	773 R	58.6%	41.3%	58.7%	41.3%
589,904	FULTON	214,689	91,785	120,752	2,152	28,967 D	42.8%	56.2%	43.2%	56.8%

GEORGIA

PRESIDENT 1988

1980 Census Population	County	Total Vote	Republican	Democratic	Other	Rep.-Dem. Plurality	Percentage Total Vote Rep.	Total Vote Dem.	Major Vote Rep.	Major Vote Dem.
11,110	GILMER	4,746	3,353	1,363	30	1,990 R	70.6%	28.7%	71.1%	28.9%
2,382	GLASCOCK	790	580	210		370 R	73.4%	26.6%	73.4%	26.6%
54,981	GLYNN	17,611	11,126	6,339	146	4,787 R	63.2%	36.0%	63.7%	36.3%
30,070	GORDON	8,445	6,051	2,369	25	3,682 R	71.7%	28.1%	71.9%	28.1%
19,845	GRADY	4,892	2,989	1,883	20	1,106 R	61.1%	38.5%	61.4%	38.6%
11,391	GREENE	3,260	1,432	1,818	10	386 D	43.9%	55.8%	44.1%	55.9%
166,903	GWINNETT	87,940	66,372	20,948	620	45,424 R	75.5%	23.8%	76.0%	24.0%
25,020	HABERSHAM	7,014	4,871	2,114	29	2,757 R	69.4%	30.1%	69.7%	30.3%
75,649	HALL	25,344	17,415	7,782	147	9,633 R	68.7%	30.7%	69.1%	30.9%
9,466	HANCOCK	2,589	621	1,947	21	1,326 D	24.0%	75.2%	24.2%	75.8%
18,422	HARALSON	6,950	4,529	2,404	17	2,125 R	65.2%	34.6%	65.3%	34.7%
15,464	HARRIS	5,339	3,414	1,905	20	1,509 R	63.9%	35.7%	64.2%	35.8%
18,585	HART	5,547	3,044	2,476	27	568 R	54.9%	44.6%	55.1%	44.9%
6,520	HEARD	2,432	1,551	874	7	677 R	63.8%	35.9%	64.0%	36.0%
36,309	HENRY	15,304	10,882	4,348	74	6,534 R	71.1%	28.4%	71.5%	28.5%
77,605	HOUSTON	24,597	15,748	8,664	185	7,084 R	64.0%	35.2%	64.5%	35.5%
8,988	IRWIN	2,151	1,226	918	7	308 R	57.0%	42.7%	57.2%	42.8%
25,343	JACKSON	7,045	4,407	2,607	31	1,800 R	62.6%	37.0%	62.8%	37.2%
7,553	JASPER	2,676	1,474	1,188	14	286 R	55.1%	44.4%	55.4%	44.6%
11,473	JEFF DAVIS	3,305	2,050	1,242	13	808 R	62.0%	37.6%	62.3%	37.7%
18,403	JEFFERSON	5,151	2,788	2,346	17	442 R	54.1%	45.5%	54.3%	45.7%
8,841	JENKINS	2,248	1,288	953	7	335 R	57.3%	42.4%	57.5%	42.5%
8,660	JOHNSON	2,494	1,567	927		640 R	62.8%	37.2%	62.8%	37.2%
16,579	JONES	6,302	3,618	2,662	22	956 R	57.4%	42.2%	57.6%	42.4%
12,215	LAMAR	3,519	2,035	1,416	68	619 R	57.8%	40.2%	59.0%	41.0%
5,654	LANIER	1,427	725	698	4	27 R	50.8%	48.9%	50.9%	49.1%
36,990	LAURENS	11,970	6,929	4,879	162	2,050 R	57.9%	40.8%	58.7%	41.3%
11,684	LEE	3,883	2,875	995	13	1,880 R	74.0%	25.6%	74.3%	25.7%
37,583	LIBERTY	6,050	3,100	2,906	44	194 R	51.2%	48.0%	51.6%	48.4%
6,716	LINCOLN	2,324	1,417	893	14	524 R	61.0%	38.4%	61.3%	38.7%
4,524	LONG	1,551	858	681	12	177 R	55.3%	43.9%	55.8%	44.2%
67,972	LOWNDES	17,333	10,855	6,427	51	4,428 R	62.6%	37.1%	62.8%	37.2%
10,762	LUMPKIN	4,000	2,688	1,286	26	1,402 R	67.2%	32.2%	67.6%	32.4%
18,546	MCDUFFIE	4,968	3,231	1,704	33	1,527 R	65.0%	34.3%	65.5%	34.5%
8,046	MCINTOSH	2,824	1,273	1,527	24	254 D	45.1%	54.1%	45.5%	54.5%
14,003	MACON	3,697	1,412	2,268	17	856 D	38.2%	61.3%	38.4%	61.6%
17,747	MADISON	5,389	3,724	1,639	26	2,085 R	69.1%	30.4%	69.4%	30.6%
5,297	MARION	1,652	804	844	4	40 D	48.7%	51.1%	48.8%	51.2%
21,229	MERIWETHER	6,044	3,101	2,934	9	167 R	51.3%	48.5%	51.4%	48.6%
7,038	MILLER	1,625	1,105	515	5	590 R	68.0%	31.7%	68.2%	31.8%
21,114	MITCHELL	4,860	2,590	2,260	10	330 R	53.3%	46.5%	53.4%	46.6%
14,610	MONROE	4,558	2,570	1,970	18	600 R	56.4%	43.2%	56.6%	43.4%
7,011	MONTGOMERY	2,136	1,228	903	5	325 R	57.5%	42.3%	57.6%	42.4%
11,572	MORGAN	3,628	2,108	1,508	12	600 R	58.1%	41.6%	58.3%	41.7%
19,685	MURRAY	5,700	3,996	1,679	25	2,317 R	70.1%	29.5%	70.4%	29.6%
170,108	MUSCOGEE	42,000	23,058	18,772	170	4,286 R	54.9%	44.7%	55.1%	44.9%
34,489	NEWTON	8,969	5,809	3,111	49	2,698 R	64.8%	34.7%	65.1%	34.9%
12,427	OCONEE	6,282	4,265	1,990	27	2,275 R	67.9%	31.7%	68.2%	31.8%
8,929	OGLETHORPE	3,116	1,951	1,154	11	797 R	62.6%	37.0%	62.8%	37.2%
26,110	PAULDING	10,091	7,329	2,717	45	4,612 R	72.6%	26.9%	73.0%	27.0%
19,151	PEACH	5,796	2,782	2,972	42	190 D	48.0%	51.3%	48.3%	51.7%
11,652	PICKENS	4,474	3,021	1,430	23	1,591 R	67.5%	32.0%	67.9%	32.1%
11,897	PIERCE	3,509	1,947	1,558	4	389 R	55.5%	44.4%	55.5%	44.5%
8,937	PIKE	3,274	2,074	1,176	24	898 R	63.3%	35.9%	63.8%	36.2%
32,386	POLK	8,461	5,454	2,977	30	2,477 R	64.5%	35.2%	64.7%	35.3%
8,950	PULASKI	2,888	1,400	1,476	12	76 D	48.5%	51.1%	48.7%	51.3%
10,295	PUTNAM	3,656	2,111	1,532	13	579 R	57.7%	41.9%	57.9%	42.1%
2,357	QUITMAN	738	296	436	6	140 D	40.1%	59.1%	40.4%	59.6%
10,466	RABUN	3,608	2,278	1,301	29	977 R	63.1%	36.1%	63.6%	36.4%
9,599	RANDOLPH	2,695	1,319	1,369	7	50 D	48.9%	50.8%	49.1%	50.9%

GEORGIA

PRESIDENT 1988

1980 Census Population	County	Total Vote	Republican	Democratic	Other	Rep.-Dem. Plurality	Percentage Total Vote Rep.	Total Vote Dem.	Major Vote Rep.	Major Vote Dem.
181,629	RICHMOND	48,258	27,566	20,489	203	7,077 R	57.1%	42.5%	57.4%	42.6%
36,747	ROCKDALE	16,826	12,413	4,330	83	8,083 R	73.8%	25.7%	74.1%	25.9%
3,433	SCHLEY	1,078	635	439	4	196 R	58.9%	40.7%	59.1%	40.9%
14,043	SCREVEN	3,659	2,178	1,461	20	717 R	59.5%	39.9%	59.9%	40.1%
9,057	SEMINOLE	2,645	1,469	1,171	5	298 R	55.5%	44.3%	55.6%	44.4%
47,899	SPALDING	12,138	7,730	4,318	90	3,412 R	63.7%	35.6%	64.2%	35.8%
21,763	STEPHENS	6,550	4,329	2,185	36	2,144 R	66.1%	33.4%	66.5%	33.5%
5,896	STEWART	1,973	832	1,136	5	304 D	42.2%	57.6%	42.3%	57.7%
29,360	SUMTER	7,668	4,289	3,332	47	957 R	55.9%	43.5%	56.3%	43.7%
6,536	TALBOT	2,060	802	1,248	10	446 D	38.9%	60.6%	39.1%	60.9%
2,032	TALIAFERRO	777	306	469	2	163 D	39.4%	60.4%	39.5%	60.5%
18,134	TATTNALL	4,878	3,172	1,694	12	1,478 R	65.0%	34.7%	65.2%	34.8%
7,902	TAYLOR	2,284	1,145	1,134	5	11 R	50.1%	49.6%	50.2%	49.8%
11,445	TELFAIR	3,595	1,805	1,765	25	40 R	50.2%	49.1%	50.6%	49.4%
12,017	TERRELL	2,905	1,517	1,383	5	134 R	52.2%	47.6%	52.3%	47.7%
38,098	THOMAS	10,145	6,572	3,530	43	3,042 R	64.8%	34.8%	65.1%	34.9%
32,862	TIFT	7,234	4,760	2,446	28	2,314 R	65.8%	33.8%	66.1%	33.9%
22,592	TOOMBS	5,619	4,433	1,152	34	3,281 R	78.9%	20.5%	79.4%	20.6%
5,638	TOWNS	2,738	1,783	942	13	841 R	65.1%	34.4%	65.4%	34.6%
6,087	TREUTLEN	1,696	970	726		244 R	57.2%	42.8%	57.2%	42.8%
50,003	TROUP	14,089	9,484	4,562	43	4,922 R	67.3%	32.4%	67.5%	32.5%
9,510	TURNER	2,597	1,312	1,122	163	190 R	50.5%	43.2%	53.9%	46.1%
9,354	TWIGGS	3,005	1,261	1,730	14	469 D	42.0%	57.6%	42.2%	57.8%
9,390	UNION	3,664	2,396	1,258	10	1,138 R	65.4%	34.3%	65.6%	34.4%
25,998	UPSON	7,318	4,614	2,666	38	1,948 R	63.1%	36.4%	63.4%	36.6%
56,470	WALKER	15,280	10,487	4,753	40	5,734 R	68.6%	31.1%	68.8%	31.2%
31,211	WALTON	9,112	5,974	3,091	47	2,883 R	65.6%	33.9%	65.9%	34.1%
37,180	WARE	9,163	4,819	4,292	52	527 R	52.6%	46.8%	52.9%	47.1%
6,583	WARREN	2,003	897	1,091	15	194 D	44.8%	54.5%	45.1%	54.9%
18,842	WASHINGTON	5,383	2,752	2,615	16	137 R	51.1%	48.6%	51.3%	48.7%
20,750	WAYNE	5,766	3,340	2,417	9	923 R	57.9%	41.9%	58.0%	42.0%
2,341	WEBSTER	790	361	427	2	66 D	45.7%	54.1%	45.8%	54.2%
5,155	WHEELER	1,373	709	658	6	51 R	51.6%	47.9%	51.9%	48.1%
10,120	WHITE	3,696	2,648	1,028	20	1,620 R	71.6%	27.8%	72.0%	28.0%
65,789	WHITFIELD	17,451	12,761	4,618	72	8,143 R	73.1%	26.5%	73.4%	26.6%
7,682	WILCOX	2,319	1,235	1,079	5	156 R	53.3%	46.5%	53.4%	46.6%
10,951	WILKES	3,370	1,810	1,549	11	261 R	53.7%	46.0%	53.9%	46.1%
10,368	WILKINSON	3,413	1,546	1,831	36	285 D	45.3%	53.6%	45.8%	54.2%
18,064	WORTH	4,009	2,668	1,311	30	1,357 R	66.6%	32.7%	67.1%	32.9%
5,463,105	TOTAL	1,809,672	1,081,331	714,792	13,549	366,539 R	59.8%	39.5%	60.2%	39.8%

GEORGIA

CONGRESS

CD	Year	Total Vote	Republican Vote	Republican Candidate	Democratic Vote	Democratic Candidate	Other Vote	Rep.-Dem. Plurality	Total Vote Rep.	Total Vote Dem.	Major Vote Rep.	Major Vote Dem.
1	1988	141,083	46,552	MEREDITH, JOHN C.	94,531	THOMAS, LINDSAY		47,979 D	33.0%	67.0%	33.0%	67.0%
1	1986	69,442			69,440	THOMAS, LINDSAY	2	69,440 D		100.0%		100.0%
1	1984	154,545	28,460	DOWNING, ERIE L.	126,082	THOMAS, LINDSAY	3	97,622 D	18.4%	81.6%	18.4%	81.6%
1	1982	102,425	36,799	JONES, HERB	65,625	THOMAS, LINDSAY	1	28,826 D	35.9%	64.1%	35.9%	64.1%
2	1988	137,836	52,807	HUDGENS, RALPH T.	85,029	HATCHER, CHARLES		32,222 D	38.3%	61.7%	38.3%	61.7%
2	1986	72,490			72,482	HATCHER, CHARLES	8	72,482 D		100.0%		100.0%
2	1984	110,566			110,561	HATCHER, CHARLES	5	110,561 D		100.0%		100.0%
2	1982	73,905			73,897	HATCHER, CHARLES	8	73,897 D		100.0%		100.0%
3	1988	97,663			97,663	RAY, RICHARD		97,663 D		100.0%		100.0%
3	1986	76,062			75,850	RAY, RICHARD	212	75,850 D		99.7%		100.0%
3	1984	136,473	25,410	CANTU, MITCHELL	111,061	RAY, RICHARD	2	85,651 D	18.6%	81.4%	18.6%	81.4%
3	1982	105,171	30,537	ELLIOTT, TYRON	74,626	RAY, RICHARD	8	44,089 D	29.0%	71.0%	29.0%	71.0%
4	1988	246,139	97,745	SWINDALL, PATRICK L.	148,394	JONES, BEN		50,649 D	39.7%	60.3%	39.7%	60.3%
4	1986	162,266	86,366	SWINDALL, PATRICK L.	75,892	JONES, BEN	8	10,474 R	53.2%	46.8%	53.2%	46.8%
4	1984	226,835	120,456	SWINDALL, PATRICK L.	106,376	LEVITAS, ELLIOTT H.	3	14,080 R	53.1%	46.9%	53.1%	46.9%
4	1982	59,185	20,418	WINDER, DICK	38,758	LEVITAS, ELLIOTT H.	9	18,340 D	34.5%	65.5%	34.5%	65.5%
5	1988	172,887	37,693	TIBBS, J. W.	135,194	LEWIS, JOHN		97,501 D	21.8%	78.2%	21.8%	78.2%
5	1986	123,800	30,562	SCOTT, PORTIA A.	93,229	LEWIS, JOHN	9	62,667 D	24.7%	75.3%	24.7%	75.3%
5	1984	151,250			151,233	FOWLER, WYCHE	17	151,233 D		100.0%		100.0%
5	1982	65,955	3,633	JONES, PAUL	53,264	FOWLER, WYCHE	9,058	49,631 D	5.5%	80.8%	6.4%	93.6%
6	1988	187,011	110,169	GINGRICH, NEWT	76,824	WORLEY, DAVE	18	33,345 R	58.9%	41.1%	58.9%	41.1%
6	1986	126,941	75,583	GINGRICH, NEWT	51,352	BRAY, CRANDLE	6	24,231 R	59.5%	40.5%	59.5%	40.5%
6	1984	168,717	116,655	GINGRICH, NEWT	52,061	JOHNSON, GERALD L.	1	64,594 R	69.1%	30.9%	69.1%	30.9%
6	1982	112,812	62,352	GINGRICH, NEWT	50,459	WOOD, JIM	1	11,893 R	55.3%	44.7%	55.3%	44.7%
7	1988	208,481	73,425	LAMUTT, ROBERT	135,056	DARDEN, GEORGE		61,631 D	35.2%	64.8%	35.2%	64.8%
7	1986	133,534	44,891	MORECRAFT, JOE	88,636	DARDEN, GEORGE	7	43,745 D	33.6%	66.4%	33.6%	66.4%
7	1984	193,020	86,431	BRONSON, BILL	106,586	DARDEN, GEORGE	3	20,155 D	44.8%	55.2%	44.8%	55.2%
7	1982	117,224	45,569	SELLERS, DAVE	71,647	MCDONALD, LARRY	8	26,078 D	38.9%	61.1%	38.9%	61.1%
8	1988	102,696			102,696	ROWLAND, J. ROY		102,696 D		100.0%		100.0%
8	1986	95,206	12,952	MCDOWELL, EDDIE	82,254	ROWLAND, J. ROY		69,302 D	13.6%	86.4%	13.6%	86.4%
8	1984	100,940			100,936	ROWLAND, J. ROY	4	100,936 D		100.0%		100.0%
8	1982	75,035			75,009	ROWLAND, J. ROY	26	75,009 D		100.0%		100.0%
9	1988	193,705	71,905	HOFFMAN, JOE	121,800	JENKINS, ED		49,895 D	37.1%	62.9%	37.1%	62.9%
9	1986	84,320			84,303	JENKINS, ED	17	84,303 D		100.0%		100.0%
9	1984	162,156	52,731	COFER, FRANK	109,422	JENKINS, ED	3	56,691 D	32.5%	67.5%	32.5%	67.5%
9	1982	112,422	25,907	SHERWOOD, CHARLES	86,514	JENKINS, ED	1	60,607 D	23.0%	77.0%	23.0%	77.0%
10	1988	184,677	66,521	MYERS, MARK	118,156	BARNARD, DOUG		51,635 D	36.0%	64.0%	36.0%	64.0%
10	1986	118,267	38,714	HILL, JIM	79,548	BARNARD, DOUG	5	40,834 D	32.7%	67.3%	32.7%	67.3%
10	1984	116,374			116,364	BARNARD, DOUG	10	116,364 D		100.0%		100.0%
10	1982	80,323			80,311	BARNARD, DOUG	12	80,311 D		100.0%		100.0%

GEORGIA

1988 GENERAL ELECTION

President Other vote was 8,435 Libertarian (Paul); 5,099 New Alliance (Fulani); 15 scattered write-in. Total for the other vote column includes these 15 write-in votes not available by county.

Congress Other vote was 11 Cheney (write-in) and 7 Pearson (write-in) in CD 6.

1988 PRIMARIES

AUGUST 9 REPUBLICAN

Congress Unopposed in six CD's. No candidate in CD's 3 and 8. Contested as follows:

CD 7 7,205 Kevin Johns; 6,709 Robert Lamutt; 6,239 David R. Yood; 3,718 Robert Rivard.
CD 9 9,369 Joe Hoffman; 8,190 Julian Hutchins.

AUGUST 9 DEMOCRATIC

Congress Unopposed in six CD's. Contested as follows:

CD 2 77,789 Charles Hatcher; 38,726 Julian Holland.
CD 4 32,982 Ben Jones; 10,933 Nick Moraitakis; 8,944 John Stembler.
CD 6 34,374 Dave Worley; 27,268 Gene Owens.
CD 8 101,845 J. Roy Rowland; 16,161 R. Bayne Stone.

AUGUST 30 REPUBLICAN RUN-OFF

Congress

CD 7 6,243 Robert Lamutt; 5,620 Kevin Johns.

HAWAII

GOVERNOR

John Waihee (D). Elected 1986 to a four-year term.

SENATORS

Daniel K. Inouye (D). Re-elected 1986 to a six-year term. Previously elected 1980, 1974, 1968, 1962.

Spark M. Matsunaga (D). Re-elected 1988 to a six-year term. Previously elected 1982, 1976.

REPRESENTATIVES

1. Patricia Saiki (R)
2. Daniel K. Akaka (D)

POSTWAR VOTE FOR PRESIDENT

								Percentage			
	Total	Republican		Democratic		Other		Total Vote		Major Vote	
Year	Vote	Vote	Candidate	Vote	Candidate	Vote	Plurality	Rep.	Dem.	Rep.	Dem.
1988	354,461	158,625	Bush, George	192,364	Dukakis, Michael S.	3,472	33,739 D	44.8%	54.3%	45.2%	54.8%
1984	335,846	185,050	Reagan, Ronald	147,154	Mondale, Walter F.	3,642	37,896 R	55.1%	43.8%	55.7%	44.3%
1980	303,287	130,112	Reagan, Ronald	135,879	Carter, Jimmy	37,296	5,767 D	42.9%	44.8%	48.9%	51.1%
1976	291,301	140,003	Ford, Gerald R.	147,375	Carter, Jimmy	3,923	7,372 D	48.1%	50.6%	48.7%	51.3%
1972	270,274	168,865	Nixon, Richard M.	101,409	McGovern, George S.		67,456 R	62.5%	37.5%	62.5%	37.5%
1968	236,218	91,425	Nixon, Richard M.	141,324	Humphrey, Hubert H.	3,469	49,899 D	38.7%	59.8%	39.3%	60.7%
1964	207,271	44,022	Goldwater, Barry M.	163,249	Johnson, Lyndon B.		119,227 D	21.2%	78.8%	21.2%	78.8%
1960	184,705	92,295	Nixon, Richard M.	92,410	Kennedy, John F.		115 D	50.0%	50.0%	50.0%	50.0%

Hawaii was formally admitted to statehood in August 1959.

POSTWAR VOTE FOR GOVERNOR

								Percentage			
	Total	Republican		Democratic		Other	Rep.-Dem.	Total Vote		Major Vote	
Year	Vote	Vote	Candidate	Vote	Candidate	Vote	Plurality	Rep.	Dem.	Rep.	Dem.
1986	334,115	160,460	Anderson, D. G.	173,655	Waihee, John		13,195 D	48.0%	52.0%	48.0%	52.0%
1982 **	311,853	81,507	Anderson, D. G.	141,043	Ariyoshi, George R.	89,303	59,536 D	26.1%	45.2%	36.6%	63.4%
1978	281,587	124,610	Leopold, John	153,394	Ariyoshi, George R.	3,583	28,784 D	44.3%	54.5%	44.8%	55.2%
1974	249,650	113,388	Crossley, Randolph	136,262	Ariyoshi, George R.		22,874 D	45.4%	54.6%	45.4%	54.6%
1970	239,061	101,249	King, Samuel P.	137,812	Burns, John A.		36,563 D	42.4%	57.6%	42.4%	57.6%
1966	213,164	104,324	Crossley, Randolph	108,840	Burns, John A.		4,516 D	48.9%	51.1%	48.9%	51.1%
1962	196,015	81,707	Quinn, William F.	114,308	Burns, John A.		32,601 D	41.7%	58.3%	41.7%	58.3%
1959 S	168,662	86,213	Quinn, William F.	82,074	Burns, John A.	375	4,139 R	51.1%	48.7%	51.2%	48.8%

The 1959 election was for a short term pending the regular vote in 1962. In 1982 other vote was Independent Democrat (Frank F. Fasi) who ran second.

HAWAII

POSTWAR VOTE FOR SENATOR

Year	Total Vote	Republican Vote	Republican Candidate	Democratic Vote	Democratic Candidate	Other Vote	Rep.-Dem. Plurality	Percentage Total Vote Rep.	Percentage Total Vote Dem.	Percentage Major Vote Rep.	Percentage Major Vote Dem.
1988	323,876	66,987	Hustace, Maria M.	247,941	Matsunaga, Spark M.	8,948	180,954 D	20.7%	76.6%	21.3%	78.7%
1986	328,797	86,910	Hutchinson, Frank	241,887	Inouye, Daniel K.		154,977 D	26.4%	73.6%	26.4%	73.6%
1982	306,410	52,071	Brown, Clarence J.	245,386	Matsunaga, Spark M.	8,953	193,315 D	17.0%	80.1%	17.5%	82.5%
1980	288,006	53,068	Brown, Cooper	224,485	Inouye, Daniel K.	10,453	171,417 D	18.4%	77.9%	19.1%	80.9%
1976	302,092	122,724	Quinn, William F.	162,305	Matsunaga, Spark M.	17,063	39,581 D	40.6%	53.7%	43.1%	56.9%
1974	250,221		—	207,454	Inouye, Daniel K.	42,767	207,454 D		82.9%		100.0%
1970	240,760	124,163	Fong, Hiram L.	116,597	Heftel, Cecil		7,566 R	51.6%	48.4%	51.6%	48.4%
1968	226,927	34,008	Thiessen, Wayne C.	189,248	Inouye, Daniel K.	3,671	155,240 D	15.0%	83.4%	15.2%	84.8%
1964	208,814	110,747	Fong, Hiram L.	96,789	Gill, Thomas P.	1,278	13,958 R	53.0%	46.4%	53.4%	46.6%
1962	196,361	60,067	Dillingham, Ben F.	136,294	Inouye, Daniel K.		76,227 D	30.6%	69.4%	30.6%	69.4%
1959 **	164,808	87,161	Fong, Hiram L.	77,647	Fasi, Frank F.		9,514 R	52.9%	47.1%	52.9%	47.1%
1959 S	163,875	79,123	Tsukiyama, W. C.	83,700	Long, Oren E.	1,052	4,577 D	48.3%	51.1%	48.6%	51.4%

The two 1959 elections were held to indeterminate terms and the Senate later determined by lot that Senator Long would serve a short term, Senator Fong a long term.

HAWAII

Districts Established April 9, 1984

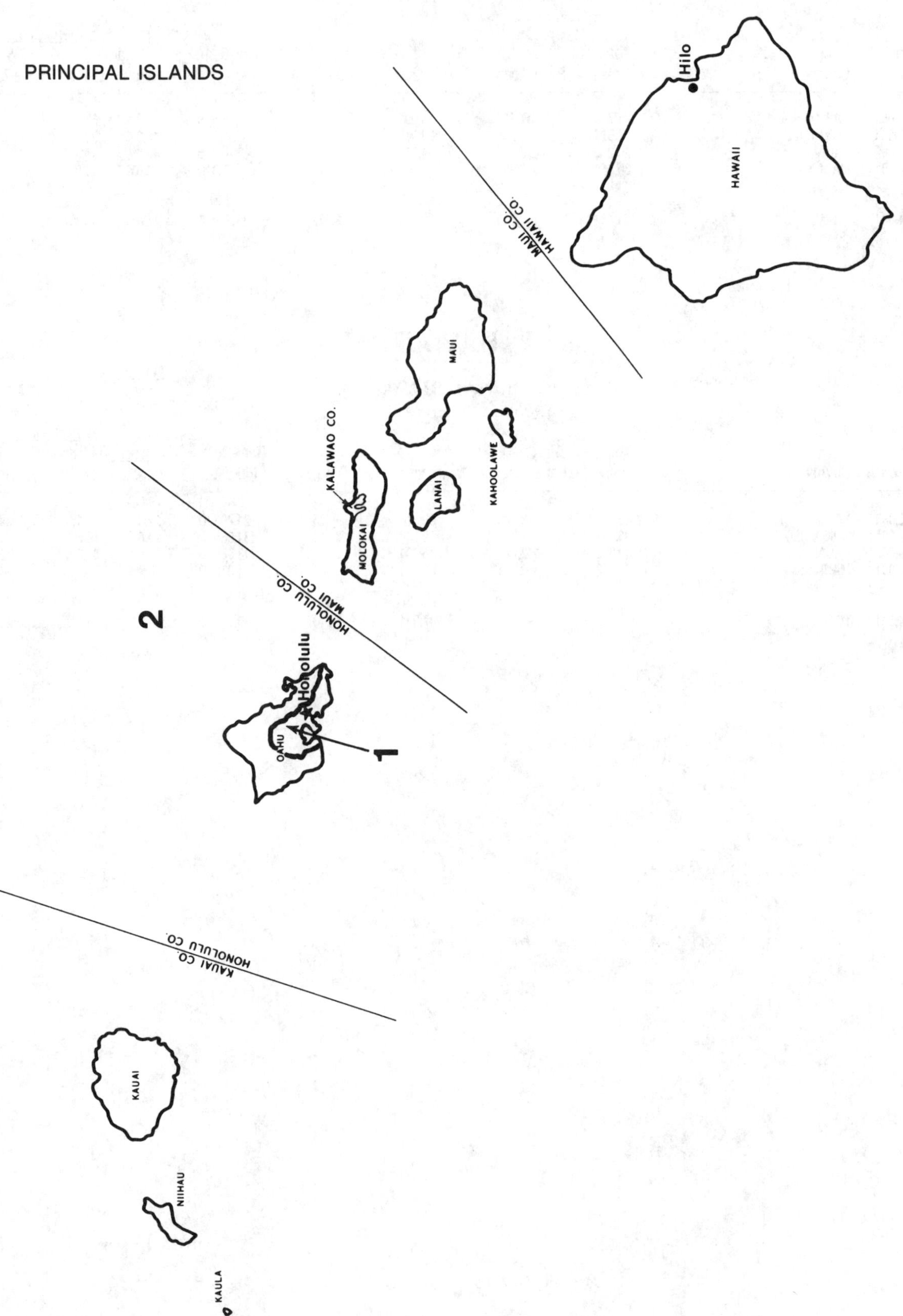

HAWAII

PRESIDENT 1988

1980 Census Population	County	Total Vote	Republican	Democratic	Other	Rep.-Dem. Plurality	Percentage Total Vote Rep.	Percentage Total Vote Dem.	Percentage Major Vote Rep.	Percentage Major Vote Dem.
92,053	HAWAII	41,768	17,125	24,091	552	6,966 D	41.0%	57.7%	41.5%	58.5%
762,565	HONOLULU	261,577	120,258	138,971	2,348	18,713 D	46.0%	53.1%	46.4%	53.6%
39,082	KAUAI	20,266	8,298	11,770	198	3,472 D	40.9%	58.1%	41.3%	58.7%
70,991	MAUI	30,850	12,944	17,532	374	4,588 D	42.0%	56.8%	42.5%	57.5%
964,691	TOTAL	354,461	158,625	192,364	3,472	33,739 D	44.8%	54.3%	45.2%	54.8%

HAWAII

SENATOR 1988

1980 Census Population	County	Total Vote	Republican	Democratic	Other	Rep.-Dem. Plurality	Percentage Total Vote Rep.	Percentage Total Vote Dem.	Percentage Major Vote Rep.	Percentage Major Vote Dem.
92,053	HAWAII	40,313	8,868	30,270	1,175	21,402 D	22.0%	75.1%	22.7%	77.3%
762,565	HONOLULU	235,017	48,781	179,819	6,417	131,038 D	20.8%	76.5%	21.3%	78.7%
39,082	KAUAI	19,330	2,427	16,391	512	13,964 D	12.6%	84.8%	12.9%	87.1%
70,991	MAUI	29,216	6,911	21,461	844	14,550 D	23.7%	73.5%	24.4%	75.6%
964,691	TOTAL	323,876	66,987	247,941	8,948	180,954 D	20.7%	76.6%	21.3%	78.7%

HAWAII

CONGRESS

CD	Year	Total Vote	Republican Vote	Republican Candidate	Democratic Vote	Democratic Candidate	Other Vote	Rep.-Dem. Plurality	Percentage Total Vote Rep.	Percentage Total Vote Dem.	Percentage Major Vote Rep.	Percentage Major Vote Dem.
1	1988	177,020	96,848	SAIKI, PATRICIA	76,394	BITTERMAN, MARY	3,778	20,454 R	54.7%	43.2%	55.9%	44.1%
1	1986	168,377	99,683	SAIKI, PATRICIA	63,061	HANNEMANN, MUFI	5,633	36,622 R	59.2%	37.5%	61.3%	38.7%
1	1984	138,865	20,608	BEARD, WILLARD F.	114,884	HEFTEL, CECIL	3,373	94,276 D	14.8%	82.7%	15.2%	84.8%
2	1988	162,808			144,802	AKAKA, DANIEL K.	18,006	144,802 D		88.9%		100.0%
2	1986	162,819	35,371	HUSTACE, MARIA M.	123,830	AKAKA, DANIEL K.	3,618	88,459 D	21.7%	76.1%	22.2%	77.8%
2	1984	136,741	20,000	SHIPLEY, ARBIS D.	112,377	AKAKA, DANIEL K.	4,364	92,377 D	14.6%	82.2%	15.1%	84.9%

HAWAII

Kalawao county, an area of 14 square miles on Molokai Island with a population of 144, consists entirely of the Kalaupapa Hansen's disease settlement. The population and voting data for this settlement are included in the Maui county statistics.

1988 GENERAL ELECTION

President Other vote was 1,999 Libertarian (Paul); 1,003 New Alliance (Fulani); 470 National Economic Recovery (LaRouche).

Senator Other vote was Libertarian (Schoolland).

Congress Other vote was Libertarian (Harris) in CD 1; Libertarian (Mallan) in CD 2.

1988 PRIMARIES

SEPTEMBER 17 REPUBLICAN

Senator 18,124 Maria M. Hustace; 13,590 Leonard Mednick; 5,526 Susanne Sydney.

Congress Unopposed in CD 1. No candidate in CD 2.

SEPTEMBER 17 DEMOCRATIC

Senator 180,853 Spark M. Matsunaga; 27,360 Robert Zimmerman.

Congress Unopposed in CD 2. Contested as follows:

CD 1 51,942 Mary Bitterman; 35,579 Leigh-Wai Doo; 15,258 John Radcliffe.

SEPTEMBER 17 LIBERTARIAN

Senator Ken Schoolland, unopposed.

Congress Unopposed in both CD's.

IDAHO

GOVERNOR

Cecil D. Andrus (D). Elected 1986 to a four-year term. Previously elected 1974, 1970.

SENATORS

James A. McClure (R). Re-elected 1984 to a six-year term. Previously elected 1978, 1972.

Steven D. Symms (R). Re-elected 1986 to a six-year term. Previously elected 1980.

REPRESENTATIVES

1. Larry Craig (R) 2. Richard Stallings (D)

POSTWAR VOTE FOR PRESIDENT

								Percentage			
	Total	Republican		Democratic		Other		Total Vote		Major Vote	
Year	Vote	Vote	Candidate	Vote	Candidate	Vote	Plurality	Rep.	Dem.	Rep.	Dem.
1988	408,968	253,881	Bush, George	147,272	Dukakis, Michael S.	7,815	106,609 R	62.1%	36.0%	63.3%	36.7%
1984	411,144	297,523	Reagan, Ronald	108,510	Mondale, Walter F.	5,111	189,013 R	72.4%	26.4%	73.3%	26.7%
1980	437,431	290,699	Reagan, Ronald	110,192	Carter, Jimmy	36,540	180,507 R	66.5%	25.2%	72.5%	27.5%
1976	344,071	204,151	Ford, Gerald R.	126,549	Carter, Jimmy	13,371	77,602 R	59.3%	36.8%	61.7%	38.3%
1972	310,379	199,384	Nixon, Richard M.	80,826	McGovern, George S.	30,169	118,558 R	64.2%	26.0%	71.2%	28.8%
1968	291,183	165,369	Nixon, Richard M.	89,273	Humphrey, Hubert H.	36,541	76,096 R	56.8%	30.7%	64.9%	35.1%
1964	292,477	143,557	Goldwater, Barry M.	148,920	Johnson, Lyndon B.		5,363 D	49.1%	50.9%	49.1%	50.9%
1960	300,450	161,597	Nixon, Richard M.	138,853	Kennedy, John F.		22,744 R	53.8%	46.2%	53.8%	46.2%
1956	272,989	166,979	Eisenhower, Dwight D.	105,868	Stevenson, Adlai E.	142	61,111 R	61.2%	38.8%	61.2%	38.8%
1952	276,254	180,707	Eisenhower, Dwight D.	95,081	Stevenson, Adlai E.	466	85,626 R	65.4%	34.4%	65.5%	34.5%
1948	214,816	101,514	Dewey, Thomas E.	107,370	Truman, Harry S.	5,932	5,856 D	47.3%	50.0%	48.6%	51.4%

POSTWAR VOTE FOR GOVERNOR

								Percentage			
	Total	Republican		Democratic		Other	Rep.-Dem.	Total Vote		Major Vote	
Year	Vote	Vote	Candidate	Vote	Candidate	Vote	Plurality	Rep.	Dem.	Rep.	Dem.
1986	387,426	189,794	Leroy, David H.	193,429	Andrus, Cecil D.	4,203	3,635 D	49.0%	49.9%	49.5%	50.5%
1982	326,522	161,157	Batt, Philip	165,365	Evans, John V.		4,208 D	49.4%	50.6%	49.4%	50.6%
1978	288,566	114,149	Larsen, Allan	169,540	Evans, John V.	4,877	55,391 D	39.6%	58.8%	40.2%	59.8%
1974	259,632	68,731	Murphy, Jack M.	184,142	Andrus, Cecil D.	6,759	115,411 D	26.5%	70.9%	27.2%	72.8%
1970	245,112	117,108	Samuelson, Don	128,004	Andrus, Cecil D.		10,896 D	47.8%	52.2%	47.8%	52.2%
1966	252,593	104,586	Samuelson, Don	93,744	Andrus, Cecil D.	54,263	10,842 R	41.4%	37.1%	52.7%	47.3%
1962	255,454	139,578	Smylie, Robert E.	115,876	Smith, Vernon K.		23,702 R	54.6%	45.4%	54.6%	45.4%
1958	239,046	121,810	Smylie, Robert E.	117,236	Derr, A. M.		4,574 R	51.0%	49.0%	51.0%	49.0%
1954	228,685	124,038	Smylie, Robert E.	104,647	Hamilton, Clark		19,391 R	54.2%	45.8%	54.2%	45.8%
1950	204,792	107,642	Jordan, Len B.	97,150	Wright, Calvin E.		10,492 R	52.6%	47.4%	52.6%	47.4%
1946	181,364	102,233	Robins, C. A.	79,131	Williams, Arnold		23,102 R	56.4%	43.6%	56.4%	43.6%

IDAHO

POSTWAR VOTE FOR SENATOR

Year	Total Vote	Republican Vote	Republican Candidate	Democratic Vote	Democratic Candidate	Other Vote	Rep.-Dem. Plurality	Percentage Total Vote Rep.	Percentage Total Vote Dem.	Percentage Major Vote Rep.	Percentage Major Vote Dem.
1986	382,024	196,958	Symms, Steven D.	185,066	Evans, John V.		11,892 R	51.6%	48.4%	51.6%	48.4%
1984	406,168	293,193	McClure, James A.	105,591	Busch, Peter M.	7,384	187,602 R	72.2%	26.0%	73.5%	26.5%
1980	439,647	218,701	Symms, Steven D.	214,439	Church, Frank	6,507	4,262 R	49.7%	48.8%	50.5%	49.5%
1978	284,047	194,412	McClure, James A.	89,635	Jensen, Dwight		104,777 R	68.4%	31.6%	68.4%	31.6%
1974	258,847	109,072	Smith, Robert L.	145,140	Church, Frank	4,635	36,068 D	42.1%	56.1%	42.9%	57.1%
1972	309,602	161,804	McClure, James A.	140,913	Davis, William E.	6,885	20,891 R	52.3%	45.5%	53.5%	46.5%
1968	287,876	114,394	Hansen, George V.	173,482	Church, Frank		59,088 D	39.7%	60.3%	39.7%	60.3%
1966	252,456	139,819	Jordan, Len B.	112,637	Harding, Ralph R.		27,182 R	55.4%	44.6%	55.4%	44.6%
1962	258,786	117,129	Hawley, Jack	141,657	Church, Frank		24,528 D	45.3%	54.7%	45.3%	54.7%
1962 S	257,677	131,279	Jordan, Len B.	126,398	Pfost, Gracie		4,881 R	50.9%	49.1%	50.9%	49.1%
1960	292,096	152,648	Dworshak, Henry C.	139,448	McLaughlin, Bob		13,200 R	52.3%	47.7%	52.3%	47.7%
1956	265,292	102,781	Welker, Herman	149,096	Church, Frank	13,415	46,315 D	38.7%	56.2%	40.8%	59.2%
1954	226,408	142,269	Dworshak, Henry C.	84,139	Taylor, Glen H.		58,130 R	62.8%	37.2%	62.8%	37.2%
1950	201,417	124,237	Welker, Herman	77,180	Clark, D. Worth		47,057 R	61.7%	38.3%	61.7%	38.3%
1950 S	201,970	104,068	Dworshak, Henry C.	97,902	Burtenshaw, Claude		6,166 R	51.5%	48.5%	51.5%	48.5%
1948	214,188	103,868	Dworshak, Henry C.	107,000	Miller, Bert H.	3,320	3,132 D	48.5%	50.0%	49.3%	50.7%
1946 S	180,152	105,523	Dworshak, Henry C.	74,629	Donart, George E.		30,894 R	58.6%	41.4%	58.6%	41.4%

The 1946 election and one each of the 1962 and 1950 elections were for short terms to fill vacancies.

IDAHO

Districts Established July 30, 1981

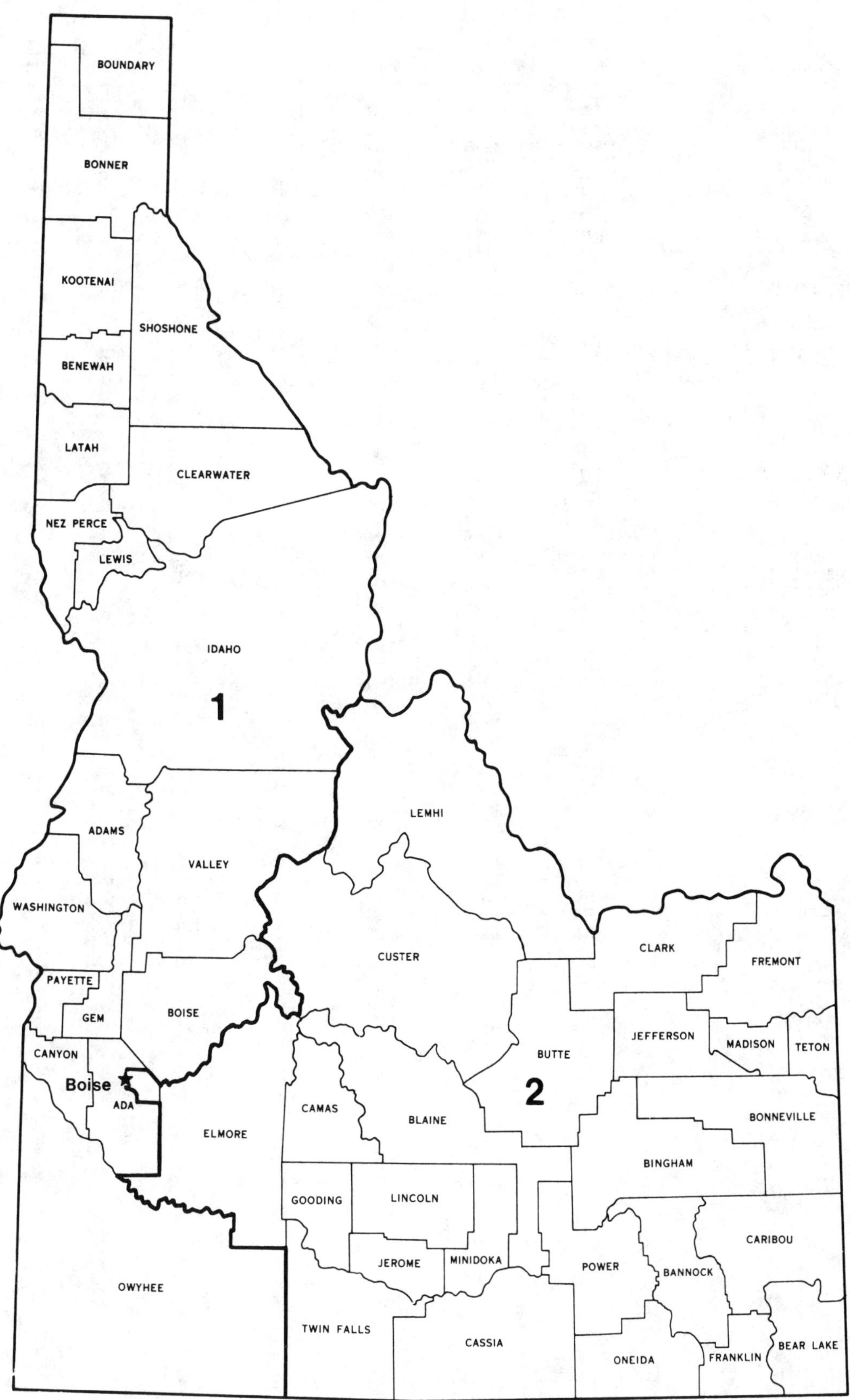

IDAHO

PRESIDENT 1988

1980 Census Population	County	Total Vote	Republican	Democratic	Other	Rep.-Dem. Plurality	Percentage Total Vote Rep.	Total Vote Dem.	Major Vote Rep.	Major Vote Dem.
173,036	ADA	87,334	54,951	30,525	1,858	24,426 R	62.9%	35.0%	64.3%	35.7%
3,347	ADAMS	1,799	1,107	643	49	464 R	61.5%	35.7%	63.3%	36.7%
65,421	BANNOCK	28,601	14,986	13,074	541	1,912 R	52.4%	45.7%	53.4%	46.6%
6,931	BEAR LAKE	2,980	2,084	867	29	1,217 R	69.9%	29.1%	70.6%	29.4%
8,292	BENEWAH	3,238	1,650	1,518	70	132 R	51.0%	46.9%	52.1%	47.9%
36,489	BINGHAM	14,705	10,131	4,346	228	5,785 R	68.9%	29.6%	70.0%	30.0%
9,841	BLAINE	5,755	3,130	2,498	127	632 R	54.4%	43.4%	55.6%	44.4%
2,999	BOISE	1,710	1,044	620	46	424 R	61.1%	36.3%	62.7%	37.3%
24,163	BONNER	11,455	5,721	5,555	179	166 R	49.9%	48.5%	50.7%	49.3%
65,980	BONNEVILLE	30,147	22,613	7,032	502	15,581 R	75.0%	23.3%	76.3%	23.7%
7,289	BOUNDARY	3,202	1,800	1,336	66	464 R	56.2%	41.7%	57.4%	42.6%
3,342	BUTTE	1,444	899	521	24	378 R	62.3%	36.1%	63.3%	36.7%
818	CAMAS	437	288	136	13	152 R	65.9%	31.1%	67.9%	32.1%
83,756	CANYON	32,396	21,426	10,207	763	11,219 R	66.1%	31.5%	67.7%	32.3%
8,695	CARIBOU	3,144	2,239	867	38	1,372 R	71.2%	27.6%	72.1%	27.9%
19,427	CASSIA	7,288	5,345	1,833	110	3,512 R	73.3%	25.2%	74.5%	25.5%
798	CLARK	421	281	133	7	148 R	66.7%	31.6%	67.9%	32.1%
10,390	CLEARWATER	3,617	1,659	1,861	97	202 D	45.9%	51.5%	47.1%	52.9%
3,385	CUSTER	1,896	1,253	616	27	637 R	66.1%	32.5%	67.0%	33.0%
21,565	ELMORE	5,919	3,756	2,078	85	1,678 R	63.5%	35.1%	64.4%	35.6%
8,895	FRANKLIN	3,871	2,992	806	73	2,186 R	77.3%	20.8%	78.8%	21.2%
10,813	FREMONT	4,652	3,401	1,178	73	2,223 R	73.1%	25.3%	74.3%	25.7%
11,972	GEM	5,142	2,926	2,064	152	862 R	56.9%	40.1%	58.6%	41.4%
11,874	GOODING	4,876	2,908	1,872	96	1,036 R	59.6%	38.4%	60.8%	39.2%
14,769	IDAHO	5,871	3,541	2,198	132	1,343 R	60.3%	37.4%	61.7%	38.3%
15,304	JEFFERSON	6,649	5,295	1,198	156	4,097 R	79.6%	18.0%	81.5%	18.5%
14,840	JEROME	5,955	3,830	1,985	140	1,845 R	64.3%	33.3%	65.9%	34.1%
59,770	KOOTENAI	27,130	15,093	11,621	416	3,472 R	55.6%	42.8%	56.5%	43.5%
28,749	LATAH	13,136	6,367	6,544	225	177 D	48.5%	49.8%	49.3%	50.7%
7,460	LEMHI	3,590	2,378	1,157	55	1,221 R	66.2%	32.2%	67.3%	32.7%
4,118	LEWIS	1,612	786	807	19	21 D	48.8%	50.1%	49.3%	50.7%
3,436	LINCOLN	1,525	918	574	33	344 R	60.2%	37.6%	61.5%	38.5%
19,480	MADISON	7,302	6,197	1,009	96	5,188 R	84.9%	13.8%	86.0%	14.0%
19,718	MINIDOKA	7,033	4,623	2,290	120	2,333 R	65.7%	32.6%	66.9%	33.1%
33,220	NEZ PERCE	15,020	7,027	7,754	239	727 D	46.8%	51.6%	47.5%	52.5%
3,258	ONEIDA	1,810	1,269	508	33	761 R	70.1%	28.1%	71.4%	28.6%
8,272	OWYHEE	2,634	1,707	848	79	859 R	64.8%	32.2%	66.8%	33.2%
15,722	PAYETTE	5,809	3,786	1,900	123	1,886 R	65.2%	32.7%	66.6%	33.4%
6,844	POWER	2,981	1,838	1,095	48	743 R	61.7%	36.7%	62.7%	37.3%
19,226	SHOSHONE	5,586	2,134	3,379	73	1,245 D	38.2%	60.5%	38.7%	61.3%
2,897	TETON	1,527	982	531	14	451 R	64.3%	34.8%	64.9%	35.1%
52,927	TWIN FALLS	20,734	13,243	7,078	413	6,165 R	63.9%	34.1%	65.2%	34.8%
5,604	VALLEY	3,195	1,897	1,251	47	646 R	59.4%	39.2%	60.3%	39.7%
8,803	WASHINGTON	3,840	2,380	1,359	101	1,021 R	62.0%	35.4%	63.7%	36.3%
943,935	TOTAL	408,968	253,881	147,272	7,815	106,609 R	62.1%	36.0%	63.3%	36.7%

IDAHO

CONGRESS

CD	Year	Total Vote	Republican Vote	Republican Candidate	Democratic Vote	Democratic Candidate	Other Vote	Rep.-Dem. Plurality	Percentage Total Vote Rep.	Percentage Total Vote Dem.	Percentage Major Vote Rep.	Percentage Major Vote Dem.
1	1988	205,549	135,221	CRAIG, LARRY	70,328	GIVENS, JEANNE		64,893 R	65.8%	34.2%	65.8%	34.2%
1	1986	186,196	121,625	CRAIG, LARRY	59,723	CURRIE, BILL	4,848	61,902 R	65.3%	32.1%	67.1%	32.9%
1	1984	202,676	139,085	CRAIG, LARRY	63,591	HELLAR, BILL		75,494 R	68.6%	31.4%	68.6%	31.4%
1	1982	160,665	86,277	CRAIG, LARRY	74,388	LAROCCO, LARRY		11,889 R	53.7%	46.3%	53.7%	46.3%
2	1988	201,885	68,226	WATKINS, DANE H.	127,956	STALLINGS, RICHARD	5,703	59,730 D	33.8%	63.4%	34.8%	65.2%
2	1986	189,563	86,528	RICHARDSON, MEL	103,035	STALLINGS, RICHARD		16,507 D	45.6%	54.4%	45.6%	54.4%
2	1984	202,404	101,117	HANSEN, GEORGE V.	101,287	STALLINGS, RICHARD		170 D	50.0%	50.0%	50.0%	50.0%
2	1982	160,481	83,873	HANSEN, GEORGE V.	76,608	STALLINGS, RICHARD		7,265 R	52.3%	47.7%	52.3%	47.7%

IDAHO

1988 GENERAL ELECTION

President Other vote was 5,313 Libertarian (Paul); 2,502 Independent (Fulani).

Congress Other vote was Libertarian (Bramwell) in CD 2.

1988 PRIMARIES

MAY 24 REPUBLICAN

Congress Unopposed in CD 1. Contested as follows:

CD 2 20,548 Dane H. Watkins; 14,356 Janet L. Reid.

MAY 24 DEMOCRATIC

Congress Unopposed in CD 2. Contested as follows:

CD 1 18,165 Jeanne Givens; 6,227 David W. Shepherd; 4,638 Bruce O. Robinson.

ILLINOIS

GOVERNOR

James R. Thompson (R). Re-elected 1986 to a four-year term. Previously elected 1982, 1978 and in 1976 to a two-year term.

SENATORS

Alan J. Dixon (D). Re-elected 1986 to a six-year term. Previously elected 1980.

Paul Simon (D). Elected 1984 to a six-year term.

REPRESENTATIVES

1. Charles A. Hayes (D)
2. Gus Savage (D)
3. Martin A. Russo (D)
4. George E. Sangmeister (D)
5. William O. Lipinski (D)
6. Henry J. Hyde (R)
7. Cardiss Collins (D)
8. Daniel Rostenkowski (D)
9. Sindey R. Yates (D)
10. John E. Porter (R)
11. Frank Annunzio (D)
12. Philip M. Crane (R)
13. Harris W. Fawell (R)
14. J. Dennis Hastert (R)
15. Edward R. Madigan (R)
16. Lynn Martin (R)
17. Lane Evans (D)
18. Robert H. Michel (R)
19. Terry L. Bruce (D)
20. Richard J. Durbin (D)
21. Jerry F. Costello (D)
22. Glenn Poshard (D)

POSTWAR VOTE FOR PRESIDENT

								Percentage			
	Total	Republican		Democratic		Other		Total Vote		Major Vote	
Year	Vote	Vote	Candidate	Vote	Candidate	Vote	Plurality	Rep.	Dem.	Rep.	Dem.
1988	4,559,120	2,310,939	Bush, George	2,215,940	Dukakis, Michael S.	32,241	94,999 R	50.7%	48.6%	51.0%	49.0%
1984	4,819,088	2,707,103	Reagan, Ronald	2,086,499	Mondale, Walter F.	25,486	620,604 R	56.2%	43.3%	56.5%	43.5%
1980	4,749,721	2,358,049	Reagan, Ronald	1,981,413	Carter, Jimmy	410,259	376,636 R	49.6%	41.7%	54.3%	45.7%
1976	4,718,914	2,364,269	Ford, Gerald R.	2,271,295	Carter, Jimmy	83,350	92,974 R	50.1%	48.1%	51.0%	49.0%
1972	4,723,236	2,788,179	Nixon, Richard M.	1,913,472	McGovern, George S.	21,585	874,707 R	59.0%	40.5%	59.3%	40.7%
1968	4,619,749	2,174,774	Nixon, Richard M.	2,039,814	Humphrey, Hubert H.	405,161	134,960 R	47.1%	44.2%	51.6%	48.4%
1964	4,702,841	1,905,946	Goldwater, Barry M.	2,796,833	Johnson, Lyndon B.	62	890,887 D	40.5%	59.5%	40.5%	59.5%
1960	4,757,409	2,368,988	Nixon, Richard M.	2,377,846	Kennedy, John F.	10,575	8,858 D	49.8%	50.0%	49.9%	50.1%
1956	4,407,407	2,623,327	Eisenhower, Dwight D.	1,775,682	Stevenson, Adlai E.	8,398	847,645 R	59.5%	40.3%	59.6%	40.4%
1952	4,481,058	2,457,327	Eisenhower, Dwight D.	2,013,920	Stevenson, Adlai E.	9,811	443,407 R	54.8%	44.9%	55.0%	45.0%
1948	3,984,046	1,961,103	Dewey, Thomas E.	1,994,715	Truman, Harry S.	28,228	33,612 D	49.2%	50.1%	49.6%	50.4%

ILLINOIS

POSTWAR VOTE FOR GOVERNOR

Year	Total Vote	Republican Vote	Republican Candidate	Democratic Vote	Democratic Candidate	Other Vote	Rep.-Dem. Plurality	Percentage Total Vote Rep.	Total Vote Dem.	Major Vote Rep.	Major Vote Dem.
1986 **	3,143,978	1,655,849	Thompson, James R.	208,830	[See note below]	1,279,299	1,447,019 R	52.7%	6.6%	88.8%	11.2%
1982	3,673,681	1,816,101	Thompson, James R.	1,811,027	Stevenson, Adlai E., III	46,553	5,074 R	49.4%	49.3%	50.1%	49.9%
1978	3,150,095	1,859,684	Thompson, James R.	1,263,134	Bakalis, Michael	27,277	596,550 R	59.0%	40.1%	59.6%	40.4%
1976 S	4,638,997	3,000,395	Thompson, James R.	1,610,258	Howlett, Michael J.	28,344	1,390,137 R	64.7%	34.7%	65.1%	34.9%
1972	4,678,804	2,293,809	Ogilvie, Richard B.	2,371,303	Walker, Daniel	13,692	77,494 D	49.0%	50.7%	49.2%	50.8%
1968	4,506,000	2,307,295	Ogilvie, Richard B.	2,179,501	Shapiro, Samuel H.	19,204	127,794 R	51.2%	48.4%	51.4%	48.6%
1964	4,657,500	2,239,095	Percy, Charles H.	2,418,394	Kerner, Otto	11	179,299 D	48.1%	51.9%	48.1%	51.9%
1960	4,674,187	2,070,479	Stratton, William G.	2,594,731	Kerner, Otto	8,977	524,252 D	44.3%	55.5%	44.4%	55.6%
1956	4,314,611	2,171,786	Stratton, William G.	2,134,909	Austin, Richard B.	7,916	36,877 R	50.3%	49.5%	50.4%	49.6%
1952	4,415,864	2,317,363	Stratton, William G.	2,089,721	Dixon, Sherwood	8,780	227,642 R	52.5%	47.3%	52.6%	47.4%
1948	3,940,257	1,678,007	Green, Dwight H.	2,250,074	Stevenson, Adlai E.	12,176	572,067 D	42.6%	57.1%	42.7%	57.3%

The 1976 vote was for a two-year term to permit shifting the vote for Governor to non-Presidential years. In 1986 there was no Democratic candidate for Governor on the ballot, Mark Fairchild being the "paired" Democrat for Lt. Governor and the Democratic vote above was cast for this ticket of "no name" and Fairchild. Other vote in this election was 1,256,626 Adlai E. Stevenson III (Solidarity) who received 40.0% of the total vote and came in second; 15,646 Gary L. Shilts (Libertarian); 6,843 Diane Roling (Socialist Workers) and 184 scattered.

POSTWAR VOTE FOR SENATOR

Year	Total Vote	Republican Vote	Republican Candidate	Democratic Vote	Democratic Candidate	Other Vote	Rep.-Dem. Plurality	Percentage Total Vote Rep.	Total Vote Dem.	Major Vote Rep.	Major Vote Dem.
1986	3,122,883	1,053,734	Koehler, Judy	2,033,783	Dixon, Alan J.	35,366	980,049 D	33.7%	65.1%	34.1%	65.9%
1984	4,787,473	2,308,039	Percy, Charles H.	2,397,303	Simon, Paul	82,131	89,264 D	48.2%	50.1%	49.1%	50.9%
1980	4,580,029	1,946,296	O'Neal, David C.	2,565,302	Dixon, Alan J.	68,431	619,006 D	42.5%	56.0%	43.1%	56.9%
1978	3,184,764	1,698,711	Percy, Charles H.	1,448,187	Seith, Alex	37,866	250,524 R	53.3%	45.5%	54.0%	46.0%
1974	2,914,666	1,084,884	Burditt, George M.	1,811,496	Stevenson, Adlai E., III	18,286	726,612 D	37.2%	62.2%	37.5%	62.5%
1972	4,608,380	2,867,078	Percy, Charles H.	1,721,031	Pucinski, Roman C.	20,271	1,146,047 R	62.2%	37.3%	62.5%	37.5%
1970 S	3,599,272	1,519,718	Smith, Ralph T.	2,065,054	Stevenson, Adlai E., III	14,500	545,336 D	42.2%	57.4%	42.4%	57.6%
1968	4,449,757	2,358,947	Dirksen, Everett M.	2,073,242	Clark, William G.	17,568	285,705 R	53.0%	46.6%	53.2%	46.8%
1966	3,822,725	2,100,449	Percy, Charles H.	1,678,147	Douglas, Paul H.	44,129	422,302 R	54.9%	43.9%	55.6%	44.4%
1962	3,709,216	1,961,202	Dirksen, Everett M.	1,748,007	Yates, Sidney R.	7	213,195 R	52.9%	47.1%	52.9%	47.1%
1960	4,632,796	2,093,846	Witwer, Samuel W.	2,530,943	Douglas, Paul H.	8,007	437,097 D	45.2%	54.6%	45.3%	54.7%
1956	4,264,830	2,307,352	Dirksen, Everett M.	1,949,883	Stengel, Richard	7,595	357,469 R	54.1%	45.7%	54.2%	45.8%
1954	3,368,025	1,563,683	Meek, Joseph T.	1,804,338	Douglas, Paul H.	4	240,655 D	46.4%	53.6%	46.4%	53.6%
1950	3,622,673	1,951,984	Dirksen, Everett M.	1,657,630	Lucas, Scott W.	13,059	294,354 R	53.9%	45.8%	54.1%	45.9%
1948	3,900,285	1,740,026	Brooks, C. Wayland	2,147,754	Douglas, Paul H.	12,505	407,728 D	44.6%	55.1%	44.8%	55.2%

The 1970 election was for a short term to fill a vacancy.

ILLINOIS

Districts Established November 23, 1981

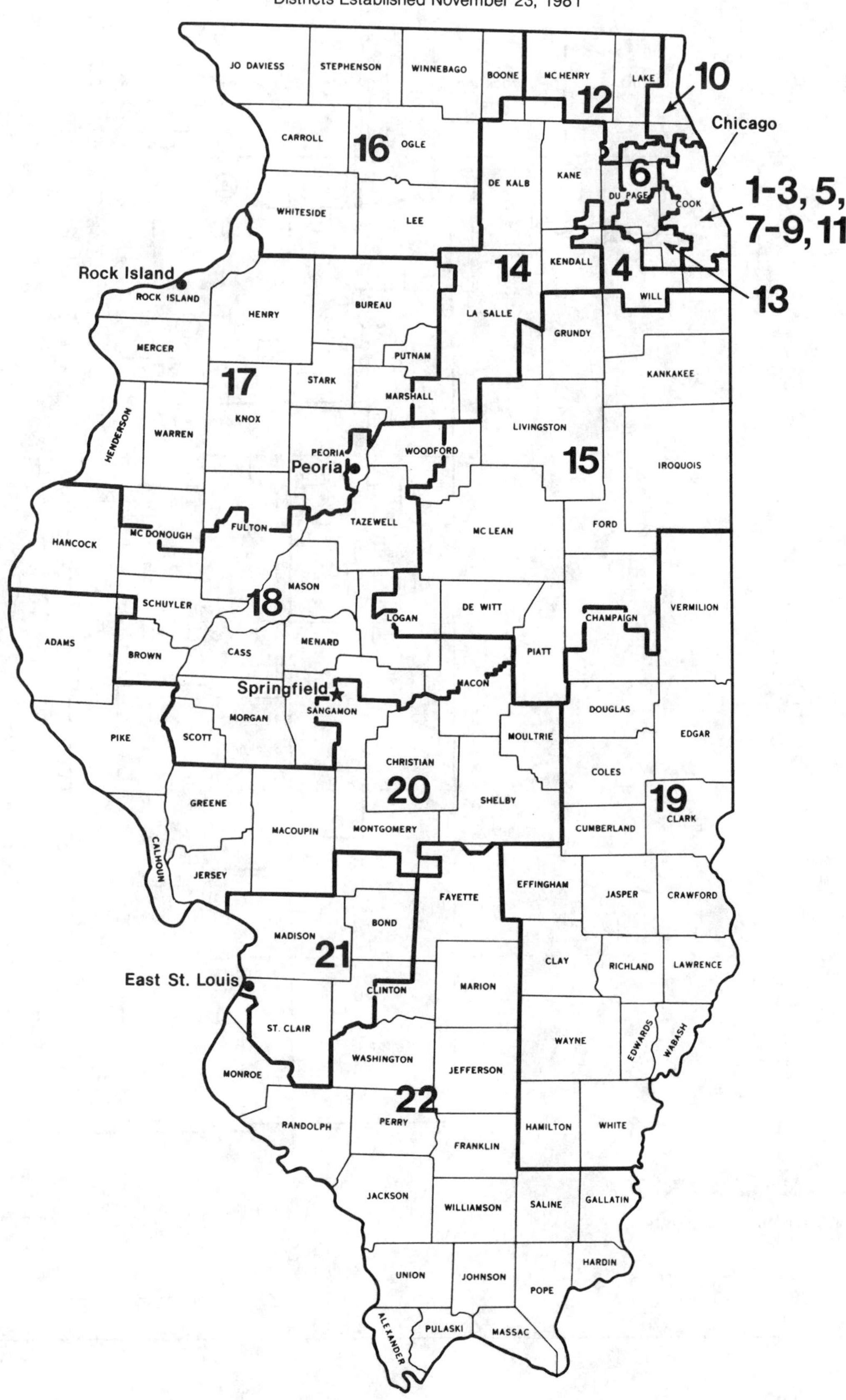

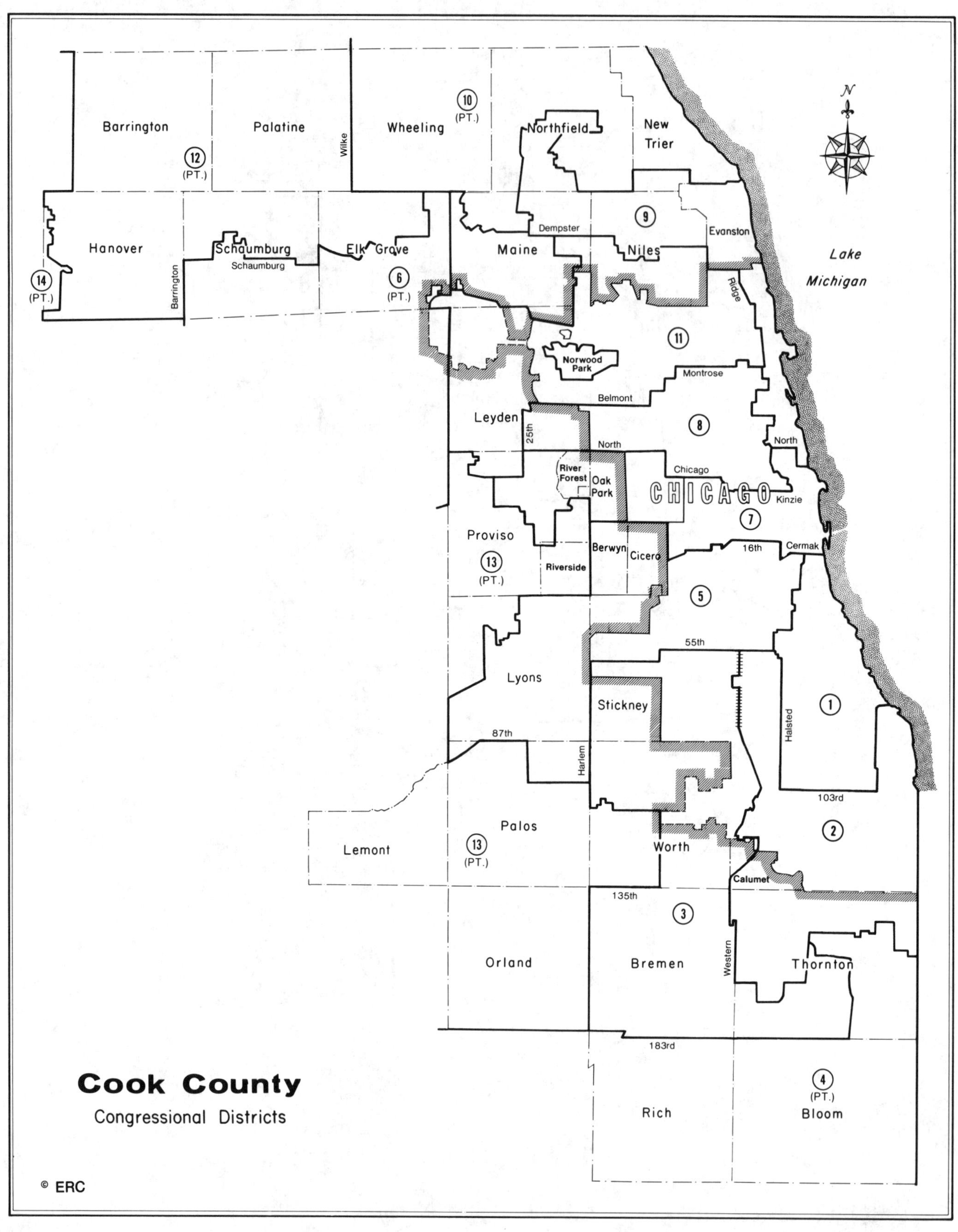

Barrington
Palatine
Wilke
Wheeling
10 (PT.)
Northfield
New Trier
12 (PT.)
Hanover
Schaumburg
Schaumburg
Elk Grove
Barrington
14 (PT.)
6 (PT.)
Maine
Dempster
9
Niles
Evanston
Lake Michigan
Ridge
11
Norwood Park
Montrose
Belmont
Leyden
25th
8
North
North
River Forest
Oak Park
Chicago
CHICAGO
Kinzie
7
Proviso
13 (PT.)
Riverside
Berwyn
Cicero
16th
Cermak
5
55th
Lyons
Stickney
1
Halsted
87th
Harlem
103rd
2
Lemont
Palos
13 (PT.)
Worth
Calumet
135th
3
Orland
Bremen
Western
Thornton
183rd
4 (PT.)
Rich
Bloom
Cook County
Congressional Districts
© ERC

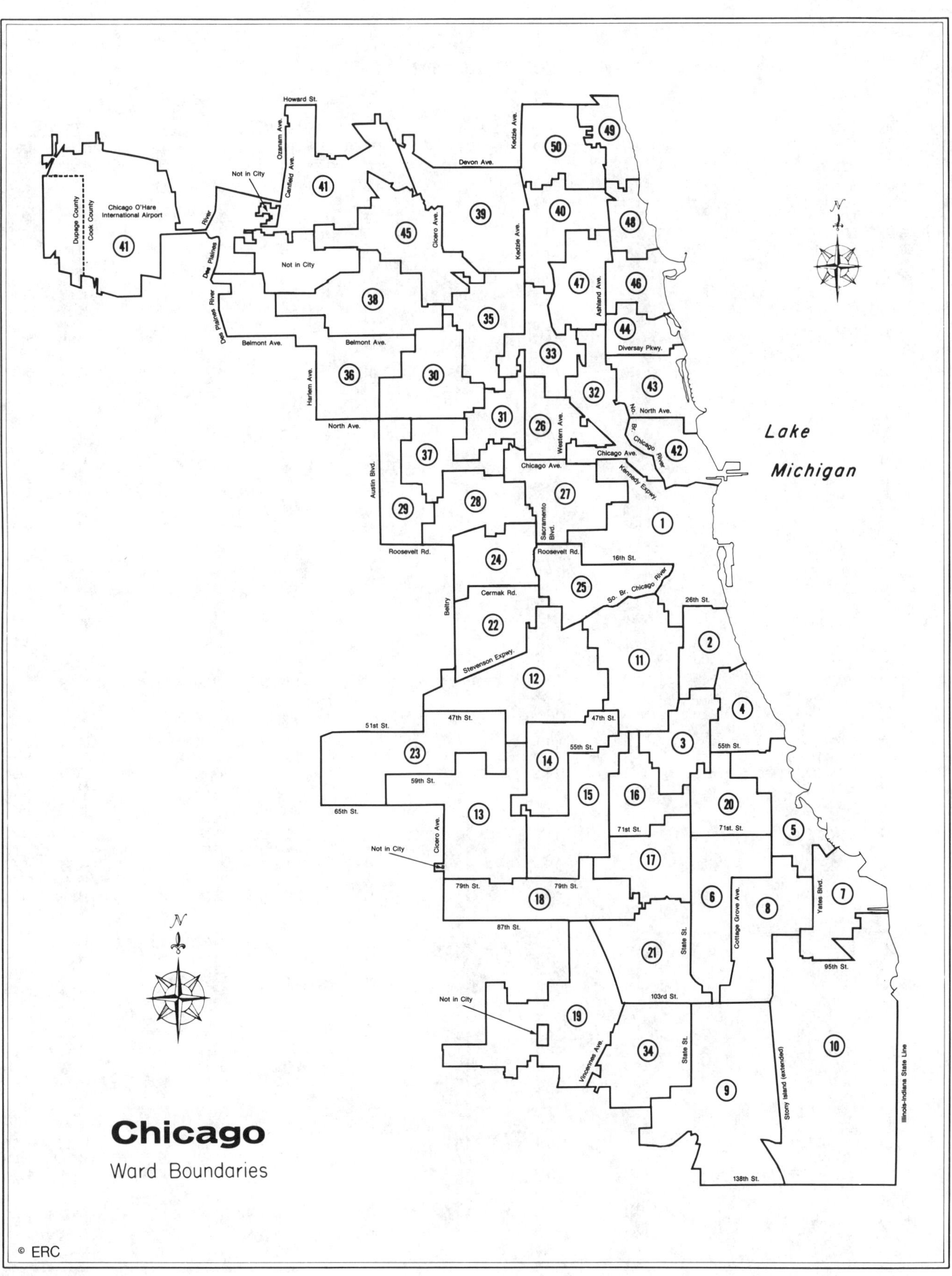

Chicago
Ward Boundaries
Lake Michigan
Chicago O'Hare International Airport
Dupage County
Cook County
Not in City
Howard St.
Ozanam Ave.
Canfield Ave.
Devon Ave.
Kedzie Ave.
Cicero Ave.
Des Plaines River
Belmont Ave.
Harlem Ave.
North Ave.
Ashland Ave.
Diversey Pkwy.
Western Ave.
No. Br. Chicago River
Chicago Ave.
Kennedy Expwy.
Austin Blvd.
Sacramento Blvd.
Roosevelt Rd.
16th St.
So. Br. Chicago River
26th St.
Cermak Rd.
Beltry
Stevenson Expwy.
47th St.
51st St.
55th St.
59th St.
65th St.
71st St.
79th St.
87th St.
95th St.
103rd St.
138th St.
Yates Blvd.
Cottage Grove Ave.
State St.
Vincennes Ave.
Stony Island (extended)
Illinois-Indiana State Line

ILLINOIS

PRESIDENT 1988

1980 Census Population	County	Total Vote	Republican	Democratic	Other	Rep.-Dem. Plurality	Percentage Total Vote Rep.	Total Vote Dem.	Major Vote Rep.	Major Vote Dem.
71,622	ADAMS	29,710	15,831	13,768	111	2,063 R	53.3%	46.3%	53.5%	46.5%
12,264	ALEXANDER	4,663	1,954	2,693	16	739 D	41.9%	57.8%	42.0%	58.0%
16,224	BOND	7,105	3,608	3,459	38	149 R	50.8%	48.7%	51.1%	48.9%
28,630	BOONE	11,222	6,923	4,234	65	2,689 R	61.7%	37.7%	62.1%	37.9%
5,411	BROWN	2,646	1,373	1,267	6	106 R	51.9%	47.9%	52.0%	48.0%
39,114	BUREAU	16,351	8,896	7,354	101	1,542 R	54.4%	45.0%	54.7%	45.3%
5,867	CALHOUN	2,790	1,238	1,544	8	306 D	44.4%	55.3%	44.5%	55.5%
18,779	CARROLL	7,512	4,464	2,990	58	1,474 R	59.4%	39.8%	59.9%	40.1%
15,084	CASS	6,267	2,916	3,316	35	400 D	46.5%	52.9%	46.8%	53.2%
168,392	CHAMPAIGN	63,499	33,247	29,733	519	3,514 R	52.4%	46.8%	52.8%	47.2%
36,446	CHRISTIAN	15,436	7,040	8,295	101	1,255 D	45.6%	53.7%	45.9%	54.1%
16,913	CLARK	7,811	4,508	3,275	28	1,233 R	57.7%	41.9%	57.9%	42.1%
15,283	CLAY	6,279	3,494	2,761	24	733 R	55.6%	44.0%	55.9%	44.1%
32,617	CLINTON	13,680	7,681	5,935	64	1,746 R	56.1%	43.4%	56.4%	43.6%
52,260	COLES	19,504	11,043	8,327	134	2,716 R	56.6%	42.7%	57.0%	43.0%
5,253,655	COOK	2,026,144	878,582	1,129,973	17,589	251,391 D	43.4%	55.8%	43.7%	56.3%
20,818	CRAWFORD	8,571	4,951	3,555	65	1,396 R	57.8%	41.5%	58.2%	41.8%
11,062	CUMBERLAND	4,600	2,667	1,904	29	763 R	58.0%	41.4%	58.3%	41.7%
74,624	DE KALB	29,190	17,182	11,811	197	5,371 R	58.9%	40.5%	59.3%	40.7%
18,108	DE WITT	6,645	3,942	2,660	43	1,282 R	59.3%	40.0%	59.7%	40.3%
19,774	DOUGLAS	7,598	4,378	3,184	36	1,194 R	57.6%	41.9%	57.9%	42.1%
658,835	DU PAGE	314,054	217,907	94,285	1,862	123,622 R	69.4%	30.0%	69.8%	30.2%
21,725	EDGAR	9,459	5,538	3,880	41	1,658 R	58.5%	41.0%	58.8%	41.2%
7,961	EDWARDS	3,450	2,212	1,218	20	994 R	64.1%	35.3%	64.5%	35.5%
30,944	EFFINGHAM	13,066	8,431	4,553	82	3,878 R	64.5%	34.8%	64.9%	35.1%
22,167	FAYETTE	10,118	5,452	4,632	34	820 R	53.9%	45.8%	54.1%	45.9%
15,265	FORD	6,145	4,059	2,026	60	2,033 R	66.1%	33.0%	66.7%	33.3%
43,201	FRANKLIN	18,783	7,677	11,023	83	3,346 D	40.9%	58.7%	41.1%	58.9%
43,687	FULTON	16,108	6,999	9,046	63	2,047 D	43.5%	56.2%	43.6%	56.4%
7,590	GALLATIN	4,063	1,580	2,455	28	875 D	38.9%	60.4%	39.2%	60.8%
16,661	GREENE	6,203	3,136	3,020	47	116 R	50.6%	48.7%	50.9%	49.1%
30,582	GRUNDY	14,361	8,743	5,525	93	3,218 R	60.9%	38.5%	61.3%	38.7%
9,172	HAMILTON	5,256	2,622	2,618	16	4 R	49.9%	49.8%	50.0%	50.0%
23,877	HANCOCK	9,378	4,568	4,740	70	172 D	48.7%	50.5%	49.1%	50.9%
5,383	HARDIN	2,824	1,504	1,308	12	196 R	53.3%	46.3%	53.5%	46.5%
9,114	HENDERSON	3,821	1,726	2,085	10	359 D	45.2%	54.6%	45.3%	54.7%
57,968	HENRY	23,048	11,358	11,594	96	236 D	49.3%	50.3%	49.5%	50.5%
32,976	IROQUOIS	13,886	9,596	4,221	69	5,375 R	69.1%	30.4%	69.5%	30.5%
61,522	JACKSON	21,185	9,687	11,334	164	1,647 D	45.7%	53.5%	46.1%	53.9%
11,318	JASPER	5,189	3,024	2,135	30	889 R	58.3%	41.1%	58.6%	41.4%
36,552	JEFFERSON	15,426	7,624	7,729	73	105 D	49.4%	50.1%	49.7%	50.3%
20,538	JERSEY	8,752	4,343	4,376	33	33 D	49.6%	50.0%	49.8%	50.2%
23,520	JO DAVIESS	9,137	4,923	4,141	73	782 R	53.9%	45.3%	54.3%	45.7%
9,624	JOHNSON	4,692	2,797	1,872	23	925 R	59.6%	39.9%	59.9%	40.1%
278,405	KANE	103,412	66,283	36,366	763	29,917 R	64.1%	35.2%	64.6%	35.4%
102,926	KANKAKEE	35,755	20,316	15,147	292	5,169 R	56.8%	42.4%	57.3%	42.7%
37,202	KENDALL	15,084	10,653	4,347	84	6,306 R	70.6%	28.8%	71.0%	29.0%
61,607	KNOX	23,700	10,842	12,752	106	1,910 D	45.7%	53.8%	46.0%	54.0%
440,372	LAKE	179,633	114,115	64,327	1,191	49,788 R	63.5%	35.8%	64.0%	36.0%
112,033	LA SALLE	44,650	22,166	22,271	213	105 D	49.6%	49.9%	49.9%	50.1%
17,807	LAWRENCE	6,823	3,655	3,140	28	515 R	53.6%	46.0%	53.8%	46.2%
36,328	LEE	13,596	8,903	4,608	85	4,295 R	65.5%	33.9%	65.9%	34.1%
41,381	LIVINGSTON	15,405	10,324	5,009	72	5,315 R	67.0%	32.5%	67.3%	32.7%
31,802	LOGAN	13,286	8,490	4,727	69	3,763 R	63.9%	35.6%	64.2%	35.8%
37,467	MCDONOUGH	12,493	7,173	5,247	73	1,926 R	57.4%	42.0%	57.8%	42.2%
147,897	MCHENRY	65,499	46,135	18,919	445	27,216 R	70.4%	28.9%	70.9%	29.1%
119,149	MCLEAN	49,511	30,572	18,659	280	11,913 R	61.7%	37.7%	62.1%	37.9%
131,375	MACON	49,489	23,862	25,364	263	1,502 D	48.2%	51.3%	48.5%	51.5%
49,384	MACOUPIN	21,669	9,362	12,195	112	2,833 D	43.2%	56.3%	43.4%	56.6%
247,691	MADISON	99,695	44,907	54,175	613	9,268 D	45.0%	54.3%	45.3%	54.7%

ILLINOIS

PRESIDENT 1988

1980 Census Population	County	Total Vote	Republican	Democratic	Other	Rep.-Dem. Plurality	Percentage Total Vote Rep.	Total Vote Dem.	Major Vote Rep.	Major Vote Dem.
43,523	MARION	17,373	8,695	8,592	86	103 R	50.0%	49.5%	50.3%	49.7%
14,479	MARSHALL	6,367	3,588	2,742	37	846 R	56.4%	43.1%	56.7%	43.3%
19,492	MASON	6,855	3,424	3,406	25	18 R	49.9%	49.7%	50.1%	49.9%
14,990	MASSAC	6,763	3,507	3,227	29	280 R	51.9%	47.7%	52.1%	47.9%
11,700	MENARD	5,705	3,560	2,103	42	1,457 R	62.4%	36.9%	62.9%	37.1%
19,286	MERCER	7,929	3,683	4,204	42	521 D	46.4%	53.0%	46.7%	53.3%
20,117	MONROE	10,851	6,275	4,529	47	1,746 R	57.8%	41.7%	58.1%	41.9%
31,686	MONTGOMERY	13,759	6,388	7,293	78	905 D	46.4%	53.0%	46.7%	53.3%
37,502	MORGAN	14,886	8,808	6,032	46	2,776 R	59.2%	40.5%	59.4%	40.6%
14,546	MOULTRIE	6,212	3,167	3,013	32	154 R	51.0%	48.5%	51.2%	48.8%
46,338	OGLE	17,394	11,644	5,641	109	6,003 R	66.9%	32.4%	67.4%	32.6%
200,466	PEORIA	73,230	37,605	35,253	372	2,352 R	51.4%	48.1%	51.6%	48.4%
21,714	PERRY	9,781	4,576	5,167	38	591 D	46.8%	52.8%	47.0%	53.0%
16,581	PIATT	7,277	4,137	3,099	41	1,038 R	56.9%	42.6%	57.2%	42.8%
18,896	PIKE	8,599	3,965	4,614	20	649 D	46.1%	53.7%	46.2%	53.8%
4,404	POPE	2,208	1,202	996	10	206 R	54.4%	45.1%	54.7%	45.3%
8,840	PULASKI	3,478	1,666	1,793	19	127 D	47.9%	51.6%	48.2%	51.8%
6,085	PUTNAM	3,139	1,516	1,601	22	85 D	48.3%	51.0%	48.6%	51.4%
35,652	RANDOLPH	15,318	7,396	7,844	78	448 D	48.3%	51.2%	48.5%	51.5%
17,587	RICHLAND	7,153	4,264	2,863	26	1,401 R	59.6%	40.0%	59.8%	40.2%
165,968	ROCK ISLAND	67,901	27,412	40,174	315	12,762 D	40.4%	59.2%	40.6%	59.4%
267,531	ST. CLAIR	97,313	41,439	55,465	409	14,026 D	42.6%	57.0%	42.8%	57.2%
28,448	SALINE	12,521	5,798	6,676	47	878 D	46.3%	53.3%	46.5%	53.5%
176,089	SANGAMON	88,403	50,175	37,729	499	12,446 R	56.8%	42.7%	57.1%	42.9%
8,365	SCHUYLER	4,066	2,178	1,866	22	312 R	53.6%	45.9%	53.9%	46.1%
6,142	SCOTT	2,790	1,535	1,243	12	292 R	55.0%	44.6%	55.3%	44.7%
23,923	SHELBY	10,078	5,370	4,650	58	720 R	53.3%	46.1%	53.6%	46.4%
7,389	STARK	3,153	1,841	1,274	38	567 R	58.4%	40.4%	59.1%	40.9%
49,536	STEPHENSON	18,945	11,342	7,460	143	3,882 R	59.9%	39.4%	60.3%	39.7%
132,078	TAZEWELL	53,727	28,861	24,603	263	4,258 R	53.7%	45.8%	54.0%	46.0%
17,765	UNION	8,479	4,244	4,197	38	47 R	50.1%	49.5%	50.3%	49.7%
95,222	VERMILION	35,067	16,943	17,918	206	975 D	48.3%	51.1%	48.6%	51.4%
13,713	WABASH	5,726	3,453	2,241	32	1,212 R	60.3%	39.1%	60.6%	39.4%
21,943	WARREN	8,254	4,584	3,617	53	967 R	55.5%	43.8%	55.9%	44.1%
15,472	WASHINGTON	6,874	4,127	2,689	58	1,438 R	60.0%	39.1%	60.5%	39.5%
18,059	WAYNE	8,660	5,481	3,135	44	2,346 R	63.3%	36.2%	63.6%	36.4%
17,864	WHITE	8,531	4,354	4,144	33	210 R	51.0%	48.6%	51.2%	48.8%
65,970	WHITESIDE	24,462	12,978	11,328	156	1,650 R	53.1%	46.3%	53.4%	46.6%
324,460	WILL	123,731	73,129	49,816	786	23,313 R	59.1%	40.3%	59.5%	40.5%
56,538	WILLIAMSON	25,130	12,274	12,712	144	438 D	48.8%	50.6%	49.1%	50.9%
250,884	WINNEBAGO	101,550	55,699	45,280	571	10,419 R	54.8%	44.6%	55.2%	44.8%
33,320	WOODFORD	14,155	9,474	4,604	77	4,870 R	66.9%	32.5%	67.3%	32.7%
11,426,518	TOTAL	4,559,120	2,310,939	2,215,940	32,241	94,999 R	50.7%	48.6%	51.0%	49.0%

CHICAGO

PRESIDENT 1988

1980 Census Population	Ward	Total Vote	Republican	Democratic	Other	Rep.-Dem. Plurality	Percentage Total Vote Rep.	Percentage Total Vote Dem.	Percentage Major Vote Rep.	Percentage Major Vote Dem.
61,716	WARD 1	21,091	6,643	14,228	220	7,585 D	31.5%	67.5%	31.8%	68.2%
60,141	WARD 2	16,461	757	15,445	259	14,688 D	4.6%	93.8%	4.7%	95.3%
60,267	WARD 3	16,108	349	15,555	204	15,206 D	2.2%	96.6%	2.2%	97.8%
60,051	WARD 4	20,293	1,457	18,470	366	17,013 D	7.2%	91.0%	7.3%	92.7%
60,215	WARD 5	22,920	1,713	20,895	312	19,182 D	7.5%	91.2%	7.6%	92.4%
60,576	WARD 6	28,711	705	27,631	375	26,926 D	2.5%	96.2%	2.5%	97.5%
59,906	WARD 7	16,837	1,292	15,363	182	14,071 D	7.7%	91.2%	7.8%	92.2%
59,928	WARD 8	26,220	628	25,255	337	24,627 D	2.4%	96.3%	2.4%	97.6%
60,425	WARD 9	19,319	831	18,269	219	17,438 D	4.3%	94.6%	4.4%	95.6%
60,184	WARD 10	25,606	10,668	14,730	208	4,062 D	41.7%	57.5%	42.0%	58.0%
58,439	WARD 11	19,686	7,591	11,947	148	4,356 D	38.6%	60.7%	38.9%	61.1%
60,674	WARD 12	18,564	8,786	9,583	195	797 D	47.3%	51.6%	47.8%	52.2%
61,249	WARD 13	31,718	18,242	13,279	197	4,963 R	57.5%	41.9%	57.9%	42.1%
61,383	WARD 14	18,422	8,127	10,110	185	1,983 D	44.1%	54.9%	44.6%	55.4%
61,567	WARD 15	19,223	2,999	16,003	221	13,004 D	15.6%	83.2%	15.8%	84.2%
59,710	WARD 16	17,496	348	16,913	235	16,565 D	2.0%	96.7%	2.0%	98.0%
58,234	WARD 17	21,153	459	20,403	291	19,944 D	2.2%	96.5%	2.2%	97.8%
60,705	WARD 18	28,673	10,316	18,152	205	7,836 D	36.0%	63.3%	36.2%	63.8%
59,786	WARD 19	31,189	16,387	14,566	236	1,821 R	52.5%	46.7%	52.9%	47.1%
59,981	WARD 20	17,844	525	17,056	263	16,531 D	2.9%	95.6%	3.0%	97.0%
59,336	WARD 21	26,752	539	25,875	338	25,336 D	2.0%	96.7%	2.0%	98.0%
59,803	WARD 22	7,194	1,627	5,422	145	3,795 D	22.6%	75.4%	23.1%	76.9%
58,596	WARD 23	29,898	17,505	12,188	205	5,317 R	58.5%	40.8%	59.0%	41.0%
63,308	WARD 24	17,815	370	17,194	251	16,824 D	2.1%	96.5%	2.1%	97.9%
60,075	WARD 25	8,708	2,110	6,511	87	4,401 D	24.2%	74.8%	24.5%	75.5%
60,612	WARD 26	12,556	2,761	9,647	148	6,886 D	22.0%	76.8%	22.3%	77.7%
60,891	WARD 27	13,553	1,217	12,151	185	10,934 D	9.0%	89.7%	9.1%	90.9%
58,626	WARD 28	15,452	336	14,919	197	14,583 D	2.2%	96.6%	2.2%	97.8%
61,446	WARD 29	16,925	909	15,770	246	14,861 D	5.4%	93.2%	5.4%	94.6%
60,108	WARD 30	18,924	7,594	11,172	158	3,578 D	40.1%	59.0%	40.5%	59.5%
59,283	WARD 31	12,826	2,715	9,965	146	7,250 D	21.2%	77.7%	21.4%	78.6%
61,459	WARD 32	15,544	4,869	10,485	190	5,616 D	31.3%	67.5%	31.7%	68.3%
58,693	WARD 33	17,002	5,933	10,924	145	4,991 D	34.9%	64.3%	35.2%	64.8%
60,092	WARD 34	23,834	549	22,998	287	22,449 D	2.3%	96.5%	2.3%	97.7%
58,780	WARD 35	18,301	8,860	9,288	153	428 D	48.4%	50.8%	48.8%	51.2%
58,942	WARD 36	27,221	15,308	11,730	183	3,578 R	56.2%	43.1%	56.6%	43.4%
60,723	WARD 37	17,357	671	16,472	214	15,801 D	3.9%	94.9%	3.9%	96.1%
59,784	WARD 38	27,741	16,258	11,314	169	4,944 R	58.6%	40.8%	59.0%	41.0%
60,669	WARD 39	22,119	11,289	10,677	153	612 R	51.0%	48.3%	51.4%	48.6%
58,685	WARD 40	18,141	7,629	10,378	134	2,749 D	42.1%	57.2%	42.4%	57.6%
60,579	WARD 41	31,946	20,372	11,406	168	8,966 R	63.8%	35.7%	64.1%	35.9%
60,173	WARD 42	28,364	12,482	15,650	232	3,168 D	44.0%	55.2%	44.4%	55.6%
60,156	WARD 43	33,144	15,087	17,795	262	2,708 D	45.5%	53.7%	45.9%	54.1%
60,163	WARD 44	28,623	9,559	18,781	283	9,222 D	33.4%	65.6%	33.7%	66.3%
58,818	WARD 45	28,155	16,467	11,545	143	4,922 R	58.5%	41.0%	58.8%	41.2%
59,848	WARD 46	21,157	6,065	14,871	221	8,806 D	28.7%	70.3%	29.0%	71.0%
60,005	WARD 47	20,805	8,419	12,214	172	3,795 D	40.5%	58.7%	40.8%	59.2%
60,135	WARD 48	20,050	6,091	13,690	269	7,599 D	30.4%	68.3%	30.8%	69.2%
60,231	WARD 49	19,612	5,145	14,228	239	9,083 D	26.2%	72.5%	26.6%	73.4%
59,916	WARD 50	24,131	8,402	15,563	166	7,161 D	34.8%	64.5%	35.1%	64.9%
	ABSENTEE	4,706	1,541	3,107	58	1,566 D	32.7%	66.0%	33.2%	66.8%
3,005,072	TOTAL	1,066,090	317,502	737,783	10,805	420,281 D	29.8%	69.2%	30.1%	69.9%

ILLINOIS

CONGRESS

CD	Year	Total Vote	Republican Vote	Republican Candidate	Democratic Vote	Democratic Candidate	Other Vote	Rep.-Dem. Plurality	Percentage Total Vote Rep.	Percentage Total Vote Dem.	Percentage Major Vote Rep.	Percentage Major Vote Dem.
1	1988	170,878	6,753	EVANS, STEPHEN J.	164,125	HAYES, CHARLES A.		157,372 D	4.0%	96.0%	4.0%	96.0%
1	1986	126,948	4,572	FAULKNER, JOSEPH C.	122,376	HAYES, CHARLES A.		117,804 D	3.6%	96.4%	3.6%	96.4%
1	1984	185,534			177,438	HAYES, CHARLES A.	8,096	177,438 D		95.6%		100.0%
1	1982	177,462	4,820	TALIAFERRO, CHARLES A.	172,641	WASHINGTON, HAROLD	1	167,821 D	2.7%	97.3%	2.7%	97.3%
2	1988	167,087	28,831	HESPEL, WILLIAM T.	138,256	SAVAGE, GUS		109,425 D	17.3%	82.7%	17.3%	82.7%
2	1986	118,417	19,149	TAYLOR, RON	99,268	SAVAGE, GUS		80,119 D	16.2%	83.8%	16.2%	83.8%
2	1984	187,215	31,865	HARMAN, DALE F.	155,349	SAVAGE, GUS	1	123,484 D	17.0%	83.0%	17.0%	83.0%
2	1982	161,794	20,670	SPARKS, KEVIN W.	140,827	SAVAGE, GUS	297	120,157 D	12.8%	87.0%	12.8%	87.2%
3	1988	212,292	80,181	MCCARTHY, JOSEPH J.	132,111	RUSSO, MARTIN A.		51,930 D	37.8%	62.2%	37.8%	62.2%
3	1986	155,567	52,618	TIERNEY, JAMES J.	102,949	RUSSO, MARTIN A.		50,331 D	33.8%	66.2%	33.8%	66.2%
3	1984	222,582	79,218	MURPHY, RICHARD D.	143,363	RUSSO, MARTIN A.	1	64,145 D	35.6%	64.4%	35.6%	64.4%
3	1982	185,659	48,268	MURPHY, RICHARD D.	137,391	RUSSO, MARTIN A.		89,123 D	26.0%	74.0%	26.0%	74.0%
4	1988	181,525	90,243	DAVIS, JACK	91,282	SANGMEISTER, GEORGE E.		1,039 D	49.7%	50.3%	49.7%	50.3%
4	1986	119,356	61,583	DAVIS, JACK	57,773	COLLINS, SHAWN		3,810 R	51.6%	48.4%	51.6%	48.4%
4	1984	190,291	121,744	O'BRIEN, GEORGE M.	68,547	MARLOW, DENNIS E.		53,197 R	64.0%	36.0%	64.0%	36.0%
4	1982	146,172	79,842	O'BRIEN, GEORGE M.	66,323	MURER, MICHAEL A.	7	13,519 R	54.6%	45.4%	54.6%	45.4%
5	1988	152,695	59,128	HOLOWINSKI, JOHN J.	93,567	LIPINSKI, WILLIAM O.		34,439 D	38.7%	61.3%	38.7%	61.3%
5	1986	117,204	34,738	SOBIESKI, DANIEL J.	82,466	LIPINSKI, WILLIAM O.		47,728 D	29.6%	70.4%	29.6%	70.4%
5	1984	167,708	61,109	PACZKOWSKI, JOHN M.	106,597	LIPINSKI, WILLIAM O.	2	45,488 D	36.4%	63.6%	36.4%	63.6%
5	1982	146,322	35,970	PARTYKA, DANIEL J.	110,351	LIPINSKI, WILLIAM O.	1	74,381 D	24.6%	75.4%	24.6%	75.4%
6	1988	208,229	153,425	HYDE, HENRY J.	54,804	ANDRLE, WILLIAM J.		98,621 R	73.7%	26.3%	73.7%	26.3%
6	1986	130,260	98,196	HYDE, HENRY J.	32,064	RENSHAW, ROBERT H.		66,132 R	75.4%	24.6%	75.4%	24.6%
6	1984	209,562	157,370	HYDE, HENRY J.	52,189	RENSHAW, ROBERT H.	3	105,181 R	75.1%	24.9%	75.1%	24.9%
6	1982	143,168	97,918	HYDE, HENRY J.	45,237	KENNEL, LEROY E.	13	52,681 R	68.4%	31.6%	68.4%	31.6%
7	1988	135,331			135,331	COLLINS, CARDISS		135,331 D		100.0%		100.0%
7	1986	113,164	21,055	KALLAS, CAROLINE K.	90,761	COLLINS, CARDISS	1,348	69,706 D	18.6%	80.2%	18.8%	81.2%
7	1984	172,908	37,411	BEVEL, JAMES L.	135,493	COLLINS, CARDISS	4	98,082 D	21.6%	78.4%	21.6%	78.4%
7	1982	154,974	20,994	CHEEKS, DANSBY	133,978	COLLINS, CARDISS	2	112,984 D	13.5%	86.5%	13.5%	86.5%
8	1988	144,324	34,659	VETTER, V. STEPHEN	107,728	ROSTENKOWSKI, DANIEL	1,937	73,069 D	24.0%	74.6%	24.3%	75.7%
8	1986	105,256	22,383	DE FAZIO, THOMAS J.	82,873	ROSTENKOWSKI, DANIEL		60,490 D	21.3%	78.7%	21.3%	78.7%
8	1984	160,417	46,030	GEORGESON, SPIRO F.	114,385	ROSTENKOWSKI, DANIEL	2	68,355 D	28.7%	71.3%	28.7%	71.3%
8	1982	148,985	24,666	HICKEY, BONNIE	124,318	ROSTENKOWSKI, DANIEL	1	99,652 D	16.6%	83.4%	16.6%	83.4%
9	1988	205,187	67,604	SOHN, HERBERT	135,583	YATES, SIDNEY R.	2,000	67,979 D	32.9%	66.1%	33.3%	66.7%
9	1986	129,453	36,715	SOHN, HERBERT	92,738	YATES, SIDNEY R.		56,023 D	28.4%	71.6%	28.4%	71.6%
9	1984	214,495	69,613	SOHN, HERBERT	144,879	YATES, SIDNEY R.	3	75,266 D	32.5%	67.5%	32.5%	67.5%
9	1982	171,529	54,851	BERTINI, CATHERINE	114,083	YATES, SIDNEY R.	2,595	59,232 D	32.0%	66.5%	32.5%	67.5%
10	1988	218,706	158,519	PORTER, JOHN E.	60,187	FRIEDMAN, EUGENE F.		98,332 R	72.5%	27.5%	72.5%	27.5%
10	1986	116,520	87,530	PORTER, JOHN E.	28,990	CLELAND, ROBERT A.		58,540 R	75.1%	24.9%	75.1%	24.9%
10	1984	211,140	153,330	PORTER, JOHN E.	57,809	BRAVER, RUTH C.	1	95,521 R	72.6%	27.4%	72.6%	27.4%
10	1982	153,868	90,750	PORTER, JOHN E.	63,115	CHAPMAN, EUGENIA S.	3	27,635 R	59.0%	41.0%	59.0%	41.0%
11	1988	204,242	72,489	GOTTLIEB, GEORGE S.	131,753	ANNUNZIO, FRANK		59,264 D	35.5%	64.5%	35.5%	64.5%
11	1986	151,311	44,341	GOTTLIEB, GEORGE S.	106,970	ANNUNZIO, FRANK		62,629 D	29.3%	70.7%	29.3%	70.7%
11	1984	220,690	82,518	THEUSCH, CHARLES J.	138,171	ANNUNZIO, FRANK	1	55,653 D	37.4%	62.6%	37.4%	62.6%
11	1982	185,722	50,967	MOYNIHAN, JAMES F.	134,755	ANNUNZIO, FRANK		83,788 D	27.4%	72.6%	27.4%	72.6%
12	1988	220,682	165,913	CRANE, PHILIP M.	54,769	LEONARDI, JOHN A.		111,144 R	75.2%	24.8%	75.2%	24.8%
12	1986	114,580	89,044	CRANE, PHILIP M.	25,536	LEONARDI, JOHN A.		63,508 R	77.7%	22.3%	77.7%	22.3%
12	1984	205,119	159,582	CRANE, PHILIP M.	45,537	LA FLAMME, EDWARD J.		114,045 R	77.8%	22.2%	77.8%	22.2%
12	1982	130,701	86,487	CRANE, PHILIP M.	40,108	DEFOSSE, DANIEL G.	4,106	46,379 R	66.2%	30.7%	68.3%	31.7%

ILLINOIS

CONGRESS

CD	Year	Total Vote	Republican Vote	Republican Candidate	Democratic Vote	Democratic Candidate	Other Vote	Rep.-Dem. Plurality	Percentage Total Vote Rep.	Percentage Total Vote Dem.	Percentage Major Vote Rep.	Percentage Major Vote Dem.
13	1988	249,416	174,992	FAWELL, HARRIS W.	74,424	CRAIG, EVELYN E.		100,568 R	70.2%	29.8%	70.2%	29.8%
13	1986	146,101	107,227	FAWELL, HARRIS W.	38,874	JEFFREY, DOMINICK J.		68,353 R	73.4%	26.6%	73.4%	26.6%
13	1984	235,234	157,603	FAWELL, HARRIS W.	77,623	DONOHUE, MICHAEL J.	8	79,980 R	67.0%	33.0%	67.0%	33.0%
13	1982	162,530	113,423	ERLENBORN, JOHN N.	49,105	BILY, ROBERT	2	64,318 R	69.8%	30.2%	69.8%	30.2%
14	1988	218,628	161,146	HASTERT, J. DENNIS	57,482	YOUHANAIE, STEPHEN		103,664 R	73.7%	26.3%	73.7%	26.3%
14	1986	147,581	77,288	HASTERT, J. DENNIS	70,293	KEARNS, MARY LOU		6,995 R	52.4%	47.6%	52.4%	47.6%
14	1984	218,738	135,967	GROTBERG, JOHN E.	82,756	MCGRATH, DAN	15	53,211 R	62.2%	37.8%	62.2%	37.8%
14	1982	152,180	98,262	CORCORAN, TOM	53,914	MCGRATH, DAN	4	44,348 R	64.6%	35.4%	64.6%	35.4%
15	1988	195,431	140,171	MADIGAN, EDWARD R.	55,260	CURL, THOMAS J.		84,911 R	71.7%	28.3%	71.7%	28.3%
15	1986	115,284	115,284	MADIGAN, EDWARD R.				115,284 R	100.0%		100.0%	
15	1984	203,613	149,096	MADIGAN, EDWARD R.	54,516	HOFFMANN, JOHN M.	1	94,580 R	73.2%	26.8%	73.2%	26.8%
15	1982	158,344	105,038	MADIGAN, EDWARD R.	53,303	HALL, TIM L.	3	51,735 R	66.3%	33.7%	66.3%	33.7%
16	1988	200,796	128,365	MARTIN, LYNN	72,431	MAHAN, STEVEN E.		55,934 R	63.9%	36.1%	63.9%	36.1%
16	1986	139,069	92,982	MARTIN, LYNN	46,087	BOHNSACK, KENNETH F.		46,895 R	66.9%	33.1%	66.9%	33.1%
16	1984	218,538	127,684	MARTIN, LYNN	90,850	SCHWERDTFEGER, CARL R.	4	36,834 R	58.4%	41.6%	58.4%	41.6%
16	1982	156,287	89,405	MARTIN, LYNN	66,877	SCHWERDTFEGER, CARL R.	5	22,528 R	57.2%	42.8%	57.2%	42.8%
17	1988	203,690	71,560	STEWART, WILLIAM E.	132,130	EVANS, LANE		60,570 D	35.1%	64.9%	35.1%	64.9%
17	1986	153,543	68,101	MCHARD, SAM	85,442	EVANS, LANE		17,341 D	44.4%	55.6%	44.4%	55.6%
17	1984	226,345	98,069	MCMILLAN, KENNETH G.	128,273	EVANS, LANE	3	30,204 D	43.3%	56.7%	43.3%	56.7%
17	1982	178,887	84,347	MCMILLAN, KENNETH G.	94,483	EVANS, LANE	57	10,136 D	47.2%	52.8%	47.2%	52.8%
18	1988	209,221	114,458	MICHEL, ROBERT H.	94,763	STEPHENS, G. DOUGLAS		19,695 R	54.7%	45.3%	54.7%	45.3%
18	1986	150,639	94,308	MICHEL, ROBERT H.	56,331	DAWSON, JIM		37,977 R	62.6%	37.4%	62.6%	37.4%
18	1984	223,106	136,183	MICHEL, ROBERT H.	86,884	BRADLEY, GERALD A.	39	49,299 R	61.0%	38.9%	61.1%	38.9%
18	1982	188,694	97,406	MICHEL, ROBERT H.	91,281	STEPHENS, G. DOUGLAS	7	6,125 R	51.6%	48.4%	51.6%	48.4%
19	1988	206,870	73,981	KERANS, ROBERT F.	132,889	BRUCE, TERRY L.		58,908 D	35.8%	64.2%	35.8%	64.2%
19	1986	167,291	56,186	SALVI, AL	111,105	BRUCE, TERRY L.		54,919 D	33.6%	66.4%	33.6%	66.4%
19	1984	225,103	107,463	CRANE, DANIEL B.	117,634	BRUCE, TERRY L.	6	10,171 D	47.7%	52.3%	47.7%	52.3%
19	1982	182,064	94,833	CRANE, DANIEL B.	87,231	GWINN, JOHN		7,602 R	52.1%	47.9%	52.1%	47.9%
20	1988	222,644	69,303	JURGENS, PAUL E.	153,341	DURBIN, RICHARD J.		84,038 D	31.1%	68.9%	31.1%	68.9%
20	1986	185,847	59,291	MCCARTHY, KEVIN B.	126,556	DURBIN, RICHARD J.		67,265 D	31.9%	68.1%	31.9%	68.1%
20	1984	236,821	91,728	AUSTIN, RICHARD G.	145,092	DURBIN, RICHARD J.	1	53,364 D	38.7%	61.3%	38.7%	61.3%
20	1982	200,109	99,348	FINDLEY, PAUL	100,758	DURBIN, RICHARD J.	3	1,410 D	49.6%	50.4%	49.6%	50.4%
21	1988	201,221	95,385	GAFFNER, ROBERT H.	105,836	COSTELLO, JERRY F.		10,451 D	47.4%	52.6%	47.4%	52.6%
21	1986	130,501	64,779	GAFFNER, ROBERT H.	65,722	PRICE, MELVIN		943 D	49.6%	50.4%	49.6%	50.4%
21	1984	211,194	84,148	GAFFNER, ROBERT H.	127,046	PRICE, MELVIN		42,898 D	39.8%	60.2%	39.8%	60.2%
21	1982	140,608	46,764	GAFFNER, ROBERT H.	89,500	PRICE, MELVIN	4,344	42,736 D	33.3%	63.7%	34.3%	65.7%
22	1988	214,854	75,462	KELLEY, PATRICK J.	139,392	POSHARD, GLENN		63,930 D	35.1%	64.9%	35.1%	64.9%
22	1986	183,318	85,733	PATCHETT, RANDY	97,585	GRAY, KENNETH J.		11,852 D	46.8%	53.2%	46.8%	53.2%
22	1984	232,728	115,775	PATCHETT, RANDY	116,952	GRAY, KENNETH J.	1	1,177 D	49.7%	50.3%	49.7%	50.3%
22	1982	186,972	63,279	PRINEAS, PETER G.	123,693	SIMON, PAUL		60,414 D	33.8%	66.2%	33.8%	66.2%

ILLINOIS

1988 GENERAL ELECTION

President Other vote was 14,944 Libertarian (Paul); 10,276 Solidarity (Fulani); 7,021 Independent (Winn).

Congress Other vote was Communist (Almberg) in CD 8; Solidarity (Fields) in CD 9.

CHICAGO

President Other vote was 4,628 Solidarity (Fulani); 4,352 Libertarian (Paul); 1,825 Independent (Winn).

1988 PRIMARIES

MARCH 15 REPUBLICAN

Congress Unopposed in fourteen CD's. Edward G. Howlett, the unopposed candidate in CD 7, withdrew after the primary and no substitution was made. Contested as follows:

CD 2 6,732 William T. Hespel; 1,876 Ron Taylor; 1,065 Robert Ellis.
CD 5 12,207 John J. Holowinski; 5,969 Aloysius A. Majerczyk.
CD 9 9,597 Herbert Sohn; 7,857 Jeanette Sarkesian.
CD 11 14,237 George S. Gottlieb; 5,102 Elias R. Zenkich.
CD 13 36,233 Harris W. Fawell; 10,806 George T. Hamilton.
CD 18 45,228 Robert H. Michel; 7,496 James E. Unsicker.
CD 19 21,900 Robert F. Kerans; 16,501 Charles R. Fuqua.
CD 22 20,711 Patrick J. Kelley; 10,472 Peter G. Prineas.

MARCH 15 DEMOCRATIC

Congress Unopposed in twelve CD's. Contested as follows:

CD 1 97,168 Charles A. Hayes; 13,930 Inez M. Gardner.
CD 2 56,405 Gus Savage; 26,797 Emil Jones; 14,641 Melvin J. Reynolds; 5,688 Niles Sherman; 4,042 Ernest Washington.
CD 3 76,930 Martin A. Russo; 7,793 Maurice E. Johnson.
CD 4 27,064 George E. Sangmeister; 7,537 George M. Laurence.
CD 6 12,316 William J. Andrle; 7,602 Thomas W. Glosenger.
CD 7 69,624 Cardiss Collins; 8,408 Keith A. Klopfenstein.
CD 13 22,165 Evelyn E. Craig; 7,341 Dominick J. Jeffrey.
CD 16 12,735 Steven E. Mahan; 11,575 Kenneth F. Bohnsack.
CD 18 33,395 G. Douglas Stephens; 4,553 Justin Z. West.
CD 21 35,279 Jerry F. Costello; 20,500 Pete Fields; 19,223 Mike Mansfield; 1,305 Steve Maragides.

INDIANA

GOVERNOR

Evan Bayh (D). Elected 1988 to a four-year term.

SENATORS

Daniel R. Coats (R). Appointed December 1988 to fill the vacancy created when Senator J. Danforth Quayle (R) resigned to become Vice-President. Special election to be held in 1990 for the two remaining years of the term.

Richard G. Lugar (R). Re-elected 1988 to a six-year term. Previously elected 1982, 1976.

REPRESENTATIVES

1. Peter J. Visclosky (D)
2. Philip R. Sharp (D)
3. John P. Hiler (R)
4. Daniel R. Coats (R) (see page 1)
5. Jim Jontz (D)
6. Dan Burton (R)
7. John T. Myers (R)
8. Francis McCloskey (D)
9. Lee H. Hamilton (D)
10. Andrew Jacobs, Jr. (D)

POSTWAR VOTE FOR PRESIDENT

								Percentage			
	Total	Republican		Democratic		Other		Total Vote		Major Vote	
Year	Vote	Vote	Candidate	Vote	Candidate	Vote	Plurality	Rep.	Dem.	Rep.	Dem.
1988	2,168,621	1,297,763	Bush, George	860,643	Dukakis, Michael S.	10,215	437,120 R	59.8%	39.7%	60.1%	39.9%
1984	2,233,069	1,377,230	Reagan, Ronald	841,481	Mondale, Walter F.	14,358	535,749 R	61.7%	37.7%	62.1%	37.9%
1980	2,242,033	1,255,656	Reagan, Ronald	844,197	Carter, Jimmy	142,180	411,459 R	56.0%	37.7%	59.8%	40.2%
1976	2,220,362	1,183,958	Ford, Gerald R.	1,014,714	Carter, Jimmy	21,690	169,244 R	53.3%	45.7%	53.8%	46.2%
1972	2,125,529	1,405,154	Nixon, Richard M.	708,568	McGovern, George S.	11,807	696,586 R	66.1%	33.3%	66.5%	33.5%
1968	2,123,597	1,067,885	Nixon, Richard M.	806,659	Humphrey, Hubert H.	249,053	261,226 R	50.3%	38.0%	57.0%	43.0%
1964	2,091,606	911,118	Goldwater, Barry M.	1,170,848	Johnson, Lyndon B.	9,640	259,730 D	43.6%	56.0%	43.8%	56.2%
1960	2,135,360	1,175,120	Nixon, Richard M.	952,358	Kennedy, John F.	7,882	222,762 R	55.0%	44.6%	55.2%	44.8%
1956	1,974,607	1,182,811	Eisenhower, Dwight D.	783,908	Stevenson, Adlai E.	7,888	398,903 R	59.9%	39.7%	60.1%	39.9%
1952	1,955,049	1,136,259	Eisenhower, Dwight D.	801,530	Stevenson, Adlai E.	17,260	334,729 R	58.1%	41.0%	58.6%	41.4%
1948	1,656,212	821,079	Dewey, Thomas E.	807,831	Truman, Harry S.	27,302	13,248 R	49.6%	48.8%	50.4%	49.6%

POSTWAR VOTE FOR GOVERNOR

								Percentage			
	Total	Republican		Democratic		Other	Rep.-Dem.	Total Vote		Major Vote	
Year	Vote	Vote	Candidate	Vote	Candidate	Vote	Plurality	Rep.	Dem.	Rep.	Dem.
1988	2,140,781	1,002,207	Mutz, John M.	1,138,574	Bayh, Evan		136,367 D	46.8%	53.2%	46.8%	53.2%
1984	2,197,988	1,146,497	Orr, Robert D.	1,036,922	Townsend, W. Wayne	14,569	109,575 R	52.2%	47.2%	52.5%	47.5%
1980	2,178,403	1,257,383	Orr, Robert D.	913,116	Hillenbrand, John A.	7,904	344,267 R	57.7%	41.9%	57.9%	42.1%
1976	2,175,324	1,236,555	Bowen, Otis R.	927,243	Conrad, Larry A.	11,526	309,312 R	56.8%	42.6%	57.1%	42.9%
1972	2,120,847	1,203,903	Bowen, Otis R.	900,489	Welsh, Matthew E.	16,455	303,414 R	56.8%	42.5%	57.2%	42.8%
1968	2,049,072	1,080,271	Whitcomb, Edgar D.	965,816	Rock, Robert L.	2,985	114,455 R	52.7%	47.1%	52.8%	47.2%
1964	2,072,915	901,342	Ristine, Richard O.	1,164,620	Branigin, Roger D.	6,953	263,278 D	43.5%	56.2%	43.6%	56.4%
1960	2,128,965	1,049,540	Parker, Crawford F.	1,072,717	Welsh, Matthew E.	6,708	23,177 D	49.3%	50.4%	49.5%	50.5%
1956	1,954,290	1,086,868	Handley, Harold W.	859,393	Tucker, Ralph	8,029	227,475 R	55.6%	44.0%	55.8%	44.2%
1952	1,931,869	1,075,685	Craig, George N.	841,984	Watkins, John A.	14,200	233,701 R	55.7%	43.6%	56.1%	43.9%
1948	1,652,321	745,892	Creighton, Hobart	884,995	Schricker, Henry F.	21,434	139,103 D	45.1%	53.6%	45.7%	54.3%

INDIANA

POSTWAR VOTE FOR SENATOR

Year	Total Vote	Republican Vote	Republican Candidate	Democratic Vote	Democratic Candidate	Other Vote	Rep.-Dem. Plurality	Percentage Total Vote Rep.	Percentage Total Vote Dem.	Percentage Major Vote Rep.	Percentage Major Vote Dem.
1988	2,099,303	1,430,525	Lugar, Richard G.	668,778	Wickes, Jack		761,747 R	68.1%	31.9%	68.1%	31.9%
1986	1,545,563	936,143	Quayle, J. Danforth	595,192	Long, Jill L.	14,228	340,951 R	60.6%	38.5%	61.1%	38.9%
1982	1,817,287	978,301	Lugar, Richard G.	828,400	Fithian, Floyd	10,586	149,901 R	53.8%	45.6%	54.1%	45.9%
1980	2,198,376	1,182,414	Quayle, J. Danforth	1,015,962	Bayh, Birch		166,452 R	53.8%	46.2%	53.8%	46.2%
1976	2,171,187	1,275,833	Lugar, Richard G.	878,522	Hartke, R. Vance	16,832	397,311 R	58.8%	40.5%	59.2%	40.8%
1974	1,752,978	814,117	Lugar, Richard G.	889,269	Bayh, Birch	49,592	75,152 D	46.4%	50.7%	47.8%	52.2%
1970	1,737,697	866,707	Roudebush, Richard	870,990	Hartke, R. Vance		4,283 D	49.9%	50.1%	49.9%	50.1%
1968	2,053,118	988,571	Ruckelshaus, William	1,060,456	Bayh, Birch	4,091	71,885 D	48.1%	51.7%	48.2%	51.8%
1964	2,076,963	941,519	Bontrager, D. Russell	1,128,505	Hartke, R. Vance	6,939	186,986 D	45.3%	54.3%	45.5%	54.5%
1962	1,800,038	894,547	Capehart, Homer E.	905,491	Bayh, Birch		10,944 D	49.7%	50.3%	49.7%	50.3%
1958	1,724,598	731,635	Handley, Harold W.	973,636	Hartke, R. Vance	19,327	242,001 D	42.4%	56.5%	42.9%	57.1%
1956	1,963,986	1,084,262	Capehart, Homer E.	871,781	Wickard, Claude	7,943	212,481 R	55.2%	44.4%	55.4%	44.6%
1952	1,946,118	1,020,605	Jenner, William E.	911,169	Schricker, Henry F.	14,344	109,436 R	52.4%	46.8%	52.8%	47.2%
1950	1,598,724	844,303	Capehart, Homer E.	741,025	Campbell, Alex M.	13,396	103,278 R	52.8%	46.4%	53.3%	46.7%
1946	1,347,434	739,809	Jenner, William E.	584,288	Townsend, M. Clifford	23,337	155,521 R	54.9%	43.4%	55.9%	44.1%

INDIANA

Districts Established September 1, 1981

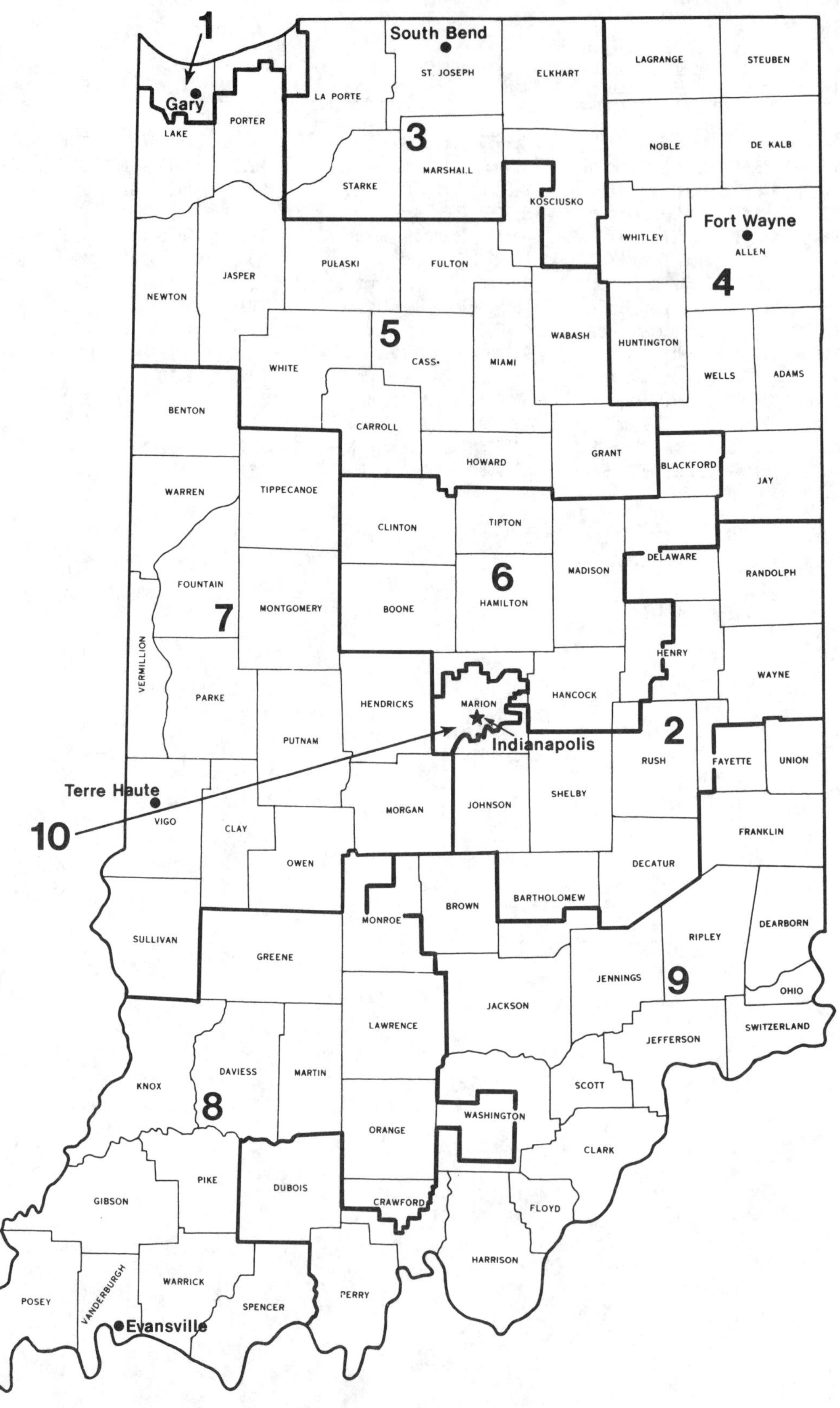

INDIANA

PRESIDENT 1988

1980 Census Population	County	Total Vote	Republican	Democratic	Other	Rep.-Dem. Plurality	Percentage Total Vote Rep.	Percentage Total Vote Dem.	Percentage Major Vote Rep.	Percentage Major Vote Dem.
29,619	ADAMS	11,997	8,137	3,811	49	4,326 R	67.8%	31.8%	68.1%	31.9%
294,335	ALLEN	114,935	74,638	39,238	1,059	35,400 R	64.9%	34.1%	65.5%	34.5%
65,088	BARTHOLOMEW	26,291	17,364	8,804	123	8,560 R	66.0%	33.5%	66.4%	33.6%
10,218	BENTON	4,069	2,698	1,349	22	1,349 R	66.3%	33.2%	66.7%	33.3%
15,570	BLACKFORD	5,608	3,336	2,253	19	1,083 R	59.5%	40.2%	59.7%	40.3%
36,446	BOONE	15,806	11,608	4,168	30	7,440 R	73.4%	26.4%	73.6%	26.4%
12,377	BROWN	5,501	3,348	2,115	38	1,233 R	60.9%	38.4%	61.3%	38.7%
19,722	CARROLL	7,964	4,981	2,952	31	2,029 R	62.5%	37.1%	62.8%	37.2%
40,936	CASS	16,851	10,970	5,784	97	5,186 R	65.1%	34.3%	65.5%	34.5%
88,838	CLARK	31,192	16,544	14,528	120	2,016 R	53.0%	46.6%	53.2%	46.8%
24,862	CLAY	9,629	5,852	3,724	53	2,128 R	60.8%	38.7%	61.1%	38.9%
31,545	CLINTON	13,021	8,570	4,412	39	4,158 R	65.8%	33.9%	66.0%	34.0%
9,820	CRAWFORD	4,596	2,532	2,036	28	496 R	55.1%	44.3%	55.4%	44.6%
27,836	DAVIESS	10,294	6,768	3,483	43	3,285 R	65.7%	33.8%	66.0%	34.0%
34,291	DEARBORN	13,309	8,195	5,066	48	3,129 R	61.6%	38.1%	61.8%	38.2%
23,841	DECATUR	9,272	6,245	2,979	48	3,266 R	67.4%	32.1%	67.7%	32.3%
33,606	DE KALB	13,716	9,018	4,657	41	4,361 R	65.7%	34.0%	65.9%	34.1%
128,587	DELAWARE	48,112	27,348	20,548	216	6,800 R	56.8%	42.7%	57.1%	42.9%
34,238	DUBOIS	16,048	9,995	5,954	99	4,041 R	62.3%	37.1%	62.7%	37.3%
137,330	ELKHART	48,200	33,793	14,236	171	19,557 R	70.1%	29.5%	70.4%	29.6%
28,272	FAYETTE	10,108	5,949	4,118	41	1,831 R	58.9%	40.7%	59.1%	40.9%
61,169	FLOYD	25,393	14,291	11,024	78	3,267 R	56.3%	43.4%	56.5%	43.5%
19,033	FOUNTAIN	8,441	5,113	3,279	49	1,834 R	60.6%	38.8%	60.9%	39.1%
19,612	FRANKLIN	7,271	4,777	2,472	22	2,305 R	65.7%	34.0%	65.9%	34.1%
19,335	FULTON	8,051	5,234	2,788	29	2,446 R	65.0%	34.6%	65.2%	34.8%
33,156	GIBSON	14,684	7,610	7,031	43	579 R	51.8%	47.9%	52.0%	48.0%
80,934	GRANT	29,371	18,441	10,799	131	7,642 R	62.8%	36.8%	63.1%	36.9%
30,416	GREENE	13,746	7,689	5,979	78	1,710 R	55.9%	43.5%	56.3%	43.7%
82,027	HAMILTON	45,615	36,654	8,853	108	27,801 R	80.4%	19.4%	80.5%	19.5%
43,939	HANCOCK	18,780	13,374	5,355	51	8,019 R	71.2%	28.5%	71.4%	28.6%
27,276	HARRISON	11,661	6,702	4,933	26	1,769 R	57.5%	42.3%	57.6%	42.4%
69,804	HENDRICKS	29,803	22,090	7,643	70	14,447 R	74.1%	25.6%	74.3%	25.7%
53,336	HENRY	19,116	11,280	7,779	57	3,501 R	59.0%	40.7%	59.2%	40.8%
86,896	HOWARD	31,620	19,971	11,518	131	8,453 R	63.2%	36.4%	63.4%	36.6%
35,596	HUNTINGTON	15,594	11,675	3,873	46	7,802 R	74.9%	24.8%	75.1%	24.9%
36,523	JACKSON	15,088	9,470	5,550	68	3,920 R	62.8%	36.8%	63.0%	37.0%
26,138	JASPER	9,292	6,009	3,237	46	2,772 R	64.7%	34.8%	65.0%	35.0%
23,239	JAY	8,620	5,363	3,212	45	2,151 R	62.2%	37.3%	62.5%	37.5%
30,419	JEFFERSON	12,268	6,949	5,221	98	1,728 R	56.6%	42.6%	57.1%	42.9%
22,854	JENNINGS	9,348	5,636	3,667	45	1,969 R	60.3%	39.2%	60.6%	39.4%
77,240	JOHNSON	33,778	24,654	9,001	123	15,653 R	73.0%	26.6%	73.3%	26.7%
41,838	KNOX	16,881	9,813	7,006	62	2,807 R	58.1%	41.5%	58.3%	41.7%
59,555	KOSCIUSKO	23,163	17,761	5,321	81	12,440 R	76.7%	23.0%	76.9%	23.1%
25,550	LAGRANGE	6,546	4,495	2,029	22	2,466 R	68.7%	31.0%	68.9%	31.1%
522,965	LAKE	185,735	79,929	105,026	780	25,097 D	43.0%	56.5%	43.2%	56.8%
108,632	LA PORTE	38,285	20,537	17,585	163	2,952 R	53.6%	45.9%	53.9%	46.1%
42,472	LAWRENCE	16,599	10,742	5,787	70	4,955 R	64.7%	34.9%	65.0%	35.0%
139,336	MADISON	57,241	32,596	24,443	202	8,153 R	56.9%	42.7%	57.1%	42.9%
765,233	MARION	315,095	184,519	128,627	1,949	55,892 R	58.6%	40.8%	58.9%	41.1%
39,155	MARSHALL	16,038	10,490	5,488	60	5,002 R	65.4%	34.2%	65.7%	34.3%
11,001	MARTIN	5,219	3,066	2,132	21	934 R	58.7%	40.9%	59.0%	41.0%
39,820	MIAMI	13,236	8,533	4,613	90	3,920 R	64.5%	34.9%	64.9%	35.1%
98,785	MONROE	37,038	20,756	15,855	427	4,901 R	56.0%	42.8%	56.7%	43.3%
35,501	MONTGOMERY	14,472	10,793	3,623	56	7,170 R	74.6%	25.0%	74.9%	25.1%
51,999	MORGAN	19,736	14,284	5,375	77	8,909 R	72.4%	27.2%	72.7%	27.3%
14,844	NEWTON	5,035	3,274	1,744	17	1,530 R	65.0%	34.6%	65.2%	34.8%
35,443	NOBLE	12,089	7,889	4,143	57	3,746 R	65.3%	34.3%	65.6%	34.4%
5,114	OHIO	2,531	1,412	1,113	6	299 R	55.8%	44.0%	55.9%	44.1%
18,677	ORANGE	8,015	5,245	2,739	31	2,506 R	65.4%	34.2%	65.7%	34.3%
15,841	OWEN	6,363	3,837	2,484	42	1,353 R	60.3%	39.0%	60.7%	39.3%

INDIANA

PRESIDENT 1988

1980 Census Population	County	Total Vote	Republican	Democratic	Other	Rep.-Dem. Plurality	Percentage Total Vote Rep.	Total Vote Dem.	Major Vote Rep.	Major Vote Dem.
16,372	PARKE	7,053	4,458	2,563	32	1,895 R	63.2%	36.3%	63.5%	36.5%
19,346	PERRY	9,580	4,720	4,804	56	84 D	49.3%	50.1%	49.6%	50.4%
13,465	PIKE	6,371	3,294	3,037	40	257 R	51.7%	47.7%	52.0%	48.0%
119,816	PORTER	49,345	29,790	19,390	165	10,400 R	60.4%	39.3%	60.6%	39.4%
26,414	POSEY	10,490	5,987	4,468	35	1,519 R	57.1%	42.6%	57.3%	42.7%
13,258	PULASKI	5,917	3,677	2,213	27	1,464 R	62.1%	37.4%	62.4%	37.6%
29,163	PUTNAM	11,021	7,119	3,850	52	3,269 R	64.6%	34.9%	64.9%	35.1%
29,997	RANDOLPH	10,908	6,856	3,990	62	2,866 R	62.9%	36.6%	63.2%	36.8%
24,398	RIPLEY	10,051	6,414	3,605	32	2,809 R	63.8%	35.9%	64.0%	36.0%
19,604	RUSH	7,583	5,112	2,451	20	2,661 R	67.4%	32.3%	67.6%	32.4%
241,617	ST. JOSEPH	97,864	49,481	48,056	327	1,425 R	50.6%	49.1%	50.7%	49.3%
20,422	SCOTT	6,854	3,455	3,378	21	77 R	50.4%	49.3%	50.6%	49.4%
39,887	SHELBY	15,621	10,176	5,382	63	4,794 R	65.1%	34.5%	65.4%	34.6%
19,361	SPENCER	9,055	4,964	4,061	30	903 R	54.8%	44.8%	55.0%	45.0%
21,997	STARKE	8,606	4,458	4,104	44	354 R	51.8%	47.7%	52.1%	47.9%
24,694	STEUBEN	10,000	6,855	3,114	31	3,741 R	68.6%	31.1%	68.8%	31.2%
21,107	SULLIVAN	8,597	4,246	4,320	31	74 D	49.4%	50.3%	49.6%	50.4%
7,153	SWITZERLAND	3,059	1,572	1,479	8	93 R	51.4%	48.3%	51.5%	48.5%
121,702	TIPPECANOE	44,364	27,897	16,256	211	11,641 R	62.9%	36.6%	63.2%	36.8%
16,819	TIPTON	7,666	5,148	2,485	33	2,663 R	67.2%	32.4%	67.4%	32.6%
6,860	UNION	2,770	1,814	946	10	868 R	65.5%	34.2%	65.7%	34.3%
167,515	VANDERBURGH	70,453	38,928	31,270	255	7,658 R	55.3%	44.4%	55.5%	44.5%
18,229	VERMILLION	7,772	3,674	4,044	54	370 D	47.3%	52.0%	47.6%	52.4%
112,385	VIGO	41,293	21,929	19,192	172	2,737 R	53.1%	46.5%	53.3%	46.7%
36,640	WABASH	13,384	9,153	4,168	63	4,985 R	68.4%	31.1%	68.7%	31.3%
8,976	WARREN	3,799	2,243	1,542	14	701 R	59.0%	40.6%	59.3%	40.7%
41,474	WARRICK	18,564	10,504	7,999	61	2,505 R	56.6%	43.1%	56.8%	43.2%
21,932	WASHINGTON	8,416	4,998	3,370	48	1,628 R	59.4%	40.0%	59.7%	40.3%
76,058	WAYNE	26,702	16,388	10,209	105	6,179 R	61.4%	38.2%	61.6%	38.4%
25,401	WELLS	11,188	7,712	3,437	39	4,275 R	68.9%	30.7%	69.2%	30.8%
23,867	WHITE	9,513	6,220	3,256	37	2,964 R	65.4%	34.2%	65.6%	34.4%
26,215	WHITLEY	11,386	7,679	3,642	65	4,037 R	67.4%	32.0%	67.8%	32.2%
5,490,224	TOTAL	2,168,621	1,297,763	860,643	10,215	437,120 R	59.8%	39.7%	60.1%	39.9%

INDIANA

GOVERNOR 1988

1980 Census Population	County	Total Vote	Republican	Democratic	Other	Rep.-Dem. Plurality	Percentage Total Vote Rep.	Total Vote Dem.	Major Vote Rep.	Major Vote Dem.
29,619	ADAMS	12,013	5,353	6,660		1,307 D	44.6%	55.4%	44.6%	55.4%
294,335	ALLEN	113,577	58,950	54,627		4,323 R	51.9%	48.1%	51.9%	48.1%
65,088	BARTHOLOMEW	26,181	13,899	12,282		1,617 R	53.1%	46.9%	53.1%	46.9%
10,218	BENTON	4,002	2,033	1,969		64 R	50.8%	49.2%	50.8%	49.2%
15,570	BLACKFORD	5,592	2,384	3,208		824 D	42.6%	57.4%	42.6%	57.4%
36,446	BOONE	15,642	9,556	6,086		3,470 R	61.1%	38.9%	61.1%	38.9%
12,377	BROWN	5,455	2,587	2,868		281 D	47.4%	52.6%	47.4%	52.6%
19,722	CARROLL	7,827	3,831	3,996		165 D	48.9%	51.1%	48.9%	51.1%
40,936	CASS	16,650	7,826	8,824		998 D	47.0%	53.0%	47.0%	53.0%
88,838	CLARK	30,098	11,331	18,767		7,436 D	37.6%	62.4%	37.6%	62.4%
24,862	CLAY	9,653	3,560	6,093		2,533 D	36.9%	63.1%	36.9%	63.1%
31,545	CLINTON	12,840	6,680	6,160		520 R	52.0%	48.0%	52.0%	48.0%
9,820	CRAWFORD	4,560	1,874	2,686		812 D	41.1%	58.9%	41.1%	58.9%
27,836	DAVIESS	10,256	5,021	5,235		214 D	49.0%	51.0%	49.0%	51.0%
34,291	DEARBORN	12,763	5,994	6,769		775 D	47.0%	53.0%	47.0%	53.0%
23,841	DECATUR	9,345	4,526	4,819		293 D	48.4%	51.6%	48.4%	51.6%
33,606	DE KALB	11,433	6,672	4,761		1,911 R	58.4%	41.6%	58.4%	41.6%
128,587	DELAWARE	48,226	21,154	27,072		5,918 D	43.9%	56.1%	43.9%	56.1%
34,238	DUBOIS	15,727	6,129	9,598		3,469 D	39.0%	61.0%	39.0%	61.0%
137,330	ELKHART	48,079	25,985	22,094		3,891 R	54.0%	46.0%	54.0%	46.0%
28,272	FAYETTE	9,876	4,491	5,385		894 D	45.5%	54.5%	45.5%	54.5%
61,169	FLOYD	24,935	10,327	14,608		4,281 D	41.4%	58.6%	41.4%	58.6%
19,033	FOUNTAIN	8,438	4,025	4,413		388 D	47.7%	52.3%	47.7%	52.3%
19,612	FRANKLIN	7,213	3,107	4,106		999 D	43.1%	56.9%	43.1%	56.9%
19,335	FULTON	8,049	3,649	4,400		751 D	45.3%	54.7%	45.3%	54.7%
33,156	GIBSON	14,710	5,101	9,609		4,508 D	34.7%	65.3%	34.7%	65.3%
80,934	GRANT	29,234	14,609	14,625		16 D	50.0%	50.0%	50.0%	50.0%
30,416	GREENE	13,587	5,256	8,331		3,075 D	38.7%	61.3%	38.7%	61.3%
82,027	HAMILTON	44,771	31,456	13,315		18,141 R	70.3%	29.7%	70.3%	29.7%
43,939	HANCOCK	18,737	10,337	8,400		1,937 R	55.2%	44.8%	55.2%	44.8%
27,276	HARRISON	11,714	4,060	7,654		3,594 D	34.7%	65.3%	34.7%	65.3%
69,804	HENDRICKS	29,553	18,455	11,098		7,357 R	62.4%	37.6%	62.4%	37.6%
53,336	HENRY	19,107	8,449	10,658		2,209 D	44.2%	55.8%	44.2%	55.8%
86,896	HOWARD	31,561	15,768	15,793		25 D	50.0%	50.0%	50.0%	50.0%
35,596	HUNTINGTON	15,469	8,225	7,244		981 R	53.2%	46.8%	53.2%	46.8%
36,523	JACKSON	14,959	6,469	8,490		2,021 D	43.2%	56.8%	43.2%	56.8%
26,138	JASPER	8,854	4,479	4,375		104 R	50.6%	49.4%	50.6%	49.4%
23,239	JAY	8,649	3,948	4,701		753 D	45.6%	54.4%	45.6%	54.4%
30,419	JEFFERSON	12,067	5,111	6,956		1,845 D	42.4%	57.6%	42.4%	57.6%
22,854	JENNINGS	9,217	3,812	5,405		1,593 D	41.4%	58.6%	41.4%	58.6%
77,240	JOHNSON	33,768	19,408	14,360		5,048 R	57.5%	42.5%	57.5%	42.5%
41,838	KNOX	16,672	6,539	10,133		3,594 D	39.2%	60.8%	39.2%	60.8%
59,555	KOSCIUSKO	23,075	13,464	9,611		3,853 R	58.3%	41.7%	58.3%	41.7%
25,550	LAGRANGE	6,554	3,139	3,415		276 D	47.9%	52.1%	47.9%	52.1%
522,965	LAKE	177,387	56,900	120,487		63,587 D	32.1%	67.9%	32.1%	67.9%
108,632	LA PORTE	38,177	14,129	24,048		9,919 D	37.0%	63.0%	37.0%	63.0%
42,472	LAWRENCE	16,321	7,635	8,686		1,051 D	46.8%	53.2%	46.8%	53.2%
139,336	MADISON	57,173	26,114	31,059		4,945 D	45.7%	54.3%	45.7%	54.3%
765,233	MARION	311,617	161,593	150,024		11,569 R	51.9%	48.1%	51.9%	48.1%
39,155	MARSHALL	15,886	8,133	7,753		380 R	51.2%	48.8%	51.2%	48.8%
11,001	MARTIN	5,142	1,980	3,162		1,182 D	38.5%	61.5%	38.5%	61.5%
39,820	MIAMI	13,301	6,696	6,605		91 R	50.3%	49.7%	50.3%	49.7%
98,785	MONROE	36,182	17,457	18,725		1,268 D	48.2%	51.8%	48.2%	51.8%
35,501	MONTGOMERY	14,458	8,528	5,930		2,598 R	59.0%	41.0%	59.0%	41.0%
51,999	MORGAN	19,592	11,439	8,153		3,286 R	58.4%	41.6%	58.4%	41.6%
14,844	NEWTON	5,037	2,457	2,580		123 D	48.8%	51.2%	48.8%	51.2%
35,443	NOBLE	11,972	5,333	6,639		1,306 D	44.5%	55.5%	44.5%	55.5%
5,114	OHIO	2,533	1,111	1,422		311 D	43.9%	56.1%	43.9%	56.1%
18,677	ORANGE	7,993	3,861	4,132		271 D	48.3%	51.7%	48.3%	51.7%
15,841	OWEN	6,297	2,784	3,513		729 D	44.2%	55.8%	44.2%	55.8%

INDIANA

GOVERNOR 1988

1980 Census Population	County	Total Vote	Republican	Democratic	Other	Rep.-Dem. Plurality	Percentage Total Vote Rep.	Total Vote Dem.	Major Vote Rep.	Major Vote Dem.
16,372	PARKE	7,080	3,097	3,983		886 D	43.7%	56.3%	43.7%	56.3%
19,346	PERRY	9,545	3,229	6,316		3,087 D	33.8%	66.2%	33.8%	66.2%
13,465	PIKE	6,414	2,284	4,130		1,846 D	35.6%	64.4%	35.6%	64.4%
119,816	PORTER	49,355	21,662	27,693		6,031 D	43.9%	56.1%	43.9%	56.1%
26,414	POSEY	10,468	4,050	6,418		2,368 D	38.7%	61.3%	38.7%	61.3%
13,258	PULASKI	5,825	2,741	3,084		343 D	47.1%	52.9%	47.1%	52.9%
29,163	PUTNAM	11,067	5,335	5,732		397 D	48.2%	51.8%	48.2%	51.8%
29,997	RANDOLPH	10,926	5,242	5,684		442 D	48.0%	52.0%	48.0%	52.0%
24,398	RIPLEY	9,753	4,609	5,144		535 D	47.3%	52.7%	47.3%	52.7%
19,604	RUSH	7,618	3,742	3,876		134 D	49.1%	50.9%	49.1%	50.9%
241,617	ST. JOSEPH	95,999	39,484	56,515		17,031 D	41.1%	58.9%	41.1%	58.9%
20,422	SCOTT	6,344	2,468	3,876		1,408 D	38.9%	61.1%	38.9%	61.1%
39,887	SHELBY	15,469	7,731	7,738		7 D	50.0%	50.0%	50.0%	50.0%
19,361	SPENCER	8,994	4,051	4,943		892 D	45.0%	55.0%	45.0%	55.0%
21,997	STARKE	8,368	3,140	5,228		2,088 D	37.5%	62.5%	37.5%	62.5%
24,694	STEUBEN	9,878	4,935	4,943		8 D	50.0%	50.0%	50.0%	50.0%
21,107	SULLIVAN	8,484	2,503	5,981		3,478 D	29.5%	70.5%	29.5%	70.5%
7,153	SWITZERLAND	2,931	1,142	1,789		647 D	39.0%	61.0%	39.0%	61.0%
121,702	TIPPECANOE	44,214	24,552	19,662		4,890 R	55.5%	44.5%	55.5%	44.5%
16,819	TIPTON	7,562	4,015	3,547		468 R	53.1%	46.9%	53.1%	46.9%
6,860	UNION	2,744	1,488	1,256		232 R	54.2%	45.8%	54.2%	45.8%
167,515	VANDERBURGH	70,226	30,889	39,337		8,448 D	44.0%	56.0%	44.0%	56.0%
18,229	VERMILLION	7,800	2,192	5,608		3,416 D	28.1%	71.9%	28.1%	71.9%
112,385	VIGO	41,747	13,783	27,964		14,181 D	33.0%	67.0%	33.0%	67.0%
36,640	WABASH	13,268	6,889	6,379		510 R	51.9%	48.1%	51.9%	48.1%
8,976	WARREN	3,804	1,743	2,061		318 D	45.8%	54.2%	45.8%	54.2%
41,474	WARRICK	18,594	7,874	10,720		2,846 D	42.3%	57.7%	42.3%	57.7%
21,932	WASHINGTON	8,138	3,573	4,565		992 D	43.9%	56.1%	43.9%	56.1%
76,058	WAYNE	26,174	12,980	13,194		214 D	49.6%	50.4%	49.6%	50.4%
25,401	WELLS	11,252	5,663	5,589		74 R	50.3%	49.7%	50.3%	49.7%
23,867	WHITE	9,564	4,585	4,979		394 D	47.9%	52.1%	47.9%	52.1%
26,215	WHITLEY	11,420	5,357	6,063		706 D	46.9%	53.1%	46.9%	53.1%
5,490,224	TOTAL	2,140,781	1,002,207	1,138,574		136,367 D	46.8%	53.2%	46.8%	53.2%

INDIANA

SENATOR 1988

1980 Census Population	County	Total Vote	Republican	Democratic	Other	Rep.-Dem. Plurality	Percentage Total Vote Rep.	Total Vote Dem.	Major Vote Rep.	Major Vote Dem.
29,619	ADAMS	11,960	9,107	2,853		6,254 R	76.1%	23.9%	76.1%	23.9%
294,335	ALLEN	110,923	81,684	29,239		52,445 R	73.6%	26.4%	73.6%	26.4%
65,088	BARTHOLOMEW	25,604	18,946	6,658		12,288 R	74.0%	26.0%	74.0%	26.0%
10,218	BENTON	3,847	2,881	966		1,915 R	74.9%	25.1%	74.9%	25.1%
15,570	BLACKFORD	5,563	3,769	1,794		1,975 R	67.8%	32.2%	67.8%	32.2%
36,446	BOONE	15,657	12,241	3,416		8,825 R	78.2%	21.8%	78.2%	21.8%
12,377	BROWN	5,356	3,737	1,619		2,118 R	69.8%	30.2%	69.8%	30.2%
19,722	CARROLL	7,877	5,436	2,441		2,995 R	69.0%	31.0%	69.0%	31.0%
40,936	CASS	16,433	11,938	4,495		7,443 R	72.6%	27.4%	72.6%	27.4%
88,838	CLARK	28,626	17,550	11,076		6,474 R	61.3%	38.7%	61.3%	38.7%
24,862	CLAY	9,561	6,553	3,008		3,545 R	68.5%	31.5%	68.5%	31.5%
31,545	CLINTON	12,587	9,045	3,542		5,503 R	71.9%	28.1%	71.9%	28.1%
9,820	CRAWFORD	4,438	2,410	2,028		382 R	54.3%	45.7%	54.3%	45.7%
27,836	DAVIESS	10,130	7,372	2,758		4,614 R	72.8%	27.2%	72.8%	27.2%
34,291	DEARBORN	12,470	8,330	4,140		4,190 R	66.8%	33.2%	66.8%	33.2%
23,841	DECATUR	8,382	6,202	2,180		4,022 R	74.0%	26.0%	74.0%	26.0%
33,606	DE KALB	13,349	9,553	3,796		5,757 R	71.6%	28.4%	71.6%	28.4%
128,587	DELAWARE	47,829	33,015	14,814		18,201 R	69.0%	31.0%	69.0%	31.0%
34,238	DUBOIS	15,406	10,716	4,690		6,026 R	69.6%	30.4%	69.6%	30.4%
137,330	ELKHART	47,868	38,452	9,416		29,036 R	80.3%	19.7%	80.3%	19.7%
28,272	FAYETTE	9,701	6,218	3,483		2,735 R	64.1%	35.9%	64.1%	35.9%
61,169	FLOYD	24,583	15,646	8,937		6,709 R	63.6%	36.4%	63.6%	36.4%
19,033	FOUNTAIN	8,445	5,870	2,575		3,295 R	69.5%	30.5%	69.5%	30.5%
19,612	FRANKLIN	6,481	4,498	1,983		2,515 R	69.4%	30.6%	69.4%	30.6%
19,335	FULTON	8,030	5,970	2,060		3,910 R	74.3%	25.7%	74.3%	25.7%
33,156	GIBSON	14,701	9,041	5,660		3,381 R	61.5%	38.5%	61.5%	38.5%
80,934	GRANT	28,320	19,878	8,442		11,436 R	70.2%	29.8%	70.2%	29.8%
30,416	GREENE	13,136	8,063	5,073		2,990 R	61.4%	38.6%	61.4%	38.6%
82,027	HAMILTON	43,815	38,240	5,575		32,665 R	87.3%	12.7%	87.3%	12.7%
43,939	HANCOCK	18,694	14,831	3,863		10,968 R	79.3%	20.7%	79.3%	20.7%
27,276	HARRISON	11,607	7,753	3,854		3,899 R	66.8%	33.2%	66.8%	33.2%
69,804	HENDRICKS	29,225	23,017	6,208		16,809 R	78.8%	21.2%	78.8%	21.2%
53,336	HENRY	18,982	12,935	6,047		6,888 R	68.1%	31.9%	68.1%	31.9%
86,896	HOWARD	29,089	20,473	8,616		11,857 R	70.4%	29.6%	70.4%	29.6%
35,596	HUNTINGTON	15,265	12,051	3,214		8,837 R	78.9%	21.1%	78.9%	21.1%
36,523	JACKSON	14,449	9,859	4,590		5,269 R	68.2%	31.8%	68.2%	31.8%
26,138	JASPER	8,676	6,189	2,487		3,702 R	71.3%	28.7%	71.3%	28.7%
23,239	JAY	8,632	6,176	2,456		3,720 R	71.5%	28.5%	71.5%	28.5%
30,419	JEFFERSON	11,664	7,433	4,231		3,202 R	63.7%	36.3%	63.7%	36.3%
22,854	JENNINGS	8,848	5,897	2,951		2,946 R	66.6%	33.4%	66.6%	33.4%
77,240	JOHNSON	31,383	25,227	6,156		19,071 R	80.4%	19.6%	80.4%	19.6%
41,838	KNOX	16,158	10,819	5,339		5,480 R	67.0%	33.0%	67.0%	33.0%
59,555	KOSCIUSKO	23,031	19,215	3,816		15,399 R	83.4%	16.6%	83.4%	16.6%
25,550	LAGRANGE	6,521	5,012	1,509		3,503 R	76.9%	23.1%	76.9%	23.1%
522,965	LAKE	171,174	82,555	88,619		6,064 D	48.2%	51.8%	48.2%	51.8%
108,632	LA PORTE	37,561	24,657	12,904		11,753 R	65.6%	34.4%	65.6%	34.4%
42,472	LAWRENCE	16,039	11,108	4,931		6,177 R	69.3%	30.7%	69.3%	30.7%
139,336	MADISON	57,026	37,331	19,695		17,636 R	65.5%	34.5%	65.5%	34.5%
765,233	MARION	307,673	202,837	104,836		98,001 R	65.9%	34.1%	65.9%	34.1%
39,155	MARSHALL	15,744	11,651	4,093		7,558 R	74.0%	26.0%	74.0%	26.0%
11,001	MARTIN	5,058	3,044	2,014		1,030 R	60.2%	39.8%	60.2%	39.8%
39,820	MIAMI	12,952	9,350	3,602		5,748 R	72.2%	27.8%	72.2%	27.8%
98,785	MONROE	35,771	25,874	9,897		15,977 R	72.3%	27.7%	72.3%	27.7%
35,501	MONTGOMERY	14,312	11,805	2,507		9,298 R	82.5%	17.5%	82.5%	17.5%
51,999	MORGAN	19,260	14,612	4,648		9,964 R	75.9%	24.1%	75.9%	24.1%
14,844	NEWTON	4,646	3,332	1,314		2,018 R	71.7%	28.3%	71.7%	28.3%
35,443	NOBLE	11,874	8,697	3,177		5,520 R	73.2%	26.8%	73.2%	26.8%
5,114	OHIO	2,310	1,413	897		516 R	61.2%	38.8%	61.2%	38.8%
18,677	ORANGE	7,407	5,206	2,201		3,005 R	70.3%	29.7%	70.3%	29.7%
15,841	OWEN	6,192	4,143	2,049		2,094 R	66.9%	33.1%	66.9%	33.1%

INDIANA

SENATOR 1988

1980 Census Population	County	Total Vote	Republican	Democratic	Other	Rep.-Dem. Plurality	Percentage Total Vote Rep.	Total Vote Dem.	Major Vote Rep.	Major Vote Dem.
16,372	PARKE	7,043	4,863	2,180		2,683 R	69.0%	31.0%	69.0%	31.0%
19,346	PERRY	9,415	4,940	4,475		465 R	52.5%	47.5%	52.5%	47.5%
13,465	PIKE	6,367	3,894	2,473		1,421 R	61.2%	38.8%	61.2%	38.8%
119,816	PORTER	49,260	34,496	14,764		19,732 R	70.0%	30.0%	70.0%	30.0%
26,414	POSEY	10,426	7,195	3,231		3,964 R	69.0%	31.0%	69.0%	31.0%
13,258	PULASKI	5,699	3,914	1,785		2,129 R	68.7%	31.3%	68.7%	31.3%
29,163	PUTNAM	11,015	8,146	2,869		5,277 R	74.0%	26.0%	74.0%	26.0%
29,997	RANDOLPH	10,880	7,901	2,979		4,922 R	72.6%	27.4%	72.6%	27.4%
24,398	RIPLEY	9,495	6,374	3,121		3,253 R	67.1%	32.9%	67.1%	32.9%
19,604	RUSH	7,087	5,327	1,760		3,567 R	75.2%	24.8%	75.2%	24.8%
241,617	ST. JOSEPH	93,834	59,314	34,520		24,794 R	63.2%	36.8%	63.2%	36.8%
20,422	SCOTT	6,537	3,406	3,131		275 R	52.1%	47.9%	52.1%	47.9%
39,887	SHELBY	15,200	11,024	4,176		6,848 R	72.5%	27.5%	72.5%	27.5%
19,361	SPENCER	8,997	5,170	3,827		1,343 R	57.5%	42.5%	57.5%	42.5%
21,997	STARKE	8,140	4,858	3,282		1,576 R	59.7%	40.3%	59.7%	40.3%
24,694	STEUBEN	9,434	7,109	2,325		4,784 R	75.4%	24.6%	75.4%	24.6%
21,107	SULLIVAN	7,974	4,684	3,290		1,394 R	58.7%	41.3%	58.7%	41.3%
7,153	SWITZERLAND	2,689	1,468	1,221		247 R	54.6%	45.4%	54.6%	45.4%
121,702	TIPPECANOE	43,402	33,059	10,343		22,716 R	76.2%	23.8%	76.2%	23.8%
16,819	TIPTON	7,359	5,445	1,914		3,531 R	74.0%	26.0%	74.0%	26.0%
6,860	UNION	2,533	1,869	664		1,205 R	73.8%	26.2%	73.8%	26.2%
167,515	VANDERBURGH	69,863	47,159	22,704		24,455 R	67.5%	32.5%	67.5%	32.5%
18,229	VERMILLION	7,729	4,433	3,296		1,137 R	57.4%	42.6%	57.4%	42.6%
112,385	VIGO	40,426	25,434	14,992		10,442 R	62.9%	37.1%	62.9%	37.1%
36,640	WABASH	12,921	9,659	3,262		6,397 R	74.8%	25.2%	74.8%	25.2%
8,976	WARREN	3,789	2,583	1,206		1,377 R	68.2%	31.8%	68.2%	31.8%
41,474	WARRICK	18,503	12,561	5,942		6,619 R	67.9%	32.1%	67.9%	32.1%
21,932	WASHINGTON	7,965	5,417	2,548		2,869 R	68.0%	32.0%	68.0%	32.0%
76,058	WAYNE	25,633	18,012	7,621		10,391 R	70.3%	29.7%	70.3%	29.7%
25,401	WELLS	11,233	8,661	2,572		6,089 R	77.1%	22.9%	77.1%	22.9%
23,867	WHITE	8,773	6,604	2,169		4,435 R	75.3%	24.7%	75.3%	24.7%
26,215	WHITLEY	11,381	8,683	2,698		5,985 R	76.3%	23.7%	76.3%	23.7%
5,490,224	TOTAL	2,099,303	1,430,525	668,778		761,747 R	68.1%	31.9%	68.1%	31.9%

INDIANA

CONGRESS

CD	Year	Total Vote	Republican Vote	Republican Candidate	Democratic Vote	Democratic Candidate	Other Vote	Rep.-Dem. Plurality	Percentage Total Vote Rep.	Percentage Total Vote Dem.	Percentage Major Vote Rep.	Percentage Major Vote Dem.
1	1988	179,327	41,076	CRUMPACKER, OWEN W.	138,251	VISCLOSKY, PETER J.		97,175 D	22.9%	77.1%	22.9%	77.1%
1	1986	118,441	30,395	COSTAS, WILLIAM	86,983	VISCLOSKY, PETER J.	1,063	56,588 D	25.7%	73.4%	25.9%	74.1%
1	1984	207,964	59,986	GRENCHIK, JOSEPH B.	147,035	VISCLOSKY, PETER J.	943	87,049 D	28.8%	70.7%	29.0%	71.0%
1	1982	155,096	66,921	KRIEGER, THOMAS	87,369	HALL, KATIE	806	20,448 D	43.1%	56.3%	43.4%	56.6%
2	1988	219,761	102,846	PENCE, MIKE	116,915	SHARP, PHILIP R.		14,069 D	46.8%	53.2%	46.8%	53.2%
2	1986	165,625	62,013	LYNCH, DONALD J.	102,456	SHARP, PHILIP R.	1,156	40,443 D	37.4%	61.9%	37.7%	62.3%
2	1984	222,663	103,061	MACKENZIE, KEN	118,965	SHARP, PHILIP R.	637	15,904 D	46.3%	53.4%	46.4%	53.6%
2	1982	190,891	83,593	VAN NATTA, RALPH	107,298	SHARP, PHILIP R.		23,705 D	43.8%	56.2%	43.8%	56.2%
3	1988	214,243	116,309	HILER, JOHN P.	97,934	WARD, THOMAS W.		18,375 R	54.3%	45.7%	54.3%	45.7%
3	1986	152,509	75,979	HILER, JOHN P.	75,932	WARD, THOMAS W.	598	47 R	49.8%	49.8%	50.0%	50.0%
3	1984	219,752	115,139	HILER, JOHN P.	103,961	BARNES, MICHAEL P.	652	11,178 R	52.4%	47.3%	52.6%	47.4%
3	1982	170,004	86,958	HILER, JOHN P.	83,046	BODINE, RICHARD C.		3,912 R	51.2%	48.8%	51.2%	48.8%
4	1988	213,758	132,843	COATS, DANIEL R.	80,915	LONG, JILL L.		51,928 R	62.1%	37.9%	62.1%	37.9%
4	1986	143,572	99,865	COATS, DANIEL R.	43,105	SCHER, GREGORY A.	602	56,760 R	69.6%	30.0%	69.9%	30.1%
4	1984	213,119	129,674	COATS, DANIEL R.	82,053	BARNARD, MICHAEL H.	1,392	47,621 R	60.8%	38.5%	61.2%	38.8%
4	1982	171,238	110,155	COATS, DANIEL R.	60,054	MILLER, ROGER M.	1,029	50,101 R	64.3%	35.1%	64.7%	35.3%
5	1988	206,403	90,163	WILLIAMS, PATRICIA L.	116,240	JONTZ, JIM		26,077 D	43.7%	56.3%	43.7%	56.3%
5	1986	157,006	75,507	BUTCHER, JAMES R.	80,772	JONTZ, JIM	727	5,265 D	48.1%	51.4%	48.3%	51.7%
5	1984	211,355	143,560	HILLIS, ELWOOD H.	66,631	MAXWELL, ALLEN	1,164	76,929 R	67.9%	31.5%	68.3%	31.7%
5	1982	172,707	105,469	HILLIS, ELWOOD H.	67,238	MAXWELL, ALLEN		38,231 R	61.1%	38.9%	61.1%	38.9%
6	1988	263,511	192,064	BURTON, DAN	71,447	HOLLAND, GEORGE T.		120,617 R	72.9%	27.1%	72.9%	27.1%
6	1986	173,165	118,363	BURTON, DAN	53,431	MCKENNA, THOMAS F.	1,371	64,932 R	68.4%	30.9%	68.9%	31.1%
6	1984	245,864	178,814	BURTON, DAN	65,772	CAMPBELL, HOWARD O.	1,278	113,042 R	72.7%	26.8%	73.1%	26.9%
6	1982	201,864	131,100	BURTON, DAN	70,764	GRABIANOWSKI, GEORGE E.		60,336 R	64.9%	35.1%	64.9%	35.1%
7	1988	211,316	130,578	MYERS, JOHN T.	80,738	WATERFILL, MARK R.		49,840 R	61.8%	38.2%	61.8%	38.2%
7	1986	157,163	104,965	MYERS, JOHN T.	49,675	SMITH, EUGENE	2,523	55,290 R	66.8%	31.6%	67.9%	32.1%
7	1984	219,694	147,787	MYERS, JOHN T.	69,097	SMITH, ARTHUR E.	2,810	78,690 R	67.3%	31.5%	68.1%	31.9%
7	1982	186,133	115,884	MYERS, JOHN T.	70,249	BONNEY, STEPHEN S.		45,635 R	62.3%	37.7%	62.3%	37.7%
8	1988	228,676	87,321	MYERS, JOHN L.	141,355	MCCLOSKEY, FRANCIS		54,034 D	38.2%	61.8%	38.2%	61.8%
8	1986	201,157	93,586	MCINTYRE, RICHARD D.	106,662	MCCLOSKEY, FRANCIS	909	13,076 D	46.5%	53.0%	46.7%	53.3%
8	1984	234,092	116,641	MCINTYRE, RICHARD D.	116,645	MCCLOSKEY, FRANCIS	806	4 D	49.8%	49.8%	50.0%	50.0%
8	1982	195,725	94,127	DECKARD, H. JOEL	100,592	MCCLOSKEY, FRANCIS	1,006	6,465 D	48.1%	51.4%	48.3%	51.7%
9	1988	208,139	60,946	COATES, FLOYD E.	147,193	HAMILTON, LEE H.		86,247 D	29.3%	70.7%	29.3%	70.7%
9	1986	167,703	46,398	KILROY, ROBERT W.	120,586	HAMILTON, LEE H.	719	74,188 D	27.7%	71.9%	27.8%	72.2%
9	1984	210,340	72,652	COATES, FLOYD E.	137,018	HAMILTON, LEE H.	670	64,366 D	34.5%	65.1%	34.7%	65.3%
9	1982	180,539	58,532	COATES, FLOYD E.	121,094	HAMILTON, LEE H.	913	62,562 D	32.4%	67.1%	32.6%	67.4%
10	1988	174,824	68,978	CUMMINGS, JAMES C.	105,846	JACOBS, ANDREW, JR.		36,868 D	39.5%	60.5%	39.5%	60.5%
10	1986	119,166	49,064	EYNON, JIM	68,817	JACOBS, ANDREW, JR.	1,285	19,753 D	41.2%	57.7%	41.6%	58.4%
10	1984	195,493	79,342	WATKINS, JOSEPH P.	115,274	JACOBS, ANDREW, JR.	877	35,932 D	40.6%	59.0%	40.8%	59.2%
10	1982	171,863	56,992	CARROLL, MICHAEL	114,674	JACOBS, ANDREW, JR.	197	57,682 D	33.2%	66.7%	33.2%	66.8%

INDIANA

1988 GENERAL ELECTION

President Other vote was New Alliance (Fulani).

Governor

Senator

Congress

1988 PRIMARIES

MAY 3 REPUBLICAN

Governor John M. Mutz, unopposed.

Senator Richard G. Lugar, unopposed.

Congress Unopposed in five CD's. Contested as follows:

CD 1 6,184 Owen W. Crumpacker; 5,617 David W. Shaw; 2,373 Lawrence J. Skubish.
CD 2 36,536 Mike Pence; 14,978 Raymond E. Schwab.
CD 5 27,506 Patricia L. Williams; 11,437 Wayne L. Burden; 7,236 Daniel C. Langmesser.
CD 8 17,810 John L. Myers; 14,379 Dick Harris; 5,415 Richard E. Mourdock; 2,159 John L. Smith; 685 Sky Wyttenbach.
CD 10 14,542 James C. Cummings; 6,446 Keith Allen Beaven; 2,591 F. Perry Ray.

MAY 3 DEMOCRATIC

Governor 493,198 Evan Bayh; 66,242 Stephen J. Daily; 34,360 Frank L. O'Bannon.

Senator Jack Wickes, unopposed.

Congress Unopposed in three CD's. Contested as follows:

CD 1 75,785 Peter J. Visclosky; 14,527 Sandra K. Smith.
CD 3 47,830 Thomas W. Ward; 6,744 R. McAlister Ellis.
CD 4 27,192 Jill L. Long; 3,814 David D. Welker; 3,608 Thomas W. Sheets; 2,478 Stephen G. Hope; 2,418 J. Carolyn Williams; 966 Ralph Spelbring.
CD 5 44,788 Jim Jontz; 3,752 S. Gopal Raju.
CD 7 16,009 Mark R. Waterfill; 12,117 George F. Fowler; 9,815 Sam Goldsmith; 7,985 John K. Purcell; 3,245 Carl Richard Greening; 1,750 Wes G. Ripperger.
CD 8 62,944 Francis McCloskey; 8,101 John W. Taylor.
CD 10 40,116 Andrew Jacobs, Jr.; 3,393 Joe L. Turner.

IOWA

GOVERNOR

Terry E. Branstad (R). Re-elected 1986 to a four-year term. Previously elected 1982.

SENATORS

Charles E. Grassley (R). Re-elected 1986 to a six-year term. Previously elected 1980.

Tom Harkin (D). Elected 1984 to a six-year term.

REPRESENTATIVES

1. James A. Leach (R)
2. Tom Tauke (R)
3. David R. Nagle (D)
4. Neal Smith (D)
5. Jim R. Lightfoot (R)
6. Fred Grandy (R)

POSTWAR VOTE FOR PRESIDENT

		Republican		Democratic				Percentage			
	Total					Other		Total Vote		Major Vote	
Year	Vote	Vote	Candidate	Vote	Candidate	Vote	Plurality	Rep.	Dem.	Rep.	Dem.
1988	1,225,614	545,355	Bush, George	670,557	Dukakis, Michael S.	9,702	125,202 D	44.5%	54.7%	44.9%	55.1%
1984	1,319,805	703,088	Reagan, Ronald	605,620	Mondale, Walter F.	11,097	97,468 R	53.3%	45.9%	53.7%	46.3%
1980	1,317,661	676,026	Reagan, Ronald	508,672	Carter, Jimmy	132,963	167,354 R	51.3%	38.6%	57.1%	42.9%
1976	1,279,306	632,863	Ford, Gerald R.	619,931	Carter, Jimmy	26,512	12,932 R	49.5%	48.5%	50.5%	49.5%
1972	1,225,944	706,207	Nixon, Richard M.	496,206	McGovern, George S.	23,531	210,001 R	57.6%	40.5%	58.7%	41.3%
1968	1,167,931	619,106	Nixon, Richard M.	476,699	Humphrey, Hubert H.	72,126	142,407 R	53.0%	40.8%	56.5%	43.5%
1964	1,184,539	449,148	Goldwater, Barry M.	733,030	Johnson, Lyndon B.	2,361	283,882 D	37.9%	61.9%	38.0%	62.0%
1960	1,273,810	722,381	Nixon, Richard M.	550,565	Kennedy, John F.	864	171,816 R	56.7%	43.2%	56.7%	43.3%
1956	1,234,564	729,187	Eisenhower, Dwight D.	501,858	Stevenson, Adlai E.	3,519	227,329 R	59.1%	40.7%	59.2%	40.8%
1952	1,268,773	808,906	Eisenhower, Dwight D.	451,513	Stevenson, Adlai E.	8,354	357,393 R	63.8%	35.6%	64.2%	35.8%
1948	1,038,264	494,018	Dewey, Thomas E.	522,380	Truman, Harry S.	21,866	28,362 D	47.6%	50.3%	48.6%	51.4%

POSTWAR VOTE FOR GOVERNOR

		Republican		Democratic				Percentage			
	Total					Other	Rep.-Dem.	Total Vote		Major Vote	
Year	Vote	Vote	Candidate	Vote	Candidate	Vote	Plurality	Rep.	Dem.	Rep.	Dem.
1986	910,623	472,712	Branstad, Terry E.	436,987	Junkins, Lowell L.	924	35,725 R	51.9%	48.0%	52.0%	48.0%
1982	1,038,229	548,313	Branstad, Terry E.	483,291	Conlin, Roxanne	6,625	65,022 R	52.8%	46.5%	53.2%	46.8%
1978	843,190	491,713	Ray, Robert	345,519	Fitzgerald, Jerome D.	5,958	146,194 R	58.3%	41.0%	58.7%	41.3%
1974 * *	920,458	534,518	Ray, Robert	377,553	Schaben, James, F.	8,387	156,965 R	58.1%	41.0%	58.6%	41.4%
1972	1,210,222	707,177	Ray, Robert	487,282	Franzenburg, Paul	15,763	219,895 R	58.4%	40.3%	59.2%	40.8%
1970	791,241	403,394	Ray, Robert	368,911	Fulton, Robert	18,936	34,483 R	51.0%	46.6%	52.2%	47.8%
1968	1,136,489	614,328	Ray, Robert	521,216	Franzenburg, Paul	945	93,112 R	54.1%	45.9%	54.1%	45.9%
1966	893,175	394,518	Murray, William G.	494,259	Hughes, Harold E.	4,398	99,741 D	44.2%	55.3%	44.4%	55.6%
1964	1,167,734	365,131	Hultman, Evan	794,610	Hughes, Harold E.	7,993	429,479 D	31.3%	68.0%	31.5%	68.5%
1962	819,854	388,955	Erbe, Norman A.	430,899	Hughes, Harold E.		41,944 D	47.4%	52.6%	47.4%	52.6%
1960	1,237,089	645,026	Erbe, Norman A.	592,063	McManus, E. J.		52,963 R	52.1%	47.9%	52.1%	47.9%
1958	859,095	394,071	Murray, William G.	465,024	Loveless, Herschel C.		70,953 D	45.9%	54.1%	45.9%	54.1%
1956	1,204,235	587,383	Hoegh, Leo A.	616,852	Loveless, Herschel C.		29,469 D	48.8%	51.2%	48.8%	51.2%
1954	848,592	435,944	Hoegh, Leo A.	410,255	Herring, Clyde E.	2,393	25,689 R	51.4%	48.3%	51.5%	48.5%
1952	1,230,045	638,388	Beardsley, William	587,671	Loveless, Herschel C.	3,986	50,717 R	51.9%	47.8%	52.1%	47.9%
1950	857,213	506,642	Beardsley, William	347,176	Gillette, Lester S.	3,395	159,466 R	59.1%	40.5%	59.3%	40.7%
1948	994,833	553,900	Beardsley, William	434,432	Switzer, Carroll O.	6,501	119,468 R	55.7%	43.7%	56.0%	44.0%
1946	631,681	362,592	Blue, Robert D.	266,190	Miles, Frank	2,899	96,402 R	57.4%	42.1%	57.7%	42.3%

The term of office of Iowa's Governor was increased from two to four years effective with the 1974 election.

IOWA

POSTWAR VOTE FOR SENATOR

Year	Total Vote	Republican Vote	Republican Candidate	Democratic Vote	Democratic Candidate	Other Vote	Rep.-Dem. Plurality	Percentage Total Vote Rep.	Percentage Total Vote Dem.	Percentage Major Vote Rep.	Percentage Major Vote Dem.
1986	891,762	588,880	Grassley, Charles E.	299,406	Roehrick, John P.	3,476	289,474 R	66.0%	33.6%	66.3%	33.7%
1984	1,292,700	564,381	Jepsen, Roger W.	716,883	Harkin, Tom	11,436	152,502 D	43.7%	55.5%	44.0%	56.0%
1980	1,277,034	683,014	Grassley, Charles E.	581,545	Culver, John C.	12,475	101,469 R	53.5%	45.5%	54.0%	46.0%
1978	824,654	421,598	Jepsen, Roger W.	395,066	Clark, Richard	7,990	26,532 R	51.1%	47.9%	51.6%	48.4%
1974	889,561	420,546	Stanley, David M.	462,947	Culver, John C.	6,068	42,401 D	47.3%	52.0%	47.6%	52.4%
1972	1,203,333	530,525	Miller, Jack	662,637	Clark, Richard	10,171	132,112 D	44.1%	55.1%	44.5%	55.5%
1968	1,144,086	568,469	Stanley, David M.	574,884	Hughes, Harold E.	733	6,415 D	49.7%	50.2%	49.7%	50.3%
1966	857,496	522,339	Miller, Jack	324,114	Smith, E. B.	11,043	198,225 R	60.9%	37.8%	61.7%	38.3%
1962	807,972	431,364	Hickenlooper, Bourke B.	376,602	Smith, E. B.	6	54,762 R	53.4%	46.6%	53.4%	46.6%
1960	1,237,582	642,463	Miller, Jack	595,119	Loveless, Herschel C.		47,344 R	51.9%	48.1%	51.9%	48.1%
1956	1,178,655	635,499	Hickenlooper, Bourke B.	543,156	Evans, R. M.		92,343 R	53.9%	46.1%	53.9%	46.1%
1954	847,355	442,409	Martin, Thomas E.	402,712	Gillette, Guy	2,234	39,697 R	52.2%	47.5%	52.3%	47.7%
1950	858,523	470,613	Hickenlooper, Bourke B.	383,766	Loveland, A. J.	4,144	86,847 R	54.8%	44.7%	55.1%	44.9%
1948	1,000,412	415,778	Wilson, George A.	578,226	Gillette, Guy	6,408	162,448 D	41.6%	57.8%	41.8%	58.2%

IOWA

Districts Established August 20, 1981

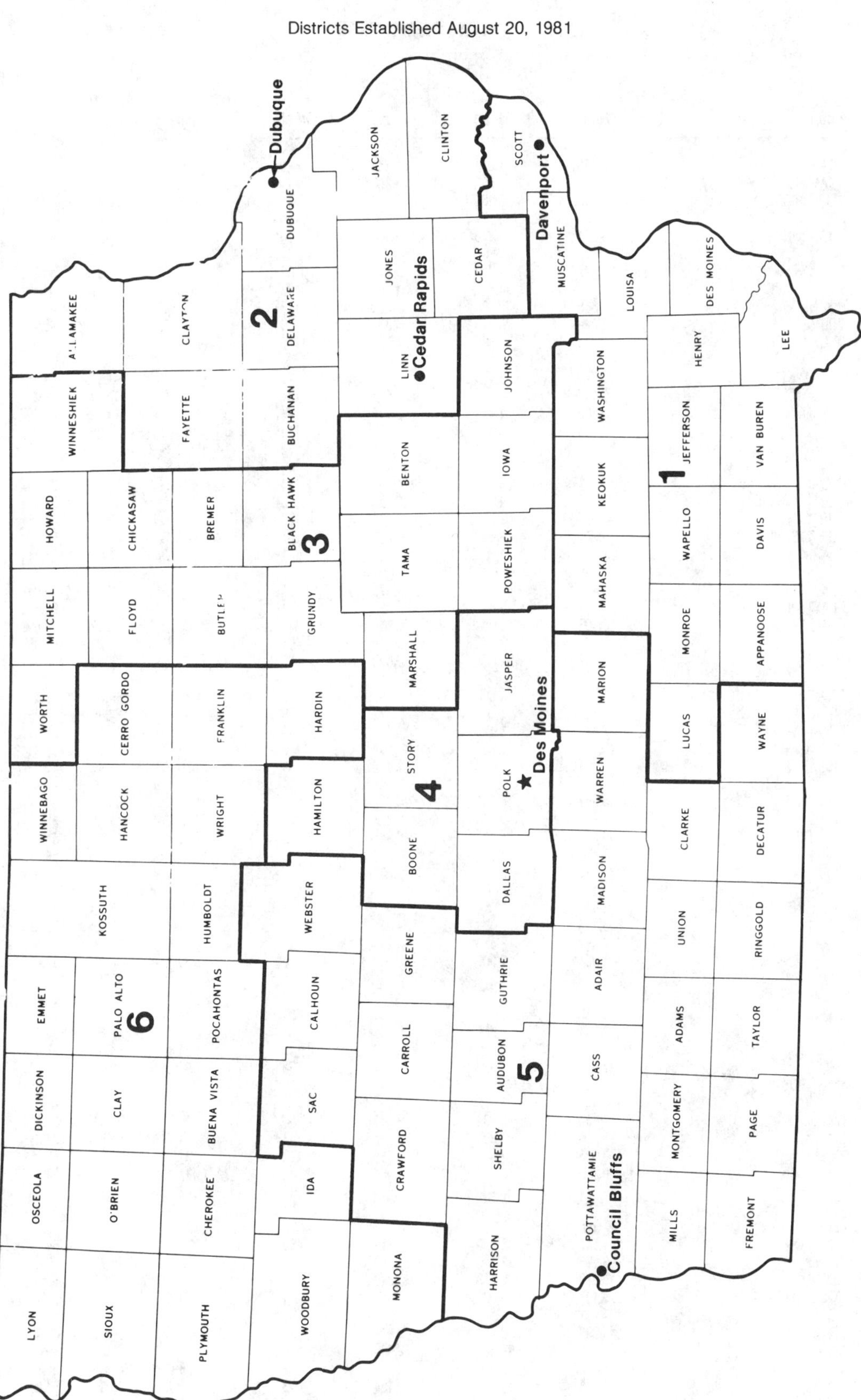

IOWA

PRESIDENT 1988

1980 Census Population	County	Total Vote	Republican	Democratic	Other	Rep.-Dem. Plurality	Percentage Total Vote Rep.	Total Vote Dem.	Major Vote Rep.	Major Vote Dem.
9,509	ADAIR	4,123	1,833	2,261	29	428 D	44.5%	54.8%	44.8%	55.2%
5,731	ADAMS	2,380	1,080	1,283	17	203 D	45.4%	53.9%	45.7%	54.3%
15,108	ALLAMAKEE	5,995	3,186	2,768	41	418 R	53.1%	46.2%	53.5%	46.5%
15,511	APPANOOSE	6,088	2,779	3,209	100	430 D	45.6%	52.7%	46.4%	53.6%
8,559	AUDUBON	3,371	1,478	1,863	30	385 D	43.8%	55.3%	44.2%	55.8%
23,649	BENTON	9,977	4,011	5,873	93	1,862 D	40.2%	58.9%	40.6%	59.4%
137,961	BLACK HAWK	56,171	24,112	31,657	402	7,545 D	42.9%	56.4%	43.2%	56.8%
26,184	BOONE	11,686	4,381	7,232	73	2,851 D	37.5%	61.9%	37.7%	62.3%
24,820	BREMER	10,099	5,079	4,961	59	118 R	50.3%	49.1%	50.6%	49.4%
22,900	BUCHANAN	8,321	3,495	4,778	48	1,283 D	42.0%	57.4%	42.2%	57.8%
20,774	BUENA VISTA	8,825	4,170	4,580	75	410 D	47.3%	51.9%	47.7%	52.3%
17,668	BUTLER	6,146	3,523	2,593	30	930 R	57.3%	42.2%	57.6%	42.4%
13,542	CALHOUN	5,505	2,474	2,990	41	516 D	44.9%	54.3%	45.3%	54.7%
22,951	CARROLL	9,273	3,701	5,437	135	1,736 D	39.9%	58.6%	40.5%	59.5%
16,932	CASS	6,968	3,962	2,934	72	1,028 R	56.9%	42.1%	57.5%	42.5%
18,635	CEDAR	7,479	3,373	4,032	74	659 D	45.1%	53.9%	45.6%	54.4%
48,458	CERRO GORDO	22,365	9,358	12,857	150	3,499 D	41.8%	57.5%	42.1%	57.9%
16,238	CHEROKEE	6,855	3,218	3,574	63	356 D	46.9%	52.1%	47.4%	52.6%
15,437	CHICKASAW	6,136	2,549	3,530	57	981 D	41.5%	57.5%	41.9%	58.1%
8,612	CLARKE	3,934	1,631	2,262	41	631 D	41.5%	57.5%	41.9%	58.1%
19,576	CLAY	7,870	3,641	4,173	56	532 D	46.3%	53.0%	46.6%	53.4%
21,098	CLAYTON	8,242	3,839	4,320	83	481 D	46.6%	52.4%	47.1%	52.9%
57,122	CLINTON	23,002	10,243	12,549	210	2,306 D	44.5%	54.6%	44.9%	55.1%
18,935	CRAWFORD	7,311	3,375	3,868	68	493 D	46.2%	52.9%	46.6%	53.4%
29,513	DALLAS	12,419	4,858	7,501	60	2,643 D	39.1%	60.4%	39.3%	60.7%
9,104	DAVIS	3,849	1,563	2,246	40	683 D	40.6%	58.4%	41.0%	59.0%
9,794	DECATUR	3,627	1,406	2,192	29	786 D	38.8%	60.4%	39.1%	60.9%
18,933	DELAWARE	7,432	3,425	3,947	60	522 D	46.1%	53.1%	46.5%	53.5%
46,203	DES MOINES	19,374	7,652	11,593	129	3,941 D	39.5%	59.8%	39.8%	60.2%
15,629	DICKINSON	7,101	3,678	3,342	81	336 R	51.8%	47.1%	52.4%	47.6%
93,745	DUBUQUE	38,547	14,530	23,797	220	9,267 D	37.7%	61.7%	37.9%	62.1%
13,336	EMMET	4,977	2,173	2,778	26	605 D	43.7%	55.8%	43.9%	56.1%
25,488	FAYETTE	10,287	4,921	5,304	62	383 D	47.8%	51.6%	48.1%	51.9%
19,597	FLOYD	7,733	3,266	4,377	90	1,111 D	42.2%	56.6%	42.7%	57.3%
13,036	FRANKLIN	4,951	2,320	2,594	37	274 D	46.9%	52.4%	47.2%	52.8%
9,401	FREMONT	3,527	1,946	1,547	34	399 R	55.2%	43.9%	55.7%	44.3%
12,119	GREENE	5,164	2,091	3,011	62	920 D	40.5%	58.3%	41.0%	59.0%
14,366	GRUNDY	5,682	3,433	2,211	38	1,222 R	60.4%	38.9%	60.8%	39.2%
11,983	GUTHRIE	4,983	2,005	2,910	68	905 D	40.2%	58.4%	40.8%	59.2%
17,862	HAMILTON	7,494	3,277	4,156	61	879 D	43.7%	55.5%	44.1%	55.9%
13,833	HANCOCK	5,593	2,731	2,831	31	100 D	48.8%	50.6%	49.1%	50.9%
21,776	HARDIN	9,001	3,856	5,088	57	1,232 D	42.8%	56.5%	43.1%	56.9%
16,348	HARRISON	6,027	3,108	2,883	36	225 R	51.6%	47.8%	51.9%	48.1%
18,890	HENRY	7,758	3,951	3,754	53	197 R	50.9%	48.4%	51.3%	48.7%
11,114	HOWARD	4,325	1,970	2,330	25	360 D	45.5%	53.9%	45.8%	54.2%
12,246	HUMBOLDT	5,357	2,594	2,713	50	119 D	48.4%	50.6%	48.9%	51.1%
8,908	IDA	3,779	1,951	1,787	41	164 R	51.6%	47.3%	52.2%	47.8%
15,429	IOWA	6,685	3,247	3,338	100	91 D	48.6%	49.9%	49.3%	50.7%
22,503	JACKSON	8,233	3,237	4,864	132	1,627 D	39.3%	59.1%	40.0%	60.0%
36,425	JASPER	15,733	6,703	8,940	90	2,237 D	42.6%	56.8%	42.8%	57.2%
16,316	JEFFERSON	7,296	3,614	3,594	88	20 R	49.5%	49.3%	50.1%	49.9%
81,717	JOHNSON	44,647	15,453	28,759	435	13,306 D	34.6%	64.4%	35.0%	65.0%
20,401	JONES	8,185	3,496	4,641	48	1,145 D	42.7%	56.7%	43.0%	57.0%
12,921	KEOKUK	5,230	2,278	2,899	53	621 D	43.6%	55.4%	44.0%	56.0%
21,891	KOSSUTH	9,107	3,938	5,088	81	1,150 D	43.2%	55.9%	43.6%	56.4%
43,106	LEE	17,290	6,228	10,911	151	4,683 D	36.0%	63.1%	36.3%	63.7%
169,775	LINN	76,718	33,129	42,993	596	9,864 D	43.2%	56.0%	43.5%	56.5%
12,055	LOUISA	4,380	2,060	2,268	52	208 D	47.0%	51.8%	47.6%	52.4%
10,313	LUCAS	4,243	1,776	2,454	13	678 D	41.9%	57.8%	42.0%	58.0%
12,896	LYON	5,264	3,517	1,706	41	1,811 R	66.8%	32.4%	67.3%	32.7%

IOWA

PRESIDENT 1988

1980 Census Population	County	Total Vote	Republican	Democratic	Other	Rep.-Dem. Plurality	Percentage Total Vote Rep.	Percentage Total Vote Dem.	Percentage Major Vote Rep.	Percentage Major Vote Dem.
12,597	MADISON	5,862	2,410	3,421	31	1,011 D	41.1%	58.4%	41.3%	58.7%
22,867	MAHASKA	9,320	4,798	4,451	71	347 R	51.5%	47.8%	51.9%	48.1%
29,669	MARION	12,954	5,914	6,922	118	1,008 D	45.7%	53.4%	46.1%	53.9%
41,652	MARSHALL	17,549	7,657	9,760	132	2,103 D	43.6%	55.6%	44.0%	56.0%
13,406	MILLS	5,369	3,212	2,092	65	1,120 R	59.8%	39.0%	60.6%	39.4%
12,329	MITCHELL	5,251	2,338	2,870	43	532 D	44.5%	54.7%	44.9%	55.1%
11,692	MONONA	4,491	2,068	2,408	15	340 D	46.0%	53.6%	46.2%	53.8%
9,209	MONROE	3,667	1,313	2,338	16	1,025 D	35.8%	63.8%	36.0%	64.0%
13,413	MONTGOMERY	5,100	3,166	1,898	36	1,268 R	62.1%	37.2%	62.5%	37.5%
40,436	MUSCATINE	14,102	6,904	7,059	139	155 D	49.0%	50.1%	49.4%	50.6%
16,972	O'BRIEN	7,072	4,241	2,768	63	1,473 R	60.0%	39.1%	60.5%	39.5%
8,371	OSCEOLA	3,264	1,951	1,277	36	674 R	59.8%	39.1%	60.4%	39.6%
19,063	PAGE	6,803	4,583	2,185	35	2,398 R	67.4%	32.1%	67.7%	32.3%
12,721	PALO ALTO	5,463	2,041	3,377	45	1,336 D	37.4%	61.8%	37.7%	62.3%
24,743	PLYMOUTH	9,607	5,316	4,220	71	1,096 R	55.3%	43.9%	55.7%	44.3%
11,369	POCAHONTAS	4,652	1,871	2,722	59	851 D	40.2%	58.5%	40.7%	59.3%
303,170	POLK	143,144	57,854	84,476	814	26,622 D	40.4%	59.0%	40.6%	59.4%
86,561	POTTAWATTAMIE	32,405	17,193	14,958	254	2,235 R	53.1%	46.2%	53.5%	46.5%
19,306	POWESHIEK	8,625	3,683	4,876	66	1,193 D	42.7%	56.5%	43.0%	57.0%
6,112	RINGGOLD	2,731	1,110	1,609	12	499 D	40.6%	58.9%	40.8%	59.2%
14,118	SAC	5,077	2,411	2,613	53	202 D	47.5%	51.5%	48.0%	52.0%
160,022	SCOTT	66,035	31,025	34,415	595	3,390 D	47.0%	52.1%	47.4%	52.6%
15,043	SHELBY	5,860	3,019	2,806	35	213 R	51.5%	47.9%	51.8%	48.2%
30,813	SIOUX	13,288	10,270	2,923	95	7,347 R	77.3%	22.0%	77.8%	22.2%
72,326	STORY	33,105	13,782	19,051	272	5,269 D	41.6%	57.5%	42.0%	58.0%
19,533	TAMA	8,012	3,362	4,584	66	1,222 D	42.0%	57.2%	42.3%	57.7%
8,353	TAYLOR	3,332	1,647	1,671	14	24 D	49.4%	50.2%	49.6%	50.4%
13,858	UNION	6,041	2,751	3,236	54	485 D	45.5%	53.6%	45.9%	54.1%
8,626	VAN BUREN	3,334	1,692	1,612	30	80 R	50.7%	48.4%	51.2%	48.8%
40,241	WAPELLO	15,673	5,350	10,177	146	4,827 D	34.1%	64.9%	34.5%	65.5%
34,878	WARREN	16,131	6,424	9,627	80	3,203 D	39.8%	59.7%	40.0%	60.0%
20,141	WASHINGTON	7,616	3,741	3,776	99	35 D	49.1%	49.6%	49.8%	50.2%
8,199	WAYNE	3,477	1,467	1,988	22	521 D	42.2%	57.2%	42.5%	57.5%
45,953	WEBSTER	17,393	6,926	10,267	200	3,341 D	39.8%	59.0%	40.3%	59.7%
13,010	WINNEBAGO	5,703	2,863	2,804	36	59 R	50.2%	49.2%	50.5%	49.5%
21,876	WINNESHIEK	8,725	4,194	4,443	88	249 D	48.1%	50.9%	48.6%	51.4%
100,884	WOODBURY	39,225	18,790	20,153	282	1,363 D	47.9%	51.4%	48.3%	51.7%
9,075	WORTH	3,982	1,488	2,440	54	952 D	37.4%	61.3%	37.9%	62.1%
16,319	WRIGHT	6,054	2,658	3,353	43	695 D	43.9%	55.4%	44.2%	55.8%
2,913,808	TOTAL	1,225,614	545,355	670,557	9,702	125,202 D	44.5%	54.7%	44.9%	55.1%

IOWA

CONGRESS

CD	Year	Total Vote	Republican Vote	Republican Candidate	Democratic Vote	Democratic Candidate	Other Vote	Rep.-Dem. Plurality	Percentage Total Vote Rep.	Percentage Total Vote Dem.	Percentage Major Vote Rep.	Percentage Major Vote Dem.
1	1988	185,716	112,746	LEACH, JAMES A.	71,280	GLUBA, WILLIAM E.	1,690	41,466 R	60.7%	38.4%	61.3%	38.7%
1	1986	130,825	86,834	LEACH, JAMES A.	43,985	WHITAKER, JOHN R.	6	42,849 R	66.4%	33.6%	66.4%	33.6%
1	1984	196,489	131,182	LEACH, JAMES A.	65,293	READY, KEVIN	14	65,889 R	66.8%	33.2%	66.8%	33.2%
1	1982	151,332	89,585	LEACH, JAMES A.	61,734	GLUBA, WILLIAM E.	13	27,851 R	59.2%	40.8%	59.2%	40.8%
2	1988	200,041	113,543	TAUKE, TOM	86,438	TABOR, ERIC	60	27,105 R	56.8%	43.2%	56.8%	43.2%
2	1986	144,630	88,708	TAUKE, TOM	55,903	TABOR, ERIC	19	32,805 R	61.3%	38.7%	61.3%	38.7%
2	1984	214,255	136,893	TAUKE, TOM	77,335	WELSH, JOE	27	59,558 R	63.9%	36.1%	63.9%	36.1%
2	1982	169,037	99,478	TAUKE, TOM	69,539	APPEL, BRENT	20	29,939 R	58.8%	41.1%	58.9%	41.1%
3	1988	203,932	74,682	REDFERN, DONALD B.	129,204	NAGLE, DAVID R.	46	54,522 D	36.6%	63.4%	36.6%	63.4%
3	1986	152,920	69,386	MCINTEE, JOHN	83,504	NAGLE, DAVID R.	30	14,118 D	45.4%	54.6%	45.4%	54.6%
3	1984	220,375	133,737	EVANS, COOPER	86,574	JOHNSTON, JOE	64	47,163 R	60.7%	39.3%	60.7%	39.3%
3	1982	187,675	104,072	EVANS, COOPER	83,581	CUTLER, LYNN G.	22	20,491 R	55.5%	44.5%	55.5%	44.5%
4	1988	219,223	62,056	LUNDE, PAUL	157,065	SMITH, NEAL	102	95,009 D	28.3%	71.6%	28.3%	71.7%
4	1986	156,952	49,641	LOCKARD, ROBERT R.	107,271	SMITH, NEAL	40	57,630 D	31.6%	68.3%	31.6%	68.4%
4	1984	225,674	88,717	LOCKARD, ROBERT R.	136,922	SMITH, NEAL	35	48,205 D	39.3%	60.7%	39.3%	60.7%
4	1982	179,972	60,534	READINGER, DAVE	118,849	SMITH, NEAL	589	58,315 D	33.6%	66.0%	33.7%	66.3%
5	1988	184,368	117,761	LIGHTFOOT, JIM R.	66,599	FREUND, GENE	8	51,162 R	63.9%	36.1%	63.9%	36.1%
5	1986	143,589	85,025	LIGHTFOOT, JIM R.	58,552	HUGHES, SCOTT	12	26,473 R	59.2%	40.8%	59.2%	40.8%
5	1984	206,072	104,632	LIGHTFOOT, JIM R.	101,435	FITZGERALD, JERRY	5	3,197 R	50.8%	49.2%	50.8%	49.2%
5	1982	158,563	65,200	DANKER, ARLYN E.	93,333	HARKIN, TOM	30	28,133 D	41.1%	58.9%	41.1%	58.9%
6	1988	195,478	125,859	GRANDY, FRED	69,614	O'BRIEN, DAVE	5	56,245 R	64.4%	35.6%	64.4%	35.6%
6	1986	160,679	81,861	GRANDY, FRED	78,807	HODGSON, CLAYTON	11	3,054 R	50.9%	49.0%	51.0%	49.0%
6	1984	205,894	78,182	RENSINK, DARREL	127,706	BEDELL, BERKLEY	6	49,524 D	38.0%	62.0%	38.0%	62.0%
6	1982	158,184	56,487	BREMER, AL	101,690	BEDELL, BERKLEY	7	45,203 D	35.7%	64.3%	35.7%	64.3%

IOWA

1988 GENERAL ELECTION

President Other vote was 3,526 LaRouche (by petition); 2,494 Libertarian (Paul); 755 Patriotic (Duke); 540 New Alliance (Fulani); 334 Socialist (Kenoyer); 235 Workers League (Winn); 205 Socialist Workers (Warren); 1,613 scattered write-in.

Congress Other vote was 1,670 Stav-River (no party) and 20 scattered in CD 1; scattered in all other CD's.

1988 PRIMARIES

JUNE 7 REPUBLICAN

Congress Unopposed in five CD's. Contested as follows:

CD 3 11,489 Donald B. Redfern; 7,310 Marvin Simpson; 6 scattered write-in.

JUNE 7 DEMOCRATIC

Congress Contested as follows:

CD 1 12,996 William E. Gluba; 5,661 Ronald R. Kirk; 13 scattered write-in.
CD 2 16,527 Eric Tabor; 2,069 Juan Cortez; 24 scattered write-in.
CD 3 15,803 David R. Nagle; 1,396 James R. Cox; 13 scattered write-in.
CD 4 12,101 Neal Smith; 1,293 Maurice W. Stoutenberg; 12 scattered write-in.
CD 5 8,343 Gene Freund; 5,883 Jon E. Dvorak; 9 scattered write-in.
CD 6 10,558 Dave O'Brien; 2,180 Michael D. Earll; 1,630 Garry DeYoung; 979 Mathilda Timmermans.

KANSAS

GOVERNOR

Mike Hayden (R). Elected 1986 to a four-year term.

SENATORS

Robert Dole (R). Re-elected 1986 to a six-year term. Previously elected 1980, 1974, 1968.

Nancy Landon Kassebaum (R). Re-elected 1984 to a six-year term. Previously elected 1978.

REPRESENTATIVES

1. Pat Roberts (R)
2. Jim Slattery (D)
3. Jan Meyers (R)
4. Dan Glickman (D)
5. Robert Whittaker (R)

POSTWAR VOTE FOR PRESIDENT

		Republican		Democratic				Percentage			
	Total					Other		Total Vote		Major Vote	
Year	Vote	Vote	Candidate	Vote	Candidate	Vote	Plurality	Rep.	Dem.	Rep.	Dem.
1988	993,044	554,049	Bush, George	422,636	Dukakis, Michael S.	16,359	131,413 R	55.8%	42.6%	56.7%	43.3%
1984	1,021,991	677,296	Reagan, Ronald	333,149	Mondale, Walter F.	11,546	344,147 R	66.3%	32.6%	67.0%	33.0%
1980	979,795	566,812	Reagan, Ronald	326,150	Carter, Jimmy	86,833	240,662 R	57.9%	33.3%	63.5%	36.5%
1976	957,845	502,752	Ford, Gerald R.	430,421	Carter, Jimmy	24,672	72,331 R	52.5%	44.9%	53.9%	46.1%
1972	916,095	619,812	Nixon, Richard M.	270,287	McGovern, George S.	25,996	349,525 R	67.7%	29.5%	69.6%	30.4%
1968	872,783	478,674	Nixon, Richard M.	302,996	Humphrey, Hubert H.	91,113	175,678 R	54.8%	34.7%	61.2%	38.8%
1964	857,901	386,579	Goldwater, Barry M.	464,028	Johnson, Lyndon B.	7,294	77,449 D	45.1%	54.1%	45.4%	54.6%
1960	928,825	561,474	Nixon, Richard M.	363,213	Kennedy, John F.	4,138	198,261 R	60.4%	39.1%	60.7%	39.3%
1956	866,243	566,878	Eisenhower, Dwight D.	296,317	Stevenson, Adlai E.	3,048	270,561 R	65.4%	34.2%	65.7%	34.3%
1952	896,166	616,302	Eisenhower, Dwight D.	273,296	Stevenson, Adlai E.	6,568	343,006 R	68.8%	30.5%	69.3%	30.7%
1948	788,819	423,039	Dewey, Thomas E.	351,902	Truman, Harry S.	13,878	71,137 R	53.6%	44.6%	54.6%	45.4%

POSTWAR VOTE FOR GOVERNOR

		Republican		Democratic				Percentage			
	Total					Other	Rep.-Dem.	Total Vote		Major Vote	
Year	Vote	Vote	Candidate	Vote	Candidate	Vote	Plurality	Rep.	Dem.	Rep.	Dem.
1986	840,605	436,267	Hayden, Mike	404,338	Docking, Thomas R.		31,929 R	51.9%	48.1%	51.9%	48.1%
1982	763,263	339,356	Hardage, Sam	405,772	Carlin, John	18,135	66,416 D	44.5%	53.2%	45.5%	54.5%
1978	736,246	348,015	Bennett, Robert F.	363,835	Carlin, John	24,396	15,820 D	47.3%	49.4%	48.9%	51.1%
1974 **	783,875	387,792	Bennett, Robert F.	384,115	Miller, Vern	11,968	3,677 R	49.5%	49.0%	50.2%	49.8%
1972	921,552	341,440	Kay, Morris	571,256	Docking, Robert	8,856	229,816 D	37.1%	62.0%	37.4%	62.6%
1970	745,196	333,227	Frizzell, Kent	404,611	Docking, Robert	7,358	71,384 D	44.7%	54.3%	45.2%	54.8%
1968	862,473	410,673	Harman, Rick	447,269	Docking, Robert	4,531	36,596 D	47.6%	51.9%	47.9%	52.1%
1966	692,955	304,325	Avery, William H.	380,030	Docking, Robert	8,600	75,705 D	43.9%	54.8%	44.5%	55.5%
1964	850,414	432,667	Avery, William H.	400,264	Wiles, Harry G.	17,483	32,403 R	50.9%	47.1%	51.9%	48.1%
1962	638,798	341,257	Anderson, John	291,285	Saffels, Dale E.	6,256	49,972 R	53.4%	45.6%	54.0%	46.0%
1960	922,522	511,534	Anderson, John	402,261	Docking, George	8,727	109,273 R	55.4%	43.6%	56.0%	44.0%
1958	735,939	313,036	Reed, Clyde M.	415,506	Docking, George	7,397	102,470 D	42.5%	56.5%	43.0%	57.0%
1956	864,935	364,340	Shaw, Warren W.	479,701	Docking, George	20,894	115,361 D	42.1%	55.5%	43.2%	56.8%
1954	622,633	329,868	Hall, Fred	286,218	Docking, George	6,547	43,650 R	53.0%	46.0%	53.5%	46.5%
1952	872,139	491,338	Arn, Edward F.	363,482	Rooney, Charles	17,319	127,856 R	56.3%	41.7%	57.5%	42.5%
1950	619,310	333,001	Arn, Edward F.	275,494	Anderson, Kenneth	10,815	57,507 R	53.8%	44.5%	54.7%	45.3%
1948	760,407	433,396	Carlson, Frank	307,485	Carpenter, Randolph	19,526	125,911 R	57.0%	40.4%	58.5%	41.5%
1946	577,694	309,064	Carlson, Frank	254,283	Woodring, Harry H.	14,347	54,781 R	53.5%	44.0%	54.9%	45.1%

The term of office of Kansas' Governor was increased from two to four years effective with the 1974 election.

KANSAS

POSTWAR VOTE FOR SENATOR

		Republican		Democratic				Percentage			
	Total					Other	Rep.-Dem.	Total Vote		Major Vote	
Year	Vote	Vote	Candidate	Vote	Candidate	Vote	Plurality	Rep.	Dem.	Rep.	Dem.
1986	823,566	576,902	Dole, Robert	246,664	MacDonald, Guy		330,238 R	70.0%	30.0%	70.0%	30.0%
1984	996,729	757,402	Kassebaum, Nancy Landon	211,664	Maher, James	27,663	545,738 R	76.0%	21.2%	78.2%	21.8%
1980	938,957	598,686	Dole, Robert	340,271	Simpson, John		258,415 R	63.8%	36.2%	63.8%	36.2%
1978	748,839	403,354	Kassebaum, Nancy Landon	317,602	Roy, William R.	27,883	85,752 R	53.9%	42.4%	55.9%	44.1%
1974	794,437	403,983	Dole, Robert	390,451	Roy, William R.	3	13,532 R	50.9%	49.1%	50.9%	49.1%
1972	871,722	622,591	Pearson, James B.	200,764	Tetzlaff, Arch O.	48,367	421,827 R	71.4%	23.0%	75.6%	24.4%
1968	817,096	490,911	Dole, Robert	315,911	Robinson, William I.	10,274	175,000 R	60.1%	38.7%	60.8%	39.2%
1966	671,345	350,077	Pearson, James B.	303,223	Breeding, J. Floyd	18,045	46,854 R	52.1%	45.2%	53.6%	46.4%
1962	622,232	388,500	Carlson, Frank	223,630	Smith, K. L.	10,102	164,870 R	62.4%	35.9%	63.5%	36.5%
1962 S	613,250	344,689	Pearson, James B.	260,756	Aylward, Paul L.	7,805	83,933 R	56.2%	42.5%	56.9%	43.1%
1960	888,592	485,499	Schoeppel, Andrew F.	388,895	Theis, Frank	14,198	96,604 R	54.6%	43.8%	55.5%	44.5%
1956	825,280	477,822	Carlson, Frank	333,939	Hart, George	13,519	143,883 R	57.9%	40.5%	58.9%	41.1%
1954	618,063	348,144	Schoeppel, Andrew F.	258,575	McGill, George	11,344	89,569 R	56.3%	41.8%	57.4%	42.6%
1950	619,104	335,880	Carlson, Frank	271,365	Aiken, Paul	11,859	64,515 R	54.3%	43.8%	55.3%	44.7%
1948	716,342	393,412	Schoeppel, Andrew F.	305,987	McGill, George	16,943	87,425 R	54.9%	42.7%	56.3%	43.7%

One of the 1962 elections was for a short term to fill a vacancy.

KANSAS

Districts Established June 2, 1982

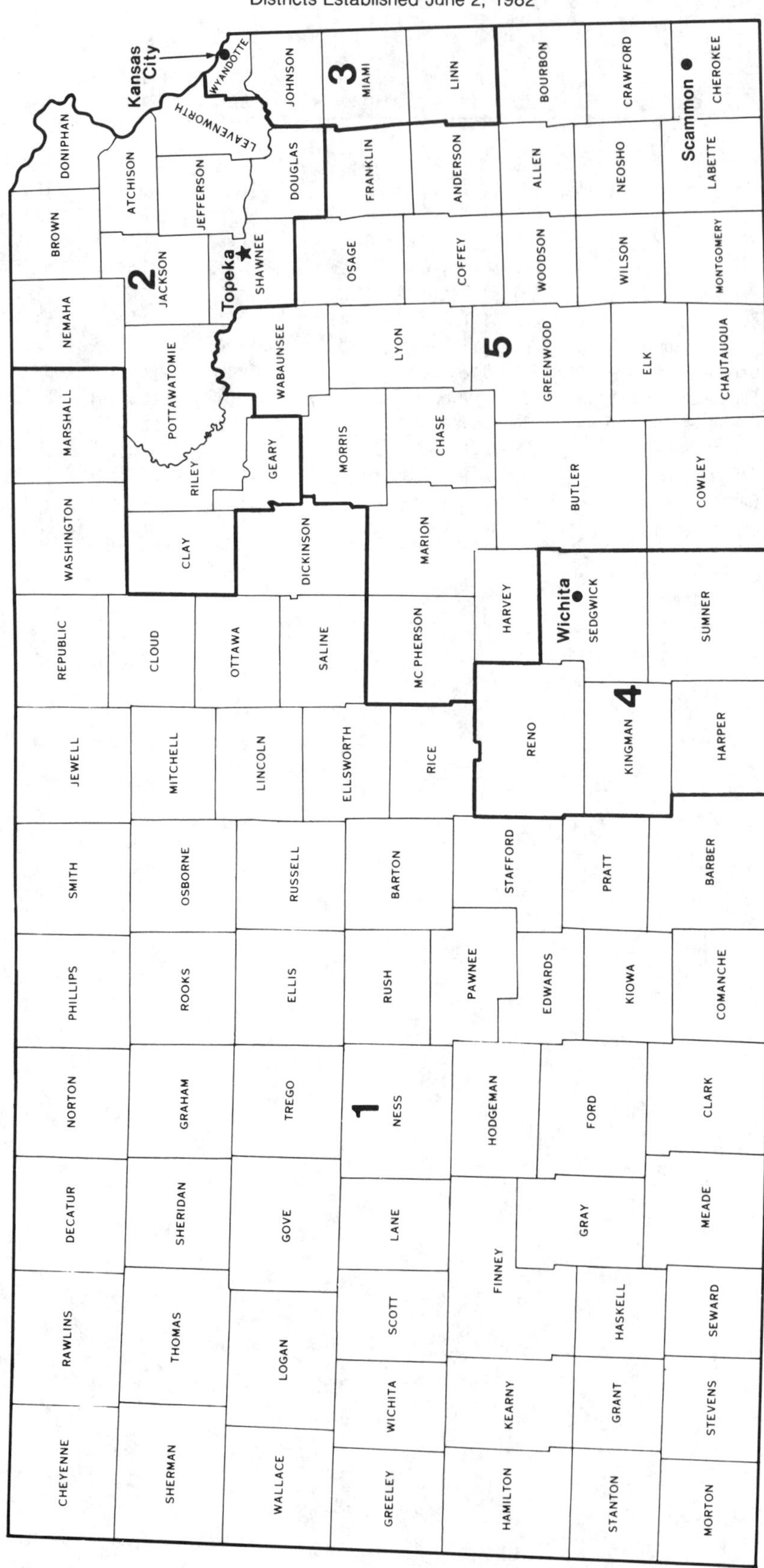

KANSAS

PRESIDENT 1988

1980 Census Population	County	Total Vote	Republican	Democratic	Other	Rep.-Dem. Plurality	Percentage Total Vote Rep.	Total Vote Dem.	Major Vote Rep.	Major Vote Dem.
15,654	ALLEN	5,898	3,429	2,392	77	1,037 R	58.1%	40.6%	58.9%	41.1%
8,749	ANDERSON	3,283	1,781	1,466	36	315 R	54.2%	44.7%	54.9%	45.1%
18,397	ATCHISON	6,614	3,243	3,177	194	66 R	49.0%	48.0%	50.5%	49.5%
6,548	BARBER	2,706	1,539	1,118	49	421 R	56.9%	41.3%	57.9%	42.1%
31,343	BARTON	13,075	7,741	5,024	310	2,717 R	59.2%	38.4%	60.6%	39.4%
15,969	BOURBON	6,332	3,660	2,623	49	1,037 R	57.8%	41.4%	58.3%	41.7%
11,955	BROWN	4,812	3,059	1,719	34	1,340 R	63.6%	35.7%	64.0%	36.0%
44,782	BUTLER	19,056	10,976	7,690	390	3,286 R	57.6%	40.4%	58.8%	41.2%
3,309	CHASE	1,458	884	538	36	346 R	60.6%	36.9%	62.2%	37.8%
5,016	CHAUTAUQUA	1,934	1,247	661	26	586 R	64.5%	34.2%	65.4%	34.6%
22,304	CHEROKEE	8,402	4,281	4,069	52	212 R	51.0%	48.4%	51.3%	48.7%
3,678	CHEYENNE	1,743	1,105	594	44	511 R	63.4%	34.1%	65.0%	35.0%
2,599	CLARK	1,315	876	409	30	467 R	66.6%	31.1%	68.2%	31.8%
9,802	CLAY	4,157	2,997	1,112	48	1,885 R	72.1%	26.8%	72.9%	27.1%
12,494	CLOUD	5,128	3,043	2,022	63	1,021 R	59.3%	39.4%	60.1%	39.9%
9,370	COFFEY	3,870	2,581	1,246	43	1,335 R	66.7%	32.2%	67.4%	32.6%
2,554	COMANCHE	1,123	738	375	10	363 R	65.7%	33.4%	66.3%	33.7%
36,824	COWLEY	14,286	7,778	6,186	322	1,592 R	54.4%	43.3%	55.7%	44.3%
37,916	CRAWFORD	14,850	6,940	7,783	127	843 D	46.7%	52.4%	47.1%	52.9%
4,509	DECATUR	2,148	1,291	793	64	498 R	60.1%	36.9%	61.9%	38.1%
20,175	DICKINSON	8,092	5,121	2,870	101	2,251 R	63.3%	35.5%	64.1%	35.9%
9,268	DONIPHAN	3,514	2,162	1,312	40	850 R	61.5%	37.3%	62.2%	37.8%
67,640	DOUGLAS	32,361	16,149	15,752	460	397 R	49.9%	48.7%	50.6%	49.4%
4,271	EDWARDS	1,843	993	792	58	201 R	53.9%	43.0%	55.6%	44.4%
3,918	ELK	1,706	1,075	608	23	467 R	63.0%	35.6%	63.9%	36.1%
26,098	ELLIS	10,672	5,194	5,289	189	95 D	48.7%	49.6%	49.5%	50.5%
6,640	ELLSWORTH	3,000	1,711	1,219	70	492 R	57.0%	40.6%	58.4%	41.6%
23,825	FINNEY	8,947	5,381	3,408	158	1,973 R	60.1%	38.1%	61.2%	38.8%
24,315	FORD	9,697	5,685	3,817	195	1,868 R	58.6%	39.4%	59.8%	40.2%
22,062	FRANKLIN	8,465	4,777	3,592	96	1,185 R	56.4%	42.4%	57.1%	42.9%
29,852	GEARY	6,573	3,782	2,721	70	1,061 R	57.5%	41.4%	58.2%	41.8%
3,726	GOVE	1,684	966	663	55	303 R	57.4%	39.4%	59.3%	40.7%
3,995	GRAHAM	1,868	1,139	702	27	437 R	61.0%	37.6%	61.9%	38.1%
6,977	GRANT	2,597	1,654	907	36	747 R	63.7%	34.9%	64.6%	35.4%
5,138	GRAY	1,917	1,180	696	41	484 R	61.6%	36.3%	62.9%	37.1%
1,845	GREELEY	853	506	317	30	189 R	59.3%	37.2%	61.5%	38.5%
8,764	GREENWOOD	3,716	2,217	1,421	78	796 R	59.7%	38.2%	60.9%	39.1%
2,514	HAMILTON	1,335	801	517	17	284 R	60.0%	38.7%	60.8%	39.2%
7,778	HARPER	3,268	1,941	1,235	92	706 R	59.4%	37.8%	61.1%	38.9%
30,531	HARVEY	12,711	6,893	5,503	315	1,390 R	54.2%	43.3%	55.6%	44.4%
3,814	HASKELL	1,430	964	427	39	537 R	67.4%	29.9%	69.3%	30.7%
2,269	HODGEMAN	1,212	732	439	41	293 R	60.4%	36.2%	62.5%	37.5%
11,644	JACKSON	5,075	2,759	2,261	55	498 R	54.4%	44.6%	55.0%	45.0%
15,207	JEFFERSON	6,492	3,605	2,810	77	795 R	55.5%	43.3%	56.2%	43.8%
5,241	JEWELL	2,274	1,546	684	44	862 R	68.0%	30.1%	69.3%	30.7%
270,269	JOHNSON	152,199	95,591	55,183	1,425	40,408 R	62.8%	36.3%	63.4%	36.6%
3,435	KEARNY	1,625	1,073	524	28	549 R	66.0%	32.2%	67.2%	32.8%
8,960	KINGMAN	3,754	2,205	1,420	129	785 R	58.7%	37.8%	60.8%	39.2%
4,046	KIOWA	1,795	1,276	485	34	791 R	71.1%	27.0%	72.5%	27.5%
25,682	LABETTE	9,684	5,125	4,433	126	692 R	52.9%	45.8%	53.6%	46.4%
2,472	LANE	1,250	768	450	32	318 R	61.4%	36.0%	63.1%	36.9%
54,809	LEAVENWORTH	18,870	9,913	8,797	160	1,116 R	52.5%	46.6%	53.0%	47.0%
4,145	LINCOLN	2,060	1,229	796	35	433 R	59.7%	38.6%	60.7%	39.3%
8,234	LINN	3,691	2,163	1,497	31	666 R	58.6%	40.6%	59.1%	40.9%
3,478	LOGAN	1,535	988	503	44	485 R	64.4%	32.8%	66.3%	33.7%
35,108	LYON	12,334	6,820	5,314	200	1,506 R	55.3%	43.1%	56.2%	43.8%
26,855	MCPHERSON	11,164	6,563	4,354	247	2,209 R	58.8%	39.0%	60.1%	39.9%
13,522	MARION	5,850	3,685	2,024	141	1,661 R	63.0%	34.6%	64.5%	35.5%
12,787	MARSHALL	5,790	3,140	2,560	90	580 R	54.2%	44.2%	55.1%	44.9%
4,788	MEADE	2,028	1,322	664	42	658 R	65.2%	32.7%	66.6%	33.4%

KANSAS

PRESIDENT 1988

1980 Census Population	County	Total Vote	Republican	Democratic	Other	Rep.-Dem. Plurality	Percentage Total Vote Rep.	Total Vote Dem.	Major Vote Rep.	Major Vote Dem.
21,618	MIAMI	9,306	4,807	4,427	72	380 R	51.7%	47.6%	52.1%	47.9%
8,117	MITCHELL	3,462	2,257	1,145	60	1,112 R	65.2%	33.1%	66.3%	33.7%
42,281	MONTGOMERY	14,628	9,067	5,429	132	3,638 R	62.0%	37.1%	62.5%	37.5%
6,419	MORRIS	2,894	1,682	1,165	47	517 R	58.1%	40.3%	59.1%	40.9%
3,454	MORTON	1,669	1,074	569	26	505 R	64.3%	34.1%	65.4%	34.6%
11,211	NEMAHA	5,182	2,849	2,261	72	588 R	55.0%	43.6%	55.8%	44.2%
18,967	NEOSHO	7,222	3,739	3,402	81	337 R	51.8%	47.1%	52.4%	47.6%
4,498	NESS	2,174	1,230	887	57	343 R	56.6%	40.8%	58.1%	41.9%
6,689	NORTON	2,847	1,923	855	69	1,068 R	67.5%	30.0%	69.2%	30.8%
15,319	OSAGE	6,435	3,496	2,840	99	656 R	54.3%	44.1%	55.2%	44.8%
5,959	OSBORNE	2,544	1,541	943	60	598 R	60.6%	37.1%	62.0%	38.0%
5,971	OTTAWA	2,834	1,836	953	45	883 R	64.8%	33.6%	65.8%	34.2%
8,065	PAWNEE	3,373	1,825	1,474	74	351 R	54.1%	43.7%	55.3%	44.7%
7,406	PHILLIPS	3,315	2,316	960	39	1,356 R	69.9%	29.0%	70.7%	29.3%
14,782	POTTAWATOMIE	6,549	3,897	2,544	108	1,353 R	59.5%	38.8%	60.5%	39.5%
10,275	PRATT	4,245	2,505	1,651	89	854 R	59.0%	38.9%	60.3%	39.7%
4,105	RAWLINS	1,983	1,318	612	53	706 R	66.5%	30.9%	68.3%	31.7%
64,983	RENO	24,954	12,753	11,545	656	1,208 R	51.1%	46.3%	52.5%	47.5%
7,569	REPUBLIC	3,462	2,346	1,069	47	1,277 R	67.8%	30.9%	68.7%	31.3%
11,900	RICE	4,645	2,503	2,033	109	470 R	53.9%	43.8%	55.2%	44.8%
63,505	RILEY	17,007	9,507	7,283	217	2,224 R	55.9%	42.8%	56.6%	43.4%
7,006	ROOKS	3,007	1,938	1,012	57	926 R	64.4%	33.7%	65.7%	34.3%
4,516	RUSH	2,153	1,045	1,020	88	25 R	48.5%	47.4%	50.6%	49.4%
8,868	RUSSELL	3,926	2,403	1,448	75	955 R	61.2%	36.9%	62.4%	37.6%
48,905	SALINE	19,618	11,371	7,998	249	3,373 R	58.0%	40.8%	58.7%	41.3%
5,782	SCOTT	2,375	1,590	717	68	873 R	66.9%	30.2%	68.9%	31.1%
366,531	SEDGWICK	155,745	86,124	65,618	4,003	20,506 R	55.3%	42.1%	56.8%	43.2%
17,071	SEWARD	5,797	4,089	1,655	53	2,434 R	70.5%	28.5%	71.2%	28.8%
154,916	SHAWNEE	70,197	35,489	33,940	768	1,549 R	50.6%	48.3%	51.1%	48.9%
3,544	SHERIDAN	1,556	901	600	55	301 R	57.9%	38.6%	60.0%	40.0%
7,759	SHERMAN	3,065	1,929	1,082	54	847 R	62.9%	35.3%	64.1%	35.9%
5,947	SMITH	2,988	1,951	1,004	33	947 R	65.3%	33.6%	66.0%	34.0%
5,694	STAFFORD	2,738	1,532	1,121	85	411 R	56.0%	40.9%	57.7%	42.3%
2,339	STANTON	950	592	310	48	282 R	62.3%	32.6%	65.6%	34.4%
4,736	STEVENS	2,307	1,642	612	53	1,030 R	71.2%	26.5%	72.8%	27.2%
24,928	SUMNER	10,042	5,394	4,417	231	977 R	53.7%	44.0%	55.0%	45.0%
8,451	THOMAS	3,870	2,342	1,408	120	934 R	60.5%	36.4%	62.5%	37.5%
4,165	TREGO	1,831	979	795	57	184 R	53.5%	43.4%	55.2%	44.8%
6,867	WABAUNSEE	2,967	1,737	1,166	64	571 R	58.5%	39.3%	59.8%	40.2%
2,045	WALLACE	941	655	257	29	398 R	69.6%	27.3%	71.8%	28.2%
8,543	WASHINGTON	3,380	2,269	1,063	48	1,206 R	67.1%	31.4%	68.1%	31.9%
3,041	WICHITA	1,148	721	399	28	322 R	62.8%	34.8%	64.4%	35.6%
12,128	WILSON	4,346	2,743	1,545	58	1,198 R	63.1%	35.5%	64.0%	36.0%
4,600	WOODSON	1,847	1,062	761	24	301 R	57.5%	41.2%	58.3%	41.7%
172,335	WYANDOTTE	58,399	19,097	38,678	624	19,581 D	32.7%	66.2%	33.1%	66.9%
2,363,679	TOTAL	993,044	554,049	422,636	16,359	131,413 R	55.8%	42.6%	56.7%	43.3%

KANSAS

CONGRESS

CD	Year	Total Vote	Republican Vote	Republican Candidate	Democratic Vote	Democratic Candidate	Other Vote	Rep.-Dem. Plurality	Percentage Total Vote Rep.	Percentage Total Vote Dem.	Percentage Major Vote Rep.	Percentage Major Vote Dem.
1	1988	168,754	168,700	ROBERTS, PAT			54	168,700 R	100.0%		100.0%	
1	1986	184,656	141,297	ROBERTS, PAT	43,359	LYON, DALE		97,938 R	76.5%	23.5%	76.5%	23.5%
1	1984	210,763	159,931	ROBERTS, PAT	49,015	RINGER, DARRELL T.	1,817	110,916 R	75.9%	23.3%	76.5%	23.5%
1	1982	169,133	115,749	ROBERTS, PAT	51,079	ROTH, KENT	2,305	64,670 R	68.4%	30.2%	69.4%	30.6%
2	1988	185,296	49,498	MEINHARDT, PHIL	135,694	SLATTERY, JIM	104	86,196 D	26.7%	73.2%	26.7%	73.3%
2	1986	156,766	46,029	KLINE, PHILL	110,737	SLATTERY, JIM		64,708 D	29.4%	70.6%	29.4%	70.6%
2	1984	187,052	73,045	VAN SLYKE, JIM	112,263	SLATTERY, JIM	1,744	39,218 D	39.1%	60.0%	39.4%	60.6%
2	1982	150,228	63,942	KAY, MORRIS	86,286	SLATTERY, JIM		22,344 D	42.6%	57.4%	42.6%	57.4%
3	1988	204,221	150,223	MEYERS, JAN	53,959	KUNST, LIONEL	39	96,264 R	73.6%	26.4%	73.6%	26.4%
3	1986	109,266	109,266	MEYERS, JAN				109,266 R	100.0%		100.0%	
3	1984	213,902	117,159	MEYERS, JAN	85,441	REARDON, JOHN E.	11,302	31,718 R	54.8%	39.9%	57.8%	42.2%
3	1982	138,696	82,117	WINN, LARRY	53,140	KOSTAR, WILLIAM L.	3,439	28,977 R	59.2%	38.3%	60.7%	39.3%
4	1988	191,957	69,165	THOMPSON, LEE	122,777	GLICKMAN, DAN	15	53,612 D	36.0%	64.0%	36.0%	64.0%
4	1986	172,342	61,178	KNIGHT, BOB	111,164	GLICKMAN, DAN		49,986 D	35.5%	64.5%	35.5%	64.5%
4	1984	186,693	47,776	KRAUSE, WILLIAM V.	138,917	GLICKMAN, DAN		91,141 D	25.6%	74.4%	25.6%	74.4%
4	1982	145,167	35,478	CAYWOOD, GERALD	107,326	GLICKMAN, DAN	2,363	71,848 D	24.4%	73.9%	24.8%	75.2%
5	1988	182,079	127,722	WHITTAKER, ROBERT	54,327	BARNES, JOHN A.	30	73,395 R	70.1%	29.8%	70.2%	29.8%
5	1986	164,340	116,800	WHITTAKER, ROBERT	47,540	MYERS, KYM E.		69,260 R	71.1%	28.9%	71.1%	28.9%
5	1984	195,915	144,075	WHITTAKER, ROBERT	49,435	BARNES, JOHN A.	2,405	94,640 R	73.5%	25.2%	74.5%	25.5%
5	1982	153,121	103,551	WHITTAKER, ROBERT	47,676	ROWE, LEE	1,894	55,875 R	67.6%	31.1%	68.5%	31.5%

KANSAS

1988 GENERAL ELECTION

President Other vote was 12,553 Independent (Paul); 3,806 Independent (Fulani).

Congress Other vote was scattered in all CD's.

1988 PRIMARIES

AUGUST 2 REPUBLICAN

Congress Unopposed in three CD's. Contested as follows:

CD 2 26,054 Phil Meinhardt; 14,543 Stanley W. Eckert.
CD 3 25,993 Jan Meyers; 4,570 Charles B. Masterson.

AUGUST 2 DEMOCRATIC

Congress Unopposed in three CD's. No candidate in CD 1. Contested as follows:

CD 5 19,179 John A. Barnes; 7,325 James Rinker.

KENTUCKY

GOVERNOR

Wallace G. Wilkinson (D). Elected 1987 to a four-year term.

SENATORS

Wendell H. Ford (D). Re-elected 1986 to a six-year term. Previously elected 1980, 1974.

Mitch McConnell (R). Elected 1984 to a six-year term.

REPRESENTATIVES

1. Carroll Hubbard (D)
2. William H. Natcher (D)
3. Romano L. Mazzoli (D)
4. Jim Bunning (R)
5. Harold Rogers (R)
6. Larry J. Hopkins (R)
7. Carl C. Perkins (D)

POSTWAR VOTE FOR PRESIDENT

Year	Total Vote	Republican Vote	Republican Candidate	Democratic Vote	Democratic Candidate	Other Vote	Plurality	Percentage Total Vote Rep.	Total Vote Dem.	Major Vote Rep.	Major Vote Dem.
1988	1,322,517	734,281	Bush, George	580,368	Dukakis, Michael S.	7,868	153,913 R	55.5%	43.9%	55.9%	44.1%
1984	1,369,345	821,702	Reagan, Ronald	539,539	Mondale, Walter F.	8,104	282,163 R	60.0%	39.4%	60.4%	39.6%
1980	1,294,627	635,274	Reagan, Ronald	616,417	Carter, Jimmy	42,936	18,857 R	49.1%	47.6%	50.8%	49.2%
1976	1,167,142	531,852	Ford, Gerald R.	615,717	Carter, Jimmy	19,573	83,865 D	45.6%	52.8%	46.3%	53.7%
1972	1,067,499	676,446	Nixon, Richard M.	371,159	McGovern, George S.	19,894	305,287 R	63.4%	34.8%	64.6%	35.4%
1968	1,055,893	462,411	Nixon, Richard M.	397,541	Humphrey, Hubert H.	195,941	64,870 R	43.8%	37.6%	53.8%	46.2%
1964	1,046,105	372,977	Goldwater, Barry M.	669,659	Johnson, Lyndon B.	3,469	296,682 D	35.7%	64.0%	35.8%	64.2%
1960	1,124,462	602,607	Nixon, Richard M.	521,855	Kennedy, John F.		80,752 R	53.6%	46.4%	53.6%	46.4%
1956	1,053,805	572,192	Eisenhower, Dwight D.	476,453	Stevenson, Adlai E.	5,160	95,739 R	54.3%	45.2%	54.6%	45.4%
1952	993,148	495,029	Eisenhower, Dwight D.	495,729	Stevenson, Adlai E.	2,390	700 D	49.8%	49.9%	50.0%	50.0%
1948	822,658	341,210	Dewey, Thomas E.	466,756	Truman, Harry S.	14,692	125,546 D	41.5%	56.7%	42.2%	57.8%

POSTWAR VOTE FOR GOVERNOR

Year	Total Vote	Republican Vote	Republican Candidate	Democratic Vote	Democratic Candidate	Other Vote	Rep.-Dem. Plurality	Percentage Total Vote Rep.	Total Vote Dem.	Major Vote Rep.	Major Vote Dem.
1987	777,815	273,141	Harper, John	504,674	Wilkinson, Wallace G.		231,533 D	35.1%	64.9%	35.1%	64.9%
1983	1,030,671	454,650	Bunning, Jim	561,674	Collins, Martha Layne	14,347	107,024 D	44.1%	54.5%	44.7%	55.3%
1979	939,366	381,278	Nunn, Louie B.	558,088	Brown, J. Y., Jr.		176,810 D	40.6%	59.4%	40.6%	59.4%
1975	748,157	277,998	Gable, Robert E.	470,159	Carroll, Julian		192,161 D	37.2%	62.8%	37.2%	62.8%
1971	930,790	412,653	Emberton, Thomas	470,720	Ford, Wendell H.	47,417	58,067 D	44.3%	50.6%	46.7%	53.3%
1967	886,946	454,123	Nunn, Louie B.	425,674	Ward, Henry	7,149	28,449 R	51.2%	48.0%	51.6%	48.4%
1963	886,047	436,496	Nunn, Louie B.	449,551	Breathitt, Edward T.		13,055 D	49.3%	50.7%	49.3%	50.7%
1959	853,005	336,456	Robsion, John M.	516,549	Combs, Bert T.		180,093 D	39.4%	60.6%	39.4%	60.6%
1955	778,488	322,671	Denney, Edwin R.	451,647	Chandler, Albert B.	4,170	128,976 D	41.4%	58.0%	41.7%	58.3%
1951	634,359	288,014	Siler, Eugene	346,345	Wetherby, Lawrence		58,331 D	45.4%	54.6%	45.4%	54.6%
1947	672,372	287,130	Dummit, Eldon S.	385,242	Clements, Earle C.		98,112 D	42.7%	57.3%	42.7%	57.3%

KENTUCKY

POSTWAR VOTE FOR SENATOR

		Republican		Democratic				Percentage			
	Total					Other	Rep.-Dem.	Total Vote		Major Vote	
Year	Vote	Vote	Candidate	Vote	Candidate	Vote	Plurality	Rep.	Dem.	Rep.	Dem.
1986	677,280	173,330	Andrews, Jackson M.	503,775	Ford, Wendell H.	175	330,445 D	25.6%	74.4%	25.6%	74.4%
1984	1,292,407	644,990	McConnell, Mitch	639,721	Huddleston, Walter	7,696	5,269 R	49.9%	49.5%	50.2%	49.8%
1980	1,106,890	386,029	Foust, Mary Louise	720,861	Ford, Wendell H.		334,832 D	34.9%	65.1%	34.9%	65.1%
1978	476,783	175,766	Guenthner, Louie	290,730	Huddleston, Walter	10,287	114,964 D	36.9%	61.0%	37.7%	62.3%
1974	745,994	328,982	Cook, Marlow W.	399,406	Ford, Wendell H.	17,606	70,424 D	44.1%	53.5%	45.2%	54.8%
1972	1,037,861	494,337	Nunn, Louie B.	528,550	Huddleston, Walter	14,974	34,213 D	47.6%	50.9%	48.3%	51.7%
1968	942,865	484,260	Cook, Marlow W.	448,960	Peden, Katherine	9,645	35,300 R	51.4%	47.6%	51.9%	48.1%
1966	749,884	483,805	Cooper, John Sherman	266,079	Brown, J. Y.		217,726 R	64.5%	35.5%	64.5%	35.5%
1962	820,088	432,648	Morton, Thruston B.	387,440	Wyatt, Wilson W.		45,208 R	52.8%	47.2%	52.8%	47.2%
1960	1,088,377	644,087	Cooper, John Sherman	444,290	Johnson, Keen		199,797 R	59.2%	40.8%	59.2%	40.8%
1956	1,006,825	506,903	Morton, Thruston B.	499,922	Clements, Earle C.		6,981 R	50.3%	49.7%	50.3%	49.7%
1956 S	1,011,645	538,505	Cooper, John Sherman	473,140	Wetherby, Lawrence		65,365 R	53.2%	46.8%	53.2%	46.8%
1954	797,057	362,948	Cooper, John Sherman	434,109	Barkley, Alben W.		71,161 D	45.5%	54.5%	45.5%	54.5%
1952 S	960,228	494,576	Cooper, John Sherman	465,652	Underwood, Thomas R.		28,924 R	51.5%	48.5%	51.5%	48.5%
1950	612,617	278,368	Dawson, Charles L.	334,249	Clements, Earle C.		55,881 D	45.4%	54.6%	45.4%	54.6%
1948	794,469	383,776	Cooper, John Sherman	408,256	Chapman, Virgil	2,437	24,480 D	48.3%	51.4%	48.5%	51.5%
1946 S	615,119	327,652	Cooper, John Sherman	285,829	Brown, J. Y.	1,638	41,823 R	53.3%	46.5%	53.4%	46.6%

One of the 1956 elections and those in 1952 and 1946 were for short terms to fill vacancies.

KENTUCKY

Districts Established March 10, 1982

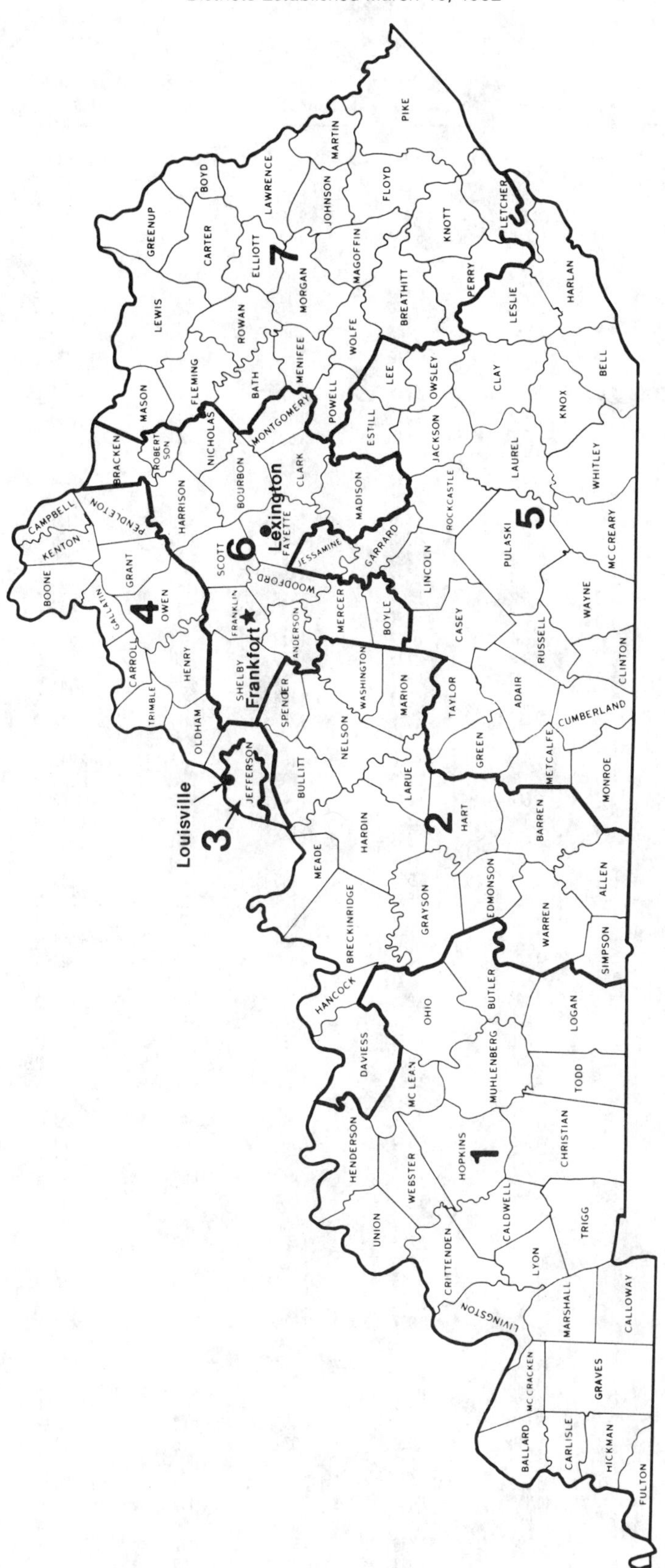

KENTUCKY

PRESIDENT 1988

1980 Census Population	County	Total Vote	Republican	Democratic	Other	Rep.-Dem. Plurality	Percentage Total Vote Rep.	Total Vote Dem.	Major Vote Rep.	Major Vote Dem.
15,233	ADAIR	6,113	4,346	1,723	44	2,623 R	71.1%	28.2%	71.6%	28.4%
14,128	ALLEN	4,923	3,342	1,573	8	1,769 R	67.9%	32.0%	68.0%	32.0%
12,567	ANDERSON	5,450	3,225	2,176	49	1,049 R	59.2%	39.9%	59.7%	40.3%
8,798	BALLARD	3,629	1,460	2,162	7	702 D	40.2%	59.6%	40.3%	59.7%
34,009	BARREN	11,506	6,653	4,799	54	1,854 R	57.8%	41.7%	58.1%	41.9%
10,025	BATH	3,724	1,614	2,099	11	485 D	43.3%	56.4%	43.5%	56.5%
34,330	BELL	11,193	5,759	5,182	252	577 R	51.5%	46.3%	52.6%	47.4%
45,842	BOONE	18,157	12,667	5,382	108	7,285 R	69.8%	29.6%	70.2%	29.8%
19,405	BOURBON	6,175	3,308	2,793	74	515 R	53.6%	45.2%	54.2%	45.8%
55,513	BOYD	18,988	9,379	9,552	57	173 D	49.4%	50.3%	49.5%	50.5%
25,066	BOYLE	8,354	4,746	3,575	33	1,171 R	56.8%	42.8%	57.0%	43.0%
7,738	BRACKEN	2,824	1,630	1,176	18	454 R	57.7%	41.6%	58.1%	41.9%
17,004	BREATHITT	5,580	2,149	3,387	44	1,238 D	38.5%	60.7%	38.8%	61.2%
16,861	BRECKINRIDGE	6,623	3,841	2,765	17	1,076 R	58.0%	41.7%	58.1%	41.9%
43,346	BULLITT	15,013	8,859	6,005	149	2,854 R	59.0%	40.0%	59.6%	40.4%
11,064	BUTLER	4,539	3,278	1,245	16	2,033 R	72.2%	27.4%	72.5%	27.5%
13,473	CALDWELL	5,577	2,952	2,564	61	388 R	52.9%	46.0%	53.5%	46.5%
30,031	CALLOWAY	11,546	6,225	5,287	34	938 R	53.9%	45.8%	54.1%	45.9%
83,317	CAMPBELL	29,104	19,387	9,553	164	9,834 R	66.6%	32.8%	67.0%	33.0%
5,487	CARLISLE	2,564	1,104	1,428	32	324 D	43.1%	55.7%	43.6%	56.4%
9,270	CARROLL	3,636	1,702	1,913	21	211 D	46.8%	52.6%	47.1%	52.9%
25,060	CARTER	8,944	4,325	4,570	49	245 D	48.4%	51.1%	48.6%	51.4%
14,818	CASEY	5,117	3,857	1,216	44	2,641 R	75.4%	23.8%	76.0%	24.0%
66,878	CHRISTIAN	15,008	9,250	5,704	54	3,546 R	61.6%	38.0%	61.9%	38.1%
28,322	CLARK	9,622	5,329	4,252	41	1,077 R	55.4%	44.2%	55.6%	44.4%
22,752	CLAY	5,884	4,156	1,709	19	2,447 R	70.6%	29.0%	70.9%	29.1%
9,321	CLINTON	4,175	3,248	899	28	2,349 R	77.8%	21.5%	78.3%	21.7%
9,207	CRITTENDEN	3,666	2,211	1,443	12	768 R	60.3%	39.4%	60.5%	39.5%
7,289	CUMBERLAND	2,995	2,231	753	11	1,478 R	74.5%	25.1%	74.8%	25.2%
85,949	DAVIESS	32,445	17,356	14,815	274	2,541 R	53.5%	45.7%	53.9%	46.1%
9,962	EDMONSON	3,828	2,555	1,243	30	1,312 R	66.7%	32.5%	67.3%	32.7%
6,908	ELLIOTT	2,357	550	1,797	10	1,247 D	23.3%	76.2%	23.4%	76.6%
14,495	ESTILL	4,794	3,077	1,692	25	1,385 R	64.2%	35.3%	64.5%	35.5%
204,165	FAYETTE	81,525	48,065	32,554	906	15,511 R	59.0%	39.9%	59.6%	40.4%
12,323	FLEMING	4,522	2,409	2,086	27	323 R	53.3%	46.1%	53.6%	46.4%
48,764	FLOYD	17,764	5,296	12,327	141	7,031 D	29.8%	69.4%	30.1%	69.9%
41,830	FRANKLIN	19,271	9,805	9,271	195	534 R	50.9%	48.1%	51.4%	48.6%
8,971	FULTON	3,016	1,474	1,531	11	57 D	48.9%	50.8%	49.1%	50.9%
4,842	GALLATIN	1,952	881	1,060	11	179 D	45.1%	54.3%	45.4%	54.6%
10,853	GARRARD	4,455	2,681	1,710	64	971 R	60.2%	38.4%	61.1%	38.9%
13,308	GRANT	4,801	2,835	1,896	70	939 R	59.1%	39.5%	59.9%	40.1%
34,049	GRAVES	13,545	6,274	7,153	118	879 D	46.3%	52.8%	46.7%	53.3%
20,854	GRAYSON	7,842	5,186	2,575	81	2,611 R	66.1%	32.8%	66.8%	33.2%
11,043	GREEN	4,751	3,139	1,595	17	1,544 R	66.1%	33.6%	66.3%	33.7%
39,132	GREENUP	13,558	6,559	6,956	43	397 D	48.4%	51.3%	48.5%	51.5%
7,742	HANCOCK	3,243	1,733	1,478	32	255 R	53.4%	45.6%	54.0%	46.0%
88,917	HARDIN	20,599	13,240	7,262	97	5,978 R	64.3%	35.3%	64.6%	35.4%
41,889	HARLAN	12,576	5,166	7,341	69	2,175 D	41.1%	58.4%	41.3%	58.7%
15,166	HARRISON	5,753	2,983	2,748	22	235 R	51.9%	47.8%	52.1%	47.9%
15,402	HART	5,468	2,927	2,519	22	408 R	53.5%	46.1%	53.7%	46.3%
40,849	HENDERSON	14,620	6,911	7,648	61	737 D	47.3%	52.3%	47.5%	52.5%
12,740	HENRY	4,866	2,286	2,544	36	258 D	47.0%	52.3%	47.3%	52.7%
6,065	HICKMAN	2,315	1,142	1,158	15	16 D	49.3%	50.0%	49.7%	50.3%
46,174	HOPKINS	15,505	7,979	7,453	73	526 R	51.5%	48.1%	51.7%	48.3%
11,996	JACKSON	4,610	3,926	678	6	3,248 R	85.2%	14.7%	85.3%	14.7%
685,004	JEFFERSON	268,629	139,711	127,936	982	11,775 R	52.0%	47.6%	52.2%	47.8%
26,146	JESSAMINE	10,116	7,057	2,955	104	4,102 R	69.8%	29.2%	70.5%	29.5%
24,432	JOHNSON	8,211	4,619	3,538	54	1,081 R	56.3%	43.1%	56.6%	43.4%
137,058	KENTON	45,793	30,738	14,838	217	15,900 R	67.1%	32.4%	67.4%	32.6%
17,940	KNOTT	6,926	1,691	5,185	50	3,494 D	24.4%	74.9%	24.6%	75.4%

KENTUCKY

PRESIDENT 1988

1980 Census Population	County	Total Vote	Republican	Democratic	Other	Rep.-Dem. Plurality	Percentage Total Vote Rep.	Percentage Total Vote Dem.	Percentage Major Vote Rep.	Percentage Major Vote Dem.
30,239	KNOX	7,882	4,903	2,919	60	1,984 R	62.2%	37.0%	62.7%	37.3%
11,922	LARUE	4,423	2,590	1,822	11	768 R	58.6%	41.2%	58.7%	41.3%
38,982	LAUREL	12,994	9,296	3,620	78	5,676 R	71.5%	27.9%	72.0%	28.0%
14,121	LAWRENCE	4,508	2,294	2,198	16	96 R	50.9%	48.8%	51.1%	48.9%
7,754	LEE	2,590	1,588	984	18	604 R	61.3%	38.0%	61.7%	38.3%
14,882	LESLIE	4,409	3,280	1,105	24	2,175 R	74.4%	25.1%	74.8%	25.2%
30,687	LETCHER	8,344	3,601	4,697	46	1,096 D	43.2%	56.3%	43.4%	56.6%
14,545	LEWIS	4,696	3,108	1,568	20	1,540 R	66.2%	33.4%	66.5%	33.5%
19,053	LINCOLN	6,232	3,530	2,677	25	853 R	56.6%	43.0%	56.9%	43.1%
9,219	LIVINGSTON	3,909	1,834	2,052	23	218 D	46.9%	52.5%	47.2%	52.8%
24,138	LOGAN	7,705	4,295	3,379	31	916 R	55.7%	43.9%	56.0%	44.0%
6,490	LYON	2,422	1,077	1,337	8	260 D	44.5%	55.2%	44.6%	55.4%
61,310	MCCRACKEN	24,643	12,160	12,208	275	48 D	49.3%	49.5%	49.9%	50.1%
15,634	MCCREARY	5,193	3,477	1,644	72	1,833 R	67.0%	31.7%	67.9%	32.1%
10,090	MCLEAN	4,111	1,829	2,269	13	440 D	44.5%	55.2%	44.6%	55.4%
53,352	MADISON	16,766	9,958	6,672	136	3,286 R	59.4%	39.8%	59.9%	40.1%
13,515	MAGOFFIN	5,080	2,158	2,895	27	737 D	42.5%	57.0%	42.7%	57.3%
17,910	MARION	5,673	2,500	3,152	21	652 D	44.1%	55.6%	44.2%	55.8%
25,637	MARSHALL	11,171	5,256	5,888	27	632 D	47.1%	52.7%	47.2%	52.8%
13,925	MARTIN	4,196	2,587	1,581	28	1,006 R	61.7%	37.7%	62.1%	37.9%
17,765	MASON	5,895	3,158	2,721	16	437 R	53.6%	46.2%	53.7%	46.3%
22,854	MEADE	6,545	3,441	3,079	25	362 R	52.6%	47.0%	52.8%	47.2%
5,117	MENIFEE	1,788	670	1,096	22	426 D	37.5%	61.3%	37.9%	62.1%
19,011	MERCER	6,843	3,904	2,832	107	1,072 R	57.1%	41.4%	58.0%	42.0%
9,484	METCALFE	3,915	2,179	1,705	31	474 R	55.7%	43.6%	56.1%	43.9%
12,353	MONROE	5,266	4,214	1,025	27	3,189 R	80.0%	19.5%	80.4%	19.6%
20,046	MONTGOMERY	6,537	3,435	3,082	20	353 R	52.5%	47.1%	52.7%	47.3%
12,103	MORGAN	3,817	1,452	2,329	36	877 D	38.0%	61.0%	38.4%	61.6%
32,238	MUHLENBERG	12,322	5,369	6,912	41	1,543 D	43.6%	56.1%	43.7%	56.3%
27,584	NELSON	10,179	5,283	4,788	108	495 R	51.9%	47.0%	52.5%	47.5%
7,157	NICHOLAS	2,559	1,271	1,242	46	29 R	49.7%	48.5%	50.6%	49.4%
21,765	OHIO	8,545	4,910	3,612	23	1,298 R	57.5%	42.3%	57.6%	42.4%
27,795	OLDHAM	12,792	8,716	4,025	51	4,691 R	68.1%	31.5%	68.4%	31.6%
8,924	OWEN	3,311	1,468	1,823	20	355 D	44.3%	55.1%	44.6%	55.4%
5,709	OWSLEY	1,613	1,266	345	2	921 R	78.5%	21.4%	78.6%	21.4%
10,989	PENDLETON	4,091	2,487	1,576	28	911 R	60.8%	38.5%	61.2%	38.8%
33,763	PERRY	10,772	5,154	5,557	61	403 D	47.8%	51.6%	48.1%	51.9%
81,123	PIKE	26,416	9,976	16,339	101	6,363 D	37.8%	61.9%	37.9%	62.1%
11,101	POWELL	4,258	2,128	2,113	17	15 R	50.0%	49.6%	50.2%	49.8%
45,803	PULASKI	18,342	13,482	4,788	72	8,694 R	73.5%	26.1%	73.8%	26.2%
2,265	ROBERTSON	1,035	511	515	9	4 D	49.4%	49.8%	49.8%	50.2%
13,973	ROCKCASTLE	4,948	3,880	1,041	27	2,839 R	78.4%	21.0%	78.8%	21.2%
19,049	ROWAN	6,077	3,093	2,968	16	125 R	50.9%	48.8%	51.0%	49.0%
13,708	RUSSELL	5,777	4,292	1,455	30	2,837 R	74.3%	25.2%	74.7%	25.3%
21,813	SCOTT	7,908	4,482	3,380	46	1,102 R	56.7%	42.7%	57.0%	43.0%
23,328	SHELBY	8,871	4,998	3,834	39	1,164 R	56.3%	43.2%	56.6%	43.4%
14,673	SIMPSON	4,859	2,699	2,138	22	561 R	55.5%	44.0%	55.8%	44.2%
5,929	SPENCER	2,505	1,368	1,121	16	247 R	54.6%	44.8%	55.0%	45.0%
21,178	TAYLOR	8,280	5,362	2,879	39	2,483 R	64.8%	34.8%	65.1%	34.9%
11,874	TODD	3,958	2,282	1,632	44	650 R	57.7%	41.2%	58.3%	41.7%
9,384	TRIGG	4,434	2,427	1,991	16	436 R	54.7%	44.9%	54.9%	45.1%
6,253	TRIMBLE	2,440	1,083	1,342	15	259 D	44.4%	55.0%	44.7%	55.3%
17,821	UNION	5,628	2,292	3,316	20	1,024 D	40.7%	58.9%	40.9%	59.1%
71,828	WARREN	26,484	16,703	9,684	97	7,019 R	63.1%	36.6%	63.3%	36.7%
10,764	WASHINGTON	4,454	2,445	1,950	59	495 R	54.9%	43.8%	55.6%	44.4%
17,022	WAYNE	5,747	3,672	2,057	18	1,615 R	63.9%	35.8%	64.1%	35.9%
14,832	WEBSTER	5,202	2,159	3,019	24	860 D	41.5%	58.0%	41.7%	58.3%
33,396	WHITLEY	11,188	7,337	3,794	57	3,543 R	65.6%	33.9%	65.9%	34.1%
6,698	WOLFE	2,480	916	1,516	48	600 D	36.9%	61.1%	37.7%	62.3%
17,778	WOODFORD	7,204	4,512	2,653	39	1,859 R	62.6%	36.8%	63.0%	37.0%
3,660,777	TOTAL	1,322,517	734,281	580,368	7,868	153,913 R	55.5%	43.9%	55.9%	44.1%

KENTUCKY

GOVERNOR 1987

1980 Census Population	County	Total Vote	Republican	Democratic	Other	Rep.-Dem. Plurality	Percentage Total Vote Rep.	Total Vote Dem.	Major Vote Rep.	Major Vote Dem.
15,233	ADAIR	4,593	1,695	2,898		1,203 D	36.9%	63.1%	36.9%	63.1%
14,128	ALLEN	2,660	1,151	1,509		358 D	43.3%	56.7%	43.3%	56.7%
12,567	ANDERSON	3,592	1,109	2,483		1,374 D	30.9%	69.1%	30.9%	69.1%
8,798	BALLARD	2,279	285	1,994		1,709 D	12.5%	87.5%	12.5%	87.5%
34,009	BARREN	6,182	1,881	4,301		2,420 D	30.4%	69.6%	30.4%	69.6%
10,025	BATH	2,610	438	2,172		1,734 D	16.8%	83.2%	16.8%	83.2%
34,330	BELL	8,684	2,661	6,023		3,362 D	30.6%	69.4%	30.6%	69.4%
45,842	BOONE	9,116	2,893	6,223		3,330 D	31.7%	68.3%	31.7%	68.3%
19,405	BOURBON	3,911	1,296	2,615		1,319 D	33.1%	66.9%	33.1%	66.9%
55,513	BOYD	13,063	4,600	8,463		3,863 D	35.2%	64.8%	35.2%	64.8%
25,066	BOYLE	5,265	2,043	3,222		1,179 D	38.8%	61.2%	38.8%	61.2%
7,738	BRACKEN	2,027	532	1,495		963 D	26.2%	73.8%	26.2%	73.8%
17,004	BREATHITT	3,416	431	2,985		2,554 D	12.6%	87.4%	12.6%	87.4%
16,861	BRECKINRIDGE	3,863	1,227	2,636		1,409 D	31.8%	68.2%	31.8%	68.2%
43,346	BULLITT	8,885	5,609	3,276		2,333 R	63.1%	36.9%	63.1%	36.9%
11,064	BUTLER	2,289	1,035	1,254		219 D	45.2%	54.8%	45.2%	54.8%
13,473	CALDWELL	2,944	811	2,133		1,322 D	27.5%	72.5%	27.5%	72.5%
30,031	CALLOWAY	6,187	2,094	4,093		1,999 D	33.8%	66.2%	33.8%	66.2%
83,317	CAMPBELL	17,690	5,718	11,972		6,254 D	32.3%	67.7%	32.3%	67.7%
5,487	CARLISLE	1,826	201	1,625		1,424 D	11.0%	89.0%	11.0%	89.0%
9,270	CARROLL	2,037	426	1,611		1,185 D	20.9%	79.1%	20.9%	79.1%
25,060	CARTER	5,596	1,813	3,783		1,970 D	32.4%	67.6%	32.4%	67.6%
14,818	CASEY	4,197	815	3,382		2,567 D	19.4%	80.6%	19.4%	80.6%
66,878	CHRISTIAN	9,238	2,283	6,955		4,672 D	24.7%	75.3%	24.7%	75.3%
28,322	CLARK	5,987	2,118	3,869		1,751 D	35.4%	64.6%	35.4%	64.6%
22,752	CLAY	4,390	1,192	3,198		2,006 D	27.2%	72.8%	27.2%	72.8%
9,321	CLINTON	2,633	1,088	1,545		457 D	41.3%	58.7%	41.3%	58.7%
9,207	CRITTENDEN	2,397	758	1,639		881 D	31.6%	68.4%	31.6%	68.4%
7,289	CUMBERLAND	1,986	824	1,162		338 D	41.5%	58.5%	41.5%	58.5%
85,949	DAVIESS	18,661	4,491	14,170		9,679 D	24.1%	75.9%	24.1%	75.9%
9,962	EDMONSON	1,819	852	967		115 D	46.8%	53.2%	46.8%	53.2%
6,908	ELLIOTT	1,814	228	1,586		1,358 D	12.6%	87.4%	12.6%	87.4%
14,495	ESTILL	2,896	1,256	1,640		384 D	43.4%	56.6%	43.4%	56.6%
204,165	FAYETTE	44,268	22,547	21,721		826 R	50.9%	49.1%	50.9%	49.1%
12,323	FLEMING	3,041	956	2,085		1,129 D	31.4%	68.6%	31.4%	68.6%
48,764	FLOYD	8,149	1,315	6,834		5,519 D	16.1%	83.9%	16.1%	83.9%
41,830	FRANKLIN	15,795	4,832	10,963		6,131 D	30.6%	69.4%	30.6%	69.4%
8,971	FULTON	1,905	253	1,652		1,399 D	13.3%	86.7%	13.3%	86.7%
4,842	GALLATIN	1,248	215	1,033		818 D	17.2%	82.8%	17.2%	82.8%
10,853	GARRARD	3,065	1,383	1,682		299 D	45.1%	54.9%	45.1%	54.9%
13,308	GRANT	2,882	801	2,081		1,280 D	27.8%	72.2%	27.8%	72.2%
34,049	GRAVES	7,818	1,297	6,521		5,224 D	16.6%	83.4%	16.6%	83.4%
20,854	GRAYSON	6,003	2,343	3,660		1,317 D	39.0%	61.0%	39.0%	61.0%
11,043	GREEN	3,132	1,341	1,791		450 D	42.8%	57.2%	42.8%	57.2%
39,132	GREENUP	8,096	2,762	5,334		2,572 D	34.1%	65.9%	34.1%	65.9%
7,742	HANCOCK	2,188	575	1,613		1,038 D	26.3%	73.7%	26.3%	73.7%
88,917	HARDIN	11,840	4,056	7,784		3,728 D	34.3%	65.7%	34.3%	65.7%
41,889	HARLAN	7,872	1,908	5,964		4,056 D	24.2%	75.8%	24.2%	75.8%
15,166	HARRISON	3,799	1,058	2,741		1,683 D	27.8%	72.2%	27.8%	72.2%
15,402	HART	3,982	1,183	2,799		1,616 D	29.7%	70.3%	29.7%	70.3%
40,849	HENDERSON	7,606	1,774	5,832		4,058 D	23.3%	76.7%	23.3%	76.7%
12,740	HENRY	3,232	793	2,439		1,646 D	24.5%	75.5%	24.5%	75.5%
6,065	HICKMAN	1,567	230	1,337		1,107 D	14.7%	85.3%	14.7%	85.3%
46,174	HOPKINS	8,969	2,417	6,552		4,135 D	26.9%	73.1%	26.9%	73.1%
11,996	JACKSON	1,628	909	719		190 R	55.8%	44.2%	55.8%	44.2%
685,004	JEFFERSON	139,930	63,348	76,582		13,234 D	45.3%	54.7%	45.3%	54.7%
26,146	JESSAMINE	5,756	2,512	3,244		732 D	43.6%	56.4%	43.6%	56.4%
24,432	JOHNSON	4,643	1,842	2,801		959 D	39.7%	60.3%	39.7%	60.3%
137,058	KENTON	30,176	10,327	19,849		9,522 D	34.2%	65.8%	34.2%	65.8%
17,940	KNOTT	2,978	515	2,463		1,948 D	17.3%	82.7%	17.3%	82.7%

KENTUCKY

GOVERNOR 1987

1980 Census Population	County	Total Vote	Republican	Democratic	Other	Rep.-Dem. Plurality	Percentage Total Vote Rep.	Total Vote Dem.	Major Vote Rep.	Major Vote Dem.
30,239	KNOX	6,794	2,735	4,059		1,324 D	40.3%	59.7%	40.3%	59.7%
11,922	LARUE	2,408	794	1,614		820 D	33.0%	67.0%	33.0%	67.0%
38,982	LAUREL	6,501	3,134	3,367		233 D	48.2%	51.8%	48.2%	51.8%
14,121	LAWRENCE	2,582	937	1,645		708 D	36.3%	63.7%	36.3%	63.7%
7,754	LEE	2,014	713	1,301		588 D	35.4%	64.6%	35.4%	64.6%
14,882	LESLIE	2,235	920	1,315		395 D	41.2%	58.8%	41.2%	58.8%
30,687	LETCHER	4,248	1,212	3,036		1,824 D	28.5%	71.5%	28.5%	71.5%
14,545	LEWIS	3,977	1,817	2,160		343 D	45.7%	54.3%	45.7%	54.3%
19,053	LINCOLN	3,844	1,161	2,683		1,522 D	30.2%	69.8%	30.2%	69.8%
9,219	LIVINGSTON	2,380	410	1,970		1,560 D	17.2%	82.8%	17.2%	82.8%
24,138	LOGAN	4,447	1,246	3,201		1,955 D	28.0%	72.0%	28.0%	72.0%
6,490	LYON	1,588	281	1,307		1,026 D	17.7%	82.3%	17.7%	82.3%
61,310	MCCRACKEN	14,864	2,819	12,045		9,226 D	19.0%	81.0%	19.0%	81.0%
15,634	MCCREARY	2,918	1,288	1,630		342 D	44.1%	55.9%	44.1%	55.9%
10,090	MCLEAN	2,448	565	1,883		1,318 D	23.1%	76.9%	23.1%	76.9%
53,352	MADISON	10,236	4,637	5,599		962 D	45.3%	54.7%	45.3%	54.7%
13,515	MAGOFFIN	4,466	1,239	3,227		1,988 D	27.7%	72.3%	27.7%	72.3%
17,910	MARION	3,828	700	3,128		2,428 D	18.3%	81.7%	18.3%	81.7%
25,637	MARSHALL	5,774	1,132	4,642		3,510 D	19.6%	80.4%	19.6%	80.4%
13,925	MARTIN	2,458	897	1,561		664 D	36.5%	63.5%	36.5%	63.5%
17,765	MASON	4,110	1,292	2,818		1,526 D	31.4%	68.6%	31.4%	68.6%
22,854	MEADE	3,928	1,043	2,885		1,842 D	26.6%	73.4%	26.6%	73.4%
5,117	MENIFEE	1,097	205	892		687 D	18.7%	81.3%	18.7%	81.3%
19,011	MERCER	4,906	1,550	3,356		1,806 D	31.6%	68.4%	31.6%	68.4%
9,484	METCALFE	2,504	617	1,887		1,270 D	24.6%	75.4%	24.6%	75.4%
12,353	MONROE	2,225	990	1,235		245 D	44.5%	55.5%	44.5%	55.5%
20,046	MONTGOMERY	4,743	1,383	3,360		1,977 D	29.2%	70.8%	29.2%	70.8%
12,103	MORGAN	3,466	666	2,800		2,134 D	19.2%	80.8%	19.2%	80.8%
32,238	MUHLENBERG	7,506	1,852	5,654		3,802 D	24.7%	75.3%	24.7%	75.3%
27,584	NELSON	5,892	1,553	4,339		2,786 D	26.4%	73.6%	26.4%	73.6%
7,157	NICHOLAS	1,685	457	1,228		771 D	27.1%	72.9%	27.1%	72.9%
21,765	OHIO	6,153	2,306	3,847		1,541 D	37.5%	62.5%	37.5%	62.5%
27,795	OLDHAM	6,298	3,382	2,916		466 R	53.7%	46.3%	53.7%	46.3%
8,924	OWEN	2,123	493	1,630		1,137 D	23.2%	76.8%	23.2%	76.8%
5,709	OWSLEY	1,275	338	937		599 D	26.5%	73.5%	26.5%	73.5%
10,989	PENDLETON	2,487	725	1,762		1,037 D	29.2%	70.8%	29.2%	70.8%
33,763	PERRY	5,468	1,574	3,894		2,320 D	28.8%	71.2%	28.8%	71.2%
81,123	PIKE	12,148	3,556	8,592		5,036 D	29.3%	70.7%	29.3%	70.7%
11,101	POWELL	2,913	723	2,190		1,467 D	24.8%	75.2%	24.8%	75.2%
45,803	PULASKI	9,951	3,989	5,962		1,973 D	40.1%	59.9%	40.1%	59.9%
2,265	ROBERTSON	669	199	470		271 D	29.7%	70.3%	29.7%	70.3%
13,973	ROCKCASTLE	2,806	1,443	1,363		80 R	51.4%	48.6%	51.4%	48.6%
19,049	ROWAN	3,474	1,182	2,292		1,110 D	34.0%	66.0%	34.0%	66.0%
13,708	RUSSELL	3,516	1,039	2,477		1,438 D	29.6%	70.4%	29.6%	70.4%
21,813	SCOTT	5,022	1,955	3,067		1,112 D	38.9%	61.1%	38.9%	61.1%
23,328	SHELBY	5,505	1,940	3,565		1,625 D	35.2%	64.8%	35.2%	64.8%
14,673	SIMPSON	2,757	586	2,171		1,585 D	21.3%	78.7%	21.3%	78.7%
5,929	SPENCER	1,448	462	986		524 D	31.9%	68.1%	31.9%	68.1%
21,178	TAYLOR	5,001	1,533	3,468		1,935 D	30.7%	69.3%	30.7%	69.3%
11,874	TODD	1,737	373	1,364		991 D	21.5%	78.5%	21.5%	78.5%
9,384	TRIGG	2,864	557	2,307		1,750 D	19.4%	80.6%	19.4%	80.6%
6,253	TRIMBLE	1,405	375	1,030		655 D	26.7%	73.3%	26.7%	73.3%
17,821	UNION	3,238	504	2,734		2,230 D	15.6%	84.4%	15.6%	84.4%
71,828	WARREN	16,559	5,151	11,408		6,257 D	31.1%	68.9%	31.1%	68.9%
10,764	WASHINGTON	3,603	1,134	2,469		1,335 D	31.5%	68.5%	31.5%	68.5%
17,022	WAYNE	5,102	2,325	2,777		452 D	45.6%	54.4%	45.6%	54.4%
14,832	WEBSTER	3,453	704	2,749		2,045 D	20.4%	79.6%	20.4%	79.6%
33,396	WHITLEY	6,236	2,873	3,363		490 D	46.1%	53.9%	46.1%	53.9%
6,698	WOLFE	1,585	272	1,313		1,041 D	17.2%	82.8%	17.2%	82.8%
17,778	WOODFORD	4,646	1,857	2,789		932 D	40.0%	60.0%	40.0%	60.0%
3,660,777	TOTAL	777,815	273,141	504,674		231,533 D	35.1%	64.9%	35.1%	64.9%

KENTUCKY

CONGRESS

CD	Year	Total Vote	Republican Vote	Republican Candidate	Democratic Vote	Democratic Candidate	Other Vote	Rep.-Dem. Plurality	Percentage Total Vote Rep.	Percentage Total Vote Dem.	Percentage Major Vote Rep.	Percentage Major Vote Dem.
1	1988	123,410			117,288	HUBBARD, CARROLL	6,122	117,288 D		95.0%		100.0%
1	1986	64,332			64,315	HUBBARD, CARROLL	17	64,315 D		100.0%		100.0%
1	1984	112,180			112,180	HUBBARD, CARROLL		112,180 D		100.0%		100.0%
1	1982	48,356			48,342	HUBBARD, CARROLL	14	48,342 D		100.0%		100.0%
2	1988	152,099	59,907	TORI, MARTIN A.	92,184	NATCHER, WILLIAM H.	8	32,277 D	39.4%	60.6%	39.4%	60.6%
2	1986	57,652			57,644	NATCHER, WILLIAM H.	8	57,644 D		100.0%		100.0%
2	1984	149,742	56,700	MORRISON, TIMOTHY A.	93,042	NATCHER, WILLIAM H.		36,342 D	37.9%	62.1%	37.9%	62.1%
2	1982	67,143	17,561	WATSON, MARK T.	49,571	NATCHER, WILLIAM H.	11	32,010 D	26.2%	73.8%	26.2%	73.8%
3	1988	189,368	57,387	DUNNAGAN, PHILIP	131,981	MAZZOLI, ROMANO L.		74,594 D	30.3%	69.7%	30.3%	69.7%
3	1986	112,233	29,348	HOLMES, LEE	81,943	MAZZOLI, ROMANO L.	942	52,595 D	26.1%	73.0%	26.4%	73.6%
3	1984	215,138	68,185	WARNER, SUZANNE M.	145,680	MAZZOLI, ROMANO L.	1,273	77,495 D	31.7%	67.7%	31.9%	68.1%
3	1982	142,597	45,900	BROWN, CARL	92,849	MAZZOLI, ROMANO L.	3,848	46,949 D	32.2%	65.1%	33.1%	66.9%
4	1988	196,184	145,609	BUNNING, JIM	50,575	BELILES, RICHARD V.		95,034 R	74.2%	25.8%	74.2%	25.8%
4	1986	122,763	67,626	BUNNING, JIM	53,906	MANN, TERRY L.	1,231	13,720 R	55.1%	43.9%	55.6%	44.4%
4	1984	202,038	108,398	SNYDER, M. G.	93,640	MULLOY, WILLIAM P.		14,758 R	53.7%	46.3%	53.7%	46.3%
4	1982	136,750	74,109	SNYDER, M. G.	61,937	MANN, TERRY L.	704	12,172 R	54.2%	45.3%	54.5%	45.5%
5	1988	104,501	104,467	ROGERS, HAROLD			34	104,467 R	100.0%		100.0%	
5	1986	56,764	56,760	ROGERS, HAROLD			4	56,760 R	100.0%		100.0%	
5	1984	164,947	125,164	ROGERS, HAROLD	39,783	MCINTOSH, SHERMAN W.		85,381 R	75.9%	24.1%	75.9%	24.1%
5	1982	81,217	52,928	ROGERS, HAROLD	28,285	DAVENPORT, DOYE	4	24,643 R	65.2%	34.8%	65.2%	34.8%
6	1988	174,277	128,898	HOPKINS, LARRY J.	45,339	PATTON, MILTON	40	83,559 R	74.0%	26.0%	74.0%	26.0%
6	1986	102,224	75,906	HOPKINS, LARRY J.	26,315	HAMMOND, JERRY	3	49,591 R	74.3%	25.7%	74.3%	25.7%
6	1984	177,108	126,525	HOPKINS, LARRY J.	49,657	HAMMOND, JERRY	926	76,868 R	71.4%	28.0%	71.8%	28.2%
6	1982	120,360	68,418	HOPKINS, LARRY J.	49,839	MILLS, DON	2,103	18,579 R	56.8%	41.4%	57.9%	42.1%
7	1988	165,112	68,165	SCOTT, WILLIAM T.	96,946	PERKINS, CARL C.	1	28,781 D	41.3%	58.7%	41.3%	58.7%
7	1986	113,828	23,209	POLLEY, JAMES T.	90,619	PERKINS, CARL C.		67,410 D	20.4%	79.6%	20.4%	79.6%
7	1984	166,569	43,890	RUSSELL, AUBREY	122,679	PERKINS, CARL C.		78,789 D	26.3%	73.7%	26.3%	73.7%
7	1982	103,899	21,436	HAMBY, TOM	82,463	PERKINS, CARL D.		61,027 D	20.6%	79.4%	20.6%	79.4%

KENTUCKY

1987 GENERAL ELECTION

Governor

1988 GENERAL ELECTION

President Other vote was 4,494 Populist (Duke); 2,118 Libertarian (Paul); 1,256 New Alliance (Fulani).

Congress Other vote was 6,106 Independent (Hatchett) and 16 scattered in CD 1; scattered in CD's 2, 5, 6 and 7.

1987 PRIMARIES

MAY 26 REPUBLICAN

Governor 37,432 John Harper; 22,396 Joseph E. Johnson; 21,067 Leonard W. Beasley; 9,475 Thurman J. Hamlin.

MAY 26 DEMOCRATIC

Governor 221,138 Wallace G. Wilkinson; 163,204 John Y. Brown, Jr.; 114,439 Steven L. Beshear; 84,613 Grady Stumbo; 42,137 Julian M. Carroll; 3,788 Stanley Luttrell; 2,638 Dinwiddie Lampton; 1,761 Anne Moore.

1988 PRIMARIES

MAY 24 REPUBLICAN

Congress Unopposed in five CD's. No candidate in CD 1. Contested as follows:

CD 3 3,673 Philip Dunnagan; 1,696 Tommy Klein; 839 Lee Holmes; 831 Herschel Wooldridge.

MAY 24 DEMOCRATIC

Congress Unopposed in three CD's. No candidate in CD 5. Contested as follows:

CD 1 63,136 Carroll Hubbard; 23,153 Lacey T. Smith.
CD 2 26,918 William H. Natcher; 8,324 Bob Evans.
CD 3 31,288 Romano L. Mazzoli; 20,207 Jeffrey Hutter.

LOUISIANA

GOVERNOR

Charles Roemer (D). Elected October 1987 to a four-year term.

SENATORS

John B. Breaux (D). Elected 1986 to a six-year term.

J. Bennett Johnston (D). Re-elected 1984 to a six-year term. Previously elected 1978, 1972.

REPRESENTATIVES

1. Bob Livingston (R)
2. Lindy Boggs (D)
3. W. J.Tauzin (D)
4. Jim McCrery (R)
5. Jerry Huckaby (D)
6. Richard H. Baker (R)
7. James A. Hayes (D)
8. Clyde C. Holloway (R)

POSTWAR VOTE FOR PRESIDENT

		Republican		Democratic					Percentage		
								Total Vote		Major Vote	
Year	Total Vote	Vote	Candidate	Vote	Candidate	Other Vote	Plurality	Rep.	Dem.	Rep.	Dem.
1988	1,628,202	883,702	Bush, George	717,460	Dukakis, Michael S.	27,040	166,242 R	54.3%	44.1%	55.2%	44.8%
1984	1,706,822	1,037,299	Reagan, Ronald	651,586	Mondale, Walter F.	17,937	385,713 R	60.8%	38.2%	61.4%	38.6%
1980	1,548,591	792,853	Reagan, Ronald	708,453	Carter, Jimmy	47,285	84,400 R	51.2%	45.7%	52.8%	47.2%
1976	1,278,439	587,446	Ford, Gerald R.	661,365	Carter, Jimmy	29,628	73,919 D	46.0%	51.7%	47.0%	53.0%
1972	1,051,491	686,852	Nixon, Richard M.	298,142	McGovern, George S.	66,497	388,710 R	65.3%	28.4%	69.7%	30.3%
1968 * *	1,097,450	257,535	Nixon, Richard M.	309,615	Humphrey, Hubert H.	530,300	220,685 A	23.5%	28.2%	45.4%	54.6%
1964	896,293	509,225	Goldwater, Barry M.	387,068	Johnson, Lyndon B.		122,157 R	56.8%	43.2%	56.8%	43.2%
1960	807,891	230,980	Nixon, Richard M.	407,339	Kennedy, John F.	169,572	176,359 D	28.6%	50.4%	36.2%	63.8%
1956	617,544	329,047	Eisenhower, Dwight D.	243,977	Stevenson, Adlai E.	44,520	85,070 R	53.3%	39.5%	57.4%	42.6%
1952	651,952	306,925	Eisenhower, Dwight D.	345,027	Stevenson, Adlai E.		38,102 D	47.1%	52.9%	47.1%	52.9%
1948 * *	416,336	72,657	Dewey, Thomas E.	136,344	Truman, Harry S.	207,335	67,946 SR	17.5%	32.7%	34.8%	65.2%

In 1968 other vote was American (Wallace). In 1948 other vote was 204,290 States Rights; 3,035 Progressive and 10 scattered.

LOUISIANA

POSTWAR VOTE FOR GOVERNOR

Year	Total Vote	Republican Vote	Republican Candidate	Democratic Vote	Democratic Candidate	Other Vote	Rep.-Dem. Plurality	Percentage Total Vote Rep.	Percentage Total Vote Dem.	Percentage Major Vote Rep.	Percentage Major Vote Dem.
1987 * *					Roemer, Charles						
1983 * *					Edwards, Edwin W.						
1979	1,371,825	690,691	Treen, David C.	681,134	Lambert, Louis		9,557 R	50.3%	49.7%	50.3%	49.7%
1975	430,095		—	430,095	Edwards, Edwin W.		430,095 D		100.0%		100.0%
1972	1,121,570	480,424	Treen, David C.	641,146	Edwards, Edwin W.		160,722 D	42.8%	57.2%	42.8%	57.2%
1968	372,762		—	372,762	McKeithen, John J.		372,762 D		100.0%		100.0%
1964	773,390	297,753	Lyons, C. H.	469,589	McKeithen, John J.	6,048	171,836 D	38.5%	60.7%	38.8%	61.2%
1960	506,562	86,135	Grevemberg, F. C.	407,907	Davis, Jimmie H.	12,520	321,772 D	17.0%	80.5%	17.4%	82.6%
1956	172,291		—	172,291	Long, Earl K.		172,291 D		100.0%		100.0%
1952	123,681	4,958	Bagwell, Harrison G.	118,723	Kennon, Robert F.		113,765 D	4.0%	96.0%	4.0%	96.0%
1948	76,566		—	76,566	Long, Earl K.		76,566 D		100.0%		100.0%

For the 1987 and 1983 elections, no run-off general elections were required (see note section).

POSTWAR VOTE FOR SENATOR

Year	Total Vote	Republican Vote	Republican Candidate	Democratic Vote	Democratic Candidate	Other Vote	Rep.-Dem. Plurality	Percentage Total Vote Rep.	Percentage Total Vote Dem.	Percentage Major Vote Rep.	Percentage Major Vote Dem.
1986	1,369,897	646,311	Moore, W. Henson	723,586	Breaux, John B.		77,275 D	47.2%	52.8%	47.2%	52.8%
1984 * *					Johnston, J. Bennett						
1980 * *					Long, Russell B.						
1978 * *					Johnston, J. Bennett						
1974	434,643		—	434,643	Long, Russell B.		434,643 D		100.0%		100.0%
1972	1,084,904	206,846	Toledano, Ben C.	598,987	Johnston, J. Bennett	279,071	392,141 D	19.1%	55.2%	25.7%	74.3%
1968	518,586		—	518,586	Long, Russell B.		518,586 D		100.0%		100.0%
1966	437,695		—	437,695	Ellender, Allen J.		437,695 D		100.0%		100.0%
1962	421,904	103,066	O'Hearn, Taylor W.	318,838	Long, Russell B.		215,772 D	24.4%	75.6%	24.4%	75.6%
1960	541,928	109,698	Reese, George W.	432,228	Ellender, Allen J.	2	322,530 D	20.2%	79.8%	20.2%	79.8%
1956	335,564		—	335,564	Long, Russell B.		335,564 D		100.0%		100.0%
1954	207,115		—	207,115	Ellender, Allen J.		207,115 D		100.0%		100.0%
1950	251,838	30,931	Gerth, Charles S.	220,907	Long, Russell B.		189,976 D	12.3%	87.7%	12.3%	87.7%
1948	330,124		—	330,115	Ellender, Allen J.	9	330,115 D		100.0%		100.0%
1948 S	408,667	102,331	Clarke, Clem S.	306,336	Long, Russell B.		204,005 D	25.0%	75.0%	25.0%	75.0%

One of the 1948 elections was for a short term to fill a vacancy. For the 1978, 1980 and 1984 elections, no run-off general elections were required (see note section).

LOUISIANA

Districts Established December 19, 1983

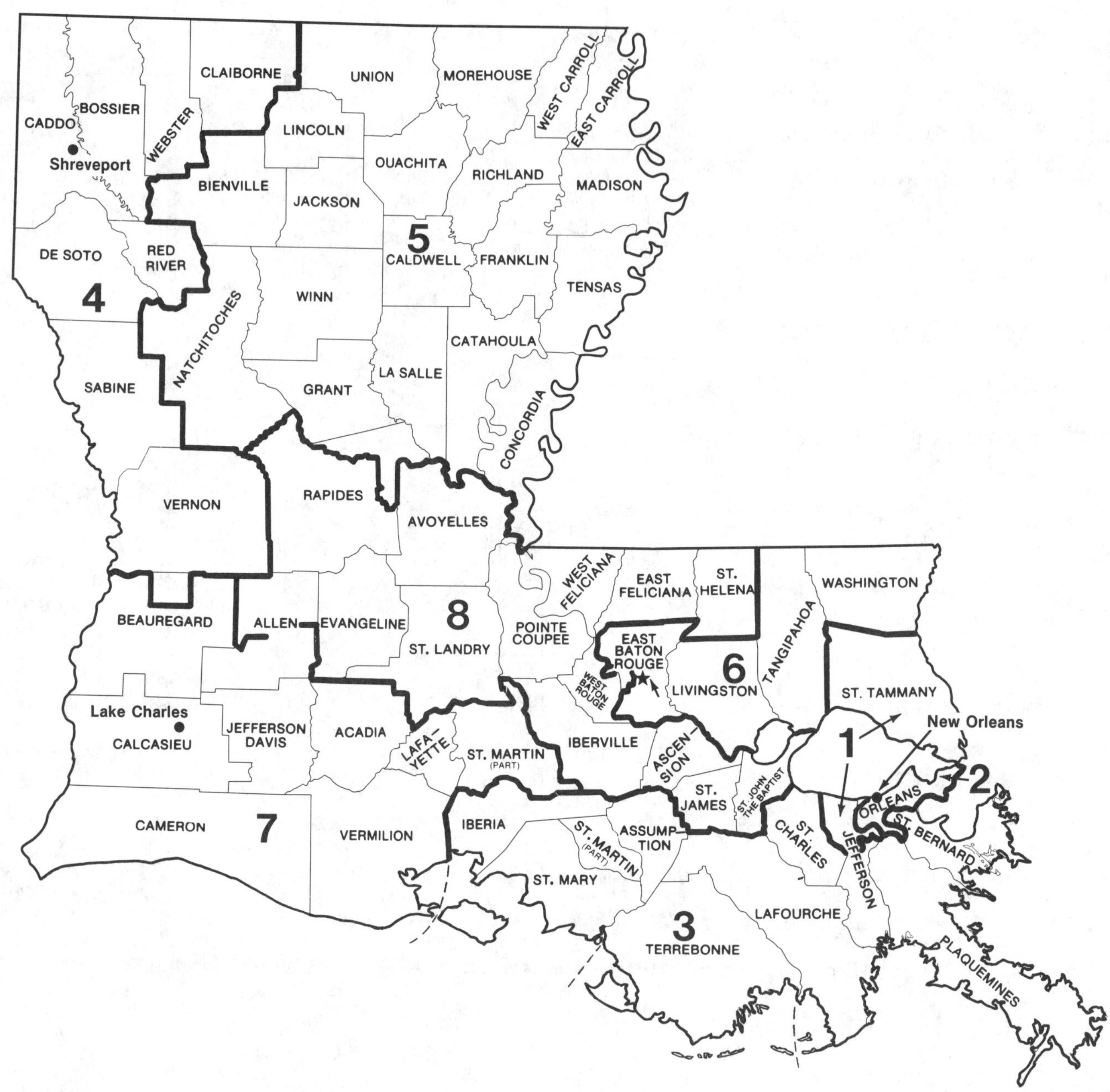

LOUISIANA

PRESIDENT 1988

1980 Census Population	Parish	Total Vote	Republican	Democratic	Other	Rep.-Dem. Plurality	Percentage Total Vote Rep.	Percentage Total Vote Dem.	Percentage Major Vote Rep.	Percentage Major Vote Dem.
56,427	ACADIA	23,110	11,319	11,510	281	191 D	49.0%	49.8%	49.6%	50.4%
21,390	ALLEN	8,989	3,674	5,204	111	1,530 D	40.9%	57.9%	41.4%	58.6%
50,068	ASCENSION	23,240	10,726	12,147	367	1,421 D	46.2%	52.3%	46.9%	53.1%
22,084	ASSUMPTION	9,995	4,017	5,610	368	1,593 D	40.2%	56.1%	41.7%	58.3%
41,393	AVOYELLES	15,600	7,659	7,353	588	306 R	49.1%	47.1%	51.0%	49.0%
29,692	BEAUREGARD	11,284	6,466	4,704	114	1,762 R	57.3%	41.7%	57.9%	42.1%
16,387	BIENVILLE	7,537	3,680	3,705	152	25 D	48.8%	49.2%	49.8%	50.2%
80,721	BOSSIER	30,085	20,807	9,035	243	11,772 R	69.2%	30.0%	69.7%	30.3%
252,358	CADDO	94,402	54,498	39,204	700	15,294 R	57.7%	41.5%	58.2%	41.8%
167,223	CALCASIEU	64,100	29,649	33,932	519	4,283 D	46.3%	52.9%	46.6%	53.4%
10,761	CALDWELL	4,559	2,997	1,423	139	1,574 R	65.7%	31.2%	67.8%	32.2%
9,336	CAMERON	4,070	1,775	2,257	38	482 D	43.6%	55.5%	44.0%	56.0%
12,287	CATAHOULA	4,950	2,862	1,916	172	946 R	57.8%	38.7%	59.9%	40.1%
17,095	CLAIBORNE	7,007	3,756	3,158	93	598 R	53.6%	45.1%	54.3%	45.7%
22,981	CONCORDIA	8,761	5,037	3,461	263	1,576 R	57.5%	39.5%	59.3%	40.7%
25,727	DE SOTO	10,516	5,022	5,366	128	344 D	47.8%	51.0%	48.3%	51.7%
366,191	EAST BATON ROUGE	147,584	86,791	59,270	1,523	27,521 R	58.8%	40.2%	59.4%	40.6%
11,772	EAST CARROLL	3,460	1,536	1,809	115	273 D	44.4%	52.3%	45.9%	54.1%
19,015	EAST FELICIANA	7,349	3,527	3,659	163	132 D	48.0%	49.8%	49.1%	50.9%
33,343	EVANGELINE	15,400	7,437	7,693	270	256 D	48.3%	50.0%	49.2%	50.8%
24,141	FRANKLIN	8,876	5,520	3,043	313	2,477 R	62.2%	34.3%	64.5%	35.5%
16,703	GRANT	7,245	4,402	2,628	215	1,774 R	60.8%	36.3%	62.6%	37.4%
63,752	IBERIA	28,331	15,438	12,166	727	3,272 R	54.5%	42.9%	55.9%	44.1%
32,159	IBERVILLE	14,836	5,855	8,678	303	2,823 D	39.5%	58.5%	40.3%	59.7%
17,321	JACKSON	7,249	4,251	2,842	156	1,409 R	58.6%	39.2%	59.9%	40.1%
454,592	JEFFERSON	166,370	110,942	53,035	2,393	57,907 R	66.7%	31.9%	67.7%	32.3%
32,168	JEFFERSON DAVIS	12,791	5,851	6,799	141	948 D	45.7%	53.2%	46.3%	53.7%
150,017	LAFAYETTE	61,658	36,648	24,133	877	12,515 R	59.4%	39.1%	60.3%	39.7%
82,483	LAFOURCHE	32,179	16,152	15,013	1,014	1,139 R	50.2%	46.7%	51.8%	48.2%
17,004	LA SALLE	6,359	4,559	1,622	178	2,937 R	71.7%	25.5%	73.8%	26.2%
39,763	LINCOLN	14,657	8,853	5,427	377	3,426 R	60.4%	37.0%	62.0%	38.0%
58,806	LIVINGSTON	25,743	15,779	9,659	305	6,120 R	61.3%	37.5%	62.0%	38.0%
15,975	MADISON	4,911	2,334	2,416	161	82 D	47.5%	49.2%	49.1%	50.9%
34,803	MOREHOUSE	12,140	7,335	4,496	309	2,839 R	60.4%	37.0%	62.0%	38.0%
39,863	NATCHITOCHES	13,733	7,224	6,151	358	1,073 R	52.6%	44.8%	54.0%	46.0%
557,515	ORLEANS	183,800	64,763	116,851	2,186	52,088 D	35.2%	63.6%	35.7%	64.3%
139,241	OUACHITA	50,292	33,858	15,429	1,005	18,429 R	67.3%	30.7%	68.7%	31.3%
26,049	PLAQUEMINES	10,293	6,084	3,997	212	2,087 R	59.1%	38.8%	60.4%	39.6%
24,045	POINTE COUPEE	10,930	4,333	6,308	289	1,975 D	39.6%	57.7%	40.7%	59.3%
135,282	RAPIDES	48,891	29,977	17,928	986	12,049 R	61.3%	36.7%	62.6%	37.4%
10,433	RED RIVER	4,586	2,266	2,254	66	12 R	49.4%	49.1%	50.1%	49.9%
22,187	RICHLAND	8,315	5,226	2,833	256	2,393 R	62.9%	34.1%	64.8%	35.2%
25,280	SABINE	8,541	4,767	3,532	242	1,235 R	55.8%	41.4%	57.4%	42.6%
64,097	ST. BERNARD	31,736	19,609	11,406	721	8,203 R	61.8%	35.9%	63.2%	36.8%
37,259	ST. CHARLES	17,995	9,685	7,973	337	1,712 R	53.8%	44.3%	54.8%	45.2%
9,827	ST. HELENA	5,153	2,006	3,013	134	1,007 D	38.9%	58.5%	40.0%	60.0%
21,495	ST. JAMES	10,719	3,799	6,707	213	2,908 D	35.4%	62.6%	36.2%	63.8%
31,924	ST. JOHN THE BAPTIST	16,219	7,464	8,366	389	902 D	46.0%	51.6%	47.2%	52.8%
84,128	ST. LANDRY	35,457	15,790	19,091	576	3,301 D	44.5%	53.8%	45.3%	54.7%
40,214	ST. MARTIN	18,129	7,541	10,148	440	2,607 D	41.6%	56.0%	42.6%	57.4%
64,253	ST. MARY	22,318	11,540	10,364	414	1,176 R	51.7%	46.4%	52.7%	47.3%
110,869	ST. TAMMANY	54,823	38,334	15,638	851	22,696 R	69.9%	28.5%	71.0%	29.0%
80,698	TANGIPAHOA	30,688	16,669	13,527	492	3,142 R	54.3%	44.1%	55.2%	44.8%
8,525	TENSAS	3,290	1,645	1,556	89	89 R	50.0%	47.3%	51.4%	48.6%
94,393	TERREBONNE	32,212	18,745	12,686	781	6,059 R	58.2%	39.4%	59.6%	40.4%
21,167	UNION	9,369	5,900	3,210	259	2,690 R	63.0%	34.3%	64.8%	35.2%
48,458	VERMILION	21,966	9,224	12,180	562	2,956 D	42.0%	55.4%	43.1%	56.9%
53,475	VERNON	12,761	7,453	4,998	310	2,455 R	58.4%	39.2%	59.9%	40.1%
44,207	WASHINGTON	18,094	9,374	8,369	351	1,005 R	51.8%	46.3%	52.8%	47.2%
43,631	WEBSTER	17,805	10,204	7,434	167	2,770 R	57.3%	41.8%	57.9%	42.1%

LOUISIANA

PRESIDENT 1988

1980 Census Population	Parish	Total Vote	Republican	Democratic	Other	Rep.-Dem. Plurality	Percentage Total Vote Rep.	Total Vote Dem.	Major Vote Rep.	Major Vote Dem.
19,086	WEST BATON ROUGE	8,801	3,972	4,686	143	714 D	45.1%	53.2%	45.9%	54.1%
12,922	WEST CARROLL	4,797	3,077	1,607	113	1,470 R	64.1%	33.5%	65.7%	34.3%
12,186	WEST FELICIANA	4,089	1,854	2,146	89	292 D	45.3%	52.5%	46.4%	53.7%
17,253	WINN	7,057	4,165	2,699	193	1,466 R	59.0%	38.2%	60.7%	39.3%
4,205,900	TOTAL	1,628,202	883,702	717,460	27,040	166,242 R	54.3%	44.1%	55.2%	44.8%

LOUISIANA

GOVERNOR 1987
(PRIMARY ELECTION)

1980 Census Population	Parish	Total Vote	Roemer	Edwards	Livingston	Tauzin	Other	Percentage of Total Vote CR	EWE	BL	WJT
56,427	ACADIA	26,417	7,607	8,650	3,197	4,268	2,695	28.8%	32.7%	12.1%	16.2%
21,390	ALLEN	9,652	3,334	2,948	1,312	858	1,200	34.5%	30.5%	13.6%	8.9%
50,068	ASCENSION	23,567	8,180	6,648	3,025	3,172	2,542	34.7%	28.2%	12.8%	13.5%
22,084	ASSUMPTION	11,043	2,067	3,456	832	3,822	866	18.7%	31.3%	7.5%	34.6%
41,393	AVOYELLES	17,509	5,900	5,336	1,994	1,609	2,670	33.7%	30.5%	11.4%	9.2%
29,692	BEAUREGARD	11,517	5,471	1,810	2,091	806	1,339	47.5%	15.7%	18.2%	7.0%
16,387	BIENVILLE	8,376	4,189	2,943	457	147	640	50.0%	35.1%	5.5%	1.8%
80,721	BOSSIER	28,144	21,551	3,999	1,499	387	708	76.6%	14.2%	5.3%	1.4%
252,358	CADDO	84,223	55,846	19,714	4,819	2,122	1,722	66.3%	23.4%	5.7%	2.5%
167,223	CALCASIEU	59,997	23,901	13,728	9,691	7,276	5,401	39.8%	22.9%	16.2%	12.1%
10,761	CALDWELL	5,347	1,932	976	1,038	158	1,243	36.1%	18.3%	19.4%	3.0%
9,336	CAMERON	5,081	1,778	1,505	484	776	538	35.0%	29.6%	9.5%	15.3%
12,287	CATAHOULA	6,149	2,129	1,527	753	220	1,520	34.6%	24.8%	12.2%	3.6%
17,095	CLAIBORNE	7,017	3,683	2,407	345	87	495	52.5%	34.3%	4.9%	1.2%
22,981	CONCORDIA	9,082	2,468	2,731	1,263	313	2,307	27.2%	30.1%	13.9%	3.4%
25,727	DE SOTO	10,968	6,036	3,812	355	161	604	55.0%	34.8%	3.2%	1.5%
366,191	EAST BATON ROUGE	132,857	54,089	31,322	27,058	8,445	11,943	40.7%	23.6%	20.4%	6.4%
11,772	EAST CARROLL	4,210	861	1,977	575	146	651	20.5%	47.0%	13.7%	3.5%
19,015	EAST FELICIANA	8,064	2,012	3,587	1,271	456	738	25.0%	44.5%	15.8%	5.7%
33,343	EVANGELINE	16,121	5,270	4,696	1,656	2,409	2,090	32.7%	29.1%	10.3%	14.9%
24,141	FRANKLIN	10,363	3,754	2,614	1,486	213	2,296	36.2%	25.2%	14.3%	2.1%
16,703	GRANT	7,799	3,328	1,610	1,369	264	1,228	42.7%	20.6%	17.6%	3.4%
63,752	IBERIA	27,351	7,676	5,891	4,586	6,675	2,523	28.1%	21.5%	16.8%	24.4%
32,159	IBERVILLE	16,738	4,272	6,972	1,440	2,240	1,814	25.5%	41.7%	8.6%	13.4%
17,321	JACKSON	7,869	3,395	2,189	1,180	178	927	43.1%	27.8%	15.0%	2.3%
454,592	JEFFERSON	141,326	30,066	33,642	49,351	10,886	17,381	21.3%	23.8%	34.9%	7.7%
32,168	JEFFERSON DAVIS	13,597	4,290	3,571	2,015	2,192	1,529	31.6%	26.3%	14.8%	16.1%
150,017	LAFAYETTE	56,245	18,150	13,038	10,552	8,372	6,133	32.3%	23.2%	18.8%	14.9%
82,483	LAFOURCHE	33,013	4,367	6,034	4,171	16,623	1,818	13.2%	18.3%	12.6%	50.4%
17,004	LA SALLE	7,581	3,540	1,037	1,132	169	1,703	46.7%	13.7%	14.9%	2.2%
39,763	LINCOLN	13,874	7,040	3,627	1,894	398	915	50.7%	26.1%	13.7%	2.9%
58,806	LIVINGSTON	29,520	11,418	7,802	5,107	1,926	3,267	38.7%	26.4%	17.3%	6.5%
15,975	MADISON	5,386	1,282	2,173	719	420	792	23.8%	40.3%	13.3%	7.8%
34,803	MOREHOUSE	11,819	3,813	2,841	2,561	514	2,090	32.3%	24.0%	21.7%	4.3%
39,863	NATCHITOCHES	14,880	7,106	4,613	1,425	611	1,125	47.8%	31.0%	9.6%	4.1%
557,515	ORLEANS	151,062	22,389	68,155	34,483	8,134	17,901	14.8%	45.1%	22.8%	5.4%
139,241	OUACHITA	46,681	17,383	10,144	11,753	1,771	5,630	37.2%	21.7%	25.2%	3.8%
26,049	PLAQUEMINES	10,017	1,752	3,538	2,303	1,019	1,405	17.5%	35.3%	23.0%	10.2%
24,045	POINTE COUPEE	11,173	3,199	4,626	1,177	1,130	1,041	28.6%	41.4%	10.5%	10.1%
135,282	RAPIDES	45,215	16,958	10,592	9,745	1,859	6,061	37.5%	23.4%	21.6%	4.1%
10,433	RED RIVER	5,362	3,106	1,641	200	157	258	57.9%	30.6%	3.7%	2.9%
22,187	RICHLAND	8,682	2,888	2,379	1,664	210	1,541	33.3%	27.4%	19.2%	2.4%
25,280	SABINE	9,776	6,599	1,892	634	175	476	67.5%	19.4%	6.5%	1.8%
64,097	ST. BERNARD	31,829	5,262	9,731	10,538	2,826	3,472	16.5%	30.6%	33.1%	8.9%
37,259	ST. CHARLES	17,164	3,439	4,828	3,331	3,759	1,807	20.0%	28.1%	19.4%	21.9%
9,827	ST. HELENA	6,141	1,645	2,839	636	330	691	26.8%	46.2%	10.4%	5.4%
21,495	ST. JAMES	11,477	2,031	4,676	873	2,676	1,221	17.7%	40.7%	7.6%	23.3%
31,924	ST. JOHN THE BAPTIST	16,030	3,397	6,011	2,518	1,860	2,244	21.2%	37.5%	15.7%	11.6%
84,128	ST. LANDRY	35,439	10,507	13,307	4,176	4,630	2,819	29.6%	37.5%	11.8%	13.1%
40,214	ST. MARTIN	19,769	3,916	7,031	2,517	3,746	2,559	19.8%	35.6%	12.7%	18.9%
64,253	ST. MARY	23,276	6,195	5,456	2,967	6,202	2,456	26.6%	23.4%	12.7%	26.6%
110,869	ST. TAMMANY	48,009	12,319	9,493	19,651	1,940	4,606	25.7%	19.8%	40.9%	4.0%
80,698	TANGIPAHOA	32,182	10,859	10,239	5,637	1,680	3,767	33.7%	31.8%	17.5%	5.2%
8,525	TENSAS	3,558	762	1,506	607	83	600	21.4%	42.3%	17.1%	2.3%
94,393	TERREBONNE	32,623	6,346	6,947	5,751	11,107	2,472	19.5%	21.3%	17.6%	34.0%
21,167	UNION	10,096	4,202	2,429	1,698	248	1,519	41.6%	24.1%	16.8%	2.5%
48,458	VERMILION	24,851	5,963	7,516	2,986	5,741	2,645	24.0%	30.2%	12.0%	23.1%
53,475	VERNON	13,865	7,557	2,721	1,666	497	1,424	54.5%	19.6%	12.0%	3.6%
44,207	WASHINGTON	18,520	5,704	5,827	3,061	1,057	2,871	30.8%	31.5%	16.5%	5.7%
43,631	WEBSTER	16,789	10,896	3,969	864	273	787	64.9%	23.6%	5.1%	1.6%

LOUISIANA

GOVERNOR 1987
(PRIMARY ELECTION)

1980 Census Population	Parish	Total Vote	Roemer	Edwards	Livingston	Tauzin	Other	Percentage of Total Vote CR	EWE	BL	WJT
19,086	WEST BATON ROUGE	8,533	2,630	3,269	949	877	808	30.8%	38.3%	11.1%	10.3%
12,922	WEST CARROLL	5,396	1,751	1,408	1,014	144	1,079	32.4%	26.1%	18.8%	2.7%
12,186	WEST FELICIANA	4,350	990	1,903	628	434	395	22.8%	43.7%	14.4%	10.0%
17,253	WINN	8,163	3,632	2,302	1,050	195	984	44.5%	28.2%	12.9%	2.4%
4,205,900	TOTAL	1,558,730	516,078	437,801	287,780	154,079	162,992	33.1%	28.1%	18.5%	9.9%

LOUISIANA

CONGRESS

CD	Year	Total Vote	Republican Vote	Republican Candidate	Democratic Vote	Democratic Candidate	Other Vote	Rep.-Dem. Plurality	Percentage Total Vote Rep.	Percentage Total Vote Dem.	Percentage Major Vote Rep.	Percentage Major Vote Dem.
1	1988			LIVINGSTON, BOB								
1	1986			LIVINGSTON, BOB								
1	1984			LIVINGSTON, BOB								
2	1988					BOGGS, LINDY						
2	1986					BOGGS, LINDY						
2	1984					BOGGS, LINDY						
3	1988					TAUZIN, W. J.						
3	1986					TAUZIN, W. J.						
3	1984					TAUZIN, W. J.						
4	1988			MCCRERY, JIM								
4	1986					ROEMER, CHARLES						
4	1984					ROEMER, CHARLES						
4	1982					ROEMER, CHARLES						
5	1988					HUCKABY, JERRY						
5	1986					HUCKABY, JERRY						
5	1984					HUCKABY, JERRY						
5	1982					HUCKABY, JERRY						
6	1988			BAKER, RICHARD H.								
6	1986			BAKER, RICHARD H.								
6	1984			MOORE, W. HENSON								
6	1982			MOORE, W. HENSON								
7	1988					HAYES, JAMES A.						
7	1986	191,498			191,498	HAYES AND LOWENTHAL		191,498 D		100.0%		100.0%
7	1984					BREAUX, JOHN B.						
7	1982					BREAUX, JOHN B.						
8	1988	204,805	116,241	HOLLOWAY, CLYDE C.	88,564	WILLIAMS, FAYE		27,677 R	56.8%	43.2%	56.8%	43.2%
8	1986	199,140	102,276	HOLLOWAY, CLYDE C.	96,864	WILLIAMS, FAYE		5,412 R	51.4%	48.6%	51.4%	48.6%
8	1984					LONG, GILLIS W.						
8	1982					LONG, GILLIS W.						

LOUISIANA

1987 GENERAL ELECTION

Governor Incumbent Governor Edwin W. Edwards withdrew after running second in the primary and no run-off general election was required. The data carried in the table for Governor 1987 are for the primary contest between the candidates listed below, with the vote by parish for the four top candidates and their percentage of the total vote. In the percentage section the following abbreviations are used: CR (Charles Roemer), EWE (Edwin W. Edwards), BL (Bob Livingston) and WJT (W. J. Tauzin).

1988 GENERAL ELECTION

President Other vote was 18,612 Populist (Duke); 4,115 Libertarian (Paul); 2,355 New Alliance (Fulani); 1,958 National Economic Recovery (LaRouche).

Congress See primary note section below. Since candidates who are unopposed in the primary or who receive a majority in the primary are elected unopposed, CD 8 was the only district to have candidate names on the ballot and votes canvassed.

PRIMARIES

Louisiana holds an open primary election with candidates from all parties running on the same ballot. Any candidate who receives a majority is elected. If no candidate receives 50 percent, there is a run-off election between the top two finishers, without regard to party affiliation, in November.

OCTOBER 24, 1987

Governor 516,078 Charles Roemer (D); 437,801 Edwin W. Edwards (D); 287,780 Bob Livingston (R); 154,079 W. J. Tauzin (D); 138,223 James H. Brown (D); 18,738 Speedy O. Long (D); 3,767 Earl J. Amedee (D); 2,264 Ken Lewis (D). Incumbent Governor Edwards withdrew after this primary and no run-off election was held in November.

OCTOBER 1, 1988

Congress Unopposed in two CD's. Contested as follows:

CD 1 67,679 Bob Livingston (R); 13,091 George Mustakas (D); 5,457 Eric Honig (D).
CD 2 63,762 Lindy Boggs (D); 7,505 Roger C. Johnson (R).
CD 3 72,110 W. J. Tauzin (D); 8,602 Millard Clement (D).
CD 4 72,228 Jim McCrery (R); 28,027 Adeline Roemer (D); 5,103 Robert Briggs (D).
CD 5 51,113 Jerry Huckaby (D); 14,343 Jack Wright (D); 6,403 Bradley T. Roark (R).
CD 8 58,831 Clyde C. Holloway (R); 46,088 Faye Williams (D); 14,814 Robert L. Freeman (D); 14,009 J. E. Jumonville (D); 1,205 John K. Snyder (D).

MAINE

GOVERNOR

John R. McKernan (R). Elected 1986 to a four-year term.

SENATORS

William S. Cohen (R). Re-elected 1984 to a six-year term. Previously elected 1978.

George J. Mitchell (D). Re-elected 1988 to a six-year term. Previously elected 1982. Appointed May 1980 to fill our the term vacated by the resignation of Senator Edmund S. Muskie to become Secretary of State.

REPRESENTATIVES

1. Joseph E. Brennan (D) 2. Olympia J. Snowe (R)

POSTWAR VOTE FOR PRESIDENT

									Percentage			
	Total	Republican		Democratic		Other			Total Vote		Major Vote	
Year	Vote	Vote	Candidate	Vote	Candidate	Vote	Plurality		Rep.	Dem.	Rep.	Dem.
1988	555,035	307,131	Bush, George	243,569	Dukakis, Michael S.	4,335	63,562	R	55.3%	43.9%	55.8%	44.2%
1984	553,144	336,500	Reagan, Ronald	214,515	Mondale, Walter F.	2,129	121,985	R	60.8%	38.8%	61.1%	38.9%
1980	523,011	238,522	Reagan, Ronald	220,974	Carter, Jimmy	63,515	17,548	R	45.6%	42.3%	51.9%	48.1%
1976	483,216	236,320	Ford, Gerald R.	232,279	Carter, Jimmy	14,617	4,041	R	48.9%	48.1%	50.4%	49.6%
1972	417,042	256,458	Nixon, Richard M.	160,584	McGovern, George S.		95,874	R	61.5%	38.5%	61.5%	38.5%
1968	392,936	169,254	Nixon, Richard M.	217,312	Humphrey, Hubert H.	6,370	48,058	D	43.1%	55.3%	43.8%	56.2%
1964	380,965	118,701	Goldwater, Barry M.	262,264	Johnson, Lyndon B.		143,563	D	31.2%	68.8%	31.2%	68.8%
1960	421,767	240,608	Nixon, Richard M.	181,159	Kennedy, John F.		59,449	R	57.0%	43.0%	57.0%	43.0%
1956	351,706	249,238	Eisenhower, Dwight D.	102,468	Stevenson, Adlai E.		146,770	R	70.9%	29.1%	70.9%	29.1%
1952	351,786	232,353	Eisenhower, Dwight D.	118,806	Stevenson, Adlai E.	627	113,547	R	66.0%	33.8%	66.2%	33.8%
1948	264,787	150,234	Dewey, Thomas E.	111,916	Truman, Harry S.	2,637	38,318	R	56.7%	42.3%	57.3%	42.7%

POSTWAR VOTE FOR GOVERNOR

									Percentage			
	Total	Republican		Democratic		Other	Rep.-Dem.		Total Vote		Major Vote	
Year	Vote	Vote	Candidate	Vote	Candidate	Vote	Plurality		Rep.	Dem.	Rep.	Dem.
1986 **	426,861	170,312	McKernan, John R.	128,744	Tierney, James	127,805	41,568	R	39.9%	30.2%	56.9%	43.1%
1982	460,295	172,949	Cragin, Charles L.	281,066	Brennan, Joseph E.	6,280	108,117	D	37.6%	61.1%	38.1%	61.9%
1978	370,258	126,862	Palmer, Linwood E.	176,493	Brennan, Joseph E.	66,903	49,631	D	34.3%	47.7%	41.8%	58.2%
1974 **	363,945	84,176	Erwin, James S.	132,219	Mitchell, George J.	147,550	48,043	D	23.1%	36.3%	38.9%	61.1%
1970	325,386	162,248	Erwin, James S.	163,138	Curtis, Kenneth M.		890	D	49.9%	50.1%	49.9%	50.1%
1966	323,838	151,802	Reed, John H.	172,036	Curtis, Kenneth M.		20,234	D	46.9%	53.1%	46.9%	53.1%
1962	292,725	146,604	Reed, John H.	146,121	Dolloff, Maynard C.		483	R	50.1%	49.9%	50.1%	49.9%
1960 S	417,315	219,768	Reed, John H.	197,547	Coffin, Frank M.		22,221	R	52.7%	47.3%	52.7%	47.3%
1958 **	280,295	134,572	Hildreth, Horace A.	145,723	Clauson, Clinton A.		11,151	D	48.0%	52.0%	48.0%	52.0%
1956	304,649	124,395	Trafton, Willis A.	180,254	Muskie, Edmund S.		55,859	D	40.8%	59.2%	40.8%	59.2%
1954	248,971	113,298	Cross, Burton M.	135,673	Muskie, Edmund S.		22,375	D	45.5%	54.5%	45.5%	54.5%
1952	248,441	128,532	Cross, Burton M.	82,538	Oliver, James C.	37,371	45,994	R	51.7%	33.2%	60.9%	39.1%
1950	241,177	145,823	Payne, Frederick G.	94,304	Grant, Earl S.	1,050	51,519	R	60.5%	39.1%	60.7%	39.3%
1948	222,500	145,956	Payne, Frederick G.	76,544	Lausier, Louis B.		69,412	R	65.6%	34.4%	65.6%	34.4%
1946	179,951	110,327	Hildreth, Horace A.	69,624	Clark, F. Davis		40,703	R	61.3%	38.7%	61.3%	38.7%

The term of office of Maine's Governor was increased from two to four years effective with the 1958 election. The 1960 election was for a short term to fill a vacancy. In 1974 James B. Longley, an Independent candidate, polled 142,464 votes (39.1% of the total vote) and won the election with a 10,245 plurality. In 1986 other vote was 64,317 Sherry F. Huber (Independent); 63,474 John E. Menario (Independent) and 14 scattered.

MAINE

POSTWAR VOTE FOR SENATOR

Year	Total Vote	Republican Vote	Republican Candidate	Democratic Vote	Democratic Candidate	Other Vote	Rep.-Dem. Plurality	Percentage Total Vote Rep.	Percentage Total Vote Dem.	Percentage Major Vote Rep.	Percentage Major Vote Dem.
1988	557,375	104,758	Wyman, Jasper S.	452,590	Mitchell, George J.	27	347,832 D	18.8%	81.2%	18.8%	81.2%
1984	551,406	404,414	Cohen, William S.	142,626	Mitchell, Elizabeth H.	4,366	261,788 R	73.3%	25.9%	73.9%	26.1%
1982	459,715	179,882	Emery, David F.	279,819	Mitchell, George J.	14	99,937 D	39.1%	60.9%	39.1%	60.9%
1978	375,172	212,294	Cohen, William S.	127,327	Hathaway, William D.	35,551	84,967 R	56.6%	33.9%	62.5%	37.5%
1976	486,254	193,489	Monks, Robert A. G.	292,704	Muskie, Edmund S.	61	99,215 D	39.8%	60.2%	39.8%	60.2%
1972	421,310	197,040	Smith, Margaret Chase	224,270	Hathaway, William D.		27,230 D	46.8%	53.2%	46.8%	53.2%
1970	323,860	123,906	Bishop, Neil S.	199,954	Muskie, Edmund S.		76,048 D	38.3%	61.7%	38.3%	61.7%
1966	319,535	188,291	Smith, Margaret Chase	131,136	Violette, Elmer H.	108	57,155 R	58.9%	41.0%	58.9%	41.1%
1964	380,551	127,040	McIntire, Clifford	253,511	Muskie, Edmund S.		126,471 D	33.4%	66.6%	33.4%	66.6%
1960	416,699	256,890	Smith, Margaret Chase	159,809	Cormier, Lucia M.		97,081 R	61.6%	38.4%	61.6%	38.4%
1958	284,226	111,522	Payne, Frederick G.	172,704	Muskie, Edmund S.		61,182 D	39.2%	60.8%	39.2%	60.8%
1954	246,605	144,530	Smith, Margaret Chase	102,075	Fullam, Paul A.		42,455 R	58.6%	41.4%	58.6%	41.4%
1952	237,164	139,205	Payne, Frederick G.	82,665	Dube, Roger P.	15,294	56,540 R	58.7%	34.9%	62.7%	37.3%
1948	223,256	159,182	Smith, Margaret Chase	64,074	Scolten, Adrian H.		95,108 R	71.3%	28.7%	71.3%	28.7%
1946	175,014	111,215	Brewster, Owen	63,799	MacDonald, Peter		47,416 R	63.5%	36.5%	63.5%	36.5%

MAINE

Districts Established March 28, 1983

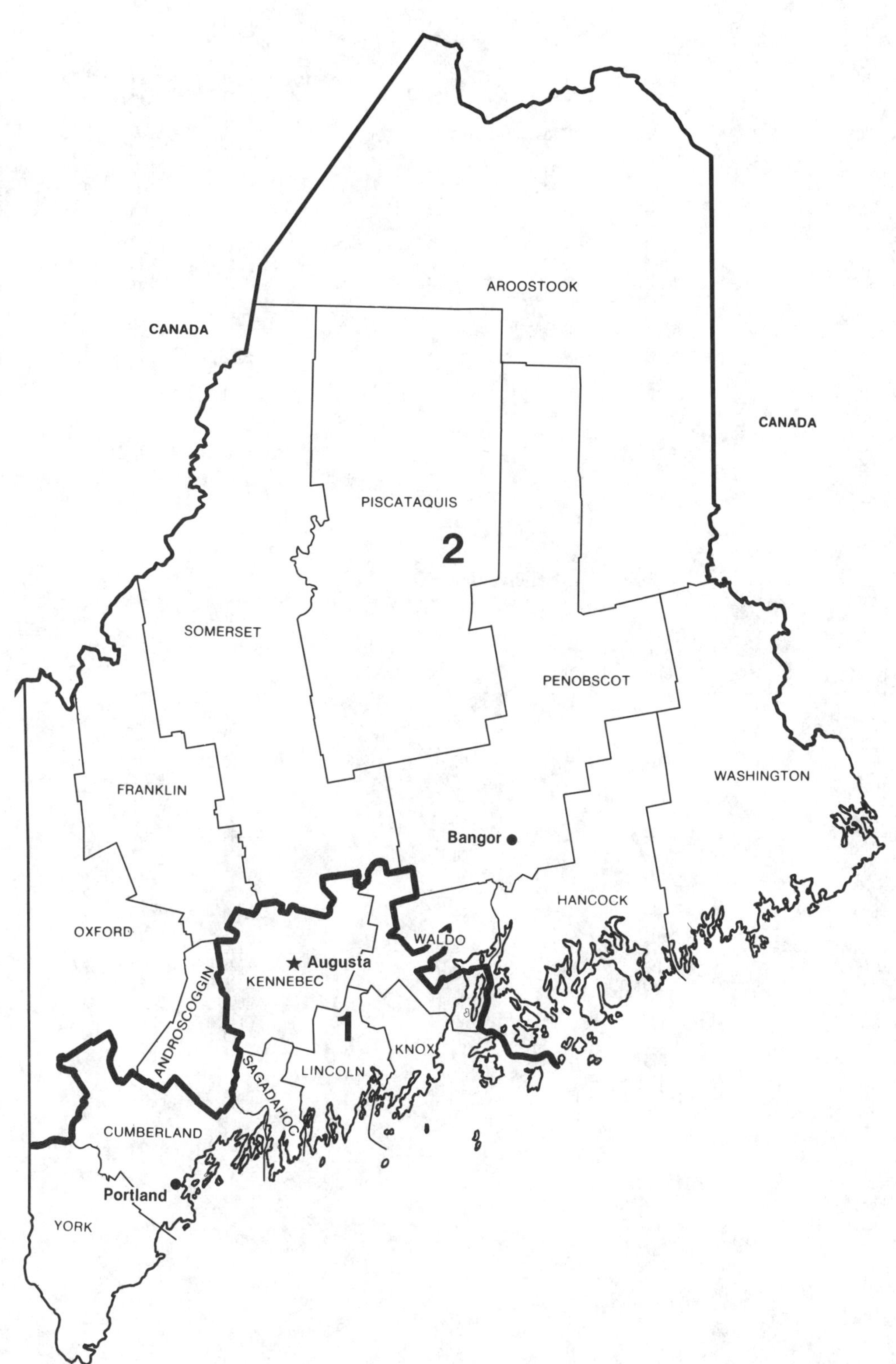

MAINE

PRESIDENT 1988

1980 Census Population	County	Total Vote	Republican	Democratic	Other	Rep.-Dem. Plurality	Percentage Total Vote Rep.	Total Vote Dem.	Major Vote Rep.	Major Vote Dem.
99,657	ANDROSCOGGIN	44,585	23,061	21,165	359	1,896 R	51.7%	47.5%	52.1%	47.9%
91,331	AROOSTOOK	32,246	17,213	14,850	183	2,363 R	53.4%	46.1%	53.7%	46.3%
215,789	CUMBERLAND	119,075	63,028	55,220	827	7,808 R	52.9%	46.4%	53.3%	46.7%
27,098	FRANKLIN	13,256	7,180	5,960	116	1,220 R	54.2%	45.0%	54.6%	45.4%
41,781	HANCOCK	23,107	12,957	9,929	221	3,028 R	56.1%	43.0%	56.6%	43.4%
109,889	KENNEBEC	51,745	27,734	23,578	433	4,156 R	53.6%	45.6%	54.0%	46.0%
32,941	KNOX	17,650	10,156	7,343	151	2,813 R	57.5%	41.6%	58.0%	42.0%
25,691	LINCOLN	15,920	9,837	5,939	144	3,898 R	61.8%	37.3%	62.4%	37.6%
48,968	OXFORD	24,266	13,568	10,523	175	3,045 R	55.9%	43.4%	56.3%	43.7%
137,015	PENOBSCOT	63,754	34,912	28,429	413	6,483 R	54.8%	44.6%	55.1%	44.9%
17,634	PISCATAQUIS	8,217	4,788	3,323	106	1,465 R	58.3%	40.4%	59.0%	41.0%
28,795	SAGADAHOC	15,158	8,825	6,212	121	2,613 R	58.2%	41.0%	58.7%	41.3%
45,028	SOMERSET	20,201	11,430	8,603	168	2,827 R	56.6%	42.6%	57.1%	42.9%
28,414	WALDO	14,778	8,236	6,402	140	1,834 R	55.7%	43.3%	56.3%	43.7%
34,963	WASHINGTON	13,828	7,872	5,831	125	2,041 R	56.9%	42.2%	57.4%	42.6%
139,666	YORK	77,249	46,334	30,262	653	16,072 R	60.0%	39.2%	60.5%	39.5%
1,124,660	TOTAL	555,035	307,131	243,569	4,335	63,562 R	55.3%	43.9%	55.8%	44.2%

MAINE

SENATOR 1988

1980 Census Population	County	Total Vote	Republican	Democratic	Other	Rep.-Dem. Plurality	Percentage Total Vote Rep.	Total Vote Dem.	Major Vote Rep.	Major Vote Dem.
99,657	ANDROSCOGGIN	45,581	7,512	38,068	1	30,556 D	16.5%	83.5%	16.5%	83.5%
91,331	AROOSTOOK	32,203	5,480	26,723		21,243 D	17.0%	83.0%	17.0%	83.0%
215,789	CUMBERLAND	119,733	19,122	100,610	1	81,488 D	16.0%	84.0%	16.0%	84.0%
27,098	FRANKLIN	13,343	2,756	10,587		7,831 D	20.7%	79.3%	20.7%	79.3%
41,781	HANCOCK	22,870	4,415	18,453	2	14,038 D	19.3%	80.7%	19.3%	80.7%
109,889	KENNEBEC	51,929	9,230	42,694	5	33,464 D	17.8%	82.2%	17.8%	82.2%
32,941	KNOX	17,708	3,647	14,061		10,414 D	20.6%	79.4%	20.6%	79.4%
25,691	LINCOLN	15,690	3,541	12,148	1	8,607 D	22.6%	77.4%	22.6%	77.4%
48,968	OXFORD	24,327	5,072	19,255		14,183 D	20.8%	79.2%	20.8%	79.2%
137,015	PENOBSCOT	63,953	10,993	52,953	7	41,960 D	17.2%	82.8%	17.2%	82.8%
17,634	PISCATAQUIS	8,273	1,739	6,534		4,795 D	21.0%	79.0%	21.0%	79.0%
28,795	SAGADAHOC	15,452	2,679	12,773		10,094 D	17.3%	82.7%	17.3%	82.7%
45,028	SOMERSET	20,460	4,622	15,837	1	11,215 D	22.6%	77.4%	22.6%	77.4%
28,414	WALDO	14,791	3,564	11,224	3	7,660 D	24.1%	75.9%	24.1%	75.9%
34,963	WASHINGTON	13,868	3,061	10,805	2	7,744 D	22.1%	77.9%	22.1%	77.9%
139,666	YORK	77,194	17,325	59,865	4	42,540 D	22.4%	77.6%	22.4%	77.6%
1,124,660	TOTAL	557,375	104,758	452,590	27	347,832 D	18.8%	81.2%	18.8%	81.2%

MAINE

PRESIDENT 1988

1980 Census Population	City/Town	Total Vote	Republican	Democratic	Other	Rep.-Dem. Plurality	Percentage Total Vote Rep.	Percentage Total Vote Dem.	Percentage Major Vote Rep.	Percentage Major Vote Dem.
23,128	AUBURN	10,657	5,947	4,629	81	1,318 R	55.8%	43.4%	56.2%	43.8%
21,819	AUGUSTA	9,862	5,182	4,576	104	606 R	52.5%	46.4%	53.1%	46.9%
31,643	BANGOR	13,812	7,194	6,534	84	660 R	52.1%	47.3%	52.4%	47.6%
10,246	BATH	4,421	2,543	1,838	40	705 R	57.5%	41.6%	58.0%	42.0%
6,243	BELFAST	2,784	1,588	1,171	25	417 R	57.0%	42.1%	57.6%	42.4%
19,638	BIDDEFORD	9,448	4,375	5,017	56	642 D	46.3%	53.1%	46.6%	53.4%
9,017	BREWER	4,716	2,908	1,784	24	1,124 R	61.7%	37.8%	62.0%	38.0%
17,366	BRUNSWICK	8,729	4,270	4,406	53	136 D	48.9%	50.5%	49.2%	50.8%
5,775	BUXTON	3,201	1,964	1,224	13	740 R	61.4%	38.2%	61.6%	38.4%
7,838	CAPE ELIZABETH	5,382	3,227	2,099	56	1,128 R	60.0%	39.0%	60.6%	39.4%
9,916	CARIBOU	3,400	1,968	1,415	17	553 R	57.9%	41.6%	58.2%	41.8%
5,284	CUMBERLAND TOWN	3,473	2,275	1,182	16	1,093 R	65.5%	34.0%	65.8%	34.2%
5,179	ELLSWORTH	2,775	1,818	936	21	882 R	65.5%	33.7%	66.0%	34.0%
6,113	FAIRFIELD	2,660	1,325	1,307	28	18 R	49.8%	49.1%	50.3%	49.7%
6,853	FALMOUTH	4,650	2,871	1,754	25	1,117 R	61.7%	37.7%	62.1%	37.9%
6,730	FARMINGTON	2,991	1,754	1,212	25	542 R	58.6%	40.5%	59.1%	40.9%
5,863	FREEPORT	3,686	2,049	1,600	37	449 R	55.6%	43.4%	56.2%	43.8%
6,485	GARDINER	3,029	1,609	1,395	25	214 R	53.1%	46.1%	53.6%	46.4%
10,101	GORHAM	5,629	3,405	2,178	46	1,227 R	60.5%	38.7%	61.0%	39.0%
5,250	HAMPDEN	3,102	1,885	1,209	8	676 R	60.8%	39.0%	60.9%	39.1%
6,766	HOULTON	2,701	1,796	886	19	910 R	66.5%	32.8%	67.0%	33.0%
5,080	JAY	2,395	784	1,593	18	809 D	32.7%	66.5%	33.0%	67.0%
6,621	KENNEBUNK	4,705	3,313	1,328	64	1,985 R	70.4%	28.2%	71.4%	28.6%
9,314	KITTERY	4,196	2,298	1,854	44	444 R	54.8%	44.2%	55.3%	44.7%
40,481	LEWISTON	16,644	7,265	9,225	154	1,960 D	43.6%	55.4%	44.1%	55.9%
8,719	LIMESTONE	933	559	367	7	192 R	59.9%	39.3%	60.4%	39.6%
5,066	LINCOLN TOWN	2,172	1,305	857	10	448 R	60.1%	39.5%	60.4%	39.6%
8,769	LISBON	3,722	2,200	1,491	31	709 R	59.1%	40.1%	59.6%	40.4%
5,282	MADAWASKA	1,961	512	1,440	9	928 D	26.1%	73.4%	26.2%	73.8%
7,567	MILLINOCKET	3,422	1,478	1,896	48	418 D	43.2%	55.4%	43.8%	56.2%
5,162	OAKLAND	2,212	1,232	973	7	259 R	55.7%	44.0%	55.9%	44.1%
6,291	OLD ORCHARD BEACH	3,970	2,144	1,794	32	350 R	54.0%	45.2%	54.4%	45.6%
8,422	OLD TOWN	3,890	1,640	2,220	30	580 D	42.2%	57.1%	42.5%	57.5%
10,578	ORONO	4,561	2,093	2,432	36	339 D	45.9%	53.3%	46.3%	53.7%
61,572	PORTLAND	30,110	11,676	18,234	200	6,558 D	38.8%	60.6%	39.0%	61.0%
11,172	PRESQUE ISLE	4,056	2,458	1,582	16	876 R	60.6%	39.0%	60.8%	39.2%
7,919	ROCKLAND	3,081	1,850	1,198	33	652 R	60.0%	38.9%	60.7%	39.3%
8,240	RUMFORD	3,545	1,300	2,216	29	916 D	36.7%	62.5%	37.0%	63.0%
12,921	SACO	7,053	3,852	3,169	32	683 R	54.6%	44.9%	54.9%	45.1%
18,020	SANFORD	8,068	4,541	3,456	71	1,085 R	56.3%	42.8%	56.8%	43.2%
11,347	SCARBOROUGH	6,536	4,095	2,397	44	1,698 R	62.7%	36.7%	63.1%	36.9%
8,098	SKOWHEGAN	3,442	1,836	1,579	27	257 R	53.3%	45.9%	53.8%	46.2%
22,712	SOUTH PORTLAND	11,642	5,744	5,820	78	76 D	49.3%	50.0%	49.7%	50.3%
5,946	STANDISH	3,311	2,056	1,216	39	840 R	62.1%	36.7%	62.8%	37.2%
6,431	TOPSHAM	3,625	2,115	1,495	15	620 R	58.3%	41.2%	58.6%	41.4%
17,779	WATERVILLE	7,257	3,158	4,031	68	873 D	43.5%	55.5%	43.9%	56.1%
8,211	WELLS	3,937	2,727	1,189	21	1,538 R	69.3%	30.2%	69.6%	30.4%
14,976	WESTBROOK	7,791	4,086	3,648	57	438 R	52.4%	46.8%	52.8%	47.2%
11,282	WINDHAM	5,816	3,579	2,216	21	1,363 R	61.5%	38.1%	61.8%	38.2%
8,057	WINSLOW	3,611	1,732	1,867	12	135 D	48.0%	51.7%	48.1%	51.9%
5,889	WINTHROP	1,951	1,135	800	16	335 R	58.2%	41.0%	58.7%	41.3%
6,585	YARMOUTH	4,494	2,649	1,825	20	824 R	58.9%	40.6%	59.2%	40.8%
8,465	YORK TOWN	5,734	3,637	2,029	68	1,608 R	63.4%	35.4%	64.2%	35.8%

MAINE

SENATOR 1988

1980 Census Population	City/Town	Total Vote	Republican	Democratic	Other	Rep.-Dem. Plurality	Percentage Total Vote Rep.	Total Vote Dem.	Major Vote Rep.	Major Vote Dem.
23,128	AUBURN	10,878	1,955	8,923		6,968 D	18.0%	82.0%	18.0%	82.0%
21,819	AUGUSTA	9,776	1,420	8,356		6,936 D	14.5%	85.5%	14.5%	85.5%
31,643	BANGOR	13,855	2,158	11,697		9,539 D	15.6%	84.4%	15.6%	84.4%
10,246	BATH	4,590	749	3,841		3,092 D	16.3%	83.7%	16.3%	83.7%
6,243	BELFAST	2,775	536	2,239		1,703 D	19.3%	80.7%	19.3%	80.7%
19,638	BIDDEFORD	9,295	1,016	8,279		7,263 D	10.9%	89.1%	10.9%	89.1%
9,017	BREWER	4,743	869	3,874		3,005 D	18.3%	81.7%	18.3%	81.7%
17,366	BRUNSWICK	8,800	1,551	7,249		5,698 D	17.6%	82.4%	17.6%	82.4%
5,775	BUXTON	3,236	663	2,573		1,910 D	20.5%	79.5%	20.5%	79.5%
7,838	CAPE ELIZABETH	5,366	977	4,388	1	3,411 D	18.2%	81.8%	18.2%	81.8%
9,916	CARIBOU	3,352	609	2,743		2,134 D	18.2%	81.8%	18.2%	81.8%
5,284	CUMBERLAND TOWN	3,491	712	2,779		2,067 D	20.4%	79.6%	20.4%	79.6%
5,179	ELLSWORTH	2,519	403	2,116		1,713 D	16.0%	84.0%	16.0%	84.0%
6,113	FAIRFIELD	2,715	525	2,190		1,665 D	19.3%	80.7%	19.3%	80.7%
6,853	FALMOUTH	4,654	921	3,733		2,812 D	19.8%	80.2%	19.8%	80.2%
6,730	FARMINGTON	2,980	684	2,296		1,612 D	23.0%	77.0%	23.0%	77.0%
5,863	FREEPORT	3,730	620	3,110		2,490 D	16.6%	83.4%	16.6%	83.4%
6,485	GARDINER	3,020	472	2,546	2	2,074 D	15.6%	84.3%	15.6%	84.4%
10,101	GORHAM	5,689	1,042	4,647		3,605 D	18.3%	81.7%	18.3%	81.7%
5,250	HAMPDEN	3,109	492	2,617		2,125 D	15.8%	84.2%	15.8%	84.2%
6,766	HOULTON	2,692	623	2,069		1,446 D	23.1%	76.9%	23.1%	76.9%
5,080	JAY	2,507	276	2,231		1,955 D	11.0%	89.0%	11.0%	89.0%
6,621	KENNEBUNK	4,709	1,295	3,410	4	2,115 D	27.5%	72.4%	27.5%	72.5%
9,314	KITTERY	4,150	1,206	2,944		1,738 D	29.1%	70.9%	29.1%	70.9%
40,481	LEWISTON	17,341	2,192	15,148	1	12,956 D	12.6%	87.4%	12.6%	87.4%
8,719	LIMESTONE	936	149	787		638 D	15.9%	84.1%	15.9%	84.1%
5,066	LINCOLN TOWN	2,207	448	1,759		1,311 D	20.3%	79.7%	20.3%	79.7%
8,769	LISBON	3,736	767	2,969		2,202 D	20.5%	79.5%	20.5%	79.5%
5,282	MADAWASKA	1,979	138	1,841		1,703 D	7.0%	93.0%	7.0%	93.0%
7,567	MILLINOCKET	3,494	463	3,028	3	2,565 D	13.3%	86.7%	13.3%	86.7%
5,162	OAKLAND	2,282	439	1,843		1,404 D	19.2%	80.8%	19.2%	80.8%
6,291	OLD ORCHARD BEACH	3,960	670	3,290		2,620 D	16.9%	83.1%	16.9%	83.1%
8,422	OLD TOWN	3,916	500	3,416		2,916 D	12.8%	87.2%	12.8%	87.2%
10,578	ORONO	4,503	546	3,957		3,411 D	12.1%	87.9%	12.1%	87.9%
61,572	PORTLAND	30,534	3,404	27,130		23,726 D	11.1%	88.9%	11.1%	88.9%
11,172	PRESQUE ISLE	3,958	609	3,349		2,740 D	15.4%	84.6%	15.4%	84.6%
7,919	ROCKLAND	3,063	614	2,449		1,835 D	20.0%	80.0%	20.0%	80.0%
8,240	RUMFORD	3,549	484	3,065		2,581 D	13.6%	86.4%	13.6%	86.4%
12,921	SACO	7,259	1,032	6,227		5,195 D	14.2%	85.8%	14.2%	85.8%
18,020	SANFORD	8,088	1,350	6,738		5,388 D	16.7%	83.3%	16.7%	83.3%
11,347	SCARBOROUGH	6,542	1,227	5,315		4,088 D	18.8%	81.2%	18.8%	81.2%
8,098	SKOWHEGAN	3,578	804	2,774		1,970 D	22.5%	77.5%	22.5%	77.5%
22,712	SOUTH PORTLAND	11,613	1,468	10,145		8,677 D	12.6%	87.4%	12.6%	87.4%
5,946	STANDISH	3,320	591	2,729		2,138 D	17.8%	82.2%	17.8%	82.2%
6,431	TOPSHAM	3,692	643	3,049		2,406 D	17.4%	82.6%	17.4%	82.6%
17,779	WATERVILLE	7,270	1,124	6,146		5,022 D	15.5%	84.5%	15.5%	84.5%
8,211	WELLS	3,957	1,058	2,899		1,841 D	26.7%	73.3%	26.7%	73.3%
14,976	WESTBROOK	7,674	1,124	6,550		5,426 D	14.6%	85.4%	14.6%	85.4%
11,282	WINDHAM	5,834	1,111	4,723		3,612 D	19.0%	81.0%	19.0%	81.0%
8,057	WINSLOW	3,737	598	3,139		2,541 D	16.0%	84.0%	16.0%	84.0%
5,889	WINTHROP	1,946	372	1,574		1,202 D	19.1%	80.9%	19.1%	80.9%
6,585	YARMOUTH	4,523	750	3,773		3,023 D	16.6%	83.4%	16.6%	83.4%
8,465	YORK TOWN	5,692	1,834	3,858		2,024 D	32.2%	67.8%	32.2%	67.8%

MAINE

CONGRESS

CD	Year	Total Vote	Republican Vote	Republican Candidate	Democratic Vote	Democratic Candidate	Other Vote	Rep.-Dem. Plurality	Percentage Total Vote Rep.	Percentage Total Vote Dem.	Percentage Major Vote Rep.	Percentage Major Vote Dem.
1	1988	302,163	111,125	O'MEARA, EDWARD S.	190,989	BRENNAN, JOSEPH E.	49	79,864 D	36.8%	63.2%	36.8%	63.2%
1	1986	229,233	100,260	IVES, H. ROLLIN	121,848	BRENNAN, JOSEPH E.	7,125	21,588 D	43.7%	53.2%	45.1%	54.9%
1	1984	287,765	182,785	MCKERNAN, JOHN R.	104,972	HOBBINS, BARRY J.	8	77,813 R	63.5%	36.5%	63.5%	36.5%
2	1988	252,721	167,226	SNOWE, OLYMPIA J.	85,346	HAYES, KENNETH P.	149	81,880 R	66.2%	33.8%	66.2%	33.8%
2	1986	192,397	148,770	SNOWE, OLYMPIA J.	43,614	CHARETTE, RICHARD R.	13	105,156 R	77.3%	22.7%	77.3%	22.7%
2	1984	253,773	192,166	SNOWE, OLYMPIA J.	57,347	BULL, CHIPMAN C.	4,260	134,819 R	75.7%	22.6%	77.0%	23.0%

MAINE

1988 GENERAL ELECTION

In addition to the county-by-county figures, data are presented for selected Maine communities. Since not all jurisdictions of the state are listed in this special tabulation, state-wide totals are shown only with the county-by-county statistics.

President Other vote was 2,700 Libertarian (Paul); 1,405 New Alliance (Fulani); 230 scattered write-in.

Senator Other vote was scattered write-in. Original unamended returns gave the Republican (Wyman) state-wide vote as 104,105. The vote in Old Orchard Beach was corrected from 17 to 670 thereby increasing the York county vote and the state-wide vote for Wyman by 653.

Congress Other vote was scattered in both CD's.

1988 PRIMARIES

JUNE 14 REPUBLICAN

Senator Jasper S. Wyman, unopposed.

Congress Unopposed in CD 2. Contested as follows:

CD 1 16,584 Edward S. O'Meara; 15,360 Linda Bean-Jones; 12 scattered write-in.

JUNE 14 DEMOCRATIC

Senator George J. Mitchell, unopposed.

Congress Unopposed in both CD's.

MARYLAND

GOVERNOR

William D. Schaefer (D). Elected 1986 to a four-year term.

SENATORS

Barbara A. Mikulski (D). Elected 1986 to a six-year term.

Paul S. Sarbanes (D). Re-elected 1988 to a six-year term. Previously elected 1982, 1976.

REPRESENTATIVES

1. Roy Dyson (D)
2. Helen D. Bentley (R)
3. Benjamin L. Cardin (D)
4. Thomas McMillen (D)
5. Steny H. Hoyer (D)
6. Beverly B. Byron (D)
7. Kweisi Mfume (D)
8. Constance A. Morella (R)

POSTWAR VOTE FOR PRESIDENT

								Percentage			
	Total	Republican		Democratic		Other		Total Vote		Major Vote	
Year	Vote	Vote	Candidate	Vote	Candidate	Vote	Plurality	Rep.	Dem.	Rep.	Dem.
1988	1,714,358	876,167	Bush, George	826,304	Dukakis, Michael S.	11,887	49,863 R	51.1%	48.2%	51.5%	48.5%
1984	1,675,873	879,918	Reagan, Ronald	787,935	Mondale, Walter F.	8,020	91,983 R	52.5%	47.0%	52.8%	47.2%
1980	1,540,496	680,606	Reagan, Ronald	726,161	Carter, Jimmy	133,729	45,555 D	44.2%	47.1%	48.4%	51.6%
1976	1,439,897	672,661	Ford, Gerald R.	759,612	Carter, Jimmy	7,624	86,951 D	46.7%	52.8%	47.0%	53.0%
1972	1,353,812	829,305	Nixon, Richard M.	505,781	McGovern, George S.	18,726	323,524 R	61.3%	37.4%	62.1%	37.9%
1968	1,235,039	517,995	Nixon, Richard M.	538,310	Humphrey, Hubert H.	178,734	20,315 D	41.9%	43.6%	49.0%	51.0%
1964	1,116,457	385,495	Goldwater, Barry M.	730,912	Johnson, Lyndon B.	50	345,417 D	34.5%	65.5%	34.5%	65.5%
1960	1,055,349	489,538	Nixon, Richard M.	565,808	Kennedy, John F.	3	76,270 D	46.4%	53.6%	46.4%	53.6%
1956	932,827	559,738	Eisenhower, Dwight D.	372,613	Stevenson, Adlai E.	476	187,125 R	60.0%	39.9%	60.0%	40.0%
1952	902,074	499,424	Eisenhower, Dwight D.	395,337	Stevenson, Adlai E.	7,313	104,087 R	55.4%	43.8%	55.8%	44.2%
1948	596,748	294,814	Dewey, Thomas E.	286,521	Truman, Harry S.	15,413	8,293 R	49.4%	48.0%	50.7%	49.3%

POSTWAR VOTE FOR GOVERNOR

								Percentage			
	Total	Republican		Democratic		Other	Rep.-Dem.	Total Vote		Major Vote	
Year	Vote	Vote	Candidate	Vote	Candidate	Vote	Plurality	Rep.	Dem.	Rep.	Dem.
1986	1,101,476	194,185	Mooney, Thomas J.	907,291	Schaefer, William D.		713,106 D	17.6%	82.4%	17.6%	82.4%
1982	1,139,149	432,826	Pascal, Robert A.	705,910	Hughes, Harry	413	273,084 D	38.0%	62.0%	38.0%	62.0%
1978	1,011,963	293,635	Beall, J. Glenn, Jr.	718,328	Hughes, Harry		424,693 D	29.0%	71.0%	29.0%	71.0%
1974	949,097	346,449	Gore, Louise	602,648	Mandel, Marvin		256,199 D	36.5%	63.5%	36.5%	63.5%
1970	973,099	314,336	Blain, C. Stanley	639,579	Mandel, Marvin	19,184	325,243 D	32.3%	65.7%	33.0%	67.0%
1966	918,761	455,318	Agnew, Spiro T.	373,543	Mahoney, George P.	89,900	81,775 R	49.6%	40.7%	54.9%	45.1%
1962	775,101	343,051	Small, Frank	432,045	Tawes, J. Millard	5	88,994 D	44.3%	55.7%	44.3%	55.7%
1958	763,234	278,173	Devereux, James	485,061	Tawes, J. Millard		206,888 D	36.4%	63.6%	36.4%	63.6%
1954	700,484	381,451	McKeldin, Theodore	319,033	Byrd, Harry C.		62,418 R	54.5%	45.5%	54.5%	45.5%
1950	645,631	369,807	McKeldin, Theodore	275,824	Lane, William P.		93,983 R	57.3%	42.7%	57.3%	42.7%
1946	489,836	221,752	McKeldin, Theodore	268,084	Lane, William P.		46,332 D	45.3%	54.7%	45.3%	54.7%

MARYLAND

POSTWAR VOTE FOR SENATOR

Year	Total Vote	Republican Vote	Republican Candidate	Democratic Vote	Democratic Candidate	Other Vote	Rep.-Dem. Plurality	Percentage Total Vote Rep.	Percentage Total Vote Dem.	Percentage Major Vote Rep.	Percentage Major Vote Dem.
1988	1,617,065	617,537	Keyes, Alan L.	999,166	Sarbanes, Paul S.	362	381,629 D	38.2%	61.8%	38.2%	61.8%
1986	1,112,637	437,411	Chavez, Linda	675,225	Mikulski, Barbara A.	1	237,814 D	39.3%	60.7%	39.3%	60.7%
1982	1,114,690	407,334	Hogan, Lawrence J.	707,356	Sarbanes, Paul S.		300,022 D	36.5%	63.5%	36.5%	63.5%
1980	1,286,088	850,970	Mathias, Charles	435,118	Conroy, Edward T.		415,852 R	66.2%	33.8%	66.2%	33.8%
1976	1,365,568	530,439	Beall, J. Glenn, Jr.	772,101	Sarbanes, Paul S.	63,028	241,662 D	38.8%	56.5%	40.7%	59.3%
1974	877,786	503,223	Mathias, Charles	374,563	Mikulski, Barbara A.		128,660 R	57.3%	42.7%	57.3%	42.7%
1970	956,370	484,960	Beall, J. Glenn, Jr.	460,422	Tydings, Joseph D.	10,988	24,538 R	50.7%	48.1%	51.3%	48.7%
1968	1,133,727	541,893	Mathias, Charles	443,367	Brewster, Daniel B.	148,467	98,526 R	47.8%	39.1%	55.0%	45.0%
1964	1,081,049	402,393	Beall, J. Glenn	678,649	Tydings, Joseph D.	7	276,256 D	37.2%	62.8%	37.2%	62.8%
1962	714,248	270,312	Miller, Edward T.	443,935	Brewster, Daniel B.	1	173,623 D	37.8%	62.2%	37.8%	62.2%
1958	749,291	382,021	Beall, J. Glenn	367,270	D'Alesandro, Thomas		14,751 R	51.0%	49.0%	51.0%	49.0%
1956	892,167	473,059	Butler, John Marshall	419,108	Mahoney, George P.		53,951 R	53.0%	47.0%	53.0%	47.0%
1952	856,193	449,823	Beall, J. Glenn	406,370	Mahoney, George P.		43,453 R	52.5%	47.5%	52.5%	47.5%
1950	615,614	326,291	Butler, John Marshall	283,180	Tydings, Millard E.	6,143	43,111 R	53.0%	46.0%	53.5%	46.5%
1946	472,232	235,000	Markey, David John	237,232	O'Conor, Herbert R.		2,232 D	49.8%	50.2%	49.8%	50.2%

MARYLAND

Districts Established April 13, 1982

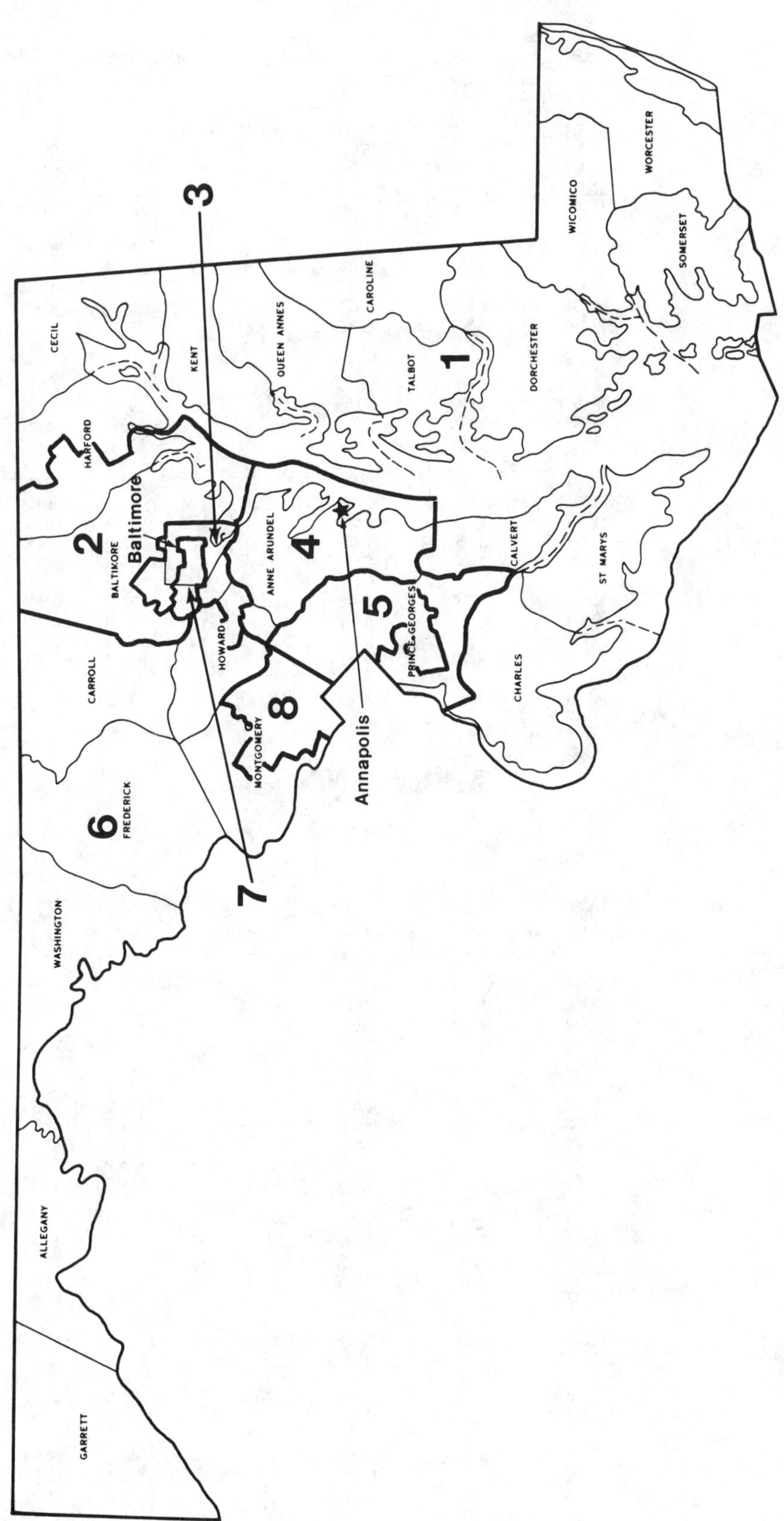

MARYLAND

PRESIDENT 1988

1980 Census Population	County	Total Vote	Republican	Democratic	Other	Rep.-Dem. Plurality	Percentage Total Vote Rep.	Total Vote Dem.	Major Vote Rep.	Major Vote Dem.
80,548	ALLEGANY	29,503	17,462	11,844	197	5,618 R	59.2%	40.1%	59.6%	40.4%
370,775	ANNE ARUNDEL	155,101	98,540	55,440	1,121	43,100 R	63.5%	35.7%	64.0%	36.0%
786,775	BALTIMORE CITY	232,367	59,089	170,813	2,465	111,724 D	25.4%	73.5%	25.7%	74.3%
655,615	BALTIMORE COUNTY	287,295	163,881	121,570	1,844	42,311 R	57.0%	42.3%	57.4%	42.6%
34,638	CALVERT	17,397	10,956	6,376	65	4,580 R	63.0%	36.6%	63.2%	36.8%
23,143	CAROLINE	7,123	4,661	2,440	22	2,221 R	65.4%	34.3%	65.6%	34.4%
96,356	CARROLL	43,747	31,224	12,368	155	18,856 R	71.4%	28.3%	71.6%	28.4%
60,430	CECIL	21,155	13,224	7,807	124	5,417 R	62.5%	36.9%	62.9%	37.1%
72,751	CHARLES	32,764	20,828	11,823	113	9,005 R	63.6%	36.1%	63.8%	36.2%
30,623	DORCHESTER	10,140	6,343	3,709	88	2,634 R	62.6%	36.6%	63.1%	36.9%
114,792	FREDERICK	49,867	32,575	17,061	231	15,514 R	65.3%	34.2%	65.6%	34.4%
26,498	GARRETT	9,282	6,665	2,557	60	4,108 R	71.8%	27.5%	72.3%	27.7%
145,930	HARFORD	58,566	38,493	19,803	270	18,690 R	65.7%	33.8%	66.0%	34.0%
118,572	HOWARD	78,530	44,153	34,007	370	10,146 R	56.2%	43.3%	56.5%	43.5%
16,695	KENT	6,732	3,761	2,925	46	836 R	55.9%	43.4%	56.3%	43.7%
579,053	MONTGOMERY	320,896	154,191	165,187	1,518	10,996 D	48.1%	51.5%	48.3%	51.7%
665,071	PRINCE GEORGES	222,881	86,545	133,816	2,520	47,271 D	38.8%	60.0%	39.3%	60.7%
25,508	QUEEN ANNES	11,703	7,803	3,857	43	3,946 R	66.7%	33.0%	66.9%	33.1%
59,895	ST. MARYS	20,290	12,767	7,434	89	5,333 R	62.9%	36.6%	63.2%	36.8%
19,188	SOMERSET	7,165	4,222	2,911	32	1,311 R	58.9%	40.6%	59.2%	40.8%
25,604	TALBOT	12,199	8,170	3,948	81	4,222 R	67.0%	32.4%	67.4%	32.6%
113,086	WASHINGTON	40,638	25,912	14,408	318	11,504 R	63.8%	35.5%	64.3%	35.7%
64,540	WICOMICO	25,755	16,272	9,413	70	6,859 R	63.2%	36.5%	63.4%	36.6%
30,889	WORCESTER	13,262	8,430	4,787	45	3,643 R	63.6%	36.1%	63.8%	36.2%
4,216,975	TOTAL	1,714,358	876,167	826,304	11,887	49,863 R	51.1%	48.2%	51.5%	48.5%

MARYLAND

SENATOR 1988

1980 Census Population	County	Total Vote	Republican	Democratic	Other	Rep.-Dem. Plurality	Percentage Total Vote Rep.	Total Vote Dem.	Major Vote Rep.	Major Vote Dem.
80,548	ALLEGANY	25,245	10,254	14,991		4,737 D	40.6%	59.4%	40.6%	59.4%
370,775	ANNE ARUNDEL	142,709	65,053	77,647	9	12,594 D	45.6%	54.4%	45.6%	54.4%
786,775	BALTIMORE CITY	219,318	44,231	175,059	28	130,828 D	20.2%	79.8%	20.2%	79.8%
655,615	BALTIMORE COUNTY	268,968	111,251	157,701	16	46,450 D	41.4%	58.6%	41.4%	58.6%
34,638	CALVERT	15,805	7,890	7,915		25 D	49.9%	50.1%	49.9%	50.1%
23,143	CAROLINE	6,384	2,841	3,543		702 D	44.5%	55.5%	44.5%	55.5%
96,356	CARROLL	41,860	22,551	19,305	4	3,246 R	53.9%	46.1%	53.9%	46.1%
60,430	CECIL	18,636	8,022	10,607	7	2,585 D	43.0%	56.9%	43.1%	56.9%
72,751	CHARLES	28,818	12,580	16,238		3,658 D	43.7%	56.3%	43.7%	56.3%
30,623	DORCHESTER	8,860	3,881	4,979		1,098 D	43.8%	56.2%	43.8%	56.2%
114,792	FREDERICK	48,430	24,423	23,997	10	426 R	50.4%	49.5%	50.4%	49.6%
26,498	GARRETT	7,551	3,669	3,882		213 D	48.6%	51.4%	48.6%	51.4%
145,930	HARFORD	61,188	27,992	33,192	4	5,200 D	45.7%	54.2%	45.8%	54.2%
118,572	HOWARD	77,143	33,602	43,521	20	9,919 D	43.6%	56.4%	43.6%	56.4%
16,695	KENT	5,837	2,349	3,488		1,139 D	40.2%	59.8%	40.2%	59.8%
579,053	MONTGOMERY	317,845	119,155	198,484	206	79,329 D	37.5%	62.4%	37.5%	62.5%
665,071	PRINCE GEORGES	206,018	62,476	143,485	57	81,009 D	30.3%	69.6%	30.3%	69.7%
25,508	QUEEN ANNES		10,632	4,996	5,636	640 D	47.0%	53.0%	47.0%	53.0%
59,895	ST. MARYS	17,764	7,285	10,478	1	3,193 D	41.0%	59.0%	41.0%	59.0%
19,188	SOMERSET	6,144	2,944	3,200		256 D	47.9%	52.1%	47.9%	52.1%
25,604	TALBOT	10,958	5,435	5,523		88 D	49.6%	50.4%	49.6%	50.4%
113,086	WASHINGTON	35,187	17,674	17,513		161 R	50.2%	49.8%	50.2%	49.8%
64,540	WICOMICO	23,874	11,406	12,468		1,062 D	47.8%	52.2%	47.8%	52.2%
30,889	WORCESTER	11,891	5,577	6,314		737 D	46.9%	53.1%	46.9%	53.1%
4,216,975	TOTAL	1,617,065	617,537	999,166	362	381,629 D	38.2%	61.8%	38.2%	61.8%

MARYLAND

CONGRESS

CD	Year	Total Vote	Republican Vote	Republican Candidate	Democratic Vote	Democratic Candidate	Other Vote	Rep.-Dem. Plurality	Percentage Total Vote Rep.	Percentage Total Vote Dem.	Percentage Major Vote Rep.	Percentage Major Vote Dem.
1	1988	190,716	94,588	GILCHREST, WAYNE T.	96,128	DYSON, ROY		1,540 D	49.6%	50.4%	49.6%	50.4%
1	1986	131,877	43,764	WILLIAMS, HARLAN C.	88,113	DYSON, ROY		44,349 D	33.2%	66.8%	33.2%	66.8%
1	1984	165,538	68,865	WILLIAMS, HARLAN C.	96,673	DYSON, ROY		27,808 D	41.6%	58.4%	41.6%	58.4%
1	1982	129,159	39,656	HOPKINS, C. A. PORTER	89,503	DYSON, ROY		49,847 D	30.7%	69.3%	30.7%	69.3%
2	1988	221,070	157,956	BENTLEY, HELEN D.	63,114	BARTENFELDER, JOSEPH		94,842 R	71.5%	28.5%	71.5%	28.5%
2	1986	164,946	96,745	BENTLEY, HELEN D.	68,200	TOWNSEND, KATHLEEN K.	1	28,545 R	58.7%	41.3%	58.7%	41.3%
2	1984	217,089	111,517	BENTLEY, HELEN D.	105,571	LONG, CLARENCE D.	1	5,946 R	51.4%	48.6%	51.4%	48.6%
2	1982	158,380	75,062	BENTLEY, HELEN D.	83,318	LONG, CLARENCE D.		8,256 D	47.4%	52.6%	47.4%	52.6%
3	1988	183,512	49,733	PIERPONT, ROSS Z.	133,779	CARDIN, BENJAMIN L.		84,046 D	27.1%	72.9%	27.1%	72.9%
3	1986	126,613	26,452	PIERPONT, ROSS Z.	100,161	CARDIN, BENJAMIN L.		73,709 D	20.9%	79.1%	20.9%	79.1%
3	1984	195,261	59,493	PIERPONT, ROSS Z.	133,189	MIKULSKI, BARBARA A.	2,579	73,696 D	30.5%	68.2%	30.9%	69.1%
3	1982	148,301	38,259	SCHERR, H. ROBERT	110,042	MIKULSKI, BARBARA A.		71,783 D	25.8%	74.2%	25.8%	74.2%
4	1988	188,312	59,688	MCCLANAHAN, BRADLYN	128,624	MCMILLEN, THOMAS		68,936 D	31.7%	68.3%	31.7%	68.3%
4	1986	129,714	64,643	NEALL, ROBERT R.	65,071	MCMILLEN, THOMAS		428 D	49.8%	50.2%	49.8%	50.2%
4	1984	172,743	114,430	HOLT, MARJORIE S.	58,312	GREENEBAUM, HOWARD	1	56,118 R	66.2%	33.8%	66.2%	33.8%
4	1982	123,564	75,617	HOLT, MARJORIE S.	47,947	AIKEN, PATRICIA O'B.		27,670 R	61.2%	38.8%	61.2%	38.8%
5	1988	163,346	34,909	SELLNER, JOHN E.	128,437	HOYER, STENY H.		93,528 D	21.4%	78.6%	21.4%	78.6%
5	1986	100,200	18,102	SELLNER, JOHN E.	82,098	HOYER, STENY H.		63,996 D	18.1%	81.9%	18.1%	81.9%
5	1984	161,149	44,839	RITCHIE, JOHN E.	116,310	HOYER, STENY H.		71,471 D	27.8%	72.2%	27.8%	72.2%
5	1982	105,470	21,533	GUTHRIE, WILLIAM P.	83,937	HOYER, STENY H.		62,404 D	20.4%	79.6%	20.4%	79.6%
6	1988	221,281	54,528	HALSEY, KENNETH W.	166,753	BYRON, BEVERLY B.		112,225 D	24.6%	75.4%	24.6%	75.4%
6	1986	142,575	39,600	VANDENBERGE, JOHN	102,975	BYRON, BEVERLY B.		63,375 D	27.8%	72.2%	27.8%	72.2%
6	1984	189,442	66,056	FICKER, ROBIN	123,383	BYRON, BEVERLY B.	3	57,327 D	34.9%	65.1%	34.9%	65.1%
6	1982	137,917	35,321	BARTLETT, ROSCOE	102,596	BYRON, BEVERLY B.		67,275 D	25.6%	74.4%	25.6%	74.4%
7	1988	117,650			117,650	MFUME, KWEISI		117,650 D		100.0%		100.0%
7	1986	91,398	12,170	CROSSE, ST. GEORGE I. B.	79,226	MFUME, KWEISI	2	67,056 D	13.3%	86.7%	13.3%	86.7%
7	1984	139,489			139,488	MITCHELL, PARREN J.	1	139,488 D		100.0%		100.0%
7	1982	117,699	14,203	JONES, M. LEONORA	103,496	MITCHELL, PARREN J.		89,293 D	12.1%	87.9%	12.1%	87.9%
8	1988	275,097	172,619	MORELLA, CONSTANCE A.	102,478	FRANCHOT, PETER		70,141 R	62.7%	37.3%	62.7%	37.3%
8	1986	175,742	92,917	MORELLA, CONSTANCE A.	82,825	BAINUM, STEWART		10,092 R	52.9%	47.1%	52.9%	47.1%
8	1984	254,569	70,715	CECCONE, ALBERT	181,947	BARNES, MICHAEL D.	1,907	111,232 D	27.8%	71.5%	28.0%	72.0%
8	1982	170,671	48,910	SPENCER, ELIZABETH W.	121,761	BARNES, MICHAEL D.		72,851 D	28.7%	71.3%	28.7%	71.3%

MARYLAND

1988 GENERAL ELECTION

President Other vote was 6,748 Libertarian (Paul); 5,115 New Alliance (Fulani); 24 scattered write-in.

Senator Other vote was 349 Ahman (write-in); 13 Ali (write-in).

Congress

1988 PRIMARIES

MARCH 8 REPUBLICAN

Senator 68,268 Thomas L. Blair; 19,720 James G. Bennett; 16,305 Patrick L. McDonough; 10,725 E. Robert Zarwell; 9,601 Albert Ceccone; 8,405 John C. Webb; 8,031 Horace S. Rich; 5,356 Herbert Rosenberg; 3,520 Monroe Cornish. Mr. Blair withdrew after the primary and Alan L. Keyes was substituted by the state central committee.

Congress Unopposed in three CD's. No candidate in CD 7. Contested as follows:

CD 1 8,190 Wayne T. Gilchrest; 6,804 John V. Meyers.
CD 3 3,775 Ross Z. Pierpont; 2,721 Fredric M. Parker; 2,712 Douglas C. Harris; 998 Roy F. Carraher.
CD 4 8,024 Bradlyn McClanahan; 5,228 Claude W. Roxborough; 3,906 Patrick L. Stevens.
CD 5 5,390 John E. Sellner; 3,801 Gregory K. Washington.

MARCH 8 DEMOCRATIC

Senator 309,919 Paul S. Sarbanes; 25,932 B. Emerson Sweatt; 25,450 A. Robert Kaufman.

Congress Unopposed in two CD's. Contested as follows:

CD 1 39,207 Roy Dyson; 6,379 Morris C. Durham.
CD 2 26,622 Joseph Bartenfelder; 13,958 Blaine Taylor.
CD 3 52,848 Benjamin L. Cardin; 8,451 Charles Walker.
CD 4 39,661 Thomas McMillen; 3,941 Edward B. Quirk; 1,877 John Rea.
CD 6 38,123 Beverly B. Byron; 9,101 Anthony P. Puca.
CD 8 36,734 Peter Franchot; 16,748 Rosemary Glynn; 4,984 James W. Walker; 4,833 Ralph K. Shur; 1,725 George W. Benns.

MASSACHUSETTS

GOVERNOR

Michael S. Dukakis (D). Re-elected 1986 to a four year term. Previously elected 1982, 1974.

SENATORS

Edward M. Kennedy (D). Re-elected 1988 to a six-year term. Previously elected 1982, 1976, 1970, 1964 and in 1962 to fill out term vacated by the resignation of Senator John F. Kennedy.

John F. Kerry (D). Elected 1984 to a six-year term.

REPRESENTATIVES

1. Silvio O. Conte (R)
2. Richard E. Neal (D)
3. Joseph D. Early (D)
4. Barney Frank (D)
5. Chester G. Atkins (D)
6. Nicholas Mavroules (D)
7. Edward J. Markey (D)
8. Joseph P. Kennedy (D)
9. John J. Moakley (D)
10. Gerry E. Studds (D)
11. Brian J. Donnelly (D)

POSTWAR VOTE FOR PRESIDENT

Year	Total Vote	Republican Vote	Republican Candidate	Democratic Vote	Democratic Candidate	Other Vote	Plurality	Percentage Total Vote Rep.	Percentage Total Vote Dem.	Percentage Major Vote Rep.	Percentage Major Vote Dem.
1988	2,632,805	1,194,635	Bush, George	1,401,415	Dukakis, Michael S.	36,755	206,780 D	45.4%	53.2%	46.0%	54.0%
1984	2,559,453	1,310,936	Reagan, Ronald	1,239,606	Mondale, Walter F.	8,911	71,330 R	51.2%	48.4%	51.4%	48.6%
1980	2,524,298	1,057,631	Reagan, Ronald	1,053,802	Carter, Jimmy	412,865	3,829 R	41.9%	41.7%	50.1%	49.9%
1976	2,547,558	1,030,276	Ford, Gerald R.	1,429,475	Carter, Jimmy	87,807	399,199 D	40.4%	56.1%	41.9%	58.1%
1972	2,458,756	1,112,078	Nixon, Richard M.	1,332,540	McGovern, George S.	14,138	220,462 D	45.2%	54.2%	45.5%	54.5%
1968	2,331,752	766,844	Nixon, Richard M.	1,469,218	Humphrey, Hubert H.	95,690	702,374 D	32.9%	63.0%	34.3%	65.7%
1964	2,344,798	549,727	Goldwater, Barry M.	1,786,422	Johnson, Lyndon B.	8,649	1,236,695 D	23.4%	76.2%	23.5%	76.5%
1960	2,469,480	976,750	Nixon, Richard M.	1,487,174	Kennedy, John F.	5,556	510,424 D	39.6%	60.2%	39.6%	60.4%
1956	2,348,506	1,393,197	Eisenhower, Dwight D.	948,190	Stevenson, Adlai E.	7,119	445,007 R	59.3%	40.4%	59.5%	40.5%
1952	2,383,398	1,292,325	Eisenhower, Dwight D.	1,083,525	Stevenson, Adlai E.	7,548	208,800 R	54.2%	45.5%	54.4%	45.6%
1948	2,107,146	909,370	Dewey, Thomas E.	1,151,788	Truman, Harry S.	45,988	242,418 D	43.2%	54.7%	44.1%	55.9%

POSTWAR VOTE FOR GOVERNOR

Year	Total Vote	Republican Vote	Republican Candidate	Democratic Vote	Democratic Candidate	Other Vote	Rep.-Dem. Plurality	Percentage Total Vote Rep.	Percentage Total Vote Dem.	Percentage Major Vote Rep.	Percentage Major Vote Dem.
1986	1,684,079	525,364	Kariotis, George	1,157,786	Dukakis, Michael S.	929	632,422 D	31.2%	68.7%	31.2%	68.8%
1982	2,050,254	749,679	Sears, John W.	1,219,109	Dukakis, Michael S.	81,466	469,430 D	36.6%	59.5%	38.1%	61.9%
1978	1,962,251	926,072	Hatch, Francis W.	1,030,294	King, Edward J.	5,885	104,222 D	47.2%	52.5%	47.3%	52.7%
1974	1,854,798	784,353	Sargent, Francis W.	992,284	Dukakis, Michael S.	78,161	207,931 D	42.3%	53.5%	44.1%	55.9%
1970	1,867,906	1,058,623	Sargent, Francis W.	799,269	White, Kevin H.	10,014	259,354 R	56.7%	42.8%	57.0%	43.0%
1966 **	2,041,177	1,277,358	Volpe, John A.	752,720	McCormack, Edward J.	11,099	524,638 R	62.6%	36.9%	62.9%	37.1%
1964	2,340,130	1,176,462	Volpe, John A.	1,153,416	Bellotti, Francis X.	10,252	23,046 R	50.3%	49.3%	50.5%	49.5%
1962	2,109,089	1,047,891	Volpe, John A.	1,053,322	Peabody, Endicott	7,876	5,431 D	49.7%	49.9%	49.9%	50.1%
1960	2,417,133	1,269,295	Volpe, John A.	1,130,810	Ward, Joseph D.	17,028	138,485 R	52.5%	46.8%	52.9%	47.1%
1958	1,899,117	818,463	Gibbons, Charles	1,067,020	Furcolo, Foster	13,634	248,557 D	43.1%	56.2%	43.4%	56.6%
1956	2,339,884	1,096,759	Whittier, Sumner G.	1,234,618	Furcolo, Foster	8,507	137,859 D	46.9%	52.8%	47.0%	53.0%
1954	1,903,774	985,339	Herter, Christian A.	910,087	Murphy, Robert F.	8,348	75,252 R	51.8%	47.8%	52.0%	48.0%
1952	2,356,298	1,175,955	Herter, Christian A.	1,161,499	Dever, Paul A.	18,844	14,456 R	49.9%	49.3%	50.3%	49.7%
1950	1,910,180	824,069	Coolidge, Arthur W.	1,074,570	Dever, Paul A.	11,541	250,501 D	43.1%	56.3%	43.4%	56.6%
1948	2,099,250	849,895	Bradford, Robert F.	1,239,247	Dever, Paul A.	10,108	389,352 D	40.5%	59.0%	40.7%	59.3%
1946	1,683,452	911,152	Bradford, Robert F.	762,743	Tobin, Maurice	9,557	148,409 R	54.1%	45.3%	54.4%	45.6%

The term of office of Massachusetts' Governor was increased from two to four years effective with the 1966 election.

MASSACHUSETTS

POSTWAR VOTE FOR SENATOR

		Republican		Democratic				Percentage			
	Total					Other	Rep.-Dem.	Total Vote		Major Vote	
Year	Vote	Vote	Candidate	Vote	Candidate	Vote	Plurality	Rep.	Dem.	Rep.	Dem.
1988	2,606,225	884,267	Malone, Joseph	1,693,344	Kennedy, Edward M.	28,614	809,077 D	33.9%	65.0%	34.3%	65.7%
1984	2,530,195	1,136,806	Shamie, Raymond	1,392,981	Kerry, John F.	408	256,175 D	44.9%	55.1%	44.9%	55.1%
1982	2,050,769	784,602	Shamie, Raymond	1,247,084	Kennedy, Edward M.	19,083	462,482 D	38.3%	60.8%	38.6%	61.4%
1978	1,985,700	890,584	Brooke, Edward W.	1,093,283	Tsongas, Paul E.	1,833	202,699 D	44.8%	55.1%	44.9%	55.1%
1976	2,491,255	722,641	Robertson, Michael	1,726,657	Kennedy, Edward M.	41,957	1,004,016 D	29.0%	69.3%	29.5%	70.5%
1972	2,370,676	1,505,932	Brooke, Edward W.	823,278	Droney, John J.	41,466	682,654 R	63.5%	34.7%	64.7%	35.3%
1970	1,935,607	715,978	Spaulding, Josiah A.	1,202,856	Kennedy, Edward M.	16,773	486,878 D	37.0%	62.1%	37.3%	62.7%
1966	1,999,949	1,213,473	Brooke, Edward W.	774,761	Peabody, Endicott	11,715	438,712 R	60.7%	38.7%	61.0%	39.0%
1964	2,312,028	587,663	Whitmore, Howard	1,716,907	Kennedy, Edward M.	7,458	1,129,244 D	25.4%	74.3%	25.5%	74.5%
1962 S	2,097,085	877,669	Lodge, George C.	1,162,611	Kennedy, Edward M.	56,805	284,942 D	41.9%	55.4%	43.0%	57.0%
1960	2,417,813	1,358,556	Saltonstall, Leverett	1,050,725	O'Connor, Thomas J.	8,532	307,831 R	56.2%	43.5%	56.4%	43.6%
1958	1,862,041	488,318	Celeste, Vincent J.	1,362,926	Kennedy, John F.	10,797	874,608 D	26.2%	73.2%	26.4%	73.6%
1954	1,892,710	956,605	Saltonstall, Leverett	927,899	Furcolo, Foster	8,206	28,706 R	50.5%	49.0%	50.8%	49.2%
1952	2,360,425	1,141,247	Lodge, Henry Cabot	1,211,984	Kennedy, John F.	7,194	70,737 D	48.3%	51.3%	48.5%	51.5%
1948	2,055,798	1,088,475	Saltonstall, Leverett	954,398	Fitzgerald, John I.	12,925	134,077 R	52.9%	46.4%	53.3%	46.7%
1946	1,662,063	989,736	Lodge, Henry Cabot	660,200	Walsh, David I.	12,127	329,536 R	59.5%	39.7%	60.0%	40.0%

The 1962 election was for a short term to fill a vacancy.

MASSACHUSETTS

Districts Established December 3, 1981

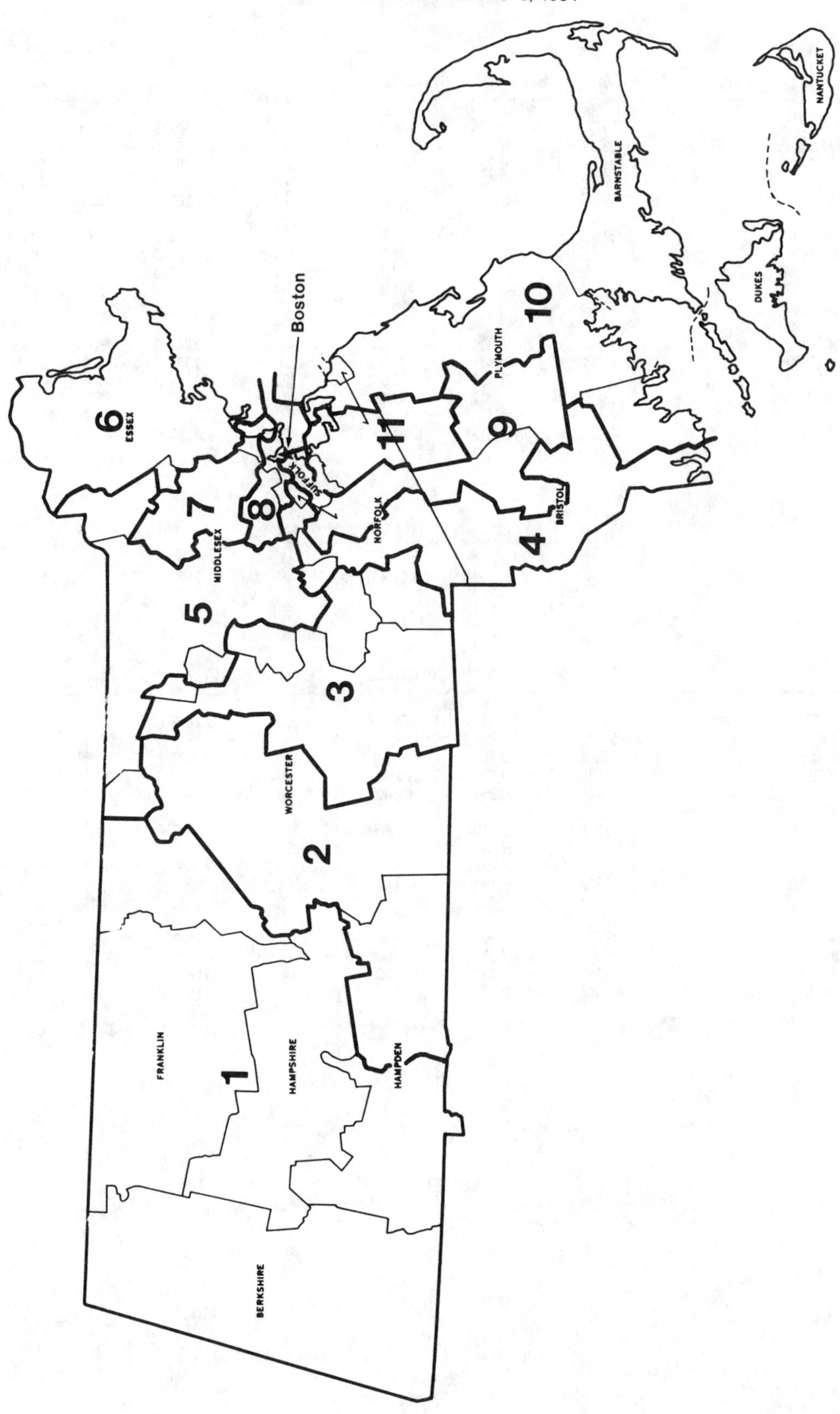

MASSACHUSETTS

PRESIDENT 1988

1980 Census Population	County	Total Vote	Republican	Democratic	Other	Rep.-Dem. Plurality	Percentage Total Vote Rep.	Total Vote Dem.	Major Vote Rep.	Major Vote Dem.
147,925	BARNSTABLE	99,872	49,676	48,747	1,449	929 R	49.7%	48.8%	50.5%	49.5%
145,110	BERKSHIRE	62,859	24,116	38,217	526	14,101 D	38.4%	60.8%	38.7%	61.3%
474,641	BRISTOL	193,530	83,797	107,854	1,879	24,057 D	43.3%	55.7%	43.7%	56.3%
8,942	DUKES	7,025	2,441	4,495	89	2,054 D	34.7%	64.0%	35.2%	64.8%
633,632	ESSEX	305,500	148,614	151,816	5,070	3,202 D	48.6%	49.7%	49.5%	50.5%
64,317	FRANKLIN	33,123	13,475	19,310	338	5,835 D	40.7%	58.3%	41.1%	58.9%
443,018	HAMPDEN	173,420	74,872	97,332	1,216	22,460 D	43.2%	56.1%	43.5%	56.5%
138,813	HAMPSHIRE	64,915	24,331	39,834	750	15,503 D	37.5%	61.4%	37.9%	62.1%
1,367,034	MIDDLESEX	662,628	290,352	361,563	10,713	71,211 D	43.8%	54.6%	44.5%	55.5%
5,087	NANTUCKET	3,731	1,469	2,209	53	740 D	39.4%	59.2%	39.9%	60.1%
606,587	NORFOLK	315,056	150,306	160,289	4,461	9,983 D	47.7%	50.9%	48.4%	51.6%
405,437	PLYMOUTH	193,480	105,684	84,587	3,209	21,097 R	54.6%	43.7%	55.5%	44.5%
650,142	SUFFOLK	224,410	77,137	143,677	3,596	66,540 D	34.4%	64.0%	34.9%	65.1%
646,352	WORCESTER	293,256	148,365	141,485	3,406	6,880 R	50.6%	48.2%	51.2%	48.8%
5,737,037	TOTAL	2,632,805	1,194,635	1,401,415	36,755	206,780 D	45.4%	53.2%	46.0%	54.0%

MASSACHUSETTS

SENATOR 1988

1980 Census Population	County	Total Vote	Republican	Democratic	Other	Rep.-Dem. Plurality	Percentage Total Vote Rep.	Total Vote Dem.	Major Vote Rep.	Major Vote Dem.
147,925	BARNSTABLE	99,684	39,087	59,702	895	20,615 D	39.2%	59.9%	39.6%	60.4%
145,110	BERKSHIRE	61,640	14,855	45,853	932	30,998 D	24.1%	74.4%	24.5%	75.5%
474,641	BRISTOL	191,389	55,883	133,402	2,104	77,519 D	29.2%	69.7%	29.5%	70.5%
8,942	DUKES	6,930	1,830	4,981	119	3,151 D	26.4%	71.9%	26.9%	73.1%
633,632	ESSEX	304,268	108,356	192,802	3,110	84,446 D	35.6%	63.4%	36.0%	64.0%
64,317	FRANKLIN	32,977	10,151	22,459	367	12,308 D	30.8%	68.1%	31.1%	68.9%
443,018	HAMPDEN	170,103	57,461	110,251	2,391	52,790 D	33.8%	64.8%	34.3%	65.7%
138,813	HAMPSHIRE	64,190	19,298	43,958	934	24,660 D	30.1%	68.5%	30.5%	69.5%
1,367,034	MIDDLESEX	656,735	221,790	427,993	6,952	206,203 D	33.8%	65.2%	34.1%	65.9%
5,087	NANTUCKET	3,688	1,148	2,482	58	1,334 D	31.1%	67.3%	31.6%	68.4%
606,587	NORFOLK	312,831	115,008	195,038	2,785	80,030 D	36.8%	62.3%	37.1%	62.9%
405,437	PLYMOUTH	192,487	74,602	115,967	1,918	41,365 D	38.8%	60.2%	39.1%	60.9%
650,142	SUFFOLK	218,261	61,688	153,357	3,216	91,669 D	28.3%	70.3%	28.7%	71.3%
646,352	WORCESTER	291,042	103,110	185,099	2,833	81,989 D	35.4%	63.6%	35.8%	64.2%
5,737,037	TOTAL	2,606,225	884,267	1,693,344	28,614	809,077 D	33.9%	65.0%	34.3%	65.7%

MASSACHUSETTS

PRESIDENT 1988

1980 Census Population	City/Town	Total Vote	Republican	Democratic	Other	Rep.-Dem. Plurality	Percentage Total Vote Rep.	Percentage Total Vote Dem.	Percentage Major Vote Rep.	Percentage Major Vote Dem.
26,271	AGAWAM	11,625	5,526	6,022	77	496 D	47.5%	51.8%	47.9%	52.1%
33,229	AMHERST	12,229	2,925	9,097	207	6,172 D	23.9%	74.4%	24.3%	75.7%
26,370	ANDOVER	15,387	8,730	6,416	241	2,314 R	56.7%	41.7%	57.6%	42.4%
48,219	ARLINGTON	26,082	9,903	15,712	467	5,809 D	38.0%	60.2%	38.7%	61.3%
34,196	ATTLEBORO	14,087	7,739	6,199	149	1,540 R	54.9%	44.0%	55.5%	44.5%
30,898	BARNSTABLE TOWN	20,247	10,026	9,971	250	55 R	49.5%	49.2%	50.1%	49.9%
26,100	BELMONT	14,811	6,487	8,117	207	1,630 D	43.8%	54.8%	44.4%	55.6%
37,655	BEVERLY	18,662	8,903	9,397	362	494 D	47.7%	50.4%	48.7%	51.3%
36,727	BILLERICA	15,524	8,152	7,061	311	1,091 R	52.5%	45.5%	53.6%	46.4%
562,994	BOSTON	187,626	62,202	122,349	3,075	60,147 D	33.2%	65.2%	33.7%	66.3%
36,337	BRAINTREE	18,108	9,398	8,481	229	917 R	51.9%	46.8%	52.6%	47.4%
95,172	BROCKTON	31,329	16,056	14,776	497	1,280 R	51.2%	47.2%	52.1%	47.9%
55,062	BROOKLINE	28,014	7,145	20,553	316	13,408 D	25.5%	73.4%	25.8%	74.2%
23,486	BURLINGTON	11,740	6,073	5,458	209	615 R	51.7%	46.5%	52.7%	47.3%
95,322	CAMBRIDGE	41,589	8,770	32,027	792	23,257 D	21.1%	77.0%	21.5%	78.5%
31,174	CHELMSFORD	16,921	9,785	6,874	262	2,911 R	57.8%	40.6%	58.7%	41.3%
25,431	CHELSEA	8,962	3,067	5,790	105	2,723 D	34.2%	64.6%	34.6%	65.4%
55,112	CHICOPEE	22,893	8,682	14,067	144	5,385 D	37.9%	61.4%	38.2%	61.8%
24,100	DANVERS	12,387	6,927	5,265	195	1,662 R	55.9%	42.5%	56.8%	43.2%
23,966	DARTMOUTH	11,664	5,009	6,563	92	1,554 D	42.9%	56.3%	43.3%	56.7%
25,298	DEDHAM	13,003	6,440	6,341	222	99 R	49.5%	48.8%	50.4%	49.6%
21,249	DRACUT	11,475	6,340	4,895	240	1,445 R	55.3%	42.7%	56.4%	43.6%
37,195	EVERETT	15,501	6,324	8,970	207	2,646 D	40.8%	57.9%	41.3%	58.7%
92,574	FALL RIVER	28,794	8,394	20,184	216	11,790 D	29.2%	70.1%	29.4%	70.6%
23,640	FALMOUTH	14,806	6,751	7,893	162	1,142 D	45.6%	53.3%	46.1%	53.9%
39,580	FITCHBURG	14,085	6,332	7,552	201	1,220 D	45.0%	53.6%	45.6%	54.4%
65,113	FRAMINGHAM	28,934	12,745	15,826	363	3,081 D	44.0%	54.7%	44.6%	55.4%
27,768	GLOUCESTER	13,248	5,671	7,440	137	1,769 D	42.8%	56.2%	43.3%	56.7%
46,865	HAVERHILL	20,539	9,302	10,826	411	1,524 D	45.3%	52.7%	46.2%	53.8%
20,339	HINGHAM	11,844	6,595	5,073	176	1,522 R	55.7%	42.8%	56.5%	43.5%
44,678	HOLYOKE	15,495	5,746	9,644	105	3,898 D	37.1%	62.2%	37.3%	62.7%
63,175	LAWRENCE	17,798	8,265	9,255	278	990 D	46.4%	52.0%	47.2%	52.8%
34,508	LEOMINSTER	15,287	8,042	7,106	139	936 R	52.6%	46.5%	53.1%	46.9%
29,479	LEXINGTON	17,771	7,252	10,252	267	3,000 D	40.8%	57.7%	41.4%	58.6%
92,418	LOWELL	30,921	13,998	16,391	532	2,393 D	45.3%	53.0%	46.1%	53.9%
78,471	LYNN	31,264	12,182	18,540	542	6,358 D	39.0%	59.3%	39.7%	60.3%
53,386	MALDEN	22,630	8,692	13,616	322	4,924 D	38.4%	60.2%	39.0%	61.0%
20,126	MARBLEHEAD	12,321	6,322	5,858	141	464 R	51.3%	47.5%	51.9%	48.1%
30,617	MARLBOROUGH	14,112	7,116	6,813	183	303 R	50.4%	48.3%	51.1%	48.9%
20,916	MARSHFIELD	11,127	5,845	5,112	170	733 R	52.5%	45.9%	53.3%	46.7%
58,076	MEDFORD	28,127	11,471	16,286	370	4,815 D	40.8%	57.9%	41.3%	58.7%
30,055	MELROSE	15,632	7,495	7,912	225	417 D	47.9%	50.6%	48.6%	51.4%
36,701	METHUEN	18,306	10,233	7,765	308	2,468 R	55.9%	42.4%	56.9%	43.1%
23,390	MILFORD	10,990	5,014	5,814	162	800 D	45.6%	52.9%	46.3%	53.7%
25,860	MILTON	15,155	7,765	7,197	193	568 R	51.2%	47.5%	51.9%	48.1%
29,461	NATICK	16,343	7,215	8,945	183	1,730 D	44.1%	54.7%	44.6%	55.4%
27,901	NEEDHAM	16,979	8,465	8,273	241	192 R	49.9%	48.7%	50.6%	49.4%
98,478	NEW BEDFORD	32,799	9,901	22,609	289	12,708 D	30.2%	68.9%	30.5%	69.5%
83,622	NEWTON	43,458	13,892	29,039	527	15,147 D	32.0%	66.8%	32.4%	67.6%
29,286	NORTHAMPTON	14,132	4,201	9,753	178	5,552 D	29.7%	69.0%	30.1%	69.9%
20,129	NORTH ANDOVER	11,568	6,697	4,682	189	2,015 R	57.9%	40.5%	58.9%	41.1%
21,095	NORTH ATTLEBOROUGH	9,924	5,903	3,911	110	1,992 R	59.5%	39.4%	60.1%	39.9%
29,711	NORWOOD	14,681	7,178	7,231	272	53 D	48.9%	49.3%	49.8%	50.2%
45,976	PEABODY	22,802	10,186	12,203	413	2,017 D	44.7%	53.5%	45.5%	54.5%
51,974	PITTSFIELD	21,610	7,683	13,780	147	6,097 D	35.6%	63.8%	35.8%	64.2%
35,913	PLYMOUTH TOWN	19,349	10,166	8,898	285	1,268 R	52.5%	46.0%	53.3%	46.7%
84,743	QUINCY	39,892	18,403	20,911	578	2,508 D	46.1%	52.4%	46.8%	53.2%
28,218	RANDOLPH	14,335	5,504	8,590	241	3,086 D	38.4%	59.9%	39.1%	60.9%
22,678	READING	12,761	6,478	6,027	256	451 R	50.8%	47.2%	51.8%	48.2%
42,423	REVERE	18,248	7,508	10,471	269	2,963 D	41.1%	57.4%	41.8%	58.2%

MASSACHUSETTS

PRESIDENT 1988

1980 Census Population	City/Town	Total Vote	Republican	Democratic	Other	Rep.-Dem. Plurality	Percentage Total Vote Rep.	Percentage Total Vote Dem.	Percentage Major Vote Rep.	Percentage Major Vote Dem.
38,220	SALEM	17,363	6,702	10,339	322	3,637 D	38.6%	59.5%	39.3%	60.7%
24,746	SAUGUS	12,364	5,929	6,253	182	324 D	48.0%	50.6%	48.7%	51.3%
22,674	SHREWSBURY	12,225	6,592	5,510	123	1,082 R	53.9%	45.1%	54.5%	45.5%
77,372	SOMERVILLE	31,176	8,931	21,612	633	12,681 D	28.6%	69.3%	29.2%	70.8%
152,319	SPRINGFIELD	46,674	16,244	30,113	317	13,869 D	34.8%	64.5%	35.0%	65.0%
21,424	STONEHAM	11,165	5,260	5,644	261	384 D	47.1%	50.6%	48.2%	51.8%
26,710	STOUGHTON	12,322	5,810	6,340	172	530 D	47.2%	51.5%	47.8%	52.2%
45,001	TAUNTON	16,949	7,805	8,953	191	1,148 D	46.0%	52.8%	46.6%	53.4%
24,635	TEWKSBURY	12,291	6,593	5,476	222	1,117 R	53.6%	44.6%	54.6%	45.4%
24,895	WAKEFIELD	13,288	6,546	6,503	239	43 R	49.3%	48.9%	50.2%	49.8%
58,200	WALTHAM	23,720	10,845	12,555	320	1,710 D	45.7%	52.9%	46.3%	53.7%
34,384	WATERTOWN	16,860	6,011	10,535	314	4,524 D	35.7%	62.5%	36.3%	63.7%
27,209	WELLESLEY	14,520	7,537	6,803	180	734 R	51.9%	46.9%	52.6%	47.4%
27,042	WEST SPRINGFIELD	11,788	5,752	5,969	67	217 D	48.8%	50.6%	49.1%	50.9%
36,465	WESTFIELD	15,166	7,403	7,638	125	235 D	48.8%	50.4%	49.2%	50.8%
55,601	WEYMOUTH	26,448	12,727	13,304	417	577 D	48.1%	50.3%	48.9%	51.1%
20,701	WINCHESTER	12,159	6,167	5,839	153	328 R	50.7%	48.0%	51.4%	48.6%
19,294	WINTHROP	9,574	4,360	5,067	147	707 D	45.5%	52.9%	46.3%	53.7%
36,626	WOBURN	17,316	8,112	8,900	304	788 D	46.8%	51.4%	47.7%	52.3%
161,799	WORCESTER CITY	59,322	24,355	34,369	598	10,014 D	41.1%	57.9%	41.5%	58.5%

MASSACHUSETTS

SENATOR 1988

1980 Census Population	City/Town	Total Vote	Republican	Democratic	Other	Rep.-Dem. Plurality	Percentage Total Vote Rep.	Total Vote Dem.	Major Vote Rep.	Major Vote Dem.
26,271	AGAWAM	11,392	4,213	7,024	155	2,811 D	37.0%	61.7%	37.5%	62.5%
33,229	AMHERST	11,770	2,306	9,217	247	6,911 D	19.6%	78.3%	20.0%	80.0%
26,370	ANDOVER	15,267	6,730	8,383	154	1,653 D	44.1%	54.9%	44.5%	55.5%
48,219	ARLINGTON	25,959	7,860	17,835	264	9,975 D	30.3%	68.7%	30.6%	69.4%
34,196	ATTLEBORO	13,871	4,667	9,020	184	4,353 D	33.6%	65.0%	34.1%	65.9%
30,898	BARNSTABLE TOWN	20,183	7,880	12,152	151	4,272 D	39.0%	60.2%	39.3%	60.7%
26,100	BELMONT	14,762	5,476	9,155	131	3,679 D	37.1%	62.0%	37.4%	62.6%
37,655	BEVERLY	18,524	6,686	11,614	224	4,928 D	36.1%	62.7%	36.5%	63.5%
36,727	BILLERICA	15,551	5,757	9,611	183	3,854 D	37.0%	61.8%	37.5%	62.5%
562,994	BOSTON	181,895	50,734	128,483	2,678	77,749 D	27.9%	70.6%	28.3%	71.7%
36,337	BRAINTREE	18,134	7,228	10,785	121	3,557 D	39.9%	59.5%	40.1%	59.9%
95,172	BROCKTON	31,207	10,504	20,393	310	9,889 D	33.7%	65.3%	34.0%	66.0%
55,062	BROOKLINE	27,358	5,888	21,163	307	15,275 D	21.5%	77.4%	21.8%	78.2%
23,486	BURLINGTON	11,519	4,454	6,943	122	2,489 D	38.7%	60.3%	39.1%	60.9%
95,322	CAMBRIDGE	41,011	7,127	33,220	664	26,093 D	17.4%	81.0%	17.7%	82.3%
31,174	CHELMSFORD	16,800	7,333	9,305	162	1,972 D	43.6%	55.4%	44.1%	55.9%
25,431	CHELSEA	8,870	2,205	6,564	101	4,359 D	24.9%	74.0%	25.1%	74.9%
55,112	CHICOPEE	22,863	6,679	15,958	226	9,279 D	29.2%	69.8%	29.5%	70.5%
24,100	DANVERS	12,369	5,087	7,174	108	2,087 D	41.1%	58.0%	41.5%	58.5%
23,966	DARTMOUTH	11,363	3,308	7,920	135	4,612 D	29.1%	69.7%	29.5%	70.5%
25,298	DEDHAM	12,885	5,221	7,553	111	2,332 D	40.5%	58.6%	40.9%	59.1%
21,249	DRACUT	11,436	4,296	6,998	142	2,702 D	37.6%	61.2%	38.0%	62.0%
37,195	EVERETT	15,372	4,756	10,405	211	5,649 D	30.9%	67.7%	31.4%	68.6%
92,574	FALL RIVER	28,279	6,398	21,541	340	15,143 D	22.6%	76.2%	22.9%	77.1%
23,640	FALMOUTH	14,723	5,004	9,562	157	4,558 D	34.0%	64.9%	34.4%	65.6%
39,580	FITCHBURG	14,049	4,491	9,418	140	4,927 D	32.0%	67.0%	32.3%	67.7%
65,113	FRAMINGHAM	28,736	9,375	19,128	233	9,753 D	32.6%	66.6%	32.9%	67.1%
27,768	GLOUCESTER	13,173	4,015	9,040	118	5,025 D	30.5%	68.6%	30.8%	69.2%
46,865	HAVERHILL	20,389	6,517	13,678	194	7,161 D	32.0%	67.1%	32.3%	67.7%
20,339	HINGHAM	11,809	5,153	6,580	76	1,427 D	43.6%	55.7%	43.9%	56.1%
44,678	HOLYOKE	14,834	4,446	10,157	231	5,711 D	30.0%	68.5%	30.4%	69.6%
63,175	LAWRENCE	17,843	5,555	12,074	214	6,519 D	31.1%	67.7%	31.5%	68.5%
34,508	LEOMINSTER	15,276	5,471	9,694	111	4,223 D	35.8%	63.5%	36.1%	63.9%
29,479	LEXINGTON	17,429	6,100	11,141	188	5,041 D	35.0%	63.9%	35.4%	64.6%
92,418	LOWELL	30,601	9,336	20,920	345	11,584 D	30.5%	68.4%	30.9%	69.1%
78,471	LYNN	31,318	8,703	22,211	404	13,508 D	27.8%	70.9%	28.2%	71.8%
53,386	MALDEN	22,110	6,247	15,633	230	9,386 D	28.3%	70.7%	28.6%	71.4%
20,126	MARBLEHEAD	12,240	4,883	7,258	99	2,375 D	39.9%	59.3%	40.2%	59.8%
30,617	MARLBOROUGH	14,063	5,006	8,936	121	3,930 D	35.6%	63.5%	35.9%	64.1%
20,916	MARSHFIELD	11,079	4,259	6,715	105	2,456 D	38.4%	60.6%	38.8%	61.2%
58,076	MEDFORD	27,995	8,769	18,953	273	10,184 D	31.3%	67.7%	31.6%	68.4%
30,055	MELROSE	15,408	5,875	9,377	156	3,502 D	38.1%	60.9%	38.5%	61.5%
36,701	METHUEN	18,247	6,915	11,150	182	4,235 D	37.9%	61.1%	38.3%	61.7%
23,390	MILFORD	10,902	3,286	7,528	88	4,242 D	30.1%	69.1%	30.4%	69.6%
25,860	MILTON	15,071	6,033	8,906	132	2,873 D	40.0%	59.1%	40.4%	59.6%
29,461	NATICK	16,211	5,635	10,447	129	4,812 D	34.8%	64.4%	35.0%	65.0%
27,901	NEEDHAM	16,797	6,982	9,674	141	2,692 D	41.6%	57.6%	41.9%	58.1%
98,478	NEW BEDFORD	32,767	6,644	25,837	286	19,193 D	20.3%	78.9%	20.5%	79.5%
83,622	NEWTON	42,714	10,794	31,554	366	20,760 D	25.3%	73.9%	25.5%	74.5%
29,286	NORTHAMPTON	14,047	3,536	10,274	237	6,738 D	25.2%	73.1%	25.6%	74.4%
20,129	NORTH ANDOVER	11,533	4,976	6,475	82	1,499 D	43.1%	56.1%	43.5%	56.5%
21,095	NORTH ATTLEBOROUGH	9,858	3,881	5,888	89	2,007 D	39.4%	59.7%	39.7%	60.3%
29,711	NORWOOD	14,643	5,449	9,051	143	3,602 D	37.2%	61.8%	37.6%	62.4%
45,976	PEABODY	22,678	6,887	15,599	192	8,712 D	30.4%	68.8%	30.6%	69.4%
51,974	PITTSFIELD	21,057	4,480	16,178	399	11,698 D	21.3%	76.8%	21.7%	78.3%
35,913	PLYMOUTH TOWN	18,996	6,840	11,900	256	5,060 D	36.0%	62.6%	36.5%	63.5%
84,743	QUINCY	39,631	14,279	24,967	385	10,688 D	36.0%	63.0%	36.4%	63.6%
28,218	RANDOLPH	14,174	3,795	10,247	132	6,452 D	26.8%	72.3%	27.0%	73.0%
22,678	READING	12,733	5,176	7,443	114	2,267 D	40.7%	58.5%	41.0%	59.0%
42,423	REVERE	18,090	5,467	12,304	319	6,837 D	30.2%	68.0%	30.8%	69.2%

MASSACHUSETTS

SENATE 1988

1980 Census Population	City/Town	Total Vote	Republican	Democratic	Other	Rep.-Dem. Plurality	Percentage Total Vote Rep.	Percentage Total Vote Dem.	Percentage Major Vote Rep.	Percentage Major Vote Dem.
38,220	SALEM	17,276	4,742	12,352	182	7,610 D	27.4%	71.5%	27.7%	72.3%
24,746	SAUGUS	12,410	4,380	7,900	130	3,520 D	35.3%	63.7%	35.7%	64.3%
22,674	SHREWSBURY	12,159	4,784	7,277	98	2,493 D	39.3%	59.8%	39.7%	60.3%
77,372	SOMERVILLE	30,882	6,521	23,891	470	17,370 D	21.1%	77.4%	21.4%	78.6%
152,319	SPRINGFIELD	45,177	12,325	31,943	909	19,618 D	27.3%	70.7%	27.8%	72.2%
21,424	STONEHAM	11,137	4,274	6,746	117	2,472 D	38.4%	60.6%	38.8%	61.2%
26,710	STOUGHTON	12,198	3,932	8,183	83	4,251 D	32.2%	67.1%	32.5%	67.5%
45,001	TAUNTON	16,660	4,948	11,498	214	6,550 D	29.7%	69.0%	30.1%	69.9%
24,635	TEWKSBURY	12,249	4,552	7,550	147	2,998 D	37.2%	61.6%	37.6%	62.4%
24,895	WAKEFIELD	13,220	4,805	8,297	118	3,492 D	36.3%	62.8%	36.7%	63.3%
58,200	WALTHAM	23,425	8,887	14,303	235	5,416 D	37.9%	61.1%	38.3%	61.7%
34,384	WATERTOWN	16,946	4,979	11,761	206	6,782 D	29.4%	69.4%	29.7%	70.3%
27,209	WELLESLEY	14,374	6,446	7,801	127	1,355 D	44.8%	54.3%	45.2%	54.8%
27,042	WEST SPRINGFIELD	11,559	4,524	6,844	191	2,320 D	39.1%	59.2%	39.8%	60.2%
36,465	WESTFIELD	15,066	5,685	9,237	144	3,552 D	37.7%	61.3%	38.1%	61.9%
55,601	WEYMOUTH	26,528	9,628	16,642	258	7,014 D	36.3%	62.7%	36.7%	63.3%
20,701	WINCHESTER	12,036	5,083	6,846	107	1,763 D	42.2%	56.9%	42.6%	57.4%
19,294	WINTHROP	9,406	3,282	6,006	118	2,724 D	34.9%	63.9%	35.3%	64.7%
36,626	WOBURN	17,087	5,979	10,917	191	4,938 D	35.0%	63.9%	35.4%	64.6%
161,799	WORCESTER CITY	58,743	16,932	41,199	612	24,267 D	28.8%	70.1%	29.1%	70.9%

MASSACHUSETTS

CONGRESS

CD	Year	Total Vote	Republican Vote	Republican Candidate	Democratic Vote	Democratic Candidate	Other Vote	Rep.-Dem. Plurality	Percentage Total Vote Rep.	Percentage Total Vote Dem.	Percentage Major Vote Rep.	Percentage Major Vote Dem.
1	1988	225,291	186,356	CONTE, SILVIO O.	38,907	ARDEN, JOHN R.	28	147,449 R	82.7%	17.3%	82.7%	17.3%
1	1986	146,090	113,653	CONTE, SILVIO O.	32,396	WEINER, ROBERT S.	41	81,257 R	77.8%	22.2%	77.8%	22.2%
1	1984	223,037	162,646	CONTE, SILVIO O.	60,372	WENTWORTH, MARY L.	19	102,274 R	72.9%	27.1%	72.9%	27.1%
1	1982	146,197	145,417	*CONTE, SILVIO O.			780	145,417 R	99.5%		100.0%	
2	1988	194,760			156,262	NEAL, RICHARD E.	38,498	156,262 D		80.2%		100.0%
2	1986	138,062	47,022	LEES, BRIAN P.	91,033	BOLAND, EDWARD P.	7	44,011 D	34.1%	65.9%	34.1%	65.9%
2	1984	193,254	60,463	SWANK, THOMAS P.	132,693	BOLAND, EDWARD P.	98	72,230 D	31.3%	68.7%	31.3%	68.7%
2	1982	162,773	44,544	SWANK, THOMAS P.	118,215	BOLAND, EDWARD P.	14	73,671 D	27.4%	72.6%	27.4%	72.6%
3	1988	191,387			191,009	EARLY, JOSEPH D.	378	191,009 D		99.8%		100.0%
3	1986	120,279			120,222	EARLY, JOSEPH D.	57	120,222 D		100.0%		100.0%
3	1984	220,254	71,765	REDDING, KENNETH J.	148,461	EARLY, JOSEPH D.	28	76,696 D	32.6%	67.4%	32.6%	67.4%
3	1982	142,740			142,611	EARLY, JOSEPH D.	129	142,611 D		99.9%		100.0%
4	1988	241,414	71,661	TUCKER, DEBRA R.	169,729	FRANK, BARNEY	24	98,068 D	29.7%	70.3%	29.7%	70.3%
4	1986	151,265			134,387	FRANK, BARNEY	16,878	134,387 D		88.8%		100.0%
4	1984	233,032	60,121	FORTE, JIM	172,903	FRANK, BARNEY	8	112,782 D	25.8%	74.2%	25.8%	74.2%
4	1982	204,615	82,804	HECKLER, MARGARET M.	121,802	FRANK, BARNEY	9	38,998 D	40.5%	59.5%	40.5%	59.5%
5	1988	216,290			181,877	ATKINS, CHESTER G.	34,413	181,877 D		84.1%		100.0%
5	1986	113,747			113,690	ATKINS, CHESTER G.	57	113,690 D		99.9%		100.0%
5	1984	224,927	104,912	HYATT, GREGORY S.	120,008	ATKINS, CHESTER G.	7	15,096 D	46.6%	53.4%	46.6%	53.4%
5	1982	165,598			140,177	SHANNON, JAMES M.	25,421	140,177 D		84.6%		100.0%
6	1988	255,067	77,186	MCCARTHY, PAUL	177,643	MAVROULES, NICHOLAS	238	100,457 D	30.3%	69.6%	30.3%	69.7%
6	1986	131,137			131,051	MAVROULES, NICHOLAS	86	131,051 D		99.9%		100.0%
6	1984	239,649	63,363	LEBER, FREDERICK S.	168,662	MAVROULES, NICHOLAS	7,624	105,299 D	26.4%	70.4%	27.3%	72.7%
6	1982	203,584	85,849	TRIMARCO, THOMAS H.	117,723	MAVROULES, NICHOLAS	12	31,874 D	42.2%	57.8%	42.2%	57.8%
7	1988	188,710			188,647	MARKEY, EDWARD J.	63	188,647 D		100.0%		100.0%
7	1986	124,245			124,183	MARKEY, EDWARD J.	62	124,183 D		100.0%		100.0%
7	1984	234,190	66,930	RALPH, S. LESTER	167,211	MARKEY, EDWARD J.	49	100,281 D	28.6%	71.4%	28.6%	71.4%
7	1982	194,369	43,063	BASILE, DAVID M.	151,305	MARKEY, EDWARD J.	1	108,242 D	22.2%	77.8%	22.2%	77.8%
8	1988	206,189	40,316	FISCUS, GLENN W.	165,745	KENNEDY, JOSEPH P.	128	125,429 D	19.6%	80.4%	19.6%	80.4%
8	1986	145,358	40,259	ABT, CLARK C.	104,651	KENNEDY, JOSEPH P.	448	64,392 D	27.7%	72.0%	27.8%	72.2%
8	1984	195,603			179,617	O'NEILL, THOMAS P.	15,986	179,617 D		91.8%		100.0%
8	1982	164,672	41,370	MCNAMARA, FRANK L.	123,296	O'NEILL, THOMAS P.	6	81,926 D	25.1%	74.9%	25.1%	74.9%
9	1988	161,042			160,799	MOAKLEY, JOHN J.	243	160,799 D		99.8%		100.0%
9	1986	131,330			110,026	MOAKLEY, JOHN J.	21,304	110,026 D		83.8%		100.0%
9	1984	153,252			153,132	MOAKLEY, JOHN J.	120	153,132 D		99.9%		100.0%
9	1982	160,225	55,030	COCHRAN, DEBORAH R.	102,665	MOAKLEY, JOHN J.	2,530	47,635 D	34.3%	64.1%	34.9%	65.1%
10	1988	280,767	93,564	BRYAN, JON L.	187,178	STUDDS, GERRY E.	25	93,614 D	33.3%	66.7%	33.3%	66.7%
10	1986	186,726	49,451	BARROS, RICARDO M.	121,578	STUDDS, GERRY E.	15,697	72,127 D	26.5%	65.1%	28.9%	71.1%
10	1984	256,824	113,745	CRAMPTON, LEWIS	143,062	STUDDS, GERRY E.	17	29,317 D	44.3%	55.7%	44.3%	55.7%
10	1982	201,436	63,014	CONWAY, JOHN E.	138,418	STUDDS, GERRY E.	4	75,404 D	31.3%	68.7%	31.3%	68.7%
11	1988	209,988	40,277	GILLERAN, MICHAEL C.	169,692	DONNELLY, BRIAN J.	19	129,415 D	19.2%	80.8%	19.2%	80.8%
11	1986	114,929			114,926	DONNELLY, BRIAN J.	3	114,926 D		100.0%		100.0%
11	1984	172,025			172,010	DONNELLY, BRIAN J.	15	172,010 D		100.0%		100.0%
11	1982	144,157			144,132	DONNELLY, BRIAN J.	25	144,132 D		100.0%		100.0%

MASSACHUSETTS

1988 GENERAL ELECTION

In addition to the county-by-county figures, data are presented for selected Massachusetts communities. Since not all jurisdictions of the state are listed in this special tabulation, state-wide totals are shown only with the county-by-county statistics.

President Other vote was 24,251 Libertarian (Paul); 9,561 New Alliance (Fulani); 18 Dodge (write-in); 15 Kenoyer (write-in); 2,910 scattered write-in.

Senator Other vote was 15,208 New Alliance (Fridley); 13,199 Libertarian (Nason); 207 scattered write-in.

Congress An asterisk in the Congressional vote table indicates a candidate received votes from another party endorsing his/her candidacy. Other vote was 38,446 Peace, Jobs and Justice (Godena) and 52 scattered in CD 2; 34,341 Libertarian (Hudson) and 72 scattered in CD 5; scattered write-in in all other CD's. In CD 3, early unamended returns gave the Democratic (Early) vote as 191,005. In CD 5, early unamended returns gave the Democratic (Atkins) vote as 181,860 and the Libertarian (Hudson) vote as 34,339.

1988 PRIMARIES

SEPTEMBER 15 REPUBLICAN

Senator Joseph Malone, unopposed.

Congress Unopposed in five CD's. No candidate in CD's 2, 3, 5, 7 and 9. Contested as follows:

CD 10 6,620 Jon L. Bryan; 5,233 Martha Keyes; 18 scattered write-in.

SEPTEMBER 15 DEMOCRATIC

Senator Edward M. Kennedy, unopposed.

Congress Unopposed in ten CD's. Contested as follows:

CD 11 40,122 Brian J. Donnelly; 6,709 David J. Peterson; 2 scattered write-in.

MICHIGAN

GOVERNOR

James J. Blanchard (D). Re-elected 1986 to a four-year term. Previously elected 1982.

SENATORS

Carl Levin (D). Re-elected 1984 to a six-year term. Previously elected 1978.

Donald W. Riegle (D). Re-elected 1988 to a six-year term. Previously elected 1982, 1976.

REPRESENTATIVES

1. John Conyers (D)
2. Carl D. Pursell (R)
3. Howard Wolpe (D)
4. Frederick Upton (R)
5. Paul Henry (R)
6. M. Robert Carr (D)
7. Dale E. Kildee (D)
8. J. Robert Traxler (D)
9. Guy Vander Jagt (R)
10. Bill Schuette (R)
11. Robert W. Davis (R)
12. David E. Bonior (D)
13. George W. Crockett (D)
14. Dennis M. Hertel (D)
15. William D. Ford (D)
16. John D. Dingell, Jr.(D)
17. Sander Levin (D)
18. William S. Broomfield (R)

POSTWAR VOTE FOR PRESIDENT

								Percentage			
	Total	Republican		Democratic		Other		Total Vote		Major Vote	
Year	Vote	Vote	Candidate	Vote	Candidate	Vote	Plurality	Rep.	Dem.	Rep.	Dem.
1988	3,669,163	1,965,486	Bush, George	1,675,783	Dukakis, Michael S.	27,894	289,703 R	53.6%	45.7%	54.0%	46.0%
1984	3,801,658	2,251,571	Reagan, Ronald	1,529,638	Mondale, Walter F.	20,449	721,933 R	59.2%	40.2%	59.5%	40.5%
1980	3,909,725	1,915,225	Reagan, Ronald	1,661,532	Carter, Jimmy	332,968	253,693 R	49.0%	42.5%	53.5%	46.5%
1976	3,653,749	1,893,742	Ford, Gerald R.	1,696,714	Carter, Jimmy	63,293	197,028 R	51.8%	46.4%	52.7%	47.3%
1972	3,489,727	1,961,721	Nixon, Richard M.	1,459,435	McGovern, George S.	68,571	502,286 R	56.2%	41.8%	57.3%	42.7%
1968	3,306,250	1,370,665	Nixon, Richard M.	1,593,082	Humphrey, Hubert H.	342,503	222,417 D	41.5%	48.2%	46.2%	53.8%
1964	3,203,102	1,060,152	Goldwater, Barry M.	2,136,615	Johnson, Lyndon B.	6,335	1,076,463 D	33.1%	66.7%	33.2%	66.8%
1960	3,318,097	1,620,428	Nixon, Richard M.	1,687,269	Kennedy, John F.	10,400	66,841 D	48.8%	50.9%	49.0%	51.0%
1956	3,080,468	1,713,647	Eisenhower, Dwight D.	1,359,898	Stevenson, Adlai E.	6,923	353,749 R	55.6%	44.1%	55.8%	44.2%
1952	2,798,592	1,551,529	Eisenhower, Dwight D.	1,230,657	Stevenson, Adlai E.	16,406	320,872 R	55.4%	44.0%	55.8%	44.2%
1948	2,109,609	1,038,595	Dewey, Thomas E.	1,003,448	Truman, Harry S.	67,566	35,147 R	49.2%	47.6%	50.9%	49.1%

MICHIGAN

POSTWAR VOTE FOR GOVERNOR

Year	Total Vote	Republican Vote	Republican Candidate	Democratic Vote	Democratic Candidate	Other Vote	Rep.-Dem. Plurality	Total Vote Rep.	Total Vote Dem.	Major Vote Rep.	Major Vote Dem.
1986	2,396,564	753,647	Lucas, William	1,632,138	Blanchard, James J.	10,779	878,491 D	31.4%	68.1%	31.6%	68.4%
1982	3,040,008	1,369,582	Headlee, Richard H.	1,561,291	Blanchard, James J.	109,135	191,709 D	45.1%	51.4%	46.7%	53.3%
1978	2,867,212	1,628,485	Milliken, William G.	1,237,256	Fitzgerald, William	1,471	391,229 R	56.8%	43.2%	56.8%	43.2%
1974	2,657,017	1,356,865	Milliken, William G.	1,242,247	Levin, Sander	57,905	114,618 R	51.1%	46.8%	52.2%	47.8%
1970	2,656,162	1,339,047	Milliken, William G.	1,294,638	Levin, Sander	22,477	44,409 R	50.4%	48.7%	50.8%	49.2%
1966 **	2,461,909	1,490,430	Romney, George W.	963,383	Ferency, Zolton A.	8,096	527,047 R	60.5%	39.1%	60.7%	39.3%
1964	3,158,102	1,764,355	Romney, George W.	1,381,442	Staebler, Neil	12,305	382,913 R	55.9%	43.7%	56.1%	43.9%
1962	2,764,839	1,420,086	Romney, George W.	1,339,513	Swainson, John B.	5,240	80,573 R	51.4%	48.4%	51.5%	48.5%
1960	3,255,991	1,602,022	Bagwell, Paul D.	1,643,634	Swainson, John B.	10,335	41,612 D	49.2%	50.5%	49.4%	50.6%
1958	2,312,184	1,078,089	Bagwell, Paul D.	1,225,533	Williams, G. Mennen	8,562	147,444 D	46.6%	53.0%	46.8%	53.2%
1956	3,049,651	1,376,376	Cobo, Albert E.	1,666,689	Williams, G. Mennen	6,586	290,313 D	45.1%	54.7%	45.2%	54.8%
1954	2,187,027	963,300	Leonard, Donald S.	1,216,308	Williams, G. Mennen	7,419	253,008 D	44.0%	55.6%	44.2%	55.8%
1952	2,865,980	1,423,275	Alger, Fred M.	1,431,893	Williams, G. Mennen	10,812	8,618 D	49.7%	50.0%	49.8%	50.2%
1950	1,879,382	933,998	Kelly, Harry F.	935,152	Williams, G. Mennen	10,232	1,154 D	49.7%	49.8%	50.0%	50.0%
1948	2,113,122	964,810	Sigler, Kim	1,128,664	Williams, G. Mennen	19,648	163,854 D	45.7%	53.4%	46.1%	53.9%
1946	1,665,475	1,003,878	Sigler, Kim	644,540	Van Wagoner, Murray	17,057	359,338 R	60.3%	38.7%	60.9%	39.1%

The term of office of Michigan's Governor was increased from two to four years effective with the 1966 election.

POSTWAR VOTE FOR SENATOR

Year	Total Vote	Republican Vote	Republican Candidate	Democratic Vote	Democratic Candidate	Other Vote	Rep.-Dem. Plurality	Total Vote Rep.	Total Vote Dem.	Major Vote Rep.	Major Vote Dem.
1988	3,505,985	1,348,219	Dunn, Jim	2,116,865	Riegle, Donald W.	40,901	768,646 D	38.5%	60.4%	38.9%	61.1%
1984	3,700,938	1,745,302	Lousma, Jack	1,915,831	Levin, Carl	39,805	170,529 D	47.2%	51.8%	47.7%	52.3%
1982	2,994,334	1,223,288	Ruppe, Philip E.	1,728,793	Riegle, Donald W.	42,253	505,505 D	40.9%	57.7%	41.4%	58.6%
1978	2,846,630	1,362,165	Griffin, Robert P.	1,484,193	Levin, Carl	272	122,028 D	47.9%	52.1%	47.9%	52.1%
1976	3,490,664	1,635,087	Esch, Marvin L.	1,831,031	Riegle, Donald W.	24,546	195,944 D	46.8%	52.5%	47.2%	52.8%
1972	3,406,906	1,781,065	Griffin, Robert P.	1,577,178	Kelley, Frank J.	48,663	203,887 R	52.3%	46.3%	53.0%	47.0%
1970	2,610,839	858,470	Romney, Lenore	1,744,716	Hart, Philip A.	7,653	886,246 D	32.9%	66.8%	33.0%	67.0%
1966	2,439,365	1,363,530	Griffin, Robert P.	1,069,484	Williams, G. Mennen	6,351	294,046 R	55.9%	43.8%	56.0%	44.0%
1964	3,101,667	1,096,272	Peterson, Elly M.	1,996,912	Hart, Philip A.	8,483	900,640 D	35.3%	64.4%	35.4%	64.6%
1960	3,226,647	1,548,873	Bentley, Alvin M.	1,669,179	McNamara, Patrick V.	8,595	120,306 D	48.0%	51.7%	48.1%	51.9%
1958	2,271,644	1,046,963	Potter, Charles E.	1,216,966	Hart, Philip A.	7,715	170,003 D	46.1%	53.6%	46.2%	53.8%
1954	2,144,840	1,049,420	Ferguson, Homer	1,088,550	McNamara, Patrick V.	6,870	39,130 D	48.9%	50.8%	49.1%	50.9%
1952	2,821,133	1,428,352	Potter, Charles E.	1,383,416	Moody, Blair	9,365	44,936 R	50.6%	49.0%	50.8%	49.2%
1948	2,062,097	1,045,156	Ferguson, Homer	1,000,329	Hook, Frank E.	16,612	44,827 R	50.7%	48.5%	51.1%	48.9%
1946	1,618,720	1,085,570	Vandenberg, Arthur	517,923	Lee, James H.	15,227	567,647 R	67.1%	32.0%	67.7%	32.3%

MICHIGAN

Districts Established May 24, 1982

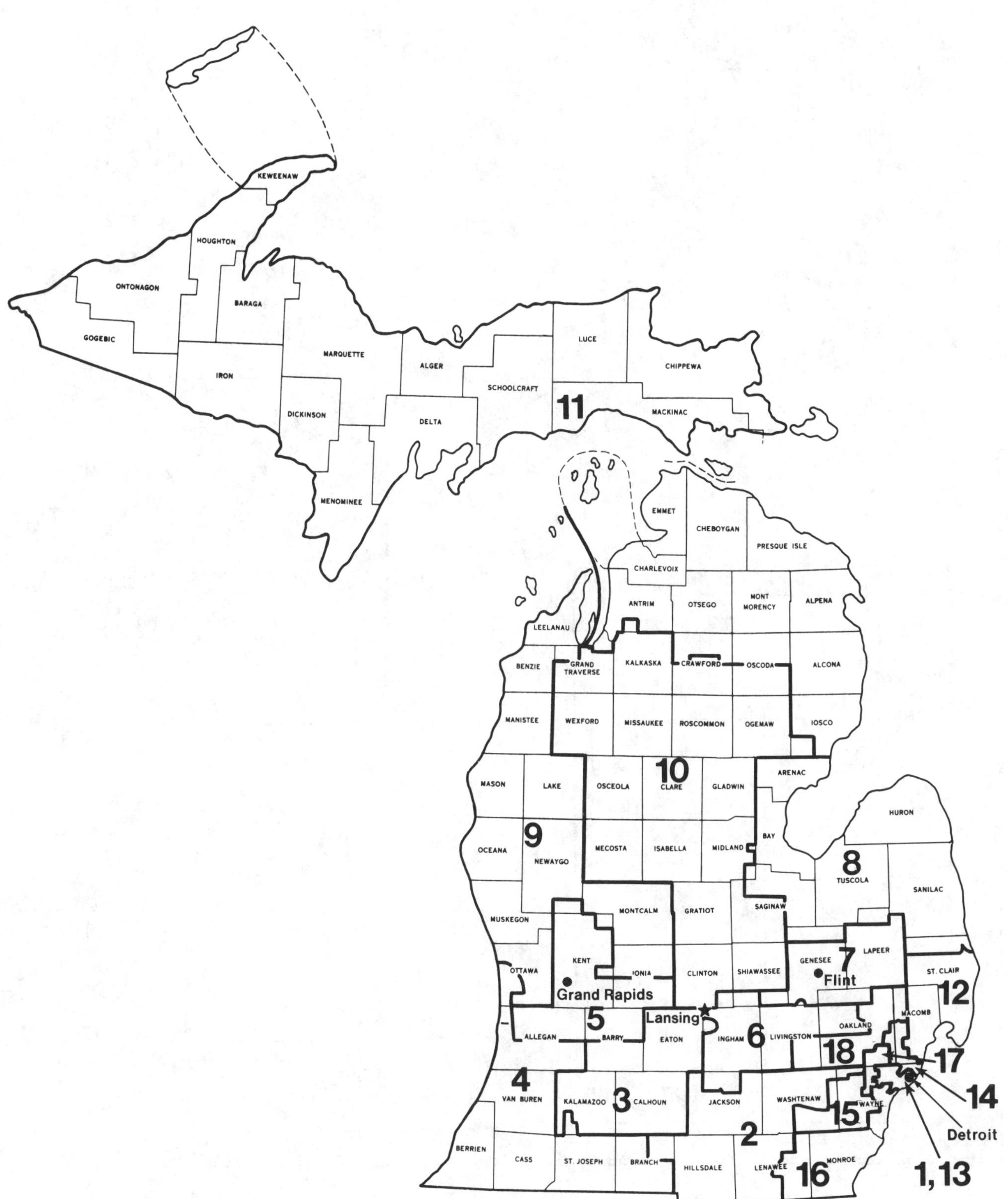

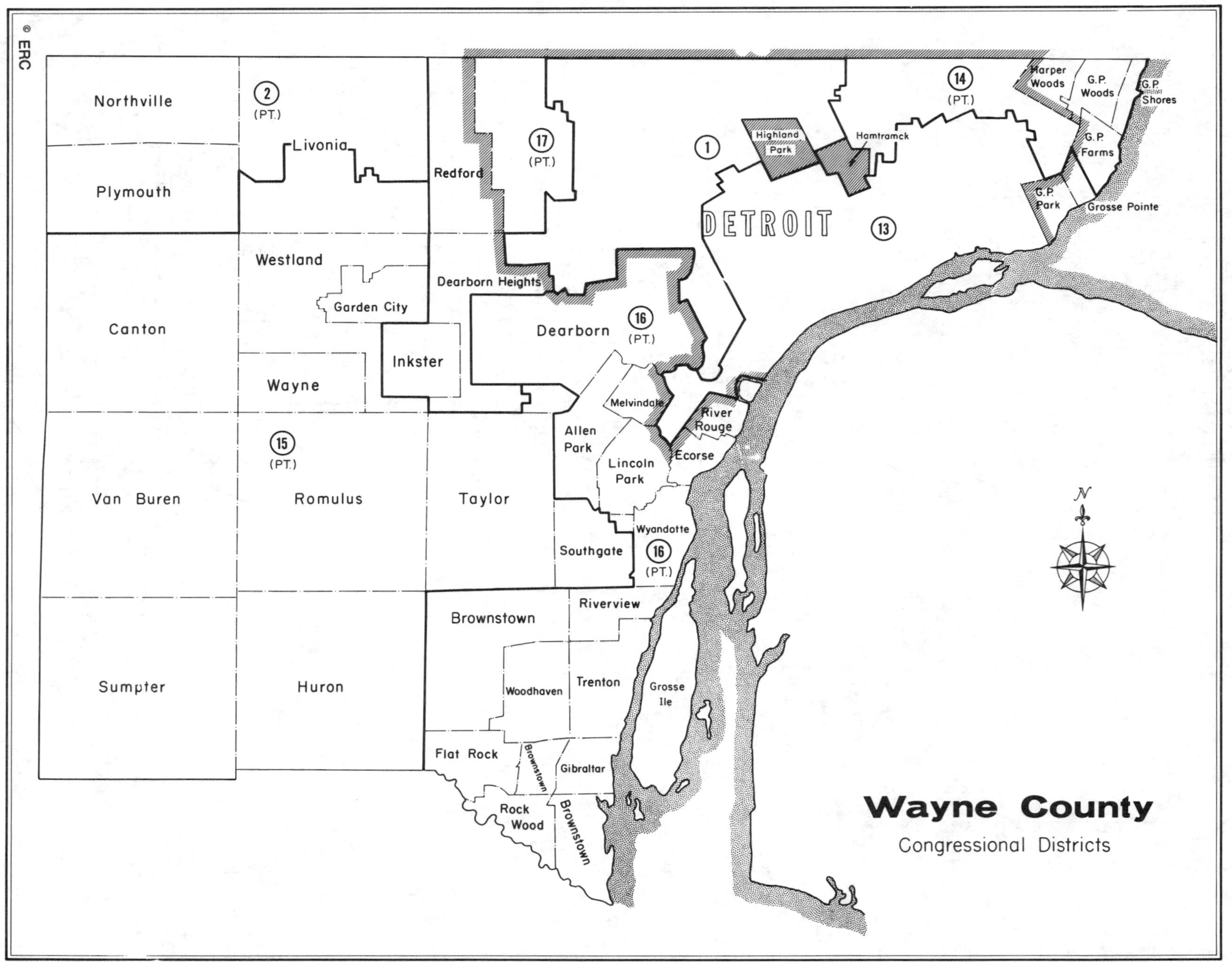

Wayne County
Congressional Districts
DETROIT
1
13
14 (PT.)
16 (PT.)
17 (PT.)
2 (PT.)
15 (PT.)
Harper Woods
G.P. Woods
G.P. Shores
G.P. Farms
G.P. Park
Grosse Pointe
Hamtramck
Highland Park
River Rouge
Ecorse
Wyandotte
Melvindale
Lincoln Park
Allen Park
Dearborn
Dearborn Heights
Redford
Southgate
Riverview
Grosse Ile
Trenton
Gibraltar
Brownstown
Woodhaven
Rock Wood
Flat Rock
Taylor
Inkster
Garden City
Livonia
Westland
Wayne
Romulus
Huron
Northville
Plymouth
Canton
Van Buren
Sumpter
N

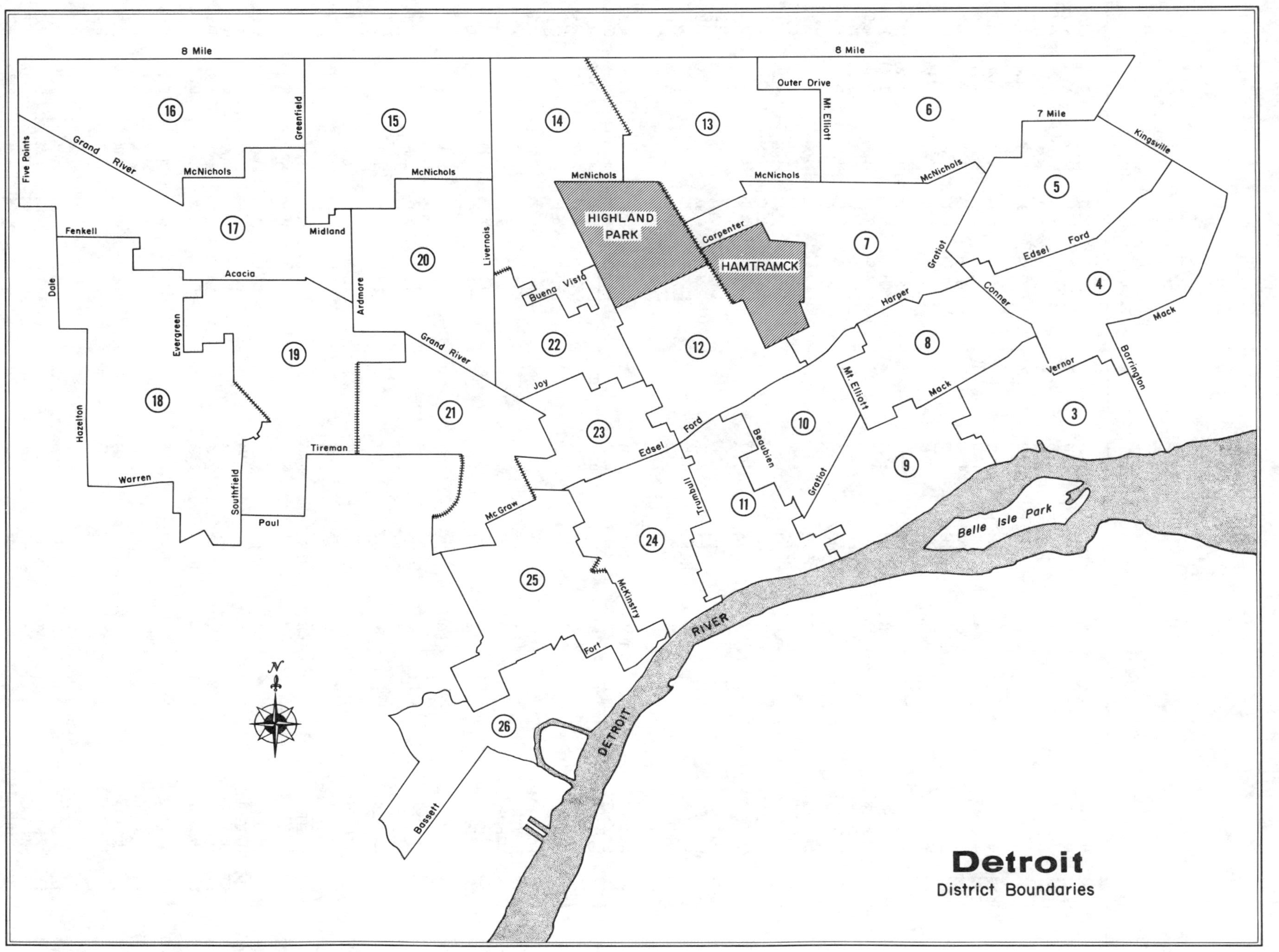
Detroit
District Boundaries
Belle Isle Park
DETROIT RIVER
HIGHLAND PARK
HAMTRAMCK
8 Mile
7 Mile
Kingsville
Mack
Barrington
Vernor
Edsel Ford
Conner
McNichols
Gratiot
Harper
Mt. Elliott
Outer Drive
Carpenter
Beaubien
Trumbull
McKinstry
Fort
Buena Vista
Joy
McGraw
Livernois
Grand River
Ardmore
Midland
Greenfield
Tireman
Paul
Southfield
Acacia
Evergreen
Warren
Hazelton
Fenkell
Dale
Five Points
Bassett
N
3
4
5
6
7
8
9
10
11
12
13
14
15
16
17
18
19
20
21
22
23
24
25
26

MICHIGAN

PRESIDENT 1988

1980 Census Population	County	Total Vote	Republican	Democratic	Other	Rep.-Dem. Plurality	Percentage Total Vote Rep.	Total Vote Dem.	Major Vote Rep.	Major Vote Dem.
9,740	ALCONA	4,905	2,966	1,918	21	1,048 R	60.5%	39.1%	60.7%	39.3%
9,225	ALGER	4,059	1,830	2,210	19	380 D	45.1%	54.4%	45.3%	54.7%
81,555	ALLEGAN	33,188	22,163	10,785	240	11,378 R	66.8%	32.5%	67.3%	32.7%
32,315	ALPENA	13,054	6,664	6,341	49	323 R	51.0%	48.6%	51.2%	48.8%
16,194	ANTRIM	8,444	5,231	3,159	54	2,072 R	61.9%	37.4%	62.3%	37.7%
14,706	ARENAC	6,300	3,064	3,211	25	147 D	48.6%	51.0%	48.8%	51.2%
8,484	BARAGA	3,404	1,630	1,753	21	123 D	47.9%	51.5%	48.2%	51.8%
45,781	BARRY	20,681	12,546	7,983	152	4,563 R	60.7%	38.6%	61.1%	38.9%
119,881	BAY	49,152	20,710	28,225	217	7,515 D	42.1%	57.4%	42.3%	57.7%
11,205	BENZIE	5,732	3,240	2,437	55	803 R	56.5%	42.5%	57.1%	42.9%
171,276	BERRIEN	60,183	37,799	21,948	436	15,851 R	62.8%	36.5%	63.3%	36.7%
40,188	BRANCH	14,531	9,225	5,231	75	3,994 R	63.5%	36.0%	63.8%	36.2%
141,557	CALHOUN	49,787	26,771	22,717	299	4,054 R	53.8%	45.6%	54.1%	45.9%
49,499	CASS	17,756	10,229	7,444	83	2,785 R	57.6%	41.9%	57.9%	42.1%
19,907	CHARLEVOIX	9,762	5,802	3,875	85	1,927 R	59.4%	39.7%	60.0%	40.0%
20,649	CHEBOYGAN	9,380	5,395	3,943	42	1,452 R	57.5%	42.0%	57.8%	42.2%
29,029	CHIPPEWA	12,068	6,786	5,222	60	1,564 R	56.2%	43.3%	56.5%	43.5%
23,822	CLARE	10,448	5,661	4,710	77	951 R	54.2%	45.1%	54.6%	45.4%
55,893	CLINTON	24,837	15,497	9,225	115	6,272 R	62.4%	37.1%	62.7%	37.3%
9,465	CRAWFORD	4,973	3,097	1,825	51	1,272 R	62.3%	36.7%	62.9%	37.1%
38,947	DELTA	16,065	7,114	8,891	60	1,777 D	44.3%	55.3%	44.4%	55.6%
25,341	DICKINSON	12,343	6,158	6,129	56	29 R	49.9%	49.7%	50.1%	49.9%
88,337	EATON	39,806	24,193	15,322	291	8,871 R	60.8%	38.5%	61.2%	38.8%
22,992	EMMET	11,386	7,105	4,170	111	2,935 R	62.4%	36.6%	63.0%	37.0%
450,449	GENESEE	176,859	70,922	104,880	1,057	33,958 D	40.1%	59.3%	40.3%	59.7%
19,957	GLADWIN	8,986	4,746	4,164	76	582 R	52.8%	46.3%	53.3%	46.7%
19,686	GOGEBIC	8,691	3,509	5,151	31	1,642 D	40.4%	59.3%	40.5%	59.5%
54,899	GRAND TRAVERSE	27,525	17,191	10,098	236	7,093 R	62.5%	36.7%	63.0%	37.0%
40,448	GRATIOT	14,230	8,447	5,719	64	2,728 R	59.4%	40.2%	59.6%	40.4%
42,071	HILLSDALE	15,479	10,571	4,763	145	5,808 R	68.3%	30.8%	68.9%	31.1%
37,872	HOUGHTON	13,694	7,098	6,510	86	588 R	51.8%	47.5%	52.2%	47.8%
36,459	HURON	15,214	9,419	5,714	81	3,705 R	61.9%	37.6%	62.2%	37.8%
275,520	INGHAM	115,435	58,363	55,984	1,088	2,379 R	50.6%	48.5%	51.0%	49.0%
51,815	IONIA	20,369	12,028	8,160	181	3,868 R	59.1%	40.1%	59.6%	40.4%
28,349	IOSCO	12,225	7,234	4,929	62	2,305 R	59.2%	40.3%	59.5%	40.5%
13,635	IRON	6,674	2,866	3,774	34	908 D	42.9%	56.5%	43.2%	56.8%
54,110	ISABELLA	18,482	10,362	7,960	160	2,402 R	56.1%	43.1%	56.6%	43.4%
151,495	JACKSON	56,127	33,885	21,865	377	12,020 R	60.4%	39.0%	60.8%	39.2%
212,378	KALAMAZOO	90,235	50,205	39,457	573	10,748 R	55.6%	43.7%	56.0%	44.0%
10,952	KALKASKA	5,504	3,369	2,092	43	1,277 R	61.2%	38.0%	61.7%	38.3%
444,506	KENT	206,842	131,910	73,467	1,465	58,443 R	63.8%	35.5%	64.2%	35.8%
1,963	KEWEENAW	1,170	536	631	3	95 D	45.8%	53.9%	45.9%	54.1%
7,711	LAKE	3,698	1,713	1,958	27	245 D	46.3%	52.9%	46.7%	53.3%
70,038	LAPEER	27,697	16,670	10,736	291	5,934 R	60.2%	38.8%	60.8%	39.2%
14,007	LEELANAU	8,619	5,215	3,331	73	1,884 R	60.5%	38.6%	61.0%	39.0%
89,948	LENAWEE	33,048	19,115	13,690	243	5,425 R	57.8%	41.4%	58.3%	41.7%
100,289	LIVINGSTON	45,546	31,331	13,749	466	17,582 R	68.8%	30.2%	69.5%	30.5%
6,659	LUCE	2,417	1,528	864	25	664 R	63.2%	35.7%	63.9%	36.1%
10,178	MACKINAC	5,242	3,127	2,093	22	1,034 R	59.7%	39.9%	59.9%	40.1%
694,600	MACOMB	291,116	175,632	112,856	2,628	62,776 R	60.3%	38.8%	60.9%	39.1%
23,019	MANISTEE	10,209	5,368	4,765	76	603 R	52.6%	46.7%	53.0%	47.0%
74,101	MARQUETTE	27,267	11,704	15,418	145	3,714 D	42.9%	56.5%	43.2%	56.8%
26,365	MASON	11,413	6,800	4,531	82	2,269 R	59.6%	39.7%	60.0%	40.0%
36,961	MECOSTA	12,981	8,181	4,736	64	3,445 R	63.0%	36.5%	63.3%	36.7%
26,201	MENOMINEE	10,406	5,440	4,918	48	522 R	52.3%	47.3%	52.5%	47.5%
73,578	MIDLAND	33,817	19,994	13,452	371	6,542 R	59.1%	39.8%	59.8%	40.2%
10,009	MISSAUKEE	5,224	3,566	1,621	37	1,945 R	68.3%	31.0%	68.7%	31.3%
134,659	MONROE	48,324	26,189	21,847	288	4,342 R	54.2%	45.2%	54.5%	45.5%
47,555	MONTCALM	18,754	10,963	7,664	127	3,299 R	58.5%	40.9%	58.9%	41.1%
7,492	MONTMORENCY	4,100	2,514	1,563	23	951 R	61.3%	38.1%	61.7%	38.3%

MICHIGAN

PRESIDENT 1988

1980 Census Population	County	Total Vote	Republican	Democratic	Other	Rep.-Dem. Plurality	Percentage Total Vote Rep.	Percentage Total Vote Dem.	Percentage Major Vote Rep.	Percentage Major Vote Dem.
157,589	MUSKEGON	62,907	33,567	28,977	363	4,590 R	53.4%	46.1%	53.7%	46.3%
34,917	NEWAYGO	15,385	9,896	5,389	100	4,507 R	64.3%	35.0%	64.7%	35.3%
1,011,793	OAKLAND	462,488	283,359	174,745	4,384	108,614 R	61.3%	37.8%	61.9%	38.1%
22,002	OCEANA	9,114	5,693	3,356	65	2,337 R	62.5%	36.8%	62.9%	37.1%
16,436	OGEMAW	8,150	4,091	4,012	47	79 R	50.2%	49.2%	50.5%	49.5%
9,861	ONTONAGON	4,562	2,023	2,517	22	494 D	44.3%	55.2%	44.6%	55.4%
18,928	OSCEOLA	8,121	5,218	2,860	43	2,358 R	64.3%	35.2%	64.6%	35.4%
6,858	OSCODA	3,167	1,972	1,170	25	802 R	62.3%	36.9%	62.8%	37.2%
14,993	OTSEGO	7,298	4,620	2,635	43	1,985 R	63.3%	36.1%	63.7%	36.3%
157,174	OTTAWA	80,729	61,515	18,769	445	42,746 R	76.2%	23.2%	76.6%	23.4%
14,267	PRESQUE ISLE	6,679	3,614	3,025	40	589 R	54.1%	45.3%	54.4%	45.6%
16,374	ROSCOMMON	10,303	5,866	4,394	43	1,472 R	56.9%	42.6%	57.2%	42.8%
228,059	SAGINAW	88,566	42,401	45,616	549	3,215 D	47.9%	51.5%	48.2%	51.8%
138,802	ST. CLAIR	53,658	32,336	20,909	413	11,427 R	60.3%	39.0%	60.7%	39.3%
56,083	ST. JOSEPH	20,196	13,084	7,017	95	6,067 R	64.8%	34.7%	65.1%	34.9%
40,789	SANILAC	16,207	10,653	5,445	109	5,208 R	65.7%	33.6%	66.2%	33.8%
8,575	SCHOOLCRAFT	3,886	1,802	2,071	13	269 D	46.4%	53.3%	46.5%	53.5%
71,140	SHIAWASSEE	28,748	15,506	13,056	186	2,450 R	53.9%	45.4%	54.3%	45.7%
56,961	TUSCOLA	21,254	12,093	9,060	101	3,033 R	56.9%	42.6%	57.2%	42.8%
66,814	VAN BUREN	25,400	14,522	10,668	210	3,854 R	57.2%	42.0%	57.6%	42.4%
264,748	WASHTENAW	117,920	55,029	61,799	1,092	6,770 D	46.7%	52.4%	47.1%	52.9%
2,337,891	WAYNE	748,156	291,996	450,222	5,938	158,226 D	39.0%	60.2%	39.3%	60.7%
25,102	WEXFORD	10,406	6,043	4,287	76	1,756 R	58.1%	41.2%	58.5%	41.5%
9,262,078	TOTAL	3,669,163	1,965,486	1,675,783	27,894	289,703 R	53.6%	45.7%	54.0%	46.0%

MICHIGAN

SENATOR 1988

1980 Census Population	County	Total Vote	Republican	Democratic	Other	Rep.-Dem. Plurality	Percentage Total Vote Rep.	Percentage Total Vote Dem.	Percentage Major Vote Rep.	Percentage Major Vote Dem.
9,740	ALCONA	4,432	2,034	2,378	20	344 D	45.9%	53.7%	46.1%	53.9%
9,225	ALGER	3,665	966	2,672	27	1,706 D	26.4%	72.9%	26.6%	73.4%
81,555	ALLEGAN	31,140	18,096	12,722	322	5,374 R	58.1%	40.9%	58.7%	41.3%
32,315	ALPENA	11,908	4,007	7,805	96	3,798 D	33.6%	65.5%	33.9%	66.1%
16,194	ANTRIM	7,503	3,429	4,014	60	585 D	45.7%	53.5%	46.1%	53.9%
14,706	ARENAC	5,840	1,849	3,964	27	2,115 D	31.7%	67.9%	31.8%	68.2%
8,484	BARAGA	3,002	757	2,219	26	1,462 D	25.2%	73.9%	25.4%	74.6%
45,781	BARRY	19,388	9,679	9,557	152	122 R	49.9%	49.3%	50.3%	49.7%
119,881	BAY	46,367	11,438	34,674	255	23,236 D	24.7%	74.8%	24.8%	75.2%
11,205	BENZIE	5,338	2,419	2,884	35	465 D	45.3%	54.0%	45.6%	54.4%
171,276	BERRIEN	57,718	32,311	24,608	799	7,703 R	56.0%	42.6%	56.8%	43.2%
40,188	BRANCH	13,493	7,066	6,327	100	739 R	52.4%	46.9%	52.8%	47.2%
141,557	CALHOUN	48,007	18,253	29,375	379	11,122 D	38.0%	61.2%	38.3%	61.7%
49,499	CASS	16,531	8,588	7,827	116	761 R	52.0%	47.3%	52.3%	47.7%
19,907	CHARLEVOIX	9,613	3,896	5,578	139	1,682 D	40.5%	58.0%	41.1%	58.9%
20,649	CHEBOYGAN	8,179	3,128	5,003	48	1,875 D	38.2%	61.2%	38.5%	61.5%
29,029	CHIPPEWA	10,634	3,564	6,992	78	3,428 D	33.5%	65.8%	33.8%	66.2%
23,822	CLARE	10,209	3,764	6,336	109	2,572 D	36.9%	62.1%	37.3%	62.7%
55,893	CLINTON	23,357	11,441	11,704	212	263 D	49.0%	50.1%	49.4%	50.6%
9,465	CRAWFORD	4,798	1,849	2,874	75	1,025 D	38.5%	59.9%	39.1%	60.9%
38,947	DELTA	14,336	3,823	10,423	90	6,600 D	26.7%	72.7%	26.8%	73.2%
25,341	DICKINSON	10,729	3,266	7,379	84	4,113 D	30.4%	68.8%	30.7%	69.3%
88,337	EATON	37,851	17,599	19,767	485	2,168 D	46.5%	52.2%	47.1%	52.9%
22,992	EMMET	11,169	4,669	6,374	126	1,705 D	41.8%	57.1%	42.3%	57.7%
450,449	GENESEE	175,446	44,508	129,276	1,662	84,768 D	25.4%	73.7%	25.6%	74.4%
19,957	GLADWIN	8,730	2,846	5,777	107	2,931 D	32.6%	66.2%	33.0%	67.0%
19,686	GOGEBIC	7,704	1,871	5,761	72	3,890 D	24.3%	74.8%	24.5%	75.5%
54,899	GRAND TRAVERSE	25,758	12,079	13,481	198	1,402 D	46.9%	52.3%	47.3%	52.7%
40,448	GRATIOT	13,689	6,145	7,449	95	1,304 D	44.9%	54.4%	45.2%	54.8%
42,071	HILLSDALE	14,309	8,248	5,902	159	2,346 R	57.6%	41.2%	58.3%	41.7%
37,872	HOUGHTON	12,404	3,993	8,320	91	4,327 D	32.2%	67.1%	32.4%	67.6%
36,459	HURON	13,433	5,747	7,571	115	1,824 D	42.8%	56.4%	43.2%	56.8%
275,520	INGHAM	113,742	40,640	70,805	2,297	30,165 D	35.7%	62.3%	36.5%	63.5%
51,815	IONIA	18,929	8,703	10,008	218	1,305 D	46.0%	52.9%	46.5%	53.5%
28,349	IOSCO	11,593	4,818	6,704	71	1,886 D	41.6%	57.8%	41.8%	58.2%
13,635	IRON	6,001	1,550	4,415	36	2,865 D	25.8%	73.6%	26.0%	74.0%
54,110	ISABELLA	17,813	6,835	10,729	249	3,894 D	38.4%	60.2%	38.9%	61.1%
151,495	JACKSON	54,217	25,514	28,109	594	2,595 D	47.1%	51.8%	47.6%	52.4%
212,378	KALAMAZOO	85,652	37,581	47,254	817	9,673 D	43.9%	55.2%	44.3%	55.7%
10,952	KALKASKA	5,040	2,011	2,998	31	987 D	39.9%	59.5%	40.1%	59.9%
444,506	KENT	200,894	103,728	94,486	2,680	9,242 R	51.6%	47.0%	52.3%	47.7%
1,963	KEWEENAW	1,057	277	777	3	500 D	26.2%	73.5%	26.3%	73.7%
7,711	LAKE	3,652	1,097	2,503	52	1,406 D	30.0%	68.5%	30.5%	69.5%
70,038	LAPEER	27,452	11,090	15,973	389	4,883 D	40.4%	58.2%	41.0%	59.0%
14,007	LEELANAU	7,987	3,782	4,141	64	359 D	47.4%	51.8%	47.7%	52.3%
89,948	LENAWEE	29,833	12,974	16,596	263	3,622 D	43.5%	55.6%	43.9%	56.1%
100,289	LIVINGSTON	44,240	22,820	20,706	714	2,114 R	51.6%	46.8%	52.4%	47.6%
6,659	LUCE	2,030	851	1,157	22	306 D	41.9%	57.0%	42.4%	57.6%
10,178	MACKINAC	4,637	1,709	2,903	25	1,194 D	36.9%	62.6%	37.1%	62.9%
694,600	MACOMB	277,383	108,200	165,614	3,569	57,414 D	39.0%	59.7%	39.5%	60.5%
23,019	MANISTEE	9,386	3,622	5,692	72	2,070 D	38.6%	60.6%	38.9%	61.1%
74,101	MARQUETTE	25,513	6,234	19,046	233	12,812 D	24.4%	74.7%	24.7%	75.3%
26,365	MASON	11,183	4,434	6,590	159	2,156 D	39.6%	58.9%	40.2%	59.8%
36,961	MECOSTA	12,193	6,090	6,029	74	61 R	49.9%	49.4%	50.3%	49.7%
26,201	MENOMINEE	8,814	3,342	5,407	65	2,065 D	37.9%	61.3%	38.2%	61.8%
73,578	MIDLAND	33,339	14,241	18,434	664	4,193 D	42.7%	55.3%	43.6%	56.4%
10,009	MISSAUKEE	5,122	2,584	2,480	58	104 R	50.4%	48.4%	51.0%	49.0%
134,659	MONROE	44,369	15,704	28,323	342	12,619 D	35.4%	63.8%	35.7%	64.3%
47,555	MONTCALM	17,348	8,178	9,020	150	842 D	47.1%	52.0%	47.6%	52.4%
7,492	MONTMORENCY	3,588	1,497	2,061	30	564 D	41.7%	57.4%	42.1%	57.9%

MICHIGAN

SENATOR 1988

1980 Census Population	County	Total Vote	Republican	Democratic	Other	Rep.-Dem. Plurality	Percentage Total Vote Rep.	Total Vote Dem.	Major Vote Rep.	Major Vote Dem.
157,589	MUSKEGON	59,147	22,369	36,433	345	14,064 D	37.8%	61.6%	38.0%	62.0%
34,917	NEWAYGO	14,327	7,237	7,003	87	234 R	50.5%	48.9%	50.8%	49.2%
1,011,793	OAKLAND	443,421	196,289	240,497	6,635	44,208 D	44.3%	54.2%	44.9%	55.1%
22,002	OCEANA	8,442	3,915	4,483	44	568 D	46.4%	53.1%	46.6%	53.4%
16,436	OGEMAW	7,766	2,466	5,235	65	2,769 D	31.8%	67.4%	32.0%	68.0%
9,861	ONTONAGON	4,108	951	3,112	45	2,161 D	23.1%	75.8%	23.4%	76.6%
18,928	OSCEOLA	7,478	3,915	3,510	53	405 R	52.4%	46.9%	52.7%	47.3%
6,858	OSCODA	3,094	1,284	1,774	36	490 D	41.5%	57.3%	42.0%	58.0%
14,993	OTSEGO	6,671	2,815	3,792	64	977 D	42.2%	56.8%	42.6%	57.4%
157,174	OTTAWA	76,868	52,357	23,790	721	28,567 R	68.1%	30.9%	68.8%	31.2%
14,267	PRESQUE ISLE	6,464	1,966	4,450	48	2,484 D	30.4%	68.8%	30.6%	69.4%
16,374	ROSCOMMON	9,495	3,773	5,661	61	1,888 D	39.7%	59.6%	40.0%	60.0%
228,059	SAGINAW	86,013	26,578	58,683	752	32,105 D	30.9%	68.2%	31.2%	68.8%
138,802	ST. CLAIR	51,648	21,342	29,806	500	8,464 D	41.3%	57.7%	41.7%	58.3%
56,083	ST. JOSEPH	18,365	10,255	7,970	140	2,285 R	55.8%	43.4%	56.3%	43.7%
40,789	SANILAC	15,172	7,682	7,386	104	296 R	50.6%	48.7%	51.0%	49.0%
8,575	SCHOOLCRAFT	3,356	895	2,434	27	1,539 D	26.7%	72.5%	26.9%	73.1%
71,140	SHIAWASSEE	27,235	10,097	16,880	258	6,783 D	37.1%	62.0%	37.4%	62.6%
56,961	TUSCOLA	19,948	7,412	12,413	123	5,001 D	37.2%	62.2%	37.4%	62.6%
66,814	VAN BUREN	23,464	11,374	11,876	214	502 D	48.5%	50.6%	48.9%	51.1%
264,748	WASHTENAW	111,507	37,954	71,900	1,653	33,946 D	34.0%	64.5%	34.5%	65.5%
2,337,891	WAYNE	722,453	187,913	525,959	8,581	338,046 D	26.0%	72.8%	26.3%	73.7%
25,102	WEXFORD	9,856	3,946	5,865	45	1,919 D	40.0%	59.5%	40.2%	59.8%
9,262,078	TOTAL	3,505,985	1,348,219	2,116,865	40,901	768,646 D	38.5%	60.4%	38.9%	61.1%

DETROIT

PRESIDENT 1988

1980 Census Population	District	Total Vote	Republican	Democratic	Other	Rep.-Dem. Plurality	Percentage Total Vote Rep.	Percentage Total Vote Dem.	Percentage Major Vote Rep.	Percentage Major Vote Dem.
	DISTRICT 3	5,443	336	5,081	26	4,745 D	6.2%	93.3%	6.2%	93.8%
	DISTRICT 4	12,127	3,360	8,648	119	5,288 D	27.7%	71.3%	28.0%	72.0%
	DISTRICT 5	11,963	3,091	8,765	107	5,674 D	25.8%	73.3%	26.1%	73.9%
	DISTRICT 6	12,644	4,107	8,415	122	4,308 D	32.5%	66.6%	32.8%	67.2%
	DISTRICT 7	8,399	974	7,358	67	6,384 D	11.6%	87.6%	11.7%	88.3%
	DISTRICT 8	8,518	165	8,316	37	8,151 D	1.9%	97.6%	1.9%	98.1%
	DISTRICT 9	8,606	902	7,638	66	6,736 D	10.5%	88.8%	10.6%	89.4%
	DISTRICT 10	3,545	198	3,331	16	3,133 D	5.6%	94.0%	5.6%	94.4%
	DISTRICT 11	5,063	693	4,300	70	3,607 D	13.7%	84.9%	13.9%	86.1%
	DISTRICT 12	6,656	285	6,317	54	6,032 D	4.3%	94.9%	4.3%	95.7%
	DISTRICT 13	13,720	912	12,738	70	11,826 D	6.6%	92.8%	6.7%	93.3%
	DISTRICT 14	12,490	916	11,465	109	10,549 D	7.3%	91.8%	7.4%	92.6%
	DISTRICT 15	21,743	730	20,902	111	20,172 D	3.4%	96.1%	3.4%	96.6%
	DISTRICT 16	16,645	1,874	14,658	113	12,784 D	11.3%	88.1%	11.3%	88.7%
	DISTRICT 17	16,913	2,781	13,998	134	11,217 D	16.4%	82.8%	16.6%	83.4%
	DISTRICT 18	13,422	4,567	8,697	158	4,130 D	34.0%	64.8%	34.4%	65.6%
	DISTRICT 19	13,570	1,446	12,032	92	10,586 D	10.7%	88.7%	10.7%	89.3%
	DISTRICT 20	14,620	417	14,115	88	13,698 D	2.9%	96.5%	2.9%	97.1%
	DISTRICT 21	13,115	923	12,111	81	11,188 D	7.0%	92.3%	7.1%	92.9%
	DISTRICT 22	9,765	241	9,475	49	9,234 D	2.5%	97.0%	2.5%	97.5%
	DISTRICT 23	7,991	179	7,785	27	7,606 D	2.2%	97.4%	2.2%	97.8%
	DISTRICT 24	4,323	429	3,836	58	3,407 D	9.9%	88.7%	10.1%	89.9%
	DISTRICT 25	7,311	2,292	4,953	66	2,661 D	31.4%	67.7%	31.6%	68.4%
	DISTRICT 26	5,161	544	4,576	41	4,032 D	10.5%	88.7%	10.6%	89.4%
	ABSENTEE	53,213	11,429	41,478	306	30,049 D	21.5%	77.9%	21.6%	78.4%
1,203,339	TOTAL	306,660	43,791	260,988	2,187	217,197 D	14.3%	85.1%	14.4%	85.6%

DETROIT

SENATOR 1988

1980 Census Population	District	Total Vote	Republican	Democratic	Other	Rep.-Dem. Plurality	Percentage Total Vote Rep.	Percentage Total Vote Dem.	Percentage Major Vote Rep.	Percentage Major Vote Dem.
	DISTRICT 3	5,227	229	4,954	44	4,725 D	4.4%	94.8%	4.4%	95.6%
	DISTRICT 4	11,396	2,154	9,058	184	6,904 D	18.9%	79.5%	19.2%	80.8%
	DISTRICT 5	11,370	1,941	9,304	125	7,363 D	17.1%	81.8%	17.3%	82.7%
	DISTRICT 6	11,868	2,434	9,296	138	6,862 D	20.5%	78.3%	20.8%	79.2%
	DISTRICT 7	8,051	630	7,325	96	6,695 D	7.8%	91.0%	7.9%	92.1%
	DISTRICT 8	8,217	114	8,066	37	7,952 D	1.4%	98.2%	1.4%	98.6%
	DISTRICT 9	8,191	583	7,498	110	6,915 D	7.1%	91.5%	7.2%	92.8%
	DISTRICT 10	3,422	135	3,263	24	3,128 D	3.9%	95.4%	4.0%	96.0%
	DISTRICT 11	4,736	446	4,183	107	3,737 D	9.4%	88.3%	9.6%	90.4%
	DISTRICT 12	6,398	159	6,182	57	6,023 D	2.5%	96.6%	2.5%	97.5%
	DISTRICT 13	13,105	575	12,448	82	11,873 D	4.4%	95.0%	4.4%	95.6%
	DISTRICT 14	11,833	574	11,131	128	10,557 D	4.9%	94.1%	4.9%	95.1%
	DISTRICT 15	20,839	390	20,344	105	19,954 D	1.9%	97.6%	1.9%	98.1%
	DISTRICT 16	15,915	1,127	14,661	127	13,534 D	7.1%	92.1%	7.1%	92.9%
	DISTRICT 17	15,986	1,776	14,030	180	12,254 D	11.1%	87.8%	11.2%	88.8%
	DISTRICT 18	12,559	2,762	9,630	167	6,868 D	22.0%	76.7%	22.3%	77.7%
	DISTRICT 19	12,917	841	11,984	92	11,143 D	6.5%	92.8%	6.6%	93.4%
	DISTRICT 20	14,023	237	13,703	83	13,466 D	1.7%	97.7%	1.7%	98.3%
	DISTRICT 21	12,567	536	11,944	87	11,408 D	4.3%	95.0%	4.3%	95.7%
	DISTRICT 22	9,381	151	9,176	54	9,025 D	1.6%	97.8%	1.6%	98.4%
	DISTRICT 23	7,713	113	7,566	34	7,453 D	1.5%	98.1%	1.5%	98.5%
	DISTRICT 24	4,115	294	3,733	88	3,439 D	7.1%	90.7%	7.3%	92.7%
	DISTRICT 25	6,857	1,423	5,322	112	3,899 D	20.8%	77.6%	21.1%	78.9%
	DISTRICT 26	4,908	350	4,511	47	4,161 D	7.1%	91.9%	7.2%	92.8%
	ABSENTEE	53,121	7,275	45,426	420	38,151 D	13.7%	85.5%	13.8%	86.2%
1,203,339	TOTAL	294,715	27,249	264,738	2,728	237,489 D	9.2%	89.8%	9.3%	90.7%

MICHIGAN

CONGRESS

		Total	Republican		Democratic		Other	Rep.-Dem.	Percentage			
									Total Vote		Major Vote	
CD	Year	Vote	Vote	Candidate	Vote	Candidate	Vote	Plurality	Rep.	Dem.	Rep.	Dem.
1	1988	140,138	10,979	ASHE, BILL	127,800	CONYERS, JOHN	1,359	116,821 D	7.8%	91.2%	7.9%	92.1%
1	1986	105,784	10,407	ASHE, BILL	94,307	CONYERS, JOHN	1,070	83,900 D	9.8%	89.2%	9.9%	90.1%
1	1984	170,510	17,393	MACK, EDWARD	152,432	CONYERS, JOHN	685	135,039 D	10.2%	89.4%	10.2%	89.8%
1	1982	129,850			125,517	CONYERS, JOHN	4,333	125,517 D		96.7%		100.0%
2	1988	219,692	120,070	PURSELL, CARL D.	98,290	POLLACK, LANA	1,332	21,780 R	54.7%	44.7%	55.0%	45.0%
2	1986	134,778	79,567	PURSELL, CARL D.	55,204	BAKER, DEAN	7	24,363 R	59.0%	41.0%	59.0%	41.0%
2	1984	205,132	140,688	PURSELL, CARL D.	62,374	MCCAULEY, MIKE	2,070	78,314 R	68.6%	30.4%	69.3%	30.7%
2	1982	163,414	106,960	PURSELL, CARL D.	53,040	SALLADE, GEORGE W.	3,414	53,920 R	65.5%	32.5%	66.9%	33.2%
3	1988	196,375	83,769	ALLGAIER, CAL	112,605	WOLPE, HOWARD	1	28,836 D	42.7%	57.3%	42.7%	57.3%
3	1986	130,400	51,678	MCGREGOR, JACKIE	78,720	WOLPE, HOWARD	2	27,042 D	39.6%	60.4%	39.6%	60.4%
3	1984	201,224	94,714	MCGREGOR, JACKIE	106,505	WOLPE, HOWARD	5	11,791 D	47.1%	52.9%	47.1%	52.9%
3	1982	171,961	73,315	MILLIMAN, RICHARD L.	96,842	WOLPE, HOWARD	1,804	23,527 D	42.6%	56.3%	43.1%	56.9%
4	1988	186,703	132,270	UPTON, FREDERICK	54,428	RIVERS, NORMAN	5	77,842 R	70.8%	29.2%	70.8%	29.2%
4	1986	113,633	70,331	UPTON, FREDERICK	41,624	ROCHE, DANIEL	1,678	28,707 R	61.9%	36.6%	62.8%	37.2%
4	1984	191,087	127,907	SILJANDER, MARK D.	63,159	RODEBAUGH, CHARLES	21	64,748 R	66.9%	33.1%	66.9%	33.1%
4	1982	146,605	87,489	SILJANDER, MARK D.	56,877	MASIOKAS, DAVID A.	2,239	30,612 R	59.7%	38.8%	60.6%	39.4%
5	1988	229,440	166,569	HENRY, PAUL	62,868	CATCHICK, JAMES	3	103,701 R	72.6%	27.4%	72.6%	27.4%
5	1986	141,186	100,577	HENRY, PAUL	40,608	DECKER, TERESA	1	59,969 R	71.2%	28.8%	71.2%	28.8%
5	1984	226,678	140,131	HENRY, PAUL	85,232	MCINERNEY, GARY	1,315	54,899 R	61.8%	37.6%	62.2%	37.8%
5	1982	185,881	98,650	SAWYER, HAROLD S.	87,229	MONSMA, STEPHEN V.	2	11,421 R	53.1%	46.9%	53.1%	46.9%
6	1988	204,625	81,079	SCHULTZ, SCOTT	120,581	CARR, M. ROBERT	2,965	39,502 D	39.6%	58.9%	40.2%	59.8%
6	1986	132,217	57,283	DUNN, JIM	74,927	CARR, M. ROBERT	7	17,644 D	43.3%	56.7%	43.3%	56.7%
6	1984	203,530	95,113	RITTER, TOM	106,705	CARR, M. ROBERT	1,712	11,592 D	46.7%	52.4%	47.1%	52.9%
6	1982	164,987	78,388	DUNN, JIM	84,778	CARR, M. ROBERT	1,821	6,390 D	47.5%	51.4%	48.0%	52.0%
7	1988	199,080	47,071	COAD, JEFF	150,832	KILDEE, DALE E.	1,177	103,761 D	23.6%	75.8%	23.8%	76.2%
7	1986	127,172	24,848	CALLIHAN, TRUDIE	101,225	KILDEE, DALE E.	1,099	76,377 D	19.5%	79.6%	19.7%	80.3%
7	1984	155,748			145,070	KILDEE, DALE E.	10,678	145,070 D		93.1%		100.0%
7	1982	157,254	36,303	DARRAH, GEORGE R.	118,538	KILDEE, DALE E.	2,413	82,235 D	23.1%	75.4%	23.4%	76.6%
8	1988	194,104	54,195	BUHL, LLOYD F.	139,904	TRAXLER, J. ROBERT	5	85,709 D	27.9%	72.1%	27.9%	72.1%
8	1986	134,101	36,695	LEVI, JOHN	97,406	TRAXLER, J. ROBERT		60,711 D	27.4%	72.6%	27.4%	72.6%
8	1984	195,845	69,683	HEUSSNER, JOHN	126,161	TRAXLER, J. ROBERT	1	56,478 D	35.6%	64.4%	35.6%	64.4%
8	1982	124,737			113,515	TRAXLER, J. ROBERT	11,222	113,515 D		91.0%		100.0%
9	1988	214,594	149,748	VANDER JAGT, GUY	64,843	GAWRON, DAVID	3	84,905 R	69.8%	30.2%	69.8%	30.2%
9	1986	139,693	89,991	VANDER JAGT, GUY	49,702	ANDERSON, RICHARD		40,289 R	64.4%	35.6%	64.4%	35.6%
9	1984	212,805	150,885	VANDER JAGT, GUY	61,233	SENGER, JOHN	687	89,652 R	70.9%	28.8%	71.1%	28.9%
9	1982	173,439	112,504	VANDER JAGT, GUY	60,932	WARNER, GERALD D.	3	51,572 R	64.9%	35.1%	64.9%	35.1%
10	1988	209,863	152,646	SCHUETTE, BILL	55,398	FORBES, MATHIAS	1,819	97,248 R	72.7%	26.4%	73.4%	26.6%
10	1986	153,424	78,475	SCHUETTE, BILL	74,941	ALBOSTA, DONALD J.	8	3,534 R	51.1%	48.8%	51.2%	48.8%
10	1984	209,645	104,950	SCHUETTE, BILL	103,636	ALBOSTA, DONALD J.	1,059	1,314 R	50.1%	49.4%	50.3%	49.7%
10	1982	169,687	66,080	REED, LAWRENCE W.	102,048	ALBOSTA, DONALD J.	1,559	35,968 D	38.9%	60.1%	39.3%	60.7%
11	1988	216,417	129,085	DAVIS, ROBERT W.	86,526	IRWIN, MITCH	806	42,559 R	59.6%	40.0%	59.9%	40.1%
11	1986	145,404	91,575	DAVIS, ROBERT W.	53,180	ANDERSON, ROBERT	649	38,395 R	63.0%	36.6%	63.3%	36.7%
11	1984	216,634	126,992	DAVIS, ROBERT W.	89,640	STEWART, TOM	2	37,352 R	58.6%	41.4%	58.6%	41.4%
11	1982	175,222	106,039	DAVIS, ROBERT W.	69,181	BOURLAND, KENT	2	36,858 R	60.5%	39.5%	60.5%	39.5%
12	1988	201,798	91,780	CARL, DOUGLAS	108,158	BONIOR, DAVID E.	1,860	16,378 D	45.5%	53.6%	45.9%	54.1%
12	1986	132,089	44,442	MILLER, CANDICE	87,643	BONIOR, DAVID E.	4	43,201 D	33.6%	66.4%	33.6%	66.4%
12	1984	194,984	79,824	TYZA, EUGENE J.	113,772	BONIOR, DAVID E.	1,388	33,948 D	40.9%	58.3%	41.2%	58.8%
12	1982	157,664	52,312	CONTESTI, RAY	103,851	BONIOR, DAVID E.	1,501	51,539 D	33.2%	65.9%	33.5%	66.5%

MICHIGAN

CONGRESS

CD	Year	Total Vote	Republican Vote	Republican Candidate	Democratic Vote	Democratic Candidate	Other Vote	Rep.-Dem. Plurality	Percentage Total Vote Rep.	Percentage Total Vote Dem.	Percentage Major Vote Rep.	Percentage Major Vote Dem.
13	1988	114,700	13,196	SAVAGE, JOHN	99,751	CROCKETT, GEORGE W.	1,753	86,555 D	11.5%	87.0%	11.7%	88.3%
13	1986	89,746	12,395	GRIFFIN, MARY	76,435	CROCKETT, GEORGE W.	916	64,040 D	13.8%	85.2%	14.0%	86.0%
13	1984	152,638	20,416	MURPHY, ROBERT	132,222	CROCKETT, GEORGE W.		111,806 D	13.4%	86.6%	13.4%	86.6%
13	1982	123,195	13,732	GUPTA, LETTY	108,351	CROCKETT, GEORGE W.	1,112	94,619 D	11.1%	88.0%	11.2%	88.8%
14	1988	178,410	64,750	MCNEALY, KENNETH	111,612	HERTEL, DENNIS M.	2,048	46,862 D	36.3%	62.6%	36.7%	63.3%
14	1986	126,667	33,831	GROT, STANLEY	92,328	HERTEL, DENNIS M.	508	58,497 D	26.7%	72.9%	26.8%	73.2%
14	1984	192,142	77,427	LAUVE, JOHN	113,610	HERTEL, DENNIS M.	1,105	36,183 D	40.3%	59.1%	40.5%	59.5%
14	1982	122,613			116,421	HERTEL, DENNIS M.	6,192	116,421 D		94.9%		100.0%
15	1988	163,842	56,963	ADKINS, BURL C.	104,596	FORD, WILLIAM D.	2,283	47,633 D	34.8%	63.8%	35.3%	64.7%
15	1986	103,612	25,078	KASSEL, GLEN	77,950	FORD, WILLIAM D.	584	52,872 D	24.2%	75.2%	24.3%	75.7%
15	1984	165,152	66,172	CARLSON, GERALD	98,973	FORD, WILLIAM D.	7	32,801 D	40.1%	59.9%	40.1%	59.9%
15	1982	130,409	33,904	MORAN, MITCHELL	94,950	FORD, WILLIAM D.	1,555	61,046 D	26.0%	72.8%	26.3%	73.7%
16	1988	136,357			132,775	DINGELL, JOHN D., JR.	3,582	132,775 D		97.4%		100.0%
16	1986	130,636	28,971	GRZYWACKI, FRANK	101,659	DINGELL, JOHN D., JR.	6	72,688 D	22.2%	77.8%	22.2%	77.8%
16	1984	190,622	68,116	GRZYWACKI, FRANK	121,463	DINGELL, JOHN D., JR.	1,043	53,347 D	35.7%	63.7%	35.9%	64.1%
16	1982	154,756	39,227	HASKINS, DAVID K.	114,006	DINGELL, JOHN D., JR.	1,523	74,779 D	25.3%	73.7%	25.6%	74.4%
17	1988	193,027	55,197	FLESSLAND, DENNIS	135,493	LEVIN, SANDER	2,337	80,296 D	28.6%	70.2%	28.9%	71.1%
17	1986	137,390	30,879	WILLIAMS, CALVIN	105,031	LEVIN, SANDER	1,480	74,152 D	22.5%	76.4%	22.7%	77.3%
17	1984	133,105			133,064	LEVIN, SANDER	41	133,064 D		100.0%		100.0%
17	1982	175,480	55,620	ROSEN, GERALD E.	116,901	LEVIN, SANDER	2,959	61,281 D	31.7%	66.6%	32.2%	67.8%
18	1988	257,228	195,579	BROOMFIELD, WILLIAM S.	57,643	KOHUT, GARY	4,006	137,936 R	76.0%	22.4%	77.2%	22.8%
18	1986	149,244	110,099	BROOMFIELD, WILLIAM S.	39,144	KOHUT, GARY	1	70,955 R	73.8%	26.2%	73.8%	26.2%
18	1984	234,884	186,505	BROOMFIELD, WILLIAM S.	46,191	SMARGON, VIVIAN	2,188	140,314 R	79.4%	19.7%	80.1%	19.9%
18	1982	181,262	132,902	BROOMFIELD, WILLIAM S.	46,545	SIPHER, ALLEN J.	1,815	86,357 R	73.3%	25.7%	74.1%	25.9%

MICHIGAN

1988 GENERAL ELECTION

President Other vote was 18,336 Libertarian (Paul); 2,513 Independent (Fulani); 2,497 Independent (McCarthy); 1,958 Workers League (Winn); 819 Independent (Warren); 804 Independent (Holmes); 60 Duke (write-in); 5 Dodge (write-in); 902 scattered write-in.

Senator Other vote was 27,116 Libertarian (Jacobs); 8,908 Workers Against Concessions (Bier); 4,821 Independent (Friedman); 56 scattered write-in.

Congress Other vote was 744 Libertarian (Flint) and 615 Workers Against Concessions (Johnson) in CD 1; 1,324 Libertarian (Raaflaub) and 8 scattered in CD 2; scattered in CD's 3, 4 and 5; 1,897 Libertarian (Wright), 1,063 Workers Against Concessions (Christensen) and 5 scattered in CD 6; 1,174 Workers Against Concessions (Walkowicz) and 3 scattered in CD 7; scattered in CD's 8 and 9; 1,812 Libertarian (Bradley) and 7 scattered in CD 10; 803 Libertarian (Kline) and 3 scattered in CD 11; 1,311 Libertarian (Edwards), 548 Workers Against Concessions (Contrera) and 1 scattered in CD 12; 878 Libertarian (Harris), 874 Workers Against Concessions (Gomez) and 1 scattered in CD 13; 1,336 Libertarian (Roddis), 710 Workers Against Concessions (Breeland) and 2 scattered in CD 14; 1,613 Libertarian (Blakenburg) and 670 Workers Against Concessions (Bell) in CD 15; 3,561 Workers Against Concessions (Leone) and 21 scattered in CD 16; 2,333 Libertarian (Hahn) and 4 scattered in CD 17; 4,003 Libertarian (O'Brien) and 3 scattered in CD 18.

DETROIT

Population data are not available for the Detroit districts.

President Other vote was 896 Libertarian (Paul); 637 Independent (Fulani); 219 Workers League (Winn); 172 Independent (McCarthy); 170 Independent (Holmes); 93 Independent (Warren). There were 187 scattered write-in votes in Wayne county not reported by districts in Detroit.

Senator Other vote was 1,399 Libertarian (Jacobs); 955 Workers Against Concessions (Bier); 374 Independent (Friedman). There were 13 scattered write-in votes in Wayne county not reported by districts in Detroit.

1988 PRIMARIES

AUGUST 2 REPUBLICAN

Senator 245,275 Jim Dunn; 155,984 Robert J. Huber.

Congress Unopposed in fifteen CD's. No candidate in CD 16. Contested as follows:

CD 8 12,487 Lloyd F. Buhl; 11,706 Bill Koelsch.
CD 15 2,690 Burl C. Adkins; 2,309 Glen Kassel; 2,016 Peter Bundarin; 1,282 Robert Fodor.

AUGUST 2 DEMOCRATIC

Senator Donald W. Riegle, unopposed.

Congress Unopposed in fifteen CD's. Contested as follows:

CD 2 12,056 Lana Pollack; 5,058 Dean Baker.
CD 11 29,939 Mitch Irwin; 7,019 Marcia Gould; 6,019 Sven A. Johnson.
CD 13 18,769 George W. Crockett; 15,609 Barbara R. Collins; 2,588 Michael J. Hartt; 1,806 Marlene Kler.

MINNESOTA

GOVERNOR

Rudy Perpich (D). Re-elected 1986 to a four-year term. Previously elected 1982. As Lieutenant-Governor, succeeded Governor Wendell R. Anderson on the latter's resignation, after the 1976 election, to accept appointment to the Senate on the resignation of Senator Walter F. Mondale to become Vice- President. Served as Governor December 1976 to January 1979.

SENATORS

Rudy Boschwitz (R). Re-elected 1984 to a six-year term. Previously elected 1978.

David Durenberger (R). Re-elected 1988 to a six-year term. Previously elected 1982 and in 1978 to fill out the remaining four years of the term vacated by the death of Senator Hubert H. Humphrey.

REPRESENTATIVES

1. Timothy J. Penny (D)
2. Vin Weber (R)
3. Bill Frenzel (R)
4. Bruce F. Vento (D)
5. Martin O. Sabo (D)
6. Gerry Sikorski (D)
7. Arlan Stangeland (R)
8. James L. Oberstar (D)

POSTWAR VOTE FOR PRESIDENT

								Percentage			
	Total	Republican		Democratic		Other		Total Vote		Major Vote	
Year	Vote	Vote	Candidate	Vote	Candidate	Vote	Plurality	Rep.	Dem.	Rep.	Dem.
1988	2,096,790	962,337	Bush, George	1,109,471	Dukakis, Michael S.	24,982	147,134 D	45.9%	52.9%	46.4%	53.6%
1984	2,084,449	1,032,603	Reagan, Ronald	1,036,364	Mondale, Walter F.	15,482	3,761 D	49.5%	49.7%	49.9%	50.1%
1980	2,051,980	873,268	Reagan, Ronald	954,174	Carter, Jimmy	224,538	80,906 D	42.6%	46.5%	47.8%	52.2%
1976	1,949,931	819,395	Ford, Gerald R.	1,070,440	Carter, Jimmy	60,096	251,045 D	42.0%	54.9%	43.4%	56.6%
1972	1,741,652	898,269	Nixon, Richard M.	802,346	McGovern, George S.	41,037	95,923 R	51.6%	46.1%	52.8%	47.2%
1968	1,588,506	658,643	Nixon, Richard M.	857,738	Humphrey, Hubert H.	72,125	199,095 D	41.5%	54.0%	43.4%	56.6%
1964	1,554,462	559,624	Goldwater, Barry M.	991,117	Johnson, Lyndon B.	3,721	431,493 D	36.0%	63.8%	36.1%	63.9%
1960	1,541,887	757,915	Nixon, Richard M.	779,933	Kennedy, John F.	4,039	22,018 D	49.2%	50.6%	49.3%	50.7%
1956	1,340,005	719,302	Eisenhower, Dwight D.	617,525	Stevenson, Adlai E.	3,178	101,777 R	53.7%	46.1%	53.8%	46.2%
1952	1,379,483	763,211	Eisenhower, Dwight D.	608,458	Stevenson, Adlai E.	7,814	154,753 R	55.3%	44.1%	55.6%	44.4%
1948	1,212,226	483,617	Dewey, Thomas E.	692,966	Truman, Harry S.	35,643	209,349 D	39.9%	57.2%	41.1%	58.9%

MINNESOTA

POSTWAR VOTE FOR GOVERNOR

	Total	Republican		Democratic		Other	Rep.-Dem.	Percentage Total Vote		Percentage Major Vote	
Year	Vote	Vote	Candidate	Vote	Candidate	Vote	Plurality	Rep.	Dem.	Rep.	Dem.
1986	1,415,989	606,755	Ludeman, Cal R.	790,138	Perpich, Rudy	19,096	183,383 D	42.9%	55.8%	43.4%	56.6%
1982	1,789,539	715,796	Whitney, Wheelock	1,049,104	Perpich, Rudy	24,639	333,308 D	40.0%	58.6%	40.6%	59.4%
1978	1,585,702	830,019	Quie, Albert H.	718,244	Perpich, Rudy	37,439	111,775 R	52.3%	45.3%	53.6%	46.4%
1974	1,252,898	367,722	Johnson, John W.	786,787	Anderson, Wendell R.	98,389	419,065 D	29.3%	62.8%	31.9%	68.1%
1970	1,365,443	621,780	Head, Douglas M.	737,921	Anderson, Wendell R.	5,742	116,141 D	45.5%	54.0%	45.7%	54.3%
1966	1,295,058	680,593	LeVander, Harold	607,943	Rolvaag, Karl F.	6,522	72,650 R	52.6%	46.9%	52.8%	47.2%
1962 * *	1,246,904	619,751	Andersen, Elmer L.	619,842	Rolvaag, Karl F.	7,311	91 D	49.7%	49.7%	50.0%	50.0%
1960	1,550,265	783,813	Andersen, Elmer L.	760,934	Freeman, Orville L.	5,518	22,879 R	50.6%	49.1%	50.7%	49.3%
1958	1,159,915	490,731	MacKinnon, George	658,326	Freeman, Orville L.	10,858	167,595 D	42.3%	56.8%	42.7%	57.3%
1956	1,422,161	685,196	Nelsen, Ancher	731,180	Freeman, Orville L.	5,785	45,984 D	48.2%	51.4%	48.4%	51.6%
1954	1,151,417	538,865	Anderson, C. Elmer	607,099	Freeman, Orville L.	5,453	68,234 D	46.8%	52.7%	47.0%	53.0%
1952	1,418,869	785,125	Anderson, C. Elmer	624,480	Freeman, Orville L.	9,264	160,645 R	55.3%	44.0%	55.7%	44.3%
1950	1,046,632	635,800	Youngdahl, Luther	400,637	Peterson, Harry H.	10,195	235,163 R	60.7%	38.3%	61.3%	38.7%
1948	1,210,894	643,572	Youngdahl, Luther	545,766	Halsted, Charles L.	21,556	97,806 R	53.1%	45.1%	54.1%	45.9%
1946	880,348	519,067	Youngdahl, Luther	349,565	Barker, Harold H.	11,716	169,502 R	59.0%	39.7%	59.8%	40.2%

The term of office of Minnesota's Governor was increased from two to four years effective with the 1962 election.

POSTWAR VOTE FOR SENATOR

	Total	Republican		Democratic		Other	Rep.-Dem.	Percentage Total Vote		Percentage Major Vote	
Year	Vote	Vote	Candidate	Vote	Candidate	Vote	Plurality	Rep.	Dem.	Rep.	Dem.
1988	2,093,953	1,176,210	Durenberger, David	856,694	Humphrey, Hubert H.,III	61,049	319,516 R	56.2%	40.9%	57.9%	42.1%
1984	2,066,143	1,199,926	Boschwitz, Rudy	852,844	Growe, Joan Anderson	13,373	347,082 R	58.1%	41.3%	58.5%	41.5%
1982	1,804,675	949,207	Durenberger, David	840,401	Dayton, Mark	15,067	108,806 R	52.6%	46.6%	53.0%	47.0%
1978	1,580,778	894,092	Boschwitz, Rudy	638,375	Anderson, Wendell R.	48,311	255,717 R	56.6%	40.4%	58.3%	41.7%
1978 S	1,560,724	957,908	Durenberger, David	538,675	Short, Robert E.	64,141	419,233 R	61.4%	34.5%	64.0%	36.0%
1976	1,912,068	478,611	Brekke, Gerald W.	1,290,736	Humphrey, Hubert H.	142,721	812,125 D	25.0%	67.5%	27.1%	72.9%
1972	1,731,653	742,121	Hansen, Philip	981,340	Mondale, Walter F.	8,192	239,219 D	42.9%	56.7%	43.1%	56.9%
1970	1,364,887	568,025	MacGregor, Clark	788,256	Humphrey, Hubert H.	8,606	220,231 D	41.6%	57.8%	41.9%	58.1%
1966	1,271,426	574,868	Forsythe, Robert A.	685,840	Mondale, Walter F.	10,718	110,972 D	45.2%	53.9%	45.6%	54.4%
1964	1,543,590	605,933	Whitney, Wheelock	931,353	McCarthy, Eugene J.	6,304	325,420 D	39.3%	60.3%	39.4%	60.6%
1960	1,536,839	648,586	Peterson, P. K.	884,168	Humphrey, Hubert H.	4,085	235,582 D	42.2%	57.5%	42.3%	57.7%
1958	1,150,883	536,629	Thye, Edward J.	608,847	McCarthy, Eugene J.	5,407	72,218 D	46.6%	52.9%	46.8%	53.2%
1954	1,138,952	479,619	Bjornson, Val	642,193	Humphrey, Hubert H.	17,140	162,574 D	42.1%	56.4%	42.8%	57.2%
1952	1,387,419	785,649	Thye, Edward J.	590,011	Carlson, William E.	11,759	195,638 R	56.6%	42.5%	57.1%	42.9%
1948	1,220,250	485,801	Ball, Joseph H.	729,494	Humphrey, Hubert H.	4,955	243,693 D	39.8%	59.8%	40.0%	60.0%
1946	878,731	517,775	Thye, Edward J.	349,520	Jorgenson, Theodore	11,436	168,255 R	58.9%	39.8%	59.7%	40.3%

One of the 1978 elections was for a short term to fill a vacancy.

MINNESOTA

Districts Established March 11, 1982

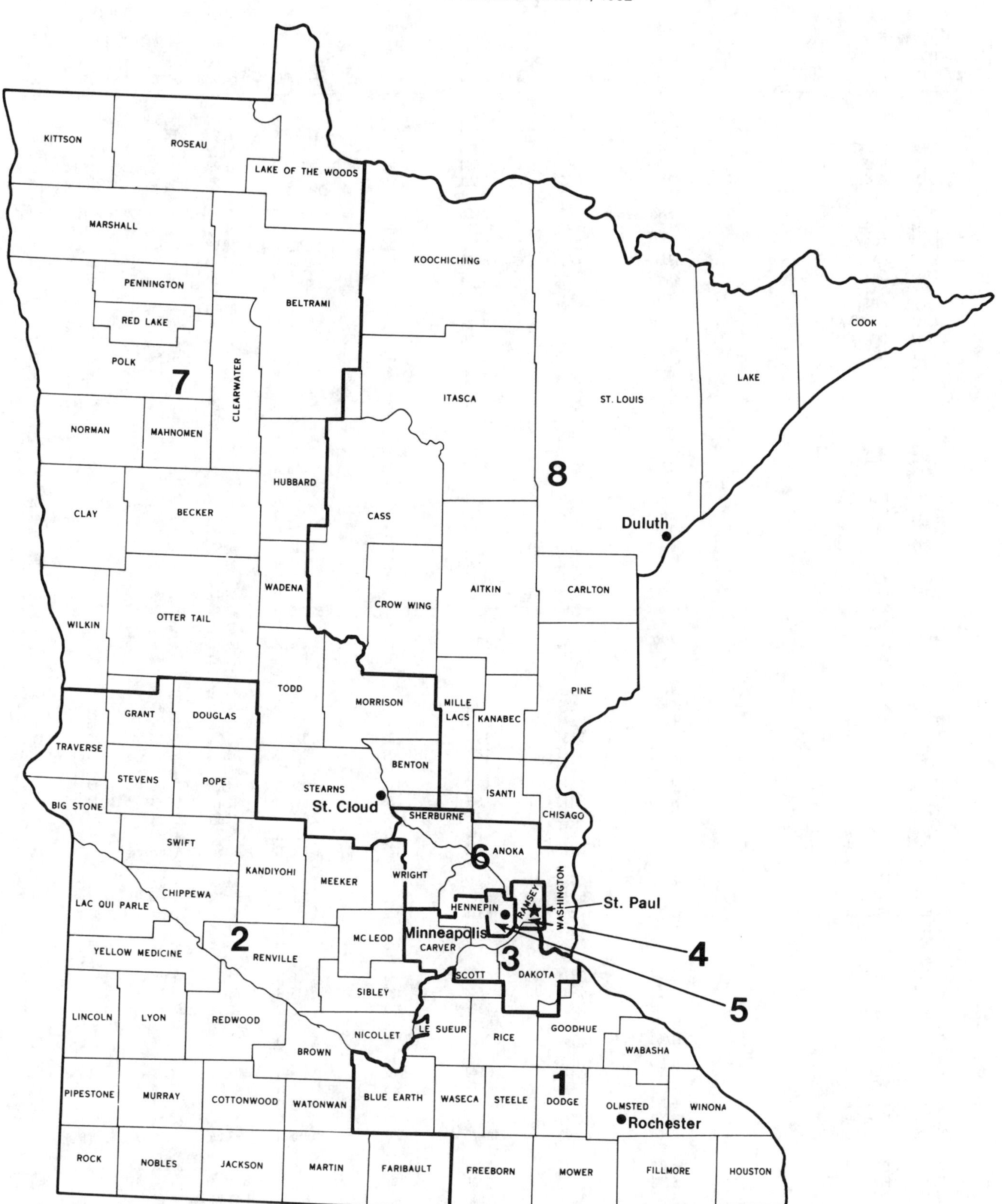

MINNESOTA

PRESIDENT 1988

1980 Census Population	County	Total Vote	Republican	Democratic	Other	Rep.-Dem. Plurality	Percentage Total Vote Rep.	Percentage Total Vote Dem.	Percentage Major Vote Rep.	Percentage Major Vote Dem.
13,404	AITKIN	6,955	3,011	3,863	81	852 D	43.3%	55.5%	43.8%	56.2%
195,998	ANOKA	105,931	46,853	57,953	1,125	11,100 D	44.2%	54.7%	44.7%	55.3%
29,336	BECKER	12,672	6,738	5,787	147	951 R	53.2%	45.7%	53.8%	46.2%
30,982	BELTRAMI	14,402	6,652	7,566	184	914 D	46.2%	52.5%	46.8%	53.2%
25,187	BENTON	12,070	6,060	5,861	149	199 R	50.2%	48.6%	50.8%	49.2%
7,716	BIG STONE	3,526	1,469	2,026	31	557 D	41.7%	57.5%	42.0%	58.0%
52,314	BLUE EARTH	24,570	11,959	12,375	236	416 D	48.7%	50.4%	49.1%	50.9%
28,645	BROWN	12,200	6,898	5,109	193	1,789 R	56.5%	41.9%	57.4%	42.6%
29,936	CARLTON	13,579	4,626	8,790	163	4,164 D	34.1%	64.7%	34.5%	65.5%
37,046	CARVER	21,262	12,560	8,439	263	4,121 R	59.1%	39.7%	59.8%	40.2%
21,050	CASS	11,141	5,895	5,127	119	768 R	52.9%	46.0%	53.5%	46.5%
14,941	CHIPPEWA	6,514	3,190	3,238	86	48 D	49.0%	49.7%	49.6%	50.4%
25,717	CHISAGO	14,196	6,163	7,875	158	1,712 D	43.4%	55.5%	43.9%	56.1%
49,327	CLAY	21,715	10,380	11,186	149	806 D	47.8%	51.5%	48.1%	51.9%
8,761	CLEARWATER	3,569	1,763	1,769	37	6 D	49.4%	49.6%	49.9%	50.1%
4,092	COOK	2,189	1,078	1,080	31	2 D	49.2%	49.3%	50.0%	50.0%
14,854	COTTONWOOD	6,560	3,390	3,095	75	295 R	51.7%	47.2%	52.3%	47.7%
41,722	CROW WING	20,929	11,017	9,674	238	1,343 R	52.6%	46.2%	53.2%	46.8%
194,279	DAKOTA	124,773	61,606	61,942	1,225	336 D	49.4%	49.6%	49.9%	50.1%
14,773	DODGE	6,854	3,848	2,925	81	923 R	56.1%	42.7%	56.8%	43.2%
27,839	DOUGLAS	13,858	7,898	5,803	157	2,095 R	57.0%	41.9%	57.6%	42.4%
19,714	FARIBAULT	8,816	4,846	3,879	91	967 R	55.0%	44.0%	55.5%	44.5%
21,930	FILLMORE	9,201	5,004	4,114	83	890 R	54.4%	44.7%	54.9%	45.1%
36,329	FREEBORN	16,219	7,226	8,836	157	1,610 D	44.6%	54.5%	45.0%	55.0%
38,749	GOODHUE	19,126	9,455	9,438	233	17 R	49.4%	49.3%	50.0%	50.0%
7,171	GRANT	3,687	1,693	1,950	44	257 D	45.9%	52.9%	46.5%	53.5%
941,411	HENNEPIN	539,788	240,209	292,909	6,670	52,700 D	44.5%	54.3%	45.1%	54.9%
18,382	HOUSTON	8,848	4,777	3,936	135	841 R	54.0%	44.5%	54.8%	45.2%
14,098	HUBBARD	7,749	4,365	3,306	78	1,059 R	56.3%	42.7%	56.9%	43.1%
23,600	ISANTI	11,477	5,246	6,075	156	829 D	45.7%	52.9%	46.3%	53.7%
43,069	ITASCA	19,076	8,358	10,517	201	2,159 D	43.8%	55.1%	44.3%	55.7%
13,690	JACKSON	5,979	2,629	3,275	75	646 D	44.0%	54.8%	44.5%	55.5%
12,161	KANABEC	5,604	2,571	2,970	63	399 D	45.9%	53.0%	46.4%	53.6%
36,763	KANDIYOHI	17,878	8,634	8,962	282	328 D	48.3%	50.1%	49.1%	50.9%
6,672	KITTSON	3,060	1,381	1,650	29	269 D	45.1%	53.9%	45.6%	54.4%
17,571	KOOCHICHING	6,795	2,842	3,867	86	1,025 D	41.8%	56.9%	42.4%	57.6%
10,592	LAC QUI PARLE	4,995	2,116	2,805	74	689 D	42.4%	56.2%	43.0%	57.0%
13,043	LAKE	5,785	1,838	3,887	60	2,049 D	31.8%	67.2%	32.1%	67.9%
3,764	LAKE OF THE WOODS	1,814	984	798	32	186 R	54.2%	44.0%	55.2%	44.8%
23,434	LE SUEUR	10,948	5,415	5,410	123	5 R	49.5%	49.4%	50.0%	50.0%
8,207	LINCOLN	3,436	1,479	1,891	66	412 D	43.0%	55.0%	43.9%	56.1%
25,207	LYON	11,762	5,969	5,657	136	312 R	50.7%	48.1%	51.3%	48.7%
29,657	MCLEOD	13,885	7,967	5,736	182	2,231 R	57.4%	41.3%	58.1%	41.9%
5,535	MAHNOMEN	2,360	1,051	1,277	32	226 D	44.5%	54.1%	45.1%	54.9%
13,027	MARSHALL	5,826	2,752	3,001	73	249 D	47.2%	51.5%	47.8%	52.2%
24,687	MARTIN	10,734	5,724	4,922	88	802 R	53.3%	45.9%	53.8%	46.2%
20,594	MEEKER	9,728	4,999	4,544	185	455 R	51.4%	46.7%	52.4%	47.6%
18,430	MILLE LACS	8,308	3,862	4,327	119	465 D	46.5%	52.1%	47.2%	52.8%
29,311	MORRISON	13,246	6,598	6,469	179	129 R	49.8%	48.8%	50.5%	49.5%
40,390	MOWER	19,050	6,969	11,893	188	4,924 D	36.6%	62.4%	36.9%	63.1%
11,507	MURRAY	5,225	2,316	2,840	69	524 D	44.3%	54.4%	44.9%	55.1%
26,929	NICOLLET	13,822	6,878	6,786	158	92 R	49.8%	49.1%	50.3%	49.7%
21,840	NOBLES	9,394	4,348	4,953	93	605 D	46.3%	52.7%	46.7%	53.3%
9,379	NORMAN	3,964	1,789	2,149	26	360 D	45.1%	54.2%	45.4%	54.6%
92,006	OLMSTED	47,609	27,683	19,423	503	8,260 R	58.1%	40.8%	58.8%	41.2%
51,937	OTTER TAIL	24,655	14,015	10,373	267	3,642 R	56.8%	42.1%	57.5%	42.5%
15,258	PENNINGTON	6,073	2,920	3,105	48	185 D	48.1%	51.1%	48.5%	51.5%
19,871	PINE	9,543	3,857	5,540	146	1,683 D	40.4%	58.1%	41.0%	59.0%
11,690	PIPESTONE	5,197	2,760	2,382	55	378 R	53.1%	45.8%	53.7%	46.3%
34,844	POLK	14,665	7,032	7,523	110	491 D	48.0%	51.3%	48.3%	51.7%

MINNESOTA

PRESIDENT 1988

1980 Census Population	County	Total Vote	Republican	Democratic	Other	Rep.-Dem. Plurality	Percentage Total Vote Rep.	Total Vote Dem.	Major Vote Rep.	Major Vote Dem.
11,657	POPE	5,783	2,627	3,074	82	447 D	45.4%	53.2%	46.1%	53.9%
459,784	RAMSEY	235,333	88,736	143,767	2,830	55,031 D	37.7%	61.1%	38.2%	61.8%
5,471	RED LAKE	2,182	918	1,229	35	311 D	42.1%	56.3%	42.8%	57.2%
19,341	REDWOOD	8,379	5,076	3,178	125	1,898 R	60.6%	37.9%	61.5%	38.5%
20,401	RENVILLE	8,932	4,356	4,454	122	98 D	48.8%	49.9%	49.4%	50.6%
46,087	RICE	21,297	9,460	11,570	267	2,110 D	44.4%	54.3%	45.0%	55.0%
10,703	ROCK	5,223	2,737	2,435	51	302 R	52.4%	46.6%	52.9%	47.1%
12,574	ROSEAU	6,214	3,500	2,630	84	870 R	56.3%	42.3%	57.1%	42.9%
222,229	ST. LOUIS	103,308	31,799	70,344	1,165	38,545 D	30.8%	68.1%	31.1%	68.9%
43,784	SCOTT	24,747	13,050	11,405	292	1,645 R	52.7%	46.1%	53.4%	46.6%
29,908	SHERBURNE	16,550	8,360	7,959	231	401 R	50.5%	48.1%	51.2%	48.8%
15,448	SIBLEY	6,952	3,655	3,154	143	501 R	52.6%	45.4%	53.7%	46.3%
108,161	STEARNS	52,166	27,529	23,798	839	3,731 R	52.8%	45.6%	53.6%	46.4%
30,328	STEELE	13,620	7,981	5,496	143	2,485 R	58.6%	40.4%	59.2%	40.8%
11,322	STEVENS	5,468	2,679	2,721	68	42 D	49.0%	49.8%	49.6%	50.4%
12,920	SWIFT	5,806	2,156	3,579	71	1,423 D	37.1%	61.6%	37.6%	62.4%
24,991	TODD	10,776	5,633	5,023	120	610 R	52.3%	46.6%	52.9%	47.1%
5,542	TRAVERSE	2,478	1,061	1,399	18	338 D	42.8%	56.5%	43.1%	56.9%
19,335	WABASHA	9,237	4,681	4,442	114	239 R	50.7%	48.1%	51.3%	48.7%
14,192	WADENA	6,309	3,733	2,484	92	1,249 R	59.2%	39.4%	60.0%	40.0%
18,448	WASECA	8,294	4,471	3,721	102	750 R	53.9%	44.9%	54.6%	45.4%
113,571	WASHINGTON	66,513	30,850	34,952	711	4,102 D	46.4%	52.5%	46.9%	53.1%
12,361	WATONWAN	5,430	2,821	2,544	65	277 R	52.0%	46.9%	52.6%	47.4%
8,454	WILKIN	3,450	1,933	1,486	31	447 R	56.0%	43.1%	56.5%	43.5%
46,256	WINONA	21,652	11,012	10,310	330	702 R	50.9%	47.6%	51.6%	48.4%
58,681	WRIGHT	29,601	14,987	14,177	437	810 R	50.6%	47.9%	51.4%	48.6%
13,653	YELLOW MEDICINE	6,298	2,925	3,282	91	357 D	46.4%	52.1%	47.1%	52.9%
4,075,970	TOTAL	2,096,790	962,337	1,109,471	24,982	147,134 D	45.9%	52.9%	46.4%	53.6%

MINNESOTA

SENATOR 1988

1980 Census Population	County	Total Vote	Republican	Democratic	Other	Rep.-Dem. Plurality	Percentage Total Vote Rep.	Percentage Total Vote Dem.	Percentage Major Vote Rep.	Percentage Major Vote Dem.
13,404	AITKIN	6,981	3,482	3,390	109	92 R	49.9%	48.6%	50.7%	49.3%
195,998	ANOKA	106,457	57,607	46,610	2,240	10,997 R	54.1%	43.8%	55.3%	44.7%
29,336	BECKER	12,744	7,392	5,209	143	2,183 R	58.0%	40.9%	58.7%	41.3%
30,982	BELTRAMI	14,420	8,024	6,115	281	1,909 R	55.6%	42.4%	56.8%	43.2%
25,187	BENTON	12,094	6,870	5,036	188	1,834 R	56.8%	41.6%	57.7%	42.3%
7,716	BIG STONE	3,535	1,635	1,868	32	233 D	46.3%	52.8%	46.7%	53.3%
52,314	BLUE EARTH	24,701	14,835	9,362	504	5,473 R	60.1%	37.9%	61.3%	38.7%
28,645	BROWN	12,247	7,679	4,425	143	3,254 R	62.7%	36.1%	63.4%	36.6%
29,936	CARLTON	13,693	5,784	7,736	173	1,952 D	42.2%	56.5%	42.8%	57.2%
37,046	CARVER	21,381	14,493	6,483	405	8,010 R	67.8%	30.3%	69.1%	30.9%
21,050	CASS	11,172	6,554	4,474	144	2,080 R	58.7%	40.0%	59.4%	40.6%
14,941	CHIPPEWA	6,611	3,596	2,928	87	668 R	54.4%	44.3%	55.1%	44.9%
25,717	CHISAGO	14,214	7,270	6,685	259	585 R	51.1%	47.0%	52.1%	47.9%
49,327	CLAY	21,764	12,820	8,754	190	4,066 R	58.9%	40.2%	59.4%	40.6%
8,761	CLEARWATER	3,590	1,957	1,586	47	371 R	54.5%	44.2%	55.2%	44.8%
4,092	COOK	2,177	1,251	871	55	380 R	57.5%	40.0%	59.0%	41.0%
14,854	COTTONWOOD	6,577	3,849	2,623	105	1,226 R	58.5%	39.9%	59.5%	40.5%
41,722	CROW WING	21,105	12,096	8,724	285	3,372 R	57.3%	41.3%	58.1%	41.9%
194,279	DAKOTA	124,416	76,305	45,215	2,896	31,090 R	61.3%	36.3%	62.8%	37.2%
14,773	DODGE	6,670	4,217	2,328	125	1,889 R	63.2%	34.9%	64.4%	35.6%
27,839	DOUGLAS	13,915	8,563	5,191	161	3,372 R	61.5%	37.3%	62.3%	37.7%
19,714	FARIBAULT	8,880	5,498	3,297	85	2,201 R	61.9%	37.1%	62.5%	37.5%
21,930	FILLMORE	9,285	5,951	3,208	126	2,743 R	64.1%	34.6%	65.0%	35.0%
36,329	FREEBORN	16,373	8,351	7,883	139	468 R	51.0%	48.1%	51.4%	48.6%
38,749	GOODHUE	19,120	11,361	7,455	304	3,906 R	59.4%	39.0%	60.4%	39.6%
7,171	GRANT	3,698	1,931	1,730	37	201 R	52.2%	46.8%	52.7%	47.3%
941,411	HENNEPIN	537,216	307,424	202,792	27,000	104,632 R	57.2%	37.7%	60.3%	39.7%
18,382	HOUSTON	8,800	5,533	3,156	111	2,377 R	62.9%	35.9%	63.7%	36.3%
14,098	HUBBARD	7,731	4,789	2,824	118	1,965 R	61.9%	36.5%	62.9%	37.1%
23,600	ISANTI	11,529	6,112	5,206	211	906 R	53.0%	45.2%	54.0%	46.0%
43,069	ITASCA	19,473	9,621	9,655	197	34 D	49.4%	49.6%	49.9%	50.1%
13,690	JACKSON	6,000	3,183	2,765	52	418 R	53.1%	46.1%	53.5%	46.5%
12,161	KANABEC	5,619	2,971	2,574	74	397 R	52.9%	45.8%	53.6%	46.4%
36,763	KANDIYOHI	17,768	9,713	7,783	272	1,930 R	54.7%	43.8%	55.5%	44.5%
6,672	KITTSON	3,079	1,553	1,508	18	45 R	50.4%	49.0%	50.7%	49.3%
17,571	KOOCHICHING	6,819	3,573	3,184	62	389 R	52.4%	46.7%	52.9%	47.1%
10,592	LAC QUI PARLE	5,009	2,468	2,497	44	29 D	49.3%	49.9%	49.7%	50.3%
13,043	LAKE	5,816	2,378	3,337	101	959 D	40.9%	57.4%	41.6%	58.4%
3,764	LAKE OF THE WOODS	1,811	1,050	746	15	304 R	58.0%	41.2%	58.5%	41.5%
23,434	LE SUEUR	11,012	6,389	4,486	137	1,903 R	58.0%	40.7%	58.7%	41.3%
8,207	LINCOLN	3,459	1,755	1,670	34	85 R	50.7%	48.3%	51.2%	48.8%
25,207	LYON	11,790	6,725	4,817	248	1,908 R	57.0%	40.9%	58.3%	41.7%
29,657	MCLEOD	13,914	8,816	4,933	165	3,883 R	63.4%	35.5%	64.1%	35.9%
5,535	MAHNOMEN	2,384	1,221	1,148	15	73 R	51.2%	48.2%	51.5%	48.5%
13,027	MARSHALL	5,838	3,206	2,603	29	603 R	54.9%	44.6%	55.2%	44.8%
24,687	MARTIN	10,903	6,662	4,113	128	2,549 R	61.1%	37.7%	61.8%	38.2%
20,594	MEEKER	9,750	5,763	3,859	128	1,904 R	59.1%	39.6%	59.9%	40.1%
18,430	MILLE LACS	8,438	4,550	3,749	139	801 R	53.9%	44.4%	54.8%	45.2%
29,311	MORRISON	13,314	7,647	5,507	160	2,140 R	57.4%	41.4%	58.1%	41.9%
40,390	MOWER	19,205	8,504	10,383	318	1,879 D	44.3%	54.1%	45.0%	55.0%
11,507	MURRAY	5,205	2,652	2,518	35	134 R	51.0%	48.4%	51.3%	48.7%
26,929	NICOLLET	13,842	8,559	4,964	319	3,595 R	61.8%	35.9%	63.3%	36.7%
21,840	NOBLES	9,463	4,720	4,658	85	62 R	49.9%	49.2%	50.3%	49.7%
9,379	NORMAN	3,994	2,025	1,948	21	77 R	50.7%	48.8%	51.0%	49.0%
92,006	OLMSTED	47,431	31,784	14,671	976	17,113 R	67.0%	30.9%	68.4%	31.6%
51,937	OTTER TAIL	24,722	15,496	8,897	329	6,599 R	62.7%	36.0%	63.5%	36.5%
15,258	PENNINGTON	6,114	3,318	2,758	38	560 R	54.3%	45.1%	54.6%	45.4%
19,871	PINE	9,552	4,642	4,751	159	109 D	48.6%	49.7%	49.4%	50.6%
11,690	PIPESTONE	5,200	2,946	2,224	30	722 R	56.7%	42.8%	57.0%	43.0%
34,844	POLK	14,791	8,155	6,523	113	1,632 R	55.1%	44.1%	55.6%	44.4%

MINNESOTA

SENATOR 1988

1980 Census Population	County	Total Vote	Republican	Democratic	Other	Rep.-Dem. Plurality	Percentage Total Vote Rep.	Percentage Total Vote Dem.	Percentage Major Vote Rep.	Percentage Major Vote Dem.
11,657	POPE	5,803	3,120	2,608	75	512 R	53.8%	44.9%	54.5%	45.5%
459,784	RAMSEY	233,591	119,758	102,811	11,022	16,947 R	51.3%	44.0%	53.8%	46.2%
5,471	RED LAKE	2,192	1,059	1,119	14	60 D	48.3%	51.0%	48.6%	51.4%
19,341	REDWOOD	8,430	5,425	2,907	98	2,518 R	64.4%	34.5%	65.1%	34.9%
20,401	RENVILLE	8,964	5,021	3,855	88	1,166 R	56.0%	43.0%	56.6%	43.4%
46,087	RICE	21,323	11,913	8,379	1,031	3,534 R	55.9%	39.3%	58.7%	41.3%
10,703	ROCK	5,210	2,959	2,205	46	754 R	56.8%	42.3%	57.3%	42.7%
12,574	ROSEAU	6,224	3,793	2,386	45	1,407 R	60.9%	38.3%	61.4%	38.6%
222,229	ST. LOUIS	102,037	41,168	58,939	1,930	17,771 D	40.3%	57.8%	41.1%	58.9%
43,784	SCOTT	24,853	16,108	8,272	473	7,836 R	64.8%	33.3%	66.1%	33.9%
29,908	SHERBURNE	16,529	9,679	6,546	304	3,133 R	58.6%	39.6%	59.7%	40.3%
15,448	SIBLEY	7,006	4,132	2,797	77	1,335 R	59.0%	39.9%	59.6%	40.4%
108,161	STEARNS	51,868	32,306	18,452	1,110	13,854 R	62.3%	35.6%	63.6%	36.4%
30,328	STEELE	13,710	8,726	4,818	166	3,908 R	63.6%	35.1%	64.4%	35.6%
11,322	STEVENS	5,471	3,161	2,229	81	932 R	57.8%	40.7%	58.6%	41.4%
12,920	SWIFT	5,861	2,619	3,194	48	575 D	44.7%	54.5%	45.1%	54.9%
24,991	TODD	10,814	6,359	4,350	105	2,009 R	58.8%	40.2%	59.4%	40.6%
5,542	TRAVERSE	2,496	1,300	1,183	13	117 R	52.1%	47.4%	52.4%	47.6%
19,335	WABASHA	9,288	5,812	3,358	118	2,454 R	62.6%	36.2%	63.4%	36.6%
14,192	WADENA	6,314	3,945	2,284	85	1,661 R	62.5%	36.2%	63.3%	36.7%
18,448	WASECA	8,384	5,167	3,045	172	2,122 R	61.6%	36.3%	62.9%	37.1%
113,571	WASHINGTON	66,706	38,731	26,244	1,731	12,487 R	58.1%	39.3%	59.6%	40.4%
12,361	WATONWAN	5,469	3,274	2,139	56	1,135 R	59.9%	39.1%	60.5%	39.5%
8,454	WILKIN	3,448	2,237	1,200	11	1,037 R	64.9%	34.8%	65.1%	34.9%
46,256	WINONA	21,198	12,958	7,810	430	5,148 R	61.1%	36.8%	62.4%	37.6%
58,681	WRIGHT	29,639	17,008	12,133	498	4,875 R	57.4%	40.9%	58.4%	41.6%
13,653	YELLOW MEDICINE	6,314	3,198	3,038	78	160 R	50.6%	48.1%	51.3%	48.7%
4,075,970	TOTAL	2,093,953	1,176,210	856,694	61,049	319,516 R	56.2%	40.9%	57.9%	42.1%

MINNESOTA

CONGRESS

CD	Year	Total Vote	Republican Vote	Republican Candidate	Democratic Vote	Democratic Candidate	Other Vote	Rep.-Dem. Plurality	Total Vote Rep.	Total Vote Dem.	Major Vote Rep.	Major Vote Dem.
1	1988	229,813	67,709	SCHRIMPF, CURT	161,118	PENNY, TIMOTHY J.	986	93,409 D	29.5%	70.1%	29.6%	70.4%
1	1986	172,877	47,750	GRAWE, PAUL H.	125,115	PENNY, TIMOTHY J.	12	77,365 D	27.6%	72.4%	27.6%	72.4%
1	1984	245,837	105,723	SPICER, KEITH	140,095	PENNY, TIMOTHY J.	19	34,372 D	43.0%	57.0%	43.0%	57.0%
1	1982	213,520	102,298	HAGEDORN, TOM	109,257	PENNY, TIMOTHY J.	1,965	6,959 D	47.9%	51.2%	48.4%	51.6%
2	1988	227,701	131,639	WEBER, VIN	96,016	PETERSON, DOUG	46	35,623 R	57.8%	42.2%	57.8%	42.2%
2	1986	194,315	100,249	WEBER, VIN	94,048	JOHNSON, DAVE	18	6,201 R	51.6%	48.4%	51.6%	48.4%
2	1984	243,097	153,308	WEBER, VIN	89,770	LUNDQUIST, TODD	19	63,538 R	63.1%	36.9%	63.1%	36.9%
2	1982	226,751	123,508	WEBER, VIN	103,243	NICHOLS, JAMES W.		20,265 R	54.5%	45.5%	54.5%	45.5%
3	1988	315,609	215,322	FRENZEL, BILL	99,770	CARLSON, DAVE	517	115,552 R	68.2%	31.6%	68.3%	31.7%
3	1986	181,729	127,434	FRENZEL, BILL	54,261	STOCK, RAY	34	73,173 R	70.1%	29.9%	70.1%	29.9%
3	1984	283,978	207,819	FRENZEL, BILL	76,132	PETERSON, DAVE	27	131,687 R	73.2%	26.8%	73.2%	26.8%
3	1982	231,311	166,891	FRENZEL, BILL	60,993	SALITERMAN, JOEL A.	3,427	105,898 R	72.2%	26.4%	73.2%	26.8%
4	1988	250,327	67,073	MAITLAND, IAN	181,227	VENTO, BRUCE F.	2,027	114,154 D	26.8%	72.4%	27.0%	73.0%
4	1986	154,635	41,926	STASSEN, HAROLD E.	112,662	VENTO, BRUCE F.	47	70,736 D	27.1%	72.9%	27.1%	72.9%
4	1984	228,071	57,450	RACHNER, MARY JANE	167,678	VENTO, BRUCE F.	2,943	110,228 D	25.2%	73.5%	25.5%	74.5%
4	1982	209,742	56,248	JAMES, BILL	153,494	VENTO, BRUCE F.		97,246 D	26.8%	73.2%	26.8%	73.2%
5	1988	241,798	60,646	GILBERTSON, RAYMOND	174,416	SABO, MARTIN O.	6,736	113,770 D	25.1%	72.1%	25.8%	74.2%
5	1986	145,031	37,583	SERRA, RICK	105,410	SABO, MARTIN O.	2,038	67,827 D	25.9%	72.7%	26.3%	73.7%
5	1984	235,470	62,642	WEIBLEN, RICHARD	165,075	SABO, MARTIN O.	7,753	102,433 D	26.6%	70.1%	27.5%	72.5%
5	1982	208,452	61,184	JOHNSON, KEITH W.	136,634	SABO, MARTIN O.	10,634	75,450 D	29.4%	65.5%	30.9%	69.1%
6	1988	259,035	89,209	PLOETZ, RAY	169,486	SIKORSKI, GERRY	340	80,277 D	34.4%	65.4%	34.5%	65.5%
6	1986	168,077	57,460	SYKORA, BARBARA Z.	110,598	SIKORSKI, GERRY	19	53,138 D	34.2%	65.8%	34.2%	65.8%
6	1984	255,692	101,058	TRUEMAN, PATRICK	154,603	SIKORSKI, GERRY	31	53,545 D	39.5%	60.5%	39.5%	60.5%
6	1982	214,980	105,734	ERDAHL, ARLEN	109,246	SIKORSKI, GERRY		3,512 D	49.2%	50.8%	49.2%	50.8%
7	1988	222,496	121,396	STANGELAND, ARLAN	101,011	HANSON, MARV	89	20,385 R	54.6%	45.4%	54.6%	45.4%
7	1986	189,264	94,024	STANGELAND, ARLAN	93,903	PETERSON, COLLIN C.	1,337	121 R	49.7%	49.6%	50.0%	50.0%
7	1984	236,839	135,087	STANGELAND, ARLAN	101,720	PETERSON, COLLIN C.	32	33,367 R	57.0%	42.9%	57.0%	43.0%
7	1982	215,316	108,254	STANGELAND, ARLAN	107,062	WENSTROM, GENE		1,192 R	50.3%	49.7%	50.3%	49.7%
8	1988	222,311	56,630	SHUSTER, JERRY	165,656	OBERSTAR, JAMES L.	25	109,026 D	25.5%	74.5%	25.5%	74.5%
8	1986	187,045	51,315	RUED, DAVE	135,718	OBERSTAR, JAMES L.	12	84,403 D	27.4%	72.6%	27.4%	72.6%
8	1984	246,483	79,181	RUED, DAVE	165,727	OBERSTAR, JAMES L.	1,575	86,546 D	32.1%	67.2%	32.3%	67.7%
8	1982	229,859	53,467	LUCE, MARJORY L.	176,392	OBERSTAR, JAMES L.		122,925 D	23.3%	76.7%	23.3%	76.7%

MINNESOTA

1988 GENERAL ELECTION

In Minnesota the Democratic party is known as the Democratic-Farmer-Labor party and the Republican party as the Independent-Republican party; candidates appear on the ballot with these designations.

President — Other vote was 5,403 Minnesota Progressive (McCarthy); 5,109 Libertarian (Paul); 2,155 Socialist Workers (Warren); 1,949 Grassroots (Herer); 1,734 New Alliance (Fulani); 1,702 National Economic Recovery (LaRouche); 1,529 Populist (Duke); 1,298 American (Dennis); 489 Workers League (Winn); 3,614 scattered write-in.

Senator — Other vote was 44,474 Progressive Issues (Mann); 9,016 Grassroots (Grimmer); 4,039 Libertarian (Overvig); 3,105 Socialist Workers (Lyons); 415 scattered write-in.

Congress — Other vote was 957 Socialist Workers (Honts) and 29 scattered in CD 1; 1,861 Socialist Workers (Terlexis) and 166 scattered in CD 4; 6,468 Grassroots (Wright) and 268 scattered in CD 5; Scattered in all other CD's.

1988 PRIMARIES

SEPTEMBER 13 REPUBLICAN

Senator — 112,413 David Durenberger; 5,464 Sharon Anderson; 2,379 John Zeleniak.

Congress — Unopposed in five CD's. Contested as follows:

CD 1 — 8,965 Curt Schrimpf; 3,571 Doug Andersen; 1,574 E. B. Henderson.
CD 5 — 3,910 Raymond Gilbertson; 3,527 Richard Weiblen.
CD 8 — 10,608 Jerry Shuster; 6,716 Mary Jane Rachner.

SEPTEMBER 13 DEMOCRATIC

Senator — 153,808 Hubert H. Humphrey, III; 15,994 Kent S. Herschbach.

Congress — Unopposed in three CD's. Contested as follows:

CD 2 — 17,204 Doug Peterson; 3,950 Andy Olson.
CD 3 — 6,903 Dave Carlson; 1,718 Joel A. Saliterman; 1,263 Stan Bentz.
CD 4 — 15,117 Bruce F. Vento; 1,168 Harold Dorland.
CD 5 — 15,240 Martin O. Sabo; 1,370 Ole Savior.
CD 7 — 16,079 Marv Hanson; 12,164 Collin C. Peterson; 1,817 Al Hanson; 1,106 Bill Kjeldahl.

MISSISSIPPI

GOVERNOR

Ray Mabus (D). Elected 1987 to a four-year term.

SENATORS

Thad Cochran (R). Re-elected 1984 to a six-year term. Previously elected 1978.

Trent Lott (R). Elected 1988 to a six-year term.

REPRESENTATIVES

1. Jamie L. Whitten (D)
2. Mike Espy (D)
3. G. V. Montgomery (D)
4. Mike Parker (D)
5. Larkin Smith (R) (see page 1)

POSTWAR VOTE FOR PRESIDENT

								Percentage			
	Total	Republican		Democratic		Other		Total Vote		Major Vote	
Year	Vote	Vote	Candidate	Vote	Candidate	Vote	Plurality	Rep.	Dem.	Rep.	Dem.
1988	931,527	557,890	Bush, George	363,921	Dukakis, Michael S.	9,716	193,969 R	59.9%	39.1%	60.5%	39.5%
1984	941,104	582,377	Reagan, Ronald	352,192	Mondale, Walter F.	6,535	230,185 R	61.9%	37.4%	62.3%	37.7%
1980	892,620	441,089	Reagan, Ronald	429,281	Carter, Jimmy	22,250	11,808 R	49.4%	48.1%	50.7%	49.3%
1976	769,361	366,846	Ford, Gerald R.	381,309	Carter, Jimmy	21,206	14,463 D	47.7%	49.6%	49.0%	51.0%
1972	645,963	505,125	Nixon, Richard M.	126,782	McGovern, George S.	14,056	378,343 R	78.2%	19.6%	79.9%	20.1%
1968 **	654,509	88,516	Nixon, Richard M.	150,644	Humphrey, Hubert H.	415,349	264,705 A	13.5%	23.0%	37.0%	63.0%
1964	409,146	356,528	Goldwater, Barry M.	52,618	Johnson, Lyndon B.		303,910 R	87.1%	12.9%	87.1%	12.9%
1960 **	298,171	73,561	Nixon, Richard M.	108,362	Kennedy, John F.	116,248	7,886 U	24.7%	36.3%	40.4%	59.6%
1956	248,104	60,685	Eisenhower, Dwight D.	144,453	Stevenson, Adlai E.	42,966	83,768 D	24.5%	58.2%	29.6%	70.4%
1952	285,532	112,966	Eisenhower, Dwight D.	172,566	Stevenson, Adlai E.		59,600 D	39.6%	60.4%	39.6%	60.4%
1948 **	192,190	5,043	Dewey, Thomas E.	19,384	Truman, Harry S.	167,763	148,154 SR	2.6%	10.1%	20.6%	79.4%

In 1968 other vote was Independent (Wallace). In 1960 other vote was Unpledged Independent Democratic. In 1948 other vote was 167,538 States Rights and 225 Progressive.

POSTWAR VOTE FOR GOVERNOR

								Percentage			
	Total	Republican		Democratic		Other	Rep.-Dem.	Total Vote		Major Vote	
Year	Vote	Vote	Candidate	Vote	Candidate	Vote	Plurality	Rep.	Dem.	Rep.	Dem.
1987	721,695	336,006	Reed, Jack	385,689	Mabus, Ray		49,683 D	46.6%	53.4%	46.6%	53.4%
1983	742,737	288,764	Bramlett, Leon	409,209	Allain, William A.	44,764	120,445 D	38.9%	55.1%	41.4%	58.6%
1979	677,322	263,702	Carmichael, Gil	413,620	Winter, William F.		149,918 D	38.9%	61.1%	38.9%	61.1%
1975	708,033	319,632	Carmichael, Gil	369,568	Finch, Cliff	18,833	49,936 D	45.1%	52.2%	46.4%	53.6%
1971	780,537		—	601,122	Waller, William L.	179,415	601,122 D		77.0%		100.0%
1967	448,697	133,379	Phillips, Rubel L.	315,318	Williams, John Bell		181,939 D	29.7%	70.3%	29.7%	70.3%
1963	363,971	138,515	Phillips, Rubel L.	225,456	Johnson, Paul B.		86,941 D	38.1%	61.9%	38.1%	61.9%
1959	57,671		—	57,671	Barnett, Ross R.		57,671 D		100.0%		100.0%
1955	40,707		—	40,707	Coleman, James P.		40,707 D		100.0%		100.0%
1951	43,422		—	43,422	White, Hugh		43,422 D		100.0%		100.0%
1947	166,095		—	161,993	Wright, Fielding L.	4,102	161,993 D		97.5%		100.0%

MISSISSIPPI

POSTWAR VOTE FOR SENATOR

									Percentage			
	Total	Republican		Democratic		Other	Rep.-Dem.		Total Vote		Major Vote	
Year	Vote	Vote	Candidate	Vote	Candidate	Vote	Plurality		Rep.	Dem.	Rep.	Dem.
1988	946,719	510,380	Lott, Trent	436,339	Dowdy, Wayne		74,041	R	53.9%	46.1%	53.9%	46.1%
1984	952,240	580,314	Cochran, Thad	371,926	Winter, William F.		208,388	R	60.9%	39.1%	60.9%	39.1%
1982	645,026	230,927	Barbour, Haley	414,099	Stennis, John		183,172	D	35.8%	64.2%	35.8%	64.2%
1978	583,936	263,089	Cochran, Thad	185,454	Dantin, Maurice	135,393	77,635	R	45.1%	31.8%	58.7%	41.3%
1976	554,433		—	554,433	Stennis, John		554,433	D		100.0%		100.0%
1972	645,746	249,779	Carmichael, Gil	375,102	Eastland, James O.	20,865	125,323	D	38.7%	58.1%	40.0%	60.0%
1970	324,215		—	286,622	Stennis, John	37,593	286,622	D		88.4%		100.0%
1966	393,900	105,150	Walker, Prentiss	258,248	Eastland, James O.	30,502	153,098	D	26.7%	65.6%	28.9%	71.1%
1964	343,364		—	343,364	Stennis, John		343,364	D		100.0%		100.0%
1960	266,148	21,807	Moore, Joe A.	244,341	Eastland, James O.		222,534	D	8.2%	91.8%	8.2%	91.8%
1958	61,039		—	61,039	Stennis, John		61,039	D		100.0%		100.0%
1954	105,526	4,678	White, James A.	100,848	Eastland, James O.		96,170	D	4.4%	95.6%	4.4%	95.6%
1952	233,919		—	233,919	Stennis, John		233,919	D		100.0%		100.0%
1948	151,478		—	151,478	Eastland, James O.		151,478	D		100.0%		100.0%
1947 S	193,709		[See note below]									
1946	46,747		—	46,747	Bilbo, Theodore		46,747	D		100.0%		100.0%

The 1947 election was for a short term to fill a vacancy and was held without party designation or nomination; John Stennis polled 52,068 votes (26.9% of the total vote) and won the election with a 6,343 plurality. Other candidate votes in this election were 45,725 W. M.Colmer; 43,642 Forrest B. Jackson; 27,159 Paul B. Johnson; 24,492 John E. Rankin and 623 R. L.Collins.

MISSISSIPPI

Districts Established January 6, 1984

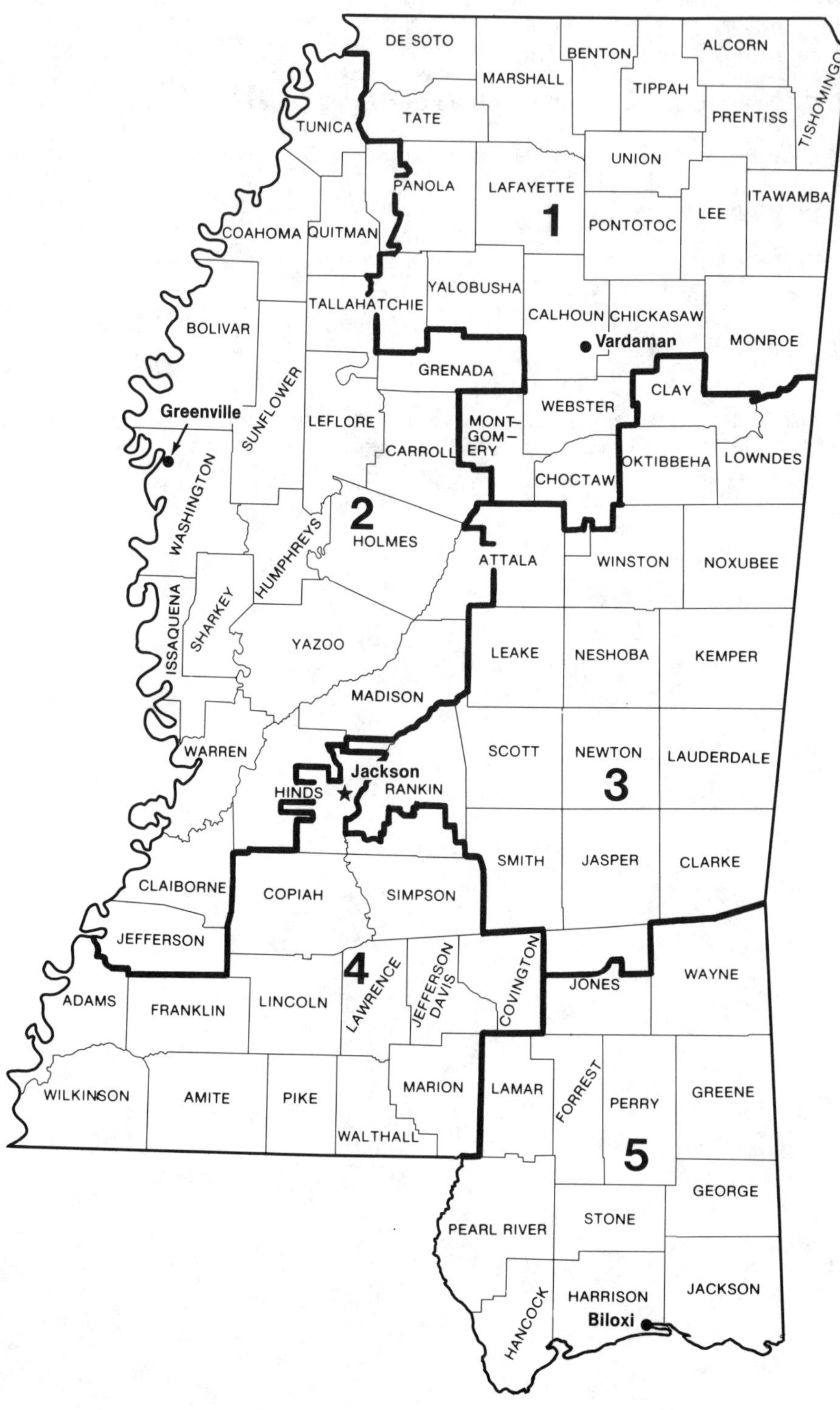

MISSISSIPPI

PRESIDENT 1988

1980 Census Population	County	Total Vote	Republican	Democratic	Other	Rep.-Dem. Plurality	Percentage Total Vote Rep.	Total Vote Dem.	Major Vote Rep.	Major Vote Dem.
38,035	ADAMS	15,994	8,116	7,732	146	384 R	50.7%	48.3%	51.2%	48.8%
33,036	ALCORN	12,102	6,641	5,335	126	1,306 R	54.9%	44.1%	55.5%	44.5%
13,369	AMITE	6,186	3,333	2,834	19	499 R	53.9%	45.8%	54.0%	46.0%
19,865	ATTALA	7,556	4,524	2,997	35	1,527 R	59.9%	39.7%	60.2%	39.8%
8,153	BENTON	3,309	1,565	1,718	26	153 D	47.3%	51.9%	47.7%	52.3%
45,965	BOLIVAR	14,085	6,105	7,606	374	1,501 D	43.3%	54.0%	44.5%	55.5%
15,664	CALHOUN	5,483	3,375	2,086	22	1,289 R	61.6%	38.0%	61.8%	38.2%
9,776	CARROLL	4,204	2,628	1,560	16	1,068 R	62.5%	37.1%	62.8%	37.2%
17,853	CHICKASAW	6,125	3,390	2,713	22	677 R	55.3%	44.3%	55.5%	44.5%
8,996	CHOCTAW	3,647	2,297	1,335	15	962 R	63.0%	36.6%	63.2%	36.8%
12,279	CLAIBORNE	4,349	1,233	3,083	33	1,850 D	28.4%	70.9%	28.6%	71.4%
16,945	CLARKE	7,098	4,522	2,576		1,946 R	63.7%	36.3%	63.7%	36.3%
21,082	CLAY	7,553	3,645	3,849	59	204 D	48.3%	51.0%	48.6%	51.4%
36,918	COAHOMA	11,278	4,939	6,139	200	1,200 D	43.8%	54.4%	44.6%	55.4%
26,503	COPIAH	9,334	5,100	4,175	59	925 R	54.6%	44.7%	55.0%	45.0%
15,927	COVINGTON	6,633	4,005	2,591	37	1,414 R	60.4%	39.1%	60.7%	39.3%
53,930	DE SOTO	20,250	14,681	5,449	120	9,232 R	72.5%	26.9%	72.9%	27.1%
66,018	FORREST	21,318	14,249	6,953	116	7,296 R	66.8%	32.6%	67.2%	32.8%
8,208	FRANKLIN	3,962	2,376	1,563	23	813 R	60.0%	39.4%	60.3%	39.7%
15,297	GEORGE	7,782	4,545	2,435	802	2,110 R	58.4%	31.3%	65.1%	34.9%
9,827	GREENE	4,970	2,837	1,637	496	1,200 R	57.1%	32.9%	63.4%	36.6%
21,043	GRENADA	9,056	5,352	3,683	21	1,669 R	59.1%	40.7%	59.2%	40.8%
24,537	HANCOCK	11,687	7,763	3,760	164	4,003 R	66.4%	32.2%	67.4%	32.6%
157,665	HARRISON	47,754	32,892	14,439	423	18,453 R	68.9%	30.2%	69.5%	30.5%
250,998	HINDS	95,006	52,749	41,058	1,199	11,691 R	55.5%	43.2%	56.2%	43.8%
22,970	HOLMES	8,126	2,737	5,350	39	2,613 D	33.7%	65.8%	33.8%	66.2%
13,931	HUMPHREYS	4,695	2,018	2,644	33	626 D	43.0%	56.3%	43.3%	56.7%
2,513	ISSAQUENA	973	424	511	38	87 D	43.6%	52.5%	45.3%	54.7%
20,518	ITAWAMBA	7,693	4,535	3,143	15	1,392 R	58.9%	40.9%	59.1%	40.9%
118,015	JACKSON	40,364	29,830	10,328	206	19,502 R	73.9%	25.6%	74.3%	25.7%
17,265	JASPER	6,572	3,368	3,184	20	184 R	51.2%	48.4%	51.4%	48.6%
9,181	JEFFERSON	3,401	702	2,693	6	1,991 D	20.6%	79.2%	20.7%	79.3%
13,846	JEFFERSON DAVIS	5,728	2,745	2,948	35	203 D	47.9%	51.5%	48.2%	51.8%
61,912	JONES	24,272	16,764	7,383	125	9,381 R	69.1%	30.4%	69.4%	30.6%
10,148	KEMPER	4,235	2,128	2,069	38	59 R	50.2%	48.9%	50.7%	49.3%
31,030	LAFAYETTE	9,852	5,841	3,967	44	1,874 R	59.3%	40.3%	59.6%	40.4%
23,821	LAMAR	11,746	9,145	2,535	66	6,610 R	77.9%	21.6%	78.3%	21.7%
77,285	LAUDERDALE	26,529	18,302	7,967	260	10,335 R	69.0%	30.0%	69.7%	30.3%
12,518	LAWRENCE	6,223	3,682	2,517	24	1,165 R	59.2%	40.4%	59.4%	40.6%
18,790	LEAKE	6,963	4,168	2,787	8	1,381 R	59.9%	40.0%	59.9%	40.1%
57,061	LEE	20,728	13,767	6,604	357	7,163 R	66.4%	31.9%	67.6%	32.4%
41,525	LEFLORE	12,579	6,409	5,830	340	579 R	50.9%	46.3%	52.4%	47.6%
30,174	LINCOLN	13,297	8,710	4,534	53	4,176 R	65.5%	34.1%	65.8%	34.2%
57,304	LOWNDES	17,331	11,258	5,993	80	5,265 R	65.0%	34.6%	65.3%	34.7%
41,613	MADISON	19,825	11,399	8,242	184	3,157 R	57.5%	41.6%	58.0%	42.0%
25,708	MARION	11,344	7,019	4,240	85	2,779 R	61.9%	37.4%	62.3%	37.7%
29,296	MARSHALL	11,751	4,668	6,982	101	2,314 D	39.7%	59.4%	40.1%	59.9%
36,404	MONROE	11,173	6,447	4,669	57	1,778 R	57.7%	41.8%	58.0%	42.0%
13,366	MONTGOMERY	4,409	2,504	1,893	12	611 R	56.8%	42.9%	56.9%	43.1%
23,789	NESHOBA	9,347	6,363	2,942	42	3,421 R	68.1%	31.5%	68.4%	31.6%
19,944	NEWTON	8,003	5,658	2,332	13	3,326 R	70.7%	29.1%	70.8%	29.2%
13,212	NOXUBEE	4,631	1,870	2,722	39	852 D	40.4%	58.8%	40.7%	59.3%
36,018	OKTIBBEHA	12,289	7,126	5,100	63	2,026 R	58.0%	41.5%	58.3%	41.7%
28,164	PANOLA	10,665	5,382	5,222	61	160 R	50.5%	49.0%	50.8%	49.2%
33,795	PEARL RIVER	14,333	10,220	3,939	174	6,281 R	71.3%	27.5%	72.2%	27.8%
9,864	PERRY	4,347	2,983	1,326	38	1,657 R	68.6%	30.5%	69.2%	30.8%
36,173	PIKE	14,239	7,637	6,531	71	1,106 R	53.6%	45.9%	53.9%	46.1%
20,918	PONTOTOC	7,740	4,939	2,772	29	2,167 R	63.8%	35.8%	64.1%	35.9%
24,025	PRENTISS	7,892	4,348	3,429	115	919 R	55.1%	43.4%	55.9%	44.1%
12,636	QUITMAN	4,351	1,832	2,497	22	665 D	42.1%	57.4%	42.3%	57.7%

MISSISSIPPI

PRESIDENT 1988

1980 Census Population	County	Total Vote	Republican	Democratic	Other	Rep.-Dem. Plurality	Percentage Total Vote Rep.	Percentage Total Vote Dem.	Percentage Major Vote Rep.	Percentage Major Vote Dem.
69,427	RANKIN	29,254	22,937	6,201	116	16,736 R	78.4%	21.2%	78.7%	21.3%
24,556	SCOTT	8,488	5,522	2,939	27	2,583 R	65.1%	34.6%	65.3%	34.7%
7,964	SHARKEY	2,970	1,277	1,609	84	332 D	43.0%	54.2%	44.2%	55.8%
23,441	SIMPSON	9,223	6,151	3,016	56	3,135 R	66.7%	32.7%	67.1%	32.9%
15,077	SMITH	6,285	4,573	1,660	52	2,913 R	72.8%	26.4%	73.4%	26.6%
9,716	STONE	4,499	3,007	1,452	40	1,555 R	66.8%	32.3%	67.4%	32.6%
34,844	SUNFLOWER	9,289	4,362	4,898	29	536 D	47.0%	52.7%	47.1%	52.9%
17,157	TALLAHATCHIE	5,547	2,633	2,881	33	248 D	47.5%	51.9%	47.8%	52.2%
20,119	TATE	7,449	4,553	2,872	24	1,681 R	61.1%	38.6%	61.3%	38.7%
18,739	TIPPAH	7,603	4,593	2,958	52	1,635 R	60.4%	38.9%	60.8%	39.2%
18,434	TISHOMINGO	7,052	3,646	3,378	28	268 R	51.7%	47.9%	51.9%	48.1%
9,652	TUNICA	2,430	896	1,510	24	614 D	36.9%	62.1%	37.2%	62.8%
21,741	UNION	8,591	5,511	3,044	36	2,467 R	64.1%	35.4%	64.4%	35.6%
13,761	WALTHALL	5,502	3,103	2,354	45	749 R	56.4%	42.8%	56.9%	43.1%
51,627	WARREN	20,170	12,507	7,437	226	5,070 R	62.0%	36.9%	62.7%	37.3%
72,344	WASHINGTON	20,687	10,229	10,222	236	7 R	49.4%	49.4%	50.0%	50.0%
19,135	WAYNE	7,414	4,496	2,889	29	1,607 R	60.6%	39.0%	60.9%	39.1%
10,300	WEBSTER	4,632	3,061	1,550	21	1,511 R	66.1%	33.5%	66.4%	33.6%
10,021	WILKINSON	4,223	1,528	2,678	17	1,150 D	36.2%	63.4%	36.3%	63.7%
19,474	WINSTON	9,229	5,317	3,851	61	1,466 R	57.6%	41.7%	58.0%	42.0%
13,139	YALOBUSHA	5,093	2,660	2,402	31	258 R	52.2%	47.2%	52.5%	47.5%
27,349	YAZOO	11,530	5,538	4,989	1,003	549 R	48.0%	43.3%	52.6%	47.4%
2,520,638	TOTAL	931,527	557,890	363,921	9,716	193,969 R	59.9%	39.1%	60.5%	39.5%

MISSISSIPPI

GOVERNOR 1987

1980 Census Population	County	Total Vote	Republican	Democratic	Other	Rep.-Dem. Plurality	Percentage Total Vote Rep.	Total Vote Dem.	Major Vote Rep.	Major Vote Dem.
38,035	ADAMS	10,799	4,465	6,334		1,869 D	41.3%	58.7%	41.3%	58.7%
33,036	ALCORN	7,838	3,029	4,809		1,780 D	38.6%	61.4%	38.6%	61.4%
13,369	AMITE	4,757	2,133	2,624		491 D	44.8%	55.2%	44.8%	55.2%
19,865	ATTALA	6,177	3,101	3,076		25 R	50.2%	49.8%	50.2%	49.8%
8,153	BENTON	2,547	941	1,606		665 D	36.9%	63.1%	36.9%	63.1%
45,965	BOLIVAR	10,693	4,060	6,633		2,573 D	38.0%	62.0%	38.0%	62.0%
15,664	CALHOUN	4,625	2,263	2,362		99 D	48.9%	51.1%	48.9%	51.1%
9,776	CARROLL	3,673	1,814	1,859		45 D	49.4%	50.6%	49.4%	50.6%
17,853	CHICKASAW	4,982	2,235	2,747		512 D	44.9%	55.1%	44.9%	55.1%
8,996	CHOCTAW	3,363	1,349	2,014		665 D	40.1%	59.9%	40.1%	59.9%
12,279	CLAIBORNE	4,814	1,365	3,449		2,084 D	28.4%	71.6%	28.4%	71.6%
16,945	CLARKE	6,577	3,253	3,324		71 D	49.5%	50.5%	49.5%	50.5%
21,082	CLAY	6,024	2,649	3,375		726 D	44.0%	56.0%	44.0%	56.0%
36,918	COAHOMA	8,912	3,494	5,418		1,924 D	39.2%	60.8%	39.2%	60.8%
26,503	COPIAH	7,753	3,078	4,675		1,597 D	39.7%	60.3%	39.7%	60.3%
15,927	COVINGTON	5,374	2,846	2,528		318 R	53.0%	47.0%	53.0%	47.0%
53,930	DE SOTO	7,920	3,207	4,713		1,506 D	40.5%	59.5%	40.5%	59.5%
66,018	FORREST	16,825	8,795	8,030		765 R	52.3%	47.7%	52.3%	47.7%
8,208	FRANKLIN	3,299	1,599	1,700		101 D	48.5%	51.5%	48.5%	51.5%
15,297	GEORGE	4,361	2,031	2,330		299 D	46.6%	53.4%	46.6%	53.4%
9,827	GREENE	3,241	1,846	1,395		451 R	57.0%	43.0%	57.0%	43.0%
21,043	GRENADA	7,313	3,038	4,275		1,237 D	41.5%	58.5%	41.5%	58.5%
24,537	HANCOCK	8,100	3,371	4,729		1,358 D	41.6%	58.4%	41.6%	58.4%
157,665	HARRISON	36,155	15,254	20,901		5,647 D	42.2%	57.8%	42.2%	57.8%
250,998	HINDS	68,968	32,718	36,250		3,532 D	47.4%	52.6%	47.4%	52.6%
22,970	HOLMES	7,416	2,347	5,069		2,722 D	31.6%	68.4%	31.6%	68.4%
13,931	HUMPHREYS	4,856	1,640	3,216		1,576 D	33.8%	66.2%	33.8%	66.2%
2,513	ISSAQUENA	875	316	559		243 D	36.1%	63.9%	36.1%	63.9%
20,518	ITAWAMBA	6,480	3,031	3,449		418 D	46.8%	53.2%	46.8%	53.2%
118,015	JACKSON	30,756	13,777	16,979		3,202 D	44.8%	55.2%	44.8%	55.2%
17,265	JASPER	6,453	2,777	3,676		899 D	43.0%	57.0%	43.0%	57.0%
9,181	JEFFERSON	3,205	639	2,566		1,927 D	19.9%	80.1%	19.9%	80.1%
13,846	JEFFERSON DAVIS	4,814	2,047	2,767		720 D	42.5%	57.5%	42.5%	57.5%
61,912	JONES	19,706	10,788	8,918		1,870 R	54.7%	45.3%	54.7%	45.3%
10,148	KEMPER	3,628	1,696	1,932		236 D	46.7%	53.3%	46.7%	53.3%
31,030	LAFAYETTE	7,162	3,887	3,275		612 R	54.3%	45.7%	54.3%	45.7%
23,821	LAMAR	8,805	5,569	3,236		2,333 R	63.2%	36.8%	63.2%	36.8%
77,285	LAUDERDALE	18,961	9,269	9,692		423 D	48.9%	51.1%	48.9%	51.1%
12,518	LAWRENCE	4,510	1,987	2,523		536 D	44.1%	55.9%	44.1%	55.9%
18,790	LEAKE	5,687	2,777	2,910		133 D	48.8%	51.2%	48.8%	51.2%
57,061	LEE	17,182	10,243	6,939		3,304 R	59.6%	40.4%	59.6%	40.4%
41,525	LEFLORE	11,210	5,311	5,899		588 D	47.4%	52.6%	47.4%	52.6%
30,174	LINCOLN	11,594	5,440	6,154		714 D	46.9%	53.1%	46.9%	53.1%
57,304	LOWNDES	13,642	7,222	6,420		802 R	52.9%	47.1%	52.9%	47.1%
41,613	MADISON	15,436	7,011	8,425		1,414 D	45.4%	54.6%	45.4%	54.6%
25,708	MARION	9,251	4,189	5,062		873 D	45.3%	54.7%	45.3%	54.7%
29,296	MARSHALL	8,234	2,577	5,657		3,080 D	31.3%	68.7%	31.3%	68.7%
36,404	MONROE	7,693	3,819	3,874		55 D	49.6%	50.4%	49.6%	50.4%
13,366	MONTGOMERY	4,006	1,740	2,266		526 D	43.4%	56.6%	43.4%	56.6%
23,789	NESHOBA	7,562	4,061	3,501		560 R	53.7%	46.3%	53.7%	46.3%
19,944	NEWTON	6,811	3,967	2,844		1,123 R	58.2%	41.8%	58.2%	41.8%
13,212	NOXUBEE	5,009	2,207	2,802		595 D	44.1%	55.9%	44.1%	55.9%
36,018	OKTIBBEHA	8,982	4,504	4,478		26 R	50.1%	49.9%	50.1%	49.9%
28,164	PANOLA	8,407	3,143	5,264		2,121 D	37.4%	62.6%	37.4%	62.6%
33,795	PEARL RIVER	9,731	4,898	4,833		65 R	50.3%	49.7%	50.3%	49.7%
9,864	PERRY	3,712	2,179	1,533		646 R	58.7%	41.3%	58.7%	41.3%
36,173	PIKE	10,790	4,449	6,341		1,892 D	41.2%	58.8%	41.2%	58.8%
20,918	PONTOTOC	6,567	3,832	2,735		1,097 R	58.4%	41.6%	58.4%	41.6%
24,025	PRENTISS	6,642	2,653	3,989		1,336 D	39.9%	60.1%	39.9%	60.1%
12,636	QUITMAN	3,828	1,437	2,391		954 D	37.5%	62.5%	37.5%	62.5%

MISSISSIPPI

GOVERNOR 1987

1980 Census Population	County	Total Vote	Republican	Democratic	Other	Rep.-Dem. Plurality	Percentage Total Vote Rep.	Total Vote Dem.	Major Vote Rep.	Major Vote Dem.
69,427	RANKIN	22,817	13,218	9,599		3,619 R	57.9%	42.1%	57.9%	42.1%
24,556	SCOTT	7,450	4,000	3,450		550 R	53.7%	46.3%	53.7%	46.3%
7,964	SHARKEY	2,930	997	1,933		936 D	34.0%	66.0%	34.0%	66.0%
23,441	SIMPSON	8,290	4,435	3,855		580 R	53.5%	46.5%	53.5%	46.5%
15,077	SMITH	5,916	3,443	2,473		970 R	58.2%	41.8%	58.2%	41.8%
9,716	STONE	4,316	1,934	2,382		448 D	44.8%	55.2%	44.8%	55.2%
34,844	SUNFLOWER	8,087	3,398	4,689		1,291 D	42.0%	58.0%	42.0%	58.0%
17,157	TALLAHATCHIE	5,342	2,191	3,151		960 D	41.0%	59.0%	41.0%	59.0%
20,119	TATE	4,010	1,638	2,372		734 D	40.8%	59.2%	40.8%	59.2%
18,739	TIPPAH	5,255	2,323	2,932		609 D	44.2%	55.8%	44.2%	55.8%
18,434	TISHOMINGO	6,584	2,246	4,338		2,092 D	34.1%	65.9%	34.1%	65.9%
9,652	TUNICA	2,206	789	1,417		628 D	35.8%	64.2%	35.8%	64.2%
21,741	UNION	6,617	3,428	3,189		239 R	51.8%	48.2%	51.8%	48.2%
13,761	WALTHALL	4,127	1,872	2,255		383 D	45.4%	54.6%	45.4%	54.6%
51,627	WARREN	14,880	6,820	8,060		1,240 D	45.8%	54.2%	45.8%	54.2%
72,344	WASHINGTON	14,879	5,990	8,889		2,899 D	40.3%	59.7%	40.3%	59.7%
19,135	WAYNE	6,651	3,570	3,081		489 R	53.7%	46.3%	53.7%	46.3%
10,300	WEBSTER	4,060	2,472	1,588		884 R	60.9%	39.1%	60.9%	39.1%
10,021	WILKINSON	1,965	828	1,137		309 D	42.1%	57.9%	42.1%	57.9%
19,474	WINSTON	7,379	3,428	3,951		523 D	46.5%	53.5%	46.5%	53.5%
13,139	YALOBUSHA	4,107	1,841	2,266		425 D	44.8%	55.2%	44.8%	55.2%
27,349	YAZOO	9,134	3,782	5,352		1,570 D	41.4%	58.6%	41.4%	58.6%
2,520,638	TOTAL	721,695	336,006	385,689		49,683 D	46.6%	53.4%	46.6%	53.4%

MISSISSIPPI

SENATOR 1988

1980 Census Population	County	Total Vote	Republican	Democratic	Other	Rep.-Dem. Plurality	Percentage Total Vote Rep.	Percentage Total Vote Dem.	Percentage Major Vote Rep.	Percentage Major Vote Dem.
38,035	ADAMS	15,805	6,929	8,876		1,947 D	43.8%	56.2%	43.8%	56.2%
33,036	ALCORN	11,957	4,676	7,281		2,605 D	39.1%	60.9%	39.1%	60.9%
13,369	AMITE	6,480	2,947	3,533		586 D	45.5%	54.5%	45.5%	54.5%
19,865	ATTALA	7,825	4,214	3,611		603 R	53.9%	46.1%	53.9%	46.1%
8,153	BENTON	3,450	1,333	2,117		784 D	38.6%	61.4%	38.6%	61.4%
45,965	BOLIVAR	13,731	6,036	7,695		1,659 D	44.0%	56.0%	44.0%	56.0%
15,664	CALHOUN	5,849	2,626	3,223		597 D	44.9%	55.1%	44.9%	55.1%
9,776	CARROLL	4,408	2,517	1,891		626 R	57.1%	42.9%	57.1%	42.9%
17,853	CHICKASAW	6,683	2,568	4,115		1,547 D	38.4%	61.6%	38.4%	61.6%
8,996	CHOCTAW	3,886	2,035	1,851		184 R	52.4%	47.6%	52.4%	47.6%
12,279	CLAIBORNE	4,448	1,185	3,263		2,078 D	26.6%	73.4%	26.6%	73.4%
16,945	CLARKE	6,942	3,961	2,981		980 R	57.1%	42.9%	57.1%	42.9%
21,082	CLAY	8,453	3,009	5,444		2,435 D	35.6%	64.4%	35.6%	64.4%
36,918	COAHOMA	10,647	4,589	6,058		1,469 D	43.1%	56.9%	43.1%	56.9%
26,503	COPIAH	9,610	4,423	5,187		764 D	46.0%	54.0%	46.0%	54.0%
15,927	COVINGTON	7,029	3,993	3,036		957 R	56.8%	43.2%	56.8%	43.2%
53,930	DE SOTO	20,940	13,348	7,592		5,756 R	63.7%	36.3%	63.7%	36.3%
66,018	FORREST	21,804	14,751	7,053		7,698 R	67.7%	32.3%	67.7%	32.3%
8,208	FRANKLIN	4,156	1,871	2,285		414 D	45.0%	55.0%	45.0%	55.0%
15,297	GEORGE	6,880	4,453	2,427		2,026 R	64.7%	35.3%	64.7%	35.3%
9,827	GREENE	4,438	3,022	1,416		1,606 R	68.1%	31.9%	68.1%	31.9%
21,043	GRENADA	9,359	4,938	4,421		517 R	52.8%	47.2%	52.8%	47.2%
24,537	HANCOCK	12,094	8,110	3,984		4,126 R	67.1%	32.9%	67.1%	32.9%
157,665	HARRISON	49,424	33,149	16,275		16,874 R	67.1%	32.9%	67.1%	32.9%
250,998	HINDS	94,557	48,412	46,145		2,267 R	51.2%	48.8%	51.2%	48.8%
22,970	HOLMES	8,395	2,621	5,774		3,153 D	31.2%	68.8%	31.2%	68.8%
13,931	HUMPHREYS	4,844	1,857	2,987		1,130 D	38.3%	61.7%	38.3%	61.7%
2,513	ISSAQUENA	922	371	551		180 D	40.2%	59.8%	40.2%	59.8%
20,518	ITAWAMBA	7,968	2,920	5,048		2,128 D	36.6%	63.4%	36.6%	63.4%
118,015	JACKSON	42,278	31,074	11,204		19,870 R	73.5%	26.5%	73.5%	26.5%
17,265	JASPER	7,085	3,501	3,584		83 D	49.4%	50.6%	49.4%	50.6%
9,181	JEFFERSON	3,532	639	2,893		2,254 D	18.1%	81.9%	18.1%	81.9%
13,846	JEFFERSON DAVIS	6,014	2,598	3,416		818 D	43.2%	56.8%	43.2%	56.8%
61,912	JONES	24,430	16,764	7,666		9,098 R	68.6%	31.4%	68.6%	31.4%
10,148	KEMPER	4,490	2,002	2,488		486 D	44.6%	55.4%	44.6%	55.4%
31,030	LAFAYETTE	10,086	5,267	4,819		448 R	52.2%	47.8%	52.2%	47.8%
23,821	LAMAR	11,949	9,096	2,853		6,243 R	76.1%	23.9%	76.1%	23.9%
77,285	LAUDERDALE	25,990	16,458	9,532		6,926 R	63.3%	36.7%	63.3%	36.7%
12,518	LAWRENCE	6,443	2,958	3,485		527 D	45.9%	54.1%	45.9%	54.1%
18,790	LEAKE	7,106	3,878	3,228		650 R	54.6%	45.4%	54.6%	45.4%
57,061	LEE	20,424	9,841	10,583		742 D	48.2%	51.8%	48.2%	51.8%
41,525	LEFLORE	12,232	6,123	6,109		14 R	50.1%	49.9%	50.1%	49.9%
30,174	LINCOLN	13,961	7,560	6,401		1,159 R	54.2%	45.8%	54.2%	45.8%
57,304	LOWNDES	17,827	10,367	7,460		2,907 R	58.2%	41.8%	58.2%	41.8%
41,613	MADISON	18,951	10,685	8,266		2,419 R	56.4%	43.6%	56.4%	43.6%
25,708	MARION	11,709	6,374	5,335		1,039 R	54.4%	45.6%	54.4%	45.6%
29,296	MARSHALL	11,362	4,118	7,244		3,126 D	36.2%	63.8%	36.2%	63.8%
36,404	MONROE	12,002	4,864	7,138		2,274 D	40.5%	59.5%	40.5%	59.5%
13,366	MONTGOMERY	4,745	2,344	2,401		57 D	49.4%	50.6%	49.4%	50.6%
23,789	NESHOBA	9,864	5,795	4,069		1,726 R	58.7%	41.3%	58.7%	41.3%
19,944	NEWTON	7,972	5,120	2,852		2,268 R	64.2%	35.8%	64.2%	35.8%
13,212	NOXUBEE	4,904	1,804	3,100		1,296 D	36.8%	63.2%	36.8%	63.2%
36,018	OKTIBBEHA	12,613	6,497	6,116		381 R	51.5%	48.5%	51.5%	48.5%
28,164	PANOLA	11,540	5,523	6,017		494 D	47.9%	52.1%	47.9%	52.1%
33,795	PEARL RIVER	13,598	9,455	4,143		5,312 R	69.5%	30.5%	69.5%	30.5%
9,864	PERRY	4,709	3,316	1,393		1,923 R	70.4%	29.6%	70.4%	29.6%
36,173	PIKE	15,077	6,072	9,005		2,933 D	40.3%	59.7%	40.3%	59.7%
20,918	PONTOTOC	8,064	3,490	4,574		1,084 D	43.3%	56.7%	43.3%	56.7%
24,025	PRENTISS	7,999	2,876	5,123		2,247 D	36.0%	64.0%	36.0%	64.0%
12,636	QUITMAN	4,681	1,716	2,965		1,249 D	36.7%	63.3%	36.7%	63.3%

MISSISSIPPI

SENATOR 1988

1980 Census Population	County	Total Vote	Republican	Democratic	Other	Rep.-Dem. Plurality	Percentage Total Vote Rep.	Percentage Total Vote Dem.	Percentage Major Vote Rep.	Percentage Major Vote Dem.
69,427	RANKIN	29,738	20,836	8,902		11,934 R	70.1%	29.9%	70.1%	29.9%
24,556	SCOTT	9,163	5,163	4,000		1,163 R	56.3%	43.7%	56.3%	43.7%
7,964	SHARKEY	2,813	1,127	1,686		559 D	40.1%	59.9%	40.1%	59.9%
23,441	SIMPSON	9,682	5,644	4,038		1,606 R	58.3%	41.7%	58.3%	41.7%
15,077	SMITH	6,802	4,393	2,409		1,984 R	64.6%	35.4%	64.6%	35.4%
9,716	STONE	4,732	3,064	1,668		1,396 R	64.8%	35.2%	64.8%	35.2%
34,844	SUNFLOWER	10,073	4,210	5,863		1,653 D	41.8%	58.2%	41.8%	58.2%
17,157	TALLAHATCHIE	6,065	2,369	3,696		1,327 D	39.1%	60.9%	39.1%	60.9%
20,119	TATE	7,888	4,297	3,591		706 R	54.5%	45.5%	54.5%	45.5%
18,739	TIPPAH	8,013	3,540	4,473		933 D	44.2%	55.8%	44.2%	55.8%
18,434	TISHOMINGO	7,285	1,983	5,302		3,319 D	27.2%	72.8%	27.2%	72.8%
9,652	TUNICA	2,427	905	1,522		617 D	37.3%	62.7%	37.3%	62.7%
21,741	UNION	8,955	4,070	4,885		815 D	45.4%	54.6%	45.4%	54.6%
13,761	WALTHALL	5,947	2,628	3,319		691 D	44.2%	55.8%	44.2%	55.8%
51,627	WARREN	18,646	10,772	7,874		2,898 R	57.8%	42.2%	57.8%	42.2%
72,344	WASHINGTON	19,706	9,483	10,223		740 D	48.1%	51.9%	48.1%	51.9%
19,135	WAYNE	7,948	5,123	2,825		2,298 R	64.5%	35.5%	64.5%	35.5%
10,300	WEBSTER	4,762	2,379	2,383		4 D	50.0%	50.0%	50.0%	50.0%
10,021	WILKINSON	4,485	1,450	3,035		1,585 D	32.3%	67.7%	32.3%	67.7%
19,474	WINSTON	9,774	4,806	4,968		162 D	49.2%	50.8%	49.2%	50.8%
13,139	YALOBUSHA	5,492	2,353	3,139		786 D	42.8%	57.2%	42.8%	57.2%
27,349	YAZOO	9,702	4,746	4,956		210 D	48.9%	51.1%	48.9%	51.1%
2,520,638	TOTAL	946,719	510,380	436,339		74,041 R	53.9%	46.1%	53.9%	46.1%

MISSISSIPPI

CONGRESS

CD	Year	Total Vote	Republican Vote	Republican Candidate	Democratic Vote	Democratic Candidate	Other Vote	Rep.-Dem. Plurality	Total Vote Rep.	Total Vote Dem.	Major Vote Rep.	Major Vote Dem.
1	1988	175,826	38,381	BUSH, JIM	137,445	WHITTEN, JAMIE L.		99,064 D	21.8%	78.2%	21.8%	78.2%
1	1986	90,137	30,267	COBB, LARRY	59,870	WHITTEN, JAMIE L.		29,603 D	33.6%	66.4%	33.6%	66.4%
1	1984	154,521			136,530	WHITTEN, JAMIE L.	17,991	136,530 D		88.4%		100.0%
2	1988	173,631	59,827	COLEMAN, JACK	112,401	ESPY, MIKE	1,403	52,574 D	34.5%	64.7%	34.7%	65.3%
2	1986	141,411	68,292	FRANKLIN, WEBB	73,119	ESPY, MIKE		4,827 D	48.3%	51.7%	48.3%	51.7%
2	1984	182,420	92,392	FRANKLIN, WEBB	89,154	CLARK, ROBERT G.	874	3,238 R	50.6%	48.9%	50.9%	49.1%
3	1988	185,380	20,729	BOURLAND, JIMMIE RAY	164,651	MONTGOMERY, G. V.		143,922 D	11.2%	88.8%	11.2%	88.8%
3	1986	80,575			80,575	MONTGOMERY, G. V.		80,575 D		100.0%		100.0%
3	1984	158,002			158,002	MONTGOMERY, G. V.		158,002 D		100.0%		100.0%
4	1988	201,063	88,433	COLLINS, THOMAS	110,184	PARKER, MIKE	2,446	21,751 D	44.0%	54.8%	44.5%	55.5%
4	1986	120,009	34,190	HEALY, GAIL	85,819	DOWDY, WAYNE		51,629 D	28.5%	71.5%	28.5%	71.5%
4	1984	205,432	91,797	ARMSTRONG, DAVID	113,635	DOWDY, WAYNE		21,838 D	44.7%	55.3%	44.7%	55.3%
5	1988	182,219	100,185	SMITH, LARKIN	82,034	TAYLOR, GENE		18,151 R	55.0%	45.0%	55.0%	45.0%
5	1986	91,431	75,288	LOTT, TRENT	16,143	ALBRITTON, LARRY L.		59,145 R	82.3%	17.7%	82.3%	17.7%
5	1984	168,477	142,637	LOTT, TRENT	25,840	COATE, ARLON		116,797 R	84.7%	15.3%	84.7%	15.3%

MISSISSIPPI

1987 GENERAL ELECTION

Governor Early unamended returns gave the Republican (Reed) vote in Itawamba county as 3,301.

1988 GENERAL ELECTION

President Other vote was 4,232 Independent (Duke); 3,329 Libertarian (Paul); 2,155 Independent (Fulani).

Senator

Congress Other vote was Independent (Benford) in CD 2; Independent (Gilchrist) in CD 4.

1987 PRIMARIES

AUGUST 4 REPUBLICAN

Governor 14,798 Jack Reed; 4,057 Doug Lemon.

AUGUST 4 DEMOCRATIC

Governor 304,559 Ray Mabus; 131,180 Mike P. Sturdivant; 105,056 William L. Waller; 98,517 John A. Eaves; 83,603 Maurice Dantin; 73,667 Ed Pittman; 5,990 Gilbert Fountain; 5,418 H. R. Toney.

AUGUST 25 DEMOCRATIC RUN-OFF

Governor 428,883 Ray Mabus; 238,039 Mike P. Sturdivant.

1988 PRIMARIES

MARCH 8 REPUBLICAN

Senator Trent Lott, unopposed.

Congress Unopposed in three CD's. Contested as follows:

CD 4 10,387 Thomas Collins; 6,862 Andy Taggart; 5,914 Mike Gunn; 4,163 Phillip Davis; 1,983 Mark Henry; 1,235 Doug Magee.

CD 5 27,260 Larkin Smith; 17,835 George R. Hall; 6,870 Glenn Mitchell; 3,506 Christopher Roosa; 515 Richard Vogel.

MARCH 8 DEMOCRATIC

Senator 189,954 Wayne Dowdy; 152,126 Dick Molpus; 13,276 Gilbert Fountain.

Congress Unopposed in one CD. Contested as follows:

CD 1 56,222 Jamie L. Whitten; 9,594 John Hargett.

CD 2 59,801 Mike Espy; 8,250 J. F. Clarke.

CD 4 23,489 Brad Pigott; 17,303 Mike Parker; 16,695 Steve Patterson; 12,037 Bobby Moak; 9,127 Clint Watkins; 8,425 Terrell Stubbs; 2,975 Deborah McNair; 1,482 Al McDonald; 1,024 Jerry Parks.

CD 5 16,948 Gene Taylor; 15,226 Glenn White; 9,046 Jim McVeay; 5,266 Doss Fowler; 3,278 Joe Stone; 1,299 Arlon Coate.

MISSISSIPPI

MARCH 29 REPUBLICAN RUN-OFF

Congress

CD 4 10,409 Thomas Collins; 6,514 Andy Taggart.
CD 5 25,470 Larkin Smith; 12,553 George R. Hall.

MARCH 29 DEMOCRATIC RUN-OFF

Congress

CD 4 34,507 Mike Parker; 22,122 Brad Pigott.
CD 5 18,933 Gene Taylor; 13,273 Glenn White.

MISSOURI

GOVERNOR

John Ashcroft (R). Re-elected 1988 to a four-year term. Previously elected 1984.

SENATORS

Christopher Bond (R). Elected 1986 to a six-year term.

John C. Danforth (R). Re-elected 1988 to a six-year term. Previously elected 1982, 1976.

REPRESENTATIVES

1. William Clay (D)
2. John Buechner (R)
3. Richard A. Gephardt (D)
4. Ike Skelton (D)
5. Alan Wheat (D)
6. E. Thomas Coleman (R)
7. Melton D. Hancock (R)
8. Bill Emerson (R)
9. Harold Volkmer (D)

POSTWAR VOTE FOR PRESIDENT

								Percentage			
	Total	Republican		Democratic		Other		Total Vote		Major Vote	
Year	Vote	Vote	Candidate	Vote	Candidate	Vote	Plurality	Rep.	Dem.	Rep.	Dem.
1988	2,093,713	1,084,953	Bush, George	1,001,619	Dukakis, Michael S.	7,141	83,334 R	51.8%	47.8%	52.0%	48.0%
1984	2,122,783	1,274,188	Reagan, Ronald	848,583	Mondale, Walter F.	12	425,605 R	60.0%	40.0%	60.0%	40.0%
1980	2,099,824	1,074,181	Reagan, Ronald	931,182	Carter, Jimmy	94,461	142,999 R	51.2%	44.3%	53.6%	46.4%
1976	1,953,600	927,443	Ford, Gerald R.	998,387	Carter, Jimmy	27,770	70,944 D	47.5%	51.1%	48.2%	51.8%
1972	1,855,803	1,153,852	Nixon, Richard M.	697,147	McGovern, George S.	4,804	456,705 R	62.2%	37.6%	62.3%	37.7%
1968	1,809,502	811,932	Nixon, Richard M.	791,444	Humphrey, Hubert H.	206,126	20,488 R	44.9%	43.7%	50.6%	49.4%
1964	1,817,879	653,535	Goldwater, Barry M.	1,164,344	Johnson, Lyndon B.		510,809 D	36.0%	64.0%	36.0%	64.0%
1960	1,934,422	962,221	Nixon, Richard M.	972,201	Kennedy, John F.		9,980 D	49.7%	50.3%	49.7%	50.3%
1956	1,832,562	914,289	Eisenhower, Dwight D.	918,273	Stevenson, Adlai E.		3,984 D	49.9%	50.1%	49.9%	50.1%
1952	1,892,062	959,429	Eisenhower, Dwight D.	929,830	Stevenson, Adlai E.	2,803	29,599 R	50.7%	49.1%	50.8%	49.2%
1948	1,578,628	655,039	Dewey, Thomas E.	917,315	Truman, Harry S.	6,274	262,276 D	41.5%	58.1%	41.7%	58.3%

POSTWAR VOTE FOR GOVERNOR

								Percentage			
	Total	Republican		Democratic		Other	Rep.-Dem.	Total Vote		Major Vote	
Year	Vote	Vote	Candidate	Vote	Candidate	Vote	Plurality	Rep.	Dem.	Rep.	Dem.
1988	2,085,928	1,339,531	Ashcroft, John	724,919	Hearnes, Betty C.	21,478	614,612 R	64.2%	34.8%	64.9%	35.1%
1984	2,108,210	1,194,506	Ashcroft, John	913,700	Rothman, Kenneth J.	4	280,806 R	56.7%	43.3%	56.7%	43.3%
1980	2,088,028	1,098,950	Bond, Christopher	981,884	Teasdale, Joseph P.	7,194	117,066 R	52.6%	47.0%	52.8%	47.2%
1976	1,933,575	958,110	Bond, Christopher	971,184	Teasdale, Joseph P.	4,281	13,074 D	49.6%	50.2%	49.7%	50.3%
1972	1,865,683	1,029,451	Bond, Christopher	832,751	Dowd, Edward L.	3,481	196,700 R	55.2%	44.6%	55.3%	44.7%
1968	1,764,602	691,797	Roos, Lawrence K.	1,072,805	Hearnes, Warren E.		381,008 D	39.2%	60.8%	39.2%	60.8%
1964	1,789,600	678,949	Shepley, Ethan	1,110,651	Hearnes, Warren E.		431,702 D	37.9%	62.1%	37.9%	62.1%
1960	1,887,331	792,131	Farmer, Edward G.	1,095,200	Dalton, John M.		303,069 D	42.0%	58.0%	42.0%	58.0%
1956	1,808,338	866,810	Hocker, Lon	941,528	Blair, James T.		74,718 D	47.9%	52.1%	47.9%	52.1%
1952	1,871,095	886,370	Elliott, Howard	983,166	Donnelly, Phil M.	1,559	96,796 D	47.4%	52.5%	47.4%	52.6%
1948	1,567,338	670,064	Thompson, Murray	893,092	Smith, Forrest	4,182	223,028 D	42.8%	57.0%	42.9%	57.1%

MISSOURI

POSTWAR VOTE FOR SENATOR

		Republican		Democratic				Percentage			
	Total					Other	Rep.-Dem.	Total Vote		Major Vote	
Year	Vote	Vote	Candidate	Vote	Candidate	Vote	Plurality	Rep.	Dem.	Rep.	Dem.
1988	2,078,875	1,407,416	Danforth, John C.	660,045	Nixon, Jeremiah W.	11,414	747,371 R	67.7%	31.8%	68.1%	31.9%
1986	1,477,327	777,612	Bond, Christopher	699,624	Woods, Harriett	91	77,988 R	52.6%	47.4%	52.6%	47.4%
1982	1,543,521	784,876	Danforth, John C.	758,629	Woods, Harriett	16	26,247 R	50.8%	49.1%	50.9%	49.1%
1980	2,066,965	985,399	McNary, Gene	1,074,859	Eagleton, Thomas F.	6,707	89,460 D	47.7%	52.0%	47.8%	52.2%
1976	1,914,777	1,090,067	Danforth, John C.	813,571	Hearnes, Warren E.	11,139	276,496 R	56.9%	42.5%	57.3%	42.7%
1974	1,224,303	480,900	Curtis, Thomas B.	735,433	Eagleton, Thomas F.	7,970	254,533 D	39.3%	60.1%	39.5%	60.5%
1970	1,283,912	617,903	Danforth, John C.	655,431	Symington, Stuart	10,578	37,528 D	48.1%	51.0%	48.5%	51.5%
1968	1,737,958	850,544	Curtis, Thomas B.	887,414	Eagleton, Thomas F.		36,870 D	48.9%	51.1%	48.9%	51.1%
1964	1,783,043	596,377	Bradshaw, Jean P.	1,186,666	Symington, Stuart		590,289 D	33.4%	66.6%	33.4%	66.6%
1962	1,222,259	555,330	Kemper, Crosby	666,929	Long, Edward V.		111,599 D	45.4%	54.6%	45.4%	54.6%
1960 S	1,880,232	880,576	Hocker, Lon	999,656	Long, Edward V.		119,080 D	46.8%	53.2%	46.8%	53.2%
1958	1,173,903	393,847	Palmer, Hazel	780,056	Symington, Stuart		386,209 D	33.6%	66.4%	33.6%	66.4%
1956	1,800,984	785,048	Douglas, Herbert	1,015,936	Hennings, Thomas C.		230,888 D	43.6%	56.4%	43.6%	56.4%
1952	1,868,083	858,170	Kem, James P.	1,008,523	Symington, Stuart	1,390	150,353 D	45.9%	54.0%	46.0%	54.0%
1950	1,279,414	592,922	Donnell, Forrest C.	685,732	Hennings, Thomas C.	760	92,810 D	46.3%	53.6%	46.4%	53.6%
1946	1,084,100	572,556	Kem, James P.	511,544	Briggs, Frank P.		61,012 R	52.8%	47.2%	52.8%	47.2%

The 1960 election was for a short term to fill a vacancy.

MISSOURI

Districts Established January 7, 1982

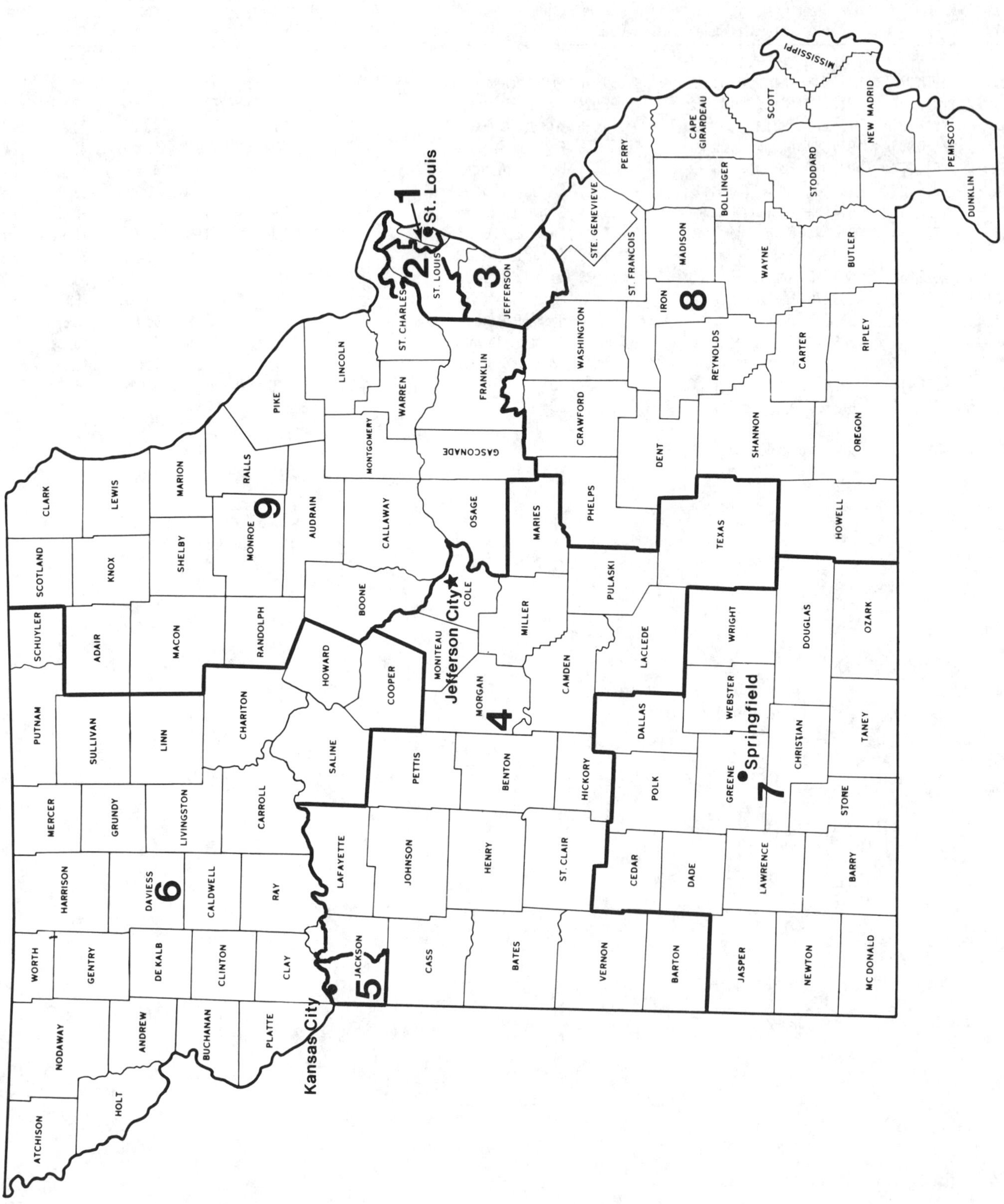

MISSOURI

PRESIDENT 1988

1980 Census Population	County	Total Vote	Republican	Democratic	Other	Rep.-Dem. Plurality	Percentage Total Vote Rep.	Total Vote Dem.	Major Vote Rep.	Major Vote Dem.
24,870	ADAIR	9,336	5,721	3,571	44	2,150 R	61.3%	38.2%	61.6%	38.4%
13,980	ANDREW	6,537	3,407	3,103	27	304 R	52.1%	47.5%	52.3%	47.7%
8,605	ATCHISON	3,239	1,761	1,468	10	293 R	54.4%	45.3%	54.5%	45.5%
26,458	AUDRAIN	10,327	5,072	5,226	29	154 D	49.1%	50.6%	49.3%	50.7%
24,408	BARRY	11,477	7,231	4,210	36	3,021 R	63.0%	36.7%	63.2%	36.8%
11,292	BARTON	4,958	3,339	1,603	16	1,736 R	67.3%	32.3%	67.6%	32.4%
15,873	BATES	6,930	3,574	3,332	24	242 R	51.6%	48.1%	51.8%	48.2%
12,183	BENTON	6,145	3,467	2,654	24	813 R	56.4%	43.2%	56.6%	43.4%
10,301	BOLLINGER	4,599	2,710	1,883	6	827 R	58.9%	40.9%	59.0%	41.0%
100,376	BOONE	47,458	22,948	24,370	140	1,422 D	48.4%	51.4%	48.5%	51.5%
87,888	BUCHANAN	34,089	15,336	18,601	152	3,265 D	45.0%	54.6%	45.2%	54.8%
37,693	BUTLER	13,738	7,968	5,751	19	2,217 R	58.0%	41.9%	58.1%	41.9%
8,660	CALDWELL	3,815	2,074	1,726	15	348 R	54.4%	45.2%	54.6%	45.4%
32,252	CALLAWAY	11,938	6,687	5,209	42	1,478 R	56.0%	43.6%	56.2%	43.8%
20,017	CAMDEN	11,759	7,773	3,930	56	3,843 R	66.1%	33.4%	66.4%	33.6%
58,837	CAPE GIRARDEAU	24,556	16,583	7,904	69	8,679 R	67.5%	32.2%	67.7%	32.3%
12,131	CARROLL	5,150	2,811	2,330	9	481 R	54.6%	45.2%	54.7%	45.3%
5,428	CARTER	2,528	1,429	1,087	12	342 R	56.5%	43.0%	56.8%	43.2%
51,029	CASS	22,961	12,799	10,092	70	2,707 R	55.7%	44.0%	55.9%	44.1%
11,894	CEDAR	4,744	2,966	1,774	4	1,192 R	62.5%	37.4%	62.6%	37.4%
10,489	CHARITON	4,555	2,193	2,347	15	154 D	48.1%	51.5%	48.3%	51.7%
22,402	CHRISTIAN	12,441	7,670	4,724	47	2,946 R	61.7%	38.0%	61.9%	38.1%
8,493	CLARK	3,431	1,493	1,925	13	432 D	43.5%	56.1%	43.7%	56.3%
136,488	CLAY	60,287	30,293	29,620	374	673 R	50.2%	49.1%	50.6%	49.4%
15,916	CLINTON	6,961	3,282	3,653	26	371 D	47.1%	52.5%	47.3%	52.7%
56,663	COLE	26,441	18,023	8,359	59	9,664 R	68.2%	31.6%	68.3%	31.7%
14,643	COOPER	6,266	3,737	2,510	19	1,227 R	59.6%	40.1%	59.8%	40.2%
18,300	CRAWFORD	6,987	3,856	3,107	24	749 R	55.2%	44.5%	55.4%	44.6%
7,383	DADE	3,476	2,154	1,315	7	839 R	62.0%	37.8%	62.1%	37.9%
12,096	DALLAS	5,223	2,898	2,298	27	600 R	55.5%	44.0%	55.8%	44.2%
8,905	DAVIESS	3,518	1,765	1,743	10	22 R	50.2%	49.5%	50.3%	49.7%
8,222	DE KALB	3,843	1,863	1,970	10	107 D	48.5%	51.3%	48.6%	51.4%
14,517	DENT	5,417	2,975	2,421	21	554 R	54.9%	44.7%	55.1%	44.9%
11,594	DOUGLAS	4,976	3,225	1,735	16	1,490 R	64.8%	34.9%	65.0%	35.0%
36,324	DUNKLIN	10,320	5,026	5,281	13	255 D	48.7%	51.2%	48.8%	51.2%
71,233	FRANKLIN	28,621	16,611	11,891	119	4,720 R	58.0%	41.5%	58.3%	41.7%
13,181	GASCONADE	5,856	4,216	1,621	19	2,595 R	72.0%	27.7%	72.2%	27.8%
7,887	GENTRY	3,433	1,554	1,872	7	318 D	45.3%	54.5%	45.4%	54.6%
185,302	GREENE	87,959	52,211	35,475	273	16,736 R	59.4%	40.3%	59.5%	40.5%
11,959	GRUNDY	4,733	2,668	2,052	13	616 R	56.4%	43.4%	56.5%	43.5%
9,890	HARRISON	4,064	2,271	1,776	17	495 R	55.9%	43.7%	56.1%	43.9%
19,672	HENRY	8,328	4,167	4,135	26	32 R	50.0%	49.7%	50.2%	49.8%
6,367	HICKORY	3,732	2,043	1,677	12	366 R	54.7%	44.9%	54.9%	45.1%
6,882	HOLT	2,855	1,583	1,258	14	325 R	55.4%	44.1%	55.7%	44.3%
10,008	HOWARD	4,322	1,865	2,446	11	581 D	43.2%	56.6%	43.3%	56.7%
28,807	HOWELL	11,645	7,277	4,324	44	2,953 R	62.5%	37.1%	62.7%	37.3%
11,084	IRON	4,170	1,877	2,283	10	406 D	45.0%	54.7%	45.1%	54.9%
629,266	JACKSON	256,621	107,810	147,964	847	40,154 D	42.0%	57.7%	42.2%	57.8%
86,958	JASPER	31,187	19,934	11,159	94	8,775 R	63.9%	35.8%	64.1%	35.9%
146,183	JEFFERSON	57,255	29,279	27,738	238	1,541 R	51.1%	48.4%	51.4%	48.6%
39,059	JOHNSON	12,921	7,512	5,373	36	2,139 R	58.1%	41.6%	58.3%	41.7%
5,508	KNOX	2,472	1,212	1,255	5	43 D	49.0%	50.8%	49.1%	50.9%
24,323	LACLEDE	9,536	6,070	3,442	24	2,628 R	63.7%	36.1%	63.8%	36.2%
29,925	LAFAYETTE	12,514	6,825	5,654	35	1,171 R	54.5%	45.2%	54.7%	45.3%
28,973	LAWRENCE	11,379	6,911	4,432	36	2,479 R	60.7%	38.9%	60.9%	39.1%
10,901	LEWIS	4,273	1,803	2,460	10	657 D	42.2%	57.6%	42.3%	57.7%
22,193	LINCOLN	9,938	5,305	4,605	28	700 R	53.4%	46.3%	53.5%	46.5%
15,495	LINN	6,230	3,061	3,150	19	89 D	49.1%	50.6%	49.3%	50.7%
15,739	LIVINGSTON	6,548	3,462	3,077	9	385 R	52.9%	47.0%	52.9%	47.1%
14,917	MCDONALD	6,153	3,812	2,299	42	1,513 R	62.0%	37.4%	62.4%	37.6%

MISSOURI

PRESIDENT 1988

1980 Census Population	County	Total Vote	Republican	Democratic	Other	Rep.-Dem. Plurality	Percentage Total Vote Rep.	Percentage Total Vote Dem.	Percentage Major Vote Rep.	Percentage Major Vote Dem.
16,313	MACON	6,639	3,406	3,215	18	191 R	51.3%	48.4%	51.4%	48.6%
10,725	MADISON	4,703	2,528	2,167	8	361 R	53.8%	46.1%	53.8%	46.2%
7,551	MARIES	3,480	1,919	1,552	9	367 R	55.1%	44.6%	55.3%	44.7%
28,638	MARION	10,677	5,034	5,617	26	583 D	47.1%	52.6%	47.3%	52.7%
4,685	MERCER	1,756	875	877	4	2 D	49.8%	49.9%	49.9%	50.1%
18,532	MILLER	8,228	5,662	2,555	11	3,107 R	68.8%	31.1%	68.9%	31.1%
15,726	MISSISSIPPI	5,042	2,218	2,814	10	596 D	44.0%	55.8%	44.1%	55.9%
12,068	MONITEAU	5,446	3,502	1,936	8	1,566 R	64.3%	35.5%	64.4%	35.6%
9,716	MONROE	4,014	1,542	2,461	11	919 D	38.4%	61.3%	38.5%	61.5%
11,537	MONTGOMERY	4,794	2,714	2,064	16	650 R	56.6%	43.1%	56.8%	43.2%
13,807	MORGAN	6,586	3,958	2,604	24	1,354 R	60.1%	39.5%	60.3%	39.7%
22,945	NEW MADRID	7,208	3,387	3,812	9	425 D	47.0%	52.9%	47.0%	53.0%
40,555	NEWTON	16,497	10,617	5,798	82	4,819 R	64.4%	35.1%	64.7%	35.3%
21,996	NODAWAY	8,387	4,103	4,240	44	137 D	48.9%	50.6%	49.2%	50.8%
10,238	OREGON	3,766	1,717	2,042	7	325 D	45.6%	54.2%	45.7%	54.3%
12,014	OSAGE	5,665	3,885	1,771	9	2,114 R	68.6%	31.3%	68.7%	31.3%
7,961	OZARK	3,744	2,404	1,329	11	1,075 R	64.2%	35.5%	64.4%	35.6%
24,987	PEMISCOT	6,364	3,066	3,288	10	222 D	48.2%	51.7%	48.3%	51.7%
16,784	PERRY	5,986	3,836	2,136	14	1,700 R	64.1%	35.7%	64.2%	35.8%
36,378	PETTIS	15,200	9,648	5,486	66	4,162 R	63.5%	36.1%	63.8%	36.2%
33,633	PHELPS	14,253	8,329	5,867	57	2,462 R	58.4%	41.2%	58.7%	41.3%
17,568	PIKE	7,101	3,271	3,816	14	545 D	46.1%	53.7%	46.2%	53.8%
46,341	PLATTE	23,134	11,838	11,225	71	613 R	51.2%	48.5%	51.3%	48.7%
18,822	POLK	8,471	5,030	3,419	22	1,611 R	59.4%	40.4%	59.5%	40.5%
42,011	PULASKI	8,114	4,642	3,446	26	1,196 R	57.2%	42.5%	57.4%	42.6%
6,092	PUTNAM	2,176	1,365	803	8	562 R	62.7%	36.9%	63.0%	37.0%
8,911	RALLS	3,990	1,494	2,489	7	995 D	37.4%	62.4%	37.5%	62.5%
25,460	RANDOLPH	9,695	4,384	5,291	20	907 D	45.2%	54.6%	45.3%	54.7%
21,378	RAY	8,662	3,763	4,879	20	1,116 D	43.4%	56.3%	43.5%	56.5%
7,230	REYNOLDS	3,035	1,162	1,864	9	702 D	38.3%	61.4%	38.4%	61.6%
12,458	RIPLEY	4,620	2,647	1,961	12	686 R	57.3%	42.4%	57.4%	42.6%
144,107	ST. CHARLES	79,548	50,005	29,286	257	20,719 R	62.9%	36.8%	63.1%	36.9%
8,622	ST. CLAIR	4,183	2,312	1,864	7	448 R	55.3%	44.6%	55.4%	44.6%
42,600	ST. FRANCOIS	16,127	7,923	8,158	46	235 D	49.1%	50.6%	49.3%	50.7%
453,085	ST. LOUIS CITY	151,758	40,906	110,076	776	69,170 D	27.0%	72.5%	27.1%	72.9%
973,896	ST. LOUIS COUNTY	480,897	262,784	216,534	1,579	46,250 R	54.6%	45.0%	54.8%	45.2%
15,180	STE. GENEVIEVE	6,164	2,532	3,612	20	1,080 D	41.1%	58.6%	41.2%	58.8%
24,919	SALINE	9,696	4,625	5,039	32	414 D	47.7%	52.0%	47.9%	52.1%
4,979	SCHUYLER	2,080	1,063	1,013	4	50 R	51.1%	48.7%	51.2%	48.8%
5,415	SCOTLAND	2,372	1,248	1,117	7	131 R	52.6%	47.1%	52.8%	47.2%
39,647	SCOTT	13,948	8,013	5,914	21	2,099 R	57.4%	42.4%	57.5%	42.5%
7,885	SHANNON	3,500	1,696	1,796	8	100 D	48.5%	51.3%	48.6%	51.4%
7,826	SHELBY	3,408	1,586	1,818	4	232 D	46.5%	53.3%	46.6%	53.4%
29,009	STODDARD	10,538	5,822	4,701	15	1,121 R	55.2%	44.6%	55.3%	44.7%
15,587	STONE	8,004	5,080	2,889	35	2,191 R	63.5%	36.1%	63.7%	36.3%
7,434	SULLIVAN	3,467	1,897	1,562	8	335 R	54.7%	45.1%	54.8%	45.2%
20,467	TANEY	10,978	7,043	3,888	47	3,155 R	64.2%	35.4%	64.4%	35.6%
21,070	TEXAS	8,506	4,584	3,887	35	697 R	53.9%	45.7%	54.1%	45.9%
19,806	VERNON	7,572	4,149	3,402	21	747 R	54.8%	44.9%	54.9%	45.1%
14,900	WARREN	7,411	4,452	2,935	24	1,517 R	60.1%	39.6%	60.3%	39.7%
17,983	WASHINGTON	7,000	3,240	3,744	16	504 D	46.3%	53.5%	46.4%	53.6%
11,277	WAYNE	5,112	2,648	2,456	8	192 R	51.8%	48.0%	51.9%	48.1%
20,414	WEBSTER	9,035	5,123	3,890	22	1,233 R	56.7%	43.1%	56.8%	43.2%
3,008	WORTH	1,411	677	732	2	55 D	48.0%	51.9%	48.0%	52.0%
16,188	WRIGHT	6,394	4,151	2,232	11	1,919 R	64.9%	34.9%	65.0%	35.0%
4,916,686	TOTAL	2,093,713	1,084,953	1,001,619	7,141	83,334 R	51.8%	47.8%	52.0%	48.0%

MISSOURI

GOVERNOR 1988

1980 Census Population	County	Total Vote	Republican	Democratic	Other	Rep.-Dem. Plurality	Percentage Total Vote Rep.	Percentage Total Vote Dem.	Percentage Major Vote Rep.	Percentage Major Vote Dem.
24,870	ADAIR	9,302	7,099	2,099	104	5,000 R	76.3%	22.6%	77.2%	22.8%
13,980	ANDREW	6,507	4,517	1,961	29	2,556 R	69.4%	30.1%	69.7%	30.3%
8,605	ATCHISON	3,194	2,160	1,024	10	1,136 R	67.6%	32.1%	67.8%	32.2%
26,458	AUDRAIN	10,332	6,615	3,649	68	2,966 R	64.0%	35.3%	64.4%	35.6%
24,408	BARRY	11,462	8,422	3,020	20	5,402 R	73.5%	26.3%	73.6%	26.4%
11,292	BARTON	5,010	3,882	1,093	35	2,789 R	77.5%	21.8%	78.0%	22.0%
15,873	BATES	6,905	4,256	2,637	12	1,619 R	61.6%	38.2%	61.7%	38.3%
12,183	BENTON	6,109	3,990	2,083	36	1,907 R	65.3%	34.1%	65.7%	34.3%
10,301	BOLLINGER	4,605	2,930	1,672	3	1,258 R	63.6%	36.3%	63.7%	36.3%
100,376	BOONE	46,922	29,200	16,772	950	12,428 R	62.2%	35.7%	63.5%	36.5%
87,888	BUCHANAN	34,303	21,800	11,989	514	9,811 R	63.6%	35.0%	64.5%	35.5%
37,693	BUTLER	13,551	9,060	4,488	3	4,572 R	66.9%	33.1%	66.9%	33.1%
8,660	CALDWELL	3,817	2,527	1,249	41	1,278 R	66.2%	32.7%	66.9%	33.1%
32,252	CALLAWAY	11,933	7,326	4,468	139	2,858 R	61.4%	37.4%	62.1%	37.9%
20,017	CAMDEN	11,786	8,849	2,830	107	6,019 R	75.1%	24.0%	75.8%	24.2%
58,837	CAPE GIRARDEAU	24,738	17,336	7,298	104	10,038 R	70.1%	29.5%	70.4%	29.6%
12,131	CARROLL	5,139	3,508	1,623	8	1,885 R	68.3%	31.6%	68.4%	31.6%
5,428	CARTER	2,496	1,590	896	10	694 R	63.7%	35.9%	64.0%	36.0%
51,029	CASS	22,918	15,031	7,677	210	7,354 R	65.6%	33.5%	66.2%	33.8%
11,894	CEDAR	4,753	3,482	1,244	27	2,238 R	73.3%	26.2%	73.7%	26.3%
10,489	CHARITON	4,530	2,720	1,805	5	915 R	60.0%	39.8%	60.1%	39.9%
22,402	CHRISTIAN	12,518	9,569	2,828	121	6,741 R	76.4%	22.6%	77.2%	22.8%
8,493	CLARK	3,428	2,255	1,170	3	1,085 R	65.8%	34.1%	65.8%	34.2%
136,488	CLAY	59,073	38,655	19,976	442	18,679 R	65.4%	33.8%	65.9%	34.1%
15,916	CLINTON	7,035	4,323	2,635	77	1,688 R	61.4%	37.5%	62.1%	37.9%
56,663	COLE	26,393	17,859	8,301	233	9,558 R	67.7%	31.5%	68.3%	31.7%
14,643	COOPER	6,292	4,404	1,836	52	2,568 R	70.0%	29.2%	70.6%	29.4%
18,300	CRAWFORD	6,997	4,636	2,312	49	2,324 R	66.3%	33.0%	66.7%	33.3%
7,383	DADE	3,484	2,685	789	10	1,896 R	77.1%	22.6%	77.3%	22.7%
12,096	DALLAS	5,228	3,806	1,403	19	2,403 R	72.8%	26.8%	73.1%	26.9%
8,905	DAVIESS	3,520	2,360	1,151	9	1,209 R	67.0%	32.7%	67.2%	32.8%
8,222	DE KALB	3,838	2,463	1,359	16	1,104 R	64.2%	35.4%	64.4%	35.6%
14,517	DENT	5,409	3,438	1,932	39	1,506 R	63.6%	35.7%	64.0%	36.0%
11,594	DOUGLAS	4,919	3,671	1,225	23	2,446 R	74.6%	24.9%	75.0%	25.0%
36,324	DUNKLIN	10,010	5,822	4,178	10	1,644 R	58.2%	41.7%	58.2%	41.8%
71,233	FRANKLIN	29,027	19,839	8,925	263	10,914 R	68.3%	30.7%	69.0%	31.0%
13,181	GASCONADE	5,832	4,495	1,298	39	3,197 R	77.1%	22.3%	77.6%	22.4%
7,887	GENTRY	3,417	2,034	1,374	9	660 R	59.5%	40.2%	59.7%	40.3%
185,302	GREENE	87,903	67,153	19,884	866	47,269 R	76.4%	22.6%	77.2%	22.8%
11,959	GRUNDY	4,747	3,332	1,399	16	1,933 R	70.2%	29.5%	70.4%	29.6%
9,890	HARRISON	4,060	2,779	1,272	9	1,507 R	68.4%	31.3%	68.6%	31.4%
19,672	HENRY	8,306	4,908	3,334	64	1,574 R	59.1%	40.1%	59.5%	40.5%
6,367	HICKORY	3,522	2,405	1,101	16	1,304 R	68.3%	31.3%	68.6%	31.4%
6,882	HOLT	2,861	2,017	836	8	1,181 R	70.5%	29.2%	70.7%	29.3%
10,008	HOWARD	4,120	2,323	1,781	16	542 R	56.4%	43.2%	56.6%	43.4%
28,807	HOWELL	11,606	8,321	3,214	71	5,107 R	71.7%	27.7%	72.1%	27.9%
11,084	IRON	4,115	2,290	1,817	8	473 R	55.7%	44.2%	55.8%	44.2%
629,266	JACKSON	255,949	143,905	108,609	3,435	35,296 R	56.2%	42.4%	57.0%	43.0%
86,958	JASPER	31,171	23,515	7,393	263	16,122 R	75.4%	23.7%	76.1%	23.9%
146,183	JEFFERSON	57,273	35,559	21,104	610	14,455 R	62.1%	36.8%	62.8%	37.2%
39,059	JOHNSON	12,910	8,914	3,868	128	5,046 R	69.0%	30.0%	69.7%	30.3%
5,508	KNOX	2,469	1,667	799	3	868 R	67.5%	32.4%	67.6%	32.4%
24,323	LACLEDE	9,641	7,202	2,367	72	4,835 R	74.7%	24.6%	75.3%	24.7%
29,925	LAFAYETTE	12,470	8,148	4,232	90	3,916 R	65.3%	33.9%	65.8%	34.2%
28,973	LAWRENCE	11,390	8,278	3,047	65	5,231 R	72.7%	26.8%	73.1%	26.9%
10,901	LEWIS	4,171	2,529	1,635	7	894 R	60.6%	39.2%	60.7%	39.3%
22,193	LINCOLN	9,869	6,400	3,446	23	2,954 R	64.8%	34.9%	65.0%	35.0%
15,495	LINN	6,238	3,730	2,457	51	1,273 R	59.8%	39.4%	60.3%	39.7%
15,739	LIVINGSTON	6,495	4,265	2,220	10	2,045 R	65.7%	34.2%	65.8%	34.2%
14,917	MCDONALD	6,154	4,434	1,660	60	2,774 R	72.1%	27.0%	72.8%	27.2%

MISSOURI

GOVERNOR 1988

1980 Census Population	County	Total Vote	Republican	Democratic	Other	Rep.-Dem. Plurality	Percentage Total Vote Rep.	Percentage Total Vote Dem.	Percentage Major Vote Rep.	Percentage Major Vote Dem.
16,313	MACON	6,589	4,304	2,245	40	2,059 R	65.3%	34.1%	65.7%	34.3%
10,725	MADISON	4,714	2,989	1,717	8	1,272 R	63.4%	36.4%	63.5%	36.5%
7,551	MARIES	3,514	2,147	1,341	26	806 R	61.1%	38.2%	61.6%	38.4%
28,638	MARION	10,689	6,762	3,872	55	2,890 R	63.3%	36.2%	63.6%	36.4%
4,685	MERCER	1,728	1,152	574	2	578 R	66.7%	33.2%	66.7%	33.3%
18,532	MILLER	8,168	6,130	2,020	18	4,110 R	75.0%	24.7%	75.2%	24.8%
15,726	MISSISSIPPI	5,027	1,638	3,379	10	1,741 D	32.6%	67.2%	32.6%	67.4%
12,068	MONITEAU	5,436	3,802	1,614	20	2,188 R	69.9%	29.7%	70.2%	29.8%
9,716	MONROE	3,963	2,140	1,820	3	320 R	54.0%	45.9%	54.0%	46.0%
11,537	MONTGOMERY	4,773	3,224	1,538	11	1,686 R	67.5%	32.2%	67.7%	32.3%
13,807	MORGAN	6,577	4,572	1,988	17	2,584 R	69.5%	30.2%	69.7%	30.3%
22,945	NEW MADRID	7,055	3,594	3,449	12	145 R	50.9%	48.9%	51.0%	49.0%
40,555	NEWTON	16,200	12,167	3,954	79	8,213 R	75.1%	24.4%	75.5%	24.5%
21,996	NODAWAY	8,600	6,041	2,485	74	3,556 R	70.2%	28.9%	70.9%	29.1%
10,238	OREGON	3,732	1,978	1,739	15	239 R	53.0%	46.6%	53.2%	46.8%
12,014	OSAGE	5,670	4,096	1,561	13	2,535 R	72.2%	27.5%	72.4%	27.6%
7,961	OZARK	3,654	2,721	920	13	1,801 R	74.5%	25.2%	74.7%	25.3%
24,987	PEMISCOT	6,234	3,033	3,171	30	138 D	48.7%	50.9%	48.9%	51.1%
16,784	PERRY	6,017	4,459	1,534	24	2,925 R	74.1%	25.5%	74.4%	25.6%
36,378	PETTIS	15,185	10,920	4,142	123	6,778 R	71.9%	27.3%	72.5%	27.5%
33,633	PHELPS	14,197	9,610	4,438	149	5,172 R	67.7%	31.3%	68.4%	31.6%
17,568	PIKE	6,995	4,568	2,411	16	2,157 R	65.3%	34.5%	65.5%	34.5%
46,341	PLATTE	23,026	15,259	7,443	324	7,816 R	66.3%	32.3%	67.2%	32.8%
18,822	POLK	8,447	6,159	2,256	32	3,903 R	72.9%	26.7%	73.2%	26.8%
42,011	PULASKI	7,968	5,544	2,410	14	3,134 R	69.6%	30.2%	69.7%	30.3%
6,092	PUTNAM	2,132	1,616	515	1	1,101 R	75.8%	24.2%	75.8%	24.2%
8,911	RALLS	3,967	2,166	1,796	5	370 R	54.6%	45.3%	54.7%	45.3%
25,460	RANDOLPH	9,630	5,526	4,082	22	1,444 R	57.4%	42.4%	57.5%	42.5%
21,378	RAY	8,636	4,859	3,714	63	1,145 R	56.3%	43.0%	56.7%	43.3%
7,230	REYNOLDS	3,029	1,528	1,490	11	38 R	50.4%	49.2%	50.6%	49.4%
12,458	RIPLEY	4,534	2,840	1,689	5	1,151 R	62.6%	37.3%	62.7%	37.3%
144,107	ST. CHARLES	79,842	58,376	20,793	673	37,583 R	73.1%	26.0%	73.7%	26.3%
8,622	ST. CLAIR	4,161	2,729	1,424	8	1,305 R	65.6%	34.2%	65.7%	34.3%
42,600	ST. FRANCOIS	16,130	9,401	6,604	125	2,797 R	58.3%	40.9%	58.7%	41.3%
453,085	ST. LOUIS CITY	151,329	59,083	88,813	3,433	29,730 D	39.0%	58.7%	39.9%	60.1%
973,896	ST. LOUIS COUNTY	478,102	327,062	145,256	5,784	181,806 R	68.4%	30.4%	69.2%	30.8%
15,180	STE. GENEVIEVE	6,176	3,437	2,691	48	746 R	55.7%	43.6%	56.1%	43.9%
24,919	SALINE	9,611	6,105	3,487	19	2,618 R	63.5%	36.3%	63.6%	36.4%
4,979	SCHUYLER	2,066	1,321	743	2	578 R	63.9%	36.0%	64.0%	36.0%
5,415	SCOTLAND	2,367	1,591	772	4	819 R	67.2%	32.6%	67.3%	32.7%
39,647	SCOTT	13,888	7,845	6,035	8	1,810 R	56.5%	43.5%	56.5%	43.5%
7,885	SHANNON	3,483	2,078	1,393	12	685 R	59.7%	40.0%	59.9%	40.1%
7,826	SHELBY	3,402	2,004	1,397	1	607 R	58.9%	41.1%	58.9%	41.1%
29,009	STODDARD	10,424	6,634	3,784	6	2,850 R	63.6%	36.3%	63.7%	36.3%
15,587	STONE	7,988	6,157	1,763	68	4,394 R	77.1%	22.1%	77.7%	22.3%
7,434	SULLIVAN	3,449	2,211	1,235	3	976 R	64.1%	35.8%	64.2%	35.8%
20,467	TANEY	10,951	8,298	2,551	102	5,747 R	75.8%	23.3%	76.5%	23.5%
21,070	TEXAS	8,605	5,644	2,880	81	2,764 R	65.6%	33.5%	66.2%	33.8%
19,806	VERNON	7,538	5,014	2,507	17	2,507 R	66.5%	33.3%	66.7%	33.3%
14,900	WARREN	7,399	5,145	2,219	35	2,926 R	69.5%	30.0%	69.9%	30.1%
17,983	WASHINGTON	6,956	3,978	2,966	12	1,012 R	57.2%	42.6%	57.3%	42.7%
11,277	WAYNE	5,065	3,047	2,014	4	1,033 R	60.2%	39.8%	60.2%	39.8%
20,414	WEBSTER	8,921	6,419	2,472	30	3,947 R	72.0%	27.7%	72.2%	27.8%
3,008	WORTH	1,404	931	471	2	460 R	66.3%	33.5%	66.4%	33.6%
16,188	WRIGHT	6,413	4,789	1,598	26	3,191 R	74.7%	24.9%	75.0%	25.0%
4,916,686	TOTAL	2,085,928	1,339,531	724,919	21,478	614,612 R	64.2%	34.8%	64.9%	35.1%

MISSOURI

SENATOR 1988

1980 Census Population	County	Total Vote	Republican	Democratic	Other	Rep.-Dem. Plurality	Percentage: Total Vote Rep.	Percentage: Total Vote Dem.	Percentage: Major Vote Rep.	Percentage: Major Vote Dem.
24,870	ADAIR	9,346	7,435	1,849	62	5,586 R	79.6%	19.8%	80.1%	19.9%
13,980	ANDREW	6,489	4,807	1,667	15	3,140 R	74.1%	25.7%	74.3%	25.7%
8,605	ATCHISON	3,182	2,240	934	8	1,306 R	70.4%	29.4%	70.6%	29.4%
26,458	AUDRAIN	10,280	6,593	3,644	43	2,949 R	64.1%	35.4%	64.4%	35.6%
24,408	BARRY	11,362	8,675	2,672	15	6,003 R	76.4%	23.5%	76.5%	23.5%
11,292	BARTON	5,009	4,118	878	13	3,240 R	82.2%	17.5%	82.4%	17.6%
15,873	BATES	6,884	4,373	2,501	10	1,872 R	63.5%	36.3%	63.6%	36.4%
12,183	BENTON	6,092	4,226	1,842	24	2,384 R	69.4%	30.2%	69.6%	30.4%
10,301	BOLLINGER	4,537	3,181	1,353	3	1,828 R	70.1%	29.8%	70.2%	29.8%
100,376	BOONE	47,011	33,786	12,763	462	21,023 R	71.9%	27.1%	72.6%	27.4%
87,888	BUCHANAN	33,944	23,827	9,872	245	13,955 R	70.2%	29.1%	70.7%	29.3%
37,693	BUTLER	13,401	9,609	3,788	4	5,821 R	71.7%	28.3%	71.7%	28.3%
8,660	CALDWELL	3,836	2,697	1,111	28	1,586 R	70.3%	29.0%	70.8%	29.2%
32,252	CALLAWAY	11,877	8,305	3,505	67	4,800 R	69.9%	29.5%	70.3%	29.7%
20,017	CAMDEN	11,764	9,470	2,211	83	7,259 R	80.5%	18.8%	81.1%	18.9%
58,837	CAPE GIRARDEAU	24,628	19,805	4,744	79	15,061 R	80.4%	19.3%	80.7%	19.3%
12,131	CARROLL	5,111	3,567	1,541	3	2,026 R	69.8%	30.2%	69.8%	30.2%
5,428	CARTER	2,440	1,741	690	9	1,051 R	71.4%	28.3%	71.6%	28.4%
51,029	CASS	22,943	15,938	6,890	115	9,048 R	69.5%	30.0%	69.8%	30.2%
11,894	CEDAR	4,740	3,591	1,125	24	2,466 R	75.8%	23.7%	76.1%	23.9%
10,489	CHARITON	4,498	2,815	1,682	1	1,133 R	62.6%	37.4%	62.6%	37.4%
22,402	CHRISTIAN	12,509	9,893	2,548	68	7,345 R	79.1%	20.4%	79.5%	20.5%
8,493	CLARK	3,411	2,236	1,170	5	1,066 R	65.6%	34.3%	65.6%	34.4%
136,488	CLAY	57,876	38,965	18,611	300	20,354 R	67.3%	32.2%	67.7%	32.3%
15,916	CLINTON	7,009	4,711	2,258	40	2,453 R	67.2%	32.2%	67.6%	32.4%
56,663	COLE	26,414	20,630	5,694	90	14,936 R	78.1%	21.6%	78.4%	21.6%
14,643	COOPER	6,288	4,673	1,595	20	3,078 R	74.3%	25.4%	74.6%	25.4%
18,300	CRAWFORD	6,959	4,611	2,318	30	2,293 R	66.3%	33.3%	66.5%	33.5%
7,383	DADE	3,453	2,703	743	7	1,960 R	78.3%	21.5%	78.4%	21.6%
12,096	DALLAS	5,194	3,873	1,308	13	2,565 R	74.6%	25.2%	74.8%	25.2%
8,905	DAVIESS	3,499	2,432	1,060	7	1,372 R	69.5%	30.3%	69.6%	30.4%
8,222	DE KALB	3,834	2,533	1,291	10	1,242 R	66.1%	33.7%	66.2%	33.8%
14,517	DENT	5,400	3,621	1,748	31	1,873 R	67.1%	32.4%	67.4%	32.6%
11,594	DOUGLAS	4,829	3,722	1,090	17	2,632 R	77.1%	22.6%	77.3%	22.7%
36,324	DUNKLIN	9,646	6,033	3,604	9	2,429 R	62.5%	37.4%	62.6%	37.4%
71,233	FRANKLIN	28,981	20,522	8,276	183	12,246 R	70.8%	28.6%	71.3%	28.7%
13,181	GASCONADE	5,853	4,817	1,002	34	3,815 R	82.3%	17.1%	82.8%	17.2%
7,887	GENTRY	3,385	2,179	1,200	6	979 R	64.4%	35.5%	64.5%	35.5%
185,302	GREENE	87,687	68,259	18,890	538	49,369 R	77.8%	21.5%	78.3%	21.7%
11,959	GRUNDY	4,701	3,389	1,303	9	2,086 R	72.1%	27.7%	72.2%	27.8%
9,890	HARRISON	4,001	2,877	1,117	7	1,760 R	71.9%	27.9%	72.0%	28.0%
19,672	HENRY	8,298	5,159	3,097	42	2,062 R	62.2%	37.3%	62.5%	37.5%
6,367	HICKORY	3,479	2,462	1,007	10	1,455 R	70.8%	28.9%	71.0%	29.0%
6,882	HOLT	2,843	2,135	696	12	1,439 R	75.1%	24.5%	75.4%	24.6%
10,008	HOWARD	4,107	2,605	1,496	6	1,109 R	63.4%	36.4%	63.5%	36.5%
28,807	HOWELL	11,480	8,727	2,703	50	6,024 R	76.0%	23.5%	76.4%	23.6%
11,084	IRON	4,069	2,468	1,593	8	875 R	60.7%	39.1%	60.8%	39.2%
629,266	JACKSON	255,338	154,653	98,927	1,758	55,726 R	60.6%	38.7%	61.0%	39.0%
86,958	JASPER	31,122	24,633	6,342	147	18,291 R	79.1%	20.4%	79.5%	20.5%
146,183	JEFFERSON	57,279	34,252	22,650	377	11,602 R	59.8%	39.5%	60.2%	39.8%
39,059	JOHNSON	12,902	9,523	3,309	70	6,214 R	73.8%	25.6%	74.2%	25.8%
5,508	KNOX	2,463	1,701	760	2	941 R	69.1%	30.9%	69.1%	30.9%
24,323	LACLEDE	9,622	7,532	2,042	48	5,490 R	78.3%	21.2%	78.7%	21.3%
29,925	LAFAYETTE	12,445	8,783	3,618	44	5,165 R	70.6%	29.1%	70.8%	29.2%
28,973	LAWRENCE	11,371	8,601	2,706	64	5,895 R	75.6%	23.8%	76.1%	23.9%
10,901	LEWIS	4,155	2,617	1,532	6	1,085 R	63.0%	36.9%	63.1%	36.9%
22,193	LINCOLN	9,845	6,673	3,160	12	3,513 R	67.8%	32.1%	67.9%	32.1%
15,495	LINN	6,239	3,992	2,224	23	1,768 R	64.0%	35.6%	64.2%	35.8%
15,739	LIVINGSTON	6,495	4,538	1,951	6	2,587 R	69.9%	30.0%	69.9%	30.1%
14,917	MCDONALD	6,135	4,595	1,502	38	3,093 R	74.9%	24.5%	75.4%	24.6%

MISSOURI

SENATOR 1988

1980 Census Population	County	Total Vote	Republican	Democratic	Other	Rep.-Dem. Plurality	Percentage: Total Vote Rep.	Percentage: Total Vote Dem.	Percentage: Major Vote Rep.	Percentage: Major Vote Dem.
16,313	MACON	6,565	4,707	1,839	19	2,868 R	71.7%	28.0%	71.9%	28.1%
10,725	MADISON	4,616	3,163	1,446	7	1,717 R	68.5%	31.3%	68.6%	31.4%
7,551	MARIES	3,519	2,339	1,168	12	1,171 R	66.5%	33.2%	66.7%	33.3%
28,638	MARION	10,637	7,073	3,533	31	3,540 R	66.5%	33.2%	66.7%	33.3%
4,685	MERCER	1,720	1,193	526	1	667 R	69.4%	30.6%	69.4%	30.6%
18,532	MILLER	8,128	6,499	1,621	8	4,878 R	80.0%	19.9%	80.0%	20.0%
15,726	MISSISSIPPI	4,804	2,873	1,916	15	957 R	59.8%	39.9%	60.0%	40.0%
12,068	MONITEAU	5,405	4,129	1,268	8	2,861 R	76.4%	23.5%	76.5%	23.5%
9,716	MONROE	3,960	2,194	1,762	4	432 R	55.4%	44.5%	55.5%	44.5%
11,537	MONTGOMERY	4,727	3,396	1,321	10	2,075 R	71.8%	27.9%	72.0%	28.0%
13,807	MORGAN	6,517	4,758	1,746	13	3,012 R	73.0%	26.8%	73.2%	26.8%
22,945	NEW MADRID	6,899	4,208	2,682	9	1,526 R	61.0%	38.9%	61.1%	38.9%
40,555	NEWTON	15,892	12,286	3,541	65	8,745 R	77.3%	22.3%	77.6%	22.4%
21,996	NODAWAY	8,601	6,454	2,117	30	4,337 R	75.0%	24.6%	75.3%	24.7%
10,238	OREGON	3,651	2,077	1,565	9	512 R	56.9%	42.9%	57.0%	43.0%
12,014	OSAGE	5,655	4,510	1,139	6	3,371 R	79.8%	20.1%	79.8%	20.2%
7,961	OZARK	3,583	2,767	806	10	1,961 R	77.2%	22.5%	77.4%	22.6%
24,987	PEMISCOT	6,163	3,583	2,554	26	1,029 R	58.1%	41.4%	58.4%	41.6%
16,784	PERRY	6,015	4,814	1,178	23	3,636 R	80.0%	19.6%	80.3%	19.7%
36,378	PETTIS	15,152	11,444	3,647	61	7,797 R	75.5%	24.1%	75.8%	24.2%
33,633	PHELPS	14,162	10,477	3,602	83	6,875 R	74.0%	25.4%	74.4%	25.6%
17,568	PIKE	6,911	4,778	2,126	7	2,652 R	69.1%	30.8%	69.2%	30.8%
46,341	PLATTE	23,072	16,187	6,706	179	9,481 R	70.2%	29.1%	70.7%	29.3%
18,822	POLK	8,427	6,244	2,167	16	4,077 R	74.1%	25.7%	74.2%	25.8%
42,011	PULASKI	7,902	5,640	2,246	16	3,394 R	71.4%	28.4%	71.5%	28.5%
6,092	PUTNAM	2,136	1,641	492	3	1,149 R	76.8%	23.0%	76.9%	23.1%
8,911	RALLS	3,935	2,238	1,692	5	546 R	56.9%	43.0%	56.9%	43.1%
25,460	RANDOLPH	9,624	5,965	3,642	17	2,323 R	62.0%	37.8%	62.1%	37.9%
21,378	RAY	8,610	5,087	3,489	34	1,598 R	59.1%	40.5%	59.3%	40.7%
7,230	REYNOLDS	2,916	1,653	1,256	7	397 R	56.7%	43.1%	56.8%	43.2%
12,458	RIPLEY	4,436	3,011	1,421	4	1,590 R	67.9%	32.0%	67.9%	32.1%
144,107	ST. CHARLES	79,814	61,342	18,049	423	43,293 R	76.9%	22.6%	77.3%	22.7%
8,622	ST. CLAIR	4,149	2,759	1,376	14	1,383 R	66.5%	33.2%	66.7%	33.3%
42,600	ST. FRANCOIS	16,071	10,273	5,737	61	4,536 R	63.9%	35.7%	64.2%	35.8%
453,085	ST. LOUIS CITY	151,359	62,826	87,252	1,281	24,426 D	41.5%	57.6%	41.9%	58.1%
973,896	ST. LOUIS COUNTY	478,001	336,336	138,542	3,123	197,794 R	70.4%	29.0%	70.8%	29.2%
15,180	STE. GENEVIEVE	6,144	3,646	2,466	32	1,180 R	59.3%	40.1%	59.7%	40.3%
24,919	SALINE	9,570	6,314	3,237	19	3,077 R	66.0%	33.8%	66.1%	33.9%
4,979	SCHUYLER	2,071	1,346	725		621 R	65.0%	35.0%	65.0%	35.0%
5,415	SCOTLAND	2,353	1,645	705	3	940 R	69.9%	30.0%	70.0%	30.0%
39,647	SCOTT	13,650	9,271	4,367	12	4,904 R	67.9%	32.0%	68.0%	32.0%
7,885	SHANNON	3,420	2,132	1,284	4	848 R	62.3%	37.5%	62.4%	37.6%
7,826	SHELBY	3,398	2,072	1,326		746 R	61.0%	39.0%	61.0%	39.0%
29,009	STODDARD	10,201	7,312	2,888	1	4,424 R	71.7%	28.3%	71.7%	28.3%
15,587	STONE	7,964	6,316	1,593	55	4,723 R	79.3%	20.0%	79.9%	20.1%
7,434	SULLIVAN	3,453	2,281	1,171	1	1,110 R	66.1%	33.9%	66.1%	33.9%
20,467	TANEY	10,919	8,512	2,341	66	6,171 R	78.0%	21.4%	78.4%	21.6%
21,070	TEXAS	8,583	5,922	2,617	44	3,305 R	69.0%	30.5%	69.4%	30.6%
19,806	VERNON	7,492	5,213	2,270	9	2,943 R	69.6%	30.3%	69.7%	30.3%
14,900	WARREN	7,347	5,479	1,847	21	3,632 R	74.6%	25.1%	74.8%	25.2%
17,983	WASHINGTON	6,866	4,174	2,684	8	1,490 R	60.8%	39.1%	60.9%	39.1%
11,277	WAYNE	5,078	3,340	1,735	3	1,605 R	65.8%	34.2%	65.8%	34.2%
20,414	WEBSTER	8,964	6,590	2,350	24	4,240 R	73.5%	26.2%	73.7%	26.3%
3,008	WORTH	1,393	989	403	1	586 R	71.0%	28.9%	71.0%	29.0%
16,188	WRIGHT	6,285	4,811	1,463	11	3,348 R	76.5%	23.3%	76.7%	23.3%
4,916,686	TOTAL	2,078,875	1,407,416	660,045	11,414	747,371 R	67.7%	31.8%	68.1%	31.9%

MISSOURI

CONGRESS

CD	Year	Total Vote	Republican Vote	Republican Candidate	Democratic Vote	Democratic Candidate	Other Vote	Rep.-Dem. Plurality	Total Vote Rep.	Total Vote Dem.	Major Vote Rep.	Major Vote Dem.
1	1988	196,658	53,109	SCHWAN, JOSEPH A.	140,751	CLAY, WILLIAM	2,798	87,642 D	27.0%	71.6%	27.4%	72.6%
1	1986	137,643	46,599	WITTMANN, ROBERT J.	91,044	CLAY, WILLIAM		44,445 D	33.9%	66.1%	33.9%	66.1%
1	1984	215,974	68,538	RATHBONE, ERIC	147,436	CLAY, WILLIAM		78,898 D	31.7%	68.3%	31.7%	68.3%
1	1982	155,255	52,599	WHITE, WILLIAM E.	102,656	CLAY, WILLIAM		50,057 D	33.9%	66.1%	33.9%	66.1%
2	1988	281,109	186,450	BUECHNER, JOHN	91,645	FEIGENBAUM, ROBERT H.	3,014	94,805 R	66.3%	32.6%	67.0%	33.0%
2	1986	194,548	101,010	BUECHNER, JOHN	93,538	YOUNG, ROBERT A.		7,472 R	51.9%	48.1%	51.9%	48.1%
2	1984	268,616	127,710	BUECHNER, JOHN	139,123	YOUNG, ROBERT A.	1,783	11,413 D	47.5%	51.8%	47.9%	52.1%
2	1982	178,203	77,433	DIELMANN, HAROLD L.	100,770	YOUNG, ROBERT A.		23,337 D	43.5%	56.5%	43.5%	56.5%
3	1988	239,203	86,763	HEARNE, MARK F.	150,205	GEPHARDT, RICHARD A.	2,235	63,442 D	36.3%	62.8%	36.6%	63.4%
3	1986	168,785	52,382	AMELUNG, ROY C.	116,403	GEPHARDT, RICHARD A.		64,021 D	31.0%	69.0%	31.0%	69.0%
3	1984	193,537			193,537	GEPHARDT, RICHARD A.		193,537 D		100.0%		100.0%
3	1982	168,954	37,388	FORISTEL, RICHARD	131,566	GEPHARDT, RICHARD A.		94,178 D	22.1%	77.9%	22.1%	77.9%
4	1988	231,873	65,393	EYERLY, DAVID	166,480	SKELTON, IKE		101,087 D	28.2%	71.8%	28.2%	71.8%
4	1986	129,471			129,471	SKELTON, IKE		129,471 D		100.0%		100.0%
4	1984	225,058	74,434	RUSSELL, CARL D.	150,624	SKELTON, IKE		76,190 D	33.1%	66.9%	33.1%	66.9%
4	1982	175,953	79,565	BAILEY, WENDELL	96,388	SKELTON, IKE		16,823 D	45.2%	54.8%	45.2%	54.8%
5	1988	212,139	60,453	LOBB, MARY ELLEN	149,166	WHEAT, ALAN	2,520	88,713 D	28.5%	70.3%	28.8%	71.2%
5	1986	142,574	39,340	FISHER, GREG	101,030	WHEAT, ALAN	2,204	61,690 D	27.6%	70.9%	28.0%	72.0%
5	1984	228,230	72,477	KENWORTHY, JIM	150,675	WHEAT, ALAN	5,078	78,198 D	31.8%	66.0%	32.5%	67.5%
5	1982	165,989	66,664	SHARP, JOHN A.	96,059	WHEAT, ALAN	3,266	29,395 D	40.2%	57.9%	41.0%	59.0%
6	1988	229,011	135,883	COLEMAN, E. THOMAS	93,128	HUGHES, DOUG R.		42,755 R	59.3%	40.7%	59.3%	40.7%
6	1986	169,020	95,865	COLEMAN, E. THOMAS	73,155	HUGHES, DOUG R.		22,710 R	56.7%	43.3%	56.7%	43.3%
6	1984	232,913	150,996	COLEMAN, E. THOMAS	81,917	HENSLEY, KENNETH C.		69,079 R	64.8%	35.2%	64.8%	35.2%
6	1982	177,046	97,993	COLEMAN, E. THOMAS	79,053	RUSSELL, JIM		18,940 R	55.3%	44.7%	55.3%	44.7%
7	1988	240,911	127,939	HANCOCK, MELTON D.	111,244	BACON, MAX	1,728	16,695 R	53.1%	46.2%	53.5%	46.5%
7	1986	170,501	114,210	TAYLOR, GENE	56,291	YOUNG, KEN		57,919 R	67.0%	33.0%	67.0%	33.0%
7	1984	236,453	164,586	TAYLOR, GENE	71,867	YOUNG, KEN		92,719 R	69.6%	30.4%	69.6%	30.4%
7	1982	180,940	91,391	TAYLOR, GENE	89,549	GEISLER, DAVID A.		1,842 R	50.5%	49.5%	50.5%	49.5%
8	1988	202,402	117,601	EMERSON, BILL	84,801	CRYTS, WAYNE		32,800 R	58.1%	41.9%	58.1%	41.9%
8	1986	150,674	79,142	EMERSON, BILL	71,532	CRYTS, WAYNE		7,610 R	52.5%	47.5%	52.5%	47.5%
8	1984	205,108	134,186	EMERSON, BILL	70,922	BLUE, BILL		63,264 R	65.4%	34.6%	65.4%	34.6%
8	1982	162,906	86,493	EMERSON, BILL	76,413	FORD, JERRY		10,080 R	53.1%	46.9%	53.1%	46.9%
9	1988	236,880	76,008	DUDLEY, KEN A.	160,872	VOLKMER, HAROLD		84,864 D	32.1%	67.9%	32.1%	67.9%
9	1986	166,911	70,972	UTHLAUT, RALPH	95,939	VOLKMER, HAROLD		24,967 D	42.5%	57.5%	42.5%	57.5%
9	1984	233,688	110,100	FRANCKE, CARRIE	123,588	VOLKMER, HAROLD		13,488 D	47.1%	52.9%	47.1%	52.9%
9	1982	163,170	63,942	MEAD, LARRY E.	99,228	VOLKMER, HAROLD		35,286 D	39.2%	60.8%	39.2%	60.8%

MISSOURI

1988 GENERAL ELECTION

President — Other vote was 6,656 New Alliance (Fulani); 434 Paul (write-in); 44 Duke (write-in); 1 Dennis (write-in); 6 scattered write-in.

Governor — Other vote was 21,467 Libertarian (Roberts); 11 scattered write-in.

Senator — Other vote was 11,410 Libertarian (Guze); 4 scattered write-in.

Congress — Other vote was Libertarian (Inman) in CD 1; Libertarian (Lohmann) in CD 2; 2,128 Libertarian (Sloan) and 107 Ulett (write-in) in CD 3; Libertarian (Hurley) in CD 5; Libertarian (Lurvey) in CD 7.

1988 PRIMARIES

AUGUST 2 REPUBLICAN

Governor — John Ashcroft, unopposed.

Senator — John C. Danforth, unopposed.

Congress — Unopposed in five CD's. Contested as follows:

CD 3 — 11,772 Mark F. Hearne; 5,806 Roger F. VonderBrueg; 3,686 Wallace Anderson; 3,248 Roy C. Amelung; 1,011 Bernard L. Mazurkiewicz; 730 F. Leslie Boos.
CD 6 — 28,762 E. Thomas Coleman; 3,278 Robert L. Buck.
CD 7 — 37,067 Melton D. Hancock; 33,940 Gary Nodler; 20,354 Dennis Smith; 4,176 Cecil W. Huff.
CD 9 — 19,485 Ken A. Dudley; 7,128 Alonzo L. Coose.

AUGUST 2 DEMOCRATIC

Governor — 375,564 Betty C. Hearnes; 85,409 Lavoy Reed.

Senator — Jeremiah W. Nixon, unopposed

Congress — Unopposed in four CD's. Contested as follows:

CD 2 — 20,728 Robert H. Feigenbaum; 8,121 Clement Burns; 2,954 Marvin Tarkow.
CD 3 — 45,784 Richard A. Gephardt; 4,073 James Vires; 3,442 James W. Whitt; 2,747 Edward P. Roche.
CD 6 — 42,386 Doug R. Hughes; 18,605 John Gallagher.
CD 7 — 15,754 Max Bacon; 12,946 Keith Jaspers; 4,153 Ken Young.
CD 8 — 52,236 Wayne Cryts; 10,120 H. Riley Bock; 7,606 Thad Bullock; 6,702 Johnny Dover.

MONTANA

GOVERNOR

Stan Stephens (R). Elected 1988 to a four-year term.

SENATORS

Max S. Baucus (D). Re-elected 1984 to a six-year term. Previously elected 1978.

Conrad Burns (R). Elected 1988 to a six-year term.

REPRESENTATIVES

1. Pat Williams (D)
2. Ron Marlenee (R)

POSTWAR VOTE FOR PRESIDENT

		Republican		Democratic				Percentage			
	Total					Other		Total Vote		Major Vote	
Year	Vote	Vote	Candidate	Vote	Candidate	Vote	Plurality	Rep.	Dem.	Rep.	Dem.
1988	365,674	190,412	Bush, George	168,936	Dukakis, Michael S.	6,326	21,476 R	52.1%	46.2%	53.0%	47.0%
1984	384,377	232,450	Reagan, Ronald	146,742	Mondale, Walter F.	5,185	85,708 R	60.5%	38.2%	61.3%	38.7%
1980	363,952	206,814	Reagan, Ronald	118,032	Carter, Jimmy	39,106	88,782 R	56.8%	32.4%	63.7%	36.3%
1976	328,734	173,703	Ford, Gerald R.	149,259	Carter, Jimmy	5,772	24,444 R	52.8%	45.4%	53.8%	46.2%
1972	317,603	183,976	Nixon, Richard M.	120,197	McGovern, George S.	13,430	63,779 R	57.9%	37.8%	60.5%	39.5%
1968	274,404	138,835	Nixon, Richard M.	114,117	Humphrey, Hubert H.	21,452	24,718 R	50.6%	41.6%	54.9%	45.1%
1964	278,628	113,032	Goldwater, Barry M.	164,246	Johnson, Lyndon B.	1,350	51,214 D	40.6%	58.9%	40.8%	59.2%
1960	277,579	141,841	Nixon, Richard M.	134,891	Kennedy, John F.	847	6,950 R	51.1%	48.6%	51.3%	48.7%
1956	271,171	154,933	Eisenhower, Dwight D.	116,238	Stevenson, Adlai E.		38,695 R	57.1%	42.9%	57.1%	42.9%
1952	265,037	157,394	Eisenhower, Dwight D.	106,213	Stevenson, Adlai E.	1,430	51,181 R	59.4%	40.1%	59.7%	40.3%
1948	224,278	96,770	Dewey, Thomas E.	119,071	Truman, Harry S.	8,437	22,301 D	43.1%	53.1%	44.8%	55.2%

POSTWAR VOTE FOR GOVERNOR

		Republican		Democratic				Percentage			
	Total					Other	Rep.-Dem.	Total Vote		Major Vote	
Year	Vote	Vote	Candidate	Vote	Candidate	Vote	Plurality	Rep.	Dem.	Rep.	Dem.
1988	367,021	190,604	Stephens, Stan	169,313	Judge, Thomas L.	7,104	21,291 R	51.9%	46.1%	53.0%	47.0%
1984	378,970	100,070	Goodover, Pat M.	266,578	Schwinden, Ted	12,322	166,508 D	26.4%	70.3%	27.3%	72.7%
1980	360,466	160,892	Ramirez, Jack	199,574	Schwinden, Ted		38,682 D	44.6%	55.4%	44.6%	55.4%
1976	316,720	115,848	Woodahl, Robert	195,420	Judge, Thomas L.	5,452	79,572 D	36.6%	61.7%	37.2%	62.8%
1972	318,754	146,231	Smith, Ed	172,523	Judge, Thomas L.		26,292 D	45.9%	54.1%	45.9%	54.1%
1968	278,112	116,432	Babcock, Tim M.	150,481	Anderson, Forrest H.	11,199	34,049 D	41.9%	54.1%	43.6%	56.4%
1964	280,975	144,113	Babcock, Tim M.	136,862	Renne, Roland		7,251 R	51.3%	48.7%	51.3%	48.7%
1960	279,881	154,230	Nutter, Donald G.	125,651	Cannon, Paul		28,579 R	55.1%	44.9%	55.1%	44.9%
1956	270,366	138,878	Aronson, J. Hugo	131,488	Olsen, Arnold H.		7,390 R	51.4%	48.6%	51.4%	48.6%
1952	263,792	134,423	Aronson, J. Hugo	129,369	Bonner, John W.		5,054 R	51.0%	49.0%	51.0%	49.0%
1948	222,964	97,792	Ford, Sam C.	124,267	Bonner, John W.	905	26,475 D	43.9%	55.7%	44.0%	56.0%

MONTANA

POSTWAR VOTE FOR SENATOR

Year	Total Vote	Republican Vote	Republican Candidate	Democratic Vote	Democratic Candidate	Other Vote	Rep.-Dem. Plurality	Percentage Total Vote Rep.	Percentage Total Vote Dem.	Percentage Major Vote Rep.	Percentage Major Vote Dem.
1988	365,254	189,445	Burns, Conrad	175,809	Melcher, John		13,636 R	51.9%	48.1%	51.9%	48.1%
1984	379,155	154,308	Cozzens, Chuck	215,704	Baucus, Max S.	9,143	61,396 D	40.7%	56.9%	41.7%	58.3%
1982	321,062	133,789	Williams, Larry	174,861	Melcher, John	12,412	41,072 D	41.7%	54.5%	43.3%	56.7%
1978	287,942	127,589	Williams, Larry	160,353	Baucus, Max S.		32,764 D	44.3%	55.7%	44.3%	55.7%
1976	321,445	115,213	Burger, Stanley C.	206,232	Melcher, John		91,019 D	35.8%	64.2%	35.8%	64.2%
1972	314,925	151,316	Hibbard, Henry S.	163,609	Metcalf, Lee		12,293 D	48.0%	52.0%	48.0%	52.0%
1970	247,869	97,809	Wallace, Harold E.	150,060	Mansfield, Mike		52,251 D	39.5%	60.5%	39.5%	60.5%
1966	259,863	121,697	Babcock, Tim M.	138,166	Metcalf, Lee		16,469 D	46.8%	53.2%	46.8%	53.2%
1964	280,010	99,367	Blewett, Alex	180,643	Mansfield, Mike		81,276 D	35.5%	64.5%	35.5%	64.5%
1960	276,612	136,281	Fjare, Orvin B.	140,331	Metcalf, Lee		4,050 D	49.3%	50.7%	49.3%	50.7%
1958	229,483	54,573	Welch. Lou W.	174,910	Mansfield, Mike		120,337 D	23.8%	76.2%	23.8%	76.2%
1954	227,454	112,863	D'Ewart, Wesley A.	114,591	Murray, James E.		1,728 D	49.6%	50.4%	49.6%	50.4%
1952	262,297	127,360	Ecton, Zales N.	133,109	Mansfield, Mike	1,828	5,749 D	48.6%	50.7%	48.9%	51.1%
1948	221,003	94,458	David, Tom J.	125,193	Murray, James E.	1,352	30,735 D	42.7%	56.6%	43.0%	57.0%
1946	190,566	101,901	Ecton, Zales N.	86,476	Erickson, Leif	2,189	15,425 R	53.5%	45.4%	54.1%	45.9%

MONTANA

Districts Established March 4, 1983

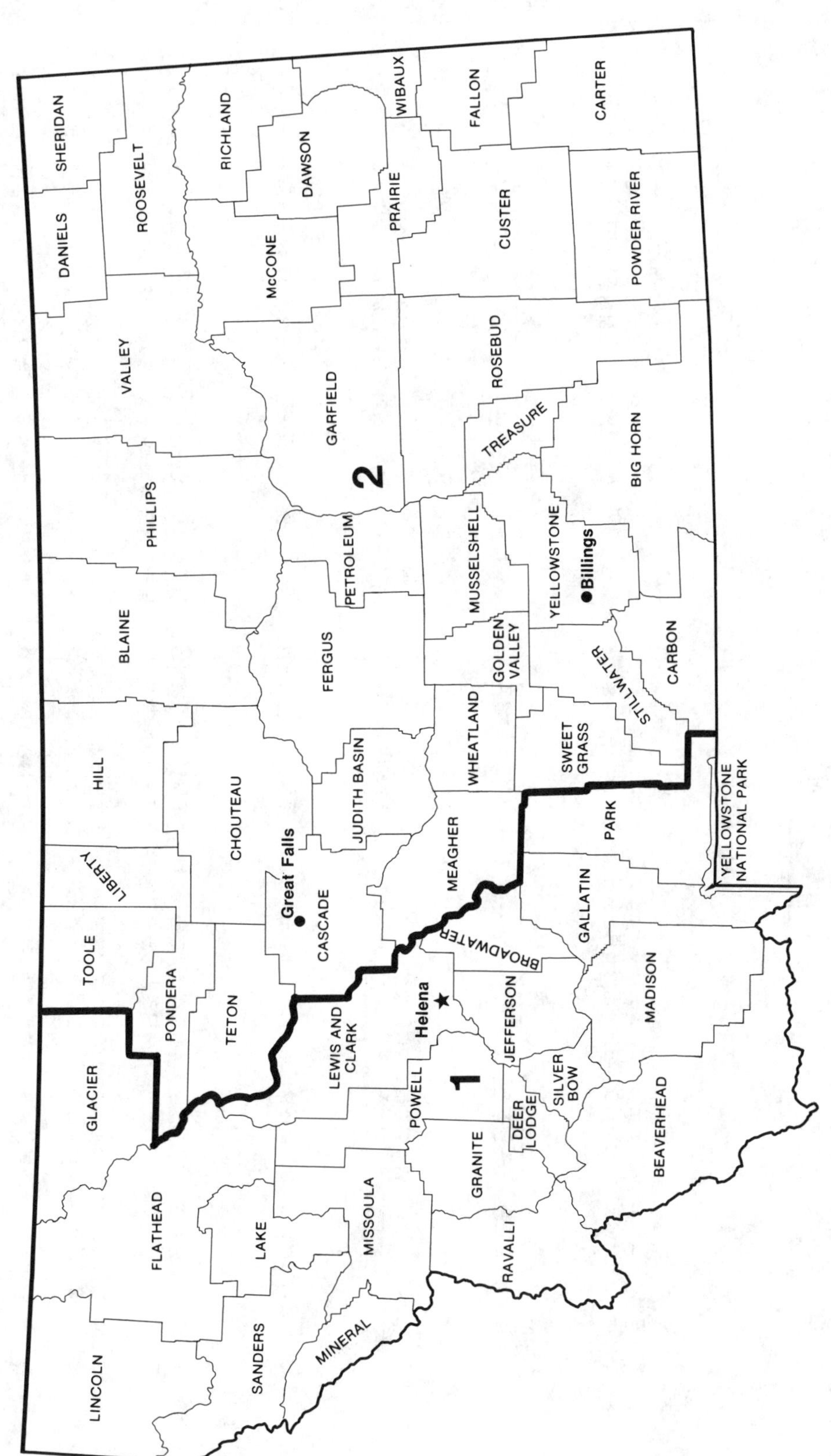

MONTANA

PRESIDENT 1988

1980 Census Population	County	Total Vote	Republican	Democratic	Other	Rep.-Dem. Plurality	Percentage Total Vote Rep.	Total Vote Dem.	Major Vote Rep.	Major Vote Dem.
8,186	BEAVERHEAD	3,998	2,668	1,274	56	1,394 R	66.7%	31.9%	67.7%	32.3%
11,096	BIG HORN	3,984	1,711	2,233	40	522 D	42.9%	56.0%	43.4%	56.6%
6,999	BLAINE	2,912	1,402	1,460	50	58 D	48.1%	50.1%	49.0%	51.0%
3,267	BROADWATER	1,683	1,054	592	37	462 R	62.6%	35.2%	64.0%	36.0%
8,099	CARBON	4,470	2,360	2,039	71	321 R	52.8%	45.6%	53.6%	46.4%
1,799	CARTER	942	686	242	14	444 R	72.8%	25.7%	73.9%	26.1%
80,696	CASCADE	32,124	15,946	15,718	460	228 R	49.6%	48.9%	50.4%	49.6%
6,092	CHOUTEAU	3,219	1,980	1,166	73	814 R	61.5%	36.2%	62.9%	37.1%
13,109	CUSTER	5,462	3,007	2,343	112	664 R	55.1%	42.9%	56.2%	43.8%
2,835	DANIELS	1,395	802	571	22	231 R	57.5%	40.9%	58.4%	41.6%
11,805	DAWSON	4,886	2,658	2,120	108	538 R	54.4%	43.4%	55.6%	44.4%
12,518	DEER LODGE	4,406	1,168	3,185	53	2,017 D	26.5%	72.3%	26.8%	73.2%
3,763	FALLON	1,636	1,002	612	22	390 R	61.2%	37.4%	62.1%	37.9%
13,076	FERGUS	6,116	3,948	2,052	116	1,896 R	64.6%	33.6%	65.8%	34.2%
51,966	FLATHEAD	25,225	14,461	10,202	562	4,259 R	57.3%	40.4%	58.6%	41.4%
42,865	GALLATIN	23,205	13,214	9,527	464	3,687 R	56.9%	41.1%	58.1%	41.9%
1,656	GARFIELD	851	631	196	24	435 R	74.1%	23.0%	76.3%	23.7%
10,628	GLACIER	4,004	1,728	2,151	125	423 D	43.2%	53.7%	44.5%	55.5%
1,026	GOLDEN VALLEY	543	335	203	5	132 R	61.7%	37.4%	62.3%	37.7%
2,700	GRANITE	1,326	789	511	26	278 R	59.5%	38.5%	60.7%	39.3%
17,985	HILL	7,791	3,467	4,219	105	752 D	44.5%	54.2%	45.1%	54.9%
7,029	JEFFERSON	3,837	2,007	1,746	84	261 R	52.3%	45.5%	53.5%	46.5%
2,646	JUDITH BASIN	1,516	902	590	24	312 R	59.5%	38.9%	60.5%	39.5%
19,056	LAKE	9,150	4,883	4,109	158	774 R	53.4%	44.9%	54.3%	45.7%
43,039	LEWIS AND CLARK	23,334	10,946	11,932	456	986 D	46.9%	51.1%	47.8%	52.2%
2,329	LIBERTY	1,208	771	418	19	353 R	63.8%	34.6%	64.8%	35.2%
17,752	LINCOLN	7,294	3,500	3,601	193	101 D	48.0%	49.4%	49.3%	50.7%
2,702	MCCONE	1,399	814	567	18	247 R	58.2%	40.5%	58.9%	41.1%
5,448	MADISON	2,980	2,045	878	57	1,167 R	68.6%	29.5%	70.0%	30.0%
2,154	MEAGHER	1,009	656	337	16	319 R	65.0%	33.4%	66.1%	33.9%
3,675	MINERAL	1,428	616	789	23	173 D	43.1%	55.3%	43.8%	56.2%
76,016	MISSOULA	35,669	15,965	19,178	526	3,213 D	44.8%	53.8%	45.4%	54.6%
4,428	MUSSELSHELL	2,204	1,280	898	26	382 R	58.1%	40.7%	58.8%	41.2%
12,660	PARK	6,465	3,823	2,526	116	1,297 R	59.1%	39.1%	60.2%	39.8%
655	PETROLEUM	302	204	91	7	113 R	67.5%	30.1%	69.2%	30.8%
5,367	PHILLIPS	2,426	1,462	905	59	557 R	60.3%	37.3%	61.8%	38.2%
6,731	PONDERA	3,114	1,795	1,245	74	550 R	57.6%	40.0%	59.0%	41.0%
2,520	POWDER RIVER	1,232	815	395	22	420 R	66.2%	32.1%	67.4%	32.6%
6,958	POWELL	2,795	1,574	1,174	47	400 R	56.3%	42.0%	57.3%	42.7%
1,836	PRAIRIE	900	541	343	16	198 R	60.1%	38.1%	61.2%	38.8%
22,493	RAVALLI	12,490	7,418	4,763	309	2,655 R	59.4%	38.1%	60.9%	39.1%
12,243	RICHLAND	4,546	2,628	1,824	94	804 R	57.8%	40.1%	59.0%	41.0%
10,467	ROOSEVELT	4,118	1,957	2,083	78	126 D	47.5%	50.6%	48.4%	51.6%
9,899	ROSEBUD	3,792	1,822	1,869	101	47 D	48.0%	49.3%	49.4%	50.6%
8,675	SANDERS	4,200	2,152	1,959	89	193 R	51.2%	46.6%	52.3%	47.7%
5,414	SHERIDAN	2,763	1,381	1,354	28	27 R	50.0%	49.0%	50.5%	49.5%
38,092	SILVER BOW	16,687	5,043	11,422	222	6,379 D	30.2%	68.4%	30.6%	69.4%
5,598	STILLWATER	3,379	1,920	1,407	52	513 R	56.8%	41.6%	57.7%	42.3%
3,216	SWEET GRASS	1,733	1,242	462	29	780 R	71.7%	26.7%	72.9%	27.1%
6,491	TETON	3,244	1,876	1,303	65	573 R	57.8%	40.2%	59.0%	41.0%
5,559	TOOLE	2,634	1,505	1,070	59	435 R	57.1%	40.6%	58.4%	41.6%
981	TREASURE	536	291	231	14	60 R	54.3%	43.1%	55.7%	44.3%
10,250	VALLEY	4,706	2,467	2,163	76	304 R	52.4%	46.0%	53.3%	46.7%
2,359	WHEATLAND	1,130	667	443	20	224 R	59.0%	39.2%	60.1%	39.9%
1,476	WIBAUX	629	358	258	13	100 R	56.9%	41.0%	58.1%	41.9%
108,035	YELLOWSTONE	50,647	28,069	21,987	591	6,082 R	55.4%	43.4%	56.1%	43.9%
786,690	TOTAL	365,674	190,412	168,936	6,326	21,476 R	52.1%	46.2%	53.0%	47.0%

MONTANA

GOVERNOR 1988

1980 Census Population	County	Total Vote	Republican	Democratic	Other	Rep.-Dem. Plurality	Percentage Total Vote Rep.	Total Vote Dem.	Major Vote Rep.	Major Vote Dem.
8,186	BEAVERHEAD	4,034	2,414	1,557	63	857 R	59.8%	38.6%	60.8%	39.2%
11,096	BIG HORN	4,080	1,636	2,364	80	728 D	40.1%	57.9%	40.9%	59.1%
6,999	BLAINE	2,970	1,388	1,541	41	153 D	46.7%	51.9%	47.4%	52.6%
3,267	BROADWATER	1,698	1,041	636	21	405 R	61.3%	37.5%	62.1%	37.9%
8,099	CARBON	4,466	2,379	2,013	74	366 R	53.3%	45.1%	54.2%	45.8%
1,799	CARTER	930	629	284	17	345 R	67.6%	30.5%	68.9%	31.1%
80,696	CASCADE	32,471	16,224	15,777	470	447 R	50.0%	48.6%	50.7%	49.3%
6,092	CHOUTEAU	3,278	1,961	1,256	61	705 R	59.8%	38.3%	61.0%	39.0%
13,109	CUSTER	5,485	2,672	2,704	109	32 D	48.7%	49.3%	49.7%	50.3%
2,835	DANIELS	1,375	824	538	13	286 R	59.9%	39.1%	60.5%	39.5%
11,805	DAWSON	4,912	2,399	2,447	66	48 D	48.8%	49.8%	49.5%	50.5%
12,518	DEER LODGE	4,578	1,117	3,385	76	2,268 D	24.4%	73.9%	24.8%	75.2%
3,763	FALLON	1,605	817	753	35	64 R	50.9%	46.9%	52.0%	48.0%
13,076	FERGUS	6,195	3,575	2,504	116	1,071 R	57.7%	40.4%	58.8%	41.2%
51,966	FLATHEAD	25,364	14,841	9,963	560	4,878 R	58.5%	39.3%	59.8%	40.2%
42,865	GALLATIN	22,897	13,139	9,270	488	3,869 R	57.4%	40.5%	58.6%	41.4%
1,656	GARFIELD	856	537	304	15	233 R	62.7%	35.5%	63.9%	36.1%
10,628	GLACIER	4,082	1,607	2,326	149	719 D	39.4%	57.0%	40.9%	59.1%
1,026	GOLDEN VALLEY	549	337	199	13	138 R	61.4%	36.2%	62.9%	37.1%
2,700	GRANITE	1,340	811	499	30	312 R	60.5%	37.2%	61.9%	38.1%
17,985	HILL	7,916	3,866	3,936	114	70 D	48.8%	49.7%	49.6%	50.4%
7,029	JEFFERSON	3,869	1,985	1,807	77	178 R	51.3%	46.7%	52.3%	47.7%
2,646	JUDITH BASIN	1,539	790	735	14	55 R	51.3%	47.8%	51.8%	48.2%
19,056	LAKE	9,202	5,152	3,864	186	1,288 R	56.0%	42.0%	57.1%	42.9%
43,039	LEWIS AND CLARK	23,513	11,174	11,869	470	695 D	47.5%	50.5%	48.5%	51.5%
2,329	LIBERTY	1,222	837	373	12	464 R	68.5%	30.5%	69.2%	30.8%
17,752	LINCOLN	7,221	3,134	3,885	202	751 D	43.4%	53.8%	44.7%	55.3%
2,702	MCCONE	1,419	727	672	20	55 R	51.2%	47.4%	52.0%	48.0%
5,448	MADISON	2,999	1,971	974	54	997 R	65.7%	32.5%	66.9%	33.1%
2,154	MEAGHER	1,012	609	390	13	219 R	60.2%	38.5%	61.0%	39.0%
3,675	MINERAL	1,430	588	805	37	217 D	41.1%	56.3%	42.2%	57.8%
76,016	MISSOULA	35,827	17,731	17,162	934	569 R	49.5%	47.9%	50.8%	49.2%
4,428	MUSSELSHELL	2,185	1,218	935	32	283 R	55.7%	42.8%	56.6%	43.4%
12,660	PARK	6,390	3,680	2,575	135	1,105 R	57.6%	40.3%	58.8%	41.2%
655	PETROLEUM	309	186	113	10	73 R	60.2%	36.6%	62.2%	37.8%
5,367	PHILLIPS	2,470	1,392	1,034	44	358 R	56.4%	41.9%	57.4%	42.6%
6,731	PONDERA	3,143	1,760	1,340	43	420 R	56.0%	42.6%	56.8%	43.2%
2,520	POWDER RIVER	1,213	737	457	19	280 R	60.8%	37.7%	61.7%	38.3%
6,958	POWELL	2,787	1,344	1,358	85	14 D	48.2%	48.7%	49.7%	50.3%
1,836	PRAIRIE	906	496	396	14	100 R	54.7%	43.7%	55.6%	44.4%
22,493	RAVALLI	12,448	7,708	4,500	240	3,208 R	61.9%	36.2%	63.1%	36.9%
12,243	RICHLAND	4,544	2,540	1,941	63	599 R	55.9%	42.7%	56.7%	43.3%
10,467	ROOSEVELT	4,118	1,799	2,231	88	432 D	43.7%	54.2%	44.6%	55.4%
9,899	ROSEBUD	3,809	1,668	2,040	101	372 D	43.8%	53.6%	45.0%	55.0%
8,675	SANDERS	4,175	2,060	2,007	108	53 R	49.3%	48.1%	50.7%	49.3%
5,414	SHERIDAN	2,769	1,508	1,243	18	265 R	54.5%	44.9%	54.8%	45.2%
38,092	SILVER BOW	16,853	5,382	11,107	364	5,725 D	31.9%	65.9%	32.6%	67.4%
5,598	STILLWATER	3,400	1,821	1,526	53	295 R	53.6%	44.9%	54.4%	45.6%
3,216	SWEET GRASS	1,738	1,270	451	17	819 R	73.1%	25.9%	73.8%	26.2%
6,491	TETON	3,236	1,837	1,368	31	469 R	56.8%	42.3%	57.3%	42.7%
5,559	TOOLE	2,656	1,504	1,096	56	408 R	56.6%	41.3%	57.8%	42.2%
981	TREASURE	541	306	222	13	84 R	56.6%	41.0%	58.0%	42.0%
10,250	VALLEY	4,643	2,225	2,263	155	38 D	47.9%	48.7%	49.6%	50.4%
2,359	WHEATLAND	1,148	652	479	17	173 R	56.8%	41.7%	57.6%	42.4%
1,476	WIBAUX	635	305	326	4	21 D	48.0%	51.3%	48.3%	51.7%
108,035	YELLOWSTONE	50,571	28,294	21,513	764	6,781 R	55.9%	42.5%	56.8%	43.2%
786,690	TOTAL	367,021	190,604	169,313	7,104	21,291 R	51.9%	46.1%	53.0%	47.0%

MONTANA

SENATOR 1988

1980 Census Population	County	Total Vote	Republican	Democratic	Other	Rep.-Dem. Plurality	Percentage Total Vote Rep.	Total Vote Dem.	Major Vote Rep.	Major Vote Dem.
8,186	BEAVERHEAD	4,060	2,918	1,142		1,776 R	71.9%	28.1%	71.9%	28.1%
11,096	BIG HORN	4,093	1,843	2,250		407 D	45.0%	55.0%	45.0%	55.0%
6,999	BLAINE	2,974	1,212	1,762		550 D	40.8%	59.2%	40.8%	59.2%
3,267	BROADWATER	1,650	1,072	578		494 R	65.0%	35.0%	65.0%	35.0%
8,099	CARBON	4,504	2,287	2,217		70 R	50.8%	49.2%	50.8%	49.2%
1,799	CARTER	958	594	364		230 R	62.0%	38.0%	62.0%	38.0%
80,696	CASCADE	32,499	15,251	17,248		1,997 D	46.9%	53.1%	46.9%	53.1%
6,092	CHOUTEAU	3,308	1,637	1,671		34 D	49.5%	50.5%	49.5%	50.5%
13,109	CUSTER	5,496	2,782	2,714		68 R	50.6%	49.4%	50.6%	49.4%
2,835	DANIELS	1,403	726	677		49 R	51.7%	48.3%	51.7%	48.3%
11,805	DAWSON	4,945	2,556	2,389		167 R	51.7%	48.3%	51.7%	48.3%
12,518	DEER LODGE	4,659	1,600	3,059		1,459 D	34.3%	65.7%	34.3%	65.7%
3,763	FALLON	1,669	917	752		165 R	54.9%	45.1%	54.9%	45.1%
13,076	FERGUS	6,163	3,573	2,590		983 R	58.0%	42.0%	58.0%	42.0%
51,966	FLATHEAD	24,717	14,873	9,844		5,029 R	60.2%	39.8%	60.2%	39.8%
42,865	GALLATIN	23,198	13,796	9,402		4,394 R	59.5%	40.5%	59.5%	40.5%
1,656	GARFIELD	873	543	330		213 R	62.2%	37.8%	62.2%	37.8%
10,628	GLACIER	4,073	1,885	2,188		303 D	46.3%	53.7%	46.3%	53.7%
1,026	GOLDEN VALLEY	551	321	230		91 R	58.3%	41.7%	58.3%	41.7%
2,700	GRANITE	1,342	896	446		450 R	66.8%	33.2%	66.8%	33.2%
17,985	HILL	7,815	3,401	4,414		1,013 D	43.5%	56.5%	43.5%	56.5%
7,029	JEFFERSON	3,890	2,238	1,652		586 R	57.5%	42.5%	57.5%	42.5%
2,646	JUDITH BASIN	1,546	830	716		114 R	53.7%	46.3%	53.7%	46.3%
19,056	LAKE	9,066	4,850	4,216		634 R	53.5%	46.5%	53.5%	46.5%
43,039	LEWIS AND CLARK	23,362	11,987	11,375		612 R	51.3%	48.7%	51.3%	48.7%
2,329	LIBERTY	1,210	686	524		162 R	56.7%	43.3%	56.7%	43.3%
17,752	LINCOLN	5,804	3,216	2,588		628 R	55.4%	44.6%	55.4%	44.6%
2,702	MCCONE	1,438	777	661		116 R	54.0%	46.0%	54.0%	46.0%
5,448	MADISON	2,935	2,095	840		1,255 R	71.4%	28.6%	71.4%	28.6%
2,154	MEAGHER	994	649	345		304 R	65.3%	34.7%	65.3%	34.7%
3,675	MINERAL	1,436	636	800		164 D	44.3%	55.7%	44.3%	55.7%
76,016	MISSOULA	35,604	16,731	18,873		2,142 D	47.0%	53.0%	47.0%	53.0%
4,428	MUSSELSHELL	2,225	1,182	1,043		139 R	53.1%	46.9%	53.1%	46.9%
12,660	PARK	6,352	3,927	2,425		1,502 R	61.8%	38.2%	61.8%	38.2%
655	PETROLEUM	307	183	124		59 R	59.6%	40.4%	59.6%	40.4%
5,367	PHILLIPS	2,481	1,295	1,186		109 R	52.2%	47.8%	52.2%	47.8%
6,731	PONDERA	3,182	1,694	1,488		206 R	53.2%	46.8%	53.2%	46.8%
2,520	POWDER RIVER	1,247	746	501		245 R	59.8%	40.2%	59.8%	40.2%
6,958	POWELL	2,812	1,743	1,069		674 R	62.0%	38.0%	62.0%	38.0%
1,836	PRAIRIE	914	463	451		12 R	50.7%	49.3%	50.7%	49.3%
22,493	RAVALLI	12,423	7,779	4,644		3,135 R	62.6%	37.4%	62.6%	37.4%
12,243	RICHLAND	4,623	2,758	1,865		893 R	59.7%	40.3%	59.7%	40.3%
10,467	ROOSEVELT	4,174	1,773	2,401		628 D	42.5%	57.5%	42.5%	57.5%
9,899	ROSEBUD	3,840	1,494	2,346		852 D	38.9%	61.1%	38.9%	61.1%
8,675	SANDERS	4,202	2,235	1,967		268 R	53.2%	46.8%	53.2%	46.8%
5,414	SHERIDAN	2,823	1,295	1,528		233 D	45.9%	54.1%	45.9%	54.1%
38,092	SILVER BOW	16,868	5,779	11,089		5,310 D	34.3%	65.7%	34.3%	65.7%
5,598	STILLWATER	3,416	1,779	1,637		142 R	52.1%	47.9%	52.1%	47.9%
3,216	SWEET GRASS	1,754	1,167	587		580 R	66.5%	33.5%	66.5%	33.5%
6,491	TETON	3,276	1,749	1,527		222 R	53.4%	46.6%	53.4%	46.6%
5,559	TOOLE	2,648	1,429	1,219		210 R	54.0%	46.0%	54.0%	46.0%
981	TREASURE	543	229	314		85 D	42.2%	57.8%	42.2%	57.8%
10,250	VALLEY	4,426	2,269	2,157		112 R	51.3%	48.7%	51.3%	48.7%
2,359	WHEATLAND	1,163	621	542		79 R	53.4%	46.6%	53.4%	46.6%
1,476	WIBAUX	662	315	347		32 D	47.6%	52.4%	47.6%	52.4%
108,035	YELLOWSTONE	50,658	26,163	24,495		1,668 R	51.6%	48.4%	51.6%	48.4%
786,690	TOTAL	365,254	189,445	175,809		13,636 R	51.9%	48.1%	51.9%	48.1%

MONTANA

CONGRESS

CD	Year	Total Vote	Republican Vote	Republican Candidate	Democratic Vote	Democratic Candidate	Other Vote	Rep.-Dem. Plurality	Percentage Total Vote Rep.	Percentage Total Vote Dem.	Percentage Major Vote Rep.	Percentage Major Vote Dem.
1	1988	189,683	74,405	FENLASON, JIM	115,278	WILLIAMS, PAT		40,873 D	39.2%	60.8%	39.2%	60.8%
1	1986	159,731	61,230	ALLEN, DON	98,501	WILLIAMS, PAT		37,271 D	38.3%	61.7%	38.3%	61.7%
1	1984	193,452	61,794	CARLSON, GARY K.	126,998	WILLIAMS, PAT	4,660	65,204 D	31.9%	65.6%	32.7%	67.3%
2	1988	175,534	97,465	MARLENEE, RON	78,069	O'BRIEN, BUCK		19,396 R	55.5%	44.5%	55.5%	44.5%
2	1986	158,131	84,548	MARLENEE, RON	73,583	O'BRIEN, BUCK		10,965 R	53.5%	46.5%	53.5%	46.5%
2	1984	177,377	116,932	MARLENEE, RON	60,445	BLAYLOCK, CHET		56,487 R	65.9%	34.1%	65.9%	34.1%

MONTANA

Population total includes 275 persons living in Yellowstone National Park and not under any county jurisdiction.

1988 GENERAL ELECTION

President Other vote was 5,047 Libertarian (Paul); 1,279 New Alliance (Fulani). Early unamended returns gave the Democratic (Dukakis) vote as 168,956; Rosebud county was adjusted by 20 votes.

Governor Other vote was Libertarian (Morris). Early unamended returns gave the Republican (Stephens) vote in Richland county as 4,540.

Senator Early unamended returns gave the Republican (Burns) vote in Meagher county as 449. There appears to be an undercount of the vote in Lincoln county, but the final, official returns are presented here.

Congress

1988 PRIMARIES

JUNE 7 REPUBLICAN

Governor 44,022 Stan Stephens; 37,875 Cal Winslow; 6,024 Jim Waltermire (died two months prior to the primary).

Senator 63,330 Conrad Burns; 11,427 Tom Faranda.

Congress Unopposed in both CD's.

JUNE 7 DEMOCRATIC

Governor 46,412 Thomas L. Judge; 32,124 Frank Morrison; 26,827 Mike Greely; 7,297 Ted Neuman; 3,360 Martin Beckman; 2,038 Curly Thornton.

Senator 88,457 John Melcher; 30,212 Robert C. Kelleher.

Congress Unopposed in both CD's.

NEBRASKA

GOVERNOR

Kay Orr (R). Elected 1986 to a four-year term.

SENATORS

J. J.Exon (D). Re-elected 1984 to a six-year term. Previously elected 1978.

Bob Kerrey (D). Elected 1988 to a six-year term.

REPRESENTATIVES

1. Douglas K. Bereuter (R)
2. Peter Hoagland (D)
3. Virginia Smith (R)

POSTWAR VOTE FOR PRESIDENT

								Percentage			
	Total	Republican		Democratic		Other		Total Vote		Major Vote	
Year	Vote	Vote	Candidate	Vote	Candidate	Vote	Plurality	Rep.	Dem.	Rep.	Dem.
1988	661,465	397,956	Bush, George	259,235	Dukakis, Michael S.	4,274	138,721 R	60.2%	39.2%	60.6%	39.4%
1984	652,090	460,054	Reagan, Ronald	187,866	Mondale, Walter F.	4,170	272,188 R	70.6%	28.8%	71.0%	29.0%
1980	640,854	419,937	Reagan, Ronald	166,851	Carter, Jimmy	54,066	253,086 R	65.5%	26.0%	71.6%	28.4%
1976	607,668	359,705	Ford, Gerald R.	233,692	Carter, Jimmy	14,271	126,013 R	59.2%	38.5%	60.6%	39.4%
1972	576,289	406,298	Nixon, Richard M.	169,991	McGovern, George S.		236,307 R	70.5%	29.5%	70.5%	29.5%
1968	536,851	321,163	Nixon, Richard M.	170,784	Humphrey, Hubert H.	44,904	150,379 R	59.8%	31.8%	65.3%	34.7%
1964	584,154	276,847	Goldwater, Barry M.	307,307	Johnson, Lyndon B.		30,460 D	47.4%	52.6%	47.4%	52.6%
1960	613,095	380,553	Nixon, Richard M.	232,542	Kennedy, John F.		148,011 R	62.1%	37.9%	62.1%	37.9%
1956	577,137	378,108	Eisenhower, Dwight D.	199,029	Stevenson, Adlai E.		179,079 R	65.5%	34.5%	65.5%	34.5%
1952	609,660	421,603	Eisenhower, Dwight D.	188,057	Stevenson, Adlai E.		233,546 R	69.2%	30.8%	69.2%	30.8%
1948	488,940	264,774	Dewey, Thomas E.	224,165	Truman, Harry S.	1	40,609 R	54.2%	45.8%	54.2%	45.8%

POSTWAR VOTE FOR GOVERNOR

								Percentage			
	Total	Republican		Democratic		Other	Rep.-Dem.	Total Vote		Major Vote	
Year	Vote	Vote	Candidate	Vote	Candidate	Vote	Plurality	Rep.	Dem.	Rep.	Dem.
1986	564,422	298,325	Orr, Kay	265,156	Boosalis, Helen	941	33,169 R	52.9%	47.0%	52.9%	47.1%
1982	547,902	270,203	Thone, Charles	277,436	Kerrey, Bob	263	7,233 D	49.3%	50.6%	49.3%	50.7%
1978	492,423	275,473	Thone, Charles	216,754	Whelan, Gerald T.	196	58,719 R	55.9%	44.0%	56.0%	44.0%
1974	451,306	159,780	Marvel, Richard D.	267,012	Exon, J. J.	24,514	107,232 D	35.4%	59.2%	37.4%	62.6%
1970	461,619	201,994	Tiemann, Norbert T.	248,552	Exon, J. J.	11,073	46,558 D	43.8%	53.8%	44.8%	55.2%
1966 **	486,396	299,245	Tiemann, Norbert T.	186,985	Sorensen, Philip C.	166	112,260 R	61.5%	38.4%	61.5%	38.5%
1964	578,090	231,029	Burney, Dwight W.	347,026	Morrison, Frank B.	35	115,997 D	40.0%	60.0%	40.0%	60.0%
1962	464,585	221,885	Seaton, Fred A.	242,669	Morrison, Frank B.	31	20,784 D	47.8%	52.2%	47.8%	52.2%
1960	598,971	287,302	Cooper, John R.	311,344	Morrison, Frank B.	325	24,042 D	48.0%	52.0%	48.0%	52.0%
1958	421,067	209,705	Anderson, Victor E.	211,345	Brooks, Ralph G.	17	1,640 D	49.8%	50.2%	49.8%	50.2%
1956	567,933	308,293	Anderson, Victor E.	228,048	Sorrell, Frank	31,592	80,245 R	54.3%	40.2%	57.5%	42.5%
1954	414,841	250,080	Anderson, Victor E.	164,753	Ritchie, William	8	85,327 R	60.3%	39.7%	60.3%	39.7%
1952	595,714	366,009	Crosby, Robert B.	229,700	Raecke, Walter R.	5	136,309 R	61.4%	38.6%	61.4%	38.6%
1950	449,720	247,081	Peterson, Val	202,638	Raecke, Walter R.	1	44,443 R	54.9%	45.1%	54.9%	45.1%
1948	476,352	286,119	Peterson, Val	190,214	Sorrell, Frank	19	95,905 R	60.1%	39.9%	60.1%	39.9%
1946	380,835	249,468	Peterson, Val	131,367	Sorrell, Frank		118,101 R	65.5%	34.5%	65.5%	34.5%

The term of office of Nebraska's Governor was increased from two to four years effective with the 1966 election.

NEBRASKA

POSTWAR VOTE FOR SENATOR

Year	Total Vote	Republican Vote	Republican Candidate	Democratic Vote	Democratic Candidate	Other Vote	Rep.-Dem. Plurality	Percentage Total Vote Rep.	Percentage Total Vote Dem.	Percentage Major Vote Rep.	Percentage Major Vote Dem.
1988	667,860	278,250	Karnes, David	378,717	Kerrey, Bob	10,893	100,467 D	41.7%	56.7%	42.4%	57.6%
1984	639,668	307,147	Hoch, Nancy	332,217	Exon, J. J.	304	25,070 D	48.0%	51.9%	48.0%	52.0%
1982	545,647	155,760	Keck, Jim	363,350	Zorinsky, Edward	26,537	207,590 D	28.5%	66.6%	30.0%	70.0%
1978	494,368	159,806	Shasteen, Donald	334,276	Exon, J. J.	286	174,470 D	32.3%	67.6%	32.3%	67.7%
1976	598,314	284,284	McCollister, John Y.	313,809	Zorinsky, Edward	221	29,525 D	47.5%	52.4%	47.5%	52.5%
1972	568,580	301,841	Curtis, Carl T.	265,922	Carpenter, Terry	817	35,919 R	53.1%	46.8%	53.2%	46.8%
1970	458,966	240,894	Hruska, Roman L.	217,681	Morrison, Frank B.	391	23,213 R	52.5%	47.4%	52.5%	47.5%
1966	485,101	296,116	Curtis, Carl T.	187,950	Morrison, Frank B.	1,035	108,166 R	61.0%	38.7%	61.2%	38.8%
1964	563,401	345,772	Hruska, Roman L.	217,605	Arndt, Raymond W.	24	128,167 R	61.4%	38.6%	61.4%	38.6%
1960	598,743	352,748	Curtis, Carl T.	245,837	Conrad, Robert	158	106,911 R	58.9%	41.1%	58.9%	41.1%
1958	417,385	232,227	Hruska, Roman L.	185,152	Morrison, Frank B.	6	47,075 R	55.6%	44.4%	55.6%	44.4%
1954	418,691	255,695	Curtis, Carl T.	162,990	Neville, Keith	6	92,705 R	61.1%	38.9%	61.1%	38.9%
1954 S	411,225	250,341	Hruska, Roman L.	160,881	Green, James F.	3	89,460 R	60.9%	39.1%	60.9%	39.1%
1952	591,749	408,971	Butler, Hugh	164,660	Long, Stanley D.	18,118	244,311 R	69.1%	27.8%	71.3%	28.7%
1952 S	581,750	369,841	Griswold, Dwight	211,898	Ritchie, William	11	157,943 R	63.6%	36.4%	63.6%	36.4%
1948	471,895	267,575	Wherry, Kenneth S.	204,320	Carpenter, Terry		63,255 R	56.7%	43.3%	56.7%	43.3%
1946	382,958	271,208	Butler, Hugh	111,750	Mekota, John E.		159,458 R	70.8%	29.2%	70.8%	29.2%

One each of the 1954 and 1952 elections was for a short term to fill a vacancy.

NEBRASKA

Districts Established May 28, 1981

NEBRASKA

PRESIDENT 1988

1980 Census Population	County	Total Vote	Republican	Democratic	Other	Rep.-Dem. Plurality	Percentage Total Vote Rep.	Total Vote Dem.	Major Vote Rep.	Major Vote Dem.
30,656	ADAMS	12,287	8,063	4,145	79	3,918 R	65.6%	33.7%	66.0%	34.0%
8,675	ANTELOPE	3,559	2,626	933	0	1,693 R	73.8%	26.2%	73.8%	26.2%
513	ARTHUR	269	210	58	1	152 R	78.1%	21.6%	78.4%	21.6%
918	BANNER	477	361	112	4	249 R	75.7%	23.5%	76.3%	23.7%
867	BLAINE	411	338	72	1	266 R	82.2%	17.5%	82.4%	17.6%
7,391	BOONE	3,150	2,160	976	14	1,184 R	68.6%	31.0%	68.9%	31.1%
13,696	BOX BUTTE	5,764	3,253	2,466	45	787 R	56.4%	42.8%	56.9%	43.1%
3,331	BOYD	1,467	967	480	20	487 R	65.9%	32.7%	66.8%	33.2%
4,377	BROWN	1,782	1,335	435	12	900 R	74.9%	24.4%	75.4%	24.6%
34,797	BUFFALO	14,825	9,980	4,700	145	5,280 R	67.3%	31.7%	68.0%	32.0%
8,813	BURT	3,531	2,050	1,458	23	592 R	58.1%	41.3%	58.4%	41.6%
9,330	BUTLER	3,816	2,083	1,715	18	368 R	54.6%	44.9%	54.8%	45.2%
20,297	CASS	8,378	4,658	3,674	46	984 R	55.6%	43.9%	55.9%	44.1%
11,375	CEDAR	4,238	2,462	1,759	17	703 R	58.1%	41.5%	58.3%	41.7%
4,758	CHASE	2,082	1,446	597	39	849 R	69.5%	28.7%	70.8%	29.2%
6,758	CHERRY	2,896	2,240	642	14	1,598 R	77.3%	22.2%	77.7%	22.3%
10,057	CHEYENNE	4,223	2,862	1,333	28	1,529 R	67.8%	31.6%	68.2%	31.8%
8,106	CLAY	3,470	2,352	1,097	21	1,255 R	67.8%	31.6%	68.2%	31.8%
9,890	COLFAX	3,898	2,329	1,542	27	787 R	59.7%	39.6%	60.2%	39.8%
11,664	CUMING	4,463	3,201	1,238	24	1,963 R	71.7%	27.7%	72.1%	27.9%
13,877	CUSTER	5,725	4,202	1,496	27	2,706 R	73.4%	26.1%	73.7%	26.3%
16,573	DAKOTA	5,696	2,744	2,941	11	197 D	48.2%	51.6%	48.3%	51.7%
9,609	DAWES	3,767	2,618	1,122	27	1,496 R	69.5%	29.8%	70.0%	30.0%
22,304	DAWSON	7,755	5,529	2,184	42	3,345 R	71.3%	28.2%	71.7%	28.3%
2,462	DEUEL	1,080	769	302	9	467 R	71.2%	28.0%	71.8%	28.2%
7,137	DIXON	2,977	1,802	1,166	9	636 R	60.5%	39.2%	60.7%	39.3%
35,847	DODGE	14,592	8,412	6,116	64	2,296 R	57.6%	41.9%	57.9%	42.1%
397,038	DOUGLAS	177,355	99,806	76,444	1,105	23,362 R	56.3%	43.1%	56.6%	43.4%
2,861	DUNDY	1,178	828	333	17	495 R	70.3%	28.3%	71.3%	28.7%
7,920	FILLMORE	3,413	1,952	1,433	28	519 R	57.2%	42.0%	57.7%	42.3%
4,377	FRANKLIN	2,085	1,294	768	23	526 R	62.1%	36.8%	62.8%	37.2%
3,647	FRONTIER	1,459	1,057	384	18	673 R	72.4%	26.3%	73.4%	26.6%
6,486	FURNAS	2,645	1,830	791	24	1,039 R	69.2%	29.9%	69.8%	30.2%
24,456	GAGE	9,185	5,114	4,008	63	1,106 R	55.7%	43.6%	56.1%	43.9%
2,802	GARDEN	1,362	986	366	10	620 R	72.4%	26.9%	72.9%	27.1%
2,363	GARFIELD	1,057	803	234	20	569 R	76.0%	22.1%	77.4%	22.6%
2,140	GOSPER	1,034	694	331	9	363 R	67.1%	32.0%	67.7%	32.3%
877	GRANT	392	301	89	2	212 R	76.8%	22.7%	77.2%	22.8%
3,462	GREELEY	1,438	763	670	5	93 R	53.1%	46.6%	53.2%	46.8%
47,690	HALL	18,950	12,020	6,822	108	5,198 R	63.4%	36.0%	63.8%	36.2%
9,301	HAMILTON	4,331	3,019	1,289	23	1,730 R	69.7%	29.8%	70.1%	29.9%
4,292	HARLAN	2,154	1,403	725	26	678 R	65.1%	33.7%	65.9%	34.1%
1,356	HAYES	682	512	160	10	352 R	75.1%	23.5%	76.2%	23.8%
4,079	HITCHCOCK	1,630	1,132	480	18	652 R	69.4%	29.4%	70.2%	29.8%
13,552	HOLT	5,466	4,081	1,327	58	2,754 R	74.7%	24.3%	75.5%	24.5%
990	HOOKER	471	378	91	2	287 R	80.3%	19.3%	80.6%	19.4%
6,773	HOWARD	2,743	1,526	1,186	31	340 R	55.6%	43.2%	56.3%	43.7%
9,817	JEFFERSON	4,322	2,470	1,819	33	651 R	57.1%	42.1%	57.6%	42.4%
5,285	JOHNSON	2,354	1,182	1,162	10	20 R	50.2%	49.4%	50.4%	49.6%
7,053	KEARNEY	3,213	2,120	1,056	37	1,064 R	66.0%	32.9%	66.8%	33.2%
9,364	KEITH	3,976	2,879	1,067	30	1,812 R	72.4%	26.8%	73.0%	27.0%
1,301	KEYA PAHA	595	446	145	4	301 R	75.0%	24.4%	75.5%	24.5%
4,882	KIMBALL	1,890	1,321	540	29	781 R	69.9%	28.6%	71.0%	29.0%
11,457	KNOX	4,147	2,644	1,477	26	1,167 R	63.8%	35.6%	64.2%	35.8%
192,884	LANCASTER	89,447	44,605	44,260	582	345 R	49.9%	49.5%	50.2%	49.8%
36,455	LINCOLN	14,556	8,395	6,070	91	2,325 R	57.7%	41.7%	58.0%	42.0%
983	LOGAN	468	373	93	2	280 R	79.7%	19.9%	80.0%	20.0%
859	LOUP	399	295	97	7	198 R	73.9%	24.3%	75.3%	24.7%
593	MCPHERSON	292	229	60	3	169 R	78.4%	20.5%	79.2%	20.8%
31,382	MADISON	11,973	9,135	2,779	59	6,356 R	76.3%	23.2%	76.7%	23.3%

NEBRASKA

PRESIDENT 1988

1980 Census Population	County	Total Vote	Republican	Democratic	Other	Rep.-Dem. Plurality	Percentage Total Vote Rep.	Percentage Total Vote Dem.	Percentage Major Vote Rep.	Percentage Major Vote Dem.
8,945	MERRICK	3,592	2,376	1,192	24	1,184 R	66.1%	33.2%	66.6%	33.4%
6,085	MORRILL	2,328	1,554	753	21	801 R	66.8%	32.3%	67.4%	32.6%
4,740	NANCE	1,990	1,185	794	11	391 R	59.5%	39.9%	59.9%	40.1%
8,367	NEMAHA	3,785	2,293	1,457	35	836 R	60.6%	38.5%	61.1%	38.9%
6,726	NUCKOLLS	2,891	1,750	1,114	27	636 R	60.5%	38.5%	61.1%	38.9%
15,183	OTOE	6,366	3,724	2,616	26	1,108 R	58.5%	41.1%	58.7%	41.3%
3,937	PAWNEE	1,758	975	767	16	208 R	55.5%	43.6%	56.0%	44.0%
3,637	PERKINS	1,602	1,117	467	18	650 R	69.7%	29.2%	70.5%	29.5%
9,769	PHELPS	4,387	3,316	1,047	24	2,269 R	75.6%	23.9%	76.0%	24.0%
8,481	PIERCE	3,399	2,474	914	11	1,560 R	72.8%	26.9%	73.0%	27.0%
28,852	PLATTE	12,385	9,029	3,285	71	5,744 R	72.9%	26.5%	73.3%	26.7%
6,320	POLK	2,723	1,768	944	11	824 R	64.9%	34.7%	65.2%	34.8%
12,615	RED WILLOW	4,873	3,325	1,505	43	1,820 R	68.2%	30.9%	68.8%	31.2%
11,315	RICHARDSON	4,658	2,702	1,926	30	776 R	58.0%	41.3%	58.4%	41.6%
2,383	ROCK	956	756	198	2	558 R	79.1%	20.7%	79.2%	20.8%
13,131	SALINE	5,500	2,352	3,119	29	767 D	42.8%	56.7%	43.0%	57.0%
86,015	SARPY	31,261	20,179	10,936	146	9,243 R	64.6%	35.0%	64.9%	35.1%
18,716	SAUNDERS	8,033	4,454	3,524	55	930 R	55.4%	43.9%	55.8%	44.2%
38,344	SCOTTS BLUFF	13,142	8,594	4,454	94	4,140 R	65.4%	33.9%	65.9%	34.1%
15,789	SEWARD	6,199	3,467	2,682	50	785 R	55.9%	43.3%	56.4%	43.6%
7,544	SHERIDAN	2,898	2,251	612	35	1,639 R	77.7%	21.1%	78.6%	21.4%
4,226	SHERMAN	1,770	914	839	17	75 R	51.6%	47.4%	52.1%	47.9%
1,845	SIOUX	767	568	194	5	374 R	74.1%	25.3%	74.5%	25.5%
6,549	STANTON	2,356	1,709	637	10	1,072 R	72.5%	27.0%	72.8%	27.2%
7,582	THAYER	3,326	1,981	1,322	23	659 R	59.6%	39.7%	60.0%	40.0%
973	THOMAS	466	383	81	2	302 R	82.2%	17.4%	82.5%	17.5%
7,186	THURSTON	2,340	1,105	1,225	10	120 D	47.2%	52.4%	47.4%	52.6%
5,633	VALLEY	2,502	1,603	873	26	730 R	64.1%	34.9%	64.7%	35.3%
15,508	WASHINGTON	7,155	4,567	2,552	36	2,015 R	63.8%	35.7%	64.2%	35.8%
9,858	WAYNE	3,614	2,473	1,111	30	1,362 R	68.4%	30.7%	69.0%	31.0%
4,858	WEBSTER	2,226	1,314	891	21	423 R	59.0%	40.0%	59.6%	40.4%
1,060	WHEELER	455	309	141	5	168 R	67.9%	31.0%	68.7%	31.3%
14,798	YORK	6,522	4,744	1,748	30	2,996 R	72.7%	26.8%	73.1%	26.9%
1,569,825	TOTAL	661,465	397,956	259,235	4,274	138,721 R	60.2%	39.2%	60.6%	39.4%

NEBRASKA

SENATOR 1988

1980 Census Population	County	Total Vote	Republican	Democratic	Other	Rep.-Dem. Plurality	Percentage Total Vote Rep.	Total Vote Dem.	Major Vote Rep.	Major Vote Dem.
30,656	ADAMS	12,638	5,704	6,841	93	1,137 D	45.1%	54.1%	45.5%	54.5%
8,675	ANTELOPE	3,702	2,056	1,617	29	439 R	55.5%	43.7%	56.0%	44.0%
513	ARTHUR	272	181	90	1	91 R	66.5%	33.1%	66.8%	33.2%
918	BANNER	490	316	172	2	144 R	64.5%	35.1%	64.8%	35.2%
867	BLAINE	426	303	118	5	185 R	71.1%	27.7%	72.0%	28.0%
7,391	BOONE	3,208	1,636	1,545	27	91 R	51.0%	48.2%	51.4%	48.6%
13,696	BOX BUTTE	5,890	2,796	3,049	45	253 D	47.5%	51.8%	47.8%	52.2%
3,331	BOYD	1,506	852	642	12	210 R	56.6%	42.6%	57.0%	43.0%
4,377	BROWN	1,810	1,147	647	16	500 R	63.4%	35.7%	63.9%	36.1%
34,797	BUFFALO	14,981	6,789	7,998	194	1,209 D	45.3%	53.4%	45.9%	54.1%
8,813	BURT	3,637	1,400	2,199	38	799 D	38.5%	60.5%	38.9%	61.1%
9,330	BUTLER	3,879	1,416	2,415	48	999 D	36.5%	62.3%	37.0%	63.0%
20,297	CASS	8,439	2,852	5,473	114	2,621 D	33.8%	64.9%	34.3%	65.7%
11,375	CEDAR	4,284	1,964	2,283	37	319 D	45.8%	53.3%	46.2%	53.8%
4,758	CHASE	2,102	1,170	916	16	254 R	55.7%	43.6%	56.1%	43.9%
6,758	CHERRY	2,923	1,958	945	20	1,013 R	67.0%	32.3%	67.4%	32.6%
10,057	CHEYENNE	4,260	2,535	1,707	18	828 R	59.5%	40.1%	59.8%	40.2%
8,106	CLAY	3,548	1,633	1,898	17	265 D	46.0%	53.5%	46.2%	53.8%
9,890	COLFAX	3,990	1,613	2,332	45	719 D	40.4%	58.4%	40.9%	59.1%
11,664	CUMING	4,520	2,354	2,126	40	228 R	52.1%	47.0%	52.5%	47.5%
13,877	CUSTER	5,740	3,421	2,268	51	1,153 R	59.6%	39.5%	60.1%	39.9%
16,573	DAKOTA	5,769	2,194	3,544	31	1,350 D	38.0%	61.4%	38.2%	61.8%
9,609	DAWES	3,726	2,380	1,306	40	1,074 R	63.9%	35.1%	64.6%	35.4%
22,304	DAWSON	7,689	4,084	3,565	40	519 R	53.1%	46.4%	53.4%	46.6%
2,462	DEUEL	1,122	661	447	14	214 R	58.9%	39.8%	59.7%	40.3%
7,137	DIXON	3,031	1,503	1,498	30	5 R	49.6%	49.4%	50.1%	49.9%
35,847	DODGE	14,711	5,258	9,348	105	4,090 D	35.7%	63.5%	36.0%	64.0%
397,038	DOUGLAS	177,868	62,606	110,173	5,089	47,567 D	35.2%	61.9%	36.2%	63.8%
2,861	DUNDY	1,180	624	550	6	74 R	52.9%	46.6%	53.2%	46.8%
7,920	FILLMORE	3,448	1,516	1,887	45	371 D	44.0%	54.7%	44.5%	55.5%
4,377	FRANKLIN	2,083	896	1,175	12	279 D	43.0%	56.4%	43.3%	56.7%
3,647	FRONTIER	1,489	864	615	10	249 R	58.0%	41.3%	58.4%	41.6%
6,486	FURNAS	2,687	1,277	1,389	21	112 D	47.5%	51.7%	47.9%	52.1%
24,456	GAGE	9,375	3,362	5,918	95	2,556 D	35.9%	63.1%	36.2%	63.8%
2,802	GARDEN	1,359	859	480	20	379 R	63.2%	35.3%	64.2%	35.8%
2,363	GARFIELD	1,075	674	385	16	289 R	62.7%	35.8%	63.6%	36.4%
2,140	GOSPER	1,054	471	576	7	105 D	44.7%	54.6%	45.0%	55.0%
877	GRANT	395	291	102	2	189 R	73.7%	25.8%	74.0%	26.0%
3,462	GREELEY	1,469	589	868	12	279 D	40.1%	59.1%	40.4%	59.6%
47,690	HALL	19,140	8,400	10,568	172	2,168 D	43.9%	55.2%	44.3%	55.7%
9,301	HAMILTON	4,359	2,145	2,193	21	48 D	49.2%	50.3%	49.4%	50.6%
4,292	HARLAN	2,193	977	1,194	22	217 D	44.6%	54.4%	45.0%	55.0%
1,356	HAYES	686	396	283	7	113 R	57.7%	41.3%	58.3%	41.7%
4,079	HITCHCOCK	1,675	845	806	24	39 R	50.4%	48.1%	51.2%	48.8%
13,552	HOLT	5,471	3,441	2,002	28	1,439 R	62.9%	36.6%	63.2%	36.8%
990	HOOKER	473	333	137	3	196 R	70.4%	29.0%	70.9%	29.1%
6,773	HOWARD	2,808	1,164	1,621	23	457 D	41.5%	57.7%	41.8%	58.2%
9,817	JEFFERSON	4,418	1,866	2,507	45	641 D	42.2%	56.7%	42.7%	57.3%
5,285	JOHNSON	2,382	800	1,565	17	765 D	33.6%	65.7%	33.8%	66.2%
7,053	KEARNEY	3,279	1,424	1,825	30	401 D	43.4%	55.7%	43.8%	56.2%
9,364	KEITH	3,985	2,476	1,481	28	995 R	62.1%	37.2%	62.6%	37.4%
1,301	KEYA PAHA	604	432	156	16	276 R	71.5%	25.8%	73.5%	26.5%
4,882	KIMBALL	1,894	1,208	671	15	537 R	63.8%	35.4%	64.3%	35.7%
11,457	KNOX	4,327	2,116	2,180	31	64 D	48.9%	50.4%	49.3%	50.7%
192,884	LANCASTER	89,893	29,973	57,689	2,231	27,716 D	33.3%	64.2%	34.2%	65.8%
36,455	LINCOLN	14,826	7,024	7,711	91	687 D	47.4%	52.0%	47.7%	52.3%
983	LOGAN	485	330	150	5	180 R	68.0%	30.9%	68.8%	31.3%
859	LOUP	405	212	183	10	29 R	52.3%	45.2%	53.7%	46.3%
593	MCPHERSON	298	231	62	5	169 R	77.5%	20.8%	78.8%	21.2%
31,382	MADISON	12,223	6,742	5,391	90	1,351 R	55.2%	44.1%	55.6%	44.4%

NEBRASKA

SENATOR 1988

1980 Census Population	County	Total Vote	Republican	Democratic	Other	Rep.-Dem. Plurality	Percentage Total Vote Rep.	Total Vote Dem.	Major Vote Rep.	Major Vote Dem.
8,945	MERRICK	3,644	1,753	1,856	35	103 D	48.1%	50.9%	48.6%	51.4%
6,085	MORRILL	2,371	1,463	899	9	564 R	61.7%	37.9%	61.9%	38.1%
4,740	NANCE	2,025	846	1,171	8	325 D	41.8%	57.8%	41.9%	58.1%
8,367	NEMAHA	3,843	1,397	2,408	38	1,011 D	36.4%	62.7%	36.7%	63.3%
6,726	NUCKOLLS	2,867	1,259	1,593	15	334 D	43.9%	55.6%	44.1%	55.9%
15,183	OTOE	6,476	2,387	4,010	79	1,623 D	36.9%	61.9%	37.3%	62.7%
3,937	PAWNEE	1,798	623	1,155	20	532 D	34.6%	64.2%	35.0%	65.0%
3,637	PERKINS	1,618	947	661	10	286 R	58.5%	40.9%	58.9%	41.1%
9,769	PHELPS	4,532	2,311	2,176	45	135 R	51.0%	48.0%	51.5%	48.5%
8,481	PIERCE	3,435	1,929	1,485	21	444 R	56.2%	43.2%	56.5%	43.5%
28,852	PLATTE	12,516	5,917	6,481	118	564 D	47.3%	51.8%	47.7%	52.3%
6,320	POLK	2,764	1,164	1,578	22	414 D	42.1%	57.1%	42.5%	57.5%
12,615	RED WILLOW	4,905	2,536	2,338	31	198 R	51.7%	47.7%	52.0%	48.0%
11,315	RICHARDSON	4,736	2,001	2,691	44	690 D	42.3%	56.8%	42.6%	57.4%
2,383	ROCK	985	658	320	7	338 R	66.8%	32.5%	67.3%	32.7%
13,131	SALINE	5,587	1,481	4,041	65	2,560 D	26.5%	72.3%	26.8%	73.2%
86,015	SARPY	31,291	12,026	18,916	349	6,890 D	38.4%	60.5%	38.9%	61.1%
18,716	SAUNDERS	8,151	2,807	5,220	124	2,413 D	34.4%	64.0%	35.0%	65.0%
38,344	SCOTTS BLUFF	13,503	7,931	5,506	66	2,425 R	58.7%	40.8%	59.0%	41.0%
15,789	SEWARD	6,235	2,186	3,977	72	1,791 D	35.1%	63.8%	35.5%	64.5%
7,544	SHERIDAN	2,924	2,149	749	26	1,400 R	73.5%	25.6%	74.2%	25.8%
4,226	SHERMAN	1,810	739	1,047	24	308 D	40.8%	57.8%	41.4%	58.6%
1,845	SIOUX	772	539	231	2	308 R	69.8%	29.9%	70.0%	30.0%
6,549	STANTON	2,367	1,185	1,154	28	31 R	50.1%	48.8%	50.7%	49.3%
7,582	THAYER	3,443	1,486	1,935	22	449 D	43.2%	56.2%	43.4%	56.6%
973	THOMAS	474	325	145	4	180 R	68.6%	30.6%	69.1%	30.9%
7,186	THURSTON	2,314	810	1,456	48	646 D	35.0%	62.9%	35.7%	64.3%
5,633	VALLEY	2,562	1,311	1,229	22	82 R	51.2%	48.0%	51.6%	48.4%
15,508	WASHINGTON	7,203	2,920	4,231	52	1,311 D	40.5%	58.7%	40.8%	59.2%
9,858	WAYNE	3,689	2,026	1,626	37	400 R	54.9%	44.1%	55.5%	44.5%
4,858	WEBSTER	2,271	878	1,376	17	498 D	38.7%	60.6%	39.0%	61.0%
1,060	WHEELER	465	230	230	5		49.5%	49.5%	50.0%	50.0%
14,798	YORK	6,685	3,290	3,344	51	54 D	49.2%	50.0%	49.6%	50.4%
1,569,825	TOTAL	667,860	278,250	378,717	10,893	100,467 D	41.7%	56.7%	42.4%	57.6%

NEBRASKA

CONGRESS

CD	Year	Total Vote	Republican Vote	Republican Candidate	Democratic Vote	Democratic Candidate	Other Vote	Rep.-Dem. Plurality	Percentage Total Vote Rep.	Percentage Total Vote Dem.	Percentage Major Vote Rep.	Percentage Major Vote Dem.
1	1988	218,502	146,231	BEREUTER, DOUGLAS K.	72,167	JONES, CORKY	104	74,064 R	66.9%	33.0%	67.0%	33.0%
1	1986	188,986	121,772	BEREUTER, DOUGLAS K.	67,137	BURNS, STEVE	77	54,635 R	64.4%	35.5%	64.5%	35.5%
1	1984	214,364	158,836	BEREUTER, DOUGLAS K.	55,508	BAUER, MONICA	20	103,328 R	74.1%	25.9%	74.1%	25.9%
1	1982	183,368	137,675	BEREUTER, DOUGLAS K.	45,676	DONALDSON, CURT	17	91,999 R	75.1%	24.9%	75.1%	24.9%
2	1988	222,275	109,193	SCHENKEN, JERRY	112,174	HOAGLAND, PETER	908	2,981 D	49.1%	50.5%	49.3%	50.7%
2	1986	170,267	99,569	DAUB, HAROLD J.	70,372	CALINGER, WALTER M.	326	29,197 R	58.5%	41.3%	58.6%	41.4%
2	1984	214,883	139,384	DAUB, HAROLD J.	75,210	CAVANAUGH, THOMAS F.	289	64,174 R	64.9%	35.0%	65.0%	35.0%
2	1982	163,349	92,639	DAUB, HAROLD J.	70,431	FELLMAN, RICHARD M.	279	22,208 R	56.7%	43.1%	56.8%	43.2%
3	1988	215,501	170,302	SMITH, VIRGINIA	45,183	RACEK, JOHN D.	16	125,119 R	79.0%	21.0%	79.0%	21.0%
3	1986	196,184	136,985	SMITH, VIRGINIA	59,182	SIDWELL, SCOTT E.	17	77,803 R	69.8%	30.2%	69.8%	30.2%
3	1984	220,814	183,901	SMITH, VIRGINIA	36,899	VICKERS, TOM	14	147,002 R	83.3%	16.7%	83.3%	16.7%
3	1982	172,364	171,853	SMITH, VIRGINIA			511	171,853 R	99.7%		100.0%	

NEBRASKA

1988 GENERAL ELECTION

President Other vote was 2,534 Libertarian (Paul); 1,740 New Alliance (Fulani).

Senator Other vote was 10,372 New Alliance (Chambers); 521 scattered write-in.

Congress Other vote was 9 Burke (write-in)and 95 scattered in CD 1; scattered in CD's 2 and 3.

1988 PRIMARIES

MAY 10 REPUBLICAN

Senator 117,439 David Karnes; 96,436 Harold J. Daub; 350 scattered write-in.

Congress Unopposed in two CD's. Contested as follows:

CD 2 23,314 Jerry Schenken; 18,414 Chris Abboud; 18,312 Ally Milder; 2,010 Carl Jennings; 120 scattered write-in.

MAY 10 DEMOCRATIC

Senator 156,498 Bob Kerrey; 14,248 Ken L. Michaelis; 423 scattered write-in.

Congress Unopposed in CD 3. Contested as follows:

CD 1 31,857 Corky Jones; 13,967 Marlin R. Pals; 184 scattered write-in.
CD 2 33,394 Peter Hoagland; 28,635 Cece Zorinsky; 2,922 David A. Wilken; 905 Jess M. Pritchett; 139 scattered write-in.

MAY 10 NEW ALLIANCE

Senator No candidate names on the ballot. Ernest Chambers received the nomination by write-in votes.

Congress No candidate names on the ballot in any of the three CD's.

NEVADA

GOVERNOR

Robert J. Miller (D). Elected Lieutenant-Governor 1986 and became Governor January 1989 on the resignation of Governor Richard H. Bryan (D) following his election November 1988 to the U.S. Senate.

SENATORS

Richard H. Bryan (D). Elected 1988 to a six-year term.

Harry Reid (D). Elected 1986 to a six-year term.

REPRESENTATIVES

1. James Bilbray (D)
2. Barbara Vucanovich (R)

POSTWAR VOTE FOR PRESIDENT

Year	Total Vote	Republican Vote	Republican Candidate	Democratic Vote	Democratic Candidate	Other Vote	Plurality	Percentage Total Vote Rep.	Total Vote Dem.	Major Vote Rep.	Major Vote Dem.
1988	350,067	206,040	Bush, George	132,738	Dukakis, Michael S.	11,289	73,302 R	58.9%	37.9%	60.8%	39.2%
1984	286,667	188,770	Reagan, Ronald	91,655	Mondale, Walter F.	6,242	97,115 R	65.8%	32.0%	67.3%	32.7%
1980	247,885	155,017	Reagan, Ronald	66,666	Carter, Jimmy	26,202	88,351 R	62.5%	26.9%	69.9%	30.1%
1976	201,876	101,273	Ford, Gerald R.	92,479	Carter, Jimmy	8,124	8,794 R	50.2%	45.8%	52.3%	47.7%
1972	181,766	115,750	Nixon, Richard M.	66,016	McGovern, George S.		49,734 R	63.7%	36.3%	63.7%	36.3%
1968	154,218	73,188	Nixon, Richard M.	60,598	Humphrey, Hubert H.	20,432	12,590 R	47.5%	39.3%	54.7%	45.3%
1964	135,433	56,094	Goldwater, Barry M.	79,339	Johnson, Lyndon B.		23,245 D	41.4%	58.6%	41.4%	58.6%
1960	107,267	52,387	Nixon, Richard M.	54,880	Kennedy, John F.		2,493 D	48.8%	51.2%	48.8%	51.2%
1956	96,689	56,049	Eisenhower, Dwight D.	40,640	Stevenson, Adlai E.		15,409 R	58.0%	42.0%	58.0%	42.0%
1952	82,190	50,502	Eisenhower, Dwight D.	31,688	Stevenson, Adlai E.		18,814 R	61.4%	38.6%	61.4%	38.6%
1948	62,117	29,357	Dewey, Thomas E.	31,291	Truman, Harry S.	1,469	1,934 D	47.3%	50.4%	48.4%	51.6%

POSTWAR VOTE FOR GOVERNOR

Year	Total Vote	Republican Vote	Republican Candidate	Democratic Vote	Democratic Candidate	Other Vote	Rep.-Dem. Plurality	Percentage Total Vote Rep.	Total Vote Dem.	Major Vote Rep.	Major Vote Dem.
1986	260,375	65,081	Cafferata, Patty	187,268	Bryan, Richard H.	8,026	122,187 D	25.0%	71.9%	25.8%	74.2%
1982	239,751	100,104	List, Robert F.	128,132	Bryan, Richard H.	11,515	28,028 D	41.8%	53.4%	43.9%	56.1%
1978	192,445	108,097	List, Robert F.	76,361	Rose, Robert E.	7,987	31,736 R	56.2%	39.7%	58.6%	41.4%
1974	169,358	28,959	Crumpler, Shirley	114,114	O'Callaghan, Mike	26,285	85,155 D	17.1%	67.4%	20.2%	79.8%
1970	146,991	64,400	Fike, Ed	70,697	O'Callaghan, Mike	11,894	6,297 D	43.8%	48.1%	47.7%	52.3%
1966	137,677	71,807	Laxalt, Paul	65,870	Sawyer, Grant		5,937 R	52.2%	47.8%	52.2%	47.8%
1962	96,929	32,145	Gragson, Oran K.	64,784	Sawyer, Grant		32,639 D	33.2%	66.8%	33.2%	66.8%
1958	84,889	34,025	Russell, Charles H.	50,864	Sawyer, Grant		16,839 D	40.1%	59.9%	40.1%	59.9%
1954	78,462	41,665	Russell, Charles H.	36,797	Pittman, Vail		4,868 R	53.1%	46.9%	53.1%	46.9%
1950	61,773	35,609	Russell, Charles H.	26,164	Pittman, Vail		9,445 R	57.6%	42.4%	57.6%	42.4%
1946	49,902	21,247	Jepson, Melvin E.	28,655	Pittman, Vail		7,408 D	42.6%	57.4%	42.6%	57.4%

NEVADA

POSTWAR VOTE FOR SENATOR

Year	Total Vote	Republican Vote	Republican Candidate	Democratic Vote	Democratic Candidate	Other Vote	Rep.-Dem. Plurality	Percentage Total Vote Rep.	Percentage Total Vote Dem.	Percentage Major Vote Rep.	Percentage Major Vote Dem.
1988	349,649	161,336	Hecht, Chic	175,548	Bryan, Richard H.	12,765	14,212 D	46.1%	50.2%	47.9%	52.1%
1986	261,932	116,606	Santini, James	130,955	Reid, Harry	14,371	14,349 D	44.5%	50.0%	47.1%	52.9%
1982	240,394	120,377	Hecht, Chic	114,720	Cannon, Howard W.	5,297	5,657 R	50.1%	47.7%	51.2%	48.8%
1980	246,436	144,224	Laxalt, Paul	92,129	Gojack, Mary	10,083	52,095 R	58.5%	37.4%	61.0%	39.0%
1976	201,980	63,471	Towell, David	127,295	Cannon, Howard W.	11,214	63,824 D	31.4%	63.0%	33.3%	66.7%
1974	169,473	79,605	Laxalt, Paul	78,981	Reid, Harry	10,887	624 R	47.0%	46.6%	50.2%	49.8%
1970	147,768	60,838	Raggio, William J.	85,187	Cannon, Howard W.	1,743	24,349 D	41.2%	57.6%	41.7%	58.3%
1968	152,690	69,068	Fike, Ed	83,622	Bible, Alan		14,554 D	45.2%	54.8%	45.2%	54.8%
1964	134,624	67,288	Laxalt, Paul	67,336	Cannon, Howard W.		48 D	50.0%	50.0%	50.0%	50.0%
1962	97,192	33,749	Wright, William B.	63,443	Bible, Alan		29,694 D	34.7%	65.3%	34.7%	65.3%
1958	84,492	35,760	Malone, George W.	48,732	Cannon, Howard W.		12,972 D	42.3%	57.7%	42.3%	57.7%
1956	96,389	45,712	Young, Clifton	50,677	Bible, Alan		4,965 D	47.4%	52.6%	47.4%	52.6%
1954 S	77,513	32,470	Brown, Ernest S.	45,043	Bible, Alan		12,573 D	41.9%	58.1%	41.9%	58.1%
1952	81,090	41,906	Malone, George W.	39,184	Mechling, Thomas B.		2,722 R	51.7%	48.3%	51.7%	48.3%
1950	61,762	25,933	Marshall, George E.	35,829	McCarran, Pat		9,896 D	42.0%	58.0%	42.0%	58.0%
1946	50,354	27,801	Malone, George W.	22,553	Bunker, Berkeley		5,248 R	55.2%	44.8%	55.2%	44.8%

The 1954 election was for a short term to fill a vacancy.

NEVADA

Districts Established June 4, 1981

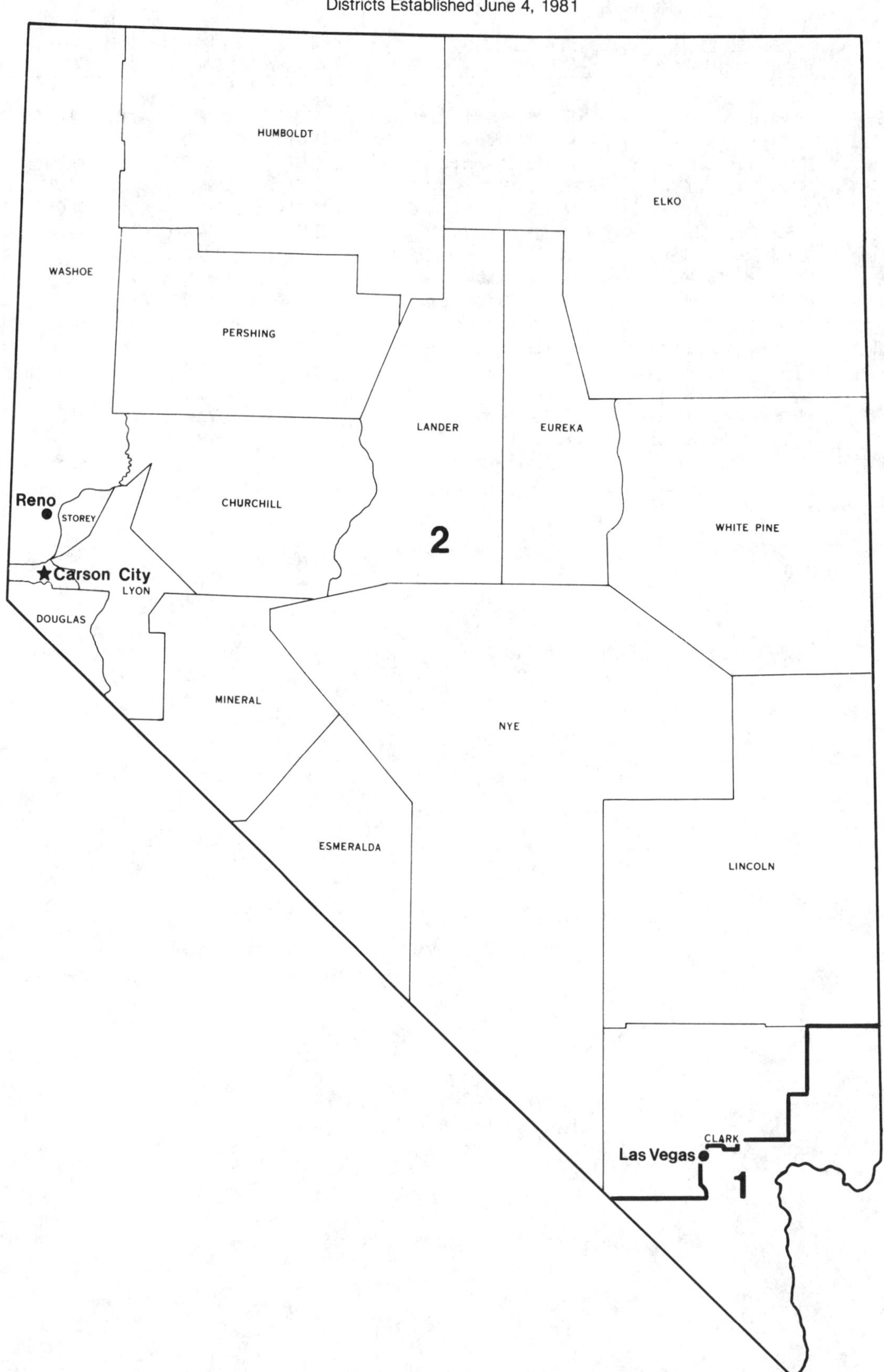

NEVADA

PRESIDENT 1988

1980 Census Population	County	Total Vote	Republican	Democratic	Other	Rep.-Dem. Plurality	Percentage Total Vote Rep.	Percentage Total Vote Dem.	Percentage Major Vote Rep.	Percentage Major Vote Dem.
32,022	CARSON CITY	15,291	9,701	5,088	502	4,613 R	63.4%	33.3%	65.6%	34.4%
13,917	CHURCHILL	6,283	4,578	1,481	224	3,097 R	72.9%	23.6%	75.6%	24.4%
463,087	CLARK	191,779	108,110	78,359	5,310	29,751 R	56.4%	40.9%	58.0%	42.0%
19,421	DOUGLAS	10,555	7,074	3,107	374	3,967 R	67.0%	29.4%	69.5%	30.5%
17,269	ELKO	8,372	5,722	2,310	340	3,412 R	68.3%	27.6%	71.2%	28.8%
777	ESMERALDA	552	380	143	29	237 R	68.8%	25.9%	72.7%	27.3%
1,198	EUREKA	582	413	151	18	262 R	71.0%	25.9%	73.2%	26.8%
9,434	HUMBOLDT	3,576	2,378	1,024	174	1,354 R	66.5%	28.6%	69.9%	30.1%
4,076	LANDER	1,714	1,214	439	61	775 R	70.8%	25.6%	73.4%	26.6%
3,732	LINCOLN	1,564	1,035	466	63	569 R	66.2%	29.8%	69.0%	31.0%
13,594	LYON	6,987	4,390	2,301	296	2,089 R	62.8%	32.9%	65.6%	34.4%
6,217	MINERAL	2,602	1,480	978	144	502 R	56.9%	37.6%	60.2%	39.8%
9,048	NYE	5,603	3,619	1,748	236	1,871 R	64.6%	31.2%	67.4%	32.6%
3,408	PERSHING	1,396	867	458	71	409 R	62.1%	32.8%	65.4%	34.6%
1,503	STOREY	1,155	651	432	72	219 R	56.4%	37.4%	60.1%	39.9%
193,623	WASHOE	88,728	52,654	32,902	3,172	19,752 R	59.3%	37.1%	61.5%	38.5%
8,167	WHITE PINE	3,328	1,774	1,351	203	423 R	53.3%	40.6%	56.8%	43.2%
800,493	TOTAL	350,067	206,040	132,738	11,289	73,302 R	58.9%	37.9%	60.8%	39.2%

NEVADA

SENATOR 1988

1980 Census Population	County	Total Vote	Republican	Democratic	Other	Rep.-Dem. Plurality	Percentage Total Vote Rep.	Percentage Total Vote Dem.	Percentage Major Vote Rep.	Percentage Major Vote Dem.
32,022	CARSON CITY	15,418	7,848	6,973	597	875 R	50.9%	45.2%	53.0%	47.0%
13,917	CHURCHILL	6,285	4,119	1,958	208	2,161 R	65.5%	31.2%	67.8%	32.2%
463,087	CLARK	191,555	81,575	103,898	6,082	22,323 D	42.6%	54.2%	44.0%	56.0%
19,421	DOUGLAS	10,508	5,804	4,291	413	1,513 R	55.2%	40.8%	57.5%	42.5%
17,269	ELKO	8,381	5,226	2,871	284	2,355 R	62.4%	34.3%	64.5%	35.5%
777	ESMERALDA	551	344	182	25	162 R	62.4%	33.0%	65.4%	34.6%
1,198	EUREKA	579	384	175	20	209 R	66.3%	30.2%	68.7%	31.3%
9,434	HUMBOLDT	3,591	2,096	1,339	156	757 R	58.4%	37.3%	61.0%	39.0%
4,076	LANDER	1,711	1,083	551	77	532 R	63.3%	32.2%	66.3%	33.7%
3,732	LINCOLN	1,568	1,102	421	45	681 R	70.3%	26.8%	72.4%	27.6%
13,594	LYON	7,032	3,736	2,994	302	742 R	53.1%	42.6%	55.5%	44.5%
6,217	MINERAL	2,599	1,437	1,049	113	388 R	55.3%	40.4%	57.8%	42.2%
9,048	NYE	5,596	3,314	2,056	226	1,258 R	59.2%	36.7%	61.7%	38.3%
3,408	PERSHING	1,386	765	565	56	200 R	55.2%	40.8%	57.5%	42.5%
1,503	STOREY	1,154	488	624	42	136 D	42.3%	54.1%	43.9%	56.1%
193,623	WASHOE	88,394	40,312	44,075	4,007	3,763 D	45.6%	49.9%	47.8%	52.2%
8,167	WHITE PINE	3,341	1,703	1,526	112	177 R	51.0%	45.7%	52.7%	47.3%
800,493	TOTAL	349,649	161,336	175,548	12,765	14,212 D	46.1%	50.2%	47.9%	52.1%

NEVADA

CONGRESS

CD	Year	Total Vote	Republican Vote	Republican Candidate	Democratic Vote	Democratic Candidate	Other Vote	Rep.-Dem. Plurality	Percentage Total Vote Rep.	Percentage Total Vote Dem.	Percentage Major Vote Rep.	Percentage Major Vote Dem.
1	1988	159,076	53,588	LUSK, LUCILLE	101,764	BILBRAY, JAMES	3,724	48,176 D	33.7%	64.0%	34.5%	65.5%
1	1986	114,317	50,342	RYAN, BOB	61,830	BILBRAY, JAMES	2,145	11,488 D	44.0%	54.1%	44.9%	55.1%
1	1984	130,518	55,391	CAVNAR, PEGGY	73,242	REID, HARRY	1,885	17,851 D	42.4%	56.1%	43.1%	56.9%
1	1982	107,576	45,675	CAVNAR, PEGGY	61,901	REID, HARRY		16,226 D	42.5%	57.5%	42.5%	57.5%
2	1988	185,097	105,981	VUCANOVICH, BARBARA	75,163	SPOO, JAMES	3,953	30,818 R	57.3%	40.6%	58.5%	41.5%
2	1986	142,912	83,479	VUCANOVICH, BARBARA	59,433	SFERRAZZA, PETE		24,046 R	58.4%	41.6%	58.4%	41.6%
2	1984	140,106	99,775	VUCANOVICH, BARBARA	36,130	BARBANO, ANDREW	4,201	63,645 R	71.2%	25.8%	73.4%	26.6%
2	1982	126,496	70,188	VUCANOVICH, BARBARA	52,265	GOJACK, MARY	4,043	17,923 R	55.5%	41.3%	57.3%	42.7%

NEVADA

1988 GENERAL ELECTION

President Other vote was 3,520 Libertarian (Paul); 835 New Alliance (Fulani); 6,934 "None of these Candidates".

Senator Other vote was 5,523 Libertarian (Frye); 7,242 "None of these Candidates".

Congress Other vote was Libertarian (O'Neill) in CD 1; Libertarian (Cromwell) in CD 2.

1988 PRIMARIES

SEPTEMBER 6 REPUBLICAN

Senator 55,473 Chic Hecht; 5,618 Larry Scheffler; 6,460 "None of these Candidates".

Congress Unopposed in CD 2. Contested as follows:

CD 1 12,139 Lucille Lusk; 10,755 James Gritz; 2,555 John E. Kraft.

SEPTEMBER 6 DEMOCRATIC

Senator 62,278 Richard H. Bryan; 4,721 Patrick M. Fitzpatrick; 2,656 Manny Beals; 1,655 Larry Kepler; 7,035 "None of these Candidates".

Congress Unopposed in both CD's.

NEW HAMPSHIRE

GOVERNOR

Judd Gregg (R). Elected 1988 to a two-year term.

SENATORS

Gordon J. Humphrey (R). Re-elected 1984 to a six-year term. Previously elected 1978.

Warren Rudman (R). Re-elected 1986 to a six-year term. Previously elected 1980.

REPRESENTATIVES

1. Robert C. Smith (R)
2. Chuck Douglas (R)

POSTWAR VOTE FOR PRESIDENT

Year	Total Vote	Republican Vote	Republican Candidate	Democratic Vote	Democratic Candidate	Other Vote	Plurality	Percentage Total Vote Rep.	Percentage Total Vote Dem.	Percentage Major Vote Rep.	Percentage Major Vote Dem.
1988	451,074	281,537	Bush, George	163,696	Dukakis, Michael S.	5,841	117,841 R	62.4%	36.3%	63.2%	36.8%
1984	389,066	267,051	Reagan, Ronald	120,395	Mondale, Walter F.	1,620	146,656 R	68.6%	30.9%	68.9%	31.1%
1980	383,990	221,705	Reagan, Ronald	108,864	Carter, Jimmy	53,421	112,841 R	57.7%	28.4%	67.1%	32.9%
1976	339,618	185,935	Ford, Gerald R.	147,635	Carter, Jimmy	6,048	38,300 R	54.7%	43.5%	55.7%	44.3%
1972	334,055	213,724	Nixon, Richard M.	116,435	McGovern, George S.	3,896	97,289 R	64.0%	34.9%	64.7%	35.3%
1968	297,298	154,903	Nixon, Richard M.	130,589	Humphrey, Hubert H.	11,806	24,314 R	52.1%	43.9%	54.3%	45.7%
1964	288,093	104,029	Goldwater, Barry M.	184,064	Johnson, Lyndon B.		80,035 D	36.1%	63.9%	36.1%	63.9%
1960	295,761	157,989	Nixon, Richard M.	137,772	Kennedy, John F.		20,217 R	53.4%	46.6%	53.4%	46.6%
1956	266,994	176,519	Eisenhower, Dwight D.	90,364	Stevenson, Adlai E.	111	86,155 R	66.1%	33.8%	66.1%	33.9%
1952	272,950	166,287	Eisenhower, Dwight D.	106,663	Stevenson, Adlai E.		59,624 R	60.9%	39.1%	60.9%	39.1%
1948	231,440	121,299	Dewey, Thomas E.	107,995	Truman, Harry S.	2,146	13,304 R	52.4%	46.7%	52.9%	47.1%

POSTWAR VOTE FOR GOVERNOR

Year	Total Vote	Republican Vote	Republican Candidate	Democratic Vote	Democratic Candidate	Other Vote	Rep.-Dem. Plurality	Percentage Total Vote Rep.	Percentage Total Vote Dem.	Percentage Major Vote Rep.	Percentage Major Vote Dem.
1988	441,923	267,064	Gregg, Judd	172,543	McEachern, Paul	2,316	94,521 R	60.4%	39.0%	60.8%	39.2%
1986	251,107	134,824	Sununu, John H.	116,142	McEachern, Paul	141	18,682 R	53.7%	46.3%	53.7%	46.3%
1984	383,910	256,574	Sununu, John H.	127,156	Spirou, Chris	180	129,418 R	66.8%	33.1%	66.9%	33.1%
1982	282,588	145,389	Sununu, John H.	132,317	Gallen, Hugh J.	4,882	13,072 R	51.4%	46.8%	52.4%	47.6%
1980	384,031	156,178	Thomson, Meldrim	226,436	Gallen, Hugh J.	1,417	70,258 D	40.7%	59.0%	40.8%	59.2%
1978	269,587	122,464	Thomson, Meldrim	133,133	Gallen, Hugh J.	13,990	10,669 D	45.4%	49.4%	47.9%	52.1%
1976	342,669	197,589	Thomson, Meldrim	145,015	Spanos, Harry V.	65	52,574 R	57.7%	42.3%	57.7%	42.3%
1974	226,665	115,933	Thomson, Meldrim	110,591	Leonard, Richard W.	141	5,342 R	51.1%	48.8%	51.2%	48.8%
1972	323,102	133,702	Thomson, Meldrim	126,107	Crowley, Roger J.	63,293	7,595 R	41.4%	39.0%	51.5%	48.5%
1970	222,441	102,298	Peterson, Walter R.	98,098	Crowley, Roger J.	22,045	4,200 R	46.0%	44.1%	51.0%	49.0%
1968	285,342	149,902	Peterson, Walter R.	135,378	Bussiere, Emile R.	62	14,524 R	52.5%	47.4%	52.5%	47.5%
1966	233,642	107,259	Gregg, Hugh	125,882	King, John W.	501	18,623 D	45.9%	53.9%	46.0%	54.0%
1964	285,863	94,824	Pillsbury, John	190,863	King, John W.	176	96,039 D	33.2%	66.8%	33.2%	66.8%
1962	230,048	94,567	Pillsbury, John	135,481	King, John W.		40,914 D	41.1%	58.9%	41.1%	58.9%
1960	290,527	161,123	Powell, Wesley	129,404	Boutin, Bernard L.		31,719 R	55.5%	44.5%	55.5%	44.5%
1958	206,745	106,790	Powell, Wesley	99,955	Boutin, Bernard L.		6,835 R	51.7%	48.3%	51.7%	48.3%
1956	258,695	141,578	Dwinell, Lane	117,117	Shaw, John		24,461 R	54.7%	45.3%	54.7%	45.3%
1954	194,631	107,287	Dwinell, Lane	87,344	Shaw, John		19,943 R	55.1%	44.9%	55.1%	44.9%
1952	265,715	167,791	Gregg, Hugh	97,924	Craig, William H.		69,867 R	63.1%	36.9%	63.1%	36.9%
1950	191,239	108,907	Adams, Sherman	82,258	Bingham, Robert P.	74	26,649 R	56.9%	43.0%	57.0%	43.0%
1948	222,571	116,212	Adams, Sherman	105,207	Hill, Herbert W.	1,152	11,005 R	52.2%	47.3%	52.5%	47.5%
1946	163,451	103,204	Dale, Charles M.	60,247	Keefe, F. Clyde		42,957 R	63.1%	36.9%	63.1%	36.9%

NEW HAMPSHIRE

POSTWAR VOTE FOR SENATOR

									Percentage			
	Total	Republican		Democratic		Other	Rep.-Dem.		Total Vote		Major Vote	
Year	Vote	Vote	Candidate	Vote	Candidate	Vote	Plurality		Rep.	Dem.	Rep.	Dem.
1986	244,797	154,090	Rudman, Warren	79,225	Peabody, Endicott	11,482	74,865	R	62.9%	32.4%	66.0%	34.0%
1984	384,406	225,828	Humphrey, Gordon J.	157,447	D'Amours, Norman E.	1,131	68,381	R	58.7%	41.0%	58.9%	41.1%
1980	375,064	195,563	Rudman, Warren	179,455	Durkin, John A.	46	16,108	R	52.1%	47.8%	52.1%	47.9%
1978	263,779	133,745	Humphrey, Gordon J.	127,945	McIntyre, Thomas J.	2,089	5,800	R	50.7%	48.5%	51.1%	48.9%
1975 S	262,682	113,007	Wyman, Louis C.	140,778	Durkin, John A.	8,897	27,771	D	43.0%	53.6%	44.5%	55.5%
1974 **	223,363	110,926	Wyman, Louis C.	110,924	Durkin, John A.	1,513	2	R	49.7%	49.7%	50.0%	50.0%
1972	324,354	139,852	Powell, Wesley	184,495	McIntyre, Thomas J.	7	44,643	D	43.1%	56.9%	43.1%	56.9%
1968	286,989	170,163	Cotton, Norris	116,816	King, John W.	10	53,347	R	59.3%	40.7%	59.3%	40.7%
1966	229,305	105,241	Thyng, Harrison R.	123,888	McIntyre, Thomas J.	176	18,647	D	45.9%	54.0%	45.9%	54.1%
1962	224,479	134,035	Cotton, Norris	90,444	Catalfo, Alfred		43,591	R	59.7%	40.3%	59.7%	40.3%
1962 S	224,811	107,199	Bass, Perkins	117,612	McIntyre, Thomas J.		10,413	D	47.7%	52.3%	47.7%	52.3%
1960	287,545	173,521	Bridges, Styles	114,024	Hill, Herbert W.		59,497	R	60.3%	39.7%	60.3%	39.7%
1956	251,943	161,424	Cotton, Norris	90,519	Pickett, Laurence M.		70,905	R	64.1%	35.9%	64.1%	35.9%
1954	194,536	117,150	Bridges, Styles	77,386	Morin, Gerard L.		39,764	R	60.2%	39.8%	60.2%	39.8%
1954 S	189,558	114,068	Cotton, Norris	75,490	Bentley, Stanley J.		38,578	R	60.2%	39.8%	60.2%	39.8%
1950	190,573	106,142	Tobey, Charles W.	72,473	Kelley, Emmet J.	11,958	33,669	R	55.7%	38.0%	59.4%	40.6%
1948	222,898	129,600	Bridges, Styles	91,760	Fortin, Alfred E.	1,538	37,840	R	58.1%	41.2%	58.5%	41.5%

One each of the 1962 and 1954 elections were for short terms to fill vacancies. Following the 1974 election, neither candidate was seated and the 1975 special election was held for the remaining years of this term.

NEW HAMPSHIRE

Districts Established March 4, 1982

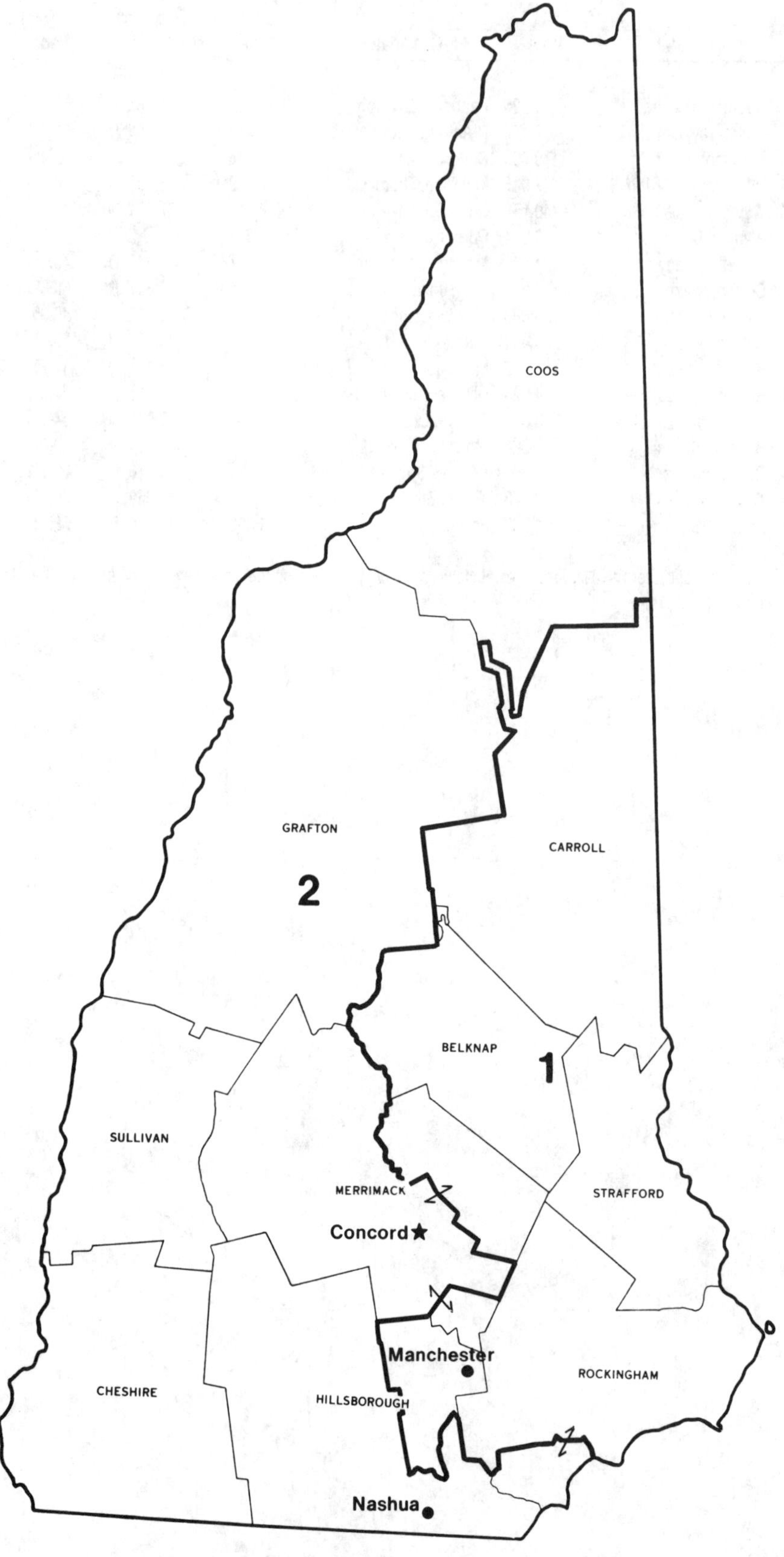

NEW HAMPSHIRE

PRESIDENT 1988

1980 Census Population	County	Total Vote	Republican	Democratic	Other	Rep.-Dem. Plurality	Percentage Total Vote Rep.	Percentage Total Vote Dem.	Percentage Major Vote Rep.	Percentage Major Vote Dem.
42,884	BELKNAP	21,280	14,454	6,603	223	7,851 R	67.9%	31.0%	68.6%	31.4%
27,931	CARROLL	18,344	12,983	5,153	208	7,830 R	70.8%	28.1%	71.6%	28.4%
62,116	CHESHIRE	27,512	15,002	12,339	171	2,663 R	54.5%	44.8%	54.9%	45.1%
35,147	COOS	13,900	8,763	4,981	156	3,782 R	63.0%	35.8%	63.8%	36.2%
65,806	GRAFTON	30,699	19,033	11,484	182	7,549 R	62.0%	37.4%	62.4%	37.6%
276,608	HILLSBOROUGH	135,778	88,261	45,799	1,718	42,462 R	65.0%	33.7%	65.8%	34.2%
98,302	MERRIMACK	48,686	29,535	18,637	514	10,898 R	60.7%	38.3%	61.3%	38.7%
190,345	ROCKINGHAM	101,747	64,034	35,775	1,938	28,259 R	62.9%	35.2%	64.2%	35.8%
85,408	STRAFFORD	37,845	20,636	16,547	662	4,089 R	54.5%	43.7%	55.5%	44.5%
36,063	SULLIVAN	15,283	8,836	6,378	69	2,458 R	57.8%	41.7%	58.1%	41.9%
920,610	TOTAL	451,074	281,537	163,696	5,841	117,841 R	62.4%	36.3%	63.2%	36.8%

NEW HAMPSHIRE

PRESIDENT 1988

1980 Census Population	City/Town	Total Vote	Republican	Democratic	Other	Rep.-Dem. Plurality	Percentage Total Vote Rep.	Percentage Total Vote Dem.	Percentage Major Vote Rep.	Percentage Major Vote Dem.
8,243	AMHERST	4,681	3,336	1,281	64	2,055 R	71.3%	27.4%	72.3%	27.7%
9,481	BEDFORD	6,805	5,237	1,499	69	3,738 R	77.0%	22.0%	77.7%	22.3%
13,084	BERLIN	4,840	2,529	2,271	40	258 R	52.3%	46.9%	52.7%	47.3%
14,557	CLAREMONT	4,788	2,513	2,254	21	259 R	52.5%	47.1%	52.7%	47.3%
30,400	CONCORD	14,265	7,439	6,698	128	741 R	52.1%	47.0%	52.6%	47.4%
7,158	CONWAY	3,514	2,430	1,058	26	1,372 R	69.2%	30.1%	69.7%	30.3%
18,875	DERRY	9,290	6,253	2,845	192	3,408 R	67.3%	30.6%	68.7%	31.3%
22,377	DOVER	10,350	5,357	4,803	190	554 R	51.8%	46.4%	52.7%	47.3%
10,652	DURHAM	3,710	1,647	2,030	33	383 D	44.4%	54.7%	44.8%	55.2%
11,024	EXETER	5,818	3,453	2,276	89	1,177 R	59.4%	39.1%	60.3%	39.7%
7,901	FRANKLIN	2,737	1,703	1,010	24	693 R	62.2%	36.9%	62.8%	37.2%
11,315	GOFFSTOWN	5,793	3,999	1,728	66	2,271 R	69.0%	29.8%	69.8%	30.2%
10,493	HAMPTON	6,364	3,536	2,678	150	858 R	55.6%	42.1%	56.9%	43.1%
9,119	HANOVER	3,654	1,472	2,156	26	684 D	40.3%	59.0%	40.6%	59.4%
7,303	HOOKSETT	3,583	2,587	959	37	1,628 R	72.2%	26.8%	73.0%	27.0%
14,022	HUDSON	7,385	4,819	2,456	110	2,363 R	65.3%	33.3%	66.2%	33.8%
21,449	KEENE	9,059	4,535	4,466	58	69 R	50.1%	49.3%	50.4%	49.6%
15,575	LACONIA	6,007	3,835	2,111	61	1,724 R	63.8%	35.1%	64.5%	35.5%
11,134	LEBANON	4,602	2,326	2,258	18	68 R	50.5%	49.1%	50.7%	49.3%
5,558	LITTLETON	2,278	1,659	606	13	1,053 R	72.8%	26.6%	73.2%	26.8%
13,598	LONDONDERRY	7,569	5,232	2,160	177	3,072 R	69.1%	28.5%	70.8%	29.2%
90,936	MANCHESTER	36,819	23,893	12,567	359	11,326 R	64.9%	34.1%	65.5%	34.5%
15,406	MERRIMACK TOWN	8,440	5,765	2,570	105	3,195 R	68.3%	30.5%	69.2%	30.8%
8,684	MILFORD	4,744	3,259	1,427	58	1,832 R	68.7%	30.1%	69.5%	30.5%
67,865	NASHUA	32,727	19,369	12,833	525	6,536 R	59.2%	39.2%	60.1%	39.9%
6,229	NEWPORT	2,155	1,314	830	11	484 R	61.0%	38.5%	61.3%	38.7%
8,090	PELHAM	3,930	2,713	1,155	62	1,558 R	69.0%	29.4%	70.1%	29.9%
5,609	PLAISTOW	2,658	1,756	863	39	893 R	66.1%	32.5%	67.0%	33.0%
5,094	PLYMOUTH	1,778	1,141	624	13	517 R	64.2%	35.1%	64.6%	35.4%
26,254	PORTSMOUTH	10,370	4,827	5,377	166	550 D	46.5%	51.9%	47.3%	52.7%
5,453	RAYMOND	2,883	1,928	881	74	1,047 R	66.9%	30.6%	68.6%	31.4%
21,560	ROCHESTER	9,081	5,368	3,591	122	1,777 R	59.1%	39.5%	59.9%	40.1%
24,124	SALEM	10,995	7,314	3,512	169	3,802 R	66.5%	31.9%	67.6%	32.4%
5,917	SEABROOK	2,928	1,855	1,047	26	808 R	63.4%	35.8%	63.9%	36.1%
10,350	SOMERSWORTH	3,967	1,999	1,885	83	114 R	50.4%	47.5%	51.5%	48.5%
5,183	SWANZEY	2,258	1,299	944	15	355 R	57.5%	41.8%	57.9%	42.1%
5,664	WINDHAM	3,891	2,755	1,024	112	1,731 R	70.8%	26.3%	72.9%	27.1%

NEW HAMPSHIRE

GOVERNOR 1988

1980 Census Population	County	Total Vote	Republican	Democratic	Other	Rep.-Dem. Plurality	Percentage Total Vote Rep.	Total Vote Dem.	Major Vote Rep.	Major Vote Dem.
42,884	BELKNAP	21,154	13,501	7,512	141	5,989 R	63.8%	35.5%	64.3%	35.7%
27,931	CARROLL	17,705	12,423	5,210	72	7,213 R	70.2%	29.4%	70.5%	29.5%
62,116	CHESHIRE	27,154	14,178	12,903	73	1,275 R	52.2%	47.5%	52.4%	47.6%
35,147	COOS	13,439	8,667	4,725	47	3,942 R	64.5%	35.2%	64.7%	35.3%
65,806	GRAFTON	30,052	18,739	11,176	137	7,563 R	62.4%	37.2%	62.6%	37.4%
276,608	HILLSBOROUGH	132,451	86,588	45,098	765	41,490 R	65.4%	34.0%	65.8%	34.2%
98,302	MERRIMACK	48,537	28,604	19,695	238	8,909 R	58.9%	40.6%	59.2%	40.8%
190,345	ROCKINGHAM	99,440	57,318	41,498	624	15,820 R	57.6%	41.7%	58.0%	42.0%
85,408	STRAFFORD	36,944	18,496	18,272	176	224 R	50.1%	49.5%	50.3%	49.7%
36,063	SULLIVAN	15,047	8,550	6,454	43	2,096 R	56.8%	42.9%	57.0%	43.0%
920,610	TOTAL	441,923	267,064	172,543	2,316	94,521 R	60.4%	39.0%	60.8%	39.2%

NEW HAMPSHIRE

GOVERNOR 1988

1980 Census Population	City/Town	Total Vote	Republican	Democratic	Other	Rep.-Dem. Plurality	Percentage Total Vote Rep.	Total Vote Dem.	Major Vote Rep.	Major Vote Dem.
8,243	AMHERST	4,632	3,454	1,162	16	2,292 R	74.6%	25.1%	74.8%	25.2%
9,481	BEDFORD	6,771	5,108	1,626	37	3,482 R	75.4%	24.0%	75.9%	24.1%
13,084	BERLIN	4,637	2,479	2,148	10	331 R	53.5%	46.3%	53.6%	46.4%
14,557	CLAREMONT	4,741	2,414	2,312	15	102 R	50.9%	48.8%	51.1%	48.9%
30,400	CONCORD	14,324	7,395	6,847	82	548 R	51.6%	47.8%	51.9%	48.1%
7,158	CONWAY	3,359	2,272	1,070	17	1,202 R	67.6%	31.9%	68.0%	32.0%
18,875	DERRY	9,174	5,720	3,365	89	2,355 R	62.4%	36.7%	63.0%	37.0%
22,377	DOVER	10,164	5,087	5,023	54	64 R	50.0%	49.4%	50.3%	49.7%
10,652	DURHAM	3,605	1,607	1,990	8	383 D	44.6%	55.2%	44.7%	55.3%
11,024	EXETER	5,673	3,042	2,610	21	432 R	53.6%	46.0%	53.8%	46.2%
7,901	FRANKLIN	2,794	1,740	1,035	19	705 R	62.3%	37.0%	62.7%	37.3%
11,315	GOFFSTOWN	5,750	3,864	1,865	21	1,999 R	67.2%	32.4%	67.4%	32.6%
10,493	HAMPTON	6,148	2,885	3,234	29	349 D	46.9%	52.6%	47.1%	52.9%
9,119	HANOVER	3,511	1,509	1,975	27	466 D	43.0%	56.3%	43.3%	56.7%
7,303	HOOKSETT	3,558	2,463	1,084	11	1,379 R	69.2%	30.5%	69.4%	30.6%
14,022	HUDSON	7,386	4,912	2,405	69	2,507 R	66.5%	32.6%	67.1%	32.9%
21,449	KEENE	8,859	4,146	4,696	17	550 D	46.8%	53.0%	46.9%	53.1%
15,575	LACONIA	5,990	3,587	2,359	44	1,228 R	59.9%	39.4%	60.3%	39.7%
11,134	LEBANON	4,525	2,286	2,222	17	64 R	50.5%	49.1%	50.7%	49.3%
5,558	LITTLETON	2,247	1,673	563	11	1,110 R	74.5%	25.1%	74.8%	25.2%
13,598	LONDONDERRY	7,447	4,913	2,467	67	2,446 R	66.0%	33.1%	66.6%	33.4%
90,936	MANCHESTER	35,998	22,389	13,492	117	8,897 R	62.2%	37.5%	62.4%	37.6%
15,406	MERRIMACK TOWN	8,408	5,654	2,686	68	2,968 R	67.2%	31.9%	67.8%	32.2%
8,684	MILFORD	4,668	3,319	1,326	23	1,993 R	71.1%	28.4%	71.5%	28.5%
67,865	NASHUA	30,911	19,341	11,280	290	8,061 R	62.6%	36.5%	63.2%	36.8%
6,229	NEWPORT	2,105	1,293	806	6	487 R	61.4%	38.3%	61.6%	38.4%
8,090	PELHAM	3,910	2,658	1,222	30	1,436 R	68.0%	31.3%	68.5%	31.5%
5,609	PLAISTOW	2,480	1,507	960	13	547 R	60.8%	38.7%	61.1%	38.9%
5,094	PLYMOUTH	1,739	1,119	612	8	507 R	64.3%	35.2%	64.6%	35.4%
26,254	PORTSMOUTH	10,064	4,010	6,005	49	1,995 D	39.8%	59.7%	40.0%	60.0%
5,453	RAYMOND	2,784	1,747	1,023	14	724 R	62.8%	36.7%	63.1%	36.9%
21,560	ROCHESTER	8,826	4,581	4,215	30	366 R	51.9%	47.8%	52.1%	47.9%
24,124	SALEM	10,931	6,795	4,034	102	2,761 R	62.2%	36.9%	62.7%	37.3%
5,917	SEABROOK	2,821	1,542	1,272	7	270 R	54.7%	45.1%	54.8%	45.2%
10,350	SOMERSWORTH	3,895	1,768	2,104	23	336 D	45.4%	54.0%	45.7%	54.3%
5,183	SWANZEY	2,250	1,218	1,027	5	191 R	54.1%	45.6%	54.3%	45.7%
5,664	WINDHAM	3,846	2,688	1,119	39	1,569 R	69.9%	29.1%	70.6%	29.4%

NEW HAMPSHIRE

CONGRESS

CD	Year	Total Vote	Republican Vote	Republican Candidate	Democratic Vote	Democratic Candidate	Other Vote	Rep.-Dem. Plurality	Percentage Total Vote Rep.	Percentage Total Vote Dem.	Percentage Major Vote Rep.	Percentage Major Vote Dem.
1	1988	218,505	131,824	SMITH, ROBERT C.	86,623	KEEFE, JOSEPH F.	58	45,201 R	60.3%	39.6%	60.3%	39.7%
1	1986	125,547	70,739	SMITH, ROBERT C.	54,787	DEMERS, JAMES M.	21	15,952 R	56.3%	43.6%	56.4%	43.6%
1	1984	190,516	111,627	SMITH, ROBERT C.	76,854	DUDLEY, DUDLEY	2,035	34,773 R	58.6%	40.3%	59.2%	40.8%
1	1982	138,911	61,876	SMITH, ROBERT C.	76,281	D'AMOURS, NORMAN E.	754	14,405 D	44.5%	54.9%	44.8%	55.2%
2	1988	210,994	119,742	DOUGLAS, CHUCK	89,677	DONCHESS, JAMES W.	1,575	30,065 R	56.8%	42.5%	57.2%	42.8%
2	1986	115,200	85,479	GREGG, JUDD	29,688	CRAIG-GREEN, LAURENCE	33	55,791 R	74.2%	25.8%	74.2%	25.8%
2	1984	182,444	138,975	GREGG, JUDD	42,257	CONVERSE, LARRY	1,212	96,718 R	76.2%	23.2%	76.7%	23.3%
2	1982	130,007	92,098	GREGG, JUDD	37,906	DUPAY, ROBERT L.	3	54,192 R	70.8%	29.2%	70.8%	29.2%

NEW HAMPSHIRE

1988 GENERAL ELECTION

President Other vote was 4,502 Libertarian (Paul); 790 New Alliance (Fulani); 549 scattered write-in.

Governor Other vote was 2,216 Libertarian (Wilson); 100 scattered write-in. Early unamended returns gave the Republican (Gregg) vote as 266,763 and the Democratic (McEachen) vote as 172,466.

Congress Other vote was scattered in CD 1; 1,454 American (Kendel) and 121 scattered in CD 2.

1988 PRIMARIES

SEPTEMBER 13 REPUBLICAN

Governor 65,777 Judd Gregg; 15,133 Robert F. Shaw; 2,361 William Lawrence.

Congress Unopposed in CD 1. Contested as follows:

CD 2 22,774 Chuck Douglas; 19,827 Betty Tamposi; 2,546 Stephen Gregg; 1,497 Alf E. Jacobson; 872 Andrew D. Tempelman; 744 Dennis Allen.

SEPTEMBER 13 DEMOCRATIC

Governor Paul McEachern, unopposed.

Congress Contested as follows:

CD 1 12,361 Joseph F. Keefe; 5,722 Scott Williams; 1,159 Robert Patton; 77 scattered write-in.
CD 2 11,030 James W. Donchess; 4,949 Barbara Underwood; 1,492 Lewis duP. Smith.

NEW JERSEY

GOVERNOR

Thomas H. Kean (R). Re-elected 1985 to a four-year term. Previously elected 1981.

SENATORS

Bill Bradley (D). Re-elected 1984 to a six-year term. Previously elected 1978.

Frank R. Lautenberg (D). Re-elected 1988 to a six-year term. Previously elected 1982.

REPRESENTATIVES

1. James J. Florio (D)
2. William J. Hughes (D)
3. Frank Pallone (D)
4. Christopher H. Smith (R)
5. Margaret S. Roukema (R)
6. Bernard J. Dwyer (D)
7. Matthew J. Rinaldo (R)
8. Robert A. Roe (D)
9. Robert G. Torricelli (D)
10. Donald M. Payne (D)
11. Dean A. Gallo (R)
12. James A. Courter (R)
13. H. James Saxton (R)
14. Frank J. Guarini (D)

POSTWAR VOTE FOR PRESIDENT

								Percentage			
	Total	Republican		Democratic		Other		Total Vote		Major Vote	
Year	Vote	Vote	Candidate	Vote	Candidate	Vote	Plurality	Rep.	Dem.	Rep.	Dem.
1988	3,099,553	1,743,192	Bush, George	1,320,352	Dukakis, Michael S.	36,009	422,840 R	56.2%	42.6%	56.9%	43.1%
1984	3,217,862	1,933,630	Reagan, Ronald	1,261,323	Mondale, Walter F.	22,909	672,307 R	60.1%	39.2%	60.5%	39.5%
1980	2,975,684	1,546,557	Reagan, Ronald	1,147,364	Carter, Jimmy	281,763	399,193 R	52.0%	38.6%	57.4%	42.6%
1976	3,014,472	1,509,688	Ford, Gerald R.	1,444,653	Carter, Jimmy	60,131	65,035 R	50.1%	47.9%	51.1%	48.9%
1972	2,997,229	1,845,502	Nixon, Richard M.	1,102,211	McGovern, George S.	49,516	743,291 R	61.6%	36.8%	62.6%	37.4%
1968	2,875,395	1,325,467	Nixon, Richard M.	1,264,206	Humphrey, Hubert H.	285,722	61,261 R	46.1%	44.0%	51.2%	48.8%
1964	2,847,663	964,174	Goldwater, Barry M.	1,868,231	Johnson, Lyndon B.	15,258	904,057 D	33.9%	65.6%	34.0%	66.0%
1960	2,773,111	1,363,324	Nixon, Richard M.	1,385,415	Kennedy, John F.	24,372	22,091 D	49.2%	50.0%	49.6%	50.4%
1956	2,484,312	1,606,942	Eisenhower, Dwight D.	850,337	Stevenson, Adlai E.	27,033	756,605 R	64.7%	34.2%	65.4%	34.6%
1952	2,418,554	1,373,613	Eisenhower, Dwight D.	1,015,902	Stevenson, Adlai E.	29,039	357,711 R	56.8%	42.0%	57.5%	42.5%
1948	1,949,555	981,124	Dewey, Thomas E.	895,455	Truman, Harry S.	72,976	85,669 R	50.3%	45.9%	52.3%	47.7%

NEW JERSEY

POSTWAR VOTE FOR GOVERNOR

Year	Total Vote	Republican Vote	Republican Candidate	Democratic Vote	Democratic Candidate	Other Vote	Rep.-Dem. Plurality	Percentage Total Vote Rep.	Percentage Total Vote Dem.	Percentage Major Vote Rep.	Percentage Major Vote Dem.
1985	1,972,624	1,372,631	Kean, Thomas H.	578,402	Shapiro, Peter	21,591	794,229 R	69.6%	29.3%	70.4%	29.6%
1981	2,317,239	1,145,999	Kean, Thomas H.	1,144,202	Florio, James J.	27,038	1,797 R	49.5%	49.4%	50.0%	50.0%
1977	2,126,264	888,880	Bateman, Raymond H.	1,184,564	Byrne, Brendan T.	52,820	295,684 D	41.8%	55.7%	42.9%	57.1%
1973	2,122,009	676,235	Sandman, Charles W.	1,414,613	Byrne, Brendan T.	31,161	738,378 D	31.9%	66.7%	32.3%	67.7%
1969	2,366,606	1,411,905	Cahill, William T.	911,003	Meyner, Robert B.	43,698	500,902 R	59.7%	38.5%	60.8%	39.2%
1965	2,229,583	915,996	Dumont, Wayne	1,279,568	Hughes, Richard J.	34,019	363,572 D	41.1%	57.4%	41.7%	58.3%
1961	2,152,662	1,049,274	Mitchell, James P.	1,084,194	Hughes, Richard J.	19,194	34,920 D	48.7%	50.4%	49.2%	50.8%
1957	2,018,488	897,321	Forbes, Malcolm S.	1,101,130	Meyner, Robert B.	20,037	203,809 D	44.5%	54.6%	44.9%	55.1%
1953	1,810,812	809,068	Troast, Paul L.	962,710	Meyner, Robert B.	39,034	153,642 D	44.7%	53.2%	45.7%	54.3%
1949 * *	1,718,788	885,882	Driscoll, Alfred	810,022	Wene, Elmer H.	22,884	75,860 R	51.5%	47.1%	52.2%	47.8%
1946	1,414,527	807,378	Driscoll, Alfred	585,960	Hansen, Lewis G.	21,189	221,418 R	57.1%	41.4%	57.9%	42.1%

The term of office of New Jersey's Governor was increased from three to four years effective with the 1949 election.

POSTWAR VOTE FOR SENATOR

Year	Total Vote	Republican Vote	Republican Candidate	Democratic Vote	Democratic Candidate	Other Vote	Rep.-Dem. Plurality	Percentage Total Vote Rep.	Percentage Total Vote Dem.	Percentage Major Vote Rep.	Percentage Major Vote Dem.
1988	2,987,634	1,349,937	Dawkins, Peter M.	1,599,905	Lautenberg, Frank R.	37,792	249,968 D	45.2%	53.6%	45.8%	54.2%
1984	3,096,456	1,080,100	Mochary, Mary V.	1,986,644	Bradley, Bill	29,712	906,544 D	34.9%	64.2%	35.2%	64.8%
1982	2,193,945	1,047,626	Fenwick, Millicent	1,117,549	Lautenberg, Frank R.	28,770	69,923 D	47.8%	50.9%	48.4%	51.6%
1978	1,957,515	844,200	Bell, Jeffrey	1,082,960	Bradley, Bill	30,355	238,760 D	43.1%	55.3%	43.8%	56.2%
1976	2,771,390	1,054,508	Norcross, David F.	1,681,140	Williams, Harrison	35,742	626,632 D	38.0%	60.7%	38.5%	61.5%
1972	2,791,907	1,743,854	Case, Clifford P.	963,573	Krebs, Paul J.	84,480	780,281 R	62.5%	34.5%	64.4%	35.6%
1970	2,142,105	903,026	Gross, Nelson G.	1,157,074	Williams, Harrison	82,005	254,048 D	42.2%	54.0%	43.8%	56.2%
1966	2,131,188	1,279,343	Case, Clifford P.	788,021	Wilentz, Warren W.	63,824	491,322 R	60.0%	37.0%	61.9%	38.1%
1964	2,710,441	1,011,610	Shanley, Bernard M.	1,678,051	Williams, Harrison	20,780	666,441 D	37.3%	61.9%	37.6%	62.4%
1960	2,664,556	1,483,832	Case, Clifford P.	1,151,385	Lord, Thorn	29,339	332,447 R	55.7%	43.2%	56.3%	43.7%
1958	1,881,329	882,287	Kean, Robert W.	966,832	Williams, Harrison	32,210	84,545 D	46.9%	51.4%	47.7%	52.3%
1954	1,770,557	861,528	Case, Clifford P.	858,158	Howell, Charles R.	50,871	3,370 R	48.7%	48.5%	50.1%	49.9%
1952	2,318,232	1,286,782	Smith, H. Alexander	1,011,187	Alexander, Archibald	20,263	275,595 R	55.5%	43.6%	56.0%	44.0%
1948	1,869,882	934,720	Hendrickson, Robert	884,414	Alexander, Archibald	50,748	50,306 R	50.0%	47.3%	51.4%	48.6%
1946	1,367,155	799,808	Smith, H. Alexander	548,458	Brunner, George E.	18,889	251,350 R	58.5%	40.1%	59.3%	40.7%

NEW JERSEY

Districts Established February 17, 1984

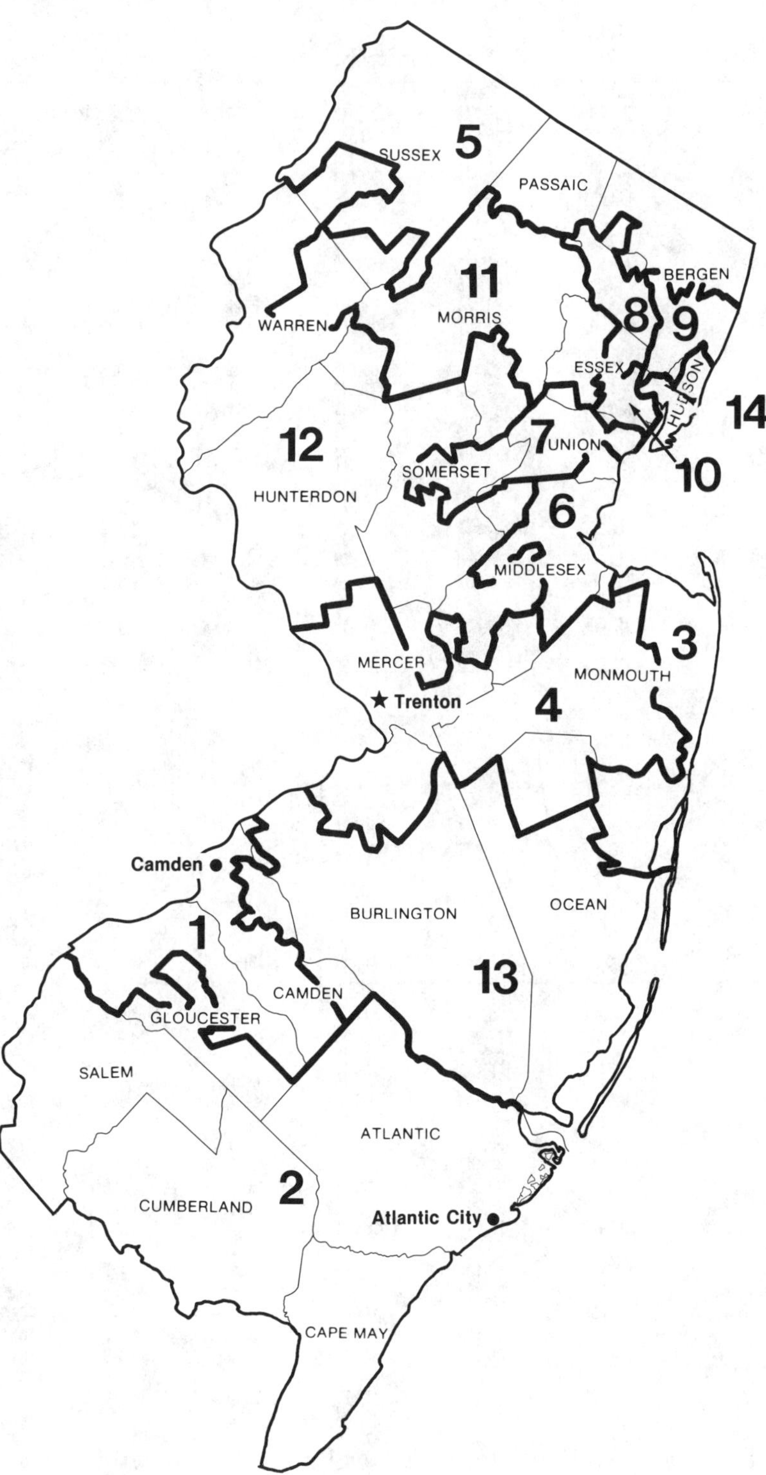

NEW JERSEY

PRESIDENT 1988

1980 Census Population	County	Total Vote	Republican	Democratic	Other	Rep.-Dem. Plurality	Percentage Total Vote Rep.	Percentage Total Vote Dem.	Percentage Major Vote Rep.	Percentage Major Vote Dem.
194,119	ATLANTIC	79,442	44,748	34,047	647	10,701 R	56.3%	42.9%	56.8%	43.2%
845,385	BERGEN	389,933	226,885	160,655	2,393	66,230 R	58.2%	41.2%	58.5%	41.5%
362,542	BURLINGTON	149,949	87,416	61,140	1,393	26,276 R	58.3%	40.8%	58.8%	41.2%
471,650	CAMDEN	192,515	100,072	90,704	1,739	9,368 R	52.0%	47.1%	52.5%	47.5%
82,266	CAPE MAY	44,117	28,738	15,105	274	13,633 R	65.1%	34.2%	65.5%	34.5%
132,866	CUMBERLAND	48,349	26,024	21,869	456	4,155 R	53.8%	45.2%	54.3%	45.7%
851,116	ESSEX	276,967	111,491	156,098	9,378	44,607 D	40.3%	56.4%	41.7%	58.3%
199,917	GLOUCESTER	88,117	51,708	35,479	930	16,229 R	58.7%	40.3%	59.3%	40.7%
556,972	HUDSON	184,463	84,334	98,507	1,622	14,173 D	45.7%	53.4%	46.1%	53.9%
87,361	HUNTERDON	46,182	31,907	13,758	517	18,149 R	69.1%	29.8%	69.9%	30.1%
307,863	MERCER	135,345	65,384	68,712	1,249	3,328 D	48.3%	50.8%	48.8%	51.2%
595,893	MIDDLESEX	264,119	143,422	117,149	3,548	26,273 R	54.3%	44.4%	55.0%	45.0%
503,173	MONMOUTH	240,957	147,320	91,844	1,793	55,476 R	61.1%	38.1%	61.6%	38.4%
407,630	MORRIS	187,249	127,420	58,721	1,108	68,699 R	68.0%	31.4%	68.5%	31.5%
346,038	OCEAN	190,558	124,587	64,474	1,497	60,113 R	65.4%	33.8%	65.9%	34.1%
447,585	PASSAIC	157,513	88,070	66,254	3,189	21,816 R	55.9%	42.1%	57.1%	42.9%
64,676	SALEM	25,606	15,240	9,956	410	5,284 R	59.5%	38.9%	60.5%	39.5%
203,129	SOMERSET	106,193	67,658	37,406	1,129	30,252 R	63.7%	35.2%	64.4%	35.6%
116,119	SUSSEX	50,160	36,086	13,676	398	22,410 R	71.9%	27.3%	72.5%	27.5%
504,094	UNION	208,153	112,967	93,158	2,028	19,809 R	54.3%	44.8%	54.8%	45.2%
84,429	WARREN	33,666	21,715	11,640	311	10,075 R	64.5%	34.6%	65.1%	34.9%
7,364,823	TOTAL	3,099,553	1,743,192	1,320,352	36,009	422,840 R	56.2%	42.6%	56.9%	43.1%

NEW JERSEY

SENATOR 1988

1980 Census Population	County	Total Vote	Republican	Democratic	Other	Rep.-Dem. Plurality	Percentage Total Vote Rep.	Percentage Total Vote Dem.	Percentage Major Vote Rep.	Percentage Major Vote Dem.
194,119	ATLANTIC	74,914	33,417	41,004	493	7,587 D	44.6%	54.7%	44.9%	55.1%
845,385	BERGEN	378,743	172,257	199,195	7,291	26,938 D	45.5%	52.6%	46.4%	53.6%
362,542	BURLINGTON	145,099	68,657	75,513	929	6,856 D	47.3%	52.0%	47.6%	52.4%
471,650	CAMDEN	187,318	75,162	110,718	1,438	35,556 D	40.1%	59.1%	40.4%	59.6%
82,266	CAPE MAY	42,292	22,349	19,720	223	2,629 R	52.8%	46.6%	53.1%	46.9%
132,866	CUMBERLAND	45,830	19,680	25,379	771	5,699 D	42.9%	55.4%	43.7%	56.3%
851,116	ESSEX	262,615	85,169	170,591	6,855	85,422 D	32.4%	65.0%	33.3%	66.7%
199,917	GLOUCESTER	86,534	39,232	46,247	1,055	7,015 D	45.3%	53.4%	45.9%	54.1%
556,972	HUDSON	175,717	65,092	108,355	2,270	43,263 D	37.0%	61.7%	37.5%	62.5%
87,361	HUNTERDON	44,440	25,615	18,281	544	7,334 R	57.6%	41.1%	58.4%	41.6%
307,863	MERCER	130,415	49,122	80,569	724	31,447 D	37.7%	61.8%	37.9%	62.1%
595,893	MIDDLESEX	256,045	112,182	141,067	2,796	28,885 D	43.8%	55.1%	44.3%	55.7%
503,173	MONMOUTH	230,287	111,318	117,063	1,906	5,745 D	48.3%	50.8%	48.7%	51.3%
407,630	MORRIS	184,137	103,843	79,237	1,057	24,606 R	56.4%	43.0%	56.7%	43.3%
346,038	OCEAN	184,485	98,161	84,812	1,512	13,349 R	53.2%	46.0%	53.6%	46.4%
447,585	PASSAIC	147,779	66,440	77,827	3,512	11,387 D	45.0%	52.7%	46.1%	53.9%
64,676	SALEM	25,581	12,562	12,485	534	77 R	49.1%	48.8%	50.2%	49.8%
203,129	SOMERSET	102,755	53,969	47,648	1,138	6,321 R	52.5%	46.4%	53.1%	46.9%
116,119	SUSSEX	49,557	29,909	19,035	613	10,874 R	60.4%	38.4%	61.1%	38.9%
504,094	UNION	199,654	88,027	109,852	1,775	21,825 D	44.1%	55.0%	44.5%	55.5%
84,429	WARREN	33,437	17,774	15,307	356	2,467 R	53.2%	45.8%	53.7%	46.3%
7,364,823	TOTAL	2,987,634	1,349,937	1,599,905	37,792	249,968 D	45.2%	53.6%	45.8%	54.2%

NEW JERSEY

CONGRESS

		Total	Republican		Democratic		Other	Rep.-Dem.	Percentage			
									Total Vote		Major Vote	
CD	Year	Vote	Vote	Candidate	Vote	Candidate	Vote	Plurality	Rep.	Dem.	Rep.	Dem.
1	1988	203,153	60,037	CRISTAUDO, FRANK A.	141,988	FLORIO, JAMES J.	1,128	81,951 D	29.6%	69.9%	29.7%	70.3%
1	1986	123,603	29,175	BUSCH, FREDERICK A.	93,497	FLORIO, JAMES J.	931	64,322 D	23.6%	75.6%	23.8%	76.2%
1	1984	211,711	58,800	BUSCH, FREDERICK A.	152,125	FLORIO, JAMES J.	786	93,325 D	27.8%	71.9%	27.9%	72.1%
2	1988	204,636	67,759	CONOVER, KIRK W.	134,505	HUGHES, WILLIAM J.	2,372	66,746 D	33.1%	65.7%	33.5%	66.5%
2	1986	122,800	35,167	BENNINGTON, ALFRED J.	83,821	HUGHES, WILLIAM J.	3,812	48,654 D	28.6%	68.3%	29.6%	70.4%
2	1984	210,072	77,231	MASSIE, RAYMOND G.	132,841	HUGHES, WILLIAM J.		55,610 D	36.8%	63.2%	36.8%	63.2%
3	1988	226,610	107,479	AZZOLINA, JOSEPH	117,024	PALLONE, FRANK	2,107	9,545 D	47.4%	51.6%	47.9%	52.1%
3	1986	125,625	51,882	KENNEDY, BRIAN T.	73,743	HOWARD, JAMES J.		21,861 D	41.3%	58.7%	41.3%	58.7%
3	1984	229,422	105,028	KENNEDY, BRIAN T.	122,291	HOWARD, JAMES J.	2,103	17,263 D	45.8%	53.3%	46.2%	53.8%
4	1988	236,194	155,283	SMITH, CHRISTOPHER H.	79,006	HOLLAND, BETTY	1,905	76,277 R	65.7%	33.4%	66.3%	33.7%
4	1986	128,778	78,699	SMITH, CHRISTOPHER H.	49,290	LAURENTI, JEFFREY	789	29,409 R	61.1%	38.3%	61.5%	38.5%
4	1984	227,203	139,295	SMITH, CHRISTOPHER H.	87,908	HEDDEN, JAMES C.		51,387 R	61.3%	38.7%	61.3%	38.7%
5	1988	231,936	175,562	ROUKEMA, MARGARET S.	54,828	MONACO, LEE	1,546	120,734 R	75.7%	23.6%	76.2%	23.8%
5	1986	126,398	94,253	ROUKEMA, MARGARET S.	32,145	JOLLEY, H. VERNON		62,108 R	74.6%	25.4%	74.6%	25.4%
5	1984	241,645	171,979	ROUKEMA, MARGARET S.	69,666	BRUNETTO, ROSE		102,313 R	71.2%	28.8%	71.2%	28.8%
6	1988	196,598	74,824	SICA, PETER J.	120,125	DWYER, BERNARD J.	1,649	45,301 D	38.1%	61.1%	38.4%	61.6%
6	1986	97,769	28,286	SCALAMONTI, JOHN D.	67,460	DWYER, BERNARD J.	2,023	39,174 D	28.9%	69.0%	29.5%	70.5%
6	1984	212,080	90,862	ADAMS, DENNIS	118,532	DWYER, BERNARD J.	2,686	27,670 D	42.8%	55.9%	43.4%	56.6%
7	1988	205,539	153,350	RINALDO, MATTHEW J.	52,189	HELY, JAMES		101,161 R	74.6%	25.4%	74.6%	25.4%
7	1986	116,716	92,254	RINALDO, MATTHEW J.	24,462	FISCHER, JUNE S.		67,792 R	79.0%	21.0%	79.0%	21.0%
7	1984	223,282	165,685	RINALDO, MATTHEW J.	56,798	FEELEY, JOHN F.	799	108,887 R	74.2%	25.4%	74.5%	25.5%
8	1988	96,036			96,036	ROE, ROBERT A.		96,036 D		100.0%		100.0%
8	1986	92,088	34,268	ZAMPINO, THOMAS P.	57,820	ROE, ROBERT A.		23,552 D	37.2%	62.8%	37.2%	62.8%
8	1984	189,395	69,973	PAGE, MARGUERITE A.	118,793	ROE, ROBERT A.	629	48,820 D	36.9%	62.7%	37.1%	62.9%
9	1988	211,494	68,363	LANE, ROGER J.	142,012	TORRICELLI, ROBERT G.	1,119	73,649 D	32.3%	67.1%	32.5%	67.5%
9	1986	129,860	40,226	JONES, ARTHUR F.	89,634	TORRICELLI, ROBERT G.		49,408 D	31.0%	69.0%	31.0%	69.0%
9	1984	238,659	89,166	ROMANO, NEIL	149,493	TORRICELLI, ROBERT G.		60,327 D	37.4%	62.6%	37.4%	62.6%
10	1988	109,473	13,848	WEBB, MICHAEL	84,681	PAYNE, DONALD M.	10,944	70,833 D	12.6%	77.4%	14.1%	85.9%
10	1986	48,643			46,666	RODINO, PETER W.	1,977	46,666 D		95.9%		100.0%
10	1984	132,956	21,712	BERKELEY, HOWARD E.	111,244	RODINO, PETER W.		89,532 D	16.3%	83.7%	16.3%	83.7%
11	1988	219,427	154,654	GALLO, DEAN A.	64,773	SHAW, JOHN C.		89,881 R	70.5%	29.5%	70.5%	29.5%
11	1986	110,317	75,037	GALLO, DEAN A.	35,280	ASKIN, FRANK		39,757 R	68.0%	32.0%	68.0%	32.0%
11	1984	239,700	133,662	GALLO, DEAN A.	106,038	MINISH, JOSEPH G.		27,624 R	55.8%	44.2%	55.8%	44.2%
12	1988	239,537	165,918	COURTER, JAMES A.	71,596	WEINSTEIN, NORMAN J.	2,023	94,322 R	69.3%	29.9%	69.9%	30.1%
12	1986	114,933	72,966	COURTER, JAMES A.	41,967	CRABIEL, DAVID B.		30,999 R	63.5%	36.5%	63.5%	36.5%
12	1984	227,833	148,042	COURTER, JAMES A.	78,167	BEARSE, PETER	1,624	69,875 R	65.0%	34.3%	65.4%	34.6%
13	1988	241,031	167,470	SAXTON, H. JAMES	73,561	SMITH, JAMES B.		93,909 R	69.5%	30.5%	69.5%	30.5%
13	1986	126,786	82,866	SAXTON, H. JAMES	43,920	WYDRA, JOHN		38,946 R	65.4%	34.6%	65.4%	34.6%
13	1984	232,483	141,136	SAXTON, H. JAMES	89,307	SMITH, JAMES B.	2,040	51,829 R	60.7%	38.4%	61.2%	38.8%
14	1988	154,440	47,293	THEEMLING, FRED J.	104,001	GUARINI, FRANK J.	3,146	56,708 D	30.6%	67.3%	31.3%	68.7%
14	1986	89,229	23,822	SIRES, ALBIO	63,057	GUARINI, FRANK J.	2,350	39,235 D	26.7%	70.7%	27.4%	72.6%
14	1984	175,217	58,265	MAGEE, EDWARD T.	115,117	GUARINI, FRANK J.	1,835	56,852 D	33.3%	65.7%	33.6%	66.4%

NEW JERSEY

1988 GENERAL ELECTION

President Other vote was 9,953 Peace and Freedom (Lewin); 8,421 Libertarian (Paul); 5,139 New Alliance (Fulani); 3,454 Consumer (McCarthy); 2,587 Socialist (Kenoyer); 2,446 Populist (Duke); 2,298 Socialist Workers (Warren); 1,020 Workers World (Holmes); 691 Workers League (Winn). Statistics presented are the final, official amended returns with adjustments in Hudson and Middlesex counties.

Senator Other vote was 20,091 Independent (Job); 12,354 Libertarian (Zeldin); 5,347 Socialist Workers (Fiske).

Congress Other vote was Libertarian (Bartucci) in CD 1; Pro-Life Conservative (Schindenwolf) in CD 2; Libertarian (Stewart) in CD 3; 1,114 Independent (Carter) and 791 Libertarian (Maiullo) in CD 4; Libertarian (Karlan) in CD 5; 1,034 Socialist Workers (Paltrineri) and 615 Libertarian (Schoen) in CD 6; Poor Man's Party (Kemly) in CD 9; 5,422 People's Choice (Imperiale), 4,539 Socialist Workers (Bridno), 551 Time for Change (Curtis) and 432 Independent (Bowser) in CD 10; Libertarian (Friedlander) in CD 12; 1,346 All Peoples Congress (Jones), 1,005 Libertarian (White), 442 Communist (Rummel) and 353 Independent (Galbo) in CD 14.

1988 PRIMARIES

JUNE 7 REPUBLICAN

Senator Peter M. Dawkins, unopposed.

Congress Unopposed in eight CD's. No candidate in CD 8. Contested as follows:

CD 2 16,157 Kirk W. Conover; 3,069 Thomas M. Warner.
CD 3 15,433 Joseph Azzolina; 3,251 Brian T. Kennedy; 1,789 Scott M. Colabella; 1,587 Brian J. Rechten; 1,000 John J. Whalen.
CD 6 5,047 Peter J. Sica; 1.953 James G. Fennessy.
CD 12 25,816 James A. Courter; 3,177 Thomas J. Young.
CD 14 5,370 James V. McNally; 1,639 Louis Russo. Mr. McNally withdrew after the primary and Fred J. Theemling was substituted by the local party committee.

JUNE 7 DEMOCRATIC

Senator 362,072 Frank R. Lautenberg; 51,938 Elnardo J. Webster; 41,303 Harold J. Young.

Congress Unopposed in ten CD's. Contested as follows:

CD 4 21,169 Betty Holland; 10,247 Saul G. Hornik.
CD 10 40,608 Donald M. Payne; 14,908 Ralph T. Grant.
CD 13 20,109 James B. Smith; 3,000 Michael DiMarco.
CD 14 35,964 Frank J. Guarini; 10,680 Robert P. Haney; 7,027 Edward A. Allen.

NEW MEXICO

GOVERNOR

Garrey E. Carruthers (R). Elected 1986 to a four-year term.

SENATORS

Jeff Bingaman (D). Re-elected 1988 to a six-year term. Previously elected 1982.

Peter V. Domenici (R). Re-elected 1984 to a six-year term. Previously elected 1978, 1972.

REPRESENTATIVES

1. Steven H. Schiff (R)
2. Joseph R. Skeen (R)
3. Bill Richardson (D)

POSTWAR VOTE FOR PRESIDENT

									Percentage			
	Total	Republican		Democratic		Other		Total Vote		Major Vote		
Year	Vote	Vote	Candidate	Vote	Candidate	Vote	Plurality	Rep.	Dem.	Rep.	Dem.	
1988	521,287	270,341	Bush, George	244,497	Dukakis, Michael S.	6,449	25,844 R	51.9%	46.9%	52.5%	47.5%	
1984	514,370	307,101	Reagan, Ronald	201,769	Mondale, Walter F.	5,500	105,332 R	59.7%	39.2%	60.3%	39.7%	
1980	456,971	250,779	Reagan, Ronald	167,826	Carter, Jimmy	38,366	82,953 R	54.9%	36.7%	59.9%	40.1%	
1976	418,409	211,419	Ford, Gerald R.	201,148	Carter, Jimmy	5,842	10,271 R	50.5%	48.1%	51.2%	48.8%	
1972	386,241	235,606	Nixon, Richard M.	141,084	McGovern, George S.	9,551	94,522 R	61.0%	36.5%	62.5%	37.5%	
1968	327,350	169,692	Nixon, Richard M.	130,081	Humphrey, Hubert H.	27,577	39,611 R	51.8%	39.7%	56.6%	43.4%	
1964	328,645	132,838	Goldwater, Barry M.	194,015	Johnson, Lyndon B.	1,792	61,177 D	40.4%	59.0%	40.6%	59.4%	
1960	311,107	153,733	Nixon, Richard M.	156,027	Kennedy, John F.	1,347	2,294 D	49.4%	50.2%	49.6%	50.4%	
1956	253,926	146,788	Eisenhower, Dwight D.	106,098	Stevenson, Adlai E.	1,040	40,690 R	57.8%	41.8%	58.0%	42.0%	
1952	238,608	132,170	Eisenhower, Dwight D.	105,661	Stevenson, Adlai E.	777	26,509 R	55.4%	44.3%	55.6%	44.4%	
1948	187,063	80,303	Dewey, Thomas E.	105,464	Truman, Harry S.	1,296	25,161 D	42.9%	56.4%	43.2%	56.8%	

POSTWAR VOTE FOR GOVERNOR

								Percentage			
	Total	Republican		Democratic		Other	Rep.-Dem.	Total Vote		Major Vote	
Year	Vote	Vote	Candidate	Vote	Candidate	Vote	Plurality	Rep.	Dem.	Rep.	Dem.
1986	394,833	209,455	Carruthers, Garrey E.	185,378	Powell. Ray B.		24,077 R	53.0%	47.0%	53.0%	47.0%
1982	407,466	191,626	Irick, John B.	215,840	Anaya, Toney		24,214 D	47.0%	53.0%	47.0%	53.0%
1978	345,577	170,848	Skeen, Joseph R.	174,631	King, Bruce	98	3,783 D	49.4%	50.5%	49.5%	50.5%
1974	328,742	160,430	Skeen, Joseph R.	164,172	Apodaca, Jerry	4,140	3,742 D	48.8%	49.9%	49.4%	50.6%
1970 **	290,375	134,640	Domenici, Peter V.	148,835	King, Bruce	6,900	14,195 D	46.4%	51.3%	47.5%	52.5%
1968	318,975	160,140	Cargo, David F.	157,230	Chavez, Fabian	1,605	2,910 R	50.2%	49.3%	50.5%	49.5%
1966	260,232	134,625	Cargo, David F.	125,587	Lusk, Thomas E.	20	9,038 R	51.7%	48.3%	51.7%	48.3%
1964	318,042	126,540	Tucker, Merle H.	191,497	Campbell, Jack M.	5	64,957 D	39.8%	60.2%	39.8%	60.2%
1962	247,135	116,184	Mechem, Edwin L.	130,933	Campbell, Jack M.	18	14,749 D	47.0%	53.0%	47.0%	53.0%
1960	305,542	153,765	Mechem, Edwin L.	151,777	Burroughs, John		1,988 R	50.3%	49.7%	50.3%	49.7%
1958	205,048	101,567	Mechem, Edwin L.	103,481	Burroughs, John		1,914 D	49.5%	50.5%	49.5%	50.5%
1956	251,751	131,488	Mechem, Edwin L.	120,263	Simms, John F.		11,225 R	52.2%	47.8%	52.2%	47.8%
1954	193,956	83,373	Stockton, Alvin	110,583	Simms, John F.		27,210 D	43.0%	57.0%	43.0%	57.0%
1952	240,150	129,116	Mechem, Edwin L.	111,034	Grantham, Everett		18,082 R	53.8%	46.2%	53.8%	46.2%
1950	180,205	96,846	Mechem, Edwin L.	83,359	Miles, John E.		13,487 R	53.7%	46.3%	53.7%	46.3%
1948	189,992	86,023	Lujan, Manuel	103,969	Mabry, Thomas J.		17,946 D	45.3%	54.7%	45.3%	54.7%
1946	132,930	62,875	Safford, Edward L.	70,055	Mabry, Thomas J.		7,180 D	47.3%	52.7%	47.3%	52.7%

The term of New Mexico's Governor was increased from two to four years effective with the 1970 election.

NEW MEXICO

POSTWAR VOTE FOR SENATOR

Year	Total Vote	Republican Vote	Republican Candidate	Democratic Vote	Democratic Candidate	Other Vote	Rep.-Dem. Plurality	Percentage Total Vote Rep.	Percentage Total Vote Dem.	Percentage Major Vote Rep.	Percentage Major Vote Dem.
1988	508,598	186,579	Valentine, William	321,983	Bingaman, Jeff	36	135,404 D	36.7%	63.3%	36.7%	63.3%
1984	502,634	361,371	Domenici, Peter V.	141,253	Pratt, Judith A.	10	220,118 R	71.9%	28.1%	71.9%	28.1%
1982	404,810	187,128	Schmitt, Harrison	217,682	Bingaman, Jeff		30,554 D	46.2%	53.8%	46.2%	53.8%
1978	343,554	183,442	Domenici, Peter V.	160,045	Anaya, Toney	67	23,397 R	53.4%	46.6%	53.4%	46.6%
1976	413,141	234,681	Schmitt, Harrison	176,382	Montoya, Joseph M.	2,078	58,299 R	56.8%	42.7%	57.1%	42.9%
1972	378,330	204,253	Domenici, Peter V.	173,815	Daniels, Jack	262	30,438 R	54.0%	45.9%	54.0%	46.0%
1970	289,906	135,004	Carter, Anderson	151,486	Montoya, Joseph M.	3,416	16,482 D	46.6%	52.3%	47.1%	52.9%
1966	258,203	120,988	Carter, Anderson	137,205	Anderson, Clinton P.	10	16,217 D	46.9%	53.1%	46.9%	53.1%
1964	325,774	147,562	Mechem, Edwin L.	178,209	Montoya, Joseph M.	3	30,647 D	45.3%	54.7%	45.3%	54.7%
1960	300,551	109,897	Colwes, William F.	190,654	Anderson, Clinton P.		80,757 D	36.6%	63.4%	36.6%	63.4%
1958	203,323	75,827	Atchley, Forrest S.	127,496	Chavez, Dennis		51,669 D	37.3%	62.7%	37.3%	62.7%
1954	194,422	83,071	Mechem, Edwin L.	111,351	Anderson, Clinton P.		28,280 D	42.7%	57.3%	42.7%	57.3%
1952	239,711	117,168	Hurley, Patrick J.	122,543	Chavez, Dennis		5,375 D	48.9%	51.1%	48.9%	51.1%
1948	188,495	80,226	Hurley, Patrick J.	108,269	Anderson, Clinton P.		28,043 D	42.6%	57.4%	42.6%	57.4%
1946	133,282	64,632	Hurley, Patrick J.	68,650	Chavez, Dennis		4,018 D	48.5%	51.5%	48.5%	51.5%

NEW MEXICO

Districts Established January 19, 1982

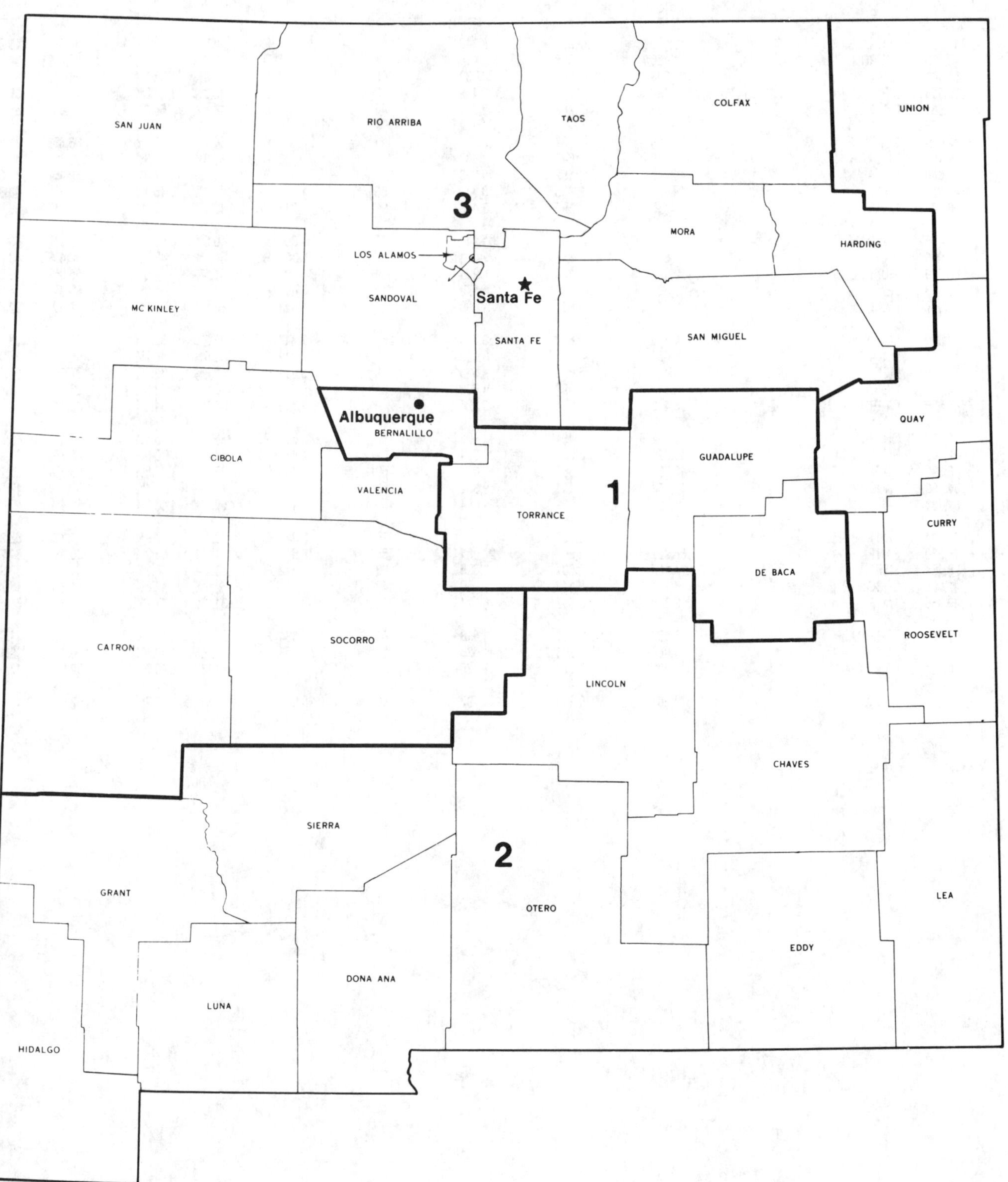

NEW MEXICO

PRESIDENT 1988

1980 Census Population	County	Total Vote	Republican	Democratic	Other	Rep.-Dem. Plurality	Percentage Total Vote Rep.	Total Vote Dem.	Major Vote Rep.	Major Vote Dem.
419,700	BERNALILLO	173,135	92,830	78,346	1,959	14,484 R	53.6%	45.3%	54.2%	45.8%
2,720	CATRON	1,486	925	490	71	435 R	62.2%	33.0%	65.4%	34.6%
51,103	CHAVES	20,303	13,367	6,730	206	6,637 R	65.8%	33.1%	66.5%	33.5%
30,364	CIBOLA	6,137	2,640	3,458	39	818 D	43.0%	56.3%	43.3%	56.7%
13,667	COLFAX	5,085	2,256	2,785	44	529 D	44.4%	54.8%	44.8%	55.2%
42,019	CURRY	12,138	8,032	3,995	111	4,037 R	66.2%	32.9%	66.8%	33.2%
2,454	DE BACA	1,136	643	480	13	163 R	56.6%	42.3%	57.3%	42.7%
96,340	DONA ANA	41,747	21,582	19,608	557	1,974 R	51.7%	47.0%	52.4%	47.6%
47,855	EDDY	18,535	9,805	8,544	186	1,261 R	52.9%	46.1%	53.4%	46.6%
26,204	GRANT	9,735	4,196	5,443	96	1,247 D	43.1%	55.9%	43.5%	56.5%
4,496	GUADALUPE	2,119	861	1,243	15	382 D	40.6%	58.7%	40.9%	59.1%
1,090	HARDING	672	377	291	4	86 R	56.1%	43.3%	56.4%	43.6%
6,049	HIDALGO	2,020	1,100	901	19	199 R	54.5%	44.6%	55.0%	45.0%
55,993	LEA	17,303	11,309	5,879	115	5,430 R	65.4%	34.0%	65.8%	34.2%
10,997	LINCOLN	5,288	3,511	1,690	87	1,821 R	66.4%	32.0%	67.5%	32.5%
17,599	LOS ALAMOS	10,153	6,622	3,275	256	3,347 R	65.2%	32.3%	66.9%	33.1%
15,585	LUNA	6,636	3,415	3,066	155	349 R	51.5%	46.2%	52.7%	47.3%
56,449	MCKINLEY	15,467	5,694	9,595	178	3,901 D	36.8%	62.0%	37.2%	62.8%
4,205	MORA	2,545	923	1,601	21	678 D	36.3%	62.9%	36.6%	63.4%
44,665	OTERO	15,478	9,984	5,284	210	4,700 R	64.5%	34.1%	65.4%	34.6%
10,577	QUAY	4,412	2,454	1,901	57	553 R	55.6%	43.1%	56.3%	43.7%
29,282	RIO ARRIBA	10,626	3,024	7,503	99	4,479 D	28.5%	70.6%	28.7%	71.3%
15,695	ROOSEVELT	5,681	3,589	2,033	59	1,556 R	63.2%	35.8%	63.8%	36.2%
34,799	SANDOVAL	19,011	9,411	9,332	268	79 R	49.5%	49.1%	50.2%	49.8%
81,433	SAN JUAN	27,750	16,202	11,094	454	5,108 R	58.4%	40.0%	59.4%	40.6%
22,751	SAN MIGUEL	9,023	2,763	6,131	129	3,366 D	30.6%	67.9%	31.1%	68.9%
75,360	SANTA FE	36,927	12,891	23,581	455	10,690 D	34.9%	63.9%	35.3%	64.7%
8,454	SIERRA	4,165	2,507	1,595	63	912 R	60.2%	38.3%	61.1%	38.9%
12,566	SOCORRO	6,217	3,114	2,960	143	154 R	50.1%	47.6%	51.3%	48.7%
19,456	TAOS	9,259	2,897	6,271	91	3,374 D	31.3%	67.7%	31.6%	68.4%
7,491	TORRANCE	3,938	2,252	1,618	68	634 R	57.2%	41.1%	58.2%	41.8%
4,725	UNION	1,960	1,291	638	31	653 R	65.9%	32.6%	66.9%	33.1%
30,751	VALENCIA	15,200	7,874	7,136	190	738 R	51.8%	46.9%	52.5%	47.5%
1,302,894	TOTAL	521,287	270,341	244,497	6,449	25,844 R	51.9%	46.9%	52.5%	47.5%

NEW MEXICO

SENATOR 1988

1980 Census Population	County	Total Vote	Republican	Democratic	Other	Rep.-Dem. Plurality	Percentage Total Vote Rep.	Total Vote Dem.	Major Vote Rep.	Major Vote Dem.
419,700	BERNALILLO	170,310	63,322	106,959	29	43,637 D	37.2%	62.8%	37.2%	62.8%
2,720	CATRON	1,422	650	772		122 D	45.7%	54.3%	45.7%	54.3%
51,103	CHAVES	19,872	9,656	10,216		560 D	48.6%	51.4%	48.6%	51.4%
30,364	CIBOLA	6,047	1,696	4,351		2,655 D	28.0%	72.0%	28.0%	72.0%
13,667	COLFAX	4,957	1,517	3,440		1,923 D	30.6%	69.4%	30.6%	69.4%
42,019	CURRY	11,620	5,503	6,117		614 D	47.4%	52.6%	47.4%	52.6%
2,454	DE BACA	1,068	436	632		196 D	40.8%	59.2%	40.8%	59.2%
96,340	DONA ANA	40,150	13,687	26,462	1	12,775 D	34.1%	65.9%	34.1%	65.9%
47,855	EDDY	18,088	7,125	10,963		3,838 D	39.4%	60.6%	39.4%	60.6%
26,204	GRANT	9,589	2,546	7,043		4,497 D	26.6%	73.4%	26.6%	73.4%
4,496	GUADALUPE	2,019	506	1,513		1,007 D	25.1%	74.9%	25.1%	74.9%
1,090	HARDING	660	241	419		178 D	36.5%	63.5%	36.5%	63.5%
6,049	HIDALGO	1,921	647	1,274		627 D	33.7%	66.3%	33.7%	66.3%
55,993	LEA	17,032	8,246	8,786		540 D	48.4%	51.6%	48.4%	51.6%
10,997	LINCOLN	5,147	2,740	2,407		333 R	53.2%	46.8%	53.2%	46.8%
17,599	LOS ALAMOS	9,976	4,307	5,669		1,362 D	43.2%	56.8%	43.2%	56.8%
15,585	LUNA	6,318	2,443	3,875		1,432 D	38.7%	61.3%	38.7%	61.3%
56,449	MCKINLEY	14,420	3,667	10,751	2	7,084 D	25.4%	74.6%	25.4%	74.6%
4,205	MORA	2,491	801	1,690		889 D	32.2%	67.8%	32.2%	67.8%
44,665	OTERO	15,020	6,808	8,212		1,404 D	45.3%	54.7%	45.3%	54.7%
10,577	QUAY	4,179	1,513	2,666		1,153 D	36.2%	63.8%	36.2%	63.8%
29,282	RIO ARRIBA	10,344	2,171	8,171	2	6,000 D	21.0%	79.0%	21.0%	79.0%
15,695	ROOSEVELT	5,438	2,432	3,006		574 D	44.7%	55.3%	44.7%	55.3%
34,799	SANDOVAL	18,641	6,762	11,877	2	5,115 D	36.3%	63.7%	36.3%	63.7%
81,433	SAN JUAN	27,221	12,418	14,803		2,385 D	45.6%	54.4%	45.6%	54.4%
22,751	SAN MIGUEL	8,665	1,912	6,753		4,841 D	22.1%	77.9%	22.1%	77.9%
75,360	SANTA FE	36,289	8,700	27,589		18,889 D	24.0%	76.0%	24.0%	76.0%
8,454	SIERRA	4,061	1,955	2,106		151 D	48.1%	51.9%	48.1%	51.9%
12,566	SOCORRO	6,058	2,122	3,936		1,814 D	35.0%	65.0%	35.0%	65.0%
19,456	TAOS	8,916	2,157	6,759		4,602 D	24.2%	75.8%	24.2%	75.8%
7,491	TORRANCE	3,822	1,597	2,225		628 D	41.8%	58.2%	41.8%	58.2%
4,725	UNION	1,795	703	1,092		389 D	39.2%	60.8%	39.2%	60.8%
30,751	VALENCIA	15,042	5,593	9,449		3,856 D	37.2%	62.8%	37.2%	62.8%
1,302,894	TOTAL	508,598	186,579	321,983	36	135,404 D	36.7%	63.3%	36.7%	63.3%

NEW MEXICO

CONGRESS

CD	Year	Total Vote	Republican Vote	Republican Candidate	Democratic Vote	Democratic Candidate	Other Vote	Rep.-Dem. Plurality	Percentage Total Vote Rep.	Percentage Total Vote Dem.	Percentage Major Vote Rep.	Percentage Major Vote Dem.
1	1988	177,962	89,985	SCHIFF, STEVEN H.	84,138	UDALL, TOM	3,839	5,847 R	50.6%	47.3%	51.7%	48.3%
1	1986	127,632	90,476	LUJAN, MANUEL, JR.	37,138	GARCIA, MANNY	18	53,338 R	70.9%	29.1%	70.9%	29.1%
1	1984	178,342	115,808	LUJAN, MANUEL, JR.	60,598	ASBURY, CHARLES T.	1,936	55,210 R	64.9%	34.0%	65.6%	34.4%
1	1982	141,993	74,459	LUJAN, MANUEL, JR.	67,534	HARTKE, JAN A.		6,925 R	52.4%	47.6%	52.4%	47.6%
2	1988	100,324	100,324	SKEEN, JOSEPH R.				100,324 R	100.0%		100.0%	
2	1986	123,711	77,787	SKEEN, JOSEPH R.	45,924	RUNNELS, MIKE		31,863 R	62.9%	37.1%	62.9%	37.1%
2	1984	156,069	116,006	SKEEN, JOSEPH R.	40,063	YORK, PETER R.		75,943 R	74.3%	25.7%	74.3%	25.7%
2	1982	121,620	71,021	SKEEN, JOSEPH R.	50,599	CHANDLER, CALEB J.		20,422 R	58.4%	41.6%	58.4%	41.6%
3	1988	170,892	45,954	SALAZAR, CECILIA M.	124,938	RICHARDSON, BILL		78,984 D	26.9%	73.1%	26.9%	73.1%
3	1986	134,312	38,552	CARGO, DAVID F.	95,760	RICHARDSON, BILL		57,208 D	28.7%	71.3%	28.7%	71.3%
3	1984	165,209	62,351	GALLEGOS, LOUIS H.	100,470	RICHARDSON, BILL	2,388	38,119 D	37.7%	60.8%	38.3%	61.7%
3	1982	131,293	46,466	CHAMBERS, MARJORIE B.	84,669	RICHARDSON, BILL	158	38,203 D	35.4%	64.5%	35.4%	64.6%

NEW MEXICO

1988 GENERAL ELECTION

President Other vote was 3,268 Libertarian (Paul); 2,237 New Alliance (Fulani); 344 Socialist Workers (Warren); 258 Workers World (Holmes); 249 Prohibition (Dodge); 93 Scattered write-in.

Senator Other vote was Cole (write-in).

Congress Other vote was Libertarian (Parkman) in CD 1.

1988 PRIMARIES

JUNE 7 REPUBLICAN

Senator 35,809 William Valentine; 23,162 Rick Montoya; 16,539 Corky Morris; 6,928 Joseph J. Carraro.

Congress Unopposed in two CD's. Contested as follows:

CD 1 14,028 Steven H. Schiff; 12,801 Edward L. Lujan; 7,393 John A. Budagher.

JUNE 7 DEMOCRATIC

Senator Jeff Bingaman, unopposed.

Congress Unopposed in CD 3. No candidate in CD 2. Contested as follows:

CD 1 14,068 Tom Udall; 11,799 Patricia A. Madrid; 11,776 Jim Baca; 8,772 Steve D. Gallegos; 4,539 Lenton Malry; 2,159 Manny Garcia; 1,158 Steven P. Kramer; 993 Fred F. Rael; 762 Alan Reed; 427 William J. Orona.

NEW YORK

GOVERNOR

Mario M. Cuomo (D). Re-elected 1986 to a four-year term. Previously elected 1982.

SENATORS

Alfonse M. D'Amato (R). Re-elected 1986 to a six-year term. Previously elected 1980.

Daniel P. Moynihan (D). Re-elected 1988 to a six-year term. Previously elected 1982, 1976.

REPRESENTATIVES

1. George J. Hochbrueckner (D)
2. Thomas J. Downey (D)
3. Robert J. Mrazek (D)
4. Norman F. Lent (R)
5. Raymond J. McGrath (R)
6. Floyd H. Flake (D)
7. Gary L. Ackerman (D)
8. James H. Scheuer (D)
9. Thomas J. Manton (D)
10. Charles E. Schumer (D)
11. Edolphus Towns (D)
12. Major R. Owens (D)
13. Stephen J. Solarz (D)
14. Guy V. Molinari (R)
15. S. William Green (R)
16. Charles B. Rangel (D)
17. Theodore S. Weiss (D)
18. Robert Garcia (D)
19. Eliot L. Engel (D)
20. Nita M. Lowey (D)
21. Hamilton Fish (R)
22. Benjamin A. Gilman (R)
23. Michael R. McNulty (D)
24. Gerald B. Solomon (R)
25. Sherwood L. Boehlert (R)
26. David O'B. Martin (R)
27. James T. Walsh (R)
28. Matthew F. McHugh (D)
29. Frank J. Horton (R)
30. Louise M. Slaughter (D)
31. L. William Paxon (R)
32. John J. LaFalce (D)
33. Henry J. Nowak (D)
34. Amory Houghton (R)

POSTWAR VOTE FOR PRESIDENT

		Republican		Democratic				Percentage			
								Total Vote		Major Vote	
Year	Total Vote	Vote	Candidate	Vote	Candidate	Other Vote	Plurality	Rep.	Dem.	Rep.	Dem.
1988	6,485,683	3,081,871	Bush, George	3,347,882	Dukakis, Michael S.	55,930	266,011 D	47.5%	51.6%	47.9%	52.1%
1984	6,806,810	3,664,763	Reagan, Ronald	3,119,609	Mondale, Walter F.	22,438	545,154 R	53.8%	45.8%	54.0%	46.0%
1980	6,201,959	2,893,831	Reagan, Ronald	2,728,372	Carter, Jimmy	579,756	165,459 R	46.7%	44.0%	51.5%	48.5%
1976	6,534,170	3,100,791	Ford, Gerald R.	3,389,558	Carter, Jimmy	43,821	288,767 D	47.5%	51.9%	47.8%	52.2%
1972	7,165,919	4,192,778	Nixon, Richard M.	2,951,084	McGovern, George S.	22,057	1,241,694 R	58.5%	41.2%	58.7%	41.3%
1968	6,791,688	3,007,932	Nixon, Richard M.	3,378,470	Humphrey, Hubert H.	405,286	370,538 D	44.3%	49.7%	47.1%	52.9%
1964	7,166,275	2,243,559	Goldwater, Barry M.	4,913,102	Johnson, Lyndon B.	9,614	2,669,543 D	31.3%	68.6%	31.3%	68.7%
1960	7,291,079	3,446,419	Nixon, Richard M.	3,830,085	Kennedy, John F.	14,575	383,666 D	47.3%	52.5%	47.4%	52.6%
1956	7,095,971	4,345,506	Eisenhower, Dwight D.	2,747,944	Stevenson, Adlai E.	2,521	1,597,562 R	61.2%	38.7%	61.3%	38.7%
1952	7,128,239	3,952,813	Eisenhower, Dwight D.	3,104,601	Stevenson, Adlai E.	70,825	848,212 R	55.5%	43.6%	56.0%	44.0%
1948	6,177,337	2,841,163	Dewey, Thomas E.	2,780,204	Truman, Harry S.	555,970	60,959 R	46.0%	45.0%	50.5%	49.5%

NEW YORK

POSTWAR VOTE FOR GOVERNOR

									Percentage			
	Total	Republican		Democratic		Other	Rep.-Dem.		Total Vote		Major Vote	
Year	Vote	Vote	Candidate	Vote	Candidate	Vote	Plurality		Rep.	Dem.	Rep.	Dem.
1986	4,294,124	1,363,810	O'Rourke, Andrew P.	2,775,229	Cuomo, Mario M.	155,085	1,411,419	D	31.8%	64.6%	32.9%	67.1%
1982	5,254,891	2,494,827	Lehrman, Lew	2,675,213	Cuomo, Mario M.	84,851	180,386	D	47.5%	50.9%	48.3%	51.7%
1978	4,768,820	2,156,404	Duryea, Perry B.	2,429,272	Carey, Hugh L.	183,144	272,868	D	45.2%	50.9%	47.0%	53.0%
1974	5,293,176	2,219,667	Wilson, Malcolm	3,028,503	Carey, Hugh L.	45,006	808,836	D	41.9%	57.2%	42.3%	57.7%
1970	6,013,064	3,151,432	Rockefeller, Nelson A.	2,421,426	Goldberg, Arthur	440,206	730,006	R	52.4%	40.3%	56.5%	43.5%
1966 **	6,031,585	2,690,626	Rockefeller, Nelson A.	2,298,363	O'Connor, Frank D.	1,042,596	392,263	R	44.6%	38.1%	53.9%	46.1%
1962	5,805,631	3,081,587	Rockefeller, Nelson A.	2,552,418	Morgenthau, Robert M.	171,626	529,169	R	53.1%	44.0%	54.7%	45.3%
1958	5,712,665	3,126,929	Rockefeller, Nelson A.	2,553,895	Harriman, Averell	31,841	573,034	R	54.7%	44.7%	55.0%	45.0%
1954	5,161,942	2,549,613	Ives, Irving M.	2,560,738	Harriman, Averell	51,591	11,125	D	49.4%	49.6%	49.9%	50.1%
1950	5,308,889	2,819,523	Dewey, Thomas E.	2,246,855	Lynch, Walter A.	242,511	572,668	R	53.1%	42.3%	55.7%	44.3%
1946	4,964,552	2,825,633	Dewey, Thomas E.	2,138,482	Mead, James M.	437	687,151	R	56.9%	43.1%	56.9%	43.1%

In 1966 other vote was 510,023 Conservative (Adams); 507,234 Liberal (F. D.Roosevelt, Jr.); 12,730 Socialist Labor (Herder); 12,506 Socialist Workers (White) and 103 scattered.

POSTWAR VOTE FOR SENATOR

									Percentage			
	Total	Republican		Democratic		Other	Rep.-Dem.		Total Vote		Major Vote	
Year	Vote	Vote	Candidate	Vote	Candidate	Vote	Plurality		Rep.	Dem.	Rep.	Dem.
1988	6,040,980	1,875,784	McMillan, Robert	4,048,649	Moynihan, Daniel P.	116,547	2,172,865	D	31.1%	67.0%	31.7%	68.3%
1986	4,179,447	2,378,197	D'Amato, Alfonse M.	1,723,216	Green, Mark	78,034	654,981	R	56.9%	41.2%	58.0%	42.0%
1982	4,967,729	1,696,766	Sullivan, Florence M.	3,232,146	Moynihan, Daniel P.	38,817	1,535,380	D	34.2%	65.1%	34.4%	65.6%
1980	6,014,914	2,699,652	D'Amato, Alfonse M.	2,618,661	Holtzman, Elizabeth	696,601	80,991	R	44.9%	43.5%	50.8%	49.2%
1976	6,319,755	2,836,633	Buckley, James L.	3,422,594	Moynihan, Daniel P.	60,528	585,961	D	44.9%	54.2%	45.3%	54.7%
1974	5,163,600	2,340,188	Javits, Jacob K.	1,973,781	Clark, Ramsey	849,631	366,407	R	45.3%	38.2%	54.2%	45.8%
1970 **	5,904,782	1,434,472	Goodell, Charles	2,171,232	Ottinger, Richard L.	2,299,078	736,760	D	24.3%	36.8%	39.8%	60.2%
1968 **	6,581,587	3,269,772	Javits, Jacob K.	2,150,695	O'Dwyer, Paul	1,161,120	1,119,077	R	49.7%	32.7%	60.3%	39.7%
1964	7,151,686	3,104,056	Keating, Kenneth B.	3,823,749	Kennedy, Robert F.	223,881	719,693	D	43.4%	53.5%	44.8%	55.2%
1962	5,700,186	3,269,417	Javits, Jacob K.	2,289,341	Donovan, James B.	141,428	980,076	R	57.4%	40.2%	58.8%	41.2%
1958	5,602,088	2,842,942	Keating, Kenneth B.	2,709,950	Hogan, Frank S.	49,196	132,992	R	50.7%	48.4%	51.2%	48.8%
1956	6,991,136	3,723,933	Javits, Jacob K.	3,265,159	Wagner, Robert F.	2,044	458,774	R	53.3%	46.7%	53.3%	46.7%
1952	6,980,259	3,853,934	Ives, Irving M.	2,521,736	Cashmore, John	604,589	1,332,198	R	55.2%	36.1%	60.4%	39.6%
1950	5,228,403	2,367,353	Hanley, Joe R.	2,632,313	Lehman, Herbert H.	228,737	264,960	D	45.3%	50.3%	47.4%	52.6%
1949 S	4,966,878	2,384,381	Dulles, John Foster	2,582,438	Lehman, Herbert H.	59	198,057	D	48.0%	52.0%	48.0%	52.0%
1946	4,867,564	2,559,365	Ives, Irving M.	2,308,112	Lehman, Herbert H.	87	251,253	R	52.6%	47.4%	52.6%	47.4%

The 1949 election was for a short term to fill a vacancy. In 1968 other vote was 1,139,402 Conservative (Buckley); 8,775 Freedom and Peace (Ferguson); 7,964 Socialist Labor (Emanuel); 4,979 Socialist Workers (Garza). In 1970 James L. Buckley, the Conservative candidate, polled 2,288,190 votes (38.8% of the total vote) and won the election with a 116,958 plurality.

NEW YORK

Districts Established September 27, 1983

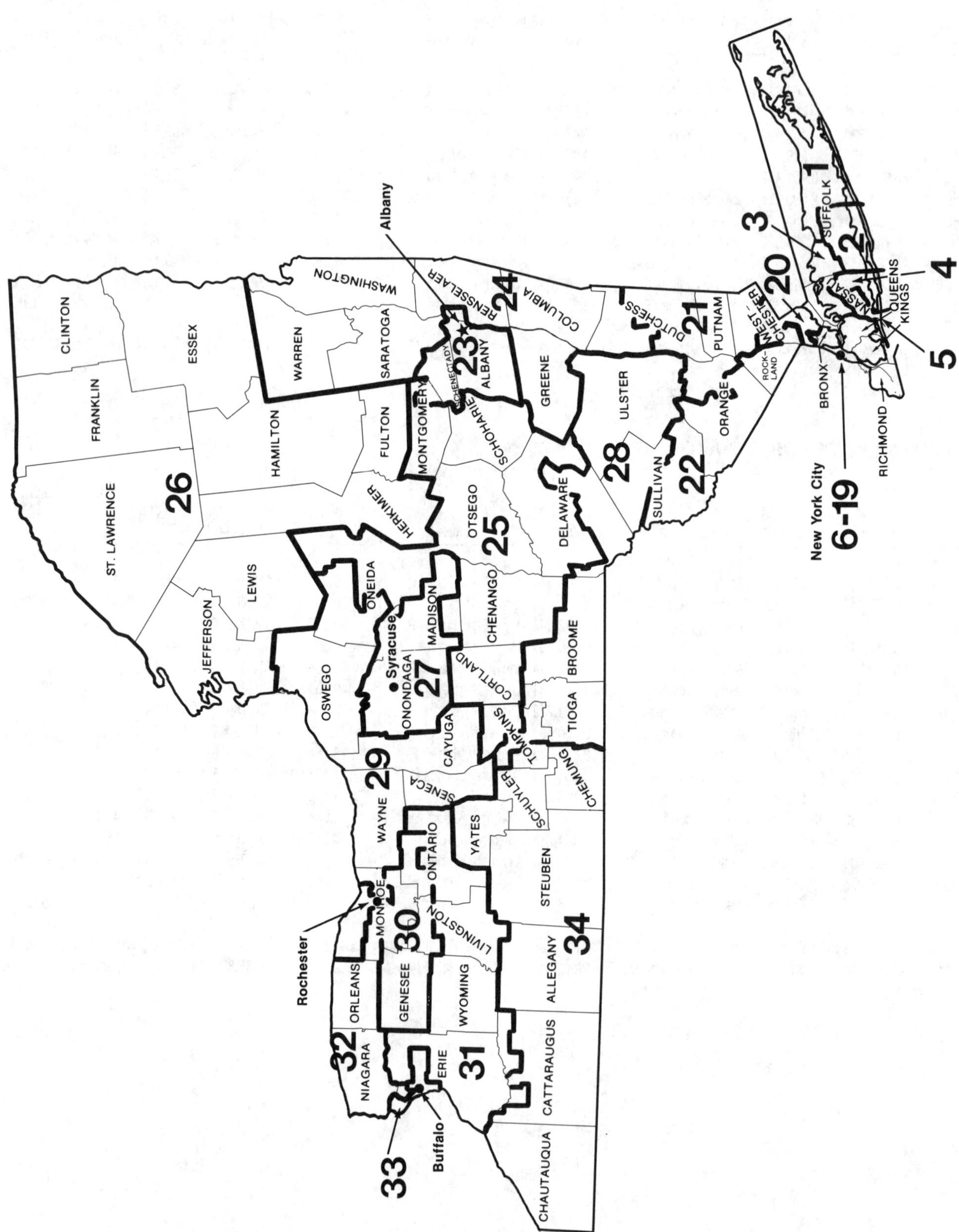

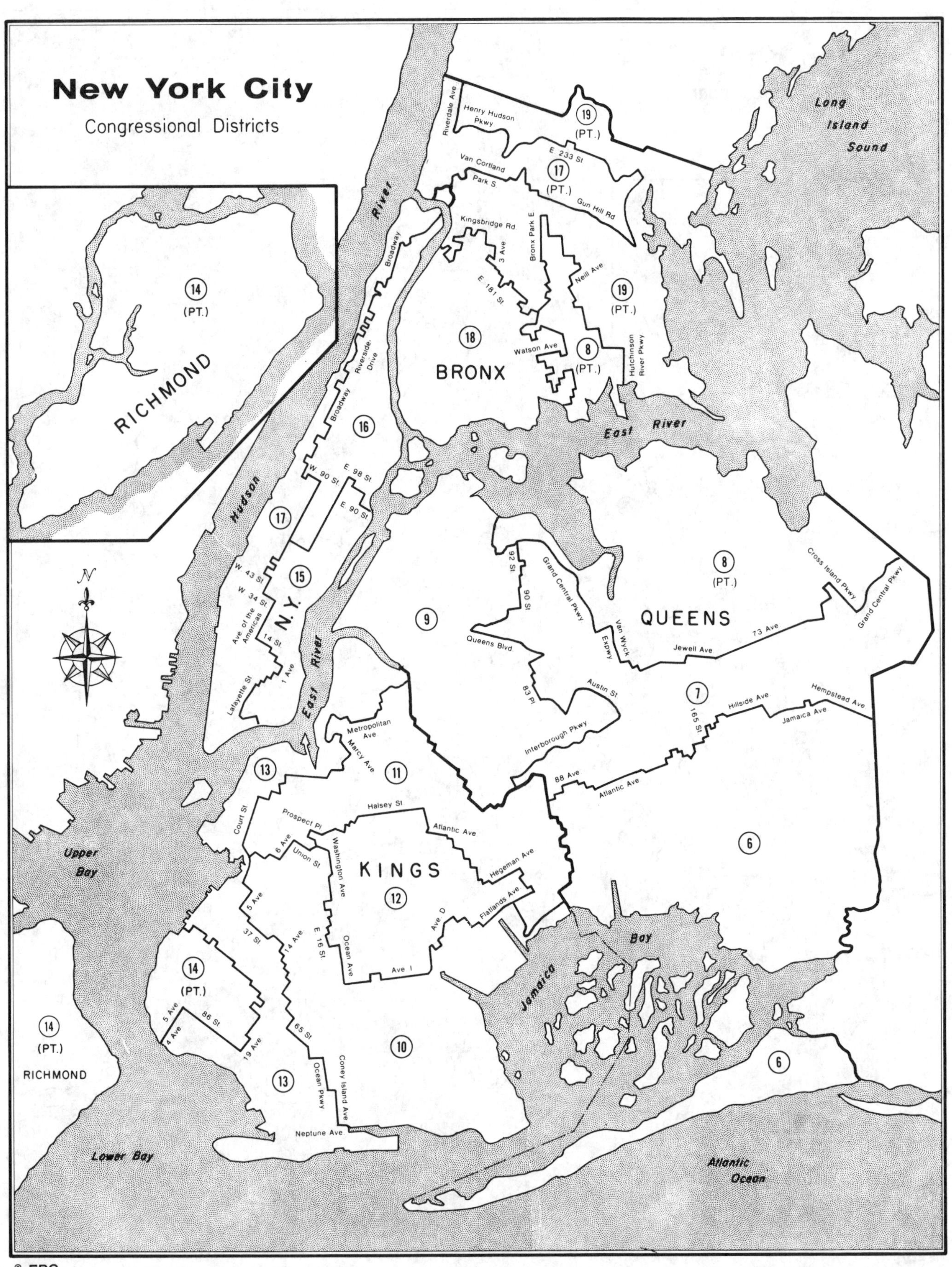
New York City
Congressional Districts
RICHMOND
14 (PT.)
BRONX
QUEENS
KINGS
N.Y.
Long Island Sound
East River
Hudson River
Upper Bay
Lower Bay
Jamaica Bay
Atlantic Ocean
19 (PT.)
17 (PT.)
18
8 (PT.)
16
17
15
9
7
6
11
12
13
10
Riverdale Ave
Henry Hudson Pkwy
E 233 St
Van Cortland Park S
Gun Hill Rd
Kingsbridge Rd
3 Ave
E 181 St
Bronx Park E
Neill Ave
Watson Ave
Hutchinson River Pkwy
Broadway
Riverside Drive
W 90 St
E 98 St
E 90 St
W 43 St
W 34 St
Ave of the Americas
14 St
1 Ave
Lafayette St
92 St
90 St
Grand Central Pkwy
Van Wyck Expwy
Jewell Ave
73 Ave
Cross Island Pkwy
Queens Blvd
83 Pl
Austin St
Interborough Pkwy
165 St
Hillside Ave
Hempstead Ave
Jamaica Ave
88 Ave
Atlantic Ave
Metropolitan Ave
Marcy Ave
Halsey St
Prospect Pl
Court St
6 Ave
Union St
Washington Ave
Hegeman Ave
Flatlands Ave
5 Ave
37 St
14 Ave
E 16 St
Ocean Ave
Ave D
Ave I
4 Ave
86 St
19 Ave
65 St
Ocean Pkwy
Coney Island Ave
Neptune Ave

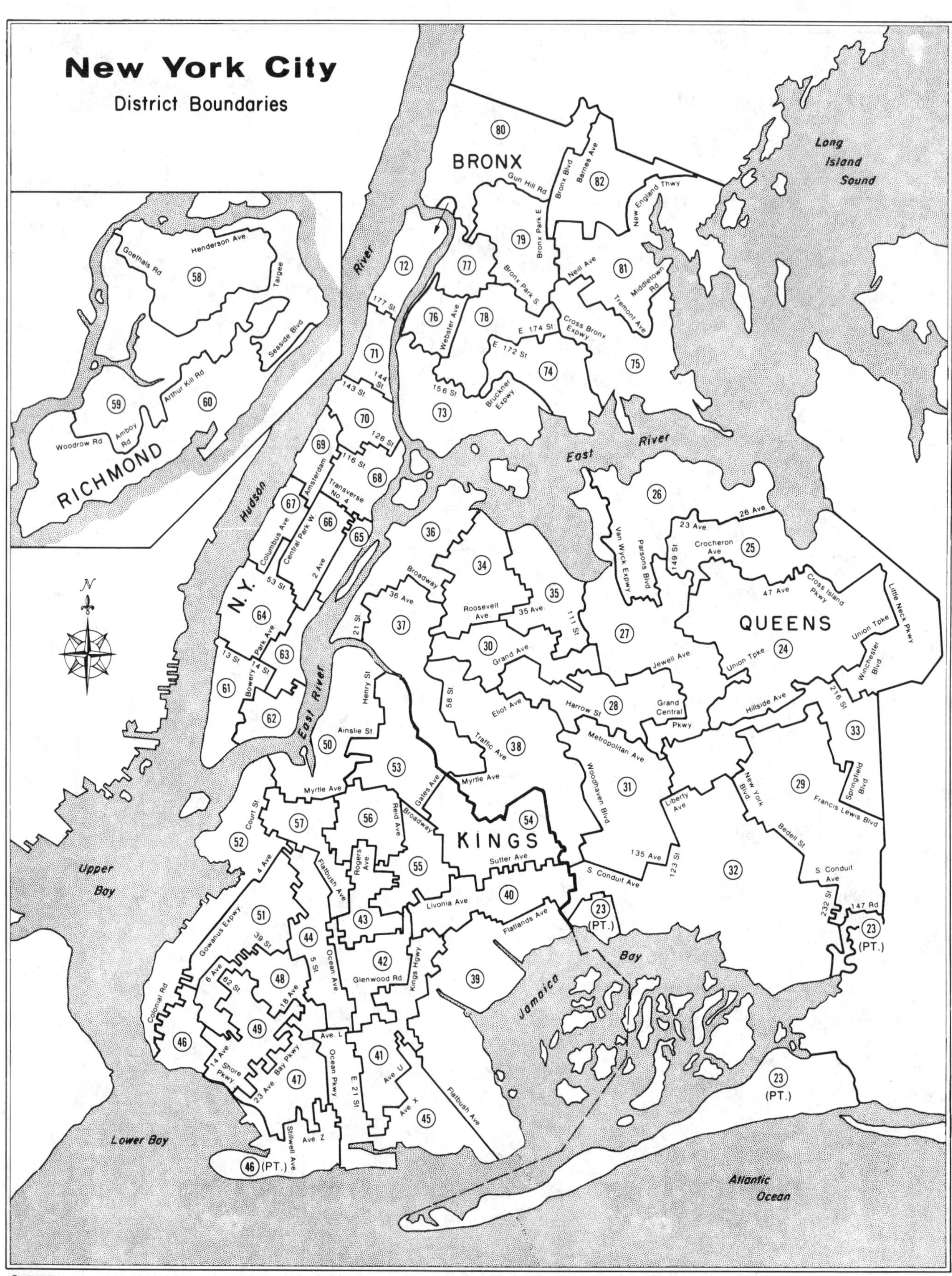
New York City
District Boundaries
BRONX
QUEENS
KINGS
N.Y.
RICHMOND
Long Island Sound
East River
Hudson River
Upper Bay
Lower Bay
Jamaica Bay
Atlantic Ocean
N

NEW YORK

PRESIDENT 1988

1980 Census Population	County	Total Vote	Republican	Democratic	Other	Rep.-Dem. Plurality	Percentage Total Vote Rep.	Percentage Total Vote Dem.	Percentage Major Vote Rep.	Percentage Major Vote Dem.
285,909	ALBANY	147,461	59,534	86,564	1,363	27,030 D	40.4%	58.7%	40.7%	59.3%
51,742	ALLEGANY	17,626	11,880	5,614	132	6,266 R	67.4%	31.9%	67.9%	32.1%
1,168,972	BRONX	298,081	76,043	218,245	3,793	142,202 D	25.5%	73.2%	25.8%	74.2%
213,648	BROOME	96,365	47,610	48,130	625	520 D	49.4%	49.9%	49.7%	50.3%
85,697	CATTARAUGUS	32,428	19,691	12,447	290	7,244 R	60.7%	38.4%	61.3%	38.7%
79,894	CAYUGA	32,285	16,934	15,044	307	1,890 R	52.5%	46.6%	53.0%	47.0%
146,925	CHAUTAUQUA	57,867	31,642	25,814	411	5,828 R	54.7%	44.6%	55.1%	44.9%
97,656	CHEMUNG	37,139	20,951	15,966	222	4,985 R	56.4%	43.0%	56.8%	43.2%
49,344	CHENANGO	19,902	11,727	8,021	154	3,706 R	58.9%	40.3%	59.4%	40.6%
80,750	CLINTON	28,563	15,702	12,670	191	3,032 R	55.0%	44.4%	55.3%	44.7%
59,487	COLUMBIA	26,924	15,111	11,585	228	3,526 R	56.1%	43.0%	56.6%	43.4%
48,820	CORTLAND	18,769	10,934	7,673	162	3,261 R	58.3%	40.9%	58.8%	41.2%
46,824	DELAWARE	19,010	11,391	7,463	156	3,928 R	59.9%	39.3%	60.4%	39.6%
245,055	DUTCHESS	101,959	62,165	38,968	826	23,197 R	61.0%	38.2%	61.5%	38.5%
1,015,472	ERIE	430,792	188,796	238,779	3,217	49,983 D	43.8%	55.4%	44.2%	55.8%
36,176	ESSEX	17,113	10,350	6,623	140	3,727 R	60.5%	38.7%	61.0%	39.0%
44,929	FRANKLIN	17,192	9,135	7,928	129	1,207 R	53.1%	46.1%	53.5%	46.5%
55,153	FULTON	20,931	11,757	9,012	162	2,745 R	56.2%	43.1%	56.6%	43.4%
59,400	GENESEE	24,332	14,182	9,945	205	4,237 R	58.3%	40.9%	58.8%	41.2%
40,861	GREENE	19,319	11,874	7,265	180	4,609 R	61.5%	37.6%	62.0%	38.0%
5,034	HAMILTON	3,317	2,320	976	21	1,344 R	69.9%	29.4%	70.4%	29.6%
66,714	HERKIMER	28,022	15,104	12,694	224	2,410 R	53.9%	45.3%	54.3%	45.7%
88,151	JEFFERSON	33,622	19,304	14,137	181	5,167 R	57.4%	42.0%	57.7%	42.3%
2,230,936	KINGS	549,019	178,961	363,916	6,142	184,955 D	32.6%	66.3%	33.0%	67.0%
25,035	LEWIS	10,138	5,787	4,252	99	1,535 R	57.1%	41.9%	57.6%	42.4%
57,006	LIVINGSTON	23,697	14,004	9,506	187	4,498 R	59.1%	40.1%	59.6%	40.4%
65,150	MADISON	25,754	14,902	10,665	187	4,237 R	57.9%	41.4%	58.3%	41.7%
702,238	MONROE	311,466	155,271	153,650	2,545	1,621 R	49.9%	49.3%	50.3%	49.7%
53,439	MONTGOMERY	22,685	11,128	11,371	186	243 D	49.1%	50.1%	49.5%	50.5%
1,321,582	NASSAU	592,418	337,430	250,130	4,858	87,300 R	57.0%	42.2%	57.4%	42.6%
1,428,285	NEW YORK	506,551	115,927	385,675	4,949	269,748 D	22.9%	76.1%	23.1%	76.9%
227,354	NIAGARA	86,868	42,537	43,801	530	1,264 D	49.0%	50.4%	49.3%	50.7%
253,466	ONEIDA	103,461	55,039	47,665	757	7,374 R	53.2%	46.1%	53.6%	46.4%
463,920	ONONDAGA	200,485	104,080	94,751	1,654	9,329 R	51.9%	47.3%	52.3%	47.7%
88,909	ONTARIO	39,435	21,780	17,341	314	4,439 R	55.2%	44.0%	55.7%	44.3%
259,603	ORANGE	104,810	65,446	38,465	899	26,981 R	62.4%	36.7%	63.0%	37.0%
38,496	ORLEANS	15,055	9,028	5,913	114	3,115 R	60.0%	39.3%	60.4%	39.6%
113,901	OSWEGO	44,211	25,362	18,430	419	6,932 R	57.4%	41.7%	57.9%	42.1%
59,075	OTSEGO	24,335	13,021	11,069	245	1,952 R	53.5%	45.5%	54.1%	45.9%
77,193	PUTNAM	36,500	24,086	12,158	256	11,928 R	66.0%	33.3%	66.5%	33.5%
1,891,325	QUEENS	546,729	217,049	325,147	4,533	108,098 D	39.7%	59.5%	40.0%	60.0%
151,966	RENSSELAER	69,197	35,412	33,066	719	2,346 R	51.2%	47.8%	51.7%	48.3%
352,121	RICHMOND	125,975	77,427	47,812	736	29,615 R	61.5%	38.0%	61.8%	38.2%
259,530	ROCKLAND	112,301	63,825	47,634	842	16,191 R	56.8%	42.4%	57.3%	42.7%
114,254	ST. LAWRENCE	39,481	20,290	18,921	270	1,369 R	51.4%	47.9%	51.7%	48.3%
153,759	SARATOGA	75,788	43,498	31,684	606	11,814 R	57.4%	41.8%	57.9%	42.1%
149,946	SCHENECTADY	70,386	33,364	36,483	539	3,119 D	47.4%	51.8%	47.8%	52.2%
29,710	SCHOHARIE	12,536	7,008	5,389	139	1,619 R	55.9%	43.0%	56.5%	43.5%
17,686	SCHUYLER	7,242	4,291	2,900	51	1,391 R	59.3%	40.0%	59.7%	40.3%
33,733	SENECA	13,571	7,221	6,215	135	1,006 R	53.2%	45.8%	53.7%	46.3%
99,217	STEUBEN	38,466	25,359	12,824	283	12,535 R	65.9%	33.3%	66.4%	33.6%
1,284,231	SUFFOLK	514,350	311,242	199,215	3,893	112,027 R	60.5%	38.7%	61.0%	39.0%
65,155	SULLIVAN	27,568	15,713	11,635	220	4,078 R	57.0%	42.2%	57.5%	42.5%
49,812	TIOGA	20,946	12,670	8,102	174	4,568 R	60.5%	38.7%	61.0%	39.0%
87,085	TOMPKINS	36,699	14,932	21,455	312	6,523 D	40.7%	58.5%	41.0%	59.0%
158,158	ULSTER	72,557	41,173	30,744	640	10,429 R	56.7%	42.4%	57.3%	42.7%
54,854	WARREN	24,622	15,860	8,580	182	7,280 R	64.4%	34.8%	64.9%	35.1%
54,795	WASHINGTON	22,515	14,103	8,201	211	5,902 R	62.6%	36.4%	63.2%	36.8%
84,581	WAYNE	33,902	20,613	12,959	330	7,654 R	60.8%	38.2%	61.4%	38.6%
866,599	WESTCHESTER	371,008	197,956	169,860	3,192	28,096 R	53.4%	45.8%	53.8%	46.2%

NEW YORK

PRESIDENT 1988

1980 Census Population	County	Total Vote	Republican	Democratic	Other	Rep.-Dem. Plurality	Percentage Total Vote Rep.	Percentage Total Vote Dem.	Percentage Major Vote Rep.	Percentage Major Vote Dem.
39,895	WYOMING	14,863	9,451	5,228	184	4,223 R	63.6%	35.2%	64.4%	35.6%
21,459	YATES	9,074	5,488	3,507	79	1,981 R	60.5%	38.6%	61.0%	39.0%
17,558,072	TOTAL	6,485,683	3,081,871	3,347,882	55,930	266,011 D	47.5%	51.6%	47.9%	52.1%

NEW YORK

SENATOR 1988

1980 Census Population	County	Total Vote	Republican	Democratic	Other	Rep.-Dem. Plurality	Percentage Total Vote Rep.	Percentage Total Vote Dem.	Percentage Major Vote Rep.	Percentage Major Vote Dem.
285,909	ALBANY	140,320	35,853	101,955	2,512	66,102 D	25.6%	72.7%	26.0%	74.0%
51,742	ALLEGANY	16,262	7,809	8,094	359	285 D	48.0%	49.8%	49.1%	50.9%
1,168,972	BRONX	262,609	40,055	217,852	4,702	177,797 D	15.3%	83.0%	15.5%	84.5%
213,648	BROOME	88,132	29,286	56,885	1,961	27,599 D	33.2%	64.5%	34.0%	66.0%
85,697	CATTARAUGUS	29,717	12,172	16,787	758	4,615 D	41.0%	56.5%	42.0%	58.0%
79,894	CAYUGA	30,283	11,142	18,515	626	7,373 D	36.8%	61.1%	37.6%	62.4%
146,925	CHAUTAUQUA	54,333	19,316	33,887	1,130	14,571 D	35.6%	62.4%	36.3%	63.7%
97,656	CHEMUNG	34,204	14,581	18,804	819	4,223 D	42.6%	55.0%	43.7%	56.3%
49,344	CHENANGO	18,673	8,623	9,594	456	971 D	46.2%	51.4%	47.3%	52.7%
80,750	CLINTON	25,881	10,337	14,739	805	4,402 D	39.9%	56.9%	41.2%	58.8%
59,487	COLUMBIA	25,133	10,604	14,025	504	3,421 D	42.2%	55.8%	43.1%	56.9%
48,820	CORTLAND	17,498	7,695	9,367	436	1,672 D	44.0%	53.5%	45.1%	54.9%
46,824	DELAWARE	17,660	7,627	9,669	364	2,042 D	43.2%	54.8%	44.1%	55.9%
245,055	DUTCHESS	95,257	41,231	51,928	2,098	10,697 D	43.3%	54.5%	44.3%	55.7%
1,015,472	ERIE	393,614	95,112	289,626	8,876	194,514 D	24.2%	73.6%	24.7%	75.3%
36,176	ESSEX	15,341	7,417	7,530	394	113 D	48.3%	49.1%	49.6%	50.4%
44,929	FRANKLIN	15,545	6,225	8,892	428	2,667 D	40.0%	57.2%	41.2%	58.8%
55,153	FULTON	19,273	7,905	10,951	417	3,046 D	41.0%	56.8%	41.9%	58.1%
59,400	GENESEE	22,446	8,534	13,394	518	4,860 D	38.0%	59.7%	38.9%	61.1%
40,861	GREENE	17,994	8,728	8,935	331	207 D	48.5%	49.7%	49.4%	50.6%
5,034	HAMILTON	3,061	1,752	1,241	68	511 R	57.2%	40.5%	58.5%	41.5%
66,714	HERKIMER	25,206	10,236	14,338	632	4,102 D	40.6%	56.9%	41.7%	58.3%
88,151	JEFFERSON	30,971	12,955	17,311	705	4,356 D	41.8%	55.9%	42.8%	57.2%
2,230,936	KINGS	495,626	84,189	402,987	8,450	318,798 D	17.0%	81.3%	17.3%	82.7%
25,035	LEWIS	9,220	3,971	5,032	217	1,061 D	43.1%	54.6%	44.1%	55.9%
57,006	LIVINGSTON	22,227	9,211	12,598	418	3,387 D	41.4%	56.7%	42.2%	57.8%
65,150	MADISON	23,566	8,633	14,434	499	5,801 D	36.6%	61.2%	37.4%	62.6%
702,238	MONROE	289,424	86,519	197,697	5,208	111,178 D	29.9%	68.3%	30.4%	69.6%
53,439	MONTGOMERY	20,876	7,133	13,217	526	6,084 D	34.2%	63.3%	35.1%	64.9%
1,321,582	NASSAU	569,875	237,326	322,191	10,358	84,865 D	41.6%	56.5%	42.4%	57.6%
1,428,285	NEW YORK	476,787	61,793	405,962	9,032	344,169 D	13.0%	85.1%	13.2%	86.8%
227,354	NIAGARA	79,879	22,569	55,566	1,744	32,997 D	28.3%	69.6%	28.9%	71.1%
253,466	ONEIDA	95,252	35,735	57,250	2,267	21,515 D	37.5%	60.1%	38.4%	61.6%
463,920	ONONDAGA	189,041	54,282	131,317	3,442	77,035 D	28.7%	69.5%	29.2%	70.8%
88,909	ONTARIO	36,954	14,427	21,974	553	7,547 D	39.0%	59.5%	39.6%	60.4%
259,603	ORANGE	98,236	38,050	57,920	2,266	19,870 D	38.7%	59.0%	39.6%	60.4%
38,496	ORLEANS	13,765	5,410	8,029	326	2,619 D	39.3%	58.3%	40.3%	59.7%
113,901	OSWEGO	40,398	16,699	22,804	895	6,105 D	41.3%	56.4%	42.3%	57.7%
59,075	OTSEGO	22,713	9,012	13,159	542	4,147 D	39.7%	57.9%	40.6%	59.4%
77,193	PUTNAM	34,251	15,835	17,593	823	1,758 D	46.2%	51.4%	47.4%	52.6%
1,891,325	QUEENS	512,439	119,525	386,168	6,746	266,643 D	23.3%	75.4%	23.6%	76.4%
151,966	RENSSELAER	65,390	23,267	40,724	1,399	17,457 D	35.6%	62.3%	36.4%	63.6%
352,121	RICHMOND	117,231	42,509	72,682	2,040	30,173 D	36.3%	62.0%	36.9%	63.1%
259,530	ROCKLAND	106,490	37,168	67,055	2,267	29,887 D	34.9%	63.0%	35.7%	64.3%
114,254	ST. LAWRENCE	36,552	13,514	22,367	671	8,853 D	37.0%	61.2%	37.7%	62.3%
153,759	SARATOGA	71,220	30,885	39,060	1,275	8,175 D	43.4%	54.8%	44.2%	55.8%
149,946	SCHENECTADY	66,830	23,327	42,321	1,182	18,994 D	34.9%	63.3%	35.5%	64.5%
29,710	SCHOHARIE	11,774	4,995	6,492	287	1,497 D	42.4%	55.1%	43.5%	56.5%
17,686	SCHUYLER	6,549	3,121	3,274	154	153 D	47.7%	50.0%	48.8%	51.2%
33,733	SENECA	12,680	4,798	7,574	308	2,776 D	37.8%	59.7%	38.8%	61.2%
99,217	STEUBEN	34,711	16,946	16,971	794	25 D	48.8%	48.9%	50.0%	50.0%
1,284,231	SUFFOLK	487,729	206,355	271,898	9,476	65,543 D	42.3%	55.7%	43.1%	56.9%
65,155	SULLIVAN	25,643	9,966	15,131	546	5,165 D	38.9%	59.0%	39.7%	60.3%
49,812	TIOGA	18,838	8,435	9,772	631	1,337 D	44.8%	51.9%	46.3%	53.7%
87,085	TOMPKINS	33,500	9,670	23,070	760	13,400 D	28.9%	68.9%	29.5%	70.5%
158,158	ULSTER	67,917	26,204	39,770	1,943	13,566 D	38.6%	58.6%	39.7%	60.3%
54,854	WARREN	22,796	10,622	11,877	297	1,255 D	46.6%	52.1%	47.2%	52.8%
54,795	WASHINGTON	20,611	9,838	10,350	423	512 D	47.7%	50.2%	48.7%	51.3%
84,581	WAYNE	31,192	13,109	17,452	631	4,343 D	42.0%	56.0%	42.9%	57.1%
866,599	WESTCHESTER	351,093	125,618	218,810	6,665	93,192 D	35.8%	62.3%	36.5%	63.5%

NEW YORK

SENATOR 1988

1980 Census Population	County	Total Vote	Republican	Democratic	Other	Rep.-Dem. Plurality	Percentage Total Vote Rep.	Total Vote Dem.	Major Vote Rep.	Major Vote Dem.
39,895	WYOMING	13,836	5,995	7,434	407	1,439 D	43.3%	53.7%	44.6%	55.4%
21,459	YATES	8,456	3,928	4,348	180	420 D	46.5%	51.4%	47.5%	52.5%
17,558,072	TOTAL	6,040,980	1,875,784	4,048,649	116,547	2,172,865 D	31.1%	67.0%	31.7%	68.3%

NEW YORK CITY

BRONX COUNTY

PRESIDENT 1988

1980 Census Population	Assembly District	Total Vote	Republican	Democratic	Other	Rep.-Dem. Plurality	Percentage Total Vote Rep.	Total Vote Dem.	Major Vote Rep.	Major Vote Dem.
116,902	DISTRICT 73	27,583	3,161	23,998	424	20,837 D	11.5%	87.0%	11.6%	88.4%
116,909	DISTRICT 74	27,242	4,504	22,367	371	17,863 D	16.5%	82.1%	16.8%	83.2%
116,924	DISTRICT 75	34,303	15,674	18,232	397	2,558 D	45.7%	53.1%	46.2%	53.8%
116,909	DISTRICT 76	21,082	2,103	18,604	375	16,501 D	10.0%	88.2%	10.2%	89.8%
116,908	DISTRICT 77	20,816	3,334	17,206	276	13,872 D	16.0%	82.7%	16.2%	83.8%
116,909	DISTRICT 78	26,705	3,207	23,104	394	19,897 D	12.0%	86.5%	12.2%	87.8%
116,909	DISTRICT 79	29,453	9,190	20,002	261	10,812 D	31.2%	67.9%	31.5%	68.5%
116,911	DISTRICT 80	39,710	14,001	25,381	328	11,380 D	35.3%	63.9%	35.6%	64.4%
116,925	DISTRICT 81	41,621	15,961	25,279	381	9,318 D	38.3%	60.7%	38.7%	61.3%
116,909	DISTRICT 82	29,566	4,908	24,072	586	19,164 D	16.6%	81.4%	16.9%	83.1%
1,169,115	TOTAL	298,081	76,043	218,245	3,793	142,202 D	25.5%	73.2%	25.8%	74.2%

NEW YORK CITY

KINGS COUNTY

PRESIDENT 1988

1980 Census Population	Assembly District	Total Vote	Republican	Democratic	Other	Rep.-Dem. Plurality	Percentage Total Vote Rep.	Total Vote Dem.	Major Vote Rep.	Major Vote Dem.
117,424	DISTRICT 39	34,627	15,318	19,142	167	3,824 D	44.2%	55.3%	44.5%	55.5%
117,423	DISTRICT 40	23,774	1,590	21,749	435	20,159 D	6.7%	91.5%	6.8%	93.2%
117,426	DISTRICT 41	39,012	16,784	21,942	286	5,158 D	43.0%	56.2%	43.3%	56.7%
117,425	DISTRICT 42	21,085	4,366	16,288	431	11,922 D	20.7%	77.2%	21.1%	78.9%
117,416	DISTRICT 43	20,575	2,791	17,231	553	14,440 D	13.6%	83.7%	13.9%	86.1%
117,435	DISTRICT 44	34,006	10,779	22,927	300	12,148 D	31.7%	67.4%	32.0%	68.0%
117,408	DISTRICT 45	37,088	16,177	20,759	152	4,582 D	43.6%	56.0%	43.8%	56.2%
117,414	DISTRICT 46	35,714	13,717	21,790	207	8,073 D	38.4%	61.0%	38.6%	61.4%
117,402	DISTRICT 47	28,886	13,825	14,934	127	1,109 D	47.9%	51.7%	48.1%	51.9%
117,414	DISTRICT 48	28,205	18,346	9,735	124	8,611 R	65.0%	34.5%	65.3%	34.7%
117,390	DISTRICT 49	26,856	15,639	11,104	113	4,535 R	58.2%	41.3%	58.5%	41.5%
117,418	DISTRICT 50	25,786	10,094	15,455	237	5,361 D	39.1%	59.9%	39.5%	60.5%
117,420	DISTRICT 51	29,370	9,978	19,109	283	9,131 D	34.0%	65.1%	34.3%	65.7%
117,416	DISTRICT 52	40,801	15,628	24,819	354	9,191 D	38.3%	60.8%	38.6%	61.4%
117,421	DISTRICT 53	23,114	4,652	18,258	204	13,606 D	20.1%	79.0%	20.3%	79.7%
117,420	DISTRICT 54	19,731	3,728	15,751	252	12,023 D	18.9%	79.8%	19.1%	80.9%
117,422	DISTRICT 55	24,527	1,333	22,657	537	21,324 D	5.4%	92.4%	5.6%	94.4%
117,420	DISTRICT 56	25,836	1,449	23,744	643	22,295 D	5.6%	91.9%	5.8%	94.2%
117,422	DISTRICT 57	30,026	2,767	26,522	737	23,755 D	9.2%	88.3%	9.4%	90.6%
2,230,936	TOTAL	549,019	178,961	363,916	6,142	184,955 D	32.6%	66.3%	33.0%	67.0%

NEW YORK CITY

NEW YORK COUNTY

PRESIDENT 1988

1980 Census Population	Assembly District	Total Vote	Republican	Democratic	Other	Rep.-Dem. Plurality	Percentage Total Vote Rep.	Total Vote Dem.	Major Vote Rep.	Major Vote Dem.
118,950	DISTRICT 61	56,188	10,575	45,180	433	34,605 D	18.8%	80.4%	19.0%	81.0%
118,951	DISTRICT 62	26,957	6,400	20,329	228	13,929 D	23.7%	75.4%	23.9%	76.1%
118,962	DISTRICT 63	52,679	15,529	36,763	387	21,234 D	29.5%	69.8%	29.7%	70.3%
118,973	DISTRICT 64	49,224	10,744	38,069	411	27,325 D	21.8%	77.3%	22.0%	78.0%
119,036	DISTRICT 65	52,646	18,502	33,919	225	15,417 D	35.1%	64.4%	35.3%	64.7%
118,984	DISTRICT 66	49,148	20,058	28,913	177	8,855 D	40.8%	58.8%	41.0%	59.0%
118,949	DISTRICT 67	55,197	11,335	43,532	330	32,197 D	20.5%	78.9%	20.7%	79.3%
118,965	DISTRICT 68	31,608	3,772	27,303	533	23,531 D	11.9%	86.4%	12.1%	87.9%
118,956	DISTRICT 69	46,974	6,407	40,036	531	33,629 D	13.6%	85.2%	13.8%	86.2%
118,963	DISTRICT 70	29,777	1,800	27,105	872	25,305 D	6.0%	91.0%	6.2%	93.8%
118,908	DISTRICT 71	27,054	2,887	23,611	556	20,724 D	10.7%	87.3%	10.9%	89.1%
118,936	DISTRICT 72	29,099	7,918	20,915	266	12,997 D	27.2%	71.9%	27.5%	72.5%
1,427,533	TOTAL	506,551	115,927	385,675	4,949	269,748 D	22.9%	76.1%	23.1%	76.9%

NEW YORK CITY

QUEENS COUNTY

PRESIDENT 1988

1980 Census Population	Assembly District	Total Vote	Republican	Democratic	Other	Rep.-Dem. Plurality	Percentage Total Vote Rep.	Total Vote Dem.	Major Vote Rep.	Major Vote Dem.
118,206	DISTRICT 23	33,523	13,875	19,298	350	5,423 D	41.4%	57.6%	41.8%	58.2%
118,191	DISTRICT 24	47,492	19,534	27,760	198	8,226 D	41.1%	58.5%	41.3%	58.7%
118,200	DISTRICT 25	44,157	24,208	19,639	310	4,569 R	54.8%	44.5%	55.2%	44.8%
118,198	DISTRICT 26	38,696	16,145	22,340	211	6,195 D	41.7%	57.7%	42.0%	58.0%
118,201	DISTRICT 27	36,046	14,319	21,545	182	7,226 D	39.7%	59.8%	39.9%	60.1%
118,218	DISTRICT 28	42,594	17,494	24,925	175	7,431 D	41.1%	58.5%	41.2%	58.8%
118,207	DISTRICT 29	36,148	3,741	31,692	715	27,951 D	10.3%	87.7%	10.6%	89.4%
118,215	DISTRICT 30	27,900	12,419	15,371	110	2,952 D	44.5%	55.1%	44.7%	55.3%
118,210	DISTRICT 31	32,253	17,793	14,277	183	3,516 R	55.2%	44.3%	55.5%	44.5%
118,206	DISTRICT 32	35,805	6,770	28,432	603	21,662 D	18.9%	79.4%	19.2%	80.8%
118,203	DISTRICT 33	26,197	5,015	20,750	432	15,735 D	19.1%	79.2%	19.5%	80.5%
118,216	DISTRICT 34	31,647	14,271	17,174	202	2,903 D	45.1%	54.3%	45.4%	54.6%
118,203	DISTRICT 35	20,522	5,276	14,970	276	9,694 D	25.7%	72.9%	26.1%	73.9%
118,217	DISTRICT 36	31,128	10,879	20,045	204	9,166 D	34.9%	64.4%	35.2%	64.8%
118,217	DISTRICT 37	27,301	12,551	14,549	201	1,998 D	46.0%	53.3%	46.3%	53.7%
118,217	DISTRICT 38	35,320	22,759	12,380	181	10,379 R	64.4%	35.1%	64.8%	35.2%
1,891,325	TOTAL	546,729	217,049	325,147	4,533	108,098 D	39.7%	59.5%	40.0%	60.0%

NEW YORK CITY

RICHMOND COUNTY

PRESIDENT 1988

1980 Census Population	Assembly District	Total Vote	Republican	Democratic	Other	Rep.-Dem. Plurality	Percentage Total Vote Rep.	Percentage Total Vote Dem.	Percentage Major Vote Rep.	Percentage Major Vote Dem.
117,373	DISTRICT 58	40,192	22,847	17,065	280	5,782 R	56.8%	42.5%	57.2%	42.8%
117,376	DISTRICT 59	39,151	21,789	17,115	247	4,674 R	55.7%	43.7%	56.0%	44.0%
117,372	DISTRICT 60	46,632	32,791	13,632	209	19,159 R	70.3%	29.2%	70.6%	29.4%
352,121	TOTAL	125,975	77,427	47,812	736	29,615 R	61.5%	38.0%	61.8%	38.2%

NEW YORK CITY

PRESIDENT 1988

1980 Census Population	County	Total Vote	Republican	Democratic	Other	Rep.-Dem. Plurality	Percentage Total Vote Rep.	Percentage Total Vote Dem.	Percentage Major Vote Rep.	Percentage Major Vote Dem.
1,169,115	BRONX	298,081	76,043	218,245	3,793	142,202 D	25.5%	73.2%	25.8%	74.2%
2,230,936	KINGS	549,019	178,961	363,916	6,142	184,955 D	32.6%	66.3%	33.0%	67.0%
1,427,533	NEW YORK	506,551	115,927	385,675	4,949	269,748 D	22.9%	76.1%	23.1%	76.9%
1,891,325	QUEENS	546,729	217,049	325,147	4,533	108,098 D	39.7%	59.5%	40.0%	60.0%
352,121	RICHMOND	125,975	77,427	47,812	736	29,615 R	61.5%	38.0%	61.8%	38.2%
7,071,030	TOTAL	2,026,355	665,407	1,340,795	20,153	675,388 D	32.8%	66.2%	33.2%	66.8%

NEW YORK CITY

BRONX COUNTY
SENATOR 1988

1980 Census Population	Assembly District	Total Vote	Republican	Democratic	Other	Rep.-Dem. Plurality	Percentage Total Vote Rep.	Percentage Total Vote Dem.	Percentage Major Vote Rep.	Percentage Major Vote Dem.
116,902	DISTRICT 73	21,728	1,518	19,734	476	18,216 D	7.0%	90.8%	7.1%	92.9%
116,909	DISTRICT 74	22,982	2,373	20,224	385	17,851 D	10.3%	88.0%	10.5%	89.5%
116,924	DISTRICT 75	31,515	8,547	22,488	480	13,941 D	27.1%	71.4%	27.5%	72.5%
116,909	DISTRICT 76	17,435	1,171	15,878	386	14,707 D	6.7%	91.1%	6.9%	93.1%
116,908	DISTRICT 77	16,769	1,769	14,606	394	12,837 D	10.5%	87.1%	10.8%	89.2%
116,909	DISTRICT 78	21,508	1,694	19,393	421	17,699 D	7.9%	90.2%	8.0%	92.0%
116,909	DISTRICT 79	26,925	4,682	21,698	545	17,016 D	17.4%	80.6%	17.7%	82.3%
116,911	DISTRICT 80	38,024	7,121	30,317	586	23,196 D	18.7%	79.7%	19.0%	81.0%
116,925	DISTRICT 81	38,797	8,464	29,734	599	21,270 D	21.8%	76.6%	22.2%	77.8%
116,909	DISTRICT 82	26,926	2,716	23,780	430	21,064 D	10.1%	88.3%	10.3%	89.7%
1,169,115	TOTAL	262,609	40,055	217,852	4,702	177,797 D	15.3%	83.0%	15.5%	84.5%

NEW YORK CITY

KINGS COUNTY
SENATOR 1988

1980 Census Population	Assembly District	Total Vote	Republican	Democratic	Other	Rep.-Dem. Plurality	Percentage Total Vote Rep.	Percentage Total Vote Dem.	Percentage Major Vote Rep.	Percentage Major Vote Dem.
117,424	DISTRICT 39	32,786	6,647	25,885	254	19,238 D	20.3%	79.0%	20.4%	79.6%
117,423	DISTRICT 40	20,531	878	19,283	370	18,405 D	4.3%	93.9%	4.4%	95.6%
117,426	DISTRICT 41	36,727	7,608	28,629	490	21,021 D	20.7%	78.0%	21.0%	79.0%
117,425	DISTRICT 42	19,110	1,972	16,771	367	14,799 D	10.3%	87.8%	10.5%	89.5%
117,416	DISTRICT 43	18,445	1,208	16,826	411	15,618 D	6.5%	91.2%	6.7%	93.3%
117,435	DISTRICT 44	31,904	4,673	26,557	674	21,884 D	14.6%	83.2%	15.0%	85.0%
117,408	DISTRICT 45	35,418	6,650	28,380	388	21,730 D	18.8%	80.1%	19.0%	81.0%
117,414	DISTRICT 46	33,297	7,165	25,749	383	18,584 D	21.5%	77.3%	21.8%	78.2%
117,402	DISTRICT 47	26,561	6,948	19,289	324	12,341 D	26.2%	72.6%	26.5%	73.5%
117,414	DISTRICT 48	25,880	6,242	19,348	290	13,106 D	24.1%	74.8%	24.4%	75.6%
117,390	DISTRICT 49	23,820	7,862	15,685	273	7,823 D	33.0%	65.8%	33.4%	66.6%
117,418	DISTRICT 50	21,868	4,089	17,403	376	13,314 D	18.7%	79.6%	19.0%	81.0%
117,420	DISTRICT 51	26,869	5,516	20,676	677	15,160 D	20.5%	77.0%	21.1%	78.9%
117,416	DISTRICT 52	38,199	9,017	28,483	699	19,466 D	23.6%	74.6%	24.0%	76.0%
117,421	DISTRICT 53	17,855	2,471	14,992	392	12,521 D	13.8%	84.0%	14.1%	85.9%
117,420	DISTRICT 54	16,222	2,124	13,767	331	11,643 D	13.1%	84.9%	13.4%	86.6%
117,422	DISTRICT 55	20,882	730	19,736	416	19,006 D	3.5%	94.5%	3.6%	96.4%
117,420	DISTRICT 56	22,319	824	20,985	510	20,161 D	3.7%	94.0%	3.8%	96.2%
117,422	DISTRICT 57	26,933	1,565	24,543	825	22,978 D	5.8%	91.1%	6.0%	94.0%
2,230,936	TOTAL	495,626	84,189	402,987	8,450	318,798 D	17.0%	81.3%	17.3%	82.7%

NEW YORK CITY

NEW YORK COUNTY
SENATOR 1988

1980 Census Population	Assembly District	Total Vote	Republican	Democratic	Other	Rep.-Dem. Plurality	Percentage Total Vote Rep.	Total Vote Dem.	Major Vote Rep.	Major Vote Dem.
118,950	DISTRICT 61	54,646	5,999	47,617	1,030	41,618 D	11.0%	87.1%	11.2%	88.8%
118,951	DISTRICT 62	23,664	2,918	20,195	551	17,277 D	12.3%	85.3%	12.6%	87.4%
118,962	DISTRICT 63	50,448	8,376	41,142	930	32,766 D	16.6%	81.6%	16.9%	83.1%
118,973	DISTRICT 64	47,271	6,228	40,097	946	33,869 D	13.2%	84.8%	13.4%	86.6%
119,036	DISTRICT 65	50,551	9,506	40,575	470	31,069 D	18.8%	80.3%	19.0%	81.0%
118,984	DISTRICT 66	47,688	10,595	36,732	361	26,137 D	22.2%	77.0%	22.4%	77.6%
118,949	DISTRICT 67	53,534	5,710	47,104	720	41,394 D	10.7%	88.0%	10.8%	89.2%
118,965	DISTRICT 68	27,130	2,050	24,316	764	22,266 D	7.6%	89.6%	7.8%	92.2%
118,956	DISTRICT 69	44,152	3,538	39,373	1,241	35,835 D	8.0%	89.2%	8.2%	91.8%
118,963	DISTRICT 70	26,839	1,091	24,904	844	23,813 D	4.1%	92.8%	4.2%	95.8%
118,908	DISTRICT 71	24,139	1,702	21,801	636	20,099 D	7.1%	90.3%	7.2%	92.8%
118,936	DISTRICT 72	26,725	4,080	22,106	539	18,026 D	15.3%	82.7%	15.6%	84.4%
1,427,533	TOTAL	476,787	61,793	405,962	9,032	344,169 D	13.0%	85.1%	13.2%	86.8%

NEW YORK CITY

QUEENS COUNTY
SENATOR 1988

1980 Census Population	Assembly District	Total Vote	Republican	Democratic	Other	Rep.-Dem. Plurality	Percentage Total Vote Rep.	Total Vote Dem.	Major Vote Rep.	Major Vote Dem.
118,206	DISTRICT 23	30,901	6,527	23,857	517	17,330 D	21.1%	77.2%	21.5%	78.5%
118,191	DISTRICT 24	45,979	10,596	34,987	396	24,391 D	23.0%	76.1%	23.2%	76.8%
118,200	DISTRICT 25	42,291	14,314	27,387	590	13,073 D	33.8%	64.8%	34.3%	65.7%
118,198	DISTRICT 26	36,939	8,993	27,552	394	18,559 D	24.3%	74.6%	24.6%	75.4%
118,201	DISTRICT 27	34,528	7,774	26,354	400	18,580 D	22.5%	76.3%	22.8%	77.2%
118,218	DISTRICT 28	40,920	7,775	32,795	350	25,020 D	19.0%	80.1%	19.2%	80.8%
118,207	DISTRICT 29	33,463	2,156	30,734	573	28,578 D	6.4%	91.8%	6.6%	93.4%
118,215	DISTRICT 30	26,231	6,772	19,198	261	12,426 D	25.8%	73.2%	26.1%	73.9%
118,210	DISTRICT 31	30,044	10,042	19,545	457	9,503 D	33.4%	65.1%	33.9%	66.1%
118,206	DISTRICT 32	32,634	3,758	28,290	586	24,532 D	11.5%	86.7%	11.7%	88.3%
118,203	DISTRICT 33	23,764	2,836	20,553	375	17,717 D	11.9%	86.5%	12.1%	87.9%
118,216	DISTRICT 34	29,789	8,379	21,011	399	12,632 D	28.1%	70.5%	28.5%	71.5%
118,203	DISTRICT 35	18,847	3,153	15,452	242	12,299 D	16.7%	82.0%	16.9%	83.1%
118,217	DISTRICT 36	28,535	6,336	21,781	418	15,445 D	22.2%	76.3%	22.5%	77.5%
118,217	DISTRICT 37	25,243	7,599	17,279	365	9,680 D	30.1%	68.5%	30.5%	69.5%
118,217	DISTRICT 38	32,331	12,515	19,393	423	6,878 D	38.7%	60.0%	39.2%	60.8%
1,891,325	TOTAL	512,439	119,525	386,168	6,746	266,643 D	23.3%	75.4%	23.6%	76.4%

NEW YORK CITY

RICHMOND COUNTY
SENATOR 1988

1980 Census Population	Assembly District	Total Vote	Republican	Democratic	Other	Rep.-Dem. Plurality	Percentage Total Vote Rep.	Percentage Total Vote Dem.	Percentage Major Vote Rep.	Percentage Major Vote Dem.
117,373	DISTRICT 58	37,596	12,011	24,918	667	12,907 D	31.9%	66.3%	32.5%	67.5%
117,376	DISTRICT 59	36,339	11,941	23,779	619	11,838 D	32.9%	65.4%	33.4%	66.6%
117,372	DISTRICT 60	43,296	18,557	23,985	754	5,428 D	42.9%	55.4%	43.6%	56.4%
352,121	TOTAL	117,231	42,509	72,682	2,040	30,173 D	36.3%	62.0%	36.9%	63.1%

NEW YORK CITY

SENATOR 1988

1980 Census Population	County	Total Vote	Republican	Democratic	Other	Rep.-Dem. Plurality	Percentage Total Vote Rep.	Percentage Total Vote Dem.	Percentage Major Vote Rep.	Percentage Major Vote Dem.
1,169,115	BRONX	262,609	40,055	217,852	4,702	177,797 D	15.3%	83.0%	15.5%	84.5%
2,230,936	KINGS	495,626	84,189	402,987	8,450	318,798 D	17.0%	81.3%	17.3%	82.7%
1,427,533	NEW YORK	476,787	61,793	405,962	9,032	344,169 D	13.0%	85.1%	13.2%	86.8%
1,891,325	QUEENS	512,439	119,525	386,168	6,746	266,643 D	23.3%	75.4%	23.6%	76.4%
352,121	RICHMOND	117,231	42,509	72,682	2,040	30,173 D	36.3%	62.0%	36.9%	63.1%
7,071,030	TOTAL	1,864,692	348,071	1,485,651	30,970	1,137,580 D	18.7%	79.7%	19.0%	81.0%

NEW YORK

CONGRESS

CD	Year	Total Vote	Republican Vote	Republican Candidate	Democratic Vote	Democratic Candidate	Other Vote	Rep.-Dem. Plurality	Total Vote Rep.	Total Vote Dem.	Major Vote Rep.	Major Vote Dem.
1	1988	207,951	102,327	*ROMAINE, EDWARD P.	105,624	*HOCHBRUECKNER, GEORGE J.		3,297 D	49.2%	50.8%	49.2%	50.8%
1	1986	131,031	55,413	*BLASS, GREGORY J.	67,139	*HOCHBRUECKNER, GEORGE J.	8,479	11,726 D	42.3%	51.2%	45.2%	54.8%
1	1984	201,580	107,029	*CARNEY, WILLIAM	94,551	*HOCHBRUECKNER, GEORGE J.		12,478 R	53.1%	46.9%	53.1%	46.9%
1	1982	138,021	88,234	*CARNEY, WILLIAM	49,787	ELDON, ETHAN C.		38,447 R	63.9%	36.1%	63.9%	36.1%
2	1988	174,618	66,972	*CARDINO, JOSEPH	107,646	*DOWNEY, THOMAS J.		40,674 D	38.4%	61.6%	38.4%	61.6%
2	1986	108,554	35,132	*BUTZKE, JEFFREY A.	69,771	*DOWNEY, THOMAS J.	3,651	34,639 D	32.4%	64.3%	33.5%	66.5%
2	1984	178,503	80,855	*ANIBOLI, PAUL	97,648	*DOWNEY, THOMAS J.		16,793 D	45.3%	54.7%	45.3%	54.7%
2	1982	126,712	42,790	*COSTELLO, PAUL G.	80,951	*DOWNEY, THOMAS J.	2,971	38,161 D	33.8%	63.9%	34.6%	65.4%
3	1988	224,306	91,122	*PREVIDI, ROBERT	128,336	MRAZEK, ROBERT J.	4,848	37,214 D	40.6%	57.2%	41.5%	58.5%
3	1986	148,792	60,367	*GUARINO, JOSEPH A.	83,985	MRAZEK, ROBERT J.	4,440	23,618 D	40.6%	56.4%	41.8%	58.2%
3	1984	235,751	112,909	*QUINN, ROBERT P.	120,191	MRAZEK, ROBERT J.	2,651	7,282 D	47.9%	51.0%	48.4%	51.6%
4	1988	215,386	151,038	*LENT, NORMAN F.	59,479	*GOBAN, FRANCIS T.	4,869	91,559 R	70.1%	27.6%	71.7%	28.3%
4	1986	142,288	92,214	*LENT, NORMAN F.	43,581	*SULLIVAN, PATRICIA	6,493	48,633 R	64.8%	30.6%	67.9%	32.1%
4	1984	224,679	154,875	*LENT, NORMAN F.	65,678	*ENGELHARD, SHELDON	4,126	89,197 R	68.9%	29.2%	70.2%	29.8%
5	1988	207,313	134,881	*MCGRATH, RAYMOND J.	68,930	KELLY, WILLIAM G.	3,502	65,951 R	65.1%	33.2%	66.2%	33.8%
5	1986	143,201	93,473	*MCGRATH, RAYMOND J.	49,728	*SULLIVAN, MICHAEL T.		43,745 R	65.3%	34.7%	65.3%	34.7%
5	1984	222,191	138,560	*MCGRATH, RAYMOND J.	78,429	*D'INNOCENZO, MICHAEL	5,202	60,131 R	62.4%	35.3%	63.9%	36.1%
6	1988	110,053			94,506	*FLAKE, FLOYD H.	15,547	94,506 D		85.9%		100.0%
6	1986	86,090	27,773	*DIETL, RICHARD	58,317	FLAKE, FLOYD H.		30,544 D	32.3%	67.7%	32.3%	67.7%
6	1984	145,138	25,040	*VELTRE, PHILIP J.	120,098	*ADDABBO, JOSEPH P.		95,058 D	17.3%	82.7%	17.3%	82.7%
7	1988	93,120			93,120	*ACKERMAN, GARY L.		93,120 D		100.0%		100.0%
7	1986	81,220	18,384	*RODRIGUEZ, EDWARD N.	62,836	ACKERMAN, GARY L.		44,452 D	22.6%	77.4%	22.6%	77.4%
7	1984	141,044	43,370	*REIFENKUGEL, GUSTAVE A.	97,674	*ACKERMAN, GARY L.		54,304 D	30.7%	69.3%	30.7%	69.3%
8	1988	100,240			100,240	*SCHEUER, JAMES H.		100,240 D		100.0%		100.0%
8	1986	78,284			70,605	*SCHEUER, JAMES H.	7,679	70,605 D		90.2%		100.0%
8	1984	166,573	62,015	*BRANDOFINO, ROBERT L.	104,558	*SCHEUER, JAMES H.		42,543 D	37.2%	62.8%	37.2%	62.8%
9	1988	72,851			72,851	MANTON, THOMAS J.		72,851 D		100.0%		100.0%
9	1986	73,126	18,040	CALISE, SALVATORE J.	50,738	MANTON, THOMAS J.	4,348	32,698 D	24.7%	69.4%	26.2%	73.8%
9	1984	135,330	63,910	*MALTESE, SERPHIN R.	71,420	MANTON, THOMAS J.		7,510 D	47.2%	52.8%	47.2%	52.8%
9	1982	102,820	20,352	WEIGANDT, JOHN L.	75,286	FERRARO, GERALDINE A.	7,182	54,934 D	19.8%	73.2%	21.3%	78.7%
10	1988	136,488	24,313	POPIELARSKI, GEORGE S.	107,056	*SCHUMER, CHARLES E.	5,119	82,743 D	17.8%	78.4%	18.5%	81.5%
10	1986	81,790			76,318	*SCHUMER, CHARLES E.	5,472	76,318 D		93.3%		100.0%
10	1984	159,992	42,009	*FOX, JOHN H.	115,867	*SCHUMER, CHARLES E.	2,116	73,858 D	26.3%	72.4%	26.6%	73.4%
11	1988	83,158	7,418	HUSSAIN, RIAZ B.	73,755	*TOWNS, EDOLPHUS	1,985	66,337 D	8.9%	88.7%	9.1%	90.9%
11	1986	46,616	4,053	HENDRICKS, NATHANIEL	41,689	*TOWNS, EDOLPHUS	874	37,636 D	8.7%	89.4%	8.9%	91.1%
11	1984	95,064	12,494	HENDRICKS, NATHANIEL	81,002	*TOWNS, EDOLPHUS	1,568	68,508 D	13.1%	85.2%	13.4%	86.6%
12	1988	79,886	5,582	*AUGUSTIN, OWEN	74,304	*OWENS, MAJOR R.		68,722 D	7.0%	93.0%	7.0%	93.0%
12	1986	46,058	2,752	AUGUSTIN, OWEN	42,138	*OWENS, MAJOR R.	1,168	39,386 D	6.0%	91.5%	6.1%	93.9%
12	1984	90,656	8,609	*CAESAR, JOSEPH N.	82,047	*OWENS, MAJOR R.		73,438 D	9.5%	90.5%	9.5%	90.5%
12	1982	49,259	3,215	KATAN, DAVID	44,586	*OWENS, MAJOR R.	1,458	41,371 D	6.5%	90.5%	6.7%	93.3%
13	1988	108,841	27,536	*CURCI, ANTHONY M.	81,305	*SOLARZ, STEPHEN J.		53,769 D	25.3%	74.7%	25.3%	74.7%
13	1986	74,136	10,941	NADROWSKI, LEON	61,089	*SOLARZ, STEPHEN J.	2,106	50,148 D	14.8%	82.4%	15.2%	84.8%
13	1984	125,347	42,737	*LEVIN, LEW Y.	82,610	*SOLARZ, STEPHEN J.		39,873 D	34.1%	65.9%	34.1%	65.9%
14	1988	156,682	99,179	*MOLINARI, GUY V.	57,503	*O'DONOVAN, JEROME X.		41,676 R	63.3%	36.7%	63.3%	36.7%
14	1986	93,972	64,647	*MOLINARI, GUY V.	27,950	WALLA, BARBARA	1,375	36,697 R	68.8%	29.7%	69.8%	30.2%
14	1984	166,817	117,041	*MOLINARI, GUY V.	49,776	SHEEHY, KEVIN		67,265 R	70.2%	29.8%	70.2%	29.8%

NEW YORK

CONGRESS

		Total	Republican		Democratic		Other	Rep.-Dem.	Percentage Total Vote		Percentage Major Vote	
CD	Year	Vote	Vote	Candidate	Vote	Candidate	Vote	Plurality	Rep.	Dem.	Rep.	Dem.
15	1988	175,483	107,599	*GREEN, S. WILLIAM	64,425	DOUKAS, PETER G.	3,459	43,174 R	61.3%	36.7%	62.5%	37.5%
15	1986	100,361	58,214	*GREEN, S. WILLIAM	42,147	*HIRSCH, GEORGE A.		16,067 R	58.0%	42.0%	58.0%	42.0%
15	1984	192,048	107,644	*GREEN, S. WILLIAM	84,404	*STEIN, ANDREW J.		23,240 R	56.1%	43.9%	56.1%	43.9%
15	1982	123,698	66,262	*GREEN, S. WILLIAM	55,483	*LALL, BETTY G.	1,953	10,779 R	53.6%	44.9%	54.4%	45.6%
16	1988	110,850			107,620	*RANGEL, CHARLES B.	3,230	107,620 D		97.1%		100.0%
16	1986	63,545			61,262	*RANGEL, CHARLES B.	2,283	61,262 D		96.4%		100.0%
16	1984	121,398			117,759	*RANGEL, CHARLES B.	3,639	117,759 D		97.0%		100.0%
16	1982	78,605			76,626	*RANGEL, CHARLES B.	1,979	76,626 D		97.5%		100.0%
17	1988	186,495	29,156	*ALBERT, MYRNA C.	157,339	*WEISS, THEODORE S.		128,183 D	15.6%	84.4%	15.6%	84.4%
17	1986	111,262	15,587	*CHORBA, THOMAS A.	95,094	*WEISS, THEODORE S.	581	79,507 D	14.0%	85.5%	14.1%	85.9%
17	1984	199,479	33,316	KATZMAN, KENNETH	162,489	*WEISS, THEODORE S.	3,674	129,173 D	16.7%	81.5%	17.0%	83.0%
17	1982	133,100	19,928	*ANTONELLI, LOUIS S.	113,172	*WEISS, THEODORE S.		93,244 D	15.0%	85.0%	15.0%	85.0%
18	1988	82,866	5,764	BROWN, FRED	75,459	*GARCIA, ROBERT	1,643	69,695 D	7.0%	91.1%	7.1%	92.9%
18	1986	46,353	2,479	CHASE, MELANIE	43,343	*GARCIA, ROBERT	531	40,864 D	5.3%	93.5%	5.4%	94.6%
18	1984	96,328	8,970	JOHNSON, CURTIS	85,960	*GARCIA, ROBERT	1,398	76,990 D	9.3%	89.2%	9.4%	90.6%
19	1988	137,743	37,454	BIAGGI, MARIO	77,158	*ENGEL, ELIOT L.	23,131	39,704 D	27.2%	56.0%	32.7%	67.3%
19	1986	97,349			87,774	*BIAGGI, MARIO	9,575	87,774 D		90.2%		100.0%
19	1984	163,539			155,067	*BIAGGI, MARIO	8,472	155,067 D		94.8%		100.0%
20	1988	203,263	96,465	*DIOGUARDI, JOSEPH J.	102,235	LOWEY, NITA M.	4,563	5,770 D	47.5%	50.3%	48.5%	51.5%
20	1986	148,920	80,220	*DIOGUARDI, JOSEPH J.	66,359	ABZUG, BELLA S.	2,341	13,861 R	53.9%	44.6%	54.7%	45.3%
20	1984	213,349	106,958	*DIOGUARDI, JOSEPH J.	102,842	TEICHER, OREN J.	3,549	4,116 R	50.1%	48.2%	51.0%	49.0%
21	1988	201,607	150,443	*FISH, HAMILTON	47,294	GRUNBERGER, LAWRENCE W.	3,870	103,149 R	74.6%	23.5%	76.1%	23.9%
21	1986	133,397	102,070	*FISH, HAMILTON	28,339	GRUNBERGER, LAWRENCE W.	2,988	73,731 R	76.5%	21.2%	78.3%	21.7%
21	1984	204,327	160,053	*FISH, HAMILTON	44,274	GRUNBERGER, LAWRENCE W.		115,779 R	78.3%	21.7%	78.3%	21.7%
21	1982	156,124	117,460	*FISH, HAMILTON	38,664	STRONG, J. MORGAN		78,796 R	75.2%	24.8%	75.2%	24.8%
22	1988	203,635	144,227	GILMAN, BENJAMIN A.	54,312	BURLINGHAM, ELEANOR F.	5,096	89,915 R	70.8%	26.7%	72.6%	27.4%
22	1986	135,656	94,244	GILMAN, BENJAMIN A.	36,852	BURLINGHAM, ELEANOR F.	4,560	57,392 R	69.5%	27.2%	71.9%	28.1%
22	1984	210,486	144,278	GILMAN, BENJAMIN A.	57,934	*LEVINE, BRUCE M.	8,274	86,344 R	68.5%	27.5%	71.3%	28.7%
22	1982	174,286	92,266	GILMAN, BENJAMIN A.	73,124	*PEYSER, PETER A.	8,896	19,142 R	52.9%	42.0%	55.8%	44.2%
23	1988	234,898	89,858	*BAKAL, PETER M.	145,040	MCNULTY, MICHAEL R.		55,182 D	38.3%	61.7%	38.3%	61.7%
23	1986	146,038			140,759	STRATTON, SAMUEL S.	5,279	140,759 D		96.4%		100.0%
23	1984	241,846	53,060	*WICKS, FRANK	188,144	STRATTON, SAMUEL S.	642	135,084 D	21.9%	77.8%	22.0%	78.0%
23	1982	216,083	41,386	*WICKS, FRANK	164,427	STRATTON, SAMUEL S.	10,270	123,041 D	19.2%	76.1%	20.1%	79.9%
24	1988	225,139	162,962	*SOLOMON, GERALD B.	62,177	BAYE, FRED		100,785 R	72.4%	27.6%	72.4%	27.6%
24	1986	166,510	117,285	*SOLOMON, GERALD B.	49,225	BLOCH, EDWARD J.		68,060 R	70.4%	29.6%	70.4%	29.6%
24	1984	224,207	164,019	*SOLOMON, GERALD B.	60,188	BLOCH, EDWARD J.		103,831 R	73.2%	26.8%	73.2%	26.8%
24	1982	189,737	140,296	*SOLOMON, GERALD B.	49,441	ESIASON, ROY		90,855 R	73.9%	26.1%	73.9%	26.1%
25	1988	130,122	130,122	BOEHLERT, SHERWOOD L.				130,122 R	100.0%		100.0%	
25	1986	151,079	104,216	BOEHLERT, SHERWOOD L.	33,864	CONWAY, KEVIN J.	12,999	70,352 R	69.0%	22.4%	75.5%	24.5%
25	1984	192,690	140,256	BOEHLERT, SHERWOOD L.	52,434	BALL, JAMES J.		87,822 R	72.8%	27.2%	72.8%	27.2%
26	1988	174,628	131,043	*MARTIN, DAVID O'B.	43,585	RAVENSCROFT, DONALD R.		87,458 R	75.0%	25.0%	75.0%	25.0%
26	1986	94,840	94,840	*MARTIN, DAVID O'B.				94,840 R	100.0%		100.0%	
26	1984	185,920	131,257	*MARTIN, DAVID O'B.	54,663	LAMMERS, BERNARD J.		76,594 R	70.6%	29.4%	70.6%	29.4%
26	1982	152,170	108,962	*MARTIN, DAVID O'B.	43,208	LANDY, DAVID P.		65,754 R	71.6%	28.4%	71.6%	28.4%
27	1988	217,426	124,928	*WALSH, JAMES T.	90,854	*POOLER, ROSEMARY S.	1,644	34,074 R	57.5%	41.8%	57.9%	42.1%
27	1986	168,026	83,430	*WORTLEY, GEORGE C.	82,491	*POOLER, ROSEMARY S.	2,105	939 R	49.7%	49.1%	50.3%	49.7%
27	1984	215,816	122,215	*WORTLEY, GEORGE C.	93,601	*BUCKEL, THOMAS C.		28,614 R	56.6%	43.4%	56.6%	43.4%

NEW YORK

CONGRESS

CD	Year	Total Vote	Republican Vote	Republican Candidate	Democratic Vote	Democratic Candidate	Other Vote	Rep.-Dem. Plurality	Percentage Total Vote Rep.	Percentage Total Vote Dem.	Percentage Major Vote Rep.	Percentage Major Vote Dem.
28	1988	152,371			141,976	MCHUGH, MATTHEW F.	10,395	141,976 D		93.2%		100.0%
28	1986	152,121	48,213	*MASTERSON, MARK R.	103,908	MCHUGH, MATTHEW F.		55,695 D	31.7%	68.3%	31.7%	68.3%
28	1984	218,061	90,324	COOK, CONSTANCE E.	123,334	MCHUGH, MATTHEW F.	4,403	33,010 D	41.4%	56.6%	42.3%	57.7%
29	1988	192,661	132,608	HORTON, FRANK J.	51,243	VOGEL, JAMES R.	8,810	81,365 R	68.8%	26.6%	72.1%	27.9%
29	1986	141,008	99,704	HORTON, FRANK J.	34,194	VOGEL, JAMES R.	7,110	65,510 R	70.7%	24.2%	74.5%	25.5%
29	1984	198,662	138,362	HORTON, FRANK J.	48,301	TOOLE, JAMES R.	11,999	90,061 R	69.6%	24.3%	74.1%	25.9%
30	1988	225,712	89,126	BOUCHARD, JOHN D.	128,364	SLAUGHTER, LOUISE M.	8,222	39,238 D	39.5%	56.9%	41.0%	59.0%
30	1986	170,179	83,402	*ECKERT, FRED J.	86,777	SLAUGHTER, LOUISE M.		3,375 D	49.0%	51.0%	49.0%	51.0%
30	1984	220,273	119,844	*ECKERT, FRED J.	100,066	CALL, W. DOUGLAS	363	19,778 R	54.4%	45.4%	54.5%	45.5%
30	1982	174,620	119,105	CONABLE, BARBER B.	48,764	BENET, BILL	6,751	70,341 R	68.2%	27.9%	71.0%	29.0%
31	1988	220,487	117,710	*PAXON, L. WILLIAM	102,777	*SWARTS, DAVID J.		14,933 R	53.4%	46.6%	53.4%	46.6%
31	1986	160,995	92,508	*KEMP, JACK F.	67,574	*KEANE, JAMES P.	913	24,934 R	57.5%	42.0%	57.8%	42.2%
31	1984	224,488	168,332	*KEMP, JACK F.	56,156	*MARTINELLI, PETER J.		112,176 R	75.0%	25.0%	75.0%	25.0%
32	1988	184,146	50,229	*EVERETT, EMIL K.	133,917	*LAFALCE, JOHN J.		83,688 D	27.3%	72.7%	27.3%	72.7%
32	1986	109,657			99,745	*LAFALCE, JOHN J.	9,912	99,745 D		91.0%		100.0%
32	1984	201,776	61,797	*MURTY, ANTHONY J.	139,979	*LAFALCE, JOHN J.		78,182 D	30.6%	69.4%	30.6%	69.4%
32	1982	127,383			116,386	*LAFALCE, JOHN J.	10,997	116,386 D		91.4%		100.0%
33	1988	139,604			139,604	*NOWAK, HENRY J.		139,604 D		100.0%		100.0%
33	1986	128,403	19,147	*WALKER, CHARLES A.	109,256	*NOWAK, HENRY J.		90,109 D	14.9%	85.1%	14.9%	85.1%
33	1984	200,078	44,880	*LEWANDOWSKI, DAVID S.	155,198	*NOWAK, HENRY J.		110,318 D	22.4%	77.6%	22.4%	77.6%
33	1982	149,977	19,791	*PILLICH, WALTER J.	126,091	*NOWAK, HENRY J.	4,095	106,300 D	13.2%	84.1%	13.6%	86.4%
34	1988	135,875	131,078	*HOUGHTON, AMORY			4,797	131,078 R	96.5%		100.0%	
34	1986	142,754	85,856	*HOUGHTON, AMORY	56,898	HIMELEIN, LARRY M.		28,958 R	60.1%	39.9%	60.1%	39.9%
34	1984	204,478	91,016	*EMERY, JILL H.	110,902	LUNDINE, STANLEY N.	2,560	19,886 D	44.5%	54.2%	45.1%	54.9%

NEW YORK

1988 GENERAL ELECTION

President The Republican candidate was also the Conservative nominee and 243,457 of his votes were received as the Conservative candidate. The Democratic candidate was also the Liberal nominee and 92,395 of his votes were received as the Liberal candidate. Other vote was 20,497 Right to Life (Marra); 15,845 New Alliance (Fulani); 12,109 Libertarian (Paul); 4,179 Workers World (Holmes); 3,287 Socialist Workers (Warren); 10 Winn (write-in); 3 Kenoyer (write-in).

Senator The Republican candidate was also the Conservative nominee and 189,226 of his votes were received as the Conservative candidate. The Democratic candidate was also the Liberal nominee and 141,471 of his votes were received as the Liberal candidate. Other vote was 64,845 Right to Life (Nathanson); 14,770 Independent Progressive (Mitchell); 13,573 Workers World (Bayoneta); 12,064 Libertarian (McMillen); 11,239 Socialist Workers (Harris); 56 scattered write-in.

Congress An asterisk in the Congressional vote table indicates a candidate received votes as the nominee of an additional party/parties. Mario Biaggi, the Democratic incumbent member in CD 19, was defeated for renomination in the Democratic primary; however he was the unopposed nominee in the Republican primary. Other vote was 3,625 Right to Life (Considine) and 1,223 Liberal (Signorelli) in CD 3; Right to Life (McGeary) in CD 4; Right to Life (Matier) in CD 5; 13,499 Conservative plus 2,048 Drug Fighter (Brandofino) in CD 6; Conservative (Gaffney) in CD 10; 1,271 Conservative (Hamel) and 714 New Alliance (Stevens) in CD 11; Liberal (Levitt) in CD 15; 1,779 Conservative (Liccione) and 1,451 New Alliance (Taylor) in CD 16; 904 New Alliance (Mendez) and 739 Conservative (Verhoff) in CD 18; 11,271 Right to Life (Martin O'Grady), 11,182 Conservative (Blumetti) and 678 Independent Progressive Line (Zagarell) in CD 19; 2,932 Right to Life (Florence O'Grady) and 1,631 Liberal (Levine) in CD 20; Right to Life (Curtin) in CD 21; Right to Life (Braun) in CD 22; Right to Life (Hoff) in CD 27; Right to Life (Dixon) in CD 28; 5,688 Conservative (Baxter) and 3,122 Right to Life (Peters) in CD 29; 6,252 Conservative (Cook) and 1,970 Right to Life (Flanagan) in CD 30; Liberal (Woodward) in CD 34.

NEW YORK CITY

The City is composed of five counties, each of which for municipal government pruposes is known as a borough. Names of the counties and boroughs are the same save in the case of New York county (Manhattan borough), Kings county (Brooklyn borough) and Richmond county (Staten Island borough).

President The Republican vote includes 54,987 votes cast for George Bush as the Conservative candidate. The Democratic vote includes 47,283 votes cast for Michael S. Dukakis as the Liberal candidate. Other vote was 10,502 New Alliance (Fulani); 4,640 Right to Life (Marra); 2,185 Libertarian (Paul); 1,661 Socialist Workers (Warren); 1,165 Workers World (Holmes).

Senator The Republican vote includes 44,436 votes cast for Robert McMillan as the Conservative candidate. The Democratic vote includes 57,997 votes cast for Daniel P. Moynihan as the Liberal candidate. Other vote was 13,067 Right to Life (Nathanson); 6,457 Independent Progressive (Mitchell); 5,128 Socialist Workers (Harris); 4,141 Workers World (Bayoneta); 2,177 Libertarian (McMillen).

1988 PRIMARIES

SEPTEMBER 15 REPUBLICAN

Senator Robert McMillan, unopposed.

Congress Unopposed in twenty-eight CD's. No candidate in CD's 6, 7, 8, 9, 28 and 33.

NEW YORK

SEPTEMBER 15 DEMOCRATIC

Senator Daniel P. Moynihan, unopposed.

Congress Unopposed in twenty-one CD's. No candidate in CD's 25 and 34. Contested as follows:

CD 11 14,570 Edolphus Towns; 4,575 Riaz B. Hussain (the unopposed Republican candidate).
CD 15 6,302 Peter G. Doukas; 5,421 John B. Levitt; 3,645 Paul P. Rao; 3,064 George T. McDonald.
CD 17 29,064 Theodore S. Weiss; 4,143 Harry C. Fotopoulos.
CD 18 16,868 Robert Garcia; 7,531 Pedro Espada; 3,433 Ismael Betancourt.
CD 19 12,181 Eliot L. Engel; 6,700 Vincent A. Marchiselli; 6,525 Mario Biaggi (the unopposed Republican candidate)
CD 20 10,533 Nita M. Lowey; 8,578 Hamilton Fish, III; 4,849 Dennis Mehiel; 2 scattered write-in.
CD 22 5,580 Eleanor F. Burlingham; 4,505 Michael T. Delia.
CD 27 10,260 Rosemary S. Pooler; 4,209 Stephen S. Bowman.
CD 29 5,025 James R. Vogel; 659 Keith R. T. Perez.
CD 31 10,688 David J. Swarts; 4,750 George F. Hasiotis.
CD 33 39,860 Henry J. Nowak; 3,706 Charles H. Carman.

SEPTEMBER 15 CONSERVATIVE

Senator Robert McMillan, unopposed.

Congress Major party candidates endorsed or nominees unopposed in all CD's in which a candidate was named except for the following CD's:

CD 27 439 James T. Walsh (the unopposed Republican candidate); 212 David G. Flagg.
CD 30 827 Thomas D. Cook; 436 John D. Bouchard.

SEPTEMBER 15 LIBERAL

Senator Daniel P. Moynihan, unopposed.

Congress Major party candidates endorsed or nominees unopposed in all CD's in which a candidate was named.

SEPTEMBER 15 RIGHT TO LIFE

Senator Adelle R. Nathanson, unopposed.

Congress Major party candidates endorsed or nominees unopposed in all CD's in which a candidate was named except for the following CD:

CD 21 75 Richard S. Curtin; 61 Karen A. Gormely-Vitale.

NORTH CAROLINA

GOVERNOR

James G. Martin (R). Re-elected 1988 to a four-year term. Previously elected 1984.

SENATORS

Jesse Helms (R). Re-elected 1984 to a six-year term. Previously elected 1978, 1972.

Terry Sanford (D). Elected 1986 to a six-year term.

REPRESENTATIVES

1. Walter B. Jones (D)
2. I. T.Valentine (D)
3. Martin Lancaster (D)
4. David E. Price (D)
5. Stephen L. Neal (D)
6. Howard Coble (R)
7. Charles G. Rose (D)
8. W. G.Hefner (D)
9. J. Alex McMillan (R)
10. Cass Ballenger (R)
11. James McC. Clarke (D)

POSTWAR VOTE FOR PRESIDENT

								Percentage			
	Total	Republican		Democratic		Other		Total Vote		Major Vote	
Year	Vote	Vote	Candidate	Vote	Candidate	Vote	Plurality	Rep.	Dem.	Rep.	Dem.
1988	2,134,370	1,237,258	Bush, George	890,167	Dukakis, Michael S.	6,945	347,091 R	58.0%	41.7%	58.2%	41.8%
1984	2,175,361	1,346,481	Reagan, Ronald	824,287	Mondale, Walter F.	4,593	522,194 R	61.9%	37.9%	62.0%	38.0%
1980	1,855,833	915,018	Reagan, Ronald	875,635	Carter, Jimmy	65,180	39,383 R	49.3%	47.2%	51.1%	48.9%
1976	1,678,914	741,960	Ford, Gerald R.	927,365	Carter, Jimmy	9,589	185,405 D	44.2%	55.2%	44.4%	55.6%
1972	1,518,612	1,054,889	Nixon, Richard M.	438,705	McGovern, George S.	25,018	616,184 R	69.5%	28.9%	70.6%	29.4%
1968 **	1,587,493	627,192	Nixon, Richard M.	464,113	Humphrey, Hubert H.	496,188	131,004 R	39.5%	29.2%	57.5%	42.5%
1964	1,424,983	624,844	Goldwater, Barry M.	800,139	Johnson, Lyndon B.		175,295 D	43.8%	56.2%	43.8%	56.2%
1960	1,368,556	655,420	Nixon, Richard M.	713,136	Kennedy, John F.		57,716 D	47.9%	52.1%	47.9%	52.1%
1956	1,165,592	575,062	Eisenhower, Dwight D.	590,530	Stevenson, Adlai E.		15,468 D	49.3%	50.7%	49.3%	50.7%
1952	1,210,910	558,107	Eisenhower, Dwight D.	652,803	Stevenson, Adlai E.		94,696 D	46.1%	53.9%	46.1%	53.9%
1948	791,209	258,572	Dewey, Thomas E.	459,070	Truman, Harry S.	73,567	200,498 D	32.7%	58.0%	36.0%	64.0%

In 1968 other vote was American (Wallace).

POSTWAR VOTE FOR GOVERNOR

								Percentage			
	Total	Republican		Democratic		Other	Rep.-Dem.	Total Vote		Major Vote	
Year	Vote	Vote	Candidate	Vote	Candidate	Vote	Plurality	Rep.	Dem.	Rep.	Dem.
1988	2,180,025	1,222,338	Martin, James G.	957,687	Jordan, Robert B.		264,651 R	56.1%	43.9%	56.1%	43.9%
1984	2,226,727	1,208,167	Martin, James G.	1,011,209	Edmisten, Rufus	7,351	196,958 R	54.3%	45.4%	54.4%	45.6%
1980	1,847,432	691,449	Lake, Beverly	1,143,145	Hunt, James B.	12,838	451,696 D	37.4%	61.9%	37.7%	62.3%
1976	1,663,824	564,102	Flaherty, David T.	1,081,293	Hunt, James B.	18,429	517,191 D	33.9%	65.0%	34.3%	65.7%
1972	1,504,785	767,470	Holshouser, James E.	729,104	Bowles, Hargrove	8,211	38,366 R	51.0%	48.5%	51.3%	48.7%
1968	1,558,308	737,075	Gardner, James C.	821,233	Scott, Robert W.		84,158 D	47.3%	52.7%	47.3%	52.7%
1964	1,396,508	606,165	Gavin, Robert L.	790,343	Moore, Dan K.		184,178 D	43.4%	56.6%	43.4%	56.6%
1960	1,350,360	613,975	Gavin, Robert L.	735,248	Sanford, Terry	1,137	121,273 D	45.5%	54.4%	45.5%	54.5%
1956	1,135,859	375,379	Hayes, Kyle	760,480	Hodges, Luther H.		385,101 D	33.0%	67.0%	33.0%	67.0%
1952	1,179,635	383,329	Seawell, H. F.	796,306	Umstead, William B.		412,977 D	32.5%	67.5%	32.5%	67.5%
1948	780,525	206,166	Pritchard, George	570,995	Scott, William Kerr	3,364	364,829 D	26.4%	73.2%	26.5%	73.5%

NORTH CAROLINA

POSTWAR VOTE FOR SENATOR

	Total	Republican		Democratic		Other	Rep.-Dem.	Percentage			
								Total Vote		Major Vote	
Year	Vote	Vote	Candidate	Vote	Candidate	Vote	Plurality	Rep.	Dem.	Rep.	Dem.
1986	1,591,330	767,668	Broyhill, James T.	823,662	Sanford, Terry		55,994 D	48.2%	51.8%	48.2%	51.8%
1984	2,239,051	1,156,768	Helms, Jesse	1,070,488	Hunt, James B.	11,795	86,280 R	51.7%	47.8%	51.9%	48.1%
1980	1,797,665	898,064	East, John P.	887,653	Morgan, Robert	11,948	10,411 R	50.0%	49.4%	50.3%	49.7%
1978	1,135,814	619,151	Helms, Jesse	516,663	Ingram, John		102,488 R	54.5%	45.5%	54.5%	45.5%
1974	1,020,367	377,618	Stevens, William E.	633,775	Morgan, Robert	8,974	256,157 D	37.0%	62.1%	37.3%	62.7%
1972	1,472,541	795,248	Helms, Jesse	677,293	Galifianakis, Nick		117,955 R	54.0%	46.0%	54.0%	46.0%
1968	1,437,340	566,934	Somers, Robert V.	870,406	Ervin, Sam J.		303,472 D	39.4%	60.6%	39.4%	60.6%
1966	901,978	400,502	Shallcross, John S.	501,440	Jordan, B. Everett	36	100,938 D	44.4%	55.6%	44.4%	55.6%
1962	813,155	321,635	Greene, Claude L.	491,520	Ervin, Sam J.		169,885 D	39.6%	60.4%	39.6%	60.4%
1960	1,291,485	497,964	Hayes, Kyle	793,521	Jordan, B. Everett		295,557 D	38.6%	61.4%	38.6%	61.4%
1958 S	616,469	184,977	Clarke, Richard C.	431,492	Jordan, B. Everett		246,515 D	30.0%	70.0%	30.0%	70.0%
1956	1,098,828	367,475	Johnson, Joel A.	731,353	Ervin, Sam J.		363,878 D	33.4%	66.6%	33.4%	66.6%
1954	619,634	211,322	West, Paul C.	408,312	Scott, William Kerr		196,990 D	34.1%	65.9%	34.1%	65.9%
1954 S	410,574		—	410,574	Ervin, Sam J.		410,574 D		100.0%		100.0%
1950	548,276	171,804	Leavitt, Halsey B.	376,472	Hoey, Clyde R.		204,668 D	31.3%	68.7%	31.3%	68.7%
1950 S	544,924	177,753	Gavin, E. L.	364,912	Smith, Willis	2,259	187,159 D	32.6%	67.0%	32.8%	67.2%
1948	764,559	220,307	Wilkinson, John A.	540,762	Broughton, J. M.	3,490	320,455 D	28.8%	70.7%	28.9%	71.1%

The 1958 election and one each of the 1954 and 1950 elections were for short terms to fill vacancies.

NORTH CAROLINA

Districts Established February 11, 1982

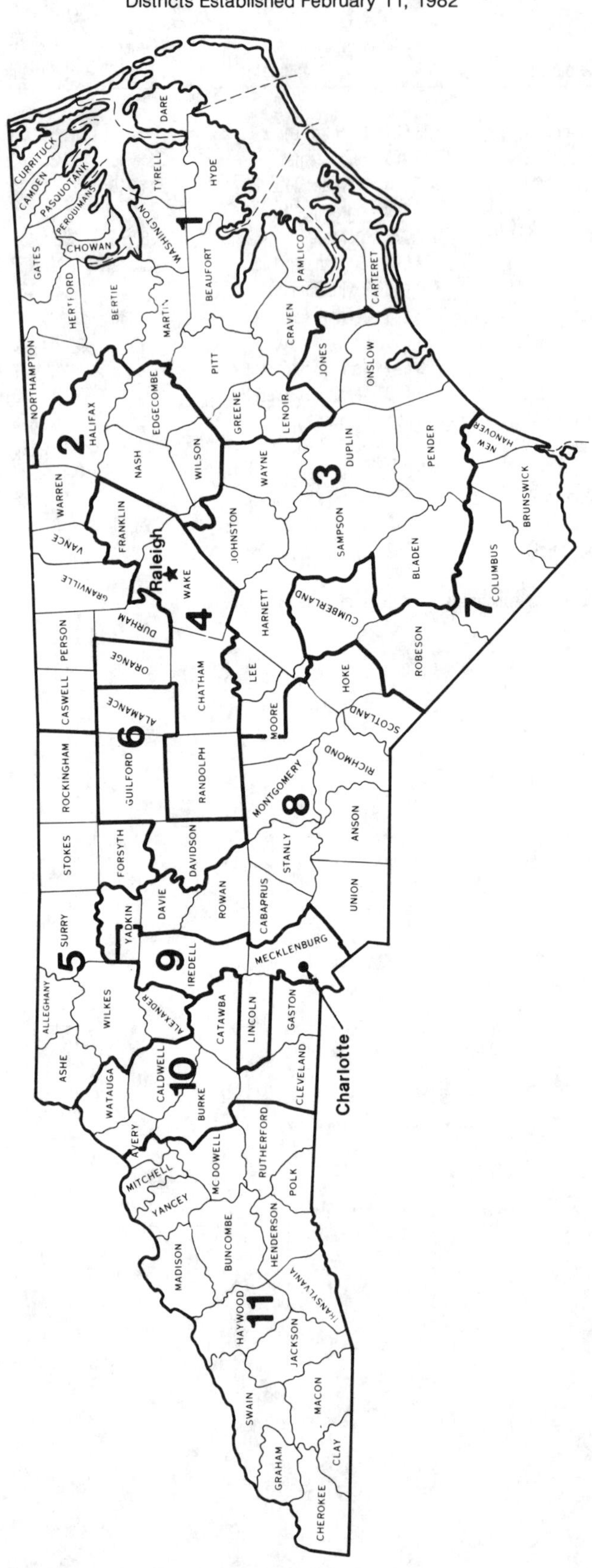

NORTH CAROLINA

PRESIDENT 1988

1980 Census Population	County	Total Vote	Republican	Democratic	Other	Rep.-Dem. Plurality	Percentage Total Vote Rep.	Total Vote Dem.	Major Vote Rep.	Major Vote Dem.
99,319	ALAMANCE	36,851	24,131	12,642	78	11,489 R	65.5%	34.3%	65.6%	34.4%
24,999	ALEXANDER	12,154	7,968	4,148	38	3,820 R	65.6%	34.1%	65.8%	34.2%
9,587	ALLEGHANY	4,264	2,174	2,087	3	87 R	51.0%	48.9%	51.0%	49.0%
25,649	ANSON	7,633	2,782	4,831	20	2,049 D	36.4%	63.3%	36.5%	63.5%
22,325	ASHE	10,083	6,019	4,034	30	1,985 R	59.7%	40.0%	59.9%	40.1%
14,409	AVERY	5,678	4,277	1,367	34	2,910 R	75.3%	24.1%	75.8%	24.2%
40,355	BEAUFORT	13,570	8,190	5,352	28	2,838 R	60.4%	39.4%	60.5%	39.5%
21,024	BERTIE	5,919	2,145	3,762	12	1,617 D	36.2%	63.6%	36.3%	63.7%
30,491	BLADEN	8,814	3,770	5,031	13	1,261 D	42.8%	57.1%	42.8%	57.2%
35,777	BRUNSWICK	17,939	10,007	7,881	51	2,126 R	55.8%	43.9%	55.9%	44.1%
160,934	BUNCOMBE	63,992	36,828	26,964	200	9,864 R	57.6%	42.1%	57.7%	42.3%
72,504	BURKE	26,819	15,933	10,848	38	5,085 R	59.4%	40.4%	59.5%	40.5%
85,895	CABARRUS	33,284	22,524	10,686	74	11,838 R	67.7%	32.1%	67.8%	32.2%
67,746	CALDWELL	23,071	15,176	7,862	33	7,314 R	65.8%	34.1%	65.9%	34.1%
5,829	CAMDEN	2,249	1,144	1,081	24	63 R	50.9%	48.1%	51.4%	48.6%
41,092	CARTERET	17,994	11,076	6,859	59	4,217 R	61.6%	38.1%	61.8%	38.2%
20,705	CASWELL	7,509	3,299	4,189	21	890 D	43.9%	55.8%	44.1%	55.9%
105,208	CATAWBA	41,838	28,872	12,922	44	15,950 R	69.0%	30.9%	69.1%	30.9%
33,415	CHATHAM	14,639	6,999	7,600	40	601 D	47.8%	51.9%	47.9%	52.1%
18,933	CHEROKEE	7,145	4,557	2,567	21	1,990 R	63.8%	35.9%	64.0%	36.0%
12,558	CHOWAN	3,654	1,884	1,756	14	128 R	51.6%	48.1%	51.8%	48.2%
6,619	CLAY	3,480	2,174	1,289	17	885 R	62.5%	37.0%	62.8%	37.2%
83,435	CLEVELAND	24,397	14,039	10,321	37	3,718 R	57.5%	42.3%	57.6%	42.4%
51,037	COLUMBUS	15,882	6,659	9,172	51	2,513 D	41.9%	57.8%	42.1%	57.9%
71,043	CRAVEN	19,417	12,057	7,313	47	4,744 R	62.1%	37.7%	62.2%	37.8%
247,160	CUMBERLAND	50,979	27,057	23,789	133	3,268 R	53.1%	46.7%	53.2%	46.8%
11,089	CURRITUCK	4,006	2,443	1,555	8	888 R	61.0%	38.8%	61.1%	38.9%
13,377	DARE	8,071	5,234	2,806	31	2,428 R	64.8%	34.8%	65.1%	34.9%
113,162	DAVIDSON	41,662	28,374	13,215	73	15,159 R	68.1%	31.7%	68.2%	31.8%
24,599	DAVIE	11,192	7,988	3,166	38	4,822 R	71.4%	28.3%	71.6%	28.4%
40,952	DUPLIN	11,726	5,774	5,945	7	171 D	49.2%	50.7%	49.3%	50.7%
152,785	DURHAM	65,883	29,928	35,441	514	5,513 D	45.4%	53.8%	45.8%	54.2%
55,988	EDGECOMBE	15,916	6,831	9,044	41	2,213 D	42.9%	56.8%	43.0%	57.0%
243,683	FORSYTH	97,735	57,688	39,726	321	17,962 R	59.0%	40.6%	59.2%	40.8%
30,055	FRANKLIN	10,960	5,499	5,438	23	61 R	50.2%	49.6%	50.3%	49.7%
162,568	GASTON	49,451	34,775	14,582	94	20,193 R	70.3%	29.5%	70.5%	29.5%
8,875	GATES	3,485	1,451	2,024	10	573 D	41.6%	58.1%	41.8%	58.2%
7,217	GRAHAM	3,419	2,091	1,313	15	778 R	61.2%	38.4%	61.4%	38.6%
34,043	GRANVILLE	10,439	4,880	5,280	279	400 D	46.7%	50.6%	48.0%	52.0%
16,117	GREENE	5,238	2,498	2,729	11	231 D	47.7%	52.1%	47.8%	52.2%
317,154	GUILFORD	117,232	66,060	50,351	821	15,709 R	56.3%	42.9%	56.7%	43.3%
55,286	HALIFAX	16,211	7,462	8,726	23	1,264 D	46.0%	53.8%	46.1%	53.9%
59,570	HARNETT	17,029	9,749	7,259	21	2,490 R	57.2%	42.6%	57.3%	42.7%
46,495	HAYWOOD	18,028	8,957	9,010	61	53 D	49.7%	50.0%	49.9%	50.1%
58,580	HENDERSON	29,125	19,711	9,338	76	10,373 R	67.7%	32.1%	67.9%	32.1%
23,368	HERTFORD	7,930	2,977	4,943	10	1,966 D	37.5%	62.3%	37.6%	62.4%
20,383	HOKE	5,333	2,020	3,281	32	1,261 D	37.9%	61.5%	38.1%	61.9%
5,873	HYDE	2,264	940	1,316	8	376 D	41.5%	58.1%	41.7%	58.3%
82,538	IREDELL	32,135	21,536	10,530	69	11,006 R	67.0%	32.8%	67.2%	32.8%
25,811	JACKSON	10,123	5,166	4,933	24	233 R	51.0%	48.7%	51.2%	48.8%
70,599	JOHNSTON	24,329	15,563	8,717	49	6,846 R	64.0%	35.8%	64.1%	35.9%
9,705	JONES	3,602	1,649	1,946	7	297 D	45.8%	54.0%	45.9%	54.1%
36,718	LEE	11,371	7,104	4,231	36	2,873 R	62.5%	37.2%	62.7%	37.3%
59,819	LENOIR	18,353	10,669	7,649	35	3,020 R	58.1%	41.7%	58.2%	41.8%
42,372	LINCOLN	18,130	11,651	6,444	35	5,207 R	64.3%	35.5%	64.4%	35.6%
35,135	MCDOWELL	10,997	6,526	4,449	22	2,077 R	59.3%	40.5%	59.5%	40.5%
20,178	MACON	9,816	6,026	3,773	17	2,253 R	61.4%	38.4%	61.5%	38.5%
16,827	MADISON	6,506	3,453	3,033	20	420 R	53.1%	46.6%	53.2%	46.8%
25,948	MARTIN	6,756	3,149	3,598	9	449 D	46.6%	53.3%	46.7%	53.3%
404,270	MECKLENBURG	178,796	106,236	71,907	653	34,329 R	59.4%	40.2%	59.6%	40.4%

NORTH CAROLINA

PRESIDENT 1988

1980 Census Population	County	Total Vote	Republican	Democratic	Other	Rep.-Dem. Plurality	Percentage Total Vote Rep.	Percentage Total Vote Dem.	Percentage Major Vote Rep.	Percentage Major Vote Dem.
14,428	MITCHELL	6,014	4,620	1,377	17	3,243 R	76.8%	22.9%	77.0%	23.0%
22,469	MONTGOMERY	8,530	4,504	3,995	31	509 R	52.8%	46.8%	53.0%	47.0%
50,505	MOORE	22,248	14,543	7,642	63	6,901 R	65.4%	34.3%	65.6%	34.4%
67,153	NASH	24,722	15,906	8,740	76	7,166 R	64.3%	35.4%	64.5%	35.5%
103,471	NEW HANOVER	39,313	23,807	15,401	105	8,406 R	60.6%	39.2%	60.7%	39.3%
22,584	NORTHAMPTON	7,033	2,415	4,599	19	2,184 D	34.3%	65.4%	34.4%	65.6%
112,784	ONSLOW	19,488	12,253	7,162	73	5,091 R	62.9%	36.8%	63.1%	36.9%
77,055	ORANGE	37,067	14,503	22,326	238	7,823 D	39.1%	60.2%	39.4%	60.6%
10,398	PAMLICO	4,506	2,297	2,188	21	109 R	51.0%	48.6%	51.2%	48.8%
28,462	PASQUOTANK	7,892	4,006	3,860	26	146 R	50.8%	48.9%	50.9%	49.1%
22,215	PENDER	9,323	4,926	4,377	20	549 R	52.8%	46.9%	53.0%	47.0%
9,486	PERQUIMANS	3,340	1,781	1,543	16	238 R	53.3%	46.2%	53.6%	46.4%
29,164	PERSON	8,628	4,832	3,777	19	1,055 R	56.0%	43.8%	56.1%	43.9%
90,146	PITT	33,127	18,245	14,777	105	3,468 R	55.1%	44.6%	55.3%	44.7%
12,984	POLK	6,423	3,874	2,534	15	1,340 R	60.3%	39.5%	60.5%	39.5%
91,728	RANDOLPH	32,571	23,881	8,641	49	15,240 R	73.3%	26.5%	73.4%	26.6%
45,481	RICHMOND	12,257	5,073	7,151	33	2,078 D	41.4%	58.3%	41.5%	58.5%
101,610	ROBESON	27,000	9,908	16,988	104	7,080 D	36.7%	62.9%	36.8%	63.2%
83,426	ROCKINGHAM	26,164	14,591	11,551	22	3,040 R	55.8%	44.1%	55.8%	44.2%
99,186	ROWAN	35,416	23,192	12,127	97	11,065 R	65.5%	34.2%	65.7%	34.3%
53,787	RUTHERFORD	17,306	10,337	6,926	43	3,411 R	59.7%	40.0%	59.9%	40.1%
49,687	SAMPSON	16,555	8,524	8,009	22	515 R	51.5%	48.4%	51.6%	48.4%
32,273	SCOTLAND	7,084	3,199	3,865	20	666 D	45.2%	54.6%	45.3%	54.7%
48,517	STANLY	18,532	11,885	6,627	20	5,258 R	64.1%	35.8%	64.2%	35.8%
33,086	STOKES	14,012	8,661	5,319	32	3,342 R	61.8%	38.0%	62.0%	38.0%
59,449	SURRY	18,660	11,393	7,245	22	4,148 R	61.1%	38.8%	61.1%	38.9%
10,283	SWAIN	3,625	1,795	1,821	9	26 D	49.5%	50.2%	49.6%	50.4%
23,417	TRANSYLVANIA	11,330	7,009	4,280	41	2,729 R	61.9%	37.8%	62.1%	37.9%
3,975	TYRRELL	1,425	637	785	3	148 D	44.7%	55.1%	44.8%	55.2%
70,380	UNION	25,896	17,015	8,820	61	8,195 R	65.7%	34.1%	65.9%	34.1%
36,748	VANCE	11,276	5,625	5,631	20	6 D	49.9%	49.9%	50.0%	50.0%
301,327	WAKE	143,504	81,613	61,352	539	20,261 R	56.9%	42.8%	57.1%	42.9%
16,232	WARREN	6,429	2,163	4,249	17	2,086 D	33.6%	66.1%	33.7%	66.3%
14,801	WASHINGTON	5,004	2,186	2,806	12	620 D	43.7%	56.1%	43.8%	56.2%
31,666	WATAUGA	14,785	8,662	6,048	75	2,614 R	58.6%	40.9%	58.9%	41.1%
97,054	WAYNE	24,474	15,292	9,135	47	6,157 R	62.5%	37.3%	62.6%	37.4%
58,657	WILKES	22,514	15,231	7,230	53	8,001 R	67.7%	32.1%	67.8%	32.2%
63,132	WILSON	19,257	10,997	8,214	46	2,783 R	57.1%	42.7%	57.2%	42.8%
28,439	YADKIN	11,137	7,918	3,195	24	4,723 R	71.1%	28.7%	71.2%	28.8%
14,934	YANCEY	8,000	4,160	3,803	37	357 R	52.0%	47.5%	52.2%	47.8%
5,881,766	TOTAL	2,134,370	1,237,258	890,167	6,945	347,091 R	58.0%	41.7%	58.2%	41.8%

NORTH CAROLINA

GOVERNOR 1988

1980 Census Population	County	Total Vote	Republican	Democratic	Other	Rep.-Dem. Plurality	Percentage Total Vote Rep.	Percentage Total Vote Dem.	Percentage Major Vote Rep.	Percentage Major Vote Dem.
99,319	ALAMANCE	37,593	23,262	14,331		8,931 R	61.9%	38.1%	61.9%	38.1%
24,999	ALEXANDER	12,108	7,395	4,713		2,682 R	61.1%	38.9%	61.1%	38.9%
9,587	ALLEGHANY	4,331	2,031	2,300		269 D	46.9%	53.1%	46.9%	53.1%
25,649	ANSON	7,569	2,320	5,249		2,929 D	30.7%	69.3%	30.7%	69.3%
22,325	ASHE	10,206	5,805	4,401		1,404 R	56.9%	43.1%	56.9%	43.1%
14,409	AVERY	5,709	4,064	1,645		2,419 R	71.2%	28.8%	71.2%	28.8%
40,355	BEAUFORT	13,889	7,633	6,256		1,377 R	55.0%	45.0%	55.0%	45.0%
21,024	BERTIE	6,273	2,106	4,167		2,061 D	33.6%	66.4%	33.6%	66.4%
30,491	BLADEN	8,949	3,544	5,405		1,861 D	39.6%	60.4%	39.6%	60.4%
35,777	BRUNSWICK	18,393	9,658	8,735		923 R	52.5%	47.5%	52.5%	47.5%
160,934	BUNCOMBE	65,849	36,968	28,881		8,087 R	56.1%	43.9%	56.1%	43.9%
72,504	BURKE	27,097	14,925	12,172		2,753 R	55.1%	44.9%	55.1%	44.9%
85,895	CABARRUS	33,646	21,485	12,161		9,324 R	63.9%	36.1%	63.9%	36.1%
67,746	CALDWELL	23,042	14,047	8,995		5,052 R	61.0%	39.0%	61.0%	39.0%
5,829	CAMDEN	2,250	948	1,302		354 D	42.1%	57.9%	42.1%	57.9%
41,092	CARTERET	18,797	10,719	8,078		2,641 R	57.0%	43.0%	57.0%	43.0%
20,705	CASWELL	7,231	2,689	4,542		1,853 D	37.2%	62.8%	37.2%	62.8%
105,208	CATAWBA	42,085	28,042	14,043		13,999 R	66.6%	33.4%	66.6%	33.4%
33,415	CHATHAM	15,091	7,201	7,890		689 D	47.7%	52.3%	47.7%	52.3%
18,933	CHEROKEE	7,620	4,516	3,104		1,412 R	59.3%	40.7%	59.3%	40.7%
12,558	CHOWAN	4,216	1,762	2,454		692 D	41.8%	58.2%	41.8%	58.2%
6,619	CLAY	3,478	2,026	1,452		574 R	58.3%	41.7%	58.3%	41.7%
83,435	CLEVELAND	25,144	13,305	11,839		1,466 R	52.9%	47.1%	52.9%	47.1%
51,037	COLUMBUS	16,488	5,833	10,655		4,822 D	35.4%	64.6%	35.4%	64.6%
71,043	CRAVEN	21,121	11,921	9,200		2,721 R	56.4%	43.6%	56.4%	43.6%
247,160	CUMBERLAND	52,523	25,670	26,853		1,183 D	48.9%	51.1%	48.9%	51.1%
11,089	CURRITUCK	4,057	2,159	1,898		261 R	53.2%	46.8%	53.2%	46.8%
13,377	DARE	8,233	4,792	3,441		1,351 R	58.2%	41.8%	58.2%	41.8%
113,162	DAVIDSON	41,943	26,735	15,208		11,527 R	63.7%	36.3%	63.7%	36.3%
24,599	DAVIE	11,138	7,606	3,532		4,074 R	68.3%	31.7%	68.3%	31.7%
40,952	DUPLIN	12,451	5,847	6,604		757 D	47.0%	53.0%	47.0%	53.0%
152,785	DURHAM	65,803	31,010	34,793		3,783 D	47.1%	52.9%	47.1%	52.9%
55,988	EDGECOMBE	16,092	6,524	9,568		3,044 D	40.5%	59.5%	40.5%	59.5%
243,683	FORSYTH	99,632	59,337	40,295		19,042 R	59.6%	40.4%	59.6%	40.4%
30,055	FRANKLIN	11,082	5,287	5,795		508 D	47.7%	52.3%	47.7%	52.3%
162,568	GASTON	50,391	32,658	17,733		14,925 R	64.8%	35.2%	64.8%	35.2%
8,875	GATES	3,400	1,158	2,242		1,084 D	34.1%	65.9%	34.1%	65.9%
7,217	GRAHAM	3,366	1,854	1,512		342 R	55.1%	44.9%	55.1%	44.9%
34,043	GRANVILLE	10,845	4,842	6,003		1,161 D	44.6%	55.4%	44.6%	55.4%
16,117	GREENE	5,150	2,090	3,060		970 D	40.6%	59.4%	40.6%	59.4%
317,154	GUILFORD	118,110	65,331	52,779		12,552 R	55.3%	44.7%	55.3%	44.7%
55,286	HALIFAX	16,421	6,947	9,474		2,527 D	42.3%	57.7%	42.3%	57.7%
59,570	HARNETT	17,280	9,245	8,035		1,210 R	53.5%	46.5%	53.5%	46.5%
46,495	HAYWOOD	18,041	8,727	9,314		587 D	48.4%	51.6%	48.4%	51.6%
58,580	HENDERSON	29,055	19,623	9,432		10,191 R	67.5%	32.5%	67.5%	32.5%
23,368	HERTFORD	8,151	2,829	5,322		2,493 D	34.7%	65.3%	34.7%	65.3%
20,383	HOKE	5,276	1,600	3,676		2,076 D	30.3%	69.7%	30.3%	69.7%
5,873	HYDE	2,208	850	1,358		508 D	38.5%	61.5%	38.5%	61.5%
82,538	IREDELL	32,598	21,481	11,117		10,364 R	65.9%	34.1%	65.9%	34.1%
25,811	JACKSON	10,380	5,138	5,242		104 D	49.5%	50.5%	49.5%	50.5%
70,599	JOHNSTON	24,669	15,324	9,345		5,979 R	62.1%	37.9%	62.1%	37.9%
9,705	JONES	3,556	1,445	2,111		666 D	40.6%	59.4%	40.6%	59.4%
36,718	LEE	12,293	7,107	5,186		1,921 R	57.8%	42.2%	57.8%	42.2%
59,819	LENOIR	18,367	9,844	8,523		1,321 R	53.6%	46.4%	53.6%	46.4%
42,372	LINCOLN	18,386	11,320	7,066		4,254 R	61.6%	38.4%	61.6%	38.4%
35,135	MCDOWELL	11,301	6,128	5,173		955 R	54.2%	45.8%	54.2%	45.8%
20,178	MACON	10,073	5,824	4,249		1,575 R	57.8%	42.2%	57.8%	42.2%
16,827	MADISON	6,381	3,194	3,187		7 R	50.1%	49.9%	50.1%	49.9%
25,948	MARTIN	7,526	3,101	4,425		1,324 D	41.2%	58.8%	41.2%	58.8%
404,270	MECKLENBURG	179,018	114,237	64,781		49,456 R	63.8%	36.2%	63.8%	36.2%

NORTH CAROLINA

GOVERNOR 1988

1980 Census Population	County	Total Vote	Republican	Democratic	Other	Rep.-Dem. Plurality	Percentage Total Vote Rep.	Total Vote Dem.	Major Vote Rep.	Major Vote Dem.
14,428	MITCHELL	6,062	4,568	1,494		3,074 R	75.4%	24.6%	75.4%	24.6%
22,469	MONTGOMERY	8,505	3,714	4,791		1,077 D	43.7%	56.3%	43.7%	56.3%
50,505	MOORE	22,477	14,284	8,193		6,091 R	63.5%	36.5%	63.5%	36.5%
67,153	NASH	24,933	15,179	9,754		5,425 R	60.9%	39.1%	60.9%	39.1%
103,471	NEW HANOVER	39,909	22,888	17,021		5,867 R	57.4%	42.6%	57.4%	42.6%
22,584	NORTHAMPTON	7,454	2,341	5,113		2,772 D	31.4%	68.6%	31.4%	68.6%
112,784	ONSLOW	19,690	11,605	8,085		3,520 R	58.9%	41.1%	58.9%	41.1%
77,055	ORANGE	36,629	16,083	20,546		4,463 D	43.9%	56.1%	43.9%	56.1%
10,398	PAMLICO	4,475	2,086	2,389		303 D	46.6%	53.4%	46.6%	53.4%
28,462	PASQUOTANK	8,482	3,569	4,913		1,344 D	42.1%	57.9%	42.1%	57.9%
22,215	PENDER	9,455	4,677	4,778		101 D	49.5%	50.5%	49.5%	50.5%
9,486	PERQUIMANS	3,285	1,484	1,801		317 D	45.2%	54.8%	45.2%	54.8%
29,164	PERSON	8,731	4,582	4,149		433 R	52.5%	47.5%	52.5%	47.5%
90,146	PITT	32,909	17,036	15,873		1,163 R	51.8%	48.2%	51.8%	48.2%
12,984	POLK	6,745	3,984	2,761		1,223 R	59.1%	40.9%	59.1%	40.9%
91,728	RANDOLPH	34,805	23,840	10,965		12,875 R	68.5%	31.5%	68.5%	31.5%
45,481	RICHMOND	12,554	4,597	7,957		3,360 D	36.6%	63.4%	36.6%	63.4%
101,610	ROBESON	27,462	8,722	18,740		10,018 D	31.8%	68.2%	31.8%	68.2%
83,426	ROCKINGHAM	26,958	13,842	13,116		726 R	51.3%	48.7%	51.3%	48.7%
99,186	ROWAN	35,793	22,008	13,785		8,223 R	61.5%	38.5%	61.5%	38.5%
53,787	RUTHERFORD	17,693	9,813	7,880		1,933 R	55.5%	44.5%	55.5%	44.5%
49,687	SAMPSON	17,490	8,810	8,680		130 R	50.4%	49.6%	50.4%	49.6%
32,273	SCOTLAND	7,149	2,652	4,497		1,845 D	37.1%	62.9%	37.1%	62.9%
48,517	STANLY	19,165	11,370	7,795		3,575 R	59.3%	40.7%	59.3%	40.7%
33,086	STOKES	14,412	8,212	6,200		2,012 R	57.0%	43.0%	57.0%	43.0%
59,449	SURRY	20,452	11,512	8,940		2,572 R	56.3%	43.7%	56.3%	43.7%
10,283	SWAIN	3,826	1,970	1,856		114 R	51.5%	48.5%	51.5%	48.5%
23,417	TRANSYLVANIA	11,436	6,858	4,578		2,280 R	60.0%	40.0%	60.0%	40.0%
3,975	TYRRELL	1,400	520	880		360 D	37.1%	62.9%	37.1%	62.9%
70,380	UNION	25,865	15,761	10,104		5,657 R	60.9%	39.1%	60.9%	39.1%
36,748	VANCE	11,818	5,329	6,489		1,160 D	45.1%	54.9%	45.1%	54.9%
301,327	WAKE	155,028	92,498	62,530		29,968 R	59.7%	40.3%	59.7%	40.3%
16,232	WARREN	6,211	2,069	4,142		2,073 D	33.3%	66.7%	33.3%	66.7%
14,801	WASHINGTON	4,945	2,021	2,924		903 D	40.9%	59.1%	40.9%	59.1%
31,666	WATAUGA	15,021	8,747	6,274		2,473 R	58.2%	41.8%	58.2%	41.8%
97,054	WAYNE	25,859	14,778	11,081		3,697 R	57.1%	42.9%	57.1%	42.9%
58,657	WILKES	22,912	14,854	8,058		6,796 R	64.8%	35.2%	64.8%	35.2%
63,132	WILSON	19,391	10,708	8,683		2,025 R	55.2%	44.8%	55.2%	44.8%
28,439	YADKIN	11,087	7,589	3,498		4,091 R	68.4%	31.6%	68.4%	31.6%
14,934	YANCEY	8,181	4,109	4,072		37 R	50.2%	49.8%	50.2%	49.8%
5,881,766	TOTAL	2,180,025	1,222,338	957,687		264,651 R	56.1%	43.9%	56.1%	43.9%

NORTH CAROLINA

CONGRESS

			Republican		Democratic				Percentage			
		Total					Other	Rep.-Dem.	Total Vote		Major Vote	
CD	Year	Vote	Vote	Candidate	Vote	Candidate	Vote	Plurality	Rep.	Dem.	Rep.	Dem.
1	1988	181,040	63,013	MOYE, HOWARD	118,027	JONES, WALTER B.		55,014 D	34.8%	65.2%	34.8%	65.2%
1	1986	131,034	39,912	MOYE, HOWARD	91,122	JONES, WALTER B.		51,210 D	30.5%	69.5%	30.5%	69.5%
1	1984	182,968	60,153	LEE, HERBERT W.	122,815	JONES, WALTER B.		62,662 D	32.9%	67.1%	32.9%	67.1%
1	1982	98,342	17,478	MCINTYRE, JAMES F.	79,954	JONES, WALTER B.	910	62,476 D	17.8%	81.3%	17.9%	82.1%
2	1988	128,832			128,832	VALENTINE, I. T.		128,832 D		100.0%		100.0%
2	1986	127,835	32,515	MCELHANEY, BUD	95,320	VALENTINE, I. T.		62,805 D	25.4%	74.6%	25.4%	74.6%
2	1984	180,604	58,312	HILL, FRANK H.	122,292	VALENTINE, I. T.		63,980 D	32.3%	67.7%	32.3%	67.7%
2	1982	111,326	34,293	MARIN, JOHN W.	59,617	VALENTINE, I. T.	17,416	25,324 D	30.8%	53.6%	36.5%	63.5%
3	1988	95,323			95,323	LANCASTER, MARTIN		95,323 D		100.0%		100.0%
3	1986	110,868	39,408	HURST, GERALD B.	71,460	LANCASTER, MARTIN		32,052 D	35.5%	64.5%	35.5%	64.5%
3	1984	156,281	56,096	MOODY, DANNY G.	100,185	WHITLEY, CHARLES		44,089 D	35.9%	64.1%	35.9%	64.1%
3	1982	108,473	39,046	MCDANIEL, EUGENE	68,936	WHITLEY, CHARLES	491	29,890 D	36.0%	63.6%	36.2%	63.8%
4	1988	227,378	95,482	FETZER, TOM	131,896	PRICE, DAVID E.		36,414 D	42.0%	58.0%	42.0%	58.0%
4	1986	165,685	73,469	COBEY, WILLIAM	92,216	PRICE, DAVID E.		18,747 D	44.3%	55.7%	44.3%	55.7%
4	1984	231,898	117,436	COBEY, WILLIAM	114,462	ANDREWS, IKE F.		2,974 R	50.6%	49.4%	50.6%	49.4%
4	1982	137,044	64,955	COBEY, WILLIAM	70,369	ANDREWS, IKE F.	1,720	5,414 D	47.4%	51.3%	48.0%	52.0%
5	1988	210,056	99,540	GRAY, LYONS	110,516	NEAL, STEPHEN L.		10,976 D	47.4%	52.6%	47.4%	52.6%
5	1986	159,671	73,261	EPPERSON, STUART	86,410	NEAL, STEPHEN L.		13,149 D	45.9%	54.1%	45.9%	54.1%
5	1984	216,430	106,599	EPPERSON, STUART	109,831	NEAL, STEPHEN L.		3,232 D	49.3%	50.7%	49.3%	50.7%
5	1982	145,707	57,083	BAGNAL, ANNE	87,819	NEAL, STEPHEN L.	805	30,736 D	39.2%	60.3%	39.4%	60.6%
6	1988	186,542	116,534	COBLE, HOWARD	70,008	GILMORE, TOM		46,526 R	62.5%	37.5%	62.5%	37.5%
6	1986	144,579	72,329	COBLE, HOWARD	72,250	BRITT, C. ROBIN		79 R	50.0%	50.0%	50.0%	50.0%
6	1984	203,473	102,925	COBLE, HOWARD	100,263	BRITT, C. ROBIN	285	2,662 R	50.6%	49.3%	50.7%	49.3%
6	1982	127,619	58,244	JOHNSTON, EUGENE	68,696	BRITT, C. ROBIN	679	10,452 D	45.6%	53.8%	45.9%	54.1%
7	1988	152,247	49,855	THOMPSON, GEORGE G.	102,392	ROSE, CHARLES G.		52,537 D	32.7%	67.3%	32.7%	67.3%
7	1986	109,760	39,289	HARRELSON, THOMAS J.	70,471	ROSE, CHARLES G.		31,182 D	35.8%	64.2%	35.8%	64.2%
7	1984	155,782	63,625	RHODES, S. THOMAS	92,157	ROSE, CHARLES G.		28,532 D	40.8%	59.2%	40.8%	59.2%
7	1982	96,534	27,015	JOHNSON, EDWARD	68,529	ROSE, CHARLES G.	990	41,514 D	28.0%	71.0%	28.3%	71.7%
8	1988	192,677	93,463	BLANTON, TED	99,214	HEFNER, W. G.		5,751 D	48.5%	51.5%	48.5%	51.5%
8	1986	139,900	58,941	HAMBY, WILLIAM G.	80,959	HEFNER, W. G.		22,018 D	42.1%	57.9%	42.1%	57.9%
8	1984	196,085	96,354	BLAKE, HARRIS D.	99,731	HEFNER, W. G.		3,377 D	49.1%	50.9%	49.1%	50.9%
8	1982	124,938	52,417	BLAKE, HARRIS D.	71,691	HEFNER, W. G.	830	19,274 D	42.0%	57.4%	42.2%	57.8%
9	1988	210,816	139,014	MCMILLAN, J. ALEX	71,802	SHOLANDER, MARK		67,212 R	65.9%	34.1%	65.9%	34.1%
9	1986	156,592	80,352	MCMILLAN, J. ALEX	76,240	MARTIN, D. G.		4,112 R	51.3%	48.7%	51.3%	48.7%
9	1984	218,519	109,420	MCMILLAN, J. ALEX	109,099	MARTIN, D. G.		321 R	50.1%	49.9%	50.1%	49.9%
9	1982	112,786	64,297	MARTIN, JAMES G.	47,258	CORNELIUS, PRESTON	1,231	17,039 R	57.0%	41.9%	57.6%	42.4%
10	1988	184,419	112,554	BALLENGER, CASS	71,865	RHYNE, JACK L.		40,689 R	61.0%	39.0%	61.0%	39.0%
10	1986	145,937	83,902	BALLENGER, CASS	62,035	ROARK, LESTER D.		21,867 R	57.5%	42.5%	57.5%	42.5%
10	1984	194,733	142,873	BROYHILL, JAMES T.	51,860	POOVEY, TED A.		91,013 R	73.4%	26.6%	73.4%	26.6%
10	1982	87,264	80,904	BROYHILL, JAMES T.			6,360	80,904 R	92.7%		100.0%	
11	1988	215,343	106,907	TAYLOR, CHARLES H.	108,436	CLARKE, JAMES MCC.		1,529 D	49.6%	50.4%	49.6%	50.4%
11	1986	180,644	89,069	HENDON, WILLIAM M.	91,575	CLARKE, JAMES MCC.		2,506 D	49.3%	50.7%	49.3%	50.7%
11	1984	220,882	112,598	HENDON, WILLIAM M.	108,284	CLARKE, JAMES MCC.		4,314 R	51.0%	49.0%	51.0%	49.0%
11	1982	171,047	84,085	HENDON, WILLIAM M.	85,410	CLARKE, JAMES MCC.	1,552	1,325 D	49.2%	49.9%	49.6%	50.4%

NORTH CAROLINA

1988 GENERAL ELECTION

President Other vote was 5,682 New Alliance (Fulani); 1,263 Paul (write-in).

Governor

Congress

1988 PRIMARIES

MAY 3 REPUBLICAN

Governor James G. Martin, unopposed.

Congress Unopposed in seven CD's. No candidate in CD 2 and 3. Contested as follows:

CD 1 6,333 Howard Moye; 1,921 William J. Wahl.
CD 7 3,702 George G. Thompson; 2,904 A. C. Parker.

MAY 3 DEMOCRATIC

Governor 403,145 Robert B. Jordan; 60,770 Billy Martin; 21,844 Carroll W. Crawford; 10,438 James Lloyd; 9,876 Bruce A. Friedman.

Congress Unopposed in nine CD's. Contested as follows:

CD 9 12,820 Mark Sholander; 12,243 David P. McKnight.
CD 10 17,573 Jack L. Rhyne; 6,596 Mildred T. Keene; 3,203 Ted A. Poovey.

NORTH DAKOTA

GOVERNOR

George Sinner (D). Re-elected 1988 to a four-year term. Previously elected 1984.

SENATORS

Quentin N. Burdick (D). Re-elected 1988 to a six-year term. Previously elected 1982, 1976, 1970, 1964 and in June 1960 to fill our term vacated by the death of Senator William Langer.

Kent Conrad (D). Elected 1986 to a six-year term.

REPRESENTATIVE

At-large. Byron L. Dorgan (D)

POSTWAR VOTE FOR PRESIDENT

Year	Total Vote	Republican Vote	Republican Candidate	Democratic Vote	Democratic Candidate	Other Vote	Plurality	Percentage Total Vote Rep.	Percentage Total Vote Dem.	Percentage Major Vote Rep.	Percentage Major Vote Dem.
1988	297,261	166,559	Bush, George	127,739	Dukakis, Michael S.	2,963	38,820 R	56.0%	43.0%	56.6%	43.4%
1984	308,971	200,336	Reagan, Ronald	104,429	Mondale, Walter F.	4,206	95,907 R	64.8%	33.8%	65.7%	34.3%
1980	301,545	193,695	Reagan, Ronald	79,189	Carter, Jimmy	28,661	114,506 R	64.2%	26.3%	71.0%	29.0%
1976	297,188	153,470	Ford, Gerald R.	136,078	Carter, Jimmy	7,640	17,392 R	51.6%	45.8%	53.0%	47.0%
1972	280,514	174,109	Nixon, Richard M.	100,384	McGovern, George S.	6,021	73,725 R	62.1%	35.8%	63.4%	36.6%
1968	247,882	138,669	Nixon, Richard M.	94,769	Humphrey, Hubert H.	14,444	43,900 R	55.9%	38.2%	59.4%	40.6%
1964	258,389	108,207	Goldwater, Barry M.	149,784	Johnson, Lyndon B.	398	41,577 D	41.9%	58.0%	41.9%	58.1%
1960	278,431	154,310	Nixon, Richard M.	123,963	Kennedy, John F.	158	30,347 R	55.4%	44.5%	55.5%	44.5%
1956	253,991	156,766	Eisenhower, Dwight D.	96,742	Stevenson, Adlai E.	483	60,024 R	61.7%	38.1%	61.8%	38.2%
1952	270,127	191,712	Eisenhower, Dwight D.	76,694	Stevenson, Adlai E.	1,721	115,018 R	71.0%	28.4%	71.4%	28.6%
1948	220,716	115,139	Dewey, Thomas E.	95,812	Truman, Harry S.	9,765	19,327 R	52.2%	43.4%	54.6%	45.4%

POSTWAR VOTE FOR GOVERNOR

Year	Total Vote	Republican Vote	Republican Candidate	Democratic Vote	Democratic Candidate	Other Vote	Rep.-Dem. Plurality	Percentage Total Vote Rep.	Percentage Total Vote Dem.	Percentage Major Vote Rep.	Percentage Major Vote Dem.
1988	299,080	119,986	Mallberg, Leon L.	179,094	Sinner, George		59,108 D	40.1%	59.9%	40.1%	59.9%
1984	314,382	140,460	Olson, Allen I.	173,922	Sinner, George		33,462 D	44.7%	55.3%	44.7%	55.3%
1980	302,621	162,230	Olson, Allen I.	140,391	Link, Arthur A.		21,839 R	53.6%	46.4%	53.6%	46.4%
1976	297,249	138,321	Elkin, Richard	153,309	Link, Arthur A.	5,619	14,988 D	46.5%	51.6%	47.4%	52.6%
1972	281,931	138,032	Larsen, Richard	143,899	Link, Arthur A.		5,867 D	49.0%	51.0%	49.0%	51.0%
1968	248,000	108,382	McCarney, Robert P.	135,955	Guy, William L.	3,663	27,573 D	43.7%	54.8%	44.4%	55.6%
1964 **	262,661	116,247	Halcrow, Donald M.	146,414	Guy, William L.		30,167 D	44.3%	55.7%	44.3%	55.7%
1962	228,509	113,251	Andrews, Mark	115,258	Guy, William L.		2,007 D	49.6%	50.4%	49.6%	50.4%
1960	275,375	122,486	Dahl, C. P.	136,148	Guy, William L.	16,741	13,662 D	44.5%	49.4%	47.4%	52.6%
1958	210,599	111,836	Davis, John E.	98,763	Lord, John F.		13,073 R	53.1%	46.9%	53.1%	46.9%
1956	252,435	147,566	Davis, John E.	104,869	Warner, Wallace E.		42,697 R	58.5%	41.5%	58.5%	41.5%
1954	193,501	124,253	Brunsdale, C. Norman	69,248	Bymers, Cornelius		55,005 R	64.2%	35.8%	64.2%	35.8%
1952	253,934	199,944	Brunsdale, C. Norman	53,990	Johnson, Ole C.		145,954 R	78.7%	21.3%	78.7%	21.3%
1950	183,772	121,822	Brunsdale, C. Norman	61,950	Byerly, Clyde G.		59,872 R	66.3%	33.7%	66.3%	33.7%
1948	214,858	131,764	Aandahl, Fred G.	80,555	Henry, Howard	2,539	51,209 R	61.3%	37.5%	62.1%	37.9%
1946	169,391	116,672	Aandahl, Fred G.	52,719	Burdick, Quentin N.		63,953 R	68.9%	31.1%	68.9%	31.1%

The term of office of North Dakota's Governor was increased from two to four years effective with the 1964 election.

NORTH DAKOTA

POSTWAR VOTE FOR SENATOR

									Percentage			
	Total	Republican		Democratic		Other	Rep.-Dem.		Total Vote		Major Vote	
Year	Vote	Vote	Candidate	Vote	Candidate	Vote	Plurality		Rep.	Dem.	Rep.	Dem.
1988	289,170	112,937	Striden, Earl	171,899	Burdick, Quentin N.	4,334	58,962	D	39.1%	59.4%	39.6%	60.4%
1986	288,998	141,797	Andrews, Mark	143,932	Conrad, Kent	3,269	2,135	D	49.1%	49.8%	49.6%	50.4%
1982	262,465	89,304	Knorr, Gene	164,873	Burdick, Quentin N.	8,288	75,569	D	34.0%	62.8%	35.1%	64.9%
1980	299,272	210,347	Andrews, Mark	86,658	Johanneson, Kent	2,267	123,689	R	70.3%	29.0%	70.8%	29.2%
1976	283,062	103,466	Stroup, Richard	175,772	Burdick, Quentin N.	3,824	72,306	D	36.6%	62.1%	37.1%	62.9%
1974	235,661	114,117	Young, Milton R.	113,931	Guy, William L.	7,613	186	R	48.4%	48.3%	50.0%	50.0%
1970	219,560	82,996	Kleppe, Tom	134,519	Burdick, Quentin N.	2,045	51,523	D	37.8%	61.3%	38.2%	61.8%
1968	239,776	154,968	Young, Milton R.	80,815	Lashkowitz, Herschel	3,993	74,153	R	64.6%	33.7%	65.7%	34.3%
1964	258,945	109,681	Kleppe, Tom	149,264	Burdick, Quentin N.		39,583	D	42.4%	57.6%	42.4%	57.6%
1962	223,737	135,705	Young, Milton R.	88,032	Lanier, William		47,673	R	60.7%	39.3%	60.7%	39.3%
1960 S	210,349	103,475	Davis, John E.	104,593	Burdick, Quentin N.	2,281	1,118	D	49.2%	49.7%	49.7%	50.3%
1958	204,635	117,070	Langer, William	84,892	Vendsel, Raymond	2,673	32,178	R	57.2%	41.5%	58.0%	42.0%
1956	244,161	155,305	Young, Milton R.	87,919	Burdick, Quentin N.	937	67,386	R	63.6%	36.0%	63.9%	36.1%
1952	237,995	157,907	Langer, William	55,347	Morrison, Harold A.	24,741	102,560	R	66.3%	23.3%	74.0%	26.0%
1950	186,716	126,209	Young, Milton R.	60,507	O'Brien, Harry		65,702	R	67.6%	32.4%	67.6%	32.4%
1946 * *	165,382	88,210	Langer, William	38,368	Larson, Abner B.	38,804	49,842	R	53.3%	23.2%	69.7%	30.3%
1946 S	136,852	75,998	Young, Milton R.	37,507	Lanier, William	23,347	38,491	R	55.5%	27.4%	67.0%	33.0%

The 1960 and 1946 special elections were held in June for short terms to fill vacancies. In 1946 other vote was Arthur Thompson (Independent) who received 23.5% of the total vote and ran second.

NORTH DAKOTA

One At Large

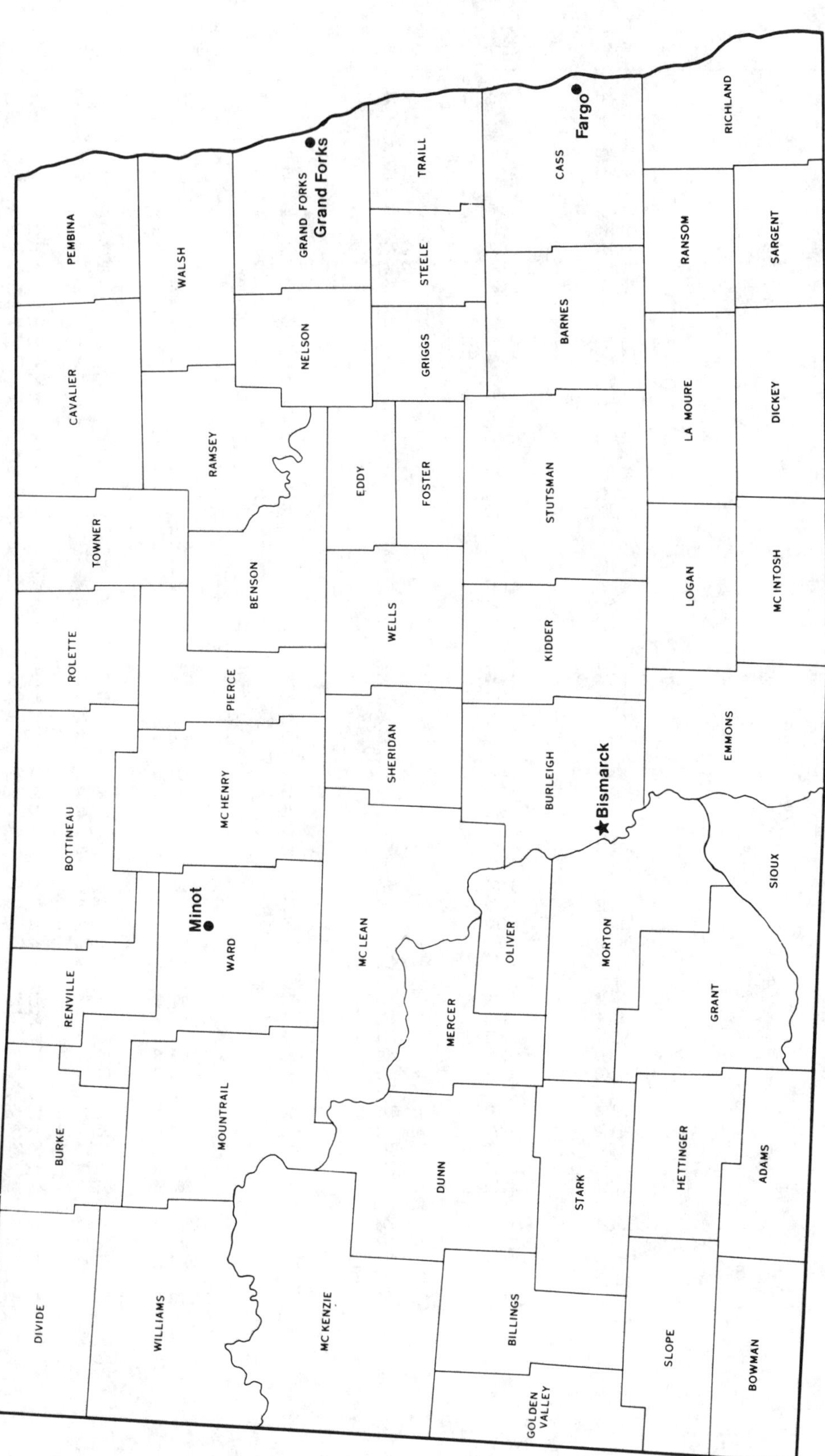

NORTH DAKOTA

PRESIDENT 1988

1980 Census Population	County	Total Vote	Republican	Democratic	Other	Rep.-Dem. Plurality	Percentage Total Vote Rep.	Total Vote Dem.	Major Vote Rep.	Major Vote Dem.
3,584	ADAMS	1,737	1,018	708	11	310 R	58.6%	40.8%	59.0%	41.0%
13,960	BARNES	6,546	3,631	2,858	57	773 R	55.5%	43.7%	56.0%	44.0%
7,944	BENSON	3,031	1,316	1,691	24	375 D	43.4%	55.8%	43.8%	56.2%
1,138	BILLINGS	659	437	211	11	226 R	66.3%	32.0%	67.4%	32.6%
9,239	BOTTINEAU	4,251	2,530	1,684	37	846 R	59.5%	39.6%	60.0%	40.0%
4,229	BOWMAN	1,867	1,111	737	19	374 R	59.5%	39.5%	60.1%	39.9%
3,822	BURKE	1,690	971	693	26	278 R	57.5%	41.0%	58.4%	41.6%
54,811	BURLEIGH	29,084	18,000	10,760	324	7,240 R	61.9%	37.0%	62.6%	37.4%
88,247	CASS	49,137	26,699	22,107	331	4,592 R	54.3%	45.0%	54.7%	45.3%
7,636	CAVALIER	3,457	2,096	1,333	28	763 R	60.6%	38.6%	61.1%	38.9%
7,207	DICKEY	3,336	2,064	1,249	23	815 R	61.9%	37.4%	62.3%	37.7%
3,494	DIVIDE	1,768	869	875	24	6 D	49.2%	49.5%	49.8%	50.2%
4,627	DUNN	2,178	1,263	892	23	371 R	58.0%	41.0%	58.6%	41.4%
3,554	EDDY	1,658	891	748	19	143 R	53.7%	45.1%	54.4%	45.6%
5,877	EMMONS	2,596	1,634	925	37	709 R	62.9%	35.6%	63.9%	36.1%
4,611	FOSTER	2,070	1,218	837	15	381 R	58.8%	40.4%	59.3%	40.7%
2,391	GOLDEN VALLEY	1,183	781	388	14	393 R	66.0%	32.8%	66.8%	33.2%
66,100	GRAND FORKS	27,531	14,801	12,494	236	2,307 R	53.8%	45.4%	54.2%	45.8%
4,274	GRANT	2,043	1,351	654	38	697 R	66.1%	32.0%	67.4%	32.6%
3,714	GRIGGS	1,885	1,020	846	19	174 R	54.1%	44.9%	54.7%	45.3%
4,275	HETTINGER	2,111	1,395	698	18	697 R	66.1%	33.1%	66.7%	33.3%
3,833	KIDDER	1,761	1,039	678	44	361 R	59.0%	38.5%	60.5%	39.5%
6,473	LA MOURE	2,901	1,642	1,223	36	419 R	56.6%	42.2%	57.3%	42.7%
3,493	LOGAN	1,671	1,111	540	20	571 R	66.5%	32.3%	67.3%	32.7%
7,858	MCHENRY	3,583	1,888	1,665	30	223 R	52.7%	46.5%	53.1%	46.9%
4,800	MCINTOSH	2,347	1,726	598	23	1,128 R	73.5%	25.5%	74.3%	25.7%
7,132	MCKENZIE	3,253	1,949	1,273	31	676 R	59.9%	39.1%	60.5%	39.5%
12,383	MCLEAN	5,396	2,906	2,428	62	478 R	53.9%	45.0%	54.5%	45.5%
9,404	MERCER	4,902	3,013	1,843	46	1,170 R	61.5%	37.6%	62.0%	38.0%
25,177	MORTON	10,447	5,588	4,708	151	880 R	53.5%	45.1%	54.3%	45.7%
7,679	MOUNTRAIL	3,458	1,443	1,977	38	534 D	41.7%	57.2%	42.2%	57.8%
5,233	NELSON	2,243	1,078	1,151	14	73 D	48.1%	51.3%	48.4%	51.6%
2,495	OLIVER	1,237	696	526	15	170 R	56.3%	42.5%	57.0%	43.0%
10,399	PEMBINA	4,149	2,471	1,616	62	855 R	59.6%	38.9%	60.5%	39.5%
6,166	PIERCE	2,477	1,422	1,008	47	414 R	57.4%	40.7%	58.5%	41.5%
13,048	RAMSEY	5,841	3,103	2,665	73	438 R	53.1%	45.6%	53.8%	46.2%
6,698	RANSOM	2,858	1,362	1,459	37	97 D	47.7%	51.0%	48.3%	51.7%
3,608	RENVILLE	1,750	893	837	20	56 R	51.0%	47.8%	51.6%	48.4%
19,207	RICHLAND	8,274	4,670	3,523	81	1,147 R	56.4%	42.6%	57.0%	43.0%
12,177	ROLETTE	3,606	1,126	2,426	54	1,300 D	31.2%	67.3%	31.7%	68.3%
5,512	SARGENT	2,436	1,119	1,306	11	187 D	45.9%	53.6%	46.1%	53.9%
2,819	SHERIDAN	1,318	885	428	5	457 R	67.1%	32.5%	67.4%	32.6%
3,620	SIOUX	1,042	325	701	16	376 D	31.2%	67.3%	31.7%	68.3%
1,157	SLOPE	530	315	202	13	113 R	59.4%	38.1%	60.9%	39.1%
23,697	STARK	10,003	6,137	3,678	188	2,459 R	61.4%	36.8%	62.5%	37.5%
3,106	STEELE	1,595	690	895	10	205 D	43.3%	56.1%	43.5%	56.5%
24,154	STUTSMAN	9,669	5,375	4,214	80	1,161 R	55.6%	43.6%	56.1%	43.9%
4,052	TOWNER	1,934	946	970	18	24 D	48.9%	50.2%	49.4%	50.6%
9,624	TRAILL	4,559	2,562	1,940	57	622 R	56.2%	42.6%	56.9%	43.1%
15,371	WALSH	5,966	3,250	2,646	70	604 R	54.5%	44.4%	55.1%	44.9%
58,392	WARD	23,228	13,179	9,906	143	3,273 R	56.7%	42.6%	57.1%	42.9%
6,979	WELLS	3,241	1,901	1,317	23	584 R	58.7%	40.6%	59.1%	40.9%
22,237	WILLIAMS	9,768	5,653	4,004	111	1,649 R	57.9%	41.0%	58.5%	41.5%
652,717	TOTAL	297,261	166,559	127,739	2,963	38,820 R	56.0%	43.0%	56.6%	43.4%

NORTH DAKOTA

GOVERNOR 1988

1980 Census Population	County	Total Vote	Republican	Democratic	Other	Rep.-Dem. Plurality	Percentage Total Vote Rep.	Total Vote Dem.	Major Vote Rep.	Major Vote Dem.
3,584	ADAMS	1,754	839	915		76 D	47.8%	52.2%	47.8%	52.2%
13,960	BARNES	6,717	2,426	4,291		1,865 D	36.1%	63.9%	36.1%	63.9%
7,944	BENSON	3,026	948	2,078		1,130 D	31.3%	68.7%	31.3%	68.7%
1,138	BILLINGS	671	292	379		87 D	43.5%	56.5%	43.5%	56.5%
9,239	BOTTINEAU	4,244	1,964	2,280		316 D	46.3%	53.7%	46.3%	53.7%
4,229	BOWMAN	1,877	873	1,004		131 D	46.5%	53.5%	46.5%	53.5%
3,822	BURKE	1,694	842	852		10 D	49.7%	50.3%	49.7%	50.3%
54,811	BURLEIGH	28,816	12,201	16,615		4,414 D	42.3%	57.7%	42.3%	57.7%
88,247	CASS	49,170	16,660	32,510		15,850 D	33.9%	66.1%	33.9%	66.1%
7,636	CAVALIER	3,442	1,357	2,085		728 D	39.4%	60.6%	39.4%	60.6%
7,207	DICKEY	3,365	1,648	1,717		69 D	49.0%	51.0%	49.0%	51.0%
3,494	DIVIDE	1,789	747	1,042		295 D	41.8%	58.2%	41.8%	58.2%
4,627	DUNN	2,255	1,028	1,227		199 D	45.6%	54.4%	45.6%	54.4%
3,554	EDDY	1,693	615	1,078		463 D	36.3%	63.7%	36.3%	63.7%
5,877	EMMONS	2,700	1,266	1,434		168 D	46.9%	53.1%	46.9%	53.1%
4,611	FOSTER	2,044	819	1,225		406 D	40.1%	59.9%	40.1%	59.9%
2,391	GOLDEN VALLEY	1,202	594	608		14 D	49.4%	50.6%	49.4%	50.6%
66,100	GRAND FORKS	27,383	10,195	17,188		6,993 D	37.2%	62.8%	37.2%	62.8%
4,274	GRANT	2,106	1,083	1,023		60 R	51.4%	48.6%	51.4%	48.6%
3,714	GRIGGS	1,900	730	1,170		440 D	38.4%	61.6%	38.4%	61.6%
4,275	HETTINGER	2,157	1,003	1,154		151 D	46.5%	53.5%	46.5%	53.5%
3,833	KIDDER	1,804	862	942		80 D	47.8%	52.2%	47.8%	52.2%
6,473	LA MOURE	3,009	1,212	1,797		585 D	40.3%	59.7%	40.3%	59.7%
3,493	LOGAN	1,714	868	846		22 R	50.6%	49.4%	50.6%	49.4%
7,858	MCHENRY	3,593	1,519	2,074		555 D	42.3%	57.7%	42.3%	57.7%
4,800	MCINTOSH	2,413	1,446	967		479 R	59.9%	40.1%	59.9%	40.1%
7,132	MCKENZIE	3,283	1,467	1,816		349 D	44.7%	55.3%	44.7%	55.3%
12,383	MCLEAN	5,559	2,439	3,120		681 D	43.9%	56.1%	43.9%	56.1%
9,404	MERCER	4,952	2,306	2,646		340 D	46.6%	53.4%	46.6%	53.4%
25,177	MORTON	10,718	4,618	6,100		1,482 D	43.1%	56.9%	43.1%	56.9%
7,679	MOUNTRAIL	3,486	1,263	2,223		960 D	36.2%	63.8%	36.2%	63.8%
5,233	NELSON	2,327	802	1,525		723 D	34.5%	65.5%	34.5%	65.5%
2,495	OLIVER	1,257	583	674		91 D	46.4%	53.6%	46.4%	53.6%
10,399	PEMBINA	4,255	1,899	2,356		457 D	44.6%	55.4%	44.6%	55.4%
6,166	PIERCE	2,592	1,101	1,491		390 D	42.5%	57.5%	42.5%	57.5%
13,048	RAMSEY	5,969	2,108	3,861		1,753 D	35.3%	64.7%	35.3%	64.7%
6,698	RANSOM	2,937	938	1,999		1,061 D	31.9%	68.1%	31.9%	68.1%
3,608	RENVILLE	1,753	671	1,082		411 D	38.3%	61.7%	38.3%	61.7%
19,207	RICHLAND	8,373	3,135	5,238		2,103 D	37.4%	62.6%	37.4%	62.6%
12,177	ROLETTE	3,689	1,011	2,678		1,667 D	27.4%	72.6%	27.4%	72.6%
5,512	SARGENT	2,502	824	1,678		854 D	32.9%	67.1%	32.9%	67.1%
2,819	SHERIDAN	1,322	764	558		206 R	57.8%	42.2%	57.8%	42.2%
3,620	SIOUX	1,054	285	769		484 D	27.0%	73.0%	27.0%	73.0%
1,157	SLOPE	544	246	298		52 D	45.2%	54.8%	45.2%	54.8%
23,697	STARK	9,488	4,463	5,025		562 D	47.0%	53.0%	47.0%	53.0%
3,106	STEELE	1,605	434	1,171		737 D	27.0%	73.0%	27.0%	73.0%
24,154	STUTSMAN	9,884	4,211	5,673		1,462 D	42.6%	57.4%	42.6%	57.4%
4,052	TOWNER	1,917	642	1,275		633 D	33.5%	66.5%	33.5%	66.5%
9,624	TRAILL	4,683	1,683	3,000		1,317 D	35.9%	64.1%	35.9%	64.1%
15,371	WALSH	6,119	2,423	3,696		1,273 D	39.6%	60.4%	39.6%	60.4%
58,392	WARD	23,112	9,383	13,729		4,346 D	40.6%	59.4%	40.6%	59.4%
6,979	WELLS	3,270	1,586	1,684		98 D	48.5%	51.5%	48.5%	51.5%
22,237	WILLIAMS	9,892	4,664	5,228		564 D	47.1%	52.9%	47.1%	52.9%
652,717	TOTAL	299,080	119,986	179,094		59,108 D	40.1%	59.9%	40.1%	59.9%

NORTH DAKOTA

SENATOR 1988

1980 Census Population	County	Total Vote	Republican	Democratic	Other	Rep.-Dem. Plurality	Percentage Total Vote Rep.	Total Vote Dem.	Major Vote Rep.	Major Vote Dem.
3,584	ADAMS	1,744	654	1,064	26	410 D	37.5%	61.0%	38.1%	61.9%
13,960	BARNES	5,926	2,182	3,660	84	1,478 D	36.8%	61.8%	37.4%	62.6%
7,944	BENSON	3,083	849	2,200	34	1,351 D	27.5%	71.4%	27.8%	72.2%
1,138	BILLINGS	662	252	389	21	137 D	38.1%	58.8%	39.3%	60.7%
9,239	BOTTINEAU	4,284	1,666	2,549	69	883 D	38.9%	59.5%	39.5%	60.5%
4,229	BOWMAN	1,871	736	1,099	36	363 D	39.3%	58.7%	40.1%	59.9%
3,822	BURKE	1,703	614	1,065	24	451 D	36.1%	62.5%	36.6%	63.4%
54,811	BURLEIGH	26,431	11,485	14,561	385	3,076 D	43.5%	55.1%	44.1%	55.9%
88,247	CASS	49,217	20,557	28,038	622	7,481 D	41.8%	57.0%	42.3%	57.7%
7,636	CAVALIER	3,470	1,223	2,193	54	970 D	35.2%	63.2%	35.8%	64.2%
7,207	DICKEY	3,374	1,704	1,618	52	86 R	50.5%	48.0%	51.3%	48.7%
3,494	DIVIDE	1,802	526	1,256	20	730 D	29.2%	69.7%	29.5%	70.5%
4,627	DUNN	2,247	811	1,402	34	591 D	36.1%	62.4%	36.6%	63.4%
3,554	EDDY	1,690	581	1,081	28	500 D	34.4%	64.0%	35.0%	65.0%
5,877	EMMONS	2,700	1,062	1,564	74	502 D	39.3%	57.9%	40.4%	59.6%
4,611	FOSTER	2,084	839	1,229	16	390 D	40.3%	59.0%	40.6%	59.4%
2,391	GOLDEN VALLEY	1,200	490	680	30	190 D	40.8%	56.7%	41.9%	58.1%
66,100	GRAND FORKS	24,454	9,352	14,821	281	5,469 D	38.2%	60.6%	38.7%	61.3%
4,274	GRANT	2,107	930	1,104	73	174 D	44.1%	52.4%	45.7%	54.3%
3,714	GRIGGS	1,934	751	1,158	25	407 D	38.8%	59.9%	39.3%	60.7%
4,275	HETTINGER	2,155	853	1,261	41	408 D	39.6%	58.5%	40.4%	59.6%
3,833	KIDDER	1,792	710	1,046	36	336 D	39.6%	58.4%	40.4%	59.6%
6,473	LA MOURE	2,992	1,261	1,698	33	437 D	42.1%	56.8%	42.6%	57.4%
3,493	LOGAN	1,709	761	906	42	145 D	44.5%	53.0%	45.7%	54.3%
7,858	MCHENRY	3,627	1,260	2,322	45	1,062 D	34.7%	64.0%	35.2%	64.8%
4,800	MCINTOSH	2,414	1,340	1,023	51	317 R	55.5%	42.4%	56.7%	43.3%
7,132	MCKENZIE	3,285	1,340	1,878	67	538 D	40.8%	57.2%	41.6%	58.4%
12,383	MCLEAN	5,554	2,128	3,344	82	1,216 D	38.3%	60.2%	38.9%	61.1%
9,404	MERCER	4,972	2,032	2,845	95	813 D	40.9%	57.2%	41.7%	58.3%
25,177	MORTON	9,669	3,503	5,987	179	2,484 D	36.2%	61.9%	36.9%	63.1%
7,679	MOUNTRAIL	3,527	1,032	2,432	63	1,400 D	29.3%	69.0%	29.8%	70.2%
5,233	NELSON	2,326	759	1,538	29	779 D	32.6%	66.1%	33.0%	67.0%
2,495	OLIVER	1,236	423	793	20	370 D	34.2%	64.2%	34.8%	65.2%
10,399	PEMBINA	4,259	1,614	2,549	96	935 D	37.9%	59.8%	38.8%	61.2%
6,166	PIERCE	2,166	867	1,270	29	403 D	40.0%	58.6%	40.6%	59.4%
13,048	RAMSEY	5,107	1,711	3,322	74	1,611 D	33.5%	65.0%	34.0%	66.0%
6,698	RANSOM	2,941	1,011	1,885	45	874 D	34.4%	64.1%	34.9%	65.1%
3,608	RENVILLE	1,766	553	1,190	23	637 D	31.3%	67.4%	31.7%	68.3%
19,207	RICHLAND	8,380	3,581	4,684	115	1,103 D	42.7%	55.9%	43.3%	56.7%
12,177	ROLETTE	3,237	627	2,564	46	1,937 D	19.4%	79.2%	19.6%	80.4%
5,512	SARGENT	2,492	834	1,638	20	804 D	33.5%	65.7%	33.7%	66.3%
2,819	SHERIDAN	1,326	659	653	14	6 R	49.7%	49.2%	50.2%	49.8%
3,620	SIOUX	1,068	239	803	26	564 D	22.4%	75.2%	22.9%	77.1%
1,157	SLOPE	537	190	332	15	142 D	35.4%	61.8%	36.4%	63.6%
23,697	STARK	9,690	3,829	5,659	202	1,830 D	39.5%	58.4%	40.4%	59.6%
3,106	STEELE	1,620	444	1,160	16	716 D	27.4%	71.6%	27.7%	72.3%
24,154	STUTSMAN	8,620	3,516	4,966	138	1,450 D	40.8%	57.6%	41.5%	58.5%
4,052	TOWNER	1,973	627	1,317	29	690 D	31.8%	66.8%	32.3%	67.7%
9,624	TRAILL	4,032	1,496	2,499	37	1,003 D	37.1%	62.0%	37.4%	62.6%
15,371	WALSH	6,165	2,085	3,984	96	1,899 D	33.8%	64.6%	34.4%	65.6%
58,392	WARD	23,369	8,997	14,041	331	5,044 D	38.5%	60.1%	39.1%	60.9%
6,979	WELLS	3,280	1,404	1,832	44	428 D	42.8%	55.9%	43.4%	56.6%
22,237	WILLIAMS	9,901	3,987	5,747	167	1,760 D	40.3%	58.0%	41.0%	59.0%
652,717	TOTAL	289,170	112,937	171,899	4,334	58,962 D	39.1%	59.4%	39.6%	60.4%

NORTH DAKOTA

CONGRESS

CD	Year	Total Vote	Republican Vote	Republican Candidate	Democratic Vote	Democratic Candidate	Other Vote	Rep.-Dem. Plurality	Percentage Total Vote Rep.	Percentage Total Vote Dem.	Percentage Major Vote Rep.	Percentage Major Vote Dem.
AL	1988	299,982	84,475	SYDNESS, STEVE	212,583	DORGAN, BYRON L.	2,924	128,108 D	28.2%	70.9%	28.4%	71.6%
AL	1986	286,361	66,989	VINJE, SYVER	216,258	DORGAN, BYRON L.	3,114	149,269 D	23.4%	75.5%	23.7%	76.3%
AL	1984	308,729	65,761	ALTENBURG, LOIS I.	242,968	DORGAN, BYRON L.		177,207 D	21.3%	78.7%	21.3%	78.7%
AL	1982	260,499	72,241	JONES, KENT	186,534	DORGAN, BYRON L.	1,724	114,293 D	27.7%	71.6%	27.9%	72.1%
AL	1980	293,076	124,707	SMYKOWSKI, JIM	166,437	DORGAN, BYRON L.	1,932	41,730 D	42.6%	56.8%	42.8%	57.2%
AL	1978	220,348	147,746	ANDREWS, MARK	68,016	HAGEN, BRUCE	4,586	79,730 R	67.1%	30.9%	68.5%	31.5%
AL	1976	289,881	181,018	ANDREWS, MARK	104,263	OMDAHL, LLOYD B.	4,600	76,755 R	62.4%	36.0%	63.5%	36.5%
AL	1974	233,688	130,184	ANDREWS, MARK	103,504	DORGAN, BYRON L.		26,680 R	55.7%	44.3%	55.7%	44.3%
AL	1972	268,721	195,360	ANDREWS, MARK	72,850	ISTA, RICHARD	511	122,510 R	72.7%	27.1%	72.8%	27.2%

NORTH DAKOTA

1988 GENERAL ELECTION

President Other vote was 1,315 Libertarian (Paul); 905 National Economic Recovery (LaRouche); 396 New Alliance (Fulani); 347 Socialist Workers (Warren).

Governor

Senator Other vote was Libertarian (Gardner).

Congress Other vote at-large was Libertarian (Brekke).

1988 PRIMARIES

JUNE 14 REPUBLICAN

Governor Leon L. Mallberg, unopposed.

Senator Earl Strinden, unopposed.

Congress Unopposed at-large.

JUNE 14 DEMOCRATIC

Governor George Sinner, unopposed.

Senator Quentin N. Burdick, unopposed.

Congress Unopposed at-large.

JUNE 14 LIBERTARIAN

Governor No candidate.

Senator Kenneth C. Gardner, unopposed.

Congress Unopposed at-large.

OHIO

GOVERNOR

Richard F. Celeste (D). Re-elected 1986 to a four-year term. Previously elected 1982.

SENATORS

John H. Glenn (D). Re-elected 1986 to a six-year term. Previously elected 1980, 1974.

Howard Metzenbaum (D). Re-elected 1988 to a six-year term. Previously elected 1982, 1976.

REPRESENTATIVES

1. Thomas A. Luken (D)
2. Willis D. Gradison (R)
3. Tony P. Hall (D)
4. Michael G. Oxley (R)
5. Paul E. Gillmor (R)
6. Bob McEwen (R)
7. Michael DeWine (R)
8. Donald E. Lukens (R)
9. Marcy Kaptur (D)
10. Clarence E. Miller (R)
11. Dennis E. Eckart (D)
12. John R. Kasich (R)
13. Donald J. Pease (D)
14. Thomas C. Sawyer (D)
15. Chalmers P. Wylie (R)
16. Ralph S. Regula (R)
17. James A. Traficant (D)
18. Douglas Applegate (D)
19. Edward F. Feighan (D)
20. Mary Rose Oakar (D)
21. Louis Stokes (D)

POSTWAR VOTE FOR PRESIDENT

								Percentage			
	Total	Republican		Democratic		Other		Total Vote		Major Vote	
Year	Vote	Vote	Candidate	Vote	Candidate	Vote	Plurality	Rep.	Dem.	Rep.	Dem.
1988	4,393,699	2,416,549	Bush, George	1,939,629	Dukakis, Michael S.	37,521	476,920 R	55.0%	44.1%	55.5%	44.5%
1984	4,547,619	2,678,560	Reagan, Ronald	1,825,440	Mondale, Walter F.	43,619	853,120 R	58.9%	40.1%	59.5%	40.5%
1980	4,283,603	2,206,545	Reagan, Ronald	1,752,414	Carter, Jimmy	324,644	454,131 R	51.5%	40.9%	55.7%	44.3%
1976	4,111,873	2,000,505	Ford, Gerald R.	2,011,621	Carter, Jimmy	99,747	11,116 D	48.7%	48.9%	49.9%	50.1%
1972	4,094,787	2,441,827	Nixon, Richard M.	1,558,889	McGovern, George S.	94,071	882,938 R	59.6%	38.1%	61.0%	39.0%
1968	3,959,698	1,791,014	Nixon, Richard M.	1,700,586	Humphrey, Hubert H.	468,098	90,428 R	45.2%	42.9%	51.3%	48.7%
1964	3,969,196	1,470,865	Goldwater, Barry M.	2,498,331	Johnson, Lyndon B.		1,027,466 D	37.1%	62.9%	37.1%	62.9%
1960	4,161,859	2,217,611	Nixon, Richard M.	1,944,248	Kennedy, John F.		273,363 R	53.3%	46.7%	53.3%	46.7%
1956	3,702,265	2,262,610	Eisenhower, Dwight D.	1,439,655	Stevenson, Adlai E.		822,955 R	61.1%	38.9%	61.1%	38.9%
1952	3,700,758	2,100,391	Eisenhower, Dwight D.	1,600,367	Stevenson, Adlai E.		500,024 R	56.8%	43.2%	56.8%	43.2%
1948	2,936,071	1,445,684	Dewey, Thomas E.	1,452,791	Truman, Harry S.	37,596	7,107 D	49.2%	49.5%	49.9%	50.1%

OHIO

POSTWAR VOTE FOR GOVERNOR

Year	Total Vote	Republican Vote	Republican Candidate	Democratic Vote	Democratic Candidate	Other Vote	Rep.-Dem. Plurality	Percentage Total Vote Rep.	Percentage Total Vote Dem.	Percentage Major Vote Rep.	Percentage Major Vote Dem.
1986	3,066,611	1,207,264	Rhodes, James A.	1,858,372	Celeste, Richard F.	975	651,108 D	39.4%	60.6%	39.4%	60.6%
1982	3,356,721	1,303,962	Brown, Clarence, Jr.	1,981,882	Celeste, Richard F.	70,877	677,920 D	38.8%	59.0%	39.7%	60.3%
1978	2,843,351	1,402,167	Rhodes, James A.	1,354,631	Celeste, Richard F.	86,553	47,536 R	49.3%	47.6%	50.9%	49.1%
1974	3,072,010	1,493,679	Rhodes, James A.	1,482,191	Gilligan, John J.	96,140	11,488 R	48.6%	48.2%	50.2%	49.8%
1970	3,184,133	1,382,659	Cloud, Roger	1,725,560	Gilligan, John J.	75,914	342,901 D	43.4%	54.2%	44.5%	55.5%
1966	2,887,331	1,795,277	Rhodes, James A.	1,092,054	Reams, Frazier, Jr.		703,223 R	62.2%	37.8%	62.2%	37.8%
1962	3,116,711	1,836,190	Rhodes, James A.	1,280,521	DiSalle, Michael V.		555,669 R	58.9%	41.1%	58.9%	41.1%
1958 * *	3,284,134	1,414,874	O'Neill, C. William	1,869,260	DiSalle, Michael V.		454,386 D	43.1%	56.9%	43.1%	56.9%
1956	3,542,091	1,984,988	O'Neill, C. William	1,557,103	DiSalle, Michael V.		427,885 R	56.0%	44.0%	56.0%	44.0%
1954	2,597,790	1,192,528	Rhodes, James A.	1,405,262	Lausche, Frank J.		212,734 D	45.9%	54.1%	45.9%	54.1%
1952	3,605,168	1,590,058	Taft, Charles P.	2,015,110	Lausche, Frank J.		425,052 D	44.1%	55.9%	44.1%	55.9%
1950	2,892,819	1,370,570	Ebright, Don H.	1,522,249	Lausche, Frank J.		151,679 D	47.4%	52.6%	47.4%	52.6%
1948	3,018,289	1,398,514	Herbert, Thomas J.	1,619,775	Lausche, Frank J.		221,261 D	46.3%	53.7%	46.3%	53.7%
1946	2,303,750	1,166,550	Herbert, Thomas J.	1,125,997	Lausche, Frank J.	11,203	40,553 R	50.6%	48.9%	50.9%	49.1%

The term of office of Ohio's Governor was increased from two to four years effective with the 1958 election.

POSTWAR VOTE FOR SENATOR

Year	Total Vote	Republican Vote	Republican Candidate	Democratic Vote	Democratic Candidate	Other Vote	Rep.-Dem. Plurality	Percentage Total Vote Rep.	Percentage Total Vote Dem.	Percentage Major Vote Rep.	Percentage Major Vote Dem.
1988	4,352,905	1,872,716	Voinovich, George	2,480,038	Metzenbaum, Howard	151	607,322 D	43.0%	57.0%	43.0%	57.0%
1986	3,121,189	1,171,893	Kindness, Thomas N.	1,949,208	Glenn, John H.	88	777,315 D	37.5%	62.5%	37.5%	62.5%
1982	3,395,463	1,396,790	Pfeifer, Paul E.	1,923,767	Metzenbaum, Howard	74,906	526,977 D	41.1%	56.7%	42.1%	57.9%
1980	4,027,303	1,137,695	Betts, James E.	2,770,786	Glenn, John H.	118,822	1,633,091 D	28.2%	68.8%	29.1%	70.9%
1976	3,920,613	1,823,774	Taft, Robert A.,Jr.	1,941,113	Metzenbaum, Howard	155,726	117,339 D	46.5%	49.5%	48.4%	51.6%
1974	2,987,951	918,133	Perk, Ralph J.	1,930,670	Glenn, John H.	139,148	1,012,537 D	30.7%	64.6%	32.2%	67.8%
1970	3,151,274	1,565,682	Taft, Robert A.,Jr.	1,495,262	Metzenbaum, Howard	90,330	70,420 R	49.7%	47.4%	51.2%	48.8%
1968	3,743,121	1,928,964	Saxbe, William B.	1,814,152	Gilligan, John J.	5	114,812 R	51.5%	48.5%	51.5%	48.5%
1964	3,830,389	1,906,781	Taft, Robert A.,Jr.	1,923,608	Young, Stephen M.		16,827 D	49.8%	50.2%	49.8%	50.2%
1962	2,994,986	1,151,173	Briley, John M.	1,843,813	Lausche, Frank J.		692,640 D	38.4%	61.6%	38.4%	61.6%
1958	3,149,410	1,497,199	Bricker, John W.	1,652,211	Young, Stephen M.		155,012 D	47.5%	52.5%	47.5%	52.5%
1956	3,525,499	1,660,910	Bender, George H.	1,864,589	Lausche, Frank J.		203,679 D	47.1%	52.9%	47.1%	52.9%
1954 S	2,512,778	1,257,874	Bender, George H.	1,254,904	Burke, Thomas A.		2,970 R	50.1%	49.9%	50.1%	49.9%
1952	3,442,291	1,878,961	Bricker, John W.	1,563,330	DiSalle, Michael V.		315,631 R	54.6%	45.4%	54.6%	45.4%
1950	2,860,102	1,645,643	Taft, Robert A.	1,214,459	Ferguson, Joseph T.		431,184 R	57.5%	42.5%	57.5%	42.5%
1946	2,237,269	1,275,774	Bricker, John W.	947,610	Huffman, James W.	13,885	328,164 R	57.0%	42.4%	57.4%	42.6%

The 1954 election was for a short term to fill a vacancy.

OHIO

Districts Established July 12, 1985

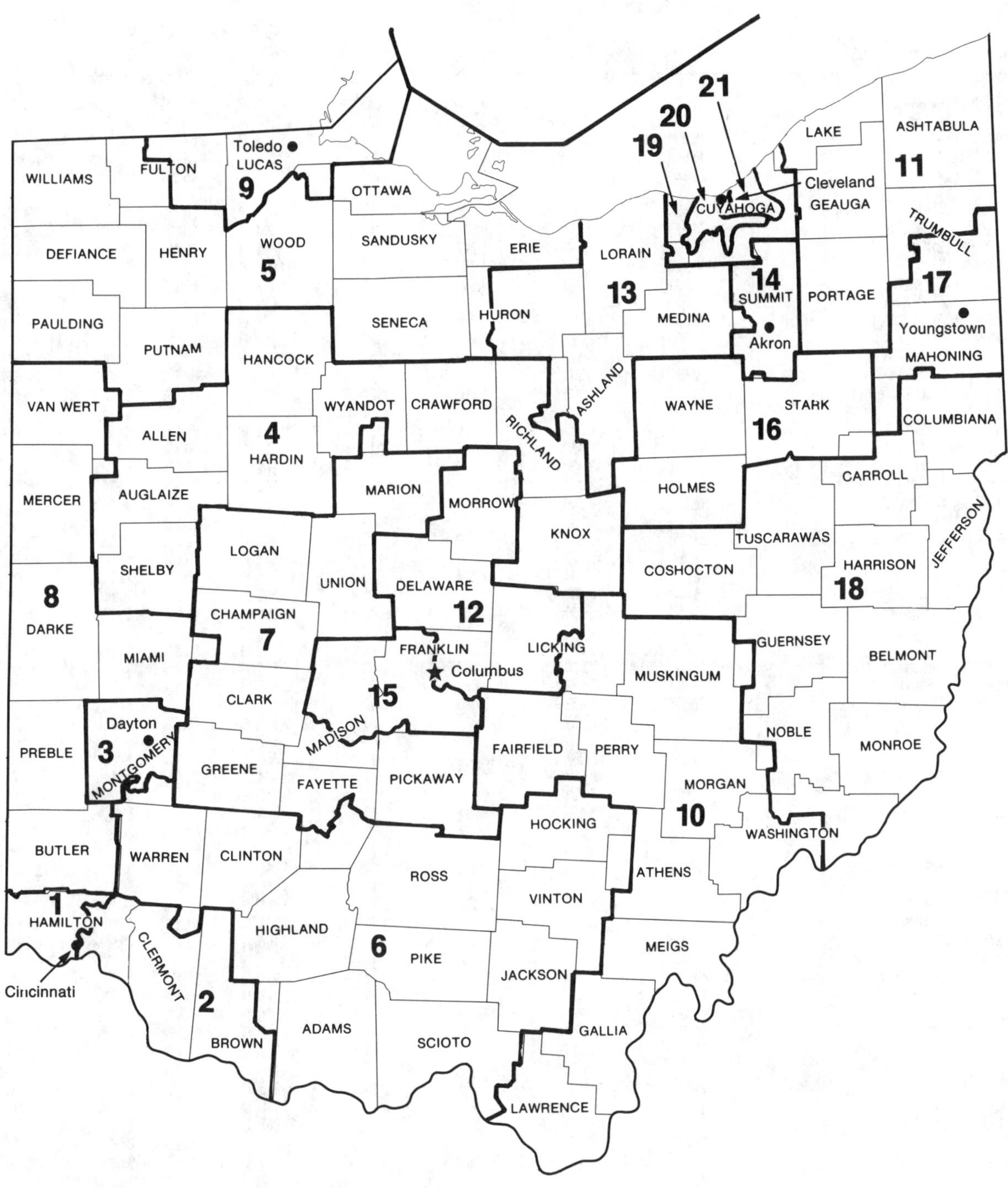

OHIO

PRESIDENT 1988

1980 Census Population	County	Total Vote	Republican	Democratic	Other	Rep.-Dem. Plurality	Percentage Total Vote Rep.	Percentage Total Vote Dem.	Percentage Major Vote Rep.	Percentage Major Vote Dem.
24,328	ADAMS	9,744	5,916	3,740	88	2,176 R	60.7%	38.4%	61.3%	38.7%
112,241	ALLEN	44,975	31,021	13,727	227	17,294 R	69.0%	30.5%	69.3%	30.7%
46,178	ASHLAND	18,939	12,726	6,072	141	6,654 R	67.2%	32.1%	67.7%	32.3%
104,215	ASHTABULA	38,556	17,654	20,536	366	2,882 D	45.8%	53.3%	46.2%	53.8%
56,399	ATHENS	20,281	9,314	10,795	172	1,481 D	45.9%	53.2%	46.3%	53.7%
42,554	AUGLAIZE	18,479	13,562	4,756	161	8,806 R	73.4%	25.7%	74.0%	26.0%
82,569	BELMONT	31,973	12,214	19,515	244	7,301 D	38.2%	61.0%	38.5%	61.5%
31,920	BROWN	12,698	7,539	5,047	112	2,492 R	59.4%	39.7%	59.9%	40.1%
258,787	BUTLER	110,208	75,725	33,770	713	41,955 R	68.7%	30.6%	69.2%	30.8%
25,598	CARROLL	10,994	6,179	4,667	148	1,512 R	56.2%	42.5%	57.0%	43.0%
33,649	CHAMPAIGN	13,368	8,995	4,272	101	4,723 R	67.3%	32.0%	67.8%	32.2%
150,236	CLARK	56,503	32,729	23,247	527	9,482 R	57.9%	41.1%	58.5%	41.5%
128,483	CLERMONT	53,085	37,417	15,352	316	22,065 R	70.5%	28.9%	70.9%	29.1%
34,603	CLINTON	12,699	8,856	3,746	97	5,110 R	69.7%	29.5%	70.3%	29.7%
113,572	COLUMBIANA	43,140	21,175	21,581	384	406 D	49.1%	50.0%	49.5%	50.5%
36,024	COSHOCTON	14,506	8,282	6,020	204	2,262 R	57.1%	41.5%	57.9%	42.1%
50,075	CRAWFORD	18,700	12,472	6,018	210	6,454 R	66.7%	32.2%	67.5%	32.5%
1,498,400	CUYAHOGA	601,117	242,439	353,401	5,277	110,962 D	40.3%	58.8%	40.7%	59.3%
55,096	DARKE	21,954	14,914	6,851	189	8,063 R	67.9%	31.2%	68.5%	31.5%
39,987	DEFIANCE	15,153	9,566	5,448	139	4,118 R	63.1%	36.0%	63.7%	36.3%
53,840	DELAWARE	28,498	20,693	7,590	215	13,103 R	72.6%	26.6%	73.2%	26.8%
79,655	ERIE	32,198	16,670	15,097	431	1,573 R	51.8%	46.9%	52.5%	47.5%
93,678	FAIRFIELD	42,051	29,208	12,504	339	16,704 R	69.5%	29.7%	70.0%	30.0%
27,467	FAYETTE	8,873	6,186	2,623	64	3,563 R	69.7%	29.6%	70.2%	29.8%
869,132	FRANKLIN	377,357	226,265	147,585	3,507	78,680 R	60.0%	39.1%	60.5%	39.5%
37,751	FULTON	15,428	10,230	5,076	122	5,154 R	66.3%	32.9%	66.8%	33.2%
30,098	GALLIA	12,349	7,399	4,834	116	2,565 R	59.9%	39.1%	60.5%	39.5%
74,474	GEAUGA	34,608	22,339	11,874	395	10,465 R	64.5%	34.3%	65.3%	34.7%
129,769	GREENE	52,856	34,432	18,025	399	16,407 R	65.1%	34.1%	65.6%	34.4%
42,024	GUERNSEY	14,563	8,507	5,926	130	2,581 R	58.4%	40.7%	58.9%	41.1%
873,224	HAMILTON	370,384	227,004	140,354	3,026	86,650 R	61.3%	37.9%	61.8%	38.2%
64,581	HANCOCK	27,643	19,896	7,435	312	12,461 R	72.0%	26.9%	72.8%	27.2%
32,719	HARDIN	11,606	7,291	4,145	170	3,146 R	62.8%	35.7%	63.8%	36.2%
18,152	HARRISON	7,252	3,298	3,881	73	583 D	45.5%	53.5%	45.9%	54.1%
28,383	HENRY	12,468	8,618	3,764	86	4,854 R	69.1%	30.2%	69.6%	30.4%
33,477	HIGHLAND	13,178	8,776	4,278	124	4,498 R	66.6%	32.5%	67.2%	32.8%
24,304	HOCKING	9,243	5,426	3,706	111	1,720 R	58.7%	40.1%	59.4%	40.6%
29,416	HOLMES	7,316	5,064	2,179	73	2,885 R	69.2%	29.8%	69.9%	30.1%
54,608	HURON	20,642	12,633	7,794	215	4,839 R	61.2%	37.8%	61.8%	38.2%
30,592	JACKSON	11,267	6,671	4,505	91	2,166 R	59.2%	40.0%	59.7%	40.3%
91,564	JEFFERSON	36,509	14,141	22,095	273	7,954 D	38.7%	60.5%	39.0%	61.0%
46,304	KNOX	19,200	12,180	6,882	138	5,298 R	63.4%	35.8%	63.9%	36.1%
212,801	LAKE	93,524	52,963	39,667	894	13,296 R	56.6%	42.4%	57.2%	42.8%
63,849	LAWRENCE	24,768	12,937	11,628	203	1,309 R	52.2%	46.9%	52.7%	47.3%
120,981	LICKING	51,767	34,540	16,793	434	17,747 R	66.7%	32.4%	67.3%	32.7%
39,155	LOGAN	15,697	11,099	4,484	114	6,615 R	70.7%	28.6%	71.2%	28.8%
274,909	LORAIN	106,926	50,410	55,600	916	5,190 D	47.1%	52.0%	47.6%	52.4%
471,741	LUCAS	185,095	83,788	99,755	1,552	15,967 D	45.3%	53.9%	45.7%	54.3%
33,004	MADISON	11,817	8,303	3,421	93	4,882 R	70.3%	28.9%	70.8%	29.2%
289,487	MAHONING	120,126	43,722	75,524	880	31,802 D	36.4%	62.9%	36.7%	63.3%
67,974	MARION	24,718	14,864	9,596	258	5,268 R	60.1%	38.8%	60.8%	39.2%
113,150	MEDINA	49,874	29,962	19,505	407	10,457 R	60.1%	39.1%	60.6%	39.4%
23,641	MEIGS	9,276	5,486	3,699	91	1,787 R	59.1%	39.9%	59.7%	40.3%
38,334	MERCER	16,286	11,162	4,978	146	6,184 R	68.5%	30.6%	69.2%	30.8%
90,381	MIAMI	36,434	24,915	11,138	381	13,777 R	68.4%	30.6%	69.1%	30.9%
17,382	MONROE	6,874	2,557	4,269	48	1,712 D	37.2%	62.1%	37.5%	62.5%
571,697	MONTGOMERY	228,943	131,596	95,737	1,610	35,859 R	57.5%	41.8%	57.9%	42.1%
14,241	MORGAN	5,859	3,713	2,085	61	1,628 R	63.4%	35.6%	64.0%	36.0%
26,480	MORROW	10,760	7,130	3,515	115	3,615 R	66.3%	32.7%	67.0%	33.0%
83,340	MUSKINGUM	31,674	19,736	11,691	247	8,045 R	62.3%	36.9%	62.8%	37.2%

OHIO

PRESIDENT 1988

1980 Census Population	County	Total Vote	Republican	Democratic	Other	Rep.-Dem. Plurality	Percentage Total Vote Rep.	Total Vote Dem.	Major Vote Rep.	Major Vote Dem.
11,310	NOBLE	5,308	3,155	2,079	74	1,076 R	59.4%	39.2%	60.3%	39.7%
40,076	OTTAWA	17,517	9,352	8,038	127	1,314 R	53.4%	45.9%	53.8%	46.2%
21,302	PAULDING	8,571	5,381	3,114	76	2,267 R	62.8%	36.3%	63.3%	36.7%
31,032	PERRY	11,731	6,602	5,011	118	1,591 R	56.3%	42.7%	56.9%	43.1%
43,662	PICKAWAY	15,794	10,796	4,905	93	5,891 R	68.4%	31.1%	68.8%	31.2%
22,802	PIKE	10,919	5,611	5,191	117	420 R	51.4%	47.5%	51.9%	48.1%
135,856	PORTAGE	52,480	26,334	25,607	539	727 R	50.2%	48.8%	50.7%	49.3%
38,223	PREBLE	15,381	10,297	4,937	147	5,360 R	66.9%	32.1%	67.6%	32.4%
32,991	PUTNAM	15,301	11,183	4,004	114	7,179 R	73.1%	26.2%	73.6%	26.4%
131,205	RICHLAND	50,047	30,047	19,617	383	10,430 R	60.0%	39.2%	60.5%	39.5%
65,004	ROSS	24,113	14,563	9,271	279	5,292 R	60.4%	38.4%	61.1%	38.9%
63,267	SANDUSKY	24,232	14,203	9,709	320	4,494 R	58.6%	40.1%	59.4%	40.6%
84,545	SCIOTO	30,760	16,029	14,442	289	1,587 R	52.1%	47.0%	52.6%	47.4%
61,901	SENECA	23,430	13,704	9,504	222	4,200 R	58.5%	40.6%	59.0%	41.0%
43,089	SHELBY	17,425	12,198	5,065	162	7,133 R	70.0%	29.1%	70.7%	29.3%
378,823	STARK	158,096	87,087	69,639	1,370	17,448 R	55.1%	44.0%	55.6%	44.4%
524,472	SUMMIT	215,589	101,155	112,612	1,822	11,457 D	46.9%	52.2%	47.3%	52.7%
241,863	TRUMBULL	98,250	38,815	58,674	761	19,859 D	39.5%	59.7%	39.8%	60.2%
84,614	TUSCARAWAS	31,589	17,145	14,185	259	2,960 R	54.3%	44.9%	54.7%	45.3%
29,536	UNION	12,071	8,846	3,130	95	5,716 R	73.3%	25.9%	73.9%	26.1%
30,458	VAN WERT	13,336	9,410	3,848	78	5,562 R	70.6%	28.9%	71.0%	29.0%
11,584	VINTON	5,081	2,652	2,385	44	267 R	52.2%	46.9%	52.7%	47.3%
99,276	WARREN	42,818	31,419	11,145	254	20,274 R	73.4%	26.0%	73.8%	26.2%
64,266	WASHINGTON	24,916	14,767	9,967	182	4,800 R	59.3%	40.0%	59.7%	40.3%
97,408	WAYNE	36,208	22,320	13,571	317	8,749 R	61.6%	37.5%	62.2%	37.8%
36,369	WILLIAMS	15,585	10,782	4,666	137	6,116 R	69.2%	29.9%	69.8%	30.2%
107,372	WOOD	44,933	26,013	18,579	341	7,434 R	57.9%	41.3%	58.3%	41.7%
22,651	WYANDOT	9,239	6,178	2,936	125	3,242 R	66.9%	31.8%	67.8%	32.2%
10,797,630	TOTAL	4,393,699	2,416,549	1,939,629	37,521	476,920 R	55.0%	44.1%	55.5%	44.5%

OHIO

SENATOR 1988

1980 Census Population	County	Total Vote	Republican	Democratic	Other	Rep.-Dem. Plurality	Percentage Total Vote Rep.	Total Vote Dem.	Major Vote Rep.	Major Vote Dem.
24,328	ADAMS	9,734	4,624	5,110		486 D	47.5%	52.5%	47.5%	52.5%
112,241	ALLEN	45,111	27,398	17,713		9,685 R	60.7%	39.3%	60.7%	39.3%
46,178	ASHLAND	18,855	10,086	8,769		1,317 R	53.5%	46.5%	53.5%	46.5%
104,215	ASHTABULA	38,627	14,772	23,855		9,083 D	38.2%	61.8%	38.2%	61.8%
56,399	ATHENS	20,158	7,577	12,581		5,004 D	37.6%	62.4%	37.6%	62.4%
42,554	AUGLAIZE	18,262	11,137	7,125		4,012 R	61.0%	39.0%	61.0%	39.0%
82,569	BELMONT	31,704	8,278	23,426		15,148 D	26.1%	73.9%	26.1%	73.9%
31,920	BROWN	12,535	5,254	7,281		2,027 D	41.9%	58.1%	41.9%	58.1%
258,787	BUTLER	109,300	56,433	52,867		3,566 R	51.6%	48.4%	51.6%	48.4%
25,598	CARROLL	10,944	4,808	6,136		1,328 D	43.9%	56.1%	43.9%	56.1%
33,649	CHAMPAIGN	13,329	6,518	6,811		293 D	48.9%	51.1%	48.9%	51.1%
150,236	CLARK	56,247	22,918	33,308	21	10,390 D	40.7%	59.2%	40.8%	59.2%
128,483	CLERMONT	52,572	27,744	24,828		2,916 R	52.8%	47.2%	52.8%	47.2%
34,603	CLINTON	12,669	6,435	6,234		201 R	50.8%	49.2%	50.8%	49.2%
113,572	COLUMBIANA	43,050	16,711	26,339		9,628 D	38.8%	61.2%	38.8%	61.2%
36,024	COSHOCTON	14,385	6,481	7,904		1,423 D	45.1%	54.9%	45.1%	54.9%
50,075	CRAWFORD	18,696	9,791	8,904	1	887 R	52.4%	47.6%	52.4%	47.6%
1,498,400	CUYAHOGA	601,028	201,368	399,651	9	198,283 D	33.5%	66.5%	33.5%	66.5%
55,096	DARKE	21,867	10,698	11,169		471 D	48.9%	51.1%	48.9%	51.1%
39,987	DEFIANCE	15,028	7,929	7,099		830 R	52.8%	47.2%	52.8%	47.2%
53,840	DELAWARE	28,295	16,880	11,415		5,465 R	59.7%	40.3%	59.7%	40.3%
79,655	ERIE	30,624	12,946	17,678		4,732 D	42.3%	57.7%	42.3%	57.7%
93,678	FAIRFIELD	42,094	22,470	19,624		2,846 R	53.4%	46.6%	53.4%	46.6%
27,467	FAYETTE	8,860	4,732	4,128		604 R	53.4%	46.6%	53.4%	46.6%
869,132	FRANKLIN	363,368	172,171	191,196	1	19,025 D	47.4%	52.6%	47.4%	52.6%
37,751	FULTON	15,307	7,673	7,634		39 R	50.1%	49.9%	50.1%	49.9%
30,098	GALLIA	12,035	5,763	6,272		509 D	47.9%	52.1%	47.9%	52.1%
74,474	GEAUGA	34,368	19,026	15,342		3,684 R	55.4%	44.6%	55.4%	44.6%
129,769	GREENE	52,268	25,112	27,156		2,044 D	48.0%	52.0%	48.0%	52.0%
42,024	GUERNSEY	14,472	6,691	7,781		1,090 D	46.2%	53.8%	46.2%	53.8%
873,224	HAMILTON	368,587	177,351	191,236		13,885 D	48.1%	51.9%	48.1%	51.9%
64,581	HANCOCK	26,857	16,699	10,158		6,541 R	62.2%	37.8%	62.2%	37.8%
32,719	HARDIN	11,572	6,150	5,422		728 R	53.1%	46.9%	53.1%	46.9%
18,152	HARRISON	7,240	2,472	4,768		2,296 D	34.1%	65.9%	34.1%	65.9%
28,383	HENRY	12,392	6,676	5,716		960 R	53.9%	46.1%	53.9%	46.1%
33,477	HIGHLAND	13,155	6,320	6,835		515 D	48.0%	52.0%	48.0%	52.0%
24,304	HOCKING	9,261	3,936	5,325		1,389 D	42.5%	57.5%	42.5%	57.5%
29,416	HOLMES	7,380	4,342	3,038		1,304 R	58.8%	41.2%	58.8%	41.2%
54,608	HURON	20,741	9,468	11,273		1,805 D	45.6%	54.4%	45.6%	54.4%
30,592	JACKSON	11,140	5,097	6,043		946 D	45.8%	54.2%	45.8%	54.2%
91,564	JEFFERSON	35,914	10,431	25,483		15,052 D	29.0%	71.0%	29.0%	71.0%
46,304	KNOX	18,861	9,285	9,576		291 D	49.2%	50.8%	49.2%	50.8%
212,801	LAKE	90,819	44,205	46,612	2	2,407 D	48.7%	51.3%	48.7%	51.3%
63,849	LAWRENCE	24,450	8,994	15,456		6,462 D	36.8%	63.2%	36.8%	63.2%
120,981	LICKING	51,787	25,895	25,892		3 R	50.0%	50.0%	50.0%	50.0%
39,155	LOGAN	15,679	8,496	7,183		1,313 R	54.2%	45.8%	54.2%	45.8%
274,909	LORAIN	107,369	40,659	66,710		26,051 D	37.9%	62.1%	37.9%	62.1%
471,741	LUCAS	175,616	55,857	119,758	1	63,901 D	31.8%	68.2%	31.8%	68.2%
33,004	MADISON	11,768	6,191	5,577		614 R	52.6%	47.4%	52.6%	47.4%
289,487	MAHONING	120,902	34,682	86,162	58	51,480 D	28.7%	71.3%	28.7%	71.3%
67,974	MARION	24,875	11,440	13,435		1,995 D	46.0%	54.0%	46.0%	54.0%
113,150	MEDINA	49,439	23,465	25,974		2,509 D	47.5%	52.5%	47.5%	52.5%
23,641	MEIGS	9,216	4,492	4,724		232 D	48.7%	51.3%	48.7%	51.3%
38,334	MERCER	16,256	9,435	6,821		2,614 R	58.0%	42.0%	58.0%	42.0%
90,381	MIAMI	36,318	17,620	18,698		1,078 D	48.5%	51.5%	48.5%	51.5%
17,382	MONROE	6,760	1,800	4,960		3,160 D	26.6%	73.4%	26.6%	73.4%
571,697	MONTGOMERY	226,157	92,558	133,598	1	41,040 D	40.9%	59.1%	40.9%	59.1%
14,241	MORGAN	5,790	2,920	2,870		50 R	50.4%	49.6%	50.4%	49.6%
26,480	MORROW	10,791	5,403	5,388		15 R	50.1%	49.9%	50.1%	49.9%
83,340	MUSKINGUM	31,105	14,869	16,236		1,367 D	47.8%	52.2%	47.8%	52.2%

OHIO

SENATOR 1988

1980 Census Population	County	Total Vote	Republican	Democratic	Other	Rep.-Dem. Plurality	Percentage Total Vote Rep.	Percentage Total Vote Dem.	Percentage Major Vote Rep.	Percentage Major Vote Dem.
11,310	NOBLE	5,268	2,376	2,892		516 D	45.1%	54.9%	45.1%	54.9%
40,076	OTTAWA	17,565	6,586	10,979		4,393 D	37.5%	62.5%	37.5%	62.5%
21,302	PAULDING	8,414	4,701	3,713		988 R	55.9%	44.1%	55.9%	44.1%
31,032	PERRY	11,762	4,601	7,161		2,560 D	39.1%	60.9%	39.1%	60.9%
43,662	PICKAWAY	15,624	8,101	7,523		578 R	51.8%	48.2%	51.8%	48.2%
22,802	PIKE	10,839	4,320	6,519		2,199 D	39.9%	60.1%	39.9%	60.1%
135,856	PORTAGE	52,372	20,610	31,762		11,152 D	39.4%	60.6%	39.4%	60.6%
38,223	PREBLE	15,332	6,887	8,444	1	1,557 D	44.9%	55.1%	44.9%	55.1%
32,991	PUTNAM	15,280	9,695	5,585		4,110 R	63.4%	36.6%	63.4%	36.6%
131,205	RICHLAND	50,506	23,740	26,766		3,026 D	47.0%	53.0%	47.0%	53.0%
65,004	ROSS	23,770	10,661	13,109		2,448 D	44.9%	55.1%	44.9%	55.1%
63,267	SANDUSKY	24,138	10,162	13,976		3,814 D	42.1%	57.9%	42.1%	57.9%
84,545	SCIOTO	30,398	12,136	18,262		6,126 D	39.9%	60.1%	39.9%	60.1%
61,901	SENECA	23,376	11,177	12,199		1,022 D	47.8%	52.2%	47.8%	52.2%
43,089	SHELBY	17,328	9,363	7,965		1,398 R	54.0%	46.0%	54.0%	46.0%
378,823	STARK	158,938	71,400	87,538		16,138 D	44.9%	55.1%	44.9%	55.1%
524,472	SUMMIT	215,176	79,048	136,127	1	57,079 D	36.7%	63.3%	36.7%	63.3%
241,863	TRUMBULL	98,276	29,664	68,557	55	38,893 D	30.2%	69.8%	30.2%	69.8%
84,614	TUSCARAWAS	32,452	13,732	18,720		4,988 D	42.3%	57.7%	42.3%	57.7%
29,536	UNION	12,090	7,101	4,989		2,112 R	58.7%	41.3%	58.7%	41.3%
30,458	VAN WERT	13,364	8,914	4,450		4,464 R	66.7%	33.3%	66.7%	33.3%
11,584	VINTON	5,015	2,010	3,005		995 D	40.1%	59.9%	40.1%	59.9%
99,276	WARREN	42,452	23,084	19,368		3,716 R	54.4%	45.6%	54.4%	45.6%
64,266	WASHINGTON	23,674	12,338	11,336		1,002 R	52.1%	47.9%	52.1%	47.9%
97,408	WAYNE	36,323	18,751	17,572		1,179 R	51.6%	48.4%	51.6%	48.4%
36,369	WILLIAMS	15,381	8,731	6,650		2,081 R	56.8%	43.2%	56.8%	43.2%
107,372	WOOD	44,608	20,323	24,285		3,962 D	45.6%	54.4%	45.6%	54.4%
22,651	WYANDOT	9,195	4,872	4,323		549 R	53.0%	47.0%	53.0%	47.0%
10,797,630	TOTAL	4,352,905	1,872,716	2,480,038	151	607,322 D	43.0%	57.0%	43.0%	57.0%

OHIO

CONGRESS

CD	Year	Total Vote	Republican Vote	Republican Candidate	Democratic Vote	Democratic Candidate	Other Vote	Rep.-Dem. Plurality	Percentage Total Vote Rep.	Percentage Total Vote Dem.	Percentage Major Vote Rep.	Percentage Major Vote Dem.
1	1988	208,420	90,738	CHABOT, STEVE	117,682	LUKEN, THOMAS A.		26,944 D	43.5%	56.5%	43.5%	56.5%
1	1986	146,577	56,100	MORR, FRED E.	90,477	LUKEN, THOMAS A.		34,377 D	38.3%	61.7%	38.3%	61.7%
2	1988	211,799	153,162	GRADISON, WILLIS D.	58,637	STIDHAM, CHUCK R.		94,525 R	72.3%	27.7%	72.3%	27.7%
2	1986	148,509	105,061	GRADISON, WILLIS D.	43,448	STINEMAN, WILLIAM F.		61,613 R	70.7%	29.3%	70.7%	29.3%
3	1988	184,617	42,664	CRUTCHER, RON	141,953	HALL, TONY P.		99,289 D	23.1%	76.9%	23.1%	76.9%
3	1986	133,478	35,167	CRUTCHER, RON	98,311	HALL, TONY P.		63,144 D	26.3%	73.7%	26.3%	73.7%
4	1988	160,637	160,099	OXLEY, MICHAEL G.			538	160,099 R	99.7%		100.0%	
4	1986	154,068	115,751	OXLEY, MICHAEL G.	26,320	CRATTY, CLEM	11,997	89,431 R	75.1%	17.1%	81.5%	18.5%
5	1988	204,130	123,838	GILLMOR, PAUL E.	80,292	MURRAY, TOM		43,546 R	60.7%	39.3%	60.7%	39.3%
5	1986	156,880	102,016	LATTA, DELBERT L.	54,864	MURRAY, TOM		47,152 R	65.0%	35.0%	65.0%	35.0%
6	1988	204,870	152,235	MCEWEN, BOB	52,635	ROBERTS, GORDON		99,600 R	74.3%	25.7%	74.3%	25.7%
6	1986	151,338	106,354	MCEWEN, BOB	42,155	ROBERTS, GORDON	2,829	64,199 R	70.3%	27.9%	71.6%	28.4%
7	1988	193,020	142,597	DEWINE, MICHAEL	50,423	SCHIRA, JACK		92,174 R	73.9%	26.1%	73.9%	26.1%
7	1986	119,238	119,238	DEWINE, MICHAEL				119,238 R	100.0%		100.0%	
8	1988	203,248	154,164	LUKENS, DONALD E.	49,084	GRIFFIN, JOHN W.		105,080 R	75.9%	24.1%	75.9%	24.1%
8	1986	144,670	98,475	LUKENS, DONALD E.	46,195	GRIFFIN, JOHN W.		52,280 R	68.1%	31.9%	68.1%	31.9%
9	1988	193,812	36,183	HAWKINS, AL	157,557	KAPTUR, MARCY	72	121,374 D	18.7%	81.3%	18.7%	81.3%
9	1986	136,289	30,643	SHUFELDT, MIKE	105,646	KAPTUR, MARCY		75,003 D	22.5%	77.5%	22.5%	77.5%
10	1988	200,566	143,673	MILLER, CLARENCE E.	56,893	BUCHANAN, JOHN M.		86,780 R	71.6%	28.4%	71.6%	28.4%
10	1986	151,717	106,870	MILLER, CLARENCE E.	44,847	BUCHANAN, JOHN M.		62,023 R	70.4%	29.6%	70.4%	29.6%
11	1988	202,628	78,028	MUELLER, MARGARET R.	124,600	ECKART, DENNIS E.		46,572 D	38.5%	61.5%	38.5%	61.5%
11	1986	144,568	35,944	MUELLER, MARGARET R.	104,740	ECKART, DENNIS E.	3,884	68,796 D	24.9%	72.5%	25.5%	74.5%
12	1988	195,905	154,727	KASICH, JOHN R.	41,178	BROWN, MARK P.		113,549 R	79.0%	21.0%	79.0%	21.0%
12	1986	160,632	117,905	KASICH, JOHN R.	42,727	JOCHIM, TIMOTHY C.		75,178 R	73.4%	26.6%	73.4%	26.6%
13	1988	196,361	59,287	BROWN, DWIGHT	137,074	PEASE, DONALD J.		77,787 D	30.2%	69.8%	30.2%	69.8%
13	1986	141,064	52,452	NIELSEN, WILLIAM D.	88,612	PEASE, DONALD J.		36,160 D	37.2%	62.8%	37.2%	62.8%
14	1988	199,307	50,356	LANG, LORETTA A.	148,951	SAWYER, THOMAS C.		98,595 D	25.3%	74.7%	25.3%	74.7%
14	1986	154,970	71,713	SLABY, LYNN	83,257	SAWYER, THOMAS C.		11,544 D	46.3%	53.7%	46.3%	53.7%
15	1988	196,295	146,854	WYLIE, CHALMERS P.	49,441	FROEHLICH, MARK S.		97,413 R	74.8%	25.2%	74.8%	25.2%
15	1986	153,495	97,745	WYLIE, CHALMERS P.	55,750	JACKSON, DAVID L.		41,995 R	63.7%	36.3%	63.7%	36.3%
16	1988	202,180	158,824	REGULA, RALPH S.	43,356	GRAVELY, MELVIN J.		115,468 R	78.6%	21.4%	78.6%	21.4%
16	1986	154,845	118,206	REGULA, RALPH S.	36,639	KENNICK, WILLIAM J.		81,567 R	76.3%	23.7%	76.3%	23.7%
17	1988	210,455	47,929	LENZ, FREDERICK W.	162,526	TRAFICANT, JAMES A.		114,597 D	22.8%	77.2%	22.8%	77.2%
17	1986	156,189	43,334	FULKS, JAMES H.	112,855	TRAFICANT, JAMES A.		69,521 D	27.7%	72.3%	27.7%	72.3%
18	1988	197,436	46,130	ABRAHAM, WILLIAM C.	151,306	APPLEGATE, DOUGLAS		105,176 D	23.4%	76.6%	23.4%	76.6%
18	1986	126,526			126,526	APPLEGATE, DOUGLAS		126,526 D		100.0%		100.0%
19	1988	238,424	70,359	ROBERTS, NOEL F.	168,065	FEIGHAN, EDWARD F.		97,706 D	29.5%	70.5%	29.5%	70.5%
19	1986	178,557	80,743	SUHADOLNIK, GARY C.	97,814	FEIGHAN, EDWARD F.		17,071 D	45.2%	54.8%	45.2%	54.8%
20	1988	177,659	30,944	SAJNA, MICHAEL	146,715	OAKAR, MARY ROSE		115,771 D	17.4%	82.6%	17.4%	82.6%
20	1986	130,770	19,794	SMITH, BILL	110,976	OAKAR, MARY ROSE		91,182 D	15.1%	84.9%	15.1%	84.9%
21	1988	173,192	24,804	ROSKI, FRANKLIN H.	148,388	STOKES, LOUIS		123,584 D	14.3%	85.7%	14.3%	85.7%
21	1986	122,472	22,594	ROSKI, FRANKLIN H.	99,878	STOKES, LOUIS		77,284 D	18.4%	81.6%	18.4%	81.6%

OHIO

1988 GENERAL ELECTION

President Other vote was 12,017 Fulani; 11,989 Paul; 7,733 LaRouche; 5,432 Winn, all appearing on the ballot without party designation and 134 Holmes (write-in); 216 scattered write-in. Adjustments to the original unamended returns were made in Sandusky county in the minor party votes for LaRouche, Paul and Winn.

Senator Other vote was Marshall (write-in).

Congress Other vote was Hicks (write-in) in CD 4; Cartier (write-in) in CD 9. In CD 5, original unamended returns gave the Democratic (Murray) vote as 80,472. In CD 12, unamended returns gave the Republican (Kasich) vote as 204,892 and the Democratic (Brown) vote as 50,782. In CD 15, unamended returns gave the Republican (Wylie) vote as 154,694 and the Democratic (Froehlich) vote as 51,172. In CD 17, unamended returns gave the Repbulican (Lenz) vote as 68,822 and the Democratic (Traficant) vote as 232,221. In CD 18, unamended returns gave the Republican (Abraham) vote as 43,628.

1988 PRIMARIES

MAY 3 REPUBLICAN

Senator George Voinovich, unopposed.

Congress Unopposed in fourteen CD's. No candidate in CD 20; in that CD Michael Sajna received 566 write-in votes and became the nominee. Contested as follows:

CD 5 28,694 Paul E. Gillmor; 28,667 Robert E. Latta; 5,769 Rex Damschroder. Data given are for the recount.
CD 9 18,946 Al Hawkins; 4,328 Ellsworth R. Fraley.
CD 10 52,243 Clarence E. Miller; 9,782 Ronald E. Shoemaker.
CD 13 13,582 Dwight Brown; 10,823 Steve D. Hambley.
CD 14 9,496 Loretta A. Lang; 8,521 John L. Smith.
CD 17 12,315 Frederick W. Lenz; 5,389 William B. Salkind.

MAY 3 DEMOCRATIC

Senator 1,070,934 Howard Metzenbaum; 210,508 Ralph A. Applegate.

Congress Unopposed in fourteen CD's. No candidate in CD 4; in that CD, Elmer L. Hicks received 45 write-in votes but did not qualify. Contested as follows:

CD 6 20,688 Gordon Roberts; 16,820 Raymond J. Mitchell.
CD 8 23,285 John W. Griffin; 9,019 A. John Mutschler.
CD 10 22,535 John M. Buchanan; 17,453 David C. Wilhelm; 5,487 Ray H. Blair.
CD 13 52,388 Donald J. Pease; 11,037 John M. Ryan.
CD 17 98,341 James A. Traficant; 16,130 Van Williams.
CD 20 64,417 Mary Rose Oakar; 19,530 Dennis J. Kucinich.

OKLAHOMA

GOVERNOR

Henry Bellmon (R). Elected 1986 to a four-year term. Previously elected 1962.

SENATORS

David L. Boren (D). Re-elected 1984 to a six-year term. Previously elected 1978.

Don Nickles (R). Re-elected 1986 to a six-year term. Previously elected 1980.

REPRESENTATIVES

1. James M. Inhofe (R)
2. Mike Synar (D)
3. Wes Watkins (D)
4. Dave McCurdy (D)
5. M. H.Edwards (R)
6. Glenn English (D)

POSTWAR VOTE FOR PRESIDENT

		Republican		Democratic				Percentage			
								Total Vote		Major Vote	
Year	Total Vote	Vote	Candidate	Vote	Candidate	Other Vote	Plurality	Rep.	Dem.	Rep.	Dem.
1988	1,171,036	678,367	Bush, George	483,423	Dukakis, Michael S.	9,246	194,944 R	57.9%	41.3%	58.4%	41.6%
1984	1,255,676	861,530	Reagan, Ronald	385,080	Mondale, Walter F.	9,066	476,450 R	68.6%	30.7%	69.1%	30.9%
1980	1,149,708	695,570	Reagan, Ronald	402,026	Carter, Jimmy	52,112	293,544 R	60.5%	35.0%	63.4%	36.6%
1976	1,092,251	545,708	Ford, Gerald R.	532,442	Carter, Jimmy	14,101	13,266 R	50.0%	48.7%	50.6%	49.4%
1972	1,029,900	759,025	Nixon, Richard M.	247,147	McGovern, George S.	23,728	511,878 R	73.7%	24.0%	75.4%	24.6%
1968	943,086	449,697	Nixon, Richard M.	301,658	Humphrey, Hubert H.	191,731	148,039 R	47.7%	32.0%	59.9%	40.1%
1964	932,499	412,665	Goldwater, Barry M.	519,834	Johnson, Lyndon B.		107,169 D	44.3%	55.7%	44.3%	55.7%
1960	903,150	533,039	Nixon, Richard M.	370,111	Kennedy, John F.		162,928 R	59.0%	41.0%	59.0%	41.0%
1956	859,350	473,769	Eisenhower, Dwight D.	385,581	Stevenson, Adlai E.		88,188 R	55.1%	44.9%	55.1%	44.9%
1952	948,984	518,045	Eisenhower, Dwight D.	430,939	Stevenson, Adlai E.		87,106 R	54.6%	45.4%	54.6%	45.4%
1948	721,599	268,817	Dewey, Thomas E.	452,782	Truman, Harry S.		183,965 D	37.3%	62.7%	37.3%	62.7%

POSTWAR VOTE FOR GOVERNOR

		Republican		Democratic				Percentage			
								Total Vote		Major Vote	
Year	Total Vote	Vote	Candidate	Vote	Candidate	Other Vote	Rep.-Dem. Plurality	Rep.	Dem.	Rep.	Dem.
1986	909,925	431,762	Bellmon, Henry	405,295	Walters, David	72,868	26,467 R	47.5%	44.5%	51.6%	48.4%
1982	883,130	332,207	Daxon, Tom	548,159	Nigh, George	2,764	215,952 D	37.6%	62.1%	37.7%	62.3%
1978	777,414	367,055	Shotts, Ron	402,240	Nigh, George	8,119	35,185 D	47.2%	51.7%	47.7%	52.3%
1974	804,848	290,459	Inhofe, James M.	514,389	Boren, David L.		223,930 D	36.1%	63.9%	36.1%	63.9%
1970	698,790	336,157	Bartlett, Dewey F.	338,338	Hall, David	24,295	2,181 D	48.1%	48.4%	49.8%	50.2%
1966	677,258	377,078	Bartlett, Dewey F.	296,328	Moore, Preston J.	3,852	80,750 R	55.7%	43.8%	56.0%	44.0%
1962	709,763	392,316	Bellmon, Henry	315,357	Atkinson, W. P.	2,090	76,959 R	55.3%	44.4%	55.4%	44.6%
1958	538,839	107,495	Ferguson, Phil	399,504	Edmondson, J. Howard	31,840	292,009 D	19.9%	74.1%	21.2%	78.8%
1954	609,194	251,808	Sparks, Reuben K.	357,386	Gary, Raymond		105,578 D	41.3%	58.7%	41.3%	58.7%
1950	644,276	313,205	Ferguson, Jo O.	329,308	Murray, Johnston	1,763	16,103 D	48.6%	51.1%	48.7%	51.3%
1946	494,599	227,426	Flynn, Olney F.	259,491	Turner, Roy J.	7,682	32,065 D	46.0%	52.5%	46.7%	53.3%

OKLAHOMA

POSTWAR VOTE FOR SENATOR

Year	Total Vote	Republican Vote	Republican Candidate	Democratic Vote	Democratic Candidate	Other Vote	Rep.-Dem. Plurality	Percentage Total Vote Rep.	Percentage Total Vote Dem.	Percentage Major Vote Rep.	Percentage Major Vote Dem.
1986	893,666	493,436	Nickles, Don	400,230	Jones, James R.		93,206 R	55.2%	44.8%	55.2%	44.8%
1984	1,197,937	280,638	Crozier, Will E.	906,131	Boren, David L.	11,168	625,493 D	23.4%	75.6%	23.6%	76.4%
1980	1,098,294	587,252	Nickles, Don	478,283	Coats, Andrew	32,759	108,969 R	53.5%	43.5%	55.1%	44.9%
1978	754,264	247,857	Kamm, Robert B.	493,953	Boren, David L.	12,454	246,096 D	32.9%	65.5%	33.4%	66.6%
1974	791,809	390,997	Bellmon, Henry	387,162	Edmondson, Ed	13,650	3,835 R	49.4%	48.9%	50.2%	49.8%
1972	1,005,148	516,934	Bartlett, Dewey F.	478,212	Edmondson, Ed	10,002	38,722 R	51.4%	47.6%	51.9%	48.1%
1968	909,119	470,120	Bellmon, Henry	419,658	Monroney, A. S.Mike	19,341	50,462 R	51.7%	46.2%	52.8%	47.2%
1966	638,742	295,585	Patterson, Pat J.	343,157	Harris, Fred R.		47,572 D	46.3%	53.7%	46.3%	53.7%
1964 S	912,174	445,392	Wilkinson, Bud	466,782	Harris, Fred R.		21,390 D	48.8%	51.2%	48.8%	51.2%
1962	664,712	307,966	Crawford, B. Hayden	353,890	Monroney, A. S.Mike	2,856	45,924 D	46.3%	53.2%	46.5%	53.5%
1960	864,475	385,646	Crawford, B. Hayden	474,116	Kerr, Robert S.	4,713	88,470 D	44.6%	54.8%	44.9%	55.1%
1956	831,142	371,146	McKeever, Douglas	459,996	Monroney, A. S.Mike		88,850 D	44.7%	55.3%	44.7%	55.3%
1954	600,120	262,013	Mock, Fred M.	335,127	Kerr, Robert S.	2,980	73,114 D	43.7%	55.8%	43.9%	56.1%
1950	631,177	285,224	Alexander, W. H.	345,953	Monroney, A. S.Mike		60,729 D	45.2%	54.8%	45.2%	54.8%
1948	708,931	265,169	Rizley, Ross	441,654	Kerr, Robert S.	2,108	176,485 D	37.4%	62.3%	37.5%	62.5%

The 1964 election was for a short term to fill a vacancy.

OKLAHOMA

Districts Established July 22, 1981

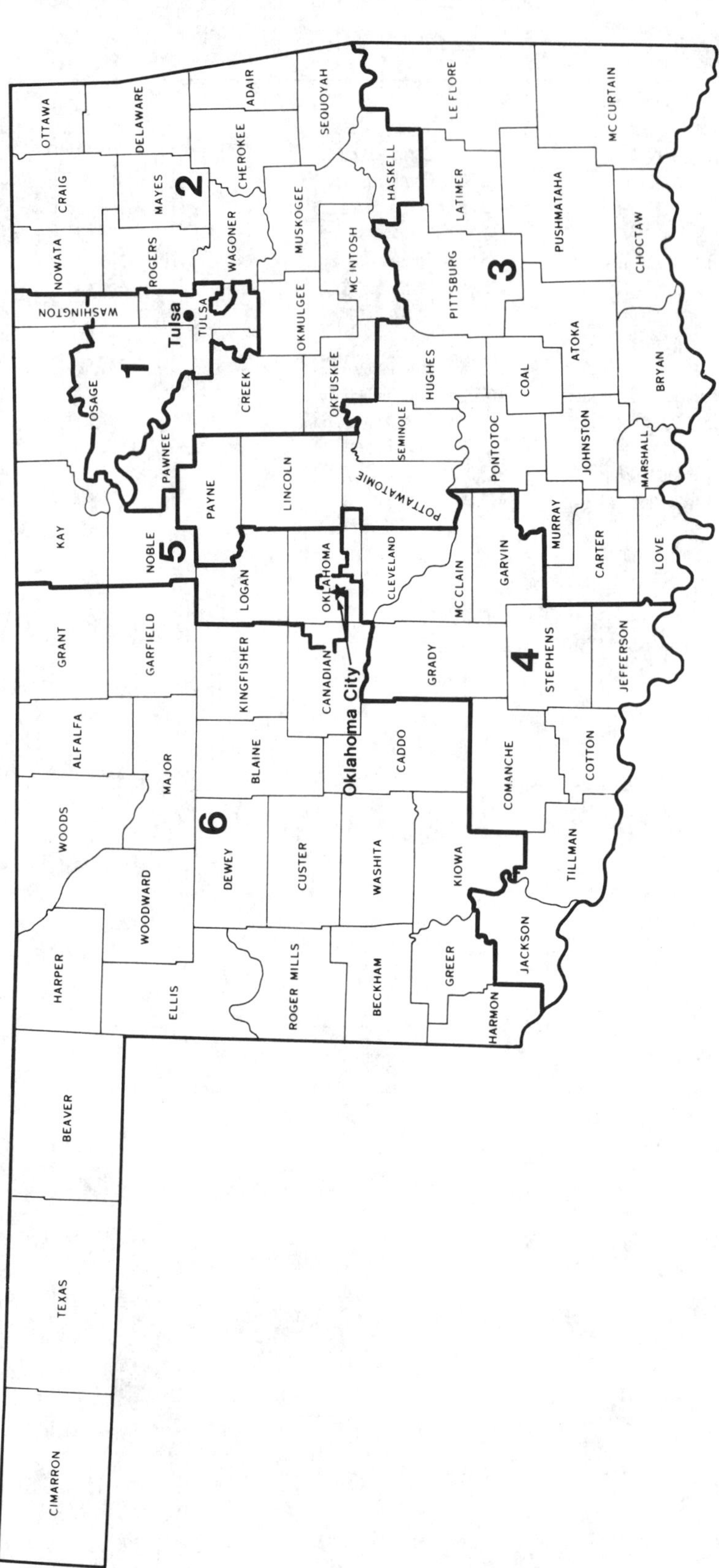

OKLAHOMA

PRESIDENT 1988

1980 Census Population	County	Total Vote	Republican	Democratic	Other	Rep.-Dem. Plurality	Percentage: Total Vote Rep.	Percentage: Total Vote Dem.	Percentage: Major Vote Rep.	Percentage: Major Vote Dem.
18,575	ADAIR	6,240	3,558	2,624	58	934 R	57.0%	42.1%	57.6%	42.4%
7,077	ALFALFA	3,132	1,960	1,117	55	843 R	62.6%	35.7%	63.7%	36.3%
12,748	ATOKA	4,570	1,971	2,565	34	594 D	43.1%	56.1%	43.5%	56.5%
6,806	BEAVER	2,834	2,013	777	44	1,236 R	71.0%	27.4%	72.2%	27.8%
19,243	BECKHAM	6,915	3,463	3,388	64	75 R	50.1%	49.0%	50.5%	49.5%
13,443	BLAINE	4,734	2,889	1,775	70	1,114 R	61.0%	37.5%	61.9%	38.1%
30,535	BRYAN	11,501	4,615	6,849	37	2,234 D	40.1%	59.6%	40.3%	59.7%
30,905	CADDO	10,177	4,689	5,387	101	698 D	46.1%	52.9%	46.5%	53.5%
56,452	CANADIAN	25,530	17,872	7,453	205	10,419 R	70.0%	29.2%	70.6%	29.4%
43,610	CARTER	16,535	8,430	7,988	117	442 R	51.0%	48.3%	51.3%	48.7%
30,684	CHEROKEE	12,424	5,838	6,483	103	645 D	47.0%	52.2%	47.4%	52.6%
17,203	CHOCTAW	5,599	2,217	3,362	20	1,145 D	39.6%	60.0%	39.7%	60.3%
3,648	CIMARRON	1,647	1,153	470	24	683 R	70.0%	28.5%	71.0%	29.0%
133,173	CLEVELAND	58,933	36,313	22,067	553	14,246 R	61.6%	37.4%	62.2%	37.8%
6,041	COAL	2,270	891	1,365	14	474 D	39.3%	60.1%	39.5%	60.5%
112,456	COMANCHE	29,099	17,464	11,441	194	6,023 R	60.0%	39.3%	60.4%	39.6%
7,338	COTTON	2,775	1,266	1,482	27	216 D	45.6%	53.4%	46.1%	53.9%
15,014	CRAIG	5,446	2,463	2,940	43	477 D	45.2%	54.0%	45.6%	54.4%
59,016	CREEK	20,982	11,308	9,512	162	1,796 R	53.9%	45.3%	54.3%	45.7%
25,995	CUSTER	10,527	6,735	3,697	95	3,038 R	64.0%	35.1%	64.6%	35.4%
23,946	DELAWARE	10,212	5,248	4,889	75	359 R	51.4%	47.9%	51.8%	48.2%
5,922	DEWEY	2,551	1,543	963	45	580 R	60.5%	37.7%	61.6%	38.4%
5,596	ELLIS	2,244	1,422	786	36	636 R	63.4%	35.0%	64.4%	35.6%
62,820	GARFIELD	23,538	15,248	8,067	223	7,181 R	64.8%	34.3%	65.4%	34.6%
27,856	GARVIN	10,656	5,109	5,438	109	329 D	47.9%	51.0%	48.4%	51.6%
39,490	GRADY	14,848	7,994	6,689	165	1,305 R	53.8%	45.0%	54.4%	45.6%
6,518	GRANT	2,980	1,690	1,249	41	441 R	56.7%	41.9%	57.5%	42.5%
7,028	GREER	2,503	1,225	1,256	22	31 D	48.9%	50.2%	49.4%	50.6%
4,519	HARMON	1,504	611	890	3	279 D	40.6%	59.2%	40.7%	59.3%
4,715	HARPER	1,900	1,281	593	26	688 R	67.4%	31.2%	68.4%	31.6%
11,010	HASKELL	4,829	1,822	2,963	44	1,141 D	37.7%	61.4%	38.1%	61.9%
14,338	HUGHES	5,327	2,037	3,259	31	1,222 D	38.2%	61.2%	38.5%	61.5%
30,356	JACKSON	8,001	4,423	3,542	36	881 R	55.3%	44.3%	55.5%	44.5%
8,183	JEFFERSON	2,846	1,063	1,767	16	704 D	37.4%	62.1%	37.6%	62.4%
10,356	JOHNSTON	3,581	1,518	2,042	21	524 D	42.4%	57.0%	42.6%	57.4%
49,852	KAY	20,564	12,646	7,751	167	4,895 R	61.5%	37.7%	62.0%	38.0%
14,187	KINGFISHER	5,852	4,011	1,777	64	2,234 R	68.5%	30.4%	69.3%	30.7%
12,711	KIOWA	4,358	2,030	2,296	32	266 D	46.6%	52.7%	46.9%	53.1%
9,840	LATIMER	4,233	1,830	2,365	38	535 D	43.2%	55.9%	43.6%	56.4%
40,698	LE FLORE	13,641	6,964	6,594	83	370 R	51.1%	48.3%	51.4%	48.6%
26,601	LINCOLN	10,740	6,409	4,225	106	2,184 R	59.7%	39.3%	60.3%	39.7%
26,881	LOGAN	11,704	6,947	4,603	154	2,344 R	59.4%	39.3%	60.1%	39.9%
7,469	LOVE	3,267	1,361	1,889	17	528 D	41.7%	57.8%	41.9%	58.1%
20,291	MCCLAIN	8,453	4,771	3,594	88	1,177 R	56.4%	42.5%	57.0%	43.0%
36,151	MCCURTAIN	9,911	4,920	4,928	63	8 D	49.6%	49.7%	50.0%	50.0%
15,562	MCINTOSH	6,742	2,665	4,041	36	1,376 D	39.5%	59.9%	39.7%	60.3%
8,772	MAJOR	3,671	2,638	982	51	1,656 R	71.9%	26.8%	72.9%	27.1%
10,550	MARSHALL	4,669	1,911	2,730	28	819 D	40.9%	58.5%	41.2%	58.8%
32,261	MAYES	12,901	6,115	6,691	95	576 D	47.4%	51.9%	47.8%	52.2%
12,147	MURRAY	4,794	2,056	2,697	41	641 D	42.9%	56.3%	43.3%	56.7%
66,939	MUSKOGEE	25,068	11,147	13,760	161	2,613 D	44.5%	54.9%	44.8%	55.2%
11,573	NOBLE	4,726	3,015	1,661	50	1,354 R	63.8%	35.1%	64.5%	35.5%
11,486	NOWATA	4,234	2,000	2,203	31	203 D	47.2%	52.0%	47.6%	52.4%
11,125	OKFUSKEE	4,098	1,851	2,209	38	358 D	45.2%	53.9%	45.6%	54.4%
568,933	OKLAHOMA	212,891	135,376	75,812	1,703	59,564 R	63.6%	35.6%	64.1%	35.9%
39,169	OKMULGEE	14,004	5,674	8,262	68	2,588 D	40.5%	59.0%	40.7%	59.3%
39,327	OSAGE	15,055	7,162	7,778	115	616 D	47.6%	51.7%	47.9%	52.1%
32,870	OTTAWA	11,729	5,026	6,658	45	1,632 D	42.9%	56.8%	43.0%	57.0%
15,310	PAWNEE	6,162	3,324	2,781	57	543 R	53.9%	45.1%	54.4%	45.6%
62,435	PAYNE	26,905	16,027	10,568	310	5,459 R	59.6%	39.3%	60.3%	39.7%

OKLAHOMA

PRESIDENT 1988

1980 Census Population	County	Total Vote	Republican	Democratic	Other	Rep.-Dem. Plurality	Percentage Total Vote Rep.	Percentage Total Vote Dem.	Percentage Major Vote Rep.	Percentage Major Vote Dem.
40,524	PITTSBURG	16,342	7,594	8,623	125	1,029 D	46.5%	52.8%	46.8%	53.2%
32,598	PONTOTOC	13,239	6,609	6,484	146	125 R	49.9%	49.0%	50.5%	49.5%
55,239	POTTAWATOMIE	21,169	12,099	8,873	197	3,226 R	57.2%	41.9%	57.7%	42.3%
11,773	PUSHMATAHA	4,301	1,841	2,430	30	589 D	42.8%	56.5%	43.1%	56.9%
4,799	ROGER MILLS	2,012	1,132	866	14	266 R	56.3%	43.0%	56.7%	43.3%
46,436	ROGERS	21,851	12,940	8,771	140	4,169 R	59.2%	40.1%	59.6%	40.4%
27,473	SEMINOLE	9,073	4,078	4,911	84	833 D	44.9%	54.1%	45.4%	54.6%
30,749	SEQUOYAH	10,729	5,710	4,951	68	759 R	53.2%	46.1%	53.6%	46.4%
43,419	STEPHENS	17,795	9,844	7,833	118	2,011 R	55.3%	44.0%	55.7%	44.3%
17,727	TEXAS	6,752	4,971	1,717	64	3,254 R	73.6%	25.4%	74.3%	25.7%
12,398	TILLMAN	3,928	1,754	2,148	26	394 D	44.7%	54.7%	45.0%	55.0%
470,593	TULSA	197,763	127,512	69,044	1,207	58,468 R	64.5%	34.9%	64.9%	35.1%
41,801	WAGONER	17,718	10,219	7,378	121	2,841 R	57.7%	41.6%	58.1%	41.9%
48,113	WASHINGTON	21,713	14,613	6,971	129	7,642 R	67.3%	32.1%	67.7%	32.3%
13,798	WASHITA	4,745	2,402	2,290	53	112 R	50.6%	48.3%	51.2%	48.8%
10,923	WOODS	4,651	2,835	1,735	81	1,100 R	61.0%	37.3%	62.0%	38.0%
21,172	WOODWARD	7,493	4,996	2,408	89	2,588 R	66.7%	32.1%	67.5%	32.5%
3,025,290	TOTAL	1,171,036	678,367	483,423	9,246	194,944 R	57.9%	41.3%	58.4%	41.6%

OKLAHOMA

CONGRESS

CD	Year	Total Vote	Republican Vote	Republican Candidate	Democratic Vote	Democratic Candidate	Other Vote	Rep.-Dem. Plurality	Percentage Total Vote Rep.	Total Vote Dem.	Major Vote Rep.	Major Vote Dem.
1	1988	196,559	103,458	INHOFE, JAMES M.	93,101	GLASSCO, KURT		10,357 R	52.6%	47.4%	52.6%	47.4%
1	1986	144,037	78,919	INHOFE, JAMES M.	61,663	ALLISON, GARY D.	3,455	17,256 R	54.8%	42.8%	56.1%	43.9%
1	1984	218,093	103,098	KEATING, FRANK	113,919	JONES, JAMES R.	1,076	10,821 D	47.3%	52.2%	47.5%	52.5%
1	1982	141,083	64,704	FREEMAN, RICHARD C.	76,379	JONES, JAMES R.		11,675 D	45.9%	54.1%	45.9%	54.1%
2	1988	209,668	73,659	PHILLIPS, IRA	136,009	SYNAR, MIKE		62,350 D	35.1%	64.9%	35.1%	64.9%
2	1986	156,338	41,795	RICE, GARY K.	114,543	SYNAR, MIKE		72,748 D	26.7%	73.3%	26.7%	73.3%
2	1984	200,013	51,889	RICE, GARY K.	148,124	SYNAR, MIKE		96,235 D	25.9%	74.1%	25.9%	74.1%
2	1982	154,193	42,298	STRIEGEL, LOU	111,895	SYNAR, MIKE		69,597 D	27.4%	72.6%	27.4%	72.6%
3	1988					WATKINS, WES						
3	1986	145,921	31,913	MILLER, PATRICK K.	114,008	WATKINS, WES		82,095 D	21.9%	78.1%	21.9%	78.1%
3	1984	177,418	39,454	MILLER, PATRICK K.	137,964	WATKINS, WES		98,510 D	22.2%	77.8%	22.2%	77.8%
3	1982	148,005	26,335	MILLER, PATRICK K.	121,670	WATKINS, WES		95,335 D	17.8%	82.2%	17.8%	82.2%
4	1988					MCCURDY, DAVE						
4	1986	124,681	29,697	HUMPHREYS, LARRY	94,984	MCCURDY, DAVE		65,287 D	23.8%	76.2%	23.8%	76.2%
4	1984	172,039	60,844	SMITH, JERRY	109,447	MCCURDY, DAVE	1,748	48,603 D	35.4%	63.6%	35.7%	64.3%
4	1982	129,504	44,351	RUTLEDGE, HOWARD	84,205	MCCURDY, DAVE	948	39,854 D	34.2%	65.0%	34.5%	65.5%
5	1988	192,850	139,182	EDWARDS, M. H.	53,668	MONTGOMERY, TERRY J.		85,514 R	72.2%	27.8%	72.2%	27.8%
5	1986	154,030	108,774	EDWARDS, M. H.	45,256	COMPTON, DONNA		63,518 R	70.6%	29.4%	70.6%	29.4%
5	1984	178,726	135,167	EDWARDS, M. H.	39,089	GREESON, ALLEN	4,470	96,078 R	75.6%	21.9%	77.6%	22.4%
5	1982	147,209	98,979	EDWARDS, M. H.	42,453	LANE, DAN	5,777	56,526 R	67.2%	28.8%	70.0%	30.0%
6	1988	168,126	45,239	BROWN, MIKE	122,887	ENGLISH, GLENN		77,648 D	26.9%	73.1%	26.9%	73.1%
6	1986					ENGLISH, GLENN						
6	1984	164,595	67,601	DODD, CRAIG	96,994	ENGLISH, GLENN		29,393 D	41.1%	58.9%	41.1%	58.9%
6	1982	136,330	33,519	MOORE, ED	102,811	ENGLISH, GLENN		69,292 D	24.6%	75.4%	24.6%	75.4%

OKLAHOMA

1988 GENERAL ELECTION

President Other vote was 6,261 Libertarian (Paul); 2,985 New Alliance (Fulani).

Congress According to state law, votes are not required to be tabulated for unopposed candidates.

1988 PRIMARIES

AUGUST 23 REPUBLICAN

Congress Unopposed in two CD's. No candidate in CD's 3 and 4. Contested as follows:

CD 2 8,279 Ira Phillips; 6,649 Marshall Farrier.
CD 5 25,311 M. H. Edwards; 5,142 Bill Maguire.

AUGUST 23 DEMOCRATIC

Congress Unopposed in CD 3. Contested as follows:

CD 1 18,196 Kurt Glassco; 3,766 Virginia Jenner; 3,737 George Gentry; 2,347 Bruce D. Gaither; 2,109 Charles R. Doty.
CD 2 62,936 Mike Synar; 27,604 Frank Shurden.
CD 4 52,366 Dave McCurdy; 10,728 Howard Bell.
CD 5 18,305 Terry J. Montgomery; 10,966 John S. Hubbell.
CD 6 51,733 Glenn English; 9,490 Batch Batchelder.

OREGON

GOVERNOR

Neil Goldschmidt (D). Elected 1986 to a four-year term.

SENATORS

Mark Hatfield (R). Re-elected 1984 to a six-year term. Previously elected 1978, 1972, 1966.

Robert W. Packwood (R). Re-elected 1986 to a six-year term. Previously elected 1980, 1974, 1968.

REPRESENTATIVES

1. Les AuCoin (D)
2. Robert F. Smith (R)
3. Ron Wyden (D)
4. Peter A. DeFazio (D)
5. Denny Smith (R)

POSTWAR VOTE FOR PRESIDENT

Year	Total Vote	Republican Vote	Republican Candidate	Democratic Vote	Democratic Candidate	Other Vote	Plurality	Percentage Total Vote Rep.	Percentage Total Vote Dem.	Percentage Major Vote Rep.	Percentage Major Vote Dem.
1988	1,201,694	560,126	Bush, George	616,206	Dukakis, Michael S.	25,362	56,080 D	46.6%	51.3%	47.6%	52.4%
1984	1,226,527	685,700	Reagan, Ronald	536,479	Mondale, Walter F.	4,348	149,221 R	55.9%	43.7%	56.1%	43.9%
1980	1,181,516	571,044	Reagan, Ronald	456,890	Carter, Jimmy	153,582	114,154 R	48.3%	38.7%	55.6%	44.4%
1976	1,029,876	492,120	Ford, Gerald R.	490,407	Carter, Jimmy	47,349	1,713 R	47.8%	47.6%	50.1%	49.9%
1972	927,946	486,686	Nixon, Richard M.	392,760	McGovern, George S.	48,500	93,926 R	52.4%	42.3%	55.3%	44.7%
1968	819,622	408,433	Nixon, Richard M.	358,866	Humphrey, Hubert H.	52,323	49,567 R	49.8%	43.8%	53.2%	46.8%
1964	786,305	282,779	Goldwater, Barry M.	501,017	Johnson, Lyndon B.	2,509	218,238 D	36.0%	63.7%	36.1%	63.9%
1960	776,421	408,060	Nixon, Richard M.	367,402	Kennedy, John F.	959	40,658 R	52.6%	47.3%	52.6%	47.4%
1956	736,132	406,393	Eisenhower, Dwight D.	329,204	Stevenson, Adlai E.	535	77,189 R	55.2%	44.7%	55.2%	44.8%
1952	695,059	420,815	Eisenhower, Dwight D.	270,579	Stevenson, Adlai E.	3,665	150,236 R	60.5%	38.9%	60.9%	39.1%
1948	524,080	260,904	Dewey, Thomas E.	243,147	Truman, Harry S.	20,029	17,757 R	49.8%	46.4%	51.8%	48.2%

POSTWAR VOTE FOR GOVERNOR

Year	Total Vote	Republican Vote	Republican Candidate	Democratic Vote	Democratic Candidate	Other Vote	Rep.-Dem. Plurality	Percentage Total Vote Rep.	Percentage Total Vote Dem.	Percentage Major Vote Rep.	Percentage Major Vote Dem.
1986	1,059,630	506,986	Paulus, Norma	549,456	Goldschmidt, Neil	3,188	42,470 D	47.8%	51.9%	48.0%	52.0%
1982	1,042,009	639,841	Atiyeh, Victor	374,316	Kulongoski, Ted	27,852	265,525 R	61.4%	35.9%	63.1%	36.9%
1978	911,143	498,452	Atiyeh, Victor	409,411	Straub, Robert W.	3,280	89,041 R	54.7%	44.9%	54.9%	45.1%
1974	770,574	324,751	Atiyeh, Victor	444,812	Straub, Robert W.	1,011	120,061 D	42.1%	57.7%	42.2%	57.8%
1970	666,394	369,964	McCall, Tom	293,892	Straub, Robert W.	2,538	76,072 R	55.5%	44.1%	55.7%	44.3%
1966	682,862	377,346	McCall, Tom	305,008	Straub, Robert W.	508	72,338 R	55.3%	44.7%	55.3%	44.7%
1962	637,407	345,497	Hatfield, Mark	265,359	Thornton, Robert Y.	26,551	80,138 R	54.2%	41.6%	56.6%	43.4%
1958	599,994	331,900	Hatfield, Mark	267,934	Holmes, Robert D.	160	63,966 R	55.3%	44.7%	55.3%	44.7%
1956 S	731,279	361,840	Smith, Elmo E.	369,439	Holmes, Robert D.		7,599 D	49.5%	50.5%	49.5%	50.5%
1954	566,701	322,522	Patterson, Paul	244,179	Carson, Joseph K.		78,343 R	56.9%	43.1%	56.9%	43.1%
1950	505,910	334,160	McKay, Douglas	171,750	Flegel, Austin F.		162,410 R	66.1%	33.9%	66.1%	33.9%
1948 S	509,633	271,295	McKay, Douglas	226,958	Wallace, Lew	11,380	44,337 R	53.2%	44.5%	54.4%	45.6%
1946	344,155	237,681	Snell, Earl	106,474	Donaugh, Carl C.		131,207 R	69.1%	30.9%	69.1%	30.9%

The 1956 and 1948 elections were for short terms to fill vacancies.

OREGON

POSTWAR VOTE FOR SENATOR

Year	Total Vote	Republican Vote	Republican Candidate	Democratic Vote	Democratic Candidate	Other Vote	Rep.-Dem. Plurality	Percentage Total Vote Rep.	Percentage Total Vote Dem.	Percentage Major Vote Rep.	Percentage Major Vote Dem.
1986	1,042,555	656,317	Packwood, Robert W.	375,735	Bauman, Rick	10,503	280,582 R	63.0%	36.0%	63.6%	36.4%
1984	1,214,735	808,152	Hatfield, Mark	406,122	Hendriksen, Margie	461	402,030 R	66.5%	33.4%	66.6%	33.4%
1980	1,140,494	594,290	Packwood, Robert W.	501,963	Kulongoski, Ted	44,241	92,327 R	52.1%	44.0%	54.2%	45.8%
1978	892,518	550,165	Hatfield, Mark	341,616	Cook, Vernon	737	208,549 R	61.6%	38.3%	61.7%	38.3%
1974	766,414	420,984	Packwood, Robert W.	338,591	Roberts, Betty	6,839	82,393 R	54.9%	44.2%	55.4%	44.6%
1972	920,833	494,671	Hatfield, Mark	425,036	Morse, Wayne L.	1,126	69,635 R	53.7%	46.2%	53.8%	46.2%
1968	814,176	408,646	Packwood, Robert W.	405,353	Morse, Wayne L.	177	3,293 R	50.2%	49.8%	50.2%	49.8%
1966	685,067	354,391	Hatfield, Mark	330,374	Duncan, Robert B.	302	24,017 R	51.7%	48.2%	51.8%	48.2%
1962	636,558	291,587	Unander, Sig	344,716	Morse, Wayne L.	255	53,129 D	45.8%	54.2%	45.8%	54.2%
1960	755,875	343,009	Smith, Elmo E.	412,757	Neuberger, Maurine	109	69,748 D	45.4%	54.6%	45.4%	54.6%
1956	732,254	335,405	McKay, Douglas	396,849	Morse, Wayne L.		61,444 D	45.8%	54.2%	45.8%	54.2%
1954	569,088	283,313	Cordon, Guy	285,775	Neuberger, Richard L.		2,462 D	49.8%	50.2%	49.8%	50.2%
1950	503,455	376,510	Morse, Wayne L.	116,780	Latourette, Howard	10,165	259,730 R	74.8%	23.2%	76.3%	23.7%
1948	498,570	299,295	Cordon, Guy	199,275	Wilson, Manley J.		100,020 R	60.0%	40.0%	60.0%	40.0%

OREGON

Districts Established July 28, 1981

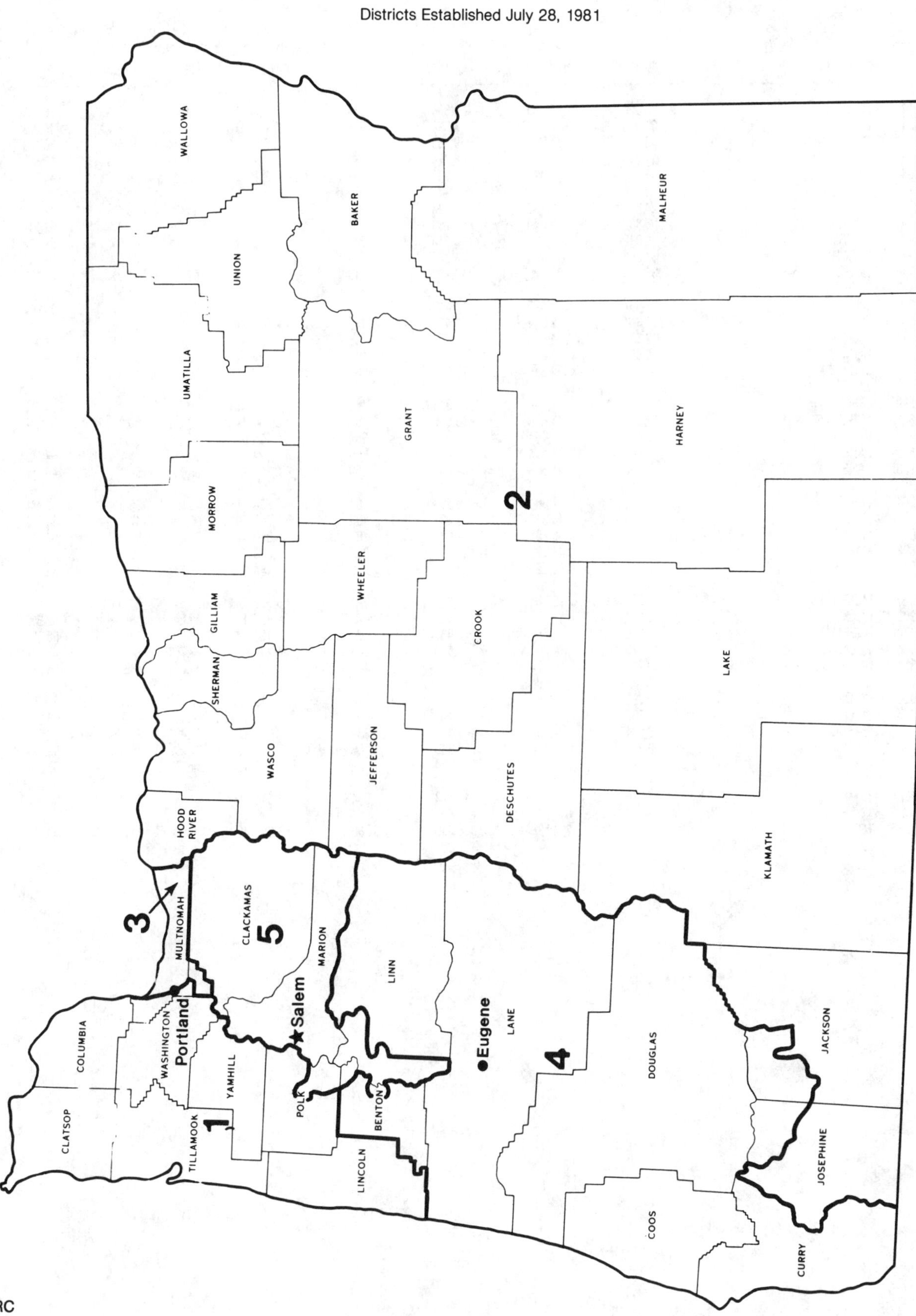

OREGON

PRESIDENT 1988

1980 Census Population	County	Total Vote	Republican	Democratic	Other	Rep.-Dem. Plurality	Percentage Total Vote Rep.	Total Vote Dem.	Major Vote Rep.	Major Vote Dem.
16,134	BAKER	6,826	3,696	2,896	234	800 R	54.1%	42.4%	56.1%	43.9%
68,211	BENTON	31,610	14,004	16,930	676	2,926 D	44.3%	53.6%	45.3%	54.7%
241,919	CLACKAMAS	123,351	61,381	59,799	2,171	1,582 R	49.8%	48.5%	50.7%	49.3%
32,489	CLATSOP	14,316	5,956	8,074	286	2,118 D	41.6%	56.4%	42.5%	57.5%
35,646	COLUMBIA	15,806	6,424	8,983	399	2,559 D	40.6%	56.8%	41.7%	58.3%
64,047	COOS	24,836	10,153	13,996	687	3,843 D	40.9%	56.4%	42.0%	58.0%
13,091	CROOK	5,882	3,049	2,719	114	330 R	51.8%	46.2%	52.9%	47.1%
16,992	CURRY	9,012	4,761	4,015	236	746 R	52.8%	44.6%	54.3%	45.7%
62,142	DESCHUTES	31,366	16,425	14,264	677	2,161 R	52.4%	45.5%	53.5%	46.5%
93,748	DOUGLAS	38,415	20,120	17,255	1,040	2,865 R	52.4%	44.9%	53.8%	46.2%
2,057	GILLIAM	897	470	417	10	53 R	52.4%	46.5%	53.0%	47.0%
8,210	GRANT	3,844	2,264	1,437	143	827 R	58.9%	37.4%	61.2%	38.8%
8,314	HARNEY	3,330	1,833	1,379	118	454 R	55.0%	41.4%	57.1%	42.9%
15,835	HOOD RIVER	6,689	3,257	3,275	157	18 D	48.7%	49.0%	49.9%	50.1%
132,456	JACKSON	61,912	32,516	28,028	1,368	4,488 R	52.5%	45.3%	53.7%	46.3%
11,599	JEFFERSON	4,995	2,509	2,346	140	163 R	50.2%	47.0%	51.7%	48.3%
58,855	JOSEPHINE	27,272	15,876	10,646	750	5,230 R	58.2%	39.0%	59.9%	40.1%
59,117	KLAMATH	22,470	13,484	8,429	557	5,055 R	60.0%	37.5%	61.5%	38.5%
7,532	LAKE	3,463	2,161	1,237	65	924 R	62.4%	35.7%	63.6%	36.4%
275,226	LANE	119,702	47,563	69,883	2,256	22,320 D	39.7%	58.4%	40.5%	59.5%
35,264	LINCOLN	17,443	7,364	9,598	481	2,234 D	42.2%	55.0%	43.4%	56.6%
89,495	LINN	36,122	18,312	17,007	803	1,305 R	50.7%	47.1%	51.8%	48.2%
26,896	MALHEUR	9,443	6,285	2,965	193	3,320 R	66.6%	31.4%	67.9%	32.1%
204,692	MARION	88,492	45,292	41,193	2,007	4,099 R	51.2%	46.5%	52.4%	47.6%
7,519	MORROW	2,970	1,529	1,375	66	154 R	51.5%	46.3%	52.7%	47.3%
562,640	MULTNOMAH	261,843	95,561	161,361	4,921	65,800 D	36.5%	61.6%	37.2%	62.8%
45,203	POLK	20,621	10,553	9,626	442	927 R	51.2%	46.7%	52.3%	47.7%
2,172	SHERMAN	1,016	555	435	26	120 R	54.6%	42.8%	56.1%	43.9%
21,164	TILLAMOOK	10,070	4,297	5,529	244	1,232 D	42.7%	54.9%	43.7%	56.3%
58,861	UMATILLA	18,981	10,254	8,327	400	1,927 R	54.0%	43.9%	55.2%	44.8%
23,921	UNION	10,090	5,061	4,682	347	379 R	50.2%	46.4%	51.9%	48.1%
7,273	WALLOWA	3,503	1,993	1,425	85	568 R	56.9%	40.7%	58.3%	41.7%
21,732	WASCO	9,834	4,462	5,141	231	679 D	45.4%	52.3%	46.5%	53.5%
245,808	WASHINGTON	129,211	67,018	59,837	2,356	7,181 R	51.9%	46.3%	52.8%	47.2%
1,513	WHEELER	673	367	274	32	93 R	54.5%	40.7%	57.3%	42.7%
55,332	YAMHILL	25,388	13,321	11,423	644	1,898 R	52.5%	45.0%	53.8%	46.2%
2,633,105	TOTAL	1,201,694	560,126	616,206	25,362	56,080 D	46.6%	51.3%	47.6%	52.4%

OREGON

CONGRESS

CD	Year	Total Vote	Republican Vote	Republican Candidate	Democratic Vote	Democratic Candidate	Other Vote	Rep.-Dem. Plurality	Percentage Total Vote Rep.	Percentage Total Vote Dem.	Percentage Major Vote Rep.	Percentage Major Vote Dem.
1	1988	258,603	78,626	MOLANDER, EARL	179,915	AUCOIN, LES	62	101,289 D	30.4%	69.6%	30.4%	69.6%
1	1986	229,495	87,874	MEEKER, ANTHONY	141,585	AUCOIN, LES	36	53,711 D	38.3%	61.7%	38.3%	61.7%
1	1984	260,667	122,247	MOSHOFSKY, BILL	138,393	AUCOIN, LES	27	16,146 D	46.9%	53.1%	46.9%	53.1%
1	1982	220,378	101,720	MOSHOFSKY, BILL	118,638	AUCOIN, LES	20	16,918 D	46.2%	53.8%	46.2%	53.8%
2	1988	200,079	125,366	SMITH, ROBERT F.	74,700	TUTTLE, LARRY	13	50,666 R	62.7%	37.3%	62.7%	37.3%
2	1986	188,716	113,566	SMITH, ROBERT F.	75,124	TUTTLE, LARRY	26	38,442 R	60.2%	39.8%	60.2%	39.8%
2	1984	232,826	132,649	SMITH, ROBERT F.	100,152	WILLIS, LARRYANN	25	32,497 R	57.0%	43.0%	57.0%	43.0%
2	1982	192,427	106,912	SMITH, ROBERT F.	85,495	WILLIS, LARRYANN	20	21,417 R	55.6%	44.4%	55.6%	44.4%
3	1988	191,825			190,684	WYDEN, RON	1,141	190,684 D		99.4%		100.0%
3	1986	209,581	29,321	PHELAN, THOMAS H.	180,067	WYDEN, RON	193	150,746 D	14.0%	85.9%	14.0%	86.0%
3	1984	239,897	66,394	DAVIS, DREW	173,438	WYDEN, RON	65	107,044 D	27.7%	72.3%	27.7%	72.3%
3	1982	203,662	44,162	PHELAN, THOMAS H.	159,416	WYDEN, RON	84	115,254 D	21.7%	78.3%	21.7%	78.3%
4	1988	150,735	42,220	HOWARD, JIM	108,483	DEFAZIO, PETER A.	32	66,263 D	28.0%	72.0%	28.0%	72.0%
4	1986	195,548	89,795	LONG, BRUCE	105,697	DEFAZIO, PETER A.	56	15,902 D	45.9%	54.1%	45.9%	54.1%
4	1984	230,687	96,487	LONG, BRUCE	134,190	WEAVER, JAMES	10	37,703 D	41.8%	58.2%	41.8%	58.2%
4	1982	195,524	80,054	ANTHONY, ROSS	115,448	WEAVER, JAMES	22	35,394 D	40.9%	59.0%	40.9%	59.1%
5	1988	222,354	111,489	SMITH, DENNY	110,782	KOPETSKI, MIKE	83	707 R	50.1%	49.8%	50.2%	49.8%
5	1986	208,204	125,906	SMITH, DENNY	82,290	ROSS, BARBARA	8	43,616 R	60.5%	39.5%	60.5%	39.5%
5	1984	239,414	130,424	SMITH, DENNY	108,919	MCFARLAND, RUTH	71	21,505 R	54.5%	45.5%	54.5%	45.5%
5	1982	202,901	103,906	SMITH, DENNY	98,952	MCFARLAND, RUTH	43	4,954 R	51.2%	48.8%	51.2%	48.8%

OREGON

1988 GENERAL ELECTION

President Other vote was 14,811 Libertarian (Paul); 6,487 Independent (Fulani); 90 Duke (write-in); 3,974 scattered write-in.

Congress Other vote was scattered in all CD's. The vote in CD 5 is for the recount.

1988 PRIMARIES

MAY 17 REPUBLICAN

Congress Unopposed in three CD's. No candidate in CD 3. Contested as follows:

CD 1 19,963 Earl Molander; 11,845 William Jolley; 8,010 Bert Miller; 4,268 John Schiess; 116 scattered write-in.

MAY 17 DEMOCRATIC

Congress Unopposed in three CD's. Contested as follows:

CD 3 84,978 Ron Wyden; 4,790 Sam Kahl; 41 scattered write-in.
CD 5 40,424 Mike Kopetski; 18,810 John Dennis; 77 scattered write-in.

PENNSYLVANIA

GOVERNOR

Robert Casey (D). Elected 1986 to a four-year term.

SENATORS

H. John Heinz (R). Re-elected 1988 to a six-year term. Previously elected 1982, 1976.

Arlen Specter (R). Re-elected 1986 to a six-year term. Previously elected 1980.

REPRESENTATIVES

1. Thomas M. Foglietta (D)
2. William H. Gray (D)
3. Robert A. Borski (D)
4. Joseph P. Kolter (D)
5. Richard T. Schulze (R)
6. Gus Yatron (D)
7. Curt Weldon (R)
8. Peter H. Kostmayer (D)
9. E. G.Shuster (R)
10. Joseph M. McDade (R)
11. Paul E. Kanjorski (D)
12. John P. Murtha (D)
13. R. Lawrence Coughlin (R)
14. William J. Coyne (D)
15. Donald L. Ritter (R)
16. Robert S. Walker (R)
17. George W. Gekas (R)
18. Douglas Walgren (D)
19. William F. Goodling (R)
20. Joseph M. Gaydos (D)
21. Thomas J. Ridge (R)
22. Austin J. Murphy (D)
23. William F. Clinger (R)

POSTWAR VOTE FOR PRESIDENT

								Percentage			
	Total	Republican		Democratic		Other		Total Vote		Major Vote	
Year	Vote	Vote	Candidate	Vote	Candidate	Vote	Plurality	Rep.	Dem.	Rep.	Dem.
1988	4,536,251	2,300,087	Bush, George	2,194,944	Dukakis, Michael S.	41,220	105,143 R	50.7%	48.4%	51.2%	48.8%
1984	4,844,903	2,584,323	Reagan, Ronald	2,228,131	Mondale, Walter F.	32,449	356,192 R	53.3%	46.0%	53.7%	46.3%
1980	4,561,501	2,261,872	Reagan, Ronald	1,937,540	Carter, Jimmy	362,089	324,332 R	49.6%	42.5%	53.9%	46.1%
1976	4,620,787	2,205,604	Ford, Gerald R.	2,328,677	Carter, Jimmy	86,506	123,073 D	47.7%	50.4%	48.6%	51.4%
1972	4,592,106	2,714,521	Nixon, Richard M.	1,796,951	McGovern, George S.	80,634	917,570 R	59.1%	39.1%	60.2%	39.8%
1968	4,747,928	2,090,017	Nixon, Richard M.	2,259,405	Humphrey, Hubert H.	398,506	169,388 D	44.0%	47.6%	48.1%	51.9%
1964	4,822,690	1,673,657	Goldwater, Barry M.	3,130,954	Johnson, Lyndon B.	18,079	1,457,297 D	34.7%	64.9%	34.8%	65.2%
1960	5,006,541	2,439,956	Nixon, Richard M.	2,556,282	Kennedy, John F.	10,303	116,326 D	48.7%	51.1%	48.8%	51.2%
1956	4,576,503	2,585,252	Eisenhower, Dwight D.	1,981,769	Stevenson, Adlai E.	9,482	603,483 R	56.5%	43.3%	56.6%	43.4%
1952	4,580,969	2,415,789	Eisenhower, Dwight D.	2,146,269	Stevenson, Adlai E.	18,911	269,520 R	52.7%	46.9%	53.0%	47.0%
1948	3,735,348	1,902,197	Dewey, Thomas E.	1,752,426	Truman, Harry S.	80,725	149,771 R	50.9%	46.9%	52.0%	48.0%

PENNSYLVANIA

POSTWAR VOTE FOR GOVERNOR

Year	Total Vote	Republican Vote	Republican Candidate	Democratic Vote	Democratic Candidate	Other Vote	Rep.-Dem. Plurality	Percentage Total Vote Rep.	Percentage Total Vote Dem.	Percentage Major Vote Rep.	Percentage Major Vote Dem.
1986	3,388,275	1,638,268	Scranton, William W., III	1,717,484	Casey, Robert	32,523	79,216 D	48.4%	50.7%	48.8%	51.2%
1982	3,683,985	1,872,784	Thornburgh, Richard L.	1,772,353	Ertel, Allen E.	38,848	100,431 R	50.8%	48.1%	51.4%	48.6%
1978	3,741,969	1,966,042	Thornburgh, Richard L.	1,737,888	Flaherty, Peter	38,039	228,154 R	52.5%	46.4%	53.1%	46.9%
1974	3,491,234	1,578,917	Lewis, Andrew L.	1,878,252	Shapp, Milton	34,065	299,335 D	45.2%	53.8%	45.7%	54.3%
1970	3,700,060	1,542,854	Broderick, Raymond	2,043,029	Shapp, Milton	114,177	500,175 D	41.7%	55.2%	43.0%	57.0%
1966	4,050,668	2,110,349	Shafer, Raymond P.	1,868,719	Shapp, Milton	71,600	241,630 R	52.1%	46.1%	53.0%	47.0%
1962	4,378,042	2,424,918	Scranton, William W.	1,938,627	Dilworth, Richardson	14,497	486,291 R	55.4%	44.3%	55.6%	44.4%
1958	3,986,918	1,948,769	McGonigle, A. T.	2,024,852	Lawrence, David	13,297	76,083 D	48.9%	50.8%	49.0%	51.0%
1954	3,720,457	1,717,070	Wood, Lloyd H.	1,996,266	Leader, George M.	7,121	279,196 D	46.2%	53.7%	46.2%	53.8%
1950	3,540,059	1,796,119	Fine, John S.	1,710,355	Dilworth, Richardson	33,585	85,764 R	50.7%	48.3%	51.2%	48.8%
1946	3,123,994	1,828,462	Duff, James H.	1,270,947	Rice, John S.	24,585	557,515 R	58.5%	40.7%	59.0%	41.0%

POSTWAR VOTE FOR SENATOR

Year	Total Vote	Republican Vote	Republican Candidate	Democratic Vote	Democratic Candidate	Other Vote	Rep.-Dem. Plurality	Percentage Total Vote Rep.	Percentage Total Vote Dem.	Percentage Major Vote Rep.	Percentage Major Vote Dem.
1988	4,366,598	2,901,715	Heinz, H. John	1,416,764	Vignola, Joseph C.	48,119	1,484,951 R	66.5%	32.4%	67.2%	32.8%
1986	3,378,226	1,906,537	Specter, Arlen	1,448,219	Edgar, Robert W.	23,470	458,318 R	56.4%	42.9%	56.8%	43.2%
1982	3,604,108	2,136,418	Heinz, H. John	1,412,965	Wecht, Cyril H.	54,725	723,453 R	59.3%	39.2%	60.2%	39.8%
1980	4,418,042	2,230,404	Specter, Arlen	2,122,391	Flaherty, Peter	65,247	108,013 R	50.5%	48.0%	51.2%	48.8%
1976	4,546,353	2,381,891	Heinz, H. John	2,126,977	Green, William J., III	37,485	254,914 R	52.4%	46.8%	52.8%	47.2%
1974	3,477,812	1,843,317	Schweiker, Richard S.	1,596,121	Flaherty, Peter	38,374	247,196 R	53.0%	45.9%	53.6%	46.4%
1970	3,644,305	1,874,106	Scott, Hugh	1,653,774	Sesler, William G.	116,425	220,332 R	51.4%	45.4%	53.1%	46.9%
1968	4,624,218	2,399,762	Schweiker, Richard S.	2,117,662	Clark, Joseph S.	106,794	282,100 R	51.9%	45.8%	53.1%	46.9%
1964	4,803,835	2,429,858	Scott, Hugh	2,359,223	Blatt, Genevieve	14,754	70,635 R	50.6%	49.1%	50.7%	49.3%
1962	4,383,475	2,134,649	Van Zandt, James E.	2,238,383	Clark, Joseph S.	10,443	103,734 D	48.7%	51.1%	48.8%	51.2%
1958	3,988,622	2,042,586	Scott, Hugh	1,929,821	Leader, George M.	16,215	112,765 R	51.2%	48.4%	51.4%	48.6%
1956	4,529,874	2,250,671	Duff, James H.	2,268,641	Clark, Joseph S.	10,562	17,970 D	49.7%	50.1%	49.8%	50.2%
1952	4,519,761	2,331,034	Martin, Edward	2,168,546	Bard, Guy Kurtz	20,181	162,488 R	51.6%	48.0%	51.8%	48.2%
1950	3,548,703	1,820,400	Duff, James H.	1,694,076	Myers, Francis J.	34,227	126,324 R	51.3%	47.7%	51.8%	48.2%
1946	3,127,860	1,853,458	Martin, Edward	1,245,338	Guffey, Joseph F.	29,064	608,120 R	59.3%	39.8%	59.8%	40.2%

PENNSYLVANIA

Districts Established March 3, 1982

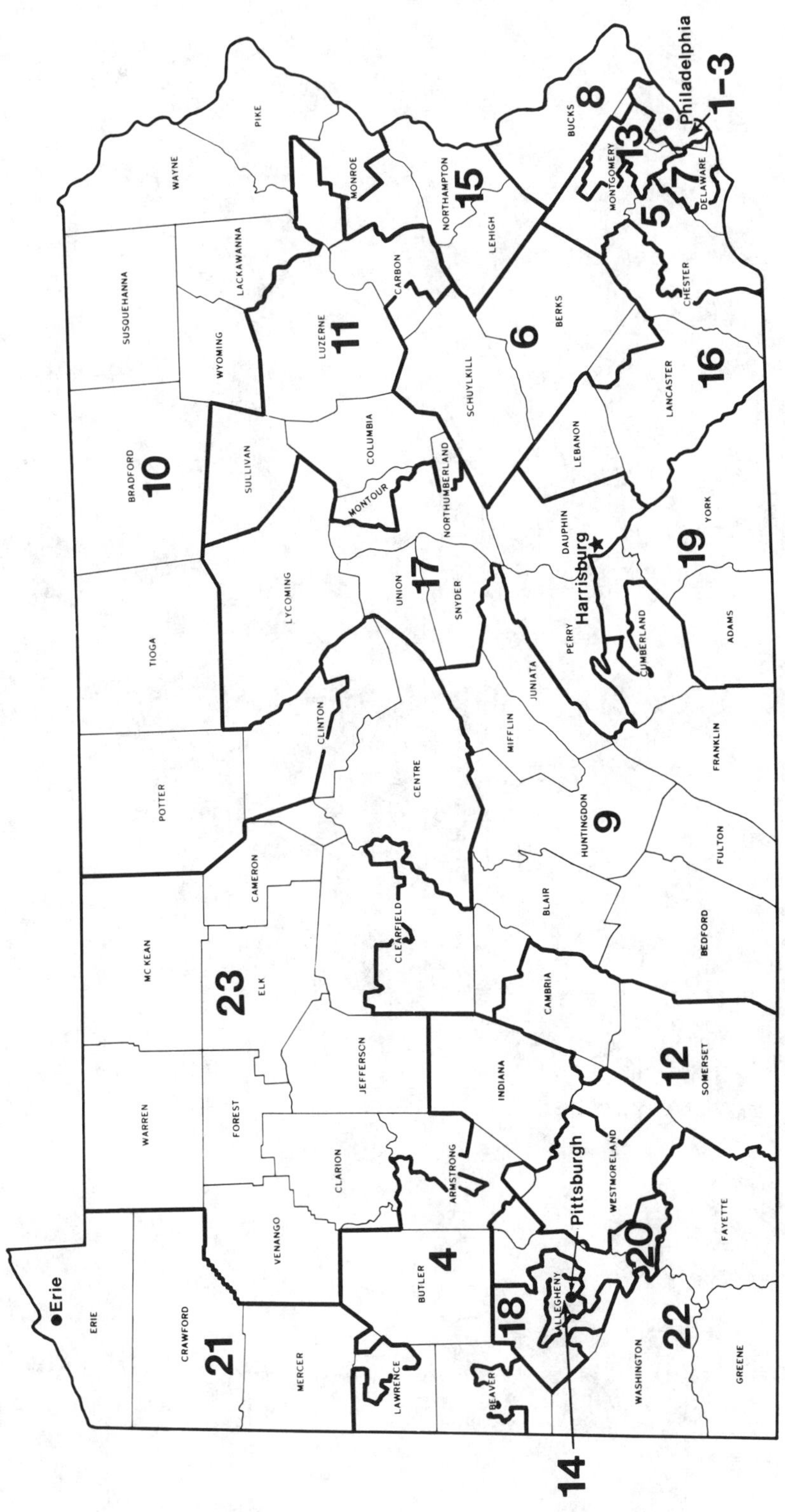

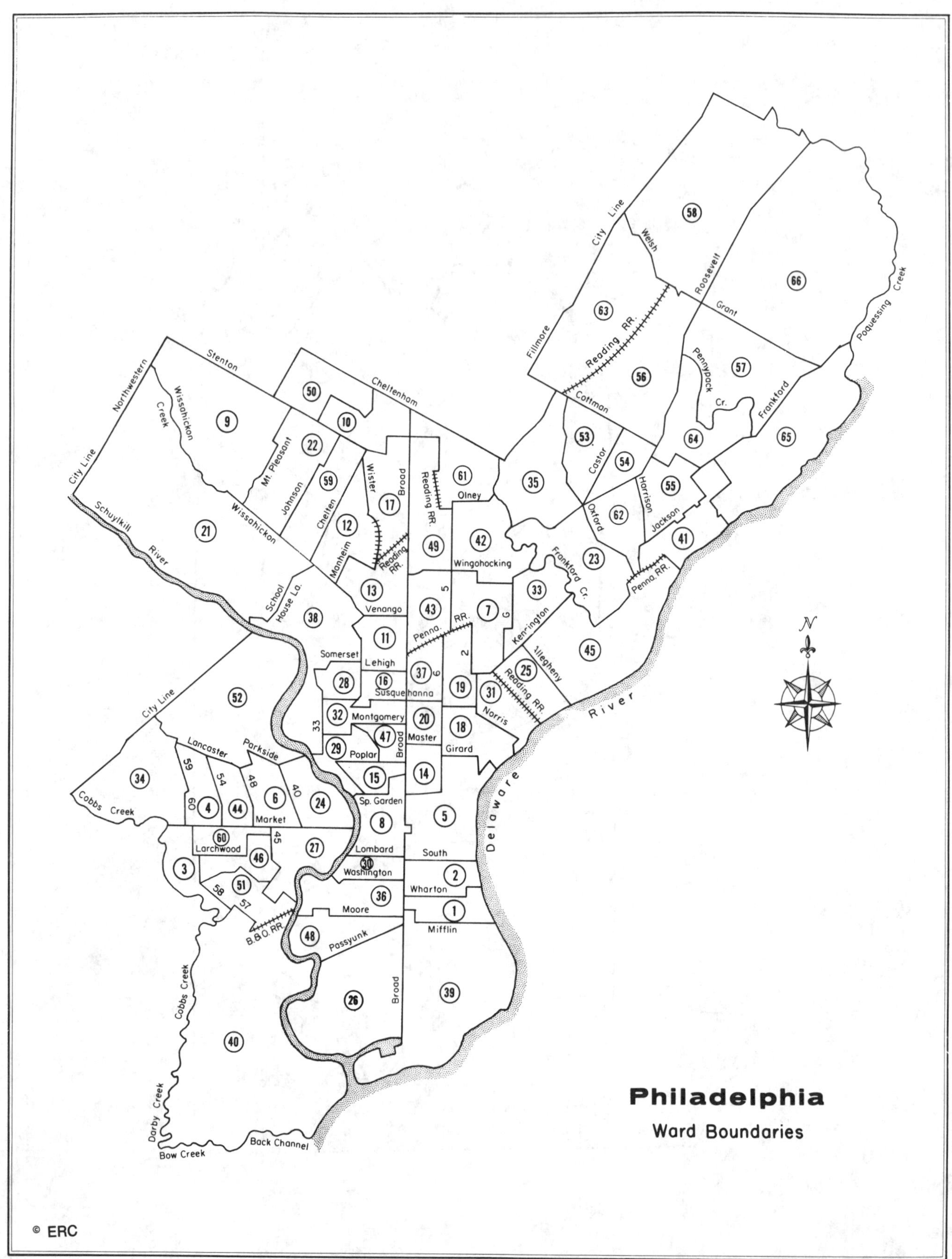
Philadelphia
Ward Boundaries
© ERC

PENNSYLVANIA

PRESIDENT 1988

1980 Census Population	County	Total Vote	Republican	Democratic	Other	Rep.-Dem. Plurality	Percentage Total Vote Rep.	Percentage Total Vote Dem.	Percentage Major Vote Rep.	Percentage Major Vote Dem.
68,292	ADAMS	24,105	15,650	8,299	156	7,351 R	64.9%	34.4%	65.3%	34.7%
1,450,085	ALLEGHENY	586,151	231,137	348,814	6,200	117,677 D	39.4%	59.5%	39.9%	60.1%
77,768	ARMSTRONG	25,683	11,509	13,892	282	2,383 D	44.8%	54.1%	45.3%	54.7%
204,441	BEAVER	76,469	25,764	50,327	378	24,563 D	33.7%	65.8%	33.9%	66.1%
46,784	BEDFORD	16,969	11,123	5,754	92	5,369 R	65.5%	33.9%	65.9%	34.1%
312,509	BERKS	112,444	70,153	41,040	1,251	29,113 R	62.4%	36.5%	63.1%	36.9%
136,621	BLAIR	41,662	25,623	15,588	451	10,035 R	61.5%	37.4%	62.2%	37.8%
62,919	BRADFORD	20,337	13,568	6,635	134	6,933 R	66.7%	32.6%	67.2%	32.8%
479,211	BUCKS	212,640	127,563	82,472	2,605	45,091 R	60.0%	38.8%	60.7%	39.3%
147,912	BUTLER	50,667	27,777	22,341	549	5,436 R	54.8%	44.1%	55.4%	44.6%
183,263	CAMBRIA	64,552	25,626	38,517	409	12,891 D	39.7%	59.7%	40.0%	60.0%
6,674	CAMERON	2,655	1,731	901	23	830 R	65.2%	33.9%	65.8%	34.2%
53,285	CARBON	19,547	10,232	9,104	211	1,128 R	52.3%	46.6%	52.9%	47.1%
112,760	CENTRE	42,527	23,875	18,357	295	5,518 R	56.1%	43.2%	56.5%	43.5%
316,660	CHESTER	139,585	93,522	44,853	1,210	48,669 R	67.0%	32.1%	67.6%	32.4%
43,362	CLARION	13,751	8,026	5,616	109	2,410 R	58.4%	40.8%	58.8%	41.2%
83,578	CLEARFIELD	26,713	14,296	12,235	182	2,061 R	53.5%	45.8%	53.9%	46.1%
38,971	CLINTON	11,613	5,735	5,759	119	24 D	49.4%	49.6%	49.9%	50.1%
61,967	COLUMBIA	20,021	12,114	7,767	140	4,347 R	60.5%	38.8%	60.9%	39.1%
88,869	CRAWFORD	30,628	17,249	13,021	358	4,228 R	56.3%	42.5%	57.0%	43.0%
178,541	CUMBERLAND	72,433	47,292	24,613	528	22,679 R	65.3%	34.0%	65.8%	34.2%
232,317	DAUPHIN	84,677	48,917	35,079	681	13,838 R	57.8%	41.4%	58.2%	41.8%
555,007	DELAWARE	246,305	147,656	96,144	2,505	51,512 R	59.9%	39.0%	60.6%	39.4%
38,338	ELK	12,744	6,737	5,879	128	858 R	52.9%	46.1%	53.4%	46.6%
279,780	ERIE	103,300	48,306	53,913	1,081	5,607 D	46.8%	52.2%	47.3%	52.7%
159,417	FAYETTE	50,349	16,915	33,098	336	16,183 D	33.6%	65.7%	33.8%	66.2%
5,072	FOREST	2,065	1,159	895	11	264 R	56.1%	43.3%	56.4%	43.6%
113,629	FRANKLIN	39,644	27,086	12,368	190	14,718 R	68.3%	31.2%	68.7%	31.3%
12,842	FULTON	4,646	3,086	1,532	28	1,554 R	66.4%	33.0%	66.8%	33.2%
40,476	GREENE	14,095	4,879	9,126	90	4,247 D	34.6%	64.7%	34.8%	65.2%
42,253	HUNTINGDON	13,631	8,800	4,752	79	4,048 R	64.6%	34.9%	64.9%	35.1%
92,281	INDIANA	31,739	14,983	16,514	242	1,531 D	47.2%	52.0%	47.6%	52.4%
48,303	JEFFERSON	16,109	9,743	6,235	131	3,508 R	60.5%	38.7%	61.0%	39.0%
19,188	JUNIATA	7,764	4,881	2,834	49	2,047 R	62.9%	36.5%	63.3%	36.7%
227,908	LACKAWANNA	88,741	42,083	45,591	1,067	3,508 D	47.4%	51.4%	48.0%	52.0%
362,346	LANCASTER	137,029	96,979	38,982	1,068	57,997 R	70.8%	28.4%	71.3%	28.7%
107,150	LAWRENCE	37,904	15,829	21,884	191	6,055 D	41.8%	57.7%	42.0%	58.0%
108,582	LEBANON	36,608	24,415	11,912	281	12,503 R	66.7%	32.5%	67.2%	32.8%
272,349	LEHIGH	100,107	56,363	42,801	943	13,562 R	56.3%	42.8%	56.8%	43.2%
343,079	LUZERNE	118,092	59,059	58,553	480	506 R	50.0%	49.6%	50.2%	49.8%
118,416	LYCOMING	38,735	24,792	13,528	415	11,264 R	64.0%	34.9%	64.7%	35.3%
50,635	MCKEAN	14,747	9,323	5,300	124	4,023 R	63.2%	35.9%	63.8%	36.2%
128,299	MERCER	45,880	21,301	24,278	301	2,977 D	46.4%	52.9%	46.7%	53.3%
46,908	MIFFLIN	13,075	8,170	4,790	115	3,380 R	62.5%	36.6%	63.0%	37.0%
69,409	MONROE	27,371	17,185	9,859	327	7,326 R	62.8%	36.0%	63.5%	36.5%
643,621	MONTGOMERY	282,870	170,294	109,834	2,742	60,460 R	60.2%	38.8%	60.8%	39.2%
16,675	MONTOUR	5,696	3,617	2,031	48	1,586 R	63.5%	35.7%	64.0%	36.0%
225,418	NORTHAMPTON	82,978	42,748	39,264	966	3,484 R	51.5%	47.3%	52.1%	47.9%
100,381	NORTHUMBERLAND	34,800	20,207	14,255	338	5,952 R	58.1%	41.0%	58.6%	41.4%
35,718	PERRY	12,533	8,545	3,910	78	4,635 R	68.2%	31.2%	68.6%	31.4%
1,688,210	PHILADELPHIA	674,977	219,053	449,566	6,358	230,513 D	32.5%	66.6%	32.8%	67.2%
18,271	PIKE	9,917	6,659	3,097	161	3,562 R	67.1%	31.2%	68.3%	31.7%
17,726	POTTER	6,592	4,432	2,119	41	2,313 R	67.2%	32.1%	67.7%	32.3%
160,630	SCHUYLKILL	57,842	32,666	24,797	379	7,869 R	56.5%	42.9%	56.8%	43.2%
33,584	SNYDER	11,779	9,054	2,658	67	6,396 R	76.9%	22.6%	77.3%	22.7%
81,243	SOMERSET	30,768	16,809	13,815	144	2,994 R	54.6%	44.9%	54.9%	45.1%
6,349	SULLIVAN	2,922	1,808	1,091	23	717 R	61.9%	37.3%	62.4%	37.6%
37,876	SUSQUEHANNA	14,056	9,077	4,871	108	4,206 R	64.6%	34.7%	65.1%	34.9%
40,973	TIOGA	14,350	9,471	4,807	72	4,664 R	66.0%	33.5%	66.3%	33.7%
32,870	UNION	11,136	7,912	3,163	61	4,749 R	71.0%	28.4%	71.4%	28.6%

PENNSYLVANIA

PRESIDENT 1988

1980 Census Population	County	Total Vote	Republican	Democratic	Other	Rep.-Dem. Plurality	Percentage Total Vote Rep.	Total Vote Dem.	Major Vote Rep.	Major Vote Dem.
64,444	VENANGO	20,263	11,468	8,624	171	2,844 R	56.6%	42.6%	57.1%	42.9%
47,449	WARREN	15,995	8,991	6,790	214	2,201 R	56.2%	42.5%	57.0%	43.0%
217,074	WASHINGTON	76,553	28,651	47,527	375	18,876 D	37.4%	62.1%	37.6%	62.4%
35,237	WAYNE	13,862	9,926	3,775	161	6,151 R	71.6%	27.2%	72.4%	27.6%
392,294	WESTMORELAND	139,290	61,472	76,710	1,108	15,238 D	44.1%	55.1%	44.5%	55.5%
26,433	WYOMING	9,447	6,607	2,797	43	3,810 R	69.9%	29.6%	70.3%	29.7%
312,963	YORK	111,116	72,408	37,691	1,017	34,717 R	65.2%	33.9%	65.8%	34.2%
11,863,895	TOTAL	4,536,251	2,300,087	2,194,944	41,220	105,143 R	50.7%	48.4%	51.2%	48.8%

PENNSYLVANIA

SENATOR 1988

1980 Census Population	County	Total Vote	Republican	Democratic	Other	Rep.-Dem. Plurality	Percentage Total Vote Rep.	Total Vote Dem.	Major Vote Rep.	Major Vote Dem.
68,292	ADAMS	23,697	18,171	5,290	236	12,881 R	76.7%	22.3%	77.5%	22.5%
1,450,085	ALLEGHENY	557,259	366,278	182,846	8,135	183,432 R	65.7%	32.8%	66.7%	33.3%
77,768	ARMSTRONG	25,727	18,708	5,967	1,052	12,741 R	72.7%	23.2%	75.8%	24.2%
204,441	BEAVER	76,158	47,706	27,810	642	19,896 R	62.6%	36.5%	63.2%	36.8%
46,784	BEDFORD	16,909	13,020	3,756	133	9,264 R	77.0%	22.2%	77.6%	22.4%
312,509	BERKS	108,089	78,474	28,340	1,275	50,134 R	72.6%	26.2%	73.5%	26.5%
136,621	BLAIR	41,555	33,171	7,826	558	25,345 R	79.8%	18.8%	80.9%	19.1%
62,919	BRADFORD	19,507	15,916	3,375	216	12,541 R	81.6%	17.3%	82.5%	17.5%
479,211	BUCKS	206,276	144,645	59,289	2,342	85,356 R	70.1%	28.7%	70.9%	29.1%
147,912	BUTLER	50,357	39,020	10,358	979	28,662 R	77.5%	20.6%	79.0%	21.0%
183,263	CAMBRIA	64,353	41,691	22,022	640	19,669 R	64.8%	34.2%	65.4%	34.6%
6,674	CAMERON	2,576	1,879	672	25	1,207 R	72.9%	26.1%	73.7%	26.3%
53,285	CARBON	18,369	12,160	6,024	185	6,136 R	66.2%	32.8%	66.9%	33.1%
112,760	CENTRE	41,703	30,975	10,145	583	20,830 R	74.3%	24.3%	75.3%	24.7%
316,660	CHESTER	137,756	108,419	28,025	1,312	80,394 R	78.7%	20.3%	79.5%	20.5%
43,362	CLARION	13,733	10,854	2,729	150	8,125 R	79.0%	19.9%	79.9%	20.1%
83,578	CLEARFIELD	26,498	18,374	7,915	209	10,459 R	69.3%	29.9%	69.9%	30.1%
38,971	CLINTON	11,137	7,476	3,453	208	4,023 R	67.1%	31.0%	68.4%	31.6%
61,967	COLUMBIA	19,690	14,840	4,649	201	10,191 R	75.4%	23.6%	76.1%	23.9%
88,869	CRAWFORD	29,347	22,461	6,475	411	15,986 R	76.5%	22.1%	77.6%	22.4%
178,541	CUMBERLAND	70,684	56,731	13,411	542	43,320 R	80.3%	19.0%	80.9%	19.1%
232,317	DAUPHIN	82,288	61,564	20,040	684	41,524 R	74.8%	24.4%	75.4%	24.6%
555,007	DELAWARE	239,265	169,247	67,980	2,038	101,267 R	70.7%	28.4%	71.3%	28.7%
38,338	ELK	12,764	8,922	3,727	115	5,195 R	69.9%	29.2%	70.5%	29.5%
279,780	ERIE	98,048	72,054	24,563	1,431	47,491 R	73.5%	25.1%	74.6%	25.4%
159,417	FAYETTE	47,828	25,891	21,264	673	4,627 R	54.1%	44.5%	54.9%	45.1%
5,072	FOREST	2,063	1,564	483	16	1,081 R	75.8%	23.4%	76.4%	23.6%
113,629	FRANKLIN	38,619	30,410	7,888	321	22,522 R	78.7%	20.4%	79.4%	20.6%
12,842	FULTON	4,538	3,271	1,224	43	2,047 R	72.1%	27.0%	72.8%	27.2%
40,476	GREENE	13,755	8,596	5,064	95	3,532 R	62.5%	36.8%	62.9%	37.1%
42,253	HUNTINGDON	13,338	10,574	2,670	94	7,904 R	79.3%	20.0%	79.8%	20.2%
92,281	INDIANA	31,633	23,129	8,170	334	14,959 R	73.1%	25.8%	73.9%	26.1%
48,303	JEFFERSON	16,127	12,472	3,518	137	8,954 R	77.3%	21.8%	78.0%	22.0%
19,188	JUNIATA	7,761	5,899	1,827	35	4,072 R	76.0%	23.5%	76.4%	23.6%
227,908	LACKAWANNA	81,044	54,732	25,093	1,219	29,639 R	67.5%	31.0%	68.6%	31.4%
362,346	LANCASTER	133,712	107,433	25,180	1,099	82,253 R	80.3%	18.8%	81.0%	19.0%
107,150	LAWRENCE	37,399	23,704	13,380	315	10,324 R	63.4%	35.8%	63.9%	36.1%
108,582	LEBANON	35,624	28,367	6,984	273	21,383 R	79.6%	19.6%	80.2%	19.8%
272,349	LEHIGH	95,865	66,475	28,438	952	38,037 R	69.3%	29.7%	70.0%	30.0%
343,079	LUZERNE	109,186	72,092	36,272	822	35,820 R	66.0%	33.2%	66.5%	33.5%
118,416	LYCOMING	37,407	28,973	7,893	541	21,080 R	77.5%	21.1%	78.6%	21.4%
50,635	MCKEAN	14,051	10,475	3,433	143	7,042 R	74.5%	24.4%	75.3%	24.7%
128,299	MERCER	43,173	27,378	15,388	407	11,990 R	63.4%	35.6%	64.0%	36.0%
46,908	MIFFLIN	12,616	9,586	2,920	110	6,666 R	76.0%	23.1%	76.7%	23.3%
69,409	MONROE	26,486	19,158	6,981	347	12,177 R	72.3%	26.4%	73.3%	26.7%
643,621	MONTGOMERY	275,845	199,086	74,411	2,348	124,675 R	72.2%	27.0%	72.8%	27.2%
16,675	MONTOUR	5,646	4,347	1,227	72	3,120 R	77.0%	21.7%	78.0%	22.0%
225,418	NORTHAMPTON	78,395	48,903	28,401	1,091	20,502 R	62.4%	36.2%	63.3%	36.7%
100,381	NORTHUMBERLAND	32,295	22,647	9,114	534	13,533 R	70.1%	28.2%	71.3%	28.7%
35,718	PERRY	12,559	10,573	1,889	97	8,684 R	84.2%	15.0%	84.8%	15.2%
1,688,210	PHILADELPHIA	633,077	245,923	380,696	6,458	134,773 D	38.8%	60.1%	39.2%	60.8%
18,271	PIKE	9,458	6,970	2,331	157	4,639 R	73.7%	24.6%	74.9%	25.1%
17,726	POTTER	6,229	4,551	1,612	66	2,939 R	73.1%	25.9%	73.8%	26.2%
160,630	SCHUYLKILL	57,388	41,674	15,253	461	26,421 R	72.6%	26.6%	73.2%	26.8%
33,584	SNYDER	11,558	10,074	1,414	70	8,660 R	87.2%	12.2%	87.7%	12.3%
81,243	SOMERSET	30,780	22,805	7,795	180	15,010 R	74.1%	25.3%	74.5%	25.5%
6,349	SULLIVAN	2,903	2,101	789	13	1,312 R	72.4%	27.2%	72.7%	27.3%
37,876	SUSQUEHANNA	14,805	11,747	2,896	162	8,851 R	79.3%	19.6%	80.2%	19.8%
40,973	TIOGA	14,189	10,924	3,173	92	7,751 R	77.0%	22.4%	77.5%	22.5%
32,870	UNION	10,860	9,144	1,624	92	7,520 R	84.2%	15.0%	84.9%	15.1%

PENNSYLVANIA

SENATOR 1988

1980 Census Population	County	Total Vote	Republican	Democratic	Other	Rep.-Dem. Plurality	Percentage Total Vote Rep.	Percentage Total Vote Dem.	Percentage Major Vote Rep.	Percentage Major Vote Dem.
64,444	VENANGO	20,289	15,383	4,642	264	10,741 R	75.8%	22.9%	76.8%	23.2%
47,449	WARREN	15,073	11,003	3,840	230	7,163 R	73.0%	25.5%	74.1%	25.9%
217,074	WASHINGTON	75,709	49,976	25,073	660	24,903 R	66.0%	33.1%	66.6%	33.4%
35,237	WAYNE	13,145	10,782	2,186	177	8,596 R	82.0%	16.6%	83.1%	16.9%
392,294	WESTMORELAND	132,810	87,838	43,365	1,607	44,473 R	66.1%	32.7%	66.9%	33.1%
26,433	WYOMING	9,319	7,895	1,376	48	6,519 R	84.7%	14.8%	85.2%	14.8%
312,963	YORK	108,296	84,434	22,900	962	61,534 R	78.0%	21.1%	78.7%	21.3%
11,863,895	TOTAL	4,366,598	2,901,715	1,416,764	48,119	1,484,951 R	66.5%	32.4%	67.2%	32.8%

PHILADELPHIA

PRESIDENT 1988

1980 Census Population	Ward	Total Vote	Republican	Democratic	Other	Rep.-Dem. Plurality	Percentage Total Vote Rep.	Total Vote Dem.	Major Vote Rep.	Major Vote Dem.
20,177	WARD 1	8,261	4,205	4,012	44	193 R	50.9%	48.6%	51.2%	48.8%
22,751	WARD 2	9,776	3,613	6,090	73	2,477 D	37.0%	62.3%	37.2%	62.8%
24,119	WARD 3	10,527	369	10,058	100	9,689 D	3.5%	95.5%	3.5%	96.5%
22,303	WARD 4	9,680	282	9,318	80	9,036 D	2.9%	96.3%	2.9%	97.1%
21,593	WARD 5	11,096	3,417	7,578	101	4,161 D	30.8%	68.3%	31.1%	68.9%
18,520	WARD 6	6,044	241	5,717	86	5,476 D	4.0%	94.6%	4.0%	96.0%
22,651	WARD 7	6,049	2,528	3,453	68	925 D	41.8%	57.1%	42.3%	57.7%
28,580	WARD 8	14,717	4,157	10,430	130	6,273 D	28.2%	70.9%	28.5%	71.5%
16,994	WARD 9	8,483	3,050	5,371	62	2,321 D	36.0%	63.3%	36.2%	63.8%
29,871	WARD 10	12,632	489	11,999	144	11,510 D	3.9%	95.0%	3.9%	96.1%
18,921	WARD 11	7,011	267	6,675	69	6,408 D	3.8%	95.2%	3.8%	96.2%
25,839	WARD 12	9,568	748	8,687	133	7,939 D	7.8%	90.8%	7.9%	92.1%
24,273	WARD 13	8,791	551	8,149	91	7,598 D	6.3%	92.7%	6.3%	93.7%
12,560	WARD 14	3,437	223	3,165	49	2,942 D	6.5%	92.1%	6.6%	93.4%
16,990	WARD 15	7,586	2,240	5,264	82	3,024 D	29.5%	69.4%	29.9%	70.1%
18,656	WARD 16	6,849	239	6,531	79	6,292 D	3.5%	95.4%	3.5%	96.5%
27,667	WARD 17	11,119	528	10,489	102	9,961 D	4.7%	94.3%	4.8%	95.2%
17,121	WARD 18	5,265	2,026	3,161	78	1,135 D	38.5%	60.0%	39.1%	60.9%
19,150	WARD 19	4,838	751	4,045	42	3,294 D	15.5%	83.6%	15.7%	84.3%
11,680	WARD 20	3,413	228	3,148	37	2,920 D	6.7%	92.2%	6.8%	93.2%
48,965	WARD 21	20,783	11,693	8,891	199	2,802 R	56.3%	42.8%	56.8%	43.2%
26,193	WARD 22	11,875	967	10,810	98	9,843 D	8.1%	91.0%	8.2%	91.8%
23,829	WARD 23	8,392	3,960	4,338	94	378 D	47.2%	51.7%	47.7%	52.3%
17,473	WARD 24	5,950	638	5,244	68	4,606 D	10.7%	88.1%	10.8%	89.2%
22,200	WARD 25	8,584	4,437	4,050	97	387 R	51.7%	47.2%	52.3%	47.7%
27,679	WARD 26	10,510	6,575	3,872	63	2,703 R	62.6%	36.8%	62.9%	37.1%
25,228	WARD 27	8,170	1,998	6,068	104	4,070 D	24.5%	74.3%	24.8%	75.2%
17,501	WARD 28	6,657	171	6,442	44	6,271 D	2.6%	96.8%	2.6%	97.4%
16,538	WARD 29	6,033	304	5,667	62	5,363 D	5.0%	93.9%	5.1%	94.9%
14,225	WARD 30	5,822	648	5,074	100	4,426 D	11.1%	87.2%	11.3%	88.7%
18,277	WARD 31	6,359	3,295	3,014	50	281 R	51.8%	47.4%	52.2%	47.8%
30,101	WARD 32	9,773	365	9,287	121	8,922 D	3.7%	95.0%	3.8%	96.2%
22,916	WARD 33	9,316	5,075	4,152	89	923 R	54.5%	44.6%	55.0%	45.0%
39,985	WARD 34	17,824	4,891	12,790	143	7,899 D	27.4%	71.8%	27.7%	72.3%
32,175	WARD 35	14,097	8,341	5,609	147	2,732 R	59.2%	39.8%	59.8%	40.2%
35,472	WARD 36	14,497	2,325	12,012	160	9,687 D	16.0%	82.9%	16.2%	83.8%
20,306	WARD 37	6,338	359	5,938	41	5,579 D	5.7%	93.7%	5.7%	94.3%
23,399	WARD 38	8,919	1,798	7,057	64	5,259 D	20.2%	79.1%	20.3%	79.7%
47,439	WARD 39	19,400	10,678	8,610	112	2,068 R	55.0%	44.4%	55.4%	44.6%
50,806	WARD 40	18,519	7,794	10,601	124	2,807 D	42.1%	57.2%	42.4%	57.6%
23,528	WARD 41	9,760	5,577	4,089	94	1,488 R	57.1%	41.9%	57.7%	42.3%
29,145	WARD 42	8,712	4,117	4,510	85	393 D	47.3%	51.8%	47.7%	52.3%
27,147	WARD 43	7,542	980	6,505	57	5,525 D	13.0%	86.3%	13.1%	86.9%
17,276	WARD 44	6,965	281	6,611	73	6,330 D	4.0%	94.9%	4.1%	95.9%
24,576	WARD 45	10,017	5,338	4,533	146	805 R	53.3%	45.3%	54.1%	45.9%
24,939	WARD 46	9,796	703	8,971	122	8,268 D	7.2%	91.6%	7.3%	92.7%
11,264	WARD 47	3,411	160	3,209	42	3,049 D	4.7%	94.1%	4.7%	95.3%
22,391	WARD 48	8,884	4,097	4,726	61	629 D	46.1%	53.2%	46.4%	53.6%
33,401	WARD 49	9,523	1,134	8,273	116	7,139 D	11.9%	86.9%	12.1%	87.9%
31,271	WARD 50	13,385	750	12,491	144	11,741 D	5.6%	93.3%	5.7%	94.3%
28,662	WARD 51	9,743	356	9,286	101	8,930 D	3.7%	95.3%	3.7%	96.3%
28,926	WARD 52	12,333	1,583	10,617	133	9,034 D	12.8%	86.1%	13.0%	87.0%
21,786	WARD 53	11,548	5,122	6,332	94	1,210 D	44.4%	54.8%	44.7%	55.3%
19,800	WARD 54	10,184	3,514	6,610	60	3,096 D	34.5%	64.9%	34.7%	65.3%
27,590	WARD 55	13,368	7,809	5,435	124	2,374 R	58.4%	40.7%	59.0%	41.0%
35,662	WARD 56	18,247	7,992	10,195	60	2,203 D	43.8%	55.9%	43.9%	56.1%
29,362	WARD 57	13,117	7,182	5,819	116	1,363 R	54.8%	44.4%	55.2%	44.8%
47,404	WARD 58	22,097	11,994	9,937	166	2,057 R	54.3%	45.0%	54.7%	45.3%
24,998	WARD 59	9,566	756	8,690	120	7,934 D	7.9%	90.8%	8.0%	92.0%
21,070	WARD 60	9,224	330	8,797	97	8,467 D	3.6%	95.4%	3.6%	96.4%

PHILADELPHIA

PRESIDENT 1988

1980 Census Population	Ward	Total Vote	Republican	Democratic	Other	Rep.-Dem. Plurality	Percentage Total Vote Rep.	Total Vote Dem.	Major Vote Rep.	Major Vote Dem.
27,764	WARD 61	9,956	4,808	5,035	113	227 D	48.3%	50.6%	48.8%	51.2%
26,749	WARD 62	11,826	6,440	5,274	112	1,166 R	54.5%	44.6%	55.0%	45.0%
24,050	WARD 63	11,788	6,814	4,880	94	1,934 R	57.8%	41.4%	58.3%	41.7%
16,800	WARD 64	8,911	5,483	3,344	84	2,139 R	61.5%	37.5%	62.1%	37.9%
27,290	WARD 65	10,476	5,436	4,930	110	506 R	51.9%	47.1%	52.4%	47.6%
54,236	WARD 66	21,638	13,833	7,601	204	6,232 R	63.9%	35.1%	64.5%	35.5%
1,688,210	TOTAL	674,977	219,053	449,566	6,358	230,513 D	32.5%	66.6%	32.8%	67.2%

PHILADELPHIA

SENATOR 1988

1980 Census Population	Ward	Total Vote	Republican	Democratic	Other	Rep.-Dem. Plurality	Percentage Total Vote Rep.	Total Vote Dem.	Major Vote Rep.	Major Vote Dem.
20,177	WARD 1	7,776	3,932	3,792	52	140 R	50.6%	48.8%	50.9%	49.1%
22,751	WARD 2	9,322	3,817	5,406	99	1,589 D	40.9%	58.0%	41.4%	58.6%
24,119	WARD 3	9,936	1,014	8,836	86	7,822 D	10.2%	88.9%	10.3%	89.7%
22,303	WARD 4	8,929	805	8,040	84	7,235 D	9.0%	90.0%	9.1%	90.9%
21,593	WARD 5	10,292	4,750	5,404	138	654 D	46.2%	52.5%	46.8%	53.2%
18,520	WARD 6	5,353	508	4,793	52	4,285 D	9.5%	89.5%	9.6%	90.4%
22,651	WARD 7	5,629	2,531	3,020	78	489 D	45.0%	53.7%	45.6%	54.4%
28,580	WARD 8	14,264	6,183	7,910	171	1,727 D	43.3%	55.5%	43.9%	56.1%
16,994	WARD 9	8,188	4,210	3,894	84	316 R	51.4%	47.6%	51.9%	48.1%
29,871	WARD 10	11,849	1,184	10,540	125	9,356 D	10.0%	89.0%	10.1%	89.9%
18,921	WARD 11	6,414	561	5,790	63	5,229 D	8.7%	90.3%	8.8%	91.2%
25,839	WARD 12	8,871	1,289	7,409	173	6,120 D	14.5%	83.5%	14.8%	85.2%
24,273	WARD 13	8,169	945	7,121	103	6,176 D	11.6%	87.2%	11.7%	88.3%
12,560	WARD 14	3,156	384	2,715	57	2,331 D	12.2%	86.0%	12.4%	87.6%
16,990	WARD 15	6,987	2,860	4,020	107	1,160 D	40.9%	57.5%	41.6%	58.4%
18,656	WARD 16	6,395	437	5,868	90	5,431 D	6.8%	91.8%	6.9%	93.1%
27,667	WARD 17	10,422	1,063	9,257	102	8,194 D	10.2%	88.8%	10.3%	89.7%
17,121	WARD 18	4,725	1,971	2,681	73	710 D	41.7%	56.7%	42.4%	57.6%
19,150	WARD 19	4,282	684	3,558	40	2,874 D	16.0%	83.1%	16.1%	83.9%
11,680	WARD 20	3,181	341	2,809	31	2,468 D	10.7%	88.3%	10.8%	89.2%
48,965	WARD 21	19,256	12,162	6,893	201	5,269 R	63.2%	35.8%	63.8%	36.2%
26,193	WARD 22	11,492	2,347	8,937	208	6,590 D	20.4%	77.8%	20.8%	79.2%
23,829	WARD 23	7,869	3,961	3,809	99	152 R	50.3%	48.4%	51.0%	49.0%
17,473	WARD 24	5,522	907	4,546	69	3,639 D	16.4%	82.3%	16.6%	83.4%
22,200	WARD 25	7,992	4,494	3,413	85	1,081 R	56.2%	42.7%	56.8%	43.2%
27,679	WARD 26	9,669	5,527	4,077	65	1,450 R	57.2%	42.2%	57.5%	42.5%
25,228	WARD 27	7,361	2,632	4,606	123	1,974 D	35.8%	62.6%	36.4%	63.6%
17,501	WARD 28	6,174	382	5,749	43	5,367 D	6.2%	93.1%	6.2%	93.8%
16,538	WARD 29	5,631	462	5,110	59	4,648 D	8.2%	90.7%	8.3%	91.7%
14,225	WARD 30	5,339	1,107	4,151	81	3,044 D	20.7%	77.7%	21.1%	78.9%
18,277	WARD 31	5,931	3,197	2,686	48	511 R	53.9%	45.3%	54.3%	45.7%
30,101	WARD 32	8,604	648	7,813	143	7,165 D	7.5%	90.8%	7.7%	92.3%
22,916	WARD 33	8,672	5,123	3,472	77	1,651 R	59.1%	40.0%	59.6%	40.4%
39,985	WARD 34	16,680	5,569	10,988	123	5,419 D	33.4%	65.9%	33.6%	66.4%
32,175	WARD 35	13,555	9,089	4,304	162	4,785 R	67.1%	31.8%	67.9%	32.1%
35,472	WARD 36	13,951	2,662	11,159	130	8,497 D	19.1%	80.0%	19.3%	80.7%
20,306	WARD 37	5,890	449	5,404	37	4,955 D	7.6%	91.7%	7.7%	92.3%
23,399	WARD 38	8,377	2,332	5,954	91	3,622 D	27.8%	71.1%	28.1%	71.9%
47,439	WARD 39	17,663	9,368	8,171	124	1,197 R	53.0%	46.3%	53.4%	46.6%
50,806	WARD 40	17,843	8,199	9,509	135	1,310 D	46.0%	53.3%	46.3%	53.7%
23,528	WARD 41	9,201	5,624	3,507	70	2,117 R	61.1%	38.1%	61.6%	38.4%
29,145	WARD 42	8,286	4,329	3,875	82	454 R	52.2%	46.8%	52.8%	47.2%
27,147	WARD 43	6,863	1,135	5,661	67	4,526 D	16.5%	82.5%	16.7%	83.3%
17,276	WARD 44	6,420	670	5,690	60	5,020 D	10.4%	88.6%	10.5%	89.5%
24,576	WARD 45	9,406	5,196	4,100	110	1,096 R	55.2%	43.6%	55.9%	44.1%
24,939	WARD 46	9,303	1,495	7,681	127	6,186 D	16.1%	82.6%	16.3%	83.7%
11,264	WARD 47	3,319	228	3,044	47	2,816 D	6.9%	91.7%	7.0%	93.0%
22,391	WARD 48	8,265	3,485	4,701	79	1,216 D	42.2%	56.9%	42.6%	57.4%
33,401	WARD 49	8,950	1,628	7,216	106	5,588 D	18.2%	80.6%	18.4%	81.6%
31,271	WARD 50	12,648	1,694	10,819	135	9,125 D	13.4%	85.5%	13.5%	86.5%
28,662	WARD 51	9,463	885	8,477	101	7,592 D	9.4%	89.6%	9.5%	90.5%
28,926	WARD 52	11,774	2,809	8,862	103	6,053 D	23.9%	75.3%	24.1%	75.9%
21,786	WARD 53	10,893	5,972	4,837	84	1,135 R	54.8%	44.4%	55.3%	44.7%
19,800	WARD 54	9,701	4,364	5,253	84	889 D	45.0%	54.1%	45.4%	54.6%
27,590	WARD 55	12,553	8,028	4,435	90	3,593 R	64.0%	35.3%	64.4%	35.6%
35,662	WARD 56	17,472	9,535	7,819	118	1,716 R	54.6%	44.8%	54.9%	45.1%
29,362	WARD 57	12,471	7,888	4,467	116	3,421 R	63.3%	35.8%	63.8%	36.2%
47,404	WARD 58	20,831	13,474	7,217	140	6,257 R	64.7%	34.6%	65.1%	34.9%
24,998	WARD 59	8,870	1,486	7,226	158	5,740 D	16.8%	81.5%	17.1%	82.9%
21,070	WARD 60	8,491	851	7,554	86	6,703 D	10.0%	89.0%	10.1%	89.9%

PHILADELPHIA

SENATOR 1988

1980 Census Population	Ward	Total Vote	Republican	Democratic	Other	Rep.-Dem. Plurality	Percentage Total Vote Rep.	Percentage Total Vote Dem.	Percentage Major Vote Rep.	Percentage Major Vote Dem.
27,764	WARD 61	9,364	5,071	4,171	122	900 R	54.2%	44.5%	54.9%	45.1%
26,749	WARD 62	11,059	6,578	4,379	102	2,199 R	59.5%	39.6%	60.0%	40.0%
24,050	WARD 63	11,209	7,433	3,700	76	3,733 R	66.3%	33.0%	66.8%	33.2%
16,800	WARD 64	8,608	5,849	2,707	52	3,142 R	67.9%	31.4%	68.4%	31.6%
27,290	WARD 65	9,782	5,731	3,978	73	1,753 R	58.6%	40.7%	59.0%	41.0%
54,236	WARD 66	20,264	14,399	5,706	159	8,693 R	71.1%	28.2%	71.6%	28.4%
1,688,210	TOTAL	633,077	245,923	380,696	6,458	134,773 D	38.8%	60.1%	39.2%	60.8%

PENNSYLVANIA

CONGRESS

CD	Year	Total Vote	Republican Vote	Republican Candidate	Democratic Vote	Democratic Candidate	Other Vote	Rep.-Dem. Plurality	Percentage Total Vote Rep.	Percentage Total Vote Dem.	Percentage Major Vote Rep.	Percentage Major Vote Dem.
1	1988	167,825	39,749	O'BRIEN, WILLIAM J.	128,076	FOGLIETTA, THOMAS M.		88,327 D	23.7%	76.3%	23.7%	76.3%
1	1986	118,035	29,811	MUCCIOLO, ANTHONY J.	88,224	FOGLIETTA, THOMAS M.		58,413 D	25.3%	74.7%	25.3%	74.7%
1	1984	197,682	49,559	DI BIASE, CARMINE	148,123	FOGLIETTA, THOMAS M.		98,564 D	25.1%	74.9%	25.1%	74.9%
1	1982	143,416	38,155	MARINO, MICHAEL	103,626	FOGLIETTA, THOMAS M.	1,635	65,471 D	26.6%	72.3%	26.9%	73.1%
2	1988	196,687	12,365	HARSCH, RICHARD L.	184,322	GRAY, WILLIAM H.		171,957 D	6.3%	93.7%	6.3%	93.7%
2	1986	130,495			128,399	GRAY, WILLIAM H.	2,096	128,399 D		98.4%		100.0%
2	1984	220,295	18,224	SHARPER, RONALD J.	200,484	GRAY, WILLIAM H.	1,587	182,260 D	8.3%	91.0%	8.3%	91.7%
2	1982	158,675			120,744	GRAY, WILLIAM H.	37,931	120,744 D		76.1%		100.0%
3	1988	214,499	78,909	MATTHEWS, MARK	135,590	BORSKI, ROBERT A.		56,681 D	36.8%	63.2%	36.8%	63.2%
3	1986	174,497	66,693	ROVNER, ROBERT A.	107,804	BORSKI, ROBERT A.		41,111 D	38.2%	61.8%	38.2%	61.8%
3	1984	238,786	85,358	BECKER, FLORA L.	152,598	BORSKI, ROBERT A.	830	67,240 D	35.7%	63.9%	35.9%	64.1%
3	1982	193,954	94,497	DOUGHERTY, CHARLES F.	97,161	BORSKI, ROBERT A.	2,296	2,664 D	48.7%	50.1%	49.3%	50.7%
4	1988	177,699	52,402	JOHNSTON, GORDON R.	124,041	KOLTER, JOSEPH P.	1,256	71,639 D	29.5%	69.8%	29.7%	70.3%
4	1986	142,594	55,165	LINDSAY, AL	86,133	KOLTER, JOSEPH P.	1,296	30,968 D	38.7%	60.4%	39.0%	61.0%
4	1984	200,809	86,769	KUNDER, JAMES	114,040	KOLTER, JOSEPH P.		27,271 D	43.2%	56.8%	43.2%	56.8%
4	1982	167,102	64,539	ATKINSON, EUGENE V.	100,481	KOLTER, JOSEPH P.	2,082	35,942 D	38.6%	60.1%	39.1%	60.9%
5	1988	196,211	153,453	SCHULZE, RICHARD T.	42,758	HADLEY, DONALD		110,695 R	78.2%	21.8%	78.2%	21.8%
5	1986	133,241	87,593	SCHULZE, RICHARD T.	45,648	RINGGOLD, TIM		41,945 R	65.7%	34.3%	65.7%	34.3%
5	1984	195,551	141,965	SCHULZE, RICHARD T.	53,586	FANTI, LOUIS J.		88,379 R	72.6%	27.4%	72.6%	27.4%
5	1982	134,818	90,648	SCHULZE, RICHARD T.	44,170	BURGER, BOB		46,478 R	67.2%	32.8%	67.2%	32.8%
6	1988	180,745	65,278	ERWIN, JAMES R.	114,119	YATRON, GUS	1,348	48,841 D	36.1%	63.1%	36.4%	63.6%
6	1986	142,000	43,858	BERTASAVAGE, NORMAN W.	98,142	YATRON, GUS		54,284 D	30.9%	69.1%	30.9%	69.1%
6	1984	181,165			181,165	*YATRON, GUS		181,165 D		100.0%		100.0%
6	1982	150,385	42,155	MARTIN, HARRY B.	108,230	YATRON, GUS		66,075 D	28.0%	72.0%	28.0%	72.0%
7	1988	229,132	155,387	WELDON, CURT	73,745	LANDAU, DAVID		81,642 R	67.8%	32.2%	67.8%	32.2%
7	1986	179,675	110,118	WELDON, CURT	69,557	SPINGLER, BILL		40,561 R	61.3%	38.7%	61.3%	38.7%
7	1984	248,504	124,046	WELDON, CURT	124,458	EDGAR, ROBERT W.		412 D	49.9%	50.1%	49.9%	50.1%
7	1982	190,798	85,023	JOACHIM, STEVE	105,775	EDGAR, ROBERT W.		20,752 D	44.6%	55.4%	44.6%	55.4%
8	1988	225,566	93,648	HOWARD, ED	128,153	KOSTMAYER, PETER H.	3,765	34,505 D	41.5%	56.8%	42.2%	57.8%
8	1986	155,778	70,047	CHRISTIAN, DAVID A.	85,731	KOSTMAYER, PETER H.		15,684 D	45.0%	55.0%	45.0%	55.0%
8	1984	221,344	108,696	CHRISTIAN, DAVID A.	112,648	KOSTMAYER, PETER H.		3,952 D	49.1%	50.9%	49.1%	50.9%
8	1982	165,535	80,928	COYNE, JAMES K.	83,242	KOSTMAYER, PETER H.	1,365	2,314 D	48.9%	50.3%	49.3%	50.7%
9	1988	158,702	158,702	*SHUSTER, E. G.				158,702 R	100.0%		100.0%	
9	1986	120,890	120,890	*SHUSTER, E. G.				120,890 R	100.0%		100.0%	
9	1984	177,986	118,437	SHUSTER, E. G.	59,549	KULP, NANCY		58,888 R	66.5%	33.5%	66.5%	33.5%
9	1982	141,905	92,322	SHUSTER, E. G.	49,583	DUNCAN, EUGENE J.		42,739 R	65.1%	34.9%	65.1%	34.9%
10	1988	191,275	140,096	MCDADE, JOSEPH M.	51,179	CORDARO, ROBERT C.		88,917 R	73.2%	26.8%	73.2%	26.8%
10	1986	158,851	118,603	MCDADE, JOSEPH M.	40,248	BOLUS, ROBERT C.		78,355 R	74.7%	25.3%	74.7%	25.3%
10	1984	194,737	150,166	MCDADE, JOSEPH M.	44,571	BASALYGA, GENE		105,595 R	77.1%	22.9%	77.1%	22.9%
10	1982	153,485	103,617	MCDADE, JOSEPH M.	49,868	RAFALKO, ROBERT J.		53,749 R	67.5%	32.5%	67.5%	32.5%
11	1988	120,706			120,706	KANJORSKI, PAUL E.		120,706 D		100.0%		100.0%
11	1986	159,190	46,785	HOLTZMAN, MARC	112,405	KANJORSKI, PAUL E.		65,620 D	29.4%	70.6%	29.4%	70.6%
11	1984	185,122	76,692	HUDOCK, ROBERT P.	108,430	KANJORSKI, PAUL E.		31,738 D	41.4%	58.6%	41.4%	58.6%
11	1982	168,856	78,485	NELLIGAN, JAMES L.	90,371	HARRISON, FRANK		11,886 D	46.5%	53.5%	46.5%	53.5%
12	1988	133,081			133,081	MURTHA, JOHN P.		133,081 D		100.0%		100.0%
12	1986	144,072	46,937	HOLTZMAN, KATHY	97,135	MURTHA, JOHN P.		50,198 D	32.6%	67.4%	32.6%	67.4%
12	1984	194,494	57,446	FULLARD, THOMAS J.	134,384	MURTHA, JOHN P.	2,664	76,938 D	29.5%	69.1%	29.9%	70.1%
12	1982	157,640	54,212	TUSCANO, WILLIAM N.	96,369	MURTHA, JOHN P.	7,059	42,157 D	34.4%	61.1%	36.0%	64.0%

PENNSYLVANIA

CONGRESS

CD	Year	Total Vote	Republican Vote	Republican Candidate	Democratic Vote	Democratic Candidate	Other Vote	Rep.-Dem. Plurality	Percentage Total Vote Rep.	Total Vote Dem.	Major Vote Rep.	Major Vote Dem.
13	1988	228,615	152,191	COUGHLIN, R. LAWRENCE	76,424	TOMKIN, BERNARD		75,767 R	66.6%	33.4%	66.6%	33.4%
13	1986	172,082	100,701	COUGHLIN, R. LAWRENCE	71,381	HOEFFEL, JOSEPH M.		29,320 R	58.5%	41.5%	58.5%	41.5%
13	1984	238,704	133,948	COUGHLIN, R. LAWRENCE	104,756	HOEFFEL, JOSEPH M.		29,192 R	56.1%	43.9%	56.1%	43.9%
13	1982	169,824	109,198	COUGHLIN, R. LAWRENCE	59,709	CUNNINGHAM, MARTIN J.	917	49,489 R	64.3%	35.2%	64.6%	35.4%
14	1988	171,900	36,719	CALIGIURI, RICHARD E.	135,181	COYNE, WILLIAM J.		98,462 D	21.4%	78.6%	21.4%	78.6%
14	1986	116,859			104,726	COYNE, WILLIAM J.	12,133	104,726 D		89.6%		100.0%
14	1984	213,797	42,616	CLARK, JOHN R.	163,818	COYNE, WILLIAM J.	7,363	121,202 D	19.9%	76.6%	20.6%	79.4%
14	1982	161,577	32,780	CLARK, JOHN R.	120,980	COYNE, WIL LIAM J.	7,817	88,200 D	20.3%	74.9%	21.3%	78.7%
15	1988	186,078	106,951	RITTER, DONALD L.	79,127	REIBMAN, ED		27,824 R	57.5%	42.5%	57.5%	42.5%
15	1986	131,801	74,829	RITTER, DONALD L.	56,972	SIMONETTA, JOE		17,857 R	56.8%	43.2%	56.8%	43.2%
15	1984	189,828	110,338	RITTER, DONALD L.	79,490	WELLS-SCHOOLEY, JANE		30,848 R	58.1%	41.9%	58.1%	41.9%
15	1982	137,457	79,455	RITTER, DONALD L.	58,002	ORLOSKI, RICHARD J.		21,453 R	57.8%	42.2%	57.8%	42.2%
16	1988	185,113	136,944	WALKER, ROBERT S.	48,169	GUYLL, ERNEST E.		88,775 R	74.0%	26.0%	74.0%	26.0%
16	1986	135,183	100,784	WALKER, ROBERT S.	34,399	HAGELGANS, JAMES D.		66,385 R	74.6%	25.4%	74.6%	25.4%
16	1984	177,992	138,477	WALKER, ROBERT S.	39,515	BARD, MARTIN L.		98,962 R	77.8%	22.2%	77.8%	22.2%
16	1982	130,398	93,034	WALKER, ROBERT S.	37,364	MOWERY, JEAN D.		55,670 R	71.3%	28.7%	71.3%	28.7%
17	1988	166,289	166,289	*GEKAS, GEORGE W.				166,289 R	100.0%		100.0%	
17	1986	137,184	101,027	GEKAS, GEORGE W.	36,157	OGDEN, MICHAEL S.		64,870 R	73.6%	26.4%	73.6%	26.4%
17	1984	178,651	129,716	GEKAS, GEORGE W.	48,935	ANDERSON, STEPHEN A.		80,781 R	72.6%	27.4%	72.6%	27.4%
17	1982	146,265	84,291	GEKAS, GEORGE W.	61,974	HOCHENDONER, LARRY J.		22,317 R	57.6%	42.4%	57.6%	42.4%
18	1988	218,488	80,975	NEWMAN, JOHN A.	136,924	WALGREN, DOUGLAS	589	55,949 D	37.1%	62.7%	37.2%	62.8%
18	1986	165,328	61,164	BUCKMAN, ERNIE	104,164	WALGREN, DOUGLAS		43,000 D	37.0%	63.0%	37.0%	63.0%
18	1984	238,489	87,521	MAXWELL, JOHN G.	149,628	WALGREN, DOUGLAS	1,340	62,107 D	36.7%	62.7%	36.9%	63.1%
18	1982	187,683	84,428	JACOB, TED	101,807	WALGREN, DOUGLAS	1,448	17,379 D	45.0%	54.2%	45.3%	54.7%
19	1988	188,200	145,381	GOODLING, WILLIAM F.	42,819	RITCHEY, PAUL E.		102,562 R	77.2%	22.8%	77.2%	22.8%
19	1986	137,278	100,055	GOODLING, WILLIAM F.	37,223	THORNTON, RICHARD F.		62,832 R	72.9%	27.1%	72.9%	27.1%
19	1984	186,742	141,196	GOODLING, WILLIAM F.	44,117	RARIG, JOHN	1,429	97,079 R	75.6%	23.6%	76.2%	23.8%
19	1982	142,950	101,163	GOODLING, WILLIAM F.	41,787	BECKER, LARRY		59,376 R	70.8%	29.2%	70.8%	29.2%
20	1988	139,616			137,472	GAYDOS, JOSEPH M.	2,144	137,472 D		98.5%		100.0%
20	1986	138,752			136,638	*GAYDOS, JOSEPH M.	2,114	136,638 D		98.5%		100.0%
20	1984	208,998	50,247	LLOYD, DANIEL	158,751	GAYDOS, JOSEPH M.		108,504 D	24.0%	76.0%	24.0%	76.0%
20	1982	167,428	38,212	RAY, TERRY T.	127,281	GAYDOS, JOSEPH M.	1,935	89,069 D	22.8%	76.0%	23.1%	76.9%
21	1988	180,120	141,832	RIDGE, THOMAS J.	38,288	ELDER, GEORGE R.	H.	103,544 R	78.7%	21.3%	78.7%	21.3%
21	1986	137,472	111,148	RIDGE, THOMAS J.	26,324	BLACKWELL, JOYLYN		84,824 R	80.9%	19.1%	80.9%	19.1%
21	1984	192,109	125,730	RIDGE, THOMAS J.	65,594	YOUNG, JAMES A.	785	60,136 R	65.4%	34.1%	65.7%	34.3%
21	1982	159,631	80,180	RIDGE, THOMAS J.	79,451	ANDREZESKI, ANTHONY		729 R	50.2%	49.8%	50.2%	49.8%
22	1988	170,467	47,039	HODGKISS, WILLIAM	123,428	MURPHY, AUSTIN J.		76,389 D	27.6%	72.4%	27.6%	72.4%
22	1986	131,650			131,650	*MURPHY, AUSTIN J.		131,650 D		100.0%		100.0%
22	1984	194,428	39,752	PRYOR, NANCY S.	153,514	MURPHY, AUSTIN J.	1,162	113,762 D	20.4%	79.0%	20.6%	79.4%
22	1982	157,215	32,176	PATERRA, FRANK J.	123,716	MURPHY, AUSTIN J.	1,323	91,540 D	20.5%	78.7%	20.6%	79.4%
23	1988	170,160	105,575	CLINGER, WILLIAM F.	63,476	SHAKESPEARE, HOWARD	1,109	42,099 R	62.0%	37.3%	62.5%	37.5%
23	1986	143,470	79,595	CLINGER, WILLIAM F.	63,875	WACHOB, BILL		15,720 R	55.5%	44.5%	55.5%	44.5%
23	1984	183,909	94,952	CLINGER, WILLIAM F.	88,957	WACHOB, BILL		5,995 R	51.6%	48.4%	51.6%	48.4%
23	1982	141,721	92,424	CLINGER, WILLIAM F.	49,297	CALLA, JOSEPH J.		43,127 R	65.2%	34.8%	65.2%	34.8%

PENNSYLVANIA

1988 GENERAL ELECTION

President Other vote was 19,158 Consumer (McCarthy); 12,051 Libertarian (Paul); 4,379 New Alliance (Fulani); 3,444 Populist (Duke); 2,188 Workers World (Winn).

Senator Other vote was 25,273 Consumer (Richardson); 11,822 Libertarian (Haller); 6,455 Populist (Cross); 4,569 New Alliance (Blancato).

Congress An asterisk in the Congressional vote table indicates a candidate received votes as the nominee of an additional party. Other vote was Populist (Kaltenhauser) in CD 4; Perugini for Congress (Perugini) in CD 6; Libertarian (Ernsberger) in CD 8; Populist (Bailey) in CD 18; Populist (Wilson) in CD 20; Populist (Smolik) in CD 23.

PHILADELPHIA

Philadelphia city and county are coterminous.

President Other vote was 2,082 New Alliance (Fulani); 1,820 Libertarian (Paul); 1,773 Consumer (McCarthy); 349 Workers World (Winn); 334 Populist (Duke).

Senator Other vote was 3,247 Consumer (Richardson); 1,461 Libertarian (Haller); 1,140 New Alliance (Blancato); 610 Populist (Cross).

1988 PRIMARIES

APRIL 26 REPUBLICAN

Senator H. John Heinz, unopposed.

Congress Unopposed in seventeen CD's. No candidate in CD's 11, 20 and 22. In CD 22 William Hodgkiss received 1,274 write-in votes and became the nominee. Jonathan M. Jacobs, the unopposed candidate in CD 12, withdrew after the primary and no substitution was made. Contested as follows:

CD 4 22,318 Gordon R. Johnston; 11,387 John Loth.
CD 8 27,555 Ed Howard; 7,903 Henry F. Schickling.
CD 18 23,863 John A. Newman; 15,061 Drew Ley.

APRIL 26 DEMOCRATIC

Senator 492,153 Joseph C. Vignola; 371,443 Susan S. Kefover; 145,614 Steve Douglas; 76,020 John J. Logue.

Congress Unopposed in thirteen CD's. No candidate in CD's 9 and 17. In CD 9 E. G. Shuster, the Republican nominee, received 3,491 write-in votes and became the nominee of both parties. In CD 17 George W. Gekas, the Republican nominee, received 2,001 write-in votes and became the nominee of both parties. Contested as follows:

CD 3 61,440 Robert A. Borski; 5,801 John J. Hughes.
CD 5 10,605 Donald Hadley; 8,646 Robert W. Houchins.
CD 7 23,719 David Landau; 5,419 Claudia Billington.
CD 8 34,298 Peter H. Kostmayer; 3,947 Edward T. Czyzyk.
CD 10 26,083 Robert C. Cordaro; 9,492 George Eddleston.
CD 15 25,011 Ed Reibman; 15,036 Richard J. Orloski; 5,791 Charles Buss.
CD 22 64,187 Austin J. Murphy; 23,193 Thomas J. Fullard.
CD 23 20,202 Howard Shakespeare; 18,504 Joseph J. Calla.

RHODE ISLAND

GOVERNOR

Edward DiPrete (R). Re-elected 1988 to a two-year term. Previously elected 1986, 1984.

SENATORS

John H. Chafee (R). Re-elected 1988 to a six-year term. Previously elected 1982, 1976.

Claiborne Pell (D). Re-elected 1984 to a six-year term. Previously elected 1978, 1972, 1966, 1960.

REPRESENTATIVES

1. Ronald K. Machtley (R)
2. Claudine Schneider (R)

POSTWAR VOTE FOR PRESIDENT

									Percentage			
	Total	Republican		Democratic		Other			Total Vote		Major Vote	
Year	Vote	Vote	Candidate	Vote	Candidate	Vote	Plurality		Rep.	Dem.	Rep.	Dem.
1988	404,620	177,761	Bush, George	225,123	Dukakis, Michael S.	1,736	47,362	D	43.9%	55.6%	44.1%	55.9%
1984	410,492	212,080	Reagan, Ronald	197,106	Mondale, Walter F.	1,306	14,974	R	51.7%	48.0%	51.8%	48.2%
1980	416,072	154,793	Reagan, Ronald	198,342	Carter, Jimmy	62,937	43,549	D	37.2%	47.7%	43.8%	56.2%
1976	411,170	181,249	Ford, Gerald R.	227,636	Carter, Jimmy	2,285	46,387	D	44.1%	55.4%	44.3%	55.7%
1972	415,808	220,383	Nixon, Richard M.	194,645	McGovern, George S.	780	25,738	R	53.0%	46.8%	53.1%	46.9%
1968	385,000	122,359	Nixon, Richard M.	246,518	Humphrey, Hubert H.	16,123	124,159	D	31.8%	64.0%	33.2%	66.8%
1964	390,091	74,615	Goldwater, Barry M.	315,463	Johnson, Lyndon B.	13	240,848	D	19.1%	80.9%	19.1%	80.9%
1960	405,535	147,502	Nixon, Richard M.	258,032	Kennedy, John F.	1	110,530	D	36.4%	63.6%	36.4%	63.6%
1956	387,609	225,819	Eisenhower, Dwight D.	161,790	Stevenson, Adlai E.		64,029	R	58.3%	41.7%	58.3%	41.7%
1952	414,498	210,935	Eisenhower, Dwight D.	203,293	Stevenson, Adlai E.	270	7,642	R	50.9%	49.0%	50.9%	49.1%
1948	327,702	135,787	Dewey, Thomas E.	188,736	Truman, Harry S.	3,179	52,949	D	41.4%	57.6%	41.8%	58.2%

RHODE ISLAND

POSTWAR VOTE FOR GOVERNOR

Year	Total Vote	Republican Vote	Republican Candidate	Democratic Vote	Democratic Candidate	Other Vote	Rep.-Dem. Plurality	Percentage Total Vote Rep.	Percentage Total Vote Dem.	Percentage Major Vote Rep.	Percentage Major Vote Dem.
1988	400,516	203,550	DiPrete, Edward	196,936	Sundlun, Bruce G.	30	6,614 R	50.8%	49.2%	50.8%	49.2%
1986	322,724	208,822	DiPrete, Edward	104,508	Sundlun, Bruce G.	9,394	104,314 R	64.7%	32.4%	66.6%	33.4%
1984	408,375	245,059	DiPrete, Edward	163,311	Solomon, Anthony J.	5	81,748 R	60.0%	40.0%	60.0%	40.0%
1982	337,259	79,602	Marzullo, Vincent	247,208	Garrahy, J. Joseph	10,449	167,606 D	23.6%	73.3%	24.4%	75.6%
1980	405,916	106,729	Cianci, Vincent A.	299,174	Garrahy, J. Joseph	13	192,445 D	26.3%	73.7%	26.3%	73.7%
1978	314,363	96,596	Almond, Lincoln	197,386	Garrahy, J. Joseph	20,381	100,790 D	30.7%	62.8%	32.9%	67.1%
1976	398,683	178,254	Taft, James L.	218,561	Garrahy, J. Joseph	1,868	40,307 D	44.7%	54.8%	44.9%	55.1%
1974	321,660	69,224	Nugent, James W.	252,436	Noel, Philip W.		183,212 D	21.5%	78.5%	21.5%	78.5%
1972	412,866	194,315	DeSimone, Herbert F.	216,953	Noel, Philip W.	1,598	22,638 D	47.1%	52.5%	47.2%	52.8%
1970	346,342	171,549	DeSimone, Herbert F.	173,420	Licht, Frank	1,373	1,871 D	49.5%	50.1%	49.7%	50.3%
1968	383,725	187,958	Chafee, John H.	195,766	Licht, Frank	1	7,808 D	49.0%	51.0%	49.0%	51.0%
1966	332,064	210,202	Chafee, John H.	121,862	Hobbs, Horace E.		88,340 R	63.3%	36.7%	63.3%	36.7%
1964	391,668	239,501	Chafee, John H.	152,165	Gallogly, Edward P.	2	87,336 R	61.1%	38.9%	61.1%	38.9%
1962	327,506	163,952	Chafee, John H.	163,554	Notte, John A.		398 R	50.1%	49.9%	50.1%	49.9%
1960	401,362	174,044	Del Sesto, Christopher	227,318	Notte, John A.		53,274 D	43.4%	56.6%	43.4%	56.6%
1958	346,780	176,505	Del Sesto, Christopher	170,275	Roberts, Dennis J.		6,230 R	50.9%	49.1%	50.9%	49.1%
1956	383,919	191,604	Del Sesto, Christopher	192,315	Roberts, Dennis J.		711 D	49.9%	50.1%	49.9%	50.1%
1954	328,670	137,131	Lewis, Dean J.	189,595	Roberts, Dennis J.	1,944	52,464 D	41.7%	57.7%	42.0%	58.0%
1952	409,689	194,102	Archambault, Raoul	215,587	Roberts, Dennis J.		21,485 D	47.4%	52.6%	47.4%	52.6%
1950	296,809	120,684	Lachapelle, E. T.	176,125	Roberts, Dennis J.		55,441 D	40.7%	59.3%	40.7%	59.3%
1948	323,863	124,441	Ruerat, Albert P.	198,056	Pastore, John O.	1,366	73,615 D	38.4%	61.2%	38.6%	61.4%
1946	275,341	126,456	Murphy, John G.	148,885	Pastore, John O.		22,429 D	45.9%	54.1%	45.9%	54.1%

POSTWAR VOTE FOR SENATOR

Year	Total Vote	Republican Vote	Republican Candidate	Democratic Vote	Democratic Candidate	Other Vote	Rep.-Dem. Plurality	Percentage Total Vote Rep.	Percentage Total Vote Dem.	Percentage Major Vote Rep.	Percentage Major Vote Dem.
1988	397,996	217,273	Chafee, John H.	180,717	Licht, Richard A.	6	36,556 R	54.6%	45.4%	54.6%	45.4%
1984	395,285	108,492	Leonard, Barbara	286,780	Pell, Claiborne	13	178,288 D	27.4%	72.6%	27.4%	72.6%
1982	342,779	175,495	Chafee, John H.	167,283	Michaelson, Julius C.	1	8,212 R	51.2%	48.8%	51.2%	48.8%
1978	305,618	76,061	Reynolds, James G.	229,557	Pell, Claiborne		153,496 D	24.9%	75.1%	24.9%	75.1%
1976	398,906	230,329	Chafee, John H.	167,665	Lorber, Richard P.	912	62,664 R	57.7%	42.0%	57.9%	42.1%
1972	413,432	188,990	Chafee, John H.	221,942	Pell, Claiborne	2,500	32,952 D	45.7%	53.7%	46.0%	54.0%
1970	341,222	107,351	McLaughlin, John	230,469	Pastore, John O.	3,402	123,118 D	31.5%	67.5%	31.8%	68.2%
1966	324,173	104,838	Briggs, Ruth M.	219,331	Pell, Claiborne	4	114,493 D	32.3%	67.7%	32.3%	67.7%
1964	386,322	66,715	Lagueux, Ronald R.	319,607	Pastore, John O.		252,892 D	17.3%	82.7%	17.3%	82.7%
1960	399,983	124,408	Archambault, Raoul	275,575	Pell, Claiborne		151,167 D	31.1%	68.9%	31.1%	68.9%
1958	344,519	122,353	Ewing, Bayard	222,166	Pastore, John O.		99,813 D	35.5%	64.5%	35.5%	64.5%
1954	326,624	132,970	Sundlun, Walter I.	193,654	Green, Theodore F.		60,684 D	40.7%	59.3%	40.7%	59.3%
1952	410,978	185,850	Ewing, Bayard	225,128	Pastore, John O.		39,278 D	45.2%	54.8%	45.2%	54.8%
1950 S	297,909	114,184	Levy, Austin T.	183,725	Pastore, John O.		69,541 D	38.3%	61.7%	38.3%	61.7%
1948	320,420	130,262	Hazard, Thomas P.	190,158	Green, Theodore F.		59,896 D	40.7%	59.3%	40.7%	59.3%
1946	273,528	122,780	Dyer, W. Gurnee	150,748	McGrath, J. Howard		27,968 D	44.9%	55.1%	44.9%	55.1%

The 1950 election was for a short term to fill a vacancy.

RHODE ISLAND

Districts Established April 9, 1982

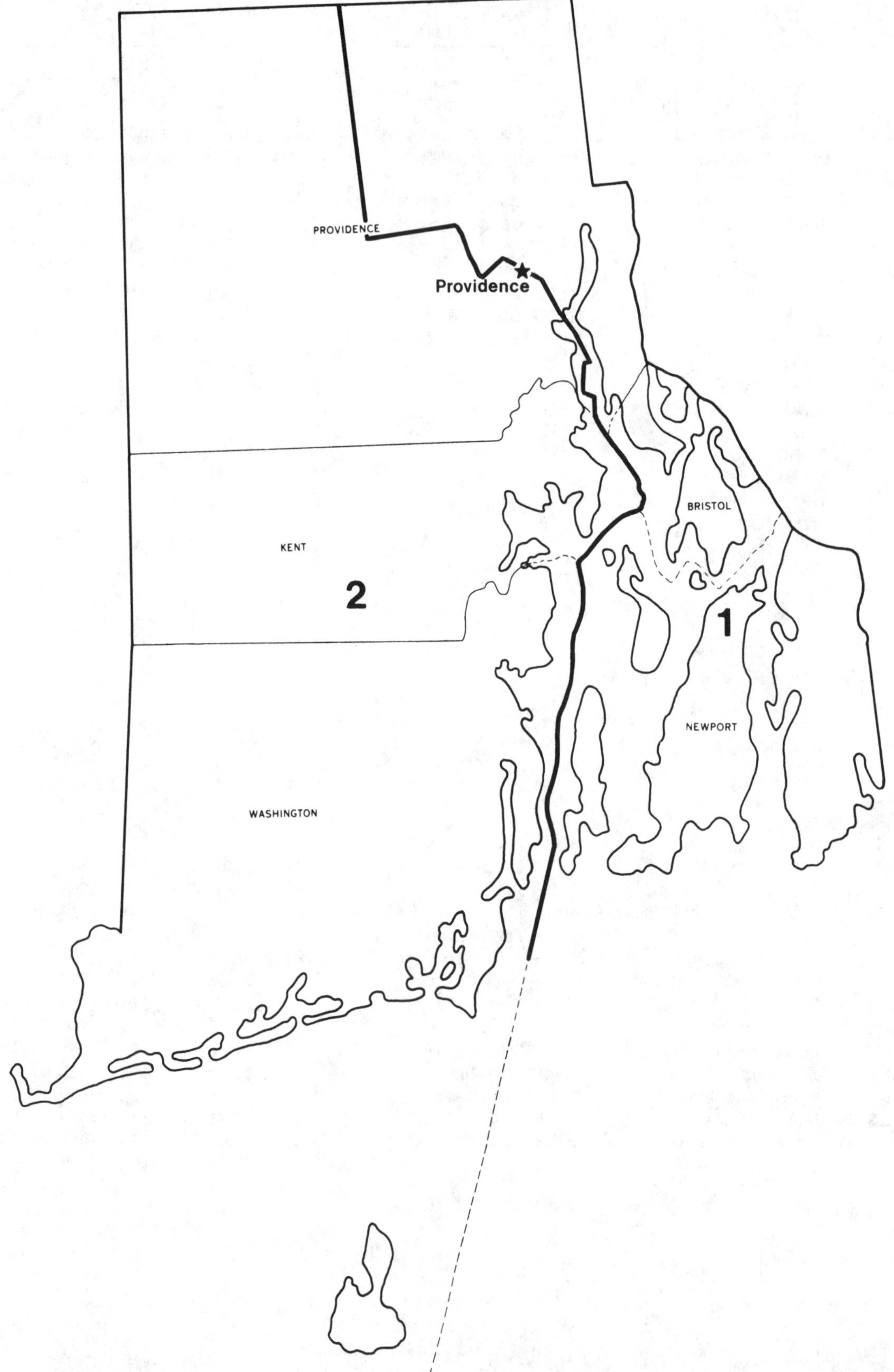

RHODE ISLAND

PRESIDENT 1988

1980 Census Population	County	Total Vote	Republican	Democratic	Other	Rep.-Dem. Plurality	Percentage Total Vote Rep.	Total Vote Dem.	Major Vote Rep.	Major Vote Dem.
46,942	BRISTOL	21,883	10,626	11,168	89	542 D	48.6%	51.0%	48.8%	51.2%
154,163	KENT	71,801	34,314	37,221	266	2,907 D	47.8%	51.8%	48.0%	52.0%
81,383	NEWPORT	34,664	16,923	17,597	144	674 D	48.8%	50.8%	49.0%	51.0%
571,349	PROVIDENCE	231,159	94,248	135,927	984	41,679 D	40.8%	58.8%	40.9%	59.1%
93,317	WASHINGTON	45,062	21,650	23,210	202	1,560 D	48.0%	51.5%	48.3%	51.7%
947,154	TOTAL	404,620	177,761	225,123	1,736	47,362 D	43.9%	55.6%	44.1%	55.9%

RHODE ISLAND

GOVERNOR 1988

1980 Census Population	County	Total Vote	Republican	Democratic	Other	Rep.-Dem. Plurality	Percentage Total Vote Rep.	Total Vote Dem.	Major Vote Rep.	Major Vote Dem.
46,942	BRISTOL	21,733	12,327	9,406		2,921 R	56.7%	43.3%	56.7%	43.3%
154,163	KENT	71,587	36,565	35,022		1,543 R	51.1%	48.9%	51.1%	48.9%
81,383	NEWPORT	33,931	17,370	16,561		809 R	51.2%	48.8%	51.2%	48.8%
571,349	PROVIDENCE	228,644	112,783	115,861		3,078 D	49.3%	50.7%	49.3%	50.7%
93,317	WASHINGTON	44,591	24,505	20,086		4,419 R	55.0%	45.0%	55.0%	45.0%
947,154	TOTAL	400,516	203,550	196,936	30	6,614 R	50.8%	49.2%	50.8%	49.2%

RHODE ISLAND

SENATOR 1988

1980 Census Population	County	Total Vote	Republican	Democratic	Other	Rep.-Dem. Plurality	Percentage Total Vote Rep.	Total Vote Dem.	Major Vote Rep.	Major Vote Dem.
46,942	BRISTOL	21,642	13,088	8,554		4,534 R	60.5%	39.5%	60.5%	39.5%
154,163	KENT	71,478	41,938	29,540		12,398 R	58.7%	41.3%	58.7%	41.3%
81,383	NEWPORT	33,629	20,082	13,547		6,535 R	59.7%	40.3%	59.7%	40.3%
571,349	PROVIDENCE	226,841	114,037	112,804		1,233 R	50.3%	49.7%	50.3%	49.7%
93,317	WASHINGTON	44,400	28,128	16,272		11,856 R	63.4%	36.6%	63.4%	36.6%
947,154	TOTAL	397,996	217,273	180,717	6	36,556 R	54.6%	45.4%	54.6%	45.4%

RHODE ISLAND

PRESIDENT 1988

1980 Census Population	City/Town	Total Vote	Republican	Democratic	Other	Rep.-Dem. Plurality	Percentage Total Vote Rep.	Percentage Total Vote Dem.	Percentage Major Vote Rep.	Percentage Major Vote Dem.
16,174	BARRINGTON	8,908	4,968	3,909	31	1,059 R	55.8%	43.9%	56.0%	44.0%
20,128	BRISTOL TOWN	8,323	3,538	4,746	39	1,208 D	42.5%	57.0%	42.7%	57.3%
13,164	BURRILLVILLE	5,181	2,479	2,681	21	202 D	47.8%	51.7%	48.0%	52.0%
16,995	CENTRAL FALLS	4,475	1,493	2,964	18	1,471 D	33.4%	66.2%	33.5%	66.5%
4,800	CHARLESTOWN	2,623	1,325	1,284	14	41 R	50.5%	49.0%	50.8%	49.2%
27,065	COVENTRY	12,756	6,348	6,362	46	14 D	49.8%	49.9%	49.9%	50.1%
71,992	CRANSTON	36,968	17,129	19,711	128	2,582 D	46.3%	53.3%	46.5%	53.5%
27,069	CUMBERLAND	13,173	6,281	6,854	38	573 D	47.7%	52.0%	47.8%	52.2%
10,211	EAST GREENWICH	6,045	3,637	2,386	22	1,251 R	60.2%	39.5%	60.4%	39.6%
50,980	EAST PROVIDENCE	20,218	8,181	11,948	89	3,767 D	40.5%	59.1%	40.6%	59.4%
4,453	EXETER	2,075	1,095	972	8	123 R	52.8%	46.8%	53.0%	47.0%
3,370	FOSTER	1,757	862	888	7	26 D	49.1%	50.5%	49.3%	50.7%
7,550	GLOCESTER	3,676	1,881	1,774	21	107 R	51.2%	48.3%	51.5%	48.5%
6,406	HOPKINTON	2,640	1,405	1,227	8	178 R	53.2%	46.5%	53.4%	46.6%
4,040	JAMESTOWN	2,765	1,304	1,448	13	144 D	47.2%	52.4%	47.4%	52.6%
24,907	JOHNSTON	12,194	5,391	6,769	34	1,378 D	44.2%	55.5%	44.3%	55.7%
16,949	LINCOLN	8,834	4,527	4,269	38	258 R	51.2%	48.3%	51.5%	48.5%
3,085	LITTLE COMPTON	1,838	989	843	6	146 R	53.8%	45.9%	54.0%	46.0%
17,216	MIDDLETOWN	6,139	3,173	2,936	30	237 R	51.7%	47.8%	51.9%	48.1%
12,088	NARRAGANSETT	6,482	2,936	3,513	33	577 D	45.3%	54.2%	45.5%	54.5%
29,259	NEWPORT CITY	10,099	4,493	5,567	39	1,074 D	44.5%	55.1%	44.7%	55.3%
620	NEW SHOREHAM	814	361	447	6	86 D	44.3%	54.9%	44.7%	55.3%
21,938	NORTH KINGSTOWN	11,040	5,848	5,146	46	702 R	53.0%	46.6%	53.2%	46.8%
29,188	NORTH PROVIDENCE	16,120	6,666	9,410	44	2,744 D	41.4%	58.4%	41.5%	58.5%
9,972	NORTH SMITHFIELD	5,082	2,557	2,513	12	44 R	50.3%	49.4%	50.4%	49.6%
71,204	PAWTUCKET	25,442	9,359	15,985	98	6,626 D	36.8%	62.8%	36.9%	63.1%
14,257	PORTSMOUTH	7,416	3,911	3,469	36	442 R	52.7%	46.8%	53.0%	47.0%
156,804	PROVIDENCE CITY	50,418	15,310	34,806	302	19,496 D	30.4%	69.0%	30.5%	69.5%
4,018	RICHMOND	2,215	1,034	1,174	7	140 D	46.7%	53.0%	46.8%	53.2%
8,405	SCITUATE	4,604	2,737	1,834	33	903 R	59.4%	39.8%	59.9%	40.1%
16,886	SMITHFIELD	8,159	3,955	4,163	41	208 D	48.5%	51.0%	48.7%	51.3%
20,414	SOUTH KINGSTOWN	8,619	3,790	4,778	51	988 D	44.0%	55.4%	44.2%	55.8%
13,526	TIVERTON	6,407	3,053	3,334	20	281 D	47.7%	52.0%	47.8%	52.2%
10,640	WARREN	4,652	2,120	2,513	19	393 D	45.6%	54.0%	45.8%	54.2%
87,123	WARWICK	39,863	18,052	21,662	149	3,610 D	45.3%	54.3%	45.5%	54.5%
18,580	WESTERLY	8,554	3,856	4,669	29	813 D	45.1%	54.6%	45.2%	54.8%
2,738	WEST GREENWICH	1,692	989	697	6	292 R	58.5%	41.2%	58.7%	41.3%
27,026	WEST WARWICK	11,445	5,288	6,114	43	826 D	46.2%	53.4%	46.4%	53.6%
45,914	WOONSOCKET	14,858	5,440	9,358	60	3,918 D	36.6%	63.0%	36.8%	63.2%
947,154	TOTAL	404,620	177,761	225,123	1,736	47,362 D	43.9%	55.6%	44.1%	55.9%

RHODE ISLAND

GOVERNOR 1988

1980 Census Population	City/Town	Total Vote	Republican	Democratic	Other	Rep.-Dem. Plurality	Percentage Total Vote Rep.	Percentage Total Vote Dem.	Percentage Major Vote Rep.	Percentage Major Vote Dem.
16,174	BARRINGTON	8,779	5,202	3,577		1,625 R	59.3%	40.7%	59.3%	40.7%
20,128	BRISTOL TOWN	8,312	4,667	3,645		1,022 R	56.1%	43.9%	56.1%	43.9%
13,164	BURRILLVILLE	5,137	2,823	2,314		509 R	55.0%	45.0%	55.0%	45.0%
16,995	CENTRAL FALLS	4,391	1,650	2,741		1,091 D	37.6%	62.4%	37.6%	62.4%
4,800	CHARLESTOWN	2,583	1,522	1,061		461 R	58.9%	41.1%	58.9%	41.1%
27,065	COVENTRY	12,706	7,033	5,673		1,360 R	55.4%	44.6%	55.4%	44.6%
71,992	CRANSTON	36,834	21,924	14,910		7,014 R	59.5%	40.5%	59.5%	40.5%
27,069	CUMBERLAND	12,988	6,724	6,264		460 R	51.8%	48.2%	51.8%	48.2%
10,211	EAST GREENWICH	6,002	3,554	2,448		1,106 R	59.2%	40.8%	59.2%	40.8%
50,980	EAST PROVIDENCE	19,928	9,535	10,393		858 D	47.8%	52.2%	47.8%	52.2%
4,453	EXETER	2,075	1,129	946		183 R	54.4%	45.6%	54.4%	45.6%
3,370	FOSTER	1,744	995	749		246 R	57.1%	42.9%	57.1%	42.9%
7,550	GLOCESTER	3,666	2,024	1,642		382 R	55.2%	44.8%	55.2%	44.8%
6,406	HOPKINTON	2,625	1,617	1,008		609 R	61.6%	38.4%	61.6%	38.4%
4,040	JAMESTOWN	2,771	1,335	1,436		101 D	48.2%	51.8%	48.2%	51.8%
24,907	JOHNSTON	12,163	5,915	6,248		333 D	48.6%	51.4%	48.6%	51.4%
16,949	LINCOLN	8,823	4,746	4,077		669 R	53.8%	46.2%	53.8%	46.2%
3,085	LITTLE COMPTON	1,797	1,021	776		245 R	56.8%	43.2%	56.8%	43.2%
17,216	MIDDLETOWN	6,058	3,107	2,951		156 R	51.3%	48.7%	51.3%	48.7%
12,088	NARRAGANSETT	6,433	3,275	3,158		117 R	50.9%	49.1%	50.9%	49.1%
29,259	NEWPORT CITY	9,854	4,689	5,165		476 D	47.6%	52.4%	47.6%	52.4%
620	NEW SHOREHAM	803	452	351		101 R	56.3%	43.7%	56.3%	43.7%
21,938	NORTH KINGSTOWN	10,978	5,963	5,015		948 R	54.3%	45.7%	54.3%	45.7%
29,188	NORTH PROVIDENCE	16,001	7,625	8,376		751 D	47.7%	52.3%	47.7%	52.3%
9,972	NORTH SMITHFIELD	5,036	2,838	2,198		640 R	56.4%	43.6%	56.4%	43.6%
71,204	PAWTUCKET	25,140	10,948	14,192		3,244 D	43.5%	56.5%	43.5%	56.5%
14,257	PORTSMOUTH	7,287	4,024	3,263		761 R	55.2%	44.8%	55.2%	44.8%
156,804	PROVIDENCE CITY	49,432	20,687	28,745		8,058 D	41.8%	58.2%	41.8%	58.2%
4,018	RICHMOND	2,189	1,161	1,028		133 R	53.0%	47.0%	53.0%	47.0%
8,405	SCITUATE	4,565	2,787	1,778		1,009 R	61.1%	38.9%	61.1%	38.9%
16,886	SMITHFIELD	8,150	4,277	3,873		404 R	52.5%	47.5%	52.5%	47.5%
20,414	SOUTH KINGSTOWN	8,547	4,607	3,940		667 R	53.9%	46.1%	53.9%	46.1%
13,526	TIVERTON	6,164	3,194	2,970		224 R	51.8%	48.2%	51.8%	48.2%
10,640	WARREN	4,642	2,458	2,184		274 R	53.0%	47.0%	53.0%	47.0%
87,123	WARWICK	39,821	19,021	20,800		1,779 D	47.8%	52.2%	47.8%	52.2%
18,580	WESTERLY	8,358	4,779	3,579		1,200 R	57.2%	42.8%	57.2%	42.8%
2,738	WEST GREENWICH	1,678	970	708		262 R	57.8%	42.2%	57.8%	42.2%
27,026	WEST WARWICK	11,380	5,987	5,393		594 R	52.6%	47.4%	52.6%	47.4%
45,914	WOONSOCKET	14,646	7,285	7,361		76 D	49.7%	50.3%	49.7%	50.3%
947,154	TOTAL	400,516	203,550	196,936	30	6,614 R	50.8%	49.2%	50.8%	49.2%

RHODE ISLAND

SENATOR 1988

1980 Census Population	City/Town	Total Vote	Republican	Democratic	Other	Rep.-Dem. Plurality	Percentage Total Vote Rep.	Total Vote Dem.	Major Vote Rep.	Major Vote Dem.
16,174	BARRINGTON	8,771	6,087	2,684		3,403 R	69.4%	30.6%	69.4%	30.6%
20,128	BRISTOL TOWN	8,222	4,451	3,771		680 R	54.1%	45.9%	54.1%	45.9%
13,164	BURRILLVILLE	5,116	2,620	2,496		124 R	51.2%	48.8%	51.2%	48.8%
16,995	CENTRAL FALLS	4,331	1,674	2,657		983 D	38.7%	61.3%	38.7%	61.3%
4,800	CHARLESTOWN	2,559	1,661	898		763 R	64.9%	35.1%	64.9%	35.1%
27,065	COVENTRY	12,696	7,350	5,346		2,004 R	57.9%	42.1%	57.9%	42.1%
71,992	CRANSTON	36,415	20,499	15,916		4,583 R	56.3%	43.7%	56.3%	43.7%
27,069	CUMBERLAND	12,898	7,228	5,670		1,558 R	56.0%	44.0%	56.0%	44.0%
10,211	EAST GREENWICH	6,008	4,394	1,614		2,780 R	73.1%	26.9%	73.1%	26.9%
50,980	EAST PROVIDENCE	19,794	10,370	9,424		946 R	52.4%	47.6%	52.4%	47.6%
4,453	EXETER	2,080	1,344	736		608 R	64.6%	35.4%	64.6%	35.4%
3,370	FOSTER	1,754	1,160	594		566 R	66.1%	33.9%	66.1%	33.9%
7,550	GLOCESTER	3,646	2,302	1,344		958 R	63.1%	36.9%	63.1%	36.9%
6,406	HOPKINTON	2,620	1,596	1,024		572 R	60.9%	39.1%	60.9%	39.1%
4,040	JAMESTOWN	2,742	1,843	899		944 R	67.2%	32.8%	67.2%	32.8%
24,907	JOHNSTON	11,991	5,764	6,227		463 D	48.1%	51.9%	48.1%	51.9%
16,949	LINCOLN	8,805	5,307	3,498		1,809 R	60.3%	39.7%	60.3%	39.7%
3,085	LITTLE COMPTON	1,801	1,174	627		547 R	65.2%	34.8%	65.2%	34.8%
17,216	MIDDLETOWN	6,020	3,646	2,374		1,272 R	60.6%	39.4%	60.6%	39.4%
12,088	NARRAGANSETT	6,379	4,088	2,291		1,797 R	64.1%	35.9%	64.1%	35.9%
29,259	NEWPORT CITY	9,735	5,798	3,937		1,861 R	59.6%	40.4%	59.6%	40.4%
620	NEW SHOREHAM	804	605	199		406 R	75.2%	24.8%	75.2%	24.8%
21,938	NORTH KINGSTOWN	10,936	7,339	3,597		3,742 R	67.1%	32.9%	67.1%	32.9%
29,188	NORTH PROVIDENCE	15,840	7,760	8,080		320 D	49.0%	51.0%	49.0%	51.0%
9,972	NORTH SMITHFIELD	5,009	2,785	2,224		561 R	55.6%	44.4%	55.6%	44.4%
71,204	PAWTUCKET	24,908	11,642	13,266		1,624 D	46.7%	53.3%	46.7%	53.3%
14,257	PORTSMOUTH	7,231	4,517	2,714		1,803 R	62.5%	37.5%	62.5%	37.5%
156,804	PROVIDENCE CITY	49,109	21,453	27,656		6,203 D	43.7%	56.3%	43.7%	56.3%
4,018	RICHMOND	2,185	1,314	871		443 R	60.1%	39.9%	60.1%	39.9%
8,405	SCITUATE	4,552	3,172	1,380		1,792 R	69.7%	30.3%	69.7%	30.3%
16,886	SMITHFIELD	8,103	4,638	3,465		1,173 R	57.2%	42.8%	57.2%	42.8%
20,414	SOUTH KINGSTOWN	8,524	5,638	2,886		2,752 R	66.1%	33.9%	66.1%	33.9%
13,526	TIVERTON	6,100	3,104	2,996		108 R	50.9%	49.1%	50.9%	49.1%
10,640	WARREN	4,649	2,550	2,099		451 R	54.9%	45.1%	54.9%	45.1%
87,123	WARWICK	39,715	23,049	16,666		6,383 R	58.0%	42.0%	58.0%	42.0%
18,580	WESTERLY	8,313	4,543	3,770		773 R	54.6%	45.4%	54.6%	45.4%
2,738	WEST GREENWICH	1,668	1,061	607		454 R	63.6%	36.4%	63.6%	36.4%
27,026	WEST WARWICK	11,391	6,084	5,307		777 R	53.4%	46.6%	53.4%	46.6%
45,914	WOONSOCKET	14,570	5,663	8,907		3,244 D	38.9%	61.1%	38.9%	61.1%
947,154	TOTAL	397,996	217,273	180,717	6	36,556 R	54.6%	45.4%	54.6%	45.4%

RHODE ISLAND

CONGRESS

CD	Year	Total Vote	Republican Vote	Republican Candidate	Democratic Vote	Democratic Candidate	Other Vote	Rep.-Dem. Plurality	Percentage Total Vote Rep.	Percentage Total Vote Dem.	Percentage Major Vote Rep.	Percentage Major Vote Dem.
1	1988	189,647	105,506	MACHTLEY, RONALD K.	84,141	ST. GERMAIN, FERNAND		21,365 R	55.6%	44.4%	55.6%	44.4%
1	1986	147,474	62,397	HOLMES, JOHN A.	85,077	ST. GERMAIN, FERNAND		22,680 D	42.3%	57.7%	42.3%	57.7%
1	1984	190,511	59,926	REGO, ALFRED	130,585	ST. GERMAIN, FERNAND		70,659 D	31.5%	68.5%	31.5%	68.5%
1	1982	160,131	61,253	STALLWOOD, BURTON	97,254	ST. GERMAIN, FERNAND	1,624	36,001 D	38.3%	60.7%	38.6%	61.4%
2	1988	201,347	145,218	SCHNEIDER, CLAUDINE	56,129	MORGENTHAU, RUTH S.		89,089 R	72.1%	27.9%	72.1%	27.9%
2	1986	158,189	113,603	SCHNEIDER, CLAUDINE	44,586	FERRY, DONALD J.		69,017 R	71.8%	28.2%	71.8%	28.2%
2	1984	199,508	135,151	SCHNEIDER, CLAUDINE	64,357	SINAPI, RICHARD		70,794 R	67.7%	32.3%	67.7%	32.3%
2	1982	173,051	96,282	SCHNEIDER, CLAUDINE	76,769	AUKERMAN, JAMES V.		19,513 R	55.6%	44.4%	55.6%	44.4%

RHODE ISLAND

1988 GENERAL ELECTION

In addition to the county-by-county figures, data are presented by cities and towns.

President — Other vote was 825 Libertarian (Paul); 280 New Alliance (Fulani); 195 Peace and Freedom (Lewin); 159 Populist (Duke); 130 Socialist Workers (Warren); 96 Socialist (Kenoyer); 51 scattered write-in.

Governor — Total in the other vote column represents scattered write-in votes not available by county or city/town.

Senator — Total in the other vote column represents scattered write-in votes not available by county or city/town.

Congress — There were 10 scattered write-in votes not available by CD's.

1988 PRIMARIES

SEPTEMBER 14 REPUBLICAN

Governor — Edward DiPrete, unopposed.

Senator — John H. Chafee, unopposed.

Congress — Unopposed in both CD's.

SEPTEMBER 14 DEMOCRATIC

Governor — 68,065 Bruce G. Sundlun; 7,328 Peter VanDaam.

Senator — Richard A. Licht, unopposed.

Congress — Contested as follows:

CD 1 — 26,727 Fernand St. Germain; 21,748 Scott Wolf.
CD 2 — 19,007 Ruth S. Morgenthau; 8,629 Paul Iacono.

SOUTH CAROLINA

GOVERNOR

Carroll Campbell (R). Elected 1986 to a four-year term.

SENATORS

Ernest F. Hollings (D). Re-elected 1986 to a six-year term. Previously elected 1980, 1974, 1968 and in 1966 to fill out term vacated by the death of Senator Olin D. Johnston.

Strom Thurmond (R). Re-elected 1984 to a six-year term. Previously elected 1978, 1972, 1966, 1960 and in 1956 to fill out term vacated by his own resignation in April 1956; had been elected to this term in 1954 as an Independent Democrat. Changed party affiliation from Democrat to Republican in September 1964.

REPRESENTATIVES

1. Arthur Ravenel (R)
2. Floyd Spence (R)
3. Butler Derrick (D)
4. Elizabeth J. Patterson (D)
5. John Spratt (D)
6. Robert M. Tallon (D)

POSTWAR VOTE FOR PRESIDENT

								Percentage			
	Total	Republican		Democratic		Other		Total Vote		Major Vote	
Year	Vote	Vote	Candidate	Vote	Candidate	Vote	Plurality	Rep.	Dem.	Rep.	Dem.
1988	986,009	606,443	Bush, George	370,554	Dukakis, Michael S.	9,012	235,889 R	61.5%	37.6%	62.1%	37.9%
1984	968,529	615,539	Reagan, Ronald	344,459	Mondale, Walter F.	8,531	271,080 R	63.6%	35.6%	64.1%	35.9%
1980	894,071	441,841	Reagan, Ronald	430,385	Carter, Jimmy	21,845	11,456 R	49.4%	48.1%	50.7%	49.3%
1976	802,583	346,149	Ford, Gerald R.	450,807	Carter, Jimmy	5,627	104,658 D	43.1%	56.2%	43.4%	56.6%
1972	673,960	477,044	Nixon, Richard M.	186,824	McGovern, George S.	10,092	290,220 R	70.8%	27.7%	71.9%	28.1%
1968 * *	666,978	254,062	Nixon, Richard M.	197,486	Humphrey, Hubert H.	215,430	38,632 R	38.1%	29.6%	56.3%	43.7%
1964	524,779	309,048	Goldwater, Barry M.	215,723	Johnson, Lyndon B.	8	93,325 R	58.9%	41.1%	58.9%	41.1%
1960	386,688	188,558	Nixon, Richard M.	198,129	Kennedy, John F.	1	9,571 D	48.8%	51.2%	48.8%	51.2%
1956 * *	300,583	75,700	Eisenhower, Dwight D.	136,372	Stevenson, Adlai E.	88,511	47,863 D	25.2%	45.4%	35.7%	64.3%
1952	341,087	168,082	Eisenhower, Dwight D.	173,004	Stevenson, Adlai E.	1	4,922 D	49.3%	50.7%	49.3%	50.7%
1948 * *	142,571	5,386	Dewey, Thomas E.	34,423	Truman, Harry S.	102,762	68,184 SR	3.8%	24.1%	13.5%	86.5%

In 1968 other vote was Independent (Wallace). In 1956 other vote was 88,509 Independent (Uncommitted States Rights) and 2 scattered. In 1948 other vote was 102,607 States Rights; 154 Progressive and 1 Socialist.

POSTWAR VOTE FOR GOVERNOR

								Percentage			
	Total	Republican		Democratic		Other	Rep.-Dem.	Total Vote		Major Vote	
Year	Vote	Vote	Candidate	Vote	Candidate	Vote	Plurality	Rep.	Dem.	Rep.	Dem.
1986	753,751	384,565	Campbell, Carroll	361,325	Daniel, Mike	7,861	23,240 R	51.0%	47.9%	51.6%	48.4%
1982	671,625	202,806	Workman, W. D.	468,819	Riley, Richard W.		266,013 D	30.2%	69.8%	30.2%	69.8%
1978	627,182	236,946	Young, Edward L.	384,898	Riley, Richard W.	5,338	147,952 D	37.8%	61.4%	38.1%	61.9%
1974	523,199	266,109	Edwards, James B.	248,938	Dorn, W. J.Bryan	8,152	17,171 R	50.9%	47.6%	51.7%	48.3%
1970	484,857	221,233	Watson, Albert W.	250,551	West, John C.	13,073	29,318 D	45.6%	51.7%	46.9%	53.1%
1966	439,942	184,088	Rogers, Joseph O.	255,854	McNair, Robert E.		71,766 D	41.8%	58.2%	41.8%	58.2%
1962	253,721		—	253,704	Russell, Donald S.	17	253,704 D		100.0%		100.0%
1958	77,740		—	77,714	Hollings, Ernest F.	26	77,714 D		100.0%		100.0%
1954	214,212		—	214,204	Timmerman, George B.	8	214,204 D		100.0%		100.0%
1950	50,642		—	50,633	Byrnes, James F.	9	50,633 D		100.0%		100.0%
1946	26,520		—	26,520	Thurmond, Strom		26,520 D		100.0%		100.0%

SOUTH CAROLINA

POSTWAR VOTE FOR SENATOR

Year	Total Vote	Republican Vote	Republican Candidate	Democratic Vote	Democratic Candidate	Other Vote	Rep.-Dem. Plurality	Percentage Total Vote Rep.	Percentage Total Vote Dem.	Percentage Major Vote Rep.	Percentage Major Vote Dem.
1986	737,962	262,886	McMaster, Henry D.	465,500	Hollings, Ernest F.	9,576	202,614 D	35.6%	63.1%	36.1%	63.9%
1984	965,130	644,815	Thurmond, Strom	306,982	Purvis, Melvin	13,333	337,833 R	66.8%	31.8%	67.7%	32.3%
1980	870,594	257,946	Mays, Marshall T.	612,554	Hollings, Ernest F.	94	354,608 D	29.6%	70.4%	29.6%	70.4%
1978	632,852	351,733	Thurmond, Strom	281,119	Ravenel, Charles D.		70,614 R	55.6%	44.4%	55.6%	44.4%
1974	512,397	146,645	Bush, Gwenyfred	356,126	Hollings, Ernest F.	9,626	209,481 D	28.6%	69.5%	29.2%	70.8%
1972	672,246	426,601	Thurmond, Strom	245,457	Zeigler, Eugene N.	188	181,144 R	63.5%	36.5%	63.5%	36.5%
1968	652,855	248,780	Parker, Marshall	404,060	Hollings, Ernest F.	15	155,280 D	38.1%	61.9%	38.1%	61.9%
1966	436,252	271,297	Thurmond, Strom	164,955	Morrah, Bradley		106,342 R	62.2%	37.8%	62.2%	37.8%
1966 S	435,822	212,032	Parker, Marshall	223,790	Hollings, Ernest F.		11,758 D	48.7%	51.3%	48.7%	51.3%
1962	312,647	133,930	Workman, W. D.	178,712	Johnston, Olin D.	5	44,782 D	42.8%	57.2%	42.8%	57.2%
1960	330,266		—	330,164	Thurmond, Strom	102	330,164 D		100.0%		100.0%
1956	279,845	49,695	Crawford, Leon P.	230,150	Johnston, Olin D.		180,455 D	17.8%	82.2%	17.8%	82.2%
1956 S	251,907		—	251,907	Thurmond, Strom		251,907 D		100.0%		100.0%
1954 * *	227,232		—	83,525	Brown, Edgar A.	143,707	83,525 D		36.8%		100.0%
1950	50,277		—	50,240	Johnston, Olin D.	37	50,240 D		99.9%		100.0%
1948	141,006	5,008	Gerald, J. Bates	135,998	Maybank, Burnet R.		130,990 D	3.6%	96.4%	3.6%	96.4%

One each of the 1966 and 1956 elections was for a short term to fill a vacancy. In 1954, Strom Thurmond polled 143,444 votes as an Independent Democratic write-in candidate (63.1% of the total vote) and won the election with a 59,919 pluarlity.

SOUTH CAROLINA

Districts Established April 30, 1982

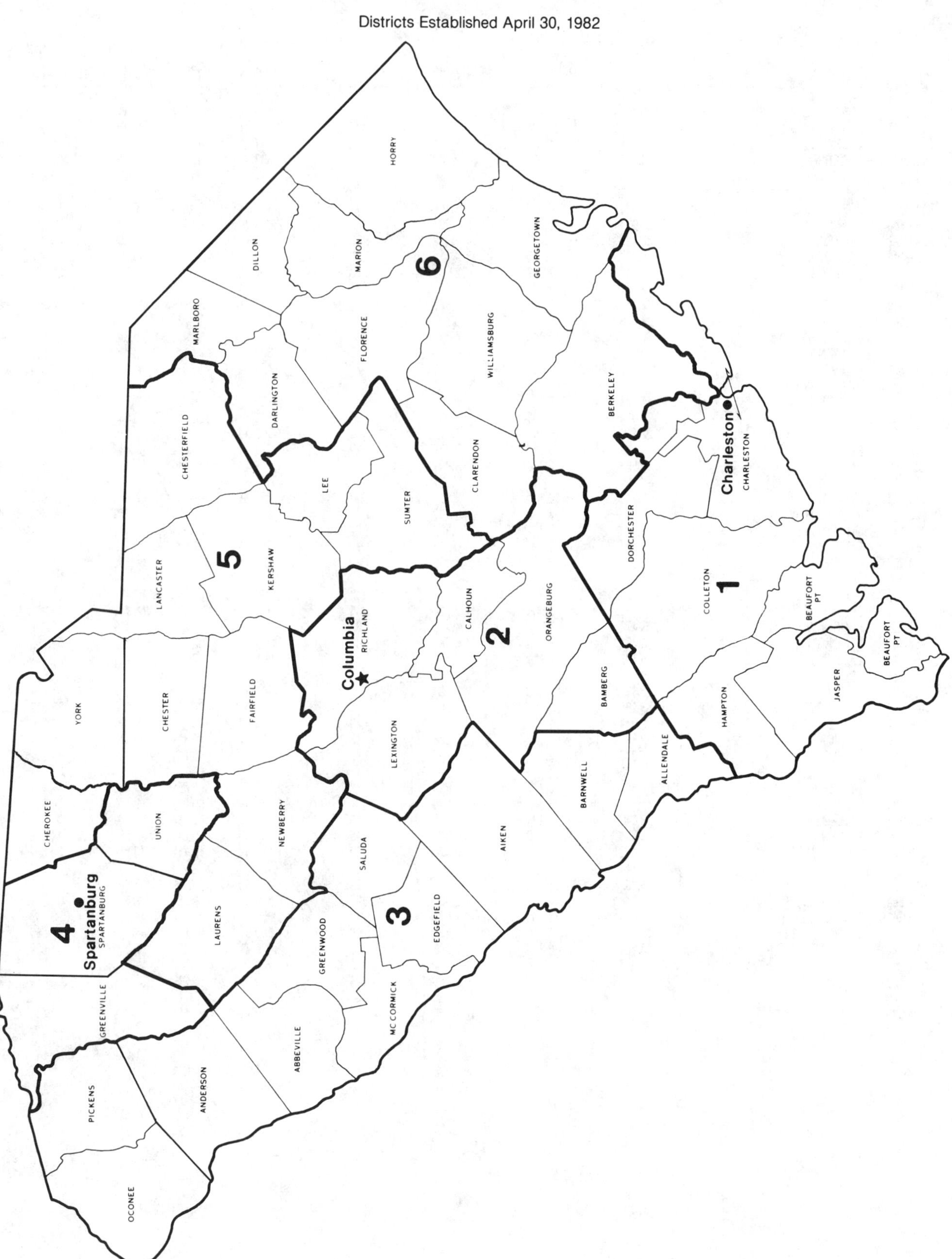

SOUTH CAROLINA

PRESIDENT 1988

1980 Census Population	County	Total Vote	Republican	Democratic	Other	Rep.-Dem. Plurality	Percentage Total Vote Rep.	Total Vote Dem.	Major Vote Rep.	Major Vote Dem.
22,627	ABBEVILLE	7,401	3,738	3,629	34	109 R	50.5%	49.0%	50.7%	49.3%
105,625	AIKEN	38,507	27,665	10,598	244	17,067 R	71.8%	27.5%	72.3%	27.7%
10,700	ALLENDALE	3,114	1,295	1,796	23	501 D	41.6%	57.7%	41.9%	58.1%
133,235	ANDERSON	38,383	25,939	12,281	163	13,658 R	67.6%	32.0%	67.9%	32.1%
18,118	BAMBERG	5,255	2,403	2,830	22	427 D	45.7%	53.9%	45.9%	54.1%
19,868	BARNWELL	7,075	4,467	2,564	44	1,903 R	63.1%	36.2%	63.5%	36.5%
65,364	BEAUFORT	25,021	16,184	8,691	146	7,493 R	64.7%	34.7%	65.1%	34.9%
94,727	BERKELEY	26,297	16,779	9,312	206	7,467 R	63.8%	35.4%	64.3%	35.7%
12,206	CALHOUN	4,787	2,585	2,175	27	410 R	54.0%	45.4%	54.3%	45.7%
276,974	CHARLESTON	82,916	49,149	32,977	790	16,172 R	59.3%	39.8%	59.8%	40.2%
40,983	CHEROKEE	12,151	7,763	4,322	66	3,441 R	63.9%	35.6%	64.2%	35.8%
30,148	CHESTER	7,748	3,968	3,737	43	231 R	51.2%	48.2%	51.5%	48.5%
38,161	CHESTERFIELD	9,735	4,999	4,699	37	300 R	51.4%	48.3%	51.5%	48.5%
27,464	CLARENDON	9,397	4,337	5,030	30	693 D	46.2%	53.5%	46.3%	53.7%
31,776	COLLETON	9,547	4,962	4,508	77	454 R	52.0%	47.2%	52.4%	47.6%
62,717	DARLINGTON	17,843	9,854	7,625	364	2,229 R	55.2%	42.7%	56.4%	43.6%
31,083	DILLON	7,069	3,793	3,251	25	542 R	53.7%	46.0%	53.8%	46.2%
58,761	DORCHESTER	22,232	14,756	7,371	105	7,385 R	66.4%	33.2%	66.7%	33.3%
17,528	EDGEFIELD	6,863	3,814	3,020	29	794 R	55.6%	44.0%	55.8%	44.2%
20,700	FAIRFIELD	6,583	2,714	3,827	42	1,113 D	41.2%	58.1%	41.5%	58.5%
110,163	FLORENCE	32,214	19,490	12,531	193	6,959 R	60.5%	38.9%	60.9%	39.1%
42,461	GEORGETOWN	12,506	7,032	5,402	72	1,630 R	56.2%	43.2%	56.6%	43.4%
287,913	GREENVILLE	95,126	67,371	27,188	567	40,183 R	70.8%	28.6%	71.2%	28.8%
57,847	GREENWOOD	15,704	9,096	6,511	97	2,585 R	57.9%	41.5%	58.3%	41.7%
18,159	HAMPTON	6,306	2,826	3,435	45	609 D	44.8%	54.5%	45.1%	54.9%
101,419	HORRY	38,409	24,843	13,316	250	11,527 R	64.7%	34.7%	65.1%	34.9%
14,504	JASPER	4,929	2,004	2,894	31	890 D	40.7%	58.7%	40.9%	59.1%
39,015	KERSHAW	13,473	8,877	4,494	102	4,383 R	65.9%	33.4%	66.4%	33.6%
53,361	LANCASTER	15,393	9,152	6,181	60	2,971 R	59.5%	40.2%	59.7%	40.3%
52,214	LAURENS	15,702	9,731	5,930	41	3,801 R	62.0%	37.8%	62.1%	37.9%
18,929	LEE	6,359	2,936	3,423		487 D	46.2%	53.8%	46.2%	53.8%
140,353	LEXINGTON	53,238	41,467	11,366	405	30,101 R	77.9%	21.3%	78.5%	21.5%
7,797	MCCORMICK	2,914	1,172	1,722	20	550 D	40.2%	59.1%	40.5%	59.5%
34,179	MARION	9,486	4,403	5,008	75	605 D	46.4%	52.8%	46.8%	53.2%
31,634	MARLBORO	6,870	2,921	3,937	12	1,016 D	42.5%	57.3%	42.6%	57.4%
31,242	NEWBERRY	10,305	6,427	3,825	53	2,602 R	62.4%	37.1%	62.7%	37.3%
48,611	OCONEE	14,585	10,184	4,299	102	5,885 R	69.8%	29.5%	70.3%	29.7%
82,276	ORANGEBURG	28,049	13,281	14,655	113	1,374 D	47.3%	52.2%	47.5%	52.5%
79,292	PICKENS	23,696	17,448	6,103	145	11,345 R	73.6%	25.8%	74.1%	25.9%
269,735	RICHLAND	83,123	43,841	36,420	2,862	7,421 R	52.7%	43.8%	54.6%	45.4%
16,150	SALUDA	5,232	3,225	1,984	23	1,241 R	61.6%	37.9%	61.9%	38.1%
201,861	SPARTANBURG	64,568	40,801	22,964	803	17,837 R	63.2%	35.6%	64.0%	36.0%
88,243	SUMTER	22,801	13,161	9,502	138	3,659 R	57.7%	41.7%	58.1%	41.9%
30,751	UNION	10,465	6,019	4,420	26	1,599 R	57.5%	42.2%	57.7%	42.3%
38,226	WILLIAMSBURG	13,324	5,914	7,343	67	1,429 D	44.4%	55.1%	44.6%	55.4%
106,720	YORK	33,308	21,657	11,458	193	10,199 R	65.0%	34.4%	65.4%	34.6%
3,121,820	TOTAL	986,009	606,443	370,554	9,012	235,889 R	61.5%	37.6%	62.1%	37.9%

SOUTH CAROLINA

CONGRESS

CD	Year	Total Vote	Republican Vote	Republican Candidate	Democratic Vote	Democratic Candidate	Other Vote	Rep.-Dem. Plurality	Percentage Total Vote Rep.	Percentage Total Vote Dem.	Percentage Major Vote Rep.	Percentage Major Vote Dem.
1	1988	159,263	101,572	RAVENEL, ARTHUR	57,691	TILLMAN, WHEELER		43,881 R	63.8%	36.2%	63.8%	36.2%
1	1986	115,232	59,969	RAVENEL, ARTHUR	55,262	STUCKEY, JIMMY	1	4,707 R	52.0%	48.0%	52.0%	48.0%
1	1984	167,310	103,288	HARTNETT, THOMAS F.	64,022	PENDARVIS, ED		39,266 R	61.7%	38.3%	61.7%	38.3%
1	1982	117,832	63,945	HARTNETT, THOMAS F.	52,916	MCLEOD, W. MULLINS	971	11,029 R	54.3%	44.9%	54.7%	45.3%
2	1988	179,999	94,960	SPENCE, FLOYD	83,978	LEVENTIS, JIM	1,061	10,982 R	52.8%	46.7%	53.1%	46.9%
2	1986	137,052	73,455	SPENCE, FLOYD	63,592	ZEIGLER, FRED	5	9,863 R	53.6%	46.4%	53.6%	46.4%
2	1984	174,027	108,085	SPENCE, FLOYD	63,932	MOSELY, KEN	2,010	44,153 R	62.1%	36.7%	62.8%	37.2%
2	1982	122,318	71,569	SPENCE, FLOYD	50,749	MOSELY, KEN		20,820 R	58.5%	41.5%	58.5%	41.5%
3	1988	165,825	75,571	JORDAN, HENRY S.	89,071	DERRICK, BUTLER	1,183	13,500 D	45.6%	53.7%	45.9%	54.1%
3	1986	115,683	36,495	DICKISON, RICHARD	79,109	DERRICK, BUTLER	79	42,614 D	31.5%	68.4%	31.6%	68.4%
3	1984	152,166	61,739	TAYLOR, CLARENCE E.	88,917	DERRICK, BUTLER	1,510	27,178 D	40.6%	58.4%	41.0%	59.0%
3	1982	85,339			77,125	DERRICK, BUTLER	8,214	77,125 D		90.4%		100.0%
4	1988	173,027	82,793	WHITE, KNOX	90,234	PATTERSON, ELIZABETH J.		7,441 D	47.8%	52.2%	47.8%	52.2%
4	1986	130,407	61,648	WORKMAN, W. D.,III	67,012	PATTERSON, ELIZABETH J.	1,747	5,364 D	47.3%	51.4%	47.9%	52.1%
4	1984	164,424	105,139	CAMPBELL, CARROLL	57,854	SMITH, JEFF	1,431	47,285 R	63.9%	35.2%	64.5%	35.5%
4	1982	110,196	69,802	CAMPBELL, CARROLL	40,394	TYUS, MARION E.		29,408 R	63.3%	36.7%	63.3%	36.7%
5	1988	154,581	46,622	CARLEY, ROBERT K.	107,959	SPRATT, JOHN		61,337 D	30.2%	69.8%	30.2%	69.8%
5	1986	96,149			95,859	SPRATT, JOHN	290	95,859 D		99.7%		100.0%
5	1984	107,291			98,513	SPRATT, JOHN	8,778	98,513 D		91.8%		100.0%
5	1982	102,536	33,191	WILKERSON, JOHN S.	69,345	SPRATT, JOHN		36,154 D	32.4%	67.6%	32.4%	67.6%
6	1988	158,677	37,958	CUNNINGHAM, ROBBIE	120,719	TALLON, ROBERT M.		82,761 D	23.9%	76.1%	23.9%	76.1%
6	1986	122,343	29,922	CUNNINGHAM, ROBBIE	92,398	TALLON, ROBERT M.	23	62,476 D	24.5%	75.5%	24.5%	75.5%
6	1984	162,384	63,005	EARGLE, LOIS	97,329	TALLON, ROBERT M.	2,050	34,324 D	38.8%	59.9%	39.3%	60.7%
6	1982	119,235	56,653	NAPIER, JOHN L.	62,582	TALLON, ROBERT M.		5,929 D	47.5%	52.5%	47.5%	52.5%

SOUTH CAROLINA

1988 GENERAL ELECTION

President Other vote was 4,935 Libertarian (Paul); 4,077 United Citizens (Fulani).

Congress Other vote was Libertarian (Sommer) in CD 2; Libertarian (Heaton) in CD 3.

1988 PRIMARIES

JUNE 14 REPUBLICAN

Congress Unopposed in four CD's. Contested as follows:

CD 4 15,096 Knox White; 11,424 Ted Adams.
CD 6 2,283 Robbie Cunningham; 2,218 Doug Cooke.

JUNE 14 DEMOCRATIC

Congress Unopposed in five CD's. Contested as follows:

CD 6 65,608 Robert M. Tallon; 8,448 Luther Lightly.

SOUTH DAKOTA

GOVERNOR

George S. Mickelson (R). Elected 1986 to a four-year term.

SENATORS

Thomas A. Daschle (D). Elected 1986 to a six-year term.

Larry Pressler (R). Re-elected 1984 to a six-year term. Previously elected 1978.

REPRESENTATIVE

At-Large. Tim Johnson (D)

POSTWAR VOTE FOR PRESIDENT

								Percentage			
	Total	Republican		Democratic		Other		Total Vote		Major Vote	
Year	Vote	Vote	Candidate	Vote	Candidate	Vote	Plurality	Rep.	Dem.	Rep.	Dem.
1988	312,991	165,415	Bush, George	145,560	Dukakis, Michael S.	2,016	19,855 R	52.8%	46.5%	53.2%	46.8%
1984	317,867	200,267	Reagan, Ronald	116,113	Mondale, Walter F.	1,487	84,154 R	63.0%	36.5%	63.3%	36.7%
1980	327,703	198,343	Reagan, Ronald	103,855	Carter, Jimmy	25,505	94,488 R	60.5%	31.7%	65.6%	34.4%
1976	300,678	151,505	Ford, Gerald R.	147,068	Carter, Jimmy	2,105	4,437 R	50.4%	48.9%	50.7%	49.3%
1972	307,415	166,476	Nixon, Richard M.	139,945	McGovern, George S.	994	26,531 R	54.2%	45.5%	54.3%	45.7%
1968	281,264	149,841	Nixon, Richard M.	118,023	Humphrey, Hubert H.	13,400	31,818 R	53.3%	42.0%	55.9%	44.1%
1964	293,118	130,108	Goldwater, Barry M.	163,010	Johnson, Lyndon B.		32,902 D	44.4%	55.6%	44.4%	55.6%
1960	306,487	178,417	Nixon, Richard M.	128,070	Kennedy, John F.		50,347 R	58.2%	41.8%	58.2%	41.8%
1956	293,857	171,569	Eisenhower, Dwight D.	122,288	Stevenson, Adlai E.		49,281 R	58.4%	41.6%	58.4%	41.6%
1952	294,283	203,857	Eisenhower, Dwight D.	90,426	Stevenson, Adlai E.		113,431 R	69.3%	30.7%	69.3%	30.7%
1948	250,105	129,651	Dewey, Thomas E.	117,653	Truman, Harry S.	2,801	11,998 R	51.8%	47.0%	52.4%	47.6%

POSTWAR VOTE FOR GOVERNOR

								Percentage			
	Total	Republican		Democratic		Other	Rep.-Dem.	Total Vote		Major Vote	
Year	Vote	Vote	Candidate	Vote	Candidate	Vote	Plurality	Rep.	Dem.	Rep.	Dem.
1986	294,441	152,543	Mickelson, George S.	141,898	Herseth, R. Lars		10,645 R	51.8%	48.2%	51.8%	48.2%
1982	278,562	197,426	Janklow, William J.	81,136	O'Connor, Michael J.		116,290 R	70.9%	29.1%	70.9%	29.1%
1978	259,795	147,116	Janklow, William J.	112,679	McKellips, Roger		34,437 R	56.6%	43.4%	56.6%	43.4%
1974 **	278,228	129,077	Olson, John E.	149,151	Kneip, Richard F.		20,074 D	46.4%	53.6%	46.4%	53.6%
1972	308,177	123,165	Thompson, Carveth	185,012	Kneip, Richard F.		61,847 D	40.0%	60.0%	40.0%	60.0%
1970	239,963	108,347	Farrar, Frank	131,616	Kneip, Richard F.		23,269 D	45.2%	54.8%	45.2%	54.8%
1968	276,906	159,646	Farrar, Frank	117,260	Chamberlin, Robert		42,386 R	57.7%	42.3%	57.7%	42.3%
1966	228,214	131,710	Boe, Nils A.	96,504	Chamberlin, Robert		35,206 R	57.7%	42.3%	57.7%	42.3%
1964	290,570	150,151	Boe, Nils A.	140,419	Lindley, John F.		9,732 R	51.7%	48.3%	51.7%	48.3%
1962	256,120	143,682	Gubbrud, Archie M.	112,438	Herseth, Ralph		31,244 R	56.1%	43.9%	56.1%	43.9%
1960	304,625	154,530	Gubbrud, Archie M.	150,095	Herseth, Ralph		4,435 R	50.7%	49.3%	50.7%	49.3%
1958	258,281	125,520	Saunders, Phil	132,761	Herseth, Ralph		7,241 D	48.6%	51.4%	48.6%	51.4%
1956	292,017	158,819	Foss, Joe J.	133,198	Herseth, Ralph		25,621 R	54.4%	45.6%	54.4%	45.6%
1954	236,255	133,878	Foss, Joe J.	102,377	Martin, Ed C.		31,501 R	56.7%	43.3%	56.7%	43.3%
1952	289,515	203,102	Anderson, Sigurd	86,413	Iverson, Sherman A.		116,689 R	70.2%	29.8%	70.2%	29.8%
1950	253,316	154,254	Anderson, Sigurd	99,062	Robbie, Joseph		55,192 R	60.9%	39.1%	60.9%	39.1%
1948	245,372	149,883	Mickelson, George	95,489	Volz, Harold J.		54,394 R	61.1%	38.9%	61.1%	38.9%
1946	162,292	108,998	Mickelson, George	53,294	Haeder, Richard		55,704 R	67.2%	32.8%	67.2%	32.8%

The term of office of South Dakota's Governor was increased from two to four years effective with the 1974 election.

SOUTH DAKOTA

POSTWAR VOTE FOR SENATOR

Year	Total Vote	Republican Vote	Republican Candidate	Democratic Vote	Democratic Candidate	Other Vote	Rep.-Dem. Plurality	Percentage Total Vote Rep.	Percentage Total Vote Dem.	Percentage Major Vote Rep.	Percentage Major Vote Dem.
1986	295,830	143,173	Abdnor, James	152,657	Daschle, Thomas A.		9,484 D	48.4%	51.6%	48.4%	51.6%
1984	315,713	235,176	Pressler, Larry	80,537	Cunningham, George V.		154,639 R	74.5%	25.5%	74.5%	25.5%
1980	327,478	190,594	Abdnor, James	129,018	McGovern, George S.	7,866	61,576 R	58.2%	39.4%	59.6%	40.4%
1978	255,599	170,832	Pressler, Larry	84,767	Barnett, Don		86,065 R	66.8%	33.2%	66.8%	33.2%
1974	278,884	130,955	Thorsness, Leo K.	147,929	McGovern, George S.		16,974 D	47.0%	53.0%	47.0%	53.0%
1972	306,386	131,613	Hirsch, Robert W.	174,773	Abourezk, James		43,160 D	43.0%	57.0%	43.0%	57.0%
1968	279,912	120,951	Gubbrud, Archie M.	158,961	McGovern, George S.		38,010 D	43.2%	56.8%	43.2%	56.8%
1966	227,080	150,517	Mundt, Karl E.	76,563	Wright, Donn H.		73,954 R	66.3%	33.7%	66.3%	33.7%
1962	254,319	126,861	Bottum, Joe H.	127,458	McGovern, George S.		597 D	49.9%	50.1%	49.9%	50.1%
1960	305,442	160,181	Mundt, Karl E.	145,261	McGovern, George S.		14,920 R	52.4%	47.6%	52.4%	47.6%
1956	290,622	147,621	Case, Francis	143,001	Holum, Kenneth		4,620 R	50.8%	49.2%	50.8%	49.2%
1954	235,745	135,071	Mundt, Karl E.	100,674	Holum, Kenneth		34,397 R	57.3%	42.7%	57.3%	42.7%
1950	251,362	160,670	Case, Francis	90,692	Engel, John A.		69,978 R	63.9%	36.1%	63.9%	36.1%
1948	242,833	144,084	Mundt, Karl E.	98,749	Engel, John A.		45,335 R	59.3%	40.7%	59.3%	40.7%

SOUTH DAKOTA

One At Large

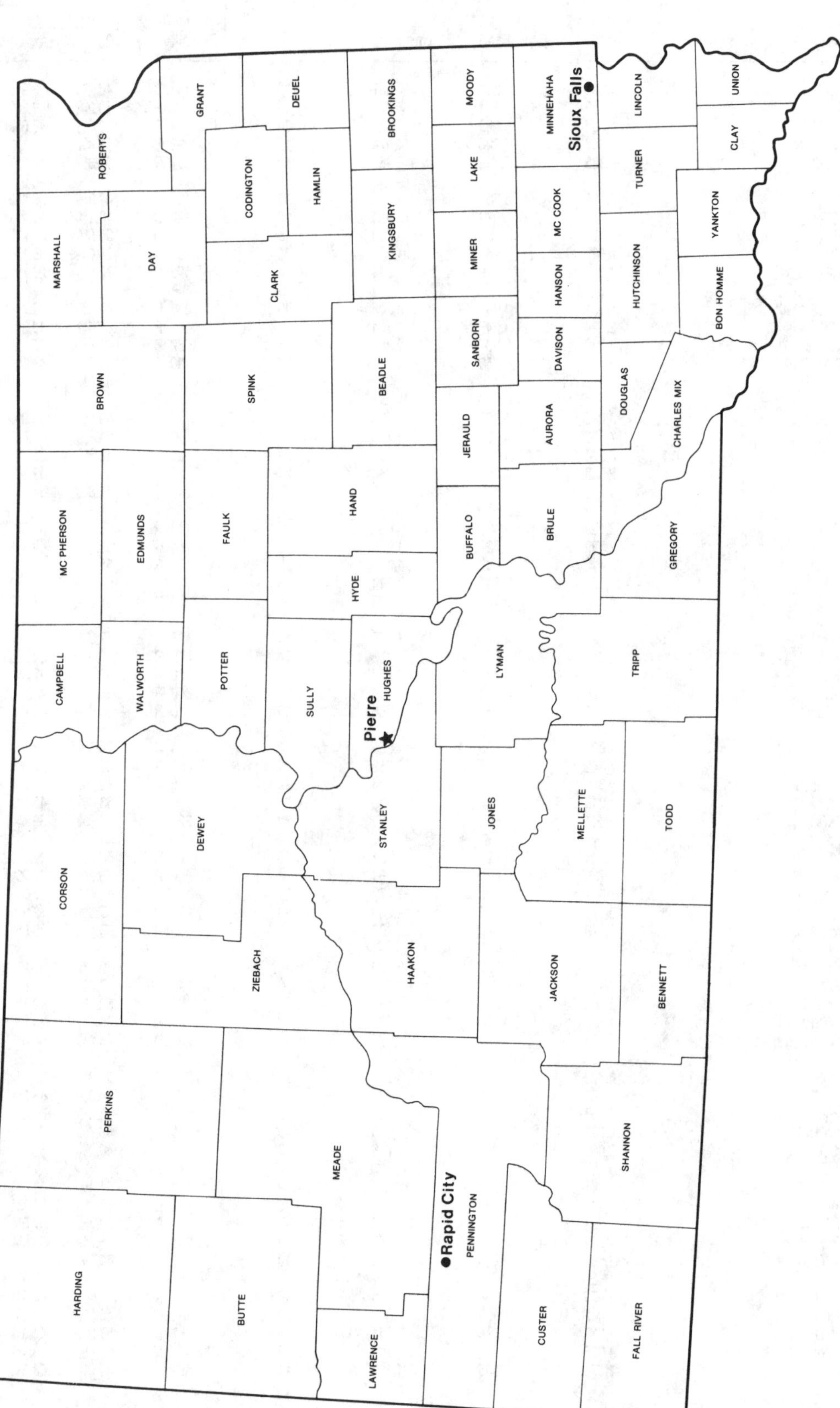

SOUTH DAKOTA

PRESIDENT 1988

1980 Census Population	County	Total Vote	Republican	Democratic	Other	Rep.-Dem. Plurality	Percentage: Total Vote Rep.	Percentage: Total Vote Dem.	Percentage: Major Vote Rep.	Percentage: Major Vote Dem.
3,628	AURORA	1,854	856	987	11	131 D	46.2%	53.2%	46.4%	53.6%
19,195	BEADLE	9,180	4,611	4,523	46	88 R	50.2%	49.3%	50.5%	49.5%
3,044	BENNETT	1,262	663	579	20	84 R	52.5%	45.9%	53.4%	46.6%
8,059	BONHOMME	3,417	1,826	1,574	17	252 R	53.4%	46.1%	53.7%	46.3%
24,332	BROOKINGS	10,305	5,394	4,860	51	534 R	52.3%	47.2%	52.6%	47.4%
36,962	BROWN	17,302	8,537	8,673	92	136 D	49.3%	50.1%	49.6%	50.4%
5,245	BRULE	1,974	971	991	12	20 D	49.2%	50.2%	49.5%	50.5%
1,795	BUFFALO	490	151	334	5	183 D	30.8%	68.2%	31.1%	68.9%
8,372	BUTTE	3,582	2,291	1,256	35	1,035 R	64.0%	35.1%	64.6%	35.4%
2,243	CAMPBELL	1,252	909	334	9	575 R	72.6%	26.7%	73.1%	26.9%
9,680	CHARLES MIX	4,184	1,966	2,205	13	239 D	47.0%	52.7%	47.1%	52.9%
4,894	CLARK	2,424	1,247	1,164	13	83 R	51.4%	48.0%	51.7%	48.3%
13,689	CLAY	5,200	2,307	2,859	34	552 D	44.4%	55.0%	44.7%	55.3%
20,885	CODINGTON	9,714	5,050	4,570	94	480 R	52.0%	47.0%	52.5%	47.5%
5,196	CORSON	1,448	710	722	16	12 D	49.0%	49.9%	49.6%	50.4%
6,000	CUSTER	3,036	1,806	1,180	50	626 R	59.5%	38.9%	60.5%	39.5%
17,820	DAVISON	7,786	4,024	3,705	57	319 R	51.7%	47.6%	52.1%	47.9%
8,133	DAY	3,774	1,616	2,137	21	521 D	42.8%	56.6%	43.1%	56.9%
5,289	DEUEL	2,528	1,251	1,246	31	5 R	49.5%	49.3%	50.1%	49.9%
5,366	DEWEY	1,789	765	1,007	17	242 D	42.8%	56.3%	43.2%	56.8%
4,181	DOUGLAS	2,139	1,438	695	6	743 R	67.2%	32.5%	67.4%	32.6%
5,159	EDMUNDS	2,599	1,327	1,259	13	68 R	51.1%	48.4%	51.3%	48.7%
8,439	FALL RIVER	3,417	2,002	1,380	35	622 R	58.6%	40.4%	59.2%	40.8%
3,327	FAULK	1,561	842	714	5	128 R	53.9%	45.7%	54.1%	45.9%
9,013	GRANT	4,172	2,148	1,988	36	160 R	51.5%	47.7%	51.9%	48.1%
6,015	GREGORY	2,722	1,566	1,138	18	428 R	57.5%	41.8%	57.9%	42.1%
2,794	HAAKON	1,351	958	379	14	579 R	70.9%	28.1%	71.7%	28.3%
5,261	HAMLIN	2,651	1,380	1,258	13	122 R	52.1%	47.5%	52.3%	47.7%
4,948	HAND	2,578	1,461	1,101	16	360 R	56.7%	42.7%	57.0%	43.0%
3,415	HANSON	1,572	786	776	10	10 R	50.0%	49.4%	50.3%	49.7%
1,700	HARDING	900	633	259	8	374 R	70.3%	28.8%	71.0%	29.0%
14,220	HUGHES	7,442	4,545	2,853	44	1,692 R	61.1%	38.3%	61.4%	38.6%
9,350	HUTCHINSON	4,316	2,700	1,594	22	1,106 R	62.6%	36.9%	62.9%	37.1%
2,069	HYDE	1,019	546	436	37	110 R	53.6%	42.8%	55.6%	44.4%
3,437	JACKSON	1,141	671	450	20	221 R	58.8%	39.4%	59.9%	40.1%
2,929	JERAULD	1,534	777	751	6	26 R	50.7%	49.0%	50.9%	49.1%
1,463	JONES	786	521	261	4	260 R	66.3%	33.2%	66.6%	33.4%
6,679	KINGSBURY	3,087	1,592	1,472	23	120 R	51.6%	47.7%	52.0%	48.0%
10,724	LAKE	5,122	2,439	2,663	20	224 D	47.6%	52.0%	47.8%	52.2%
18,339	LAWRENCE	9,379	5,570	3,705	104	1,865 R	59.4%	39.5%	60.1%	39.9%
13,942	LINCOLN	6,757	3,537	3,190	30	347 R	52.3%	47.2%	52.6%	47.4%
3,864	LYMAN	1,480	843	631	6	212 R	57.0%	42.6%	57.2%	42.8%
6,444	MCCOOK	3,002	1,501	1,492	9	9 R	50.0%	49.7%	50.2%	49.8%
4,027	MCPHERSON	1,936	1,358	571	7	787 R	70.1%	29.5%	70.4%	29.6%
5,404	MARSHALL	2,525	1,142	1,372	11	230 D	45.2%	54.3%	45.4%	54.6%
20,717	MEADE	8,473	5,189	3,212	72	1,977 R	61.2%	37.9%	61.8%	38.2%
2,249	MELLETTE	852	460	385	7	75 R	54.0%	45.2%	54.4%	45.6%
3,739	MINER	1,755	795	955	5	160 D	45.3%	54.4%	45.4%	54.6%
109,435	MINNEHAHA	56,095	26,765	29,135	195	2,370 D	47.7%	51.9%	47.9%	52.1%
6,692	MOODY	2,889	1,161	1,715	13	554 D	40.2%	59.4%	40.4%	59.6%
70,361	PENNINGTON	31,757	19,510	12,068	179	7,442 R	61.4%	38.0%	61.8%	38.2%
4,700	PERKINS	2,197	1,326	851	20	475 R	60.4%	38.7%	60.9%	39.1%
3,674	POTTER	1,893	1,175	701	17	474 R	62.1%	37.0%	62.6%	37.4%
10,911	ROBERTS	4,311	2,012	2,267	32	255 D	46.7%	52.6%	47.0%	53.0%
3,213	SANBORN	1,595	815	770	10	45 R	51.1%	48.3%	51.4%	48.6%
11,323	SHANNON	1,479	256	1,206	17	950 D	17.3%	81.5%	17.5%	82.5%
9,201	SPINK	4,062	1,969	2,071	22	102 D	48.5%	51.0%	48.7%	51.3%
2,533	STANLEY	1,219	698	511	10	187 R	57.3%	41.9%	57.7%	42.3%
1,990	SULLY	1,006	571	393	42	178 R	56.8%	39.1%	59.2%	40.8%
7,328	TODD	1,676	535	1,117	24	582 D	31.9%	66.6%	32.4%	67.6%

SOUTH DAKOTA

PRESIDENT 1988

1980 Census Population	County	Total Vote	Republican	Democratic	Other	Rep.-Dem. Plurality	Percentage Total Vote Rep.	Percentage Total Vote Dem.	Percentage Major Vote Rep.	Percentage Major Vote Dem.
7,268	TRIPP	3,356	2,113	1,219	24	894 R	63.0%	36.3%	63.4%	36.6%
9,255	TURNER	4,239	2,436	1,780	23	656 R	57.5%	42.0%	57.8%	42.2%
10,938	UNION	4,550	1,907	2,612	31	705 D	41.9%	57.4%	42.2%	57.8%
7,011	WALWORTH	3,060	1,940	1,094	26	846 R	63.4%	35.8%	63.9%	36.1%
18,952	YANKTON	8,043	4,186	3,777	80	409 R	52.0%	47.0%	52.6%	47.4%
2,308	ZIEBACH	795	362	427	6	65 D	45.5%	53.7%	45.9%	54.1%
690,768	TOTAL	312,991	165,415	145,560	2,016	19,855 R	52.8%	46.5%	53.2%	46.8%

SOUTH DAKOTA

CONGRESS

CD	Year	Total Vote	Republican Vote	Republican Candidate	Democratic Vote	Democratic Candidate	Other Vote	Rep.-Dem. Plurality	Percentage Total Vote Rep.	Percentage Total Vote Dem.	Percentage Major Vote Rep.	Percentage Major Vote Dem.
AL	1988	311,916	88,157	VOLK, DAVID	223,759	JOHNSON, TIM		135,602 D	28.3%	71.7%	28.3%	71.7%
AL	1986	289,723	118,261	BELL, DALE	171,462	JOHNSON, TIM		53,201 D	40.8%	59.2%	40.8%	59.2%
AL	1984	316,222	134,821	BELL, DALE	181,401	DASCHLE, THOMAS A.		46,580 D	42.6%	57.4%	42.6%	57.4%
AL	1982	275,652	133,530	ROBERTS, CLINT	142,122	DASCHLE, THOMAS A.		8,592 D	48.4%	51.6%	48.4%	51.6%

SOUTH DAKOTA

1988 GENERAL ELECTION

President Other vote was 1,060 Libertarian (Paul); 730 New Alliance (Fulani); 226 Socialist Workers (Warren).

Congress

1988 PRIMARIES

JUNE 7 REPUBLICAN

Congress Unopposed at-large.

JUNE 7 DEMOCRATIC

Congress Unopposed at-large.

TENNESSEE

GOVERNOR

Ned McWherter (D). Elected 1986 to a four-year term.

SENATORS

Albert Gore, Jr. (D). Elected 1984 to a six-year term.

James R. Sasser (D). Re-elected 1988 to a six-year term. Previously elected 1982, 1976.

REPRESENTATIVES

1. James H. Quillen (R)
2. John J. Duncan, Jr. (R)
3. Marilyn Lloyd (D)
4. Jim Cooper (D)
5. Bob Clement (D)
6. Bart Gordon (D)
7. Don Sundquist (R)
8. John Tanner (D)
9. Harold E. Ford (D)

POSTWAR VOTE FOR PRESIDENT

								Percentage			
	Total	Republican		Democratic		Other		Total Vote		Major Vote	
Year	Vote	Vote	Candidate	Vote	Candidate	Vote	Plurality	Rep.	Dem.	Rep.	Dem.
1988	1,636,250	947,233	Bush, George	679,794	Dukakis, Michael S.	9,223	267,439 R	57.9%	41.5%	58.2%	41.8%
1984	1,711,994	990,212	Reagan, Ronald	711,714	Mondale, Walter F.	10,068	278,498 R	57.8%	41.6%	58.2%	41.8%
1980	1,617,616	787,761	Reagan, Ronald	783,051	Carter, Jimmy	46,804	4,710 R	48.7%	48.4%	50.1%	49.9%
1976	1,476,345	633,969	Ford, Gerald R.	825,879	Carter, Jimmy	16,497	191,910 D	42.9%	55.9%	43.4%	56.6%
1972	1,201,182	813,147	Nixon, Richard M.	357,293	McGovern, George S.	30,742	455,854 R	67.7%	29.7%	69.5%	30.5%
1968 **	1,248,617	472,592	Nixon, Richard M.	351,233	Humphrey, Hubert H.	424,792	47,800 R	37.8%	28.1%	57.4%	42.6%
1964	1,143,946	508,965	Goldwater, Barry M.	634,947	Johnson, Lyndon B.	34	125,982 D	44.5%	55.5%	44.5%	55.5%
1960	1,051,792	556,577	Nixon, Richard M.	481,453	Kennedy, John F.	13,762	75,124 R	52.9%	45.8%	53.6%	46.4%
1956	939,404	462,288	Eisenhower, Dwight D.	456,507	Stevenson, Adlai E.	20,609	5,781 R	49.2%	48.6%	50.3%	49.7%
1952	892,553	446,147	Eisenhower, Dwight D.	443,710	Stevenson, Adlai E.	2,696	2,437 R	50.0%	49.7%	50.1%	49.9%
1948	550,283	202,914	Dewey, Thomas E.	270,402	Truman, Harry S.	76,967	67,488 D	36.9%	49.1%	42.9%	57.1%

In 1968 other vote was American (Wallace).

POSTWAR VOTE FOR GOVERNOR

								Percentage			
	Total	Republican		Democratic		Other	Rep.-Dem.	Total Vote		Major Vote	
Year	Vote	Vote	Candidate	Vote	Candidate	Vote	Plurality	Rep.	Dem.	Rep.	Dem.
1986	1,210,339	553,449	Dunn, Winfield	656,602	McWherter, Ned	288	103,153 D	45.7%	54.2%	45.7%	54.3%
1982	1,238,927	737,963	Alexander, Lamar	500,937	Tyree, Randy	27	237,026 R	59.6%	40.4%	59.6%	40.4%
1978	1,189,695	661,959	Alexander, Lamar	523,495	Butcher, Jake	4,241	138,464 R	55.6%	44.0%	55.8%	44.2%
1974	1,040,714	455,467	Alexander, Lamar	576,833	Blanton, Ray	8,414	121,366 D	43.8%	55.4%	44.1%	55.9%
1970	1,108,247	575,777	Dunn, Winfield	509,521	Hooker, John J.	22,949	66,256 R	52.0%	46.0%	53.1%	46.9%
1966 **	656,566		—	532,998	Ellington, Buford	123,568	532,998 D		81.2%		100.0%
1962 **	621,064	100,190	Patty, Hubert D.	315,648	Clement, Frank G.	205,226	215,458 D	16.1%	50.8%	24.1%	75.9%
1958 **	432,545	35,938	Wall, Thomas P.	248,874	Ellington, Buford	147,733	212,936 D	8.3%	57.5%	12.6%	87.4%
1954 **	322,586		—	281,291	Clement, Frank G.	41,295	281,291 D		87.2%		100.0%
1952	806,771	166,377	Witt, R. Beecher	640,290	Clement, Frank G.	104	473,913 D	20.6%	79.4%	20.6%	79.4%
1950	236,194		—	184,437	Browning, Gordon	51,757	184,437 D		78.1%		100.0%
1948	543,881	179,957	Acuff, Roy	363,903	Browning, Gordon	21	183,946 D	33.1%	66.9%	33.1%	66.9%
1946	229,456	73,222	Lowe, W. O.	149,937	McCord, Jim Nance	6,297	76,715 D	31.9%	65.3%	32.8%	67.2%

The term of office of Tennessee's Governor was increased from two to four years effective with the 1954 election. In 1958 Jim Nance McCord (Independent) received 136,399 votes (31.5% of the total vote) and ran second. In 1962 other vote was 203,765 William R. Anderson (Independent) who ran second; 1,441 E. B.Bowles (Independent) and 20 scattered. In 1966 other vote was 64,602 H. L.Crawford (Independent); 50,221 Charles Moffett (Independent); 8,407 Charles G. Vick (Independent) and 338 scattered.

TENNESSEE

POSTWAR VOTE FOR SENATOR

Year	Total Vote	Republican Vote	Republican Candidate	Democratic Vote	Democratic Candidate	Other Vote	Rep.-Dem. Plurality	Percentage Total Vote Rep.	Percentage Total Vote Dem.	Percentage Major Vote Rep.	Percentage Major Vote Dem.
1988	1,567,181	541,033	Anderson, Bill	1,020,061	Sasser, James R.	6,087	479,028 D	34.5%	65.1%	34.7%	65.3%
1984	1,648,064	557,016	Ashe, Victor	1,000,607	Gore, Albert, Jr.	90,441	443,591 D	33.8%	60.7%	35.8%	64.2%
1982	1,259,785	479,642	Beard, Robin L.	780,113	Sasser, James R.	30	300,471 D	38.1%	61.9%	38.1%	61.9%
1978	1,157,094	642,644	Baker, Howard H., Jr.	466,228	Eskind, Jane	48,222	176,416 R	55.5%	40.3%	58.0%	42.0%
1976	1,432,046	673,231	Brock, William E.	751,180	Sasser, James R.	7,635	77,949 D	47.0%	52.5%	47.3%	52.7%
1972	1,164,195	716,539	Baker, Howard H., Jr.	440,599	Blanton, Ray	7,057	275,940 R	61.5%	37.8%	61.9%	38.1%
1970	1,097,041	562,645	Brock, William E.	519,858	Gore, Albert	14,538	42,787 R	51.3%	47.4%	52.0%	48.0%
1966	866,961	483,063	Baker, Howard H., Jr.	383,843	Clement, Frank G.	55	99,220 R	55.7%	44.3%	55.7%	44.3%
1964	1,064,018	493,475	Kuykendall, Daniel H.	570,542	Gore, Albert	1	77,067 D	46.4%	53.6%	46.4%	53.6%
1964 S	1,091,093	517,330	Baker, Howard H., Jr.	568,905	Bass, Ross	4,858	51,575 D	47.4%	52.1%	47.6%	52.4%
1960	828,519	234,053	Frazier, A. Bradley	594,460	Kefauver, Estes	6	360,407 D	28.2%	71.7%	28.2%	71.8%
1958	401,666	76,371	Atkins, Hobart F.	317,324	Gore, Albert	7,971	240,953 D	19.0%	79.0%	19.4%	80.6%
1954	356,094	106,971	Wall, Thomas P.	249,121	Kefauver, Estes	2	142,150 D	30.0%	70.0%	30.0%	70.0%
1952	735,219	153,479	Atkins, Hobart F.	545,432	Gore, Albert	36,308	391,953 D	20.9%	74.2%	22.0%	78.0%
1948	499,218	166,947	Reece, B. Carroll	326,142	Kefauver, Estes	6,129	159,195 D	33.4%	65.3%	33.9%	66.1%
1946	218,714	57,238	Ladd, William B.	145,654	McKellar, Kenneth	15,822	88,416 D	26.2%	66.6%	28.2%	71.8%

One of the 1964 elections was for a short term to fill a vacancy.

TENNESSEE

Districts Established June 18, 1981

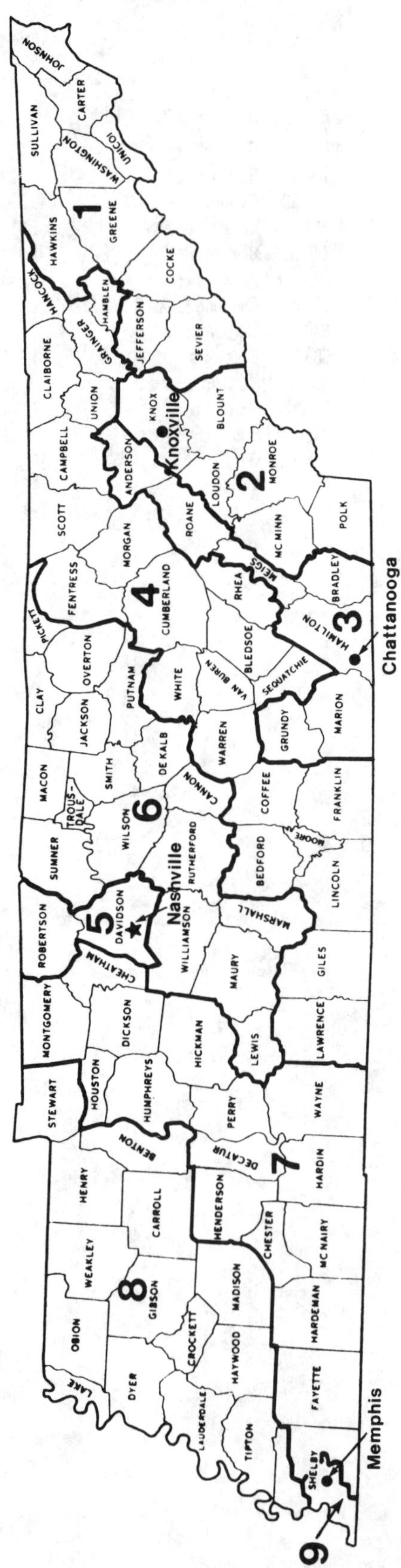

TENNESSEE

PRESIDENT 1988

1980 Census Population	County	Total Vote	Republican	Democratic	Other	Rep.-Dem. Plurality	Percentage Total Vote Rep.	Total Vote Dem.	Major Vote Rep.	Major Vote Dem.
67,346	ANDERSON	24,788	15,056	9,589	143	5,467 R	60.7%	38.7%	61.1%	38.9%
27,916	BEDFORD	8,939	4,856	4,046	37	810 R	54.3%	45.3%	54.5%	45.5%
14,901	BENTON	5,009	2,167	2,826	16	659 D	43.3%	56.4%	43.4%	56.6%
9,478	BLEDSOE	3,147	1,858	1,274	15	584 R	59.0%	40.5%	59.3%	40.7%
77,770	BLOUNT	29,776	20,027	9,602	147	10,425 R	67.3%	32.2%	67.6%	32.4%
67,547	BRADLEY	22,031	15,829	6,122	80	9,707 R	71.8%	27.8%	72.1%	27.9%
34,923	CAMPBELL	9,416	5,197	4,188	31	1,009 R	55.2%	44.5%	55.4%	44.6%
10,234	CANNON	3,348	1,604	1,726	18	122 D	47.9%	51.6%	48.2%	51.8%
28,285	CARROLL	9,830	5,635	4,151	44	1,484 R	57.3%	42.2%	57.6%	42.4%
50,205	CARTER	16,778	12,036	4,634	108	7,402 R	71.7%	27.6%	72.2%	27.8%
21,616	CHEATHAM	7,250	4,132	3,067	51	1,065 R	57.0%	42.3%	57.4%	42.6%
12,727	CHESTER	4,555	2,781	1,757	17	1,024 R	61.1%	38.6%	61.3%	38.7%
24,595	CLAIBORNE	7,082	4,071	2,977	34	1,094 R	57.5%	42.0%	57.8%	42.2%
7,676	CLAY	2,493	1,291	1,183	19	108 R	51.8%	47.5%	52.2%	47.8%
28,792	COCKE	7,579	5,430	2,115	34	3,315 R	71.6%	27.9%	72.0%	28.0%
38,311	COFFEE	13,615	7,837	5,686	92	2,151 R	57.6%	41.8%	58.0%	42.0%
14,941	CROCKETT	3,970	2,214	1,742	14	472 R	55.8%	43.9%	56.0%	44.0%
28,676	CUMBERLAND	11,594	7,557	3,964	73	3,593 R	65.2%	34.2%	65.6%	34.4%
477,811	DAVIDSON	188,946	98,599	89,270	1,077	9,329 R	52.2%	47.2%	52.5%	47.5%
10,857	DECATUR	4,191	2,286	1,880	25	406 R	54.5%	44.9%	54.9%	45.1%
13,589	DE KALB	4,581	2,098	2,452	31	354 D	45.8%	53.5%	46.1%	53.9%
30,037	DICKSON	10,536	5,343	5,129	64	214 R	50.7%	48.7%	51.0%	49.0%
34,663	DYER	10,243	6,508	3,690	45	2,818 R	63.5%	36.0%	63.8%	36.2%
25,305	FAYETTE	6,921	3,573	3,292	56	281 R	51.6%	47.6%	52.0%	48.0%
14,826	FENTRESS	4,992	3,103	1,856	33	1,247 R	62.2%	37.2%	62.6%	37.4%
31,983	FRANKLIN	10,886	5,381	5,442	63	61 D	49.4%	50.0%	49.7%	50.3%
49,467	GIBSON	16,038	8,415	7,542	81	873 R	52.5%	47.0%	52.7%	47.3%
24,625	GILES	7,478	3,518	3,918	42	400 D	47.0%	52.4%	47.3%	52.7%
16,751	GRAINGER	4,174	2,734	1,423	17	1,311 R	65.5%	34.1%	65.8%	34.2%
54,422	GREENE	17,132	11,947	5,077	108	6,870 R	69.7%	29.6%	70.2%	29.8%
13,787	GRUNDY	3,857	1,429	2,415	13	986 D	37.0%	62.6%	37.2%	62.8%
49,300	HAMBLEN	15,565	10,418	5,061	86	5,357 R	66.9%	32.5%	67.3%	32.7%
287,740	HAMILTON	109,709	68,111	40,990	608	27,121 R	62.1%	37.4%	62.4%	37.6%
6,887	HANCOCK	2,082	1,303	737	42	566 R	62.6%	35.4%	63.9%	36.1%
23,873	HARDEMAN	7,138	3,547	3,526	65	21 R	49.7%	49.4%	50.1%	49.9%
22,280	HARDIN	7,089	4,252	2,808	29	1,444 R	60.0%	39.6%	60.2%	39.8%
43,751	HAWKINS	14,646	9,356	5,212	78	4,144 R	63.9%	35.6%	64.2%	35.8%
20,318	HAYWOOD	5,640	2,687	2,923	30	236 D	47.6%	51.8%	47.9%	52.1%
21,390	HENDERSON	7,819	5,418	2,296	105	3,122 R	69.3%	29.4%	70.2%	29.8%
28,656	HENRY	9,975	4,784	5,138	53	354 D	48.0%	51.5%	48.2%	51.8%
15,151	HICKMAN	4,918	2,246	2,643	29	397 D	45.7%	53.7%	45.9%	54.1%
6,871	HOUSTON	2,367	882	1,467	18	585 D	37.3%	62.0%	37.5%	62.5%
15,957	HUMPHREYS	5,188	2,132	3,037	19	905 D	41.1%	58.5%	41.2%	58.8%
9,398	JACKSON	3,144	1,168	1,962	14	794 D	37.2%	62.4%	37.3%	62.7%
31,284	JEFFERSON	10,069	6,832	3,168	69	3,664 R	67.9%	31.5%	68.3%	31.7%
13,745	JOHNSON	5,079	3,715	1,329	35	2,386 R	73.1%	26.2%	73.7%	26.3%
319,694	KNOX	115,521	73,092	41,829	600	31,263 R	63.3%	36.2%	63.6%	36.4%
7,455	LAKE	1,750	806	935	9	129 D	46.1%	53.4%	46.3%	53.7%
24,555	LAUDERDALE	6,639	3,308	3,296	35	12 R	49.8%	49.6%	50.1%	49.9%
34,110	LAWRENCE	11,183	6,273	4,903	7	1,370 R	56.1%	43.8%	56.1%	43.9%
9,700	LEWIS	2,761	1,324	1,419	18	95 D	48.0%	51.4%	48.3%	51.7%
26,483	LINCOLN	8,017	4,288	3,672	57	616 R	53.5%	45.8%	53.9%	46.1%
28,553	LOUDON	10,679	7,122	3,480	77	3,642 R	66.7%	32.6%	67.2%	32.8%
41,878	MCMINN	13,078	8,462	4,568	48	3,894 R	64.7%	34.9%	64.9%	35.1%
22,525	MCNAIRY	8,191	4,625	3,510	56	1,115 R	56.5%	42.9%	56.9%	43.1%
15,700	MACON	4,531	2,962	1,538	31	1,424 R	65.4%	33.9%	65.8%	34.2%
74,546	MADISON	28,039	16,952	11,001	86	5,951 R	60.5%	39.2%	60.6%	39.4%
24,416	MARION	8,618	4,407	4,175	36	232 R	51.1%	48.4%	51.4%	48.6%
19,698	MARSHALL	5,791	2,975	2,795	21	180 R	51.4%	48.3%	51.6%	48.4%
51,095	MAURY	14,788	8,397	6,280	111	2,117 R	56.8%	42.5%	57.2%	42.8%

TENNESSEE

PRESIDENT 1988

1980 Census Population	County	Total Vote	Republican	Democratic	Other	Rep.-Dem. Plurality	Percentage Total Vote Rep.	Total Vote Dem.	Major Vote Rep.	Major Vote Dem.
7,431	MEIGS	2,568	1,507	1,048	13	459 R	58.7%	40.8%	59.0%	41.0%
28,700	MONROE	10,393	6,355	4,000	38	2,355 R	61.1%	38.5%	61.4%	38.6%
83,342	MONTGOMERY	21,855	12,599	9,145	111	3,454 R	57.6%	41.8%	57.9%	42.1%
4,510	MOORE	1,530	786	731	13	55 R	51.4%	47.8%	51.8%	48.2%
16,604	MORGAN	4,546	2,576	1,941	29	635 R	56.7%	42.7%	57.0%	43.0%
32,781	OBION	10,858	6,037	4,785	36	1,252 R	55.6%	44.1%	55.8%	44.2%
17,575	OVERTON	4,397	1,873	2,511	13	638 D	42.6%	57.1%	42.7%	57.3%
6,111	PERRY	2,076	854	1,208	14	354 D	41.1%	58.2%	41.4%	58.6%
4,358	PICKETT	1,756	1,118	634	4	484 R	63.7%	36.1%	63.8%	36.2%
13,602	POLK	4,391	2,297	2,073	21	224 R	52.3%	47.2%	52.6%	47.4%
47,690	PUTNAM	16,285	9,547	6,606	132	2,941 R	58.6%	40.6%	59.1%	40.9%
24,235	RHEA	7,776	5,144	2,595	37	2,549 R	66.2%	33.4%	66.5%	33.5%
48,425	ROANE	17,497	10,881	6,535	81	4,346 R	62.2%	37.3%	62.5%	37.5%
37,021	ROBERTSON	11,672	5,714	5,884	74	170 D	49.0%	50.4%	49.3%	50.7%
84,058	RUTHERFORD	32,801	20,397	12,245	159	8,152 R	62.2%	37.3%	62.5%	37.5%
19,259	SCOTT	4,193	2,562	1,611	20	951 R	61.1%	38.4%	61.4%	38.6%
8,605	SEQUATCHIE	2,869	1,659	1,196	14	463 R	57.8%	41.7%	58.1%	41.9%
41,418	SEVIER	15,631	11,920	3,643	68	8,277 R	76.3%	23.3%	76.6%	23.4%
777,113	SHELBY	308,988	157,457	149,759	1,772	7,698 R	51.0%	48.5%	51.3%	48.7%
14,935	SMITH	4,686	2,138	2,522	26	384 D	45.6%	53.8%	45.9%	54.1%
8,665	STEWART	3,296	1,302	1,979	15	677 D	39.5%	60.0%	39.7%	60.3%
143,968	SULLIVAN	50,977	32,996	17,396	585	15,600 R	64.7%	34.1%	65.5%	34.5%
85,790	SUMNER	31,389	19,523	11,702	164	7,821 R	62.2%	37.3%	62.5%	37.5%
32,930	TIPTON	9,918	6,052	3,824	42	2,228 R	61.0%	38.6%	61.3%	38.7%
6,137	TROUSDALE	2,173	969	1,193	11	224 D	44.6%	54.9%	44.8%	55.2%
16,362	UNICOI	5,486	3,664	1,794	28	1,870 R	66.8%	32.7%	67.1%	32.9%
11,707	UNION	3,564	2,110	1,431	23	679 R	59.2%	40.2%	59.6%	40.4%
4,728	VAN BUREN	1,580	780	796	4	16 D	49.4%	50.4%	49.5%	50.5%
32,653	WARREN	9,218	4,529	4,646	43	117 D	49.1%	50.4%	49.4%	50.6%
88,755	WASHINGTON	29,887	19,615	10,087	185	9,528 R	65.6%	33.8%	66.0%	34.0%
13,946	WAYNE	4,951	3,405	1,516	30	1,889 R	68.8%	30.6%	69.2%	30.8%
32,896	WEAKLEY	9,989	5,701	4,239	49	1,462 R	57.1%	42.4%	57.4%	42.6%
19,567	WHITE	5,249	2,646	2,562	41	84 R	50.4%	48.8%	50.8%	49.2%
58,108	WILLIAMSON	28,823	20,847	7,864	112	12,983 R	72.3%	27.3%	72.6%	27.4%
56,064	WILSON	21,793	13,317	8,360	116	4,957 R	61.1%	38.4%	61.4%	38.6%
4,591,120	TOTAL	1,636,250	947,233	679,794	9,223	267,439 R	57.9%	41.5%	58.2%	41.8%

TENNESSEE

SENATOR 1988

1980 Census Population	County	Total Vote	Republican	Democratic	Other	Rep.-Dem. Plurality	Percentage Total Vote Rep.	Total Vote Dem.	Major Vote Rep.	Major Vote Dem.
67,346	ANDERSON	23,488	8,459	14,997	32	6,538 D	36.0%	63.8%	36.1%	63.9%
27,916	BEDFORD	8,464	2,182	6,275	7	4,093 D	25.8%	74.1%	25.8%	74.2%
14,901	BENTON	5,049	998	4,042	9	3,044 D	19.8%	80.1%	19.8%	80.2%
9,478	BLEDSOE	3,182	1,353	1,824	5	471 D	42.5%	57.3%	42.6%	57.4%
77,770	BLOUNT	28,095	13,016	15,039	40	2,023 D	46.3%	53.5%	46.4%	53.6%
67,547	BRADLEY	22,455	10,578	11,834	43	1,256 D	47.1%	52.7%	47.2%	52.8%
34,923	CAMPBELL	8,783	2,919	5,852	12	2,933 D	33.2%	66.6%	33.3%	66.7%
10,234	CANNON	3,183	728	2,445	10	1,717 D	22.9%	76.8%	22.9%	77.1%
28,285	CARROLL	8,954	2,759	6,188	7	3,429 D	30.8%	69.1%	30.8%	69.2%
50,205	CARTER	15,266	6,751	8,484	31	1,733 D	44.2%	55.6%	44.3%	55.7%
21,616	CHEATHAM	6,775	1,870	4,890	15	3,020 D	27.6%	72.2%	27.7%	72.3%
12,727	CHESTER	4,274	1,612	2,659	3	1,047 D	37.7%	62.2%	37.7%	62.3%
24,595	CLAIBORNE	6,853	2,273	4,568	12	2,295 D	33.2%	66.7%	33.2%	66.8%
7,676	CLAY	2,197	673	1,522	2	849 D	30.6%	69.3%	30.7%	69.3%
28,792	COCKE	6,653	3,119	3,523	11	404 D	46.9%	53.0%	47.0%	53.0%
38,311	COFFEE	13,037	4,069	8,955	13	4,886 D	31.2%	68.7%	31.2%	68.8%
14,941	CROCKETT	3,964	1,093	2,866	5	1,773 D	27.6%	72.3%	27.6%	72.4%
28,676	CUMBERLAND	10,956	4,872	6,074	10	1,202 D	44.5%	55.4%	44.5%	55.5%
477,811	DAVIDSON	183,277	55,900	126,569	808	70,669 D	30.5%	69.1%	30.6%	69.4%
10,857	DECATUR	3,972	1,086	2,885	1	1,799 D	27.3%	72.6%	27.3%	72.7%
13,589	DE KALB	4,302	1,019	3,279	4	2,260 D	23.7%	76.2%	23.7%	76.3%
30,037	DICKSON	9,947	2,621	7,312	14	4,691 D	26.3%	73.5%	26.4%	73.6%
34,663	DYER	10,030	3,015	6,992	23	3,977 D	30.1%	69.7%	30.1%	69.9%
25,305	FAYETTE	6,860	2,109	4,727	24	2,618 D	30.7%	68.9%	30.9%	69.1%
14,826	FENTRESS	4,180	1,295	2,871	14	1,576 D	31.0%	68.7%	31.1%	68.9%
31,983	FRANKLIN	10,297	2,721	7,549	27	4,828 D	26.4%	73.3%	26.5%	73.5%
49,467	GIBSON	14,777	3,350	11,403	24	8,053 D	22.7%	77.2%	22.7%	77.3%
24,625	GILES	6,866	1,787	5,060	19	3,273 D	26.0%	73.7%	26.1%	73.9%
16,751	GRAINGER	3,857	1,727	2,126	4	399 D	44.8%	55.1%	44.8%	55.2%
54,422	GREENE	15,899	6,982	8,895	22	1,913 D	43.9%	55.9%	44.0%	56.0%
13,787	GRUNDY	3,634	672	2,957	5	2,285 D	18.5%	81.4%	18.5%	81.5%
49,300	HAMBLEN	14,427	6,125	8,280	22	2,155 D	42.5%	57.4%	42.5%	57.5%
287,740	HAMILTON	109,782	49,296	60,154	332	10,858 D	44.9%	54.8%	45.0%	55.0%
6,887	HANCOCK	1,751	760	987	4	227 D	43.4%	56.4%	43.5%	56.5%
23,873	HARDEMAN	6,472	1,624	4,828	20	3,204 D	25.1%	74.6%	25.2%	74.8%
22,280	HARDIN	6,436	2,196	4,234	6	2,038 D	34.1%	65.8%	34.2%	65.8%
43,751	HAWKINS	13,792	5,589	8,184	19	2,595 D	40.5%	59.3%	40.6%	59.4%
20,318	HAYWOOD	5,632	1,462	4,150	20	2,688 D	26.0%	73.7%	26.1%	73.9%
21,390	HENDERSON	7,230	2,915	4,309	6	1,394 D	40.3%	59.6%	40.4%	59.6%
28,656	HENRY	9,158	2,044	7,104	10	5,060 D	22.3%	77.6%	22.3%	77.7%
15,151	HICKMAN	4,649	1,079	3,564	6	2,485 D	23.2%	76.7%	23.2%	76.8%
6,871	HOUSTON	2,281	436	1,840	5	1,404 D	19.1%	80.7%	19.2%	80.8%
15,957	HUMPHREYS	5,076	1,000	4,067	9	3,067 D	19.7%	80.1%	19.7%	80.3%
9,398	JACKSON	2,997	506	2,485	6	1,979 D	16.9%	82.9%	16.9%	83.1%
31,284	JEFFERSON	9,317	4,251	5,060	6	809 D	45.6%	54.3%	45.7%	54.3%
13,745	JOHNSON	4,600	2,118	2,459	23	341 D	46.0%	53.5%	46.3%	53.7%
319,694	KNOX	111,963	45,081	66,540	342	21,459 D	40.3%	59.4%	40.4%	59.6%
7,455	LAKE	1,459	268	1,187	4	919 D	18.4%	81.4%	18.4%	81.6%
24,555	LAUDERDALE	6,733	1,555	5,164	14	3,609 D	23.1%	76.7%	23.1%	76.9%
34,110	LAWRENCE	10,403	3,612	6,778	13	3,166 D	34.7%	65.2%	34.8%	65.2%
9,700	LEWIS	2,660	643	2,007	10	1,364 D	24.2%	75.5%	24.3%	75.7%
26,483	LINCOLN	7,106	1,765	5,327	14	3,562 D	24.8%	75.0%	24.9%	75.1%
28,553	LOUDON	9,992	4,087	5,886	19	1,799 D	40.9%	58.9%	41.0%	59.0%
41,878	MCMINN	13,152	5,875	7,262	15	1,387 D	44.7%	55.2%	44.7%	55.3%
22,525	MCNAIRY	7,630	2,419	5,205	6	2,786 D	31.7%	68.2%	31.7%	68.3%
15,700	MACON	4,095	1,370	2,721	4	1,351 D	33.5%	66.4%	33.5%	66.5%
74,546	MADISON	28,021	9,130	18,824	67	9,694 D	32.6%	67.2%	32.7%	67.3%
24,416	MARION	8,733	2,646	6,079	8	3,433 D	30.3%	69.6%	30.3%	69.7%
19,698	MARSHALL	5,494	1,416	4,073	5	2,657 D	25.8%	74.1%	25.8%	74.2%
51,095	MAURY	13,898	4,457	9,431	10	4,974 D	32.1%	67.9%	32.1%	67.9%

TENNESSEE

SENATOR 1988

1980 Census Population	County	Total Vote	Republican	Democratic	Other	Rep.-Dem. Plurality	Percentage Total Vote Rep.	Total Vote Dem.	Major Vote Rep.	Major Vote Dem.
7,431	MEIGS	2,410	991	1,412	7	421 D	41.1%	58.6%	41.2%	58.8%
28,700	MONROE	10,057	4,713	5,337	7	624 D	46.9%	53.1%	46.9%	53.1%
83,342	MONTGOMERY	20,621	6,617	13,959	45	7,342 D	32.1%	67.7%	32.2%	67.8%
4,510	MOORE	1,412	370	1,039	3	669 D	26.2%	73.6%	26.3%	73.7%
16,604	MORGAN	4,288	1,297	2,983	8	1,686 D	30.2%	69.6%	30.3%	69.7%
32,781	OBION	8,958	1,836	7,105	17	5,269 D	20.5%	79.3%	20.5%	79.5%
17,575	OVERTON	4,143	834	3,304	5	2,470 D	20.1%	79.7%	20.2%	79.8%
6,111	PERRY	1,997	391	1,602	4	1,211 D	19.6%	80.2%	19.6%	80.4%
4,358	PICKETT	1,524	703	818	3	115 D	46.1%	53.7%	46.2%	53.8%
13,602	POLK	4,266	1,528	2,738		1,210 D	35.8%	64.2%	35.8%	64.2%
47,690	PUTNAM	15,043	4,304	10,719	20	6,415 D	28.6%	71.3%	28.6%	71.4%
24,235	RHEA	7,394	3,434	3,951	9	517 D	46.4%	53.4%	46.5%	53.5%
48,425	ROANE	16,749	6,152	10,583	14	4,431 D	36.7%	63.2%	36.8%	63.2%
37,021	ROBERTSON	11,040	2,645	8,374	21	5,729 D	24.0%	75.9%	24.0%	76.0%
84,058	RUTHERFORD	31,831	10,687	21,070	74	10,383 D	33.6%	66.2%	33.7%	66.3%
19,259	SCOTT	3,772	1,379	2,385	8	1,006 D	36.6%	63.2%	36.6%	63.4%
8,605	SEQUATCHIE	2,664	876	1,786	2	910 D	32.9%	67.0%	32.9%	67.1%
41,418	SEVIER	14,326	7,642	6,657	27	985 R	53.3%	46.5%	53.4%	46.6%
777,113	SHELBY	296,609	88,768	204,815	3,026	116,047 D	29.9%	69.1%	30.2%	69.8%
14,935	SMITH	4,372	914	3,455	3	2,541 D	20.9%	79.0%	20.9%	79.1%
8,665	STEWART	3,163	707	2,454	2	1,747 D	22.4%	77.6%	22.4%	77.6%
143,968	SULLIVAN	49,193	19,046	29,928	219	10,882 D	38.7%	60.8%	38.9%	61.1%
85,790	SUMNER	29,793	9,903	19,851	39	9,948 D	33.2%	66.6%	33.3%	66.7%
32,930	TIPTON	9,978	3,104	6,853	21	3,749 D	31.1%	68.7%	31.2%	68.8%
6,137	TROUSDALE	1,984	337	1,643	4	1,306 D	17.0%	82.8%	17.0%	83.0%
16,362	UNICOI	5,180	2,241	2,933	6	692 D	43.3%	56.6%	43.3%	56.7%
11,707	UNION	3,319	1,321	1,993	5	672 D	39.8%	60.0%	39.9%	60.1%
4,728	VAN BUREN	1,485	289	1,195	1	906 D	19.5%	80.5%	19.5%	80.5%
32,653	WARREN	8,730	2,293	6,417	20	4,124 D	26.3%	73.5%	26.3%	73.7%
88,755	WASHINGTON	28,101	10,512	17,527	62	7,015 D	37.4%	62.4%	37.5%	62.5%
13,946	WAYNE	4,268	1,932	2,329	7	397 D	45.3%	54.6%	45.3%	54.7%
32,896	WEAKLEY	9,824	2,559	7,239	26	4,680 D	26.0%	73.7%	26.1%	73.9%
19,567	WHITE	5,281	1,305	3,967	9	2,662 D	24.7%	75.1%	24.8%	75.2%
58,108	WILLIAMSON	28,103	13,294	14,764	45	1,470 D	47.3%	52.5%	47.4%	52.6%
56,064	WILSON	20,838	6,776	14,025	37	7,249 D	32.5%	67.3%	32.6%	67.4%
4,591,120	TOTAL	1,567,181	541,033	1,020,061	6,087	479,028 D	34.5%	65.1%	34.7%	65.3%

TENNESSEE

CONGRESS

CD	Year	Total Vote	Republican Vote	Republican Candidate	Democratic Vote	Democratic Candidate	Other Vote	Rep.-Dem. Plurality	Percentage Total Vote Rep.	Percentage Total Vote Dem.	Percentage Major Vote Rep.	Percentage Major Vote Dem.
1	1988	148,998	119,526	QUILLEN, JAMES H.	29,469	SMITH, SIDNEY S.	3	90,057 R	80.2%	19.8%	80.2%	19.8%
1	1986	116,570	80,289	QUILLEN, JAMES H.	36,278	RUSSELL, JOHN B.	3	44,011 R	68.9%	31.1%	68.9%	31.1%
1	1984	113,442	113,407	QUILLEN, JAMES H.			35	113,407 R	100.0%		100.0%	
1	1982	120,858	89,497	QUILLEN, JAMES H.	27,580	CABLE, JESSIE J.	3,781	61,917 R	74.1%	22.8%	76.4%	23.6%
2	1988	177,174	99,631	DUNCAN, JOHN J., JR.	77,540	TAYLOR, DUDLEY W.	3	22,091 R	56.2%	43.8%	56.2%	43.8%
2	1986	126,486	96,396	DUNCAN, JOHN J.	30,088	BOWEN, JOHN F.	2	66,308 R	76.2%	23.8%	76.2%	23.8%
2	1984	171,453	132,604	DUNCAN, JOHN J.	38,846	BOWEN, JOHN F.	3	93,758 R	77.3%	22.7%	77.3%	22.7%
2	1982	109,057	109,045	DUNCAN, JOHN J.			12	109,045 R	100.0%		100.0%	
3	1988	188,638	80,372	COKER, HAROLD L.	108,264	LLOYD, MARILYN	2	27,892 D	42.6%	57.4%	42.6%	57.4%
3	1986	139,120	64,084	GOLDEN, JIM	75,034	LLOYD, MARILYN	2	10,950 D	46.1%	53.9%	46.1%	53.9%
3	1984	189,683	90,216	DAVIS, JOHN	99,465	LLOYD, MARILYN	2	9,249 D	47.6%	52.4%	47.6%	52.4%
3	1982	137,493	49,885	BYERS, GLEN	84,967	BOUQUARD, MARILYN LLOYD	2,641	35,082 D	36.3%	61.8%	37.0%	63.0%
4	1988	94,151			94,129	COOPER, JIM	22	94,129 D		100.0%		100.0%
4	1986	87,005			86,997	COOPER, JIM	8	86,997 D		100.0%		100.0%
4	1984	124,863	31,011	SEIGNEUR, JAMES B.	93,848	COOPER, JIM	4	62,837 D	24.8%	75.2%	24.8%	75.2%
4	1982	141,322	47,865	BAKER, CISSY	93,453	COOPER, JIM	4	45,588 D	33.9%	66.1%	33.9%	66.1%
5	1988	155,140			155,068	CLEMENT, BOB	72	155,068 D		100.0%		100.0%
5	1986	147,147	58,701	HOLCOMB, TERRY	85,126	BONER, BILL	3,320	26,425 D	39.9%	57.9%	40.8%	59.2%
5	1984	138,286			138,233	BONER, BILL	53	138,233 D		100.0%		100.0%
5	1982	136,349	27,061	STEINHICE, LAUREL	109,282	BONER, BILL	6	82,221 D	19.8%	80.1%	19.8%	80.2%
6	1988	161,687	38,033	EMBRY, WALLACE	123,652	GORDON, BART	2	85,619 D	23.5%	76.5%	23.5%	76.5%
6	1986	133,004	30,823	VAIL, FRED	102,180	GORDON, BART	1	71,357 D	23.2%	76.8%	23.2%	76.8%
6	1984	165,565	61,559	SIMPKINS, JOE	103,989	GORDON, BART	17	42,430 D	37.2%	62.8%	37.2%	62.8%
6	1982	104,105			104,094	GORE, ALBERT, JR.	11	104,094 D		100.0%		100.0%
7	1988	177,266	142,025	SUNDQUIST, DON	35,237	BLOODWORTH, KEN	4	106,788 R	80.1%	19.9%	80.1%	19.9%
7	1986	129,878	93,902	SUNDQUIST, DON	35,966	HILER, M. LLOYD	10	57,936 R	72.3%	27.7%	72.3%	27.7%
7	1984	107,278	107,257	SUNDQUIST, DON			21	107,257 R	100.0%		100.0%	
7	1982	146,197	73,835	SUNDQUIST, DON	72,359	CLEMENT, BOB	3	1,476 R	50.5%	49.5%	50.5%	49.5%
8	1988	151,465	56,893	BRYANT, ED	94,571	TANNER, JOHN	1	37,678 D	37.6%	62.4%	37.6%	62.4%
8	1986	126,503	24,792	CAMPBELL, DAN H.	101,699	JONES, ED	12	76,907 D	19.6%	80.4%	19.6%	80.4%
8	1984	118,668			118,653	JONES, ED	15	118,653 D		100.0%		100.0%
8	1982	125,472	31,527	BENSON, BRUCE	93,945	JONES, ED		62,418 D	25.1%	74.9%	25.1%	74.9%
9	1988	154,802			126,280	FORD, HAROLD E.	28,522	126,280 D		81.6%		100.0%
9	1986	99,516			83,006	FORD, HAROLD E.	16,510	83,006 D		83.4%		100.0%
9	1984	186,497	53,064	THOMPSON, WILLIAM B.	133,428	FORD, HAROLD E.	5	80,364 D	28.5%	71.5%	28.5%	71.5%
9	1982	154,830	40,812	CRAWFORD, JOE	112,143	FORD, HAROLD E.	1,875	71,331 D	26.4%	72.4%	26.7%	73.3%

TENNESSEE

1988 GENERAL ELECTION

President Other vote was 2,041 Independent (Paul); 1,807 Independent (Dodge); 1,807 Independent (Duke); 1,334 Independent (Fulani); 873 Independent (LaRouche); 718 Independent (Warren); 358 Independent (Kenoyer); 285 scattered write-in.

Senator Other vote was 6,042 Independent (Khalil-Ullah Al-Muhaymin); 45 scattered write-in.

Congress Other vote was Independent (Richmond) in CD 9; scattered in all other CD's.

1988 PRIMARIES

AUGUST 4 REPUBLICAN

Senator 115,341 Bill Anderson; 34,413 Alice W. Algood; 8,358 Hubert D. Patty; 11 scattered write-in.

Congress Unopposed in four CD's. No candidate in CD's 4, 5 and 9. Contested as follows:

CD 2 33,246 John J. Duncan, Jr.; 5,015 Robert D. Proffitt.
CD 8 7,252 Ed Bryant; 4,262 Richard Jacobs; 984 Dan Campbell.

AUGUST 4 DEMOCRATIC

Senator James R. Sasser, unopposed.

Congress Unopposed in four CD's. Contested as follows:

CD 2 7,725 Dudley W. Taylor; 5,663 John F. Bowen; 5,261 Robert R. Scott; 1 scattered write-in.
CD 3 31,007 Marilyn Lloyd; 2,168 Walter Ward; 1,815 Lamar Lasley; 1 scattered write-in.
CD 7 13,650 Ken Bloodworth; 7,433 Francis Tapp; 2 scattered write-in.
CD 8 45,271 John Tanner; 10,468 Bob Conger; 7,202 Ray Blanton; 5,311 Ivy Scarborough.
CD 9 35,589 Harold E. Ford; 8,720 Mark F. Flanagan.

TEXAS

GOVERNOR

William P. Clements (R). Elected 1986 to a four-year term. Previously elected 1978.

SENATORS

Lloyd Bentsen (D). Re-elected 1988 to a six-year term. Previously elected 1982, 1976, 1970.

Phil Gramm (R). Elected 1984 to a six-year term.

REPRESENTATIVES

1. James L. Chapman (D)
2. Charles Wilson (D)
3. Steve Bartlett (R)
4. Ralph M. Hall (D)
5. John Bryant (D)
6. Joe L. Barton (R)
7. W. R.Archer (R)
8. Jack Fields (R)
9. Jack B. Brooks (D)
10. Jake Pickle (D)
11. J. Marvin Leath (D)
12. James C. Wright (D) (see page 1)
13. Bill Sarpalius (D)
14. Greg Laughlin (D)
15. Eligio de la Garza (D)
16. Ronald Coleman (D)
17. Charles W. Stenholm (D)
18. Mickey Leland (D) (see page 1)
19. Larry Combest (R)
20. Henry B. Gonzalez (D)
21. Lamar Smith (R)
22. Thomas D. DeLay (R)
23. Albert G. Bustamante (D)
24. Martin Frost (D)
25. Mike Andrews (D)
26. Dick Armey (R)
27. Solomon P. Ortiz (D)

POSTWAR VOTE FOR PRESIDENT

Year	Total Vote	Republican Vote	Republican Candidate	Democratic Vote	Democratic Candidate	Other Vote	Plurality	Percentage Total Vote Rep.	Percentage Total Vote Dem.	Percentage Major Vote Rep.	Percentage Major Vote Dem.
1988	5,427,410	3,036,829	Bush, George	2,352,748	Dukakis, Michael S.	37,833	684,081 R	56.0%	43.3%	56.3%	43.7%
1984	5,397,571	3,433,428	Reagan, Ronald	1,949,276	Mondale, Walter F.	14,867	1,484,152 R	63.6%	36.1%	63.8%	36.2%
1980	4,541,636	2,510,705	Reagan, Ronald	1,881,147	Carter, Jimmy	149,784	629,558 R	55.3%	41.4%	57.2%	42.8%
1976	4,071,884	1,953,300	Ford, Gerald R.	2,082,319	Carter, Jimmy	36,265	129,019 D	48.0%	51.1%	48.4%	51.6%
1972	3,471,281	2,298,896	Nixon, Richard M.	1,154,289	McGovern, George S.	18,096	1,144,607 R	66.2%	33.3%	66.6%	33.4%
1968 **	3,079,216	1,227,844	Nixon, Richard M.	1,266,804	Humphrey, Hubert H.	584,568	38,960 D	39.9%	41.1%	49.2%	50.8%
1964	2,626,811	958,566	Goldwater, Barry M.	1,663,185	Johnson, Lyndon B.	5,060	704,619 D	36.5%	63.3%	36.6%	63.4%
1960	2,311,084	1,121,310	Nixon, Richard M.	1,167,567	Kennedy, John F.	22,207	46,257 D	48.5%	50.5%	49.0%	51.0%
1956	1,955,168	1,080,619	Eisenhower, Dwight D.	859,958	Stevenson, Adlai E.	14,591	220,661 R	55.3%	44.0%	55.7%	44.3%
1952	2,075,946	1,102,878	Eisenhower, Dwight D.	969,228	Stevenson, Adlai E.	3,840	133,650 R	53.1%	46.7%	53.2%	46.8%
1948	1,249,577	303,467	Dewey, Thomas E.	824,235	Truman, Harry S.	121,875	520,768 D	24.3%	66.0%	26.9%	73.1%

In 1968 other vote was 584,269 American (Wallace) and 299 scattered.

TEXAS

POSTWAR VOTE FOR GOVERNOR

Year	Total Vote	Republican Vote	Republican Candidate	Democratic Vote	Democratic Candidate	Other Vote	Rep.-Dem. Plurality	Total Vote Rep.	Total Vote Dem.	Major Vote Rep.	Major Vote Dem.
1986	3,441,460	1,813,779	Clements, William P.	1,584,515	White, Mark	43,166	229,264 R	52.7%	46.0%	53.4%	46.6%
1982	3,191,091	1,465,937	Clements, William P.	1,697,870	White, Mark	27,284	231,933 D	45.9%	53.2%	46.3%	53.7%
1978	2,369,764	1,183,839	Clements, William P.	1,166,979	Hill, John	18,946	16,860 R	50.0%	49.2%	50.4%	49.6%
1974 **	1,654,984	514,725	Granberry, Jim	1,016,334	Briscoe, Dolph	123,925	501,609 D	31.1%	61.4%	33.6%	66.4%
1972	3,410,128	1,534,060	Grover, Henry C.	1,633,970	Briscoe, Dolph	242,098	99,910 D	45.0%	47.9%	48.4%	51.6%
1970	2,235,847	1,037,723	Eggers, Paul W.	1,197,726	Smith, Preston	398	160,003 D	46.4%	53.6%	46.4%	53.6%
1968	2,916,509	1,254,333	Eggers, Paul W.	1,662,019	Smith, Preston	157	407,686 D	43.0%	57.0%	43.0%	57.0%
1966	1,425,861	368,025	Kennerly, T. E.	1,037,517	Connally, John B.	20,319	669,492 D	25.8%	72.8%	26.2%	73.8%
1964	2,544,753	661,675	Crichton, Jack	1,877,793	Connally, John B.	5,285	1,216,118 D	26.0%	73.8%	26.1%	73.9%
1962	1,569,181	715,025	Cox, Jack	847,036	Connally, John B.	7,120	132,011 D	45.6%	54.0%	45.8%	54.2%
1960	2,250,718	612,963	Steger, William M.	1,637,755	Daniel, Price		1,024,792 D	27.2%	72.8%	27.2%	72.8%
1958	789,133	94,098	Mayer, Edwin S.	695,035	Daniel, Price		600,937 D	11.9%	88.1%	11.9%	88.1%
1956	1,828,161	271,088	Bryant, William R.	1,433,051	Daniel, Price	124,022	1,161,963 D	14.8%	78.4%	15.9%	84.1%
1954	636,892	66,154	Adams, Tod R.	569,533	Shivers, Allan	1,205	503,379 D	10.4%	89.4%	10.4%	89.6%
1952	1,881,202		—	1,844,530	Shivers, Allan	36,672	1,844,530 D		98.1%		100.0%
1950	394,747	39,737	Currie, Ralph W.	355,010	Shivers, Allan		315,273 D	10.1%	89.9%	10.1%	89.9%
1948	1,208,860	177,399	Lane, Alvin H.	1,024,160	Jester, Beauford	7,301	846,761 D	14.7%	84.7%	14.8%	85.2%
1946	378,744	33,231	Nolte, Eugene	345,513	Jester, Beauford		312,282 D	8.8%	91.2%	8.8%	91.2%

The term of office of Texas' Governor was increased from two to four years effective with the 1974 election.

POSTWAR VOTE FOR SENATOR

Year	Total Vote	Republican Vote	Republican Candidate	Democratic Vote	Democratic Candidate	Other Vote	Rep.-Dem. Plurality	Total Vote Rep.	Total Vote Dem.	Major Vote Rep.	Major Vote Dem.
1988	5,323,606	2,129,228	Boulter, Beau	3,149,806	Bentsen, Lloyd	44,572	1,020,578 D	40.0%	59.2%	40.3%	59.7%
1984	5,319,178	3,116,348	Gramm, Phil	2,202,557	Doggett, Lloyd	273	913,791 R	58.6%	41.4%	58.6%	41.4%
1982	3,103,167	1,256,759	Collins, James M.	1,818,223	Bentsen, Lloyd	28,185	561,464 D	40.5%	58.6%	40.9%	59.1%
1978	2,312,540	1,151,376	Tower, John G.	1,139,149	Krueger, Robert	22,015	12,227 R	49.8%	49.3%	50.3%	49.7%
1976	3,874,516	1,636,370	Steelman, Alan	2,199,956	Bentsen, Lloyd	38,190	563,586 D	42.2%	56.8%	42.7%	57.3%
1972	3,413,903	1,822,877	Tower, John G.	1,511,985	Sanders, Barefoot	79,041	310,892 R	53.4%	44.3%	54.7%	45.3%
1970	2,231,671	1,035,794	Bush, George	1,194,069	Bentsen, Lloyd	1,808	158,275 D	46.4%	53.5%	46.5%	53.5%
1966	1,493,182	842,501	Tower, John G.	643,855	Carr, Waggoner	6,826	198,646 R	56.4%	43.1%	56.7%	43.3%
1964	2,603,856	1,134,337	Bush, George	1,463,958	Yarborough, Ralph	5,561	329,621 D	43.6%	56.2%	43.7%	56.3%
1961 S	886,091	448,217	Tower, John G.	437,874	Blakley, William A.		10,343 R	50.6%	49.4%	50.6%	49.4%
1960	2,253,784	926,653	Tower, John G.	1,306,625	Johnson, Lyndon B.	20,506	379,972 D	41.1%	58.0%	41.5%	58.5%
1958	787,128	185,926	Whittenburg, Roy	587,030	Yarborough, Ralph	14,172	401,104 D	23.6%	74.6%	24.1%	75.9%
1957 S	957,298		[See note below]								
1954	636,475	94,131	Watson, Carlos G.	539,319	Johnson, Lyndon B.	3,025	445,188 D	14.8%	84.7%	14.9%	85.1%
1952	1,895,192		—	1,895,192	Daniel, Price		1,895,192 D		100.0%		100.0%
1948	1,061,563	349,665	Porter, Jack	702,985	Johnson, Lyndon B.	8,913	353,320 D	32.9%	66.2%	33.2%	66.8%
1946	380,681	43,750	Sells, Murray C.	336,931	Connally, Tom		293,181 D	11.5%	88.5%	11.5%	88.5%

The May 1961 and April 1957 elections were for short terms to fill vacancies. Though neither vote was held with official party designations, the 1961 vote above was a run-off contest between unofficial party candidates. In 1957 there was a single ballot without run-off and Ralph Yarborough polled 364,605 votes (38.1% of the total vote) and won the election with a 73,802 plurality.

TEXAS

Districts Established June 19, 1983

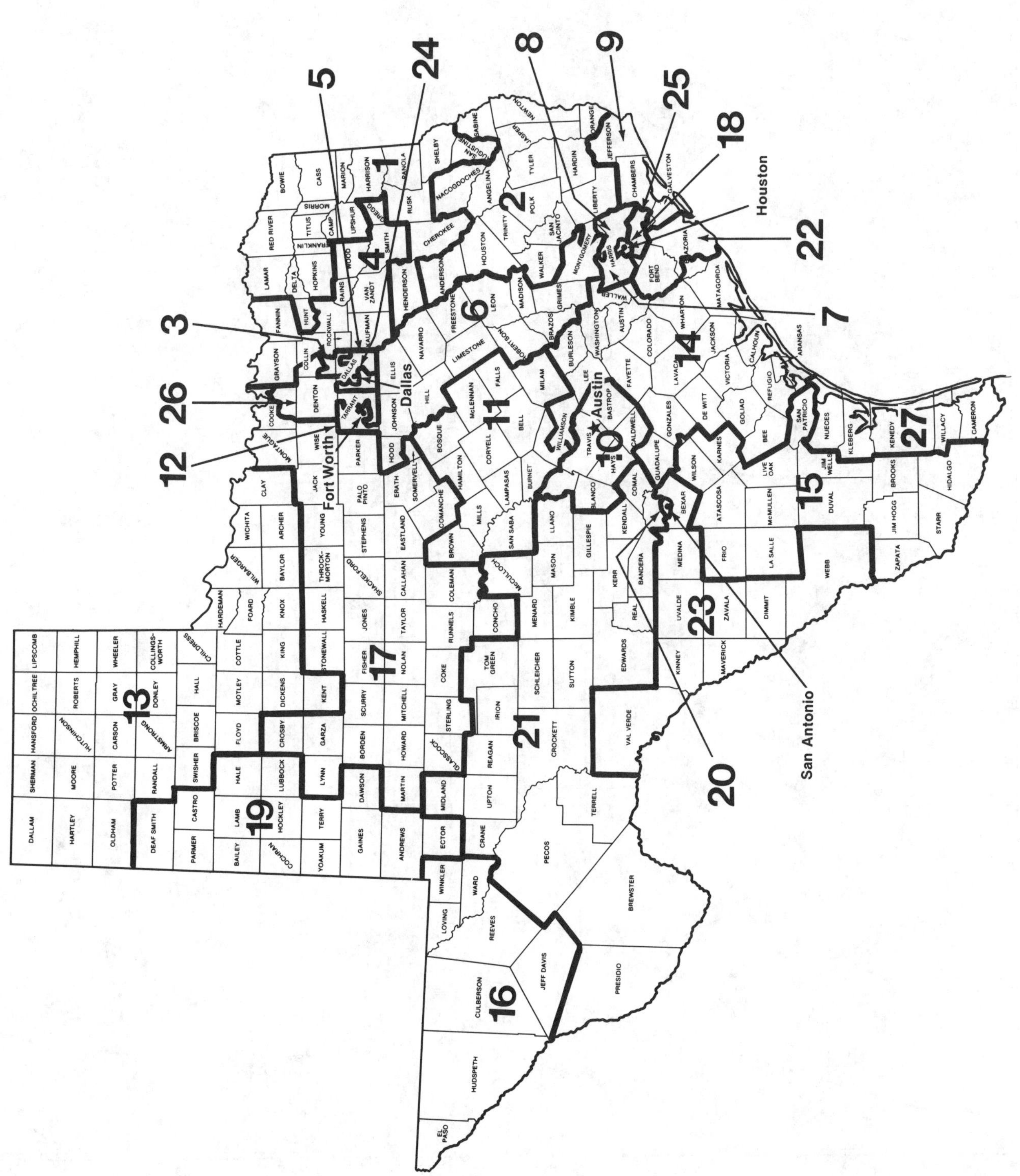

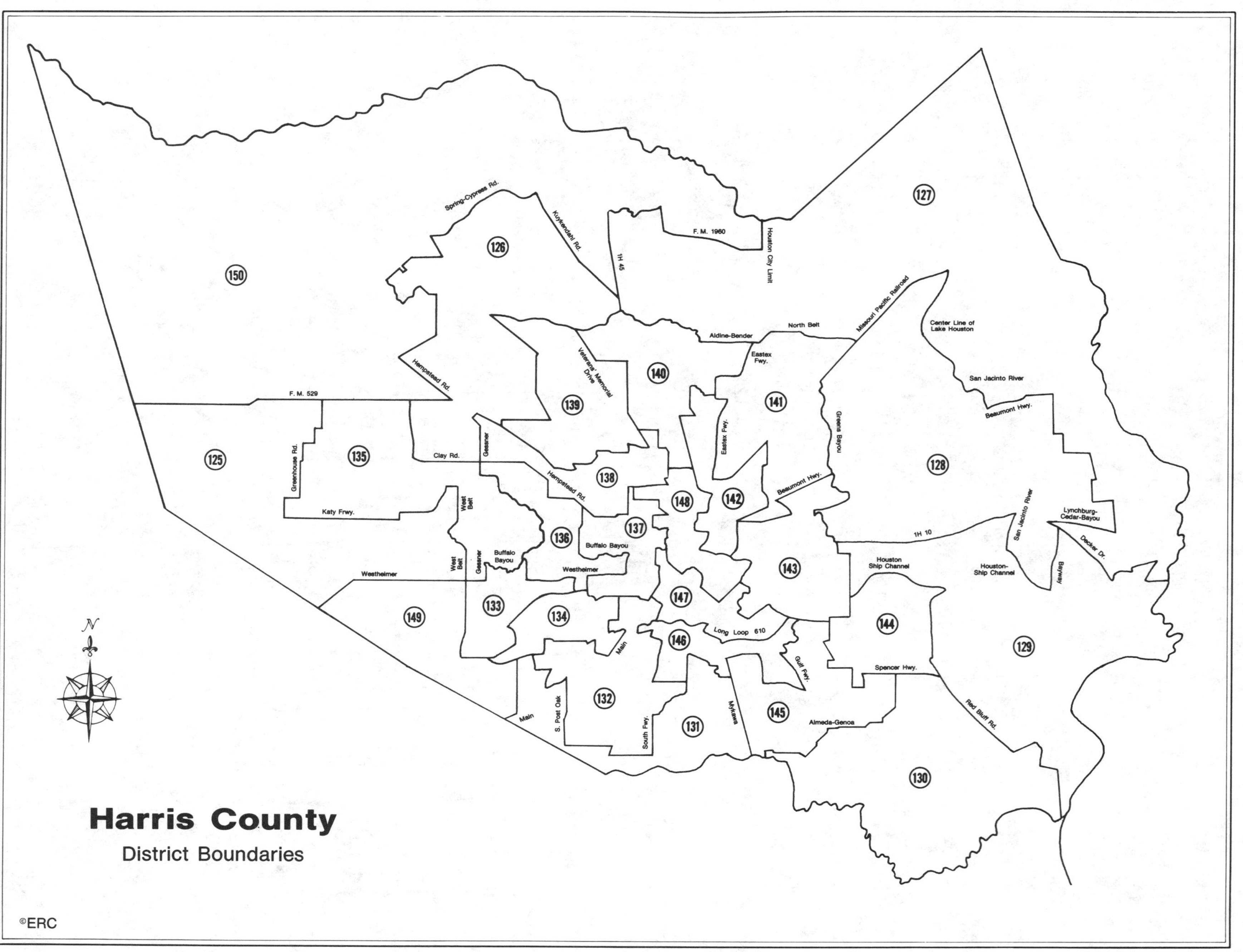
Harris County
District Boundaries
©ERC
N
150
126
127
125
135
139
140
141
128
138
142
148
137
136
143
147
133
134
146
144
149
129
132
131
145
130
Spring-Cypress Rd.
Kuykendahl Rd.
IH 45
F. M. 1960
Houston City Limit
Missouri Pacific Railroad
North Belt
Aldine-Bender
Eastex Fwy.
Center Line of Lake Houston
San Jacinto River
Beaumont Hwy.
Hempstead Rd.
Veterans' Memorial Drive
F. M. 529
Greenhouse Rd.
Katy Frwy.
Clay Rd.
Gessner
Eastex Fwy.
Greens Bayou
Hempstead Rd.
Beaumont Hwy.
San Jacinto River
Lynchburg-Cedar-Bayou
Decker Dr.
West Belt
IH 10
Buffalo Bayou
Houston Ship Channel
Houston-Ship Channel
Bayway
West Belt
Gessner
Buffalo Bayou
Westheimer
Westheimer
Long Loop 610
Main
Gulf Fwy.
Spencer Hwy.
Red Bluff Rd.
Main
S. Post Oak
South Fwy.
Mykawa
Almeda-Genoa

TEXAS

PRESIDENT 1988

1980 Census Population	County	Total Vote	Republican	Democratic	Other	Rep.-Dem. Plurality	Percentage Total Vote Rep.	Percentage Total Vote Dem.	Percentage Major Vote Rep.	Percentage Major Vote Dem.
38,381	ANDERSON	14,045	7,858	6,128	59	1,730 R	55.9%	43.6%	56.2%	43.8%
13,323	ANDREWS	4,191	3,052	1,122	17	1,930 R	72.8%	26.8%	73.1%	26.9%
64,172	ANGELINA	23,852	12,738	10,849	265	1,889 R	53.4%	45.5%	54.0%	46.0%
14,260	ARANSAS	6,196	3,858	2,305	33	1,553 R	62.3%	37.2%	62.6%	37.4%
7,266	ARCHER	3,646	2,010	1,627	9	383 R	55.1%	44.6%	55.3%	44.7%
1,994	ARMSTRONG	1,040	720	314	6	406 R	69.2%	30.2%	69.6%	30.4%
25,055	ATASCOSA	9,504	4,777	4,657	70	120 R	50.3%	49.0%	50.6%	49.4%
17,726	AUSTIN	7,160	4,524	2,593	43	1,931 R	63.2%	36.2%	63.6%	36.4%
8,168	BAILEY	2,343	1,459	876	8	583 R	62.3%	37.4%	62.5%	37.5%
7,084	BANDERA	4,761	3,435	1,251	75	2,184 R	72.1%	26.3%	73.3%	26.7%
24,726	BASTROP	14,092	5,991	8,004	97	2,013 D	42.5%	56.8%	42.8%	57.2%
4,919	BAYLOR	2,070	914	1,153	3	239 D	44.2%	55.7%	44.2%	55.8%
26,030	BEE	9,281	4,620	4,616	45	4 R	49.8%	49.7%	50.0%	50.0%
157,889	BELL	47,551	29,382	17,751	418	11,631 R	61.8%	37.3%	62.3%	37.7%
988,800	BEXAR	369,749	193,192	174,036	2,521	19,156 R	52.2%	47.1%	52.6%	47.4%
4,681	BLANCO	2,719	1,680	1,012	27	668 R	61.8%	37.2%	62.4%	37.6%
859	BORDEN	454	283	169	2	114 R	62.3%	37.2%	62.6%	37.4%
13,401	BOSQUE	6,147	3,458	2,670	19	788 R	56.3%	43.4%	56.4%	43.6%
75,301	BOWIE	27,941	15,454	12,331	156	3,123 R	55.3%	44.1%	55.6%	44.4%
169,587	BRAZORIA	59,081	34,028	23,436	1,617	10,592 R	57.6%	39.7%	59.2%	40.8%
93,588	BRAZOS	44,690	29,369	14,885	436	14,484 R	65.7%	33.3%	66.4%	33.6%
7,573	BREWSTER	3,313	1,708	1,569	36	139 R	51.6%	47.4%	52.1%	47.9%
2,579	BRISCOE	1,048	464	574	10	110 D	44.3%	54.8%	44.7%	55.3%
8,428	BROOKS	3,489	608	2,859	22	2,251 D	17.4%	81.9%	17.5%	82.5%
33,057	BROWN	11,606	6,810	4,763	33	2,047 R	58.7%	41.0%	58.8%	41.2%
12,313	BURLESON	5,339	2,242	3,085	12	843 D	42.0%	57.8%	42.1%	57.9%
17,803	BURNET	9,508	5,120	4,343	45	777 R	53.8%	45.7%	54.1%	45.9%
23,637	CALDWELL	8,262	3,553	4,649	60	1,096 D	43.0%	56.3%	43.3%	56.7%
19,574	CALHOUN	6,524	3,183	3,314	27	131 D	48.8%	50.8%	49.0%	51.0%
10,992	CALLAHAN	4,921	2,887	2,017	17	870 R	58.7%	41.0%	58.9%	41.1%
209,727	CAMERON	55,552	24,263	30,972	317	6,709 D	43.7%	55.8%	43.9%	56.1%
9,275	CAMP	4,042	1,908	2,121	13	213 D	47.2%	52.5%	47.4%	52.6%
6,672	CARSON	3,148	2,100	1,034	14	1,066 R	66.7%	32.8%	67.0%	33.0%
29,430	CASS	11,262	5,305	5,941	16	636 D	47.1%	52.8%	47.2%	52.8%
10,556	CASTRO	3,049	1,604	1,436	9	168 R	52.6%	47.1%	52.8%	47.2%
18,538	CHAMBERS	6,781	3,694	3,035	52	659 R	54.5%	44.8%	54.9%	45.1%
38,127	CHEROKEE	13,165	7,520	5,604	41	1,916 R	57.1%	42.6%	57.3%	42.7%
6,950	CHILDRESS	2,267	1,201	1,060	6	141 R	53.0%	46.8%	53.1%	46.9%
9,582	CLAY	4,340	2,043	2,288	9	245 D	47.1%	52.7%	47.2%	52.8%
4,825	COCHRAN	1,462	771	681	10	90 R	52.7%	46.6%	53.1%	46.9%
3,196	COKE	1,542	863	674	5	189 R	56.0%	43.7%	56.1%	43.9%
10,439	COLEMAN	4,321	2,340	1,978	3	362 R	54.2%	45.8%	54.2%	45.8%
144,576	COLLIN	91,230	67,776	22,934	520	44,842 R	74.3%	25.1%	74.7%	25.3%
4,648	COLLINGSWORTH	1,683	872	809	2	63 R	51.8%	48.1%	51.9%	48.1%
18,823	COLORADO	6,600	3,723	2,847	30	876 R	56.4%	43.1%	56.7%	43.3%
36,446	COMAL	19,980	13,994	5,716	270	8,278 R	70.0%	28.6%	71.0%	29.0%
12,617	COMANCHE	4,761	2,120	2,622	19	502 D	44.5%	55.1%	44.7%	55.3%
2,915	CONCHO	1,263	617	643	3	26 D	48.9%	50.9%	49.0%	51.0%
27,656	COOKE	11,452	7,196	4,217	39	2,979 R	62.8%	36.8%	63.1%	36.9%
56,767	CORYELL	11,627	7,461	4,026	140	3,435 R	64.2%	34.6%	65.0%	35.0%
2,947	COTTLE	1,083	379	690	14	311 D	35.0%	63.7%	35.5%	64.5%
4,600	CRANE	1,818	1,219	596	3	623 R	67.1%	32.8%	67.2%	32.8%
4,608	CROCKETT	1,819	932	881	6	51 R	51.2%	48.4%	51.4%	48.6%
8,859	CROSBY	2,562	1,121	1,435	6	314 D	43.8%	56.0%	43.9%	56.1%
3,315	CULBERSON	982	417	557	8	140 D	42.5%	56.7%	42.8%	57.2%
6,531	DALLAM	1,862	1,205	645	12	560 R	64.7%	34.6%	65.1%	34.9%
1,556,390	DALLAS	594,538	347,094	243,198	4,246	103,896 R	58.4%	40.9%	58.8%	41.2%
16,184	DAWSON	5,317	3,154	2,155	8	999 R	59.3%	40.5%	59.4%	40.6%
21,165	DEAF SMITH	5,726	3,744	1,930	52	1,814 R	65.4%	33.7%	66.0%	34.0%
4,839	DELTA	2,101	849	1,244	8	395 D	40.4%	59.2%	40.6%	59.4%

TEXAS

PRESIDENT 1988

1980 Census Population	County	Total Vote	Republican	Democratic	Other	Rep.-Dem. Plurality	Percentage Total Vote Rep.	Total Vote Dem.	Major Vote Rep.	Major Vote Dem.
143,126	DENTON	84,210	57,444	26,204	562	31,240 R	68.2%	31.1%	68.7%	31.3%
18,903	DE WITT	6,255	3,628	2,579	48	1,049 R	58.0%	41.2%	58.5%	41.5%
3,539	DICKENS	1,141	435	696	10	261 D	38.1%	61.0%	38.5%	61.5%
11,367	DIMMIT	3,651	900	2,735	16	1,835 D	24.7%	74.9%	24.8%	75.2%
4,075	DONLEY	1,713	1,043	661	9	382 R	60.9%	38.6%	61.2%	38.8%
12,517	DUVAL	5,097	907	4,177	13	3,270 D	17.8%	82.0%	17.8%	82.2%
19,480	EASTLAND	7,166	3,929	3,215	22	714 R	54.8%	44.9%	55.0%	45.0%
115,374	ECTOR	34,152	23,155	10,825	172	12,330 R	67.8%	31.7%	68.1%	31.9%
2,033	EDWARDS	930	556	368	6	188 R	59.8%	39.6%	60.2%	39.8%
59,743	ELLIS	27,749	16,422	11,169	158	5,253 R	59.2%	40.3%	59.5%	40.5%
479,899	EL PASO	118,781	55,573	62,622	586	7,049 D	46.8%	52.7%	47.0%	53.0%
22,560	ERATH	9,570	5,427	4,113	30	1,314 R	56.7%	43.0%	56.9%	43.1%
17,946	FALLS	5,237	2,344	2,877	16	533 D	44.8%	54.9%	44.9%	55.1%
24,285	FANNIN	9,214	4,024	5,163	27	1,139 D	43.7%	56.0%	43.8%	56.2%
18,832	FAYETTE	7,971	4,551	3,390	30	1,161 R	57.1%	42.5%	57.3%	42.7%
5,891	FISHER	2,240	721	1,516	3	795 D	32.2%	67.7%	32.2%	67.8%
9,834	FLOYD	3,138	1,741	1,391	6	350 R	55.5%	44.3%	55.6%	44.4%
2,158	FOARD	820	306	513	1	207 D	37.3%	62.6%	37.4%	62.6%
130,846	FORT BEND	63,784	39,818	23,351	615	16,467 R	62.4%	36.6%	63.0%	37.0%
6,893	FRANKLIN	2,896	1,439	1,453	4	14 D	49.7%	50.2%	49.8%	50.2%
14,830	FREESTONE	6,092	3,159	2,916	17	243 R	51.9%	47.9%	52.0%	48.0%
13,785	FRIO	4,538	1,505	3,016	17	1,511 D	33.2%	66.5%	33.3%	66.7%
13,150	GAINES	3,606	2,265	1,310	31	955 R	62.8%	36.3%	63.4%	36.6%
195,940	GALVESTON	74,042	34,913	38,633	496	3,720 D	47.2%	52.2%	47.5%	52.5%
5,336	GARZA	2,190	1,183	989	18	194 R	54.0%	45.2%	54.5%	45.5%
13,532	GILLESPIE	7,313	5,662	1,588	63	4,074 R	77.4%	21.7%	78.1%	21.9%
1,304	GLASSCOCK	528	384	143	1	241 R	72.7%	27.1%	72.9%	27.1%
5,193	GOLIAD	2,792	1,427	1,358	7	69 R	51.1%	48.6%	51.2%	48.8%
16,883	GONZALES	5,916	2,983	2,897	36	86 R	50.4%	49.0%	50.7%	49.3%
26,386	GRAY	9,781	7,259	2,460	62	4,799 R	74.2%	25.2%	74.7%	25.3%
89,796	GRAYSON	33,287	18,825	14,347	115	4,478 R	56.6%	43.1%	56.7%	43.3%
99,487	GREGG	39,387	26,465	12,486	436	13,979 R	67.2%	31.7%	67.9%	32.1%
13,580	GRIMES	5,582	2,820	2,735	27	85 R	50.5%	49.0%	50.8%	49.2%
46,708	GUADALUPE	20,609	13,265	7,111	233	6,154 R	64.4%	34.5%	65.1%	34.9%
37,592	HALE	9,811	6,284	3,502	25	2,782 R	64.1%	35.7%	64.2%	35.8%
5,594	HALL	1,743	714	1,029		315 D	41.0%	59.0%	41.0%	59.0%
8,297	HAMILTON	3,086	1,718	1,355	13	363 R	55.7%	43.9%	55.9%	44.1%
6,209	HANSFORD	2,421	1,967	443	11	1,524 R	81.2%	18.3%	81.6%	18.4%
6,368	HARDEMAN	2,001	855	1,143	3	288 D	42.7%	57.1%	42.8%	57.2%
40,721	HARDIN	15,173	6,897	8,245	31	1,348 D	45.5%	54.3%	45.5%	54.5%
2,409,547	HARRIS	814,160	464,217	342,919	7,024	121,298 R	57.0%	42.1%	57.5%	42.5%
52,265	HARRISON	21,285	11,957	8,974	354	2,983 R	56.2%	42.2%	57.1%	42.9%
3,987	HARTLEY	1,747	1,229	505	13	724 R	70.3%	28.9%	70.9%	29.1%
7,725	HASKELL	2,915	1,193	1,715	7	522 D	40.9%	58.8%	41.0%	59.0%
40,594	HAYS	23,264	11,716	11,187	361	529 R	50.4%	48.1%	51.2%	48.8%
5,304	HEMPHILL	1,705	1,170	527	8	643 R	68.6%	30.9%	68.9%	31.1%
42,606	HENDERSON	20,918	11,005	9,819	94	1,186 R	52.6%	46.9%	52.8%	47.2%
283,229	HIDALGO	83,870	29,246	54,330	294	25,084 D	34.9%	64.8%	35.0%	65.0%
25,024	HILL	9,198	4,796	4,381	21	415 R	52.1%	47.6%	52.3%	47.7%
23,230	HOCKLEY	7,250	4,368	2,850	32	1,518 R	60.2%	39.3%	60.5%	39.5%
17,714	HOOD	11,716	7,400	4,255	61	3,145 R	63.2%	36.3%	63.5%	36.5%
25,247	HOPKINS	10,142	5,133	4,984	25	149 R	50.6%	49.1%	50.7%	49.3%
22,299	HOUSTON	7,764	3,882	3,846	36	36 R	50.0%	49.5%	50.2%	49.8%
33,142	HOWARD	10,517	6,024	4,445	48	1,579 R	57.3%	42.3%	57.5%	42.5%
2,728	HUDSPETH	816	405	406	5	1 D	49.6%	49.8%	49.9%	50.1%
55,248	HUNT	21,238	12,331	8,820	87	3,511 R	58.1%	41.5%	58.3%	41.7%
26,304	HUTCHINSON	10,526	7,526	2,950	50	4,576 R	71.5%	28.0%	71.8%	28.2%
1,386	IRION	867	539	326	2	213 R	62.2%	37.6%	62.3%	37.7%
7,408	JACK	3,074	1,542	1,521	11	21 R	50.2%	49.5%	50.3%	49.7%
13,352	JACKSON	5,115	2,954	2,141	20	813 R	57.8%	41.9%	58.0%	42.0%

TEXAS

PRESIDENT 1988

1980 Census Population	County	Total Vote	Republican	Democratic	Other	Rep.-Dem. Plurality	Percentage Total Vote Rep.	Total Vote Dem.	Major Vote Rep.	Major Vote Dem.
30,781	JASPER	11,629	4,985	6,613	31	1,628 D	42.9%	56.9%	43.0%	57.0%
1,647	JEFF DAVIS	870	524	325	21	199 R	60.2%	37.4%	61.7%	38.3%
250,938	JEFFERSON	91,693	35,754	55,649	290	19,895 D	39.0%	60.7%	39.1%	60.9%
5,168	JIM HOGG	2,143	510	1,630	3	1,120 D	23.8%	76.1%	23.8%	76.2%
36,498	JIM WELLS	12,886	4,335	8,495	56	4,160 D	33.6%	65.9%	33.8%	66.2%
67,649	JOHNSON	30,171	17,509	12,507	155	5,002 R	58.0%	41.5%	58.3%	41.7%
17,268	JONES	5,916	3,000	2,898	18	102 R	50.7%	49.0%	50.9%	49.1%
13,593	KARNES	4,933	2,383	2,529	21	146 D	48.3%	51.3%	48.5%	51.5%
39,015	KAUFMAN	15,916	8,466	7,358	92	1,108 R	53.2%	46.2%	53.5%	46.5%
10,635	KENDALL	6,398	4,875	1,446	77	3,429 R	76.2%	22.6%	77.1%	22.9%
543	KENEDY	196	76	119	1	43 D	38.8%	60.7%	39.0%	61.0%
1,145	KENT	674	274	398	2	124 D	40.7%	59.1%	40.8%	59.2%
28,780	KERR	14,937	11,207	3,587	143	7,620 R	75.0%	24.0%	75.8%	24.2%
4,063	KIMBLE	1,617	1,061	551	5	510 R	65.6%	34.1%	65.8%	34.2%
425	KING	175	111	64		47 R	63.4%	36.6%	63.4%	36.6%
2,279	KINNEY	1,450	771	669	10	102 R	53.2%	46.1%	53.5%	46.5%
33,358	KLEBERG	9,946	4,443	5,367	136	924 D	44.7%	54.0%	45.3%	54.7%
5,329	KNOX	1,782	765	1,013	4	248 D	42.9%	56.8%	43.0%	57.0%
42,156	LAMAR	15,598	8,021	7,553	24	468 R	51.4%	48.4%	51.5%	48.5%
18,669	LAMB	5,316	3,064	2,230	22	834 R	57.6%	41.9%	57.9%	42.1%
12,005	LAMPASAS	4,966	3,000	1,954	12	1,046 R	60.4%	39.3%	60.6%	39.4%
5,514	LA SALLE	2,352	693	1,651	8	958 D	29.5%	70.2%	29.6%	70.4%
19,004	LAVACA	7,962	4,377	3,531	54	846 R	55.0%	44.3%	55.3%	44.7%
10,952	LEE	5,067	2,513	2,527	27	14 D	49.6%	49.9%	49.9%	50.1%
9,594	LEON	5,115	2,778	2,316	21	462 R	54.3%	45.3%	54.5%	45.5%
47,088	LIBERTY	16,973	8,524	8,343	106	181 R	50.2%	49.2%	50.5%	49.5%
20,224	LIMESTONE	6,763	3,257	3,476	30	219 D	48.2%	51.4%	48.4%	51.6%
3,766	LIPSCOMB	1,499	1,111	377	11	734 R	74.1%	25.2%	74.7%	25.3%
9,606	LIVE OAK	3,880	2,277	1,573	30	704 R	58.7%	40.5%	59.1%	40.9%
10,144	LLANO	6,202	3,550	2,629	23	921 R	57.2%	42.4%	57.5%	42.5%
91	LOVING	77	54	23		31 R	70.1%	29.9%	70.1%	29.9%
211,651	LUBBOCK	73,292	50,760	22,202	330	28,558 R	69.3%	30.3%	69.6%	30.4%
8,605	LYNN	2,367	1,279	1,086	2	193 R	54.0%	45.9%	54.1%	45.9%
8,735	MCCULLOCH	3,293	1,618	1,665	10	47 D	49.1%	50.6%	49.3%	50.7%
170,755	MCLENNAN	66,423	38,606	27,545	272	11,061 R	58.1%	41.5%	58.4%	41.6%
789	MCMULLEN	398	302	94	2	208 R	75.9%	23.6%	76.3%	23.7%
10,649	MADISON	3,747	1,896	1,835	16	61 R	50.6%	49.0%	50.8%	49.2%
10,360	MARION	4,129	1,857	2,255	17	398 D	45.0%	54.6%	45.2%	54.8%
4,684	MARTIN	1,651	1,017	632	2	385 R	61.6%	38.3%	61.7%	38.3%
3,683	MASON	1,655	975	671	9	304 R	58.9%	40.5%	59.2%	40.8%
37,828	MATAGORDA	12,566	6,787	5,675	104	1,112 R	54.0%	45.2%	54.5%	45.5%
31,398	MAVERICK	6,003	1,592	4,395	16	2,803 D	26.5%	73.2%	26.6%	73.4%
23,164	MEDINA	10,029	5,722	4,227	80	1,495 R	57.1%	42.1%	57.5%	42.5%
2,346	MENARD	1,171	552	614	5	62 D	47.1%	52.4%	47.3%	52.7%
82,636	MIDLAND	39,326	30,618	8,487	221	22,131 R	77.9%	21.6%	78.3%	21.7%
22,732	MILAM	8,396	3,512	4,865	19	1,353 D	41.8%	57.9%	41.9%	58.1%
4,477	MILLS	1,888	1,043	842	3	201 R	55.2%	44.6%	55.3%	44.7%
9,088	MITCHELL	3,376	1,596	1,773	7	177 D	47.3%	52.5%	47.4%	52.6%
17,410	MONTAGUE	7,186	3,475	3,689	22	214 D	48.4%	51.3%	48.5%	51.5%
128,487	MONTGOMERY	59,146	40,360	18,394	392	21,966 R	68.2%	31.1%	68.7%	31.3%
16,575	MOORE	5,281	3,710	1,537	34	2,173 R	70.3%	29.1%	70.7%	29.3%
14,629	MORRIS	5,630	2,104	3,522	4	1,418 D	37.4%	62.6%	37.4%	62.6%
1,950	MOTLEY	692	429	262	1	167 R	62.0%	37.9%	62.1%	37.9%
46,786	NACOGDOCHES	18,883	11,767	6,886	230	4,881 R	62.3%	36.5%	63.1%	36.9%
35,323	NAVARRO	13,232	6,445	6,749	38	304 D	48.7%	51.0%	48.8%	51.2%
13,254	NEWTON	5,309	1,659	3,640	10	1,981 D	31.2%	68.6%	31.3%	68.7%
17,359	NOLAN	5,609	2,734	2,853	22	119 D	48.7%	50.9%	48.9%	51.1%
268,215	NUECES	95,932	46,337	49,209	386	2,872 D	48.3%	51.3%	48.5%	51.5%
9,588	OCHILTREE	3,517	2,928	579	10	2,349 R	83.3%	16.5%	83.5%	16.5%
2,283	OLDHAM	1,004	691	303	10	388 R	68.8%	30.2%	69.5%	30.5%

TEXAS

PRESIDENT 1988

1980 Census Population	County	Total Vote	Republican	Democratic	Other	Rep.-Dem. Plurality	Total Vote Rep.	Total Vote Dem.	Major Vote Rep.	Major Vote Dem.
83,838	ORANGE	29,908	11,959	17,834	115	5,875 D	40.0%	59.6%	40.1%	59.9%
24,062	PALO PINTO	8,634	4,649	3,930	55	719 R	53.8%	45.5%	54.2%	45.8%
20,724	PANOLA	8,780	4,642	4,123	15	519 R	52.9%	47.0%	53.0%	47.0%
44,609	PARKER	22,723	14,090	8,517	116	5,573 R	62.0%	37.5%	62.3%	37.7%
11,038	PARMER	2,839	2,061	764	14	1,297 R	72.6%	26.9%	73.0%	27.0%
14,618	PECOS	4,460	2,483	1,960	17	523 R	55.7%	43.9%	55.9%	44.1%
24,407	POLK	11,929	5,831	5,943	155	112 D	48.9%	49.8%	49.5%	50.5%
98,637	POTTER	26,131	16,400	9,563	168	6,837 R	62.8%	36.6%	63.2%	36.8%
5,188	PRESIDIO	1,771	586	1,176	9	590 D	33.1%	66.4%	33.3%	66.7%
4,839	RAINS	2,736	1,281	1,448	7	167 D	46.8%	52.9%	46.9%	53.1%
75,062	RANDALL	36,666	27,986	8,492	188	19,494 R	76.3%	23.2%	76.7%	23.3%
4,135	REAGAN	1,355	935	418	2	517 R	69.0%	30.8%	69.1%	30.9%
2,469	REAL	1,291	795	483	13	312 R	61.6%	37.4%	62.2%	37.8%
16,101	RED RIVER	5,652	2,475	3,165	12	690 D	43.8%	56.0%	43.9%	56.1%
15,801	REEVES	4,554	1,724	2,812	18	1,088 D	37.9%	61.7%	38.0%	62.0%
9,289	REFUGIO	3,724	1,883	1,831	10	52 R	50.6%	49.2%	50.7%	49.3%
1,187	ROBERTS	581	441	135	5	306 R	75.9%	23.2%	76.6%	23.4%
14,653	ROBERTSON	5,832	2,184	3,630	18	1,446 D	37.4%	62.2%	37.6%	62.4%
14,528	ROCKWALL	9,939	7,214	2,659	66	4,555 R	72.6%	26.8%	73.1%	26.9%
11,872	RUNNELS	4,147	2,417	1,720	10	697 R	58.3%	41.5%	58.4%	41.6%
41,382	RUSK	14,313	9,117	5,140	56	3,977 R	63.7%	35.9%	63.9%	36.1%
8,702	SABINE	3,987	1,925	2,053	9	128 D	48.3%	51.5%	48.4%	51.6%
8,785	SAN AUGUSTINE	4,084	1,946	2,118	20	172 D	47.6%	51.9%	47.9%	52.1%
11,434	SAN JACINTO	5,688	2,691	2,972	25	281 D	47.3%	52.3%	47.5%	52.5%
58,013	SAN PATRICIO	19,458	9,159	9,920	379	761 D	47.1%	51.0%	48.0%	52.0%
6,204	SAN SABA	2,277	1,099	1,165	13	66 D	48.3%	51.2%	48.5%	51.5%
2,820	SCHLEICHER	1,157	653	494	10	159 R	56.4%	42.7%	56.9%	43.1%
18,192	SCURRY	5,894	3,749	2,119	26	1,630 R	63.6%	36.0%	63.9%	36.1%
3,915	SHACKELFORD	1,554	865	681	8	184 R	55.7%	43.8%	56.0%	44.0%
23,084	SHELBY	8,273	3,999	4,261	13	262 D	48.3%	51.5%	48.4%	51.6%
3,174	SHERMAN	1,499	1,145	340	14	805 R	76.4%	22.7%	77.1%	22.9%
128,366	SMITH	53,592	34,658	18,719	215	15,939 R	64.7%	34.9%	64.9%	35.1%
4,154	SOMERVELL	2,296	1,304	983	9	321 R	56.8%	42.8%	57.0%	43.0%
27,266	STARR	8,211	1,218	6,958	35	5,740 D	14.8%	84.7%	14.9%	85.1%
9,926	STEPHENS	3,874	2,342	1,519	13	823 R	60.5%	39.2%	60.7%	39.3%
1,206	STERLING	656	464	188	4	276 R	70.7%	28.7%	71.2%	28.8%
2,406	STONEWALL	1,147	421	724	2	303 D	36.7%	63.1%	36.8%	63.2%
5,130	SUTTON	1,570	996	571	3	425 R	63.4%	36.4%	63.6%	36.4%
9,723	SWISHER	3,179	1,271	1,893	15	622 D	40.0%	59.5%	40.2%	59.8%
860,880	TARRANT	396,237	242,660	151,310	2,267	91,350 R	61.2%	38.2%	61.6%	38.4%
110,932	TAYLOR	42,024	28,563	13,073	388	15,490 R	68.0%	31.1%	68.6%	31.4%
1,595	TERRELL	689	296	390	3	94 D	43.0%	56.6%	43.1%	56.9%
14,581	TERRY	4,600	2,645	1,941	14	704 R	57.5%	42.2%	57.7%	42.3%
2,053	THROCKMORTON	998	455	534	9	79 D	45.6%	53.5%	46.0%	54.0%
21,442	TITUS	8,620	4,247	4,357	16	110 D	49.3%	50.5%	49.4%	50.6%
84,784	TOM GREEN	34,012	21,463	12,283	266	9,180 R	63.1%	36.1%	63.6%	36.4%
419,573	TRAVIS	236,084	105,915	127,783	2,386	21,868 D	44.9%	54.1%	45.3%	54.7%
9,450	TRINITY	5,137	2,448	2,657	32	209 D	47.7%	51.7%	48.0%	52.0%
16,223	TYLER	7,292	3,070	4,198	24	1,128 D	42.1%	57.6%	42.2%	57.8%
28,595	UPSHUR	11,265	5,991	5,242	32	749 R	53.2%	46.5%	53.3%	46.7%
4,619	UPTON	1,740	1,189	544	7	645 R	68.3%	31.3%	68.6%	31.4%
22,441	UVALDE	8,001	4,266	3,684	51	582 R	53.3%	46.0%	53.7%	46.3%
35,910	VAL VERDE	10,211	5,109	5,044	58	65 R	50.0%	49.4%	50.3%	49.7%
31,426	VAN ZANDT	13,559	7,371	6,153	35	1,218 R	54.4%	45.4%	54.5%	45.5%
68,807	VICTORIA	24,253	15,056	8,923	274	6,133 R	62.1%	36.8%	62.8%	37.2%
41,789	WALKER	14,391	8,473	5,826	92	2,647 R	58.9%	40.5%	59.3%	40.7%
19,798	WALLER	7,624	3,607	3,957	60	350 D	47.3%	51.9%	47.7%	52.3%
13,976	WARD	4,590	2,709	1,858	23	851 R	59.0%	40.5%	59.3%	40.7%
21,998	WASHINGTON	9,037	6,041	2,960	36	3,081 R	66.8%	32.8%	67.1%	32.9%
99,258	WEBB	23,832	7,528	16,227	77	8,699 D	31.6%	68.1%	31.7%	68.3%

TEXAS

PRESIDENT 1988

1980 Census Population	County	Total Vote	Republican	Democratic	Other	Rep.-Dem. Plurality	Percentage Total Vote Rep.	Total Vote Dem.	Major Vote Rep.	Major Vote Dem.
40,242	WHARTON	12,991	6,978	5,935	78	1,043 R	53.7%	45.7%	54.0%	46.0%
7,137	WHEELER	2,777	1,703	1,067	7	636 R	61.3%	38.4%	61.5%	38.5%
121,082	WICHITA	41,590	23,324	17,956	310	5,368 R	56.1%	43.2%	56.5%	43.5%
15,931	WILBARGER	4,929	2,669	2,248	12	421 R	54.1%	45.6%	54.3%	45.7%
17,495	WILLACY	4,940	1,750	3,165	25	1,415 D	35.4%	64.1%	35.6%	64.4%
76,521	WILLIAMSON	47,230	27,322	19,589	319	7,733 R	57.8%	41.5%	58.2%	41.8%
16,756	WILSON	8,425	4,436	3,953	36	483 R	52.7%	46.9%	52.9%	47.1%
9,944	WINKLER	2,611	1,656	947	8	709 R	63.4%	36.3%	63.6%	36.4%
26,575	WISE	11,395	6,064	5,288	43	776 R	53.2%	46.4%	53.4%	46.6%
24,697	WOOD	11,366	6,216	4,553	597	1,663 R	54.7%	40.1%	57.7%	42.3%
8,299	YOAKUM	2,507	1,762	727	18	1,035 R	70.3%	29.0%	70.8%	29.2%
19,083	YOUNG	7,193	4,156	3,007	30	1,149 R	57.8%	41.8%	58.0%	42.0%
6,628	ZAPATA	3,135	958	2,171	6	1,213 D	30.6%	69.3%	30.6%	69.4%
11,666	ZAVALA	3,973	628	3,338	7	2,710 D	15.8%	84.0%	15.8%	84.2%
14,229,191	TOTAL	5,427,410	3,036,829	2,352,748	37,833	684,081 R	56.0%	43.3%	56.3%	43.7%

TEXAS

SENATOR 1988

1980 Census Population	County	Total Vote	Republican	Democratic	Other	Rep.-Dem. Plurality	Percentage Total Vote Rep.	Total Vote Dem.	Major Vote Rep.	Major Vote Dem.
38,381	ANDERSON	14,002	5,378	8,506	118	3,128 D	38.4%	60.7%	38.7%	61.3%
13,323	ANDREWS	4,345	2,281	2,034	30	247 R	52.5%	46.8%	52.9%	47.1%
64,172	ANGELINA	23,603	8,153	15,044	406	6,891 D	34.5%	63.7%	35.1%	64.9%
14,260	ARANSAS	6,169	2,780	3,340	49	560 D	45.1%	54.1%	45.4%	54.6%
7,266	ARCHER	3,590	1,543	2,042	5	499 D	43.0%	56.9%	43.0%	57.0%
1,994	ARMSTRONG	1,026	542	474	10	68 R	52.8%	46.2%	53.3%	46.7%
25,055	ATASCOSA	9,342	3,251	5,978	113	2,727 D	34.8%	64.0%	35.2%	64.8%
17,726	AUSTIN	6,961	3,174	3,758	29	584 D	45.6%	54.0%	45.8%	54.2%
8,168	BAILEY	2,269	1,074	1,186	9	112 D	47.3%	52.3%	47.5%	52.5%
7,084	BANDERA	4,534	2,483	1,996	55	487 R	54.8%	44.0%	55.4%	44.6%
24,726	BASTROP	13,582	3,367	10,067	148	6,700 D	24.8%	74.1%	25.1%	74.9%
4,919	BAYLOR	2,032	699	1,327	6	628 D	34.4%	65.3%	34.5%	65.5%
26,030	BEE	9,138	3,282	5,811	45	2,529 D	35.9%	63.6%	36.1%	63.9%
157,889	BELL	44,751	20,841	23,442	468	2,601 D	46.6%	52.4%	47.1%	52.9%
988,800	BEXAR	355,104	139,956	211,845	3,303	71,889 D	39.4%	59.7%	39.8%	60.2%
4,681	BLANCO	2,607	1,071	1,516	20	445 D	41.1%	58.2%	41.4%	58.6%
859	BORDEN	430	200	229	1	29 D	46.5%	53.3%	46.6%	53.4%
13,401	BOSQUE	6,003	2,611	3,369	23	758 D	43.5%	56.1%	43.7%	56.3%
75,301	BOWIE	27,219	9,318	17,490	411	8,172 D	34.2%	64.3%	34.8%	65.2%
169,587	BRAZORIA	57,319	23,914	32,467	938	8,553 D	41.7%	56.6%	42.4%	57.6%
93,588	BRAZOS	43,706	17,774	25,490	442	7,716 D	40.7%	58.3%	41.1%	58.9%
7,573	BREWSTER	3,217	1,084	2,088	45	1,004 D	33.7%	64.9%	34.2%	65.8%
2,579	BRISCOE	1,045	319	724	2	405 D	30.5%	69.3%	30.6%	69.4%
8,428	BROOKS	3,474	333	3,115	26	2,782 D	9.6%	89.7%	9.7%	90.3%
33,057	BROWN	11,614	4,764	6,783	67	2,019 D	41.0%	58.4%	41.3%	58.7%
12,313	BURLESON	5,208	1,341	3,844	23	2,503 D	25.7%	73.8%	25.9%	74.1%
17,803	BURNET	9,170	3,323	5,794	53	2,471 D	36.2%	63.2%	36.4%	63.6%
23,637	CALDWELL	7,811	2,127	5,612	72	3,485 D	27.2%	71.8%	27.5%	72.5%
19,574	CALHOUN	6,519	2,187	4,276	56	2,089 D	33.5%	65.6%	33.8%	66.2%
10,992	CALLAHAN	4,635	1,888	2,729	18	841 D	40.7%	58.9%	40.9%	59.1%
209,727	CAMERON	51,206	17,304	33,574	328	16,270 D	33.8%	65.6%	34.0%	66.0%
9,275	CAMP	3,915	1,136	2,769	10	1,633 D	29.0%	70.7%	29.1%	70.9%
6,672	CARSON	3,102	1,526	1,563	13	37 D	49.2%	50.4%	49.4%	50.6%
29,430	CASS	10,755	3,070	7,660	25	4,590 D	28.5%	71.2%	28.6%	71.4%
10,556	CASTRO	3,029	1,180	1,838	11	658 D	39.0%	60.7%	39.1%	60.9%
18,538	CHAMBERS	6,767	2,379	4,310	78	1,931 D	35.2%	63.7%	35.6%	64.4%
38,127	CHEROKEE	12,658	4,755	7,839	64	3,084 D	37.6%	61.9%	37.8%	62.2%
6,950	CHILDRESS	2,240	1,027	1,205	8	178 D	45.8%	53.8%	46.0%	54.0%
9,582	CLAY	4,122	1,571	2,543	8	972 D	38.1%	61.7%	38.2%	61.8%
4,825	COCHRAN	1,437	537	894	6	357 D	37.4%	62.2%	37.5%	62.5%
3,196	COKE	1,498	523	971	4	448 D	34.9%	64.8%	35.0%	65.0%
10,439	COLEMAN	4,217	1,579	2,633	5	1,054 D	37.4%	62.4%	37.5%	62.5%
144,576	COLLIN	90,878	50,602	39,508	768	11,094 R	55.7%	43.5%	56.2%	43.8%
4,648	COLLINGSWORTH	1,660	638	1,021	1	383 D	38.4%	61.5%	38.5%	61.5%
18,823	COLORADO	6,420	2,552	3,850	18	1,298 D	39.8%	60.0%	39.9%	60.1%
36,446	COMAL	19,775	10,911	8,561	303	2,350 R	55.2%	43.3%	56.0%	44.0%
12,617	COMANCHE	4,647	1,413	3,225	9	1,812 D	30.4%	69.4%	30.5%	69.5%
2,915	CONCHO	1,237	339	895	3	556 D	27.4%	72.4%	27.5%	72.5%
27,656	COOKE	11,026	5,350	5,621	55	271 D	48.5%	51.0%	48.8%	51.2%
56,767	CORYELL	11,416	5,334	6,008	74	674 D	46.7%	52.6%	47.0%	53.0%
2,947	COTTLE	1,077	299	777	1	478 D	27.8%	72.1%	27.8%	72.2%
4,600	CRANE	1,774	810	955	9	145 D	45.7%	53.8%	45.9%	54.1%
4,608	CROCKETT	1,707	486	1,213	8	727 D	28.5%	71.1%	28.6%	71.4%
8,859	CROSBY	2,475	794	1,677	4	883 D	32.1%	67.8%	32.1%	67.9%
3,315	CULBERSON	885	216	664	5	448 D	24.4%	75.0%	24.5%	75.5%
6,531	DALLAM	1,821	907	903	11	4 R	49.8%	49.6%	50.1%	49.9%
1,556,390	DALLAS	584,029	256,302	322,712	5,015	66,410 D	43.9%	55.3%	44.3%	55.7%
16,184	DAWSON	4,991	2,070	2,902	19	832 D	41.5%	58.1%	41.6%	58.4%
21,165	DEAF SMITH	5,730	2,806	2,879	45	73 D	49.0%	50.2%	49.4%	50.6%
4,839	DELTA	2,041	518	1,514	9	996 D	25.4%	74.2%	25.5%	74.5%

TEXAS

SENATOR 1988

1980 Census Population	County	Total Vote	Republican	Democratic	Other	Rep.-Dem. Plurality	Percentage Total Vote Rep.	Percentage Total Vote Dem.	Percentage Major Vote Rep.	Percentage Major Vote Dem.
143,126	DENTON	83,820	43,263	39,661	896	3,602 R	51.6%	47.3%	52.2%	47.8%
18,903	DE WITT	6,077	2,774	3,266	37	492 D	45.6%	53.7%	45.9%	54.1%
3,539	DICKENS	1,123	328	790	5	462 D	29.2%	70.3%	29.3%	70.7%
11,367	DIMMIT	3,432	571	2,843	18	2,272 D	16.6%	82.8%	16.7%	83.3%
4,075	DONLEY	1,692	818	863	11	45 D	48.3%	51.0%	48.7%	51.3%
12,517	DUVAL	4,891	598	4,272	21	3,674 D	12.2%	87.3%	12.3%	87.7%
19,480	EASTLAND	6,891	2,802	4,055	34	1,253 D	40.7%	58.8%	40.9%	59.1%
115,374	ECTOR	35,117	17,706	17,166	245	540 R	50.4%	48.9%	50.8%	49.2%
2,033	EDWARDS	781	342	436	3	94 D	43.8%	55.8%	44.0%	56.0%
59,743	ELLIS	27,578	11,750	15,658	170	3,908 D	42.6%	56.8%	42.9%	57.1%
479,899	EL PASO	119,576	34,393	84,022	1,161	49,629 D	28.8%	70.3%	29.0%	71.0%
22,560	ERATH	9,368	3,770	5,549	49	1,779 D	40.2%	59.2%	40.5%	59.5%
17,946	FALLS	4,881	1,769	3,102	10	1,333 D	36.2%	63.6%	36.3%	63.7%
24,285	FANNIN	9,082	2,611	6,422	49	3,811 D	28.7%	70.7%	28.9%	71.1%
18,832	FAYETTE	7,743	2,819	4,896	28	2,077 D	36.4%	63.2%	36.5%	63.5%
5,891	FISHER	2,050	409	1,636	5	1,227 D	20.0%	79.8%	20.0%	80.0%
9,834	FLOYD	3,128	1,498	1,622	8	124 D	47.9%	51.9%	48.0%	52.0%
2,158	FOARD	823	237	583	3	346 D	28.8%	70.8%	28.9%	71.1%
130,846	FORT BEND	63,440	27,068	35,925	447	8,857 D	42.7%	56.6%	43.0%	57.0%
6,893	FRANKLIN	2,776	828	1,939	9	1,111 D	29.8%	69.8%	29.9%	70.1%
14,830	FREESTONE	5,974	2,327	3,623	24	1,296 D	39.0%	60.6%	39.1%	60.9%
13,785	FRIO	4,415	1,087	3,305	23	2,218 D	24.6%	74.9%	24.7%	75.3%
13,150	GAINES	3,771	1,715	2,024	32	309 D	45.5%	53.7%	45.9%	54.1%
195,940	GALVESTON	73,132	24,095	48,452	585	24,357 D	32.9%	66.3%	33.2%	66.8%
5,336	GARZA	2,004	817	1,177	10	360 D	40.8%	58.7%	41.0%	59.0%
13,532	GILLESPIE	7,243	4,567	2,604	72	1,963 R	63.1%	36.0%	63.7%	36.3%
1,304	GLASSCOCK	512	240	269	3	29 D	46.9%	52.5%	47.2%	52.8%
5,193	GOLIAD	2,610	994	1,601	15	607 D	38.1%	61.3%	38.3%	61.7%
16,883	GONZALES	5,592	1,845	3,708	39	1,863 D	33.0%	66.3%	33.2%	66.8%
26,386	GRAY	9,867	6,020	3,732	115	2,288 R	61.0%	37.8%	61.7%	38.3%
89,796	GRAYSON	33,384	13,258	19,825	301	6,567 D	39.7%	59.4%	40.1%	59.9%
99,487	GREGG	36,796	17,874	18,383	539	509 D	48.6%	50.0%	49.3%	50.7%
13,580	GRIMES	5,404	1,756	3,621	27	1,865 D	32.5%	67.0%	32.7%	67.3%
46,708	GUADALUPE	20,467	9,915	10,316	236	401 D	48.4%	50.4%	49.0%	51.0%
37,592	HALE	9,783	4,866	4,876	41	10 D	49.7%	49.8%	49.9%	50.1%
5,594	HALL	1,722	527	1,192	3	665 D	30.6%	69.2%	30.7%	69.3%
8,297	HAMILTON	3,004	1,264	1,731	9	467 D	42.1%	57.6%	42.2%	57.8%
6,209	HANSFORD	2,490	1,506	975	9	531 R	60.5%	39.2%	60.7%	39.3%
6,368	HARDEMAN	1,966	657	1,305	4	648 D	33.4%	66.4%	33.5%	66.5%
40,721	HARDIN	14,539	3,854	10,621	64	6,767 D	26.5%	73.1%	26.6%	73.4%
2,409,547	HARRIS	797,358	317,656	473,429	6,273	155,773 D	39.8%	59.4%	40.2%	59.8%
52,265	HARRISON	19,531	7,175	11,991	365	4,816 D	36.7%	61.4%	37.4%	62.6%
3,987	HARTLEY	1,732	939	778	15	161 R	54.2%	44.9%	54.7%	45.3%
7,725	HASKELL	2,871	738	2,126	7	1,388 D	25.7%	74.1%	25.8%	74.2%
40,594	HAYS	23,018	6,922	15,569	527	8,647 D	30.1%	67.6%	30.8%	69.2%
5,304	HEMPHILL	1,679	891	779	9	112 R	53.1%	46.4%	53.4%	46.6%
42,606	HENDERSON	20,779	8,270	12,349	160	4,079 D	39.8%	59.4%	40.1%	59.9%
283,229	HIDALGO	80,602	21,030	59,198	374	38,168 D	26.1%	73.4%	26.2%	73.8%
25,024	HILL	9,003	3,573	5,407	23	1,834 D	39.7%	60.1%	39.8%	60.2%
23,230	HOCKLEY	7,370	3,531	3,773	66	242 D	47.9%	51.2%	48.3%	51.7%
17,714	HOOD	11,619	5,737	5,788	94	51 D	49.4%	49.8%	49.8%	50.2%
25,247	HOPKINS	9,797	2,939	6,834	24	3,895 D	30.0%	69.8%	30.1%	69.9%
22,299	HOUSTON	7,386	2,328	5,020	38	2,692 D	31.5%	68.0%	31.7%	68.3%
33,142	HOWARD	10,899	4,447	6,375	77	1,928 D	40.8%	58.5%	41.1%	58.9%
2,728	HUDSPETH	747	215	527	5	312 D	28.8%	70.5%	29.0%	71.0%
55,248	HUNT	21,028	8,849	12,034	145	3,185 D	42.1%	57.2%	42.4%	57.6%
26,304	HUTCHINSON	10,574	5,994	4,491	89	1,503 R	56.7%	42.5%	57.2%	42.8%
1,386	IRION	838	273	563	2	290 D	32.6%	67.2%	32.7%	67.3%
7,408	JACK	2,969	1,012	1,949	8	937 D	34.1%	65.6%	34.2%	65.8%
13,352	JACKSON	4,893	2,076	2,791	26	715 D	42.4%	57.0%	42.7%	57.3%

TEXAS

SENATOR 1988

1980 Census Population	County	Total Vote	Republican	Democratic	Other	Rep.-Dem. Plurality	Percentage Total Vote Rep.	Total Vote Dem.	Major Vote Rep.	Major Vote Dem.
30,781	JASPER	11,553	2,916	8,559	78	5,643 D	25.2%	74.1%	25.4%	74.6%
1,647	JEFF DAVIS	819	321	479	19	158 D	39.2%	58.5%	40.1%	59.9%
250,938	JEFFERSON	91,049	21,819	68,487	743	46,668 D	24.0%	75.2%	24.2%	75.8%
5,168	JIM HOGG	2,041	230	1,807	4	1,577 D	11.3%	88.5%	11.3%	88.7%
36,498	JIM WELLS	12,799	2,635	10,110	54	7,475 D	20.6%	79.0%	20.7%	79.3%
67,649	JOHNSON	30,123	13,045	16,846	232	3,801 D	43.3%	55.9%	43.6%	56.4%
17,268	JONES	5,691	1,914	3,746	31	1,832 D	33.6%	65.8%	33.8%	66.2%
13,593	KARNES	4,755	1,621	3,119	15	1,498 D	34.1%	65.6%	34.2%	65.8%
39,015	KAUFMAN	16,035	6,177	9,697	161	3,520 D	38.5%	60.5%	38.9%	61.1%
10,635	KENDALL	6,149	3,736	2,321	92	1,415 R	60.8%	37.7%	61.7%	38.3%
543	KENEDY	180	32	148		116 D	17.8%	82.2%	17.8%	82.2%
1,145	KENT	648	178	467	3	289 D	27.5%	72.1%	27.6%	72.4%
28,780	KERR	14,705	9,130	5,433	142	3,697 R	62.1%	36.9%	62.7%	37.3%
4,063	KIMBLE	1,515	707	800	8	93 D	46.7%	52.8%	46.9%	53.1%
425	KING	173	84	89		5 D	48.6%	51.4%	48.6%	51.4%
2,279	KINNEY	1,296	465	823	8	358 D	35.9%	63.5%	36.1%	63.9%
33,358	KLEBERG	9,428	2,839	6,422	167	3,583 D	30.1%	68.1%	30.7%	69.3%
5,329	KNOX	1,753	520	1,229	4	709 D	29.7%	70.1%	29.7%	70.3%
42,156	LAMAR	15,216	4,693	10,486	37	5,793 D	30.8%	68.9%	30.9%	69.1%
18,669	LAMB	5,188	2,330	2,841	17	511 D	44.9%	54.8%	45.1%	54.9%
12,005	LAMPASAS	4,663	1,875	2,752	36	877 D	40.2%	59.0%	40.5%	59.5%
5,514	LA SALLE	2,193	422	1,760	11	1,338 D	19.2%	80.3%	19.3%	80.7%
19,004	LAVACA	7,589	2,805	4,742	42	1,937 D	37.0%	62.5%	37.2%	62.8%
10,952	LEE	4,726	1,424	3,270	32	1,846 D	30.1%	69.2%	30.3%	69.7%
9,594	LEON	4,947	1,803	3,125	19	1,322 D	36.4%	63.2%	36.6%	63.4%
47,088	LIBERTY	16,802	5,802	10,883	117	5,081 D	34.5%	64.8%	34.8%	65.2%
20,224	LIMESTONE	6,658	2,478	4,162	18	1,684 D	37.2%	62.5%	37.3%	62.7%
3,766	LIPSCOMB	1,489	929	549	11	380 R	62.4%	36.9%	62.9%	37.1%
9,606	LIVE OAK	3,760	1,541	2,187	32	646 D	41.0%	58.2%	41.3%	58.7%
10,144	LLANO	6,302	2,709	3,564	29	855 D	43.0%	56.6%	43.2%	56.8%
91	LOVING	72	34	38		4 D	47.2%	52.8%	47.2%	52.8%
211,651	LUBBOCK	75,504	42,901	32,163	440	10,738 R	56.8%	42.6%	57.2%	42.8%
8,605	LYNN	2,329	856	1,467	6	611 D	36.8%	63.0%	36.8%	63.2%
8,735	MCCULLOCH	3,162	1,026	2,116	20	1,090 D	32.4%	66.9%	32.7%	67.3%
170,755	MCLENNAN	66,211	30,683	35,136	392	4,453 D	46.3%	53.1%	46.6%	53.4%
789	MCMULLEN	371	202	166	3	36 R	54.4%	44.7%	54.9%	45.1%
10,649	MADISON	3,601	1,141	2,450	10	1,309 D	31.7%	68.0%	31.8%	68.2%
10,360	MARION	3,955	1,186	2,749	20	1,563 D	30.0%	69.5%	30.1%	69.9%
4,684	MARTIN	1,562	609	950	3	341 D	39.0%	60.8%	39.1%	60.9%
3,683	MASON	1,588	666	916	6	250 D	41.9%	57.7%	42.1%	57.9%
37,828	MATAGORDA	12,405	4,497	7,815	93	3,318 D	36.3%	63.0%	36.5%	63.5%
31,398	MAVERICK	5,654	914	4,716	24	3,802 D	16.2%	83.4%	16.2%	83.8%
23,164	MEDINA	9,673	3,956	5,645	72	1,689 D	40.9%	58.4%	41.2%	58.8%
2,346	MENARD	1,110	364	743	3	379 D	32.8%	66.9%	32.9%	67.1%
82,636	MIDLAND	39,087	24,556	14,252	279	10,304 R	62.8%	36.5%	63.3%	36.7%
22,732	MILAM	8,220	2,305	5,888	27	3,583 D	28.0%	71.6%	28.1%	71.9%
4,477	MILLS	1,824	737	1,082	5	345 D	40.4%	59.3%	40.5%	59.5%
9,088	MITCHELL	3,189	910	2,245	34	1,335 D	28.5%	70.4%	28.8%	71.2%
17,410	MONTAGUE	7,073	2,469	4,585	19	2,116 D	34.9%	64.8%	35.0%	65.0%
128,487	MONTGOMERY	58,826	29,828	28,521	477	1,307 R	50.7%	48.5%	51.1%	48.9%
16,575	MOORE	5,318	2,823	2,451	44	372 R	53.1%	46.1%	53.5%	46.5%
14,629	MORRIS	5,424	1,108	4,304	12	3,196 D	20.4%	79.4%	20.5%	79.5%
1,950	MOTLEY	668	361	304	3	57 R	54.0%	45.5%	54.3%	45.7%
46,786	NACOGDOCHES	18,643	7,390	10,865	388	3,475 D	39.6%	58.3%	40.5%	59.5%
35,323	NAVARRO	12,970	4,769	8,169	32	3,400 D	36.8%	63.0%	36.9%	63.1%
13,254	NEWTON	5,081	853	4,209	19	3,356 D	16.8%	82.8%	16.9%	83.1%
17,359	NOLAN	5,601	1,802	3,763	36	1,961 D	32.2%	67.2%	32.4%	67.6%
268,215	NUECES	91,182	29,594	60,920	668	31,326 D	32.5%	66.8%	32.7%	67.3%
9,588	OCHILTREE	3,457	2,392	1,048	17	1,344 R	69.2%	30.3%	69.5%	30.5%
2,283	OLDHAM	987	475	508	4	33 D	48.1%	51.5%	48.3%	51.7%

TEXAS

SENATOR 1988

1980 Census Population	County	Total Vote	Republican	Democratic	Other	Rep.-Dem. Plurality	Percentage Total Vote Rep.	Percentage Total Vote Dem.	Percentage Major Vote Rep.	Percentage Major Vote Dem.
83,838	ORANGE	29,657	7,016	22,374	267	15,358 D	23.7%	75.4%	23.9%	76.1%
24,062	PALO PINTO	8,446	3,383	5,012	51	1,629 D	40.1%	59.3%	40.3%	59.7%
20,724	PANOLA	8,633	2,754	5,850	29	3,096 D	31.9%	67.8%	32.0%	68.0%
44,609	PARKER	22,637	10,200	12,254	183	2,054 D	45.1%	54.1%	45.4%	54.6%
11,038	PARMER	2,790	1,490	1,286	14	204 R	53.4%	46.1%	53.7%	46.3%
14,618	PECOS	4,599	1,688	2,882	29	1,194 D	36.7%	62.7%	36.9%	63.1%
24,407	POLK	11,698	4,046	7,443	209	3,397 D	34.6%	63.6%	35.2%	64.8%
98,637	POTTER	26,113	13,356	12,491	266	865 R	51.1%	47.8%	51.7%	48.3%
5,188	PRESIDIO	1,686	361	1,314	11	953 D	21.4%	77.9%	21.6%	78.4%
4,839	RAINS	2,626	882	1,734	10	852 D	33.6%	66.0%	33.7%	66.3%
75,062	RANDALL	36,874	22,658	13,987	229	8,671 R	61.4%	37.9%	61.8%	38.2%
4,135	REAGAN	1,308	568	736	4	168 D	43.4%	56.3%	43.6%	56.4%
2,469	REAL	1,185	553	621	11	68 D	46.7%	52.4%	47.1%	52.9%
16,101	RED RIVER	5,416	1,361	4,041	14	2,680 D	25.1%	74.6%	25.2%	74.8%
15,801	REEVES	4,607	1,200	3,375	32	2,175 D	26.0%	73.3%	26.2%	73.8%
9,289	REFUGIO	3,582	1,155	2,415	12	1,260 D	32.2%	67.4%	32.4%	67.6%
1,187	ROBERTS	575	345	226	4	119 R	60.0%	39.3%	60.4%	39.6%
14,653	ROBERTSON	5,717	1,491	4,212	14	2,721 D	26.1%	73.7%	26.1%	73.9%
14,528	ROCKWALL	9,956	5,322	4,546	88	776 R	53.5%	45.7%	53.9%	46.1%
11,872	RUNNELS	3,995	1,397	2,585	13	1,188 D	35.0%	64.7%	35.1%	64.9%
41,382	RUSK	14,011	5,970	7,898	143	1,928 D	42.6%	56.4%	43.0%	57.0%
8,702	SABINE	3,736	1,115	2,602	19	1,487 D	29.8%	69.6%	30.0%	70.0%
8,785	SAN AUGUSTINE	3,767	997	2,741	29	1,744 D	26.5%	72.8%	26.7%	73.3%
11,434	SAN JACINTO	5,508	1,888	3,592	28	1,704 D	34.3%	65.2%	34.5%	65.5%
58,013	SAN PATRICIO	18,097	6,038	11,678	381	5,640 D	33.4%	64.5%	34.1%	65.9%
6,204	SAN SABA	2,162	683	1,462	17	779 D	31.6%	67.6%	31.8%	68.2%
2,820	SCHLEICHER	1,111	398	702	11	304 D	35.8%	63.2%	36.2%	63.8%
18,192	SCURRY	6,144	2,754	3,355	35	601 D	44.8%	54.6%	45.1%	54.9%
3,915	SHACKELFORD	1,595	605	983	7	378 D	37.9%	61.6%	38.1%	61.9%
23,084	SHELBY	7,954	1,886	6,033	35	4,147 D	23.7%	75.8%	23.8%	76.2%
3,174	SHERMAN	1,460	840	607	13	233 R	57.5%	41.6%	58.1%	41.9%
128,366	SMITH	54,148	25,954	27,769	425	1,815 D	47.9%	51.3%	48.3%	51.7%
4,154	SOMERVELL	2,160	814	1,326	20	512 D	37.7%	61.4%	38.0%	62.0%
27,266	STARR	7,877	729	7,128	20	6,399 D	9.3%	90.5%	9.3%	90.7%
9,926	STEPHENS	3,741	1,538	2,185	18	647 D	41.1%	58.4%	41.3%	58.7%
1,206	STERLING	613	275	336	2	61 D	44.9%	54.8%	45.0%	55.0%
2,406	STONEWALL	1,212	358	848	6	490 D	29.5%	70.0%	29.7%	70.3%
5,130	SUTTON	1,485	562	915	8	353 D	37.8%	61.6%	38.1%	61.9%
9,723	SWISHER	3,163	851	2,301	11	1,450 D	26.9%	72.7%	27.0%	73.0%
860,880	TARRANT	392,508	178,721	210,852	2,935	32,131 D	45.5%	53.7%	45.9%	54.1%
110,932	TAYLOR	41,365	19,557	21,273	535	1,716 D	47.3%	51.4%	47.9%	52.1%
1,595	TERRELL	620	174	443	3	269 D	28.1%	71.5%	28.2%	71.8%
14,581	TERRY	4,445	1,960	2,471	14	511 D	44.1%	55.6%	44.2%	55.8%
2,053	THROCKMORTON	989	323	665	1	342 D	32.7%	67.2%	32.7%	67.3%
21,442	TITUS	8,331	2,177	6,140	14	3,963 D	26.1%	73.7%	26.2%	73.8%
84,784	TOM GREEN	33,727	13,700	19,573	454	5,873 D	40.6%	58.0%	41.2%	58.8%
419,573	TRAVIS	233,255	60,029	170,403	2,823	110,374 D	25.7%	73.1%	26.1%	73.9%
9,450	TRINITY	4,875	1,412	3,431	32	2,019 D	29.0%	70.4%	29.2%	70.8%
16,223	TYLER	6,907	1,633	5,230	44	3,597 D	23.6%	75.7%	23.8%	76.2%
28,595	UPSHUR	10,825	3,709	7,074	42	3,365 D	34.3%	65.3%	34.4%	65.6%
4,619	UPTON	1,650	679	954	17	275 D	41.2%	57.8%	41.6%	58.4%
22,441	UVALDE	7,491	2,727	4,710	54	1,983 D	36.4%	62.9%	36.7%	63.3%
35,910	VAL VERDE	9,831	3,376	6,412	43	3,036 D	34.3%	65.2%	34.5%	65.5%
31,426	VAN ZANDT	13,216	5,140	8,025	51	2,885 D	38.9%	60.7%	39.0%	61.0%
68,807	VICTORIA	23,137	10,610	12,226	301	1,616 D	45.9%	52.8%	46.5%	53.5%
41,789	WALKER	13,960	5,373	8,491	96	3,118 D	38.5%	60.8%	38.8%	61.2%
19,798	WALLER	7,607	2,470	5,068	69	2,598 D	32.5%	66.6%	32.8%	67.2%
13,976	WARD	4,714	1,853	2,827	34	974 D	39.3%	60.0%	39.6%	60.4%
21,998	WASHINGTON	8,870	4,241	4,588	41	347 D	47.8%	51.7%	48.0%	52.0%
99,258	WEBB	23,293	3,782	19,312	199	15,530 D	16.2%	82.9%	16.4%	83.6%

TEXAS

SENATOR 1988

1980 Census Population	County	Total Vote	Republican	Democratic	Other	Rep.-Dem. Plurality	Percentage Total Vote Rep.	Total Vote Dem.	Major Vote Rep.	Major Vote Dem.
40,242	WHARTON	12,982	4,496	8,398	88	3,902 D	34.6%	64.7%	34.9%	65.1%
7,137	WHEELER	2,739	1,361	1,371	7	10 D	49.7%	50.1%	49.8%	50.2%
121,082	WICHITA	41,419	18,174	22,869	376	4,695 D	43.9%	55.2%	44.3%	55.7%
15,931	WILBARGER	4,859	1,846	3,004	9	1,158 D	38.0%	61.8%	38.1%	61.9%
17,495	WILLACY	4,738	1,200	3,513	25	2,313 D	25.3%	74.1%	25.5%	74.5%
76,521	WILLIAMSON	46,918	16,288	30,211	419	13,923 D	34.7%	64.4%	35.0%	65.0%
16,756	WILSON	8,036	2,921	5,069	46	2,148 D	36.3%	63.1%	36.6%	63.4%
9,944	WINKLER	2,706	1,231	1,462	13	231 D	45.5%	54.0%	45.7%	54.3%
26,575	WISE	11,034	4,265	6,722	47	2,457 D	38.7%	60.9%	38.8%	61.2%
24,697	WOOD	10,547	4,290	6,217	40	1,927 D	40.7%	58.9%	40.8%	59.2%
8,299	YOAKUM	2,618	1,429	1,171	18	258 R	54.6%	44.7%	55.0%	45.0%
19,083	YOUNG	7,031	2,896	4,105	30	1,209 D	41.2%	58.4%	41.4%	58.6%
6,628	ZAPATA	2,952	598	2,340	14	1,742 D	20.3%	79.3%	20.4%	79.6%
11,666	ZAVALA	3,778	394	3,377	7	2,983 D	10.4%	89.4%	10.4%	89.6%
14,229,191	TOTAL	5,323,606	2,129,228	3,149,806	44,572	1,020,578 D	40.0%	59.2%	40.3%	59.7%

HARRIS COUNTY

PRESIDENT 1988

1980 Census Population	District	Total Vote	Republican	Democratic	Other	Rep.-Dem. Plurality	Percentage Total Vote Rep.	Percentage Total Vote Dem.	Percentage Major Vote Rep.	Percentage Major Vote Dem.
	DISTRICT 125	43,888	34,213	9,349	326	24,864 R	78.0%	21.3%	78.5%	21.5%
	DISTRICT 126	48,161	35,508	12,308	345	23,200 R	73.7%	25.6%	74.3%	25.7%
	DISTRICT 127	36,753	26,070	10,453	230	15,617 R	70.9%	28.4%	71.4%	28.6%
	DISTRICT 128	22,722	10,435	12,118	169	1,683 D	45.9%	53.3%	46.3%	53.7%
	DISTRICT 129	22,163	13,049	8,927	187	4,122 R	58.9%	40.3%	59.4%	40.6%
	DISTRICT 130	38,905	27,095	11,394	416	15,701 R	69.6%	29.3%	70.4%	29.6%
	DISTRICT 131	24,808	6,302	18,247	259	11,945 D	25.4%	73.6%	25.7%	74.3%
	DISTRICT 132	33,260	14,120	18,758	382	4,638 D	42.5%	56.4%	42.9%	57.1%
	DISTRICT 133	21,527	14,057	7,220	250	6,837 R	65.3%	33.5%	66.1%	33.9%
	DISTRICT 134	27,708	17,383	9,988	337	7,395 R	62.7%	36.0%	63.5%	36.5%
	DISTRICT 135	37,679	29,384	8,003	292	21,381 R	78.0%	21.2%	78.6%	21.4%
	DISTRICT 136	28,048	21,280	6,527	241	14,753 R	75.9%	23.3%	76.5%	23.5%
	DISTRICT 137	23,496	10,503	12,599	394	2,096 D	44.7%	53.6%	45.5%	54.5%
	DISTRICT 138	22,298	11,035	11,085	178	50 D	49.5%	49.7%	49.9%	50.1%
	DISTRICT 139	28,045	12,339	15,513	193	3,174 D	44.0%	55.3%	44.3%	55.7%
	DISTRICT 140	16,137	8,116	7,911	110	205 R	50.3%	49.0%	50.6%	49.4%
	DISTRICT 141	20,463	1,866	18,428	169	16,562 D	9.1%	90.1%	9.2%	90.8%
	DISTRICT 142	18,885	1,584	17,164	137	15,580 D	8.4%	90.9%	8.4%	91.6%
	DISTRICT 143	16,022	3,740	12,192	90	8,452 D	23.3%	76.1%	23.5%	76.5%
	DISTRICT 144	17,672	9,687	7,815	170	1,872 R	54.8%	44.2%	55.3%	44.7%
	DISTRICT 145	22,081	11,360	10,474	247	886 R	51.4%	47.4%	52.0%	48.0%
	DISTRICT 146	20,095	3,926	15,982	187	12,056 D	19.5%	79.5%	19.7%	80.3%
	DISTRICT 147	14,839	2,349	12,290	200	9,941 D	15.8%	82.8%	16.0%	84.0%
	DISTRICT 148	14,322	4,085	10,085	152	6,000 D	28.5%	70.4%	28.8%	71.2%
	DISTRICT 149	37,716	23,796	13,546	374	10,250 R	63.1%	35.9%	63.7%	36.3%
	DISTRICT 150	45,960	34,020	11,607	333	22,413 R	74.0%	25.3%	74.6%	25.4%
	ABSENTEE	110,490	76,915	32,936	639	43,979 R	69.6%	29.8%	70.0%	30.0%
2,409,547	TOTAL	814,160	464,217	342,919	7,024	121,298 R	57.0%	42.1%	57.5%	42.5%

HARRIS COUNTY

SENATOR 1988

1980 Census Population	District	Total Vote	Republican	Democratic	Other	Rep.-Dem. Plurality	Percentage Total Vote Rep.	Percentage Total Vote Dem.	Percentage Major Vote Rep.	Percentage Major Vote Dem.
	DISTRICT 125	43,031	23,053	19,645	333	3,408 R	53.6%	45.7%	54.0%	46.0%
	DISTRICT 126	47,214	24,154	22,732	328	1,422 R	51.2%	48.1%	51.5%	48.5%
	DISTRICT 127	35,813	17,765	17,840	208	75 D	49.6%	49.8%	49.9%	50.1%
	DISTRICT 128	22,072	6,570	15,341	161	8,771 D	29.8%	69.5%	30.0%	70.0%
	DISTRICT 129	21,693	8,572	12,919	202	4,347 D	39.5%	59.6%	39.9%	60.1%
	DISTRICT 130	38,056	17,536	20,148	372	2,612 D	46.1%	52.9%	46.5%	53.5%
	DISTRICT 131	24,445	4,279	20,000	166	15,721 D	17.5%	81.8%	17.6%	82.4%
	DISTRICT 132	32,790	8,965	23,549	276	14,584 D	27.3%	71.8%	27.6%	72.4%
	DISTRICT 133	21,064	9,593	11,246	225	1,653 D	45.5%	53.4%	46.0%	54.0%
	DISTRICT 134	27,255	11,275	15,718	262	4,443 D	41.4%	57.7%	41.8%	58.2%
	DISTRICT 135	37,054	19,988	16,802	264	3,186 R	53.9%	45.3%	54.3%	45.7%
	DISTRICT 136	27,505	14,111	13,179	215	932 R	51.3%	47.9%	51.7%	48.3%
	DISTRICT 137	23,017	6,558	16,088	371	9,530 D	28.5%	69.9%	29.0%	71.0%
	DISTRICT 138	21,803	7,529	14,095	179	6,566 D	34.5%	64.6%	34.8%	65.2%
	DISTRICT 139	27,493	8,238	19,078	177	10,840 D	30.0%	69.4%	30.2%	69.8%
	DISTRICT 140	15,650	5,399	10,126	125	4,727 D	34.5%	64.7%	34.8%	65.2%
	DISTRICT 141	20,038	1,266	18,669	103	17,403 D	6.3%	93.2%	6.4%	93.6%
	DISTRICT 142	18,538	1,056	17,409	73	16,353 D	5.7%	93.9%	5.7%	94.3%
	DISTRICT 143	15,763	2,403	13,265	95	10,862 D	15.2%	84.2%	15.3%	84.7%
	DISTRICT 144	17,407	6,523	10,694	190	4,171 D	37.5%	61.4%	37.9%	62.1%
	DISTRICT 145	21,713	7,723	13,797	193	6,074 D	35.6%	63.5%	35.9%	64.1%
	DISTRICT 146	19,770	2,825	16,832	113	14,007 D	14.3%	85.1%	14.4%	85.6%
	DISTRICT 147	14,560	1,585	12,876	99	11,291 D	10.9%	88.4%	11.0%	89.0%
	DISTRICT 148	14,024	2,647	11,232	145	8,585 D	18.9%	80.1%	19.1%	80.9%
	DISTRICT 149	36,902	15,638	20,908	356	5,270 D	42.4%	56.7%	42.8%	57.2%
	DISTRICT 150	44,922	23,578	20,997	347	2,581 R	52.5%	46.7%	52.9%	47.1%
	ABSENTEE	107,723	58,827	48,244	652	10,583 R	54.6%	44.8%	54.9%	45.1%
2,409,547	TOTAL	797,358	317,656	473,429	6,273	155,773 D	39.8%	59.4%	40.2%	59.8%

TEXAS

CONGRESS

CD	Year	Total Vote	Republican Vote	Republican Candidate	Democratic Vote	Democratic Candidate	Other Vote	Rep.-Dem. Plurality	Percentage Total Vote Rep.	Percentage Total Vote Dem.	Percentage Major Vote Rep.	Percentage Major Vote Dem.
1	1988	196,923	74,357	MCQUEEN, HORACE	122,566	CHAPMAN, JAMES L.		48,209 D	37.8%	62.2%	37.8%	62.2%
1	1986	84,445			84,445	CHAPMAN, JAMES L.		84,445 D		100.0%		100.0%
1	1984	139,829			139,829	HALL, SAM B.		139,829 D		100.0%		100.0%
1	1982	103,283			100,685	HALL, SAM B.	2,598	100,685 D		97.5%		100.0%
2	1988	166,089			145,614	WILSON, CHARLES	20,475	145,614 D		87.7%		100.0%
2	1986	118,353	35,986	GORDON, JULIAN	78,529	WILSON, CHARLES	3,838	42,543 D	30.4%	66.4%	31.4%	68.6%
2	1984	191,067	77,842	DUGAS, LOUIS	113,225	WILSON, CHARLES		35,383 D	40.7%	59.3%	40.7%	59.3%
2	1982	97,346			91,762	WILSON, CHARLES	5,584	91,762 D		94.3%		100.0%
3	1988	278,509	227,882	BARTLETT, STEVE	50,627	COWDEN, BLAKE		177,255 R	81.8%	18.2%	81.8%	18.2%
3	1986	152,385	143,381	BARTLETT, STEVE			9,004	143,381 R	94.1%		100.0%	
3	1984	275,709	228,819	BARTLETT, STEVE	46,890	WESTBROOK, JIM		181,929 R	83.0%	17.0%	83.0%	17.0%
4	1988	209,868	67,337	SUTTON, RANDY	139,379	HALL, RALPH M.	3,152	72,042 D	32.1%	66.4%	32.6%	67.4%
4	1986	136,118	38,578	BLOW, THOMAS	97,540	HALL, RALPH M.		58,962 D	28.3%	71.7%	28.3%	71.7%
4	1984	208,341	87,553	BLOW, THOMAS	120,749	HALL, RALPH M.	39	33,196 D	42.0%	58.0%	42.0%	58.0%
4	1982	127,496	32,221	COLLUMB, PETER J.	94,134	HALL, RALPH M.	1,141	61,913 D	25.3%	73.8%	25.5%	74.5%
5	1988	157,039	59,877	WILLIAMS, LON	95,376	BRYANT, JOHN	1,786	35,499 D	38.1%	60.7%	38.6%	61.4%
5	1986	98,104	39,945	CARTER, TOM	57,410	BRYANT, JOHN	749	17,465 D	40.7%	58.5%	41.0%	59.0%
5	1984	94,391			94,391	BRYANT, JOHN		94,391 D		100.0%		100.0%
5	1982	80,530	27,121	DEVANY, JOE	52,214	BRYANT, JOHN	1,195	25,093 D	33.7%	64.8%	34.2%	65.8%
6	1988	243,478	164,692	BARTON, JOE L.	78,786	KENDRICK, N. P.		85,906 R	67.6%	32.4%	67.6%	32.4%
6	1986	154,460	86,190	BARTON, JOE L.	68,270	GEREN, PETE		17,920 R	55.8%	44.2%	55.8%	44.2%
6	1984	232,281	131,482	BARTON, JOE L.	100,799	KUBIAK, DAN		30,683 R	56.6%	43.4%	56.6%	43.4%
7	1988	234,027	185,203	ARCHER, W. R.	48,824	RICHARDS, DIANNE		136,379 R	79.1%	20.9%	79.1%	20.9%
7	1986	148,395	129,673	ARCHER, W. R.	17,635	KNIFFEN, HARRY	1,087	112,038 R	87.4%	11.9%	88.0%	12.0%
7	1984	246,315	213,480	ARCHER, W. R.	32,835	WILLIBEY, BILLY		180,645 R	86.7%	13.3%	86.7%	13.3%
7	1982	127,922	108,718	ARCHER, W. R.	17,866	SCOGGINS, DENNIS G.	1,338	90,852 R	85.0%	14.0%	85.9%	14.1%
8	1988	90,503	90,503	FIELDS, JACK				90,503 R	100.0%		100.0%	
8	1986	96,903	66,280	FIELDS, JACK	30,617	MANN, BLAINE	6	35,663 R	68.4%	31.6%	68.4%	31.6%
8	1984	175,103	113,031	FIELDS, JACK	62,072	BUFORD, DON		50,959 R	64.6%	35.4%	64.6%	35.4%
8	1982	89,218	50,630	FIELDS, JACK	38,041	ALLEE, HENRY E.	547	12,589 R	56.7%	42.6%	57.1%	42.9%
9	1988	137,270			137,270	BROOKS, JACK B.		137,270 D		100.0%		100.0%
9	1986	119,119	45,834	DUPERIER, LISA	73,285	BROOKS, JACK B.		27,451 D	38.5%	61.5%	38.5%	61.5%
9	1984	204,865	84,306	MAHAN, JIM	120,559	BROOKS, JACK B.		36,253 D	41.2%	58.8%	41.2%	58.8%
9	1982	116,897	35,422	LEWIS, JOHN W.	78,965	BROOKS, JACK B.	2,510	43,543 D	30.3%	67.6%	31.0%	69.0%
10	1988	248,494			232,213	PICKLE, JAKE	16,281	232,213 D		93.4%		100.0%
10	1986	187,863	52,000	RYLANDER, CAROLE K.	135,863	PICKLE, JAKE		83,863 D	27.7%	72.3%	27.7%	72.3%
10	1984	186,785			186,447	PICKLE, JAKE	338	186,447 D		99.8%		100.0%
10	1982	134,276			121,030	PICKLE, JAKE	13,246	121,030 D		90.1%		100.0%
11	1988	140,740			134,207	LEATH, J. MARVIN	6,533	134,207 D		95.4%		100.0%
11	1986	84,201			84,201	LEATH, J. MARVIN		84,201 D		100.0%		100.0%
11	1984	112,940			112,940	LEATH, J. MARVIN		112,940 D		100.0%		100.0%
11	1982	86,395			83,236	LEATH, J. MARVIN	3,159	83,236 D		96.3%		100.0%
12	1988	136,456			135,459	WRIGHT, JAMES C.	997	135,459 D		99.3%		100.0%
12	1986	123,451	38,620	MCNEIL, DON	84,831	WRIGHT, JAMES C.		46,211 D	31.3%	68.7%	31.3%	68.7%
12	1984	106,302			106,299	WRIGHT, JAMES C.	3	106,299 D		100.0%		100.0%
13	1988	187,450	89,105	MILNER, LARRY S.	98,345	SARPALIUS, BILL		9,240 D	47.5%	52.5%	47.5%	52.5%
13	1986	130,887	84,980	BOULTER, BEAU	45,907	SEAL, DOUG		39,073 R	64.9%	35.1%	64.9%	35.1%
13	1984	202,967	107,600	BOULTER, BEAU	95,367	HIGHTOWER, JOHN		12,233 R	53.0%	47.0%	53.0%	47.0%
13	1982	135,820	47,877	SLOVER, RON	86,376	HIGHTOWER, JOHN	1,567	38,499 D	35.3%	63.6%	35.7%	64.3%

TEXAS

CONGRESS

CD	Year	Total Vote	Republican Vote	Republican Candidate	Democratic Vote	Democratic Candidate	Other Vote	Rep.-Dem. Plurality	Percentage Total Vote Rep.	Percentage Total Vote Dem.	Percentage Major Vote Rep.	Percentage Major Vote Dem.
14	1988	209,216	96,042	SWEENEY, MAC	111,395	LAUGHLIN, GREG	1,779	15,353 D	45.9%	53.2%	46.3%	53.7%
14	1986	142,323	74,471	SWEENEY, MAC	67,852	LAUGHLIN, GREG		6,619 R	52.3%	47.7%	52.3%	47.7%
14	1984	203,066	104,181	SWEENEY, MAC	98,885	PATMAN, WILLIAM N.		5,296 R	51.3%	48.7%	51.3%	48.7%
14	1982	126,712	48,942	WYATT, JOE	76,851	PATMAN, WILLIAM N.	919	27,909 D	38.6%	60.7%	38.9%	61.1%
15	1988	99,805			93,672	DE LA GARZA, ELIGIO	6,133	93,672 D		93.9%		100.0%
15	1986	70,777			70,777	DE LA GARZA, ELIGIO		70,777 D		100.0%		100.0%
15	1984	104,863			104,863	DE LA GARZA, ELIGIO		104,863 D		100.0%		100.0%
15	1982	80,002			76,544	DE LA GARZA, ELIGIO	3,458	76,544 D		95.7%		100.0%
16	1988	104,514			104,514	COLEMAN, RONALD		104,514 D		100.0%		100.0%
16	1986	77,011	26,421	GILLIA, ROY	50,590	COLEMAN, RONALD		24,169 D	34.3%	65.7%	34.3%	65.7%
16	1984	132,964	56,589	HAMMOND, JACK	76,375	COLEMAN, RONALD		19,786 D	42.6%	57.4%	42.6%	57.4%
16	1982	81,671	36,064	HAGGERTY, PAT	44,024	COLEMAN, RONALD	1,583	7,960 D	44.2%	53.9%	45.0%	55.0%
17	1988	149,064			149,064	STENHOLM, CHARLES W.		149,064 D		100.0%		100.0%
17	1986	97,791			97,791	STENHOLM, CHARLES W.		97,791 D		100.0%		100.0%
17	1984	143,012			143,012	STENHOLM, CHARLES W.		143,012 D		100.0%		100.0%
17	1982	112,630			109,359	STENHOLM, CHARLES W.	3,271	109,359 D		97.1%		100.0%
18	1988	101,643			94,408	LELAND, MICKEY	7,235	94,408 D		92.9%		100.0%
18	1986	70,219			63,335	LELAND, MICKEY	6,884	63,335 D		90.2%		100.0%
18	1984	139,110	26,400	BEAMAN, GLEN E.	109,626	LELAND, MICKEY	3,084	83,226 D	19.0%	78.8%	19.4%	80.6%
18	1982	82,335	12,104	PICKETT, C. LEON	68,014	LELAND, MICKEY	2,217	55,910 D	14.7%	82.6%	15.1%	84.9%
19	1988	167,000	113,068	COMBEST, LARRY	53,932	MCCATHERN, GERALD		59,136 R	67.7%	32.3%	67.7%	32.3%
19	1986	110,824	68,695	COMBEST, LARRY	42,129	MCCATHERN, GERALD		26,566 R	62.0%	38.0%	62.0%	38.0%
19	1984	176,849	102,805	COMBEST, LARRY	74,044	RICHARDS, DON R.		28,761 R	58.1%	41.9%	58.1%	41.9%
19	1982	109,970	19,062	HICKS, E. L.	89,702	HANCE, KENT	1,206	70,640 D	17.3%	81.6%	17.5%	82.5%
20	1988	133,696	36,801	TREVINO, LEE	94,527	GONZALEZ, HENRY B.	2,368	57,726 D	27.5%	70.7%	28.0%	72.0%
20	1986	55,363			55,363	GONZALEZ, HENRY B.		55,363 D		100.0%		100.0%
20	1984	100,443			100,443	GONZALEZ, HENRY B.		100,443 D		100.0%		100.0%
21	1988	218,790	203,989	SMITH, LAMAR			14,801	203,989 R	93.2%		100.0%	
21	1986	165,567	100,346	SMITH, LAMAR	63,779	SNELSON, PETE	1,442	36,567 R	60.6%	38.5%	61.1%	38.9%
21	1984	247,980	199,909	LOEFFLER, TOM	48,039	SULLIVAN, JOE	32	151,870 R	80.6%	19.4%	80.6%	19.4%
22	1988	186,484	125,733	DELAY, THOMAS D.	58,471	WALKER, WAYNE	2,280	67,262 R	67.4%	31.4%	68.3%	31.7%
22	1986	106,538	76,459	DELAY, THOMAS D.	30,079	DIRECTOR, SUSAN		46,380 R	71.8%	28.2%	71.8%	28.2%
22	1984	191,751	125,225	DELAY, THOMAS D.	66,495	WILLIAMS, DOUG	31	58,730 R	65.3%	34.7%	65.3%	34.7%
22	1982	67,479	66,536	PAUL, RON			943	66,536 R	98.6%		100.0%	
23	1988	180,430	60,559	GONZALES, JEROME L.	116,423	BUSTAMANTE, ALBERT G.	3,448	55,864 D	33.6%	64.5%	34.2%	65.8%
23	1986	75,132			68,131	BUSTAMANTE, ALBERT G.	7,001	68,131 D		90.7%		100.0%
23	1984	95,721			95,721	BUSTAMANTE, ALBERT G.		95,721 D		100.0%		100.0%
24	1988	146,635			135,794	FROST, MARTIN	10,841	135,794 D		92.6%		100.0%
24	1986	103,191	33,819	BURK, BOB	69,368	FROST, MARTIN	4	35,549 D	32.8%	67.2%	32.8%	67.2%
24	1984	176,918	71,703	BURK, BOB	105,210	FROST, MARTIN	5	33,507 D	40.5%	59.5%	40.5%	59.5%
25	1988	159,036	44,043	LOEFFLER, GEORGE H.	113,499	ANDREWS, MIKE	1,494	69,456 D	27.7%	71.4%	28.0%	72.0%
25	1986	67,435			67,435	ANDREWS, MIKE		67,435 D		100.0%		100.0%
25	1984	177,920	63,974	PATTERSON, JERRY	113,946	ANDREWS, MIKE		49,972 D	36.0%	64.0%	36.0%	64.0%
25	1982	105,914	40,112	FAUBION, MIKE	63,974	ANDREWS, MIKE	1,828	23,862 D	37.9%	60.4%	38.5%	61.5%
26	1988	281,446	194,944	ARMEY, DICK	86,490	REYES, JO ANN	12	108,454 R	69.3%	30.7%	69.3%	30.7%
26	1986	149,386	101,735	ARMEY, DICK	47,651	RICHARDSON, GEORGE		54,084 R	68.1%	31.9%	68.1%	31.9%
26	1984	247,094	126,641	ARMEY, DICK	120,451	VANDERGRIFF, TOM	2	6,190 R	51.3%	48.7%	51.3%	48.7%

TEXAS

CONGRESS

CD	Year	Total Vote	Republican Vote	Republican Candidate	Democratic Vote	Democratic Candidate	Other Vote	Rep.-Dem. Plurality	Percentage Total Vote Rep.	Percentage Total Vote Dem.	Percentage Major Vote Rep.	Percentage Major Vote Dem.
27	1988	105,085			105,085	ORTIZ, SOLOMON P.		105,085 D		100.0%		100.0%
27	1986	64,165			64,165	ORTIZ, SOLOMON P.		64,165 D		100.0%		100.0%
27	1984	165,799	60,283	MOORE, RICHARD	105,516	ORTIZ, SOLOMON P.		45,233 D	36.4%	63.6%	36.4%	63.6%
27	1982	104,044	35,209	LUBY, JASON	66,604	ORTIZ, SOLOMON P.	2,231	31,395 D	33.8%	64.0%	34.6%	65.4%

TEXAS

1988 GENERAL ELECTION

President Other vote was 30,355 Libertarian (Paul); 7,208 New Alliance (Fulani); 110 Warren (write-in); 62 Kenoyer (write-in); 98 scattered write-in.

Senator Other vote was 43,989 Libertarian (Daiell); 344 Wright (write-in); 88 Divoky (write-in); 77 Sims (write-in); 74 Budka (write-in).

Congress In AMERICA VOTES 17, the Republican (Gordon) 1986 vote in CD 2 was listed as 55,986. Late amended returns, which were not available when AV 17 was published, corrected the vote to 35,986 with a change in Hardin county's vote from 22,236 to 2,236. Other vote in 1988 was Libertarian (Nelson) in CD 2; Libertarian (Dunn) in CD 4; Libertarian (Ashby) in CD 5; Libertarian (May) in CD 10; Libertarian (King) in CD 11; 767 Ryan (write-in) and 230 Johnson (write-in) in CD 12; Libertarian (Kelley) in CD 14; Libertarian (Hendrix) in CD 15; Libertarian (Snead) in CD 18; Libertarian (Doyle) in CD 20; Libertarian (Robinson) in CD 21; 2,276 Libertarian (Harper) and 4 Sims (write-in) in CD 22; Libertarian (Garza) in CD 23; Libertarian (Sadovy) in CD 24; Libertarian (Southwick) in CD 25; Turner (write-in) in CD 26.

HARRIS COUNTY

Population data not available by districts.

President Other vote was 5,205 Libertarian (Paul); 1,802 New Alliance (Fulani); 8 Warren (write-in); 3 Kenoyer (write-in) 6 scattered write-in. Write-in votes are included in the total of the other vote column but are not available by districts.

Senator Other vote was 6,230 Libertarian (Daiell); 25 Wright (write-in); 10 Budka (write-in); 6 Divoky (write-in); 2 Sims (write-in). Write-in votes are included in the total of the other vote column but are not available by districts.

1988 PRIMARIES

MARCH 8 REPUBLICAN

Senator 275,080 Wes Gilbreath; 228,676 Beau Boulter; 138,031 Milton E. Fox; 107,560 Ned Snead.

Congress Unopposed in twelve CD's. No candidate in CD's 2, 9, 10, 11, 12, 15, 16, 17, 18, 24 and 27. Contested as follows:

CD 5 17,356 Lon Williams; 6,482 Kay Cohlmia.
CD 13 10,129 Larry S. Milner; 7,953 Robert Price; 7,830 Jim Brandon; 6,464 Chip Staniswalis; 5,031 Ron Buffum; 3,737 Alan Pickering.
CD 20 6,399 Lee Trevino; 5,389 Terry Peters.
CD 25 13,066 George H. Loeffler; 3,936 Lon P. Arnett.

MARCH 8 DEMOCRATIC

Senator 1,365,736 Lloyd Bentsen; 244,805 Joe Sullivan.

Congress Unopposed in twenty CD's. No candidate in CD 8 and 21. Contested as follows:

CD 6 21,245 N. P. Kendrick; 20,275 John E. Welch; 16,651 W. Alton Parish.
CD 13 37,745 Bill Sarpalius; 19,629 Ed Lehman; 10,755 Randy Hollums.
CD 14 59,213 Greg Laughlin; 22,770 Michael L. Herzik.
CD 18 38,963 Mickey Leland; 8,321 Elizabeth Spates.
CD 22 12,049 Wayne Walker; 8,775 Richard Konrad; 7,715 Ray Lemmon.

TEXAS

APRIL 12 REPUBLICAN RUN-OFF

Senator 111,134 Beau Boulter; 73,573 Wes Gilbreath.

Congress

CD 13 12,013 Larry S. Milner; 9,322 Robert Price.

APRIL 12 DEMOCRATIC RUN-OFF

Congress

CD 6 12,209 N. P. Kendrick; 11,838 John E. Welch.
CD 22 3,757 Wayne Walker; 3,667 Richard Konrad.

UTAH

GOVERNOR

Norman H. Bangerter (R). Re-elected 1988 to a four-year term. Previously elected 1984.

SENATORS

E. J.Garn (R). Re-elected 1986 to a six-year term. Previously elected 1980, 1974.

Orrin G. Hatch (R). Re-elected 1988 to a six-year term. Previously elected 1982, 1976.

REPRESENTATIVES

1. James V. Hansen (R)
2. Wayne Owens (D)
3. Howard C. Nielson (R)

POSTWAR VOTE FOR PRESIDENT

Year	Total Vote	Republican Vote	Republican Candidate	Democratic Vote	Democratic Candidate	Other Vote	Plurality	Percentage Total Vote Rep.	Percentage Total Vote Dem.	Percentage Major Vote Rep.	Percentage Major Vote Dem.
1988	647,008	428,442	Bush, George	207,343	Dukakis, Michael S.	11,223	221,099 R	66.2%	32.0%	67.4%	32.6%
1984	629,656	469,105	Reagan, Ronald	155,369	Mondale, Walter F.	5,182	313,736 R	74.5%	24.7%	75.1%	24.9%
1980	604,222	439,687	Reagan, Ronald	124,266	Carter, Jimmy	40,269	315,421 R	72.8%	20.6%	78.0%	22.0%
1976	541,198	337,908	Ford, Gerald R.	182,110	Carter, Jimmy	21,180	155,798 R	62.4%	33.6%	65.0%	35.0%
1972	478,476	323,643	Nixon, Richard M.	126,284	McGovern, George S.	28,549	197,359 R	67.6%	26.4%	71.9%	28.1%
1968	422,568	238,728	Nixon, Richard M.	156,665	Humphrey, Hubert H.	27,175	82,063 R	56.5%	37.1%	60.4%	39.6%
1964	401,413	181,785	Goldwater, Barry M.	219,628	Johnson, Lyndon B.		37,843 D	45.3%	54.7%	45.3%	54.7%
1960	374,709	205,361	Nixon, Richard M.	169,248	Kennedy, John F.	100	36,113 R	54.8%	45.2%	54.8%	45.2%
1956	333,995	215,631	Eisenhower, Dwight D.	118,364	Stevenson, Adlai E.		97,267 R	64.6%	35.4%	64.6%	35.4%
1952	329,554	194,190	Eisenhower, Dwight D.	135,364	Stevenson, Adlai E.		58,826 R	58.9%	41.1%	58.9%	41.1%
1948	276,306	124,402	Dewey, Thomas E.	149,151	Truman, Harry S.	2,753	24,749 D	45.0%	54.0%	45.5%	54.5%

POSTWAR VOTE FOR GOVERNOR

Year	Total Vote	Republican Vote	Republican Candidate	Democratic Vote	Democratic Candidate	Other Vote	Rep.-Dem. Plurality	Percentage Total Vote Rep.	Percentage Total Vote Dem.	Percentage Major Vote Rep.	Percentage Major Vote Dem.
1988 **	649,114	260,462	Bangerter, Norman H.	249,321	Wilson, Ted	139,331	11,141 R	40.1%	38.4%	51.1%	48.9%
1984	629,619	351,792	Bangerter, Norman H.	275,669	Owens, Wayne	2,158	76,123 R	55.9%	43.8%	56.1%	43.9%
1980	600,019	266,578	Wright, Bob	330,974	Matheson, Scott M.	2,467	64,396 D	44.4%	55.2%	44.6%	55.4%
1976	539,649	248,027	Romney, Vernon B.	280,706	Matheson, Scott M.	10,916	32,679 D	46.0%	52.0%	46.9%	53.1%
1972	476,447	144,449	Strike, Nicholas L.	331,998	Rampton, Calvin L.		187,549 D	30.3%	69.7%	30.3%	69.7%
1968	421,012	131,729	Buehner, Carl W.	289,283	Rampton, Calvin L.		157,554 D	31.3%	68.7%	31.3%	68.7%
1964	398,256	171,300	Melich, Mitchell	226,956	Rampton, Calvin L.		55,656 D	43.0%	57.0%	43.0%	57.0%
1960	371,489	195,634	Clyde, George D.	175,855	Barlocker, W. A.		19,779 R	52.7%	47.3%	52.7%	47.3%
1956 **	332,889	127,164	Clyde, George D.	111,297	Romney, L. C.	94,428	15,867 R	38.2%	33.4%	53.3%	46.7%
1952	327,704	180,516	Lee, J. Bracken	147,188	Glade, Earl J.		33,328 R	55.1%	44.9%	55.1%	44.9%
1948	275,067	151,253	Lee, J. Bracken	123,814	Maw, Herbert B.		27,439 R	55.0%	45.0%	55.0%	45.0%

In 1956 other vote was Independent (Lee). In 1988 other vote was 136,651 Independent (Cook); 1,661 Libertarian (Burton) and 1,019 American (Pedersen).

UTAH

POSTWAR VOTE FOR SENATOR

Year	Total Vote	Republican Vote	Republican Candidate	Democratic Vote	Democratic Candidate	Other Vote	Rep.-Dem. Plurality	Percentage Total Vote Rep.	Percentage Total Vote Dem.	Percentage Major Vote Rep.	Percentage Major Vote Dem.
1988	640,702	430,089	Hatch, Orrin G.	203,364	Moss, Brian H.	7,249	226,725 R	67.1%	31.7%	67.9%	32.1%
1986	435,111	314,608	Garn, E. J.	115,523	Oliver, Craig	4,980	199,085 R	72.3%	26.6%	73.1%	26.9%
1982	530,802	309,332	Hatch, Orrin G.	219,482	Wilson, Ted	1,988	89,850 R	58.3%	41.3%	58.5%	41.5%
1980	594,298	437,675	Garn, E. J.	151,454	Berman, Dan	5,169	286,221 R	73.6%	25.5%	74.3%	25.7%
1976	540,108	290,221	Hatch, Orrin G.	241,948	Moss, Frank E.	7,939	48,273 R	53.7%	44.8%	54.5%	45.5%
1974	420,642	210,299	Garn, E. J.	185,377	Owens, Wayne	24,966	24,922 R	50.0%	44.1%	53.1%	46.9%
1970	374,303	159,004	Burton, Laurence J.	210,207	Moss, Frank E.	5,092	51,203 D	42.5%	56.2%	43.1%	56.9%
1968	419,262	225,075	Bennett, Wallace F.	192,168	Weilenmann, Milton	2,019	32,907 R	53.7%	45.8%	53.9%	46.1%
1964	397,384	169,562	Wilkinson, Ernest L.	227,822	Moss, Frank E.		58,260 D	42.7%	57.3%	42.7%	57.3%
1962	318,411	166,755	Bennett, Wallace F.	151,656	King, David S.		15,099 R	52.4%	47.6%	52.4%	47.6%
1958 **	291,311	101,471	Watkins, Arthur V.	112,827	Moss, Frank E.	77,013	11,356 D	34.8%	38.7%	47.4%	52.6%
1956	330,381	178,261	Bennett, Wallace F.	152,120	Hopkin, Alonzo F.		26,141 R	54.0%	46.0%	54.0%	46.0%
1952	327,033	177,435	Watkins, Arthur V.	149,598	Granger, Walter K.		27,837 R	54.3%	45.7%	54.3%	45.7%
1950	264,440	142,427	Bennett, Wallace F.	121,198	Thomas, Elbert D.	815	21,229 R	53.9%	45.8%	54.0%	46.0%
1946	197,399	101,142	Watkins, Arthur V.	96,257	Murdock, Abe		4,885 R	51.2%	48.8%	51.2%	48.8%

In 1958 other vote was Independent (Lee).

UTAH

Districts Established January 1, 1982

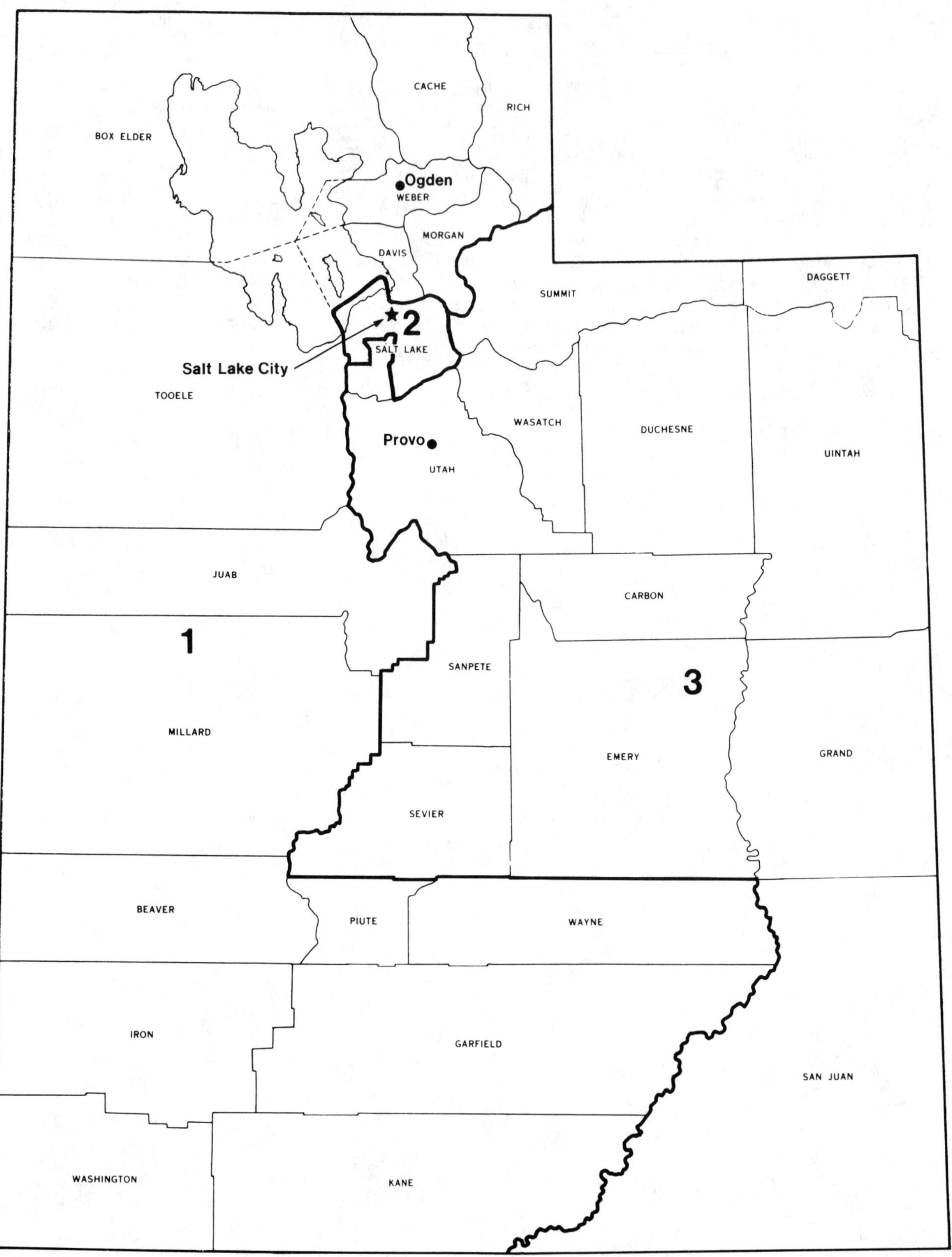

UTAH

PRESIDENT 1988

1980 Census Population	County	Total Vote	Republican	Democratic	Other	Rep.-Dem. Plurality	Percentage Total Vote Rep.	Total Vote Dem.	Major Vote Rep.	Major Vote Dem.
4,378	BEAVER	2,112	1,286	816	10	470 R	60.9%	38.6%	61.2%	38.8%
33,222	BOX ELDER	15,461	12,585	2,736	140	9,849 R	81.4%	17.7%	82.1%	17.9%
57,176	CACHE	27,963	21,766	5,871	326	15,895 R	77.8%	21.0%	78.8%	21.2%
22,179	CARBON	8,603	3,019	5,521	63	2,502 D	35.1%	64.2%	35.4%	64.6%
769	DAGGETT	412	272	132	8	140 R	66.0%	32.0%	67.3%	32.7%
146,540	DAVIS	68,384	50,469	16,868	1,047	33,601 R	73.8%	24.7%	74.9%	25.1%
12,565	DUCHESNE	4,403	3,118	1,227	58	1,891 R	70.8%	27.9%	71.8%	28.2%
11,451	EMERY	4,144	2,322	1,788	34	534 R	56.0%	43.1%	56.5%	43.5%
3,673	GARFIELD	1,855	1,470	370	15	1,100 R	79.2%	19.9%	79.9%	20.1%
8,241	GRAND	3,248	1,895	1,287	66	608 R	58.3%	39.6%	59.6%	40.4%
17,349	IRON	7,868	6,038	1,736	94	4,302 R	76.7%	22.1%	77.7%	22.3%
5,530	JUAB	2,523	1,505	974	44	531 R	59.7%	38.6%	60.7%	39.3%
4,024	KANE	2,255	1,788	398	69	1,390 R	79.3%	17.6%	81.8%	18.2%
8,970	MILLARD	4,710	3,515	1,124	71	2,391 R	74.6%	23.9%	75.8%	24.2%
4,917	MORGAN	2,567	1,889	647	31	1,242 R	73.6%	25.2%	74.5%	25.5%
1,329	PIUTE	687	476	206	5	270 R	69.3%	30.0%	69.8%	30.2%
2,100	RICH	860	621	234	5	387 R	72.2%	27.2%	72.6%	27.4%
619,066	SALT LAKE	276,903	163,557	107,453	5,893	56,104 R	59.1%	38.8%	60.4%	39.6%
12,253	SAN JUAN	3,837	2,377	1,407	53	970 R	61.9%	36.7%	62.8%	37.2%
14,620	SANPETE	6,517	4,579	1,822	116	2,757 R	70.3%	28.0%	71.5%	28.5%
14,727	SEVIER	6,221	4,747	1,403	71	3,344 R	76.3%	22.6%	77.2%	22.8%
10,198	SUMMIT	6,503	3,881	2,536	86	1,345 R	59.7%	39.0%	60.5%	39.5%
26,033	TOOELE	9,804	5,539	4,166	99	1,373 R	56.5%	42.5%	57.1%	42.9%
20,506	UINTAH	7,218	5,341	1,799	78	3,542 R	74.0%	24.9%	74.8%	25.2%
218,106	UTAH	88,227	68,134	18,533	1,560	49,601 R	77.2%	21.0%	78.6%	21.4%
8,523	WASATCH	3,997	2,487	1,451	59	1,036 R	62.2%	36.3%	63.2%	36.8%
26,065	WASHINGTON	16,565	13,306	3,054	205	10,252 R	80.3%	18.4%	81.3%	18.7%
1,911	WAYNE	1,143	784	353	6	431 R	68.6%	30.9%	69.0%	31.0%
144,616	WEBER	62,018	39,676	21,431	911	18,245 R	64.0%	34.6%	64.9%	35.1%
1,461,037	TOTAL	647,008	428,442	207,343	11,223	221,099 R	66.2%	32.0%	67.4%	32.6%

UTAH

GOVERNOR 1988

1980 Census Population	County	Total Vote	Republican	Democratic	Other	Rep.-Dem. Plurality	Percentage Total Vote Rep.	Total Vote Dem.	Major Vote Rep.	Major Vote Dem.
4,378	BEAVER	2,111	869	998	244	129 D	41.2%	47.3%	46.5%	53.5%
33,222	BOX ELDER	16,093	7,880	5,421	2,792	2,459 R	49.0%	33.7%	59.2%	40.8%
57,176	CACHE	27,995	13,916	10,326	3,753	3,590 R	49.7%	36.9%	57.4%	42.6%
22,179	CARBON	8,570	1,265	6,102	1,203	4,837 D	14.8%	71.2%	17.2%	82.8%
769	DAGGETT	415	171	189	55	18 D	41.2%	45.5%	47.5%	52.5%
146,540	DAVIS	68,547	29,729	21,407	17,411	8,322 R	43.4%	31.2%	58.1%	41.9%
12,565	DUCHESNE	4,378	1,471	1,597	1,310	126 D	33.6%	36.5%	47.9%	52.1%
11,451	EMERY	4,150	1,397	2,185	568	788 D	33.7%	52.7%	39.0%	61.0%
3,673	GARFIELD	1,853	1,310	362	181	948 R	70.7%	19.5%	78.3%	21.7%
8,241	GRAND	3,207	1,049	1,507	651	458 D	32.7%	47.0%	41.0%	59.0%
17,349	IRON	7,780	4,361	2,550	869	1,811 R	56.1%	32.8%	63.1%	36.9%
5,530	JUAB	2,526	928	1,158	440	230 D	36.7%	45.8%	44.5%	55.5%
4,024	KANE	2,225	1,499	491	235	1,008 R	67.4%	22.1%	75.3%	24.7%
8,970	MILLARD	4,655	2,030	1,529	1,096	501 R	43.6%	32.8%	57.0%	43.0%
4,917	MORGAN	2,560	1,066	818	676	248 R	41.6%	32.0%	56.6%	43.4%
1,329	PIUTE	675	364	247	64	117 R	53.9%	36.6%	59.6%	40.4%
2,100	RICH	866	408	315	143	93 R	47.1%	36.4%	56.4%	43.6%
619,066	SALT LAKE	278,607	97,642	120,102	60,863	22,460 D	35.0%	43.1%	44.8%	55.2%
12,253	SAN JUAN	3,785	1,658	1,752	375	94 D	43.8%	46.3%	48.6%	51.4%
14,620	SANPETE	6,552	3,000	2,384	1,168	616 R	45.8%	36.4%	55.7%	44.3%
14,727	SEVIER	6,214	2,831	1,910	1,473	921 R	45.6%	30.7%	59.7%	40.3%
10,198	SUMMIT	6,396	2,120	3,129	1,147	1,009 D	33.1%	48.9%	40.4%	59.6%
26,033	TOOELE	9,675	3,113	4,724	1,838	1,611 D	32.2%	48.8%	39.7%	60.3%
20,506	UINTAH	7,207	2,698	2,368	2,141	330 R	37.4%	32.9%	53.3%	46.7%
218,106	UTAH	88,195	44,329	26,129	17,737	18,200 R	50.3%	29.6%	62.9%	37.1%
8,523	WASATCH	3,966	1,624	1,654	688	30 D	40.9%	41.7%	49.5%	50.5%
26,065	WASHINGTON	16,533	9,588	4,203	2,742	5,385 R	58.0%	25.4%	69.5%	30.5%
1,911	WAYNE	1,127	692	353	82	339 R	61.4%	31.3%	66.2%	33.8%
144,616	WEBER	62,251	21,454	23,411	17,386	1,957 D	34.5%	37.6%	47.8%	52.2%
1,461,037	TOTAL	649,114	260,462	249,321	139,331	11,141 R	40.1%	38.4%	51.1%	48.9%

UTAH

SENATOR 1988

1980 Census Population	County	Total Vote	Republican	Democratic	Other	Rep.-Dem. Plurality	Percentage Total Vote Rep.	Total Vote Dem.	Major Vote Rep.	Major Vote Dem.
4,378	BEAVER	2,110	1,358	729	23	629 R	64.4%	34.5%	65.1%	34.9%
33,222	BOX ELDER	15,013	12,048	2,930	35	9,118 R	80.3%	19.5%	80.4%	19.6%
57,176	CACHE	27,919	22,103	5,608	208	16,495 R	79.2%	20.1%	79.8%	20.2%
22,179	CARBON	8,484	3,325	5,096	63	1,771 D	39.2%	60.1%	39.5%	60.5%
769	DAGGETT	387	267	118	2	149 R	69.0%	30.5%	69.4%	30.6%
146,540	DAVIS	68,240	49,784	17,734	722	32,050 R	73.0%	26.0%	73.7%	26.3%
12,565	DUCHESNE	4,233	3,200	1,012	21	2,188 R	75.6%	23.9%	76.0%	24.0%
11,451	EMERY	4,053	2,411	1,618	24	793 R	59.5%	39.9%	59.8%	40.2%
3,673	GARFIELD	1,771	1,446	320	5	1,126 R	81.6%	18.1%	81.9%	18.1%
8,241	GRAND	3,102	1,977	1,114	11	863 R	63.7%	35.9%	64.0%	36.0%
17,349	IRON	7,575	5,931	1,604	40	4,327 R	78.3%	21.2%	78.7%	21.3%
5,530	JUAB	2,454	1,552	897	5	655 R	63.2%	36.6%	63.4%	36.6%
4,024	KANE	2,146	1,796	346	4	1,450 R	83.7%	16.1%	83.8%	16.2%
8,970	MILLARD	4,630	3,546	1,070	14	2,476 R	76.6%	23.1%	76.8%	23.2%
4,917	MORGAN	2,508	1,819	686	3	1,133 R	72.5%	27.4%	72.6%	27.4%
1,329	PIUTE	663	497	165	1	332 R	75.0%	24.9%	75.1%	24.9%
2,100	RICH	829	617	211	1	406 R	74.4%	25.5%	74.5%	25.5%
619,066	SALT LAKE	274,650	166,095	104,608	3,947	61,487 R	60.5%	38.1%	61.4%	38.6%
12,253	SAN JUAN	3,712	2,430	1,251	31	1,179 R	65.5%	33.7%	66.0%	34.0%
14,620	SANPETE	6,479	4,760	1,642	77	3,118 R	73.5%	25.3%	74.4%	25.6%
14,727	SEVIER	6,161	4,764	1,319	78	3,445 R	77.3%	21.4%	78.3%	21.7%
10,198	SUMMIT	6,382	3,926	2,395	61	1,531 R	61.5%	37.5%	62.1%	37.9%
26,033	TOOELE	9,333	5,553	3,746	34	1,807 R	59.5%	40.1%	59.7%	40.3%
20,506	UINTAH	7,126	5,366	1,668	92	3,698 R	75.3%	23.4%	76.3%	23.7%
218,106	UTAH	87,550	67,719	18,911	920	48,808 R	77.3%	21.6%	78.2%	21.8%
8,523	WASATCH	3,875	2,594	1,267	14	1,327 R	66.9%	32.7%	67.2%	32.8%
26,065	WASHINGTON	16,470	13,332	3,015	123	10,317 R	80.9%	18.3%	81.6%	18.4%
1,911	WAYNE	1,097	807	289	1	518 R	73.6%	26.3%	73.6%	26.4%
144,616	WEBER	61,750	39,066	21,995	689	17,071 R	63.3%	35.6%	64.0%	36.0%
1,461,037	TOTAL	640,702	430,089	203,364	7,249	226,725 R	67.1%	31.7%	67.9%	32.1%

UTAH

CONGRESS

CD	Year	Total Vote	Republican Vote	Republican Candidate	Democratic Vote	Democratic Candidate	Other Vote	Rep.-Dem. Plurality	Total Vote Rep.	Total Vote Dem.	Major Vote Rep.	Major Vote Dem.
1	1988	218,869	130,893	HANSEN, JAMES V.	87,976	MCKAY, GUNN		42,917 R	59.8%	40.2%	59.8%	40.2%
1	1986	159,331	82,151	HANSEN, JAMES V.	77,180	MCKAY, GUNN		4,971 R	51.6%	48.4%	51.6%	48.4%
1	1984	200,717	142,952	HANSEN, JAMES V.	56,619	ABRAMS, MILTON C.	1,146	86,333 R	71.2%	28.2%	71.6%	28.4%
1	1982	177,422	111,416	HANSEN, JAMES V.	66,006	DIRKS, A. STEPHEN		45,410 R	62.8%	37.2%	62.8%	37.2%
2	1988	195,338	80,212	SNELGROVE, RICHARD	112,129	OWENS, WAYNE	2,997	31,917 D	41.1%	57.4%	41.7%	58.3%
2	1986	139,390	60,967	SHIMIZU, TOM	76,921	OWENS, WAYNE	1,502	15,954 D	43.7%	55.2%	44.2%	55.8%
2	1984	213,793	105,540	MONSON, DAVID S.	105,044	FARLEY, FRANCES	3,209	496 R	49.4%	49.1%	50.1%	49.9%
2	1982	171,090	92,109	MARRIOTT, DAN	78,981	FARLEY, FRANCES		13,128 R	53.8%	46.2%	53.8%	46.2%
3	1988	194,461	129,951	NIELSON, HOWARD C.	60,018	STRINGHAM, ROBERT W.	4,492	69,933 R	66.8%	30.9%	68.4%	31.6%
3	1986	130,074	86,599	NIELSON, HOWARD C.	42,582	GARDINER, DALE F.	893	44,017 R	66.6%	32.7%	67.0%	33.0%
3	1984	186,572	138,918	NIELSON, HOWARD C.	46,560	BAIRD, BRUCE R.	1,094	92,358 R	74.5%	25.0%	74.9%	25.1%
3	1982	141,139	108,478	NIELSON, HOWARD C.			32,661	108,478 R	76.9%		100.0%	

UTAH

1988 GENERAL ELECTION

President	Other vote was 7,473 Libertarian (Paul); 2,158 American (Dennis); 455 New Alliance (Fulani); 427 National Economic Recovery (LaRouche); 372 Independent (Youngkeit); 209 Socialist Workers (Warren); 129 Socialist (Kenoyer).
Governor	Other vote was 136,651 Independent (Cook); 1,661 Libertarian (Burton); 1,019 American (Pendersen).
Senator	Other vote was 6,016 American (Smith); 1,233 Socialist Workers (Arth).
Congress	Other vote was Libertarian (Lee) in CD 2; 3,285 American (Christensen) and 1,207 Socialist Workers (Stranahan) in CD 3.

1988 PRIMARIES

SEPTEMBER 13 REPUBLICAN

Governor	Norman H. Bangerter, nominated by convention.
Senator	Orrin G. Hatch, nominated by convention.
Congress	Nominated by convention in all three CD's.

SEPTEMBER 13 DEMOCRATIC

Governor	Ted Wilson, nominated by convention.
Senator	Brian H. Moss, nominated by convention.
Congress	Nominated by convention in CD's 1 and 2. Contested as follows:
CD 3	7,061 Robert W. Stringham; 6,510 Craig Oliver.

VERMONT

GOVERNOR

Madeleine M. Kunin (D). Re-elected 1988 to a two year term. Previously elected January 1987 by the State Legislature and in 1984 by popular vote.

SENATORS

James M. Jeffords (R). Elected 1988 to a six-year term.

Patrick J. Leahy (D). Re-elected 1986 to a six-year term. Previously elected 1980, 1974.

REPRESENTATIVE

At-Large. Peter Smith (R)

POSTWAR VOTE FOR PRESIDENT

								Percentage			
	Total	Republican		Democratic		Other		Total Vote		Major Vote	
Year	Vote	Vote	Candidate	Vote	Candidate	Vote	Plurality	Rep.	Dem.	Rep.	Dem.
1988	243,328	124,331	Bush, George	115,775	Dukakis, Michael S.	3,222	8,556 R	51.1%	47.6%	51.8%	48.2%
1984	234,561	135,865	Reagan, Ronald	95,730	Mondale, Walter F.	2,966	40,135 R	57.9%	40.8%	58.7%	41.3%
1980	213,299	94,628	Reagan, Ronald	81,952	Carter, Jimmy	36,719	12,676 R	44.4%	38.4%	53.6%	46.4%
1976	187,765	102,085	Ford, Gerald R.	80,954	Carter, Jimmy	4,726	21,131 R	54.4%	43.1%	55.8%	44.2%
1972	186,947	117,149	Nixon, Richard M.	68,174	McGovern, George S.	1,624	48,975 R	62.7%	36.5%	63.2%	36.8%
1968	161,404	85,142	Nixon, Richard M.	70,255	Humphrey, Hubert H.	6,007	14,887 R	52.8%	43.5%	54.8%	45.2%
1964	163,089	54,942	Goldwater, Barry M.	108,127	Johnson, Lyndon B.	20	53,185 D	33.7%	66.3%	33.7%	66.3%
1960	167,324	98,131	Nixon, Richard M.	69,186	Kennedy, John F.	7	28,945 R	58.6%	41.3%	58.6%	41.4%
1956	152,978	110,390	Eisenhower, Dwight D.	42,549	Stevenson, Adlai E.	39	67,841 R	72.2%	27.8%	72.2%	27.8%
1952	153,557	109,717	Eisenhower, Dwight D.	43,355	Stevenson, Adlai E.	485	66,362 R	71.5%	28.2%	71.7%	28.3%
1948	123,382	75,926	Dewey, Thomas E.	45,557	Truman, Harry S.	1,899	30,369 R	61.5%	36.9%	62.5%	37.5%

VERMONT

POSTWAR VOTE FOR GOVERNOR

Year	Total Vote	Republican Vote	Republican Candidate	Democratic Vote	Democratic Candidate	Other Vote	Rep.-Dem. Plurality	Total Vote Rep.	Total Vote Dem.	Major Vote Rep.	Major Vote Dem.
1988	242,879	105,191	Bernhardt, Michael	134,438	Kunin, Madeleine M.	3,250	29,247 D	43.3%	55.4%	43.9%	56.1%
1986 *	196,716	75,162	Smith, Peter	92,379	Kunin, Madeleine M.	29,175	17,217 D	38.2%	47.0%	44.9%	55.1%
1984	233,753	113,264	Easton, John J.	116,938	Kunin, Madeleine M.	3,551	3,674 D	48.5%	50.0%	49.2%	50.8%
1982	169,251	93,111	Snelling, Richard A.	74,394	Kunin, Madeleine M.	1,746	18,717 R	55.0%	44.0%	55.6%	44.4%
1980	210,381	123,229	Snelling, Richard A.	77,363	Diamond, J. Jerome	9,789	45,866 R	58.6%	36.8%	61.4%	38.6%
1978	124,482	78,181	Snelling, Richard A.	42,482	Granai, Edwin C.	3,819	35,699 R	62.8%	34.1%	64.8%	35.2%
1976	185,929	99,268	Snelling, Richard A.	75,262	Hackel, Stella B.	11,399	24,006 R	53.4%	40.5%	56.9%	43.1%
1974	141,156	53,672	Kennedy, Walter L.	79,842	Salmon, Thomas P.	7,642	26,170 D	38.0%	56.6%	40.2%	59.8%
1972	189,237	82,491	Hackett, Luther F.	104,533	Salmon, Thomas P.	2,213	22,042 D	43.6%	55.2%	44.1%	55.9%
1970	153,528	87,458	Davis, Deane C.	66,028	O'Brien, Leo	42	21,430 R	57.0%	43.0%	57.0%	43.0%
1968	161,089	89,387	Davis, Deane C.	71,656	Daley, John J.	46	17,731 R	55.5%	44.5%	55.5%	44.5%
1966	136,262	57,577	Snelling, Richard A.	78,669	Hoff, Philip H.	16	21,092 D	42.3%	57.7%	42.3%	57.7%
1964	164,199	57,576	Foote, Ralph A.	106,611	Hoff, Philip H.	12	49,035 D	35.1%	64.9%	35.1%	64.9%
1962	121,422	60,035	Keyser, F. Ray	61,383	Hoff, Philip H.	4	1,348 D	49.4%	50.6%	49.4%	50.6%
1960	164,632	92,861	Keyser, F. Ray	71,755	Niquette, Russell F.	16	21,106 R	56.4%	43.6%	56.4%	43.6%
1958	123,728	62,222	Stafford, Robert T.	61,503	Leddy, Bernard J.	3	719 R	50.3%	49.7%	50.3%	49.7%
1956	153,809	88,379	Johnson, Joseph B.	65,420	Branon, E. Frank	10	22,959 R	57.5%	42.5%	57.5%	42.5%
1954	114,360	59,778	Johnson, Joseph B.	54,554	Branon, E. Frank	28	5,224 R	52.3%	47.7%	52.3%	47.7%
1952	150,862	78,338	Emerson, Lee E.	60,051	Larrow, Robert W.	12,473	18,287 R	51.9%	39.8%	56.6%	43.4%
1950	87,155	64,915	Emerson, Lee E.	22,227	Moran, J. Edward	13	42,688 R	74.5%	25.5%	74.5%	25.5%
1948	120,183	86,394	Gibson, Ernest W., Jr.	33,588	Ryan, Charles F.	201	52,806 R	71.9%	27.9%	72.0%	28.0%
1946	72,044	57,849	Gibson, Ernest W., Jr.	14,096	Coburn, Berthold	99	43,753 R	80.3%	19.6%	80.4%	19.6%

In 1986, in the absence of a majority for any candidate, the State Legislature elected Madeleine M. Kunin to a two-year term.

POSTWAR VOTE FOR SENATOR

Year	Total Vote	Republican Vote	Republican Candidate	Democratic Vote	Democratic Candidate	Other Vote	Rep.-Dem. Plurality	Total Vote Rep.	Total Vote Dem.	Major Vote Rep.	Major Vote Dem.
1988	240,108	163,183	Jeffords, James M.	71,460	Gray, William	5,465	91,723 R	68.0%	29.8%	69.5%	30.5%
1986	196,532	67,798	Snelling, Richard A.	124,123	Leahy, Patrick J.	4,611	56,325 D	34.5%	63.2%	35.3%	64.7%
1982	168,003	84,450	Stafford, Robert T.	79,340	Guest, James A.	4,213	5,110 R	50.3%	47.2%	51.6%	48.4%
1980	209,124	101,421	Ledbetter, Stewart M.	104,176	Leahy, Patrick J.	3,527	2,755 D	48.5%	49.8%	49.3%	50.7%
1976	189,060	94,481	Stafford, Robert T.	85,682	Salmon, Thomas P.	8,897	8,799 R	50.0%	45.3%	52.4%	47.6%
1974	142,772	66,223	Mallary, Richard W.	70,629	Leahy, Patrick J.	5,920	4,406 D	46.4%	49.5%	48.4%	51.6%
1972 S	71,348	45,888	Stafford, Robert T.	23,842	Major, Randolph T.	1,618	22,046 R	64.3%	33.4%	65.8%	34.2%
1970	154,899	91,198	Prouty, Winston L.	62,271	Hoff, Philip H.	1,430	28,927 R	58.9%	40.2%	59.4%	40.6%
1968 **	157,375	157,154	Aiken, George D.		—	221	157,154 R	99.9%		100.0%	
1964	164,350	87,879	Prouty, Winston L.	76,457	Fayette, Frederick J.	14	11,422 R	53.5%	46.5%	53.5%	46.5%
1962	121,571	81,241	Aiken, George D.	40,134	Johnson, W. Robert	196	41,107 R	66.8%	33.0%	66.9%	33.1%
1958	124,442	64,900	Prouty, Winston L.	59,536	Fayette, Frederick J.	6	5,364 R	52.2%	47.8%	52.2%	47.8%
1956	155,289	103,101	Aiken, George D.	52,184	O'Shea, Bernard G.	4	50,917 R	66.4%	33.6%	66.4%	33.6%
1952	154,052	111,406	Flanders, Ralph E.	42,630	Johnston, Allan R.	16	68,776 R	72.3%	27.7%	72.3%	27.7%
1950	89,171	69,543	Aiken, George D.	19,608	Bigelow, James E.	20	49,935 R	78.0%	22.0%	78.0%	22.0%
1946	73,340	54,729	Flanders, Ralph E.	18,594	McDevitt, Charles P.	17	36,135 R	74.6%	25.4%	74.6%	25.4%

In 1968 the Republican candidate won both major party nominations. The January 1972 election was for a short term to fill a vacancy.

VERMONT

One At Large

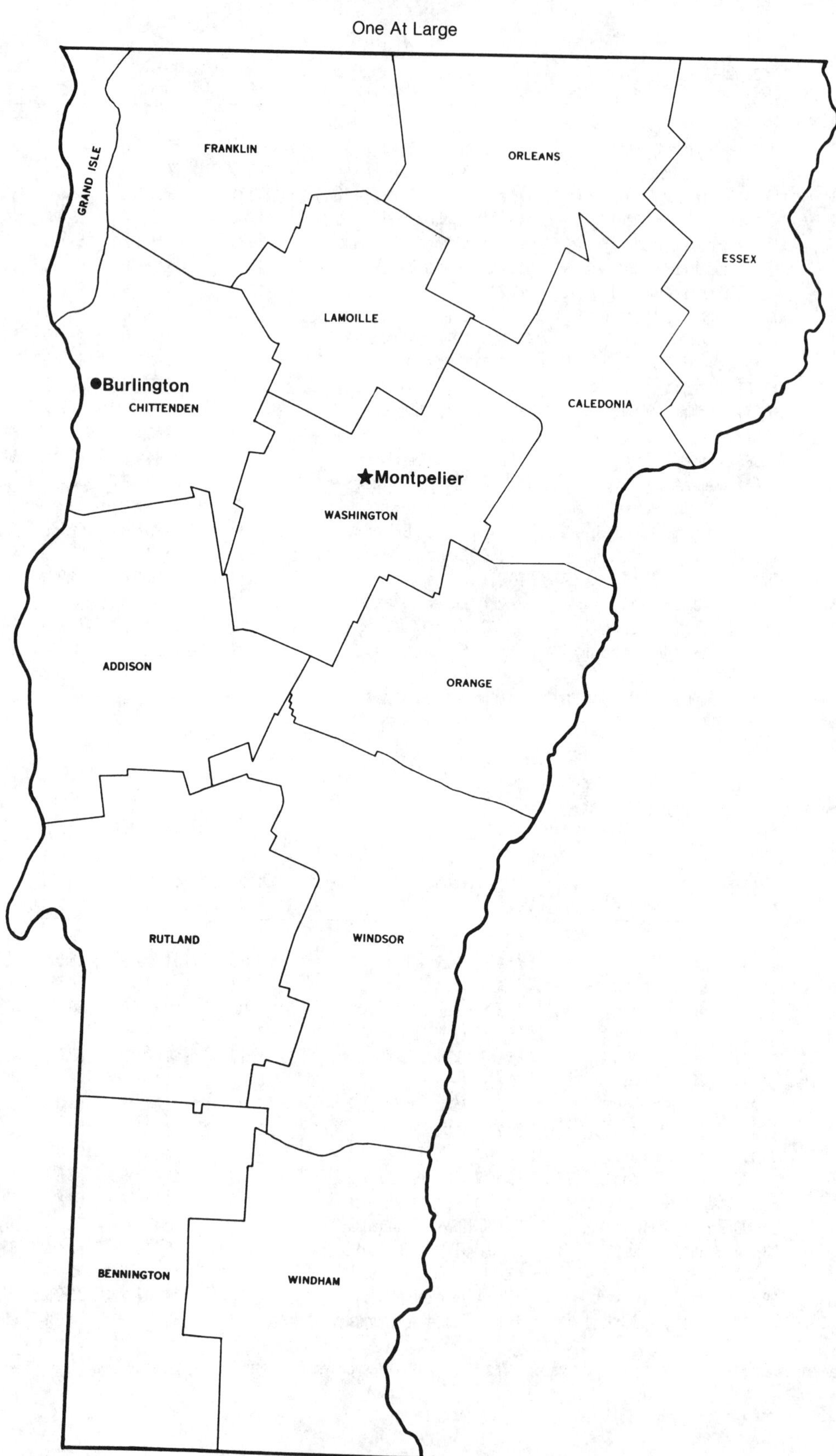

VERMONT

PRESIDENT 1988

1980 Census Population	County	Total Vote	Republican	Democratic	Other	Rep.-Dem. Plurality	Percentage Total Vote Rep.	Percentage Total Vote Dem.	Percentage Major Vote Rep.	Percentage Major Vote Dem.
29,406	ADDISON	13,791	6,773	6,791	227	18 D	49.1%	49.2%	49.9%	50.1%
33,345	BENNINGTON	15,725	8,387	7,174	164	1,213 R	53.3%	45.6%	53.9%	46.1%
25,808	CALEDONIA	11,312	6,915	4,251	146	2,664 R	61.1%	37.6%	61.9%	38.1%
115,534	CHITTENDEN	57,346	27,380	29,185	781	1,805 D	47.7%	50.9%	48.4%	51.6%
6,313	ESSEX	2,391	1,535	837	19	698 R	64.2%	35.0%	64.7%	35.3%
34,788	FRANKLIN	14,834	7,293	7,372	169	79 D	49.2%	49.7%	49.7%	50.3%
4,613	GRAND ISLE	2,728	1,316	1,369	43	53 D	48.2%	50.2%	49.0%	51.0%
16,767	LAMOILLE	8,133	4,433	3,561	139	872 R	54.5%	43.8%	55.5%	44.5%
22,739	ORANGE	11,318	6,151	4,977	190	1,174 R	54.3%	44.0%	55.3%	44.7%
23,440	ORLEANS	9,611	5,257	4,224	130	1,033 R	54.7%	43.9%	55.4%	44.6%
58,347	RUTLAND	26,260	14,482	11,496	282	2,986 R	55.1%	43.8%	55.7%	44.3%
52,393	WASHINGTON	26,294	13,253	12,690	351	563 R	50.4%	48.3%	51.1%	48.9%
36,933	WINDHAM	18,654	8,572	9,839	243	1,267 D	46.0%	52.7%	46.6%	53.4%
51,030	WINDSOR	24,930	12,584	12,009	337	575 R	50.5%	48.2%	51.2%	48.8%
511,456	TOTAL	243,328	124,331	115,775	3,222	8,556 R	51.1%	47.6%	51.8%	48.2%

VERMONT

PRESIDENT 1988

1980 Census Population	City/Town	Total Vote	Republican	Democratic	Other	Rep.-Dem. Plurality	Percentage Total Vote Rep.	Percentage Total Vote Dem.	Percentage Major Vote Rep.	Percentage Major Vote Dem.
9,824	BARRE CITY	4,286	2,100	2,132	54	32 D	49.0%	49.7%	49.6%	50.4%
7,090	BARRE TOWN	3,504	2,084	1,387	33	697 R	59.5%	39.6%	60.0%	40.0%
15,815	BENNINGTON TOWN	5,978	2,748	3,180	50	432 D	46.0%	53.2%	46.4%	53.6%
11,886	BRATTLEBORO	5,236	2,044	3,136	56	1,092 D	39.0%	59.9%	39.5%	60.5%
37,712	BURLINGTON	16,373	6,382	9,748	243	3,366 D	39.0%	59.5%	39.6%	60.4%
12,629	COLCHESTER	5,522	2,914	2,543	65	371 R	52.8%	46.1%	53.4%	46.6%
14,392	ESSEX TOWN	7,272	4,165	3,027	80	1,138 R	57.3%	41.6%	57.9%	42.1%
7,963	HARTFORD	3,636	1,873	1,721	42	152 R	51.5%	47.3%	52.1%	47.9%
7,574	MIDDLEBURY	3,059	1,276	1,741	42	465 D	41.7%	56.9%	42.3%	57.7%
6,829	MILTON	2,919	1,708	1,170	41	538 R	58.5%	40.1%	59.3%	40.7%
8,241	MONTPELIER	4,434	2,013	2,351	70	338 D	45.4%	53.0%	46.1%	53.9%
5,435	NORTHFIELD	2,483	1,526	932	25	594 R	61.5%	37.5%	62.1%	37.9%
5,538	ROCKINGHAM	2,129	925	1,182	22	257 D	43.4%	55.5%	43.9%	56.1%
18,436	RUTLAND CITY	7,292	3,631	3,590	71	41 R	49.8%	49.2%	50.3%	49.7%
7,308	ST. ALBANS CITY	2,762	1,295	1,441	26	146 D	46.9%	52.2%	47.3%	52.7%
7,938	ST. JOHNSBURY	3,193	1,974	1,188	31	786 R	61.8%	37.2%	62.4%	37.6%
5,000	SHELBURNE	3,338	1,673	1,628	37	45 R	50.1%	48.8%	50.7%	49.3%
10,679	SOUTH BURLINGTON	6,592	3,136	3,373	83	237 D	47.6%	51.2%	48.2%	51.8%
10,190	SPRINGFIELD	4,143	2,083	2,023	37	60 R	50.3%	48.8%	50.7%	49.3%
5,141	SWANTON	1,885	939	942	4	3 D	49.8%	50.0%	49.9%	50.1%
6,318	WINOOSKI	2,472	1,014	1,426	32	412 D	41.0%	57.7%	41.6%	58.4%

VERMONT

GOVERNOR 1988

1980 Census Population	County	Total Vote	Republican	Democratic	Other	Rep.-Dem. Plurality	Percentage Total Vote Rep.	Total Vote Dem.	Major Vote Rep.	Major Vote Dem.
29,406	ADDISON	13,506	6,001	7,236	269	1,235 D	44.4%	53.6%	45.3%	54.7%
33,345	BENNINGTON	15,584	7,465	7,952	167	487 D	47.9%	51.0%	48.4%	51.6%
25,808	CALEDONIA	11,292	6,557	4,603	132	1,954 R	58.1%	40.8%	58.8%	41.2%
115,534	CHITTENDEN	58,137	20,268	37,268	601	17,000 D	34.9%	64.1%	35.2%	64.8%
6,313	ESSEX	2,374	1,282	1,065	27	217 R	54.0%	44.9%	54.6%	45.4%
34,788	FRANKLIN	14,801	6,018	8,612	171	2,594 D	40.7%	58.2%	41.1%	58.9%
4,613	GRAND ISLE	2,893	1,244	1,613	36	369 D	43.0%	55.8%	43.5%	56.5%
16,767	LAMOILLE	8,102	3,830	4,173	99	343 D	47.3%	51.5%	47.9%	52.1%
22,739	ORANGE	10,961	4,926	5,842	193	916 D	44.9%	53.3%	45.7%	54.3%
23,440	ORLEANS	9,565	4,984	4,467	114	517 R	52.1%	46.7%	52.7%	47.3%
58,347	RUTLAND	26,212	13,645	12,215	352	1,430 R	52.1%	46.6%	52.8%	47.2%
52,393	WASHINGTON	26,126	11,271	14,431	424	3,160 D	43.1%	55.2%	43.9%	56.1%
36,933	WINDHAM	18,487	7,842	10,300	345	2,458 D	42.4%	55.7%	43.2%	56.8%
51,030	WINDSOR	24,839	9,858	14,661	320	4,803 D	39.7%	59.0%	40.2%	59.8%
511,456	TOTAL	242,879	105,191	134,438	3,250	29,247 D	43.3%	55.4%	43.9%	56.1%

VERMONT

GOVERNOR 1988

1980 Census Population	City/Town	Total Vote	Republican	Democratic	Other	Rep.-Dem. Plurality	Percentage Total Vote Rep.	Total Vote Dem.	Major Vote Rep.	Major Vote Dem.
9,824	BARRE CITY	4,259	1,701	2,503	55	802 D	39.9%	58.8%	40.5%	59.5%
7,090	BARRE TOWN	3,498	1,665	1,801	32	136 D	47.6%	51.5%	48.0%	52.0%
15,815	BENNINGTON TOWN	5,905	2,567	3,273	65	706 D	43.5%	55.4%	44.0%	56.0%
11,886	BRATTLEBORO	5,188	1,746	3,361	81	1,615 D	33.7%	64.8%	34.2%	65.8%
37,712	BURLINGTON	17,230	4,681	12,294	255	7,613 D	27.2%	71.4%	27.6%	72.4%
12,629	COLCHESTER	5,488	2,023	3,436	29	1,413 D	36.9%	62.6%	37.1%	62.9%
14,392	ESSEX TOWN	7,225	3,174	4,004	47	830 D	43.9%	55.4%	44.2%	55.8%
7,963	HARTFORD	3,631	1,160	2,452	19	1,292 D	31.9%	67.5%	32.1%	67.9%
7,574	MIDDLEBURY	3,026	1,110	1,793	123	683 D	36.7%	59.3%	38.2%	61.8%
6,829	MILTON	2,939	1,186	1,725	28	539 D	40.4%	58.7%	40.7%	59.3%
8,241	MONTPELIER	4,379	1,790	2,498	91	708 D	40.9%	57.0%	41.7%	58.3%
5,435	NORTHFIELD	2,451	1,201	1,225	25	24 D	49.0%	50.0%	49.5%	50.5%
5,538	ROCKINGHAM	2,113	775	1,302	36	527 D	36.7%	61.6%	37.3%	62.7%
18,436	RUTLAND CITY	7,299	3,548	3,669	82	121 D	48.6%	50.3%	49.2%	50.8%
7,308	ST. ALBANS CITY	2,744	1,044	1,674	26	630 D	38.0%	61.0%	38.4%	61.6%
7,938	ST. JOHNSBURY	3,192	1,944	1,209	39	735 R	60.9%	37.9%	61.7%	38.3%
5,000	SHELBURNE	3,321	1,237	2,060	24	823 D	37.2%	62.0%	37.5%	62.5%
10,679	SOUTH BURLINGTON	6,565	2,356	4,159	50	1,803 D	35.9%	63.4%	36.2%	63.8%
10,190	SPRINGFIELD	4,170	1,582	2,561	27	979 D	37.9%	61.4%	38.2%	61.8%
5,141	SWANTON	1,882	745	1,118	19	373 D	39.6%	59.4%	40.0%	60.0%
6,318	WINOOSKI	2,498	744	1,725	29	981 D	29.8%	69.1%	30.1%	69.9%

VERMONT

SENATOR 1988

1980 Census Population	County	Total Vote	Republican	Democratic	Other	Rep.-Dem. Plurality	Percentage Total Vote Rep.	Total Vote Dem.	Major Vote Rep.	Major Vote Dem.
29,406	ADDISON	13,593	9,327	3,879	387	5,448 R	68.6%	28.5%	70.6%	29.4%
33,345	BENNINGTON	15,249	10,328	4,598	323	5,730 R	67.7%	30.2%	69.2%	30.8%
25,808	CALEDONIA	11,095	7,922	2,925	248	4,997 R	71.4%	26.4%	73.0%	27.0%
115,534	CHITTENDEN	57,464	36,441	19,669	1,354	16,772 R	63.4%	34.2%	64.9%	35.1%
6,313	ESSEX	2,340	1,612	675	53	937 R	68.9%	28.8%	70.5%	29.5%
34,788	FRANKLIN	14,704	9,776	4,695	233	5,081 R	66.5%	31.9%	67.6%	32.4%
4,613	GRAND ISLE	2,868	1,908	917	43	991 R	66.5%	32.0%	67.5%	32.5%
16,767	LAMOILLE	8,001	5,592	2,242	167	3,350 R	69.9%	28.0%	71.4%	28.6%
22,739	ORANGE	11,072	7,673	3,135	264	4,538 R	69.3%	28.3%	71.0%	29.0%
23,440	ORLEANS	9,482	6,602	2,694	186	3,908 R	69.6%	28.4%	71.0%	29.0%
58,347	RUTLAND	25,925	19,232	6,227	466	13,005 R	74.2%	24.0%	75.5%	24.5%
52,393	WASHINGTON	25,730	17,994	7,081	655	10,913 R	69.9%	27.5%	71.8%	28.2%
36,933	WINDHAM	18,185	12,223	5,286	676	6,937 R	67.2%	29.1%	69.8%	30.2%
51,030	WINDSOR	24,400	16,553	7,437	410	9,116 R	67.8%	30.5%	69.0%	31.0%
511,456	TOTAL	240,108	163,183	71,460	5,465	91,723 R	68.0%	29.8%	69.5%	30.5%

VERMONT

SENATOR 1988

1980 Census Population	City/Town	Total Vote	Republican	Democratic	Other	Rep.-Dem. Plurality	Percentage Total Vote Rep.	Total Vote Dem.	Major Vote Rep.	Major Vote Dem.
9,824	BARRE CITY	4,223	2,875	1,282	66	1,593 R	68.1%	30.4%	69.2%	30.8%
7,090	BARRE TOWN	3,464	2,515	895	54	1,620 R	72.6%	25.8%	73.8%	26.2%
15,815	BENNINGTON TOWN	5,805	3,593	2,110	102	1,483 R	61.9%	36.3%	63.0%	37.0%
11,886	BRATTLEBORO	5,119	3,359	1,530	230	1,829 R	65.6%	29.9%	68.7%	31.3%
37,712	BURLINGTON	16,924	9,623	6,807	494	2,816 R	56.9%	40.2%	58.6%	41.4%
12,629	COLCHESTER	5,482	3,632	1,774	76	1,858 R	66.3%	32.4%	67.2%	32.8%
14,392	ESSEX TOWN	7,170	4,755	2,279	136	2,476 R	66.3%	31.8%	67.6%	32.4%
7,963	HARTFORD	3,550	2,363	1,121	66	1,242 R	66.6%	31.6%	67.8%	32.2%
7,574	MIDDLEBURY	2,984	1,951	953	80	998 R	65.4%	31.9%	67.2%	32.8%
6,829	MILTON	2,915	1,976	879	60	1,097 R	67.8%	30.2%	69.2%	30.8%
8,241	MONTPELIER	4,253	2,911	1,212	130	1,699 R	68.4%	28.5%	70.6%	29.4%
5,435	NORTHFIELD	2,405	1,788	568	49	1,220 R	74.3%	23.6%	75.9%	24.1%
5,538	ROCKINGHAM	2,085	1,349	705	31	644 R	64.7%	33.8%	65.7%	34.3%
18,436	RUTLAND CITY	7,300	5,390	1,800	110	3,590 R	73.8%	24.7%	75.0%	25.0%
7,308	ST. ALBANS CITY	2,706	1,717	957	32	760 R	63.5%	35.4%	64.2%	35.8%
7,938	ST. JOHNSBURY	3,130	2,250	816	64	1,434 R	71.9%	26.1%	73.4%	26.6%
5,000	SHELBURNE	3,279	2,239	955	85	1,284 R	68.3%	29.1%	70.1%	29.9%
10,679	SOUTH BURLINGTON	6,516	4,339	2,057	120	2,282 R	66.6%	31.6%	67.8%	32.2%
10,190	SPRINGFIELD	4,117	2,982	1,096	39	1,886 R	72.4%	26.6%	73.1%	26.9%
5,141	SWANTON	1,875	1,212	644	19	568 R	64.6%	34.3%	65.3%	34.7%
6,318	WINOOSKI	2,445	1,399	999	47	400 R	57.2%	40.9%	58.3%	41.7%

VERMONT

CONGRESS

CD	Year	Total Vote	Republican Vote	Republican Candidate	Democratic Vote	Democratic Candidate	Other Vote	Rep.-Dem. Plurality	Percentage Total Vote Rep.	Percentage Total Vote Dem.	Percentage Major Vote Rep.	Percentage Major Vote Dem.
AL	1988	240,131	98,937	SMITH, PETER	45,330	POIRIER, PAUL N.	95,864	53,607 R	41.2%	18.9%	68.6%	31.4%
AL	1986	188,954	168,403	*JEFFORDS, JAMES M.			20,551	168,403 R	89.1%		100.0%	
AL	1984	226,297	148,025	JEFFORDS, JAMES M.	60,360	POLLINA, ANTHONY	17,912	87,665 R	65.4%	26.7%	71.0%	29.0%
AL	1982	164,951	114,191	JEFFORDS, JAMES M.	38,296	KAPLAN, MARK A.	12,464	75,895 R	69.2%	23.2%	74.9%	25.1%
AL	1980	194,697	154,274	JEFFORDS, JAMES M.			40,423	154,274 R	79.2%		100.0%	
AL	1978	120,502	90,688	JEFFORDS, JAMES M.	23,228	DIETZ, S. MARIE	6,586	67,460 R	75.3%	19.3%	79.6%	20.4%
AL	1976	184,783	124,458	JEFFORDS, JAMES M.	60,202	*BURGESS, JOHN A.	123	64,256 R	67.4%	32.6%	67.4%	32.6%
AL	1974	140,899	74,561	JEFFORDS, JAMES M.	56,342	*CAIN, FRANCIS J.	9,996	18,219 R	52.9%	40.0%	57.0%	43.0%
AL	1972	186,028	120,924	MALLARY, RICHARD W.	65,062	MEYER, WILLIAM H.	42	55,862 R	65.0%	35.0%	65.0%	35.0%
AL	1970	152,557	103,806	STAFFORD, ROBERT T.	44,415	O'SHEA, BERNARD G.	4,336	59,391 R	68.0%	29.1%	70.0%	30.0%
AL	1968	157,133	156,956	*STAFFORD, ROBERT T.			177	156,956 R	99.9%		100.0%	
AL	1966	135,748	89,097	STAFFORD, ROBERT T.	46,643	RYAN, WILLIAM J.	8	42,454 R	65.6%	34.4%	65.6%	34.4%
AL	1964	163,452	92,252	STAFFORD, ROBERT T.	71,193	O'SHEA, BERNARD G.	7	21,059 R	56.4%	43.6%	56.4%	43.6%
AL	1962	121,381	68,822	STAFFORD, ROBERT T.	52,535	RAYNOLDS, HAROLD	24	16,287 R	56.7%	43.3%	56.7%	43.3%
AL	1960	166,035	94,905	STAFFORD, ROBERT T.	71,111	MEYER, WILLIAM H.	19	23,794 R	57.2%	42.8%	57.2%	42.8%
AL	1958	122,702	59,536	ARTHUR, HAROLD J.	63,131	MEYER, WILLIAM H.	35	3,595 D	48.5%	51.5%	48.5%	51.5%
AL	1956	154,536	103,736	PROUTY, WINSTON L.	50,797	ST. AMOUR, CAMILLE	3	52,939 R	67.1%	32.9%	67.1%	32.9%
AL	1954	114,289	70,143	PROUTY, WINSTON L.	44,141	BOYLAN, JOHN J.	5	26,002 R	61.4%	38.6%	61.4%	38.6%
AL	1952	153,060	109,871	PROUTY, WINSTON L.	43,187	COMINGS, HERBERT B.	2	66,684 R	71.8%	28.2%	71.8%	28.2%
AL	1950	88,851	65,248	PROUTY, WINSTON L.	22,709	COMINGS, HERBERT B.	894	42,539 R	73.4%	25.6%	74.2%	25.8%
AL	1948	121,968	74,076	PLUMLEY, CHARLES A.	47,767	READY, ROBERT W.	125	26,309 R	60.7%	39.2%	60.8%	39.2%
AL	1946	73,066	46,985	PLUMLEY, CHARLES A.	26,056	CALDBECK, MATTHEW J.	25	20,929 R	64.3%	35.7%	64.3%	35.7%

VERMONT

1988 GENERAL ELECTION

In addition to the county-by-county figures, data are presented for selected Vermont communities. Since not all jurisdictions of the state are listed in this tabulation, state-wide totals are shown only with the county-by-county statistics.

President — Other vote was 1,000 Libertarian (Paul); 275 Independent (LaRouche); 205 New Alliance (Fulani); 189 Populist (Duke); 164 Peace and Freedom (Lewin); 142 Liberty Union (Kenoyer); 113 Socialist Workers (Warren); 1,134 scattered write-in.

Governor — Other vote was 2,919 Liberty Union (Gottlieb); 331 scattered write-in.

Senator — Other vote was 2,533 Liberty Union (Levy); 2,424 Independent (Milne); 508 scattered write-in.

Congress — An asterisk in the Congressional vote table indicates a candidate received votes from another party endorsing his/her candidacy. Other vote at-large was 90,026 Independent (Sanders); 3,110 Libertarian (Hedbor); 1,455 Liberty Union (Diamondstone); 1,070 Small is Beautiful (Earle); 203 scattered write-in. Independent candidate Sanders ran second (8,911 votes behind the winner) and polled 37.5% of the total vote.

1988 PRIMARIES

SEPTEMBER 13 REPUBLICAN

Governor — Michael Bernhardt, unopposed.

Senator — 30,555 James M. Jeffords; 19,593 Mike Griffes; 128 scattered write-in.

Congress — Contested as follows:

AL — 37,211 Peter Smith; 9,954 David Gates; 828 scattered write-in.

SEPTEMBER 13 DEMOCRATIC

Governor — Madeleine M. Kunin, unopposed.

Senator — William Gray, unopposed.

Congress — Contested as follows:

AL — 11,024 Paul N. Poirier; 10,756 Peter F. Welch; 8,301 James A. Guest; 2,132 Dolores Sandoval; 261 scattered write-in.

SEPTEMBER 13 LIBERTY UNION

Governor — Richard F. Gottlieb, unopposed.

Senator — Jerry Levy, unopposed.

Congress — Unopposed at-large.

SEPTEMBER 13 LIBERTARIAN

Governor — No candidate.

Senator — No candidate.

Congress — Unopposed at-large.

VIRGINIA

GOVERNOR

Gerald L. Baliles (D). Elected 1985 to a four-year term.

SENATORS

Charles S. Robb (D). Elected 1988 to a six-year term.

John Warner (R). Re-elected 1984 to a six-year term. Previously elected 1978.

REPRESENTATIVES

1. Herbert H. Bateman (R)
2. Owen B. Pickett (D)
3. Thomas J. Bliley (R)
4. Norman Sisisky (D)
5. L. F.Payne (D)
6. James R. Olin (D)
7. D. French Slaughter (R)
8. Stanford E. Parris (R)
9. Frederick C. Boucher (D)
10. Frank R. Wolf (R)

POSTWAR VOTE FOR PRESIDENT

								Percentage			
	Total	Republican		Democratic		Other		Total Vote		Major Vote	
Year	Vote	Vote	Candidate	Vote	Candidate	Vote	Plurality	Rep.	Dem.	Rep.	Dem.
1988	2,191,609	1,309,162	Bush, George	859,799	Dukakis, Michael S.	22,648	449,363 R	59.7%	39.2%	60.4%	39.6%
1984	2,146,635	1,337,078	Reagan, Ronald	796,250	Mondale, Walter F.	13,307	540,828 R	62.3%	37.1%	62.7%	37.3%
1980	1,866,032	989,609	Reagan, Ronald	752,174	Carter, Jimmy	124,249	237,435 R	53.0%	40.3%	56.8%	43.2%
1976	1,697,094	836,554	Ford, Gerald R.	813,896	Carter, Jimmy	46,644	22,658 R	49.3%	48.0%	50.7%	49.3%
1972	1,457,019	988,493	Nixon, Richard M.	438,887	McGovern, George S.	29,639	549,606 R	67.8%	30.1%	69.3%	30.7%
1968 **	1,361,491	590,319	Nixon, Richard M.	442,387	Humphrey, Hubert H.	328,785	147,932 R	43.4%	32.5%	57.2%	42.8%
1964	1,042,267	481,334	Goldwater, Barry M.	558,038	Johnson, Lyndon B.	2,895	76,704 D	46.2%	53.5%	46.3%	53.7%
1960	771,449	404,521	Nixon, Richard M.	362,327	Kennedy, John F.	4,601	42,194 R	52.4%	47.0%	52.8%	47.2%
1956	697,978	386,459	Eisenhower, Dwight D.	267,760	Stevenson, Adlai E.	43,759	118,699 R	55.4%	38.4%	59.1%	40.9%
1952	619,689	349,037	Eisenhower, Dwight D.	268,677	Stevenson, Adlai E.	1,975	80,360 R	56.3%	43.4%	56.5%	43.5%
1948	419,256	172,070	Dewey, Thomas E.	200,786	Truman, Harry S.	46,400	28,716 D	41.0%	47.9%	46.1%	53.9%

In 1968 other vote was 321,833 American Independent (Wallace); 4,671 Socialist Labor; 1,680 Peace and Freedom and 601 Prohibition.

VIRGINIA

POSTWAR VOTE FOR GOVERNOR

								Percentage			
	Total	Republican		Democratic		Other	Rep.-Dem.	Total Vote		Major Vote	
Year	Vote	Vote	Candidate	Vote	Candidate	Vote	Plurality	Rep.	Dem.	Rep.	Dem.
1985	1,343,243	601,652	Durrette, Wyatt B.	741,438	Baliles, Gerald L.	153	139,786 D	44.8%	55.2%	44.8%	55.2%
1981	1,420,611	659,398	Coleman, J. Marshall	760,357	Robb, Charles S.	856	100,959 D	46.4%	53.5%	46.4%	53.6%
1977	1,250,940	699,302	Dalton, John	541,319	Howell, Henry	10,319	157,983 R	55.9%	43.3%	56.4%	43.6%
1973 **	1,035,495	525,075	Godwin, Mills E.		—	510,420	525,075 R	50.7%		100.0%	
1969	915,764	480,869	Holton, Linwood	415,695	Battle, William C.	19,200	65,174 R	52.5%	45.4%	53.6%	46.4%
1965	562,789	212,207	Holton, Linwood	269,526	Godwin, Mills E.	81,056	57,319 D	37.7%	47.9%	44.1%	55.9%
1961	394,490	142,567	Pearson, H. Clyde	251,861	Harrison, Albertis	62	109,294 D	36.1%	63.8%	36.1%	63.9%
1957	517,655	188,628	Dalton, Ted	326,921	Almond, J. Lindsay	2,106	138,293 D	36.4%	63.2%	36.6%	63.4%
1953	414,025	183,328	Dalton, Ted	226,998	Stanley, Thomas B.	3,699	43,670 D	44.3%	54.8%	44.7%	55.3%
1949	262,350	71,991	Johnson, Walter	184,772	Battle, John S.	5,587	112,781 D	27.4%	70.4%	28.0%	72.0%
1945	168,783	52,386	Landreth, S. Floyd	112,355	Tuck, William M.	4,042	59,969 D	31.0%	66.6%	31.8%	68.2%

In 1973 other vote was 510,103 Independent (Howell) and 317 scattered.

POSTWAR VOTE FOR SENATOR

								Percentage			
	Total	Republican		Democratic		Other	Rep.-Dem.	Total Vote		Major Vote	
Year	Vote	Vote	Candidate	Vote	Candidate	Vote	Plurality	Rep.	Dem.	Rep.	Dem.
1988	2,068,897	593,652	Dawkins, Maurice A.	1,474,086	Robb, Charles S.	1,159	880,434 D	28.7%	71.2%	28.7%	71.3%
1984	2,007,487	1,406,194	Warner, John	601,142	Harrison, Edythe C.	151	805,052 R	70.0%	29.9%	70.1%	29.9%
1982	1,415,622	724,571	Trible, Paul	690,839	Davis, Richard	212	33,732 R	51.2%	48.8%	51.2%	48.8%
1978	1,222,256	613,232	Warner, John	608,511	Miller, Andrew P.	513	4,721 R	50.2%	49.8%	50.2%	49.8%
1976 **	1,557,500		—	596,009	Zumwalt, Elmo R.	961,491	596,009 D		38.3%		100.0%
1972	1,396,268	718,337	Scott, William L.	643,963	Spong, William B.	33,968	74,374 R	51.4%	46.1%	52.7%	47.3%
1970 **	946,751	145,031	Garland, Ray	295,057	Rawlings, George C.	506,663	150,026 D	15.3%	31.2%	33.0%	67.0%
1966	733,879	245,681	Ould, James P.	429,855	Spong, William B.	58,343	184,174 D	33.5%	58.6%	36.4%	63.6%
1966 S	729,839	272,804	Traylor, Lawrence M.	389,028	Byrd, Harry Flood, Jr.	68,007	116,224 D	37.4%	53.3%	41.2%	58.8%
1964	928,363	176,624	May, Richard A.	592,260	Byrd, Harry Flood	159,479	415,636 D	19.0%	63.8%	23.0%	77.0%
1960	622,820		—	506,169	Robertson, A. Willis	116,651	506,169 D		81.3%		100.0%
1958	457,640		—	317,221	Byrd, Harry Flood	140,419	317,221 D		69.3%		100.0%
1954	306,510		—	244,844	Robertson, A. Willis	61,666	244,844 D		79.9%		100.0%
1952	543,516		—	398,677	Byrd, Harry Flood	144,839	398,677 D		73.4%		100.0%
1948	386,178	118,546	Woods, Robert	253,865	Robertson, A. Willis	13,767	135,319 D	30.7%	65.7%	31.8%	68.2%
1946	252,863	77,005	Parsons, Lester S.	163,960	Byrd, Harry Flood	11,898	86,955 D	30.5%	64.8%	32.0%	68.0%
1946 S	248,962	72,253	Woods, Robert	169,680	Robertson, A. Willis	7,029	97,427 D	29.0%	68.2%	29.9%	70.1%

One each of the 1966 and 1946 elections was for a short term to fill a vacancy. In 1970 Harry Flood Byrd, Jr., the Independent candidate, polled 506,633 votes (53.5% of the total vote) and won the election with a 211,576 plurality. In 1976 Harry Flood Byrd, Jr., polled 890,778 votes as an Independent candidate (57.2% of the total vote) and won the election with a 294,769 plurality.

VIRGINIA

Districts Established June 12, 1981

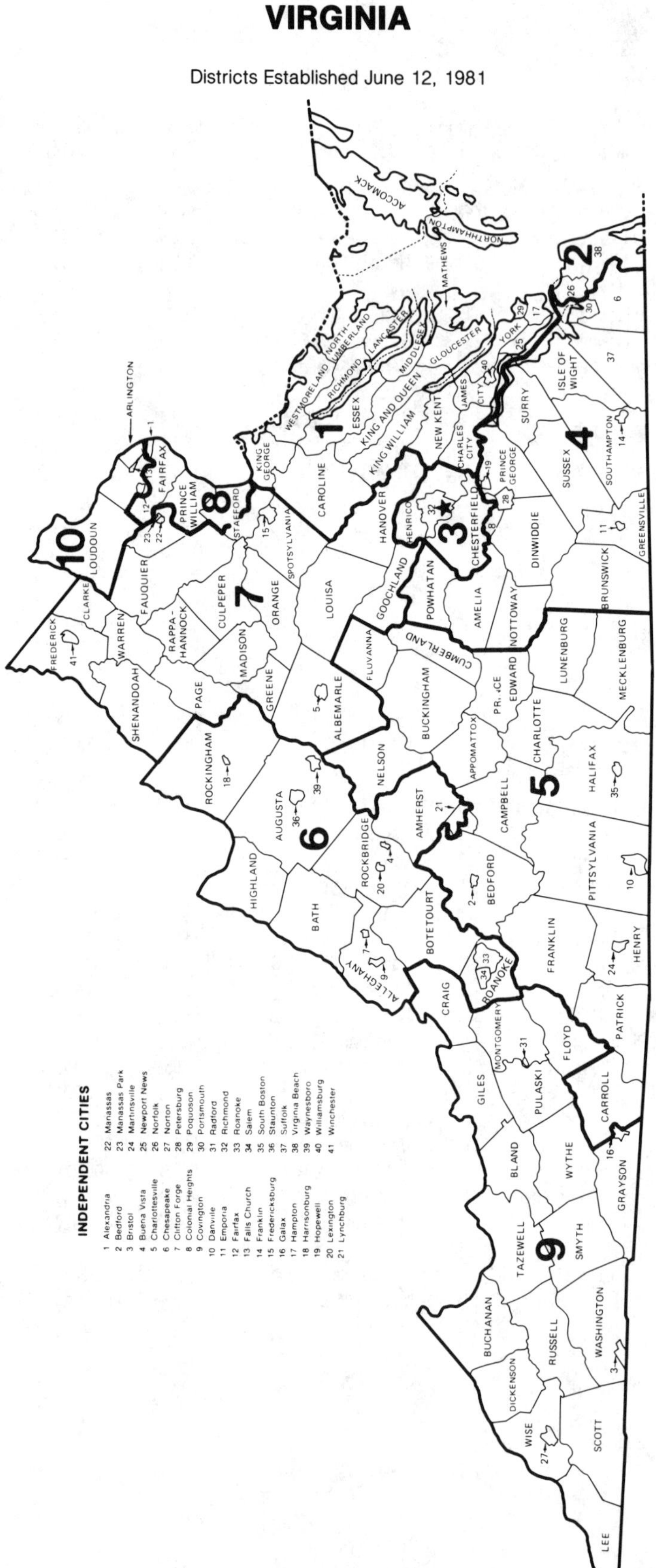

VIRGINIA

PRESIDENT 1988

1980 Census Population	County	Total Vote	Republican	Democratic	Other	Rep.-Dem. Plurality	Percentage Total Vote Rep.	Percentage Total Vote Dem.	Percentage Major Vote Rep.	Percentage Major Vote Dem.
31,268	ACCOMACK	11,542	6,926	4,443	173	2,483 R	60.0%	38.5%	60.9%	39.1%
55,783	ALBEMARLE	25,753	15,117	10,363	273	4,754 R	58.7%	40.2%	59.3%	40.7%
14,333	ALLEGHANY	4,926	2,555	2,316	55	239 R	51.9%	47.0%	52.5%	47.5%
8,405	AMELIA	3,594	2,187	1,359	48	828 R	60.9%	37.8%	61.7%	38.3%
29,122	AMHERST	10,151	6,507	3,567	77	2,940 R	64.1%	35.1%	64.6%	35.4%
11,971	APPOMATTOX	5,040	3,205	1,740	95	1,465 R	63.6%	34.5%	64.8%	35.2%
152,599	ARLINGTON	75,365	34,191	40,314	860	6,123 D	45.4%	53.5%	45.9%	54.1%
53,732	AUGUSTA	17,634	13,251	4,170	213	9,081 R	75.1%	23.6%	76.1%	23.9%
5,860	BATH	2,167	1,273	881	13	392 R	58.7%	40.7%	59.1%	40.9%
34,927	BEDFORD COUNTY	16,382	10,702	5,406	274	5,296 R	65.3%	33.0%	66.4%	33.6%
6,349	BLAND	2,546	1,556	937	53	619 R	61.1%	36.8%	62.4%	37.6%
23,270	BOTETOURT	9,591	5,687	3,763	141	1,924 R	59.3%	39.2%	60.2%	39.8%
15,632	BRUNSWICK	5,884	2,742	3,070	72	328 D	46.6%	52.2%	47.2%	52.8%
37,989	BUCHANAN	10,965	3,912	6,935	118	3,023 D	35.7%	63.2%	36.1%	63.9%
11,751	BUCKINGHAM	4,471	2,481	1,941	49	540 R	55.5%	43.4%	56.1%	43.9%
45,424	CAMPBELL	17,533	12,713	4,574	246	8,139 R	72.5%	26.1%	73.5%	26.5%
17,904	CAROLINE	6,292	3,065	3,186	41	121 D	48.7%	50.6%	49.0%	51.0%
27,270	CARROLL	9,637	6,377	3,190	70	3,187 R	66.2%	33.1%	66.7%	33.3%
6,692	CHARLES CITY	2,700	826	1,839	35	1,013 D	30.6%	68.1%	31.0%	69.0%
12,266	CHARLOTTE	4,699	2,699	1,923	77	776 R	57.4%	40.9%	58.4%	41.6%
141,372	CHESTERFIELD	78,083	58,828	18,723	532	40,105 R	75.3%	24.0%	75.9%	24.1%
9,965	CLARKE	4,020	2,502	1,478	40	1,024 R	62.2%	36.8%	62.9%	37.1%
3,948	CRAIG	2,005	1,112	864	29	248 R	55.5%	43.1%	56.3%	43.7%
22,620	CULPEPER	8,599	5,896	2,555	148	3,341 R	68.6%	29.7%	69.8%	30.2%
7,881	CUMBERLAND	3,159	1,978	1,132	49	846 R	62.6%	35.8%	63.6%	36.4%
19,806	DICKENSON	7,604	3,091	4,461	52	1,370 D	40.6%	58.7%	40.9%	59.1%
22,602	DINWIDDIE	7,659	4,165	3,405	89	760 R	54.4%	44.5%	55.0%	45.0%
8,864	ESSEX	3,365	2,038	1,294	33	744 R	60.6%	38.5%	61.2%	38.8%
596,901	FAIRFAX COUNTY	328,365	200,641	125,711	2,013	74,930 R	61.1%	38.3%	61.5%	38.5%
35,889	FAUQUIER	16,796	11,733	4,837	226	6,896 R	69.9%	28.8%	70.8%	29.2%
11,563	FLOYD	4,735	2,921	1,727	87	1,194 R	61.7%	36.5%	62.8%	37.2%
10,244	FLUVANNA	4,059	2,447	1,562	50	885 R	60.3%	38.5%	61.0%	39.0%
35,740	FRANKLIN COUNTY	13,261	7,391	5,734	136	1,657 R	55.7%	43.2%	56.3%	43.7%
34,150	FREDERICK	13,717	9,921	3,707	89	6,214 R	72.3%	27.0%	72.8%	27.2%
17,810	GILES	6,648	3,490	3,042	116	448 R	52.5%	45.8%	53.4%	46.6%
20,107	GLOUCESTER	11,181	7,646	3,372	163	4,274 R	68.4%	30.2%	69.4%	30.6%
11,761	GOOCHLAND	6,013	3,765	2,209	39	1,556 R	62.6%	36.7%	63.0%	37.0%
16,579	GRAYSON	6,451	3,968	2,441	42	1,527 R	61.5%	37.8%	61.9%	38.1%
7,625	GREENE	3,224	2,234	899	91	1,335 R	69.3%	27.9%	71.3%	28.7%
10,903	GREENSVILLE	3,733	1,610	2,083	40	473 D	43.1%	55.8%	43.6%	56.4%
30,599	HALIFAX	10,124	5,671	4,282	171	1,389 R	56.0%	42.3%	57.0%	43.0%
50,398	HANOVER	26,718	20,570	5,985	163	14,585 R	77.0%	22.4%	77.5%	22.5%
180,735	HENRICO	89,887	62,284	26,980	623	35,304 R	69.3%	30.0%	69.8%	30.2%
57,654	HENRY	18,729	10,871	7,536	322	3,335 R	58.0%	40.2%	59.1%	40.9%
2,937	HIGHLAND	1,286	807	456	23	351 R	62.8%	35.5%	63.9%	36.1%
21,603	ISLE OF WIGHT	9,621	5,779	3,747	95	2,032 R	60.1%	38.9%	60.7%	39.3%
22,763	JAMES CITY	13,773	8,945	4,642	186	4,303 R	64.9%	33.7%	65.8%	34.2%
5,968	KING AND QUEEN	2,727	1,376	1,309	42	67 R	50.5%	48.0%	51.2%	48.8%
10,543	KING GEORGE	4,146	2,587	1,519	40	1,068 R	62.4%	36.6%	63.0%	37.0%
9,334	KING WILLIAM	4,349	2,735	1,561	53	1,174 R	62.9%	35.9%	63.7%	36.3%
10,129	LANCASTER	5,043	3,380	1,551	112	1,829 R	67.0%	30.8%	68.5%	31.5%
25,956	LEE	9,045	4,080	4,906	59	826 D	45.1%	54.2%	45.4%	54.6%
57,427	LOUDOUN	30,862	20,448	10,101	313	10,347 R	66.3%	32.7%	66.9%	33.1%
17,825	LOUISA	6,702	3,831	2,789	82	1,042 R	57.2%	41.6%	57.9%	42.1%
12,124	LUNENBURG	4,496	2,530	1,870	96	660 R	56.3%	41.6%	57.5%	42.5%
10,232	MADISON	4,026	2,501	1,427	98	1,074 R	62.1%	35.4%	63.7%	36.3%
7,995	MATHEWS	4,076	2,752	1,235	89	1,517 R	67.5%	30.3%	69.0%	31.0%
29,444	MECKLENBURG	9,278	5,887	3,275	116	2,612 R	63.5%	35.3%	64.3%	35.7%
7,719	MIDDLESEX	4,018	2,571	1,361	86	1,210 R	64.0%	33.9%	65.4%	34.6%
63,516	MONTGOMERY	21,444	12,326	8,909	209	3,417 R	57.5%	41.5%	58.0%	42.0%

VIRGINIA

PRESIDENT 1988

1980 Census Population	County	Total Vote	Republican	Democratic	Other	Rep.-Dem. Plurality	Percentage: Total Vote Rep.	Percentage: Total Vote Dem.	Percentage: Major Vote Rep.	Percentage: Major Vote Dem.
12,204	NELSON	4,849	2,502	2,272	75	230 R	51.6%	46.9%	52.4%	47.6%
8,781	NEW KENT	4,384	2,917	1,427	40	1,490 R	66.5%	32.6%	67.2%	32.8%
14,625	NORTHAMPTON	4,927	2,562	2,242	123	320 R	52.0%	45.5%	53.3%	46.7%
9,828	NORTHUMBERLAND	4,581	2,984	1,506	91	1,478 R	65.1%	32.9%	66.5%	33.5%
14,666	NOTTOWAY	5,509	3,161	2,217	131	944 R	57.4%	40.2%	58.8%	41.2%
18,063	ORANGE	7,015	4,319	2,592	104	1,727 R	61.6%	36.9%	62.5%	37.5%
19,401	PAGE	7,575	5,013	2,499	63	2,514 R	66.2%	33.0%	66.7%	33.3%
17,647	PATRICK	6,229	3,990	2,093	146	1,897 R	64.1%	33.6%	65.6%	34.4%
66,147	PITTSYLVANIA	19,201	12,229	6,612	360	5,617 R	63.7%	34.4%	64.9%	35.1%
13,062	POWHATAN	5,541	4,040	1,467	34	2,573 R	72.9%	26.5%	73.4%	26.6%
16,456	PRINCE EDWARD	5,720	3,147	2,434	139	713 R	55.0%	42.6%	56.4%	43.6%
25,733	PRINCE GEORGE	7,515	4,982	2,469	64	2,513 R	66.3%	32.9%	66.9%	33.1%
144,703	PRINCE WILLIAM	59,453	39,654	19,198	601	20,456 R	66.7%	32.3%	67.4%	32.6%
35,229	PULASKI	11,719	6,844	4,686	189	2,158 R	58.4%	40.0%	59.4%	40.6%
6,093	RAPPAHANNOCK	2,686	1,657	1,003	26	654 R	61.7%	37.3%	62.3%	37.7%
6,952	RICHMOND COUNTY	2,811	1,862	924	25	938 R	66.2%	32.9%	66.8%	33.2%
72,945	ROANOKE COUNTY	35,157	22,011	12,938	208	9,073 R	62.6%	36.8%	63.0%	37.0%
17,911	ROCKBRIDGE	6,062	3,541	2,412	109	1,129 R	58.4%	39.8%	59.5%	40.5%
57,038	ROCKINGHAM	18,241	13,241	4,716	284	8,525 R	72.6%	25.9%	73.7%	26.3%
31,761	RUSSELL	10,753	4,374	6,222	157	1,848 D	40.7%	57.9%	41.3%	58.7%
25,068	SCOTT	8,785	4,986	3,616	183	1,370 R	56.8%	41.2%	58.0%	42.0%
27,559	SHENANDOAH	12,004	8,612	3,276	116	5,336 R	71.7%	27.3%	72.4%	27.6%
33,366	SMYTH	11,727	7,446	3,989	292	3,457 R	63.5%	34.0%	65.1%	34.9%
18,731	SOUTHAMPTON	6,493	3,439	3,000	54	439 R	53.0%	46.2%	53.4%	46.6%
34,435	SPOTSYLVANIA	16,593	10,978	5,486	129	5,492 R	66.2%	33.1%	66.7%	33.3%
40,470	STAFFORD	17,712	12,234	5,380	98	6,854 R	69.1%	30.4%	69.5%	30.5%
6,046	SURRY	2,899	1,246	1,602	51	356 D	43.0%	55.3%	43.8%	56.3%
10,874	SUSSEX	3,896	1,822	1,958	116	136 D	46.8%	50.3%	48.2%	51.8%
50,511	TAZEWELL	15,453	7,165	8,098	190	933 D	46.4%	52.4%	46.9%	53.1%
21,200	WARREN	7,598	4,700	2,769	129	1,931 R	61.9%	36.4%	62.9%	37.1%
46,487	WASHINGTON	16,899	10,722	5,819	358	4,903 R	63.4%	34.4%	64.8%	35.2%
14,041	WESTMORELAND	5,370	2,974	2,311	85	663 R	55.4%	43.0%	56.3%	43.7%
43,863	WISE	13,386	6,189	7,017	180	828 D	46.2%	52.4%	46.9%	53.1%
25,522	WYTHE	9,225	5,827	3,201	197	2,626 R	63.2%	34.7%	64.5%	35.5%
35,463	YORK	15,871	11,103	4,639	129	6,464 R	70.0%	29.2%	70.5%	29.5%
	City									
103,217	ALEXANDRIA	45,804	20,913	24,358	533	3,445 D	45.7%	53.2%	46.2%	53.8%
5,991	BEDFORD CITY	2,328	1,322	960	46	362 R	56.8%	41.2%	57.9%	42.1%
19,042	BRISTOL	6,895	4,407	2,446	42	1,961 R	63.9%	35.5%	64.3%	35.7%
6,717	BUENA VISTA	1,999	1,121	828	50	293 R	56.1%	41.4%	57.5%	42.5%
39,916	CHARLOTTESVILLE	13,652	5,817	7,671	164	1,854 D	42.6%	56.2%	43.1%	56.9%
114,486	CHESAPEAKE	48,855	29,738	18,828	289	10,910 R	60.9%	38.5%	61.2%	38.8%
5,046	CLIFTON FORGE	1,739	759	961	19	202 D	43.6%	55.3%	44.1%	55.9%
16,509	COLONIAL HEIGHTS	7,638	6,001	1,581	56	4,420 R	78.6%	20.7%	79.1%	20.9%
9,063	COVINGTON	2,915	1,274	1,567	74	293 D	43.7%	53.8%	44.8%	55.2%
45,642	DANVILLE	19,874	12,221	7,353	300	4,868 R	61.5%	37.0%	62.4%	37.6%
4,840	EMPORIA	2,277	1,289	977	11	312 R	56.6%	42.9%	56.9%	43.1%
19,390	FAIRFAX CITY	9,101	5,576	3,430	95	2,146 R	61.3%	37.7%	61.9%	38.1%
9,515	FALLS CHURCH	4,989	2,470	2,484	35	14 D	49.5%	49.8%	49.9%	50.1%
7,308	FRANKLIN CITY	3,210	1,557	1,630	23	73 D	48.5%	50.8%	48.9%	51.1%
15,322	FREDERICKSBURG	6,154	3,401	2,683	70	718 R	55.3%	43.6%	55.9%	44.1%
6,524	GALAX	2,200	1,278	907	15	371 R	58.1%	41.2%	58.5%	41.5%
122,617	HAMPTON	43,818	24,034	19,106	678	4,928 R	54.8%	43.6%	55.7%	44.3%
19,671	HARRISONBURG	8,288	5,376	2,799	113	2,577 R	64.9%	33.8%	65.8%	34.2%
23,397	HOPEWELL	7,360	4,672	2,566	122	2,106 R	63.5%	34.9%	64.5%	35.5%
7,292	LEXINGTON	2,024	994	997	33	3 D	49.1%	49.3%	49.9%	50.1%
66,743	LYNCHBURG	23,926	15,323	8,279	324	7,044 R	64.0%	34.6%	64.9%	35.1%
15,438	MANASSAS	8,719	5,980	2,658	81	3,322 R	68.6%	30.5%	69.2%	30.8%
6,524	MANASSAS PARK	1,446	993	434	19	559 R	68.7%	30.0%	69.6%	30.4%
18,149	MARTINSVILLE	6,264	3,360	2,794	110	566 R	53.6%	44.6%	54.6%	45.4%
144,903	NEWPORT NEWS	54,395	32,570	21,413	412	11,157 R	59.9%	39.4%	60.3%	39.7%

VIRGINIA

PRESIDENT 1988

1980 Census Population	City	Total Vote	Republican	Democratic	Other	Rep.-Dem. Plurality	Percentage Total Vote Rep.	Percentage Total Vote Dem.	Percentage Major Vote Rep.	Percentage Major Vote Dem.
266,979	NORFOLK	68,891	30,538	37,778	575	7,240 D	44.3%	54.8%	44.7%	55.3%
4,757	NORTON	1,423	608	795	20	187 D	42.7%	55.9%	43.3%	56.7%
41,055	PETERSBURG	12,591	4,231	8,177	183	3,946 D	33.6%	64.9%	34.1%	65.9%
8,726	POQUOSON	4,751	3,840	877	34	2,963 R	80.8%	18.5%	81.4%	18.6%
104,577	PORTSMOUTH	36,059	16,087	19,698	274	3,611 D	44.6%	54.6%	45.0%	55.0%
13,225	RADFORD	4,365	2,481	1,855	29	626 R	56.8%	42.5%	57.2%	42.8%
219,214	RICHMOND CITY	74,736	31,586	42,155	995	10,569 D	42.3%	56.4%	42.8%	57.2%
100,220	ROANOKE CITY	32,813	15,389	17,185	239	1,796 D	46.9%	52.4%	47.2%	52.8%
23,958	SALEM	9,527	5,694	3,760	73	1,934 R	59.8%	39.5%	60.2%	39.8%
7,093	SOUTH BOSTON	2,645	1,694	936	15	758 R	64.0%	35.4%	64.4%	35.6%
21,857	STAUNTON	8,334	5,775	2,457	102	3,318 R	69.3%	29.5%	70.2%	29.8%
47,621	SUFFOLK	17,950	9,742	8,080	128	1,662 R	54.3%	45.0%	54.7%	45.3%
262,199	VIRGINIA BEACH	111,018	76,481	33,780	757	42,701 R	68.9%	30.4%	69.4%	30.6%
15,329	WAYNESBORO	6,799	4,672	2,038	89	2,634 R	68.7%	30.0%	69.6%	30.4%
9,870	WILLIAMSBURG	3,237	1,648	1,534	55	114 R	50.9%	47.4%	51.8%	48.2%
20,217	WINCHESTER	6,862	4,497	2,300	65	2,197 R	65.5%	33.5%	66.2%	33.8%
5,346,818	TOTAL	2,191,609	1,309,162	859,799	22,648	449,363 R	59.7%	39.2%	60.4%	39.6%

VIRGINIA

SENATOR 1988

1980 Census Population	County	Total Vote	Republican	Democratic	Other	Rep.-Dem. Plurality	Percentage Total Vote Rep.	Percentage Total Vote Dem.	Percentage Major Vote Rep.	Percentage Major Vote Dem.
31,268	ACCOMACK	10,461	2,914	7,546	1	4,632 D	27.9%	72.1%	27.9%	72.1%
55,783	ALBEMARLE	24,475	7,144	17,315	16	10,171 D	29.2%	70.7%	29.2%	70.8%
14,333	ALLEGHANY	4,594	1,009	3,585		2,576 D	22.0%	78.0%	22.0%	78.0%
8,405	AMELIA	3,377	1,249	2,127	1	878 D	37.0%	63.0%	37.0%	63.0%
29,122	AMHERST	9,592	2,225	7,365	2	5,140 D	23.2%	76.8%	23.2%	76.8%
11,971	APPOMATTOX	4,594	1,219	3,375		2,156 D	26.5%	73.5%	26.5%	73.5%
152,599	ARLINGTON	72,414	18,193	54,202	19	36,009 D	25.1%	74.9%	25.1%	74.9%
53,732	AUGUSTA	16,261	6,594	9,662	5	3,068 D	40.6%	59.4%	40.6%	59.4%
5,860	BATH	2,121	552	1,569		1,017 D	26.0%	74.0%	26.0%	74.0%
34,927	BEDFORD COUNTY	15,097	4,632	10,465		5,833 D	30.7%	69.3%	30.7%	69.3%
6,349	BLAND	2,209	750	1,459		709 D	34.0%	66.0%	34.0%	66.0%
23,270	BOTETOURT	8,998	2,551	6,446	1	3,895 D	28.4%	71.6%	28.4%	71.6%
15,632	BRUNSWICK	5,381	1,253	4,126	2	2,873 D	23.3%	76.7%	23.3%	76.7%
37,989	BUCHANAN	10,179	2,188	7,991		5,803 D	21.5%	78.5%	21.5%	78.5%
11,751	BUCKINGHAM	4,096	1,270	2,824	2	1,554 D	31.0%	68.9%	31.0%	69.0%
45,424	CAMPBELL	16,010	5,406	10,603	1	5,197 D	33.8%	66.2%	33.8%	66.2%
17,904	CAROLINE	5,980	1,347	4,632	1	3,285 D	22.5%	77.5%	22.5%	77.5%
27,270	CARROLL	8,667	3,506	5,161		1,655 D	40.5%	59.5%	40.5%	59.5%
6,692	CHARLES CITY	2,564	509	2,055		1,546 D	19.9%	80.1%	19.9%	80.1%
12,266	CHARLOTTE	4,216	1,213	3,000	3	1,787 D	28.8%	71.2%	28.8%	71.2%
141,372	CHESTERFIELD	76,227	27,215	48,860	152	21,645 D	35.7%	64.1%	35.8%	64.2%
9,965	CLARKE	3,857	903	2,952	2	2,049 D	23.4%	76.5%	23.4%	76.6%
3,948	CRAIG	1,925	600	1,325		725 D	31.2%	68.8%	31.2%	68.8%
22,620	CULPEPER	7,867	2,943	4,919	5	1,976 D	37.4%	62.5%	37.4%	62.6%
7,881	CUMBERLAND	2,904	1,125	1,778	1	653 D	38.7%	61.2%	38.8%	61.2%
19,806	DICKENSON	7,069	1,871	5,196	2	3,325 D	26.5%	73.5%	26.5%	73.5%
22,602	DINWIDDIE	7,249	1,882	5,364	3	3,482 D	26.0%	74.0%	26.0%	74.0%
8,864	ESSEX	3,166	901	2,262	3	1,361 D	28.5%	71.4%	28.5%	71.5%
596,901	FAIRFAX COUNTY	317,967	86,911	230,780	276	143,869 D	27.3%	72.6%	27.4%	72.6%
35,889	FAUQUIER	15,512	5,546	9,963	3	4,417 D	35.8%	64.2%	35.8%	64.2%
11,563	FLOYD	4,300	1,480	2,820		1,340 D	34.4%	65.6%	34.4%	65.6%
10,244	FLUVANNA	3,814	1,198	2,616		1,418 D	31.4%	68.6%	31.4%	68.6%
35,740	FRANKLIN COUNTY	12,306	2,764	9,540	2	6,776 D	22.5%	77.5%	22.5%	77.5%
34,150	FREDERICK	13,205	3,767	9,436	2	5,669 D	28.5%	71.5%	28.5%	71.5%
17,810	GILES	6,185	1,620	4,563	2	2,943 D	26.2%	73.8%	26.2%	73.8%
20,107	GLOUCESTER	10,380	2,781	7,598	1	4,817 D	26.8%	73.2%	26.8%	73.2%
11,761	GOOCHLAND	5,719	2,075	3,642	2	1,567 D	36.3%	63.7%	36.3%	63.7%
16,579	GRAYSON	5,674	1,795	3,879		2,084 D	31.6%	68.4%	31.6%	68.4%
7,625	GREENE	2,868	1,185	1,682	1	497 D	41.3%	58.6%	41.3%	58.7%
10,903	GREENSVILLE	3,431	677	2,754		2,077 D	19.7%	80.3%	19.7%	80.3%
30,599	HALIFAX	8,628	2,393	6,233	2	3,840 D	27.7%	72.2%	27.7%	72.3%
50,398	HANOVER	25,193	9,464	15,708	21	6,244 D	37.6%	62.4%	37.6%	62.4%
180,735	HENRICO	87,104	29,379	57,471	254	28,092 D	33.7%	66.0%	33.8%	66.2%
57,654	HENRY	16,663	4,803	11,854	6	7,051 D	28.8%	71.1%	28.8%	71.2%
2,937	HIGHLAND	1,240	406	834		428 D	32.7%	67.3%	32.7%	67.3%
21,603	ISLE OF WIGHT	9,107	2,328	6,779		4,451 D	25.6%	74.4%	25.6%	74.4%
22,763	JAMES CITY	12,748	3,654	9,091	3	5,437 D	28.7%	71.3%	28.7%	71.3%
5,968	KING AND QUEEN	2,554	673	1,881		1,208 D	26.4%	73.6%	26.4%	73.6%
10,543	KING GEORGE	3,959	1,161	2,798		1,637 D	29.3%	70.7%	29.3%	70.7%
9,334	KING WILLIAM	4,110	1,318	2,792		1,474 D	32.1%	67.9%	32.1%	67.9%
10,129	LANCASTER	4,597	1,594	3,002	1	1,408 D	34.7%	65.3%	34.7%	65.3%
25,956	LEE	8,022	1,827	6,195		4,368 D	22.8%	77.2%	22.8%	77.2%
57,427	LOUDOUN	28,443	10,117	18,322	4	8,205 D	35.6%	64.4%	35.6%	64.4%
17,825	LOUISA	6,390	2,204	4,182	4	1,978 D	34.5%	65.4%	34.5%	65.5%
12,124	LUNENBURG	4,033	1,158	2,875		1,717 D	28.7%	71.3%	28.7%	71.3%
10,232	MADISON	3,697	1,316	2,379	2	1,063 D	35.6%	64.3%	35.6%	64.4%
7,995	MATHEWS	3,732	986	2,746		1,760 D	26.4%	73.6%	26.4%	73.6%
29,444	MECKLENBURG	7,937	2,496	5,436	5	2,940 D	31.4%	68.5%	31.5%	68.5%
7,719	MIDDLESEX	3,665	1,210	2,454	1	1,244 D	33.0%	67.0%	33.0%	67.0%
63,516	MONTGOMERY	20,253	5,720	14,529	4	8,809 D	28.2%	71.7%	28.2%	71.8%

VIRGINIA

SENATOR 1988

1980 Census Population	County	Total Vote	Republican	Democratic	Other	Rep.-Dem. Plurality	Percentage Total Vote Rep.	Total Vote Dem.	Major Vote Rep.	Major Vote Dem.
12,204	NELSON	4,505	903	3,597	5	2,694 D	20.0%	79.8%	20.1%	79.9%
8,781	NEW KENT	4,300	1,311	2,983	6	1,672 D	30.5%	69.4%	30.5%	69.5%
14,625	NORTHAMPTON	4,566	1,048	3,518		2,470 D	23.0%	77.0%	23.0%	77.0%
9,828	NORTHUMBERLAND	4,173	1,306	2,867		1,561 D	31.3%	68.7%	31.3%	68.7%
14,666	NOTTOWAY	5,113	1,562	3,548	3	1,986 D	30.5%	69.4%	30.6%	69.4%
18,063	ORANGE	6,492	2,112	4,377	3	2,265 D	32.5%	67.4%	32.5%	67.5%
19,401	PAGE	6,998	2,389	4,606	3	2,217 D	34.1%	65.8%	34.2%	65.8%
17,647	PATRICK	5,168	1,860	3,306	2	1,446 D	36.0%	64.0%	36.0%	64.0%
66,147	PITTSYLVANIA	16,194	5,657	10,533	4	4,876 D	34.9%	65.0%	34.9%	65.1%
13,062	POWHATAN	5,255	2,006	3,246	3	1,240 D	38.2%	61.8%	38.2%	61.8%
16,456	PRINCE EDWARD	5,319	1,763	3,555	1	1,792 D	33.1%	66.8%	33.2%	66.8%
25,733	PRINCE GEORGE	7,144	2,230	4,913	1	2,683 D	31.2%	68.8%	31.2%	68.8%
144,703	PRINCE WILLIAM	54,768	18,049	36,715	4	18,666 D	33.0%	67.0%	33.0%	67.0%
35,229	PULASKI	11,024	3,037	7,981	6	4,944 D	27.5%	72.4%	27.6%	72.4%
6,093	RAPPAHANNOCK	2,680	779	1,901		1,122 D	29.1%	70.9%	29.1%	70.9%
6,952	RICHMOND COUNTY	2,513	675	1,837	1	1,162 D	26.9%	73.1%	26.9%	73.1%
72,945	ROANOKE COUNTY	34,013	8,310	25,700	3	17,390 D	24.4%	75.6%	24.4%	75.6%
17,911	ROCKBRIDGE	5,627	1,511	4,116		2,605 D	26.9%	73.1%	26.9%	73.1%
57,038	ROCKINGHAM	16,486	6,626	9,858	2	3,232 D	40.2%	59.8%	40.2%	59.8%
31,761	RUSSELL	9,936	2,361	7,575		5,214 D	23.8%	76.2%	23.8%	76.2%
25,068	SCOTT	7,868	2,751	5,116	1	2,365 D	35.0%	65.0%	35.0%	65.0%
27,559	SHENANDOAH	11,222	4,012	7,210		3,198 D	35.8%	64.2%	35.8%	64.2%
33,366	SMYTH	10,353	3,056	7,297		4,241 D	29.5%	70.5%	29.5%	70.5%
18,731	SOUTHAMPTON	5,949	1,374	4,575		3,201 D	23.1%	76.9%	23.1%	76.9%
34,435	SPOTSYLVANIA	15,928	4,809	11,117	2	6,308 D	30.2%	69.8%	30.2%	69.8%
40,470	STAFFORD	16,934	5,312	11,622		6,310 D	31.4%	68.6%	31.4%	68.6%
6,046	SURRY	2,727	604	2,123		1,519 D	22.1%	77.9%	22.1%	77.9%
10,874	SUSSEX	3,557	803	2,754		1,951 D	22.6%	77.4%	22.6%	77.4%
50,511	TAZEWELL	14,001	3,185	10,816		7,631 D	22.7%	77.3%	22.7%	77.3%
21,200	WARREN	6,997	2,307	4,690		2,383 D	33.0%	67.0%	33.0%	67.0%
46,487	WASHINGTON	14,717	4,212	10,505		6,293 D	28.6%	71.4%	28.6%	71.4%
14,041	WESTMORELAND	4,993	1,286	3,706	1	2,420 D	25.8%	74.2%	25.8%	74.2%
43,863	WISE	12,460	3,068	9,392		6,324 D	24.6%	75.4%	24.6%	75.4%
25,522	WYTHE	8,382	2,768	5,614		2,846 D	33.0%	67.0%	33.0%	67.0%
35,463	YORK	15,170	4,076	11,092	2	7,016 D	26.9%	73.1%	26.9%	73.1%
	City									
103,217	ALEXANDRIA	43,241	10,783	32,449	9	21,666 D	24.9%	75.0%	24.9%	75.1%
5,991	BEDFORD CITY	2,113	589	1,524		935 D	27.9%	72.1%	27.9%	72.1%
19,042	BRISTOL	6,200	1,478	4,722		3,244 D	23.8%	76.2%	23.8%	76.2%
6,717	BUENA VISTA	1,927	468	1,458	1	990 D	24.3%	75.7%	24.3%	75.7%
39,916	CHARLOTTESVILLE	13,172	3,164	9,982	26	6,818 D	24.0%	75.8%	24.1%	75.9%
114,486	CHESAPEAKE	47,784	13,304	34,456	24	21,152 D	27.8%	72.1%	27.9%	72.1%
5,046	CLIFTON FORGE	1,601	332	1,269		937 D	20.7%	79.3%	20.7%	79.3%
16,509	COLONIAL HEIGHTS	7,153	2,137	5,010	6	2,873 D	29.9%	70.0%	29.9%	70.1%
9,063	COVINGTON	2,706	516	2,189	1	1,673 D	19.1%	80.9%	19.1%	80.9%
45,642	DANVILLE	16,519	5,526	10,992	1	5,466 D	33.5%	66.5%	33.5%	66.5%
4,840	EMPORIA	2,091	511	1,580		1,069 D	24.4%	75.6%	24.4%	75.6%
19,390	FAIRFAX CITY	8,577	2,762	5,815		3,053 D	32.2%	67.8%	32.2%	67.8%
9,515	FALLS CHURCH	4,733	1,041	3,692		2,651 D	22.0%	78.0%	22.0%	78.0%
7,308	FRANKLIN CITY	2,900	646	2,254		1,608 D	22.3%	77.7%	22.3%	77.7%
15,322	FREDERICKSBURG	5,863	1,599	4,260	4	2,661 D	27.3%	72.7%	27.3%	72.7%
6,524	GALAX	2,023	582	1,441		859 D	28.8%	71.2%	28.8%	71.2%
122,617	HAMPTON	40,355	10,406	29,942	7	19,536 D	25.8%	74.2%	25.8%	74.2%
19,671	HARRISONBURG	7,585	2,531	5,051	3	2,520 D	33.4%	66.6%	33.4%	66.6%
23,397	HOPEWELL	6,800	1,983	4,811	6	2,828 D	29.2%	70.8%	29.2%	70.8%
7,292	LEXINGTON	1,920	469	1,451		982 D	24.4%	75.6%	24.4%	75.6%
66,743	LYNCHBURG	22,309	7,383	14,919	7	7,536 D	33.1%	66.9%	33.1%	66.9%
15,438	MANASSAS	8,165	3,143	5,022		1,879 D	38.5%	61.5%	38.5%	61.5%
6,524	MANASSAS PARK	1,327	522	804	1	282 D	39.3%	60.6%	39.4%	60.6%
18,149	MARTINSVILLE	5,745	1,532	4,213		2,681 D	26.7%	73.3%	26.7%	73.3%
144,903	NEWPORT NEWS	51,581	13,238	38,341	2	25,103 D	25.7%	74.3%	25.7%	74.3%

VIRGINIA

SENATOR 1988

1980 Census Population	City	Total Vote	Republican	Democratic	Other	Rep.-Dem. Plurality	Percentage Total Vote Rep.	Total Vote Dem.	Major Vote Rep.	Major Vote Dem.
266,979	NORFOLK	66,958	13,485	53,436	37	39,951 D	20.1%	79.8%	20.2%	79.8%
4,757	NORTON	1,290	223	1,067		844 D	17.3%	82.7%	17.3%	82.7%
41,055	PETERSBURG	11,997	2,913	9,076	8	6,163 D	24.3%	75.7%	24.3%	75.7%
8,726	POQUOSON	4,526	1,428	3,098		1,670 D	31.6%	68.4%	31.6%	68.4%
104,577	PORTSMOUTH	34,776	7,234	27,542		20,308 D	20.8%	79.2%	20.8%	79.2%
13,225	RADFORD	4,171	1,133	3,038		1,905 D	27.2%	72.8%	27.2%	72.8%
219,214	RICHMOND CITY	70,355	19,594	50,704	57	31,110 D	27.9%	72.1%	27.9%	72.1%
100,220	ROANOKE CITY	31,322	6,872	24,448	2	17,576 D	21.9%	78.1%	21.9%	78.1%
23,958	SALEM	9,110	2,262	6,848		4,586 D	24.8%	75.2%	24.8%	75.2%
7,093	SOUTH BOSTON	2,312	669	1,642	1	973 D	28.9%	71.0%	28.9%	71.1%
21,857	STAUNTON	7,585	2,721	4,864		2,143 D	35.9%	64.1%	35.9%	64.1%
47,621	SUFFOLK	16,936	3,588	13,348		9,760 D	21.2%	78.8%	21.2%	78.8%
262,199	VIRGINIA BEACH	108,761	31,994	76,686	81	44,692 D	29.4%	70.5%	29.4%	70.6%
15,329	WAYNESBORO	6,330	2,339	3,991		1,652 D	37.0%	63.0%	37.0%	63.0%
9,870	WILLIAMSBURG	3,012	724	2,286	2	1,562 D	24.0%	75.9%	24.1%	75.9%
20,217	WINCHESTER	6,548	1,540	5,006	2	3,466 D	23.5%	76.5%	23.5%	76.5%
5,346,818	TOTAL	2,068,897	593,652	1,474,086	1,159	880,434 D	28.7%	71.2%	28.7%	71.3%

VIRGINIA

CONGRESS

CD	Year	Total Vote	Republican Vote	Republican Candidate	Democratic Vote	Democratic Candidate	Other Vote	Rep.-Dem. Plurality	Percentage Total Vote Rep.	Percentage Total Vote Dem.	Percentage Major Vote Rep.	Percentage Major Vote Dem.
1	1988	185,573	135,937	BATEMAN, HERBERT H.	49,614	ELLENSON, JAMES S.	22	86,323 R	73.3%	26.7%	73.3%	26.7%
1	1986	144,086	80,713	BATEMAN, HERBERT H.	63,364	SCOTT, ROBERT C.	9	17,349 R	56.0%	44.0%	56.0%	44.0%
1	1984	199,822	118,085	BATEMAN, HERBERT H.	79,577	MCGLENNON, JOHN J.	2,160	38,508 R	59.1%	39.8%	59.7%	40.3%
1	1982	142,802	76,926	BATEMAN, HERBERT H.	62,379	MCGLENNON, JOHN J.	3,497	14,547 R	53.9%	43.7%	55.2%	44.8%
2	1988	176,208	62,564	CURRY, JERRY R.	106,666	PICKETT, OWEN B.	6,978	44,102 D	35.5%	60.5%	37.0%	63.0%
2	1986	110,169	46,137	CANADA, A. J.	54,491	PICKETT, OWEN B.	9,541	8,354 D	41.9%	49.5%	45.8%	54.2%
2	1984	136,888	136,632	WHITEHURST, G. W.			256	136,632 R	99.8%		100.0%	
2	1982	78,205	78,108	WHITEHURST, G. W.			97	78,108 R	99.9%		100.0%	
3	1988	187,898	187,354	BLILEY, THOMAS J.			544	187,354 R	99.7%		100.0%	
3	1986	111,179	74,525	BLILEY, THOMAS J.	32,961	POWELL, KENNETH E.	3,693	41,564 R	67.0%	29.6%	69.3%	30.7%
3	1984	198,567	169,987	BLILEY, THOMAS J.			28,580	169,987 R	85.6%		100.0%	
3	1982	156,891	92,928	BLILEY, THOMAS J.	63,946	WALDROP, JOHN A.	17	28,982 R	59.2%	40.8%	59.2%	40.8%
4	1988	134,884			134,786	SISISKY, NORMAN	98	134,786 D		99.9%		100.0%
4	1986	64,835			64,699	SISISKY, NORMAN	136	64,699 D		99.8%		100.0%
4	1984	120,162			120,093	SISISKY, NORMAN	69	120,093 D		99.9%		100.0%
4	1982	148,406	67,708	DANIEL, ROBERT W.	80,695	SISISKY, NORMAN	3	12,987 D	45.6%	54.4%	45.6%	54.4%
5	1988	179,442	78,396	HAWKINS, CHARLES	97,242	PAYNE, L. F.	3,804	18,846 D	43.7%	54.2%	44.6%	55.4%
5	1986	89,653			73,085	DANIEL, W. C.	16,568	73,085 D		81.5%		100.0%
5	1984	117,778			117,738	DANIEL, W. C.	40	117,738 D		100.0%		100.0%
5	1982	88,324			88,293	DANIEL, W. C.	31	88,293 D		100.0%		100.0%
6	1988	185,312	66,935	JUDD, CHARLES E.	118,369	OLIN, JAMES R.	8	51,434 D	36.1%	63.9%	36.1%	63.9%
6	1986	126,310	38,051	TRAYWICK, FLO N.	88,230	OLIN, JAMES R.	29	50,179 D	30.1%	69.9%	30.1%	69.9%
6	1984	196,560	91,344	GARLAND, RAY L.	105,207	OLIN, JAMES R.	9	13,863 D	46.5%	53.5%	46.5%	53.5%
6	1982	137,140	66,537	MILLER, KEVIN G.	68,192	OLIN, JAMES R.	2,411	1,655 D	48.5%	49.7%	49.4%	50.6%
7	1988	137,476	136,988	SLAUGHTER, D. FRENCH			488	136,988 R	99.6%		100.0%	
7	1986	59,976	58,927	SLAUGHTER, D. FRENCH			1,049	58,927 R	98.3%		100.0%	
7	1984	193,156	109,110	SLAUGHTER, D. FRENCH	77,624	COSTELLO, LEWIS M.	6,422	31,486 R	56.5%	40.2%	58.4%	41.6%
7	1982	128,224	76,752	ROBINSON, J. KENNETH	46,514	DORRIER, LINDSAY G.	4,958	30,238 R	59.9%	36.3%	62.3%	37.7%
8	1988	248,400	154,761	PARRIS, STANFORD E.	93,561	BRICKLEY, DAVID G.	78	61,200 R	62.3%	37.7%	62.3%	37.7%
8	1986	117,655	72,670	PARRIS, STANFORD E.	44,965	BOREN, JAMES H.	20	27,705 R	61.8%	38.2%	61.8%	38.2%
8	1984	224,091	125,015	PARRIS, STANFORD E.	97,250	SASLAW, RICHARD L.	1,826	27,765 R	55.8%	43.4%	56.2%	43.8%
8	1982	140,070	69,620	PARRIS, STANFORD E.	68,071	HARRIS, HERBERT E.	2,379	1,549 R	49.7%	48.6%	50.6%	49.4%
9	1988	178,727	65,410	BROWN, JOHN C.	113,309	BOUCHER, FREDERICK C.	8	47,899 D	36.6%	63.4%	36.6%	63.4%
9	1986	60,466			59,864	BOUCHER, FREDERICK C.	602	59,864 D		99.0%		100.0%
9	1984	196,956	94,510	STAFFORD, C. JEFFERSON	102,446	BOUCHER, FREDERICK C.		7,936 D	48.0%	52.0%	48.0%	52.0%
9	1982	151,289	75,082	WAMPLER, WILLIAM C.	76,205	BOUCHER, FREDERICK C.	2	1,123 D	49.6%	50.4%	49.6%	50.4%
10	1988	276,908	188,550	WOLF, FRANK R.	88,284	WEINBERG, ROBERT L.	74	100,266 R	68.1%	31.9%	68.1%	31.9%
10	1986	159,023	95,724	WOLF, FRANK R.	63,292	MILLIKEN, JOHN G.	7	32,432 R	60.2%	39.8%	60.2%	39.8%
10	1984	253,625	158,528	WOLF, FRANK R.	95,074	FLANNERY, JOHN P.	23	63,454 R	62.5%	37.5%	62.5%	37.5%
10	1982	164,035	86,506	WOLF, FRANK R.	75,361	LECHNER, IRA M.	2,168	11,145 R	52.7%	45.9%	53.4%	46.6%
10	1980	216,744	110,840	WOLF, FRANK R.	105,883	FISHER, JOSEPH L.	21	4,957 R	51.1%	48.9%	51.1%	48.9%
10	1978	132,882	61,981	WOLF, FRANK R.	70,892	FISHER, JOSEPH L.	9	8,911 D	46.6%	53.3%	46.6%	53.4%
10	1976	189,489	73,616	CALLAHAN, VINCENT F.	103,689	FISHER, JOSEPH L.	12,184	30,073 D	38.8%	54.7%	41.5%	58.5%
10	1974	125,304	56,649	BROYHILL, JOEL T.	67,184	FISHER, JOSEPH L.	1,471	10,535 D	45.2%	53.6%	45.7%	54.3%
10	1972	179,778	101,138	BROYHILL, JOEL T.	78,638	MILLER, HAROLD O.	2	22,500 R	56.3%	43.7%	56.3%	43.7%

VIRGINIA

Under Virginia's local government system a number of urban areas - 41 since 1977 - are organized as cities independent of county authority.

1988 GENERAL ELECTION

President Other vote was 14,312 Independent (Fulani); 8,336 Libertarian (Paul).

Senator Other vote was scattered write-in.

Congress Other vote was 4,255 Independent (Shao), 2,691 Independent (Smith) and 32 scattered in CD 2; 3,792 Independent (Cole) and 12 scattered in CD 5; scattered in all other CD's.

1988 PRIMARIES

JUNE 14 REPUBLICAN

Senator Maurice A. Dawkins, nominated by convention.

Congress No candidate in CD's 4 and 6. Linda Arey, the candidate nominated by convention in CD 5, withdrew after the primary and Charles Hawkins was substituted by the local party committee. In CD 6 Charles E. Judd was named after the primary by the local party committee. Candidates nominated by convention in all other CD's.

JUNE 14 DEMOCRATIC

Senator Charles S. Robb, nominated by convention.

Congress No candidate in CD's 3 and 7. Candidates nominated by convention in all other CD's except CD 10 which was contested as follows:

CD 10 6,880 Robert L. Weinberg; 2,081 N. MacKenzie Canter.

WASHINGTON

GOVERNOR

Booth Gardner (D). Re-elected 1988 to a four-year term. Previously elected 1984.

SENATORS

Brock Adams (D). Elected 1986 to a six-year term.

Slade Gorton (R). Elected 1988 to a six-year term. Previously elected 1980.

REPRESENTATIVES

1. John R. Miller (R)
2. Al Swift (D)
3. Jolene Unsoeld (D)
4. Sid Morrison (R)
5. Thomas S. Foley (D)
6. Norman D. Dicks (D)
7. Jim McDermott (D)
8. Rod Chandler (R)

POSTWAR VOTE FOR PRESIDENT

		Republican		Democratic				Percentage			
	Total					Other		Total Vote		Major Vote	
Year	Vote	Vote	Candidate	Vote	Candidate	Vote	Plurality	Rep.	Dem.	Rep.	Dem.
1988	1,865,253	903,835	Bush, George	933,516	Dukakis, Michael S.	27,902	29,681 D	48.5%	50.0%	49.2%	50.8%
1984	1,883,910	1,051,670	Reagan, Ronald	807,352	Mondale, Walter F.	24,888	244,318 R	55.8%	42.9%	56.6%	43.4%
1980	1,742,394	865,244	Reagan, Ronald	650,193	Carter, Jimmy	226,957	215,051 R	49.7%	37.3%	57.1%	42.9%
1976	1,555,534	777,732	Ford, Gerald R.	717,323	Carter, Jimmy	60,479	60,409 R	50.0%	46.1%	52.0%	48.0%
1972	1,470,847	837,135	Nixon, Richard M.	568,334	McGovern, George S.	65,378	268,801 R	56.9%	38.6%	59.6%	40.4%
1968	1,304,281	588,510	Nixon, Richard M.	616,037	Humphrey, Hubert H.	99,734	27,527 D	45.1%	47.2%	48.9%	51.1%
1964	1,258,556	470,366	Goldwater, Barry M.	779,881	Johnson, Lyndon B.	8,309	309,515 D	37.4%	62.0%	37.6%	62.4%
1960	1,241,572	629,273	Nixon, Richard M.	599,298	Kennedy, John F.	13,001	29,975 R	50.7%	48.3%	51.2%	48.8%
1956	1,150,889	620,430	Eisenhower, Dwight D.	523,002	Stevenson, Adlai E.	7,457	97,428 R	53.9%	45.4%	54.3%	45.7%
1952	1,102,708	599,107	Eisenhower, Dwight D.	492,845	Stevenson, Adlai E.	10,756	106,262 R	54.3%	44.7%	54.9%	45.1%
1948	905,058	386,314	Dewey, Thomas E.	476,165	Truman, Harry S.	42,579	89,851 D	42.7%	52.6%	44.8%	55.2%

POSTWAR VOTE FOR GOVERNOR

		Republican		Democratic				Percentage			
	Total					Other	Rep.-Dem.	Total Vote		Major Vote	
Year	Vote	Vote	Candidate	Vote	Candidate	Vote	Plurality	Rep.	Dem.	Rep.	Dem.
1988	1,874,929	708,481	Williams, Bob	1,166,448	Gardner, Booth		457,967 D	37.8%	62.2%	37.8%	62.2%
1984	1,888,987	881,994	Spellman, John D.	1,006,993	Gardner, Booth		124,999 D	46.7%	53.3%	46.7%	53.3%
1980	1,730,896	981,083	Spellman, John D.	749,813	McDermott, James A.		231,270 R	56.7%	43.3%	56.7%	43.3%
1976	1,546,382	687,039	Spellman, John D.	821,797	Ray, Dixy Lee	37,546	134,758 D	44.4%	53.1%	45.5%	54.5%
1972	1,472,542	747,825	Evans, Daniel J.	630,613	Rosellini, Albert D.	94,104	117,212 R	50.8%	42.8%	54.3%	45.7%
1968	1,265,355	692,378	Evans, Daniel J.	560,262	O'Connell, John J.	12,715	132,116 R	54.7%	44.3%	55.3%	44.7%
1964	1,250,274	697,256	Evans, Daniel J.	548,692	Rosellini, Albert D.	4,326	148,564 R	55.8%	43.9%	56.0%	44.0%
1960	1,215,748	594,122	Andrews, Lloyd J.	611,987	Rosellini, Albert D.	9,639	17,865 D	48.9%	50.3%	49.3%	50.7%
1956	1,128,977	508,041	Anderson, Emmett T.	616,773	Rosellini, Albert D.	4,163	108,732 D	45.0%	54.6%	45.2%	54.8%
1952	1,078,497	567,822	Langlie, Arthur B.	510,675	Mitchell, Hugh B.		57,147 R	52.6%	47.4%	52.6%	47.4%
1948	883,141	445,958	Langlie, Arthur B.	417,035	Wallgren, Mon C.	20,148	28,923 R	50.5%	47.2%	51.7%	48.3%

WASHINGTON

POSTWAR VOTE FOR SENATOR

		Republican		Democratic				Percentage			
	Total	Republican		Democratic		Other	Rep.-Dem.	Total Vote		Major Vote	
Year	Vote	Vote	Candidate	Vote	Candidate	Vote	Plurality	Rep.	Dem.	Rep.	Dem.
1988	1,848,542	944,359	Gorton, Slade	904,183	Lowry, Mike		40,176 R	51.1%	48.9%	51.1%	48.9%
1986	1,337,367	650,931	Gorton, Slade	677,471	Adams, Brock	8,965	26,540 D	48.7%	50.7%	49.0%	51.0%
1983 S	1,213,307	672,326	Evans, Daniel J.	540,981	Lowry, Mike		131,345 R	55.4%	44.6%	55.4%	44.6%
1982	1,368,476	332,273	Jewett, Doug	943,655	Jackson, Henry M.	92,548	611,382 D	24.3%	69.0%	26.0%	74.0%
1980	1,728,369	936,317	Gorton, Slade	792,052	Magnuson, Warren G.		144,265 R	54.2%	45.8%	54.2%	45.8%
1976	1,491,111	361,546	Brown, George M.	1,071,219	Jackson, Henry M.	58,346	709,673 D	24.2%	71.8%	25.2%	74.8%
1974	1,007,847	363,626	Metcalf, Jack	611,811	Magnuson, Warren G.	32,410	248,185 D	36.1%	60.7%	37.3%	62.7%
1970	1,066,807	170,790	Elicker, Charles W.	879,385	Jackson, Henry M.	16,632	708,595 D	16.0%	82.4%	16.3%	83.7%
1968	1,236,063	435,894	Metcalf, Jack	796,183	Magnuson, Warren G.	3,986	360,289 D	35.3%	64.4%	35.4%	64.6%
1964	1,213,088	337,138	Andrews, Lloyd J.	875,950	Jackson, Henry M.		538,812 D	27.8%	72.2%	27.8%	72.2%
1962	943,229	446,204	Christensen, Richard G.	491,365	Magnuson, Warren G.	5,660	45,161 D	47.3%	52.1%	47.6%	52.4%
1958	886,822	278,271	Bantz, William B.	597,040	Jackson, Henry M.	11,511	318,769 D	31.4%	67.3%	31.8%	68.2%
1956	1,122,217	436,652	Langlie, Arthur B.	685,565	Magnuson, Warren G.		248,913 D	38.9%	61.1%	38.9%	61.1%
1952	1,058,735	460,884	Cain, Harry P.	595,288	Jackson, Henry M.	2,563	134,404 D	43.5%	56.2%	43.6%	56.4%
1950	744,783	342,464	Williams, Walter	397,719	Magnuson, Warren G.	4,600	55,255 D	46.0%	53.4%	46.3%	53.7%
1946	660,342	358,847	Cain, Harry P.	298,683	Mitchell, Hugh B.	2,812	60,164 R	54.3%	45.2%	54.6%	45.4%

The 1983 election was for a short term to fill a vacancy.

WASHINGTON

Districts Established March 29, 1983

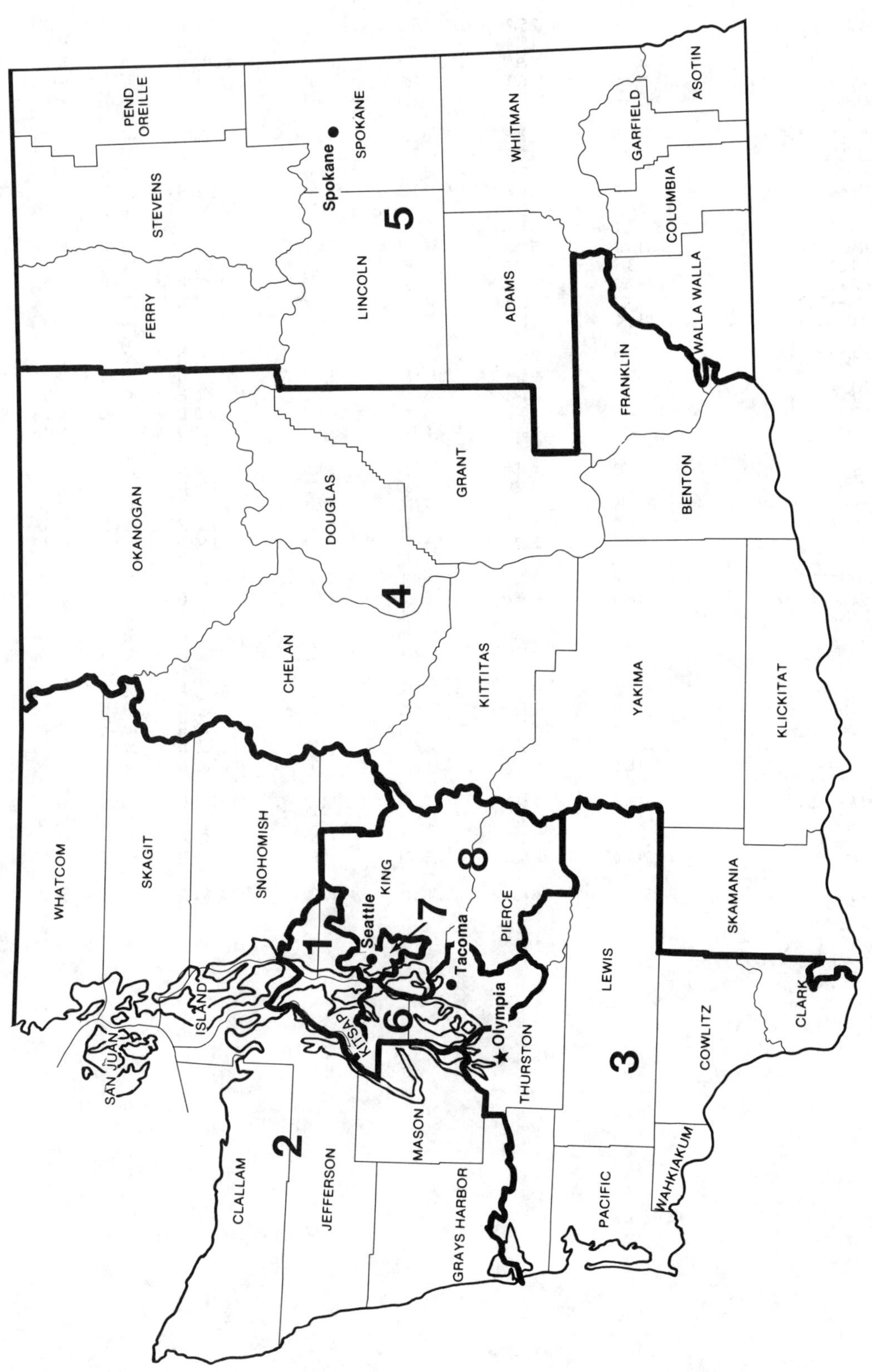

WASHINGTON

PRESIDENT 1988

1980 Census Population	County	Total Vote	Republican	Democratic	Other	Rep.-Dem. Plurality	Percentage Total Vote Rep.	Total Vote Dem.	Major Vote Rep.	Major Vote Dem.
13,267	ADAMS	4,288	2,612	1,612	64	1,000 R	60.9%	37.6%	61.8%	38.2%
16,823	ASOTIN	6,384	2,874	3,422	88	548 D	45.0%	53.6%	45.6%	54.4%
109,444	BENTON	44,016	28,688	14,817	511	13,871 R	65.2%	33.7%	65.9%	34.1%
45,061	CHELAN	20,065	11,601	8,183	281	3,418 R	57.8%	40.8%	58.6%	41.4%
51,648	CLALLAM	22,794	11,200	11,123	471	77 R	49.1%	48.8%	50.2%	49.8%
192,227	CLARK	78,306	37,285	40,021	1,000	2,736 D	47.6%	51.1%	48.2%	51.8%
4,057	COLUMBIA	1,944	1,172	730	42	442 R	60.3%	37.6%	61.6%	38.4%
79,548	COWLITZ	28,465	12,009	16,090	366	4,081 D	42.2%	56.5%	42.7%	57.3%
22,144	DOUGLAS	9,247	5,378	3,760	109	1,618 R	58.2%	40.7%	58.9%	41.1%
5,811	FERRY	2,021	972	972	77		48.1%	48.1%	50.0%	50.0%
35,025	FRANKLIN	11,452	6,488	4,772	192	1,716 R	56.7%	41.7%	57.6%	42.4%
2,468	GARFIELD	1,319	714	593	12	121 R	54.1%	45.0%	54.6%	45.4%
48,522	GRANT	18,799	10,859	7,564	376	3,295 R	57.8%	40.2%	58.9%	41.1%
66,314	GRAYS HARBOR	23,391	8,860	14,097	434	5,237 D	37.9%	60.3%	38.6%	61.4%
44,048	ISLAND	21,353	12,552	8,510	291	4,042 R	58.8%	39.9%	59.6%	40.4%
15,965	JEFFERSON	9,636	4,184	5,270	182	1,086 D	43.4%	54.7%	44.3%	55.7%
1,269,749	KING	648,957	290,574	349,663	8,720	59,089 D	44.8%	53.9%	45.4%	54.6%
147,152	KITSAP	69,649	34,743	33,748	1,158	995 R	49.9%	48.5%	50.7%	49.3%
24,877	KITTITAS	10,496	5,048	5,318	130	270 D	48.1%	50.7%	48.7%	51.3%
15,822	KLICKITAT	6,086	2,920	2,991	175	71 D	48.0%	49.1%	49.4%	50.6%
56,025	LEWIS	23,238	14,184	8,629	425	5,555 R	61.0%	37.1%	62.2%	37.8%
9,604	LINCOLN	4,645	2,689	1,884	72	805 R	57.9%	40.6%	58.8%	41.2%
31,184	MASON	15,545	7,426	7,826	293	400 D	47.8%	50.3%	48.7%	51.3%
30,639	OKANOGAN	11,740	5,856	5,630	254	226 R	49.9%	48.0%	51.0%	49.0%
17,237	PACIFIC	8,200	3,073	5,017	110	1,944 D	37.5%	61.2%	38.0%	62.0%
8,580	PEND OREILLE	3,794	1,802	1,925	67	123 D	47.5%	50.7%	48.3%	51.7%
485,643	PIERCE	194,473	94,167	96,688	3,618	2,521 D	48.4%	49.7%	49.3%	50.7%
7,838	SAN JUAN	5,814	2,660	3,008	146	348 D	45.8%	51.7%	46.9%	53.1%
64,138	SKAGIT	32,401	16,550	15,159	692	1,391 R	51.1%	46.8%	52.2%	47.8%
7,919	SKAMANIA	3,162	1,356	1,748	58	392 D	42.9%	55.3%	43.7%	56.3%
337,720	SNOHOMISH	167,165	84,158	80,694	2,313	3,464 R	50.3%	48.3%	51.1%	48.9%
341,835	SPOKANE	139,150	68,787	68,520	1,843	267 R	49.4%	49.2%	50.1%	49.9%
28,979	STEVENS	11,962	6,576	5,068	318	1,508 R	55.0%	42.4%	56.5%	43.5%
124,264	THURSTON	66,930	31,980	33,860	1,090	1,880 D	47.8%	50.6%	48.6%	51.4%
3,832	WAHKIAKUM	1,626	629	961	36	332 D	38.7%	59.1%	39.6%	60.4%
47,435	WALLA WALLA	17,403	9,683	7,448	272	2,235 R	55.6%	42.8%	56.5%	43.5%
106,701	WHATCOM	50,094	23,820	25,571	703	1,751 D	47.6%	51.0%	48.2%	51.8%
40,103	WHITMAN	15,333	7,680	7,403	250	277 R	50.1%	48.3%	50.9%	49.1%
172,508	YAKIMA	53,910	30,026	23,221	663	6,805 R	55.7%	43.1%	56.4%	43.6%
4,132,156	TOTAL	1,865,253	903,835	933,516	27,902	29,681 D	48.5%	50.0%	49.2%	50.8%

WASHINGTON

GOVERNOR 1988

1980 Census Population	County	Total Vote	Republican	Democratic	Other	Rep.-Dem. Plurality	Percentage Total Vote Rep.	Total Vote Dem.	Major Vote Rep.	Major Vote Dem.
13,267	ADAMS	4,471	2,243	2,228		15 R	50.2%	49.8%	50.2%	49.8%
16,823	ASOTIN	6,609	2,264	4,345		2,081 D	34.3%	65.7%	34.3%	65.7%
109,444	BENTON	44,740	29,333	15,407		13,926 R	65.6%	34.4%	65.6%	34.4%
45,061	CHELAN	18,998	7,961	11,037		3,076 D	41.9%	58.1%	41.9%	58.1%
51,648	CLALLAM	23,182	9,406	13,776		4,370 D	40.6%	59.4%	40.6%	59.4%
192,227	CLARK	78,158	33,086	45,072		11,986 D	42.3%	57.7%	42.3%	57.7%
4,057	COLUMBIA	1,972	1,054	918		136 R	53.4%	46.6%	53.4%	46.6%
79,548	COWLITZ	28,738	14,584	14,154		430 R	50.7%	49.3%	50.7%	49.3%
22,144	DOUGLAS	9,504	4,296	5,208		912 D	45.2%	54.8%	45.2%	54.8%
5,811	FERRY	2,031	870	1,161		291 D	42.8%	57.2%	42.8%	57.2%
35,025	FRANKLIN	11,025	6,587	4,438		2,149 R	59.7%	40.3%	59.7%	40.3%
2,468	GARFIELD	1,344	561	783		222 D	41.7%	58.3%	41.7%	58.3%
48,522	GRANT	18,213	8,830	9,383		553 D	48.5%	51.5%	48.5%	51.5%
66,314	GRAYS HARBOR	24,287	7,336	16,951		9,615 D	30.2%	69.8%	30.2%	69.8%
44,048	ISLAND	21,646	9,277	12,369		3,092 D	42.9%	57.1%	42.9%	57.1%
15,965	JEFFERSON	9,678	3,300	6,378		3,078 D	34.1%	65.9%	34.1%	65.9%
1,269,749	KING	648,950	195,378	453,572		258,194 D	30.1%	69.9%	30.1%	69.9%
147,152	KITSAP	70,299	27,683	42,616		14,933 D	39.4%	60.6%	39.4%	60.6%
24,877	KITTITAS	10,609	3,886	6,723		2,837 D	36.6%	63.4%	36.6%	63.4%
15,822	KLICKITAT	6,099	2,617	3,482		865 D	42.9%	57.1%	42.9%	57.1%
56,025	LEWIS	23,636	13,380	10,256		3,124 R	56.6%	43.4%	56.6%	43.4%
9,604	LINCOLN	4,740	2,317	2,423		106 D	48.9%	51.1%	48.9%	51.1%
31,184	MASON	15,916	6,217	9,699		3,482 D	39.1%	60.9%	39.1%	60.9%
30,639	OKANOGAN	11,902	5,078	6,824		1,746 D	42.7%	57.3%	42.7%	57.3%
17,237	PACIFIC	8,181	2,668	5,513		2,845 D	32.6%	67.4%	32.6%	67.4%
8,580	PEND OREILLE	3,834	1,517	2,317		800 D	39.6%	60.4%	39.6%	60.4%
485,643	PIERCE	188,766	69,307	119,459		50,152 D	36.7%	63.3%	36.7%	63.3%
7,838	SAN JUAN	5,790	1,976	3,814		1,838 D	34.1%	65.9%	34.1%	65.9%
64,138	SKAGIT	32,991	13,089	19,902		6,813 D	39.7%	60.3%	39.7%	60.3%
7,919	SKAMANIA	3,157	1,504	1,653		149 D	47.6%	52.4%	47.6%	52.4%
337,720	SNOHOMISH	168,480	63,123	105,357		42,234 D	37.5%	62.5%	37.5%	62.5%
341,835	SPOKANE	142,249	61,571	80,678		19,107 D	43.3%	56.7%	43.3%	56.7%
28,979	STEVENS	12,129	6,249	5,880		369 R	51.5%	48.5%	51.5%	48.5%
124,264	THURSTON	67,875	25,292	42,583		17,291 D	37.3%	62.7%	37.3%	62.7%
3,832	WAHKIAKUM	1,575	755	820		65 D	47.9%	52.1%	47.9%	52.1%
47,435	WALLA WALLA	17,705	8,789	8,916		127 D	49.6%	50.4%	49.6%	50.4%
106,701	WHATCOM	50,255	18,934	31,321		12,387 D	37.7%	62.3%	37.7%	62.3%
40,103	WHITMAN	15,363	6,026	9,337		3,311 D	39.2%	60.8%	39.2%	60.8%
172,508	YAKIMA	59,832	30,137	29,695		442 R	50.4%	49.6%	50.4%	49.6%
4,132,156	TOTAL	1,874,929	708,481	1,166,448		457,967 D	37.8%	62.2%	37.8%	62.2%

WASHINGTON

SENATOR 1988

1980 Census Population	County	Total Vote	Republican	Democratic	Other	Rep.-Dem. Plurality	Percentage Total Vote Rep.	Percentage Total Vote Dem.	Percentage Major Vote Rep.	Percentage Major Vote Dem.
13,267	ADAMS	4,462	2,856	1,606		1,250 R	64.0%	36.0%	64.0%	36.0%
16,823	ASOTIN	6,568	3,195	3,373		178 D	48.6%	51.4%	48.6%	51.4%
109,444	BENTON	44,533	35,986	8,547		27,439 R	80.8%	19.2%	80.8%	19.2%
45,061	CHELAN	19,794	12,083	7,711		4,372 R	61.0%	39.0%	61.0%	39.0%
51,648	CLALLAM	22,973	11,738	11,235		503 R	51.1%	48.9%	51.1%	48.9%
192,227	CLARK	77,953	40,518	37,435		3,083 R	52.0%	48.0%	52.0%	48.0%
4,057	COLUMBIA	1,954	1,170	784		386 R	59.9%	40.1%	59.9%	40.1%
79,548	COWLITZ	28,457	13,502	14,955		1,453 D	47.4%	52.6%	47.4%	52.6%
22,144	DOUGLAS	9,407	5,718	3,689		2,029 R	60.8%	39.2%	60.8%	39.2%
5,811	FERRY	1,985	981	1,004		23 D	49.4%	50.6%	49.4%	50.6%
35,025	FRANKLIN	10,908	7,683	3,225		4,458 R	70.4%	29.6%	70.4%	29.6%
2,468	GARFIELD	1,321	719	602		117 R	54.4%	45.6%	54.4%	45.6%
48,522	GRANT	18,162	10,897	7,265		3,632 R	60.0%	40.0%	60.0%	40.0%
66,314	GRAYS HARBOR	24,189	9,780	14,409		4,629 D	40.4%	59.6%	40.4%	59.6%
44,048	ISLAND	21,481	12,806	8,675		4,131 R	59.6%	40.4%	59.6%	40.4%
15,965	JEFFERSON	9,686	4,298	5,388		1,090 D	44.4%	55.6%	44.4%	55.6%
1,269,749	KING	628,489	289,087	339,402		50,315 D	46.0%	54.0%	46.0%	54.0%
147,152	KITSAP	66,618	36,125	30,493		5,632 R	54.2%	45.8%	54.2%	45.8%
24,877	KITTITAS	10,583	5,542	5,041		501 R	52.4%	47.6%	52.4%	47.6%
15,822	KLICKITAT	6,047	3,064	2,983		81 R	50.7%	49.3%	50.7%	49.3%
56,025	LEWIS	23,541	14,254	9,287		4,967 R	60.5%	39.5%	60.5%	39.5%
9,604	LINCOLN	4,737	2,805	1,932		873 R	59.2%	40.8%	59.2%	40.8%
31,184	MASON	15,770	7,692	8,078		386 D	48.8%	51.2%	48.8%	51.2%
30,639	OKANOGAN	11,900	6,189	5,711		478 R	52.0%	48.0%	52.0%	48.0%
17,237	PACIFIC	8,212	3,325	4,887		1,562 D	40.5%	59.5%	40.5%	59.5%
8,580	PEND OREILLE	3,725	1,870	1,855		15 R	50.2%	49.8%	50.2%	49.8%
485,643	PIERCE	189,432	96,122	93,310		2,812 R	50.7%	49.3%	50.7%	49.3%
7,838	SAN JUAN	5,743	2,811	2,932		121 D	48.9%	51.1%	48.9%	51.1%
64,138	SKAGIT	32,163	16,747	15,416		1,331 R	52.1%	47.9%	52.1%	47.9%
7,919	SKAMANIA	3,074	1,299	1,775		476 D	42.3%	57.7%	42.3%	57.7%
337,720	SNOHOMISH	168,720	88,307	80,413		7,894 R	52.3%	47.7%	52.3%	47.7%
341,835	SPOKANE	142,065	73,583	68,482		5,101 R	51.8%	48.2%	51.8%	48.2%
28,979	STEVENS	12,118	6,729	5,389		1,340 R	55.5%	44.5%	55.5%	44.5%
124,264	THURSTON	67,637	33,371	34,266		895 D	49.3%	50.7%	49.3%	50.7%
3,832	WAHKIAKUM	1,520	716	804		88 D	47.1%	52.9%	47.1%	52.9%
47,435	WALLA WALLA	17,651	10,647	7,004		3,643 R	60.3%	39.7%	60.3%	39.7%
106,701	WHATCOM	50,057	25,278	24,779		499 R	50.5%	49.5%	50.5%	49.5%
40,103	WHITMAN	15,278	8,022	7,256		766 R	52.5%	47.5%	52.5%	47.5%
172,508	YAKIMA	59,629	36,844	22,785		14,059 R	61.8%	38.2%	61.8%	38.2%
4,132,156	TOTAL	1,848,542	944,359	904,183		40,176 R	51.1%	48.9%	51.1%	48.9%

WASHINGTON

CONGRESS

CD	Year	Total Vote	Republican Vote	Republican Candidate	Democratic Vote	Democratic Candidate	Other Vote	Rep.-Dem. Plurality	Percentage Total Vote Rep.	Percentage Total Vote Dem.	Percentage Major Vote Rep.	Percentage Major Vote Dem.
1	1988	274,911	152,265	MILLER, JOHN R.	122,646	LINDQUIST, REESE		29,619 R	55.4%	44.6%	55.4%	44.6%
1	1986	190,666	97,969	MILLER, JOHN R.	92,697	LINDQUIST, REESE		5,272 R	51.4%	48.6%	51.4%	48.6%
1	1984	262,927	147,926	MILLER, JOHN R.	115,001	EVANS, BROCK		32,925 R	56.3%	43.7%	56.3%	43.7%
2	1988	175,191			175,191	SWIFT, AL		175,191 D		100.0%		100.0%
2	1986	172,917	48,077	TALMAN, THOMAS S.	124,840	SWIFT, AL		76,763 D	27.8%	72.2%	27.8%	72.2%
2	1984	242,392	93,472	KLAUDER, JIM	142,065	SWIFT, AL	6,855	48,593 D	38.6%	58.6%	39.7%	60.3%
3	1988	218,206	108,794	WIGHT, BILL	109,412	UNSOELD, JOLENE		618 D	49.9%	50.1%	49.9%	50.1%
3	1986	156,050	41,275	ILLING, JOE	114,775	BONKER, DON		73,500 D	26.4%	73.6%	26.4%	73.6%
3	1984	211,651	61,219	ELDER, HERB	150,432	BONKER, DON		89,213 D	28.9%	71.1%	28.9%	71.1%
4	1988	191,788	142,938	MORRISON, SID	48,850	GOLOB, J. RICHARD		94,088 R	74.5%	25.5%	74.5%	25.5%
4	1986	149,302	107,593	MORRISON, SID	41,709	GOEDECKE, ROBERT		65,884 R	72.1%	27.9%	72.1%	27.9%
4	1984	197,480	150,322	MORRISON, SID	47,158	EPPERSON, MARK		103,164 R	76.1%	23.9%	76.1%	23.9%
5	1988	210,311	49,657	DERBY, MARLYN A.	160,654	FOLEY, THOMAS S.		110,997 D	23.6%	76.4%	23.6%	76.4%
5	1986	162,911	41,179	WAKEFIELD, FLOYD L.	121,732	FOLEY, THOMAS S.		80,553 D	25.3%	74.7%	25.3%	74.7%
5	1984	222,426	67,438	HEBNER, JACK	154,988	FOLEY, THOMAS S.		87,550 D	30.3%	69.7%	30.3%	69.7%
6	1988	186,250	60,346	COOK, KEVIN P.	125,904	DICKS, NORMAN D.		65,558 D	32.4%	67.6%	32.4%	67.6%
6	1986	126,473	36,410	BRAATEN, KENNETH W.	90,063	DICKS, NORMAN D.		53,653 D	28.8%	71.2%	28.8%	71.2%
6	1984	188,041	60,721	LONERGAN, MIKE	124,367	DICKS, NORMAN D.	2,953	63,646 D	32.3%	66.1%	32.8%	67.2%
7	1988	227,711	53,902	EDWARDS, ROBERT	173,809	MCDERMOTT, JIM		119,907 D	23.7%	76.3%	23.7%	76.3%
7	1986	171,148	46,831	MACDONALD, DON	124,317	LOWRY, MIKE		77,486 D	27.4%	72.6%	27.4%	72.6%
7	1984	247,846	71,576	DORSE, BOB	174,560	LOWRY, MIKE	1,710	102,984 D	28.9%	70.4%	29.1%	70.9%
8	1988	246,862	174,942	CHANDLER, ROD	71,920	KEAN, JIM		103,022 R	70.9%	29.1%	70.9%	29.1%
8	1986	165,369	107,824	CHANDLER, ROD	57,545	GILES, DAVID E.		50,279 R	65.2%	34.8%	65.2%	34.8%
8	1984	235,270	146,891	CHANDLER, ROD	88,379	LAMSON, BOB		58,512 R	62.4%	37.6%	62.4%	37.6%

WASHINGTON

1988 GENERAL ELECTION

President Other vote was 17,240 Libertarian (Paul); 4,412 Independent (LaRouche); 3,520 New Alliance (Fulani); 1,440 Workers World (Holmes); 1,290 Socialist Workers (Warren).

Governor

Senator

Congress Vote in CD 3 is for the recount.

1988 PRIMARIES

Washington's primaries are completely open, with all candidates for an office carried on the ballot together; thus a voter may vote for a Republican for Governor, a Democrat for Senator, and so on. In this so-called "jungle primary", nominations go to the highest party candidate, providing the winner receives a minimum of one percent of the total votes cast for the office. Independents qualify for a place on the General Election ballot by polling the same minimum requirement.

SEPTEMBER 20 REPUBLICAN

Governor 187,797 Bob Williams; 139,274 Norm Maleng; 7,370 Paul D. Santos.

Senator 335,846 Slade Gorton; 31,512 Doug Smith; 26,224 William C. Goodloe.

Congress No candidate in CD 2.

CD 1 69,516 John R. Miller; 3,005 Kerman Kermoade.
CD 3 21,509 Bill Wight; 12,532 Bill Hughes.
CD 4 72,633 Sid Morrison (only Republican candidate).
CD 5 25,300 Marlyn A. Derby (only Republican candidate).
CD 6 28,640 Kevin P. Cook (only Republican candidate).
CD 7 7,815 Robert Edwards; 7,675 Robert W. Blake.
CD 8 76,861 Rod Chandler (only Republican candidate).

SEPTEMBER 20 DEMOCRATIC

Governor 539,243 Booth Gardner; 31,917 Jeanne Dixon; 14,782 Richard Short; 9,302 Ted P. Fix.

Senator 297,399 Mike Lowry; 241,170 Don Bonker.

Congress

CD 1 62,941 Reese Lindquist (only Democratic candidate).
CD 2 85,901 Al Swift (only Democratic candidate).
CD 3 44,838 Jolene Unsoeld; 30,112 John McKibbin; 4,112 John M. Libby.
CD 4 26,638 J. Richard Golob (only Democratic candidate).
CD 5 81,223 Thomas S. Foley (only Democratic candidate).
CD 6 62,833 Norman D. Dicks (only Democratic candidate).
CD 7 47,026 Jim McDermott; 35,046 Norm Rice; 23,149 Ruthe Ridder; 824 Frank Deacy.
CD 8 16,418 Jim Kean; 12,625 Ray Kennedy; 3,972 Demilt Morse.

WASHINGTON

SEPTEMBER 20 MINOR PARTIES/INDEPENDENTS

Governor 5,818 Baba J. Mangaoang (only Independent candidate) did not qualify.

Senator 3,312 Daniel B. Fein (only Socialist Workers candidate) did not qualify.

Congress

CD 7 663 Jim McMahan (only Workers World candidate) did not qualify.

WEST VIRGINIA

GOVERNOR

Gaston Caperton (D). Elected 1988 to a four-year term.

SENATORS

Robert C. Byrd (D). Re-elected 1988 to a six-year term. Previously elected 1982, 1976, 1970, 1964, 1958.

John D. Rockefeller (D). Elected 1984 to a six-year term.

REPRESENTATIVES

1. Alan B. Mollohan (D)
2. Harley O. Staggers, Jr. (D)
3. Robert E. Wise (D)
4. Nick J. Rahall (D)

POSTWAR VOTE FOR PRESIDENT

Year	Total Vote	Republican Vote	Republican Candidate	Democratic Vote	Democratic Candidate	Other Vote	Plurality	Percentage Total Vote Rep.	Total Vote Dem.	Major Vote Rep.	Major Vote Dem.
1988	653,311	310,065	Bush, George	341,016	Dukakis, Michael S.	2,230	30,951 D	47.5%	52.2%	47.6%	52.4%
1984	735,742	405,483	Reagan, Ronald	328,125	Mondale, Walter F.	2,134	77,358 R	55.1%	44.6%	55.3%	44.7%
1980	737,715	334,206	Reagan, Ronald	367,462	Carter, Jimmy	36,047	33,256 D	45.3%	49.8%	47.6%	52.4%
1976	750,964	314,760	Ford, Gerald R.	435,914	Carter, Jimmy	290	121,154 D	41.9%	58.0%	41.9%	58.1%
1972	762,399	484,964	Nixon, Richard M.	277,435	McGovern, George S.		207,529 R	63.6%	36.4%	63.6%	36.4%
1968	754,206	307,555	Nixon, Richard M.	374,091	Humphrey, Hubert H.	72,560	66,536 D	40.8%	49.6%	45.1%	54.9%
1964	792,040	253,953	Goldwater, Barry M.	538,087	Johnson, Lyndon B.		284,134 D	32.1%	67.9%	32.1%	67.9%
1960	837,781	395,995	Nixon, Richard M.	441,786	Kennedy, John F.		45,791 D	47.3%	52.7%	47.3%	52.7%
1956	830,831	449,297	Eisenhower, Dwight D.	381,534	Stevenson, Adlai E.		67,763 R	54.1%	45.9%	54.1%	45.9%
1952	873,548	419,970	Eisenhower, Dwight D.	453,578	Stevenson, Adlai E.		33,608 D	48.1%	51.9%	48.1%	51.9%
1948	748,750	316,251	Dewey, Thomas E.	429,188	Truman, Harry S.	3,311	112,937 D	42.2%	57.3%	42.4%	57.6%

POSTWAR VOTE FOR GOVERNOR

Year	Total Vote	Republican Vote	Republican Candidate	Democratic Vote	Democratic Candidate	Other Vote	Rep.-Dem. Plurality	Percentage Total Vote Rep.	Total Vote Dem.	Major Vote Rep.	Major Vote Dem.
1988	649,593	267,172	Moore, Arch A.	382,421	Caperton, Gaston		115,249 D	41.1%	58.9%	41.1%	58.9%
1984	741,502	394,937	Moore, Arch A.	346,565	See, Clyde M.		48,372 R	53.3%	46.7%	53.3%	46.7%
1980	742,150	337,240	Moore, Arch A.	401,863	Rockefeller, John D.	3,047	64,623 D	45.4%	54.1%	45.6%	54.4%
1976	749,270	253,420	Underwood, Cecil H.	495,661	Rockefeller, John D.	189	242,241 D	33.8%	66.2%	33.8%	66.2%
1972	774,279	423,817	Moore, Arch A.	350,462	Rockefeller, John D.		73,355 R	54.7%	45.3%	54.7%	45.3%
1968	743,845	378,315	Moore, Arch A.	365,530	Sprouse, James M.		12,785 R	50.9%	49.1%	50.9%	49.1%
1964	788,582	355,559	Underwood, Cecil H.	433,023	Smith, Hulett C.		77,464 D	45.1%	54.9%	45.1%	54.9%
1960	827,420	380,665	Neely, Harold E.	446,755	Barron, W. W.		66,090 D	46.0%	54.0%	46.0%	54.0%
1956	817,623	440,502	Underwood, Cecil H.	377,121	Mollohan, Robert H.		63,381 R	53.9%	46.1%	53.9%	46.1%
1952	882,527	427,629	Holt, Rush D.	454,898	Marland, William C.		27,269 D	48.5%	51.5%	48.5%	51.5%
1948	768,061	329,309	Boreman, Herbert	438,752	Patteson, Okey L.		109,443 D	42.9%	57.1%	42.9%	57.1%

WEST VIRGINIA

POSTWAR VOTE FOR SENATOR

									Percentage			
	Total	Republican		Democratic		Other	Rep.-Dem.		Total Vote		Major Vote	
Year	Vote	Vote	Candidate	Vote	Candidate	Vote	Plurality		Rep.	Dem.	Rep.	Dem.
1988	634,547	223,564	Wolfe, M. Jay	410,983	Byrd, Robert C.		187,419	D	35.2%	64.8%	35.2%	64.8%
1984	722,212	344,680	Raese, John R.	374,233	Rockefeller, John D.	3,299	29,553	D	47.7%	51.8%	47.9%	52.1%
1982	565,314	173,910	Benedict, Cleveland K.	387,170	Byrd, Robert C.	4,234	213,260	D	30.8%	68.5%	31.0%	69.0%
1978	493,351	244,317	Moore, Arch A.	249,034	Randolph, Jennings		4,717	D	49.5%	50.5%	49.5%	50.5%
1976	566,790		—	566,423	Byrd, Robert C.	367	566,423	D		99.9%		100.0%
1972	731,841	245,531	Leonard, Louise	486,310	Randolph, Jennings		240,779	D	33.5%	66.5%	33.5%	66.5%
1970	445,623	99,658	Dodson, Elmer H.	345,965	Byrd, Robert C.		246,307	D	22.4%	77.6%	22.4%	77.6%
1966	491,216	198,891	Love, Francis J.	292,325	Randolph, Jennings		93,434	D	40.5%	59.5%	40.5%	59.5%
1964	761,087	246,072	Benedict, Cooper P.	515,015	Byrd, Robert C.		268,943	D	32.3%	67.7%	32.3%	67.7%
1960	828,292	369,935	Underwood, Cecil H.	458,355	Randolph, Jennings	2	88,420	D	44.7%	55.3%	44.7%	55.3%
1958	644,917	263,172	Revercomb, Chapman	381,745	Byrd, Robert C.		118,573	D	40.8%	59.2%	40.8%	59.2%
1958 S	630,677	256,510	Hoblitzell, John D.	374,167	Randolph, Jennings		117,657	D	40.7%	59.3%	40.7%	59.3%
1956 S	805,174	432,123	Revercomb, Chapman	373,051	Marland, William C.		59,072	R	53.7%	46.3%	53.7%	46.3%
1954	593,329	268,066	Sweeney, Tom	325,263	Neely, Matthew M.		57,197	D	45.2%	54.8%	45.2%	54.8%
1952	876,573	406,554	Revercomb, Chapman	470,019	Kilgore, Harley M.		63,465	D	46.4%	53.6%	46.4%	53.6%
1948	763,888	328,534	Revercomb, Chapman	435,354	Neely, Matthew M.		106,820	D	43.0%	57.0%	43.0%	57.0%
1946	542,768	269,617	Sweeney, Tom	273,151	Kilgore, Harley M.		3,534	D	49.7%	50.3%	49.7%	50.3%

One of the 1958 elections and the 1956 election were for short terms to fill vacancies.

WEST VIRGINIA

Districts Established February 8, 1982

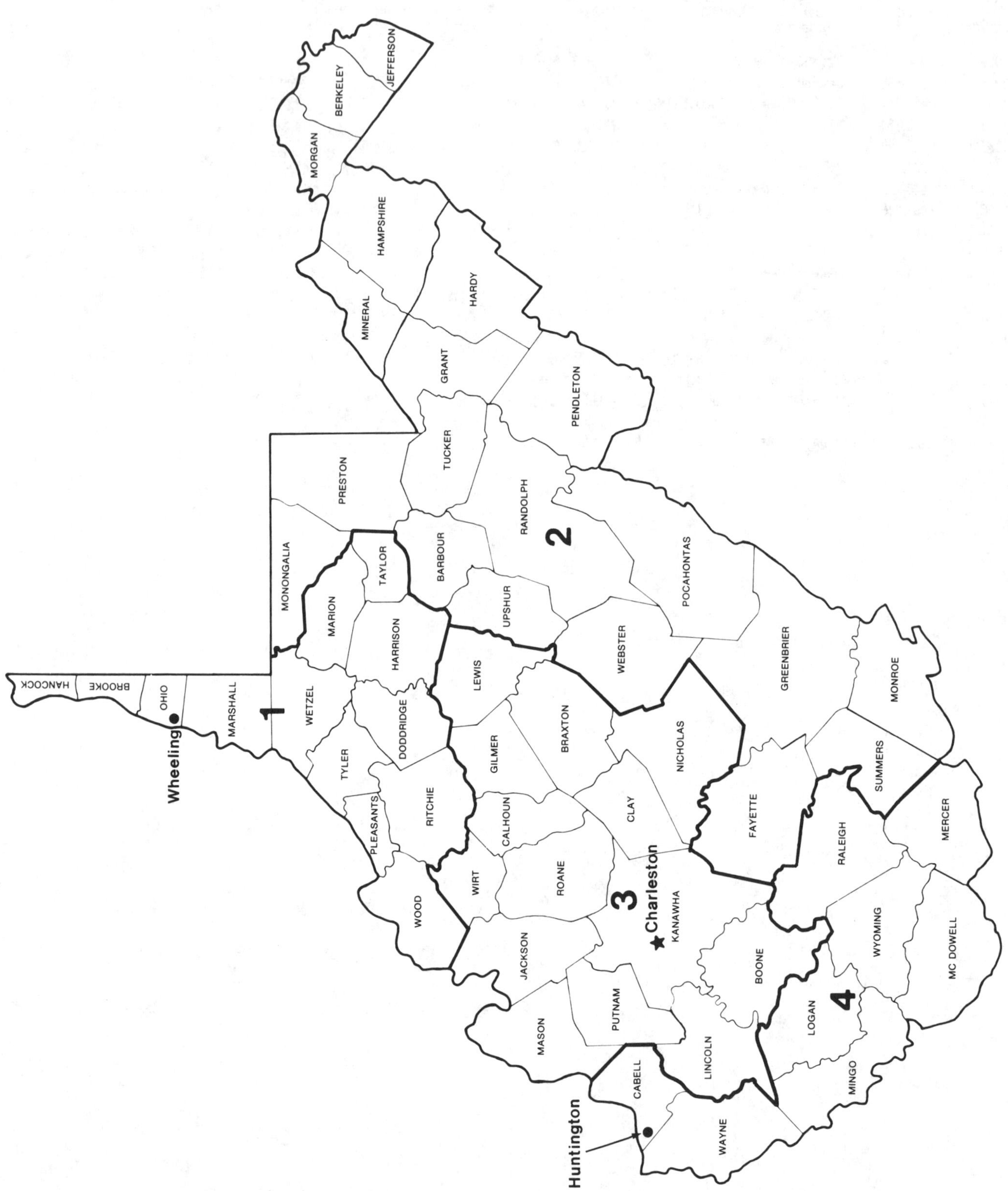

WEST VIRGINIA

Districts Established February 8, 1982

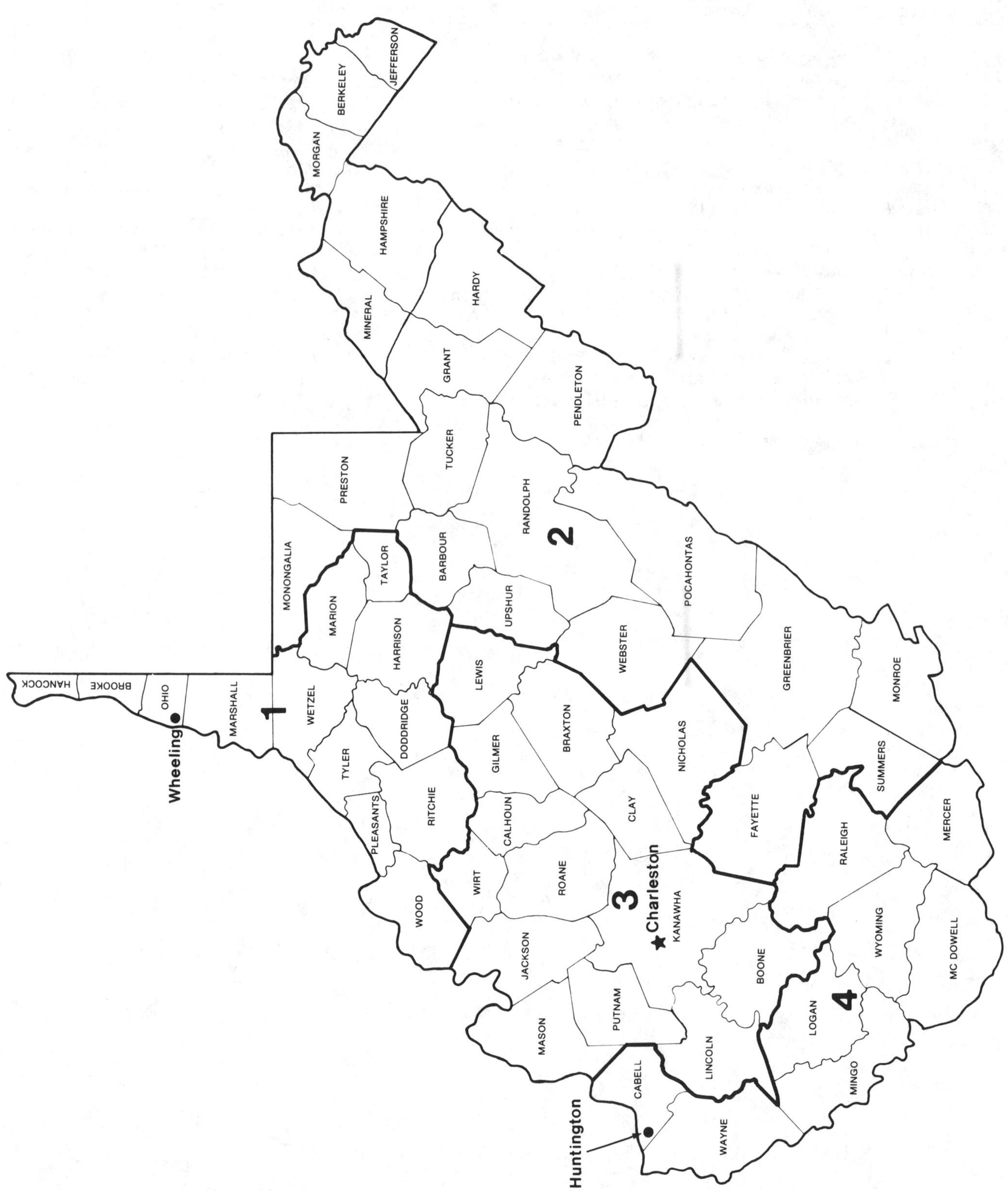

WEST VIRGINIA

PRESIDENT 1988

1980 Census Population	County	Total Vote	Republican	Democratic	Other	Rep.-Dem. Plurality	Percentage Total Vote Rep.	Percentage Total Vote Dem.	Percentage Major Vote Rep.	Percentage Major Vote Dem.
16,639	BARBOUR	6,261	3,023	3,221	17	198 D	48.3%	51.4%	48.4%	51.6%
46,775	BERKELEY	17,135	10,761	6,313	61	4,448 R	62.8%	36.8%	63.0%	37.0%
30,447	BOONE	9,345	2,786	6,539	20	3,753 D	29.8%	70.0%	29.9%	70.1%
13,894	BRAXTON	5,423	2,024	3,377	22	1,353 D	37.3%	62.3%	37.5%	62.5%
31,117	BROOKE	10,306	4,006	6,258	42	2,252 D	38.9%	60.7%	39.0%	61.0%
106,835	CABELL	32,662	17,197	15,368	97	1,829 R	52.7%	47.1%	52.8%	47.2%
8,250	CALHOUN	3,057	1,395	1,644	18	249 D	45.6%	53.8%	45.9%	54.1%
11,265	CLAY	3,811	1,536	2,263	12	727 D	40.3%	59.4%	40.4%	59.6%
7,433	DODDRIDGE	2,847	1,880	955	12	925 R	66.0%	33.5%	66.3%	33.7%
57,863	FAYETTE	16,205	5,143	11,009	53	5,866 D	31.7%	67.9%	31.8%	68.2%
8,334	GILMER	3,064	1,387	1,661	16	274 D	45.3%	54.2%	45.5%	54.5%
10,210	GRANT	4,130	3,215	893	22	2,322 R	77.8%	21.6%	78.3%	21.7%
37,665	GREENBRIER	11,521	5,395	6,091	35	696 D	46.8%	52.9%	47.0%	53.0%
14,867	HAMPSHIRE	5,363	3,253	2,085	25	1,168 R	60.7%	38.9%	60.9%	39.1%
40,418	HANCOCK	14,280	5,882	8,338	60	2,456 D	41.2%	58.4%	41.4%	58.6%
10,030	HARDY	4,288	2,581	1,689	18	892 R	60.2%	39.4%	60.4%	39.6%
77,710	HARRISON	30,418	13,364	17,005	49	3,641 D	43.9%	55.9%	44.0%	56.0%
25,794	JACKSON	10,291	5,696	4,573	22	1,123 R	55.3%	44.4%	55.5%	44.5%
30,302	JEFFERSON	9,726	5,349	4,334	43	1,015 R	55.0%	44.6%	55.2%	44.8%
231,414	KANAWHA	79,542	38,140	41,144	258	3,004 D	47.9%	51.7%	48.1%	51.9%
18,813	LEWIS	6,908	3,602	3,272	34	330 R	52.1%	47.4%	52.4%	47.6%
23,675	LINCOLN	8,529	3,457	5,049	23	1,592 D	40.5%	59.2%	40.6%	59.4%
50,679	LOGAN	15,608	4,244	11,317	47	7,073 D	27.2%	72.5%	27.3%	72.7%
49,899	MCDOWELL	9,714	2,463	7,204	47	4,741 D	25.4%	74.2%	25.5%	74.5%
65,789	MARION	23,742	9,229	14,441	72	5,212 D	38.9%	60.8%	39.0%	61.0%
41,608	MARSHALL	14,779	6,793	7,903	83	1,110 D	46.0%	53.5%	46.2%	53.8%
27,045	MASON	10,825	5,332	5,468	25	136 D	49.3%	50.5%	49.4%	50.6%
73,942	MERCER	20,430	10,221	10,152	57	69 R	50.0%	49.7%	50.2%	49.8%
27,234	MINERAL	10,111	6,015	4,059	37	1,956 R	59.5%	40.1%	59.7%	40.3%
37,336	MINGO	10,350	2,896	7,429	25	4,533 D	28.0%	71.8%	28.0%	72.0%
75,024	MONONGALIA	26,338	12,091	14,178	69	2,087 D	45.9%	53.8%	46.0%	54.0%
12,873	MONROE	5,168	2,719	2,427	22	292 R	52.6%	47.0%	52.8%	47.2%
10,711	MORGAN	4,564	3,002	1,545	17	1,457 R	65.8%	33.9%	66.0%	34.0%
28,126	NICHOLAS	8,936	3,731	5,173	32	1,442 D	41.8%	57.9%	41.9%	58.1%
61,389	OHIO	20,578	10,341	10,121	116	220 R	50.3%	49.2%	50.5%	49.5%
7,910	PENDLETON	3,503	1,901	1,595	7	306 R	54.3%	45.5%	54.4%	45.6%
8,236	PLEASANTS	3,187	1,761	1,421	5	340 R	55.3%	44.6%	55.3%	44.7%
9,919	POCAHONTAS	3,852	1,876	1,958	18	82 D	48.7%	50.8%	48.9%	51.1%
30,460	PRESTON	10,196	5,804	4,357	35	1,447 R	56.9%	42.7%	57.1%	42.9%
38,181	PUTNAM	14,841	8,163	6,640	38	1,523 R	55.0%	44.7%	55.1%	44.9%
86,821	RALEIGH	24,782	10,395	14,302	85	3,907 D	41.9%	57.7%	42.1%	57.9%
28,734	RANDOLPH	10,017	4,746	5,233	38	487 D	47.4%	52.2%	47.6%	52.4%
11,442	RITCHIE	4,338	2,874	1,446	18	1,428 R	66.3%	33.3%	66.5%	33.5%
15,952	ROANE	5,332	2,861	2,447	24	414 R	53.7%	45.9%	53.9%	46.1%
15,875	SUMMERS	5,314	2,231	3,072	11	841 D	42.0%	57.8%	42.1%	57.9%
16,584	TAYLOR	5,694	2,816	2,852	26	36 D	49.5%	50.1%	49.7%	50.3%
8,675	TUCKER	3,577	1,699	1,869	9	170 D	47.5%	52.3%	47.6%	52.4%
11,320	TYLER	3,874	2,365	1,501	8	864 R	61.0%	38.7%	61.2%	38.8%
23,427	UPSHUR	7,894	4,813	3,065	16	1,748 R	61.0%	38.8%	61.1%	38.9%
46,021	WAYNE	15,775	7,123	8,621	31	1,498 D	45.2%	54.6%	45.2%	54.8%
12,245	WEBSTER	3,217	1,016	2,185	16	1,169 D	31.6%	67.9%	31.7%	68.3%
21,874	WETZEL	7,350	3,381	3,928	41	547 D	46.0%	53.4%	46.3%	53.7%
4,922	WIRT	2,066	1,125	929	12	196 R	54.5%	45.0%	54.8%	45.2%
93,648	WOOD	32,563	19,450	12,959	154	6,491 R	59.7%	39.8%	60.0%	40.0%
35,993	WYOMING	9,684	3,516	6,138	30	2,622 D	36.3%	63.4%	36.4%	63.6%
1,949,644	TOTAL	653,311	310,065	341,016	2,230	30,951 D	47.5%	52.2%	47.6%	52.4%

WEST VIRGINIA

GOVERNOR 1988

1980 Census Population	County	Total Vote	Republican	Democratic	Other	Rep.-Dem. Plurality	Percentage: Total Vote Rep.	Percentage: Total Vote Dem.	Percentage: Major Vote Rep.	Percentage: Major Vote Dem.
16,639	BARBOUR	6,286	2,942	3,344		402 D	46.8%	53.2%	46.8%	53.2%
46,775	BERKELEY	17,082	8,220	8,862		642 D	48.1%	51.9%	48.1%	51.9%
30,447	BOONE	9,432	2,662	6,770		4,108 D	28.2%	71.8%	28.2%	71.8%
13,894	BRAXTON	5,468	1,849	3,619		1,770 D	33.8%	66.2%	33.8%	66.2%
31,117	BROOKE	10,381	3,577	6,804		3,227 D	34.5%	65.5%	34.5%	65.5%
106,835	CABELL	32,382	14,775	17,607		2,832 D	45.6%	54.4%	45.6%	54.4%
8,250	CALHOUN	3,066	1,293	1,773		480 D	42.2%	57.8%	42.2%	57.8%
11,265	CLAY	3,846	1,378	2,468		1,090 D	35.8%	64.2%	35.8%	64.2%
7,433	DODDRIDGE	2,812	1,765	1,047		718 R	62.8%	37.2%	62.8%	37.2%
57,863	FAYETTE	16,301	4,163	12,138		7,975 D	25.5%	74.5%	25.5%	74.5%
8,334	GILMER	3,054	1,313	1,741		428 D	43.0%	57.0%	43.0%	57.0%
10,210	GRANT	4,082	2,891	1,191		1,700 R	70.8%	29.2%	70.8%	29.2%
37,665	GREENBRIER	11,523	4,379	7,144		2,765 D	38.0%	62.0%	38.0%	62.0%
14,867	HAMPSHIRE	5,388	2,292	3,096		804 D	42.5%	57.5%	42.5%	57.5%
40,418	HANCOCK	13,772	4,109	9,663		5,554 D	29.8%	70.2%	29.8%	70.2%
10,030	HARDY	4,156	1,939	2,217		278 D	46.7%	53.3%	46.7%	53.3%
77,710	HARRISON	30,056	13,641	16,415		2,774 D	45.4%	54.6%	45.4%	54.6%
25,794	JACKSON	10,355	5,255	5,100		155 R	50.7%	49.3%	50.7%	49.3%
30,302	JEFFERSON	8,558	4,150	4,408		258 D	48.5%	51.5%	48.5%	51.5%
231,414	KANAWHA	78,626	29,925	48,701		18,776 D	38.1%	61.9%	38.1%	61.9%
18,813	LEWIS	6,890	3,153	3,737		584 D	45.8%	54.2%	45.8%	54.2%
23,675	LINCOLN	8,567	3,540	5,027		1,487 D	41.3%	58.7%	41.3%	58.7%
50,679	LOGAN	15,774	4,440	11,334		6,894 D	28.1%	71.9%	28.1%	71.9%
49,899	MCDOWELL	9,663	2,723	6,940		4,217 D	28.2%	71.8%	28.2%	71.8%
65,789	MARION	23,658	10,448	13,210		2,762 D	44.2%	55.8%	44.2%	55.8%
41,608	MARSHALL	14,887	7,981	6,906		1,075 R	53.6%	46.4%	53.6%	46.4%
27,045	MASON	10,871	4,610	6,261		1,651 D	42.4%	57.6%	42.4%	57.6%
73,942	MERCER	20,293	7,265	13,028		5,763 D	35.8%	64.2%	35.8%	64.2%
27,234	MINERAL	10,069	4,704	5,365		661 D	46.7%	53.3%	46.7%	53.3%
37,336	MINGO	10,406	2,319	8,087		5,768 D	22.3%	77.7%	22.3%	77.7%
75,024	MONONGALIA	26,011	8,237	17,774		9,537 D	31.7%	68.3%	31.7%	68.3%
12,873	MONROE	5,130	2,002	3,128		1,126 D	39.0%	61.0%	39.0%	61.0%
10,711	MORGAN	4,487	2,263	2,224		39 R	50.4%	49.6%	50.4%	49.6%
28,126	NICHOLAS	8,972	2,977	5,995		3,018 D	33.2%	66.8%	33.2%	66.8%
61,389	OHIO	20,563	10,323	10,240		83 R	50.2%	49.8%	50.2%	49.8%
7,910	PENDLETON	3,473	1,539	1,934		395 D	44.3%	55.7%	44.3%	55.7%
8,236	PLEASANTS	3,165	1,458	1,707		249 D	46.1%	53.9%	46.1%	53.9%
9,919	POCAHONTAS	3,833	1,589	2,244		655 D	41.5%	58.5%	41.5%	58.5%
30,460	PRESTON	10,085	4,509	5,576		1,067 D	44.7%	55.3%	44.7%	55.3%
38,181	PUTNAM	14,843	6,224	8,619		2,395 D	41.9%	58.1%	41.9%	58.1%
86,821	RALEIGH	24,855	8,018	16,837		8,819 D	32.3%	67.7%	32.3%	67.7%
28,734	RANDOLPH	10,142	5,075	5,067		8 R	50.0%	50.0%	50.0%	50.0%
11,442	RITCHIE	4,325	2,731	1,594		1,137 R	63.1%	36.9%	63.1%	36.9%
15,952	ROANE	5,379	2,699	2,680		19 R	50.2%	49.8%	50.2%	49.8%
15,875	SUMMERS	5,328	2,171	3,157		986 D	40.7%	59.3%	40.7%	59.3%
16,584	TAYLOR	5,694	2,669	3,025		356 D	46.9%	53.1%	46.9%	53.1%
8,675	TUCKER	3,619	1,815	1,804		11 R	50.2%	49.8%	50.2%	49.8%
11,320	TYLER	3,863	2,160	1,703		457 R	55.9%	44.1%	55.9%	44.1%
23,427	UPSHUR	7,916	4,342	3,574		768 R	54.9%	45.1%	54.9%	45.1%
46,021	WAYNE	15,449	6,271	9,178		2,907 D	40.6%	59.4%	40.6%	59.4%
12,245	WEBSTER	3,212	999	2,213		1,214 D	31.1%	68.9%	31.1%	68.9%
21,874	WETZEL	7,391	3,336	4,055		719 D	45.1%	54.9%	45.1%	54.9%
4,922	WIRT	2,100	974	1,126		152 D	46.4%	53.6%	46.4%	53.6%
93,648	WOOD	32,359	15,897	16,462		565 D	49.1%	50.9%	49.1%	50.9%
35,993	WYOMING	9,695	3,193	6,502		3,309 D	32.9%	67.1%	32.9%	67.1%
1,949,644	TOTAL	649,593	267,172	382,421		115,249 D	41.1%	58.9%	41.1%	58.9%

WEST VIRGINIA

SENATOR 1988

1980 Census Population	County	Total Vote	Republican	Democratic	Other	Rep.-Dem. Plurality	Percentage Total Vote Rep.	Total Vote Dem.	Major Vote Rep.	Major Vote Dem.
16,639	BARBOUR	6,249	2,299	3,950		1,651 D	36.8%	63.2%	36.8%	63.2%
46,775	BERKELEY	16,548	6,343	10,205		3,862 D	38.3%	61.7%	38.3%	61.7%
30,447	BOONE	9,178	2,378	6,800		4,422 D	25.9%	74.1%	25.9%	74.1%
13,894	BRAXTON	5,337	1,640	3,697		2,057 D	30.7%	69.3%	30.7%	69.3%
31,117	BROOKE	9,575	2,295	7,280		4,985 D	24.0%	76.0%	24.0%	76.0%
106,835	CABELL	31,527	12,846	18,681		5,835 D	40.7%	59.3%	40.7%	59.3%
8,250	CALHOUN	3,018	1,108	1,910		802 D	36.7%	63.3%	36.7%	63.3%
11,265	CLAY	3,815	1,285	2,530		1,245 D	33.7%	66.3%	33.7%	66.3%
7,433	DODDRIDGE	2,811	1,544	1,267		277 R	54.9%	45.1%	54.9%	45.1%
57,863	FAYETTE	16,069	4,277	11,792		7,515 D	26.6%	73.4%	26.6%	73.4%
8,334	GILMER	3,065	1,249	1,816		567 D	40.8%	59.2%	40.8%	59.2%
10,210	GRANT	3,846	1,745	2,101		356 D	45.4%	54.6%	45.4%	54.6%
37,665	GREENBRIER	11,365	4,238	7,127		2,889 D	37.3%	62.7%	37.3%	62.7%
14,867	HAMPSHIRE	5,197	1,816	3,381		1,565 D	34.9%	65.1%	34.9%	65.1%
40,418	HANCOCK	12,939	2,896	10,043		7,147 D	22.4%	77.6%	22.4%	77.6%
10,030	HARDY	4,159	1,145	3,014		1,869 D	27.5%	72.5%	27.5%	72.5%
77,710	HARRISON	29,083	9,981	19,102		9,121 D	34.3%	65.7%	34.3%	65.7%
25,794	JACKSON	10,080	4,807	5,273		466 D	47.7%	52.3%	47.7%	52.3%
30,302	JEFFERSON	9,379	3,420	5,959		2,539 D	36.5%	63.5%	36.5%	63.5%
231,414	KANAWHA	77,054	29,534	47,520		17,986 D	38.3%	61.7%	38.3%	61.7%
18,813	LEWIS	6,908	2,861	4,047		1,186 D	41.4%	58.6%	41.4%	58.6%
23,675	LINCOLN	8,389	2,754	5,635		2,881 D	32.8%	67.2%	32.8%	67.2%
50,679	LOGAN	15,032	3,274	11,758		8,484 D	21.8%	78.2%	21.8%	78.2%
49,899	MCDOWELL	9,241	2,104	7,137		5,033 D	22.8%	77.2%	22.8%	77.2%
65,789	MARION	23,356	7,586	15,770		8,184 D	32.5%	67.5%	32.5%	67.5%
41,608	MARSHALL	14,374	4,450	9,924		5,474 D	31.0%	69.0%	31.0%	69.0%
27,045	MASON	10,694	3,987	6,707		2,720 D	37.3%	62.7%	37.3%	62.7%
73,942	MERCER	19,935	8,745	11,190		2,445 D	43.9%	56.1%	43.9%	56.1%
27,234	MINERAL	9,933	3,189	6,744		3,555 D	32.1%	67.9%	32.1%	67.9%
37,336	MINGO	9,895	2,162	7,733		5,571 D	21.8%	78.2%	21.8%	78.2%
75,024	MONONGALIA	25,896	6,453	19,443		12,990 D	24.9%	75.1%	24.9%	75.1%
12,873	MONROE	4,936	2,015	2,921		906 D	40.8%	59.2%	40.8%	59.2%
10,711	MORGAN	4,305	1,851	2,454		603 D	43.0%	57.0%	43.0%	57.0%
28,126	NICHOLAS	8,642	2,901	5,741		2,840 D	33.6%	66.4%	33.6%	66.4%
61,389	OHIO	19,932	5,989	13,943		7,954 D	30.0%	70.0%	30.0%	70.0%
7,910	PENDLETON	3,433	1,047	2,386		1,339 D	30.5%	69.5%	30.5%	69.5%
8,236	PLEASANTS	3,139	1,105	2,034		929 D	35.2%	64.8%	35.2%	64.8%
9,919	POCAHONTAS	3,803	1,194	2,609		1,415 D	31.4%	68.6%	31.4%	68.6%
30,460	PRESTON	9,768	3,228	6,540		3,312 D	33.0%	67.0%	33.0%	67.0%
38,181	PUTNAM	14,552	6,728	7,824		1,096 D	46.2%	53.8%	46.2%	53.8%
86,821	RALEIGH	24,477	8,364	16,113		7,749 D	34.2%	65.8%	34.2%	65.8%
28,734	RANDOLPH	9,921	3,154	6,767		3,613 D	31.8%	68.2%	31.8%	68.2%
11,442	RITCHIE	4,272	2,211	2,061		150 R	51.8%	48.2%	51.8%	48.2%
15,952	ROANE	5,184	2,313	2,871		558 D	44.6%	55.4%	44.6%	55.4%
15,875	SUMMERS	5,266	1,935	3,331		1,396 D	36.7%	63.3%	36.7%	63.3%
16,584	TAYLOR	5,665	2,043	3,622		1,579 D	36.1%	63.9%	36.1%	63.9%
8,675	TUCKER	3,573	1,109	2,464		1,355 D	31.0%	69.0%	31.0%	69.0%
11,320	TYLER	3,807	1,604	2,203		599 D	42.1%	57.9%	42.1%	57.9%
23,427	UPSHUR	7,762	3,632	4,130		498 D	46.8%	53.2%	46.8%	53.2%
46,021	WAYNE	14,551	5,139	9,412		4,273 D	35.3%	64.7%	35.3%	64.7%
12,245	WEBSTER	3,194	861	2,333		1,472 D	27.0%	73.0%	27.0%	73.0%
21,874	WETZEL	7,169	2,283	4,886		2,603 D	31.8%	68.2%	31.8%	68.2%
4,922	WIRT	2,074	824	1,250		426 D	39.7%	60.3%	39.7%	60.3%
93,648	WOOD	31,691	14,600	17,091		2,491 D	46.1%	53.9%	46.1%	53.9%
35,993	WYOMING	9,484	3,023	6,461		3,438 D	31.9%	68.1%	31.9%	68.1%
1,949,644	TOTAL	634,547	223,564	410,983		187,419 D	35.2%	64.8%	35.2%	64.8%

WEST VIRGINIA

CONGRESS

CD	Year	Total Vote	Republican Vote	Republican Candidate	Democratic Vote	Democratic Candidate	Other Vote	Rep.-Dem. Plurality	Percentage Total Vote Rep.	Percentage Total Vote Dem.	Percentage Major Vote Rep.	Percentage Major Vote Dem.
1	1988	159,988	40,732	TUCK, HOWARD	119,256	MOLLOHAN, ALAN B.		78,524 D	25.5%	74.5%	25.5%	74.5%
1	1986	90,715			90,715	MOLLOHAN, ALAN B.		90,715 D		100.0%		100.0%
1	1984	192,261	87,622	ALTMEYER, JAMES	104,639	MOLLOHAN, ALAN B.		17,017 D	45.6%	54.4%	45.6%	54.4%
1	1982	149,598	70,069	MCCUSKEY, JOHN F.	79,529	MOLLOHAN, ALAN B.		9,460 D	46.8%	53.2%	46.8%	53.2%
2	1988	118,356			118,356	STAGGERS, HARLEY O., JR.		118,356 D		100.0%		100.0%
2	1986	109,909	33,554	GOLDEN, MICHELE	76,355	STAGGERS, HARLEY O., JR.		42,801 D	30.5%	69.5%	30.5%	69.5%
2	1984	179,281	78,936	BENEDICT, CLEVELAND K.	100,345	STAGGERS, HARLEY O., JR.		21,409 D	44.0%	56.0%	44.0%	56.0%
2	1982	137,317	49,413	HINKLE, J. D.	87,904	STAGGERS, HARLEY O., JR.		38,491 D	36.0%	64.0%	36.0%	64.0%
3	1988	161,670	41,478	HART, PAUL W.	120,192	WISE, ROBERT E.		78,714 D	25.7%	74.3%	25.7%	74.3%
3	1986	113,489	39,820	SHARP, TIM	73,669	WISE, ROBERT E.		33,849 D	35.1%	64.9%	35.1%	64.9%
3	1984	184,434	59,128	MILLER, MARGARET P.	125,306	WISE, ROBERT E.		66,178 D	32.1%	67.9%	32.1%	67.9%
3	1982	146,250	60,844	STATON, DAVID M.	84,619	WISE, ROBERT E.	787	23,775 D	41.6%	57.9%	41.8%	58.2%
4	1988	128,565	49,753	BREWSTER, MARIANNE R.	78,812	RAHALL, NICK J.		29,059 D	38.7%	61.3%	38.7%	61.3%
4	1986	81,707	23,490	MILLER, MARTIN	58,217	RAHALL, NICK J.		34,727 D	28.7%	71.3%	28.7%	71.3%
4	1984	148,393	49,474	SHUMATE, JESS T.	98,919	RAHALL, NICK J.		49,445 D	33.3%	66.7%	33.3%	66.7%
4	1982	113,238	22,054	HARRIS, HOMER L.	91,184	RAHALL, NICK J.		69,130 D	19.5%	80.5%	19.5%	80.5%
4	1980	153,615	36,020	COVEY, WINTON G.	117,595	RAHALL, NICK J.		81,575 D	23.4%	76.6%	23.4%	76.6%
4	1978	70,035			70,035	RAHALL, NICK J.		70,035 D		100.0%		100.0%
4	1976	161,520	28,825	GOODMAN, E. S.	73,626	RAHALL, NICK J.	59,069	44,801 D	17.8%	45.6%	28.1%	71.9%
4	1974	66,420			66,420	HECHLER, KEN		66,420 D		100.0%		100.0%
4	1972	164,842	64,242	NEAL, JOE	100,600	HECHLER, KEN		36,358 D	39.0%	61.0%	39.0%	61.0%

WEST VIRGINIA

1988 GENERAL ELECTION

President Other vote was New Alliance (Fulani).

Governor

Senator

Congress

1988 PRIMARIES

MAY 10 REPUBLICAN

Governor 78,495 Arch A. Moore; 68,973 John R. Raese.

Senator 81,286 M. Jay Wolfe; 34,273 Bernie Lumbert.

Congress Unopposed in two CD's. No candidate in CD 1 and 2. In CD 1, Howard Tuck was nominated by the local party committee after the primary.

MAY 10 DEMOCRATIC

Governor 132,435 Gaston Caperton; 94,364 Clyde M. See; 51,722 Mario J. Palumbo; 48,748 Gus R. Douglass; 14,916 Dan Tonkovich; 5,217 Larry Harless; 1,484 Paul Nuchims.

Senator 252,767 Robert C. Byrd; 60,186 Bobbie E. Myers.

Congress Unopposed in three CD's. Contested as follows:

CD 4 56,996 Nick J. Rahall; 12,920 William Sanders; 8,503 Ted T. Stacy.

WISCONSIN

GOVERNOR

Tommy G. Thompson (R). Elected 1986 to a four-year term.

SENATORS

Robert W. Kasten (R). Re-elected 1986 to a six-year term. Previously elected 1980.

Herbert H. Kohl (D). Elected 1988 to a six-year term.

REPRESENTATIVES

1. Les Aspin (D)
2. Robert Kastenmeier (D)
3. Steven Gunderson (R)
4. Gerald D. Kleczka (D)
5. Jim Moody (D)
6. Thomas E. Petri (R)
7. David R. Obey (D)
8. Toby Roth (R)
9. F. James Sensenbrenner (R)

POSTWAR VOTE FOR PRESIDENT

		Republican		Democratic				Percentage			
								Total Vote		Major Vote	
Year	Total Vote	Vote	Candidate	Vote	Candidate	Other Vote	Plurality	Rep.	Dem.	Rep.	Dem.
1988	2,191,608	1,047,499	Bush, George	1,126,794	Dukakis, Michael S.	17,315	79,295 D	47.8%	51.4%	48.2%	51.8%
1984	2,211,689	1,198,584	Reagan, Ronald	995,740	Mondale, Walter F.	17,365	202,844 R	54.2%	45.0%	54.6%	45.4%
1980	2,273,221	1,088,845	Reagan, Ronald	981,584	Carter, Jimmy	202,792	107,261 R	47.9%	43.2%	52.6%	47.4%
1976	2,104,175	1,004,987	Ford, Gerald R.	1,040,232	Carter, Jimmy	58,956	35,245 D	47.8%	49.4%	49.1%	50.9%
1972	1,852,890	989,430	Nixon, Richard M.	810,174	McGovern, George S.	53,286	179,256 R	53.4%	43.7%	55.0%	45.0%
1968	1,691,538	809,997	Nixon, Richard M.	748,804	Humphrey, Hubert H.	132,737	61,193 R	47.9%	44.3%	52.0%	48.0%
1964	1,691,815	638,495	Goldwater, Barry M.	1,050,424	Johnson, Lyndon B.	2,896	411,929 D	37.7%	62.1%	37.8%	62.2%
1960	1,729,082	895,175	Nixon, Richard M.	830,805	Kennedy, John F.	3,102	64,370 R	51.8%	48.0%	51.9%	48.1%
1956	1,550,558	954,844	Eisenhower, Dwight D.	586,768	Stevenson, Adlai E.	8,946	368,076 R	61.6%	37.8%	61.9%	38.1%
1952	1,607,370	979,744	Eisenhower, Dwight D.	622,175	Stevenson, Adlai E.	5,451	357,569 R	61.0%	38.7%	61.2%	38.8%
1948	1,276,800	590,959	Dewey, Thomas E.	647,310	Truman, Harry S.	38,531	56,351 D	46.3%	50.7%	47.7%	52.3%

WISCONSIN

POSTWAR VOTE FOR GOVERNOR

Year	Total Vote	Republican Vote	Republican Candidate	Democratic Vote	Democratic Candidate	Other Vote	Rep.-Dem. Plurality	Percentage Total Vote Rep.	Percentage Total Vote Dem.	Percentage Major Vote Rep.	Percentage Major Vote Dem.
1986	1,526,960	805,090	Thompson, Tommy G.	705,578	Earl, Anthony S.	16,292	99,512 R	52.7%	46.2%	53.3%	46.7%
1982	1,580,344	662,838	Kohler, Terry J.	896,812	Earl, Anthony S.	20,694	233,974 D	41.9%	56.7%	42.5%	57.5%
1978	1,500,996	816,056	Dreyfus, Lee S.	673,813	Schreiber, Martin J.	11,127	142,243 R	54.4%	44.9%	54.8%	45.2%
1974	1,181,976	497,195	Dyke, William D.	628,639	Lucey, Patrick J.	56,142	131,444 D	42.1%	53.2%	44.2%	55.8%
1970 **	1,343,160	602,617	Olson, Jack B.	728,403	Lucey, Patrick J.	12,140	125,786 D	44.9%	54.2%	45.3%	54.7%
1968	1,689,738	893,463	Knowles, Warren P.	791,100	LaFollette, Bronson C.	5,175	102,363 R	52.9%	46.8%	53.0%	47.0%
1966	1,170,173	626,041	Knowles, Warren P.	539,258	Lucey, Patrick J.	4,874	86,783 R	53.5%	46.1%	53.7%	46.3%
1964	1,694,887	856,779	Knowles, Warren P.	837,901	Reynolds, John W.	207	18,878 R	50.6%	49.4%	50.6%	49.4%
1962	1,265,900	625,536	Kuehn, Philip G.	637,491	Reynolds, John W.	2,873	11,955 D	49.4%	50.4%	49.5%	50.5%
1960	1,728,009	837,123	Kuehn, Philip G.	890,868	Nelson, Gaylord A.	18	53,745 D	48.4%	51.6%	48.4%	51.6%
1958	1,202,219	556,391	Thomson, Vernon W.	644,296	Nelson, Gaylord A.	1,532	87,905 D	46.3%	53.6%	46.3%	53.7%
1956	1,557,788	808,273	Thomson, Vernon W.	749,421	Proxmire, William	94	58,852 R	51.9%	48.1%	51.9%	48.1%
1954	1,158,666	596,158	Kohler, Walter J.	560,747	Proxmire, William	1,761	35,411 R	51.5%	48.4%	51.5%	48.5%
1952	1,615,214	1,009,171	Kohler, Walter J.	601,844	Proxmire, William	4,199	407,327 R	62.5%	37.3%	62.6%	37.4%
1950	1,138,148	605,649	Kohler, Walter J.	525,319	Thompson, Carl W.	7,180	80,330 R	53.2%	46.2%	53.6%	46.4%
1948	1,266,139	684,839	Rennebohm, Oscar	558,497	Thompson, Carl W.	22,803	126,342 R	54.1%	44.1%	55.1%	44.9%
1946	1,040,444	621,970	Goodland, Walter	406,499	Hoan, Daniel W.	11,975	215,471 R	59.8%	39.1%	60.5%	39.5%

The term of office of Wisconsin's Governor was increased from two to four years effective with the 1970 election.

POSTWAR VOTE FOR SENATOR

Year	Total Vote	Republican Vote	Republican Candidate	Democratic Vote	Democratic Candidate	Other Vote	Rep.-Dem. Plurality	Percentage Total Vote Rep.	Percentage Total Vote Dem.	Percentage Major Vote Rep.	Percentage Major Vote Dem.
1988	2,168,190	1,030,440	Engeleiter, Susan	1,128,625	Kohl, Herbert H.	9,125	98,185 D	47.5%	52.1%	47.7%	52.3%
1986	1,483,174	754,573	Kasten, Robert W.	702,963	Garvey, Edward R.	25,638	51,610 R	50.9%	47.4%	51.8%	48.2%
1982	1,544,981	527,355	McCallum, Scott	983,311	Proxmire, William	34,315	455,956 D	34.1%	63.6%	34.9%	65.1%
1980	2,204,202	1,106,311	Kasten, Robert W.	1,065,487	Nelson, Gaylord A.	32,404	40,824 R	50.2%	48.3%	50.9%	49.1%
1976	1,935,183	521,902	York, Stanley	1,396,970	Proxmire, William	16,311	875,068 D	27.0%	72.2%	27.2%	72.8%
1974	1,199,495	429,327	Petri, Thomas E.	740,700	Nelson, Gaylord A.	29,468	311,373 D	35.8%	61.8%	36.7%	63.3%
1970	1,338,967	381,297	Erickson, John E.	948,445	Proxmire, William	9,225	567,148 D	28.5%	70.8%	28.7%	71.3%
1968	1,654,861	633,910	Leonard, Jerris	1,020,931	Nelson, Gaylord A.	20	387,021 D	38.3%	61.7%	38.3%	61.7%
1964	1,673,776	780,116	Renk, Wilbur N.	892,013	Proxmire, William	1,647	111,897 D	46.6%	53.3%	46.7%	53.3%
1962	1,260,168	594,846	Wiley, Alexander	662,342	Nelson, Gaylord A.	2,980	67,496 D	47.2%	52.6%	47.3%	52.7%
1958	1,194,678	510,398	Steinle, Roland J.	682,440	Proxmire, William	1,840	172,042 D	42.7%	57.1%	42.8%	57.2%
1957 S	772,620	312,931	Kohler, Walter J.	435,985	Proxmire, William	23,704	123,054 D	40.5%	56.4%	41.8%	58.2%
1956	1,523,356	892,473	Wiley, Alexander	627,903	Maier, Henry W.	2,980	264,570 R	58.6%	41.2%	58.7%	41.3%
1952	1,605,228	870,444	McCarthy, Joseph R.	731,402	Fairchild, Thomas E.	3,382	139,042 R	54.2%	45.6%	54.3%	45.7%
1950	1,116,135	595,283	Wiley, Alexander	515,539	Fairchild, Thomas E.	5,313	79,744 R	53.3%	46.2%	53.6%	46.4%
1946	1,014,594	620,430	McCarthy, Joseph R.	378,772	McMurray, Howard J.	15,392	241,658 R	61.2%	37.3%	62.1%	37.9%

The 1957 election was held in August for a short term to fill a vacancy.

WISCONSIN

Districts Established March 31, 1982

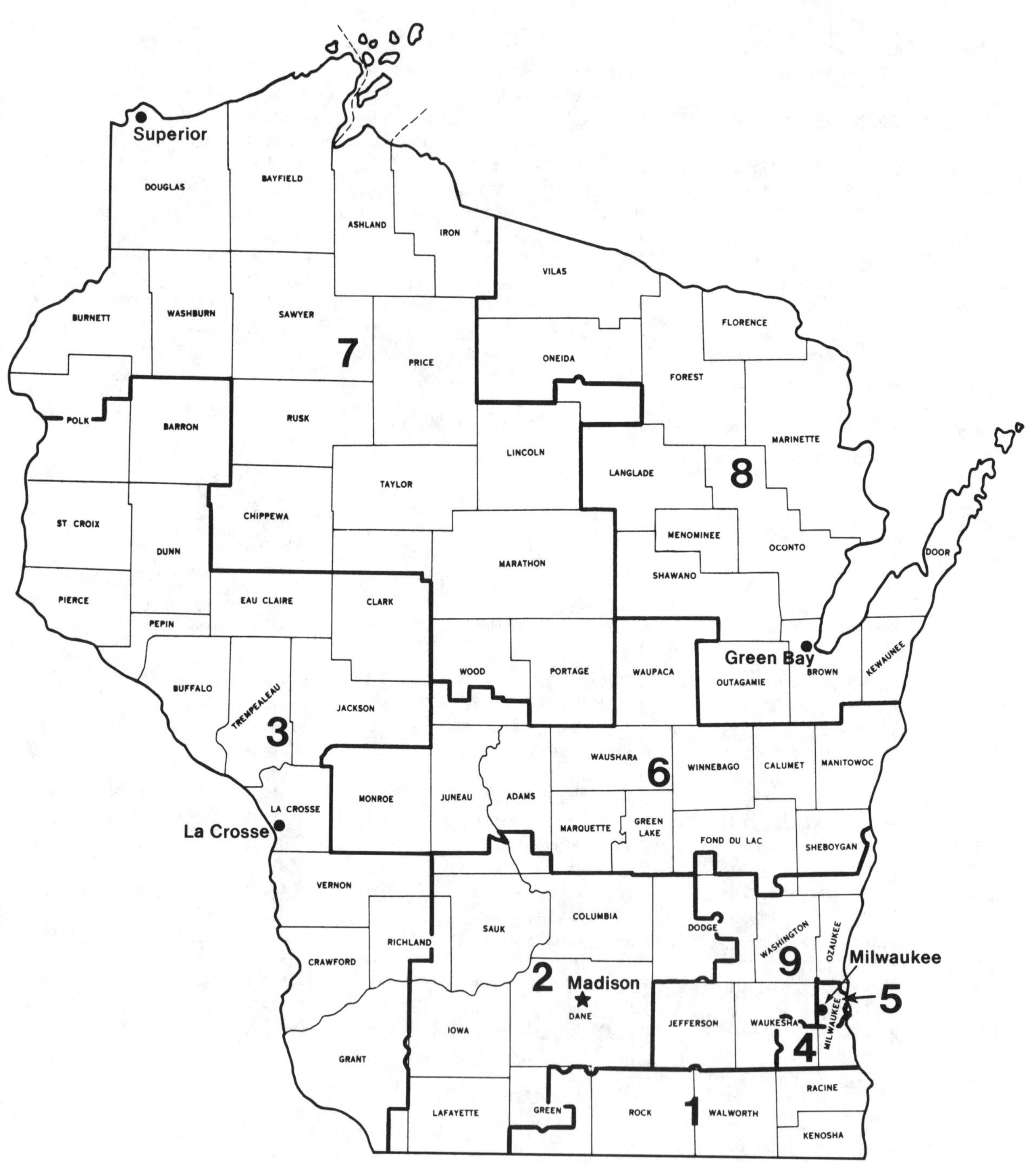

WISCONSIN

PRESIDENT 1988

1980 Census Population	County	Total Vote	Republican	Democratic	Other	Rep.-Dem. Plurality	Percentage Total Vote Rep.	Percentage Total Vote Dem.	Percentage Major Vote Rep.	Percentage Major Vote Dem.
13,457	ADAMS	6,883	3,258	3,598	27	340 D	47.3%	52.3%	47.5%	52.5%
16,783	ASHLAND	7,489	2,926	4,526	37	1,600 D	39.1%	60.4%	39.3%	60.7%
38,730	BARRON	17,579	8,527	8,951	101	424 D	48.5%	50.9%	48.8%	51.2%
13,822	BAYFIELD	7,471	3,095	4,323	53	1,228 D	41.4%	57.9%	41.7%	58.3%
175,280	BROWN	85,953	43,625	41,788	540	1,837 R	50.8%	48.6%	51.1%	48.9%
14,309	BUFFALO	6,322	2,783	3,481	58	698 D	44.0%	55.1%	44.4%	55.6%
12,340	BURNETT	6,483	2,884	3,537	62	653 D	44.5%	54.6%	44.9%	55.1%
30,867	CALUMET	14,712	8,107	6,481	124	1,626 R	55.1%	44.1%	55.6%	44.4%
52,127	CHIPPEWA	21,367	9,757	11,447	163	1,690 D	45.7%	53.6%	46.0%	54.0%
32,910	CLARK	13,058	6,296	6,642	120	346 D	48.2%	50.9%	48.7%	51.3%
43,222	COLUMBIA	19,766	10,475	9,132	159	1,343 R	53.0%	46.2%	53.4%	46.6%
16,556	CRAWFORD	6,912	3,238	3,608	66	370 D	46.8%	52.2%	47.3%	52.7%
323,545	DANE	176,158	69,143	105,414	1,601	36,271 D	39.3%	59.8%	39.6%	60.4%
75,064	DODGE	29,950	17,003	12,663	284	4,340 R	56.8%	42.3%	57.3%	42.7%
25,029	DOOR	12,430	6,907	5,425	98	1,482 R	55.6%	43.6%	56.0%	44.0%
44,421	DOUGLAS	20,468	6,440	13,907	121	7,467 D	31.5%	67.9%	31.7%	68.3%
34,314	DUNN	16,625	7,273	9,205	147	1,932 D	43.7%	55.4%	44.1%	55.9%
78,805	EAU CLAIRE	39,023	17,664	21,150	209	3,486 D	45.3%	54.2%	45.5%	54.5%
4,172	FLORENCE	2,147	1,106	1,018	23	88 R	51.5%	47.4%	52.1%	47.9%
88,964	FOND DU LAC	38,193	21,985	15,887	321	6,098 R	57.6%	41.6%	58.1%	41.9%
9,044	FOREST	4,013	1,845	2,142	26	297 D	46.0%	53.4%	46.3%	53.7%
51,736	GRANT	19,620	10,049	9,421	150	628 R	51.2%	48.0%	51.6%	48.4%
30,012	GREEN	11,908	6,636	5,153	119	1,483 R	55.7%	43.3%	56.3%	43.7%
18,370	GREEN LAKE	8,299	5,205	3,033	61	2,172 R	62.7%	36.5%	63.2%	36.8%
19,802	IOWA	8,575	4,240	4,268	67	28 D	49.4%	49.8%	49.8%	50.2%
6,730	IRON	3,717	1,599	2,090	28	491 D	43.0%	56.2%	43.3%	56.7%
16,831	JACKSON	7,523	3,555	3,924	44	369 D	47.3%	52.2%	47.5%	52.5%
66,152	JEFFERSON	26,361	14,309	11,816	236	2,493 R	54.3%	44.8%	54.8%	45.2%
21,039	JUNEAU	8,667	4,869	3,734	64	1,135 R	56.2%	43.1%	56.6%	43.4%
123,137	KENOSHA	52,149	21,661	30,089	399	8,428 D	41.5%	57.7%	41.9%	58.1%
19,539	KEWAUNEE	9,191	4,330	4,786	75	456 D	47.1%	52.1%	47.5%	52.5%
91,056	LA CROSSE	44,111	21,548	22,204	359	656 D	48.8%	50.3%	49.3%	50.7%
17,412	LAFAYETTE	7,235	3,665	3,521	49	144 R	50.7%	48.7%	51.0%	49.0%
19,978	LANGLADE	9,201	4,884	4,254	63	630 R	53.1%	46.2%	53.4%	46.6%
26,555	LINCOLN	11,185	5,257	5,819	109	562 D	47.0%	52.0%	47.5%	52.5%
82,918	MANITOWOC	36,025	16,020	19,680	325	3,660 D	44.5%	54.6%	44.9%	55.1%
111,270	MARATHON	49,543	24,482	24,658	403	176 D	49.4%	49.8%	49.8%	50.2%
39,314	MARINETTE	17,791	9,637	8,030	124	1,607 R	54.2%	45.1%	54.5%	45.5%
11,672	MARQUETTE	5,573	3,059	2,463	51	596 R	54.9%	44.2%	55.4%	44.6%
3,373	MENOMINEE	1,422	381	1,028	13	647 D	26.8%	72.3%	27.0%	73.0%
964,988	MILWAUKEE	440,296	168,363	268,287	3,646	99,924 D	38.2%	60.9%	38.6%	61.4%
35,074	MONROE	13,591	7,073	6,437	81	636 R	52.0%	47.4%	52.4%	47.6%
28,947	OCONTO	13,733	7,084	6,549	100	535 R	51.6%	47.7%	52.0%	48.0%
31,216	ONEIDA	15,670	8,130	7,414	126	716 R	51.9%	47.3%	52.3%	47.7%
128,799	OUTAGAMIE	61,304	33,113	27,771	420	5,342 R	54.0%	45.3%	54.4%	45.6%
66,981	OZAUKEE	35,852	22,899	12,661	292	10,238 R	63.9%	35.3%	64.4%	35.6%
7,477	PEPIN	3,255	1,311	1,906	38	595 D	40.3%	58.6%	40.8%	59.2%
31,149	PIERCE	14,831	6,045	8,659	127	2,614 D	40.8%	58.4%	41.1%	58.9%
32,351	POLK	16,022	6,866	8,981	175	2,115 D	42.9%	56.1%	43.3%	56.7%
57,420	PORTAGE	28,542	12,057	16,317	168	4,260 D	42.2%	57.2%	42.5%	57.5%
15,788	PRICE	7,516	3,450	3,987	79	537 D	45.9%	53.0%	46.4%	53.6%
173,132	RACINE	76,631	36,342	39,631	658	3,289 D	47.4%	51.7%	47.8%	52.2%
17,476	RICHLAND	7,718	4,026	3,643	49	383 R	52.2%	47.2%	52.5%	47.5%
139,420	ROCK	58,227	28,178	29,576	473	1,398 D	48.4%	50.8%	48.8%	51.2%
15,589	RUSK	7,017	3,063	3,888	66	825 D	43.7%	55.4%	44.1%	55.9%
43,262	ST. CROIX	21,549	9,960	11,392	197	1,432 D	46.2%	52.9%	46.6%	53.4%
43,469	SAUK	18,699	10,225	8,324	150	1,901 R	54.7%	44.5%	55.1%	44.9%
12,843	SAWYER	6,545	3,260	3,231	54	29 R	49.8%	49.4%	50.2%	49.8%
35,928	SHAWANO	15,162	8,362	6,587	213	1,775 R	55.2%	43.4%	55.9%	44.1%
100,935	SHEBOYGAN	47,234	23,471	23,429	334	42 R	49.7%	49.6%	50.0%	50.0%

WISCONSIN

PRESIDENT 1988

1980 Census Population	County	Total Vote	Republican	Democratic	Other	Rep.-Dem. Plurality	Percentage Total Vote Rep.	Total Vote Dem.	Major Vote Rep.	Major Vote Dem.
18,817	TAYLOR	8,113	4,254	3,785	74	469 R	52.4%	46.7%	52.9%	47.1%
26,158	TREMPEALEAU	11,183	4,902	6,212	69	1,310 D	43.8%	55.5%	44.1%	55.9%
25,642	VERNON	11,102	5,226	5,754	122	528 D	47.1%	51.8%	47.6%	52.4%
16,535	VILAS	9,730	5,842	3,781	107	2,061 R	60.0%	38.9%	60.7%	39.3%
71,507	WALWORTH	30,711	18,259	12,203	249	6,056 R	59.5%	39.7%	59.9%	40.1%
13,174	WASHBURN	6,521	3,074	3,393	54	319 D	47.1%	52.0%	47.5%	52.5%
84,848	WASHINGTON	40,575	24,328	15,907	340	8,421 R	60.0%	39.2%	60.5%	39.5%
280,326	WAUKESHA	148,935	90,467	57,598	870	32,869 R	60.7%	38.7%	61.1%	38.9%
42,831	WAUPACA	18,784	11,559	7,078	147	4,481 R	61.5%	37.7%	62.0%	38.0%
18,526	WAUSHARA	8,567	4,953	3,535	79	1,418 R	57.8%	41.3%	58.4%	41.6%
131,703	WINNEBAGO	64,039	35,085	28,508	446	6,577 R	54.8%	44.5%	55.2%	44.8%
72,799	WOOD	32,856	16,549	16,074	233	475 R	50.4%	48.9%	50.7%	49.3%
4,705,767	TOTAL	2,191,608	1,047,499	1,126,794	17,315	79,295 D	47.8%	51.4%	48.2%	51.8%

WISCONSIN

SENATOR 1988

1980 Census Population	County	Total Vote	Republican	Democratic	Other	Rep.-Dem. Plurality	Percentage Total Vote Rep.	Percentage Total Vote Dem.	Percentage Major Vote Rep.	Percentage Major Vote Dem.
13,457	ADAMS	6,705	3,116	3,571	18	455 D	46.5%	53.3%	46.6%	53.4%
16,783	ASHLAND	7,465	2,778	4,679	8	1,901 D	37.2%	62.7%	37.3%	62.7%
38,730	BARRON	17,085	8,966	8,103	16	863 R	52.5%	47.4%	52.5%	47.5%
13,822	BAYFIELD	7,309	2,822	4,464	23	1,642 D	38.6%	61.1%	38.7%	61.3%
175,280	BROWN	86,833	47,194	39,344	295	7,850 R	54.4%	45.3%	54.5%	45.5%
14,309	BUFFALO	6,149	3,105	3,040	4	65 R	50.5%	49.4%	50.5%	49.5%
12,340	BURNETT	6,296	2,470	3,808	18	1,338 D	39.2%	60.5%	39.3%	60.7%
30,867	CALUMET	14,486	8,261	6,177	48	2,084 R	57.0%	42.6%	57.2%	42.8%
52,127	CHIPPEWA	21,515	10,060	11,389	66	1,329 D	46.8%	52.9%	46.9%	53.1%
32,910	CLARK	12,995	6,696	6,275	24	421 R	51.5%	48.3%	51.6%	48.4%
43,222	COLUMBIA	19,273	9,514	9,732	27	218 D	49.4%	50.5%	49.4%	50.6%
16,556	CRAWFORD	6,478	3,212	3,246	20	34 D	49.6%	50.1%	49.7%	50.3%
323,545	DANE	173,175	71,351	100,517	1,307	29,166 D	41.2%	58.0%	41.5%	58.5%
75,064	DODGE	30,162	15,824	14,234	104	1,590 R	52.5%	47.2%	52.6%	47.4%
25,029	DOOR	12,598	7,490	5,076	32	2,414 R	59.5%	40.3%	59.6%	40.4%
44,421	DOUGLAS	19,541	5,098	14,235	208	9,137 D	26.1%	72.8%	26.4%	73.6%
34,314	DUNN	15,920	7,724	8,098	98	374 D	48.5%	50.9%	48.8%	51.2%
78,805	EAU CLAIRE	39,192	18,332	20,710	150	2,378 D	46.8%	52.8%	47.0%	53.0%
4,172	FLORENCE	2,076	1,028	1,045	3	17 D	49.5%	50.3%	49.6%	50.4%
88,964	FOND DU LAC	38,516	21,223	17,145	148	4,078 R	55.1%	44.5%	55.3%	44.7%
9,044	FOREST	3,880	1,505	2,369	6	864 D	38.8%	61.1%	38.8%	61.2%
51,736	GRANT	18,886	10,672	8,168	46	2,504 R	56.5%	43.2%	56.6%	43.4%
30,012	GREEN	12,176	6,713	5,426	37	1,287 R	55.1%	44.6%	55.3%	44.7%
18,370	GREEN LAKE	8,273	5,156	3,107	10	2,049 R	62.3%	37.6%	62.4%	37.6%
19,802	IOWA	8,137	3,845	4,288	4	443 D	47.3%	52.7%	47.3%	52.7%
6,730	IRON	3,520	1,500	2,019	1	519 D	42.6%	57.4%	42.6%	57.4%
16,831	JACKSON	7,429	3,663	3,757	9	94 D	49.3%	50.6%	49.4%	50.6%
66,152	JEFFERSON	26,575	13,852	12,632	91	1,220 R	52.1%	47.5%	52.3%	47.7%
21,039	JUNEAU	8,728	4,784	3,920	24	864 R	54.8%	44.9%	55.0%	45.0%
123,137	KENOSHA	46,886	18,995	27,635	256	8,640 D	40.5%	58.9%	40.7%	59.3%
19,539	KEWAUNEE	9,088	4,853	4,227	8	626 R	53.4%	46.5%	53.4%	46.6%
91,056	LA CROSSE	44,263	23,264	20,811	188	2,453 R	52.6%	47.0%	52.8%	47.2%
17,412	LAFAYETTE	7,031	3,537	3,485	9	52 R	50.3%	49.6%	50.4%	49.6%
19,978	LANGLADE	9,070	4,548	4,501	21	47 R	50.1%	49.6%	50.3%	49.7%
26,555	LINCOLN	11,356	5,671	5,641	44	30 R	49.9%	49.7%	50.1%	49.9%
82,918	MANITOWOC	35,042	16,340	18,545	157	2,205 D	46.6%	52.9%	46.8%	53.2%
111,270	MARATHON	49,439	26,020	23,181	238	2,839 R	52.6%	46.9%	52.9%	47.1%
39,314	MARINETTE	17,545	9,721	7,783	41	1,938 R	55.4%	44.4%	55.5%	44.5%
11,672	MARQUETTE	5,481	2,879	2,591	11	288 R	52.5%	47.3%	52.6%	47.4%
3,373	MENOMINEE	1,214	372	842	0	470 D	30.6%	69.4%	30.6%	69.4%
964,988	MILWAUKEE	438,396	156,384	279,893	2,119	123,509 D	35.7%	63.8%	35.8%	64.2%
35,074	MONROE	13,544	8,017	5,511	16	2,506 R	59.2%	40.7%	59.3%	40.7%
28,947	OCONTO	13,514	7,636	5,868	10	1,768 R	56.5%	43.4%	56.5%	43.5%
31,216	ONEIDA	15,702	7,349	8,333	20	984 D	46.8%	53.1%	46.9%	53.1%
128,799	OUTAGAMIE	61,044	35,564	25,210	270	10,354 R	58.3%	41.3%	58.5%	41.5%
66,981	OZAUKEE	36,113	21,038	14,978	97	6,060 R	58.3%	41.5%	58.4%	41.6%
7,477	PEPIN	3,136	1,408	1,713	15	305 D	44.9%	54.6%	45.1%	54.9%
31,149	PIERCE	14,011	7,055	6,883	73	172 R	50.4%	49.1%	50.6%	49.4%
32,351	POLK	15,574	7,038	8,508	28	1,470 D	45.2%	54.6%	45.3%	54.7%
57,420	PORTAGE	27,820	12,036	15,699	85	3,663 D	43.3%	56.4%	43.4%	56.6%
15,788	PRICE	7,329	3,304	4,011	14	707 D	45.1%	54.7%	45.2%	54.8%
173,132	RACINE	75,308	35,127	39,769	412	4,642 D	46.6%	52.8%	46.9%	53.1%
17,476	RICHLAND	7,705	4,084	3,598	23	486 R	53.0%	46.7%	53.2%	46.8%
139,420	ROCK	57,021	27,796	28,895	330	1,099 D	48.7%	50.7%	49.0%	51.0%
15,589	RUSK	6,935	3,273	3,642	20	369 D	47.2%	52.5%	47.3%	52.7%
43,262	ST. CROIX	21,391	10,892	10,313	186	579 R	50.9%	48.2%	51.4%	48.6%
43,469	SAUK	18,844	9,441	9,341	62	100 R	50.1%	49.6%	50.3%	49.7%
12,843	SAWYER	6,453	3,182	3,255	16	73 D	49.3%	50.4%	49.4%	50.6%
35,928	SHAWANO	15,007	8,298	6,640	69	1,658 R	55.3%	44.2%	55.5%	44.5%
100,935	SHEBOYGAN	47,366	20,948	26,283	135	5,335 D	44.2%	55.5%	44.4%	55.6%

WISCONSIN

SENATOR 1988

1980 Census Population	County	Total Vote	Republican	Democratic	Other	Rep.-Dem. Plurality	Percentage Total Vote Rep.	Percentage Total Vote Dem.	Percentage Major Vote Rep.	Percentage Major Vote Dem.
18,817	TAYLOR	8,001	4,333	3,654	14	679 R	54.2%	45.7%	54.3%	45.7%
26,158	TREMPEALEAU	11,014	5,332	5,679	3	347 D	48.4%	51.6%	48.4%	51.6%
25,642	VERNON	11,085	6,114	4,953	18	1,161 R	55.2%	44.7%	55.2%	44.8%
16,535	VILAS	9,740	5,138	4,576	26	562 R	52.8%	47.0%	52.9%	47.1%
71,507	WALWORTH	31,013	18,081	12,813	119	5,268 R	58.3%	41.3%	58.5%	41.5%
13,174	WASHBURN	6,382	3,008	3,348	26	340 D	47.1%	52.5%	47.3%	52.7%
84,848	WASHINGTON	40,805	22,605	18,071	129	4,534 R	55.4%	44.3%	55.6%	44.4%
280,326	WAUKESHA	148,391	83,366	64,558	467	18,808 R	56.2%	43.5%	56.4%	43.6%
42,831	WAUPACA	18,863	12,007	6,829	27	5,178 R	63.7%	36.2%	63.7%	36.3%
18,526	WAUSHARA	8,511	4,929	3,577	5	1,352 R	57.9%	42.0%	57.9%	42.1%
131,703	WINNEBAGO	62,354	35,345	26,673	336	8,672 R	56.7%	42.8%	57.0%	43.0%
72,799	WOOD	32,030	16,158	15,735	137	423 R	50.4%	49.1%	50.7%	49.3%
4,705,767	TOTAL	2,168,190	1,030,440	1,128,625	9,125	98,185 D	47.5%	52.1%	47.7%	52.3%

WISCONSIN

CONGRESS

CD	Year	Total Vote	Republican Vote	Republican Candidate	Democratic Vote	Democratic Candidate	Other Vote	Rep.-Dem. Plurality	Percentage Total Vote Rep.	Percentage Total Vote Dem.	Percentage Major Vote Rep.	Percentage Major Vote Dem.
1	1988	208,176	49,620	WEAVER, BERNARD J.	158,552	ASPIN, LES	4	108,932 D	23.8%	76.2%	23.8%	76.2%
1	1986	143,139	34,495	PETERSON, IRIS	106,288	ASPIN, LES	2,356	71,793 D	24.1%	74.3%	24.5%	75.5%
1	1984	226,264	99,080	JANSSON, PETER N.	127,184	ASPIN, LES		28,104 D	43.8%	56.2%	43.8%	56.2%
1	1982	155,804	59,309	JANSSON, PETER N.	95,055	ASPIN, LES	1,440	35,746 D	38.1%	61.0%	38.4%	61.6%
2	1988	258,977	107,457	HANEY, ANN J.	151,501	KASTENMEIER, ROBERT	19	44,044 D	41.5%	58.5%	41.5%	58.5%
2	1986	192,535	85,156	HANEY, ANN J.	106,919	KASTENMEIER, ROBERT	460	21,763 D	44.2%	55.5%	44.3%	55.7%
2	1984	251,357	91,345	WILEY, ALBERT E.	159,987	KASTENMEIER, ROBERT	25	68,642 D	36.3%	63.6%	36.3%	63.7%
2	1982	186,045	71,989	JOHNSON, JIM	112,677	KASTENMEIER, ROBERT	1,379	40,688 D	38.7%	60.6%	39.0%	61.0%
3	1988	230,467	157,513	GUNDERSON, STEVEN	72,935	KRUEGER, KARL E.	19	84,578 R	68.3%	31.6%	68.4%	31.6%
3	1986	162,869	104,393	GUNDERSON, STEVEN	58,445	MULDER, LELAND E.	31	45,948 R	64.1%	35.9%	64.1%	35.9%
3	1984	234,695	160,437	GUNDERSON, STEVEN	74,253	DAHL, CHARLES F.	5	86,184 R	68.4%	31.6%	68.4%	31.6%
3	1982	175,465	99,304	GUNDERSON, STEVEN	75,132	OFFNER, PAUL	1,029	24,172 R	56.6%	42.8%	56.9%	43.1%
4	1988	177,892			177,283	KLECZKA, GERALD D.	609	177,283 D		99.7%		100.0%
4	1986	120,803			120,354	KLECZKA, GERALD D.	449	120,354 D		99.6%		100.0%
4	1984	238,222	78,056	NOLAN, ROBERT V.	158,722	KLECZKA, GERALD D.	1,444	80,666 D	32.8%	66.6%	33.0%	67.0%
4	1982	137,024			129,557	ZABLOCKI, CLEMENT J.	7,467	129,557 D		94.6%		100.0%
5	1988	219,179	78,307	BARNHILL, HELEN I.	140,518	MOODY, JIM	354	62,211 D	35.7%	64.1%	35.8%	64.2%
5	1986	110,604			109,506	MOODY, JIM	1,098	109,506 D		99.0%		100.0%
5	1984	178,819			175,243	MOODY, JIM	3,576	175,243 D		98.0%		100.0%
5	1982	156,921	54,826	JOHNSTON, ROD K.	99,713	MOODY, JIM	2,382	44,887 D	34.9%	63.5%	35.5%	64.5%
6	1988	223,495	165,923	PETRI, THOMAS E.	57,552	GARRETT, JOSEPH	20	108,371 R	74.2%	25.8%	74.2%	25.8%
6	1986	128,639	124,328	PETRI, THOMAS E.			4,311	124,328 R	96.6%		100.0%	
6	1984	224,546	170,271	PETRI, THOMAS E.	54,266	IAQUINTA, DAVID L.	9	116,005 R	75.8%	24.2%	75.8%	24.2%
6	1982	171,283	111,348	PETRI, THOMAS E.	59,922	LOEHR, GORDON E.	13	51,426 R	65.0%	35.0%	65.0%	35.0%
7	1988	230,179	86,077	HERMENING, KEVIN J.	142,197	OBEY, DAVID R.	1,905	56,120 D	37.4%	61.8%	37.7%	62.3%
7	1986	171,712	63,408	HERMENING, KEVIN J.	106,700	OBEY, DAVID R.	1,604	43,292 D	36.9%	62.1%	37.3%	62.7%
7	1984	238,652	92,507	MICHAELSEN, MARK G.	146,131	OBEY, DAVID R.	14	53,624 D	38.8%	61.2%	38.8%	61.2%
7	1982	179,668	57,535	ZIMMERMANN, BERNARD A.	122,124	OBEY, DAVID R.	9	64,589 D	32.0%	68.0%	32.0%	68.0%
8	1988	240,013	167,275	ROTH, TOBY	72,708	BARON, ROBERT A.	30	94,567 R	69.7%	30.3%	69.7%	30.3%
8	1986	175,432	118,162	ROTH, TOBY	57,265	WILLEMS, PAUL	5	60,897 R	67.4%	32.6%	67.4%	32.6%
8	1984	237,107	161,005	ROTH, TOBY	73,090	WILLEMS, PAUL	3,012	87,915 R	67.9%	30.8%	68.8%	31.2%
8	1982	177,152	101,379	ROTH, TOBY	74,436	CLUSEN, RUTH C.	1,337	26,943 R	57.2%	42.0%	57.7%	42.3%
9	1988	247,104	185,093	SENSENBRENNER, F. JAMES	62,003	HICKEY, THOMAS J.	8	123,090 R	74.9%	25.1%	74.9%	25.1%
9	1986	177,408	138,766	SENSENBRENNER, F. JAMES	38,636	POPP, THOMAS G.	6	100,130 R	78.2%	21.8%	78.2%	21.8%
9	1984	245,716	180,247	SENSENBRENNER, F. JAMES	64,157	KRAUSE, JOHN	1,312	116,090 R	73.4%	26.1%	73.7%	26.3%
9	1982	111,570	111,503	SENSENBRENNER, F. JAMES			67	111,503 R	99.9%		100.0%	

WISCONSIN

1988 GENERAL ELECTION

President Other vote was 5,157 Libertarian (Paul); 3,056 Populist (Duke); 2,574 Socialist Workers (Warren); 2,302 National Economic Recovery (LaRouche); 1,953 New Alliance (Fulani); 2,273 scattered write-in.

Senator Other vote was 3,965 Independent Voters of Wisconsin (Zaehringer); 3,029 Socialist Workers (Grogan); 1,198 Independent (Wollenburg); 933 scattered write-in.

Congress Other vote was 1,893 Independent (Duelge) and 12 scattered in CD 7; scattered in all other CD's.

1988 PRIMARIES

SEPTEMBER 13 REPUBLICAN

Senator 209,025 Susan Engeleiter; 148,601 Stephen B. King; 9,149 Peter Y. Taylor; 87 scattered write-in.

Congress Unopposed in seven CD's. No candidate in CD 4. Contested as follows:

CD 5 13,669 Helen I. Barnhill; 6,394 Janette Marsh; 100 scattered write-in.

SEPTEMBER 13 DEMOCRATIC

Senator 249,226 Herbert H. Kohl; 203,479 Anthony S. Earl; 55,225 Edward R. Garvey; 19,819 Douglas LaFollette; 5,040 Edmond Hou-Seye; 215 scattered write-in.

Congress Unopposed in five CD's. Contested as follows:

CD 3 17,472 Karl E. Krueger; 13,447 James L. Ziegeweid; 17 scattered write-in.
CD 5 47,789 Jim Moody; 19,906 Matthew J. Flynn; 5,314 Donald Sykes; 4,966 Terrance L. Pitts; 2,517 Frederick P. Kessler; 517 Roman R. Blenski; 33 scattered write-in.
CD 6 19,476 Joseph Garrett; 8,267 Raymond F. Gose; 3 scattered write-in.
CD 9 17,464 Thomas J. Hickey; 14,301 Joseph H. Herzberg; 2 scattered write-in.

WYOMING

GOVERNOR

Mike Sullivan (D). Elected 1986 to a four-year term.

SENATORS

Alan K. Simpson (R). Re-elected 1984 to a six-year term. Previously elected 1978.

Malcolm Wallop (R). Re-elected 1988 to a six-year term. Previously elected 1982, 1976.

REPRESENTATIVES

At-Large. Richard Cheney (R) (see page 1)

POSTWAR VOTE FOR PRESIDENT

Year	Total Vote	Republican Vote	Republican Candidate	Democratic Vote	Democratic Candidate	Other Vote	Plurality	Percentage Total Vote Rep.	Percentage Total Vote Dem.	Percentage Major Vote Rep.	Percentage Major Vote Dem.
1988	176,551	106,867	Bush, George	67,113	Dukakis, Michael S.	2,571	39,754 R	60.5%	38.0%	61.4%	38.6%
1984	188,968	133,241	Reagan, Ronald	53,370	Mondale, Walter F.	2,357	79,871 R	70.5%	28.2%	71.4%	28.6%
1980	176,713	110,700	Reagan, Ronald	49,427	Carter, Jimmy	16,586	61,273 R	62.6%	28.0%	69.1%	30.9%
1976	156,343	92,717	Ford, Gerald R.	62,239	Carter, Jimmy	1,387	30,478 R	59.3%	39.8%	59.8%	40.2%
1972	145,570	100,464	Nixon, Richard M.	44,358	McGovern, George S.	748	56,106 R	69.0%	30.5%	69.4%	30.6%
1968	127,205	70,927	Nixon, Richard M.	45,173	Humphrey, Hubert H.	11,105	25,754 R	55.8%	35.5%	61.1%	38.9%
1964	142,716	61,998	Goldwater, Barry M.	80,718	Johnson, Lyndon B.		18,720 D	43.4%	56.6%	43.4%	56.6%
1960	140,782	77,451	Nixon, Richard M.	63,331	Kennedy, John F.		14,120 R	55.0%	45.0%	55.0%	45.0%
1956	124,127	74,573	Eisenhower, Dwight D.	49,554	Stevenson, Adlai E.		25,019 R	60.1%	39.9%	60.1%	39.9%
1952	129,253	81,049	Eisenhower, Dwight D.	47,934	Stevenson, Adlai E.	270	33,115 R	62.7%	37.1%	62.8%	37.2%
1948	101,425	47,947	Dewey, Thomas E.	52,354	Truman, Harry S.	1,124	4,407 D	47.3%	51.6%	47.8%	52.2%

POSTWAR VOTE FOR GOVERNOR

Year	Total Vote	Republican Vote	Republican Candidate	Democratic Vote	Democratic Candidate	Other Vote	Rep.-Dem. Plurality	Percentage Total Vote Rep.	Percentage Total Vote Dem.	Percentage Major Vote Rep.	Percentage Major Vote Dem.
1986	164,720	75,841	Simpson, Peter	88,879	Sullivan, Mike		13,038 D	46.0%	54.0%	46.0%	54.0%
1982	168,555	62,128	Morton, Warren A.	106,427	Herschler, Ed		44,299 D	36.9%	63.1%	36.9%	63.1%
1978	137,567	67,595	Ostlund, John C.	69,972	Herschler, Ed		2,377 D	49.1%	50.9%	49.1%	50.9%
1974	128,386	56,645	Jones, Dick	71,741	Herschler, Ed		15,096 D	44.1%	55.9%	44.1%	55.9%
1970	118,257	74,249	Hathaway, Stan	44,008	Rooney, John J.		30,241 R	62.8%	37.2%	62.8%	37.2%
1966	120,873	65,624	Hathaway, Stan	55,249	Wilkerson, Ernest		10,375 R	54.3%	45.7%	54.3%	45.7%
1962	119,268	64,970	Hansen, Clifford P.	54,298	Gage, Jack R.		10,672 R	54.5%	45.5%	54.5%	45.5%
1958	112,537	52,488	Simpson, Milward L.	55,070	Hickey, J. J.	4,979	2,582 D	46.6%	48.9%	48.8%	51.2%
1954	111,438	56,275	Simpson, Milward L.	55,163	Jack, William		1,112 R	50.5%	49.5%	50.5%	49.5%
1950	96,959	54,441	Barrett, Frank A.	42,518	McIntyre, John J.		11,923 R	56.1%	43.9%	56.1%	43.9%
1946	81,353	38,333	Wright, Earl	43,020	Hunt, Lester C.		4,687 D	47.1%	52.9%	47.1%	52.9%

WYOMING

POSTWAR VOTE FOR SENATOR

	Total	Republican		Democratic		Other	Rep.-Dem.	Percentage			
								Total Vote		Major Vote	
Year	Vote	Vote	Candidate	Vote	Candidate	Vote	Plurality	Rep.	Dem.	Rep.	Dem.
1988	180,964	91,143	Wallop, Malcolm	89,821	Vinich, John P.		1,322 R	50.4%	49.6%	50.4%	49.6%
1984	186,898	146,373	Simpson, Alan K.	40,525	Ryan, Victor A.		105,848 R	78.3%	21.7%	78.3%	21.7%
1982	167,191	94,725	Wallop, Malcolm	72,466	McDaniel, Rodger		22,259 R	56.7%	43.3%	56.7%	43.3%
1978	133,364	82,908	Simpson, Alan K.	50,456	Whitaker, Raymond B.		32,452 R	62.2%	37.8%	62.2%	37.8%
1976	155,368	84,810	Wallop, Malcolm	70,558	McGee, Gale		14,252 R	54.6%	45.4%	54.6%	45.4%
1972	142,067	101,314	Hansen, Clifford P.	40,753	Vinich, Mike		60,561 R	71.3%	28.7%	71.3%	28.7%
1970	120,486	53,279	Wold, John S.	67,207	McGee, Gale		13,928 D	44.2%	55.8%	44.2%	55.8%
1966	122,689	63,548	Hansen, Clifford P.	59,141	Roncalio, Teno		4,407 R	51.8%	48.2%	51.8%	48.2%
1964	141,670	65,185	Wold, John S.	76,485	McGee, Gale		11,300 D	46.0%	54.0%	46.0%	54.0%
1962 S	119,372	69,043	Simpson, Milward L.	50,329	Hickey, J. J.		18,714 R	57.8%	42.2%	57.8%	42.2%
1960	138,550	78,103	Thomson, E. Keith	60,447	Whitaker, Ray		17,656 R	56.4%	43.6%	56.4%	43.6%
1958	114,157	56,122	Barrett, Frank A.	58,035	McGee, Gale		1,913 D	49.2%	50.8%	49.2%	50.8%
1954	112,252	54,407	Harrison, William H.	57,845	O'Mahoney, Joseph C.		3,438 D	48.5%	51.5%	48.5%	51.5%
1952	130,097	67,176	Barrett, Frank A.	62,921	O'Mahoney, Joseph C.		4,255 R	51.6%	48.4%	51.6%	48.4%
1948	101,480	43,527	Robertson, Edward V.	57,953	Hunt, Lester C.		14,426 D	42.9%	57.1%	42.9%	57.1%
1946	81,557	35,714	Henderson, Harry B.	45,843	O'Mahoney, Joseph C.		10,129 D	43.8%	56.2%	43.8%	56.2%

The 1962 election was for a short term to fill a vacancy.

WYOMING

One At Large

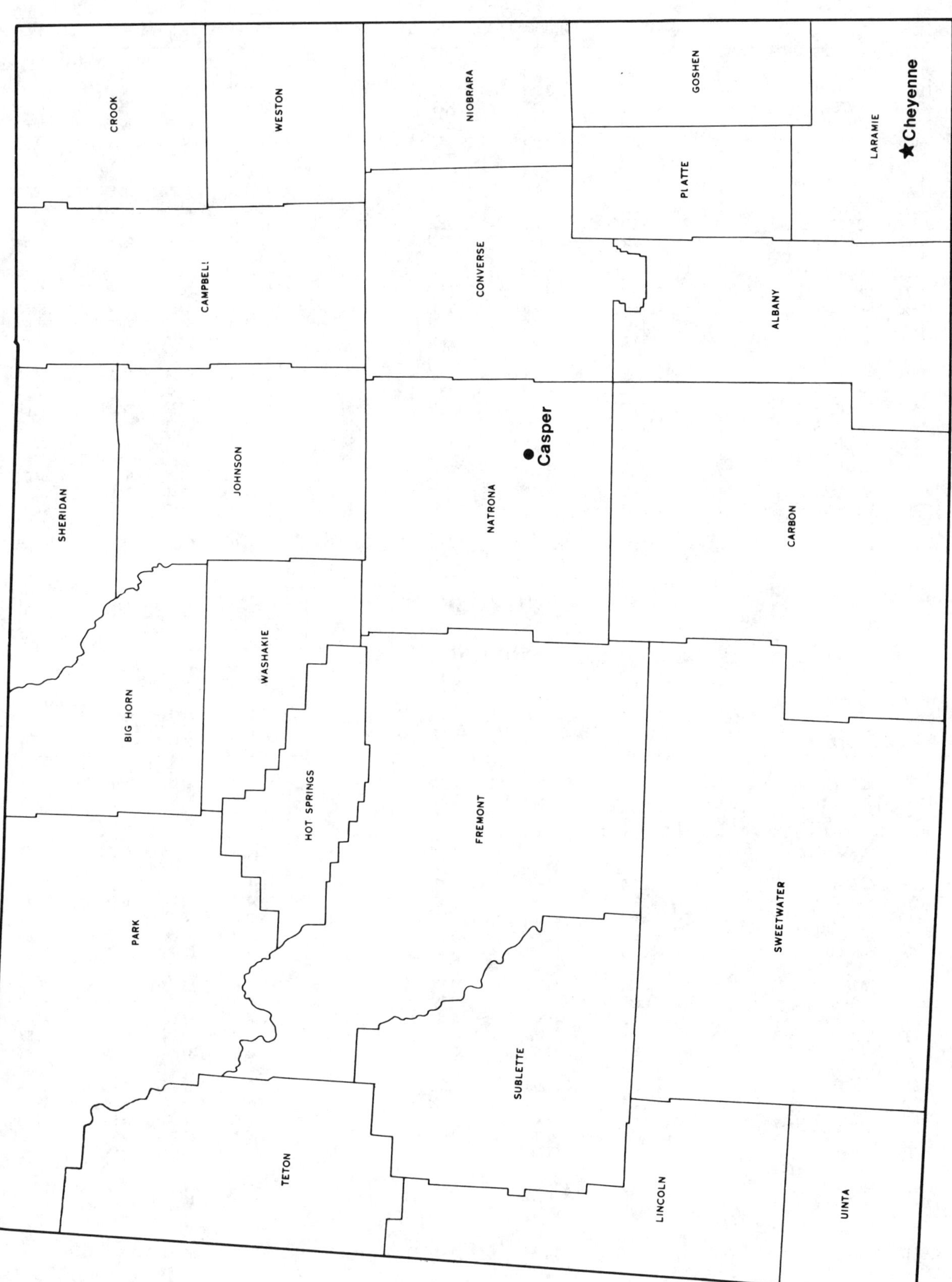

WYOMING

PRESIDENT 1988

1980 Census Population	County	Total Vote	Republican	Democratic	Other	Rep.-Dem. Plurality	Percentage Total Vote Rep.	Percentage Total Vote Dem.	Percentage Major Vote Rep.	Percentage Major Vote Dem.
29,062	ALBANY	11,335	5,653	5,486	196	167 R	49.9%	48.4%	50.7%	49.3%
11,896	BIG HORN	4,780	3,258	1,469	53	1,789 R	68.2%	30.7%	68.9%	31.1%
24,367	CAMPBELL	9,112	6,702	2,288	122	4,414 R	73.6%	25.1%	74.5%	25.5%
21,896	CARBON	5,989	3,336	2,555	98	781 R	55.7%	42.7%	56.6%	43.4%
14,069	CONVERSE	4,215	2,885	1,301	29	1,584 R	68.4%	30.9%	68.9%	31.1%
5,308	CROOK	2,540	1,939	553	48	1,386 R	76.3%	21.8%	77.8%	22.2%
38,992	FREEMONT	12,889	7,681	5,020	188	2,661 R	59.6%	38.9%	60.5%	39.5%
12,040	GOSHEN	5,005	3,075	1,875	55	1,200 R	61.4%	37.5%	62.1%	37.9%
5,710	HOT SPRINGS	2,324	1,490	800	34	690 R	64.1%	34.4%	65.1%	34.9%
6,700	JOHNSON	2,858	2,081	707	70	1,374 R	72.8%	24.7%	74.6%	25.4%
68,649	LARAMIE	27,770	15,561	11,851	358	3,710 R	56.0%	42.7%	56.8%	43.2%
12,177	LINCOLN	4,897	3,237	1,592	68	1,645 R	66.1%	32.5%	67.0%	33.0%
71,856	NATRONA	23,487	14,005	9,148	334	4,857 R	59.6%	38.9%	60.5%	39.5%
2,924	NIOBRARA	1,191	825	354	12	471 R	69.3%	29.7%	70.0%	30.0%
21,639	PARK	9,702	6,884	2,646	172	4,238 R	71.0%	27.3%	72.2%	27.8%
11,975	PLATTE	3,808	2,253	1,482	73	771 R	59.2%	38.9%	60.3%	39.7%
25,048	SHERIDAN	10,778	5,980	4,655	143	1,325 R	55.5%	43.2%	56.2%	43.8%
4,548	SUBLETTE	2,247	1,636	576	35	1,060 R	72.8%	25.6%	74.0%	26.0%
41,723	SWEETWATER	13,705	6,780	6,720	205	60 R	49.5%	49.0%	50.2%	49.8%
9,355	TETON	5,926	3,616	2,217	93	1,399 R	61.0%	37.4%	62.0%	38.0%
13,021	UINTA	5,501	3,464	1,922	115	1,542 R	63.0%	34.9%	64.3%	35.7%
9,496	WASHAKIE	3,768	2,538	1,197	33	1,341 R	67.4%	31.8%	68.0%	32.0%
7,106	WESTON	2,724	1,988	699	37	1,289 R	73.0%	25.7%	74.0%	26.0%
469,557	TOTAL	176,551	106,867	67,113	2,571	39,754 R	60.5%	38.0%	61.4%	38.6%

WYOMING

SENATOR 1988

1980 Census Population	County	Total Vote	Republican	Democratic	Other	Rep.-Dem. Plurality	Percentage Total Vote Rep.	Percentage Total Vote Dem.	Percentage Major Vote Rep.	Percentage Major Vote Dem.
29,062	ALBANY	11,453	4,913	6,540		1,627 D	42.9%	57.1%	42.9%	57.1%
11,896	BIG HORN	4,657	2,627	2,030		597 R	56.4%	43.6%	56.4%	43.6%
24,367	CAMPBELL	9,146	5,873	3,273		2,600 R	64.2%	35.8%	64.2%	35.8%
21,896	CARBON	6,458	2,855	3,603		748 D	44.2%	55.8%	44.2%	55.8%
14,069	CONVERSE	4,355	2,339	2,016		323 R	53.7%	46.3%	53.7%	46.3%
5,308	CROOK	2,560	1,823	737		1,086 R	71.2%	28.8%	71.2%	28.8%
38,992	FREEMONT	12,947	5,393	7,554		2,161 D	41.7%	58.3%	41.7%	58.3%
12,040	GOSHEN	5,190	3,150	2,040		1,110 R	60.7%	39.3%	60.7%	39.3%
5,710	HOT SPRINGS	2,318	1,200	1,118		82 R	51.8%	48.2%	51.8%	48.2%
6,700	JOHNSON	2,825	1,769	1,056		713 R	62.6%	37.4%	62.6%	37.4%
68,649	LARAMIE	30,025	13,518	16,507		2,989 D	45.0%	55.0%	45.0%	55.0%
12,177	LINCOLN	4,846	2,623	2,223		400 R	54.1%	45.9%	54.1%	45.9%
71,856	NATRONA	24,128	11,357	12,771		1,414 D	47.1%	52.9%	47.1%	52.9%
2,924	NIOBRARA	1,251	754	497		257 R	60.3%	39.7%	60.3%	39.7%
21,639	PARK	9,826	5,979	3,847		2,132 R	60.8%	39.2%	60.8%	39.2%
11,975	PLATTE	3,978	2,073	1,905		168 R	52.1%	47.9%	52.1%	47.9%
25,048	SHERIDAN	10,871	5,831	5,040		791 R	53.6%	46.4%	53.6%	46.4%
4,548	SUBLETTE	2,373	1,530	843		687 R	64.5%	35.5%	64.5%	35.5%
41,723	SWEETWATER	13,652	5,084	8,568		3,484 D	37.2%	62.8%	37.2%	62.8%
9,355	TETON	6,027	3,585	2,442		1,143 R	59.5%	40.5%	59.5%	40.5%
13,021	UINTA	5,566	2,917	2,649		268 R	52.4%	47.6%	52.4%	47.6%
9,496	WASHAKIE	3,710	2,167	1,543		624 R	58.4%	41.6%	58.4%	41.6%
7,106	WESTON	2,802	1,783	1,019		764 R	63.6%	36.4%	63.6%	36.4%
469,557	TOTAL	180,964	91,143	89,821		1,322 R	50.4%	49.6%	50.4%	49.6%

WYOMING

CONGRESS

			Republican		Democratic				Percentage			
		Total					Other	Rep.-Dem.	Total Vote		Major Vote	
CD	Year	Vote	Vote	Candidate	Vote	Candidate	Vote	Plurality	Rep.	Dem.	Rep.	Dem.
AL	1988	177,651	118,350	CHENEY, RICHARD	56,527	SHARRATT, BRYAN	2,774	61,823 R	66.6%	31.8%	67.7%	32.3%
AL	1986	159,787	111,007	CHENEY, RICHARD	48,780	GILMORE, RICK		62,227 R	69.5%	30.5%	69.5%	30.5%
AL	1984	187,904	138,234	CHENEY, RICHARD	45,857	MCFADDEN, HUGH B.	3,813	92,377 R	73.6%	24.4%	75.1%	24.9%
AL	1982	159,277	113,236	CHENEY, RICHARD	46,041	HOMMEL, THEODORE H.		67,195 R	71.1%	28.9%	71.1%	28.9%
AL	1980	169,699	116,361	CHENEY, RICHARD	53,338	ROGERS, JIM		63,023 R	68.6%	31.4%	68.6%	31.4%
AL	1978	129,377	75,855	CHENEY, RICHARD	53,522	BAGLEY, BILL		22,333 R	58.6%	41.4%	58.6%	41.4%
AL	1976	151,868	66,147	HART, LARRY	85,721	RONCALIO, TENO		19,574 D	43.6%	56.4%	43.6%	56.4%
AL	1974	126,933	57,499	STROOCK, TOM	69,434	RONCALIO, TENO		11,935 D	45.3%	54.7%	45.3%	54.7%
AL	1972	146,299	70,667	KIDD, WILLIAM	75,632	RONCALIO, TENO		4,965 D	48.3%	51.7%	48.3%	51.7%
AL	1970	116,304	57,848	ROBERTS, HARRY	58,456	RONCALIO, TENO		608 D	49.7%	50.3%	49.7%	50.3%
AL	1968	123,313	77,363	WOLD, JOHN S.	45,950	LINFORD, VELMA		31,413 R	62.7%	37.3%	62.7%	37.3%
AL	1966	119,426	62,984	HARRISON, WILLIAM H.	56,442	CHRISTIAN, AL		6,542 R	52.7%	47.3%	52.7%	47.3%
AL	1964	139,175	68,482	HARRISON, WILLIAM H.	70,693	RONCALIO, TENO		2,211 D	49.2%	50.8%	49.2%	50.8%
AL	1962	116,474	71,489	HARRISON, WILLIAM H.	44,985	MANKUS, LOUIS A.		26,504 R	61.4%	38.6%	61.4%	38.6%
AL	1960	134,331	70,241	HARRISON, WILLIAM H.	64,090	ARMSTRONG, H. T.		6,151 R	52.3%	47.7%	52.3%	47.7%
AL	1958	111,780	59,894	THOMSON, E. KEITH	51,886	WHITAKER, RAY		8,008 R	53.6%	46.4%	53.6%	46.4%
AL	1956	120,128	69,903	THOMSON, E. KEITH	50,225	O'CALLAGHAN, JERRY		19,678 R	58.2%	41.8%	58.2%	41.8%
AL	1954	108,771	61,111	THOMSON, E. KEITH	47,660	TULLY, SAM		13,451 R	56.2%	43.8%	56.2%	43.8%
AL	1952	126,720	76,161	HARRISON, WILLIAM H.	50,559	ROSE, ROBERT R.		25,602 R	60.1%	39.9%	60.1%	39.9%
AL	1950	93,348	50,865	HARRISON, WILLIAM H.	42,483	CLARK, JOHN B.		8,382 R	54.5%	45.5%	54.5%	45.5%
AL	1948	97,464	50,218	BARRETT, FRANK A.	47,246	FLANNERY, L. G.		2,972 R	51.5%	48.5%	51.5%	48.5%
AL	1946	79,438	44,482	BARRETT, FRANK A.	34,956	MCINTYRE, JOHN J.		9,526 R	56.0%	44.0%	56.0%	44.0%

WYOMING

1988 GENERAL ELECTION

President Other vote was 2,026 Libertarian (Paul); 545 New Alliance (Fulani).

Senator

Congress Other vote at-large was 1,906 Libertarian (McCune); 868 New Alliance (Hamburg).

1988 PRIMARIES

AUGUST 16 REPUBLICAN

Senator 55,752 Malcolm Wallop; 3,933 Nora M. Lewis; 3,716 I. W. Kinney; 1,898 Michael J. Dee; 1,702 Russ Hanrahan.

Congress Contested as follows:

AL 59,503 Richard Cheney; 8,511 Bob Morris.

AUGUST 16 DEMOCRATIC

Senator 23,214 John P. Vinich; 14,613 Pete Maxfield; 11,350 Lynn Simons.

Congress Unopposed at-large.

AUGUST 16 NEW ALLIANCE

Senator No candidate filed.

Congress Unopposed at-large.

AUGUST 16 LIBERTARIAN

Senator No candidate filed.

Congress No candidate filed. Craig McCune received the nomination by write-in votes.

DISTRICT OF COLUMBIA

GOVERNMENT

The District of Columbia is governed by a Mayor and City Council of thirteen.

MAYOR

Marion Barry (D). Re-elected 1986 to a four year term. Previously elected 1982, 1978.

DELEGATE

Walter E. Fauntroy (D)

POSTWAR VOTE FOR PRESIDENT

								Percentage			
	Total	Republican		Democratic		Other		Total Vote		Major Vote	
Year	Vote	Vote	Candidate	Vote	Candidate	Vote	Plurality	Rep.	Dem.	Rep.	Dem.
1988	192,877	27,590	Bush, George	159,407	Dukakis, Michael S.	5,880	131,817 D	14.3%	82.6%	14.8%	85.2%
1984	211,288	29,009	Reagan, Ronald	180,408	Mondale, Walter F.	1,871	151,399 D	13.7%	85.4%	13.9%	86.1%
1980	175,237	23,545	Reagan, Ronald	131,113	Carter, Jimmy	20,579	107,568 D	13.4%	74.8%	15.2%	84.8%
1976	168,830	27,873	Ford, Gerald R.	137,818	Carter, Jimmy	3,139	109,945 D	16.5%	81.6%	16.8%	83.2%
1972	163,421	35,226	Nixon, Richard M.	127,627	McGovern, George S.	568	92,401 D	21.6%	78.1%	21.6%	78.4%
1968	170,578	31,012	Nixon, Richard M.	139,566	Humphrey, Hubert H.		108,554 D	18.2%	81.8%	18.2%	81.8%
1964	198,597	28,801	Goldwater, Barry M.	169,796	Johnson, Lyndon B.		140,995 D	14.5%	85.5%	14.5%	85.5%

Under the 23rd Amendment to the Constitution, the District of Columbia became entitled to choose Electors beginning with the 1964 election.

POSTWAR VOTE FOR MAYOR

								Percentage			
	Total	Republican		Democratic		Other	Rep.-Dem.	Total Vote		Major Vote	
Year	Vote	Vote	Candidate	Vote	Candidate	Vote	Plurality	Rep.	Dem.	Rep.	Dem.
1986	131,802	43,676	Schwartz, Carol	80,666	Barry, Marion	7,460	36,990 D	33.1%	61.2%	35.1%	64.9%
1982	117,623	16,501	Lee, E. Brooke	95,007	Barry, Marion	6,115	78,506 D	14.0%	80.8%	14.8%	85.2%
1978	100,861	28,032	Fletcher, Arthur	69,888	Barry, Marion	2,941	41,856 D	27.8%	69.3%	28.6%	71.4%
1974	105,183	3,703	Champion, Jackson R.	84,676	Washington, Walter E.	16,804	80,973 D	3.5%	80.5%	4.2%	95.8%

POSTWAR VOTE FOR DELEGATE

								Percentage			
	Total	Republican		Democratic		Other	Rep.-Dem.	Total Vote		Major Vote	
Year	Vote	Vote	Candidate	Vote	Candidate	Vote	Plurality	Rep.	Dem.	Rep.	Dem.
1988	170,933	22,936	Reed, William	121,817	Fauntroy, Walter E.	26,180	98,881 D	13.4%	71.3%	15.8%	84.2%
1986	126,855	17,643	King, Mary L. H.	101,604	Fauntroy, Walter E.	7,608	83,961 D	13.9%	80.1%	14.8%	85.2%
1984 **	161,771		—	154,583	Fauntroy, Walter E.	7,188	154,583 D		95.6%		100.0%
1982	112,543	17,242	West, John	93,422	Fauntroy, Walter E.	1,879	76,180 D	15.3%	83.0%	15.6%	84.4%
1980	151,046	21,245	Roehr, Robert J.	112,339	Fauntroy, Walter E.	17,462	91,094 D	14.1%	74.4%	15.9%	84.1%
1978	96,306	11,677	Champion, Jackson R.	76,557	Fauntroy, Walter E.	8,072	64,880 D	12.1%	79.5%	13.2%	86.8%
1976	159,790	21,699	Hall, Daniel L.	123,464	Fauntroy, Walter E.	14,627	101,765 D	13.6%	77.3%	14.9%	85.1%
1974	104,014	9,166	Phillips, William R.	66,337	Fauntroy, Walter E.	28,511	57,171 D	8.8%	63.8%	12.1%	87.9%
1972	159,612	39,487	Chin-Lee, William	95,300	Fauntroy, Walter E.	24,825	55,813 D	24.7%	59.7%	29.3%	70.7%
1971 S	116,635	29,249	Nevius, John A.	68,166	Fauntroy, Walter E.	19,220	38,917 D	25.1%	58.4%	30.0%	70.0%

The 1971 election was held in March for a short term to the end of the 92nd Congress. In 1984 the Democratic candidate was also the nominee of the Republican and Statehood parties.

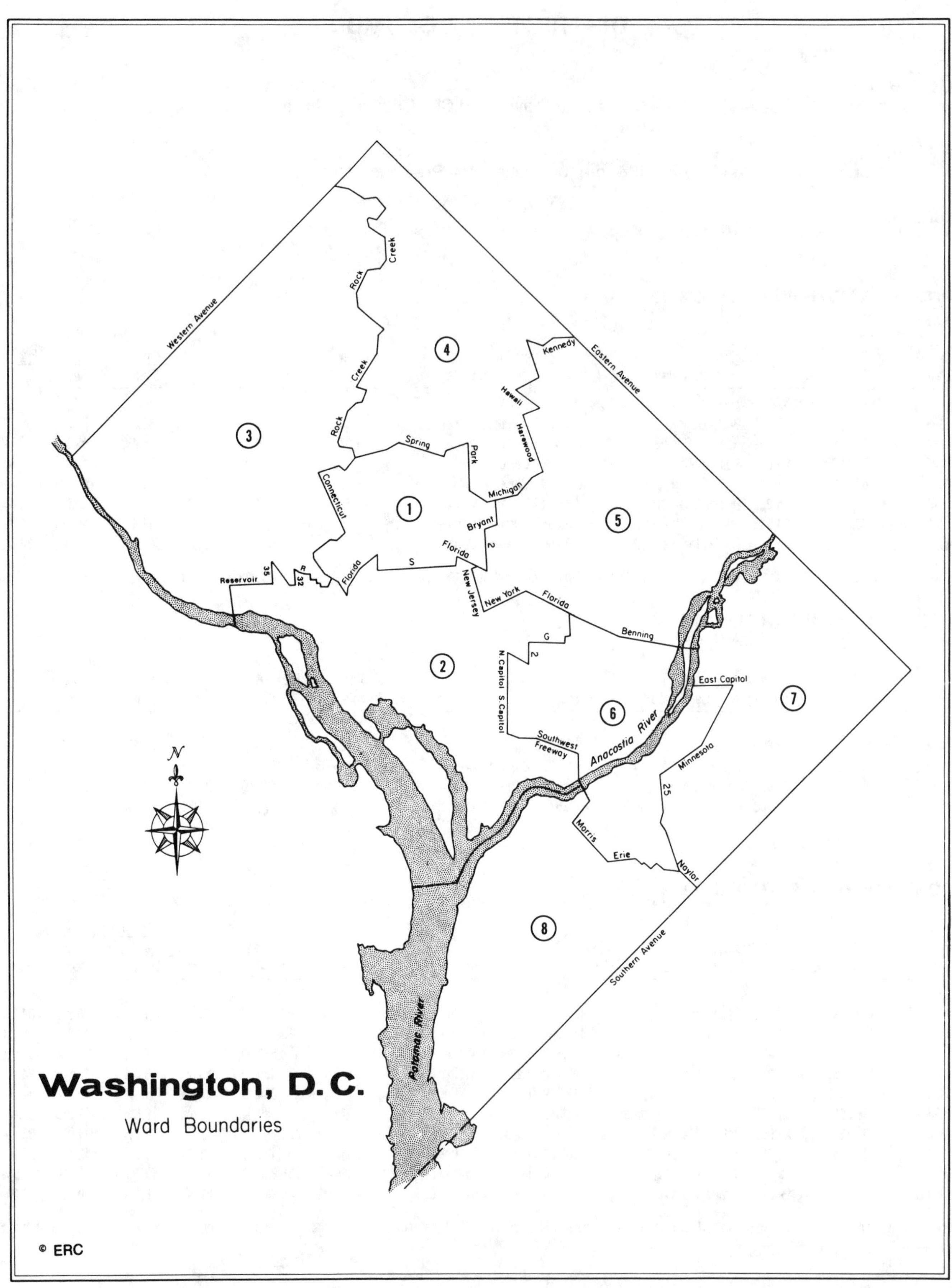

Washington, D.C.

Ward Boundaries

DISTRICT OF COLUMBIA

PRESIDENT 1988

1980 Census Population	Ward	Total Vote	Republican	Democratic	Other	Rep.-Dem. Plurality	Percentage Total Vote Rep.	Percentage Total Vote Dem.	Percentage Major Vote Rep.	Percentage Major Vote Dem.
78,700	WARD 1	21,827	2,563	18,523	741	15,960 D	11.7%	84.9%	12.2%	87.8%
81,400	WARD 2	24,135	5,231	18,270	634	13,039 D	21.7%	75.7%	22.3%	77.7%
77,800	WARD 3	35,655	11,696	23,402	557	11,706 D	32.8%	65.6%	33.3%	66.7%
81,900	WARD 4	29,022	2,116	25,763	1,143	23,647 D	7.3%	88.8%	7.6%	92.4%
82,600	WARD 5	24,855	1,432	22,532	891	21,100 D	5.8%	90.7%	6.0%	94.0%
75,700	WARD 6	23,233	2,727	19,779	727	17,052 D	11.7%	85.1%	12.1%	87.9%
82,400	WARD 7	21,592	1,108	19,689	795	18,581 D	5.1%	91.2%	5.3%	94.7%
77,900	WARD 8	11,921	526	11,009	386	10,483 D	4.4%	92.3%	4.6%	95.4%
	FEDERAL BALLOTS	637	191	440	6	249 D	30.0%	69.1%	30.3%	69.7%
638,400	TOTAL	192,877	27,590	159,407	5,880	131,817 D	14.3%	82.6%	14.8%	85.2%

DISTRICT OF COLUMBIA

DELEGATE 1988

1980 Census Population	Ward	Total Vote	Republican	Democratic	Other	Rep.-Dem. Plurality	Percentage Total Vote Rep.	Percentage Total Vote Dem.	Percentage Major Vote Rep.	Percentage Major Vote Dem.
78,700	WARD 1	18,981	2,166	12,619	4,196	10,453 D	11.4%	66.5%	14.6%	85.4%
81,400	WARD 2	21,349	4,661	12,683	4,005	8,022 D	21.8%	59.4%	26.9%	73.1%
77,800	WARD 3	29,880	10,304	12,345	7,231	2,041 D	34.5%	41.3%	45.5%	54.5%
81,900	WARD 4	26,356	1,374	22,183	2,799	20,809 D	5.2%	84.2%	5.8%	94.2%
82,600	WARD 5	22,710	985	19,594	2,131	18,609 D	4.3%	86.3%	4.8%	95.2%
75,700	WARD 6	20,734	2,467	14,711	3,556	12,244 D	11.9%	71.0%	14.4%	85.6%
82,400	WARD 7	19,594	626	17,457	1,511	16,831 D	3.2%	89.1%	3.5%	96.5%
77,900	WARD 8	10,825	242	9,903	680	9,661 D	2.2%	91.5%	2.4%	97.6%
	FEDERAL BALLOTS	504	111	322	71	211 D	22.0%	63.9%	25.6%	74.4%
638,400	TOTAL	170,933	22,936	121,817	26,180	98,881 D	13.4%	71.3%	15.8%	84.2%